Office and SharePoint 2010 User's Guide

Integrating SharePoint with Excel, Outlook, Access and Word

Michael P. Antonovich

Apress®

Office and SharePoint 2010 User's Guide: Integrating SharePoint with Excel, Outlook, Access and Word

Copyright © 2010 by Michael P. Antonovich

ISBN-13 (pbk): 978-1-4302-2760-1

ISBN-13 (electronic): 978-1-4302-2761-8

Printed and bound in the United States of America 9 8 7 6 5 4 3 2 1

President and Publisher: Paul Manning
Lead Editor: Jonathan Hassell
Technical Reviewer: Razi bin Rais
Editorial Board: Clay Andres, Steve Anglin, Mark Beckner, Ewan Buckingham, Gary Cornell, Jonathan Gennick, Jonathan Hassell, Michelle Lowman, Matthew Moodie, Duncan Parkes, Jeffrey Pepper, Frank Pohlmann, Douglas Pundick, Ben Renow-Clarke, Dominic Shakeshaft, Matt Wade, Tom Welsh
Coordinating Editor: Mary Tobin
Copy Editor: Mary Behr, Jim Compton
Production Support: Patrick Cunningham
Indexer: BIM Indexing & Proofreading Services
Artist: April Milne
Cover Designer: Anna Ishchenko

Distributed to the book trade worldwide by Springer Science+Business Media, LLC., 233 Spring Street, 6th Floor, New York, NY 10013. Phone 1-800-SPRINGER, fax (201) 348-4505, e-mail orders-ny@springer-sbm.com, or visit www.springeronline.com.

For information on translations, please e-mail rights@apress.com, or visit www.apress.com.

Apress and friends of ED books may be purchased in bulk for academic, corporate, or promotional use. eBook versions and licenses are also available for most titles. For more information, reference our Special Bulk Sales–eBook Licensing web page at www.apress.com/info/bulksales.

The source code for this book is available to readers at www.apress.com. You will need to answer questions pertaining to this book in order to successfully download the code.

For my wife of 33 years, Susan, and our wonderful daughter, Natasha. I love you both.

Contents at a Glance

Contents

About the Author

■**Michael P. Antonovich** graduated from Lehigh University with a bachelor's degree in chemical engineering in 1976 and a MBA in 1980, but his career almost from the start evolved toward computers and application development. He started working with large mainframe systems but quickly developed a keen interest in microcomputers when Apple introduced its Apple II, for which he wrote his first book in 1983. Over the years, he has learned many different systems, applications, and programming languages, but the first development environment he felt really strong about was FoxBase and later FoxPro. During the 90s, he published four books on FoxPro before the Internet and SQL Server bug bit him.

In addition to his full-time jobs developing applications, he has conducted dozens of different computer training classes for companies and universities over the years. Since his first SharePoint book, Michael has become a regular speaker at many of the SQL Saturday, Code Camp, and SharePoint Saturday events in the state of Florida, having presented nearly two dozen sessions in the last three years. He also has been serving on the Information Technology Advisory Committee of Valencia Community College.

In 2003, he joined the IT team of Orange County Public Schools as they prepared to launch a major new student tracking system. But the lure of the Internet along with a "little" product called SharePoint pulled him back into Internet development in the fall of 2006, when he took on the task of heading up the technical team to develop a new SharePoint portal for the school district that would provide all users with a single, consistent, easy-to-use interface. Since then, his team has completed the refresh and branding of all district Internet and intranet sites. They also worked with representatives from each of the over 170+ schools in the district to create new branded sites that follow a common site template providing consistency in locating information across the schools. Currently, Michael's team is preparing for a refresh of the branding for both the schools and intranet sites to enhance the consistency between sites further and to take advantage of the new SharePoint 2010 features. They are also committed to expanding the number of applications embedded or run through SharePoint employee sites to help reduce the district's paper usage and improve operating efficiencies. Orange County Public Schools is the 10th largest school district in the United States.

About the Technical Reviewer

Razi bin Rais is a Microsoft technology specialist with focus on Microsoft SharePoint Products and Technologies. Razi has extensive experience in designing, implementing and supporting enterprise solutions using Microsoft SharePoint Server. Razi has authored numerous articles published online and also worked with Microsoft MSL as a SME on several SharePoint 2010 courses. Razi is also a speaker for INETA and GITCA, and had led many sessions in several industry trade show conferences including the Microsoft TechDays, ISV innovation Days, Community Technology Updates and SharePoint Saturdays. For his community involvement and contribution, he has also been awarded the Microsoft MVP award for SharePoint Services since 2007. Razi blogs at http://razi.spaces.live.com and can be reached at razibinrais@live.com.

Acknowledgments

Even though a book may get published with a single name on the cover, many people are actually involved in getting that book into your hands. I'd like to thank Jonathan Hassell, my Apress Lead Editor, for giving me the chance to do a second SharePoint book on Office and SharePoint integration. Thanks to Razi bin Rais, my technical reviewer, for pointing out the technical things I assumed everyone would know but needed to include. To Mary Behr and Jim Compton, thanks for helping me make this text more readable and fixing my grammar mistakes, and thanks to Mary Tobin for keeping track of everything between all of us so we could get this project completed. I just want the reader to know that this team did a wonderful job catching many problems, so any errors that you may still find in this book are undoubtedly mine.

To the entire SharePoint team at Microsoft, thanks for continuing the feature expansion of such a tremendously powerful and solid development platform like SharePoint. Keep the vision. It brings together the best of the Internet with the best of Microsoft Office in a way that boosts productivity to astronomical heights. It is truly an 'office' game-changer.

To my everyday SharePoint Team of the last three years, special thanks to Mike Healey for helping all of us understand web parts, workflows and general SharePoint administration tasks. A big thanks to Suyin Ferro Rams for all the work you have done to develop applications that we can deploy through SharePoint. Thanks also to Serena Wright for guiding us as our unofficial project manager through the last three years of successfully deploying hundreds of Internet and intranet sites, and over 170 branded school sites. Finally thanks to Robert Curran, our Applications Director, who believed in our ability to succeed during the last three years as we built all of our district's sites and supported our 'One Portal – One View' vision originally proposed by Charles Thompson. As you know Robert, we are not done yet.

I also want to give a shout out of thanks to Andy Warren of End-to-End Training in Orlando, FL for getting me out of the office and involved in the original SQL Saturday (yes, my other passion is SQL Server), an activity that has led to other speaking opportunities.

A huge Thank You has to go to my wife Susan for understanding that writing a book takes a lot of time away from other things, not just for a few days, but for months. Moreover, thank you God above for making all of this possible and for giving me my wife and daughter without whom all of this would have little meaning.

Then there are the uncountable seminars, webinars, newsletters, white papers, blogs, books, and other information sites I have read over the last three years on SharePoint, Office, and SQL Server.

Finally, thanks to all the production people at Apress for their parts in making this book not only happen, but also look so good. You make the process easy.

Introduction

Since the release of SharePoint 2007, the popularity of SharePoint has grown each year. With the new release of SharePoint 2010, Microsoft has further expanded the feature set. Some of the improvements include changing the way you connect to external data sources, adding the ability to display Visio diagrams directly in the browser, publishing Access applications to a web site and more. Visually, they have made editing the content of your pages more like working in Office with the addition of the ribbon interface. It is my belief that SharePoint is the biggest change to the way you and I work in our offices since … well … since Microsoft Office. Word showed us how to write and edit more efficiently on a computer screen than we ever could with a typewriter.

Over the years, Microsoft Office has become so pervasive that it is almost impossible to get an office job today if you do not have a firm understanding of at least Microsoft Word and Microsoft Excel. Perhaps now it is time to add SharePoint to that list of job requirements. SharePoint can help organize where you save your documents as well as how you archive them into Records Centers to preserve them. Sharing documents and other files with coworkers insures that there is only a single version of the truth. The need to print documents to send them to others is all but eliminated through the ability to create and use collaboration sites and SharePoint Workspaces. Creating applications quickly and with minimal programming has been enhanced with the ability to publish Access applications in SharePoint so that anyone with a browser can access and interact with them. The new Business Connectivity Services lets you gather data from many data sources creating a single view of the information important to you and your coworkers. Of course, you can still create your corporate web sites and even internal employee intranet sites using the same tools and methodologies you learn while working with your collaboration sites.

We have all heard of that utopia of a paperless society where information flows at the speed of light from its point of creation to each user who must review, approve, and use it. However, the electronic revolution of the 1990s and 2000s did not free us from paper. Perhaps the Internet was not the solution, although it was an enabling technology that made our vision of the office of the future possible. As a result, the rising tide of paper on most information workers' desks seems to have gotten bigger. Perhaps the tools of the last two decades were just not ready. Perhaps we were simply missing that keystone software tool that brings it all together into a compelling argument.

Is SharePoint that tool? I believe that it can be the enabler that brings our dream of a paperless society into reality.

Oh, you say you have heard of SharePoint, but thought that it was just a portal for a company's web site. Yes, it is that, but that is only one part of this many-faceted tool.

SharePoint sits on top of the many technologies. It borrows a lot from web development. However, it also integrates tightly into the Microsoft Office products, giving them the ability to accomplish goals like the following:

- Create shared document libraries that users can access from anywhere they can get an Internet connection or to work on those documents offline and then synchronize their changes with the document library the next time they connect to their corporate intranet.

- Present electronic forms that people interactively complete, rather than forcing them to download and print the form, write on it, send it back, and then have someone enter the data into a computer program interface.

- Store multiple versions of documents so a revision history can be retained or to archive a copy of a document into your company's permanent records archival center.

- Display business information in Excel-style pages, dashboards and Key Performance Indicator (KPI) lists that change interactively to help managers make better decisions.

- Use agile application development with Microsoft Access to meet the needs of various departments and groups within your corporate environment and deploy that application to run on the user's browser so they can truly access it anywhere. By deploying through Access Services on SharePoint, these applications are secure, backed up, and easily maintained, since they only have a single source for the data, the forms, and the reports.

In the last three years, a large number of IT people worldwide started using SharePoint. They are creating web sites and collaboration sites by the thousands every day. And that is good. However, SharePoint will not reach its full potential until every computer user who knows how to use Microsoft Office can also use SharePoint together with their favorite Office application, such as MS Word, Outlook MS Excel, or MS Access.

This does not mean you need to know how to install SharePoint or even how to configure it (although understanding a little of the configuration would not hurt). However, it does mean that you need to know how to create and use libraries, lists, and many other features. It means that you need to learn how to use Office tools like Word, Outlook, Excel, and Access to not only create and maintain your own files on a SharePoint site, but also to store files on a centralized server at your company that you can access from anywhere you can get an Internet connection. It should no longer make a difference whether you are connecting through your home computer or using your laptop and wireless connection at a resort while on vacation. You could even be at your local library using its public computers. Perhaps you will even access your information from your cell phone or tablet computer. Anywhere. Any time. The dream of connecting to your corporate data exists today and is only a connection away.

However, there is more than just accessing your files. You can share your files easily with your colleagues or even the project consultant who works in a different city. Let's create workflows without resorting to programming so that, when you create a document, you can automatically send it to someone else for review or approval. Let's see how to consolidate lists, calendars, and tasks from multiple sources. Let's discover how to create forms for others to use directly from their browser. But most of all, let's see how you can become more productive and efficient using your favorite Microsoft Office tools together with SharePoint, without needing to spend months learning how to program first.

The revolution in the way you will work in an office began three years ago with SharePoint 2007. Are you ready? You already know how to use the basic Microsoft Office tools. Now, let me show you how to leverage those tools to enhance your productivity and free you from that paper avalanche hanging off the side of your desk.

Who This Book Is For

This book is for those of you who have been using Microsoft Office perhaps for years to get your daily work done and now are looking for ways to share your work with your coworkers and to collaborate with them. You may not really want to learn programming. You would rather leave that for others. However, you are willing to use the tools and features that programmers make available to you if it makes your job easier or helps you get your work done quicker. Sure, maybe with some programming skills and some time (perhaps a lot of time), you could make SharePoint do many other things that it just cannot do out of the box. If that is your goal, there are many other excellent books on the market that will take you down that road. However, for now you just need to get the most out of your Microsoft Office tools as quickly as possible. Are you one of those people willing to learn a new tool if it makes your job easier, faster, and perhaps even fun? If that describes you, then you are (or can become) a power user of Microsoft Office. You can become that indispensable person in your office that other people come to when they need to do something in Office and SharePoint but don't quite know how to begin.

With the release of both a new Microsoft Office 2010 suite and SharePoint Server 2010, this could be your best time to take that next step in productivity at your office. You can lead the way to increased collaboration between project and department staff members, build the content for your company intranet and Internet sites, and go green by reducing the use of paper in your office by using electronic forms redirected with workflows. Perhaps you dream of a day when you will not need a single sheet of paper on your desktop to get your work done. Perhaps your dream is to enable your coworkers to collaborate from anywhere around the world. Perhaps you dream of a day when you can work from home without having to commute hours each week to and from your office or burn more of our precious oil sitting in traffic jams. If this sounds like I am describing you, then this book is your starting point toward that future.

Contacting the Author

You can contact the author by email at mike@micmin.org. I will be establishing a blog, at www.micmin.org/blog.aspx, to go along with this book; there from time to time I will post additional tips and tricks related to collaboration between Microsoft Office and SharePoint 2010.

CHAPTER 1

■■■

An Overview of SharePoint

This book first went on sale as Microsoft introduced SharePoint 2010, a remarkable follow-up to the highly successful SharePoint 2007 product. It is hard to believe that it was only three years ago that SharePoint 2007 debuted as enterprise-level application solution for organizations deploying various combinations of internet, intranet, and extranet sites. It was so successful that Gartner placed SharePoint 2007 in its 2008 leader's quadrant for Horizontal Portal Products, Enterprise Content Management, and Information Access Technology. By heavily leveraging Microsoft's Office family products, the SharePoint environment allows teams to work together and collaborate even when separated across the country or the globe.

SharePoint 2010 continues in that fine tradition by enhancing its collaboration features. Throughout the latest release of this product, you will find many improvements over 2007; some little items, others fairly major. Together these improvements make SharePoint 2010 your platform of choice for deploying any web-based information or applications web site for your company or customers.

There are many opportunities to exploit SharePoint's features. For some, you need a fair amount of programming expertise. However, for power users of Microsoft Office, you can easily manipulate many of the features directly through the interface with little to no coding experience. In this book, I will focus on helping you extract the most benefit from SharePoint using familiar Microsoft Office tools such as Outlook, Word, Excel, PowerPoint, and Access. I will also help you explore some of the lesser-known tools such as InfoPath to build and deploy forms, Groove (renamed SharePoint Workspace) to create custom local collaboration groups that integrate with SharePoint, and SharePoint Designer for those who may want to do a little custom branding or create their own custom page layouts. Overall, this book concentrates on collaboration-type activities as opposed to Internet site development. However, many of the same techniques used in collaboration sites apply just as well when working with web pages, web parts, libraries, and lists.

In this chapter, you will first discover the basic hierarchy consisting of site collections and sites used in SharePoint site development. Think of it as creating the framework of a new building. Next, you will see how to build out that framework with pages, libraries, lists, and more. You will also learn how to set permissions for users and how to define and inherit permissions from one site to another. You will gain an understanding of how permissions affect what a user can do within a site, from creating new content to just viewing someone else's content. Next, you will build a document library and learn how to use Microsoft Word to add and edit documents stored in that library. Then I will show you how to preserve the integrity of your editing with the Check Out and Check In facility for documents. Finally, you will explore the use of versioning to keep track of changes and to control what information others can view.

Subsequent chapters explore SharePoint's other features, from lists through web pages, but in all cases, you will discover how to integrate your current knowledge of Microsoft Office tools with your SharePoint activities. My goal is not to make you a SharePoint administrator or even a SharePoint programmer; rather, my goal is to make you a power user when it comes to working with SharePoint and Microsoft Office.

For those of you who may have used Windows SharePoint Services 3.0 (WSS 3.0) for collaboration within your company, you may be pleased to know that WSS lives on but with a new name, SharePoint Foundation 2010. Although I will not single out features of SharePoint Foundation 2010, much of what I cover in collaboration applies to that product as well. In fact, Microsoft is currently expected to market at least several different versions of SharePoint 2010:

- SharePoint Server 2010: Intranet Scenarios
    - Enterprise Client Access License
    - Standard Client Access License
- SharePoint Server 2010: Internet/Extranet Scenarios
    - SharePoint Server 2010 for Internet Sites, Enterprise
    - SharePoint Server 2010 for Internet Sites, Standard
- FAST Search versions
    - FAST Search Server 2010 for SharePoint
    - FAST Search Server 2010 for Internet Business
- Entry Level/Pilot solutions
    - SharePoint Foundation 2010
    - SharePoint Online
    - SharePoint Online for Internet Sites

Site Collections, Sites, and Sub-sites

SharePoint organizes content around a container structure referred to as a site. In fact, when you first install SharePoint on a server it creates a site used to manage the entire *SharePoint farm* called Central Administration. However, other than your SharePoint administrator, most users typically never interact with Central Administration. A site can contain sub-sites and those sub-sites can contain additional sub-sites. The top-level site defines the overall site collection. You may begin your interaction at this top-level site or at one of the sub-sites in the site collection. A SharePoint installation can have multiple site collections. To support SharePoint, you may need more than a single server to support the database, indexing, searching, applications, etc. All of these servers together constitute a SharePoint farm.

SharePoint Farms

Some of you may have heard the term SharePoint farm and wondered what they were talking about. Surely, they don't grow SharePoint in the fields outside of Redmond, Washington. Rather, the SharePoint farm is a name given to the collection of all of the servers that make your SharePoint installation work. At its simplest, you could build a farm with a single server on which you have everything installed. Small companies may get along fine with a single server installation. However, as your site grows, you may find the need to move SQL Server to a separate physical server. Next, you might add separate web servers. Then, as your site continues to grow, you might need a separate server for searching or indexing your sites or perhaps a server to host other applications that you want to run from within SharePoint. As you can see, your server needs can grow from single machines to multiple machines sort of like... well... like weeds on a farm.

You create site collections only from within Central Administration. Your SharePoint administrator can create multiple site collections within what is called a web farm and may define different site collections for different purposes. All other SharePoint users typically cannot create their own site collection but must work within the one given to them from their SharePoint administrator. Therefore, I will not go into creation of site collections in detail in this book.

A site collection forms the container in which you build all sub-sites. Your organization may have one site collection or they may have many, perhaps one for each department or each division. However, no matter how many site collections you have, you build each of your other sites as sub-sites beneath one, and only one, of these site collections. Interestingly, the site collection must contain at least one site referred to as the *top-level site* of the site collection, and from within it, you can display pages, lists, and libraries. It is from within any site that you can build a sub-site, another container inside the larger container. This may remind you of nested Russian dolls, but that image is incomplete. Unlike nested Russian dolls, a site can have more than one sub-site directly beneath it. To that extent, the hierarchy is more like a family with each parent site having no children, one child, or multiple children. Figure 1-1 shows typical but very simple site hierarchy architecture in SharePoint.

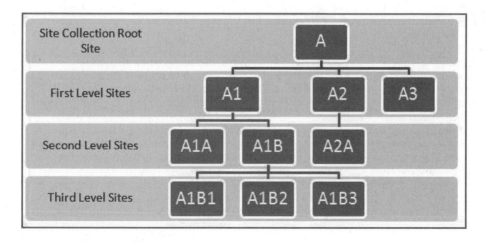

Figure 1-1. Site architecture

Another interesting thing about site collections is that each site collection can be stored within a separate database in SQL Server or you can combine multiple site collections within a single database. Storing each site collection in a separate content database makes it easy to back up and restore individual site collections. Storing multiple site collections in a single database means that there are fewer backup jobs for the DBA to manage. Using separate databases means that each database could reside on a different drive through partitioning. So is it best to place all of your site collections within a single SQL database or should you place each site collection in a separate database? The answer is not clearly one or the other. It is not that black or white. Rather it probably is a little of both. SharePoint administrators try to limit the number of site collections in each database depending on the amount of activity each site is going to get and its expected size. They do this for the following reasons:

- Improved performance within SharePoint may occur by grouping sites within one database that are read more often than updated.

- Data can be retrieved faster if you spread databases across multiple disk drives.

- Keep the number of site collections in some content databases small if the data updates frequently and the loss of data could be critical. This also makes backups and restores faster because each database is smaller.

- Special site collections created for shorter-term projects can be more easily archived and removed when they are no longer needed if you store them in their own site collection.

When considering which site collection should hold which site, you might be interested in grouping sites with similar user permissions together in one site collection so that you can manage the permissions at the top level of the site collection. You could then allow each sub-site to inherit the permissions of its parent. Only if a sub-site needs its own unique permissions would you need to break inheritance and define custom permissions.

So what goes into a site other than child sites? Each site you create supports groups of related pages, libraries, and lists. Think of this as your site's content that you can view using a web browser. In terms of content, a site typically focuses on specific topics, groups of people, or related activities. Each site has a home page, called its *default page*, which is the first page users see when going to the site. This default page usually provides navigation to the other pages in the site, either through menus or links. Each subsequent site page supports content ranging from lists to libraries to plain text and images. Once created, together they form what looks like a traditional web site.

SharePoint calls users who have the ability to change content within a site *content creators*. As a content creator within SharePoint, you have the authority to control the appearance and content of pages. No longer must you submit content changes to a web design person or web master and then wait for him to incorporate the changes into your organization's web pages. If you defined the site for collaboration, you may work with groups of people within your organization who also have permission to update lists, documents, and even content pages.

As mentioned previously, a site can have one or more *sub-sites*. While a sub-site inherits many of its properties from its parent site, you can also give it its own identity, properties, and objects. You use sub-sites to divide further the focus or topic of the higher-level site. For example, if one site represents a department, a sub-site might represent a project or a team within that department.

While you typically store all content for a site within that site, there is no reason why you cannot reference content from sub-sites. In fact, the top-level site (the first site at the root of the site collection) has several *special object collections*. One is called Site Collection Images and the other is Site Collection Documents. Both are libraries specifically designed to share files across any of the sub-sites within that site collection.

Perhaps you're thinking that creating a site from scratch sounds a little intimidating. Indeed, before SharePoint, the prospect of creating sites to support an entire organization would probably require a team of developers and months of time. However, SharePoint streamlines the process of building sites by providing a collection of *templates* for pages and for various object types that you can place on those pages to help get you started. Of course, as you progress in your SharePoint knowledge, you can add to these templates with your own or those from third-party developers. While this book focuses on collaboration sites, let's start with a quick overview of all the site types you can create out of the box with SharePoint. I'll begin with collaboration sites.

Site Collection Templates

SharePoint 2010 provides five types of site collection templates, as shown in Figure 1-2. Each template provides a unique starting point for creating a new site collection. However, just because each site collection template initially defines specific unique features and web parts, it does not limit your subsequent customization of the site. In fact, SharePoint allows you to customize a site created with one template with features and web parts found in another. You can even create your own custom templates starting from one of the supplied templates. So let's see what each site collaboration template type provides by beginning with the collaboration type templates.

Collaboration Templates

Collaboration templates help you create sites that support a high degree of interaction between the users who have access to those sites. In fact, most people who go to collaboration sites go there to add information or respond to existing information, not just to look at what is there. SharePoint 2010 provides six different templates that it classifies as collaboration style templates that it uses to create a top-level site in a new site collection. You can also use most of these as sub-sites. Figure 1-2 shows the available collaboration templates. Let's take a brief look at each of them.

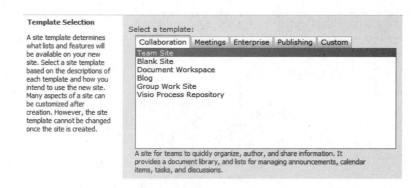

Figure 1-2. Collaboration templates

Team Site

A team site template serves as a fast, out-of-the-box starting point for content created by and for work teams. For that reason, it may become your favorite site template for building collaboration sites. It provides a common area for creating and sharing of information using document libraries and lists. It lets you establish project calendars, track individual and project tasks, and facilitate discussions among the team members.

Figure 1-3 shows the home page of a team site created by the SharePoint administrator to be the top-level site in a new site collection. I have made several additions to it so I can identify the different areas of the page that you need to become familiar with, as I will refer to them often throughout this book. As you begin work in this chapter, I will assume that your SharePoint administrator has created a team site for you to use in order to practice your new skills in this and subsequent chapters. If not, go ask for one now. I'll wait.

■ **Note** A team site created within SharePoint includes a My Site link in the My Profile drop-down menu of your user name found in the upper right of the screen. Your profile page then contains links to tags and notes that you may have created. It also contains links to your organization information, colleagues, and memberships. Of course, the amount of information stored in your profile page will depend on whether users at your organization choose to use the profile features. The **Site Actions** button appears on the upper left side of the screen for those users who have permission to use one or more of the options in the resulting drop-down menu. Users who can only view the site will not see this button. The following examples assume that you have the necessary permissions to edit site content. Anything described here that you cannot see on your site is probably due to permission settings, and you should ask your SharePoint administrator if you can get those rights at least within your practice site collection.

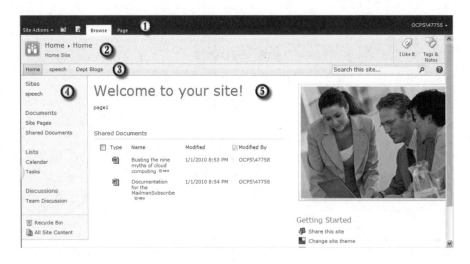

Figure 1-3. The major sections of a SharePoint page

1. The top banner of the site begins with the Site Actions drop-down menu on the left side. This menu only appears for users who have edit rights within the site. Next is the Navigate Up icon displayed as a folder with an up-pointing arrow. Clicking this option from any page shows the site hierarchy from the top-level site to the current page. You can click on any of the intermediate levels to navigate immediately to that level. The next icon looks like a page with a pencil on it; this is the Edit icon. This icon lets you edit the current page, assuming you have the necessary permissions. This icon also activates the Editing Tools for the page and opens the Format Text ribbon allowing you to immediately start making changes to text on the page. When in edit mode for the page, this icon changes to a Save link. Next is the word **Browse**, which represents the default display mode for the page. Clicking **Browse** while editing a page hides the ribbons but leaves the page in edit mode. Clicking the word **Page** opens the page in edit mode like the Edit icon but displays the Page ribbon, which includes various actions that you can perform against the page itself. Finally, on the far right of this banner SharePoint displays the name of the currently logged-in user. If you access the site anonymously, you will see the words Log In instead. Your user name serves as a drop-down menu that includes options that allow you go to your profile, change your settings, sign in as a different user, and even sign out of the site.

■ **Tip** The site developers in some organizations have multiple accounts representing different permission sets so that they can log in and view pages as other users would see them. For example, members of the IT department may have a second account that allows them to manage any site in the entire SharePoint farm.

---

2. The Title Area begins on the left with the site logo followed immediately by the name of the site and then by the name of the page. Beneath the site name, SharePoint displays the site description. On the right side of the title area, you will find several buttons depending on the options your SharePoint Administrator has turned on. The first one shown in this image allows you to add a suggested tag to the page, such as the one shown here that simply says that you like the page. If you want to tag the page with your own text string or if you would like to add a note to the page, click on the **Tags & Notes** button found on the far right. This button opens a dialog that has two tabs, one for tags and one for notes. You can add public and private tags on the first page. Tags typically consist of individual words or short phrases. Most people use tag words to identify related content. The page creator may then create a page with the new tag cloud web part, which displays the tag words in various sizes based on the frequency of their use. When a user clicks on a tag in the cloud, it displays a list of the pages where people entered those tag words so users can find related content. The second option of this button lets you create notes about the page. Notes differ from tags in that notes are more likely to consist of sentences or even paragraphs commenting on the page.

3. The Top Link Bar lists the sub-sites defined under the current site. When a user creates a new site, they have the option of whether to include the site in the top link bar of the parent site. They also have the option of whether to use the parent's top link bar or to begin a new top link bar beginning with the current site. Even though this removes the link to the parent site on the Top Link bar, the user can still return to the parent site by using the Navigate Up icon mentioned in the top banner. On the right side of the top link bar, you will find the Search and the Help buttons.

4. The Quick Launch area located along the left side of the page provides one-click access navigation to selected sites, documents, and lists. Depending on your permissions, you can customize what appears in this area and the Navigation Bar.

5. The Main Content area takes up the rest of the page. SharePoint divides this area into one or more content sections. You can add content in each area consisting of text libraries, lists, and other web parts to customize your page.

Blank Site

The blank site template is SharePoint's version of a blank sheet of paper. The person creating a site with this template must build the site's page content from scratch. Until you have developed some familiarity with the other built-in site templates and have experience customizing them with the available web parts, you may want to skip over the blank site. On the other hand, experienced site developers often prefer the blank site template because they do not have to waste time deleting or moving web parts and features that they do not want to use or that they want to appear elsewhere. Instead, they can focus on building what they do want.

Document Workspace

SharePoint provides a document workspace template designed around creating a place where a group can work collaboratively on a single document. It facilitates this through a document library along with task lists for to-do items and lists to track resources consisting of both people and things. These sites are generally temporary and when work is finished on the document, it is published to a document library on another site after which the site administrator or SharePoint Administrator deletes the workspace.

Blog

Blog sites generally exist for an individual or team to post major ideas or observations. Blog sites usually do not allow users to edit prior postings by others, but users can post comments to individual blog entries. Blog entries typically appear in reverse chronological order, making it easier for readers to see the most recent entries. Newsgroups, a close analogy to blogs, have a similar structure but typically post entries in a chronological hierarchy beginning with the initial entry.

Bloggers (blog site contributors) typically use blog sites to discuss their projects or favorite subjects, or to provide additional information or viewpoints on what they are working on or just about themselves. In fact, most of the people who created entries on newsgroups now use blog sites instead. In addition, many organizations use internal blog sites to document their work effort on projects by creating daily or weekly entries detailing the progress made since the last entry. For those *Star Trek* fans out there, you can think of a blog site as a written analogue to the Captain's Log. Maybe a future release will add voice-to-text translations for blogs.

Group Work Site

This template is another groupware alternative to allow teams to work together. It includes a group calendar to track schedules, circulation, phone-call memo lists, task lists, and a Document library.

Visio Process Repository

The Visio Process Repository template allows teams to view, share, and store Visio process diagrams. It provides, by default, a versioned document library for storing the Visio diagrams as well as lists to manage announcements, tasks, and discussions related to those diagrams.

Meeting Templates

Meeting templates comprise the second template type and provide predefined configurations that include specific web parts in the default site template to support tracking information related to meetings. SharePoint refers to these sites as *workspaces* rather than sites because they provide tools, web parts, and resources specifically oriented toward facilitating the activities of workgroups for a relatively short-term activity. Once that activity is complete, you can archive and delete the site. Meeting workspaces include lists and documents, links, and team member information.

While each meeting template has a unique combination of web parts that defines its character, always remember that you can customize the appearance of your meeting workspace to include web parts typically found in other templates. So let's look at the provided meeting templates as listed in Figure 1-4.

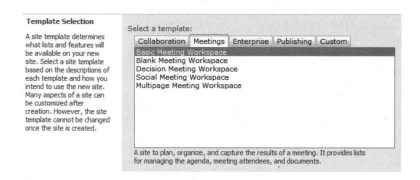

Figure 1-4. Meeting templates

Basic Meeting Workspace

Most meetings have common requirements to help members plan, conduct, and document them. Things like agendas, attendee lists, and libraries for documents reviewed in preparation for the meeting, during the meeting, or as follow-up to the meeting define a few of the important components of a basic meeting workspace.

Blank Meeting Workspace

The Blank Meeting workspace template, like its name implies, starts with no predefined pages containing specific web parts. This template best suits the experienced site designer who prefers to start with a clean site rather than spending time deleting web parts from a predefined template.

Decision Meeting Workspace

People call meetings for a variety of purposes. You might hold a meeting to brainstorm new ideas or plan the steps of a new project. You could hold informational meetings to update your staff about activities in other groups or departments. You might even call a meeting to evaluate lessons learned after a project ends. However, if your organization is anything like ours, you probably call many meetings just to make a decision.

This workspace template includes web parts to document objectives, agendas, and attendees. It includes a document library that holds documents relevant to the decision at hand. It also provides a means to create a task list prior to the meeting, document the decision, and follow up on assigned tasks.

Social Meeting Workspace

The Social Meeting workspace includes features that help plan for special events such as company picnics, awards presentations, and conferences. This workspace includes discussion boards, picture libraries, directions to the event, and lists of things to bring.

Multipage Meeting Workspace

This template includes many of the features found in a basic meeting workspace but is organized over multiple pages. Of course, the other workspace templates permit the addition of more pages as well, but you may like to start with the preconfigured pages in this template.

Enterprise Site Types

As the name implies, the Enterprise Site Types only become available with the enterprise version of SharePoint 2010. I will touch on some of these later, but for now let's preview what templates SharePoint 2010 adds for the enterprise user. Figure 1-5 shows the enterprise templates.

Figure 1-5. Enterprise templates

Document Center

The Document Center template allows you to manage documents from a central location for organizations with a large volume of content and/or a large number of documents.

Records Center

The Records Center template supports records routing and can track and route records based on rules you define. It can hold records based on a date or approval status, store records with incomplete information separately so you can address them manually, and separately store records that do not match any existing routing rules. Unlike content added to most other SharePoint sites, you cannot edit records after you add them to the records center repository.

Records Centers

Most organizations have a Records Center—a central repository where documents are sent for long-term storage. They typically retain these documents for legal or tax reasons for a specified number of years.

Users do not create records in a Records Center. They create records in document libraries or other sites. Once they no longer actively need those documents, they send them to the Records Center to be stored and managed until they are destroyed. Typically, your organization's legal department exercises some level of control over the operation of the Records Center and the rules used for retaining records.

Business Intelligence Center

The Business Intelligence Center is a site to display data in the form of BI reports, scorecards, dashboards, data connections, status lists, status indicators, etc. It is a good starting site for displaying Excel Services Workbooks and for performing analysis of data from multiple sources, creating visual charts of data, and displaying dashboards. Many organizations will find the Business Intelligence Center a useful way to build sites for management to review the status of projects.

Enterprise Search Center

The Enterprise Search Center site template creates search pages. By default, the Welcome page contains two tabs to identify different types of searches. The first is a general search. The second tab allows you to search for information about people. In addition, you can add more tabs to focus on other search criteria, search scopes, or result types.

My Site Host

You can only use the My Site Host template from the Central Administration area because it creates a container to host all other personal sites. Furthermore, you should only use this template once for each User Profile Service Application. In other words, if you get all your user information from one source like Active Directory, you need only provision this site once. On the other hand, if you use Active Directory for your employees, but perhaps another tool for extranet users, you should create two top-level host sites.

Once you create the My Site container, individual users can create their own My Site homepage (from their name drop-down) to track newsfeeds of interest to them, create content pages and libraries for their personal documents, and perhaps create their own personal blog of their work activities. Of course, one of the key advantages of storing their personal files in their My Site library is that, unlike their local hard drive, their My Site is backed up regularly.

Basic Search Center

The Basic Search Center template creates the necessary pages for general search results and advanced searches. You can easily customize this site with little to no code to provide a good search experience for users. Common features that you might change range from the basic look and feel of the search page to the number of results returned to the users from a search.

FAST Search Center

The FAST Search Center template is another one that is only available from Central Administration and is similar to Enterprise Search Center. FAST (Fast Search & Transfer) Search adds several capabilities to the standard SharePoint search including document preview that shows thumbnails of Word and PowerPoint documents right in the search results. Fast also lets you rerun the search based on a selected search result item to find similar items; it can automatically eliminate duplicate results of the same item found in different locations. Deep Results refinement lets you surface results that you might not otherwise see and you can sort on managed properties such as author and document size. The refinement options found on the left side of the results page provide drill-down capability filtered on the refinement and the general search results. Users of FAST Search can also subscribe to an RSS feed of the search results and create an alert to rerun the query at predefined intervals that can notify the user of changes in the results.

Publishing Sites (only available from Central Administration)

SharePoint 2010 adds two special site collection types that you can only create from Central Administration, shown in Figure 1-6, related to publishing content: Publishing Portal and Enterprise Wiki. Organizations use these site templates to create internet or intranet sites either for the entire organization or for specific groups within the organization. They support features such as the page editing toolbar, content editor, and several web parts specific to creating internet and intranet portals. While this book does not focus on creating web portals, it may be useful to know what publishing sites offer in case you need to use them.

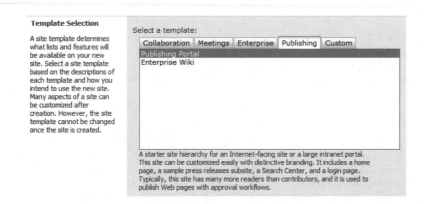

Figure 1-6. Publishing templates

Publishing Portal

The Publishing Portal's focus is as a starting point for a hierarchy of Internet-facing sites and pages. You can also use it to organize an intranet portal for use by your employees. Publishing sites typically have more readers than creators, unlike collaboration sites where the creators are the readers. Also unlike collaboration sites, you typically publish content here subject to approval before others can see it. Often SharePoint developers customize the look and feel of sites to establish a branding via themes, custom master pages, and CSS files. Organizations often use the Publishing Portal template to publish information that they want the public to see.

Enterprise Wiki

Wiki means *quick* or *fast* in Hawaiian, and therefore the Enterprise Wiki site template provides a quick way to share and discuss information. The users with content creation rights in these sites can easily edit the content and link new pages using keywords in the topic text. Wiki sites generally consist of a set of collaborative web pages to which users can easily contribute content. Links between the pages of a wiki site allow readers to branch from the main topic to related topics as they appear in the text as hyperlinks. For example, you might use a wiki to publish tricks and tips for various applications within your organization. Links might refer to similar tricks described on other pages. You can also use pages to present definitions for technical terms your organization uses, organizational information, project definitions, and additional useful pieces of information.

■ **Note** Typically, only your SharePoint Farm Administrator has the permissions necessary to create top-level site publishing templates described here.

Other Site Templates

You can use most of the site collection templates examined in the last section not only as the top-level site in a site collection, but also to define a sub-site. The exceptions to this dual use include:

- Business Intelligence Center

- My Site Host

- Publishing Portal

However, SharePoint provides additional site templates that may only appear as sub-sites depending on the type of site collection from which you begin. As you will see later, you can create sub-sites beneath any top-level site of a site collection (assuming you have site creation permissions). Figure 1-7 shows the site creation screen and some of the possible site templates available.

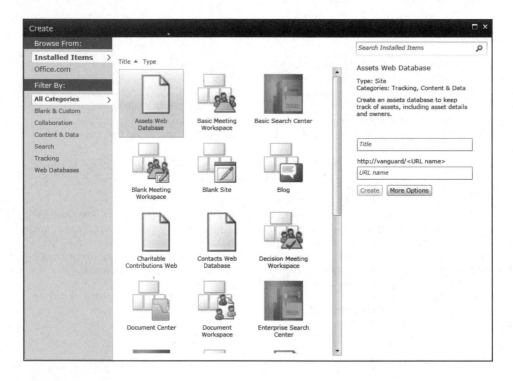

Figure 1-7. Publishing templates

If you do not have Silverlight running with your browser, your experience on this screen and many others will be different. Figure 1-8 shows a tabbed version of the **Create** page with the recommendation to install Silverlight to improve the user experience.

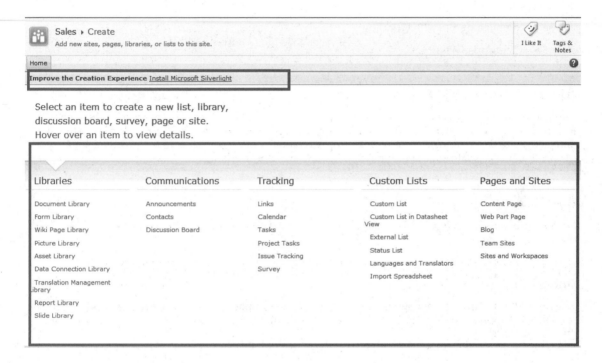

Figure 1-8. Publishing templates

For now, note that SharePoint categorizes sites differently when you create a sub-site under a top-level site or another site as compared with the organization of templates when creating a top-level site for a new site collection from within Central Administration. In fact, Figure 1-7 shows the user experience from a computer with Silverlight installed. If you have a computer that does not have Silverlight, your experience (and many other screens throughout SharePoint) will appear more like their SharePoint 2007 versions using tabs (like Figure 1-8). For the purpose of all images in this book, I will assume a machine with Silverlight installed. Note that with Silverlight, instead of a tabbed window, you can select these categories from the heading **Filter By** option in the left column of the figure. Also note that you can use many of these templates to create a top-level site in a new site collection. Some of the new templates that you can use when creating a sub-site include:

- Assets Web Database

- Charitable Contributions Web

- Contacts Web Database

- Issues Web Database

- Personalization Site
- Projects Web Database
- Publishing Site
- Publishing Site with Workflow
- Enterprise Wiki

Applications Site Types

Application site types are a new addition to SharePoint 2010. SharePoint provides several built-in but fully functional examples of how to build an application type site based on a Microsoft Access database and using Access Services. At the time of writing, five applications are included. That could change by the product release date or as additional applications become available.

Assets Web Database

You can use the Assets Web Database site template to create a sub-site to track assets, their details, their owners, and more.

Charitable Contributions

The Charitable Contributions application is another Access application running within SharePoint that tracks information about fundraising campaigns. It lets you track donations by contributor, campaign events, and tasks.

Contacts Web Database

The Contacts Web Database application lets you manage information about people. This can represent people in a team, a project, or company. You can track who each person works with and identify customers and partners.

Issues Web Database

The Issues Web Database application template provides a ready-to-use site that uses an Access application within SharePoint to track and report on software development bugs and issues. As with the other applications, SharePoint displays the Access forms and reports from this application directly within the SharePoint page.

Projects Web Database

While SharePoint 2007 provided lists to track tasks within individual projects, it was difficult to track multiple projects. The Projects Web Database application lets you not only track the tasks for multiple projects, but also to assign those tasks to individuals.

Additional Site Templates

SharePoint provides a few additional site templates that are not applications using Access. You can use two of these site templates within a top-level site created with the Publishing Portal site collection template. The third site template, the Personalization site, is optimized to work under the My Site Host site collection.

Personalization Site

The Personalization Site template allows users to create custom views of available site information. Users of a personalized site can define navigation to pages important to them, bypassing the navigation of the main site to which it belongs.

Publishing Site

SharePoint designed Publishing Sites specifically to display basic content on web pages. Developers of internet or intranet sites often use the Publishing Site template as a starting point. However, you can include document and image libraries as well as lists and other web part objects.

Publishing Site with Workflow

SharePoint bases the Publishing Site with Workflow template on the Publishing Site template but adds the ability to include workflows. Workflows might require documents to have approval before making them available for the general user to view.

Lists and Library Types

One of the most basic objects that you can add to most sites is a library. Libraries store documents, images, reports, and other objects. Some libraries serve as a general collection point for different types of documents. On the other hand, you can create other libraries for very specific purposes with only particular file types allowed. Thus, the type of library you need depends on what type of information you want to store in the library. Let's examine a few of the basic library types found in a typical collaboration site, as shown in Figure 1-9.

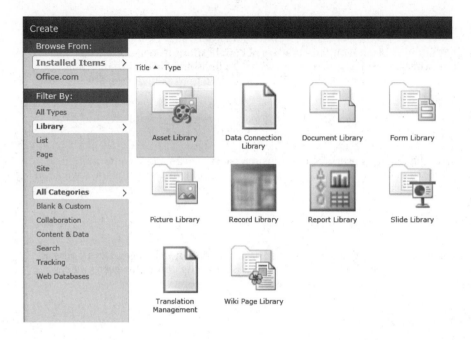

Figure 1-9. Library templates

Asset Library

The Asset Library is a new library type that provides a place to store, share, and manage many rich media assets from images to audio and video files. With SharePoint 2010's support of streaming videos, the Asset Library provides a better library type to store media files.

Data Connection Library

If you need to work with external data sources, meaning data outside of a SharePoint list, you need to create data connections to those data sources. With the new Business Connectivity Services (BCS), your data connections can both read and write data to an external data source. I will return to look at creating, storing and using data connections in several of the later chapters, including the chapters on InfoPath and Access.

Document Library

The Document Library is the most common library type. It can hold practically any file type normally found on your computer's hard disk. A document library, like a disk directory, can stores various file types with little or no relationship to each other. However, good file management applies as much to SharePoint libraries as it does to your hard disk. Just as you might create different directories for different types of files, projects, or applications, you should consider creating and managing multiple document libraries so all files in one document library have a common focus, perhaps even a common type. Of course, you can use metadata columns and filtered views to display different subsets of a document library's files and avoid the use of multiple libraries and even folders within the libraries. Chapter 4 covers more details on using document libraries.

Form Library

The Form Library stores the XML source documents for forms created with Microsoft Office InfoPath. Users with InfoPath installed on their local computer can store form definitions in any document library, but then publish them as templates to form libraries. I cover working with InfoPath and Form Libraries in more detail in Chapters 9 and 10.

Picture Library

The Picture Library provides a common place to store images used in content pages on your site. You might also use a picture library to store images or photographs for your sales or marketing staff to help them provide a consistent message. Picture libraries also provide a storage location for pictures used in web pages. By default, some site templates, such as the publishing templates, create a library called Images specifically for images used on web pages. In addition, the top-level site in a site collection creates a library called Site Collection Images. Chapter 12 covers more details about the picture library.

Report Library (SharePoint 2010 Enterprise Edition only)

The Report Library stores web pages and documents that work with web parts to track metrics, goals, and business intelligence information. Chapter 8 examines the Report Library in detail.

Record Library

The Record library is essentially a document library, but focused on storing important business information that you must often retain for legal and/or tax reasons. You will return to this library in Chapter 12 when I talk about creating a Record Center.

Slide Library

SharePoint provides the Slide Library to work specifically with Microsoft PowerPoint for the storing of individual slides. Chapter 12 explores the Slide Library in detail.

Translation Management Library (SharePoint 2010 Enterprise Edition only)

You will find the Translation Management library only in the enterprise edition of SharePoint 2010, where advanced site designers use it to manage translation workflows. A translation management workflow manages the process of routing a document to designated translators read from a Language and Translators list. The workflow notifies each translator for the document of the task. As each translator finishes the translation of their copy of the document, they can mark their part of the workflow as complete. The entire workflow is not complete until all translators for the document have finished their translations.

Wiki Page Library

The previous section briefly mentioned wiki sites and defined them as a forum for users to add their own linkable content on individual topics. Therefore, it should come as no surprise that wiki sites need a special type of library to support user collaboration. SharePoint uses the Wiki Page Library as the storage container to hold wiki page content.

These are not the only libraries that SharePoint supports. However, if you learn how to work with at least these libraries, you can work with any other libraries you may find on your SharePoint installation.

Permissions and Groups

When you, as SharePoint administrator, set up a top-level site, you need to determine who can view, edit, and design pages and content on the site. You may have a very simple site that everyone can view, or you may want to limit your site to only the people in your company, your department, or your project. You also need to decide who can contribute content to your site, who can make design change, and who can approve content for publishing sites before making it visible to the public. At first, you may think that you can do this on a person-by-person basis, but for most sites, you typically have groups of people to whom you want to assign the same rights. In fact, after careful analysis, you may only have a small number of groups that require unique rights. For that reason, SharePoint allows you to associate users together in groups and then assign permission levels to those groups. Then, when you need to assign permissions to a new user, you can simply determine in which group they should belong and assign them to that group to define their permissions automatically.

One of the first groups you will probably encounter is the site owner group. When you create a new site collection, you can associate up to two site collection administrators to it. Although you can get by with one site collection administrator, I always recommend a backup. For the top-level site of the site collection, these two administrators automatically receive owner rights. In a similar fashion, anyone who has the permission to create new sites automatically becomes an owner for any sites they create. Site owners can then add other users and groups to the site, customize or delete items within a site, and create and delete additional sub-sites under the current site. Therefore, if you, as SharePoint administrator, have turned on the My Sites functionality of SharePoint, each user is the owner of at least one site, their personal My Site.

Note that you, as SharePoint administrator, also determine whether the sites allow anonymous access as long as you enable anonymous access at the web application level. Then the site creator for every site created below the top-level site can enable or disable anonymous access as long as she enables anonymous access for its parent site.

■ **Note** Before the site collection administrator can turn on or off anonymous access to a site, the SharePoint Farm administrator must go into Central Administration and turn anonymous access on for the web application. This is done by going through the **Authentication Providers** option of the **Security** settings and selecting the **default** zone. On the resulting authentication property page, she can set the type of authentication (Windows, Form, or Web Single Sign On) and enable anonymous access, among other things.

The person who creates a site, even a top-level site, automatically becomes an owner of that site. The site owners have the permissions needed to add additional users to one or more of the site groups or create their own new groups with custom permissions. New sites begin with either the permission groups from their parent site if the site inherits its permissions during creation or a default of three groups when you create a site with unique permissions. A top-level site also begins with these three default groups as described below. Notice that each group name begins with the site name.

<Site Name> Visitors

This group defines the lowest default security group, and SharePoint associates it with the Read permission level, which allows the group members to only view pages and items. They cannot contribute content. They may have the ability to create a Self-Service Site if the SharePoint administrator activates that feature. They serve as an administrator in these sites only. For every other site, the Read permission level grants the following individual permissions:

- View Items: View list items including documents in libraries.

- Open Items: View document source with server-side file handles.

- View Versions: View past versions of list and document items.

- Create Alerts: Create alerts for changes to lists and libraries.

- View Application Pages: View forms, views, and application pages.

- Use Self-Service Site Creation: Create a web site using Self-Service Site Creation (your SharePoint Administrator may have turned this permission off depending on your company policies).

- View Pages: View pages in a web site.

- Browse User Information: View information about site users.

- Use Remote Interfaces: Use SOAP, Web DAV, the Client Object Model and SharePoint Designer to access this web site (your SharePoint Administrator may have turned this permission off depending on your company policies).

- Use Client Integration Features: Use features that launch client applications.

- Open: Allow users to open a web site, list, or folder to access items within it.

While your SharePoint administrator typically handles the creation of permission levels and security groups, you might be interested to know that SharePoint supports 32 different individual permissions, which you can combine in various ways into permission levels. The default Read permission level includes only the permissions previously listed.

<Site Name> Members

SharePoint associates this group with the predefined permission level: **Contribute**. Compared to the Visitors group, this permission level has additional rights to add, edit, and delete items to lists and libraries, including page libraries. Users in this group can work with web parts and create content. However, they may or may not be able to create new lists or libraries depending on how the SharePoint administrator defined the permission to manage lists, which, by default, SharePoint does not grant. In addition, any content they create or update may require approval by a person with approval rights before others can see it. Members of this group typically cannot approve the content they create.

\<Site Name> Owners

SharePoint associates the **Owners** group with the **Full Control** permission level. By default, this permission level includes all 32 individual permissions and you cannot edit it. Users assigned to this group can view, add, update, delete, approve, and customize all aspects of the site. They also have the ability to add new users and groups, as well as assign permissions and create new sites. If you do not want to grant quite this much access, you must create your own custom permission level.

Should you decide not to include a new user in one of the predefined site groups, you can assign them to a permission level directly using the options in the **Grant Permission** section of the page shown in Figure 1-10. Initially, SharePoint defines several permission levels, of which three are directly associated with one of the site groups just discussed:

- Full Control: Users with this permission level share the same permissions as the Site Owners and have full access to all functionality of the site.

- Design: A designer can manage lists and libraries, create pages, and customize them. They may approve pages created by the Site Member group. They can also override Check Out locks on lists and library items created by contributors. They do not have the ability to add or manage users, create or delete sub-sites, manage alerts, or enumerate permissions.

- Contribute: Contributors can view, add, update, and delete content on the site including items and documents, but they cannot approve that content on sites that require approval. Therefore, visitors to the site cannot see their changes until someone with the permission to approve them does so.

- Read: Users with this group permission can view pages and list items just like members with the View permission, and they can also download documents.

- View Only: Users with this permission level can view pages, list items, and documents. Furthermore, if the document has a server-side file handler, they can view the document only through that file handler.

- Approve: Members of this group can edit and approve pages, list items, and documents created by others before publishing them.

- Manage Hierarchy: This group's members can create sites and edit pages, list items, and documents.

- Restricted Read: This group can read pages and documents, but cannot view historical versions or user permissions.

- Records Center Web Service Submitters: Use this group specifically with the Records Center site to grant permissions to users who need to submit content to the site via Web Services.

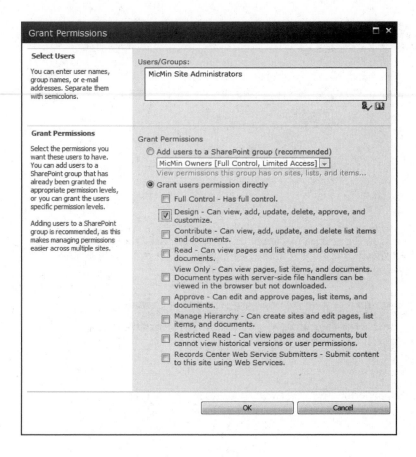

Figure 1-10. Permission options

In addition to the default groups, you can add other groups or edit the permissions of existing groups. For example, suppose you want to create a separate group that has almost all the permissions of a site owner, but you want to withhold the following permissions from this group:

- Approve Items

- Apply Themes and Borders

- Apply Style Sheets

To do this, open your site and click on the **Site Actions** drop-down menu on the upper left of the page. Then select **Site Settings**. From the **Site Settings** page, select **Site Permissions** found in the **Users and Permissions** group of the **Site Settings** page. Figure 1-11 shows this page.

Figure 1-11. Site Actions menu

The **Site Permissions** page shown in Figure 1-12 displays options to let you create new user groups; grant, edit, and remove permissions; define new permission levels; and set or reset the site collection administrators if you are in a top-level site. For now, your goal is to create a new group called Site Administrators that has a new permission level called Site Administrator.

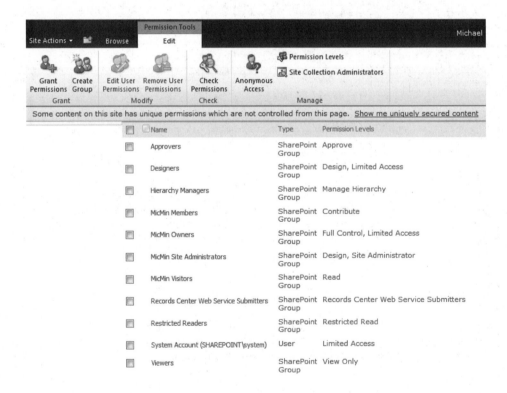

Figure 1-12. Selecting permission levels

■ **Note** If you are not in the top-level site of the site collection Figure 1-12 will appear somewhat different. If the site owner created the site by inheriting permissions, you must first click on the option **Stop Inheriting Permissions** that will appear in the **Inheritance** group.

SharePoint breaks down these options into five sections within the ribbon:

- Grant: This section includes options to create groups and grant initial permissions to a group.

- Modify: SharePoint enables the options in this section only after you select one or more of the user/groups in the list below the ribbon so that you can modify the permissions of that group. [This group only appears if you can edit the permissions.]

- Check: This option opens a separate window in which you must enter the name of the user or group you want to check. It then lists the permissions for the selected user or group and identifies whether they received permissions directly or through membership in another group.

- Manage: This section allows you to manage the permissions in any of the permission levels or to create your own. You may also be able to manage access requests and the site collection administrators for the site depending on your permissions. [This group only appears if you can edit the permissions.]

- Inheritance: This section will either let you Stop Inheriting Permissions or to Manage Parent permissions if the current sub-site inherits permissions from the parent site, or it will display a button to allow you to Inherit Permissions again from the parent if you previously broke inheritance. [This group only appears for sub-sites of the top-level site.]

Below the ribbon, you will see the groups currently defined for the site and their permission levels. You can change the permission level associated with the group by selecting the group using the check box to the immediate left of the group name and then clicking **Edit user permissions** in the **Modify** group of the ribbon. You can create new groups by clicking the **Create Group** option in the **Grant** section of the ribbon. You will return to this option to create a new group in a minute.

Before adding the new group Site Administrators, let's create the new permission level Site Administrator. You must create permission levels at the top-level site even if you only use them in one of the sub-sites. If you are not at the top-level site, when you click **Permission Levels** in the **Manage** group of the **Permission Tools** ribbon, you will not see a **Create** option. Rather, you will see in the left navigation a link to **Manage Permissions Levels on Parent Web Site**. To continue, you can click this link to return to the permission levels of the top-level site.

Next, to create a custom permission level, you have two choices: either change the permissions associated with an existing permission level or create a new permission level with your unique permissions. Then assign it to an existing or new site group. However, before you decide what to do, let's examine what permissions make up each permission level.

The **Permission Levels** page shown in Figure 1-13 displays the currently defined permission levels in the current site collection. Notice that you cannot access the **Full Control** and **Limited Access** permission levels. These levels must always exist, and their definitions cannot change. The Full Control level belongs to site owners and insures that these users always have full permissions over the site. The

Limited Access level belongs to site guests who only have limited access to specific lists or documents libraries, not the entire site.

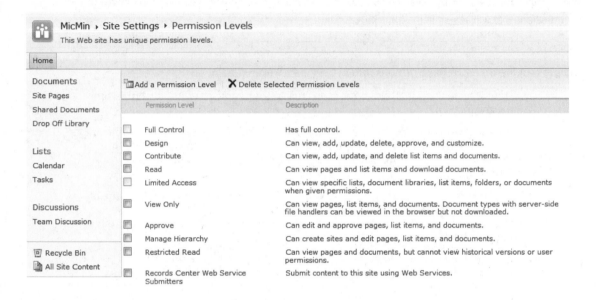

Figure 1-13. Reviewing permission levels

In your case, you want to add a new permission level called **Site Administrator**. Users with this permission will be able to do almost everything a site owner can do except approve pages and apply themes and styles. Begin by clicking the **Add a Permission Level** menu option near the top of the page to display the page shown in Figure 1-14. The first section asks you to provide a name and description for the new level. Then you can select from the possible permissions. SharePoint categorizes permissions into three major groups:

- List Permissions: Relates to list objects including libraries.

- Site Permissions: Relates to sites.

- Personal Permissions: Relates to personalization.

Note that in order to save space, the following image only displays the first portion of the **Add a Permission Level** page.

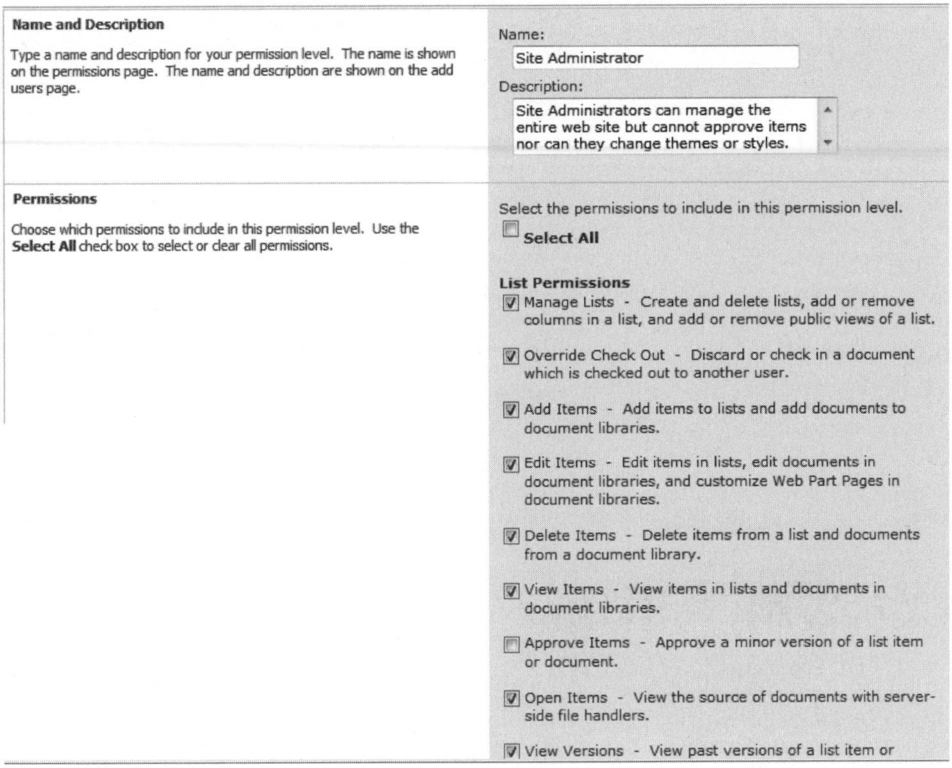

Name and Description

Type a name and description for your permission level. The name is shown on the permissions page. The name and description are shown on the add users page.

Name:

Site Administrator

Description:

Site Administrators can manage the entire web site but cannot approve items nor can they change themes or styles.

Permissions

Choose which permissions to include in this permission level. Use the **Select All** check box to select or clear all permissions.

Select the permissions to include in this permission level.

☐ **Select All**

List Permissions

☑ Manage Lists - Create and delete lists, add or remove columns in a list, and add or remove public views of a list.

☑ Override Check Out - Discard or check in a document which is checked out to another user.

☑ Add Items - Add items to lists and add documents to document libraries.

☑ Edit Items - Edit items in lists, edit documents in document libraries, and customize Web Part Pages in document libraries.

☑ Delete Items - Delete items from a list and documents from a document library.

☑ View Items - View items in lists and documents in document libraries.

☐ Approve Items - Approve a minor version of a list item or document.

☑ Open Items - View the source of documents with server-side file handlers.

☑ View Versions - View past versions of a list item or

Figure 1-14. Adding a permission level definition

Of course, you can select all permissions by either clicking each permission check box individually or by checking the **Select All** option. Then just deselect the permissions you do not want to grant for the current level definition. When satisfied with the permission settings selected for your new level, click **Create** to build the new permission level definition. Returning to the **Permission Levels** page, you now see the Site Administrator permission level as shown in Figure 1-15.

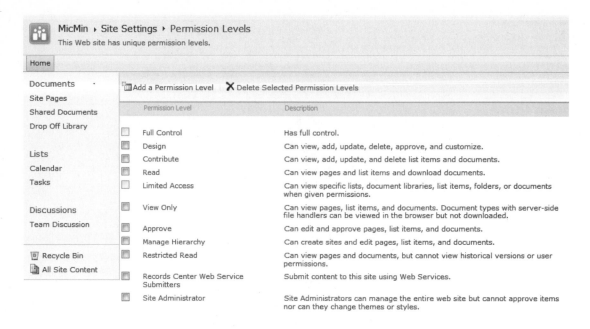

Figure 1-15. Your new permission level appears in the list.

At this point, you might go back to the Site Permissions page for your site and add a group specifically for Site Administrators using the **Create Group** option in the **Grant** section. On the **New Group** page, enter a group name `Site Administrators` along with a description. You will see other options that allow you to add an owner for the group (typically the site owner), change group settings, and handle membership requests. I will not detail these options here because your SharePoint administrator typically defines standards for most of these options for you. The important selection is the last one in which you can assign a permission level to this new group. Then finish creating the group by clicking the **Create** button at the bottom of the page, as shown in Figure 1-16.

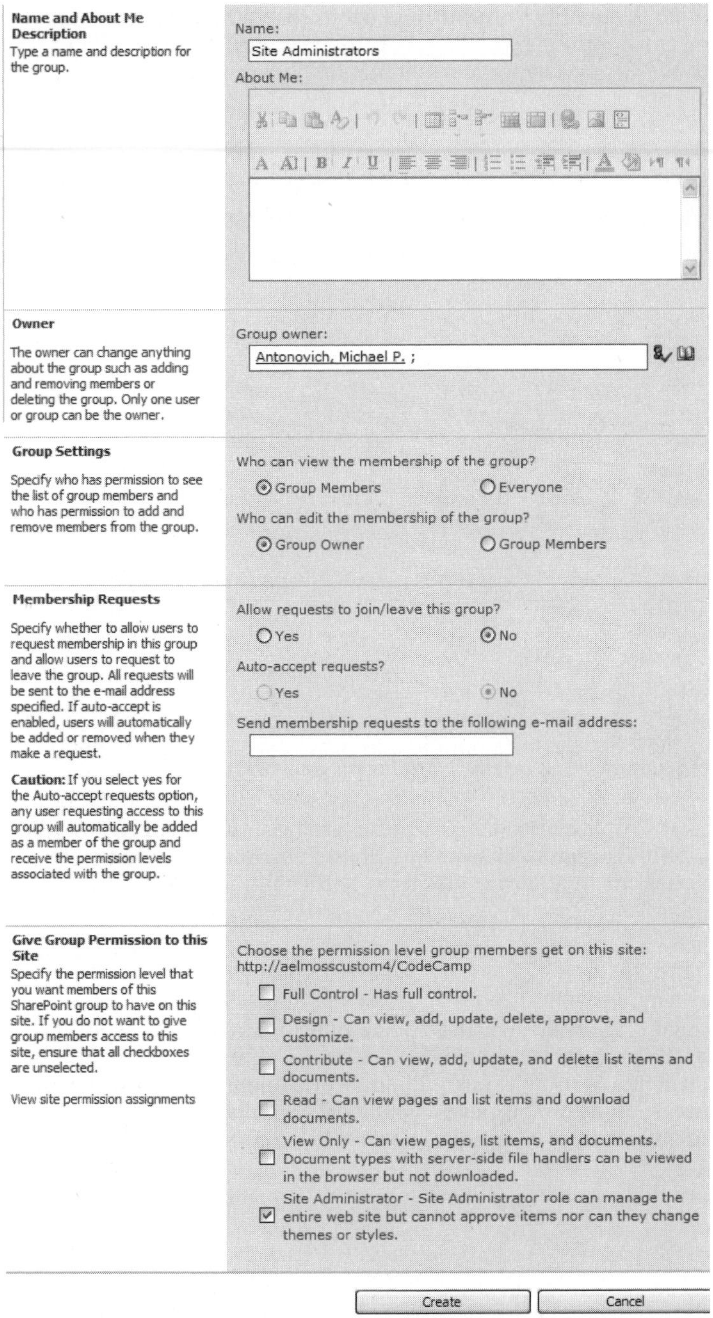

Name and About Me
Description
Type a name and description for
the group.

Name:

Site Administrators

About Me:

Owner

The owner can change anything
about the group such as adding
and removing members or
deleting the group. Only one user
or group can be the owner.

Group owner:

Antonovich, Michael P. ;

Group Settings

Specify who has permission to see
the list of group members and
who has permission to add and
remove members from the group.

Who can view the membership of the group?

⦿ Group Members   ◯ Everyone

Who can edit the membership of the group?

⦿ Group Owner   ◯ Group Members

Membership Requests

Specify whether to allow users to
request membership in this group
and allow users to request to
leave the group. All requests will
be sent to the e-mail address
specified. If auto-accept is
enabled, users will automatically
be added or removed when they
make a request.

Caution: If you select yes for
the Auto-accept requests option,
any user requesting access to this
group will automatically be added
as a member of the group and
receive the permission levels
associated with the group.

Allow requests to join/leave this group?

◯ Yes   ⦿ No

Auto-accept requests?

◯ Yes   ⦿ No

Send membership requests to the following e-mail address:

Give Group Permission to this
Site
Specify the permission level that
you want members of this
SharePoint group to have on this
site. If you do not want to give
group members access to this
site, ensure that all checkboxes
are unselected.

View site permission assignments

Choose the permission level group members get on this site:
http://aelmosscustom4/CodeCamp

☐ Full Control - Has full control.

☐ Design - Can view, add, update, delete, approve, and
customize.

☐ Contribute - Can view, add, update, and delete list items and
documents.

☐ Read - Can view pages and list items and download
documents.

☐ View Only - Can view pages, list items, and documents.
Document types with server-side file handlers can be viewed
in the browser but not downloaded.

☑ Site Administrator - Site Administrator role can manage the
entire web site but cannot approve items nor can they change
themes or styles.

[Create]   [Cancel]

Figure 1-16. Define the properties of your new group

After clicking **Create**, SharePoint finishes creating the group and opens the **People and Groups** page with the new group selected so you can continue by adding users to the group. Notice in Figure 1-17 that SharePoint automatically adds the **Group Owner** as a member of the new group.

■ **Tip** You can nest one group inside another group. This can be faster than removing users from one group and adding them to another. For those familiar with Active Directory, you can add Active Directory groups as users within a SharePoint group to associate all users in that Active Directory group with the permissions associated with the SharePoint group.

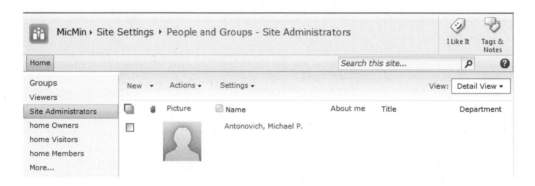

Figure 1-17. Your new group appears in the groups list on the left of People and Groups.

In summary, before adding users to a group, you need to determine what groups you need and what permissions those groups should have. Then you can work with your SharePoint administrator to create those groups with the right permissions and ensure that she adds users to the appropriate group.

Adding a Document Library

In most cases, when you first create a collaboration site, you get a default document library called **Shared Documents**. In a publishing site, SharePoint calls the default document library Documents but is essentially the same thing. However, you may want to create additional document libraries with their own names. In fact, just as you would use multiple directories on your local hard disk or your file server for different file types or projects, you might consider using multiple document libraries in SharePoint to organize your site's documents.

Why Do I Need More than one Document Library?

Document libraries can contain hundreds, even thousands, of documents. You can store different types of documents in a library, although the most common type will probably be Office documents such as Word, Excel, and PowerPoint files. However, you can also save text files, PDFs, and many other file types. You can group files by type in different folders. You can also group files by their creator in different folders. In fact, you can create folders for any criteria you might want. SharePoint 2010 also introduces the concept of Document Sets which you will learn more about in Chapter 4. Even if you don't use different folders, you can create different views of your document library to show only those documents in these groups by using a column in the library to filter the files. So why would you ever need to create more than one document library?

One of the best reasons I can offer for having more than one document library in a site occurs when different groups of people need different access rights to documents at different stages in the document's life. A good example is purchase orders. Suppose that anyone in the department can create a purchase order in the site's main shared documents library. However, once the department head signs the purchase order, you must move it to another document library where only the department head and perhaps the secretarial staff can still open and edit the document. In this new document library, the rest of the department only has view rights so that no one can modify an approved purchase order, yet the information is still accessible to everyone.

Another good reason for multiple libraries relates to defining different default document types (discussed in the next section) or content types (discussed in Chapter 10 in relation to InfoPath forms) in each library.

To create a new document library, click **View All Site Content** from the **Quick Launch** area of your collaboration site or from the **Site Actions** drop-down list if the **Quick Launch** area is not currently visible. The **All Site Content** page shows your current document libraries and lists. If someone has already created document libraries other than the **Shared Documents** library, you will see them here. Notice that you will see additional libraries to hold pages, forms, images and more in the **Document Libraries** section. Next, click the **Create** option at the top of the page to display the **Create** dialog shown in Figure 1-18.

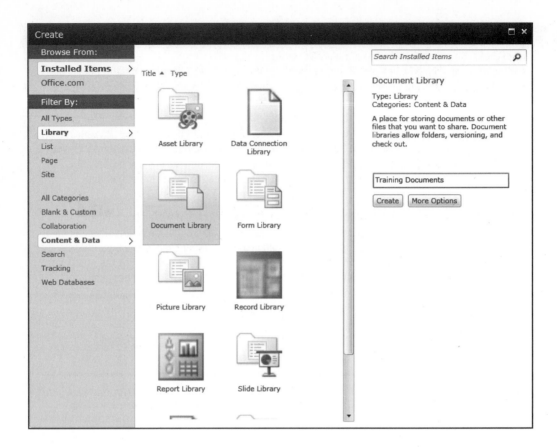

Figure 1-18. Adding a new document library

■ **Tip** You can also go directly to the Create page by clicking **More Options** from the **Site Actions** menu.

The **Create** dialog lets you create several different object types for your site. SharePoint divides these object types into four basic categories:

- Library
- List
- Page
- Site

Select the object type **Library** to display the available types of libraries you can create. With all the possible libraries displayed, you can narrow your choices by selecting a category. Figure 1-18 shows only those libraries that belong to the category **Content & Data**.

Locate and click the **Document Library** icon. The column on the right provides a short description of the library type selected and prompts you for the library name. You can use any character string as a name, but the name must be unique at least within the current site. There are additional options that you can select when defining a library. However, only the library name is mandatory. To specify the other options, click the **More Options** at the bottom of this right column.

Figure 1-19 shows the options you can define for your new document library. Besides specifying a name for your new library, you can provide a description for the library and define whether the library appears in the **Quick Launch** menu.

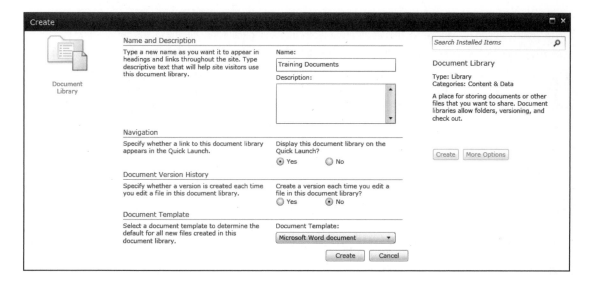

Figure 1-19. Defining document library properties

By default, new libraries do not support versions. In other words, when you make changes to documents in the library, the changes replace the previous copy stored in the library. This document mode uses the least amount of storage space, but it leaves you unable to retrieve a previous document version to compare changes or to revert back to a previous version should you accidentally delete a section of text and need to retrieve it. You will learn a little later how to fine-tune your version history to keep a limited number of prior versions, thus striking a balance between storage space and the ability to recover past versions.

The last option lets you select a default document template when creating a new document within SharePoint for this library. Each library can have only one default template, so you should select the most appropriate document template for the library. This template also defines the default content type for that library. While you can store multiple types of files within a document library, the default template defines the type of file SharePoint creates for you if you simply pressed the **New** button when displaying the library's contents.

After defining the options for your new library, click **Create** to build it. SharePoint opens the library after creating it. If you do not see one of the ribbons when the library's **All Documents** page displays, you are in what SharePoint calls **Browse** mode. You can return to this mode at any time by clicking the **Browse** tab. To open any of the other ribbons, click one of the other displayed tabs. In particular, you should see that under the tab **Library Tools**, there are two sub-tabs representing two separate ribbons. The **Documents** ribbon contains options to manage your documents such as creating new documents, uploading documents, editing documents, etc. The **Library** ribbon contains options to manage the way your new library appears on the screen including defining different views for the library, permissions, and defining additional columns, filters, and sort orders.

If you open the **Documents** ribbon, you can add documents to your library from your local or network drives by using the **Upload Document** option or you can create new documents using the default template defined when you created the library by using the **New Document** option from the **New** section of this ribbon.

■ **Tip** While you can upload documents of different types into a single library, you may consider creating a separate library for each major document type you need to store, especially if you define a custom template for your document library. There are several advantages to this. First, the user does not have to decide which content type to use; they just click **New Document**. Second, you don't have to define different views to support the different metadata that might be associated with different content types. I will cover this topic in later chapters when discussing metadata with libraries and multiple content types. For example, Chapter 10 discusses how you can publish multiple InfoPath forms as separate content types to a single library.

Knowing Your Document Templates

The Document Template section shown in Figure 1-19 allows you to define a default template to use when you create a new document directly from within the library. The default list of available templates on my computer includes the following document types:

- Microsoft Office Word 97–2003 document
- Microsoft Office Excel 97–2003 spreadsheet
- Microsoft Office PowerPoint 97–2003 presentation
- Microsoft Office Word document
- Microsoft Office Excel spreadsheet
- Microsoft Office PowerPoint presentation
- Microsoft Office OneNote section
- Microsoft Office SharePoint Designer Web page
- Basic page
- Web Part page

You might ask why this list includes some office products twice. The difference between the two Word templates is that the template named Microsoft Office Word document defaults to a Word 2007/2010 document style using the .docx format, whereas Microsoft Office Word 97-2003 defaults to the earlier .doc format. A similar difference accounts for the multiple Excel and PowerPoint entries.

Each of these predefined templates opens blank Office templates or web pages. However, your SharePoint administrator may have also preinstalled document templates. For example, a folder for expense reports may have a blank formatted expense report form created in Word or Excel. Just remember that this list of available templates does not limit what you can save within the library. They merely define a default document type when you create a new document from within the library.

Adding a Document to Your New Library

When most people start using SharePoint for collaboration, one of their first tasks is to create a document library to store files that they want to share with others. If you had your SharePoint administrator create a team site for you or if you created it yourself, you probably noticed that a **Shared Documents** library already exists in your site. This library appears under **Documents** in the **Quick Launch** menu along the left side of the main site screen.

To open the **Shared Documents library**, click it. SharePoint opens a screen that displays a list of your shared documents. Of course, a new library would not have documents in it yet. To create your first document, display the **Documents** ribbon and click the bottom half of the **New Document** button as shown in Figure 1-20.

■ **Note** Buttons that display a down-pointing arrow open a drop-down menu of multiple options. The first or top option in the menu corresponds to the default choice that SharePoint executes if you click the top half of the button instead of the bottom half.

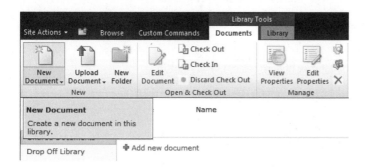

Figure 1-20. Creating a new document

SharePoint attempts to create and open a new document based on the default document template defined for this library. If this is not what you want, you can change the default template for the library even after creating the library. One way to do this is by pointing to a different file in the **Forms** folder of the library. If you have owner rights to the site, you can place any Microsoft Office document in this folder and select it as the default document template. For example, if you have a standardized expense report and want to use it in a separate document library, add a blank copy of that expense report to the **Forms** folder of the library as described in the following sidebar. Then point the document template URL for the library to that form. Then when you click **New** in this library, SharePoint displays a blank expense report for you to fill in rather than just a blank Word document.

Change the Default Template for a Document Library

Using the next 11 steps, you can change the default template for an existing document library to the Microsoft Office document of your choice or any other document type that your users' computers recognize.

1. Create the document you want to use and save it to your desktop (if it is a Word document, save it as a .docx or .dotx).

2. In SharePoint, open the library from the Quick Launch area or click **View All Site Content** if your library does not appear in the Quick Launch, and then click on your library's name.

3. Select the **Library** ribbon and then click the option **Open with Explorer** in the **Actions** section.

4. Using a separate window, browse to the template you created in step 1.

5. Right-click the file and select **Copy**.

6. Click back on the window that holds the library's **Forms** folder. If you do not see the Forms folder, select **Tools** from the menu bar and then select **Folder Options**. Click the **View** tab and then from the **Advanced Settings** list, click the option **Show hidden files and folders**. You should now see the **Forms** folder.

7. Right-click a blank area and paste the template in this folder.

8. Close the Explorer window.

9. From the **Settings** section of the **Library** ribbon, select **Library Settings**.

10. Click Advanced Settings under the General Settings column.

11. Change the template URL in the **Document Template** section to point to the file you just pasted to the forms folder. The URL should look like

    `<LibraryName>/Forms/<TemplateName>`

    where `<LibraryName>` is the library name and `<TemplateName>` is the name of the document pasted into the **Forms** folder in step 7. Notice that this is a relative reference URL.

The next time you create a new document in this library, it defaults to the new document. Chapter 10 shows how to set the default library template to an InfoPath form using content types.

Assume that you now want to create a new document on this site based on your new Microsoft Word template. Click **New Document**. Edit the new document as you would any other new Word document and, when finished, click **Save** in the **Office Button** of Word. Notice that when the **Save As** dialog box appears, it does not display files from your local directories. Rather, it displays a reference to the Shared Documents site.

Next, enter a name for the document. Notice at the bottom of the **Save As** dialog box shown in Figure 1-21 that the document type simply says **Word Document** but formats the document with the .docx extension. When I created my site and the document library, I selected **Word Document** as the default document type. Your document library default may vary. You can also click the check box before **Maintain compatibility with previous versions of Word** if you need to store documents in the .doc format. Notice also that you can update some of the document's metadata including the Authors and Title properties.

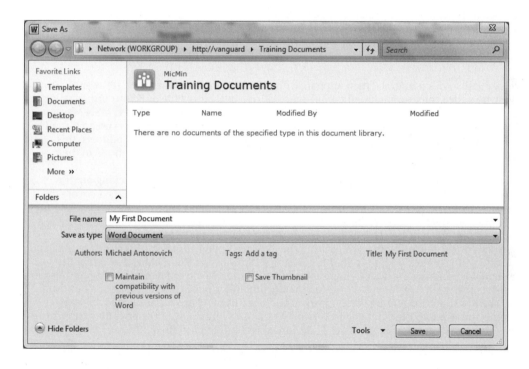

Figure 1-21. Saving your new document to SharePoint

Figure 1-22 shows that upon returning to the Shared Documents page in SharePoint, you see your new document. SharePoint displays at least three default properties for each document and perhaps more depending on the library settings. The first column, **Type**, displays an icon representing the document type. Windows Explorer uses these same icons for its file types. Clicking the icon opens the file or folder. The second column displays the document name. Notice the green text after your file name: NEW. SharePoint automatically adds this text to new documents to indicate recently added files. This indicator displays for 2 days, and then SharePoint automatically removes it. In the meantime, it helps site visitors identify new documents, which can be especially useful if you have many people adding documents to the library.

Figure 1-22. Viewing your first saved document in the library

In the third column, SharePoint displays the date and time that the file was last modified. SharePoint then displays the SharePoint name of the person who made the modification in the fourth column.

If you click the person's name, a screen appears with information about that user. If the site administrator who added the user included their e-mail address in their profile or if your organization is using any presence indicator such as Microsoft Windows Messenger version 4.6 or later, MSN Messenger version 4.6 or later, and Microsoft Office Communication server 2005 or later, you can send an e-mail to that person by clicking their e-mail address. In addition to the user's name and e-mail address, this screen can include the person's photo, department, job title, and other information defined in their profile.

The fifth column shown in Figure 1-22 appears only when the library requires checking out the document to edit it. It tracks who has this document currently locked for editing. Chapter 2 covers the purpose of this property in more detail. For now, remember that SharePoint shows this column in your library view only if you practice safe editing with Check In and Check Out.

The sixth column shown in Figure 1-22 only appears if the document library has the **Require content approval for submitted items** setting from the library's **Versioning Settings** page enabled and shows the current status of the document. In this column, a status of **Draft** indicates that either this is a new unpublished document or the document creator has made and saved changes to the last published version of the document but has not yet submitted the document for publication. A status of **Pending** indicates that she has submitted changes for approval and a status of **Approved** indicates that the current version is the approved and published version. You'll learn more about the document approval process in the "Require Document Approval to Hide Drafts—A Simple Workflow" section later in this chapter.

Adding Columns to a View

Documents have many more properties than shown in Figure 1-21. As with the Checked Out To column, SharePoint does not display some document properties unless you ask it to. In fact, whenever you see a list or library, you are looking at a view of the list or library, never the actual list or library. Views define which columns appear as well as whether you see all the items or just selected items based on a filter and sort criteria.

To add another column to the Shared Document library list, click **Library Settings** in the **Settings** group of the **Library** ribbon. Then scroll down to the **Views** section and click the **All Documents** view. The displayed page allows changes to the view name, columns, sort, filter, and other properties. For now, focus on the **Columns** group. Notice that it displays over a dozen possible columns, of which only a few have their check box selected. Scan the list until you find the column **Checked Out To**. Select this column by clicking the check box to its left.

You may have also noticed the drop-down lists to the right of each column. The numbers in these fields define the column order from left to right when displayed. To change the order, click the column you want to reposition and change the position value. SharePoint adjusts affected columns between the old and the new value to make room for the moved column. When you are done making changes to the view, click **OK** at the top or bottom of the page to save your changes.

Now when you return to the Shared Documents library, you see the new column telling you who checked out the document. As with the **Modified By** column, you can use the information stored about the user to send an e-mail to them asking when they might finish using the document.

If the person in the **Modified By** or **Checked Out To** column also uses MSN Messenger, Live Messenger, or a compatible presence awareness application such as Microsoft Office Communicator, an icon appears before the person's name. The color of the ball indicates the user's status as shown in Table 1-1. When you hover over the colored ball, it opens a menu as shown in Figure 1-23.

Table 1-1. Messenger Status Indicator

Color of Icon	Status
Green	Online
Orange/Red	Busy/In a call
Yellow	Be right back/Away/Out to lunch

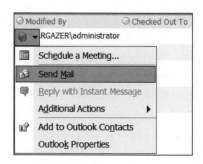

Figure 1-23. Options for Modified By person

Uploading a Document

If you previously created documents that you now want to upload to your Shared Documents site, click the **Upload Document** option in the **Library** ribbon. If you click on the lower part of the button, you see a drop-down menu that lets you upload a single document or upload multiple documents. Figure 1-24 shows the **Upload Document** screen if you choose to upload a single document.

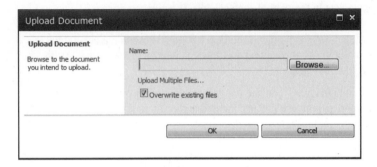

Figure 1-24. Uploading a document

In this screen, you have three options for selecting files to upload:

- You can directly enter the name of the document that you want to upload.

- You can click the Browse button to open a browse window to find and select the file to upload.

- You can click the Upload Multiple Files option to upload more than one file in a single operation.

I'll let you explore the first two options on your own since they are straightforward. However, the third option proves rather useful when uploading groups of existing documents. When you click this link, the window shown in Figure 1-25 appears. You would see this same window if you selected the **Upload Multiple Documents** option from the **Upload Documents** menu.

■ **Note** The window that appears when you select the Upload Multiple Documents could look different from Figure 1-24 if you are using Microsoft Office 2007. Note that the figures in the book are the Office 2010 version of the screens. In some cases, the functionality may exist but in a different form in Office 2007; in a few cases, it may not exist at all in earlier Office versions.

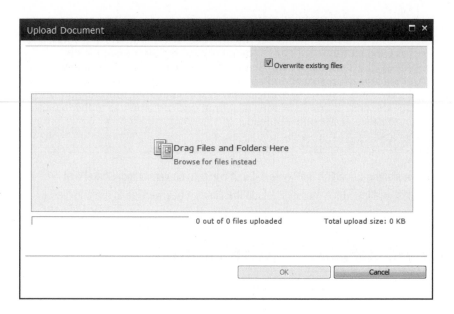

Figure 1-25. Upload multiple documents screen

■ **Caution** Although it may seem at first to be a good idea to check the option **Overwrite existing files**, this option allows you to overwrite a more recent version of a document with an older version from the upload selection without any warning.

Note that this screen consists of an area where you can drop in files that you want to upload. You can click the option **Browse for files instead** to open Windows Explorer to select your files. Of course, you can also work from an instance of Windows Explorer previously opened outside of SharePoint. In either case, navigate to the folder that contains the file(s) you want, select the files, and then click and drag them into the text area in the middle of SharePoint's **Upload Document** window. You can select files from any folder you can access, including other computers or network shares.

As mentioned above, there has been a dialog change when uploading multiple documents depending on the version of Microsoft Word installed on the client machine. The most significant improvement is the ability to upload files from more than one folder or drive at one time. Simply navigate to each folder that has a file you want to upload, and drag it to the SharePoint **Drag Files and Folders Here** section. When you have added all the files you need into this area, click the **OK** button.

Note also that you can check the box **Overwrite existing files** to replace files already in the SharePoint directory with copies from your copy location. If you do not check this option and you select a file whose name already exists in the library, SharePoint does not upload the file, even if the file selected has a more recent modified date than the version SharePoint has. Figure 1-26 shows several files after dragging them into the upload area. Note that SharePoint tells you how many files you are about to upload and the total upload size. Why is the upload size important? Most SharePoint administrators limit the size of an upload. In fact, the default limit is 50 MB. That limit does not apply to individual files in a multi-file upload, but rather to the total size of the upload.

■ **Note** The library did not have versioning turned on for Figure 1-25. If you turn on versioning, SharePoint replaces the option to overwrite existing files with a message to add the file as a new version to existing files.

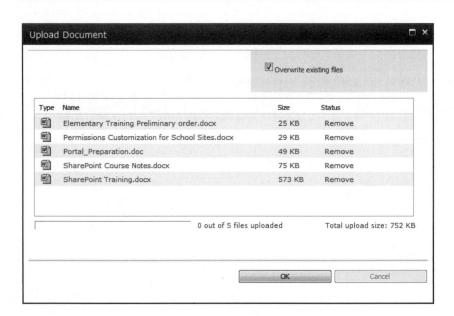

Figure 1-26. Selecting multiple files to upload

To complete your selection, click the **OK** button. SharePoint takes a few moments to retrieve and upload your files. The amount of time needed depends on the number of files you are uploading, their sizes and the speed of your network. However, SharePoint does display a progress bar as it uploads the files.

■ **Note** By default, sites limit uploads to 50MB for the entire upload, whether the upload consists of a single file or multiple files. However, this setting can be changed by your SharePoint administrator by going into **Central Administration**, selecting **Manage web applications** from the **Application Management** section, select the web application (SharePoint - 80, if you used the default install options), then open the drop-down menu for **General Settings** in the **Web Applications** ribbon, and then select **Resource Throttling**. On the Resource Throttling page, scroll down until you find the **Maximum Upload Size** options. Here you can change the 50MB limit to another value. If you exceed the 50MB upload limit because your upload includes multiple files, you may successfully upload your files as a series of smaller upload groups or even individually, as long as each upload group is less than 50MB. One additional factor that could affect your ability to upload large files is the session timeout setting controlled by IIS and your network speed.

Figure 1-27 shows the Shared Documents library after uploading the selected documents from Figure 1-26.

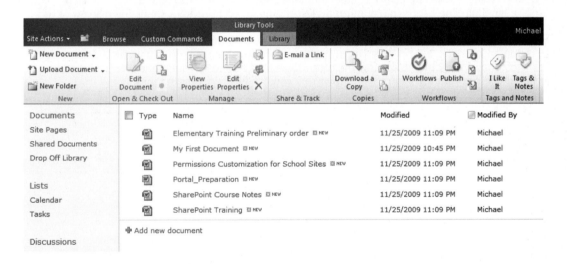

Figure 1-27. Shared Documents library after uploading multiple documents

> ■ **Tip** When you upload multiple documents, they appear initially in your library as checked out to you. If you want to check all of them in, you could use the individual item's drop-down menu by hovering over the item's name to display the drop-down button to its right and then select the command to check in the item. However, a faster method is to click the check box to the left of each library item as you select each checked-out file and then select the command **Check In** from the **Documents** ribbon.

While most of the files uploaded in Figure 1-26 came from Word 2010, I also uploaded a Word 2003 file named `Portal_Preparation` found in the middle of the list in Figure 1-27. If you do this, how can you tell a Word 2003 document from a Word 2007 document? The icons to the left of the file name do have a small difference (look at the upper left side of the icon), but an easier way exists. When you position your mouse over the document icon, a tooltip style box appears below the cursor with the full file name, and the file name also displays in the Status Bar at the bottom of the screen. Either way, the file name's extension suggests the version of Word used to save that document.

You can change the sort order of your document list by clicking the column header by which you want to sort. The first time you click the column header, SharePoint sorts that column in ascending order, and it displays a small up arrow to the right of the column name. The second time you click the column header, SharePoint sorts that column in descending order and adds a small down arrow to the right of the column name.

You can also sort a column by placing your mouse over a column header to highlight it. On the right side of the column header, a drop-down arrow appears. Click this arrow to open a menu that allows you to sort the column. In addition to sorting, the drop-down list also allows you to filter the list based on values in the selected column. Figure 1-28 shows that you can filter document types.

> ■ **Note** You cannot filter the **Name** column.

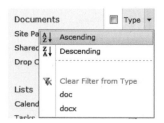

Figure 1-28. Filtering the shared documents in a library

If you select the .doc filter from the type column, the library displays only the `Portal_Preparation` document because it is a Word 2003-formatted document. SharePoint does not delete the Word 2007-formatted documents when it applies this filter, it merely hides them. Although you can only define a single filter per column, you could add an additional filter on another column, in which case SharePoint displays only documents that match the filters from both columns.

■ **Note** A column with an active filter displays a funnel to the right of the column name.

To remove filters, open the drop-down for each column that has a filter and select the **Clear Filter** option.

Displaying Documents in the Datasheet View

Before looking at how to edit a document in the library, let's look at two other ways to view your documents. You can access both methods from the **Library** ribbon at the top of the **Shared Documents** page.

Figure 1-29 shows the first alternative library view: **Datasheet View**.

■ **Note** Datasheet View requires a datasheet component compatible with SharePoint 2010. It also requires that your web browser support ActiveX controls and that you have support turned on.

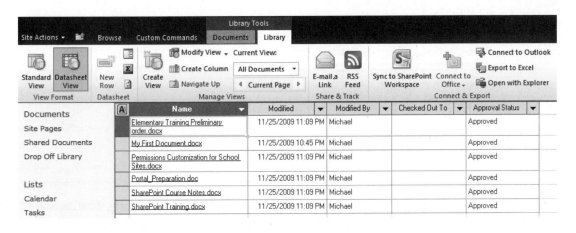

Figure 1-29. *Library displayed in Datasheet View mode*

As you can see, this view displays the same information as the **Standard View**. In **Datasheet View**, notice the icon in the upper-left corner of the table. This icon resembles the icon used by Access. In fact, SharePoint uses the Access engine to display the list of documents as a table.

This view also supports the ability to sort and filter the information displayed. However, rather than hovering over the column header with your mouse as in **Standard View**, click the down arrow to the right of the column header name, as shown in Figure 1-30, to open the menu.

Figure 1-30. Sorting and filtering in Datasheet View mode

Notice that the sort options appear at the top of the list in this figure. Beneath the sort options, you find the filter options. In addition to filtering on specific values found in the selected column, you can define a custom filter. This feature can help locate documents in large libraries when you only remember part of the file name. Figure 1-31 creates a custom filter for values of the **Name** column that begin with the word "SharePoint."

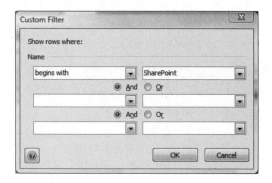

Figure 1-31. Defining a custom filter

■ **Note** You can filter on any displayed column within the library using this method. For example, if the document list displays a **Created By** column, you can filter on documents created by a specific person.

When defining a custom filter, you can specify up to three expressions for the filtered column. You can then connect each of these expressions with either an *And* or an *Or*. When you connect expressions with *And*, the expressions on either side of the connector must be true for a document to appear in the library list. When you connect expressions with *Or*, only one of the two expressions must be true for the document to appear. If you use expressions connected with both *And* and *Or* connectors, SharePoint executes the expressions from the left to the right. The *And* expression does not have precedence over the *Or* expression.

To turn a filter off, select the option (**Show All**) from the drop-down menu (Figure 1-30).

■ **Tip** Use the Datasheet View to make changes to several columns across many of the documents in the library. You can edit the data in the columns in this mode just like you edit data in an Access table view. Additional discussion on using lists appears in Chapter 2.

Displaying Documents in Windows Explorer

The last way to look at the document library in this chapter begins by opening the **Library** ribbon and choosing the option **Open with Explorer** in the **Actions** section. This command opens a separate window and displays the documents using Windows Explorer. This view supports an interesting feature. If you open a second Windows Explorer session from your desktop, you can drag and drop files between the two windows. In other words, this view provides another way to upload documents into SharePoint libraries. In Figure 1-32, you see two separate Windows Explorer sessions. The top window belongs to the SharePoint Shared Documents library and the bottom window is a Windows Explorer view of files on my E drive. The figure shows that I have just selected the file `Sites of Interest.doc` from my E drive on my local machine and I am dragging it into the **Shared Documents** library.

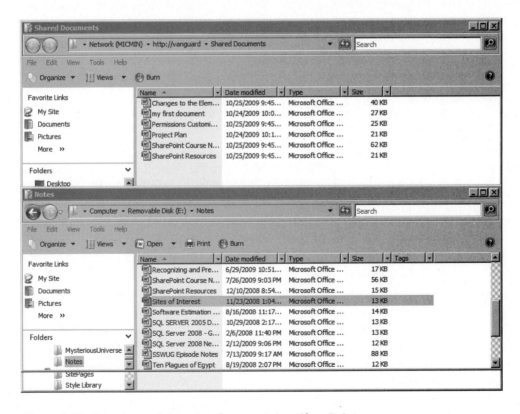

Figure 1-32. Dragging and dropping documents into SharePoint

When you return to your SharePoint window, you may need to refresh your page, but you will see that the new file now appears in the **Shared Documents** library.

■ **Tip** You can also open two different libraries in SharePoint using Windows Explorer mode to copy and paste documents between the libraries. You can also move documents from one folder in a library to another folder in the same library.

You can also use copy and paste keystrokes between libraries displayed in Windows Explorer mode by selecting documents from one library, pressing **Ctrl+C**, then navigating to the other library (or folder) and pressing **Ctrl+V** to copy the file.

Editing Documents Stored in Your Library

After you have saved several documents to your library, you probably want to edit them. You can choose from several ways to edit a document depending on your currently selected library view, Standard View or Datasheet View.

Editing a Word Document from Standard View

Suppose you want to edit one of the Word documents previously added to the library. Open the **Shared Documents** library. Position your mouse over the name of the document you want to edit. Notice that SharePoint surrounds the document name with a box and a drop-down arrow to the right. It also underlines the document name, changing it to a hyperlink. You can edit this document by either clicking the document icon or its hyperlinked name.

For now, let's assume that this SharePoint library does not require Check Out before opening the file. You will see how to require Check Out a little later when you visit the Versioning settings in the List Settings. How SharePoint tries to open your document depends on your version of Word. By default, Word 2007 tries to open documents in read-only mode. You should open documents this way if you only want to view, download, or print a copy of the document. This allows other people to open the document for editing. However, if you need to edit the document, click the **Edit Document** button that Word 2007 displays in a bar across the top of the opened document. This option allows you to switch to edit mode as shown in Figure 1-33.

Figure 1-33. Switching a document to edit mode

Once in edit mode, make your changes to the document and save them by clicking **Save** in the Office Button menu.

On the other hand, if you open the document with Word 2010 and do not require Check Out of the document, Word then supports simultaneous editing of the document by multiple people. More on this new capability appears in Chapter 4.

You can also begin editing a document by clicking the down arrow displayed to the right of the document name when you position your mouse over the name to open the document's drop-down menu. This drop-down menu shows available options. Select **Edit in Microsoft Office Word** as shown in Figure 1-34 to edit the document.

Figure 1-34. Choosing Edit in Microsoft Office Word

Editing a Document from Datasheet View

If you prefer to use the **Datasheet View** of your documents, you can still initiate editing of a document by right clicking in the **Name** field of the document you want to edit. This also opens a drop-down menu of available options. Click the **Document** option to display a submenu. This submenu, shown in Figure 1-35, provides options to open the document in **Read-Only** or **Edit** mode. You can also review the prior versions of the document if the library tracks versions.

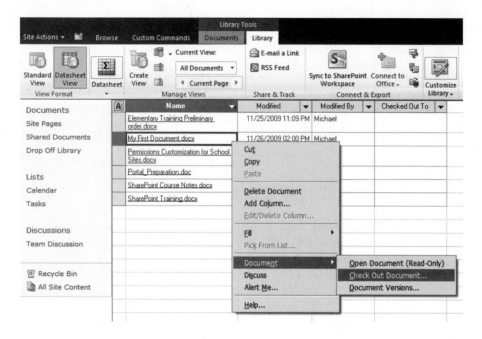

Figure 1-35. Document options in the DataSheet View

The **Check Out Document** option opens the document in **Edit** mode, assuming no one else has the document open for editing. If they do, SharePoint can only open the document in **Read-Only** mode.

So now you know several different methods of opening a document for editing. However, what happens when someone attempts to open your document while you have it open in edit mode?

Simple Locking of Documents

When you open a document in edit mode with one of the preceding methods, Word 2007 tells SharePoint to lock the document temporarily. SharePoint 2010 also locks the document if you check out the document before editing it. In either case, if another user attempts to open the document while you have it open, they receive a warning message similar to the one shown in Figure 1-36.

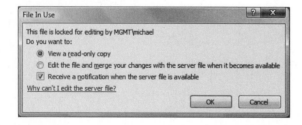

Figure 1-36. File in Use message

When SharePoint locks a file, it gives you two choices of what to do:

- Open a read-only copy.

- Edit the file and merge your changes with the server file when it becomes available.

In addition to these two options, you can choose to receive notification when the file is available. This notification is now available with both file-in-use options.

Let's assume that you really do need to edit the document, not just view or print it. In that case, opening a read-only copy is not an option. Therefore, you might select the second option. However, if you do this, you will need to open both your copy of the document and the SharePoint version of the document later using Word's Compare feature to merge your changes into the SharePoint version. This sounds like a lot of extra work, so let's assume that you just open a read-only copy of the document and then select the option to receive a notification when the server file is available.

With this option, you can ask SharePoint to notify you when the other person closes their copy of the document so you can edit it. In the meantime, you can review the current document to see if you want to make other changes or you could just open another application window to proceed to another task while you wait for access to the document. Maybe you even contact the person who has the document open and ask them to finish their changes quickly. In any case, once they check their version of the document back into the library, SharePoint sends you the message shown in Figure 1-37.

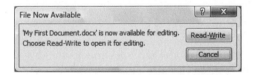

Figure 1-37. File Now Available message

When you receive this message, click the **Read-Write** button to begin editing the document, or if you no longer need to make the changes, click the **Cancel** button to make the file available to others.

For most quick changes, working in Edit mode as described in this section with the automatic locking that SharePoint provides may not pose a problem. If you are using Word 2010, this may actually be the preferred way to make minor changes to documents. However, the default SharePoint locking does not last forever. In fact, depending on the operating system used by the person editing the document, the lock may only guarantee exclusive use of the document for 10 minutes, according to Microsoft's Knowledge Base article 899709. Thus, if you need more time than that to edit the document, you could have a concurrency problem.

What Is a Concurrency Problem?

A concurrency problem occurs when two or more people edit a document at the same time but only the changes for one of them can be saved. For example, suppose you open a document using Word 2007 from the Shared Documents library. After 30 minutes, you leave for lunch without closing the document. Now Natasha from the office down the hall opens the same document. Since more than 30 minutes have passed since you opened the document, the implicit lock on the document has expired. Therefore, Natasha, unaware of your changes, opens the document, makes her quick changes, and saves them. Finally, you come back from lunch an hour later and realize that you have not closed your document. So you click **Save** and close the document.

Later that same day, Natasha goes back into the document to check one of her changes and discovers that she cannot see her changes. Furthermore, the document looks entirely different from the one she edited. She wonders who deleted her changes.

Well, you did delete her changes, but not intentionally. When you came back from lunch and saved the document, SharePoint happily overwrote the existing version in the library, the one containing Natasha's changes.

While such implicit locks may seem like an easy solution, for a quick change the use of explicit locks is a safer practice. You can explicitly lock files manually, or you can make it easy for users by forcing SharePoint to check out (lock) each document whenever someone tries to edit it. SharePoint called this process of creating explicit locks document Check Out and Check In.

Why Use Check Out and Check In?

Using Check Out locks a document before opening it for editing. This manually applied lock stays in place until you decide to check the document back in, which means you can keep a document checked out for an hour, a day, or even longer without worrying about someone else making changes to the document while you have it. Think of Check Out as getting exclusive control to a file, like checking a book out of a physical library. While you have it checked out, no one else can check it out. (Well, almost no one. I'll get to that in a moment.) However, unlike your public library, when you check out a document from a SharePoint library, other people can come in and open a read-only copy of the last saved version.

Checking out a document has other advantages. Both the **Standard View** and the **Datasheet View** can show you the name of the person who has control of the document. Therefore, if you really need to get to that document, you can just walk down the hall, call them on the phone, or instant message them to ask when they will finish editing the document so you can open it to make your changes.

However, the real benefit of checking out a document to edit it occurs when you plan on working on the document changes offline. Even Word 2010's ability to support simultaneous editors does not work when you edit the document offline.

How to Check Out a Document

To check out a file manually when using **Standard View**, open the drop-down menu for the document and select **Check Out** as shown in Figure 1-38.

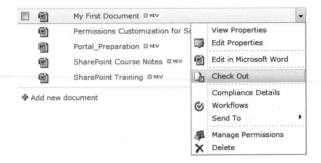

Figure 1-38. Checking out a document in Standard View

After you check out a file, you still must return to the drop-down menu to select **Edit** to open the document. However, from the time you check out a file until the time that you check it back in, you have exclusive access to the file. Remember to display the **Checked Out To** column in your **Shared Documents** view to see who has documents checked out.

■ **Note** The Checked Out To column should appear automatically in your default view when you set **Required Check Out** to Yes in the **Versioning settings** option of the **List Settings** found in the **Library** ribbon.

This Checked Out To column option does not exist if you rely on the automatic locks provided by simple document editing. Another advantage of using Check Out occurs when others attempt to edit the document you have checked out. The **File in Use** dialog box previously shown in Figure 1-36 displays the name of the user who has the file open for editing. Figure 1-39 shows an example of how the **Standard View** looks when someone has checked out the document "My First Document."

■ **Tip** Even if you use Microsoft Word 2010, which supports simultaneous editing of documents, you may still want to check out a document if you plan on working on the document offline.

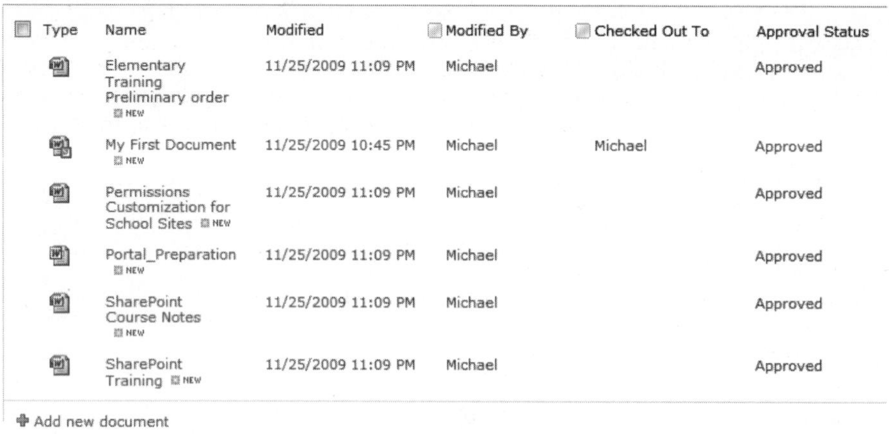

Type
Name
Modified
Modified By
Checked Out To
Approval Status
Elementary Training Preliminary order NEW
11/25/2009 11:09 PM
Michael
Approved
My First Document NEW
11/25/2009 10:45 PM
Michael
Michael
Approved
Permissions Customization for School Sites NEW
11/25/2009 11:09 PM
Michael
Approved
Portal_Preparation NEW
11/25/2009 11:09 PM
Michael
Approved
SharePoint Course Notes NEW
11/25/2009 11:09 PM
Michael
Approved
SharePoint Training NEW
11/25/2009 11:09 PM
Michael
Approved
Add new document

Figure 1-39. Checked out files listed in Standard View

If you check out a document and realize you picked the wrong document or you no longer need to save changes to that document, select the **Discard Check Out** option. This option only appears in the drop-down menu when you have a document checked out.

When you check out a document, SharePoint asks whether you want to save a copy of the document in your local drafts folder as shown in Figure 1-40. If you do not click this option, SharePoint creates a copy on the server that you can edit. However, only by saving a copy of the document in your local drafts folder when you check it out can you work on the file offline, a topic that I discuss further in Chapter 4.

Microsoft Internet Explorer
You are about to check out:
Name: My First Document.docx
From: vanguard
Use my local drafts folder
OK
Cancel
Some files can harm your computer. If this information looks suspicious, or you do not fully trust the source, do not open the file.

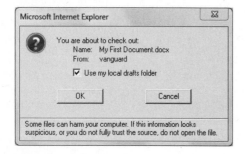

Figure 1-40. Saving a copy in your local drafts folder

■ **Note** You may need to make your SharePoint site a trusted site in your Internet Explorer Security options before you can use your local drafts folder to transfer the file back and forth between your local machine and the server.

Once you check out a document, you can edit the document for hours or even days if necessary. When you are done, make sure that you save your changes, close Word, and then check in the document. Saving your changes and closing Word does not automatically check in the document. Good office etiquette requires that you only check out a file for as long as necessary to make your changes. Keeping a file checked out longer than necessary merely prevents others from getting their work done.

If someone did not notice the checked out information in the Shared Documents listing and attempted to edit this document anyway, they would receive the warning shown in Figure 1-41.

Figure 1-41. File in Use warning

Checking Documents Back Into the Library

When you do not turn versioning on, SharePoint does not make your saved changes visible until you check the document back into the library. This functionality differs from editing a document without checking it out. In that case, every time you save the document, whether you close Microsoft Word or not, other users can see your changes.

When you do turn versioning on, each time you save your changes, SharePoint can create a minor version of the document. When you check in the document, other users with permission to edit can open the most recent document version and make further edits. Minor versions of the document may or may not be visible to users with only Read permission, depending on the **Draft Item Security** setting in the library's **Versioning** settings. Thus, you can use this setting to determine whether users with only Read permissions can see minor versions of the document. When you check out a document to your local drafts folder, SharePoint remains unaware of changes until you check the document back in because you are working with a local copy of the document. Upon checking it back in, you can assign the update a minor or a major revision number and provide revision comments.

When you close the Word session used to edit the document, a message prompt reminds you that SharePoint does not make changes visible to other users until you check the document in. If you have not finished all your changes but merely want to go to lunch, click **No**. However, if you have finished, click **Yes** to check your document back in as shown in Figure 1-42.

Figure 1-42. Prompt to check in changes

If your document library does not use versioning or if it only keeps major versions, you will see the dialog shown in Figure 1-43. In this case, you only need to supply an optional comment before saving the file.

Figure 1-43. Select Check In version and add comments via the Check In dialog box.

When you check in changes with major and minor versioning turned on, SharePoint provides several alternatives to label your new version as shown in Figure 1-44.

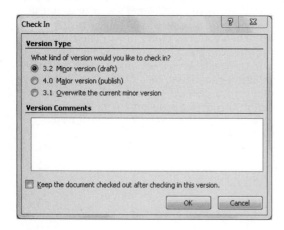

Figure 1-44. Select alternative check-in versions

By default, SharePoint labels your checked-in version with the next available version number. If your site only uses major versioning (whole numbers), SharePoint automatically increments the version by one. If your site uses minor versioning, SharePoint increments the number to the right of decimal. You must decide whether to accept the next available minor version number or instead use the next major version number. How you decide is up to you, but if you made major changes to a document and have completed those changes, you probably should go with the next major version number. Another point to remember is that users with view rights typically can see only the last major version saved based on the Draft Item Security setting of the document library. How your SharePoint administrator has set versioning in your library may also influence which option you can choose.

In addition to selecting the version for your changes, you can enter comments about the new version. In the comments section, you should include information about the changes you made, who requested them, who approved them, or what impact the change will have on your organization. You can view these comments when you display a document's version history (which you'll learn more about in the upcoming section, "Tracking Document Versions").

Overriding a Check Out

Previously, I stated that a document checked out by a user cannot be edited by anyone else. However, suppose you absolutely must get into a document, but the person who checked it out has left for a two-week Mediterranean cruise. If you have administrator rights to the Shared Documents library, you can right-click the document and select **Check In** to bring up a dialog box asking you to confirm that you want to override the Check Out as shown in Figure 1-45.

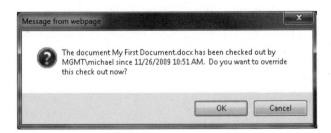

Figure 1-45. Overriding a Check Out.

When an administrator overrides a checked-out document, the user who originally checked out the document may lose some of their changes unless they edited it from their local drafts folder. Therefore, it is good office etiquette to let the other user know that you had to override their checked-out document while they were out of the office.

■ **Note** While it is possible to open your local draft copy of a document, save it in a different location, and then compare it to the current version of the document in SharePoint using Microsoft Word's document compare feature to recover any of your changes when someone else overrides your Check Out, this process is time consuming.

Tracking Document Versions

When your SharePoint administrator turns on document versioning, SharePoint stores multiple copies of each document, representing saved changes to the document. To see the versions for a document, click the down arrow when positioning your mouse over a document's name in a library and select **Version History**. Figure 1-46 displays the versions for a typical document.

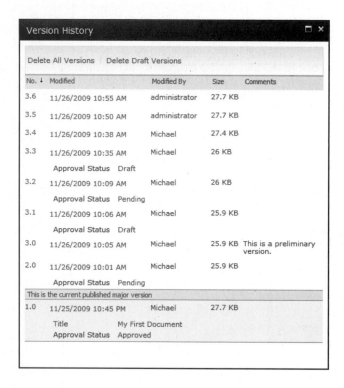

Figure 1-46. Displaying a document's version history

Notice the version history of the selected document includes both major and minor revisions. Recall that whole numbers define major versions and decimal numbers like 2.1 identify minor versions.

Depending on how you use your Shared Documents library, you may not want to track minor versions, especially if you are not using an approval process on document changes. However, if you do use an approval process, then you can hide minor versions of a document from those who can only view your documents. Users with edit rights to the library can perform additional edits on the document as long as it is not checked out. Once everyone has completed their changes to the document, you can save it with the next major version number by starting the approval workflow process. Still, only a content approver can publish a new version of a document. Until then, everyone other than content creators in that library continues to view the last published (major) version.

Your SharePoint administrator may also limit the number of both major and minor versions that SharePoint stores. After all, the more versions you retain, the more disk space you need. As an example, a SharePoint administrator may limit the library to storing only the last three major releases and perhaps the minor releases made since the last major version. Figure 1-47 shows how a SharePoint administrator might configure versions so that only users with permission to edit can view minor releases and only minor versions since the last major version are stored.

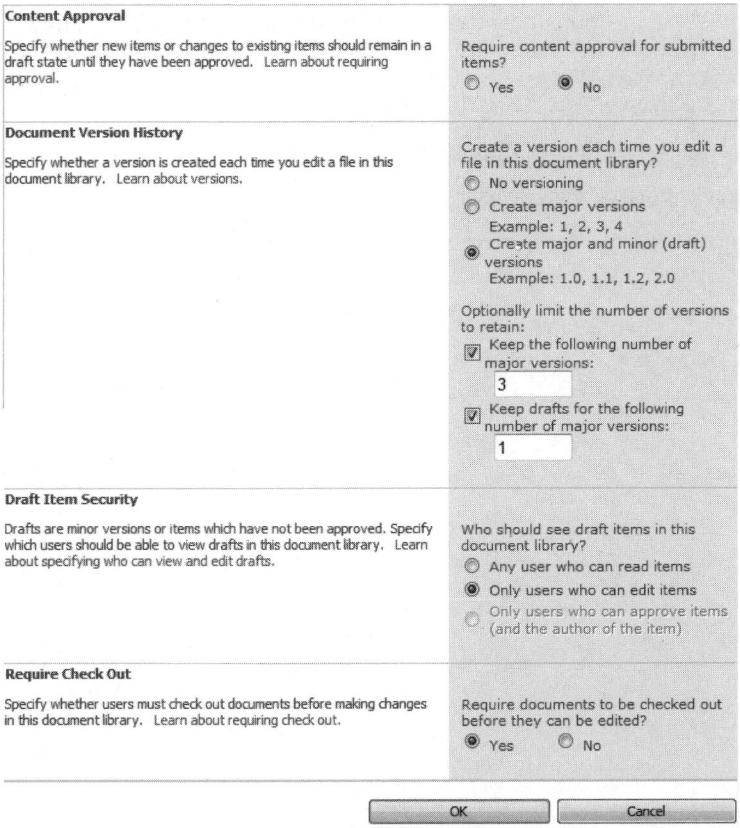

Content Approval

Specify whether new items or changes to existing items should remain in a draft state until they have been approved.   Learn about requiring approval.

Require content approval for submitted items?
- ○ Yes   ◉ No

Document Version History

Specify whether a version is created each time you edit a file in this document library.   Learn about versions.

Create a version each time you edit a file in this document library?
- ○ No versioning
- ○ Create major versions
  Example: 1, 2, 3, 4
- ◉ Create major and minor (draft) versions
  Example: 1.0, 1.1, 1.2, 2.0

Optionally limit the number of versions to retain:
- ☑ Keep the following number of major versions:
  [3]
- ☑ Keep drafts for the following number of major versions:
  [1]

Draft Item Security

Drafts are minor versions or items which have not been approved. Specify which users should be able to view drafts in this document library.   Learn about specifying who can view and edit drafts.

Who should see draft items in this document library?
- ○ Any user who can read items
- ◉ Only users who can edit items
- ○ Only users who can approve items (and the author of the item)

Require Check Out

Specify whether users must check out documents before making changes in this document library.   Learn about requiring check out.

Require documents to be checked out before they can be edited?
- ◉ Yes   ○ No

[OK]   [Cancel]

Figure 1-47. Defining versioning settings

■ **Tip** To change the version settings, open your document library and display the Library ribbon. Next, select **Library Settings** in the **Settings** group. On the **List Settings** page, select **Versioning settings** in the **General Settings** section.

Promoting a Prior Version to the Current Version

Occasionally, you may need to return to a previous version of a document. Perhaps management has rescinded the change you added to a policy document, and they want the previous policy statement reinstated. Of course, you could edit the current document and hope to reverse all changes, returning the document to its previous content. That could entail a major effort fraught with the potential of missing a change. It is far easier to simply view the version history for the document and select the prior version, making it the current version.

To do this, first check out the document from the **Standard View**. This action automatically creates a new minor version if you did not already have the document checked out. Then select **Version History** in the document's drop-down menu. Next, position your mouse over the **Modified Date/Time** of the version you want, and click the **Restore** option in the item's drop-down menu as shown in Figure 1-48.

■ **Note** If you do not first check out the document before you attempt to restore a prior version, SharePoint displays an error message informing you to check out the document.

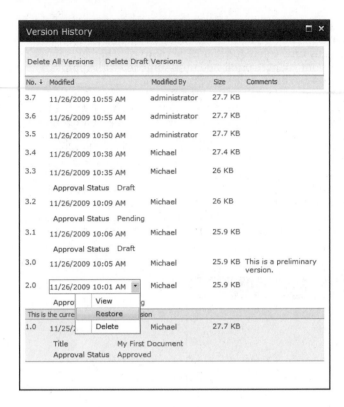

Figure 1-48. *Restoring a prior document version*

SharePoint prompts with a warning that you are replacing the current version of the document with the selected version. Click **Yes** to proceed.

When you refresh the display of the current page, you should see the selected prior version of the page.

Publishing Documents to Your Document Library

If your site requires content approval, all documents first enter a draft state. While you can set the **Draft Item Security** option in **Versioning settings** to allow any user the right to read draft items, I do not generally recommend this. Rather, you typically want to limit the ability to see draft versions to only users who can edit items in the current library or to users who can approve items in the current library. Of course, the creator of the draft can always see the draft version. This is true whether you are tracking versions of the item or not.

The situation is a little more complex when you do not require content approval. In this case, if you do not track versions, then every time you save changes to an item, those changes are immediately visible to everyone. In fact, even if you only keep major versions (published versions), everyone still sees immediately any changes you make to an item. Only when you keep major and minor versions can you choose to hide the minor versions (drafts) from all users and limit the visibility of those drafts to other users of the library.

With that basic understanding, how does that affect publishing your documents? Well, you should consider a document published immediately if you do not require content approval no matter whether you track versions or not. On the other hand, any time you require content approval, whether you track versions or not, SharePoint does not consider your changes published until someone with approval rights has approved them. During that time, you can determine who can view those drafts.

When you turn off all versioning, management of the document library becomes informal. While this practice minimizes the amount of space needed by your site, if you ever need a prior version of a document, you may be out of luck unless you can restore one from a backup copy of the SharePoint database. However, retrieving documents from a backup copy of the database requires time and a separate place to restore it. Such extra work will not earn you any bonus points with your SharePoint administrator.

The library example above has major and minor versioning enabled. To publish your most recent document, return to your Shared Documents folder and open the drop-down menu associated with that document. If it shows the document as still checked out because the **Check In** option appears, click the **Check In** option, and choose how you want to save your changes. You can save your changes as a new minor version, you can replace the current minor version, or you can publish the next major version. Figure 1-49 show these options.

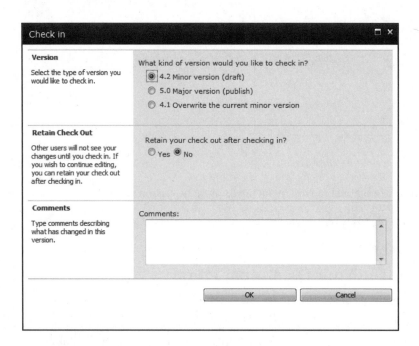

Figure 1-49. Publishing a restored document during Check In

If you choose to leave the document as a minor version, you can always return to the library later in **Standard View**, open the drop-down menu for the specific document, and click **Publish a Major Version**. When published this way, you can still add comments, as shown in Figure 1-50. Adding comments to a published document lets you identify what has changed since the last major version.

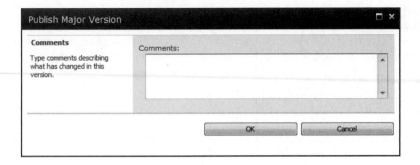

Figure 1-50. Publishing a major version

Click **OK** to submit your request to publish this version for approval. If the site does not require approval, saving a document as a major version makes it public immediately. However, if your document library requires approval, saving a major version merely sets the status of the page to **Pending** as shown in Figure 1-51.

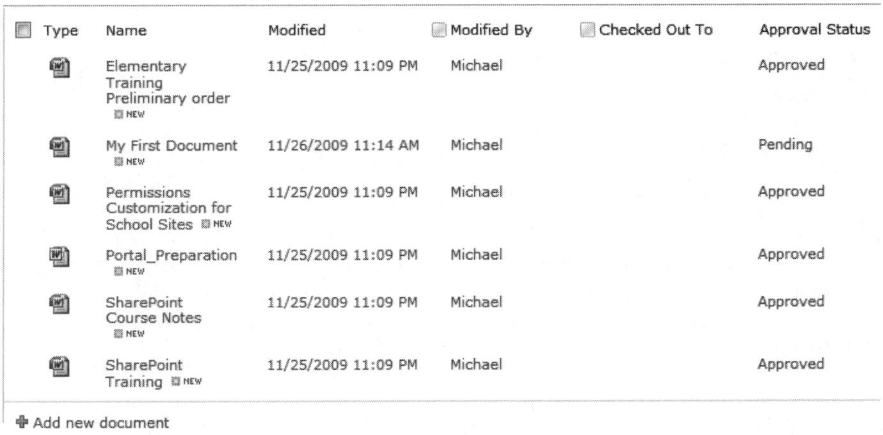

	Type	Name	Modified	Modified By	Checked Out To	Approval Status
	📄	Elementary Training Preliminary order ⊠ NEW	11/25/2009 11:09 PM	Michael		Approved
	📄	My First Document ⊠ NEW	11/26/2009 11:14 AM	Michael		Pending
	📄	Permissions Customization for School Sites ⊠ NEW	11/25/2009 11:09 PM	Michael		Approved
	📄	Portal_Preparation ⊠ NEW	11/25/2009 11:09 PM	Michael		Approved
	📄	SharePoint Course Notes ⊠ NEW	11/25/2009 11:09 PM	Michael		Approved
	📄	SharePoint Training ⊠ NEW	11/25/2009 11:09 PM	Michael		Approved

✚ Add new document

Figure 1-51. Viewing document approval status

When a SharePoint library requires approval of documents, it automatically adds the column **Approval Status**. To approve the document, log in as someone with approval permission. By the way, site owners automatically have approval permissions. If you have approval permission, go to the Shared Documents page and open the drop-down menu for the document. You now have a new option in this drop-down: **Approve/Reject**. Clicking **Approve/Reject** displays the page shown in Figure 1-52.

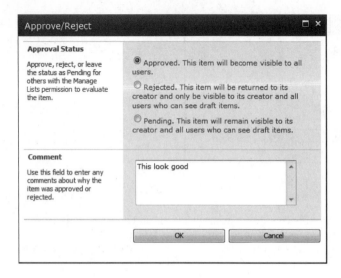

Figure 1-52. Approving a document for publishing

As you can see in this figure, approvers have three actions from which to select:

- Approved: The document becomes visible to all users.

- Rejected: The document does not become visible to other users.

- Pending: The document remains in its current state. Approvers should use this option when asking for further clarification.

No matter what action the approver selects, they can include a comment. An approver should always include comments when rejecting a document or sending it back pending additional work, information, etc. When the approver selects **Approved** and clicks **OK**, SharePoint publishes the page changing its status to **Approved**. Now all site viewers can see the updated document.

Figure 1-53 looks at the version history for this document. You see a new major release (5.0) now listed and SharePoint removes all the minor releases from version 4.0. This occurs because the version setup defined in Figure 1-47 tells SharePoint to retain only one set of minor releases, which means only the minor release since that last major release.

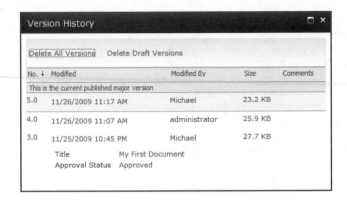

Figure 1-53. *New major release after publishing document*

Require Document Approval to Hide Drafts—A Simple Workflow

Workflows constitute an important feature of collaboration. Most business environments pass documents created by one person to two or more people for review, further editing, and ultimately approval before publishing them. In the distant past (20 years ago), organizations implemented workflows by physically transferring a document from one office to another via interoffice mail or by walking it from one office to another. More recently, e-mail replaced the need to move most documents between offices physically. However, even with e-mail, each person in the approval process must know to whom they are sending the document next. But all those e-mails and attachments clogged up everyone's inbox. Workflows automate that entire process and eliminate the load on Exchange servers created by passing the entire document as an attachment to the e-mail.

Workflows manage the stages of a document from initial draft through editing, approval, and publishing. It can determine who should receive the document next based on the specific action taken by the current person. Perhaps most important, since SharePoint carries out all steps in the workflow electronically, it is possible to locate where each document exists in the flow and where bottlenecks slow down the approval process.

For simple document approval, use the Document Library's **Versioning settings**. Open the library you want to work with and choose **Library Settings** from the **Settings** group in the Library ribbon. From the settings page, click **Versioning settings** in the **General Settings** group. Next, define the versioning settings similar to those shown in Figure 1-54. These settings turn on content approval for new and edited items.

Use major and minor version history to track multiple draft versions prior to publishing a major version. In this example, setting the number of major versions to 3 means that SharePoint only retains the three most recent approved versions of the document. Once you have four or more approved versions of a document, SharePoint automatically deletes the oldest one. Similarly, setting the draft for major versions to 1 means that SharePoint retains only drafts made to the most recent published version. As soon as you approve the document again, SharePoint deletes those drafts from that previous approved version. These settings help you conserve space used by storing multiple copies of a document while retaining the ability to recover from recent accidents.

Then set the **Draft Item Security** so that only users with edit rights to the library can view the draft documents. Finally, select the **Require Check Out** option to force SharePoint users to check out the document before editing it.

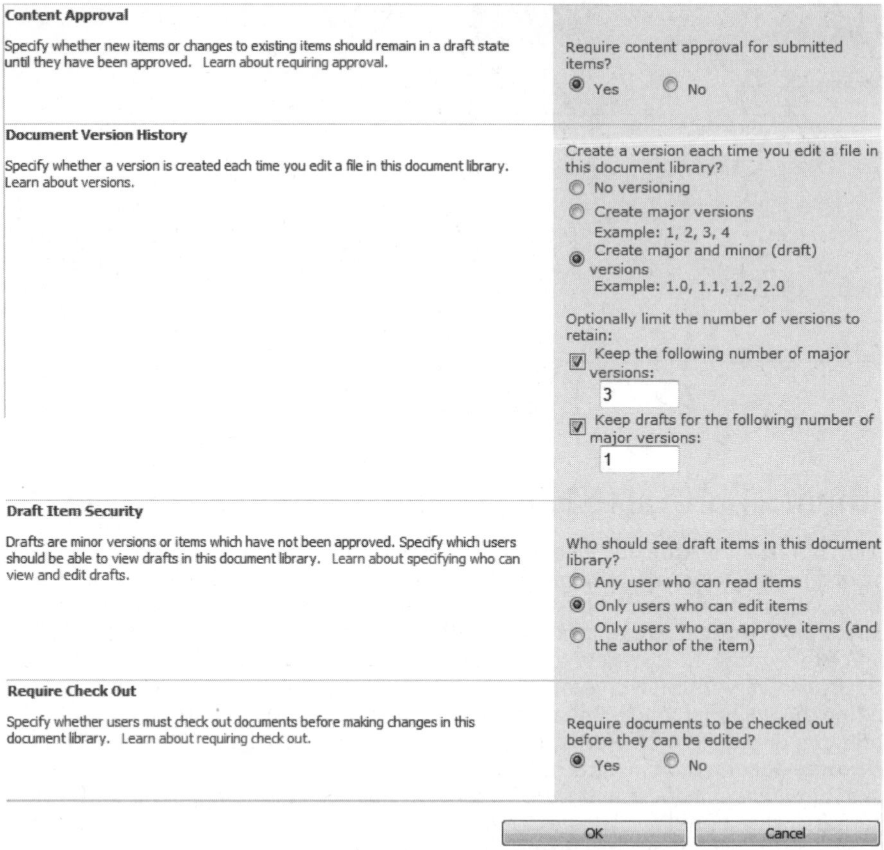

Content Approval

Specify whether new items or changes to existing items should remain in a draft state until they have been approved.   Learn about requiring approval.

Require content approval for submitted items?
- ◉ Yes   ○ No

Document Version History

Specify whether a version is created each time you edit a file in this document library. Learn about versions.

Create a version each time you edit a file in this document library?
- ○ No versioning
- ○ Create major versions
  Example: 1, 2, 3, 4
- ◉ Create major and minor (draft) versions
  Example: 1.0, 1.1, 1.2, 2.0

Optionally limit the number of versions to retain:
- ☑ Keep the following number of major versions:
  `3`
- ☑ Keep drafts for the following number of major versions:
  `1`

Draft Item Security

Drafts are minor versions or items which have not been approved. Specify which users should be able to view drafts in this document library.   Learn about specifying who can view and edit drafts.

Who should see draft items in this document library?
- ○ Any user who can read items
- ◉ Only users who can edit items
- ○ Only users who can approve items (and the author of the item)

Require Check Out

Specify whether users must check out documents before making changes in this document library.   Learn about requiring check out.

Require documents to be checked out before they can be edited?
- ◉ Yes   ○ No

[OK]   [Cancel]

Figure 1-54. Library versioning settings for document approval

A simple workflow begins with the content creator. While working on a document, SharePoint sets the document status to **Draft**. Once the content creator completes their changes for a document, they submit it for approval, which changes the status to **Pending**. An approver may approve, reject, or leave a document in a pending state (refer back to Figure 1-52). Some approvers may have permission to perform basic editing tasks, or their rights may limit them to verifying the information in the document. If the approver rejects the document, SharePoint sets the status to **Rejected**. Similarly, SharePoint changes the status of an approved document to **Approved**.

This simple workflow for a document allows documents to remain hidden while in draft mode, usually requiring a person other than the content creator to approve the document. However, at this level, SharePoint provides no dynamic notification to approvers when the user submits a document for approval. Nor does SharePoint provide notification to the content creator when the approver changes the document status to approved or rejected. Rather all parties must constantly monitor the status of documents in the various libraries. If you only have a single library, this may not seem like a major inconvenience. However, if you support several sites, each of which has multiple document libraries and lists, manually checking the status of documents and lists will probably not happen on a regular basis. In Chapter 2, you will see how to set up alerts and RSS feeds, which you could use to monitor changes to your libraries. What would make this workflow useful is e-mail notification when a task passes from one person to another. I will return to this issue in Chapter 10 to show you how to build simple workflows with e-mail notification using SharePoint Designer.

Recovering Accidental Deletions with the Recycle Bin

When you delete a document from your Shared Documents library, SharePoint prompts to confirm that you really want to delete the file. You may ask why you would need to worry about accidental deletions. I did too at first, until I realized that with more than one person having access to a site, not everyone may realize the value of the documents you decide to publish.

Should someone accidentally delete a document, SharePoint supports a recycle bin, which, like the recycle bin on your desktop, allows recovery of deleted files. For example, suppose you accidentally deleted the file My first document.docx from the Shared Documents folder and then realized that you really need to keep that document. Your first thought should be to check the **Recycle Bin** option found at the bottom of the Quick Links menu on the left of the Shared Documents page. This option, shown in Figure 1-55, displays a page listing all the documents deleted within the last 30 days.

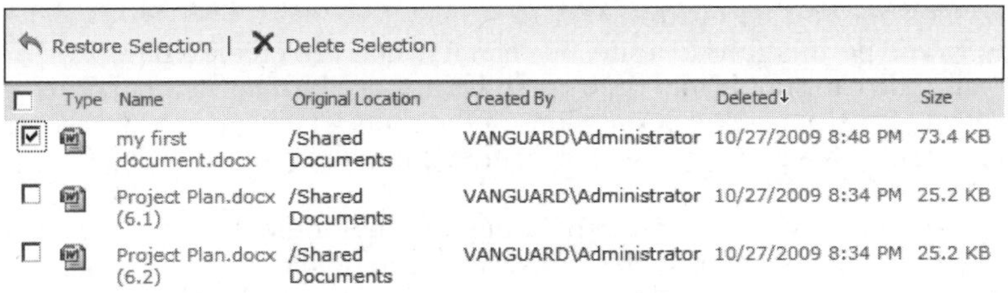

	Type	Name	Original Location	Created By	Deleted ↓	Size
☑		my first document.docx	/Shared Documents	VANGUARD\Administrator	10/27/2009 8:48 PM	73.4 KB
☐		Project Plan.docx (6.1)	/Shared Documents	VANGUARD\Administrator	10/27/2009 8:34 PM	25.2 KB
☐		Project Plan.docx (6.2)	/Shared Documents	VANGUARD\Administrator	10/27/2009 8:34 PM	25.2 KB

↶ Restore Selection | ✕ Delete Selection

Figure 1-55. The Recycle Bin collects all deleted documents.

To recover a document, click the check box to the left of the document and click the **Restore Selection** option at the top of the page.

When you delete a document, you delete all versions of that document as well. You may be surprised to learn that when you recover a document from the Recycle Bin you also recover all versions of that document as well. So, rather than thinking of files in your document library as single files, think of them as a collection of files with the same name.

■ **Tip** You can ask your SharePoint administrator to change the length of time deleted items stay in the Recycle Bin. To do so, they can go into Central Administration and select the **Application Management**. Next, select **Manage web applications** in the **Web Applications** group. Identify the web application containing the Site Collection for which you want to edit properties. By default, this would be SharePoint - 80. Click on the web application name to select it. Then open the **General Settings** drop-down menu found in the **Manage** group of the **Web Applications** ribbon and select the **General Settings** option. Scroll down the General Settings dialog until you find the **Recycle Bin** property group.

Here the SharePoint administrator can change the functionality of the Recycle Bin. For example, they can define the size of the second stage recycle bin that holds items that users delete from their Recycle Bin. Your SharePoint administrator can configure this second recycle bin as an additional percentage of the live site quota for the site collections created in the current web application. However, it should be noted that the setting to delete items after x days, where x defaults to 30 days after the item is initially deleted, applies to both the primary user recycle bin and the secondary recycle bin.

Summary

This chapter began by looking at SharePoint's hierarchical structure starting with a top-level site and then nesting additional sites within it. With the standard edition of MOSS 2010, you have collaboration and meeting site templates. The enterprise edition of MOSS augments these with enterprise and publishing templates. Remember that templates provide a starting point for building your site. You can always add features that are available in one template to other templates as well. This allows you to customize a template no matter which one you start with.

Next, you saw how to add users and permissions to a site. By default, when you create a new site under the top-level site or a sub-site, you can simply inherit the permissions used from its parent. This saves you time. However, if you need to customize the permissions or the users who have access to your site, you can add users for specific sites as well as assign them to custom group definitions having custom permission levels.

After defining which users can access a site, you can start building content for the site. You saw here how to use the document library to hold Microsoft Word files. However, it can hold other file types as well. Using Microsoft Word, you saw how to create new documents in the library as well as how to upload existing documents. Once uploaded, anyone with a compatible client application can edit a document stored in a library. However, unless the library forces you to first check out the documents or you manually check out the document, you could run into concurrency problems. Microsoft Word 2010 handles this potential problem by managing changed content at the paragraph level, but Word 2007 tries to lock the entire file. Of course, when you check out a document, you have exclusive rights to edit the entire document. Just remember to check the document back in so others can see your changes and to allow others to make further changes to the document.

Document versions allow you to track changes made to the document. You can track both major and minor versions. Keep in mind that visitors to your site may only be able to read major versions. Therefore, a good practice is to use minor versions as working documents within your team until you are ready to publish the final version as the next major version.

You can also use the document approval feature to allow documents to remain hidden until someone with approval permission can release the document. Organizations often use this model when publishing information that the public can view on Internet pages. They may grant everyone in the organization the permission to create new documents or to edit existing documents. However, until an approver reviews those documents, the public cannot see them.

Finally, the chapter closed with a brief look at the Recycle Bin. This feature helps you recover documents you accidentally delete. As you will learn in later chapters, it also works with many other SharePoint objects.

The next chapter extends this introduction to using SharePoint lists and Chapter 3 completes the introduction by looking at adding content to site pages.

CHAPTER 2

■■■

SharePoint Lists

Everything Is a List

Well, perhaps not everything. However, SharePoint stores most content information in lists, or variations of lists. This should come as no surprise, considering that SharePoint uses SQL Server as a storage container for not only all content information but also all the information used to define the appearance of your site. Of course, lists themselves translate well into the table paradigm of databases since they consist of rows and columns of information.

■ **Note** SharePoint does not save each list as a separate table. Rather, it combines information from all tables together in a special table schema, but since you are not studying how to read the SharePoint database files here, but rather how to use the SharePoint features, this difference will not matter to your understanding. One important note: directly modifying the SharePoint database files in SQL Server will terminate all Microsoft support for your installation.

One could say that SharePoint even stores the document libraries discussed in Chapter 1 in a special type of list. By adding unique attributes to those of a basic list, SharePoint can create not only other types of lists, but also libraries for documents, images, and pages. This chapter examines a selection of SharePoint's built-in lists and then explores how to create and use custom lists on collaboration pages.

■ **Tip** It is possible to store large data files outside of SharePoint using SQL Server FILESTREAM RBS Provider. While this solution is not for everyone, it could help those SharePoint users who are pushing the 4GB database limitation of SQL Server Express. Note that, although this solution does remove large files from the SQL database, it adds another point of failure since it relies on storing the file on another network file share or storage solution such as Documentum. Note that performance may take a hit due to the extra jump to get the data. If you are reaching the 4GB limit for other reasons (such as just a huge amount of normal size content), you may just want to consider upgrading your SQL Server edition.

Exploring SharePoint's Built-in List Types

Lists provide the easiest way to store information in SharePoint using a familiar paradigm. You probably have several lists going right now: important work tasks at the office, grocery items to buy on your way home, and home improvement projects for the weekend. SharePoint provides a variety of ways to keep this information electronically in predefined lists. It groups them into six categories:

- **Blank & Custom:** Blank and custom lists allow you to define your own list columns and views. They are ideal when importing data from other sources such as spreadsheets and external data sources. They also allow you to build lists structures that are significantly different from the other list templates.

- **Collaboration:** Out of the box, SharePoint provides only a single collaboration style list, the Discussion Board. This list lets you easily manage discussion threads. You can even configure the list to hide entries until someone approves them.

- **Content & Data:** This group includes those lists most often used to display content on pages.

- **Search:** This category includes lists that viewers often use to search for specific information such as events on a calendar or tasks within a project.

- **Tracking:** These lists track things such as personal and project tasks, issues, and language and translation workflows.

- **Web Databases:** Out of the box, this category has no list templates.

In the first part of this chapter you will examine most of the available lists to learn how they can be used. The second part of this chapter focuses on how to instantiate and modify these lists as well as how to publish a list through a collaboration page. Let's begin with a couple of predefined lists found in the Content & Data group so you can learn how lists work before learning how to build custom lists from a blank or custom template.

Content & Data Lists

A **Content & Data** list generally facilitates the collection and display of information on a site. You'll use it to explore the basic interaction between the columns and the items of the list. Let's assume that you are beginning from a brand new Team Site created when you started Chapter 1. You can work with one of the existing content lists by choosing **View All Site Content** from the **Site Actions** button or by clicking the **Lists** link in the **Quick Access** menu to the left of the page.

As mentioned in Chapter 1, the **All Site Content** page displays all the libraries and lists defined in the current site. Even when starting to use a new site, most site templates automatically add several default libraries and lists for you. One of the lists you should see in your team site is an **Announcements** list. Figure 2-1 shows the available lists in a default **Team Site**.

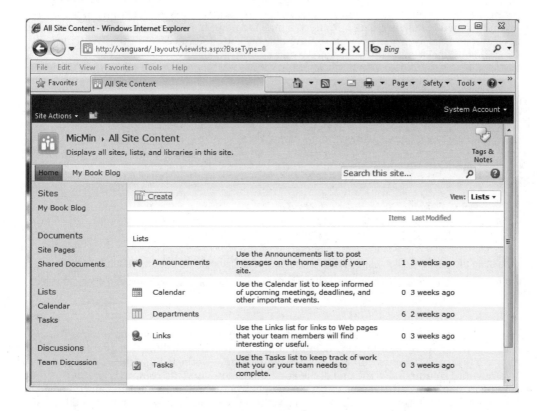

Figure 2-1. *The Create page lists the various content objects you can create.*

Both libraries and lists display the object names, the description, the number of items in the list or library, and the last date when someone made a change to the list or library. Let's begin by looking at the Announcements list that SharePoint installs with one default item. To open any list, just click on its name.

Announcements List

Several collaboration site templates include by default an announcements list. Use this list to display upcoming events, news, or activities that you want your site readers to know about. An announcement item consists of several pre-defined columns including a title, a body, and an expiration date. This list has two additional columns, Created By and Modified By,that SharePoint automatically populates when the user adds or changes an item. Let's focus on just the first three columns for now.

Figure 2-2 shows the **Announcements** list with its one default event. Each SharePoint list consists of a set of columns. Some columns appear in nearly every list. Other columns add unique capabilities to a list. In the Announcements list shown in Figure 2-2, you see four columns (you may not think of the first two as data columns even though nearly every list supports them). The first column is, in fact, a checkbox that allows you to select one or more items from the list and perform a common operation such as deleting the items, checking the items in or out, or publishing the items. The ability to perform an action on more than one item in a list or library at a time is a new SharePoint 2010 feature. Depending on how you want to use the list, you may want to turn this checkbox column off. (See the "Working with List Views" section for details on turning this feature on and off.)

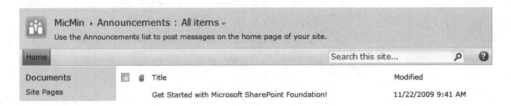

Figure 2-2. This announcements list includes attachments.

■ **Tip** When defining the view definition used to display announcements, open the **Filters** section, select the **Expires** column, and set it to be greater than or equal to **[Today]**. This filtered view hides expired announcements.

The second column shows a paperclip indicating that you can include an attachment to the list item. For example, you may add a supporting document to a list item by attaching that document. (If your list will never need attachments, you may want to define a view for the list that does not include this column.) The third column holds the title of the announcement. The Title column is another common column in nearly every list. It typically serves as a link between the list item and an edit page where you can change the information in the list. Finally, the fourth column shows the date and time of the item's last modification.

As mentioned earlier, the Announcements list has two additional columns. To see these columns, click on the Title value of the item to display a window showing the editable columns of the list. You can't directly edit the data displayed in this form unless you edit permissions for lists as discussed in Chapter 1. However, if you do have edit permissions, the **View** ribbon of this window displays the **Edit Item** icon in the **Manage** group. Click this icon to display the edit form for this list item, as shown in Figure 2-3.

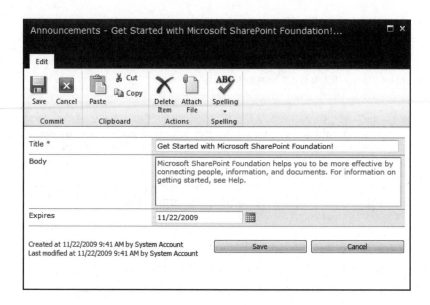

Figure 2-3. This announcements list includes expiration dates.

Note that the Title column has a red asterisk after the column name. The red asterisk indicates columns that require a value; you cannot leave it blank. Each announcement item also has a Body and an Expires date field. The Body column proves a multi-line text area where you can provide additional details about the announcement. The Expires column lets you select a date when the announcement expires. In this case, the announcement refers to the Get Started with Microsoft SharePoint Foundation announcement, which has an expired date of 11/22/2009. If you think about it, what good is an announcement of an event that displays after the event has occurred? Ideally, you would like your web site to remove past events from your announcements list automatically so that you would not need to monitor your site continually to remove them manually. Unfortunately, SharePoint will not do that even with an Expires date, at least not without creating a custom view that can compare the Expires column to the current date. However, you will learn how to do exactly that in the "Sorting and Filtering Lists" section.

For now, let's focus on the other options in the **Edit** ribbon. Let's associate another file to a list item by making it an attachment. You will find the **Attach File** option in the **Actions** group of the **Edit** ribbon. Click this option to display a dialog box that allows you to define the attachment. Before defining an attachment, however, upload the file to a library on your site. Never define an attachment to a file on your local system. However, you may want to attach to files on a network file share to conserve database space and reduce redundancy, especially if you are using SharePoint Foundation with an internal database with a 4GB database limit.

You can also cut, copy, and paste text within any column value field using the options in the Clipboard group. You can save and cancel any changes you make. You can even delete the item from the list.

■ **Note** If you delete an item from a list that has an attachment to another file in a SharePoint library, SharePoint does not delete that file. While you could handle this situation with SharePoint Event Handlers, the focus of this book is for the non-developer; therefore this solution will not be covered here.

The last item in the **Edit** ribbon is the **Spell Check** option. Click this option to spell check any text field in your list. In the Announcements list, spell check looks at the text in both the Title and Body column.

When you click anywhere within the Body text, a new set of ribbons appears at the top of the dialog. In fact, two ribbons appear under the common heading of Editing Tools. The first ribbon, **Format Text**, allows you to perform basic text editing such as font style, paragraph formatting, and text style. You can even display the HTML of the text and edit the raw formatting of the text.

■ **Caution** Only edit the HTML of a content area if you have experience working in HTML.

The second ribbon is **Insert**. It includes an option that allows you to insert tables, pictures, and links into a text field of an item. There is also an option in this ribbon to upload a file from your local machine to one of the document libraries on the site. After uploading the document, SharePoint automatically inserts a link to the document into the text at the current cursor position.

Adding Items to Your New List

Now that you know your way around an existing list, how do you add items to it? First, return to the default list view of the Announcements list as shown in Figure 2-2.

SharePoint opens a list in **Browse** mode, meaning that it displays the default list view along with the tabs for the other ribbons. You can always remove the visible ribbon commands by returning to Browse mode. Since you want to add a new announcement, you need to display the **Items** ribbon in the **List Tools** ribbon group. The **Items** ribbon allows you to add new items as well as edit and delete items. You can also change permissions for the item and view the item's history if your list or library tracks versions of each item.

In this case, click **New Item** in the **New** group to add another announcement. This action opens the edit dialog for the list item, letting you supply the column values for a new item in the list using the same dialog as shown in Figure 2-3. Click **Save** in the **Commit** group of the **Edit** ribbon to save your new announcement. After saving the announcement, you can return to the list view to see the new announcement. Figure 2-4 shows the Announcements list after adding several announcements.

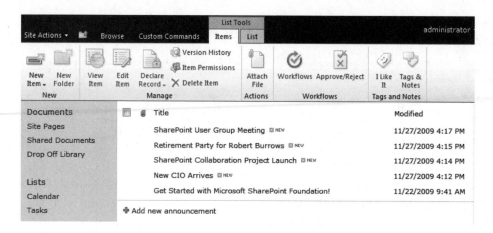

Figure 2-4. The Announcements list displaying several new announcements

One of the enhancements made to SharePoint 2010 involves the ability to edit list items not only from the default list view, but also from any page that displays the list as part of that page's content. The "Working with List Views" section later in this chapter covers this in more detail.

Contacts List

The second Content & Data list type to look at is the Contacts list. Because the team site does not automatically create a contacts list for you, you need to create this list before you begin using it. If you click **Lists** in the **Quick Access** menu, you can then click **Create** from the top of the **All Site Content** page to select the type of list you want to create. Figure 2-5 shows the available Content & Data lists. Click on the **Contacts** icon and then provide a name for the list. SharePoint requires unique names for lists and libraries. However, a list has additional properties you can set by clicking on the button **More Options**.

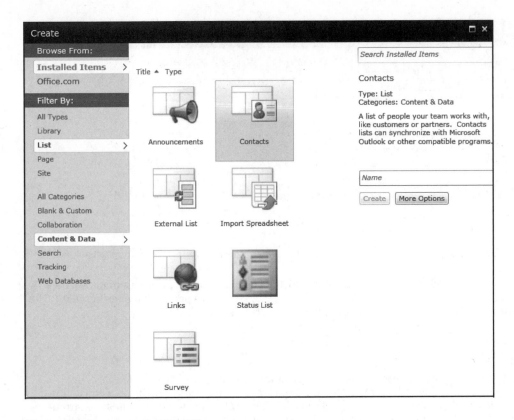

Figure 2-5. Creating a Contacts List

As you can see in Figure 2-6, the **More Options** button displays a second page in the **Create** dialog that prompts for a description of the list and asks whether you want to include a link for this list in the **Quick Launch** area. If you do not include a separate link, users can still navigate to your list by clicking the Lists heading to display the available lists within the site.

The **Description** field in this dialog displays its text in the Description column of Figure 2-1. Note that the description may be helpful to your users in determining the purpose of each of your lists. If you create a list without supplying a description, you can always return to the list to modify its properties to provide a description.

■ **Caution** SharePoint determines the size of the dialog box based on the size of the browser window so that the dialog box fits inside the window. If you start with a relatively narrow window, you may find that it truncates the details of the Create dialog. On closer examination, you should see a horizontal scroll bar at the bottom of the dialog that will let you scroll to see the contents of the dialog. However, to avoid this inconvenience, you should always begin with a maximized browser window before opening any command that displays a dialog box. The best way to insure this is to keep your browser set to Maximize.

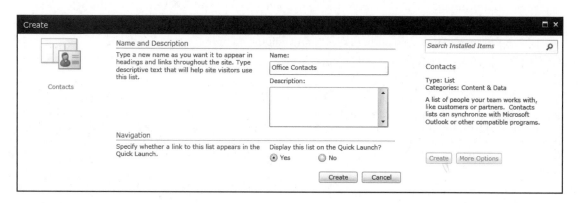

Figure 2-6. More Options for the Contacts List

After you define the properties for the list, click **Create** to begin using the list. You can see in Figure 2-7 that the list displays several columns across the top of the page including Last Name, First Name, Company, Business Phone, Home Phone, and E-mail Address. What if you do not need the Company name column because all of the contacts in your list are part of your company? And instead of Business Phone, you would rather have just their phone extension? You can easily update the columns in your contact list by going to the **List Tools** ribbon group and selecting the **List Settings** in the **List** ribbon.

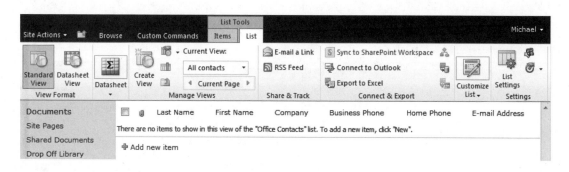

Figure 2-7. Viewing the Default Contacts Columns

The List Settings page consists of six parts:

- **List Information:** You cannot edit this section because it displays basic information about the name and location of the list.

- **General Settings:** The options in this section open dialogs that allow you to modify basic parameters defining the list.

- **Permissions and Management:** This section provides options to change permissions to the list and to manage features such as workflows and policies for the list.

- **Communications:** This section allows you to turn on or off RSS settings for the list as long as the SharePoint Farm Administrator has enabled RSS at the farm level.

- **Columns:** Use this section to review and edit the columns that define the list.

- **Views:** This section lists all currently defined views for the list.

If you are new to SharePoint, you may wonder if you must display all columns in a list. The simple answer is no. A list consists of a collection of columns (think of columns as fields) arranged by items (think of items as rows). You create or modify views for that list to display the specific columns and rows you want. First, you should notice that the list definition on the list settings page has many more columns than displayed in Figure 2-7. Therefore, before adding a new column to a list, see if there's a column you can use as-is or if you can rename one that's not in use. Only if you need a unique column should you consider adding a new column.

For example, you want a column for just the contact's business extension. Why not use the Business Phone column and redefine the column name. To do this, click on the column name to display the column properties. Change the **Column Name** from Business Phone to Business Extension. Leave the column type set to **Single line of text**. However, you may want to consider reducing the **maximum number of characters** from the default of 255 to a more realistic 3 to 5 characters depending on the size of your telephone extensions. Then scroll to the bottom of the page and click **OK**. Figure 2-8 shows the **Change Column** page for the Business Phone/Extension page.

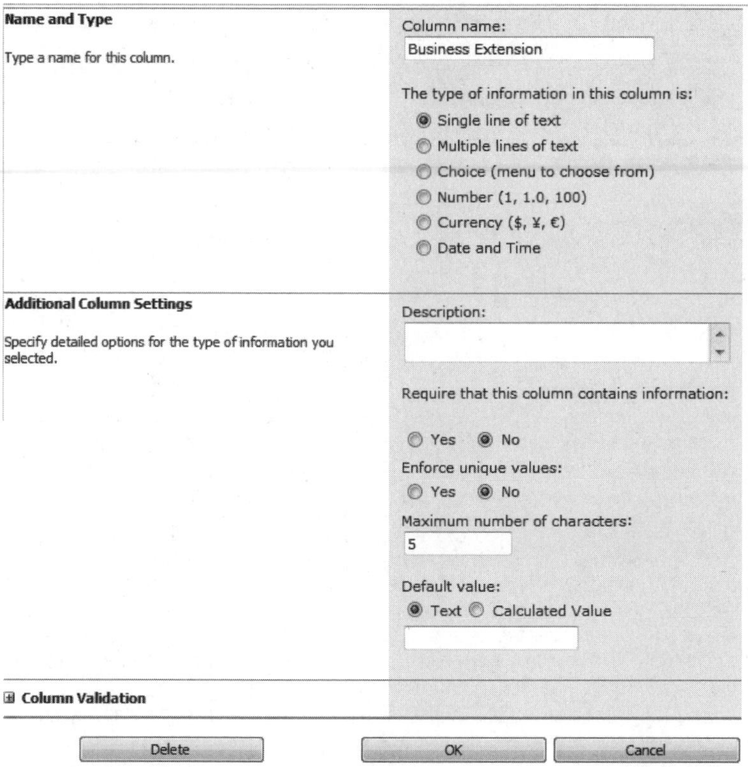

Name and Type

Type a name for this column.

Column name:

Business Extension

The type of information in this column is:

- ◉ Single line of text
- ○ Multiple lines of text
- ○ Choice (menu to choose from)
- ○ Number (1, 1.0, 100)
- ○ Currency ($, ¥, €)
- ○ Date and Time

Additional Column Settings

Specify detailed options for the type of information you selected.

Description:

Require that this column contains information:

- ○ Yes ◉ No

Enforce unique values:

- ○ Yes ◉ No

Maximum number of characters:

5

Default value:

- ◉ Text ○ Calculated Value

⊞ **Column Validation**

[Delete]   [OK]   [Cancel]

Figure 2-8. The Change Column page

Next, consider the other request not to use the column Company name. You could click on the column named Company and from the **Change Column** page, click the **Delete** button at the bottom of the page to remove this column. However, you may not want such an extreme solution. Perhaps all you really need to do is to remove the column from the list's default view. Just because you don't use a column doesn't mean that you must delete it from the list.

Return to the **List Settings** page and scroll to the bottom of the page to display the **Views** section. A list can have many views, with each one displaying a different set of columns, a different sort order, or a different filter. While you can have many views for any one list, you can only have one view designated as the default view. SharePoint uses the default view when you open the list from your available libraries and lists. To edit the view, click the **view name** to display the **view definition**, as shown in Figure 2-9.

■ **Tip** From the display of the list itself, you can quickly modify the view by selecting the command **Modify View** from the **Manage Views** group of the **List** ribbon.

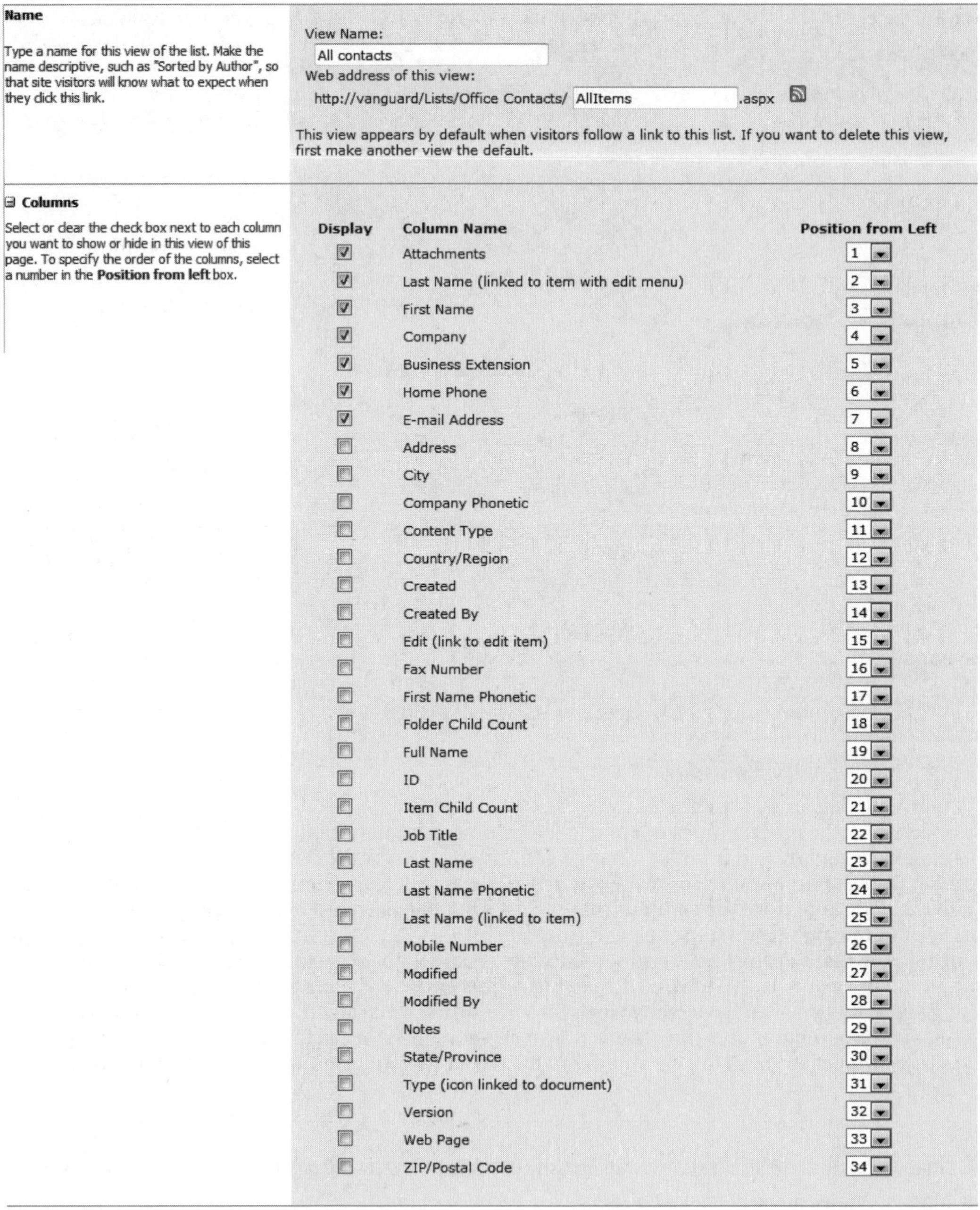

Name

Type a name for this view of the list. Make the name descriptive, such as "Sorted by Author", so that site visitors will know what to expect when they click this link.

View Name:

| All contacts |

Web address of this view:

http://vanguard/Lists/Office Contacts/ | AllItems | .aspx

This view appears by default when visitors follow a link to this list. If you want to delete this view, first make another view the default.

⊟ **Columns**

Select or clear the check box next to each column you want to show or hide in this view of this page. To specify the order of the columns, select a number in the **Position from left** box.

Display	Column Name	Position from Left
☑	Attachments	1 ▾
☑	Last Name (linked to item with edit menu)	2 ▾
☑	First Name	3 ▾
☑	Company	4 ▾
☑	Business Extension	5 ▾
☑	Home Phone	6 ▾
☑	E-mail Address	7 ▾
☐	Address	8 ▾
☐	City	9 ▾
☐	Company Phonetic	10 ▾
☐	Content Type	11 ▾
☐	Country/Region	12 ▾
☐	Created	13 ▾
☐	Created By	14 ▾
☐	Edit (link to edit item)	15 ▾
☐	Fax Number	16 ▾
☐	First Name Phonetic	17 ▾
☐	Folder Child Count	18 ▾
☐	Full Name	19 ▾
☐	ID	20 ▾
☐	Item Child Count	21 ▾
☐	Job Title	22 ▾
☐	Last Name	23 ▾
☐	Last Name Phonetic	24 ▾
☐	Last Name (linked to item)	25 ▾
☐	Mobile Number	26 ▾
☐	Modified	27 ▾
☐	Modified By	28 ▾
☐	Notes	29 ▾
☐	State/Province	30 ▾
☐	Type (icon linked to document)	31 ▾
☐	Version	32 ▾
☐	Web Page	33 ▾
☐	ZIP/Postal Code	34 ▾

Figure 2-9. Viewing the Default Contacts columns

The view definition consists of a dozen sections; you will only deal with the second, **Columns**, here.
... for the list. The check boxes to the left of the column
... displaying the view. As you can see, even a default
... columns. To include another column in the view,
... To exclude a column already displayed in the view,
... ne.
... op-down list. Each drop-down list has a different
... ottom. SharePoint lists use this column to indicate the
... splay the view. To change the order, you need only
... ew numeric value to indicate its new position.
... the rest of the columns to insert the column in the
... o move the e-mail address so that it appears
... en the drop-down list for e-mail and change its
... is, SharePoint automatically renumbers all the

... before the column **Company** since you decided not
... ttom of this dialog. After saving your changes,
... ur new view definition. You will learn more about
... of this chapter.
... fields. The first type of hyperlink field occurs on the
... nk automatically to link each item to an edit page
... ve one field that can open the edit page. By default,
... rever, you can rename the column to something more

... address column. All hyperlink columns consist of
... viewer and the second part is the actual link used to
... the link. In the case of the e-mail address, clicking
... address automatically opens your e-mail application and creates a blank message for this
contact. The contact's e-mail address in the link portion of this column must begin with `mailto:`. The
hyperlink column type can also reference a web address either within your SharePoint site or anywhere
on the Internet by prefixing the address with `http://` or `https://` as appropriate.

External List

The External list is new to SharePoint 2010. It allows you to display data from a data source outside of
SharePoint as if it were a list built within SharePoint. Thanks to the new read/write capability of Business
Connectivity Services (BCS), which replaces the Business Data Catalog (BDC) from Microsoft Office
SharePoint Server 2007, you can define a connection to almost any type of external data source, such as
another SQL Server database or an Oracle database. Once you have a connection defined, you can
instantiate any table from that data source to display and use it from within SharePoint as if it were just
another SharePoint list. You'll examine this new feature in more detail in a later chapter.

Import Spreadsheet

If you already created your data list in Excel, you can quickly and easily import that data into a SharePoint spreadsheet without re-entering all the data. Chapter 7 discusses how to import Excel data and how you can work with both SharePoint and Excel.

Links List

You might think of the Links list as one of the simpler lists in the Content & Data group. It consists of a collection of links to other pages or other web sites. Many page designers use the Links list as a container to hold the links they want to display on the web pages they build. A Links list might even provide the data for a simple menu to pages on your site or related sites.

While SharePoint provides several ways to add links to a web page, the Links list is an easy to maintain structure. However, once you have more than a dozen links, you might be tempted to start grouping your links to organize them using either separate folders or even separate lists. A better design choice adds a custom column to the list. With a custom column, you can create views that filter the links. Whether you use a separate column for each filtered view or a single column with different values or even a multi-valued column becomes a design decision. The advantage of not organizing your links in folders or in separate lists is manageability. You can easily group items in different views by defining different filtering columns. If you store everything by folders or separate lists, it is difficult to create views that combine and reuse links in different ad hoc ways.

■ **Tip** SharePoint 2010 builds collaboration pages on a Wiki page, which allows you to link pages on your site easily without using a Links list. However, for links outside of the current site, you might use the Links list or similar technique to make them easier to find and maintain.

Figure 2-10 shows two examples of a possible site menu using a Links list. The top one, called **My Links**, displays links in a custom view that includes only the URL column from a Links list. You might use a menu such as this one to link to objects that you do not include in the Quick Access area on the left side of the page or to pages outside of your site.

The second list instance uses a different view of the same Links list. In this view, the first column identifies the item type (folder or link) using different icons for each type. The second and third columns display the URL and Notes for the link respectively. The "Defining Views for Your List" section provides further details on how to customize and create views. Chapter 3 explains how to add views to a page, as shown in Figure 2-10.

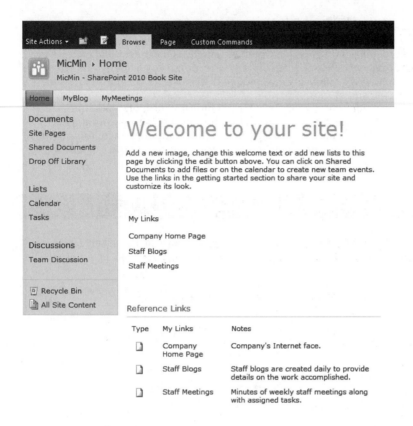

Figure 2-10. A Links list can provide hyperlinks to internal and external pages and sites.

Status List

The status list provides a way to track and display goals using colored icons that indicate how successful you have been at reaching those goals. I cover this list type in detail in the "Introduction to KPIs" Section in Chapter 8.

Survey List

The last list template in the Content & Data category is the Survey list. This list provides an example of a highly specialized list. It displays its columns as a questionnaire or a poll for the reader to complete rather than a list of columns and rows. You begin the same way when creating a new survey list by assigning a name and description to a new survey. However, surveys have two additional options that you must set when you create the list.

The first option asks whether you want to display the respondent's name in the survey. Some people like to have the respondent's name in the survey so they can contact her for additional comments related to her responses. However, if your survey asks questions such as the respondent's satisfaction with current management policies or the effectiveness of the respondent's immediate supervisor, they may not be entirely honest in their responses unless you make the survey anonymous.

The second option you must specify lets you decide whether a single user can respond to a survey only once (no stuffing the ballot boxes here please). Even if the user responds to an anonymous survey, if the survey is on a collaboration site that requires a log in, a hidden field can track the user name and thus restrict users to one response per survey.

Next, you create your survey questions. SharePoint provides 13 built-in question types from which to choose. The question types range from simple text responses to multiple choice answers and even rating scale questions using a Likert scale. Each question type has its own unique settings. You can make individual questions required. Some question types allow multiple value selections. You can also set minimum and maximum value limits to numeric questions.

The Likert Scale

A Likert scale survey attempts to determine the respondent's level of agreement with a statement by selecting a value from 1 to *n* based on how strongly he agrees or disagrees with the statement. A simple example might be as follows:

SharePoint provides a good collaboration framework for the work environment.

1. Strongly Disagree

2. Disagree

3. Neither Agree nor Disagree

4. Agree

5. Strongly Agree

Some scales do not include a central choice like the third choice above where the respondent does not really have to make a choice on one side or the other of the question. Other scales might include more values. However, the more values that separate the two extremes of the scale, the more difficulty respondents have deciding between the choices.

A concept known as *central tendency bias* refers to a respondent who avoids extreme responses. In a scale of only 1 to 5, such a bias forces a respondent's answers to the three middle values. This bias provides one argument for scales with more choices.

Two other common reactions in Likert scales include the *acquiescence bias* where respondents tend to agree with all statements and the *social desirability bias* in which respondents tend to select answers based on what they think the surveyor expects. This latter bias often appears as a problem with non-anonymous surveys in a work environment where respondents feel that their responses could affect their career.

Surveys support branching logic. Rather than building a survey in which the user answers every question, you can create a questionnaire that branches to different questions depending on how the user responds to a question, thus customizing the survey based on the individual's earlier question responses.

Figure 2-11 shows the user view of an available survey. The user initially sees only the name of the survey along with a brief description and its creation date. The user also sees the number of responses already submitted. To respond to the survey, they should click the link **Respond to this Survey** found at the top of the survey or click the title of the survey depending on where you display the survey. Both actions open a separate page to display the survey. The menu bar of this screen also has the option **Respond to this Survey** that you can use to start the survey.

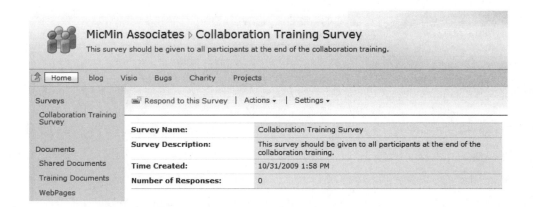

Figure 2-11. *Displaying a notification of survey availability*

When the user opens this example survey, SharePoint displays a page with the questions, as shown in Figure 2-12. Notice that for yes/no questions, SharePoint uses a check box that when checked indicates **Yes** and when left blank indicates **No**. Although you can set the default value to either **Yes** or **No** when you define the questions for the survey, neither default choice really guarantees that the respondent actually made the response. A more accurate way to ask even a simple yes/no question might use the **Choice** question type. When using this question type, include a default option **NA** to indicate that the respondent has not made a choice or simply leave the default value blank.

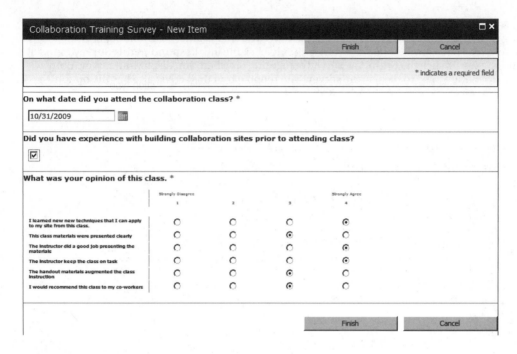

Figure 2-12. *Responding to a survey*

Steps to create survey in Figure 2-12

1. Navigate to the site where you want to create the survey.

2. Select **Site Actions ➤ View All Site Contents**.

3. Click the **Create** button from the top of the page.

4. Select from the available list types, the survey list.

5. Provide a name for the site: `Collaboration Training Survey`.

6. Click **More Options**.

7. Enter an optional description.

8. Choose whether to display the survey in the **Quick Launch** area.

9. In the **Survey Options** section, choose not to show the user names and choose not to allow multiple responses.

10. Click **Create** to begin entering survey questions.

11. Enter the first survey question: `On what date did you attend the collaboration class?`

12. From the question types, select `Date and Time`

    a. The screen now refreshes to show additional settings for this question type

13. Select `Yes` for the question **Require a response to this question**.

14. For the question **Enforce unique values**, select `No`.

15. For the question **Date and Time Format**, select `Date Only`.

16. For the **Default** value, select `(None)`.

17. Click the **Next Question** button at the bottom of the page.

18. Enter the second question: `Did you have experience building collaboration sites prior to attending class?`

19. From the question types, select `Yes/No (checkbox)`.

20. After the page refreshes, select `No` as the **Default** value in the additional settings.

21. Click the **Next Question** button at the bottom of the page.

22. For the last question, enter the text: `What was your opinion of this class.`

23. From the question types, select: `Rating Scale.`

24. After the page refreshes, select `Yes` for the prompt **Require a response to this question**.

    a. The next setting property lets you enter any number of sub-questions. To add more than one sub-question, press **Enter** at the end of each line before beginning the next sub-question.

25. Enter the first sub-question: `I learned new techniques that I can apply to my site from this class.`

26. After pressing **Enter**, type the second sub-question: `The class materials were presented clearly.`

27. After pressing **Enter**, type the third sub-question: `The instructor did a good job presenting the materials.`

28. After pressing **Enter**, type the fourth sub-question: `The instructor kept the class on task.`

29. After pressing **Enter**, type the fifth sub-question: `The handout materials augmented the class instruction.`

30. After pressing **Enter**, type the sixth sub-question: `I would recommend this class to my co-workers.`

31. Next you must select the **Number Range**: 4

32. Next specify the **Range Text** replacing `Low` with: `Strongly Disagree` and `High` with `Strong Agree`. Change the middle box to a blank since you have no middle value.

33. Deselect if necessary the **Show N/A** option.

34. Click **Finish** to complete the survey.

As mentioned previously, you can click the survey title to open a separate page displaying only the survey. This page has some options listed at the bottom. The first option asks whether the user wants to show a graphical summary of responses, as shown in Figure 2-13. This view makes it easy to interpret the survey results. Beneath that, a second option lets you show all responses. The initial list shown with this option only shows a default response identifying name that includes a simple numeric sequence indicator, the name of the responder (if not anonymous), the date the survey was taken, and whether they completed the survey.

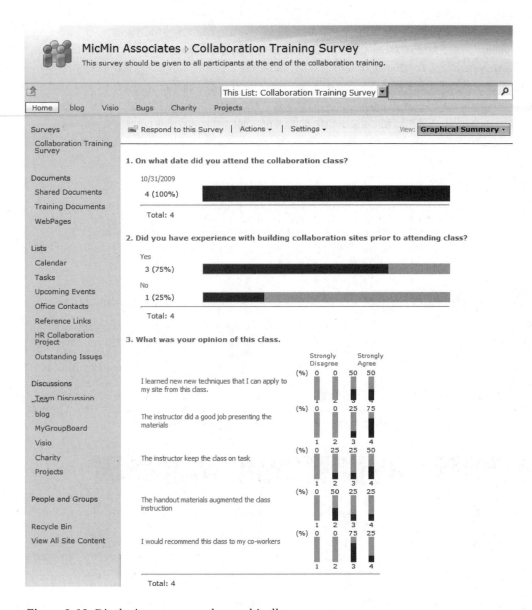

Figure 2-13. Displaying survey results graphically

■ **Note** One of the survey's Advanced Setting options allows the survey builder to determine whether other users can see everyone's responses or just their own. Of course, the survey builder as well as the site owners can always view all survey results. However, allowing potential respondents to first view prior results might distort their responses (see the sidebar "The Likert Scale" for types of bias in surveys). They may even decide that, based on the overwhelming direction of current responses, their opinion may not matter and thus not take the survey.

Collaboration Lists

Out of the box, SharePoint only provides one list classified as a collaboration list, the Discussion Board. SharePoint places this list in the collaboration category because a discussion implies more than one person, as most people do not have discussions with themselves. (Although I have to wonder if that person walking down the street talking to himself really has a Bluetooth connection for his phone.) So let's look at how the discussion board works.

Discussion Board List

The discussion board reminds some people of an Internet-style newsgroup. Both discussion boards and newsgroups support multiple messages related to each topic. Both objects allow you to group messages chronologically or by thread subject. A SharePoint discussion board supports columns such as the discussion subject and body, the name of the user who created the message, and the creation date, as well as user-defined columns. You might implement a discussion board list on topics where you want feedback from members of your organization or when you need to provide a place where they can post comments, questions, or concerns. Figure 2-14 shows a discussion board for a new collaboration project used to obtain opinions from the staff concerning features needed for collaboration.

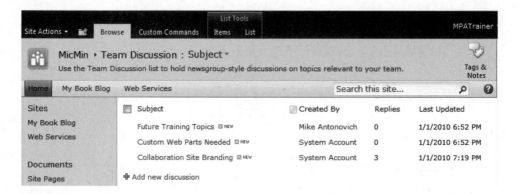

Figure 2-14. Showing subjects from a discussion board list

Figure 2-14 shows a listing of discussion topics by subject. Note that the first and second discussion threads have no replies yet, while the third topic already has three replies. To view these replies, click the subject. This action displays a new page with only the messages related to the selected subject. By default, SharePoint displays the messages in a flat view, meaning that the messages simply appear in sequence based on the Modified date column. However, there is another built-in view for this list, called the *threaded view,* which displays the messages in a hierarchy view.

■ **Note** To display a view other than the default view, use the **List** ribbon and open the drop-down list in the **Custom Views** group to display and select from available views. You can also click on the last item of the breadcrumbs in the title bar of the list to open a dropdown list of all the defined views for the current list.

In a threaded view, SharePoint indents a message reply a small amount from the message to which it replies. Multiple replies to the same message have the same indent. In Figure 2-15, user "Administrator" responded to the original message from "Michael." However, both "MPATrainer" and "Susan" responded to the Administrator's message. Note that, from this view, you can reply to any message at any level within the thread by clicking the **Reply** button to the right on the reply header.

■ **Note** When SharePoint groups the messages by thread, it sorts by **Modified date**. Therefore, you need to rely on the amount of indenting for each message to determine to which message each message replies. You can also click the link **Show Quoted Messages** at the bottom of a message to see just the messages in the current response's hierarchy.

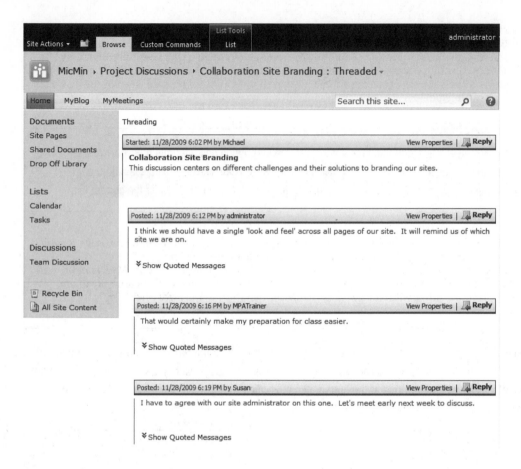

Figure 2-15. Showing threaded messages within a discussion board subject

Over time, a single message can spawn multiple branches off the main thread as people explore different issues. Using the thread view to display messages helps organize what might otherwise be a confusing chronological sequence of messages into a rational conversational sequence.

Searching Category

Although this category includes the Calendar and Project Tasks lists, I will reserve discussion of the Project Tasks list for the Tracking Category, which also includes the Project Tasks list.

Calendar List

The calendar list shares similarities to the announcements list. Both display events and activities. However, the calendar list extends this functionality showing events in a familiar month, week, or daily graphical layout similar to what you already use in Outlook. Even better, the calendar list integrates with Outlook 2003 and later. Chapter 5 explores the calendar list's capabilities more fully.

Figure 2-16 shows a basic calendar list with three upcoming events. The default view displays the date and time of the events along with the event title and description. The calendar list includes the built-in views:

- **All Events:** This view displays all past, present, and future events.

- **Current Events:** This view displays all present and future events only.

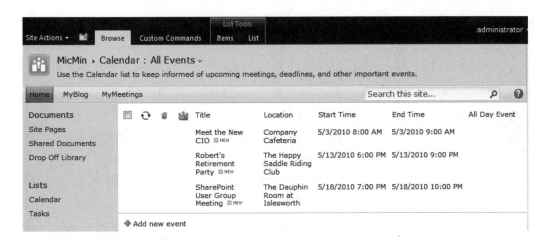

Figure 2-16. *Calendar list using the All Events view*

In addition to a list-style view, the calendar list includes special views that display calendar data by month, by week, or by day. Figure 2-17 shows an example of the month view of the same events shown in Figure 2-16.

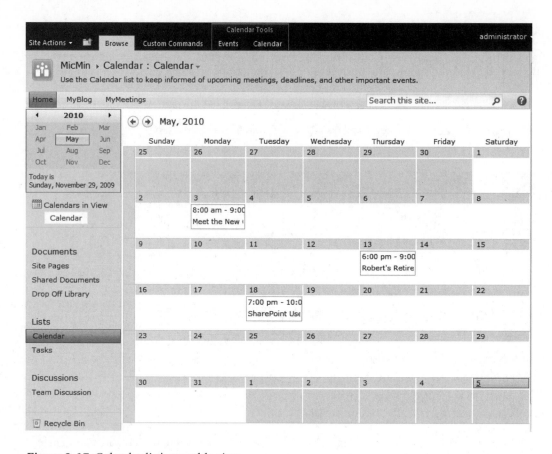

Figure 2-17. Calendar list's monthly view

The calendar list has another interesting feature. It shares its events with events in your local copy of Outlook so you can access your schedules no matter where you store your events, meetings, and appointments. For example, you might use a SharePoint site to track information about your project. Within this site, your project manager maintains a single calendar of major events related to the project. You can merge this site calendar with your Outlook calendar to build a single consolidated view of all your events. Chapter 5 explores in depth how to work with calendar lists through Outlook.

■ **Tip** Don't like the way your list view displays on a web page? Change it! Click the small down arrow to the right of the list name on the web page and select **Modify Shared Web Part**. A dialog box appears to the right of your page. You may need to scroll horizontally to see it. Find the **Selected View** property in this dialog and choose a different view from the drop-down list. Click **OK** to apply and exit this dialog box and return to the normal page view mode. The next chapter covers more on displaying views on web pages.

Tracking Lists

You can create a variety of tracking lists by clicking **More create options** from the **Site Actions** menu. Tracking lists contain information such as links to other pages or sites, calendar events, tasks, issues, or even surveys. You will find these lists under the **Tracking** group:

- Tasks

- Project Tasks

- Issue Tracking

- Agenda (available only in Meeting sites)

Tasks List

If you use the Tasks list in Outlook to manage your to-do lists or the to-do lists of your staff, you have some idea of how such lists help organize your workday. The SharePoint tasks list also includes columns that let you enter task titles, descriptions, start dates, due dates, status, and task percent completion. You can assign (depending on your permissions) tasks to other users. Then you can change the view to see all tasks, just tasks assigned to you, tasks due today, or all active tasks.

■ **Tip** You can define an alert to receive notification by e-mail when someone creates a new task and assigns it to you. But a better method is to turn on the **E-Mail Notification** option in the list's **Advanced Settings** (See **List Settings** in the **Settings** group of the **List** ribbon) to send an e-mail about the task when you assign ownership of the task using the **Assigned To** field.

What is an Alert?

An *alert* is a flag set within SharePoint to notify you via e-mail when a change occurs to the selected item. You can define when you want to receive alerts and for what types of changes you want them. Their real value is that they eliminate the need to monitor lists and libraries manually to track changes or additions. I cover alerts in more detail in the "Using Alerts to Notify You of List Changes" section later in this chapter

If you manage work for other users, the tasks list might help you organize your staff's work. Since even completed tasks remain in the list, you could create a filtered list view to show your boss all the tasks completed by your staff in the last reporting period. With a few custom fields, you could also create views to track hours expended per task. Tracking actual time to complete tasks can help you estimate required time for similar tasks in the future. You can also use this information to bill back your group's time if you manage a consulting group. By adding a field for completion dates, you could compare the difference from the task due dates to determine whether your staff can keep up with the workload or whether you need to request additional staff.

Figure 2-18 shows a simple tasks list.

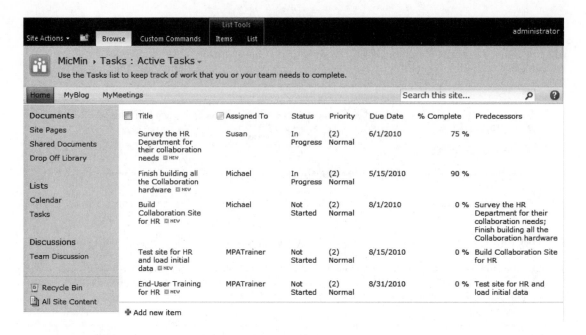

Figure 2-18. Tasks list for a project in progress

As with the calendar list, you can integrate the tasks list with Outlook. Chapter 5 explores these capabilities.

Project Tasks List

The project tasks list at first looks similar to the previous tasks list in that it supports the same basic fields. However, while the items in the tasks list might represent tasks from multiple independent projects or even tasks, the items in the project tasks list generally represents related tasks for a single project. In fact, as you enter items in this list, SharePoint uses the start and due dates to define a bar in a Gantt chart automatically as the list's default view.

Gantt Charts

You use a **Gantt chart** in project management as a way to visually show the sequence of tasks in a project along a horizontal timeline. It also shows the status of the project by shading each task line based on its percent completion, which when compared to the current date on the horizontal timeline provides a visual estimate of the project's status.

A list of the major tasks in a project appears to the left of the chart. The right side of the chart consists of a timeline depicting days or weeks in the project, depending on the time scale. Each row on the Gantt chart identifies one specific task within the project. The horizontal band to the right of the task name identifies the start and end of the project along the timeline. If one task depends on another task, lines from the end of the first task connect to the start of the next task to indicate that the second task depends on the completion of the first task. SharePoint depicts each task with two horizontal bands. The wider band represents the entire planned time span from the start date to the end date of the task. The inner band indicates the percent completion. If this inner band is missing, the task has not yet started. If the inner band started on time but extends beyond the outer band, the task was underestimated. Across the top of the chart is a calendar ribbon from which you can identify the current date. Any task in which the inner band does not reach the current date is behind schedule. Any task in which the inner band stretches beyond the current date is ahead of schedule. Thus you can visually compared the bands for each task to the current date to estimate the status of each project task.

Figure 2-19 shows a Gantt chart for a simple project: five items necessary to implement a collaboration site for the Human Resources (HR) department of an organization. Suppose that today is 5/1/2010. You could quickly see that you are ahead of schedule on these tasks. On the other hand, if today were 6/1/2010, you would clearly be behind schedule.

Figure 2-19. Project tasks list displaying a Gantt chart

Of course, this Gantt chart for a single project does not show Michael's involvement in three other projects that have a higher priority than this project. As a result, he could not devote the necessary time to this project to keep it running on schedule. The project task list does not, by itself, combine information from multiple projects to facilitate seeing relationships between projects and how that might impact resource availability. You may want to consider implementing Microsoft's Project Server 2010 along with Microsoft SharePoint Server 2010 to manage multiple projects.

Issue Tracking List

The issue tracking list also looks similar to the tasks list in that it tracks independent activities that might involve multiple projects or activities. Your organization may use an issue tracking list to track customer support calls, risk mitigation activities, or other issues that do not necessarily relate solely to one project. In addition to the fields supported by the tasks list, the issue tracking list classifies items by categories. A category might represent a department, application, project, team, or any other grouping, or it could simply indicate the severity of the issue.

■ **Tip** The Issue Tracking list defines the categories as part of the definition of the list. If you do not like the default categories, simply edit the column properties by going through List Settings and create your own categories.

You can also associate an item in the list with other items already in the list. This is a great way to tie together related issues where solving one issue may resolve or at least partially resolve another issue. Figure 2-20 shows an example of an issue tracking list created by a Customer Care group.

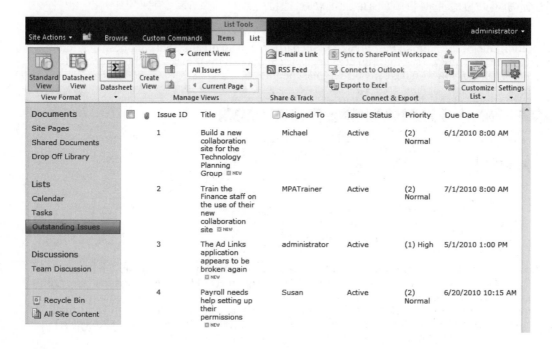

Figure 2-20. An issue tracking list tracks outstanding issues for the company.

Other Lists

SharePoint makes several other lists available when you select **Create** from the **All Site Content** page. Some lists are only available with certain site templates. For example, the first five lists shown below only exist with a meeting site.

- **Agenda:** Create an outline of meeting topics, who will cover them, and the amount of allotted time for each topic.

- **Decisions:** Used to track decisions made at the meeting.

- **Objectives:** Used to inform attendees of the meeting goals before they attend the meeting.

- **Text Box:** Used to insert custom text, instructions, messages, or quotes into a meeting.

- **Things to Bring:** List of things the meeting attendees should bring to the meeting such as handouts, projectors, laptops, power cables, etc.

Figure 2-21 shows an example of what a meeting site could look like with several of the special meeting lists on the main page. Keep in mind that once you have a meeting site definition that works for your organization, you can create a custom template of that site so you can reuse it to create other meeting sites.

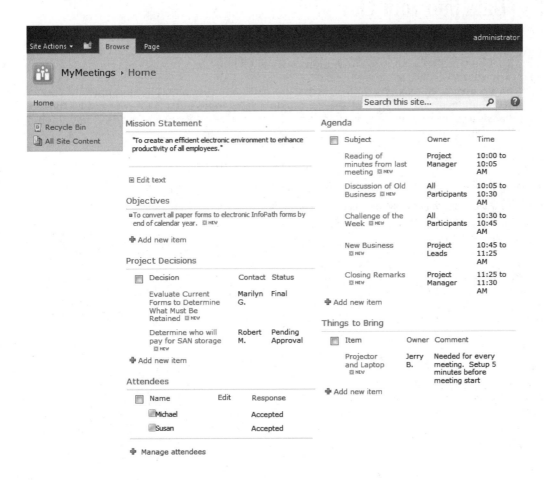

Figure 2-21. A typical meeting site with several meeting specific lists

It is typical for a site template to have specialized libraries or lists designed specifically for that site. However, you are not limited to just the lists defined by the site. You can also create custom lists. These lists begin with only the required Title column (that you can rename). You can then add your own columns to this basic list definition to create a list that meets your specific needs. The Import Spreadsheet list is a custom list that is especially useful when you need to bring data from an Excel spreadsheet into SharePoint without having to retype everything. I will cover many of its special features in subsequent chapters.

SharePoint 2010 also adds a Languages and Translators list. This list works with the Translation Management workflows and the Translation Management Library to assign translation tasks based on the languages involved.

Editing Data into Your List

Earlier in this chapter, you saw how to perform simple data editing within your list. You saw how to edit the information using one of two view styles, Standard view or Datasheet view. To begin editing data in an existing list, open the list by going to **Site Actions ➤ View All Site Content** and then clicking on the name of the list where you want to work.

Lists typically open in Standard view. Notice that one of the columns that typically appear has the name Title. As mentioned, you can rename this column to make it more suitable for your needs. The important thing is that this column links each item in the list to an edit page where the user can modify the data in the other columns.

■ **Tip** If the linked column does not appear in a different color, you can also determine which column links to the edit page by slowly passing your mouse over each column in the item (or row). A drop-down arrow appears to the right of the column value for the field linked to the edit page.

You cannot edit the column data directly in the Standard view. You must click on the value in the Title column to open a form that first displays the data for that item. You must then click **Edit item** in the header of that form to open an editable view of the data. Figure 2-22 shows the form that first displays the column data for an item along with the View ribbon and Figure 2-23 shows the form used to edit the item.

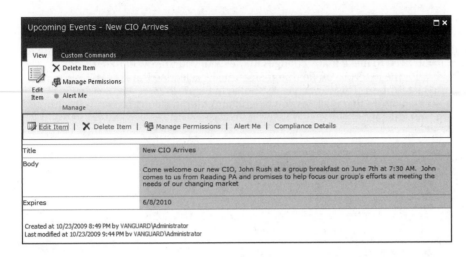

Figure 2-22. Displaying an individual item in the Upcoming Events list

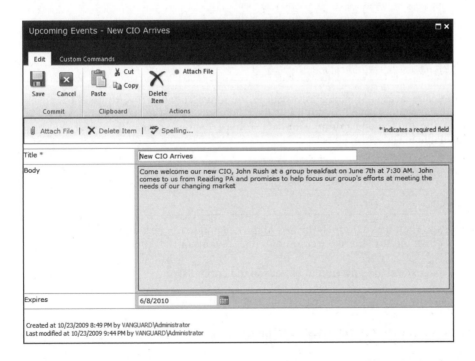

Figure 2-23. Displaying the edit form of the Upcoming Events list for an item

On this edit page, you can change the item's data and then click **Save** in the **Commit** group of the **Edit** ribbon.

If you only need to change a few values in one or two items in a list, this may be a good technique to edit the data. However, if you need to make many changes to the data, you may want to consider switching to Datasheet view for the list. You can do this at any time by selecting **Datasheet View** in the **View Format** group of the **List Ribbon**. This view style, as shown in Figure 2-24, resembles an Excel spreadsheet or an open Access table in that it allows you to edit any column value in any row by simply clicking on it and making your changes.

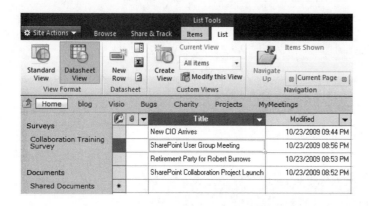

Figure 2-24. Displaying a list using DataSheet view

SharePoint automatically saves your changes every time you move from one row (or item) to another. However, the real advantage of editing multiple data elements using the Datasheet view comes from the flexibility of editing and moving around your data. Table 2-1 shows some of the major keystroke shortcuts available in Datasheet view.

Table 2-1. Keystroke Shortcuts in DataSheet View

Key	Action
Arrow keys	Left and right move through the text of the cell and to the next or previous cell. Up and down move to the same column in the previous or next row.
Ctrl+A	Used to extend the selection to all cells in the entire list.
Ctrl+C	Copies the contents of the current cell to the clipboard.
Ctrl+End	Moves to the last cell in the last row of the list.
Ctrl+Home	Moves to the first cell in the first row of the list.
Ctrl+Shift+End	Used to extend the selection to all cells from the current cell to the last cell in the list.

Key	Action
Ctrl+Shift+Home	Used to extend the selection to all cells from the current cell to the first cell in the list.
Ctrl+Spacebar	Used to extend the selection to all cells in the current column.
Ctrl+V	Pastes the contents of the clipboard to the current cell.
Ctrl+X	Cuts the contents of the current cell and places it on the clipboard.
Ctrl+Z	Undoes the last edit.
Delete	Deletes the current contents of the current cell.
End	Moves to the last cell in the row.
Enter	Moves to the same cell in the next row.
Esc	Restores the previous value to the current cell (like an Undo).
F1	Opens Help.
F2	Puts the current cell in Edit mode with the cursor at the end of the text.
F8	Opens the Datasheet Task Pane.
Home	Moves to the first cell in the row.
Page Down	Moves to the next page.
Page Up	Moves to the previous page.
Shift+Arrow Key	Used to extend the selection of cells in the direction of the arrow.
Shift+F8	Hides the Datasheet Task Pane.
Shift+F10	Opens a context menu for the current cell.
Shift+Spacebar	Used to extend the selection to all cells in the current row.
Shift +Tab	Moves one cell to the left.
Tab	Moves one cell to the right.

■ **Caution** Although it is possible to use the **Enter** key to enter data into all of the rows for one column before moving to the next column, if any of your other columns are required fields, this action fails. SharePoint tries to save each row when you exit the row and it cannot exit a row if any column that requires data remains blank. If your current view does not include all columns, this can be confusing when the required column does not appear in the view.

When you finish working in datasheet mode, you can click the **Standard View** button in the **View Format** group of the **List** ribbon.

Working with List Views

I started this chapter assuming that you have been following along using a Team site. For example, the team site automatically includes the Announcements list on the site's home page. As you made changes to the Announcements list, adding or modifying the content of individual announcements, you may have noticed that the content changed on the home page to reflect the changes you made in the list. However, it is important to know that the view of the list on the home page of the site is not the same thing as the list itself. In fact, if you were to make a change to the structure of the view from the list itself, perhaps by adding or removing a column, changing the sort order, or applying a filter, those changes would not appear in the announcements section of the home page. Only changes to the list data immediately appears in the home page view of the list.

Why do some changes appear and others do not? That is a fair question and one that perplexes many SharePoint users. The key to understanding this apparent inconsistency comes from the understanding that the list itself does not appear on a site page, only a view of that list appears. Changing the data displayed by that view does not require a change to the view definition itself. Therefore, data changes flow through the view definition to the page. However, when you change the underlying view definition, you must refresh the view definition stored within the page with the new view definition defined in the list.

Let's suppose that you only wanted to display the announcement title and not the modified date as originally shown at the beginning of this chapter. You have two ways to make this change. One way makes the change to the view definition directly stored within the page. Making the change this way has no effect on the original view definition back in the list. I call this a disjointed change because the view used on the page no longer reflects any changes made to the supposedly same view back in the list. If you want to make both views match again, you must open the view definition in the list and make the same changes there that you made to the view definition in the page. If you only made a few changes, you may be able to successfully change both views, but as the number of changes increases, the chances of missing one or more of the changes from one view to another increases.

■ **Tip** If all you need to do is change the view used on the page and do not care about the view in the list, you can easily edit the list right from the page. Place the page in edit mode. Then click anywhere in the list to display the **List Tools** ribbon group. Then click the **Modify View** option in the **Manage Views** group of the **Lists** ribbon.

The second way to make the change starts by making the change in the existing view definition in the list or by creating a new view definition in the list. Using this method makes the change in the list, but the changes do not immediate appear in the page that displays the list. To correct the page display, you must open the definition of the list on the web page and refresh the view definition. I prefer making changes to views using this second method because I only have to make the changes to one copy of the view and then simply refresh the other instance of that view on the page. The following paragraphs describe the steps needed to use this method.

First, open the original list and through the **List Settings** page, select the view you want to modify, make your changes to the view, and then save the view. In this case, to show only the **Title** column, you would need to open the **All Items** view and deselect all the columns except for the Title column. If you also want to remove the check box that appears to the left of the title column in the list, scroll down to the section **Tabular View** and deselect the check box **Allow individual item checkboxes**. Click **OK** to save the changes to the view.

Next, navigate to the page that displays the view. (I know we have not yet really discussed how to place lists on web pages. I will cover that topic in Chapter 3. If you follow the steps listed here, you should still be able to accomplish the goal.) Place the page in **Edit** mode and locate the web part that holds the list. Find and click on the small down-pointing arrow to the right of the list title. The drop-down menu that appears includes the option **Modify Shared Web Part**. Click this option to open a panel of properties for this list instance on the current page. If you do not see this panel, you may notice the horizontal scroll bar at the bottom of the page. Use the scroll if necessary to view the area to the right of your page. There you should find a panel with several options. The first two prompts include drop-down boxes. The first drop-down box allows you to select which view from the current list's views you want to use to display data on this page. SharePoint selects the default view for the list initially. However, you may want to create a custom view to limit the columns, change the sort, or apply a filter to the data that users see. In this example, select the **All Items** view to refresh the definition of the view for the page. Then click **OK** at the bottom of this panel to stop editing the web part's properties.

■ **Caution** When you apply a view to a page, SharePoint merely makes a copy of the view definition on the page. If you go to the list and subsequently change that view's definition, the page does not automatically know about the change. Rather, you must re-edit the page and re-apply the view to the page to update the latest changes to the view definition.

The second drop-down box allows you to change the Toolbar type. By default, the list does not display a link on the page to add new data to your list. You can limit additions to your list by setting the **Toolbar Type** to `No Toolbar`. (Of course, only users with the **Add** items permission can add to a list in the first place). The **Show Toolbar** option displays a header bar like you see when you open the list directly providing the ability to sort and filter the list. However, if you only want to allow users to add records easily to your list, change the **Toolbar Type** to `Summary Toolbar` and click the **OK** button in the list properties panel. SharePoint now displays a link beneath the list `Add new announcement`. Clicking it displays a blank version of the dialog shown in Figure 2-25, allowing the user to add values for a new list item. Remember, this only works if the user has permission to add announcements to the list.

Finally, you can add items to your list by opening your list directly by going through **Site Actions** to **View All Site Content** and then clicking on the desired list. Once opened, click in a blank area of the list to display the **List Tools** ribbon group. Select the **Items** ribbon and then click on the upper portion of the **New Item** option in the **New** group to show the same window, as shown in Figure 2-25.

The first field in this new window, named Title, has a red asterisk after the name. This asterisk indicates that an announcement must have a title before SharePoint can save it. Entering data into the other fields is optional.

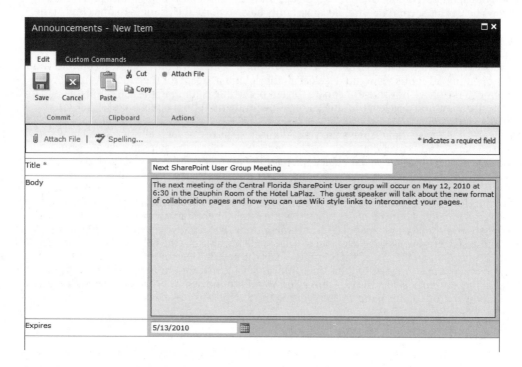

Figure 2-25. Adding a new announcement item

Click the **OK** button when you have finished entering the data for the current list item. SharePoint automatically returns you to the list page where you can see the new item in the **Announcements** list, as Figure 2-26 shows.

■ **Note** The position of the new item within the list depends on the sort order used by the default view of the list.

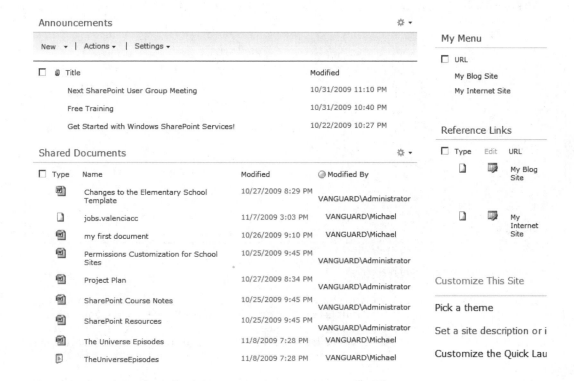

Welcome!
to your new team site, some of the things you can do here are:

Figure 2-26. Updated Announcments list displaying the newly added item

Building a Custom List

Even though SharePoint provides a wide variety of lists out of the box, you may have a requirement that no template completely satisfies. If one of the templates comes close to meeting your needs, you may want to use it and add a few additional columns, modify a few, or even delete a few to build exactly what you want. However, if your requirements differ greatly from any of the available templates you saw in the first part of this chapter, then creating a custom list from scratch can be the best choice to satisfy your specific needs.

If you have the **Create** permission for lists, you may find creating a new list easier than editing an existing one. Let's see how to begin a new list. First, click **View All Site Content** from the **Site Actions** menu. On the Create page, previously shown in Figure 2-17, select the **List** type and the **Blank &**

Custom category. From the displayed icons, select **Custom List** as shown in Figure 2-27. Like most other lists, you must provide a list name that is unique within your site. You should also provide a description that informs your site readers about the purpose of your list. To provide a description, click the **More Option** button before clicking the **Create** button.

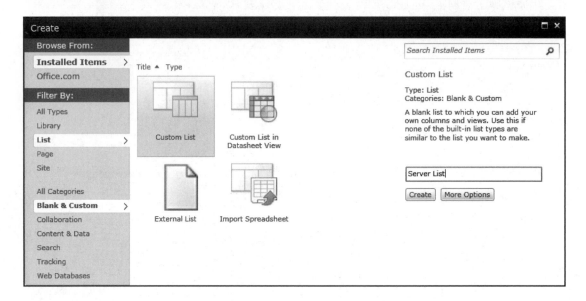

Figure 2-27. Creating a custom list

Under the navigation section, you can choose whether to include the list in the Quick Launch area. If you do not, users can still navigate to your list by clicking either **Lists** or **View All Site Content** in the Quick Launch area. Of course, it is always possible to come back later and change this setting through the **List Settings**, so do not fret too much over deciding whether to include the list in the Quick Launch area. Also, keep in mind that list instances become "web parts" that you can add to any page within a web part zone.

Next, define the columns for your list. After you click **Create**, SharePoint displays an empty list. By default, a list must have at least one column, which SharePoint names **Title**. In fact, if you only need a single column, you can use that one column, perhaps renaming it to something more appropriate. While you can rename the Title column, you cannot delete it. Even after renaming the Title column to something you do want, you will probably need to add a few more columns to that initial list.

■ **Tip** To add or rename a list column, select **List Settings** from the **Settings** group of the **List** ribbon while displaying the list. For example, within the **Columns** section, locate the Title column and click on it to edit the properties of the column. Here you can change the **Column Name** of the column and then click **OK** to save your update.

From the **List** ribbon, click **Create Column** from the **Settings** group. The top portion of the Create Column page, shown in Figure 2-28, lets you name your new column and select its field type.

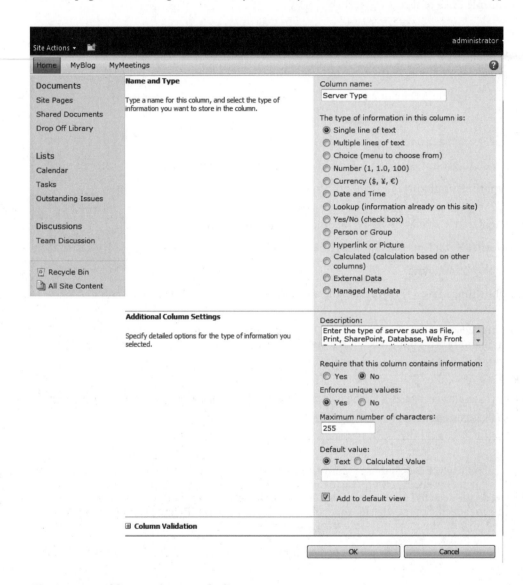

Figure 2-28. Adding a column to the list

You must define unique column names within a list instance. However, you can use the same name for columns in different list instances even within the same site. When it comes to data types, SharePoint provides a collection of column types from which to choose:

- **Single line of text:** Short text entries

- **Multiple lines of text:** Long text entries

- **Choice:** Select one or more items from a predefined list of choices

- **Number:** Any integer, real, or percentage number

- **Currency:** A number with currency formatting

- **Date and time:** A Date or a Date and Time value

- **Lookup:** Select a value from another list

- **Yes/No:** A check box

- **Person or group:** Works with Authenticated users within SharePoint

- **Hyperlink or picture:** Links to other pages, documents, web sites, or e-mail addresses

- **Calculated:** Calculation based on other columns in the current list

- **External Data:** Data outside of SharePoint accessed through the BCS

- **Managed Metadata**

- **Publishing:** Image, HTML, schedule end date, schedule start date; available only as site columns

- **Audience targeting:** Automatically added if you turn on audience targeting for a list or library. This option is not selectable as a user-defined column type.

■ **Tip** If you plan to use the column as a linking field in a master-detail relationship, it helps clarify your design intent if you use the same column names in both tables.

You will probably never use all these column types in a single list. In fact, some types only appear in lists available through SharePoint enterprise features or when using specific site templates.

Depending on the selected column type, the second half of the column definition page refreshes to display prompts for specific properties for that column. These properties include settings to make the column required, to limit the maximum length of strings, to provide minimum and maximum values for numeric fields, and more.

When defining a column, the last property determines whether this field appears on the default view for the list.

■ **Note** The default view is not the same as the form displayed by SharePoint when you add a new item to the list. The form that SharePoint creates to enter new list items or edit existing ones always displays all columns defined in the list. You cannot edit this form. However, the default view for a list consists of a unique combination of columns, filters, sort orders, and other characteristics used to display a subset of the list on a page. SharePoint optionally adds columns to the default view for you as you define the columns in your list. You can create additional views for a single list and you can change which one is the default. However, you can only define one view per list as the default view. If you add new columns after changing which view is the default view, you may end up with no view that includes all columns from the list. Of course, you can always modify a view definition to add or remove columns.

After you click **OK** to add a new column, SharePoint returns to the **List Settings** page from where you can add more columns or edit existing ones. If you have finished defining the columns for your list, you can return to the list view by clicking on the list name in the header.

Figure 2-29 shows a custom list after adding several columns, but before items have been added. At any time, you can repeat this process to add more columns. In fact, you can add several thousand columns in a standard list. After you add more than a couple columns, that last setting that asks whether to add the column to the default view becomes more important. For lists with many columns, you may only want to display the most essential ones in the default view. Readers can always click the item's title field (the one linked to the edit menu) to display a page with all the item's columns, or they can switch to a different view that displays a different subset of columns from the list.

■ **Tip** If you want to use the Datasheet view to edit your list data, you should have at least one master view that includes all columns and rows in your list. Otherwise, you may encounter problems trying to save rows that have required columns that the view does not display.

Figure 2-29. Default list view

Limits and Performance

The latest release of SharePoint does not have limits on lists and columns within lists as restrictive as prior versions. Microsoft says that SharePoint supports lists of as many as several million records. However, practical concerns related to usability still affect how you design lists. Can you imagine scrolling horizontally to view hundreds or thousands of columns? Do you really need a list with more than 2,000 columns? As a result, SharePoint uses a throttling setting to limit the number of items a user can query and display at a time. The default limit is 5,000 items for most users, and 20,000 items for super users. This is still a large number of items to format for a single web page! One possible way to override this limit via code uses the RequestThrottleOverride property in SPQuery. Another possible workaround involves creating two or more lists that you link in a master-detail relationship to retrieve only a subset of records at a time.

For those readers with a web background, talk of performance limits when displaying large lists should come as no surprise. The performance of web pages has always degraded as the size of a table displayed on the page increased. While Internet connections have improved, these improvements only push further out the size of a list or table before users notice performance issues. That's because at least two factors influence the performance of a web page. First, the sheer quantity of data clearly affects the time needed to download the entire dataset. However, the formatting of a web page can also be a very time-intensive task. The key to improving performance for large tables involves splitting tables into smaller units. You can accomplish this with a set of separately filtered views or with a view that uses paging capability to display a limited number of items at a time. Using the properties of views, you can easily limit the number of items displayed at a time. Furthermore, all views should only include the minimal number of columns needed for the current display.

Finally, if you really need lists with a large number of items, maybe what you really need is a table built in Access or SQL and then displayed in SharePoint. Chapter 6 examines ways to use Access with SharePoint.

After you finish adding the columns you need into your list, you can begin adding items by clicking **New Item** from the **New** group of the **List** ribbon. Regardless of how many columns you include in the default view, SharePoint includes all columns from the list in the form that it generates when adding a new item. Figure 2-30 shows the form created from the Custom list to maintain a corporate Server List.

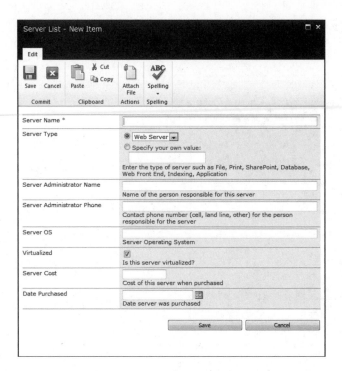

Figure 2-30. *Item entry form for the Server List*

■ **Note** The description for a column appears beneath the data entry controls on the generated Edit page.

After you see the new item data form for the first time, you may decide to change the data type description or the name of one or more of the list columns to help users understand what you want them to enter. You might even decide to change the data type of one or more columns. This example uses a choice list in the form of a drop-down list to allow the user to select the server type. Similarly, you may not want to allow the user to enter the Server Operating System (OS). Because the list of possible operating systems changes relatively infrequently, you prefer to have the user select the OS from a list that you can easily update with new operating system names as they become available. Let's see how you can modify this Server Operating System column to be a choice type column.

Modifying the Column Types in Your List

To modify a column of a SharePoint list that you or a colleague created, begin by opening the list. Let's open the Server List described in the previous section on custom lists. Select **List Settings** from the **List** ribbon.

This option opens the List Settings page for the selected list, as shown in Figure 2-31. Locate the column you want to modify in the **Columns** section of this page and click the column name. SharePoint then displays a page with possible changes you can make to the column. For many columns, you can change the column name as well as its type.

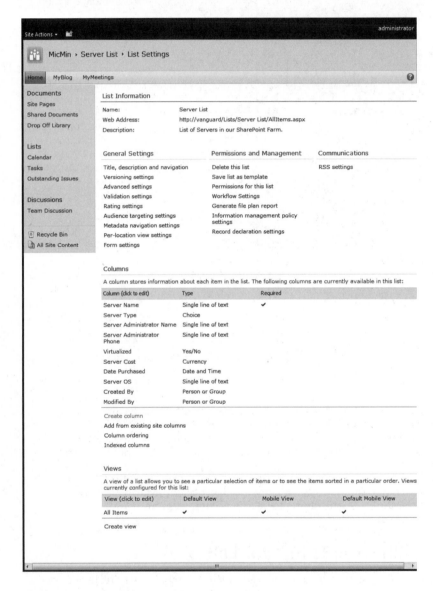

Figure 2-31. Modifying a list's settings

■ **Note** You cannot change the column type of the **Title** column. However, as mentioned previously, you can change its name. In addition, SharePoint cannot convert several column types such as multiline text fields and date time fields to other column types. Data types that you can convert to other types include the single line of text, number, currency, and yes/no column types.

Initially, you defined the Server OS column using the single line of text column type. However, this could result in problems as users incorrectly spell their entries. Even if they do correctly spell the entry, a value of Microsoft Windows 7 would not match an entry of Windows 7 or even MS Windows 7; this could cause sorting and filtering errors when trying to analyze the results. Therefore, for a column with a limited number of values that change only occasionally, a better design uses a choice type column. Fortunately, it is easy to change the single line of text column to a choice column by just changing the column type. Figure 2-32 shows the **Server OS** column definition after conversion to a choice type column. A choice type begins with a set of possible drop-down values that you supply. SharePoint can then display the choice type using a drop-down list, a set of radio buttons, or a set of check boxes.

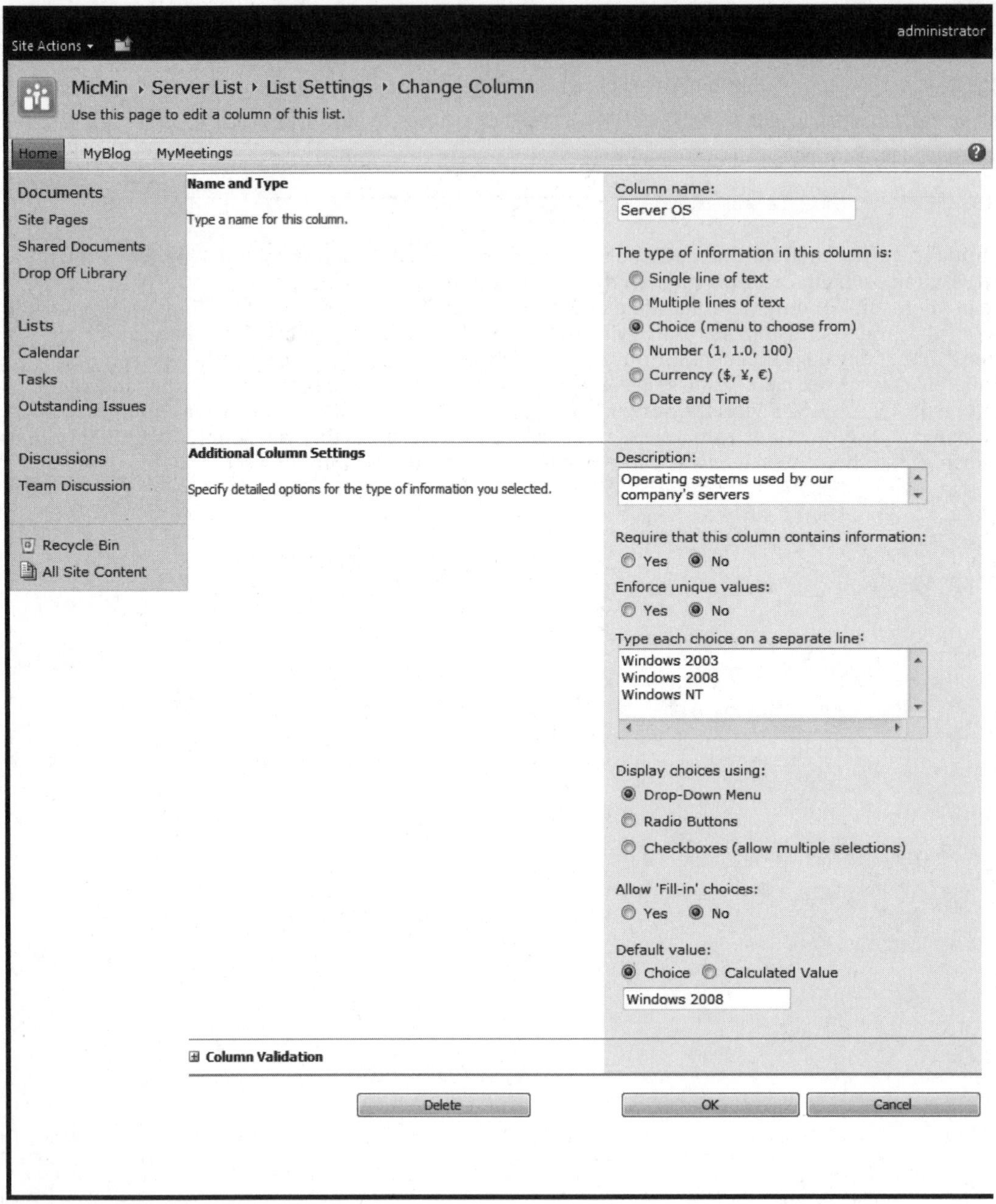

Figure 2-32. Modifying a column's type

Building Choice Lists for Columns

In many lists, the reader selects values for a column from a drop-down list. You define drop-down lists when you create the column definition using the choice type. You then display possible values in one of three ways: a drop-down menu, a set of radio buttons, or a group of check boxes.

Only the check box option allows the user to select multiple values for the column.

Developers use a drop-down list to save space when the number of choices exceeds more than four or five.

Radio buttons save keystrokes by displaying all values without needing to open a drop-down and they force the user to select only a single value.

Notice also that the settings in this figure allow the user to enter her own value rather than selecting one from the list. Use this option only if you do not know all possible values the user might enter. Also, know that misspelled entries may complicate filtering, sorting, and selecting the data later.

Finally, the choice type supports a default value. If you do not want to force a default value, leave the text box blank. An advantage of leaving the default value blank is that any value returned by the list absolutely reflects a selection made by the user.

If this is your only change, click **Save** to update the list definition. When you return to the list and add the next item, you will see the new drop-down option for the **Server OS** column shown in Figure 2-33.

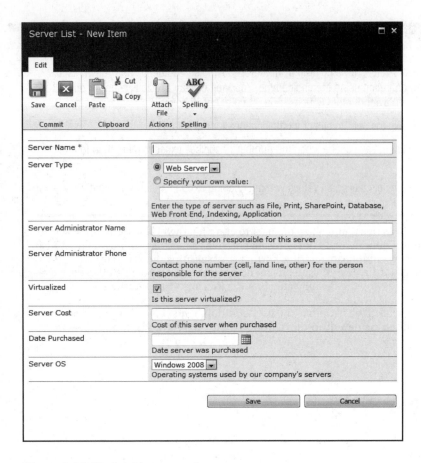

Figure 2-33. Updated item entry form

You can make changes to other columns in the same way. Note, however, that if you make changes to value limits such as maximum lengths, these restraints only apply to new data added to the list or when you edit and save an existing item. It does not automatically apply to all previous items.

■ **Caution** SharePoint allows you to change the columns of a list at any time. However, with a survey list, changing the survey questions or possible answers after several respondents have taken the survey invalidates the initial results. That reasoning should govern changes you allow to the columns of any list.

A *lookup column* is a variation of a choice column with the primary difference being where you define the possible values for the column. While you must enter the possible values into the definition of a choice column, a basic lookup column gets its values from another list. You must create this list before adding the lookup column to the current list, but you do not need to populate all of its values before defining the lookup column. Then you define the relationship between the lookup column and this other table by defining in the lookup column properties the table and column you want to use as the current column's possible values. For example, you could create a new table named Operating Systems and change the default Title column name to Operating System. In the Server list, you can define the Server Operating System column to be a lookup column type that uses the Operating System column of the Operating Systems table to define its possible values.

However, suppose you want to use the list of operating system names in more than just this one list. You can create a special type of column called a **Site Column** (see the sidebar of the same name).

■ **Tip** It is always a good practice to give users a list of possible values for any column where a limited number of possible values exist, especially if you must ensure the spelling of the entered values.

Site Columns

A *site column* differs from a regular list column in that you can access the column from any list within the site or its sub-sites. If you create a site column in the top-level site of the site collection, any list within the entire site collection can use it. If you create it in a sub-site, only those sub-sites beneath that site can see and use it.

Suppose your organization uses multiple operating systems on its computers. Rather than create an operating system column in every list, which would mean updating multiple lists when a new OS came out, you can create a site column in your top-level site to define your operating systems one time in one place. The following steps show how to create and use a site column:

1. Navigate to your top-level site.

2. Click **Site Settings** from the **Site Actions** button.

3. On the **Site Settings** page, click **Site Columns** in the **Galleries** option group.

4. Scroll through the **Site Column Gallery** page to verify that no existing site column would serve your needs or uses the same name you want to use. Note that this page organizes site columns into groups. Make sure you select **All Groups** from the **Show Group** drop-down (should be the default) when verifying the need for a new column.

5. Click **Create** to start defining a new site column.

6. Enter a name for the new site column and then choose a type. Call your column **Operating System**.

7. Choose the column type **Choice**.

8. Next, associate the new site column with an existing group or define a new group. If you have not yet created a group for your site columns, you may want to consider a group name consisting of your initials or company name.

9. In the Additional Column Settings section, begin by supplying the optional Description. Remember that the Description appears by default beneath the field in the default edit form SharePoint creates for the list.

10. Next, select Yes after the prompt **Require that this column contains information** if you want to require the user to respond to this field.

11. Although SharePoint shows you a setting to **Enforce unique values**, this setting may not make as much sense for a choice type field, so select No for this example.

12. In the next text box, enter each of the choice values.

13. The **Display choices using** setting lets you select how to display the choices. You can choose from a Drop-Down Menu, Radio Buttons, and Checkboxes. Note that only the Checkbox option allows you to select multiple selections. For this example, select Drop-Down Menu.

14. Next, decide whether users can enter their own values by clicking Yes for the setting **Allow 'Fill-in' choices**. Selecting No restricts the user to the choices previously defined.

15. Finally, choose a default value from the available choices. Clear the text box to create the column without a default value.

16. Click **OK** to create the site column definition.

17. Create a new list (or modify an existing one) in your site. For this example, modify the Server list.

18. Select **List Settings** from the **List** ribbon.

19. In the **Columns** section of the List Settings page, click **Add from existing site columns**. (If you previously added the Operating System column to this list, you need to first open the column properties so you can click the delete button to remove this column before adding the new column from the existing site columns.)

20. Find the new site column in the scrollable list of the **Available site columns** section and click the **Add** button. If you have a large number of site columns, filter the list by selecting the site column group using the drop-down list at the top of this page. This is another good reason for storing your site columns in a group named with your initials or company name.

21. Click **OK** to add the site column to the list.

22. You can edit the properties of the site column such as the name, description, etc.

Now click back on the list name found in the header at the top of the **List Settings** page. Add a new item to the list to see your site column appear when you enter, and edit item information. If you need to use the same column definition in another list, simply add the site column to create a consistent definition.

The best feature of a site column is this: If you add a new operating system to your company, and you will, you need only go back to the site column definition and update the choice list in one place to include the new OS. Immediately in all the lists that use this site column definition, you will see the new operating system without having to touch any of the other list definitions.

Another type of custom list you can build in SharePoint begins from an Excel Spreadsheet. You can find the **Import Spreadsheet** in the **Blank and Custom** category of the **List** type on the **Create** dialog from the **All Site Content** page. I will explore the use of Excel with SharePoint in more depth in Chapter 7.

■ **Tip** Even if you do not create the SharePoint list by importing an entire Excel spreadsheet, you can copy and paste selected rows or columns from the spreadsheet into a SharePoint list if you first display your SharePoint list in Datasheet view.

Using Alerts to Notify You of List Changes

Do you want to know when someone makes changes or additions to a list, but you dread having to spend time reviewing each list every day? What if SharePoint could notify you of changes or additions made to the list? Well, it can. With the **Alert Me** feature of lists and libraries, you can have SharePoint send you an e-mail whenever someone modifies or adds an item to any list.

■ **Tip** If you set an alert when you create a new list, you can monitor all changes to it.

To set up an alert for a list, first open the list. With the list displayed, click on the tab List and then select **Alert Me** from the **Share & Track** group of the ribbon, as shown in Figure 2-34.

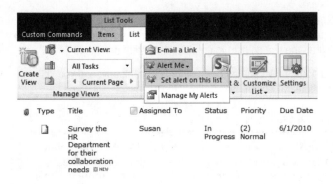

Figure 2-34. *Selecting Alert Me to create an alert*

You must name each alert you create. By default, the alert name includes just the name of the list, but since you can create more than one alert for any given list, you may want to expand this name. For example, to make it easier to identify your alerts, you might consider combining the name of the list with your initials and perhaps an indication of the type of alert such as Add or Modify. In fact, as you can see from Figure 2-35, there are many options available when you define a list and any of these options might be included in the title to help differentiate one alert from another.

■ **Tip** If you don't see the **Alert Me** option shown in Figure 2-34, make sure that the Farm Administrator has turned on alerts at the **Web Application** level. (Alerts can be found by selecting **Manage web applications** in the **Web Applications** group of the **Application Management** page. Select the **Web Application** and then choose **General Settings** from the **General Settings** command in the **Manage** group of the **Web Applications** ribbon.) Also, make sure that the account you have logged into SharePoint with has an e-mail address associated with it. Finally, have your SharePoint administrator confirm that outgoing mail has been configured. You can find these settings in **Central Administrator's System Settings ➤ E-Mail and Text Messages ➤ Configure outgoing e-mail** settings.

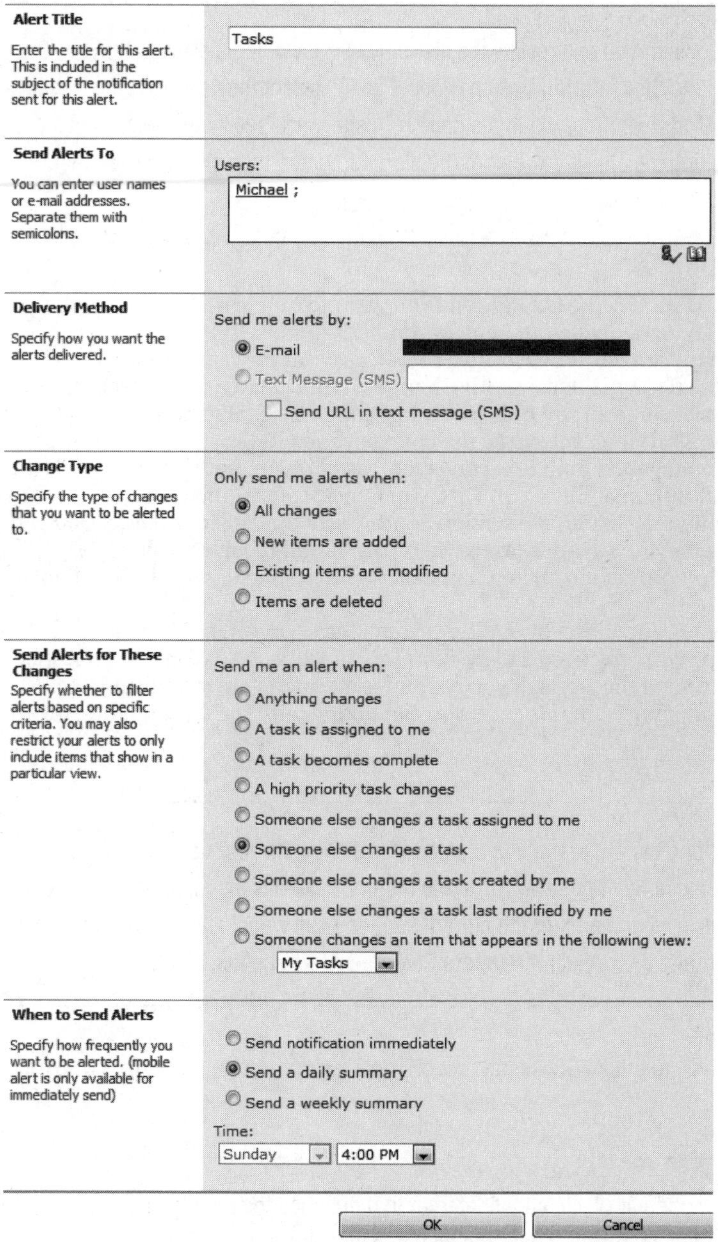

Alert Title

Enter the title for this alert. This is included in the subject of the notification sent for this alert.

Tasks

Send Alerts To

You can enter user names or e-mail addresses. Separate them with semicolons.

Users:

Michael ;

Delivery Method

Specify how you want the alerts delivered.

Send me alerts by:

● E-mail ▬▬▬▬▬▬▬▬▬

○ Text Message (SMS)

☐ Send URL in text message (SMS)

Change Type

Specify the type of changes that you want to be alerted to.

Only send me alerts when:

● All changes

○ New items are added

○ Existing items are modified

○ Items are deleted

Send Alerts for These Changes

Specify whether to filter alerts based on specific criteria. You may also restrict your alerts to only include items that show in a particular view.

Send me an alert when:

○ Anything changes

○ A task is assigned to me

○ A task becomes complete

○ A high priority task changes

○ Someone else changes a task assigned to me

● Someone else changes a task

○ Someone else changes a task created by me

○ Someone else changes a task last modified by me

○ Someone changes an item that appears in the following view:

My Tasks ▾

When to Send Alerts

Specify how frequently you want to be alerted. (mobile alert is only available for immediately send)

○ Send notification immediately

● Send a daily summary

○ Send a weekly summary

Time:

Sunday ▾ 4:00 PM ▾

OK   Cancel

Figure 2-35. Setting the properties of the alert

▪ **Tip** If you are a site administrator or owner, you can review the alerts by user by going to **Site Actions ➤ Site Settings**. Then select **User Alerts** from the **Site Administration** group. Finally, select the user from the **Display alerts for** drop-down list and click the **Update** button. When the page refreshes, you see all the selected user's alerts. You can select each alert by clicking the check box before the alert name and then click **Delete Selected Alerts** from the top of the page.

When defining an alert, you must specify the change type you want to monitor. Perhaps you only want to know when someone adds an item, deletes an item, or modifies items. Unfortunately, each of these change types is separate and you can only choose one. Therefore, your only options are to either create separate alerts for each notification type or select **All Changes** in the **Change Type** section.

You can further fine-tune an alert to e-mail you only when someone else changes an item in the list. After all, do you really need a notification when you make the change yourself? Similarly, you may only want a notification when someone changes an item that you created or an item that you were the last person to modify. If you have overall responsibility for the list, you may prefer notification of any changes made by anyone to any item in the list. In the section **Send Alerts for These Changes** you can see that there are nine different criteria you can apply as to when you should receive an alert. An interesting option is to receive an alert only when an item appears within a specific view rather than all of the items within the list.

Finally, you can decide when you want SharePoint to send your alerts. Do you really need to know about changes immediately? Perhaps you only need a daily summary of alerts. If so, you can even specify the time that you want SharePoint to send the alerts. If you only have an interest in monitoring the list, perhaps a once-a-week e-mail will satisfy you. In this case, you can define both the day and the time to receive your weekly alerts.

▪ **Tip** Want to get rid of your alerts but don't know where you created them? Click on your name in the upper right of any page within your site and select the option **My Settings**. In the menu bar across the top of this page, select **My Alerts**. The subsequent page shows all your alerts for the current site. You can select any or all of the alerts by clicking the check box before each alert and then select the **Delete Selected Alerts** option.

That is all you need do, other than to click **OK,** to start receiving alerts when data changes in your lists.

▪ **Tip** There are several third-party web parts available on the Internet that enhance the built-in capabilities of SharePoint's alert model. Your SharePoint Administrator may use one of these tools to manage alerts across all sites.

You can also manage your alerts from the **Manage My Alerts** option in the **Alert Me** drop-down in the **Share & Track** group of the **List** ribbon.

Creating RSS Feeds for Your List

RSS feeds provide another way to track additions to a list or library. RSS, which stands for *Really Simple Syndication*, has gone though several changes since the idea of content syndication across the Internet got its start. Web designers wanted a way to publish frequently updated information, such as news, that people could subscribe to and receive automatically without forcing them to return to their site. Originally, to read an RSS feed, you needed to download or purchase a program that could receive the RSS feeds and display their content as readable text. Today, you can use IE 8.0 or Microsoft Office 2010 or later versions to subscribe and read RSS feeds. In addition, you can find dozens of freeware programs that can read RSS feeds.

Setting up RSS feeds in SharePoint requires you to open your list. Then click **List Settings** in the **Settings** group of the **List** ribbon. Figure 2-36 shows the settings page for the **Upcoming Events** list. Click **RSS Settings** under the **Communications** area to define your RSS feed settings.

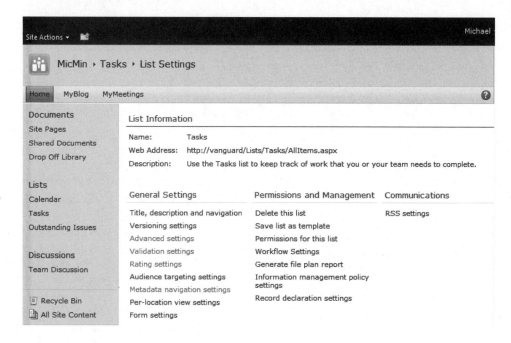

Figure 2-36. Starting a list RSS feed

When defining options for the RSS feed, you begin with a simple prompt asking whether you want to allow RSS for the current list. Of course, to create a feed, you need to select **Yes.** Under **Channel Information,** you also need to define feed properties such as the title, the description, and an optional image URL. Notice you also have the option of limiting multiline text fields to 256 characters. This option trims long feeds that may consist of entire news stories to just enough text to entice the viewer to click the item's title to read the entire story. As you will see in a moment, the title of the list item serves as a hyperlink to open the details of the item.

In the **Columns** section, you decide which columns to include in the feed. The RSS feed in Figure 2-37 includes a text column named **Body** along with the expiration date for the item. However, RSS feeds can include any or all columns from a list, including not only other custom columns you may have added, but also columns that SharePoint provides like **Title**, **Modified By**, and **Modified**.

Next, you can decide how many items to include in the feed and the maximum number of days to include an item in a feed. Both of these settings help keep your feed fresh by constantly displaying only the newest changes to your list. Be careful when setting these options; you don't want to overwhelm the reader with too many items. Finally, click **OK** on the settings screen to enable your RSS feed.

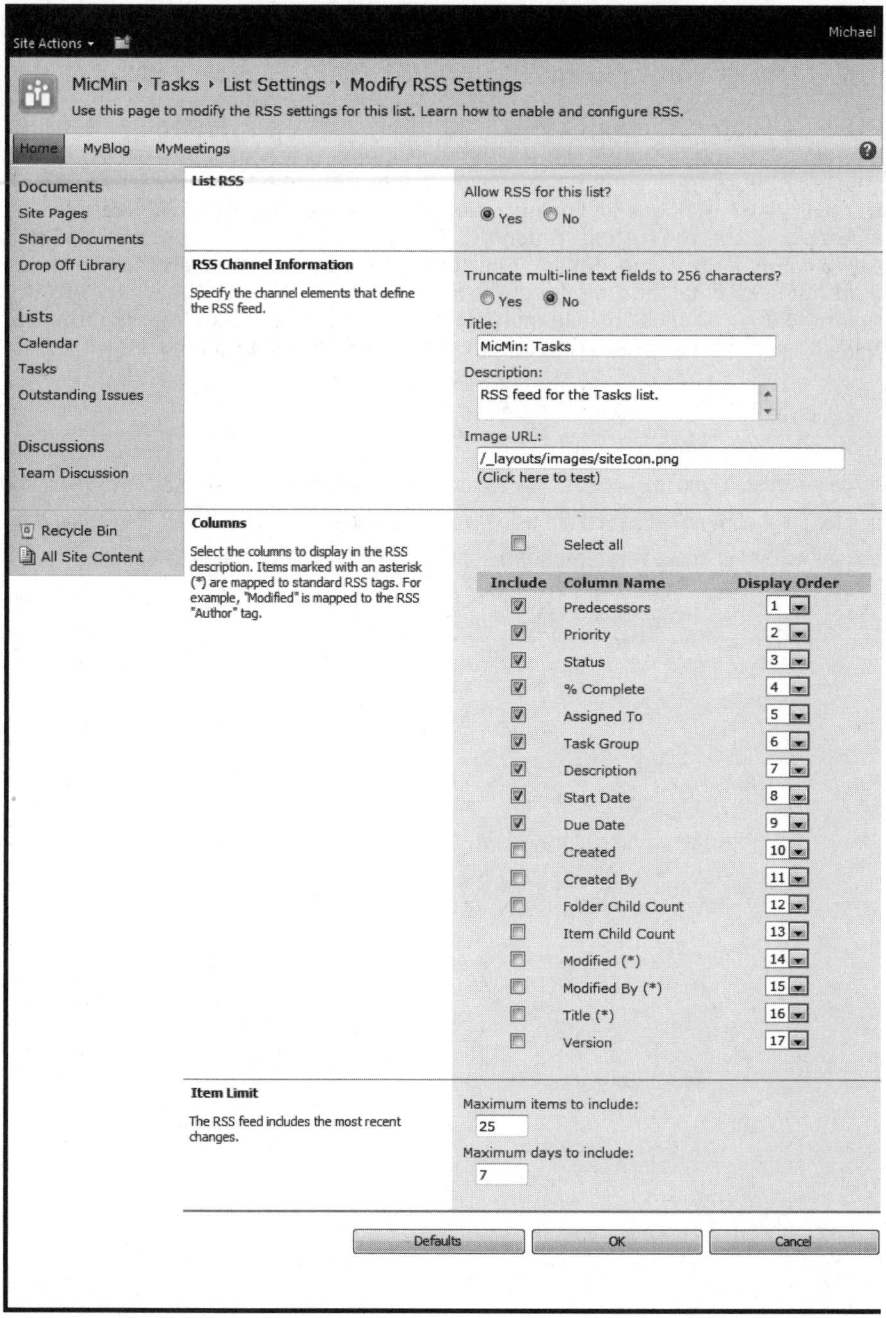

Site Actions ▾

Michael

MicMin › Tasks › List Settings › Modify RSS Settings
Use this page to modify the RSS settings for this list. Learn how to enable and configure RSS.

Home   MyBlog   MyMeetings

Documents
Site Pages
Shared Documents
Drop Off Library

Lists
Calendar
Tasks
Outstanding Issues

Discussions
Team Discussion

Recycle Bin
All Site Content

List RSS

Allow RSS for this list?
⦿ Yes   ○ No

RSS Channel Information

Specify the channel elements that define the RSS feed.

Truncate multi-line text fields to 256 characters?
○ Yes   ⦿ No

Title:
| MicMin: Tasks |

Description:
| RSS feed for the Tasks list. |

Image URL:
| /_layouts/images/siteIcon.png |
(Click here to test)

Columns

Select the columns to display in the RSS description. Items marked with an asterisk (*) are mapped to standard RSS tags. For example, "Modified" is mapped to the RSS "Author" tag.

☐ Select all

Include	Column Name	Display Order
☑	Predecessors	1
☑	Priority	2
☑	Status	3
☑	% Complete	4
☑	Assigned To	5
☑	Task Group	6
☑	Description	7
☑	Start Date	8
☑	Due Date	9
☐	Created	10
☐	Created By	11
☐	Folder Child Count	12
☐	Item Child Count	13
☐	Modified (*)	14
☐	Modified By (*)	15
☐	Title (*)	16
☐	Version	17

Item Limit

The RSS feed includes the most recent changes.

Maximum items to include:
| 25 |

Maximum days to include:
| 7 |

[Defaults]   [OK]   [Cancel]

Figure 2-37. Defining settings for the RSS feed

If you use IE 7.0 or better, you should see the RSS icon in your browser's menu bar turn from gray to orange the next time you display this list. This button remains inactive and gray when you view lists that do not support an RSS feed. However, when you navigate to a list or page that supports an RSS feed, this button turns orange.

Click the RSS feed button within IE to display a view of the RSS feed, as shown in Figure 2-38. With SharePoint lists, this view displays the site name along with the list name as the title. It then tells you that you can subscribe to the feed. Subscribing automatically downloads information from the feed to your computer, where you can display it in IE or add it to any other program that supports an RSS reader.

The sample feed view also shows the current contents of the feed. In a box in the upper right of the screen, the feed displays a count of the number of items currently in the feed. You can also sort the feed items by date, title, or author by clicking the links under the **Sort by** section. Note the small blue arrow to the left of the selected sort field. If you click the field multiple times, this arrow toggles from pointing up to pointing down and back again. This indicates the sort direction of the feed items based on the selected field.

■ **Note** If RSS feeds still do not enable, you may want to talk to your SharePoint system administrator to see if she has enabled RSS Settings for the Web Application you are using. You may also need to check your IE settings to see that the following options are set in **Tools ➤ Internet options ➤ Content ➤ Feeds and Web Slices ➤ Settings**.

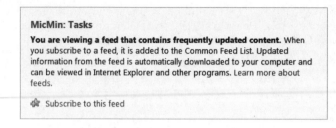

MicMin: Tasks

You are viewing a feed that contains frequently updated content. When you subscribe to a feed, it is added to the Common Feed List. Updated information from the feed is automatically downloaded to your computer and can be viewed in Internet Explorer and other programs. Learn more about feeds.

⭐ Subscribe to this feed

Displaying   5 / 5

● All   5

- -

Sort by:

▼ Date
   Title
   Author

End-User Training for HR

Today, November 29, 2009, 14 hours ago | administrator ➡

Predecessors: Test site for HR and load initial data
Priority: (2) Normal
Status: Not Started
% Complete: 0 %
Assigned To: MPATrainer
Description:
Start Date: 8/15/2010
Due Date: 8/31/2010

Test site for HR and load initial data

Today, November 29, 2009, 14 hours ago | administrator ➡

Predecessors: Build Collaboration Site for HR
Priority: (2) Normal
Status: Not Started
% Complete: 0 %
Assigned To: MPATrainer
Description:
Start Date: 7/20/2010
Due Date: 8/15/2010

Figure 2-38. Subscribing to a feed

When a user subscribes to a feed using IE, a dialog box prompts him for the name he wants to use on his computer to identify the feed. The default name includes the site name and the list name separated with a colon, as shown in Figure 2-39. However, the user can provide any name for the feed. Next, define a folder in which to store the feed. Just like favorites in IE, you can create a hierarchy of folders to organize your feeds.

Figure 2-39. Naming the feed, and placing it in a new or exising folder.

After you subscribe to the feed, you can open it by clicking the **Favorites Center** option in IE. You see, in addition to your other bookmarked URLs stored under **Favorites**, a tab named **Feeds**. Click this tab to see the folders and feeds within them. Figure 2-40 shows two folders under **Feeds**: `Microsoft Feeds` and `SharePoint Book Feeds`. Opening the `SharePoint Book Feeds` folder displays an RSS feeds added from Tasks list of the MicMin site.

Figure 2-40. Selecting the feed from within IE's Favorites Center to view the feed contents

---

■ **Note** A **Refresh** button appears to the right of each feed. The **Refresh** button consists of two green arrows pointing up and down, as shown in Figure 2-39. Click this button to refresh your RSS with the latest feeds from the RSS site.

Defining Views for Your List

Perhaps you do not like your list's default view. On the other hand, maybe you just want to create different views of the same list to use on different pages within the site or for different users. For lists like tasks lists, project tasks lists, and issue tracking lists, you might want multiple views of the list data to examine tasks or issues by person, project, status, or other criteria.

To work with views, open the **List** ribbon and look at the options in the **Custom Views** group, as shown in Figure 2-41, for the **Upcoming Events** list. The drop-down in this group displays all currently defined views for the list. You can switch from one view to another by clicking the one you want. While displaying any view, you can click **Modify this View** to make changes to the current view. If none of the existing views meets your needs, you can create a new view by clicking the **Create View** option on the left side of this option group.

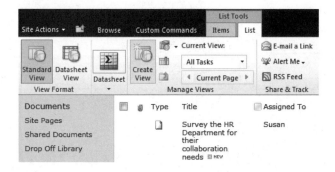

Figure 2-41. *Using the View drop-down to manage your views*

Alternatively, you can go through the **List Settings** option of the **Settings** group in the **List** ribbon to display the page shown in Figure 2-42. This option displays the **List Settings** page for the current list along with all the list options. Scroll to the bottom of this page to find the defined views. Notice that SharePoint defines one view as the default view. You can modify any view listed here by clicking its name, or you can create a new view by clicking the link **Create View**.

■ **Tip** You can delete any view, except the default view, by clicking it to display its **Edit View** page and then clicking the **Delete** button. However, what if you really want to delete the default view? You must first select one of the other views, and in the **Edit View** page promote it to be the default view. Then return to the original view, which SharePoint no longer identifies as the default, open its **Edit View** page, and **delete** it. Keep in mind that a list must have at least one view, and that one view must serve as the default view until you promote another view to be the new default view.

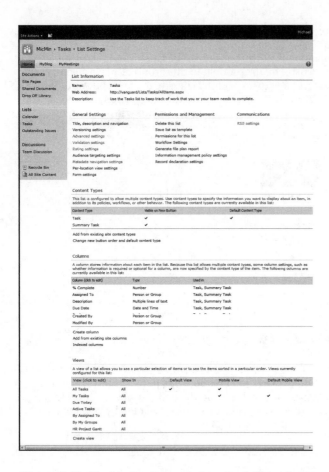

Figure 2-42. The List Settings page lets you define columns and views.

When creating a new view, SharePoint first displays a screen that lets you select the view format. SharePoint groups view formats into two starting styles, as seen in Figure 2-43. The first starting style lets you build a view from scratch by selecting your columns, sort order, and filter criteria using one of five predefined formats:

- **Standard View:** This view displays list items in a traditional style list.

- **Datasheet View:** This view displays list items in an editable spreadsheet format.

- **Calendar View:** This view displays list items in daily, weekly, or monthly calendar form and is useful if you organize your data by date.

- **Gantt View:** This view displays list items in a Gantt chart, and is useful if your data represents tasks or projects that have start dates, completion dates, and percent completions.

- **Access View:** This view works with Microsoft Office Access on the viewer's computer to show list items in forms or reports based on the columns from this list.

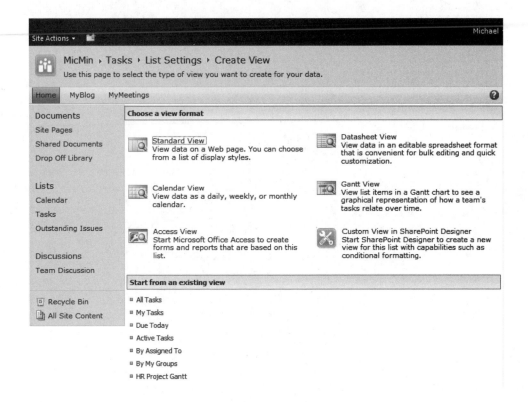

Figure 2-43. Creating the view name and columns

The second starting style lets you select one of the existing views from the current list to use as a starting point for a new view. This option saves you time if you need a series of similar views that may differ by only a few columns, sort order, or filter criteria. When starting from an existing view, you do not have to define everything from scratch; you just define or reset those properties of the new view that are different.

If you start from a new Standard view, SharePoint displays a screen like the one shown in Figure 2-44 when you create or edit a view. Actually, this figure only shows the top two sections of the view definition. In the top section, you can enter the view name. What if you decide later that you do not like the name you previously gave the view? Don't worry. Generally, you can change a view name at any time with no adverse effects. In fact, SharePoint automatically updates most references to the view name automatically when you change it. The same applies if you change the URL, as long as you store the URL in its own field such as in the Links list. However, if you embed the URL in other content, SharePoint may miss it. As a rule, try to minimize changes to URLs after you start including references to them from other parts of your site.

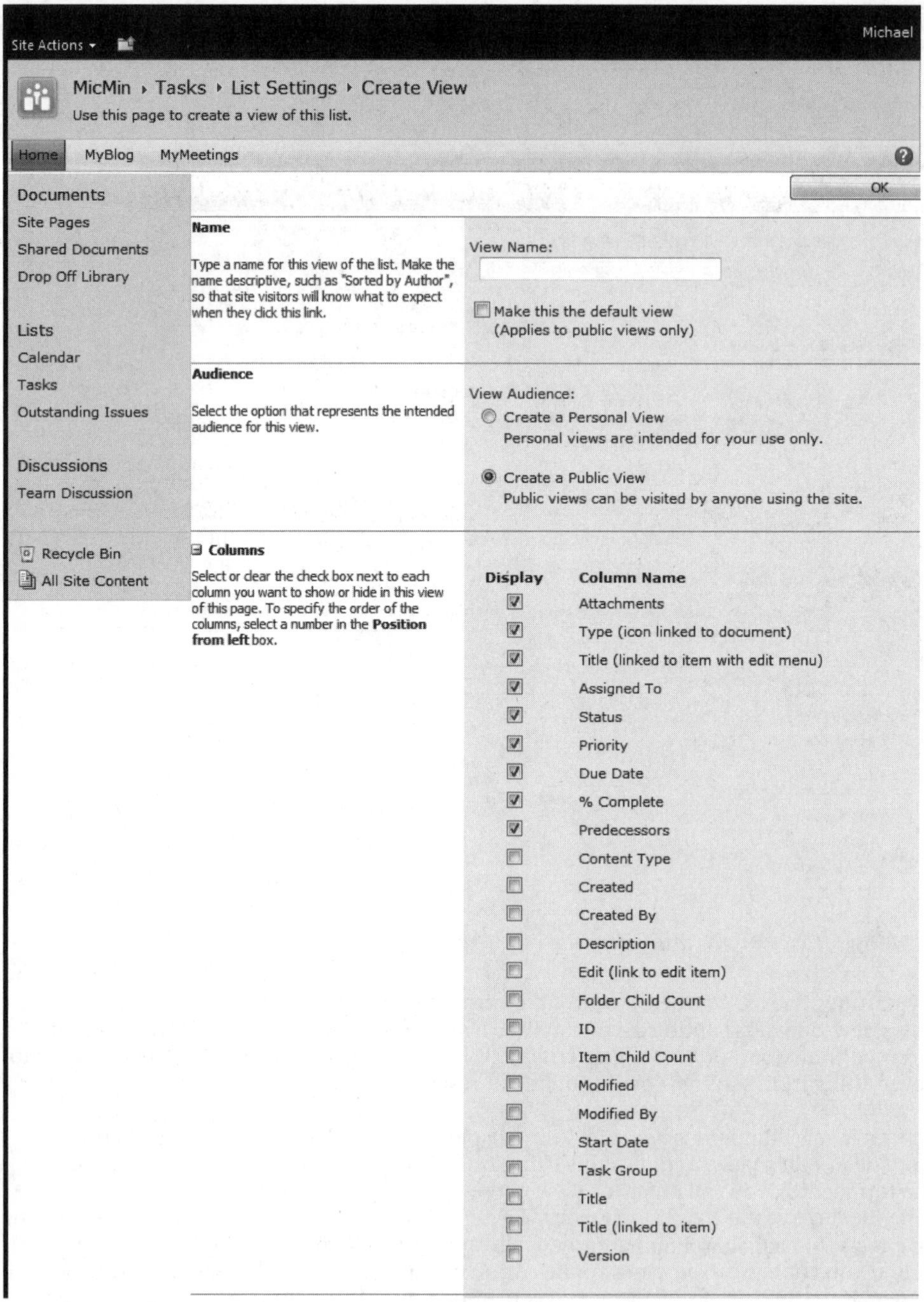

Figure 2-44. *Creating the view name and columns*

If, rather than adding a view, you decide to edit the default view, this top section reminds you that you cannot delete the current view due to the absence of a **Delete** button. If you had started from a non-default view, a **Delete** button would appear to the immediate left of the **OK** button. As mentioned in a previous tip, if you have more than one view, you can set any one of them as the default view and delete any of the rest.

The Columns section shows the available columns in the list. The check box to the left of the column name indicates whether to include the column in the current view. To add or remove a column from the view, toggle the check box. The drop-down box to the right with a number in it defines the order of the fields from left to right. To change the order of the columns, change the number in the drop-down of the column you want to move, selecting the numeric value of its new position. For example, to move the column **Attachments** to the fourth position, open its drop-down list and select the number 4. All other columns previously numbered from 2 through 4 automatically move to positions 1 through 3, making room for the repositioned **Attachments** as the 4th column.

Sorting and Filtering Lists

The third section of the **Edit View** page lets you define the sort order for the items in the view. You can sort by no more than two columns. However, you can independently sort each column in ascending or descending order. Figure 2-45 shows a view sorted first by the field **Expires** in ascending order. When more than one item has the same expiration date, it sorts by **Title** in ascending order.

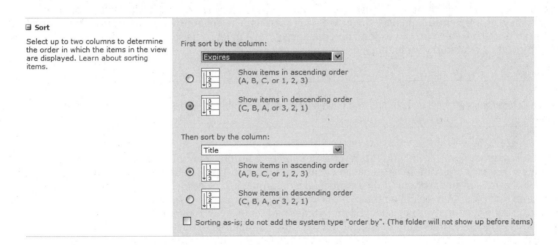

Figure 2-45. Sorting your list on up to two columns

As your list grows, you may want to define a filter for a list to focus on different item groups. For example, you could create a custom view of upcoming events that automatically hides items with expiration dates prior to today by adding a filter that compares the column **Expires** to the current date as shown in Figure 2-46.

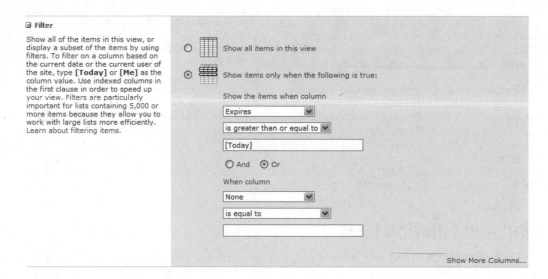

Figure 2-46. Defining a filter for your list

There are other sections on this page that define a view further. For example, the **Group By** section allows you to group items in the list using up to two columns. The advantage of using groups over merely sorting your items is that you can expand and collapse groups to let users see just a portion of the list without needing a filtered view for each group.

■ **Note Group By** works best on columns that have only a limited number of values, such as choice fields.

The **Totals** section lets you add totals on your list. For example, if your **Upcoming Events** list includes a **Department** column to associate events with their hosting department, you could count the number of events by department. If the events had a column with the associated cost of the event, you could sum that column to calculate the cost of events by department.

In the **Style** section, you can select from a predefined set of styles for your list. For example, the **Shaded** style displays items with an alternating background shading to make the list more readable.

Because lists can include folders, the **Folders** group lets you decide whether to navigate through folders or to view all items as if there were no folders. If you must use folders, you may want to create views that ignore the folders.

As your list grows, you may discover that it suddenly stops displaying some of its items. You may find the solution to that problem in the list setting **Item Limit**. First, I would not recommend that you try to display a list with thousands of items as a single screen. Even if performance does not degrade significantly, your users will not want to scroll through a list that large. Rather, use **Item Limit** along with the option to display items in batches. For example, if your list has 345 items and you specify an item limit of 100, your list begins by displaying the first 100 items. You can then select the next page of the list to display the second set of 100 items. Controls to navigate between pages of your list appear at the bottom of the list. In this way, your users can page through all items in the list, 100 items at a time, until they reach the item they want to see.

Finally, you can define views for mobile devices. These often include fewer columns and items than their PC screen cousins do. The interesting thing is that SharePoint reformats the content automatically to fit the smaller screen.

■ **Tip** Consider using filtered views to limit the number of items in a list's view. This improves user acceptance. You could also use the **Group By** (collapsed) option to limit the number of items displayed, yet easily allow users to expand the groups for which they want to see the details.

■ **Tip** When sorting or filtering a large list, index the column used by the filter. You can create indexed columns by clicking the **Indexed columns** hyperlink at the bottom of the **Columns** section of the list's **Customize** page.

Inline Editing

Inline editing of your list data is a new feature to SharePoint 2010. It allows you to edit the list data, even when it is displayed on a page, without first opening the list from **View All Site Content**. To turn this feature on, you must select the **Allow Inline Editing** check box in the **Inline Editing** section of the view properties, as shown in Figure 2-47.

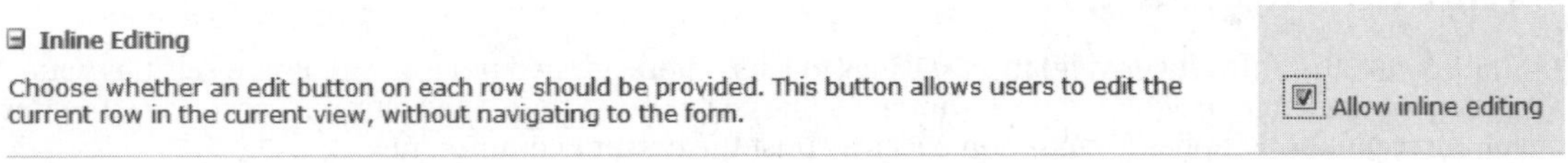

⊟ **Inline Editing**

Choose whether an edit button on each row should be provided. This button allows users to edit the current row in the current view, without navigating to the form.

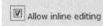 ☑ Allow inline editing

Figure 2-47. Turn on Inline Editing for a list

Now when you view the list, and position your mouse over any row, an edit icon (page with a pencil) appears at the beginning of the list. If you click this icon, all the columns in the list display as editable fields. In addition, the original icon changes to a pair of icons. The first icon shows a disk representing an option to save the changes to the item while the second icon shows a red square with a white X representing an option to cancel any changes made to the item. Figure 2-48 shows this functionality in a progression of screenshots.

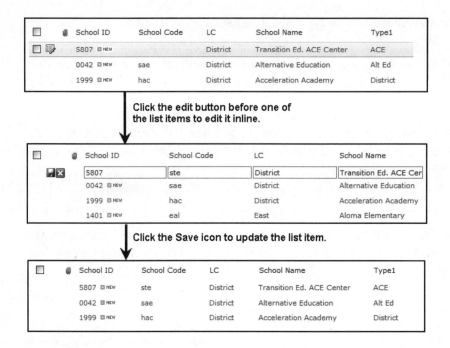

Figure 2-48. *Example of Inline Editing*

Validation Settings

SharePoint 2010 introduces validation settings to lists. There are two types of validation settings. One setting for the list item allows you to compare values from more than one column. A second setting for column validation applies a validation check against the current column only.

Item Validation

A validation expression at the list level is a formula that can include any of the columns in the list and resolves as either True or False. In order for an item to be successfully added or modified in the list, this expression must resolve to True.

For example, returning to your Task list, a very important validation might be that the Due Date for the task cannot occur before the Start Date. Since this validation involves more than one column in the list, you cannot validate either field individually at the column level. Rather, you can only validate both fields together as you attempt to save the new or modified item. To create an item level validation, follow these steps:

1. Navigate to the list where you want to add a validation (such as the Tasks list).

2. From the **List** ribbon, select **List Settings**.

3. In the **List Settings** page, select **Validation Settings** from the **General Settings** group.

4. Enter a formula that evaluates to True or False (see Figure 2-49 for an example).

5. Enter a message that SharePoint can display to the user when the validation fails (see Figure 2-50).

6. Finally, click **Save** to set your validation.

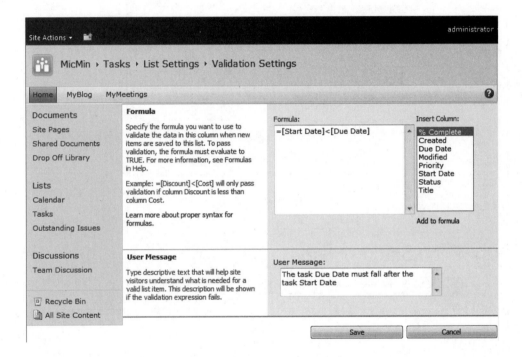

Figure 2-49. Creating an item level validation

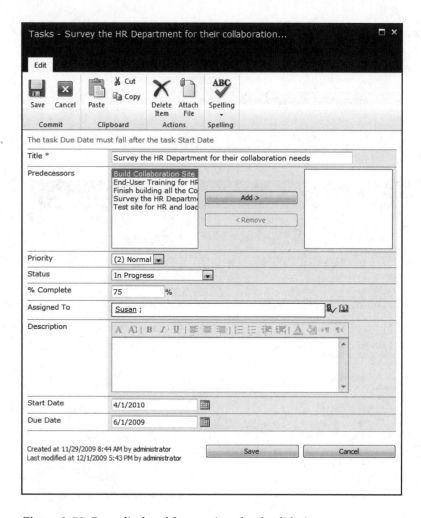

Figure 2-50. Error displayed from an item level validation

Column Validation

SharePoint 2007 had some simple column validations built into several of the column types. The most common validation was the **Required** validation. However, numeric values also supported a **Range** validation.

SharePoint 2010 expands on those validation options allowing you to define a formula to validate the column. Note that this formula cannot reference other columns.

As with the item level validation, the formula for the column validation defines a Boolean expression that returns a True or False value. In addition, you can specify a user message when the validation fails telling the user why SharePoint rejected their item update or addition.

Using the **Tasks** list one more time, let's add a column validation on the **Start Date** to check that start dates fall on or after the current date. (Open the **Task** list and go to the **List Settings** page. Then click on the **Start Date** column name in the **Columns** section of the page to edit the column properties.) Figure 2-51 shows the required column validation expression, and Figure 2-52 shows the result of attempting to enter an invalid date.

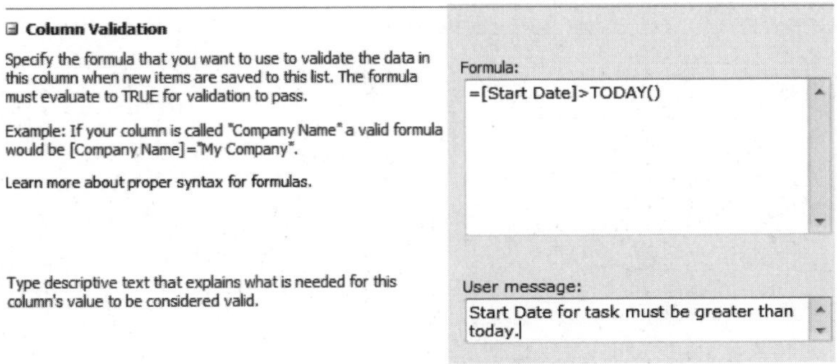

Figure 2-51. *Creating a column-level validation*

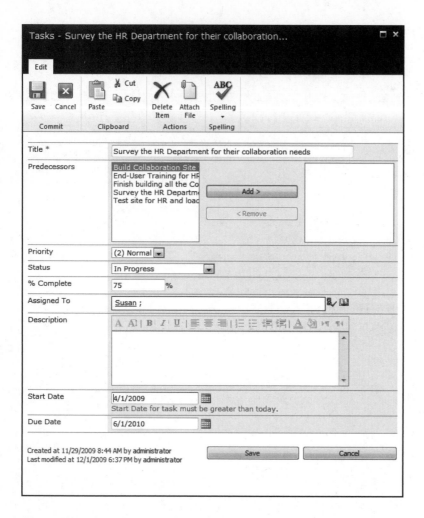

Figure 2-52. Error displayed from a column-level validation for field Start Date

■ **Note** At the time of this writing, documentation for how to define validation expressions has not been released, but my testing indicates that the validation is similar to validation in Excel cells.

Referential Integrity in List Lookups

In SharePoint 2007 collaboration, when you created a lookup relation between lists, there was no referential integrity support. In other words, as soon as you added a lookup value to an item in the current list from the lookup table, someone could go into the lookup list and change or even remove the lookup value. Furthermore, the lookup field was limited to the identifier column.

In SharePoint 2010 collaboration, you can include additional columns from the lookup list in the current list. Perhaps more importantly, you can enforce referential integrity between the two lists either by restricting deletions from the lookup table or by cascading deletes from the lookup table to the current table.

To illustrate these new features, suppose you have two tables, an Orders table and an Order Details table. To define a relationship between these two tables, first create an **Orders** table. I am not going through the specifics of how to create the Orders table here, but you should at least be aware that the column in the Orders table used to link the tables together will be **Order ID**. The Orders table must also have at least a few additional fields that you can display with your order details, such as the customer's name and the order date. However, you can have many additional columns in your Orders table.

The **Order Details** table contains columns that define the individual items ordered, including the item's name, cost, and quantity ordered. However, most importantly, the order details must have a column with the order id of the parent order. Figure 2-53 shows how to define this column as a lookup type. Notice that it defines the link to the **Orders** table and specifically to the **OrderID** field. However, unlike SharePoint 2007, which ends there, in SharePoint 2010, you can also select other columns from the lookup table that you want to display when you display the Order Details. In this figure, I have selected the columns **Order_Date** and **Customer_Name**.

In the next section, you can determine whether you want to enforce referential integrity between the two lists. If you select this option, you have two different enforcement modes. The first mode allows you to cascade deletes from the lookup table down through all the records that use the lookup value. For this example, it would be the equivalent of saying that, when you delete the order record, you also want to delete all of the order detail records associated with that order.

The second mode restricts the deletion of records from the lookup table if you use the lookup value in any other related table. For this example, it would be the equivalent of saying that you cannot delete an order record if it has order detail records. Of course, you could delete all the associated detail records first. Then you could delete the order record in the lookup table since it no longer has any related order detail records.

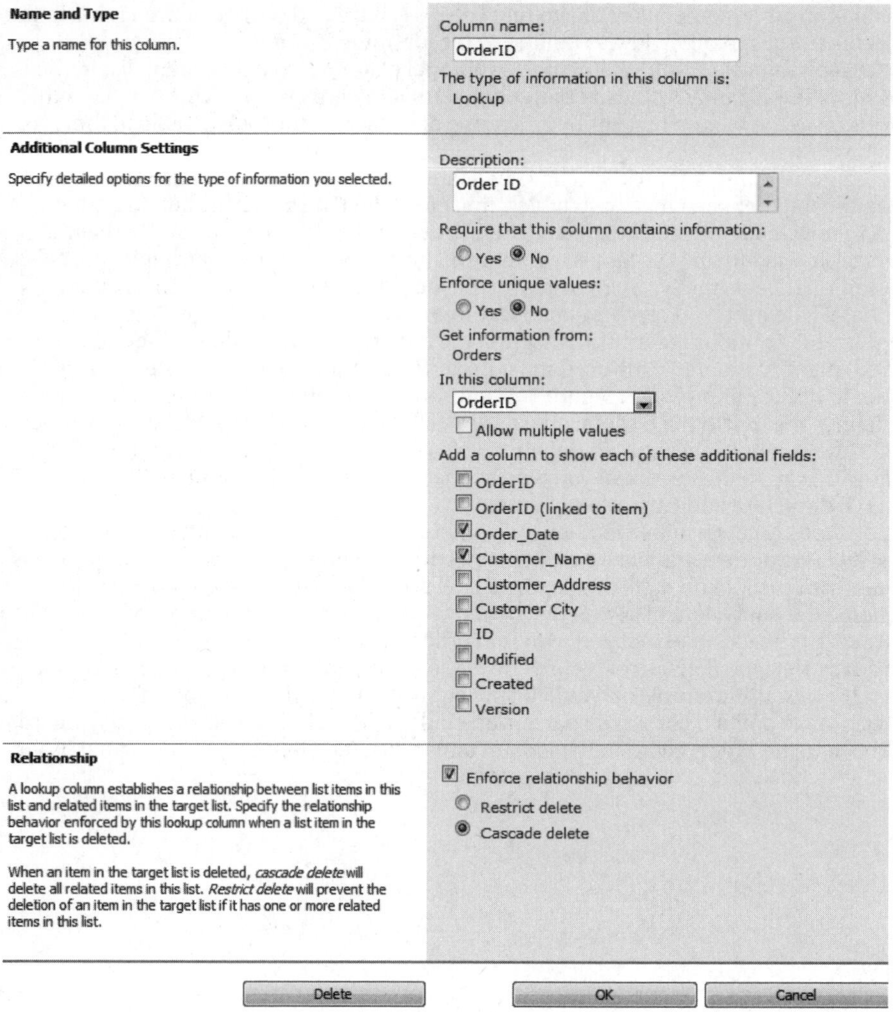

Name and Type

Type a name for this column.

Column name:

OrderID

The type of information in this column is:
Lookup

Additional Column Settings

Specify detailed options for the type of information you selected.

Description:

Order ID

Require that this column contains information:

○ Yes ● No

Enforce unique values:

○ Yes ● No

Get information from:
Orders

In this column:

OrderID

☐ Allow multiple values

Add a column to show each of these additional fields:

☐ OrderID
☐ OrderID (linked to item)
☑ Order_Date
☑ Customer_Name
☐ Customer_Address
☐ Customer City
☐ ID
☐ Modified
☐ Created
☐ Version

Relationship

A lookup column establishes a relationship between list items in this list and related items in the target list. Specify the relationship behavior enforced by this lookup column when a list item in the target list is deleted.

When an item in the target list is deleted, *cascade delete* will delete all related items in this list. *Restrict delete* will prevent the deletion of an item in the target list if it has one or more related items in this list.

☑ Enforce relationship behavior

○ Restrict delete
● Cascade delete

[Delete]   [OK]   [Cancel]

Figure 2-53. Defining the LookupUp Order ID field in the Order Details table

After defining the rest of the columns for the **Order Details** table, Figure 2-54 shows what you see when you add a detail record. Of course, you must add the **Order** record first. However, when you add an order detail record, you can select the corresponding **OrderID** from the drop-down list that consists of the **Order IDs** from the **Orders** table.

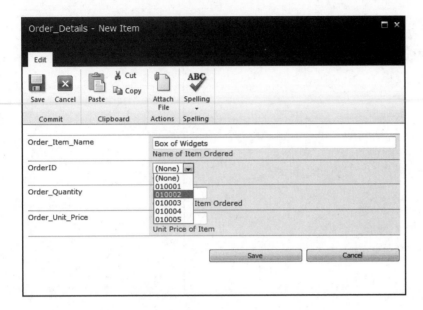

Figure 2-54. Using Lookup Field to identify the Order ID

Figure 2-54 only shows four fields in the item edit form that SharePoint generates. However, the **Order Detail** table also has a column named **Order_Extended_Price**. Since this column has been defined as a calculated column, it does not appear when adding or editing data. The formula that defines this column is:

=Order_Quantity*Order_Unit_Price

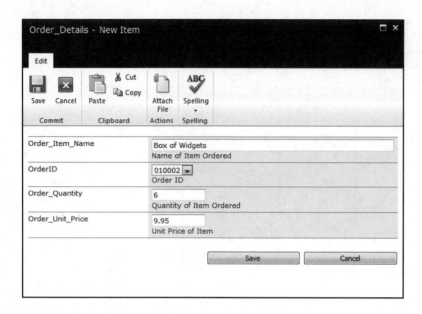

Figure 2-55. View of Order Details item with calculated Order_Unit_Price field

Figure 2-56 shows the **Order Details** table after adding several records. Notice that this view contains the **column OrderID:Order_Date** and **OrderID:Customer_Name** which it pulls from the **Orders** table from the same record as the matching **Order ID** value. Of course, you can optionally rename the columns to make them more user friendly by replacing underscores with blanks or removing the **OrderID:** references. Note that the **Extended_Price** column now appears and shows the product of the **Order_Quantity** and the **Order_Unit_Price**.

	Order_Item_Name	OrderID	OrderID:Order_Date	OrderID:Customer_Name	Order_Quantity	Order_Unit_Price	Extended_Price
	Box of Widgets ☑ NEW	010002	12/1/2009	Sara Jason	6	$9.95	$59.70
	Hammer ☑ NEW	010002	12/1/2009	Sara Jason	1	$12.95	$12.95
	Cordless Drill ☑ NEW	010001	12/1/2009	Jay Azule	1	$59.90	$59.90
	Reciprocating Saw ☑ NEW	010003	12/2/2009	Kevin Goss	1	$39.95	$39.95
	Power Sander ☑ NEW	010004	12/3/2009	Jerry Weinstein	1	$29.95	$29.95
	Gadget Bag ☑ NEW	010005	12/3/2009	Maria Natanya	2	$10.95	$21.90

Figure 2-56. Original Order Details table with Order ID 10005

If you now return to the **Orders** table and delete a record (Figure 2-57), SharePoint automatically deletes the corresponding Order Detail records related to the **Order** (Figure 2-59). However, first it prompts the user with the warning shown in Figure 2-58 that warns the user that it will delete related records and place them in the Recycle Bin.

The fact that the deleted records are placed in the Recycle Bin means that you have 30 days to change your mind, select the Order record from the Recycle Bin, and restore not only the Order record, but all the associated Order Detail records.

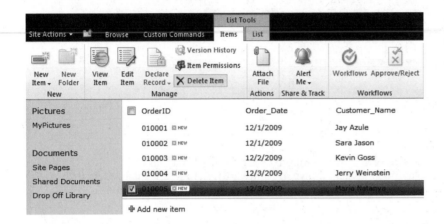

Figure 2-57. Selecting an Order item to delete

Figure 2-58. Warning that deleted orders are put in the Recycle Bin.

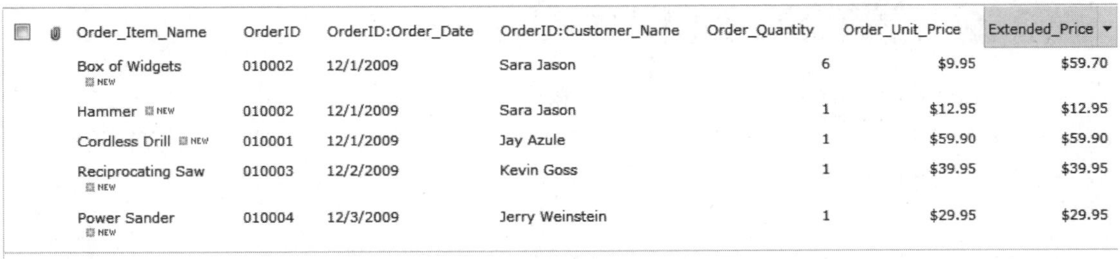

		Order_Item_Name	OrderID	OrderID:Order_Date	OrderID:Customer_Name	Order_Quantity	Order_Unit_Price	Extended_Price ▼
		Box of Widgets ⊠ NEW	010002	12/1/2009	Sara Jason	6	$9.95	$59.70
		Hammer ⊠ NEW	010002	12/1/2009	Sara Jason	1	$12.95	$12.95
		Cordless Drill ⊠ NEW	010001	12/1/2009	Jay Azule	1	$59.90	$59.90
		Reciprocating Saw ⊠ NEW	010003	12/2/2009	Kevin Goss	1	$39.95	$39.95
		Power Sander ⊠ NEW	010004	12/3/2009	Jerry Weinstein	1	$29.95	$29.95

Figure 2-59. Updated Order Details showing Order ID 10005 has been deleted.

However, what if instead of selecting **Cascade Delete** as your referential integrity relationship, you choose **Restrict Delete**, as shown in Figure 2-60?

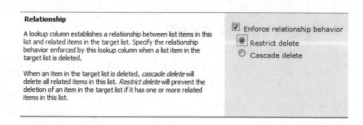

Figure 2-60. Select Restricted Delete as the referential integrity enforcement.

Again, if you return to the **Orders** list and attempt to delete an order that has one or more **Order Detail** items, SharePoint displays the message shown in Figure 2-61. At first, this might seem like SharePoint will allow you to delete the order item even through you defined the restrict delete relationship.

Figure 2-61. Error displayed when attempting to delete a order

However, if you click the **OK** button on this first dialog, a second dialog appears with the title **Error**. In the body of the dialog shown in Figure 2-62, the message tells you that it cannot delete the selected item from the Orders list because there are related items in the Order_Details list.

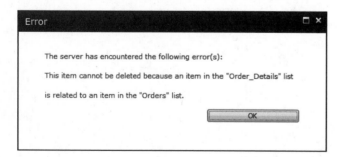

Figure 2-62. Restricting referential behavior stops the delete of the Order.

Thus, SharePoint now enforces referential integrity between two linked tables using one of two relationship modes. Of course, you can still link lists without defining a referential integrity relationship and take your chances.

Summary

This chapter began by reviewing the built-in lists that SharePoint supplies out of the box. SharePoint divides the available lists into three broad groupings. The first group, communications, includes lists that facilitate communications between users. The second group, tracking, includes lists that help users track information. The last group includes custom list templates.

I then showed you how to use existing list templates. By creating instances of these templates, you can add items to your list instances and publish the resulting list. SharePoint treats these lists as web parts that you can insert into web part zones of web and wiki-style pages.

You then saw how to customize a list by adding new columns and modifying existing columns. By creating site columns rather than just adding a new column to an individual list, you can create reusable column definitions that you can then add to any list in the current site and its sub-sites. This technique can be especially useful when defining choice columns; you only need to maintain the choice options in one place.

Next, you looked at using e-mail alerts to keep on top of changes or additions made to a list or library. You can customize how often you receive alerts and for what events you want to receive alerts.

Lists and libraries also support RSS feeds as a way to publish additions to a list or library. Both IE 7.0 and Microsoft Outlook 2007 and their subsequent versions support RSS feeds, making it easy for users to monitor updates to lists and libraries while they check their e-mail or browse the Internet.

You also learned how to define multiple views for a list. Each view can support a different combination of columns, sorts, and filters. It is also possible to group a list by a "slowing changing" column (a column that only supports a few unique values) and use an expand/collapse feature to make it easier to see subsets of your list items without creating separate views for each group.

Microsoft SharePoint 2010 collaboration adds new features for Lists and Library validation and referential integrity. Validation comes in two flavors, list and column validation. Using these validations, you can keep bad data from entering your list based on rules that you define. Finally, you saw how to use referential integrity behavior with lookup fields to protect the data by either cascading or blocking changes from the parent (lookup) table.

In later chapters, I will show how to access and work with lists directly from Microsoft Office products such as Excel, Access, and Outlook.

CHAPTER 3

■ ■ ■

Creating Content Pages

Content Pages Display Your Data

Content pages in SharePoint 2007 were, in some ways, simpler. A content page was a web page. You could use one of several page layouts. Each one had its own configuration and number of web part zones in which you could add web parts. While you can still create content pages that way in SharePoint 2010, you have another alternative, wiki-style pages. These pages feature page layouts called rich text areas that offer two benefits over the more traditional web pages. First, you can type text directly into the text areas without first needing to insert a web part such as the content editor web part. Second, you can create links from one wiki page to another just like the wiki pages in SharePoint 2007 wiki libraries. Moreover, you can insert web parts, lists, tables, images, and anything else you could put in a web page into these rich text zones.

So which page style should you use?

Before I can answer that question, let's look at both page styles and see how they are the same and how they differ.

If you look at the collaboration site that you started using in Chapter 1, SharePoint names the default page for the site: home.aspx. What you may not have noticed is that this page is actually a wiki page. Furthermore, if you open the **Site Actions** menu, there is an option, New Page. If you select this option, SharePoint generates a new wiki page and places it in a library called Site Pages. I will return to that option in a little bit. Let's first look at the other way to create a page by selecting **View All Site Content** from the **Site Actions** menu.

Adding a Web Page to Your Collaboration Site

In the previous chapters, you saw how to create libraries and lists by going to the **Site Actions** button in the upper-left corner of your site and clicking the **View All Site Content**. To create a new web page, begin the same way[1]. You will need a library in which to store your web pages. While you could store your web pages in the same library as your documents, a better design choice puts web pages in their own separate library. Therefore, let's take a side trip from creating your page to create a new library for your web pages.

---

[1] This chapter's examples add pages to non-publishing templates. However, most of the techniques apply to web pages added to publishing sites as well.

When you click **Create**, the **Create dialog** appears, which you first saw in Chapter 1. Remember that when creating a new library you should filter the objects you can create by choosing **Library** in the left navigation. Of the available library types, none says Web Page Library. That is because you can create a web page library from a document library. Simply select the **Document Library icon** and supply a unique name for the library. Then proceed to **More Options**.

■ **Tip** If you have the feature **SharePoint Server Publishing** activated, you will see a Pages library that you can use to create web pages.

As you can see in Figure 3-1, you must define a name for the library along with an optional description. I have chosen in this example not to display the document library in the Quick Launch area, but I do want to create a new version of the page every time I edit the file. You can customize the types and number of versions you would like to keep later. Finally, notice that the document template chosen for this library is not a Word document as you saw in your first document library in Chapter 1. Rather it is a Web Part page.

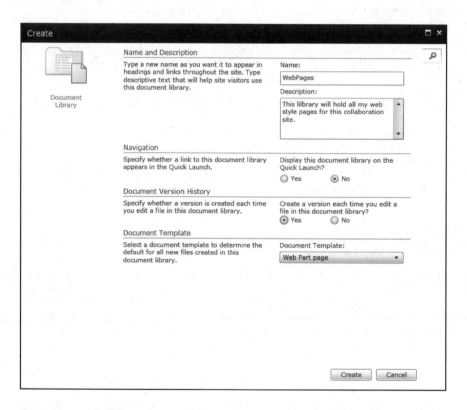

Figure 3-1. Creating a New Web Page Library

After clicking **Create**, SharePoint generates your new library and opens it as shown in Figure 3-2. When you open a library, in addition to the **Browse** and **Custom Commands** tabs, you see two new tabs representing ribbons under the heading **Library Tools**. The first tab when clicked displays the **Documents** ribbon. This ribbon holds options that let you create new documents, upload documents, check out and edit documents, view properties, and much more. The second ribbon, **Library**, focuses on managing the library. It allows you to switch between the standard and datasheet view, create and modify views of the documents in the library defining which columns to show, and sort orders and filters. However, it also has the **Library Settings** button in the **Settings** group, which you will use frequently as you progress through this chapter.

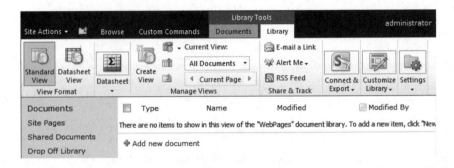

Figure 3-2. *Starting with a New Web Page Library*

To add a new page, simply click on **New Document** in the **New** group of the **Documents** ribbon. This option displays the **New Web Part Page**. For a new page, you must select two properties. The first property is the name of the page. Page names must be unique within the library. You can use the same name in different libraries even within the same site, but I would not recommend this unless it represents the same document formatted differently.

■ **Note** The **Add new document** link at the bottom of the library item list opens the Upload Document dialog.

The second property asks you to select a page layout template. Figure 3-3 shows that SharePoint supplies eight different page templates. As you click on each page template name in the list, a small figure appears on the left that shows how each template configures its web part zones. A *web part zone* is an area on the page in which you can add web parts for display. You can use other lists or even libraries as a web part on a page. There is also quite a selection of web parts provided by SharePoint to get you started. In addition, your SharePoint administrator may have downloaded additional web parts from other developers or may have developed some herself. Let's start with the relatively simple **Header, Left Column, Body** template for your first web page. By the way, I've named this page Owls.aspx for reasons that will be apparent shortly.

■ **Tip** If you see more than eight page templates in your page layout list, your SharePoint Administrator or someone in your SharePoint development team may have created new page templates using SharePoint Designer and added them to SharePoint.

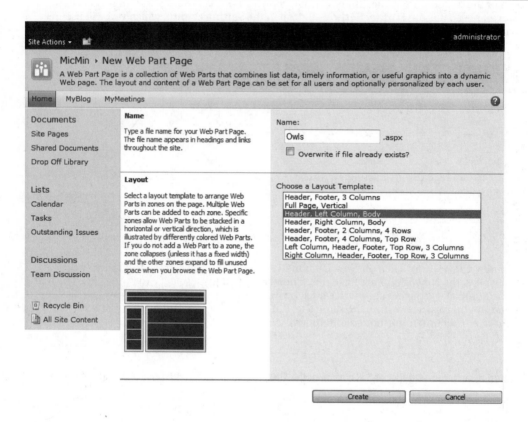

Figure 3-3. Creating a new web page using the Header, Left Column, Body Layout Template

■ **Tip** As a good practice, do not include spaces in page names. If you want to separate words within a name, use an underscore character (_) between the words. Web pages translate a space in a name to the string %20, making referencing them a little more complex. Also, it definitely looks odd.

Even with such a large selection of templates, you may not find one you like. There are two ways you can increase your template options.

- You can ask your SharePoint administrator to create a new page template for you using SharePoint Designer. This option may take some time, but after installing it, you can create web pages with it just like using any of the built-in templates. Use this method if you require a highly customized zone layout.

- You can manipulate the appearance of the various web part zones by leaving selected zones empty and/or physically changing the width or height of web parts in adjacent zones. However, this method does not let you add or redefine where zones appear.

After you click **Create**, SharePoint generates the page and opens it in Edit mode. Notice in Figure 3-4 that the **Edit** ribbon allows you to edit the properties of the page, change the page permissions, delete the page, manage page version (if you have more than one), approve the page, manage a workflow on the page, and even make the current page the default page for the site. Of course, only one page can be the default site page. The previous version of SharePoint created the default site page when you created the site and called it default.aspx; while you could change the default page for the site to another page, this option was buried in the page library settings. In SharePoint 2010, you have the ability to promote any page in your site to be the default page directly from the page edit toolbar.

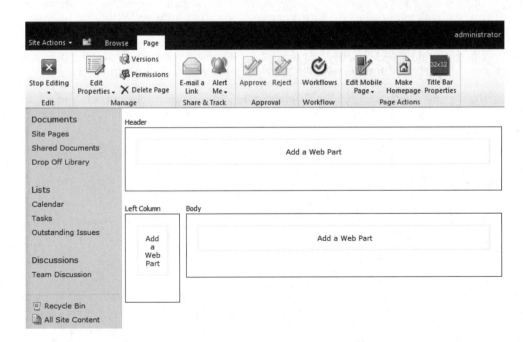

Figure 3-4. *The Page Edit Ribbon for a New Web Page*

Adding a Content to a Web Part Zone

Next, you will want to edit the content on the page. Notice that, while in Edit mode, the page has some text that identifies the Header, Left Column and Body areas. These are the areas defined by the selected Layout Template from Figure 3-3; the text only appears during Edit mode to help you identify the zones.

To add text or other information in the Header area, move your mouse into the rectangle named Header. Specifically, move your mouse into the smaller rectangle within the Header rectangle that displays the text `Add a Web Part`. You can see similar rectangles in the web part zones for the Left Column and Body zones.

If you click on the words **Add a Web Part** in the **Header** rectangle, you should see immediately below the ribbon an area that has three columns labeled: **Categories**, **Web Parts**, and **About the Web Part**. The first column, Categories, lists all of the different types of objects, called web parts, that you can place on the web page. When you click any of the categories, SharePoint updates the Web Parts column to filter the web parts displayed by that category.

For example, to add text to the Header web part, click the category **Media and Content**. This action displays four objects in the Web Parts column. The first object, Content Editor, allows you to add content to a web part zone using a rich text editor similar to WordPad. Click this web part object to select it. The About the Web Part column displays the name of the selected web part and a brief description. At the bottom of the column is a drop-down list that lets you select the web part zone where you want to place the web part. Even though you may have started by clicking the Add a Web Part text in the Header zone, you can change your mind and add the selected web part to any of the zones using this drop-down list. After selecting the web part zone, click the **Add** button to insert the web part physically onto the page at the top of the selected web part zone.

Notice that I said SharePoint adds the web part to the top of the zone. SharePoint always inserts a new web part into the top of the selected web part zone, pushing any other web parts in the zone down to make room for the new web part. You will see later in this chapter that you can easily move web parts around within the zone and between zones, so don't be too concerned if the order of the web parts as you add them to the page does not match your final desired order. You can easily fix the order.

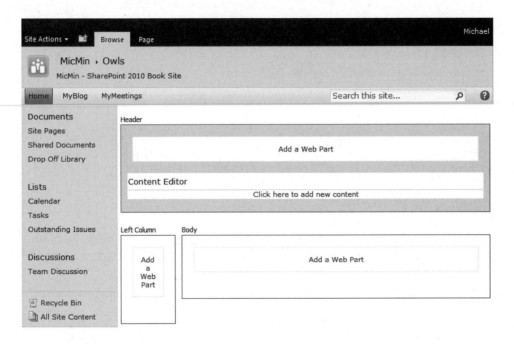

Figure 3-5. *Adding content to a new web page*

When you click Add, you will see a rectangular area beneath the **Add a Web Part** button with the name Content Editor. Beneath this title is a horizontal separating line and the words **Click here to add new content**.

When you click that phrase, the text disappears and a blinking insert cursor appears on the left side of this area. In addition, new tabs appear at the top of the page. The first tab group is named **Editing Tools** and it has two ribbons, **Format Text** and **Insert**. The second tab group is named **Web Part Tools** and has only a single ribbon **Options**, which provides several choices for defining the state and properties of the web part.

In the Content Editor, type the text `Florida Owls`. Then select the text by dragging your mouse through it. Click the **Format Text** ribbon if not already selected so you can format the text.

The text formatting features include the following:

- Fonts

- Font sizes

- Font styles (bold, italic, underlined)

- Font colors

- Text highlighting

- Alignment (left, center, and right)

- Lists (unnumbered and numbered)

- Indenting (and outdenting)

- Copy and paste of text

- Do and undo

- Tables and manipulation of tables and their cells

- Hyperlinks

- Images

One thing that you cannot easily accomplish from the new ribbon menu that you could do in SharePoint 2007 is to select a portion of the text in the content editor web part and remove all inline formatting. Many site designers found this option useful when copying text from a heavily formatted Microsoft Office Word document.

■ **Caution** While you can choose any font installed on your machine when you create your web pages, the actual font that displays depends on the fonts your viewers have on their machine. Therefore, best practices suggest that you use common fonts such as Arial, Times New Roman, Courier, or Helvetica.

Using the text formatting options, center and change the text to **18pt Arial bold**, as shown in Figure 3-6.

Figure 3-6. *Using the Format Text Ribbon in the Content Editor Web Part*

Next, open the edit drop-down menu in the Content Editor bar. This menu contains several options that I will cover later. For now, focus on the option **Edit Web Part**, as shown in Figure 3-7.

Figure 3-7. The Edit Web Part drop-down option

When you click on the **Edit Web Part** option, a panel appears on the right side of the page. If the page does not resize so you that can see this panel, look for a scroll bar on the bottom of the page and scroll to the right. This panel displays multiple groups of options. For the Content Editor Web part, these areas include the Content Editor itself, Appearance, Layout, and Advanced. Other web parts may have different option groups. Figure 3-8 shows an example of this tool panel for the Content Editor.

Figure 3-8. Panel properties for the Content Editor web part

Unlike the previous version of SharePoint, you no longer need to go to the tool panel for the Content Editor Web part to be able to create or edit the content source. You can now do this directly in the display area of the web part. However, the tool panel does begin with the option of loading your content from a text file as long as that text file has been loaded to a library within your SharePoint site. Why link to a text file for you content rather than just enter the content directly? If you have a process that automatically generates a text file as part of its output, you can display that text in a Content Editor Web part immediately if you link that text file to the Content Editor.

■ **Caution** The text is treated as HTML and ignores all white space.

The Appearance group includes options that let you change the title of the web part, its height, its width, and the state and type of Chrome used. What is chrome? *Chrome* is the header displayed at the top of the web part. SharePoint supports five chrome formats:

- Default

- None

- Title and Border

- Title Only

- Border Only

When using a Content Editor Web part to create a title for a page, a chrome type of `None` makes the most sense.

The **Layout** section identifies the zone and zone index when the web part exists. You can move a web part from one zone to another or from one position in a zone to another by simply changing the values of these two properties.

Finally, the **Advanced** section provides a variety of properties for displaying the web part. (I will skip over these for now.)

Now that you have a header for the page, you can add some content to the body section. Again, start by clicking on the text **Add a Web Part** in the **Body** zone of the page.

This time, select the **Image Viewer** web part from the **Media and Content** category and add it to the body zone. Beneath the web part header bar, the text tells you to open the tool pane to enter a URL for the image. You can click on the text `open the tool pane`, which does the same thing as clicking on **Edit Web Part** in the **Edit** drop-down menu. The link for the image can be from any web site on any web server, but the best place to store images that you want to use is in the Image library of the current site. So let's take a brief detour. (A *detour*, as described in this book, is a side task that you must complete before continuing with your main task.)

Adding an Image to an Image Library

In this case, you need to upload an image you want to use on your site to the site's Image library. Rather than back out of the work you have started, consider following these steps.

1. From the current page of your browser, copy the URL to your clipboard by clicking in the address bar and then pressing Ctrl+C.

    - Then open a new tab in your browser, or if you prefer, a new instance of your browser.

    - In the address bar of this new page, paste the contents of your clipboard. Notice that the full contents of the address bar is more than you need. Delete anything to the right of the site name where you are working and press **Enter**. For example, if the original URL was: `http://Vanguard/Project/TutorTracker/pages/default.aspx`, you only need to use: `http://Vanguard/Project/TutorTracker` in the new tab so you can navigate to your picture library.

- When the page refreshes, press **Site Actions ➤ View All Site Content** and then select your picture library. If you have not created a picture library in the current site yet, click **Create** and select **Picture Library** from the **Libraries** category. Complete the form to define the name and other properties of your picture library and click Create.

- With your picture library open, click the **Upload** button in the header of the library.

- In the **Add Picture** dialog that appears, use the **Browse** button to locate your image file and then click **OK** to upload your image to the library.

■ **Tip** Resize your pictures to the size you want to display before you upload them. If you don't own a graphics suite, you can use Microsoft Office Picture Manager found in the Office Tools folder to resize your images.

- When the picture uploads, SharePoint open the edit properties page for the image to let you specify other properties of the image such as when the picture was taken, a title, a description, and keywords that can be used to help find different images from a search.

- After defining the picture properties, click the **Save** option in the **Edit** ribbon to complete your upload.

- Now that you have at least one picture in your picture library, you can use that picture on your page. However, to use that picture, you need the URL of the picture. The easiest way to capture that URL is to click on the picture in the library to open the properties page. Then click on the preview picture shown to open just the picture in a separate page. Notice the URL in the address bar. Simply click on this URL and copy it to your clipboard.

- Now you can return from your detour back to the page you are editing. Click in the text box for the image link and paste the URL of the image.

■ **Caution** If you copied the image URL as described in these steps, make sure that you delete the default text (http://) before you paste the copied URL. Otherwise, you will have an incorrectly formatted URL.

When inserting an image on a page, you should always consider adding alternate text for those viewers who may have graphics turned off or may be using a program to read the page to them.

If you later delete the image from the picture library, the web pages will display a box with a red "x" in it, indicating that SharePoint cannot locate the image.

There are other options in the tool panel for this web part including alignment options and background color settings. In addition, you also have the Appearance, Layout, and Advanced property groups. In fact, you may want to open the **Properties** group and change **the Chrome Type** to None for this image.

When you're done modifying properties of the image, click **OK** in the tool panel.

Now you have a picture in the body section. To add some additional information about the picture, begin again by clicking **Add a Web Part** from the **Body** zone. Select the **Content Editor Web part** from the **Media and Content** category. Next, click **Add** to insert this web part in the Body zone. As Figure 3-9 shows, this new web part appears above the Image Viewer web part previously added.

Figure 3-9. Added web parts always appear at the top of the zone.

Added web parts always appear at the top of the zone. To change the sequence of the web parts within the zone, just click on the web part header that you want to move and drag it up or down within the zone. You'll notice a thick horizontal line appears in the zone to indicate where the web part will be if you were to release the mouse button. Move the content area beneath the image and enter some text about this beautiful owl.

After you have moved the content area beneath the image, click below the web part header to begin creating text. Figure 3-10 shows the Body zone with a small amount of text added beneath the picture of the owl.

Figure 3-10. Reposition the Content Editor web part below the Image Viewer

Copying Text from a Word Document

For the above example, you entered your text directly into the Content Editor Web part. Perhaps you already have a Word document containing the text you want to add to your site. You could simply copy your text from the Word document and then paste it into the Content Editor Web Part.

Note, however, that this technique copies not just the text, but also all the text formatting and styles. If you have very loose formatting standards for your content pages as opposed to strict standards for outward facing web pages to the public, you may not have to do anything more. However, if your organization imposes text formatting standards, even something as simple as the type of font to use or the font size, you may need to reformat the copied text.

■ **Note** One way to remove all special formatting from copied text is to copy the text first to Notepad and then copy the text from Notepad to the Content Editor. While this option requires an additional step, it successfully removes the special formatting that Word adds and pastes a plain text version of the content in the Content Editor, ready for formatting to match your other pages.

Let's continue with the owl page. Suppose you want to provide a little scientific information about this bird for your viewers. To do this, you need to add data into a table. Add a blank line below the current text by pressing Enter and then open the **Insert** ribbon from the **Editing Tools** ribbon group.

Notice that the first option is Table. Clicking this option displays a small dialog that looks like a grid. As you drag your mouse through the grid, individual squares (cells) change color. This indicates the size of the table in terms of columns and rows that you will create. When you have highlighted a table of 2 rows and 6 columns, click the mouse to complete your initial table size selection.

The table appears beneath the text. You can add text by clicking in any of the cells and just typing the text you want to appear. In this case, I've included a few of the scientific classification names for this owl. If you were to just accept the table with its default formatting, the data would appear as if it were in two rows with six column, but the table grid itself would not appear in the final page. This default can actually be a good way to format text on your page so that you can define different content areas without displaying obvious grid lines that define those areas. In this case, you want the table to look more like a table and display not only the grid lines, but also provide some additional formatting.

So with the table still selected (if you clicked outside of the table, just click anywhere back in the table again), open the **Design** ribbon in the **Table Tools** ribbon group. First, make sure to select the **Header Row check box** because you do have a header row for your data. However, make sure that you do not select First Column. Then click on the option **Styles** and select the **Table Style 3 – Dark**.

After you have selected the style, enter the data as shown in Figure 3-11. Open the **Edit** ribbon of the **Page** tab and click **Stop Editing** to save your changes. When completed, your page should look like Figure 3-11.

Content Editor

Florida Owls

Burrowing Owl

Burrowing owls are found in North and South America. In the east coast of North America, they primary live in Florida. They create their nests in ground burrows which thus gives them their name. While they tend to hunt mostly at dusk and dawn, they are one of the few owls that are active during the day. These birds eat insects, but they will also eat small vertebrates and invertebrates.

Class	Subclass	Order	Family	Genus	Species
Aves	Neomithes	Strigiformes	Strigidae	Athena	A.cunicularia

Figure 3-11. Adding a table to the content

Using Microsoft Word to Add a Table to Your Content

As you've seen, while you can create a table directly from within SharePoint, your formatting options are limited. When you create a table in Word, however, you can apply any of the many predefined table styles—or create your own. Figure 3-12 shows a Word table similar to the SharePoint one in Figure 3-11.

Class	Subclass	Order	Family	Genus	Species
Aves	Neomithes	Strigiformes	Strigidae	Athena	A.cunicularia

Figure 3-12. Specifying name and location for a new basic web page

In this case, if you want more control over the table's appearance, you may want to create and format your table in Word and then cut and paste it into the Content Editor Web part. This process preserves most if not all of the formatting defined in Word.

Adding a Hyperlink to Your Content

In addition to adding tables, the Content Editor Web part has the ability to add a hyperlink to another page on your site or to any site on the Internet. Suppose you find a link to additional information on burrowing owls on the Internet and want to let your visitors see that information as well. You can create a link to it from your document.

To create a hyperlink from within your content, begin by selecting the text on which you want readers to click. Then go to the **Insert** ribbon of the **Editing Tools** ribbon group and click the **Link** option in the **Links** group. As with the image dialog box, the hyperlink dialog box, shown in Figure 3-13, only has two property fields. The first field echoes the text highlighted before opening the **Insert Hyperlink** tool. You then need to enter the page URL to link to using the second field. Note that this field does not support a **Browse** button. If you don't remember the URL of the page you want to redirect users to, open a separate browser window or tab and navigate to the page. With the page open in your browser, you can click in the address bar to select the page URL and copy the link to your clipboard with Ctrl+C. Then return to your SharePoint browser tab and paste the link in the **Address** field with Ctrl+V, and click **OK**.

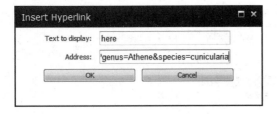

Figure 3-13. Inserting a hyperlink to an Internet site

Perhaps you noticed that the Left Column zone appears to be missing. Actually, it is not missing, it's just empty. When a zone is empty, SharePoint (and most browsers) compress that space so that other text on the page has more room. If you were to use the left column zone to create a menu of Florida owls, as shown in Figure 3-16, the body zone would reconfigure to use less horizontal space so that the left column zone can appear.

To create that menu for the left column zone, suppose you had previously created a Links list that represents the different pages on your site about Florida owls. I covered how to create lists in Chapter 2. Your Links list has three or four entries to other pages that you may have created so far. To add that list to this page, edit the page and move the mouse under the left column zone to display the zone rectangle. Click in the rectangle to display the **Page Tools' Insert** ribbon. Click on the **Existing List** option to select a list. Figure 3-14 shows the selection of the existing list named Florida Owls.

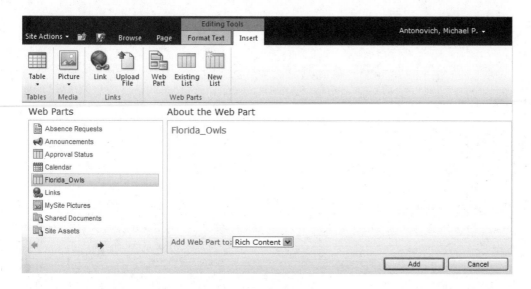

Figure 3-14. Adding an existing list to the web page

After adding this list to your page, you may see more columns than you may really want. All you really want to display is the URL column. Fortunately, because you learned in Chapter 2 how to create different views, you can create a new view that only displays the URL. Because the column name will appear on the page when you display the view, you may also want to change the name of the column to the name of the menu; so change the column name from URL to Florida Owl Pages. After doing this, you can edit the web part on the page changing the view used to display the list by setting the properties as shown in Figure 3-15. Notice that the page initially displays the list's default view. Only after you add the list to the page can you specify which view to use on the page by going to the web part's properties.

Some changes you should make while editing the web part's properties are:

- Set the view in the Selected View drop-down to the view you want to use

- Set the Chrome Type to None

- Set the Toolbar Type to No Toolbar

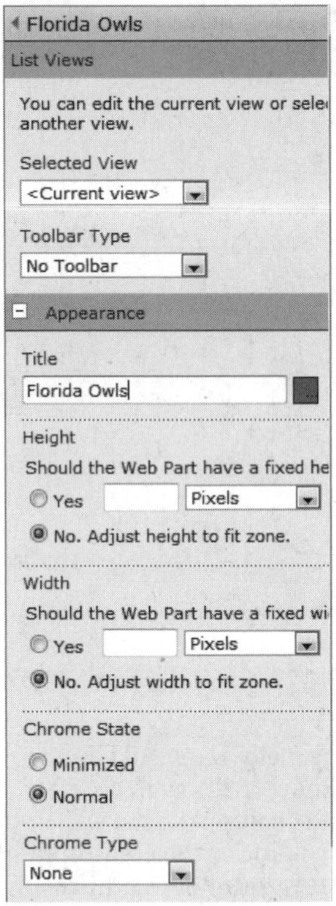

Figure 3-15. Defining Properties of the list

After making your changes to the web part properties, click **OK** to save the changes. SharePoint now displays your updated page, which should look something like Figure 3-16. Notice that with information in the Left Column zone, the Body zone is not as wide as in Figure 3-11. Actually, by choosing a longer column header as shown in this figure, I insured that the current page links did not wrap around two or more lines. If you want to see how this works, go back to the list settings and change the column name from `Florida Owl Pages` back to `URL`.

■ **Tip** Another way you can control the widths of web part zones is to modify the Width property in the Appearance section of the web part properties by setting the width to a fixed number of pixels. You can set the pixels by trial and error or you can download a simple screen utility that displays a pixel ruler on the screen. These utilities (some free, some inexpensive) are a great help in determining the number of pixels an image, column, or web part zone should use.

Figure 3-16. Final web page with image, content, and menu

■ **Tip** If you created a Links list to follow along with this example, you may have seen check boxes before each of the items. By default, SharePoint adds check boxes before each item. You can remove these check boxes when you define your menu view by opening the **Tabular View** group and turning off the option **Allow individual item checkboxes**.

Of course, there are many other things you can add to this page, but this should be enough to get you started. Now let's look at creating a similar page using the wiki page template.

Adding a Wiki Page to Your Collaboration Site

The second way to add pages to your collaboration site is to use wiki pages. In fact, this is the default page style for a Team Collaboration site. One of the key advantages of using wiki pages for collaboration is that anyone can edit the page content even if you do not want to give them edit rights to the underlying lists or libraries. For collaboration pages, this feature allows you to limit management of lists and libraries to users who have received additional training on how to work with SharePoint.

■ **Tip** If you would rather not use a wiki as the default page for your Team Collaboration site, first create a new web page. Before you exit Edit mode, click the option **Make Homepage** from the **Edit** ribbon. SharePoint does not delete the original wiki page. It still exists in the Site Pages library and you can open it with a link. However, your new web page becomes the new default page for the site.

From the main page of the collaboration team site created for you when you began Chapter 1, you can easily add not only a link to a new collaboration page, but also the page itself. Start by clicking the **Edit** tab to display the **Edit** ribbon. In the **Edit** ribbon, click the **Edit** option in the **Edit & Check Out** group. When the page refreshes, you'll see rectangles around several portions of the page. Figure 3-17 shows that the default home page has three areas, almost like the zones in the web part page you created in the first part of this chapter.

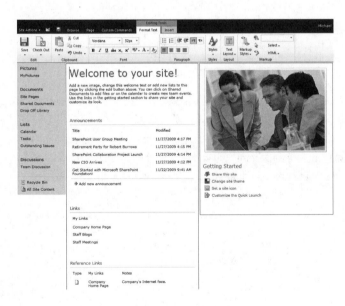

Figure 3-17. Wiki page version of a home page

If you move your mouse over a blank area in these rectangles, you may see a tool tip appear beneath your cursor that says **Rich Text Editor**. These are already text areas. You do not need to insert a web part to add content to these areas. Just click your mouse where you want to insert text and begin typing. If you do not have space to insert text between existing web parts, check out the sidebar Moving Web Parts on a wiki page.

Moving Web Parts on a Wiki Page

If you have already added web parts to the rich text area, you will find that you can only add text directly to areas outside of these web parts, not within them. If you added the web parts without adding a blank line between them, you may need to add blank lines if you want to insert text between them. Unfortunately, you cannot just click between web parts and press Enter to insert a line between them.

First, you must add a series of blank lines at the bottom of the rich text area. Then, beginning with the lowest web part, click on the web part's header and drag it to one of these new blank lines. This should effectively "bubble up" the blank lines to where you want them.

If you saved the web part with a Chrome type of **None**, you can click anywhere on the border of the web part which appears as you move your mouse over the web part. Then drag the web part as needed to arrange your blank space.

Adding blank lines while in Edit mode between web parts does not affect the display of the final page because wiki pages ignore these blank lines. So use blank lines liberally when designing your pages. I did this to the home page of the site used here so that I could add text to the top of the left column.

You can move a web part from one rich text area to another as easily as arranging the order of web parts within a rich text area. The only restriction is that you must have one or more blank lines in the destination rich text area where you want to drop the web part.

Figure 3-18 shows the web parts moved down to provide space at the top of the left column. Then I added one line of regular text. Note that I added a second line, but it is not a line of normal text. Rather, it shows how to begin a hyperlink definition within a wiki page. To start a link, type two open square brackets. As soon as you do this, a context-sensitive menu appears, listing available pages from the Site Pages library, which is the default library for your site's wiki pages. In this figure, I selected the page named MySecondPage for the link.

After you select the desired page to link, press the **Enter** Key. SharePoint automatically adds the closing square brackets to complete the statement.

Welcome to your site!

Add a new image, change this welcome text or add new lists to this page by clicking the edit button above. You can click on Shared Documents to add files or on the calendar to create new team events. Use the links in the getting started section to share your site and customize its look.

You can enter text into a wiki page by finding a blank line and just begin typing. You can even create a new page by placing the page name in square brackets as in:
[[MySecondPage]]

Announcements

Title	Modified
SharePoint User Group Meeting	11/27/2009 4:17 PM

Figure 3-18. Inserting text into a wiki page content area

Does this method only link to other wiki pages in the Site Pages library? At first glance, you might think so. After all, when you type the two opening square brackets, the list that appears only includes the names of pages in the Site Pages library. In fact, the page names displayed in the drop-down correspond to the page's Name property. Therefore, if you know the name of the wiki page you want to link to, you can enter the name directly.

So can you only reference other wiki pages? The answer is no, but let's finish this example before I get into accessing non-wiki pages.

While you did not change the displayed text associated with the link in this case, you can easily provide a different text string for SharePoint to display to the user. Simply add the pipe character (|) after the page name and then enter the alternate text you want to display. For this example, you could have entered [[MySecondPage|Page 2]] so the SharePoint would display the text Page 2 as the link. This can be especially useful if you have abbreviated page names to keep the total URL size small but would rather have a more descriptive page name displayed to the users.

Welcome to your site!

Add a new image, change this welcome text or add new lists to this page by clicking the edit button above. You can click on Shared Documents to add files or on the calendar to create new team events. Use the links in the getting started section to share your site and customize its look.

You can enter text into a wiki page by finding a blank line and just begin typing. You can even create a new page by placing the page name in square brackets as in:
MySecondPage

Announcements

Title	Modified
SharePoint User Group Meeting	11/27/2009 4:17 PM

Figure 3-19. Wiki reference to a page not yet created

Notice in Figure 3-19 that, when you save the page, the link displays with a dotted underline. This dotted underline indicates that the referenced page does not exist. If you entered the page name directly and you know the page exists, you may want to double check the Name property of the page. You may even want to make sure that the page exists in the Site Pages library of the current site and not some other site.

If the page name is correct and you know that the page does not exist yet, click on this page link. SharePoint recognizes that there is no page with this name. It therefore opens a dialog, shown in Figure 3-20, and prompts you with the question whether you want SharePoint to create a new wiki page in the Site Pages library with that name.

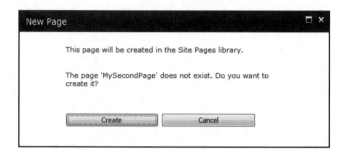

Figure 3-20. Wiki warning when about to create a new page

If you click the **Create** button, SharePoint creates a page with that name and opens the page in Edit mode, as shown in Figure 3-21. Note that a new wiki page has no default content, but it does have one rich text area that fills the entire page.

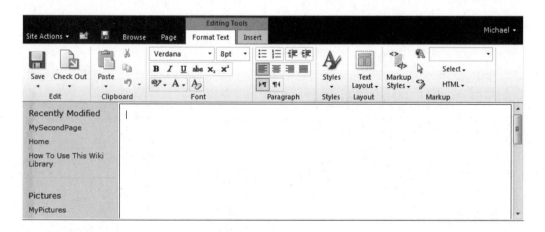

Figure 3-21. Blank new page in wiki created from link

Note that there are no web part zones. Wiki pages do not have web part zones, but don't worry. You can still use web parts in a wiki page by placing them directly in the rich text area.

Perhaps instead of just one rich text area, you want two, three, or more areas. In fact, you would like to have rich text areas laid out similarly to the web part zones you saw earlier when creating a web page. In the **Editing Tools** ribbon group, select the **Format Text** ribbon. In this ribbon, locate the **Layout** group and its sole option, **Text Layout**. If you click this option, you will see that there are several different text layouts available for wiki pages (see Figure 3-22). The thumbnail to the left of the layout name gives you a view of what those layouts look like before you select them. In most cases, you can guess what the layout will look like by reading the name. Of course, you could just select one to see what it looked like. If you have not added any content to the page yet, you can easily reopen the Text Layout drop-down menu and try a different layout until you find the one you want to use.

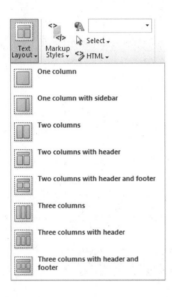

Figure 3-22. Available layouts for wiki pages

After selecting a Text Layout, SharePoint reconfigures the current wiki page and shows you the rich text areas. As a starting point to reproduce the earlier web page, create a wiki page by using the **Two columns with header** option as shown in Figure 3-23.

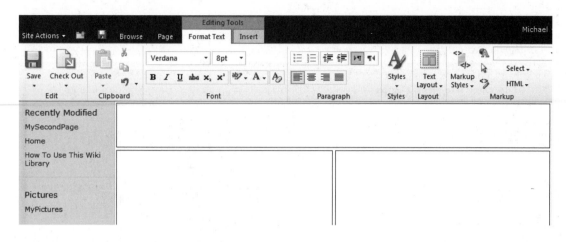

Figure 3-23. *The Two columns with header layout*

Rich text areas are not the same as web part zones. While they still automatically expand and contract to adjust to the sizes of content placed within them, merely adding text to the rich text area will not affect the current rich text area's width. You cannot manually change their widths by setting properties of the rich text area. On the other hand, if you add a list to one of the rich text areas that is wider than the area, the area will expand in an attempt to show the full list. The fact that rich text areas may not eliminate as much white space as their corresponding web page cousins can lead to pages with considerably more white space between horizontally placed rich text areas. I encountered this effect when attempting to recreate the same page content for my wiki page as we created in our earlier web part page. Although my wiki page in Figure 3-24 is close to my web part page in Figure 3-14, a close look reveals that the web page recovers extra space more effectively.

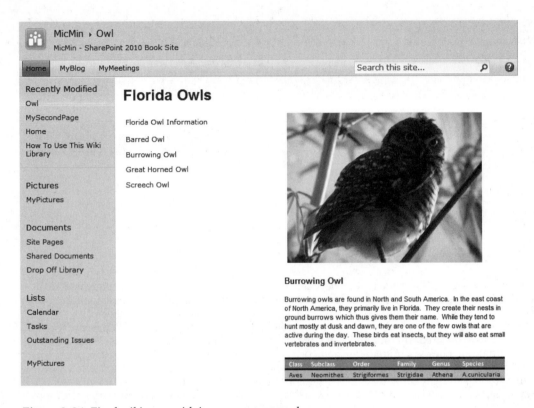

MicMin ▸ Owl
MicMin - SharePoint 2010 Book Site

Home   MyBlog   MyMeetings

Search this site...

Recently Modified
Owl
MySecondPage
Home
How To Use This Wiki
Library

Pictures
MyPictures

Documents
Site Pages
Shared Documents
Drop Off Library

Lists
Calendar
Tasks
Outstanding Issues

MyPictures

Florida Owls

Florida Owl Information

Barred Owl

Burrowing Owl

Great Horned Owl

Screech Owl

Burrowing Owl

Burrowing owls are found in North and South America. In the east coast of North America, they primarily live in Florida. They create their nests in ground burrows which thus gives them their name. While they tend to hunt mostly at dusk and dawn, they are one of the few owls that are active during the day. These birds eat insects, but they will also eat small vertebrates and invertebrates.

Class	Subclass	Order	Family	Genus	Species
Aves	Neomithes	Strigiformes	Strigidae	Athena	A.cunicularia

Figure 3-24. Final wiki page with image, content, and menu

Adding links to take you to other pages is not the only thing you can do with wiki pages. You can create links to files, lists, and views. As soon as you type the two square brackets to begin a link on a wiki page, a context-sensitive drop-down menu appears to let you choose not only other wiki pages in the site pages library but also two other options (see Figure 3-25).

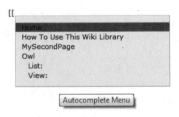

Figure 3-25. Context-sensitive drop-down of link options in a wiki page

To select an item from this list, use the up and down arrow keys on your keyboard and press the **Tab** key to select the item. SharePoint adds the page name or the word **List:** or **View:** after the square brackets. If you selected a page, you can close the link by pressing the Enter key to add the closing square brackets to the expression. However, you can define an alias name for the page that displays on the current page rather than the actual page name. To do this, press the pipe character '|' and enter the alternate name for your link. To close the link expression, you must also manually enter the two closing square brackets.

If you choose **List:** from the **Autocomplete Menu**, after you press the **Tab** key, a drop-down of all your lists will appear (if you have a relatively small number of lists). If you have a large number of lists, a message may appear telling you to "Enter more of the name to see suggestions". Enter the first one or two letters of the specific list name you want. After selecting your list, you can press the **Tab** key to select an item from the list, or you can press **Enter** to complete the link, or as with pages, you can add a pipe character and then supply an alias that SharePoint displays on the page in place of the actual list name.

The View: option starts similarly to the List: item in that you must first select the list you want. However, in this case, you do not want to press Enter after selecting the list name. Rather you want to press **Tab**. Again, SharePoint asks you to enter more of the name to see suggestions. However, this time, the prompt is referring not to the list name, but to the name of the view within the selected list. SharePoint separates the list name and view name with the slash "/" character. As with the two previous examples, you can end your selections by pressing the **Enter** key or you can add the pipe character and supply an alias name for the link.

Finally, you can reference not only regular lists with the List: option, you can access libraries as well. For example, to open a document from your Shared Documents library, select List: as before, but enter the character "s" or "sh" to display the Shared Documents name in the Autocomplete Menu. As with views, you want to press just the **Tab** key to select the library so you can continue to select the file within the library. Also like all of the previous examples, you can supply an alias name for the link.

Once you know the syntax for links on a wiki page, you can enter the link definition directly if you know the list/library and view/document information. However, using the Autocomplete Menu eliminates the potential for spelling errors.

If you were to save the page at this point and click on any of the resulting links, SharePoint would open the corresponding list, view, library, or document as defined by the link.

Figure 3-26 shows a few examples of the link options while in Edit mode. You can see that the basic format of the link is similar to the basic page link in which you begin with the page name and then you can add a pipe character '|' followed by an alias text string that appears on the page when the page displays.

```
[[List:Florida Owls]]
[[View:Florida Owls/FL Owls|My Florida Owls]]
[[List:Shared Documents/The Universe Episodes.docx|Universe Episodes]]
[[How To Use This Wiki Library|Using Wikis]]
[[Owl]]   The wiki version of the owl page
[[List:Florida Owls]]
```

Figure 3-26. Display of different types of links on a wiki page

A few paragraphs ago, I promised to tell you how you could reference non-wiki pages from within a wiki page using the wiki page link format. Just as you were able to open a document from the Shared Documents library, you can access a file in any library including page libraries. Earlier in this chapter, you created a document library named WebPages. You can begin with the List: prefix and then build a reference to a file named Owls.aspx in the WebPages library by using a string like the following:

```
[[List:WebPages/Owls|Owls]]
```

■ **Caution** SharePoint cannot use security trimming to hide links you might create on your wiki page, as shown in this section. Therefore, users may get a security warning when they click on a link that points to a list or library item to which they do not have access.

Now you know why I started Chapter 2 by saying that everything is a list. You can create content pages with both web pages and wiki pages and you can reference both page styles just as if they were another list in your site. Let's look at some additional content issues when working with collaboration pages.

Creating Master-Detail Relationships between Your Lists

■ **Caution** Creating connections between web parts as described in this section is only a function of Web Part pages, not wiki-based pages.

One of the more interesting things you can do with lists is to define master-detail relationships between two or more lists on a page. A *master-detail relationship* between lists looks a lot like the parent-child relationship between tables in a database. Basically, it means that a list designated as the master has items that relate to one or more items in a second list called the detail list.

One example of a master-detail relationship might involve a list of the departments in your organization. Since departments consist of one or more staff members, you might build a detailed staff list, including names, titles, telephone extensions, and related information.

Another example might list your employees in a master list and the projects they work on in the detail list. In fact, the staff detail list of the first example might serve as the master list for the second example.

In SharePoint, when you create a master-detail relationship between lists on a page, the master list controls the items you can see in the detail list. The master list always displays all its items. However, the item you select from the master list determines which items, if any, appear in the detail list.

Figure 3-27 shows two lists on one page. The list on the left displays a list of projects in a hypothetical company. The list on the right displays a list of staff assigned to various projects along with their main project responsibility. You probably noticed that Project Name provides a common column between these two lists. You must have a common or linking column between your two lists to create a master-detail relationship. However, these lists do not need to have the same name as in our example.

Antonov Advanced Research Projects

Research Projects						
Project Name	Project Start	Project End				
Anti-Grav Sled ⊠ NEW	4/1/2010	3/31/2011				
Heisenberg Compensator ⊠ NEW	9/1/2003	8/30/2013				
Invisibility Shield ⊠ NEW	7/1/2009	12/31/2011				
Laser Handgun ⊠ NEW	1/1/2008	9/30/2010				
Quantum Flux Capacitor ⊠ NEW	1/1/2009	12/31/2010				
Slip-Stream Drive ⊠ NEW	7/1/2010	6/30/2015				

➕ Add new item

Project Staff			
Project_Name	First_Name	Last_Name	Role
Anti-Grav Sled ⊠ NEW	Sandra	Fuller	Gravitational Researcher
Anti-Grav Sled ⊠ NEW	Phil	Jason	Project Manager
Anti-Grav Sled ⊠ NEW	Carol	Sterns	Engineering Chief
Heisenberg Compensator ⊠ NEW	Susan	Antonov	Phenomenologiist
Heisenberg Compensator ⊠ NEW	Gary	Lanahan	Physicist
Invisibility Shield ⊠ NEW	Phil	Jason	Project Manager
Invisibility Shield ⊠ NEW	Anatohly	Nikol	Optical Specialist
Invisibility Shield ⊠ NEW	Carol	Sterns	`Engineering Chief
Laser Handgun ⊠ NEW	Jenny	Abrams	Project Manager
Laser Handgun ⊠ NEW	Natasha	Gryzlov	Micro Technician
Laser Handgun ⊠ NEW	Anatohly	Nikol	Optical Specialist
Quantum Flux Capacitor ⊠ NEW	Phil	Jason	Project Manager
Quantum Flux Capacitor ⊠ NEW	Gary	Lanahan	Physicist
Quantum Flux Capacitor ⊠ NEW	Jared	Rodriguez	Head Physics Researcher
Quantum Flux Capacity ⊠ NEW	Susan	Antonov	Phenomenologist
Slip-Stream Drive ⊠ NEW	Susan	Antonov	Phenomenologist
Slip-Stream Drive ⊠ NEW	Natasha	Gryzlov	Nano-bot Designer
Slip-Stream Drive ⊠ NEW	Phil	Jason	Project Manager

➕ Add new item

Figure 3-27. Create and display two related lists on a page

Once you place both lists on the page, you can define the relationship between them starting from either list. If you begin with the Research Projects list, drop down the menu from the **Edit** button (or down-pointing arrow) in the list header. You will see the option **Connections** toward the bottom of the menu. As you position your cursor over the word Connections, a secondary menu defines the possible connection types. From this menu, move your mouse over the **Send Row of Data To** option. You use the Send Row of Data To option when you begin from the master list side of the relation. You use the **Get Filtered Values From Option** when you begin with the detail list.

Next, another menu appears listing the available lists on the current page. In this case, select **Project Staff** from the menu. Figure 3-28 shows this sequence of selections.

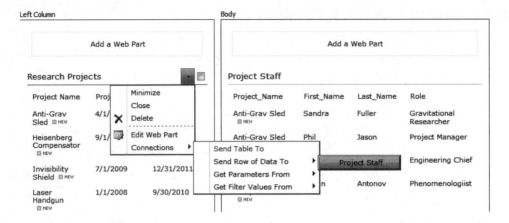

Figure 3-28. Defining the connection from the master list

Next, SharePoint displays a two-tab dialog box in which the first tab asks for the type of connection for Project Staff. Since you started by sending a row of data from the Research Projects list, you want to get filtered values from the Project Staff list. Figure 3-29 shows this dialog box.

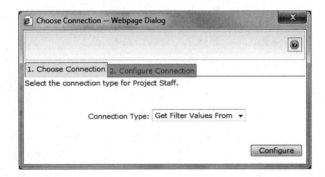

Figure 3-29. Selecting the linking field from the master list

Clicking on the **Configure Connection** tab, you must next select the column from the master or provider list to use to filter (link) the detail or consumer list. After you select the column from the master list, you must select the connecting column from the detail list. Figure 3-30 shows the selection of the Research Projects column Project Name from the provider list and the consumer list column, Project_Name from the Project Staff list.

Configure Connection -- Webpage Dialog
1. Choose Connection
2. Configure Connection
Connection Settings
Provider Field Name:
Modified By
Consumer Field Name:
Finish
Cancel

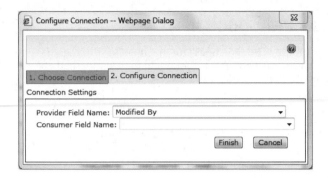

Figure 3-30. Selecting the linking field from the detail list

Click the **Finish** button to complete the relationship definition. When you exit Edit mode for the page, you see that the master list, Research Projects, displays an additional column at the beginning of the list. This column has the header Select. It places a double-headed arrow before each list item. To see the relationship between the master and detail list, click any of the double-headed arrows. The select provided item will have solid arrows while the unselected items have hollow arrows. Figure 3-27 shows the Research Projects list with the project Quantum Flux Capacitor selected. In Project Staff, note that only staff members working on the Quantum Flux Capacitor appear. Similarly, clicking the double-headed arrow before any other project filters the staff list to display only the staff for that project.

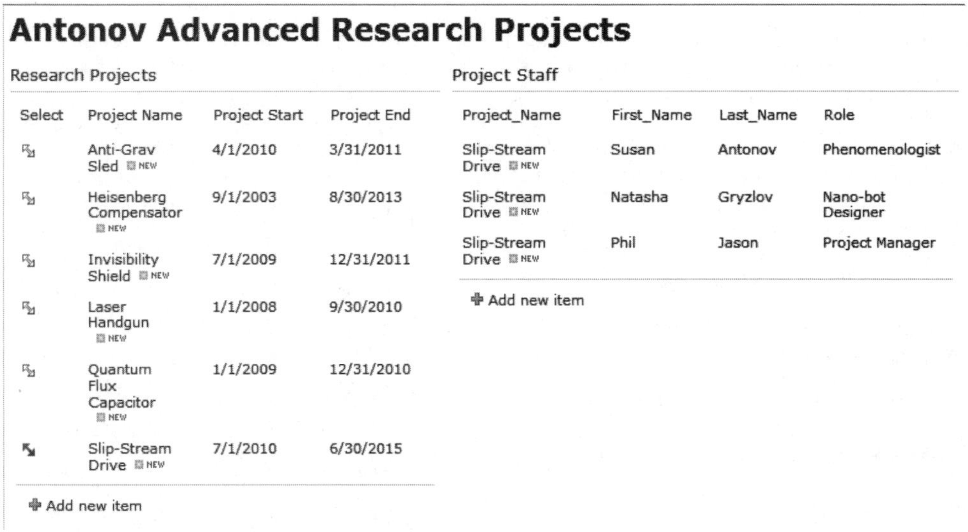

Antonov Advanced Research Projects
Research Projects
Select
Project Name
Project Start
Project End
Anti-Grav Sled NEW
4/1/2010
3/31/2011
Heisenberg Compensator NEW
9/1/2003
8/30/2013
Invisibility Shield NEW
7/1/2009
12/31/2011
Laser Handgun NEW
1/1/2008
9/30/2010
Quantum Flux Capacitor NEW
1/1/2009
12/31/2010
Slip-Stream Drive NEW
7/1/2010
6/30/2015
Add new item
Project Staff
Project_Name
First_Name
Last_Name
Role
Slip-Stream Drive NEW
Susan
Antonov
Phenomenologist
Slip-Stream Drive NEW
Natasha
Gryzlov
Nano-bot Designer
Slip-Stream Drive NEW
Phil
Jason
Project Manager
Add new item

Figure 3-31. Filtering staff by Project

Editing Pages with Check Out and Check In

In the first portion of this chapter, I did not mention the need for Check Out or Check In with regards to web or wiki pages. However, just like documents in a document library, you need to be concerned about locking your web and wiki pages while you edit them. Let's say you open a web page to make changes. While you have it open for an extended time, another staff member opens the same web page to make changes. Whoever saves their changes first loses because the second person to save the page could overwrite the changes saved by the first.

Actually, the second person to save their changes receives the dialog shown in Figure 3-32.

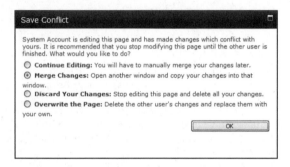

Figure 3-32. *Save Conflict notice*

Of course, just opening two copies of the page and attempting to merge changes manually can be problematic. After all, how easily can you spot all of the differences between the two page versions? Chances are good that you will miss some of the changes.

So what can you do to protect your web page while you have it open for editing? You check the page out just as you do with documents. Depending on whether your SharePoint administrator has configured your library to check out pages automatically, you may want to perform the check out as a separate step, as shown in Figure 3-33. Open the page library, use the drop-down menu for the page you want to edit, and manually select the **Check Out** option.

Figure 3-33. *Manually checking out web pages before editing*

Figure 3-33 shows the options available from the drop-down menu when you view your available pages in a page library in a publishing site. In this particular case, suppose the site does not force a check out before opening the page for editing. If you want to edit the page safely and do not know how long it will take you to edit it, you need to select the **Check Out** option first before manually editing the page. This gives you exclusive rights to edit the page as long as you keep the page checked out. If you have Microsoft Office SharePoint Designer installed on your system, you can use the option to edit your page via this tool. If you click the page name from the library to open the page and then click the **Documents** tab to open the **Documents** ribbon, you can still check the page out by clicking the **Check Out** button in the **Open & Check Out** group of the **Documents** ribbon.

Note that other options available in this group include the option to check in a page that you previously checked out. You must check in a page before others can edit the page.

You can also discard a check out. Perhaps you opened the page to check some of the content properties but did not make a change. Alternatively, maybe you made a big mistake editing the page and simply want to revert to the last saved version of the page. In these cases, discarding a check out cancels any changes you have made to the page since you checked it out.

When you check out a web page, the page icon before the name in the library displays a small box with a green arrow in it, as shown in Figure 3-33 next to the **Check Out** option. If you attempt to open and edit a checked-out page, you will get a yellow warning banner telling you that you are viewing the checked in read only version of the page (see Figure 3-34). It also tells you who has the page checked out exclusively.

Figure 3-34. *Warning that you cannot save content changes to a checked-out page*

Earlier in this section, I mentioned the possibility that your SharePoint administrator may have configured the site to check out pages automatically when you edit them. To see how she does that, return to the **Page Library** and select **Library Settings** from the **Library** ribbon. Then on the **List Settings** page, click **Versioning Settings** under the **General Settings** group of options. The resulting page, shown in Figure 3-35, has four settings groups.

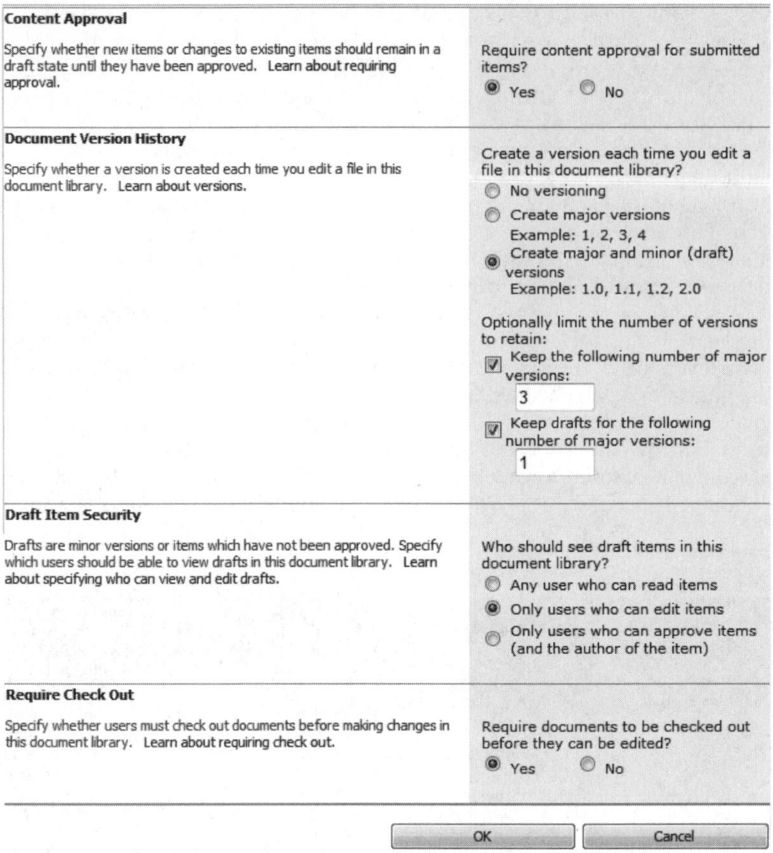

Content Approval

Specify whether new items or changes to existing items should remain in a draft state until they have been approved. Learn about requiring approval.

Require content approval for submitted items?
● Yes   ○ No

Document Version History

Specify whether a version is created each time you edit a file in this document library. Learn about versions.

Create a version each time you edit a file in this document library?
○ No versioning
○ Create major versions
   Example: 1, 2, 3, 4
● Create major and minor (draft) versions
   Example: 1.0, 1.1, 1.2, 2.0

Optionally limit the number of versions to retain:
☑ Keep the following number of major versions:
   3
☑ Keep drafts for the following number of major versions:
   1

Draft Item Security

Drafts are minor versions or items which have not been approved. Specify which users should be able to view drafts in this document library. Learn about specifying who can view and edit drafts.

Who should see draft items in this document library?
○ Any user who can read items
● Only users who can edit items
○ Only users who can approve items (and the author of the item)

Require Check Out

Specify whether users must check out documents before making changes in this document library. Learn about requiring check out.

Require documents to be checked out before they can be edited?
● Yes   ○ No

[OK]   [Cancel]

Figure 3-35. Setting your Page Library to require check out of edited pages

The first group has a single setting that asks whether you want someone to approve all new and changed items. When you select **Yes** to this setting, you must select an option from the **Draft Item Security** group. When you require approval, SharePoint places all new and edited documents in draft mode. While in draft mode, you may not want visitors to your site who have read-only rights to see the page. Perhaps you want to allow anyone with edit rights to view the new or changed pages, even if that person did not create the changes or new pages. This security mode represents a collaboration mode to editing. In the most restrictive mode, SharePoint limits access to new and changed pages to users who have approval rights so that they can approve the pages. Of course, in any of these security modes, the person who makes the changes or creates the new page has rights to view and further edit the page.

Going back to the second settings group, **Document Version History**, the SharePoint administrator can define how many versions of a page SharePoint should retain. The next section discusses versions in more detail.

Finally, the last group on the settings page, **Require Check Out**, allows the SharePoint administrator to require check out of pages before you can edit them. When set, this option checks whether you first checked the page out before you open it for editing. If you attempt to edit a page without first checking the page out, SharePoint displays the dialog box shown in Figure 3-36.

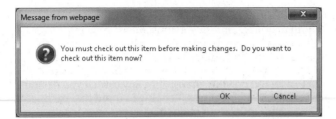

Figure 3-36. The dialog box requiring check out, as seen by a traditional Office client

If you are using a Microsoft Office Web App instead of the traditional Office client application, your screens and messages may differ from the ones shown in this book which focus on the Office client applications only. For example, this same message appears as shown in Figure 3-37 when using Office Web App.

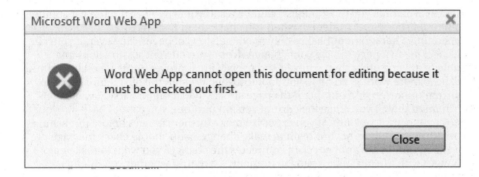

Figure 3-37. The dialog box requiring check out, as seen by Office Web App

If you click **OK** in this dialog box, SharePoint automatically checks out the page and opens it for editing. When you complete your changes, remember to check your changes back in. If you forget to check your pages in, other staff members cannot edit the page. In addition, content approvers cannot approve the page and make it available to site readers. Of course, if you have administrator rights to the site, you can override the check out of someone else. However, use this power only as a last resort, as it causes the person who had the page checked out to lose her changes.

Tracking Page Versions

By default, SharePoint does not activate versioning. In versionless mode, every change to a page updates the current version of the page. This mode uses the smallest amount of storage space for your site's pages. Whether your library maintains versioning for your pages or not, all visitors to your site can view the current major version and, depending on the Draft Item Security setting, they may see minor versions of your page unless you require content approval. Only by using content approval can you guarantee that pages under revision remain hidden from your site visitors until you submit the page for approval and a content approver publishes the page.

If your SharePoint administrator decides to allow SharePoint to save version histories, he must decide whether to retain only major versions or both major and minor versions. Major versions represent pages checked back in and approved (if content approval is required). Minor versions represent pages checked back in but not approved. You can think of minor versions as intermediate modifications or drafts to a page because either multiple people have made modifications or because you checked in your changes more than once as you worked on your changes. In any case, if you decide to keep versions, you can limit the number of versions SharePoint stores. Keeping in mind that each version uses storage space, you may want to limit the number of both major and minor versions. In Figure 3-35, the SharePoint administrator has configured SharePoint to store only the last three approved versions (major versions) and only the minor versions since the most recent major version. In other words, it only retains current works in progress as well as the last three published versions.

Publishing Pages to Your Site

When you edit a page with versioning turned on, your changes may not be visible to everyone depending on how your SharePoint administrator defined the Draft Item Security and Content Approval settings for your library. To be visible to everyone, you must publish your pages. If your site does not use versioning and approval, SharePoint publishes pages by default when you check them back in.

If your site uses versioning, SharePoint publishes only major versions of pages. However, if your site also requires approval, checking in a page to save your changes from your current session does not necessarily make it visible to anyone other than yourself and users with approver rights. Therefore, if you check in a page but still have more work to do on it, you should either assign it the next minor version number or reuse the current minor version number if the page already had a minor version when you opened it to edit. Keep in mind that, if you reuse the current version number, you cannot back out your changes by merely restoring the prior versions. If you expect to make further changes before publishing your page or if you expect other members of your team to make changes, you should check the page back in using a minor version number. If your check in completes the changes you want to make before publishing, save the changes with the next major version number. No matter whether you intend to check the page in as a major or minor version, SharePoint tracks the versions of the page and automatically assigns the next available major or minor number for you.

Perhaps you do not need to keep intermediate versions between major changes to the page. You could ask your SharePoint administrator to turn off minor versioning. This guarantees that every checked-in version is a major version.

You can also turn off all versioning if the **Page Library** is informal and you do not need to save each version. This selection saves storage space required by your site. However, if you ever need a prior version of the page, you may be out of luck unless your SharePoint administrator can restore one from a backup copy of the database. Retrieving pages from a backup copy of the database is a time-intensive task. If you do this too often, you may discover your SharePoint administrator hiding under her desk when she hears you coming toward her office.

To publish your most recent page update, you must assign the next major version number to it when you check it in. To check in your page, open the **Page Library**. Notice that the **Approval Status** value for the page you just checked in is **Draft**. This status indicates that someone modified the page since its last approved version but that they did not submit the new version for review and approval.

Next, right-click on the page. Select **Check In** from the drop-down list of options. Figure 3-38 shows the Check in dialog box. Notice that, in addition to assigning your updated page either a minor or major version number, you can determine whether you want to keep the modified page checked out, but only if you save the updated page as a minor version.

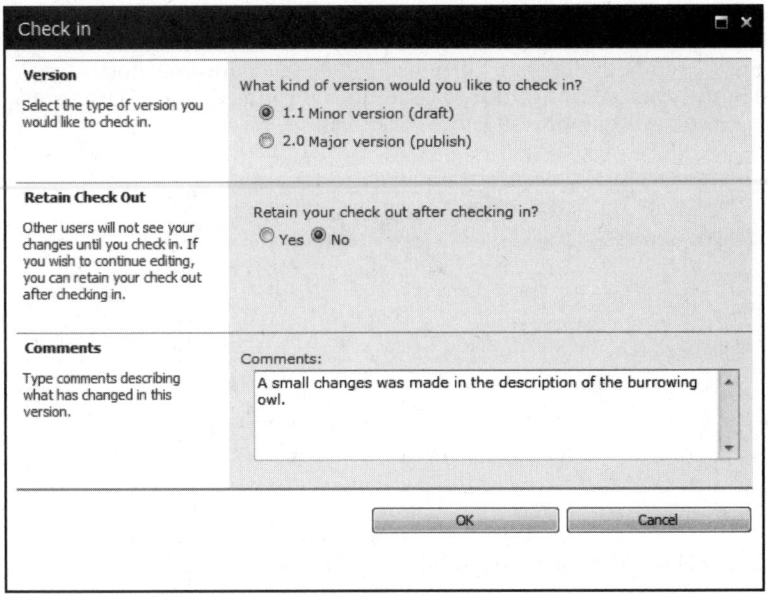

Figure 3-38. *Checking in a modified web page*

Anytime you check a page back in, you have the option of adding comments to the version. You may want to use comments to document who made the change and when and provide a change summary.

If you choose to assign the updated page a minor version for now, you can publish a major version later without making changes by going to **Site Actions ➤ View All Site Content**. Open the library, open the drop-down menu for the page you want to publish, and click **Publish a Major Version**. When published this way, you still have the option of adding comments, as shown in Figure 3-39.

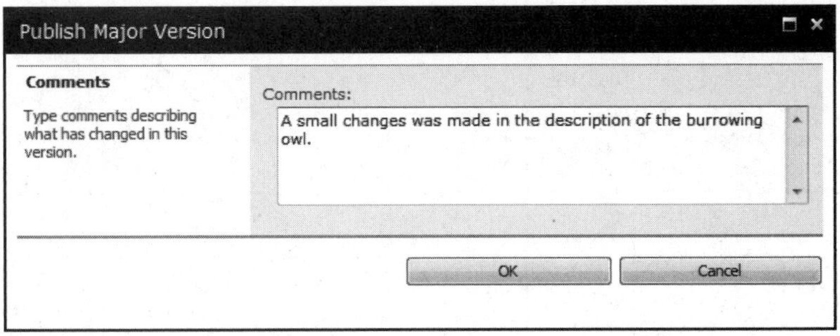

Figure 3-39. *Adding a comment when publishing a major version*

Note that, if your library requires approval of major changes before the public can view them, your page is still not visible to other users even though you just saved the page as a major version. Click **OK** to finish checking in your page. When you return to the library listing as shown in Figure 3-40, notice that SharePoint updates the **Approval Status** column from **Draft** to **Pending**, indicating that you have saved a major version of the page but that it still needs approval before others can see it.

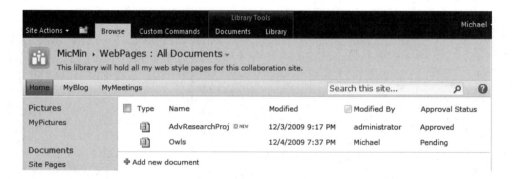

Figure 3-40. Pages checked in as major versions have a status of Pending.

To approve the page, you need to have the site administrator, site owner, or another user with approval rights open the **Page Library**. He can then click to the right of the page name to open the drop-down menu for the page and select **Approve/Reject**. Clicking this option displays the page shown in Figure 3-41.

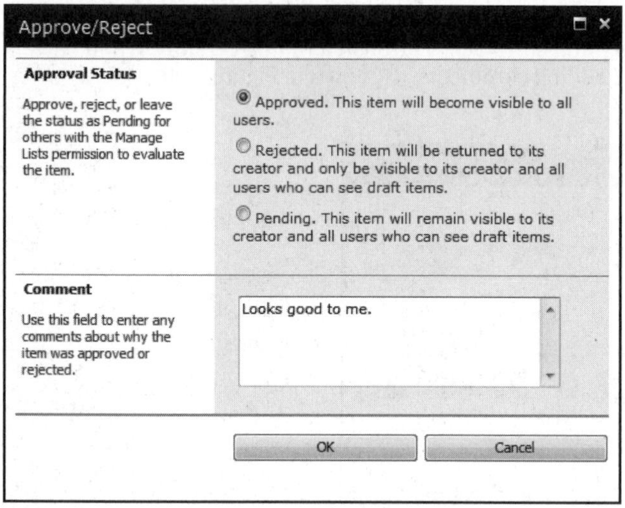

Figure 3-41. Approvers can approve or reject a major version.

As you can see in this figure, approvers have three possible actions they can select on this request:

- **Approved**: This option makes the newest page version visible to all users.

- **Rejected**: The newest page version does not become public. If the page has a previously approved version, that version remains the public version.

- **Pending**: The page remains in its current security state and is not published. The approver typically uses this option when asking for further clarification on the change.

No matter what option the approver selects, she can leave a comment. However, approvers should definitely use comments when rejecting a page or sending it back pending additional clarification or rework. When the approver clicks **OK** on this page, SharePoint executes the page action, changing the status of the page in the **Page Library** to **Approved**, **Rejected**, or **Pending** based on the selection made.

If you look at the version history for this page as shown in Figure 3-42, you'll see that SharePoint lists a new major release (2.0) after approving the page. It also removes all the minor releases from version 1.0 because the version setup defined in Figure 3-35 only requires SharePoint to save minor releases for the current major release.

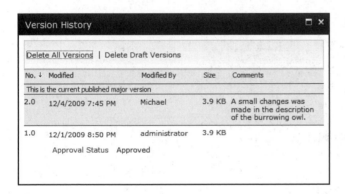

Figure 3-42. The version history for a page can tell you who made each change and when she made it.

■ **Tip** If you have Site Owner rights and can manage the site hierarchy, you can also use the Manage Content and Structure option from the Site Actions menu. This option displays the Site Content and Structure page which shows you the organization of your site. Perhaps even more important are the other items in the View drop-down from the header on the right side. This drop-down displays several additional reports you can run, including the generation of a list of documents and pages checked out to a certain person, documents and pages pending approval, all draft documents and pages, and more.

Recovering Accidental Deletions with the Recycle Bin

When you delete a page from your **Page Library**, SharePoint prompts to confirm your desire to delete it. If you only had to worry about your own accidental deletions, this dialog box may seem like more than enough protection for your pages. However, you probably have several people with edit rights on your site. In some large organizations, you may have dozens of people with edit rights, perhaps even hundreds. So what happens when they delete a page because they don't think they need it, and it's a page you worked on for hours and for which you have no other backup? I suppose you could read them the riot act, otherwise known as corporate policy. Of course, if they sit higher in the organization than you, that could limit your career potential.

Before I show you what happens when someone else accidentally deletes your page, let's see what happens when you accidentally delete one of your own pages. SharePoint provides a safety net. SharePoint 2010 supports a Recycle Bin, which, like the Recycle Bin on your desktop, temporarily stores deleted files. For example, if you were to delete your Owl page from the **WebPages Library**, rather than rant and rave about having to recreate the page, the good news is that you can recover the page with just a few mouse clicks. Begin by clicking the **Recycle Bin** option at the bottom of the **Quick Launch** menu on the left of the **Page Library** page. The Recycle Bin, shown in Figure 3-43, displays a listing of the documents you deleted within the last 30 days.

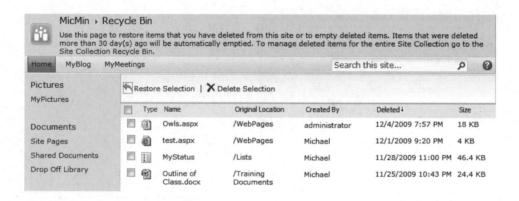

Figure 3-43. The Recycle Bin collects all deleted objects.

To recover a deleted object, click the check box to the left of the object to select it. Then click the **Restore Selection** option at the top of the page.

When you delete a page, you delete all of the versions of that page as well. SharePoint keeps all versions together as a single item in the Recycle Bin so that, when you recover an object from it, SharePoint recovers all versions of that document.

■ **Tip** You can ask your SharePoint administrator to change the length of time items stay in the Recycle Bin. She can go into Central Administration and select **Application Management**. Then by selecting **General Settings** from the **Web Applications** ribbon, she can scroll down to the **Recycle Bin** section and change the number of days SharePoint keeps items in the Recycle Bin.

The bad news is that only the person who deletes the page can recover it because the Recycle Bin is user based. Therefore, if someone else deletes your page, you will not see it in your recycle bin. However, SharePoint provides an escape clause for even this scenario. The site collection administrators can view all items deleted by anyone when they look at the Recycle Bin via the `Site Collection Recycle Bin` link found at the end of the last sentence in the header (see Figure 3-43). Therefore, all you need to do is go to the site collection administrator and ask them to restore the file for you. The site collection administrator then sees the Site Collection Recycle Bin shown in Figure 3-44.

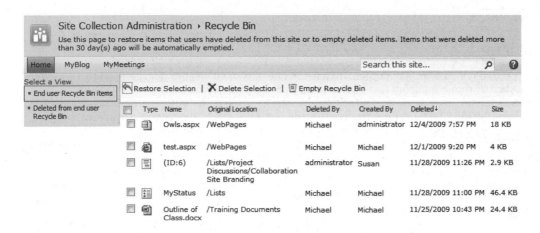

Figure 3-44. Site collection administrators can see all deleted objects in the Recycle Bin.

When you click on the Site Collection Recycle Bin link, SharePoint displays a screen that shows all of the files deleted within the last 30 days by all users of the site. Therefore, as a site collection administrator, you can recover files deleted by anyone by selecting the **check box** before the filename and then clicking the **Restore Selection** option in the header. You can also determine who deleted the file should that be important to the person requesting you to recover a lost file. Finally, notice also that you can click the **Empty Recycle Bin** option to delete any files in the Recycle Bin permanently. If you do this, you cannot recover the deleted files without resorting to a backup.

The Share and Track Features

SharePoint 2010 pages have a group of features in the Documents and the Library ribbons that allow you to share and track item from a library. Options on this ribbon include features like the Alerts and RSS

Feeds (see Figure 3-45). It also gives you the ability to e-mail a link for the current page or just copy the link so you can add it to a hyperlink on another page.

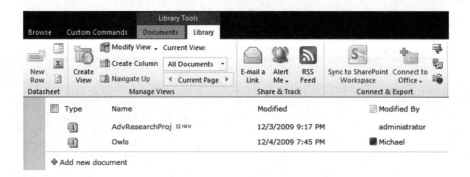

Figure 3-45. Sharing and tracking options for page libraries

E-mail a Link

Often you need to refer a page, a document, or a list to one of your colleagues. You could copy the entire text and paste it into an e-mail, but this increases the amount of data your mail server has to process, slows the mail service down, and takes up additional storage space as the same information gets stored multiple times. Perhaps the most important reason for sending a link to the page or document as opposed to copying the text is that, by sending a link, the content everyone sees is always the most current. What's to say that, as soon as you copied the contents of a page or document to send to a friend, the owner of that information does not go out and update it with new information?

Happily, SharePoint 2010 makes it easy to send a link from the content of your choice (page, list, or item) by using the **E-mail a Link** option that appears in the **Share & Track** group of many of the ribbons. Selecting this option opens a new e-mail message with the link of the corresponding page, library, list, or item already in the body of the message.

When the e-mail recipient opens the e-mail, he can click on the link to display the most up-to-date version of the content, even if he opens the link hours or days later. E-mailing links to content might also solve the problem that occurs within some companies in which attachments with specific extensions might be restricted or when there are limitations on the size of attachments added to e-mail messages.

■ **Note** SharePoint can generate a link reference for a library, list, page, or library document. However, it cannot generate a link reference for a list item.

Alerts

Alerts let you subscribe to changes on a page, delivered in a list or as an individual item. This alert subscription keeps you informed of changes by sending you an e-mail. You can even specify the frequency and the time that you want to receive those e-mails.

If you are the site owner, you might want to know when someone adds or changes content on the pages or lists for which you are responsible. If you are one of several content creators, you might only be interested in changes that others make to pages you create or maintain. If you are a visitor to a site, you might want to receive notices via e-mail every time someone posts something new to a page or list.

Figure 3-46 shows that the **Alert Me** drop-down menu in the **Share & Track** ribbon lets you create alerts for pages, lists, or items. Of course, the type of alert that you can create depends on what you last clicked on within the page. If you simply opened the page, the only option enabled in this menu is to create an alert for the current page. However, if you click in a list displayed on the page, you will see both the option to create a link to the page as well as to create a link to the list where you clicked. Finally, if you not only click in a list, but also if you click the selection check boxes that lists can display, you can subscribe only to alerts that affect that one item.

■ **Note** To enable check boxes for a list, you must modify the list's view definition and select the option **Allow individual item checkboxes** in the **Tabular View** group, resave the view definition, and apply that view definition to the page.

Figure 3-46. *Defining a page alert*

Setting an alert is much more than just defining whether you want an alert when something changes on a page, list, or item. There is a vast set of parameters you can set to determine which types of changes you see; you can even select change alerts based on who made the changes.

Figure 3-47 shows the dialog SharePoint provides to help you define your alert. It divides the dialog into several option groups. First, you must provide a name for the alert. To manage your alerts, you should consider a naming convention that tells you a little about the nature of the alert. For example, the alert name can begin with the name of the page or list that you want to monitor. However, as you will see in a moment, that may not be enough either because you can define more than one alert for any page, list, or item. Therefore, you should include the action (Add, Modify, or Delete) in the name. And even that may not be enough though, since you can create alerts for all changes; for only changes made by someone else to any page, list, or item; or for only changes made to objects you created or last modified. Using this system, possible names for an alert might include:

- `Main Site Shared Document Changes Made by Someone Else`

- `Company Calendar Additions`

When you create an alert, you can include anyone else whom you may want to notify of changes.

Although you can receive text message via SMS, many people prefer to receive an e-mail notification of the changes.

In the section where you can select the change type for which you want to be notified, note that the options in this section change depending on whether you can create an alert for a page, list, or item. Note also that the selections in the **Sent Alerts for These Changes** section are mutually exclusive since they use radio (option) buttons. You cannot choose two or more of the options at one time for a single alert. However, you could create multiple alerts, one for each change type if you need alerts on different change types.

Finally, you can select how frequently you want to receive alerts. For some alerts, you may need to know of changes immediately. However, other changes may not be as important and thus a daily or even a weekly alert may be adequate. Notice that, when you choose to receive a daily alert summary, you can specify the time of the day when you want SharePoint to send the alert. For a weekly alert, you must not only select the time of the day to receive the alert, but also the day of the week. For instance, you may want to receive an alert summary of changes at the end of the week, especially if you just want to know if changes have occurred without having to go out to the site and constantly check for changes.

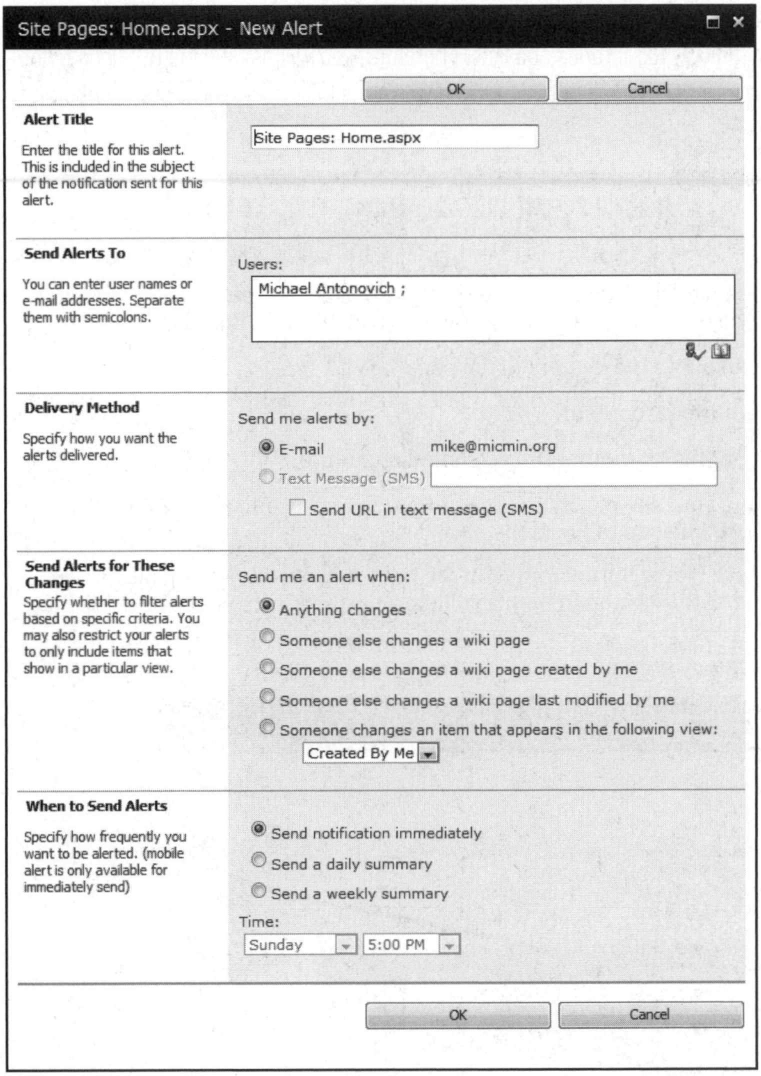

Figure 3-47. Defining the type and frequency of an alert

RSS Feeds

RSS Feeds are related to alerts in that they also help you stay aware of new additions to lists. In Chapter 2, the "Creating RSS Feeds for Your List" section covered how to set up and use RSS feeds from within your browser. As you can see in the Share & Track ribbon, you can also subscribe to an RSS feed for the current list or page library directly from the ribbon options.

■ **Note** SharePoint generates RSS feeds only for libraries and lists. Therefore, you will not see the RSS icon in the Share & Track group of a Page ribbon or a Documents ribbon, but you will see it in the **List** and **Library** ribbon for lists and libraries respectively.

The Note Board

The Note Board lets you leave a message for the current page. Your messages are public, meaning that people who can view the page can also view your messages. You can use the Note Board to:

- Leave a personal opinion about the content of the page.

- Make suggestions for additional content.

- Reference other pages on this or another site with similar content.

- If you are still developing your site pages, you might want to leave yourself some notes about what you still must do to finish the page.

To create a note, click the **Tags & Notes** button found on the right side of your site's page header area. Figure 3-48 shows an example of this button in both a collaboration site (on top) and a publishing site (on the bottom).

Figure 3-48. Adding a note to a page

This button opens the dialog shown in Figure 3-49 where you can enter your notes. In this dialog, there are two tabs, one for **Tags** and one for **Note Board**. Click the Note Board tab if necessary to select it. Note Board notes consist of plain text. They do not support special formatting options, hyperlinks, tables, or images. When you have completed your note entry, click the **Post** button.

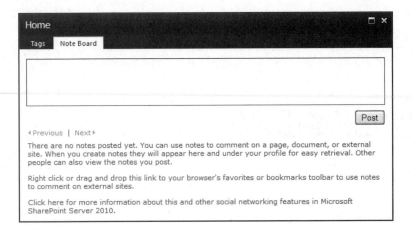

Figure 3-49. Adding a note to a page

When you post a note, anyone who can view the web page can also view the note. However, only the site owner or note creator can delete the note. The ability to delete notes is important if you use notes during site development to track tasks you must still complete on the page. The note creator can also edit the note. Figure 3-50 shows the dialog immediately after posting a note. SharePoint lists recent notes at the bottom of the dialog and provides options to edit and/or delete the note.

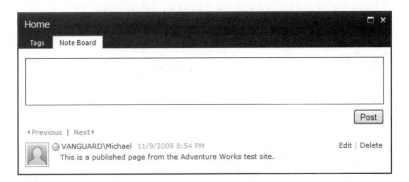

Figure 3-50. Displaying notes for a page with the options to edit or delete individual notes

Tags

You probably noticed that the dialog that lets you enter a note also lets you enter a tag by clicking the tag tab at the top of the dialog. A *note* is a free-form text entry that applies to the page, while a *tag* is more like a label attached to a page so that you can quickly group similar pages by placing the same tag on two or more pages. Tags can be private or public. Public tags effectively associate similar pages not only within a SharePoint site, but also across the entire Internet, but this does depend on how consistently other users tag pages. Private tags typically associate similar pages more accurately, but generally do not associate as many different pages since they represent tags you create only. Notice in Figure 3-51 that not only can you enter and save a tag, but you can also use an option in this dialog to add a link to your browser so you can tag external sites as well. When tagging external sites, SharePoint tracks the tag text as well as the URL of the external site so you can group similar pages both within your SharePoint site and within external web pages.

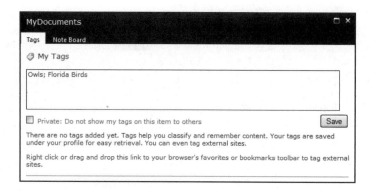

Figure 3-51. Adding a tag to a page

To view your Tags or Note Board entries, you can open **My Profile** found in the drop-down from your name in the upper right corner of the screen, as shown in Figure 3-52.

Figure 3-52. Personal drop-down menu options

Your profile consists of six tabbed pages including: Overview, Organization, Content, Tags and Notes, Colleagues, and Memberships. Click on the **Tags and Notes** tab. Figure 3-53 shows a view of the tags and notes in your **MySite**. Using the options in the upper left of this page, you can display all your tags, all your notes, or both. You can also choose between viewing just your private notes and tags and your public notes and tags.

Immediately beneath the selection of type on the left side of the page, you can select how you want to sort your tags and notes. Typically, you sort tags alphabetically so that you can quickly find all the entries for a specific tag.

The activity for the type of tag or note selected appears on the right side of the page. More specifically, the activity displayed corresponds to just the current month. Arrows on either side of the month/year let you view the activity for the previous or next month.

Each tag or note begins with a link to the page associated with that tag or note followed by its creation date. You also have a link to view related activities. If you created the tag or note, you also have the option to delete it.

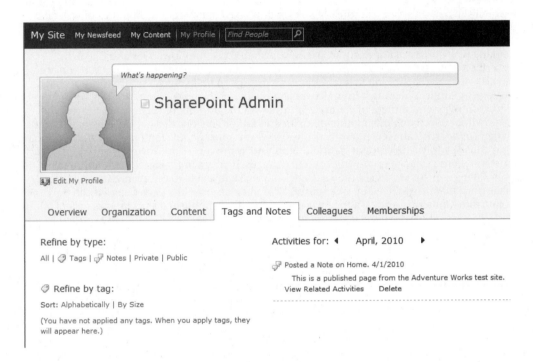

Figure 3-53. Tags and Notes page from your MySite

Summary

This chapter looked at creating wiki and web part pages within SharePoint. Both page types support similar functionality so you should have no trouble moving from one style to the other depending on the type of site you are building. If your site only supports collaboration, you may prefer the wiki-style page. On the other hand, if you publish pages of information, even within a collaboration site, that you do not want others to change, you may want to use web pages and put those pages in a separate library with different access rights.

You started by looking at the web part page. These pages contain one or more web part zones to which you can add web parts that SharePoint provides. Two web parts in particular that you examined were the content editor and image web parts. In both cases, you must be careful when entering the URL of the image or hyperlink site, because you must directly enter the value without the help of a browse feature. Furthermore, you must store your images in a picture library. You then saw that you could take a Word document and copy the text directly into the content area of a web page while preserving most of the formatting of the page. In fact, copying a table created in Word may be the best way to create a formatted table. You also saw that you could take any of the libraries or lists you created using the skills covered in Chapters 1 and 2 and add them to the page as well. After adding two or more lists to a web part page, you learned how to define a master-detail relationship between the web parts on a connecting field. After you have defined such a relationship, users can select a record from the master list to filter the records displays in the detail list to those related to the master record.

Then you created similar page as a wiki page. You saw that with wiki pages, adding content does not require a separate web part and that you can add links to other wiki pages directly into the content also without using another web part. In fact, you can link to not only other wiki pages, but other lists, libraries, and even web pages.

When working with either wiki or web part pages, you should use the Check Out and Check In features as described when working with libraries to protect the integrity of your changes until you are done. You can also use page versioning to track changes to a page so that you can return to a prior version of the page by simply selecting it from the version history of the page. When working with versions, the total storage requirement of your page grows with the number of versions you have. You can limit this growth by specifying the number of major and minor versions of a page you want to retain. You can even determine who can view minor versions. However, most people limit the viewing of minor versions to only those people with content creation rights and approvers (if approvers are used).

You learned about the value of approving content changes. If your library has content approval turned on, even saving a major version of the page does not make it visible to the average site visitor. Rather, the page must first be reviewed by an approver who must approve the page before it can be published to your site. Content approval appears most frequently on published sites used as part of an intranet or even an Internet in which the department or company wants to ensure that the content is accurate and appropriate for distribution to others.

You then saw that the Recycle Bin encountered previously for libraries also works for web pages. It allows you or the site owner to recover accidently deleted pages for up to 30 days after they have been deleted, depending on how your SharePoint administrator has configured your site.

Finally, you looked at some of the social enhancements to pages—the ability to add tags and notes to pages. Tagging of pages has become increasingly popular, and public tagging can help associate your pages with other similar content pages. SharePoint provides a web part called the Tag Cloud web part that can display this relationship.

This introduction to SharePoint, provided in the first three chapters, does not cover everything you can do with libraries, lists, and pages, but it lays a framework for the next group of chapters, which focus on how to work with these objects using several Microsoft Office tools.

■ ■ ■

CHAPTER 4

Using Your Document Library with Microsoft Office

Chapter 1 showed you how to use Microsoft Word with your SharePoint document library. However, SharePoint does not limit you to Word documents. You can store other Microsoft Office document types in your document library including Excel, PowerPoint, and OneNote. Furthermore, SharePoint does not limit you to Microsoft Office tools. You can store almost anything in SharePoint, with the only limitation being that the applications they depend on may not integrate with SharePoint as well as Office does.

However, because of SharePoint's enhanced integration with Office 2010, most of the discussion from this point forward focus on Office 2010 unless otherwise stated. Note that most features discussed here work the same across all Office 2010 tools.

Some of the topics discussed in this chapter apply specifically to Word 2010 documents and may vary considerable if one uses prior versions of Office. If you still use Office 2007, you will be happy to know that much of what I cover here also applies to that version. Unfortunately, you should not expect the integration with earlier versions of Office to be as strong as with Office 2010 or even Office 2007. Even with earlier versions, though, you can still use SharePoint as a file store for documents.

Opening a SharePoint Document from Within Microsoft Office

Beginning from Microsoft Office Word, your first challenge might be how to access SharePoint document libraries from within Word. If the document you want to open exists on a SharePoint site that you previously visited and you are using Windows XP still, you may see a reference to that library in your `My Network Places` folder of Windows Explorer. Unfortunately, neither Windows Vista nor Windows 7 automatically adds references to places you visit in SharePoint in its equivalent of My Network Places. However, you can use mapped drives in Vista and Windows 7 to point to your SharePoint site/library. For more information on setting up your My Network Places in Windows XP or mapped drives in Vista and Windows 7, see the "Referencing your SharePoint Site from Microsoft Office" sidebar. For a moment, let's assume you still use Windows XP. Open the `My Network Places` folder to display the files stored there as shown in Figure 4-1. As you can see in the figure, I already have a reference to site pages on my Vanguard server.

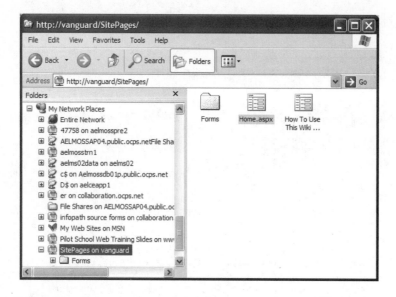

Figure 4-1. Opening a SharePoint document from Windows Explorer

Referencing Your SharePoint Site from Microsoft Office

If you are using Windows XP

In Windows XP, you can easily add to the references in My Network Places to include one that points to a SharePoint site or library by following these steps:

1. Click the **Start** button and then select **My Network Places** from the **Start** menu.

2. In the left navigation pane, click **Add a network place** in the **Network Tasks** group.

3. On the first page of the **Welcome to the Add Network Place Wizard**, just click **Next**.

4. On the page that asks **Where do you want to create this network place?** Select **Choose another network location** and click **Next**.

5. Enter the name of the URL for the site in general or the specific library you want to reference. Use a second window to open the site or library and copy the URL from the address bar. Then paste the URL in the dialog's field in the field labeled **Internet or network address**. Click **Next**.

6. On the next page of the wizard, enter a user-friendly name and click **Next**.

7. On the last page of the wizard, click **Finish**.

You can now use this entry in Network Places to navigate quickly to your site or library from within an application or even Windows Explorer.

If you are using Vista or Windows 7

To add a mapped drive to Vista or Windows 7, follow these steps:

1. Open the Start menu and choose Computer.

2. Click the **Map Network Drive** option in the **Tools** drop-down menu located at the top of the window.

3. In the dialog that appears, accept the suggested drive letter or select a different drive letter from the drop-down list.

4. In the folder text box, enter the URL of the SharePoint site or library. One way to do this is to open a browser window and navigate to the site or library. Copy the URL from the address bar and paste it in the folder text box. In my case, I would enter http://vanguard.

5. If you need to use a different user name to connect to the SharePoint server, click the link in the line **Connect using a different user name** and supply the user name and password to connect to your SharePoint site.

6. Click **Finish** to complete the mapping definition.

While you can use the mapped drive to reference your SharePoint site when you are in an application and need to open or save a document, you cannot use it as your browser to open the site.

How Can Vista Store References to Sites You Visit?

Since Vista has removed web folders, some of the steps listed here for XP will not work if you use Vista. However, with just a few changes, you can do virtually the same thing in Vista.

To create a new Internet shortcut, follow these steps:

1. Use your browser to navigate to the site you want to quickly access in the future.

2. Copy the URL to your clipboard.

3. Click the Windows **Start** icon and then click your profile name. This opens Windows Explorer to your personal profile folder.

4. On the right side of the folder contents, right-click a blank area and create a new folder named Sites.

5. Open the new folder by double-clicking it.

6. Right-click a blank area and create a new shortcut.

7. Paste the URL from the web site into the text box and click **Next**.

8. Provide a name for the shortcut and click **Finish**.

Next, to add this folder to Vista's taskbar so you can easily access its contents, follow these steps:

1. Display Vista's taskbar and right-click a blank area of the taskbar.

2. Navigate to **Toolbars** and select **New Toolbar**.

3. Click the Desktop folder in the left pane.

4. Open your profile folder.

5. Locate the folder Sites you created earlier.

6. Click Select Folder.

Now, you can do the same thing for other web sites in Vista and Windows 7. From any web site, click the icon found at the beginning of the address text box and drag it into the **Sites** toolbar in your taskbar. When you release your mouse button, Vista adds the shortcut to the **Sites** toolbar. The next time you open the **Sites** toolbar, the new shortcut appears.

Looking at your SharePoint document folders from within Windows Explorer has several advantages. First, you can rename documents in the library, move documents from one library to another, make copies of a document from one library to another, and even delete documents from the library. From a single Windows Explorer instance, you can copy and paste documents from your local hard drive or any network drive you can access to a SharePoint library. Of course, you can also copy files from that library back to your local hard disk. However, if you open a second Windows Explorer instance, you can easily drag and drop files from one folder to another, even two different SharePoint folders. Finally, to edit any Office document stored in a SharePoint library, just double-click it.

All the rules about editing documents discussed in Chapter 1 apply to documents opened directly from Windows Explorer. If the document requires you to check it out before you can modify it, you will see a bar at the top of the document asking you to check out the document, as shown in Figure 4-2.

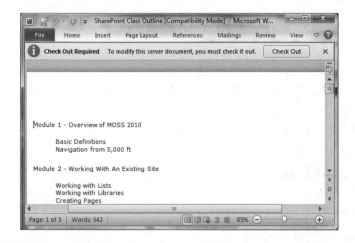

Figure 4-2. Opening a SharePoint document from Microsoft Word 2010

Of course, if you only want to read the document or print it, you do not need to check it out. Should you decide to check out the document to edit it, you have the option of editing the copy within SharePoint directly, or you can copy the document to your local computer and edit it offline, as shown in Figure 4-3. If you only have a quick change, it may not seem to make sense to download the document, make the change, and then upload the document again. However, by downloading the document, you can disconnect from the SharePoint site, edit the document, save it, and then reconnect to SharePoint to save your changes later.

Why would you need to edit a document after disconnecting from your SharePoint site? Perhaps you can only connect to your SharePoint site from your network at the office. To work on that document at home or to take it with you on that long cross-country plane flight, you need a local copy of the file on your hard disk.

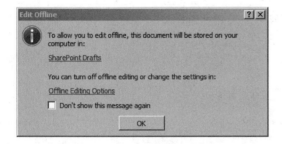

Figure 4-3. *Defining the SharePoint Drafts folder*

 Tip If you do not see Figure 4-3 when you open a document even though it requires check out, it probably means that you have configured your copy of Word to store drafts on the server. Note that this will prevent you from working offline. You can change this by going to Word Options described below.

Notice the link named **SharePoint Drafts** in Figure 4-3. If you point to this link, you can see in the pop-up tooltip the current folder on your hard drive where your computer stores SharePoint drafts. By default, Windows XP creates a folder named

`<<Drive-Letter>>:\Documents and Settings\YourUserId\MyDocuments\SharePoint Drafts\`

In Windows Vista, Windows 7, and Windows 2008 SharePoint creates a local drafts folder at

`<<Drive-Letter>>:\Users\Your_Profile_Name\Documents\SharePoint Drafts\`

In some of these operating systems, you may see \MyDocuments\ instead of \Documents\ when you browse to them using Windows Explorer. However, the Server draft location in Microsoft's Office products will save the link as \Documents\.

If you want to define a different location for your drafts, click the second link on Figure 4-3, **Offline Editing Options**. This link opens the **Word Options** dialog box (because the document is a Word document), shown in Figure 4-4. In the **Save** page of this dialog, find the section **Offline editing options**

for document management server files. In this section, select whether to save checked-out files to a server draft location on your local computer or edit them on the SharePoint server by selecting the second radio button **The Office Document Cache**. If you choose to use a local server draft location and want to change the default location defined above, you must specify its location in the **Server Drafts location** text box or use the **Browse** button to navigate to a folder you want to use.

■ **Tip** You can also get to this dialog by selecting **Options** from the **File** tab and, in the resulting dialog, select **Save** in the left panel.

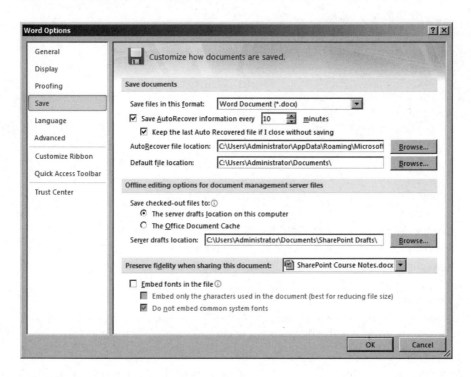

Figure 4-4. Defining offline editing options

■ **Tip** If you have not already done so, now would be a good time to define a frequency for saving an AutoRecovery copy of your document as you work on it.

If you want to define these settings ahead of time, you can open the options dialog box for any Microsoft Office 2010 product by selecting **Options** from the **File** drop-down menu.

■ **Note** If you are using Office 2007, you can find the options dialog by clicking the **Office** button. Then select **Options** from the left navigation menu just above **Exit**.

Suppose, however, that you do not see folders in Windows Explorer for your SharePoint libraries. You can still open SharePoint documents directly from within the relevant Microsoft Office 2007 tool if you know both the SharePoint site URL and the library names. Figure 4-5 shows the **Open** dialog box from within Word. Notice in the **File name** field, you can enter the name of the SharePoint site URL along with the **Shared Documents** library rather than the name of a file.

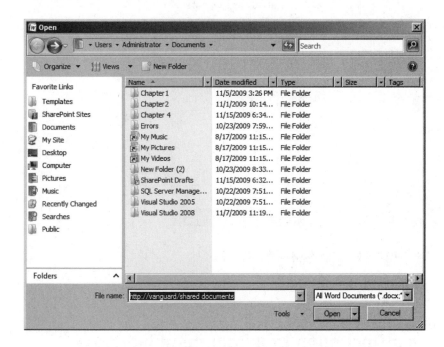

Figure 4-5. Referencing a SharePoint library in the Open dialog box

■ **Note** You must precede the site URL with either http:// or https://, depending on whether your SharePoint site uses a secure connection or not. If you do not know which to use, you can try both, or you can ask your system administrator.

Do not change the contents of the **File of type** field. Word fills in this field, as will most applications, based on the types of files the application recognizes. If you change this field to display other file types, any attempt to open those files may fail. When you click **Open** with the URL of a library specified as shown in Figure 4-5, Word displays the Word documents stored in that library, as shown in Figure 4-6.

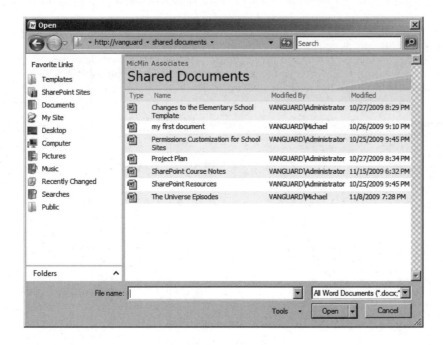

Figure 4-6. *Viewing the SharePoint library contents from within Word*

Now you can open any document by double-clicking its name. You can also click the document to select it and then click **Open**.

Editing and Saving a Document to a Document Library

In the previous section, you saw two ways to open a Word document stored in a SharePoint library without first opening a SharePoint site. You should note that security defined in SharePoint for checking out documents still applies even when you open the document from Windows Explorer or from within Word. This means you can only open the document to edit it if you have edit rights and if someone else does not have it checked out. Remember that, while these examples use Microsoft Word documents, these techniques apply to any file type recognized by SharePoint and registered in the operating system to an installed application.

Concurrency Problems

For those readers who skipped the first three chapters, the importance of using Check Out and Check In features when editing documents derives from the need to prevent concurrency problems. Concurrency problems occur when two or more people edit the same document at the same time.

The potential for concurrency problems increases as the number of users on the site increases. However, concurrency problems generally decrease as you save more content to the site because any two users are less likely to edit the same document. Unfortunately, no statistic matters much if you lose your changes because someone else worked on the same document you did and had the happy luck to save his changes *after* you saved yours, thus deleting your changes.

Word 2010 offers a new way to handle concurrency problems and allows two or more people to edit the same document at the same time. I will discuss this new feature in the "Managing Multiple Editors in a Document" section found later in this chapter.

When opening documents directly from Windows Explorer as described earlier, you receive no visual cues that someone else may have the file open for editing until you try to check it out. On the other hand, when you use a Microsoft Word, the file icon in the type column of the **Open** dialog box displays a green box with a white arrow in the lower-right corner, indicating that someone has the file checked out.

If you attempt to open a file that someone else has checked out, the **File in Use** dialog box shown in Figure 4-7 appears. Notice that this dialog box also tells you who has checked out the file.

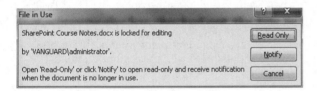

Figure 4-7. File in Use dialog box

You can choose to continue opening the file in Read Only mode. If you only need to view the document or print it, this mode does not restrict these actions. However, if you really must edit the document, click the **Notify** button. This option tells SharePoint to notify you when the document becomes available. While waiting, leave Word open, although it does not have to be the active window; you can minimize it but you cannot close it or you will not receive the notification. When the other user closes and checks in the document, a pop-up dialog box appears, as shown in Figure 4-8, notifying you that you can check out the current document version to edit it.

Figure 4-8. Notification that the file is now available for editing

When you finish editing the document, save it and close the application used to edit it. If you checked out the document, you must check it back in. Otherwise, it remains checked out to you, thereby preventing others from making changes to the document. The check out feature supports working exclusively on documents offline while letting you periodically save your changes back to SharePoint. However, you should not use it to keep the document permanently checked out.

Each of the previous examples involve opening, editing, and resaving documents that already exist in SharePoint. However, suppose you want to create a new document and save it. I will demonstrate using MS Word as the application tool, but remember that the techniques applied with one Office product typically work with others as well.

Saving a New Document

To begin, create a new document in Word 2010. For this example, call the document "Hello SharePoint." Adding your own text to the body of the document is optional. When finished, save the document by clicking the **File** tab. You could save the document by clicking **Save** and referencing your SharePoint document library just as we did in the previous section to open a SharePoint document. However, let's choose **Share** from the **File** menu and then select **Save to SharePoint**, as shown in Figure 4-9. This figure shows the **Browse for a location** button that appears if you have never saved a Word document from within Word. Clicking this button opens the same Save As dialog that you would have seen had you selected **Save As** from the **File** menu. If you have previously saved SharePoint documents, this option appears and allows you to select where you want to save your document with the options grouped in three categories:

- Current Locations: This category only appears when you begin by editing a document from a SharePoint library, and that library appears as a current location.

- Recent Locations: This category shows all the document libraries where you have recently saved files.

- My SharePoint Locations: This section references libraries in your MySite.

■ **Tip** If you previously used Word to at least open files from your SharePoint Documents folders, you may find a reference to those folders in the Recent Places of the Save As dialog.

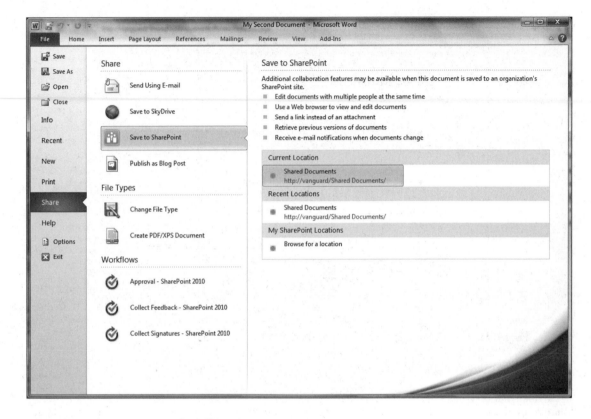

Figure 4-9. Share options in the Office menu

Saving a Document to an Existing Library

Let's continue by saving a second document, called My Second Document, by selecting **Save As** from the **File** tab. Because you previously saved a document to SharePoint, you should see a reference to **Shared Documents** on the right side of the dialog when you click on **Recent Places** on the left side of the dialog. Double-click on **Shared Documents** to open the Shared Documents library. Now specify a file name, such as My Second Document, and click **Save** as shown in Figure 4-10.

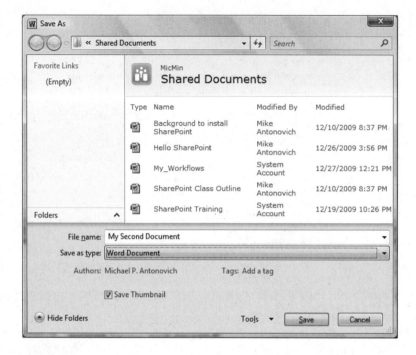

Figure 4-10. *Previously visited SharePoint libraries on a Windows XP platform*

Notice that this dialog opens the specified library, letting you save your document directly to SharePoint. If, as in this case, you have a new document, make sure that the name you want to use does not already exist in the selected library. If it does, Microsoft Word displays a dialog telling you that the file already exists. You can then replace the existing file, save your file with a different name, or merge your changes into the existing file.

If this is not the correct library, you can simply enter the URL for your site in the **File name** text box to display a list of all libraries in the site as well as a list of any sub sites. You could then navigate to the library where you want to save the document from a known site URL.

Similarly, if you have never saved anything to a document library previously and therefore have no recent locations, you can instead click on **Save** from the **File** button to again display the **Save As** dialog. As mentioned above, you can then enter the URL for your site in the **File name** text box. Again, Word shows you a list of all document libraries in the site where you can save your new document.

If you began by selecting a library or entering the URL for one, Word shows you a listing of the documents in that library. Unless you want to replace an existing document, specify a new name for the document, and click **Save** to add your document to the selected library.

What Is Metadata?

In simple terms, *metadata* is data about data. When you save a file in Windows Explorer and then view the directory, you do not see just the file name. In Windows XP and most prior versions of the Windows operating system, Windows Explorer shows the date modified, file type, and size of each file. By default, Vista's Windows Explorer also includes the date modified, type, size, and tags. These additional pieces of information represent metadata for the file; that is, they provide you with more information about the file. In addition to these fields, you can right-click the header of the directory to see additional available columns or metadata that Windows Explorer supports.

In Vista and later operating systems from Microsoft, folders that focus on different types of files might use different sets of columns. For example, if you open a folder that contains music files such as My Music, you may see column headers such as Name, Artists, Albums, #, Genre, and Rating. A photo directory might use columns like Date Taken, 35mm focal length, Camera model, Exposure time, Focal length, F-stop, and ISO speed. Some metadata receives its data values automatically such as the Modified Date, Type, and Size. However, other metadata allows you to define your own values such as Tags, Title, and Categories. In fact, there are dozens of different metadata properties available to describe the files in your directories. You can then use the metadata to group or filter your directory lists. However, most people have never used them beyond the basic default properties.

Adding Metadata to Word Documents

Metadata also exists in documents created by most Office tools such as Word, Excel, PowerPoint, and others. These programs allow you to define additional properties for your documents.

To add values to these properties in a Word 2007 document, click the **Office** button, and then point to **Prepare**. Click **Properties** in the menu that appears, and Word displays the default properties it supports in a panel across the top of the document window. Click **Advanced Properties** in the **Document Properties** drop-down menu to display the **Document Properties** dialog box from Office. Here you can create custom properties for the current document and assign them values.

What if you don't see document management options in your office ribbon? In Microsoft Word 2010, you may not see any reference to document management in any of the ribbons initially. However, you can customize the ribbon to add this feature. Begin by right-clicking on a blank area of the ribbon and select `Customize the ribbon`. In the dialog shown in Figure 4-11, select **Customize Ribbon** in the left panel if necessary. Then on the right side of the panel you see two lists named `Choose commands from` and `Customize the ribbon`.

Figure 4-11. Customizing the Ribbon

From the **Customize the Ribbon** drop-down, select the option **Main Tabs**. As shown in Figure 4-11, this shows in the list below the drop-down all the available ribbon tabs. You can create a New Tab by clicking the button **New Tab** or you can open an existing ribbon tab by clicking the square box with the plus sign before the ribbon name.

When you open a ribbon tab, the first level of options show a list of the command groups or ribbon sections. With any ribbon open, you can add a new command group or open the command group to view the commands within it. You can even add new commands to a group.

In this case, the commands needed to open the Document Properties Panel already exist. They just have not been added to a ribbon yet. You can add the document property commands to the **Home** ribbon by following these steps:

1. Expand the **Home** ribbon by clicking on the plus sign in the square box before it and click on the ribbon name, **Home**, to select it.

2. Click the **New Group** button, which creates a new group named `New Group` (Custom).

3. With the New Group Selected, click the **Rename** button and change the name to `Document Management`.

4. From the Choose commands from column, choose `All Commands`.

5. Select and drag the following commands from the list on the left to the new group **Document Management** on the right:

   - Document Management Server

   - Document Panel

   - Document Property

6. Click OK to finish customizing the ribbon.

Now when you open a document in Word 2010 and open the **Home** ribbon, you see the new **Document Management** group with its commands on the right side of the ribbon, as shown in Figure 4-12.

Figure 4-12. Updated ribbon with Document Management group

With a document open, you can click on the command **Document Panel** from the **Document Management** group. A dialog box, shown in Figure 4-13, asks whether you have a custom document Information Panel. While I will skip this option, you may want to select the check box on the bottom of the dialog that tells Word to **Always show Document Information Panel on document open and initial save**. Note that, if you do not select this option, you can always select the Document Panel from the ribbon.

Figure 4-13. Options when adding the Document Information Panel

In a few moments, the **Document Properties** panel will appear across the top of the document just below the ribbon, as shown in Figure 4-14. By default, the document properties include the following:

- Author
- Title
- Subject
- Keywords
- Category
- Status
- Comments

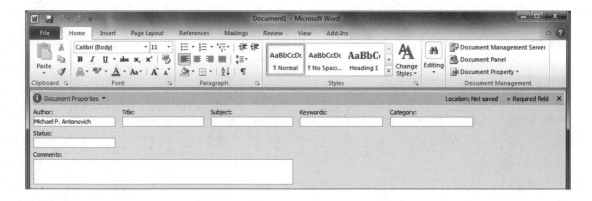

Figure 4-14. Document Properties panel within Word 2010

You can display most of these document properties as columns when you display a local directory of Word 2010 documents in Windows Explorer.

However, you are interested in how documents interact with SharePoint, not Windows Explorer. The interesting point is that you can surface a Word document's metadata within a SharePoint document library as columns in that library. Word passes the metadata values to SharePoint when you save a document or upload a new document to a properly defined document library.

■ **Caution** If you add the columns as described below to your document library after you upload your Word documents, SharePoint cannot populate values into the columns unless you re-upload the document or edit the document and reassign values to the metadata columns.

Open a new Shared Documents library on your team site and go to **Site Settings**. In the **Columns** section, you may think that you can simply create columns with the same names as the Word metadata fields. However, that does not work. Rather, you need to open the option **Add from existing site columns**, as shown in Figure 4-15.

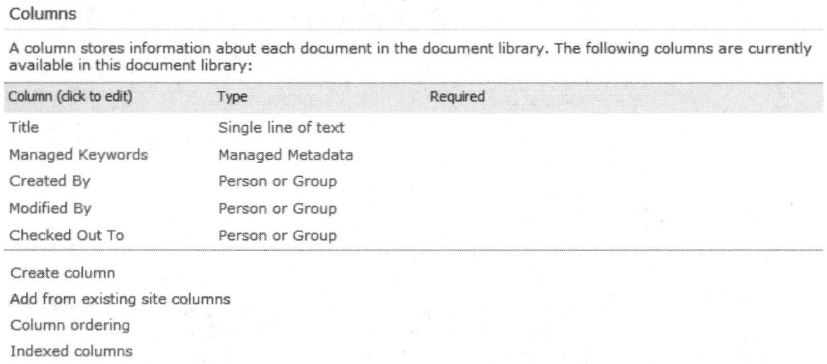

Columns

A column stores information about each document in the document library. The following columns are currently available in this document library:

Column (click to edit)	Type	Required
Title	Single line of text	
Managed Keywords	Managed Metadata	
Created By	Person or Group	
Modified By	Person or Group	
Checked Out To	Person or Group	

Create column
Add from existing site columns
Column ordering
Indexed columns

Figure 4-15. To add Word 2010 metadata to your library, use **Add from existing site columns***.*

Select **Code Document Columns** (or **All Groups** for the complete list of fields) from the **Select Site Columns from** drop-down. Then, from the **Available Site Columns** list, double-click or click the column name followed by clicking **Add** to transfer the columns to the **Columns to add** list box. You can add all the columns you need. Make sure you have selected the check box to add the columns to the default view before you click **OK**, as shown in Figure 4-16.

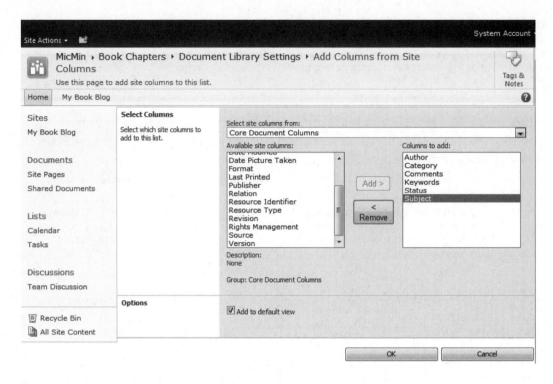

Figure 4-16. Selecting columns to match Word 2010 metadata

When you return to the view of your library list, you see the new columns. If you had previously uploaded documents to the library, these additional columns remain blank even if these documents had metadata values defined when originally created in Word. However, the next time you edit these documents and resave them to the SharePoint library, Word transfers the values to these site columns. Figure 4-17 shows an image of a SharePoint library in the background with a single document to illustrate the metadata saved in SharePoint; in the foreground of the image is the original Word document with the Document Properties panel displayed.

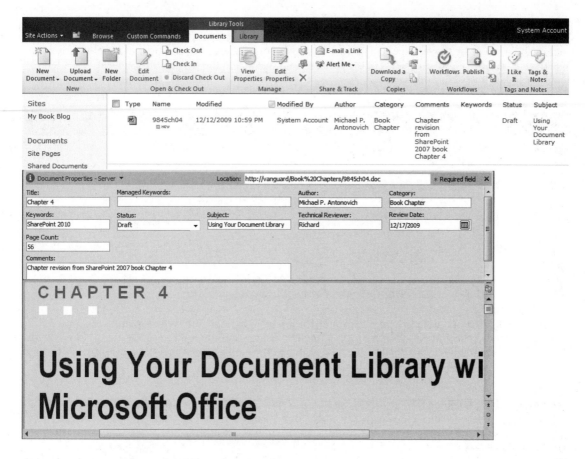

Figure 4-17. SharePoint document library shows Word 2010 metadata.

From within SharePoint, you can now use this metadata to sort or filter the items in your library. After SharePoint runs its next indexing job, you can also search for this document by values in the metadata, as long as you have selected the option to allow items from the library to appear in search results. You can find this option in the **Search** section of the **Advanced Settings** of the **Library Settings** command.

Adding Metadata to Documents from SharePoint

While SharePoint retains Word's metadata when you upload documents to a library, you can also add more metadata to the document from within SharePoint itself by adding columns to the document library. Every column in a document library then becomes metadata for each document in the library.

In the current example, suppose you add a Technical Reviewer, Review Date, and Page Count column to your SharePoint library. In addition, let's make the Page Count column a required column that must have a value greater than 0. Figure 4-18 shows your library after adding these three columns. The truncated view shows only a few of the columns. I have moved the new columns closer to the left to facilitate the format of this book.

Figure 4-18. *Adding three new columns to the SharePoint document library*

If you edit this document in Word 2007 or 2010, you get a banner across the top of the document (shown in Figure 4-19)that tells you to supply some missing or invalid required properties before you can save the document back to the server. Of course, that missing property is the Page Count, which has no initial default value but is required.

Figure 4-19. *A warning that one or more properties are invalid or missing*

When you click on the **Edit Properties** button, Word opens the **Document Properties** panel. Figure 4-20 shows that the **Page Count** column has a red asterisk on the right side. This indicates that the property is required. Notice that all of the other properties including the other two new properties for Technical Reviewer and Review Date also appear in the panel. You can update all these properties and resave the document.

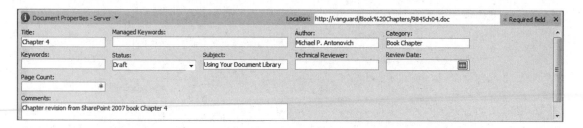

Figure 4-20. Displaying the new columns in Word's Document Properties panel

You may have also noticed that the title of this panel has changed from **Document Properties** to **Document Properties – Server**. In fact, there are two property views for the document at this point. The original Document Properties defined through Word can be seen by opening the drop-down list in the title bar (click the down-pointing arrow) and selecting **Document Properties**. The **Document Properties – Server** view shows all the properties from the SharePoint Document Library. Notice that SharePoint and Word share some properties while others are unique to SharePoint.

Only properties added to the SharePoint Document Library through the existing site columns represent columns that SharePoint can share with similarly named metadata in Microsoft Office products such as Word. SharePoint does not directly share back to Word any new columns created manually, but you can access the column through the Document Properties – Server panel.

Even though SharePoint does not share the three new columns with Word's metadata, Word respects the validation and data requirements constraints defined in SharePoint before saving a version of the document back to the library. For example, suppose you enter a Technical Review's name and Review Date, but make a mistake by entering a past year rather than the current year. Again, a popup banner appears immediately below the document properties panel to tell you that the upload failed. Unfortunately, this message does not tell us the specific field that has an invalid entry. Figure 4-21 shows the error message that appears when attempting to save this version of the document back to SharePoint. From Word, you would have to know the validation rules for the server side metadata to correct the problem and save the data.

■ **Caution** These error messages may not appear if you have created custom error pages for your office applications.

The **Advanced Properties** option in this drop-down opens the standard properties dialog box used by Word. Using this dialog box, you can access other metadata that Word supports or add new metadata fields within the current document.

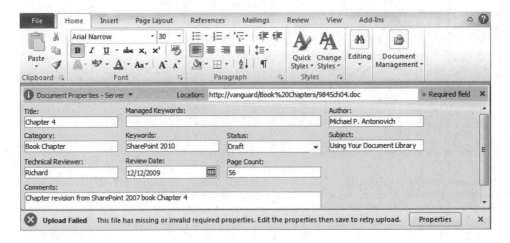

Figure 4-21. Warning of missing or invalid properties when attempting to upload a document

Now that you know that metadata can be included in everything you do in Microsoft Office, what can you do with it? Metadata can help search, filter, or sort the data it refers to, such as the items in your library. Previously, I mentioned that you could use Word's metadata in your Windows directories to sort the files in the directory. The same concept applies to the documents in a SharePoint library or the items in a list. Metadata can even help you associate documents in one library or information in a list to those in another. Finally, it can also help automate workflows by supplying values to variables used by the workflow.

Metadata can enhance your SharePoint experience, just as indexes can enhance your database experience. However, too much metadata can become a burden for users to enter, just as too many indexes can negatively affect database performance. You do not want metadata to become such a burden that users stop entering it. To illustrate the value of metadata, the next section explores the use of metadata within a custom library used to track Purchase Orders.

Using Metadata with the Document Information Panel

Your company probably uses purchase orders to buy the items it uses. On a functional level, you could use a custom shared document library to store the purchase orders after you create them. At a slightly more sophisticated level, you might take a blank purchase order form built with Word and save it as a Word template. Then you could upload that Word template into your SharePoint site and modify your purchase order library to use that template as its default document type when creating a new document. I discussed how to change your default document template in Chapter 1.

However, you can leverage SharePoint further. Suppose you create a new custom library named **Purchase Orders**. After creating the library, go into the document library settings page and rename the **Title** column to **Purchase Order Number**. While there, you can select other columns that SharePoint automatically tracks to display in your list, or you could add your own custom columns.

■ **Note Purchase Order Number** makes an ideal replacement for the **Title** column because it uniquely defines each purchase order. You should never have two purchase orders with the same number.

Because this library only holds purchase orders, you might consider adding a few special columns to track information to help sort, filter, or group your purchase orders. To illustrate this point, add the following three columns to this custom library:

- Date Created: The date someone entered the purchase order. (I am assuming that the purchase order date may be different from the item creation date.)

- Department: The department requesting the purchase order

- Purchase Amount: The total amount of the purchase order. (I will create this field as a currency field, but you may have reasons to leave it as a string or just a number.)

When defining the **Department** column, consider making it a Lookup type column using a custom list named Departments so that you can add new departments on the fly without modifying the Purchase Orders library settings. Of course, you could add more than these three columns, but these three are good enough for now.

Each of these new columns represents metadata for the purchase order. That means that they define additional information about the document. It also means that each time you create a new document in this library, you may need to define values for these columns when you save the new document. In fact, when you open a new document, Word 2010 displays these document properties in a banner-like panel across the top of the document, as shown in Figure 4-22.

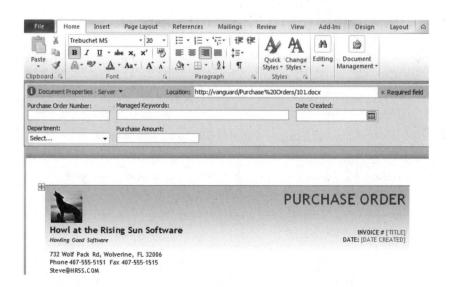

Figure 4-22. Word 2010 displays the server metadata fields in a panel at the top of the page.

Notice that the fields across the banner prompt for values for each of the custom purchase order columns. You can fill in these fields at any time from when you first open the purchase order to when you complete it. Figure 4-23 shows the purchase order library after you add the first purchase order showing the custom columns.

■ **Tip** If you plan to use metadata to sort, group, or filter your purchase orders later, return to your column definition and make each of these columns required. If you have already saved purchase orders without these columns, SharePoint does not raise an error unless you edit and resave those purchase orders after making the custom columns required.

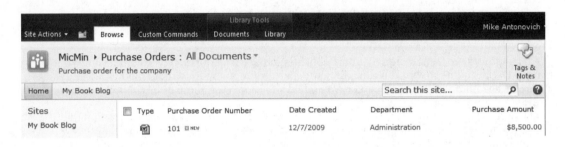

Figure 4-23. SharePoint's list displays the metadata fields added in Word's Document Properties.

Uploading Existing Documents into a Library Prompts for Required Metadata

Rather than creating a new document directly from the library, let's assume that you need to upload an existing purchase order into the library; you can accomplish this task by first opening the document in Word and then using the **Save As** dialog to point to the library as described earlier. However, if the document does not yet have values for the any required SharePoint metadata columns, SharePoint will upload but not check in the document.

To supply these values, click the command **Document Panel** in the **Document Management** group. Word displays the panel across the top of the document. You can now enter any metadata that has not already been supplied for the current document before saving it to SharePoint.

Always remember to save your document after any changes, even if you only make changes to the metadata.

Working with Document Metadata

By adding metadata to a document library, you can more easily sort, filter, and even perform simple aggregate functions across the documents it contains. The following steps are for a scenario in which you view only the purchase orders from a single department (Administration), count the number of purchase orders, and calculate a grand total amount.

1. Open the Library ribbon of the Purchase Orders library.

2. Select the **Create View** command from the **Manage Views** group.

3. From the first **Create View** page, select the **Standard View** format.

4. In the second **Create View** page, name the view Administration Purchase Orders. Do not make this the default view.

5. Create this view as a public view. You can also create a personal view that only you can see. However, for the purpose of this example, I will assume that the permissions to this library have already limited the potential audience to an appropriate subset of all users.

6. Next, select the columns you want to display. For this example, include at least the following:

   - Type Icon

   - Purchase Order Number

   - Date Created

   - Department

   - Purchase Amount

7. Define the primary sort to be **Date Created** in ascending order.

8. Define a secondary sort by ascending **Purchase Order Number** in case you have more than one purchase order a day per department.

9. Filter on column **Department** equal to Administration.

■ **Caution** Notice that, when defining a filter, you must enter the value of the filter directly, not select it from a list of possible values. Therefore, keep in mind that spelling counts. However, the value's case does not affect the result.

---

10. Expand the **Totals** section. Notice this action displays each column in the library with a drop-down of possible values.

11. Select **Count** for the **Purchase Order Number** column.

12. Select **Sum** for the **Purchase Amount** column.

13. Click **OK** to create the new view.

SharePoint returns you to the library view, as shown in Figure 4-24. Notice that the list now contains only the purchase orders for the Administration department, the **Purchase Order Number** column contains the text **Count=3**, and the **Purchase Total** column contains the text **Sum = $9,510.00**.

Figure 4-24. Using Totals to count the number of purchase orders and the value for the Administration department

This example shows how you can use metadata in a view of the document library to sort the documents, filter on a department, and then count the number of purchase orders while totaling the amounts. Notice also that, with RSS feeds turned on, you can subscribe to this library and receive notifications when someone makes additions to it through your favorite news aggregator, IE 8.0, Outlook 2010, or better. Similarly, you can also subscribe to alerts for changes. This is something that a simple Windows Explorer view of a directory of purchase order documents cannot do!

Managing Multiple Editors to a Document

Concurrency problems as described in Chapter 1 were an inevitable consequence of the way Word 2007 handled multiple editors of a document. Basically, it was an all or nothing choice. Either you locked the entire file by checking it out of SharePoint so that no one else could open it in edit mode, or you allowed multiple people to edit the document. If you choose the latter, then you had to cope with having to compare two or more versions of the document, identify the differences between them, and accept which changes you wanted to keep. Because that was such a time-consuming processing, most SharePoint administrators decided to make it easier on everyone by requiring document check out before you could edit the document.

Now Word 2010 comes out with a potentially game-changing feature, at least in the word processing arena, that allows multiple simultaneous editors to edit a document when they are using documents stored in SharePoint. Rather than locking the entire file to protect the integrity of changes made to the document, Word 2010 now supports locking individual paragraphs of a document. However, while SharePoint and Word lock those individual paragraphs, other editors can make changes to other parts of the document. Of course, as soon as you begin editing a different paragraph, Word and SharePoint lock that paragraph to any other users.

While editing a document that someone else also has open, SharePoint passes information between all users to identify which paragraphs others have edited. It places a bracket around the left side of the paragraph and adds a tag off to the left margin to identify the person performing the edit. However, it does not show the edit changes made by others in real time. These edited paragraphs remain locked until their individual editor saves their changes back to SharePoint.

You can periodically check to see if any updates to the current document have become available (in other words, saved by other users). You can then display the updated text and make changes to it.

Let's see how this works in a simple example. Suppose two people have a document open for editing at the same time. Remember that this ability to allow multiple editors to a document only works if you open the document from a library that does not require check out before editing. Now, also suppose that the System Account user has the same document open as I do and she has made a change to the first paragraph with the title Introduction. What you will see on your screen will be a light-blue solid bracket around the left side of the paragraph where the System Account made a change. It also has a flyout tag displaying the user's name, System Account, as the editor of that paragraph as shown in Figure 4-25.

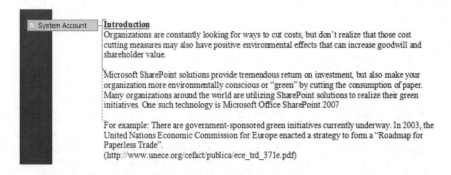

Figure 4-25. Tag indicates document paragraph has been edited by another user

You might also notice that the second paragraph has a dotted bracket around it indicating that I have made a change to that paragraph. There is no need for a tag to identify the user in this case because all paragraphs bracketed with a dotted bracket represent changes made by me.

Note also that, as soon as I initiate editing of the second paragraph, Microsoft Word places a lock on the paragraph that passes from my copy of Word 2010 through SharePoint to the System Account's copy of Word 2010 where it remains locked until I save my changes back to SharePoint and thus release the lock. If any other user tries to click inside that paragraph to make changes, Word 2010 blocks any keystrokes and displays the message `This modification is not allowed because the selection is locked`.

If the System Account really needs to edit my locked paragraph (the second paragraph), she could wait until either I save my changes or she could click on the tag identifying me as the editor of the paragraph to display a popup dialog shown in Figure 4-26. This popup displays the name, picture (if available), and presence indicator at the top of the dialog. The four icons in a row allow you to send an e-mail, an instant text message or a voice message through an instant message application such as Live Messenger, or display other options including scheduling a meeting with that person. The drop-down button on the right side of this row expands the dialog to show additional information about the editor such as his department, telephone numbers, e-mail address, and location. These options can be useful if the paragraph you need to edit remains locked for an extended period, thereby preventing you from completing your tasks.

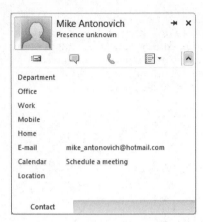

Figure 4-26. Popup identifying paragraph editor

You can also see a complete list of all users currently editing the document by clicking in the third panel from the left of the status bar at the bottom of the window. This panel displays a count of the number of simultaneous editors in the document. When clicked, it displays their names as shown in Figure 4-27. As with the tags for individually locked paragraphs, you can click on the name of any of these editors to display the same dialog box just described in Figure 4-26 to contact them.

Figure 4-27. Status bar identifies all current editors of the document.

You can also see a complete list of people currently editing the document by opening the **File** menu and selecting **Info**. In the center section of this screen, shown in Figure 4-28, is a list of all the current editors. You can click on any of the names to select them and then click the large **Send a Message** button to open an e-mail message to that person.

Figure 4-28. The Info page also identifies current users editing the document.

Also in the **Info** section of the **File** menu, Word notifies you that new updates to the document have become available, as shown in Figure 4-29. This notification occurs when any of the other editors saves their changes back to SharePoint. Only after they save their changes can you refresh your copy of the document to see those changes and make additional changes to the paragraphs previously locked.

■ **Note** You do not need to return to the **Info** page to see that updates have become available. A refresh icon (two arrows circling on each other) appears on the right side of the individual modification name tags when that editor saves their changes.

Figure 4-29. The Info page also identifies when new document updates become available.

Notice in this figure that you have to save your copy of the document in order to update it with changes from other authors. However, you do not have to check in your copy of the document. When you save your document copy, the dialog shown in Figure 4-30 appears. It tells you that you can compare the document with a previous version of the document by clicking in the **File** tab. Even if you do not do that, any insertions are immediately obvious, as Word will highlight them in green, as you can see in the icon in Figure 4-30.

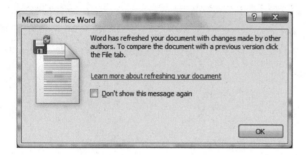

Figure 4-30. Word notifies you when document changes have been applied to your copy of the document.

To compare the current document with a prior version, open the **File** menu and select **Info**. Scroll to the bottom of the **Info** page to the section titled `Versions and Check Out`. The available document versions appear here as long as you have enabled versioning for the current library. Click on the version to which you want to compare the current document. A second Word window opens and displays the banner shown in Figure 4-31.

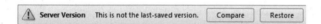

Figure 4-31. Word notifies you when document changes have been applied to your copy of the document.

Click the **Compare** button to continue with the comparison of the two versions. This opens a third window with both versions of the document in the right column and the combined version in the center column as shown in Figure 4-32.

The point of view of the comparison is what changes you must make to the current version of the document to make it look like the compared document, the one you selected from the **Info** page creating a new revised document. Therefore, items deleted by you or another editor appear as Inserted text because you would need to add that text back into the document to make it look like the older version of the document. Similarly, you would need to delete text that you added to the most recent version to match the older version. Therefore, if you want to keep your recent changes, you want to reject the suggested changes that would revert your modifications. Similarly, you could accept the changes to undo something you did that you do not want to keep. For example, if you deleted something by accident, you can simply accept the inserted text to recover the lost text. I know that sounds a little like reverse logic at first, but remember Word's viewpoint is trying to make your current document look like the comparison document, not vice versa.

To finish this example, examine each change along the left side of the window. All of the changes appear as inserts or deletes. In fact, modifications appear as a pair of changes, one insert and one delete. You can choose each individual change by clicking on it and then decide whether to accept or reject each one individually by clicking the **Accept** or **Reject** buttons in the **Review** ribbon. When you have finished reviewing all the differences and are ready to save your updated version, open the **File** menu and select **Save**. Word then displays the **Save As** dialog prefilled with the document's name and pointing to the library where the file came from. Simply click the **Save** button and Word 2010 saves your updated revised version.

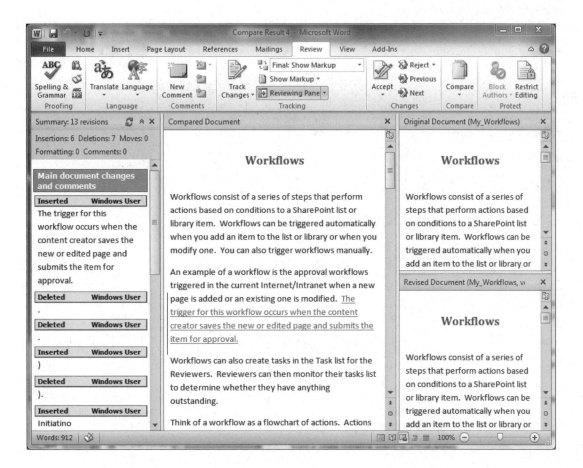

Figure 4-32. Word lets you compare document changes and choose which to accept or reject.

So why would you choose to not require check out of documents before editing them? If you have a large document for which several people have edit responsibilities, you may want to allow multiple people to edit the document simultaneously because they seldom if ever need to edit the same portion of the document anyway. This allows the work from multiple people to occur simultaneously, thereby improving efficiency. On the other hand, small documents or documents in which multiple people typically will edit the same portions would be better managed in a library that requires check out before editing to protect the edits of each individual.

Creating and Using Document Sets

Before you can use a document set in any site, you must first activate the Document Set feature. You can find this by opening **Central Administration** and clicking on **Site collection features** in the **Site Collection Administration** section.

Next, return to the site where you want to use the Document Set to create a Document Set content type. Go to **Site Actions ➤ Site Settings** and select **Site Content Types** under the **Galleries** group. Click **Create** and supply a unique name for your document set and include an optional description. Select **Document Set Content Types** from the first drop-down in the **Parent Content Types** section and then select **Document Set** from the second drop-down. In the group section, I prefer to create a separate group for the content types based on either the scope of the documents it contains or on the department or group that uses the document set. For example, a content type used for an individual project receives a name related to that project while a content type used across the entire department receives a name based on that department. Figure 4-33 shows these steps.

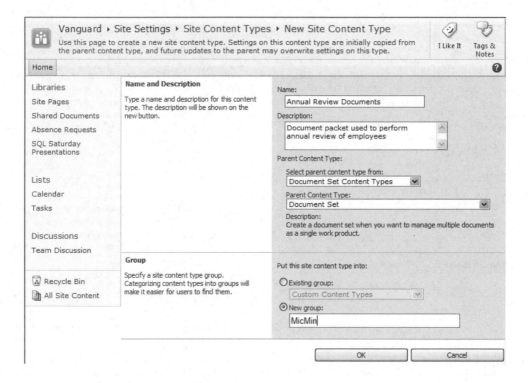

Figure 4-33. *Create a Document Set content type*

While you could use this content type as-is in a library, it would initially be empty. You could then add documents to the document set as needed. However, a more interesting use of the document set occurs when you want to create a common set of documents in each instance of the document library. Imagine that the document set created in the previous figure, Annual Review Documents, always begins with a common set of documents that the supervisor must fill in for each employee evaluation. If you add those documents to the content type, then SharePoint can create new instances of those documents in the document set each time you instantiate a new document set for a different employee.

To add documents to the document set, find your newly created content type in the list of content types in the **Site Content Types** page. Then click on the content type name. This displays a settings page for the content type as shown in Figure 4-34.

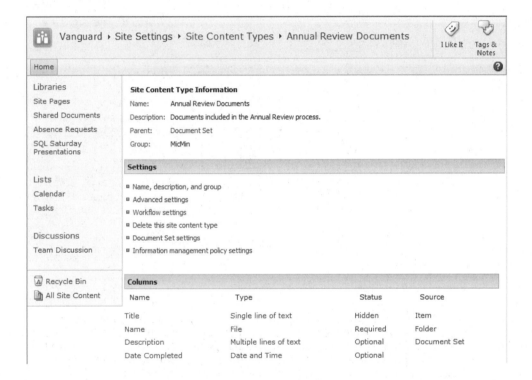

Figure 4-34. *Define settings for Document Set*

Click the **Document Set Settings** option in the **Settings** group. Figure 4-35 shows the document set settings. The first area lets you define the **Allowed Content Types** for this content type. In this case, suppose you allow **Documents** and **Images**. Of course, you could use the pick list on the left to include any of the currently defined content types for your document set. The next section lets you define the default content for the document set. These are the default documents that SharePoint creates in your document set when you instantiate it in a library. In this case, you have the four Microsoft Word documents that form the basis of the annual review. You can add any number of default documents to your document set. Of course, you can always add more documents. However, if you have a situation like this one where every instance of the document set must begin with a minimum number of documents, a document set may be just right for you.

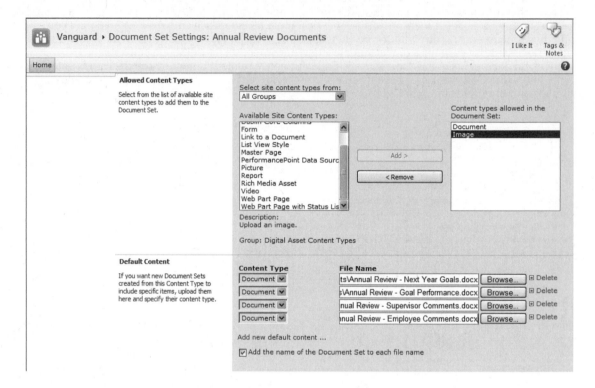

Figure 4-35. Define Allowed Content Types and Default Content

Next, navigate to the library where you will use the content type (or create a new library) and open the library settings. First, you need to enable the management of content types for this library under the **Advanced Settings** page. Then, on the **Document Library Settings** page you see a new section called **Content Types**. At the bottom of this section, click the option **Add from existing site content types**. A new screen displays the defined site content types. Initially, the list box displays all content types. However, if you added your content type to one of the existing groups or your own group, you can select the group from the first drop-down to narrow the choices in the **Available Site Content Types** list box. Either way you choose to find it, you should see the document set content type you created earlier in this section. Select it and click the **Add** button or simply double-click the content type name to move it to the **Select Content Types** list box on the right, as shown in Figure 4-36.

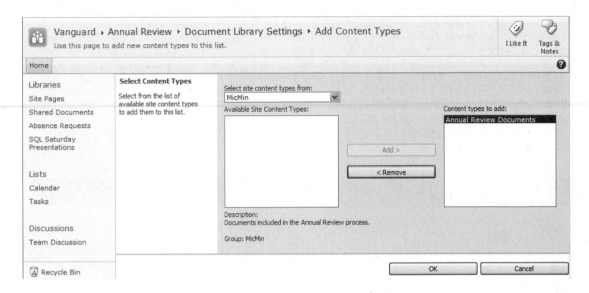

Figure 4-36. Add the document set content type to your library.

After you click **OK**, SharePoint returns you to the **Document Library Settings** page where you will see your content type listed in the **Content Types** section. Notice that SharePoint automatically includes any new content types on the **New** button. However, the original content type remains the default content type. If you would like to make your new content type (the document set) your default content type, click the option **Change New Button Order and Default Content Type** found at the bottom of this section. Figure 4-37 shows the new page where you can decide which content types you want to be visible by clicking the check box in the **Visible** column. You can also use the drop-down number list to define the position from the top for each content type. SharePoint uses the content type identified as "1" as the default content type for the current library.

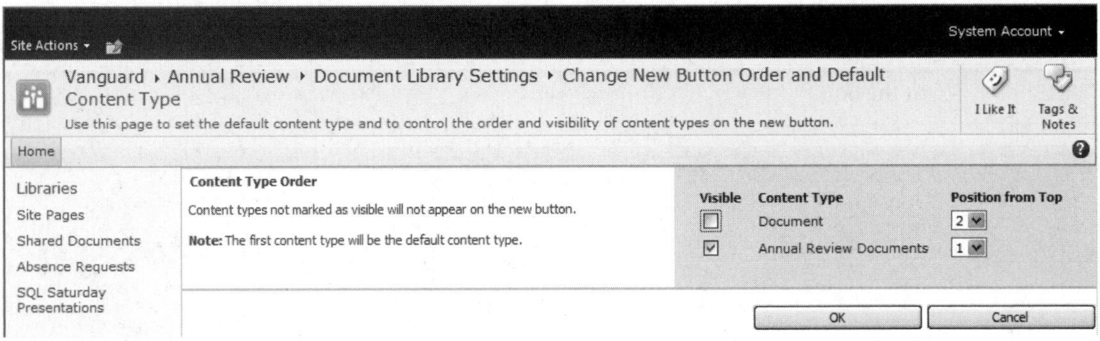

Figure 4-37. Change the option in the New drop-down.

In this figure, you can see that I have made the Annual Review Documents not only the default content type, but the only content type display by the **New Document** drop-down menu. If you open the document library (by clicking on the library name in the breadcrumbs at the top of this page), you will see that the new content type appears in the **New Document** drop-down (clicking the lower half of the **New Document** button in the **Documents** ribbon). When you select this option to create a document set, you must supply a specific name for the document set. This creates the document set allowing you to create multiple groups of this document set in the library, each with their own unique name. In this example, you could create a document set of all the documents needed to perform an annual review for each employee by naming each document set with the employee's last name, as in Figure 4-38.

Figure 4-38. Create a separate document set for each employee.

Once you have created the document set, you can open any of the sets and work with the documents individually just as if they were in a more traditional file folder. However, the productivity enhancements come about due to the ability to treat the entire multi-document set as a single object when you want to move or delete the set, start a workflow for the set, or archive the entire set to a records center. You can even manage the permissions of the document set independent of the library that contains the document set. To work with a document set, click on the document set to open its **Welcome page** as shown in Figure 4-39. From this screen, you can modify its properties or work with any of the documents defined to be part of the document type.

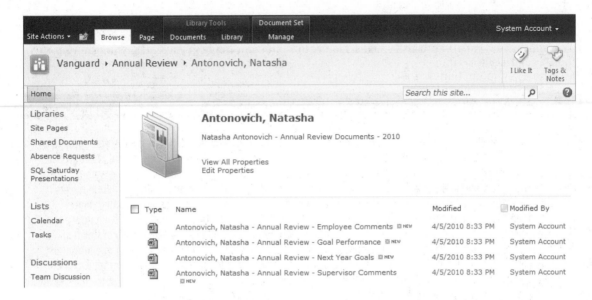

Figure 4-39. Default welcome page for the Annual Review Documents document set

This introduction to the document set will get you started. You can also add more columns to your document set, and you can customize the appearance of the Welcome page for the document set.

Searching For Your Documents

When you only have a few documents in your SharePoint site, finding the one you want is no big challenge. However, what happens after your site grows to hundreds of files in dozens of libraries, nested folders, and multiple sites? Trying to remember where you stored a document may make looking for a needle in a haystack seem easy. However, even finding a needle in a haystack can be easy with the right tool, such as a strong magnet. Similarly, you need a strong tool to find that one document out of hundreds in the libraries on your site. Fortunately, SharePoint provides that tool in the form of the Search feature.

■ **Note** Before using Search, ask your SharePoint administrator if they have configured your installation to be periodically indexed. Also find out how often the index services run. If you make an addition to your site, Search will not pick up the new document until the next time SharePoint performs a re-index of the site. Also, you can determine on a library basis whether items in the library can appear in the search results by setting the **Search** property in the **Advance Settings** section of the **Library Settings**.

The Search feature typically appears in the upper-right corner of every page in SharePoint. Of course, if someone branded your pages, they may have moved or even deleted this feature. Hopefully, they did not remove it, because the Search feature in SharePoint can help you find anything in your site quickly and easily.

What is Branding?

While you can quickly change the appearance of your SharePoint site by changing the theme you apply to it, SharePoint provides only a limited number of themes. Fortunately, it is possible with a little effort to create your own themes. If your organization has provided a limited set of themes to preserve some consistent look and feel across all sites, they may not permit you to add your own themes or customized pages made with the existing themes. You can also directly modify the appearance of individual pages using tools like SharePoint Designer among others. However, you would have to customize each new page that you add to the site manually, which would not be very efficient. While beyond the scope of this book, a better approach is to create new master pages for your site (not a simple edit of the existing master pages, but new master page files). You could also create your own CSS files to customize the appearance of the master pages, but these methods also lie beyond the scope of this book.

Creating a new set of master pages or CSS files to customize the appearance of your master pages allows you to put the changes into place one time for all pages within the site. Then all new pages created within the site automatically inherit the newly defined look and feel.

If you go to the home page of your top-level site or the default page of any sub-site, the Search feature (shown in Figure 4-40) searches the entire site and any sub-site. This is the search scope or the definition of the content that SharePoint searches. Place the words or phrases you want to search for in the text box to the right of the search scope box. Then press the button with the magnifying glass icon to start the search.

Figure 4-40. SharePoint's Search feature

The text box search string cannot exceed 255 characters. While you do have to consider simple variations of words such as whether to enter `class` or `classes`, you do not need to worry about case, as SharePoint performs all searches as case-insensitive. SharePoint ignores common words such as "`the`" or "`it`." SharePoint also ignores the order of words, making a search on `United States` the same as `states united`. So don't waste time and characters entering `flags of the United States` when you can just as easily enter `United States flags`. Note that this is true if you don't surround your search string with quotes. If you do use quotes, the search string must match not only the words but also their order.

Search now understands Boolean connectors like AND or OR between words or phrases; it will treat these words as logical connections between parts of the search but only if they are capitalized. By default, SharePoint searches for objects (documents, list items, etc.) that have all the words entered whether you put AND connections between the words or not. If you put OR between the two words, SharePoint returns all objects that have one word or the other or both.

You can also put a plus sign in front of a word to qualify the search. For example, `Software +Microsoft` returns only documents that reference software and Microsoft just like the AND connector or a simple space. Likewise, you can place a hyphen (minus sign) in front of a word to eliminate documents that contain that word. For example, `Software -Microsoft` would include documents that contained the word software but not the word Microsoft.

■ **Note** You must have at least one include expression before you can add an exclude expression such as the minus sign.

In addition, SharePoint allows you to use the wildcard asterisk (*), but only to complete a partial word. For example, a search on Sha* returns any object that contains a word that starts with the characters Sha* such as SharePoint or shampoo. Obviously, the more characters you supply, the better results your search returns. That is not all that Search can do. Table 4-1 shows a list of custom searches you can now perform with SharePoint Search, including Boolean expressions and searches against object properties such as author, modified, filename, filetype or title. Of course, these expressions were designed for a specific document library. Your queries will differ in the specific search criteria, not the style.

Table 4-1. List of Custom Searches

Expression	Description
Modified<6/1/10	Returns all objects which were last modified before June 1, 2010
Modified<=6/1/10	Returns all objects which were last modified on or before June 1, 2010
Modified>1/31/10	Returns all objects which were modified after January 31, 2010
Modified>=1/31/10	Returns all objects which were modified on or after January 31, 2010
Modified: 11/1/09..12/31/09	Returns all objects modified between November 1 and December 31 of 2009
Status:Draft	Returns all objects in which the status is Draft
"Modified by": "Mike Antonovich"	Returns all objects last modified by anyone with the name Mike Antonovich
Filename:Welcome	Returns all documents with a filename having the word Welcome in it
Filetype:docx	Returns only documents created with the .docx format (from Word 2007 or 2010)
Author:Antonovich	Returns all documents having the word Antonovich in one or more of the author's names

Finally, if you combine two or more different properties in your search, SharePoint assumes an AND connector between the properties. For example title:SharePoint filetype:docx returns Word documents saved in the .docx format and having the word SharePoint in the title. If you have two of the same properties, SharePoint assumes an OR between them. For example filetype:docx filetype:xlsx returns any Word file formatted with the .docx format or any Excel file formatted with the .xlsx format. Obviously, an AND connecting two different file types would make no sense as a single document cannot be more than one file type. You can also combine word searches with property searches as in the case of searching for a Word document with the string "2010 Budget" somewhere in the document: "2010 Budget" filetype:docx. Figure 4-41 shows an example of a combination search on an author name for Word documents.

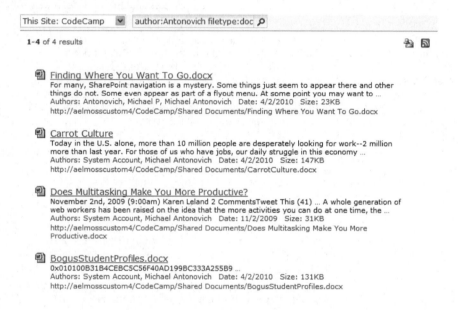

Figure 4-41. Results of a combination search for an author's name

Using Word to Contribute to Your Blog Site

Blog sites have become increasingly popular in the last few years. Many companies support blogs to provide news about their company or their company's products. They may even encourage specific individuals with a flair for writing to post blogs favorable to the company or its products. Many individuals use blogs as personal diaries. Developers and consultants use blogs to document their work and to provide a place to post downloadable information about their current projects. Speakers and authors often use blogs to post additional information for their attendees or readers such as sample code or their slide presentation.

Before you begin contributing to a blog, you must have a hosted blog site. Thousands of blog sites already exist on the Internet. Most allow visitors to the site to contribute to them after registering on their site. However, you may want to have your own blog site not associated with another company or organization. If you have a SharePoint site, and if you have permission to create sites on it, you can follow the steps in the next section to create your own blog site. If you do not have permission to create sites, talk with your SharePoint administrator to see if he can set up a blog site for your use. Of course, if your administrator built the SharePoint installation as an intranet site only, your blog will only be visible to users within your company. If that satisfies your need for fame, go for it! Otherwise, you might consider a public site such as Microsoft's Live Spaces to host your blog.

Creating a Blog Site

You can create a blog site as a sub site to any site. Some people may create a personal blog site in their My Site area. However, you may want a department or project blog. The following instructions step you through creating a blog site beneath any site:

1. Navigate to the site where you want to create your blog.

2. Select **New Site** from the **Site Actions** menu.

3. Select **Blog** from the available site types under the category **Content**.

4. Before filling anything else, click **More Options**.

5. Enter a name for your blog site along with a description.

6. Enter a web site address for the blog. Notice that SharePoint provides the first part of the address, defining the root address for the site. However, you must supply the final portion to identify the blog site.

■ **Tip** In addition to trying to keep your blog address short and easy to remember, I recommend that you use the blog title just entered, removing any special characters or blanks.

---

7. Define permissions for your blog site. You can inherit the permissions from the parent site, or you can create unique permissions to your blog site. Remember that defining unique permissions means that you will have full responsibility for creating all permissions to your blog. If you want just a personal blog for yourself, your close friends, or the other members of your department or project, unique permissions may be exactly what you need.

8. Define the navigation into and out of your site.

In the Navigation section, you define navigation into your blog site. You can determine whether a link to the blog appears in the **Quick Launch** menu and whether to display the blog site in the top link bar of the parent site. While these two navigation options provide users with ways to get to your blog site, they are not the only methods you have at your disposal. You could also add links on your site's home page pointing to your blog. If every user in your company or every product team has their own blog site, a Links list on your site's home page may be a better way to help visitors navigate to one of dozens of blog sites in your SharePoint installation.

The navigation section also includes a method to help users navigate away from your blog site. SharePoint asks whether the blog site shares the top link bar with its parent or whether it starts the top link bar all over again with just the blog site listed. By sharing the top link bar with the parent site, the user can navigate back to the parent site. However, even if you do not share the top link bar, users can still return to the top-level site by clicking the link in the **Global Links Bar** at the top of the page.

After defining the properties for your site, click the **Create** button. SharePoint creates the site and displays its main page as shown in Figure 4-42. You see a default welcome message provided by SharePoint. If you have rights to add, edit, and delete list items, you will see a column to the right of the blog entry area with administration tools for the blog.

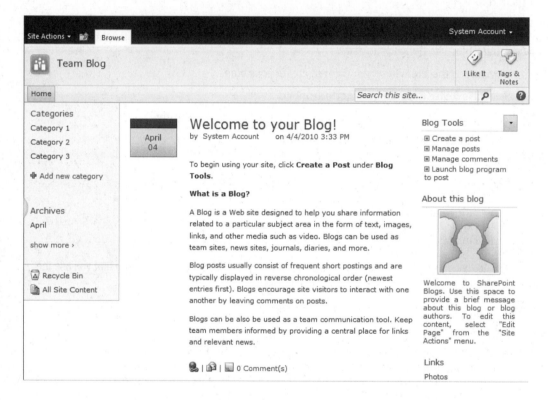

Figure 4-42. Main page of a blog

The following list itemizes the available administration options:

- **Create a Post**: Create a new blog entry

- **Manage Posts**: Edit/Delete blog entries

- **Manage Comments**: Edit/Delete comments associated with blog entries

- **Launch Blog Program to Post**: By default, this option loads Word and automatically starts defining the blog account needed for Word to publish a blog entry directly to the site.

Beneath this option is a web part called **About this blog**. This web part is actually a **Content Editor** web part and provides an image at the top followed by a welcome text message. The default image displayed is a placeholder image that is 102 pixels square and is stored at `http://vanguard/_layouts/images/`. However, you can upload an image to any image library and reference, it such as an image library created in your blog site. While you can use an image that is larger than 102 pixels, using an image that is larger than the content area you place it in could cause your page to display incorrectly. To edit the text beneath the image, click anywhere within the text and begin typing.

Beneath the **About this blog** web part, you see a **Links** web part. Use this web part to define links to other pages on your site or even in other sites. If you are building a personal blog page, these links might point to other sites of special interest.

Before you create your first blog post, you should also note that SharePoint 2010 automatically turns on RSS feeds for the posts on the blog page so your readers can subscribe to your latest entries.

Defining Categories for Your Blogs

Perhaps you noticed in the **Quick Launch** menu the three categories generically named **Category 1**, **Category 2**, and **Category 3**. Within a blog site, you may want to separate entries by category to organize them by topics or types. For example, you might use a different category to post code updates, discussions on configuration settings, or posts of instructions on how to use application features. You might even keep separate categories to post FAQs or to report bugs.

While you do not need to have all your categories predefined before people start to add posts to the blog site, you probably want to define at least a few major categories to keep all of your posts from being lumped together in one category.

■ **Tip** A person with administrator rights for the blog site can go into individual posts and reassign them to a different category. Administrators often do this when posts on a shared site with many blog contributors start to diverge from the intended purpose of the category. They may also do this to split categories into smaller groups.

To define your own initial set of categories, click **Categories** in the **Quick Launch** menu. SharePoint defines categories as a simple list of items in which the **Title** column defines the category. As with many lists, when you click a title, SharePoint opens the view that displays all columns for the selected item. Of course, the Categories list only needs one column. To change the value of any item, click **Edit Item** in the menu bar and enter your desired category text.

In a similar way, update each of the category items, adding or deleting items as necessary to build the complete list of categories you need. When finished, return to your blog site's home page by finding its reference in your breadcrumbs. Before leaving this page to create blog posts from within Word, take note of the **URL in the address bar of your browser**. Commit it to memory, copy it to the clipboard, or write it down because you will need to reference it to tell Word where to send your blog posts. You can ignore the portion of the URL at the end that says `default.aspx`.

Creating a New Blog Posting

To create your first blog post, return to Word and open the **File** menu. Click **New**. You should see **Blog post** in the **Available Templates** section. Select this template and click the **Create** button. If you never created a blog post before, you may get a dialog box asking you to register your blog account (see Figure 4-43). You can skip registration for now by clicking **Register Later**, as Word prompts you again when you attempt to post your first blog.

Figure 4-43. *Register a Blog Account dialog box*

Word then displays a blank document with a text field at the top of the page that prompts [**Enter Post Title Here**]. Click anywhere between the square brackets, and enter the title for your post. Then click beneath the horizontal line below the title and enter your blog text.

■ **Note** If you previously created accounts for your blogs, immediately below the horizontal line you will see the word **Account** followed by the name of your default blog account. If you have more than one blog account, simply click on the name of the default blog account to display a drop-down control. Click the drop-down arrow on the right side to display and select to which blog account you want to send the current document. If the blog account you have selected has categories, you can click the **Insert Category** option in the **Blog Post** ribbon. This action adds an entry below Account to let you select the category to assign your blog post to when you publish it to the currently selected account.

By creating your blog entry with Word, you can take advantage of all the formatting features Word offers. When you finish, click the **Publish** button in the **Blog** section of the **BlogPost** ribbon in Word. Figure 4-44 shows a blog post prior to publishing.

Figure 4-44. Publishing a blog entry from Word 2010

When you click **Publish** for the first time, you must register an account if you did not do so when you first selected a blog style document. Remember, you skipped registration earlier, so you must do it now. Click the **Register an Account** button in the first dialog that appears. A **New Blog Account** dialog box appears, as shown in Figure 4-45. This wizard provides a drop-down list of available blog sites to which you could publish. Maybe you already use one of these blog sites but did not know that you could publish directly to it from within Word.

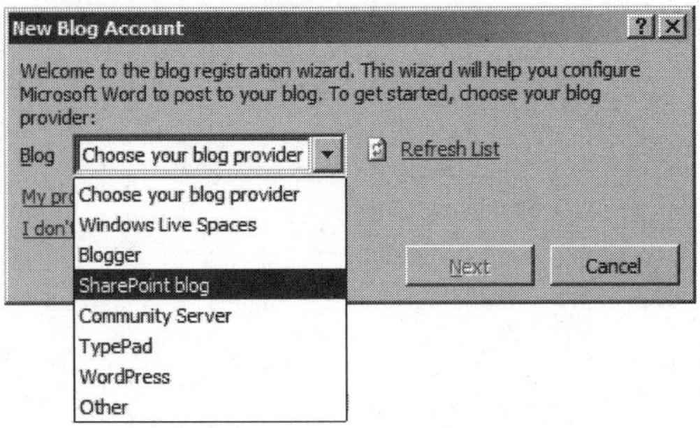

Figure 4-45. Creating a new blog account

To publish to your SharePoint blog, select **SharePoint blog** and click the **Next** button. The **New Blog Account** dialog box needs one more piece of information to post your text, the blog URL. This URL refers to the address I asked you to commit to memory or write down earlier. Enter it in the **Blog URL** text box, as shown in Figure 4-46, and click the **OK** button.

Figure 4-46. Entering your blog URL

■ **Tip** You can also get to this same point by clicking the previously mentioned Blog Tool on SharePoint's Blog page `Launch blog program to post`.

Word then alerts you that it is sending information to the blog service provider and that other people may see it. Setting up a SharePoint blog site on your company's SharePoint server exposes you to little risk, especially if your servers and you sit behind the company's firewall. So click **YES** to continue. When Word successfully registers with SharePoint, a dialog box displays, confirming its success and also informing you that you can go to the **Blog Post** ribbon within Word and click **Manage Accounts** to remove, modify, or add other accounts.

When Word returns to the document page, a banner across the top of the page tells you that it published the post to the blog site at the specified URL. Switching back to your browser, you can navigate to your blog site to see the post as shown in Figure 4-47.

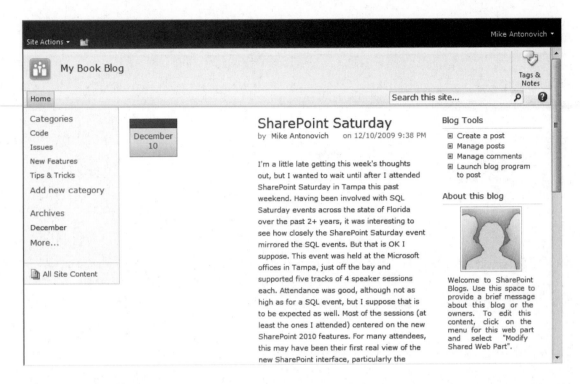

Figure 4-47. Viewing a published blog entry in SharePoint

■ **Note** If you had already pointed your browser to the blog page before starting this process, you may need to refresh the page in order to see the latest posting.

SharePoint automatically enables RSS feeds for blog sites. You can see the orange RSS feed icon in either the browser's menu bar at the top of the window or at the bottom of the page below the last blog entry. When your browser displays the orange RSS feed icon, you know that the feed has been enabled. That means that you and your users can subscribe to this RSS feed and receive notification when you or someone else posts new entries to this blog.

Commenting on a Blog Entry

To add a comment to an existing blog post, click the **Comments** link beneath the post. This adds a small form to the screen prompting for an optional title and the body of the comment, as shown in Figure 4-48. Comments automatically include the SharePoint user name of the person adding the comment as well as the date and time she added it. Comments do not display by default, but if you click the **Comments** link when the number in parentheses is greater than zero, you can view these comments and add your own.

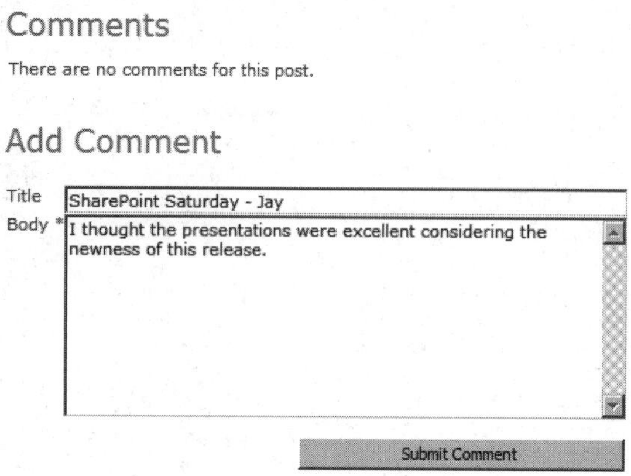

Comments

There are no comments for this post.

Add Comment

Title: SharePoint Saturday - Jay

Body *: I thought the presentations were excellent considering the newness of this release.

Submit Comment

Figure 4-48. *Adding a Comment to a blog entry*

Setting List Level Blog Permissions

SharePoint stores blogs as a list named **Posts**. As a list, you can control who has access to create and edit blogs. If you created your blog site by inheriting permissions from a parent site, then anyone with content creator rights in the parent site can contribute to your blog. However, if you need to limit the number of people who can create blog entries, you must break that inheritance.

To break inheritance of permissions, open the **Posts** list by going through **Site Actions ➤ View All Site Content**. With the Posts list open, select the **List** ribbon and click on **List Settings** in the **Settings** group. In the **Permissions and Management** column, select **Permissions** for this list. If this list still has permission inheritance turned on, a banner appears immediately below the ribbon telling you that the list inherits permissions from its parent. SharePoint provides a link to manage the parent's permissions. You can break inheritance for this list by clicking **Stop Inheriting Permissions** from the **Inheritance** group of the **Permission Tools** ribbon. This option allows you to define custom permissions for your blog.

After you stop inheriting permissions, the page refreshes and you can now change the permissions of the inherited groups and users, deleting existing groups and users, and adding new groups and users as necessary. Remember, only people with edit rights can manage posts and comments. On most public blog sites, people who can create blog posts can go back and edit their submitted entries. Typically, however, people who can only post blog comments cannot edit or delete their entries after they submit them. So be sure you want others to see what you have written before you submit your posts or comments. Finally, if you are the administrator of the blog site, you might need to delete blog or comment entries if they become inflammatory, abusive, discriminatory, or constitute a character attack.

The following steps define how you might create a new permission level that allows its members to view blogs without being able to create new blog entries or add comments.

1. Navigate to the blog site and then select **Site Permissions** under **Users and Permissions** section from the **Site Actions** button.

2. On the **Permissions** page, click **Stop Inheriting Permissions** from the **Inheritance** group of the **Permission Tools** ribbon. This option breaks the inheritance from the parent site after making a copy of the parent permissions on the current site.

3. Go to the top-level site of your current site collection and select **Site Permissions** from **Site Actions** button.

4. Click **Permission Levels** from the **Manage** group of the **Permission Tools**.

5. You can now edit the permissions in any of the existing levels or you can define unique permission levels for use anywhere within the site collection, not just your blog site. For example, you might want to place everyone except your department staff in a group that only has read rights to blogs.

6. On the **Permission Levels** page, click **Add a Permission Level**.

7. Name the permission **Blog Readers**.

8. Under **Permissions**, select only the following options:

   • View Items

   • Create Alerts

   • View Application Pages

9. In addition, under **Site Permissions**, select these options:

   • View Pages

   • Open

10. When you click **Create**, you will see that SharePoint created a new permission level named **Blog Readers**.

11. Return to the **Permissions** page of your blog site and check the check box before <<**Site Name**>> **Visitors** where <<Site Name>> represents the name of your blog site.

12. Click Edit User Permission to change the permission for this group from **Read** to **Blog Readers** and click **OK**.

Now when users assigned to the <<Site Name>> Visitors group visit the blog site, they can only view the existing blogs. They can also view the comments associated with them, but they cannot create new blog entries or add comments to existing entries. In a similar way, you can customize permissions for other groups who access your blog site.

In the future, if you may decide that you would rather inherit rights from the parent site, you can do so by returning to the **Permissions** page of the blog site and selecting **Inherit Permissions** from the **Inheritance** group of the **Permission Tools** ribbon.

Setting Item-Level Blog Permissions

In addition to setting the overall list permissions as described in the last section, blogs, like other lists and libraries, also allow you to fine-tune permissions that determine who can read, create, and edit items in the list. Let's look at the permissions that affect what a user can see and do. Begin by going to the **Blog Tools** section of the blog page and selecting **Manage Posts**. This action displays the **Posts** list, a list like many of the other lists you have examined. From the **Settings** group in the **List** ribbon select **List Settings**. Then select **Advanced Settings** under **General Settings**.

The top section of this page, shown in Figure 4-49, begins with an option to allow you to management content types. For this list, leave this option set to **No**. The next section displays item-level permissions. Notice that you can control whether users can read all posts or just their own. If users can only read their own blogs, your blog site becomes more like a private diary than a public blog.

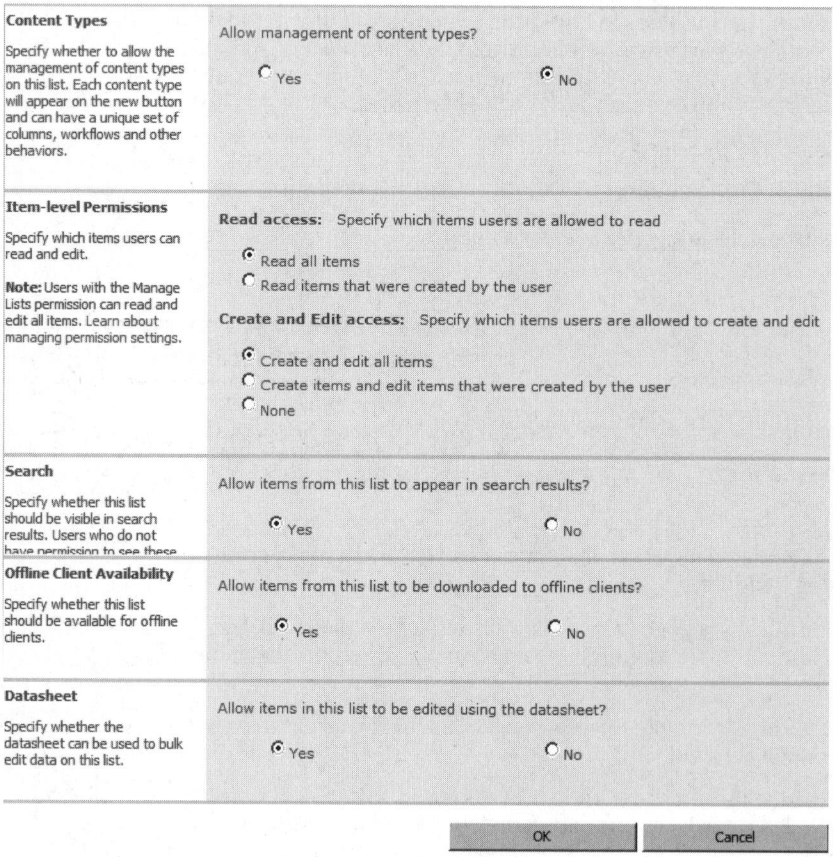

Content Types Specify whether to allow the management of content types on this list. Each content type will appear on the new button and can have a unique set of columns, workflows and other behaviors.	Allow management of content types? ○ Yes ⦿ No
Item-level Permissions Specify which items users can read and edit. **Note:** Users with the Manage Lists permission can read and edit all items. Learn about managing permission settings.	**Read access:** Specify which items users are allowed to read ⦿ Read all items ○ Read items that were created by the user **Create and Edit access:** Specify which items users are allowed to create and edit ⦿ Create and edit all items ○ Create items and edit items that were created by the user ○ None
Search Specify whether this list should be visible in search results. Users who do not have permission to see these	Allow items from this list to appear in search results? ⦿ Yes ○ No
Offline Client Availability Specify whether this list should be available for offline clients.	Allow items from this list to be downloaded to offline clients? ⦿ Yes ○ No
Datasheet Specify whether the datasheet can be used to bulk edit data on this list.	Allow items in this list to be edited using the datasheet? ⦿ Yes ○ No

                                              [OK]   [Cancel]

Figure 4-49. Advanced settings for the Posts list

More importantly, you can define whether users can create and edit all posts, only their own posts, or no posts. You may not want to allow anyone with edit permission to be able to change all blog entries no matter who created them. On the other hand, if you select none, you effectively block all attempts to edit or delete a post once you have submitted a post. Even the creator of the blog entry cannot go back to edit or deleted their own entries. Only a site administrator or site owner with the Manage Lists permission can then edit or delete posts. You control how restrictive you want to make this setting.

Next, determine whether the search engine includes blog entries in its search. You can also set whether users can download blog entries into offline clients and whether the list can appear in bulk edit mode, otherwise known as Datasheet mode. Finally, SharePoint 2010 allows you to determine whether the new, edit, and display forms appear within a separate popup dialog or whether they appear as a full-page form.

Summary

In Chapter 1, you saw how to create documents using Word for your document libraries and how to define default templates for those libraries. In this chapter, you took a deeper dive into using Microsoft Word with your SharePoint site. You saw how to work with documents in Word and then save them directly to existing SharePoint libraries and even how to create new documents from Word.

You also looked at metadata. Office products such as Word have supported the additional file properties for some time. SharePoint makes use of those properties by allowing you to associate them with columns in a library view. Once exposed as columns in a view, you can customize the view to aggregate the information found in those columns to create counts, sums, filters, etc.

You also looked at how you can use the Document Information panel to show more about the status of the document and your library site. The SharePoint Search feature helps locate documents in your libraries because it searches for words not only in the document's title, but also in the document's content as well as its metadata. You also created entries to your blog sites directly from within Word and posted those entries without logging directly into SharePoint.

Microsoft Word strongly complements SharePoint and opens the door to web-based collaboration support to people with normal Office skills. Most users knowledgeable in Word can become productive in a collaborative environment, supporting document libraries and contributing to blog sites in a short time.

In the next chapter, you will explore a different tool in the Microsoft Office Suite, Outlook. You will see how Outlook integrates its calendar and tasks with similar features in SharePoint. You will also learn how to use Outlook to synchronize documents so you can take advantage of offline editing.

CHAPTER 5

■ ■ ■

Using Outlook

This chapter focuses on using Outlook 2010. Although much of what I discuss here also works with Outlook 2007, previous versions of Outlook supported far fewer integration points with SharePoint. In fact, Office 2003 only allowed you to view copies of SharePoint lists such as the tasks list, the contacts list, and calendar list. You could not edit the data in these copied lists and send the changes back to SharePoint. While Outlook 2003 could receive alerts generated by SharePoint when someone made changes to these lists, it could not use RSS (Really Simple Syndication) feeds.

Of course, Outlook 2007 and Outlook 2010 expand on these limitations, turning Outlook into a virtual front-end client for SharePoint. Today not only can you copy lists to Outlook, but you can share changes made in Outlook with SharePoint. In addition, Outlook supports RSS feeds, workflow integration, records management, and more.

Let's begin by looking at basic sharing of lists such as SharePoint's contacts lists with Outlook.

Synchronizing Your Contacts Lists Between SharePoint and Outlook

Suppose you have one or more SharePoint sites that you regularly visit in your organization. They may be departmental or project sites, it doesn't matter. What does matter is that each of these sites has multiple contacts lists that you might need to reference on a regular basis. But going online and finding which site the contact is in each time you need a phone number, physical address, or an e-mail address just takes too long. Of course, you could just reenter the information you frequently use into Outlook yourself, but who has time for that? Besides, storing data in duplicate locations is a sure way to create data inconsistencies when one source gets updated while others do not. Fortunately, SharePoint can simplify your life.

Connecting Your SharePoint Contacts List to Outlook

To begin organizing your contacts in one place, open your favorite SharePoint site, one that has a contacts list that you frequently access. I'm going to open the list **CoWorkers** located in my team site. (Of course, you can begin with your own contacts list in one of your own team sites.)

1. Open the list in a separate window by selecting the list from the **View All Site Content** page.

2. Open the **List** ribbon from the **List Tools** group. Then in the **Connect & Export** group, located the command **Connect to Outlook**.

At this point, SharePoint attempts to connect to Outlook on your local computer. First, Internet Explorer raises a security warning to tell you that Microsoft Outlook is attempting to open content on your computer. Since you initiated this action, you should feel safe clicking the **Allow** button as shown in Figure 5-1.

Figure 5-1. *Vista and Windows 7 try to protect your computer from data connections.*

■ **Note** The warning message in Figure 5-1 pops up frequently when you follow the examples in this chapter and many of the rest. However, I will not display this dialog each time. Just keep in mind that, if you are working with your own SharePoint servers, there is no reason not to allow the website to access content on your computer. Also, this dialog may appear slightly differently if you are using Windows XP.

Outlook recognizes this attempt and raises a warning message box asking you whether you know and trust this source. To help you decide this vital security question, the message box, shown in Figure 5-2, displays the name of the site and the list. It also includes the list's URL. The buttons at the bottom of the box let you accept the connection by clicking **Yes** or reject it by clicking **No**. Of course, in this case you trust the source, so click **Yes**.

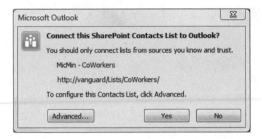

Figure 5-2. Connecting to a trusted SharePoint contacts list

In most cases, you will not need to open the **Advanced** dialog box. However, if you are curious and do click the **Advanced** button, it will display the dialog box shown in Figure 5-3. This dialog box allows you to change the folder name where Outlook stores the transferred contacts list. By default, SharePoint concatenates the site name with the contacts list name, using a hyphen between them. This usually defines a unique tasks list name in Outlook. However, you can supply your own name if you prefer. You can also provide a description for the folder. Outlook displays this description when you look at the properties of the created folder. This dialog box also displays other properties for informational purposes such as the list name, list type, and its URL.

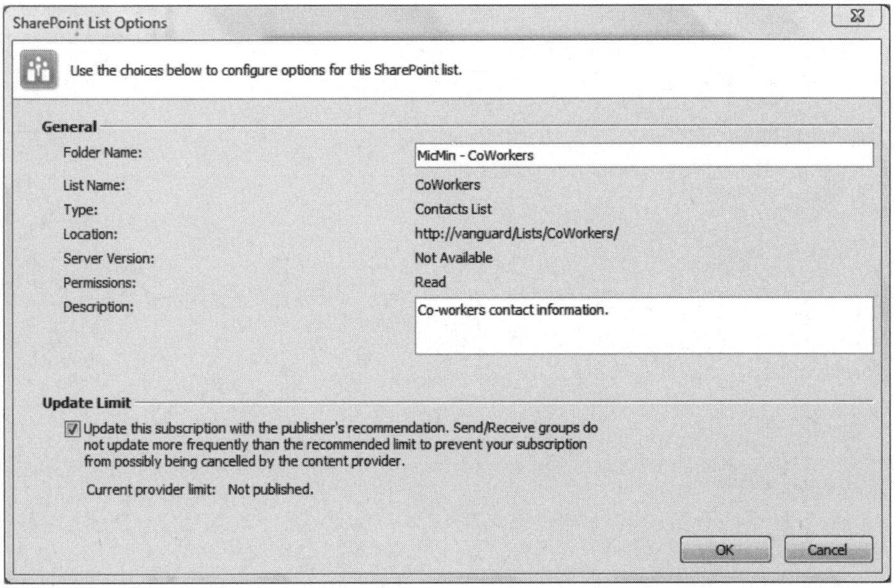

Figure 5-3. Defining the folder name and description for a shared contacts list

After you click **OK**, SharePoint transfers all items from the SharePoint list to the new folder in Outlook. If the SharePoint list has columns that do not have corresponding fields in Outlook, Outlook ignores them. Table 5-1 shows a list of the default SharePoint contact columns and their corresponding Outlook contact fields.

Table 5-1. *Mapping SharePoint Contact Columns to Outlook Columns*

SharePoint Column	Outlook Column
Last Name	Last Name
First Name	First Name
Full Name	Full Name
E-mail Address	E-mail
Company	Company
Job Title	Job Title
Business Phone	Business
Home Phone	Home
Mobile Phone	Mobile
Fax Number	Business Fax
Address	Business Address
City	Business City
State/Province	Business State/Province
Zip/Postal Code	Business Zip/Postal
Country/Region	Business Country
Web Page	Web Page
Notes	Notes
Created By	<Not mapped>
Modified By	<Not mapped>

Adding SharePoint Columns That Will Synchronize with Outlook

Perhaps you realized that Outlook supports many other fields than those shown in Table 5-1. Can you use those too? Yes, you can use them on the Outlook side without affecting the synchronization of the other data fields with SharePoint. SharePoint ignores these additional fields.

In Chapter 2, you saw that you could add columns to a list. Let's use that same technique to add some of the other fields that Outlook supports that were not in the initial SharePoint contacts list by adding the contact's home address information.

1. Begin by opening the linked contacts list in SharePoint.

2. Open the **List** ribbon and select **List Settings** from the **Settings** group.

3. In the **Columns** section, click **Add from existing site columns** at the bottom of this section.

4. Select **All Groups** from the first drop-down combo box if not already selected.

5. Scroll down through the list of fields until you find the home address fields. Select the following fields:

   - **Home Address City**

   - **Home Address Country**

   - **Home Address Postal Code**

   - **Home Address State or Province**

   - **Home Address Street**

6. Be sure to check the box **Add to default view** if you want to see these values in the list view.

7. Click **OK.**

Selecting Multiple Items

When selecting multiple items as in step 5, you can

- Select each one by clicking it and then clicking the **Add** button.

- Double-click each item.

- Click the first item. With the Shift key pressed, click the last item. (Use this technique when selecting a contiguous range of values.) Then click the **Add** button.

- Click the first item, and then while holding down the Ctrl key, click each additional item. (Use this technique when selecting items scattered throughout the list.) Then click the **Add** button.

Now when you return to your list, you can edit any or all of your contact items to add home address information. However, just because you clicked **OK** to save your changes in SharePoint doesn't mean those changes will immediately appear in Outlook. To force a refresh, open the **List** ribbon and again select the **Connect to Outlook** option from the **Connect & Export** group. This forces SharePoint and Outlook to resynchronize the changes made.

Similarly, you can make a change to contact information in Outlook. Again, the change to the fields visible or not visible in the default view of the list may not appear immediately in SharePoint. Why can't you see the changes? Actually, in this case, Outlook has passed the changes to SharePoint, but web pages do not automatically refresh. To see the updated values, click the **Refresh** button in the browser menu.

Managing Update Conflicts

What if someone updates a contact in Outlook at the same time that someone else updates the same item in SharePoint? What happens to both sets of changes? It depends on who saves his changes first. If the Outlook user saves his changes first, then you as the SharePoint user get an error message when you attempt to save your changes that says:

```
Save Conflict. Your changes conflict with those made concurrently by another user.

If you want your changes to be applied, click Back in your Web Browser,

refresh the page, and resubmit your changes.
```

What this statement does not make clear is that you may need to reapply your changes to the refreshed page. Consider that refreshing a web page updates all fields on the page including those fields just changed by the Outlook user. This, of course, erases all your changes.

If the SharePoint user saves her changes first, the Outlook user's change does not go through, but again no error message appears to tell the user that their changes were not saved due to a conflict with another user's edits.

Figure 5-4 shows an example of what a list synchronized from SharePoint looks like. Notice that Outlook places synchronized lists in a folder group named **Other Contacts** in the **Navigation** panel of the **Contacts** page. However, you can click and drag contacts lists between folder groups. If you do not like these folder groups, you can create a new folder group by right-clicking any of the folder group headers and selecting **New Folder Group**.

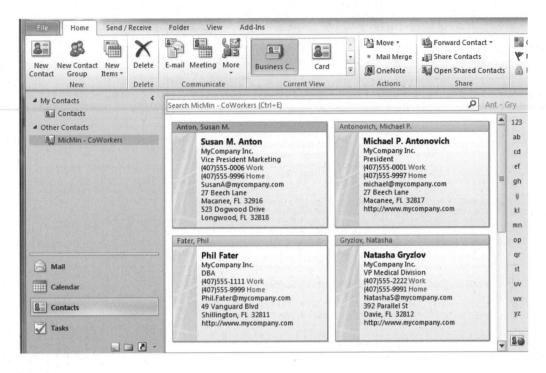

Figure 5-4. Synchronized contacts in Outlook

With each contacts list, you can right-click the list name to display its properties from the drop-down menu. The property dialog box consists of three tabbed pages. Click the **General** tab to see the description you entered back in the **SharePoint List Options** dialog box in Figure 5-3 when initially synchronizing the SharePoint list to Outlook.

You also have the ability to show or hide a contact folder from the e-mail Address Book drop-down shown in Figure 5-5. You can find the option in the third page of the properties dialog. When you click the check box before the option **Show the folder as an e-mail Address book**, you can also define another name to use for the contact list other than the one that appears in the left navigation panel.

Even if you hide the contacts list from the Address Book on the e-mail page, you can still open the Contacts page and click the desired list from the left navigation panel. Then locate the contact you want to send an e-mail. Finally, right-click the contact and select **Create ➤ E-mail** from the pop-up menu to begin an e-mail message to that person.

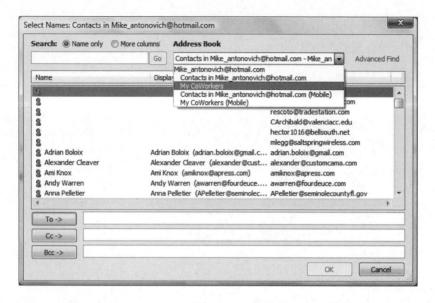

Figure 5-5. *Synchronized lists appear in Outlook's Address Book.*

Deleting Contacts

Just as you can edit contact information in either Outlook or SharePoint, you can delete contacts from either location as well. If you start from SharePoint, follow these steps:

1. Open the contacts list you want to edit.

2. Locate the contact you want to delete.

3. Hover your mouse over the contact to activate the drop-down menu button to the right of the contact.

4. Open the drop-down menu (see Figure 5-6).

Figure 5-6. *Deleting a contact from SharePoint*

5.   Click **Delete Item**.

As with documents and other lists, SharePoint prompts you with a dialog box to ensure that you really want to delete the item. Remember that even when you delete items from lists, SharePoint first places them in the site Recycle Bin for a limited time, from where you can restore them later.

■ **Note** Remember that you can ask your SharePoint administrator to change the length of time items stay in the Recycle Bin. By default, they stay there 30 days. However, your administrator can change this by going into **Central Administration** and selecting **Manage Web Applications** from the **Application Management** tab. Then select your web application, probably **SharePoint – 80** if you accepted the default name. Then, from the **General Settings** drop-down in the **Manage** group, select **General Settings**. Finally, scroll down the page to the **Recycle Bin** section to the **Recycle Bin** group and change the number of days items kept in the Recycle Bin.

If you open the **Outlook Contacts** page and view the shared SharePoint list, you will find that the contact has also been deleted from the Outlook list.

Recovering Deleted Contacts

If you accidentally delete the wrong contact, open the site Recycle Bin found at the bottom of the **Quick Launch** menu. You may need to scroll through the items previously deleted to find the contact record, or you can sort on the **Deleted** date field by clicking it. However, after you find it, click the box to the left of the name and click **Restore Selection** from the menu bar at the top of the Recycle Bin.

After 30 days (or whatever number of days your Recycle Bin has been set to), SharePoint removes the item from the site Recycle Bin so it doesn't continue to grow indefinitely. Even if you were to go into your Recycle Bin and delete an item from the bin before the 30 days have expired, you can contact your SharePoint administrator and ask him to retrieve the item from the site collection Recycle Bin. SharePoint holds deleted items here until the original 30 days (or other time period) has expired before permanently deleting the item.

Figure 5-7 shows that the deleted contact in the Recycle Bin is selected for restoration. Notice that the Recycle Bin also contains a deleted document. The Recycle Bin holds everything from lists to libraries to web pages. If you have trouble finding a deleted item, you might want to sort by item type as well as the deleted date and time to help locate the item you want.

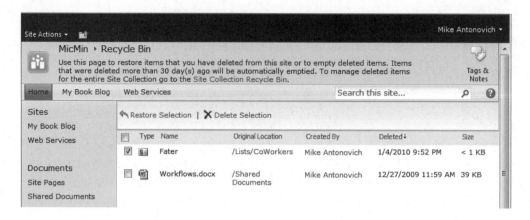

Figure 5-7. Restoring a deleted contact from the Recycle Bin

After you click the **Restore Selection** link, SharePoint prompts to confirm the item by name that you want to restore. When you click **OK**, SharePoint restores the item from the Recycle Bin, returning it to the list it originally came from. You may be surprised to learn that the process of restoring the contact from the SharePoint Recycle Bin also places the contact back in Outlook's shared list. You can verify this by opening Outlook and looking at the shared contacts list.

So what happens when you start by deleting the contact from within Outlook? In this case, SharePoint recognizes that you deleted the contact through Outlook and moves the contact information from the list to the Recycle Bin. From that point, the story remains the same. You can go into the Recycle Bin in SharePoint and restore the contact to both the SharePoint list and the Outlook contacts list.

■ **Tip** A quick way to refresh your shared contact list is to switch to one of the other Outlook pages, such as the Mail page, and then switch back to the Contact page.

Moving Contacts between Lists

SharePoint does not really provide a way to move or copy a contact from one list to another. However, if you share both contacts lists through Outlook, Outlook can accomplish this task quickly and easily by following these steps:

1. With both contacts lists synchronized in Outlook, open the list that you are going to copy the contact from in order to show the individual items it contains.

2. Click and drag the contact to the destination contacts list title in the **Navigation** panel on the left side of the screen.

3. When you release the mouse button, Outlook moves the contact from the original list and places it in the new list. You can verify this by returning to your SharePoint window and viewing the items in each contacts list. Remember to refresh the list displays if you already had them open.

■ **Tip** This ability to copy between contacts lists extends to all contacts lists in Outlook, not just those linked to SharePoint. As a result, you can use this technique as an easy way to populate a new SharePoint list from your main contacts list in Outlook.

If you work at a company that uses Exchange Server, your main Outlook contacts list already contains all the people in your organization. You can transfer that information to a custom SharePoint list for a department or project by following these steps:

1. Open SharePoint and create a new empty contacts list in the desired site.

2. Open the list after creating it.

3. Select **Connect to Outlook** from the **Connect & Export** group of the **List** ribbon

4. Open the main **Contacts** list in Outlook using the **Contacts** page.

5. Locate the people you want to add to the SharePoint list.

6. Right-click and drag the contacts to the SharePoint list name in the navigation panel.

7. Release the mouse button and select **Copy** from the pop-up menu. In this case, you don't want to move the contacts from one list to another.

8. Repeat Step 5 to copy each additional contact to the SharePoint list.

9. When finished, return to SharePoint and open the new list, or if you still have it open from before, refresh the page.

You now know how to populate a SharePoint list from Outlook without retyping the entries.

Synchronizing Your Calendars between SharePoint and Outlook

Calendars seem to be springing up everywhere. If you have been a Microsoft Office user, you probably already use Outlook's calendar to track your appointments, meetings, task due dates, and more while in the office. You may also add your personal events such as doctor appointments, birthdays, anniversaries, and your children's school events.

With the introduction of SharePoint collaboration, it has become easy for project managers and group managers to create shareable online calendars with events that affect everyone in the project or group. Like contacts lists, the more projects you belong to, the more calendars you must check on a regular basis to make sure that you do not miss an event, a deadline, or a meeting. With so many places to check for the information you need, you can easily miss something critical.

To solve this problem of having too many calendars, you can join calendars from SharePoint and Outlook into a common view. Functionally, this technique works similarly to viewing calendars from multiple people. Besides being able to view multiple calendars together on the screen, sharing calendars between SharePoint and Outlook lets you manage multiple SharePoint calendars from Outlook.

Adding a SharePoint Calendar to Outlook

To add a SharePoint calendar to Outlook, begin by opening the calendar within SharePoint, as shown in Figure 5-8.

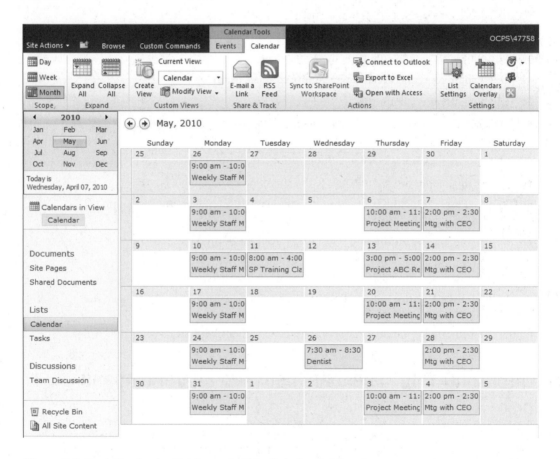

Figure 5-8. Typical calendar list shown in SharePoint's calendar view

It does not matter which calendar view you begin from, as SharePoint synchronizes all calendar items with Outlook. Information that SharePoint synchronizes includes these columns:

- Item Title

- Location

- Start Time

- End Time

- Description

- All Day Event

- Recurrence

■ **Note** While calendar events in Outlook supports scheduling options such as selecting attendees, setting reminders, and adding flags and categories, these features do not exist in SharePoint. This difference in supported elements limits what information SharePoint can synchronize.

Next, open the **Calendar** ribbon, as shown in Figure 5-9, and select the option **Connect to Outlook** from the **Actions** group.

Figure 5-9. Choose Connect to Outlook to connect a calendar list to Outlook.

As with contacts, Internet Explorer begins by popping up a pair of dialogs similar to Figure 5-1 and Figure 5-2. The first asks if you really want open Microsoft Outlook to access web content. Click the **Allow** button on this dialog. Outlook needs you to verify that you trust the source before synchronizing with a calendar list from SharePoint or any other source. If you click **Don't Allow**, the process halts.

In the dialog box shown in Figure 5-10, Outlook displays the URL of the calendar list so you can verify whether you trust the list. If so, click **Yes** to continue. Also in this dialog box, Outlook shows the name it intends to assign to the calendar. By default, the calendar name concatenates the site name with the list name separated with a hyphen.

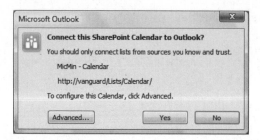

Figure 5-10. Confirm that you trust the calendar source.

If you click the **Advanced** button in this dialog box, you can specify your own calendar name as well as a description. You can view this description when you open the properties of the Calendar folder within Outlook. You might use this description to provide a more detailed explanation of the purpose of the calendar.

After Outlook creates the folder for the SharePoint calendar, you can display it within the **Calendar** page. Outlook has the ability to display two or more calendars at the same time. To display more than one calendar, open the **Navigation** panel shown in Figure 5-11 if not currently open. You can do this through Outlook's **View** menu.

Figure 5-11. The Calendar Navigation panel in Outlook

In the top portion of the **Navigation** panel, a calendar appears. Use this calendar to select the month, week, or day you want to view. Beneath this calendar is a section that contains one or more subsections. By default, the subsection named **My Calendars** represents standard calendars created within Outlook. In this subsection, you should have at least one calendar named **XXXX Calendar** where **XXXX** represents your Outlook name. This is your primary Outlook calendar. If you have created additional calendars or attached additional files to Outlook such as archived Outlook files from the current or different machines, you may see additional calendars from these archives as well.

Creating a New Outlook Calendar

You can create a new Outlook calendar for a project or other special purpose by right-clicking anywhere on the line of one of the existing calendars in the left navigation. From the drop-down menu that appears, select **New Calendar**.

1. In the dialog box that appears, supply a name for your new calendar.

2. Make sure that the **Folder Contains** drop-down has the option **Calendar Items** selected.

3. Select where you want to create the calendar. You must create it from a user account, not under another folder or calendar.

4. Once created, the new calendar appears in the **My Calendar** subsection of the **Navigation** panel.

To display the calendar, click the check box to the left of the name.

A second subsection, named **Other Calendars**, holds calendars linked to Outlook from SharePoint. I use the term "linked" here rather than "copied" to emphasize that the SharePoint calendar can be updated in either SharePoint or Outlook and have those updates displayed in the other system.

You can display any combination of the calendars from these two subsections by selecting them using the check box to the left of their names. While you can display several calendars at once, the physical width of your monitor determines how many calendars you can reasonably view. Generally, viewing more than two or three at a time makes it difficult to read the events and appointments. However, by positioning your mouse over an item in the calendar, a ToolTip-style window appears beneath your cursor with the item's time, subject and location.

Figure 5-12 shows two calendars side by side. The default Outlook calendar appears on the left, and a SharePoint calendar on the right.

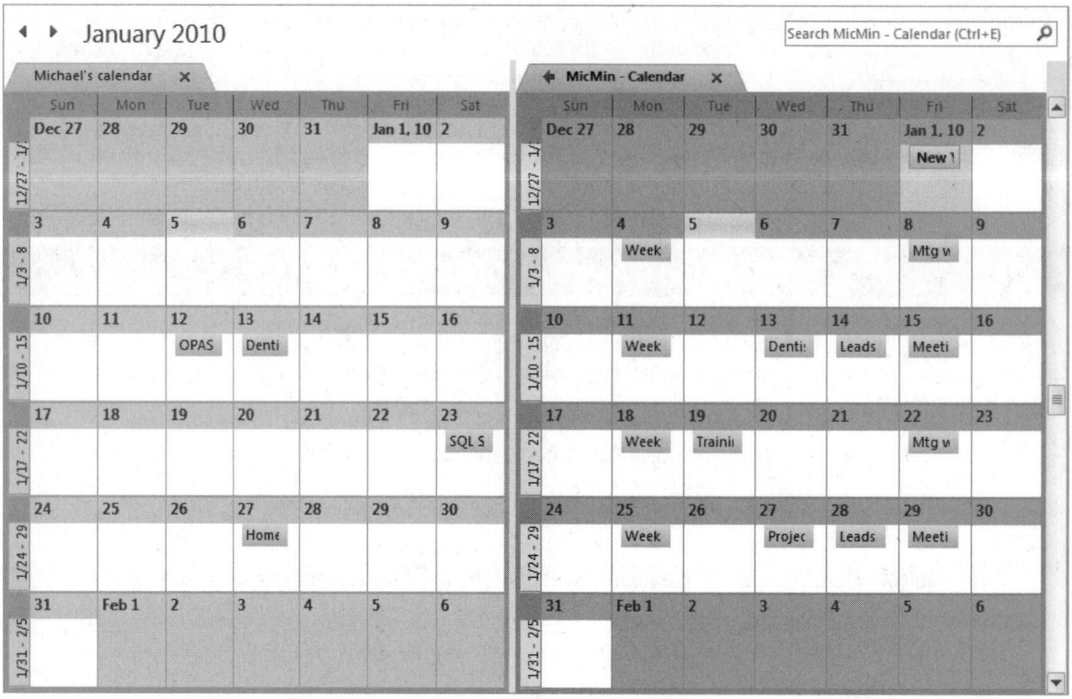

Figure 5-12. Displaying an Outlook calendar and a SharePoint calendar side by side

Outlook lets you display one day, one week, or a full month of each calendar by using the buttons across the top of the calendar area. You can quickly move between months by clicking the **Previous** and **Next** buttons, represented by left and right arrows respectively, at the top left of the calendar area. Each click moves your view one month at a time.

■ **Caution** You must be in month mode in order to move through your calendar one week at a time using the scroll wheel on your mouse.

Overlaying Calendars

While displaying two calendars side by side allows you to visually compare events and appointments on common days, you can make this process easier by overlaying the calendars on top of each other. To do this, click the arrow to the left of the calendar name tab of any calendar after the first one. When you do this, Outlook overlays the calendars to show a single view of your events and appointments.

Alternatively, you can select **Overlay** from the **Arrangement** group of the **View** ribbon, as shown in Figure 5-13.

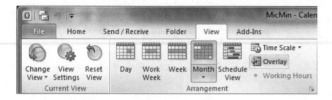

Figure 5-13. Switching view modes in the Arrangement group of the View ribbon

When Outlook overlays calendars, it displays a tab for each calendar at the top of the combined calendar. Click the tab of the calendar you want to appear on top of the others. The events and appointments of the top calendar appear in bold black text compared to the events and appointments beneath the top calendar. You should also notice that events for calendars beneath the top calendar use a font color that matches the tab color so you can easily identify to which calendar an event belongs when overlaying three or more calendars. Clicking between the tabs illustrates this point. Figure 5-14 shows two overlaid calendars. You can overlay calendars in any of the view modes: month, week, or day.

■ **Note** Grayscale images such as in this book don't really do justice to the full-color image of overlaid calendars. However, even in a grayscale image, you can identify the "on-top" calendar because it will have a darker font for the calendar text (in this case, Michael's Calendar).

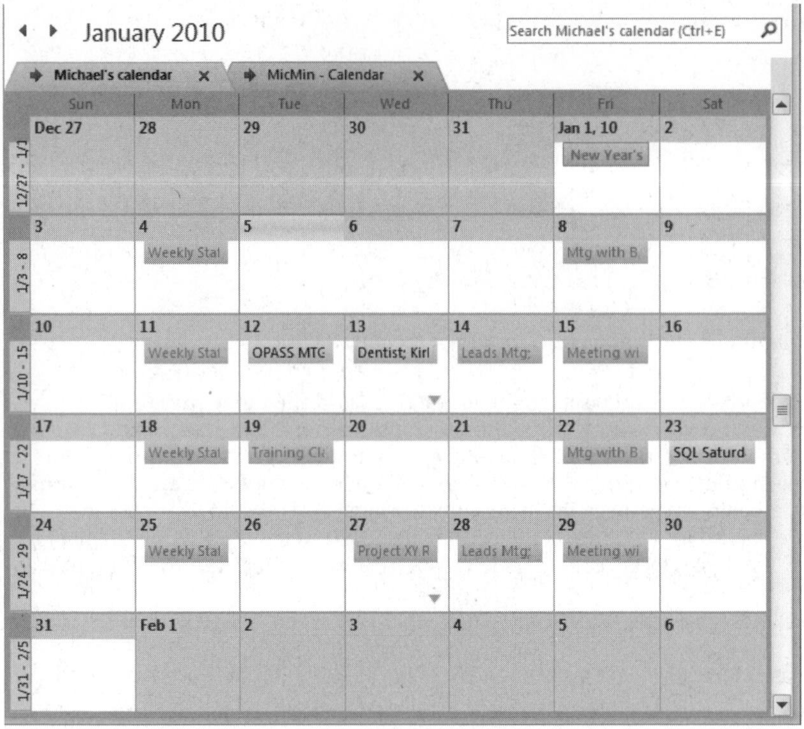

Figure 5-14. Overlaying two calendars using the month view

■ **Tip** If you can see the calendars of your coworkers, you can use this technique to overlay them to quickly spot times when you can have group meetings.

To display each calendar separately again, click the arrow to the left of any calendar name in the tab area. You can also click **Overlay** from the **Arrangement** group of the **View** ribbon to deselect this option.

Making Changes to Calendar Items

You can change the properties for an event or appointment in a synchronized SharePoint calendar by double-clicking it in Outlook to open the item's property form. Then click the **Save and Close** button to save those changes.

Outlook synchronizes changes to the original SharePoint calendar so that someone viewing the calendar item directly from SharePoint sees your changes. Similarly, changes made in the SharePoint calendar update the view in Outlook the next time you open the calendar page (or when you press F9).

■ **Caution** When editing an event or appointment from a SharePoint calendar within Outlook, you can set properties that will not synchronize back to SharePoint such as categories, flags, reminders, and several others. While Outlook saves these properties for use within Outlook, SharePoint ignores them. For example, **Categorize** in Outlook is used to visually tag appointments with different colors based on categories that you define while **Category** in SharePoint is a text property or attribute of the calendar event and has nothing to do with the physical display of the event.

Because users can update the calendar from either SharePoint or Outlook, conflict resolution for calendar data is handled the same way as when dealing with contact data described in the "Managing Update Conflicts" section of this chapter.

Copying and Moving Items between Calendars

If you have appointments in more than one calendar, you might display multiple calendars to help visually organize your day. You can also look for conflicting appointments or free time. You might even want to move appointments or events from one calendar to another.

To move an event or appointment when you have two or more calendars displayed, click and drag an item from one open calendar to the next. If you are copying an event that is part of a recurring sequence, a popup dialog asks whether you want to copy the entire series or just the selected occurrence. You can also cancel the copy from this dialog. Furthermore, if you copy an event from Outlook to SharePoint, Outlook displays a dialog (shown in Figure 5-15) that warns you that copying events from Outlook to the SharePoint list automatically removes incompatible content during synchronization. There is no corresponding warning when copying events from SharePoint to Outlook.

Figure 5-15. Outlook warning

While you can easily change the day of an appointment within a single calendar displayed in month mode, you cannot change the start or end times of the appointment by simply dragging the item; you must manually edit the times. This method, however, is much faster than reentering the appointment.

■ **Caution** Remember, anyone with access to that SharePoint calendar can see any calendar event you copy to a SharePoint calendar. It will also synchronize with their Outlook if they connect that calendar to their local Outlook. And, of course, you may not want to share your personal appointments.

You may want to create a separate calendar in Outlook to plan a project schedule. Then when you have worked out the details, you can link to a SharePoint calendar on a project collaboration site and transfer your milestone dates by dragging them from one calendar to another.

You can copy items in either direction to or from SharePoint. You could also use this technique to copy important events or appointments from a shared calendar to your personal calendar. However, once copied, the copy in your personal calendar will not show changes made to the SharePoint event or appointment or vice versa.

If, rather than copy, you want to move the item from one calendar to another, you could proceed exactly like the copy method I just outlined. After making the copy, delete the item from the original calendar. Alternatively, you can perform the operation in a single step by holding down the right mouse button while you drag the item. When you release the button, you can decide via a pop-up menu whether to copy or move the item to the new location.

■ **Tip** Need to create a project calendar but feel more comfortable working with Outlook's calendar interface? No problem. Build your project calendar in a separate Outlook calendar, link to the project calendar in SharePoint, and copy the events from your local calendar to SharePoint.

Deleting Items from the Calendar

When you delete an item from an Outlook calendar, you can restore it by selecting **Undo** from the **Edit** drop-down menu as long as you have not closed Outlook. However, after you close Outlook, you cannot recover it.

On the other hand, if you delete an item from a SharePoint calendar, even if you perform the delete on a synchronized calendar within Outlook, SharePoint places the deleted item in the site's Recycle Bin. You can recover the item by opening the Recycle Bin and selecting the item to restore, as shown in Figure 5-16. Then click the **Restore Selection** option.

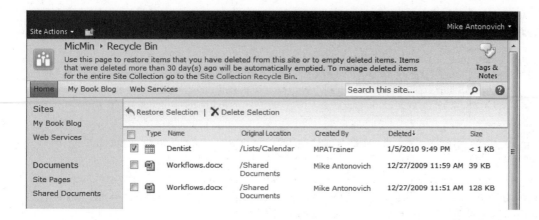

Figure 5-16. Recovering a deleted calendar item from SharePoint's Recycle Bin

After confirming that you want to restore the item, SharePoint puts the item back in the calendar. You will also see the restored item in the Outlook synchronized copy the next time you open Outlook. If you have Outlook open while restoring the item, you may need to click off the **Calendar** page, then perhaps go to the **Mail** page, and then return to the calendar page to see the restored item. You can also press F9 to perform a send-receive update.

Synchronizing Tasks between SharePoint and Outlook

Sharing tasks may be as important as sharing contacts for many people when they begin using SharePoint together with Outlook. If you already use Outlook to plan your day, you know how valuable it can be to keep all your tasks in one place where you can monitor start and due dates, group tasks by priority, categorize your tasks by percent completion, and set up reminders as deadlines approach. If you work as a consultant, you can use Outlook's **Tasks** tool to track hours for billing information. You can even use the large text area Outlook tasks provide as a task journal. For non-consultants, you might use these features to document the work effort required to complete tasks. You might even document external factors that affect your ability to meet deadlines.

No matter the specifics, using the **Tasks** feature in Outlook can help you organize and document your work. For many of these same reasons, your immediate manager or your project managers might also use the tasks list and project tasks list features of SharePoint as a convenient way to plan workloads and assign tasks to you. However, now you have a problem: you must view tasks lists scattered in several different places across one or more SharePoint installations. Your boss keeps his tasks list in the department work site, while each of the project managers you support have their own project sites with their individual tasks lists. In addition, you have your own personal tasks list stored in Outlook on your desktop. How can you keep up with changes to the individual tasks lists stored in different places to determine what you really need to focus on today? Of course, you could periodically open each list one at a time and check for new tasks or changes to your existing tasks. However, as you become busy and focus on any one task, you may forget to check the other tasks lists for the latest crisis. Fortunately, Outlook can serve as a collection point for multiple SharePoint tasks lists and can display them together with your own personal tasks list through a single page.

What About the Issue Tracking List?

Perhaps you remember from Chapter 2 that another list exists that tracks tasks: the issue tracking list. Your help desk staff might use the issue tracking list to log issues called in to them. They could use this list to assign issues that they could not directly resolve to the appropriate development staff. You might even use the issue tracking list on your personal, project, or department site to track problems.

You might think that it would be great to combine these tasks with other tasks gathered from other SharePoint tasks lists and project tasks lists. Unfortunately, SharePoint 2010 still does not support connecting to Outlook from an issue tracking list.

In the meantime, you could set up an alert in the list by clicking **Alerts** in the **Actions** menu of the list. Then in the section **Send Alerts for These Changes**, select the option **A task is assigned to me**. This will send you an e-mail when anyone adds or assigns a new task to you.

Adding Tasks Lists to Outlook

To begin organizing your tasks, open SharePoint and identify the names and locations of each tasks list you want to synchronize with Outlook. In this section, I'm going to load tasks from three tasks lists to show how Outlook gathers your tasks in one place. These tasks lists include the following:

- **Data Services Dept Tasks**: A basic tasks list created by a department manager, as shown in Figure 5-17

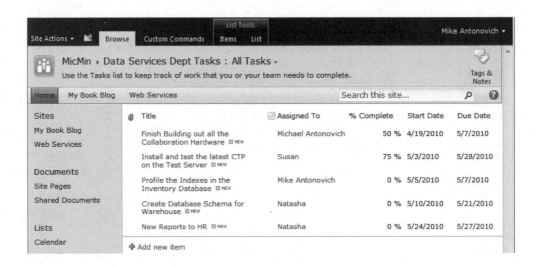

Figure 5-17. The Data Services Dept Tasks list from SharePoint

- **My Help Desk Calls**: A tasks list updated by the company's help desk, as shown in Figure 5-18.

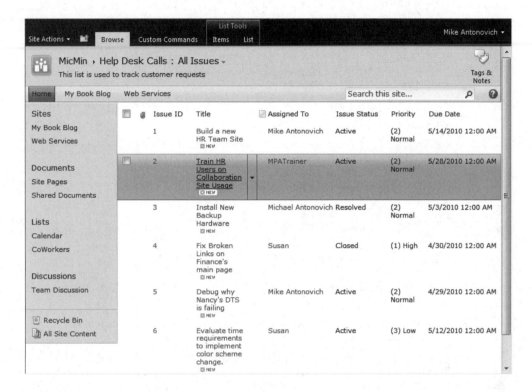

Figure 5-18. The Help Desk Calls list from SharePoint

- **Collaboration Site for HR**: A project tasks list created by the collaboration project manager, as shown in Figure 5-19.

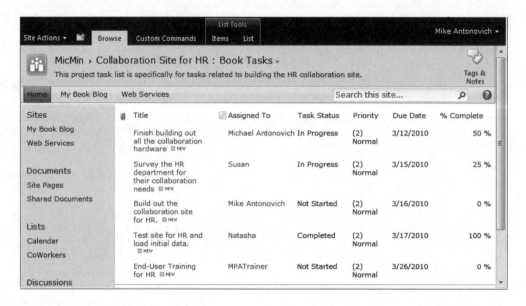

Figure 5-19. The Collaboration Site for HR list from SharePoint

1. Open the Data Services Dept Tasks list as shown previously. Be sure that the list menu appears across the top of the list.

2. Open the **List** ribbon and click **Connect to Outlook** from the **Connect & Export** group.

When you select this option, SharePoint attempts to connect to Outlook on your local computer. As you saw earlier with synchronizing contacts, Outlook tries to protect you from outside applications writing to Outlook and thus displays a warning message when it detects such an attempt (shown in Figure 5-1). In this message box, you can accept or reject the connection. In this case, trust the connection and accept the default name for the new tasks list SharePoint creates in Outlook for the transferred data.

In a similar fashion, you can open each of the other two lists and attempt to transfer them to Outlook, accepting their default names. You will find that the Help Desk Calls list based on the Issue Tracking list template will not connect to Outlook. Therefore, Figure 5-20 shows the **Navigation** panel on Outlook's **Tasks** page after attaching the other two lists.

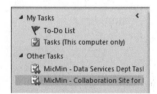

Figure 5-20. Outlook's Tasks page Navigation panel

Editing Tasks from Outlook

After you have connected to project or department tasks lists, you could edit these tasks within Outlook and have those edits appear in SharePoint, just like with contacts. However, unless you are the project manager or department manager and own the tasks list, I would recommend caution about making changes. On the one hand, your manager may want you to update selected fields such as the **% Complete**, **Finish Date**, **Completed Flag**, and **Notes** fields. On the other hand, that manager would not appreciate your changing the details of the task or the due date. At this point, SharePoint does not provide custom column-level security, so if users need edit permissions on some fields, they get edit permissions on all fields.

■ **Note** If you have SharePoint developers on your staff, they might be able to accomplish this task using SharePoint Event Receivers.

Of course, if you manage the list, not only can you edit existing tasks, but you can also create new tasks and delete tasks from within Outlook. You can even monitor the status of tasks, their progress, and their completion from within your Outlook **Tasks** page, even as your staff updates their task status through their Outlook **Tasks** pages, as long as you both link through the same SharePoint task list.

So what if you want to prevent unintended changes to your tasks by your staff? One way is to use custom permissions on the task list. Another method is to use an approval process like the one you saw earlier for documents. When turned on, the approval process hides the publishing of changes to the tasks list until a person with approval rights, such as you, approves the changes. The use of approvals provides two benefits. First, you can simply deny any unintended changes that might modify or delete the task. Second, you can review the legitimate updates to the tasks by your staff to monitor what they have accomplished.

Before you activate the approval process, make sure that you have assigned Approval permissions to managers of the lists. Then follow these steps to turn on the approval process for a tasks list:

1. Open the tasks list where you want to enable the approval process.

2. Open **List Settings** in the **Settings** group of the **List** ribbon.

3. Click **Versioning Settings** in the **General Settings** section.

4. In the **Content Approval** area, select **Yes** to require content approval.

5. You can also choose to keep both major and minor versions. I recommend keeping at least two major versions with draft versions made to the most recent approved version. These settings provide basic version protection without consuming a huge amount of additional storage space. In addition, they let you see from what the current data was changed. Change these settings in the **Item Version** history section to suit your needs.

6. In **Draft Item Security**, I recommend only allowing users with approval rights and the author to view the changes. That way everyone else sees only the most recently approved versions.

7. Click **OK** to accept these changes.

8. Click the name of your list in the breadcrumbs at the top of the page to return to the list view.

■ **Note** Draft versions of tasks may not be as common as draft versions of documents, but you may encounter them, especially when managers build tasks lists for large projects.

You can now connect the list to Outlook. Select **Connect to Outlook** from the **Actions** menu and tell Outlook that you trust the SharePoint list when the message box appears.

Sending E-mails from Tasks

You can send an e-mail when you assign a task to a person from within your SharePoint task list. By default, SharePoint turns e-mail notifications off. However, you can easily turn them on by going to your task list and choosing **List Settings** from the **Settings** group of the **List** ribbon. Then select **Advanced Settings** from the **General Settings** option group. On the **Advanced Settings** page, locate **the E-mail Notification** group and click the **Yes** radio button for the question asking whether to send an e-mail when someone assigns ownership. Click the **OK** button to exit this page and then navigate back to your task list.

Now when you add a new task to the task list, if you define the **Assigned To** property setting it to a valid user that SharePoint knows and who has an e-mail address, SharePoint sends an e-mail to that person as soon as you click **OK** to save that task.

■ **Tip** The SharePoint e-mail notification for your task list is turned on if you see a message at the top of the page when adding a new task that says **The content of this item will be sent as an e-mail message to the person or group assigned to the item.**

Using Outlook to Work Offline with Content

You can work on documents in a document library by connecting the SharePoint library to Outlook as described previously for contacts and tasks. With one additional step, you can check the document out from within SharePoint to protect your changes.

Open the library that contains the document you want to work on. If your document is in a folder within the library, open the folders until you see the document list containing the document you want.

From within the document library, right-click the documents you want to work with offline and check them out. You do not have to check out every document in the library, just the ones you plan on working with offline. This allows other users to work with the documents you have not checked out.

Select the **Connect to Outlook** option in the **Actions** menu. Outlook opens on your local computer, if not already open, and prompts you to respond whether you trust the source attempting to connect to it. Since you know the source is your SharePoint document library, check **Yes** to continue (shown in Figure 5-1 and Figure 5-2).

Outlook then creates a folder named `SharePoint Lists` if one does not already exist in your **Mail Folders** list. It then adds a folder for the site library using the naming convention `<site name> - <library name>`. Within this folder, it builds any additional folder structure needed to match the folder hierarchy within the library, down to the folder containing your document. In the last folder, the one you said to connect to Outlook from SharePoint, Outlook displays a list of all files. Figure 5-21 shows an example of the `Training` folder found within the **Shared Documents** library of a site named **MicMin**.

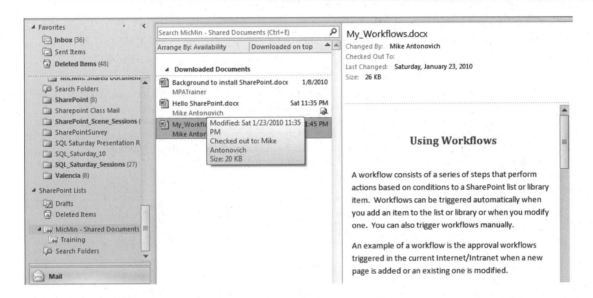

Figure 5-21. Shared Documents library referenced through Outlook

When you look at the files in this folder, how can you determine which you have checked out so you can edit them offline? If you position your mouse over the filename, the ToolTip text beneath the file tells you when the file was last modified, who currently has it checked out, and the document's size. Note that no one has the document checked out if the **Checked out to** line does not contain the name of a user immediately after it. Finally, if you double-click any file in the folder to open it, Word opens the document in **Read Only** mode first but displays the message shown in Figure 5-22 at the top of the opened document.

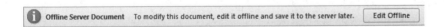

Figure 5-22. Shared Documents edited offline through Outlook

This message reminds you that the document is an offline document and that, if you edit the document, you must save it back to the server later. The connection between SharePoint and Outlook copies all the documents in the folder to your local drafts folder so you can view the files offline. You can even edit documents offline that you did not first check out. However, only documents that you do check out first before disconnecting from your network are safe to edit. By safe, I am referring to the ability to edit the document without concern about someone else editing the same document. If you want to edit the document, you must click the **Edit Offline** button shown in Figure 5-22.

■ **Tip** Outlook provides a great preview feature for Office files such as Word, Excel, and PowerPoint. When you click an e-mail message with an attachment from one of these applications, you can preview the attachment by clicking it. Similarly, when you use Outlook to work offline on SharePoint libraries with these file types, you can preview their content when you select the individual items in the linked library, as shown in Figure 5-21.

Let's assume that you want to work on the document later. After you have disconnected from your network, you can edit the local copy of the document saved in the SharePoint **Drafts** folder. You can open the document by double-clicking it through Outlook or by opening your SharePoint **Drafts** folder and double-clicking the file directly. In fact, you can open, edit, and save the document repeatedly while disconnected from the network. Word stores all your changes in the local copy of the file.

After editing a document offline, you will see the following text at the top of the document preview within Outlook.

```
Changes to this document are only available on this computer.  Open this document to check
in your changes.
```

You will also see a small icon of a page with a red arrow on the right side beneath the date, as shown in Figure 5-21.

You can upload your changes to a document that you did not check out from SharePoint the next time you connect to the network. To begin the upload, double click the document name from within Outlook. Outlook displays the message shown in Figure 5-23. Click the **Update** button to send your current version of the document to SharePoint. If you are not quite ready to send your updates to SharePoint yet, you can continue editing without updating SharePoint by clicking the **Do not update server** button.

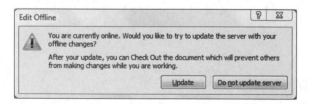

Figure 5-23. Prompt to update an unchecked out document after reconnecting to the network

If the document was checked out before editing it offline from Outlook, you can simply check it back in from within the SharePoint library the next time you connect to the network. From Outlook, you will see the following message at the top of preview window when you check out a file before disconnecting from the network.

Changes to this document are only available on this computer. To update the server with your changes, check in this document from your Web browser.

The advantage of checking out the document before disconnecting from the network is that you will have exclusive access to the document. No one else can make changes to the document while you have it checked out. Therefore, when you check the document back in, there is no chance of conflicts. If you do not check out the document first and someone else edits the document from SharePoint, you may have to reconcile your document changes with their changes.

Letting Alerts Notify You of SharePoint Changes

An alert is a feature of SharePoint that you can use for notification of changes made to libraries and lists via e-mail. This saves you the hassle of constantly returning to the library or list to see if anything was changed. With a manual check, you might spot new additions or deletions to the library or list. However, unless you were to track the modified dates of individual items in the library or list, it would be difficult to determine when someone modified them. Alerts can do this work for you. I first discussed alerts in Chapter 2 in the context of your initial exploration of lists. You can turn alerts on by opening the **Library** ribbon and clicking on the bottom half of the **Alert Me** button, as shown in Figure 5-24.

Figure 5-24. Selecting the Alert Me action

Your two options are to set an alert on the current library or to manage your alerts. Let's first look at how to create a new alert on the library.

Configuring Your Alerts

The **Set alert on this library** action opens the **New Alert** page shown in Figure 5-25. The first property you must define is the **Alert Title**. Over time, you may create hundreds of alerts within a SharePoint site. So naming the alert carefully and uniquely now helps you manage your alerts later. Note that SharePoint uses the alert title as the subject text when sending you the alert via e-mail. A unique name in the subject would certainly help you identify which alerts you need to look at first. SharePoint also uses the alert title when it lists your alerts, should you decide to delete some of them later.

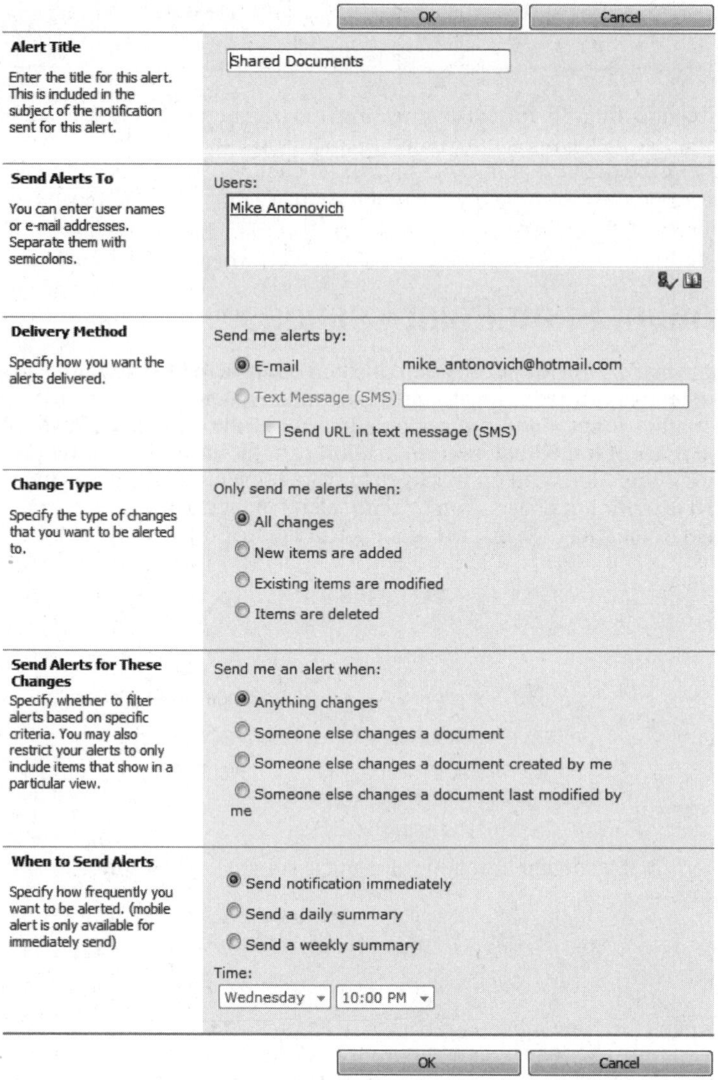

OK   Cancel

Alert Title

Enter the title for this alert.
This is included in the
subject of the notification
sent for this alert.

Shared Documents

Send Alerts To

You can enter user names
or e-mail addresses.
Separate them with
semicolons.

Users:

Mike Antonovich

Delivery Method

Specify how you want the
alerts delivered.

Send me alerts by:

◉ E-mail   mike_antonovich@hotmail.com

○ Text Message (SMS)

☐ Send URL in text message (SMS)

Change Type

Specify the type of changes
that you want to be alerted
to.

Only send me alerts when:

◉ All changes

○ New items are added

○ Existing items are modified

○ Items are deleted

**Send Alerts for These
Changes**

Specify whether to filter
alerts based on specific
criteria. You may also
restrict your alerts to only
include items that show in a
particular view.

Send me an alert when:

◉ Anything changes

○ Someone else changes a document

○ Someone else changes a document created by me

○ Someone else changes a document last modified by
me

When to Send Alerts

Specify how frequently you
want to be alerted. (mobile
alert is only available for
immediately send)

◉ Send notification immediately

○ Send a daily summary

○ Send a weekly summary

Time:

Wednesday ▾   10:00 PM ▾

OK   Cancel

Figure 5-25. Dialog box when creating a new Alert

After the alert title, you can specify who should receive the alert. By default, SharePoint places your
SharePoint user ID in this field, which links to the e-mail address defined in your user account. However,
you can create alerts for other people if you have administrator rights by adding e-mail addresses for
others separated with semicolons. If several people need to receive the same alert, you can save time
with this feature by not having to create individual alerts for each person.

Next, you need to specify for which types of changes you want to send alerts. Of course, you could send alerts for all changes, but that might create too many e-mails. You can limit alerts to just additions, modifications, or deletions. Unfortunately, you cannot select both additions and deletions, but not modifications. Radio buttons used in this section only allow mutually exclusive selections.

You can also specify whether you want to see alerts when someone other than yourself changes any document. Department and project managers may want to choose this option to keep on top of documents under their responsibility. You can also limit alerts to when someone makes changes to documents you created or modified last. With tasks lists, you can set your alert to notify you of only those tasks assigned to you.

The final section lets you define the frequency with which you want to receive the alerts. You could receive the alert as soon as the event monitored occurs. This may be important when SharePoint immediately publishes changed documents or when you are monitoring tasks assigned to you.

On the other hand, maybe you only want to receive a daily notification of events. When using this option, you can specify the time of day to receive the alert. SharePoint then delivers alerts on a 24-hour cycle. Therefore, if you specify that you want to receive alerts at 4:00 p.m. and someone updates or deletes a document at 4:30 p.m., you will not receive that alert until 4:00 p.m. the next day.

You might also choose to see alerts only once a week on a specific day and time. For example, you might want to see alerts first thing Monday mornings for changes made the previous week. As previously stated, events that occur immediately after the alert notice goes out must then wait until the end of the new cycle, even if that means waiting for 6 days, 23 hours, and 59 minutes.

You can define multiple alerts for the same list. Perhaps each one notifies you of different actions performed on the list. For example, you may want SharePoint to notify you immediately of inserts, daily of deletes, and weekly of updates.

■ **Tip** You can create custom alerts by using multiple alerts. For example, to receive change notifications every Tuesday and Thursday at noon, create two weekly alerts, one for each day. In this case, each alert works independently of the other so that events typically appear in both lists. For example, an event on Monday will appear in both the Tuesday and Thursday alerts.

So how does an alert get to you? SharePoint sends it to the e-mail address associated with your SharePoint user ID. Figure 5-26 shows an example of what a typical alert message looks like.

Figure 5-26. Sample alert sent to Outlook

■ **Note** While it is possible to modify the alert e-mails in SharePoint using the IAlertNotifyHandler interface, it requires coding knowledge that is outside the scope of this book.

Correcting/Modifying Alerts

If you make a mistake entering your alert or you just want to modify it, how can you change it? One way is to edit the alert. You can edit any alert from any list or library. Simply open the **List** or **Library** ribbon and click the lower portion of the **Alert Me** button in the **Share & Track** group. Select the option **Manage My Alerts** to display a page with all your current alerts. Note that this list of alerts includes alerts from other libraries or lists. Therefore, as mentioned above, it is important to include the name of the list or library in the name of your alert.

To change one of the alerts, click on the alert name. This displays the alert dialog with its current property settings. You can change any of these settings and click the OK button at the top or bottom of this window to update your alert definition. You also see a Delete button to the immediate left of the OK button. Click this button to remove this alert. You may start by adding alerts to many different libraries and lists in different sites. Soon, however, you may receive so many alerts that it takes much too long to review all the changes. That is a good time to review your current alerts and delete the ones you no longer need. Perhaps you could even change the frequency with which you receive alert notifications.

You can find a second way to delete your obsolete alerts back on the page that listed all your alerts. Notice that you can select any of your alerts using the check boxes in the left column. Select the alerts you no longer need and click the option **Delete Selected Alerts** from the header of the alerts list.

Finally, if you are a site administrator, you can eliminate an alert from any user by following these steps:

1. Select the **Site Settings** option after clicking the **Site Actions** button.

2. Select **User Alerts** from the **Site Administration** section. You must have administration rights to the site to see and select these options. If you do not, you must contact your administrator for his assistance.

3. In the **Display Alerts For** drop-down, select the **User ID/Name** of the person from whom you want to delete an alert and click the **Update** button to show her alerts.

■ **Note** Only users with alerts appear in this drop-down list. In addition, you can only delete these alerts, not modify them.

---

4. From the list of alerts, find the one you want to remove and click the check box to the left of the alert name. You can select multiple alerts for the person by selecting the respective check boxes.

5. Click the **Delete Selected Alerts** link at the top of the list to remove the chosen alerts.

Figure 5-27 shows the **User Alerts** page with a few alerts selected. Notice the value of using unique names here to identify which alerts to delete, especially when multiple alerts exist for the same list.

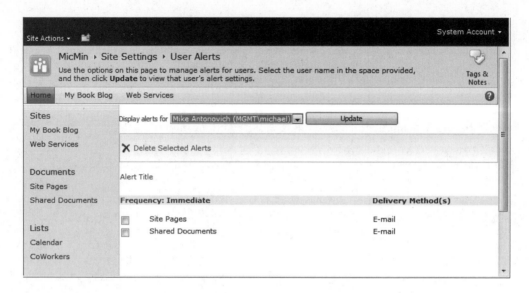

Figure 5-27. Dialog box for deleting alerts

■ **Tip** It's good practice to name alerts by the list they apply to, the events they track, and perhaps even their delivery schedule.

Using Outlook's RSS Reader to Subscribe to SharePoint RSS Feeds

Both Internet Explorer and Outlook 2007 have an RSS aggregator that displays links to your subscribed RSS feeds directly from their respective menus.

Adding an RSS Feed to Internet Explorer 7.0

To add a new RSS feed, navigate to a page in a SharePoint site that supports RSS. You can easily identify those sites by looking at the RSS feed icon in Internet Explorer 7.0's menu bar. Figure 5-28 shows the RSS feed icon.

Figure 5-28. The RSS feed icon used in Internet Explorer and web pages

Turning RSS On and Off Is a Three-Step Process

Step 1: Before you can turn RSS on for any list or library, you must first turn on RSS for the entire site. To do this, ask your site administrator to go into **Central Administration** and select **Manage Web Applications** from the **Application Management** group. Then click on the name of your web application (by default, this could be **SharePoint – 80**) to select the web application you want to set properties. Then from the **General Settings** drop-down menu in the **Manage** group of the **Web Applications** ribbon, select **General Settings**. Scroll through the displayed dialog to find the **RSS Settings** section and select **Yes** to enable the RSS feeds. In a similar fashion, you can turn off all RSS feeds for a site by selecting **No** as the RSS Setting.

Step 2: If you are the Site Administrator for your site, you can perform the next step. If you are not, you will need to solicit the help of your Site Administrator. Go to **Site Actions ➤ Site Settings**. Next, click **RSS** in the **Site Administration** group. Here you can turn RSS feeds on for the site collection, but only if RSS feeds have already been turned on for the web application that contains the site. You can also specify addition attributes of the RSS feed such as Copyright, Managing Editor and Web Master.

Step 3: Once you have turned on RSS at the Web Application level and at the site level, you can turn it on for individual lists or libraries. To do this, open the list from the list or library and click on **List Settings** or **Library Settings**. In the **Communications** section near the top of the settings page, click on **RSS settings**. On the resulting page, you can turn RSS on or off for the current list or library. You also can specify parameters that define options such as which columns to display to users trying to subscribe to your RSS feed as well as the number of items to include and the maximum number of days to include the item in the RSS feed.

When Internet Explorer displays this icon in orange, one or more elements on the page support an RSS feed. By clicking the down arrow to the right of the icon, the drop-down displays the page components that support the RSS feed. Figure 5-29 shows the **Calendar** page from a SharePoint site with an enabled RSS feed.

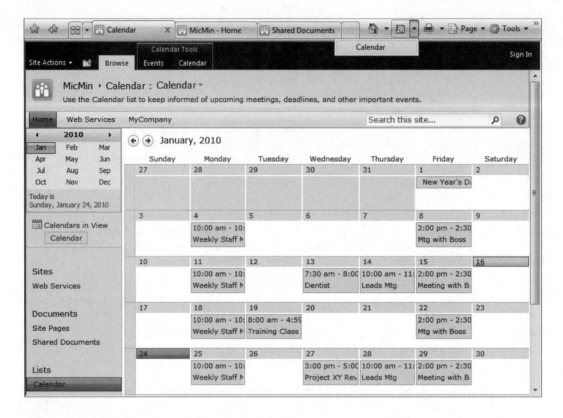

Figure 5-29. Calendar page with an active RSS feed

If the page only has a single RSS feed component, you can select it by either clicking it in this drop-down list or simply clicking the RSS icon itself. In either case, SharePoint displays a window containing information about the feed, as shown in Figure 5-30. The upper-left portion of this window identifies the source of the feed using the site name and the library name separated with a colon. The box on the right displays the number of items available in the list or library and lets you sort these items by date, title, or author. Beneath these two areas appear the current items in the list.

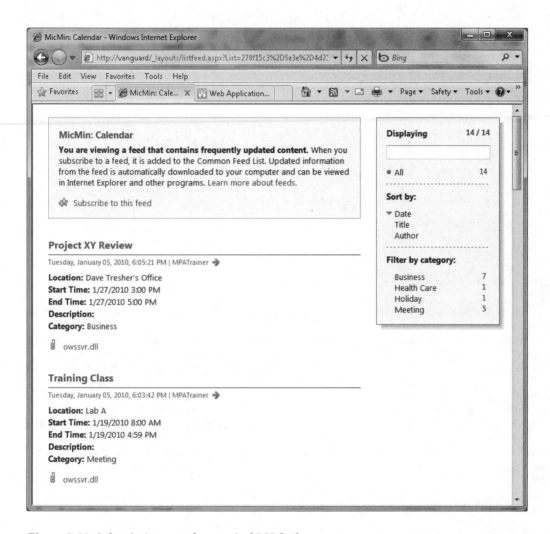

Figure 5-30. Subscription page for a typical RSS feed

To view RSS settings within Internet Explorer, go to **Tools ➤ Internet Options**. Then click the **Content** tab followed by clicking the **Settings** button in the **Feeds and Web Slices** area at the bottom of this dialog. This opens a dialog with several settings. You probably want to select a schedule of at least once a day to check your feeds. You also want to automatically mark feeds as read, turn on feed reading view, and turn on in-page Web Slice discovery. These settings are shown in Figure 5-31.

Figure 5-31. Feed and Web Slice settings

To subscribe, you could click the link **Subscribe to this feed**. While this option adds the feed to your **Favorites Center** in Internet Explorer, it may not add it to Outlook directly (see the upcoming section "Adding an RSS Feed to Outlook 2007 and 2010"). When you click the **Subscribe to this feed** link, Internet Explorer displays the subscription box, which requires the feed name and the location where you want to create the feed. By default, the feed name combines the site name and the library or list name separated by a colon. If you have never created an RSS subscription before, the **Create In** text box displays the Feeds folder. You can add your subscription directly to this top-level folder, or you can first create a new folder under **Feeds**. Of course, when you add a new folder, you can name it something appropriate to the type of feeds you intend to store in it. Figure 5-32 shows that three folders exist under **Feeds**, and you have selected the third folder, `SharePoint Book Feeds`, to hold the new subscription.

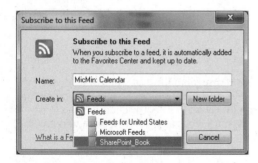

Figure 5-32. Setting properties when subscribing to an RSS feed

After you have specified a name and a folder in which to store your feed, click the **Subscribe** button. After a few moments, Internet Explorer creates the feed and displays a confirmation dialog box. This dialog box looks similar to the one shown previously in Figure 5-30, but with the **Subscribe to this feed** link changed to **View my feeds**. You can either click this link to view your feeds or click the **Favorites** button in the Internet Explorer button bar to display the **Favorites Center**. Normally, the center displays your web site favorites. However, at the top of the list, you will find the **Feeds** button. When you click this button, the center displays your subscribed feeds as shown in Figure 5-33.

Figure 5-33. RSS feeds shown in the Feeds section of Outlook's Favorites Center

Adding an RSS Feed to Outlook

You can save yourself a lot of time by letting the feeds added in IE automatically populate the feeds list in Outlook. If you want IE and Outlook to share RSS feeds, and you add a feed to IE 7.0 or better and it does not update Outlook, follow these steps:

1. Go to the **File** menu of Outlook.

2. Click **Options** to display the **Options** dialog box.

3. Click the **Advanced** option in the **General** section.

4. On the **Advanced Options** page, find the option **SynchronizeShare RSS Feeds to the Common Feed List (CFL) in Windows** in the **RSS Feeds** section and make sure that you select the check box.

5. Close Outlook and reopen it.

If you don't want to populate the RSS feeds in Outlook automatically with the feeds from IE 7.0, you must manually add RSS feeds to Outlook. There are several ways to do this. However, the fastest method is after you create the RSS subscription in Internet Explorer, you can use that feed link directly as found in the **Favorites Center**. When you finish defining a new feed or when you click one of your existing feeds, Internet Explorer opens a page with the current RSS items.

You may not have noticed that the text in your browser's URL field at the top of this page displays the feed link. You can also copy this URL to the clipboard. Then as before, right-click **RSS Feeds in Outlook** as shown in Figure 5-34, select **Add a New RSS Feed**, and paste the copied URL into the dialog box that appears.

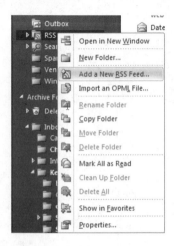

Figure 5-34. Add a New RSS Feed to Outlook's RSS Feeds

In the dialog box that Outlook displays next, you can paste the URL you copied from Internet Explorer. Then click **Add**, as shown in Figure 5-35.

Figure 5-35. Items displays from an RSS feed in Outlook

Outlook recognizes that this subscription link could be a potential risk to your system and prompts you with another dialog box asking whether you know and trust the site from which the feed originates. If you do, as in this case, you would click **Yes**. Otherwise, click **No**. After a few moments, Outlook connects to the RSS source using the supplied URL and populates your new RSS feed folder, as shown in Figure 5-36.

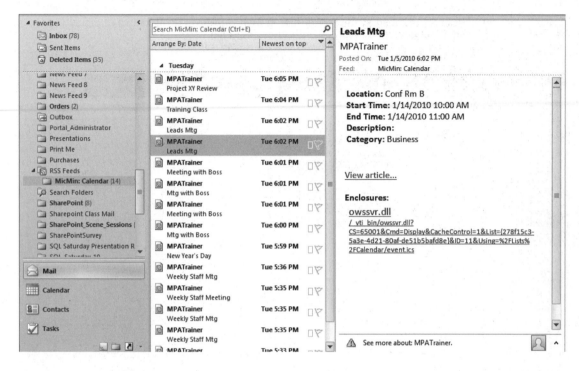

Figure 5-36. Items displays from an RSS feed in Outlook

Notice that each item in the calendar appears as a separate entry in this Outlook folder. If you click the **Arrange by** button at the top of the list, you can sort the items by any of the columns in the calendar list. You can also group the items based on the sort.

Since an RSS feed automatically updates the items shown in the subscription and bolds any item you have not yet opened, you can easily spot new items added to the list. After you open an item to view it, the text in the Outlook list reverts to normal for that item.

Deleting Items from an RSS Feed

You can delete items from the Outlook RSS list by right-clicking them and selecting **Delete**.
Unlike other lists, this has no effect on the subscription's source. However, if you really want to delete the item, you can click it to display a preview of the item and then perform one of the following actions:

- Click the link **View article** from the preview pane.

- Click the option **View Article** from the **RSS** group of the **Home** ribbon.

In either case, these actions display the SharePoint item in your browser as shown in Figure 5-37. This form uses the default view form for columns in a SharePoint list.

Figure 5-37. View form for an item's properties

At the top of this form, you have the standard options to edit or delete the current item using the **View** ribbon, assuming you have these permissions for list items in the current site. If you delete the item here, SharePoint asks you to confirm that you want to send the item to the Recycle Bin. If you click **OK**, SharePoint deletes the item from the list, but it may still appear in the RSS subscription in Outlook, at least until the next synchronization.

As with other deleted items, you can recover items deleted within SharePoint. Go to the **Recycle Bin**, select the item you want to recover, and click the **Restore Selection** button.

When viewing an RSS feed to a document library, this method still begins by showing the properties of the individual library item, as shown in Figure 5-38. To view the document associated with the item, click the document name. In this figure, clicking **Background to install SharePoint** retrieves the document from SharePoint and opens a local copy of it.

Figure 5-38. Viewing an item from a document library through an RSS feed

---

■ **Tip** Don't want the RSS feed anymore? Just right-click it and select **Delete**. If you delete the RSS feed from Outlook, it does not delete it from Internet Explorer. However, if you want to add the RSS feed back to Outlook, you may need to use the manual method discussed earlier in this section.

Viewing Other List Items Not in the RSS Feed

Remember that the RSS feed will only display relatively recent additions to the reference list or library. You will not necessarily see all the documents in the RSS feed.

■ **Note** You can specify how long documents or list items remain in the RSS feed by going to the library or list in SharePoint and selecting **Library Settings** or **List Settings** from the **Settings** group of the **Library** or **List** ribbon respectively. Then on the **Settings** page, select **RSS settings** from the **Communications** option group. On the **RSS Settings** page, find the section labeled **Item limit** at the bottom of the page.

By selecting any one item and displaying its edit page, you can navigate to the full list or library. With the item's edit page open, select the **Browse** tab at the top of the page. Then find the list or library name in the breadcrumbs. Typically, the entry immediately before the name of the current item represents the list or library from which the entry originates. Click this name to display the full list or library. From this page, you can then open and edit any item in the list or library, even those no longer referenced in the RSS feed. You can also use the Navigate Up icon to the immediate right of the Site Actions button to display the site hierarchy and return to the list or library.

■ **Tip** For libraries or lists that add new items only occasionally, you may want to limit the RSS feed based on the number of items displayed so that the list feed is never empty. If item additions occur frequently, consider using the maximum day option to determine how many items to display in the feed so that the feed stays fresh.

Sending E-mail to Lists

In this chapter, I've demonstrated several ways to use Outlook to connect to various lists and libraries in SharePoint. You also saw that SharePoint could send e-mail messages when someone adds items to a list, changes items in a list, or deletes items from a list. However, you can also send e-mail messages to groups of SharePoint users as well as several of SharePoint's lists.

Sending a Message to a List or Library

Not all SharePoint lists can receive e-mail, and even those that do handle it in different ways. Lists that can accept e-mail include

- Announcements

- Blogs

- Calendars

- Discussion boards

- Document libraries

- Form libraries

- Picture libraries

The ability to send e-mail to these lists depends on the settings your SharePoint administrator applied in the SharePoint Central Administration site. It also depends on settings added to your lists when your site administrator created the site and its lists. To enable and configure e-mail at the list or library level, you must have the **Manage Lists** permission. Site owners have this permission by default. Thus, even though these lists have the potential of receiving e-mail as defined at the site level, their current configuration may not allow receiving e-mails.

To determine whether your list can receive e-mail messages, first check the site settings for the list, assuming you have the appropriate rights. Alternatively, check with the site administrator to ask whether the list supports e-mail and what e-mail address you must use to send content to the list.

How to Enable E-mail

To add e-mail support to a SharePoint site, your SharePoint administrator must enable e-mail support at the web application level in the SharePoint's **Central Administration** site. In Central Administration, they need to navigate to the **System Settings** page and then select **Configure incoming e-mail settings** in the **E-Mail and Text Messages** section. Your SharePoint administrator is responsible for specifying these settings and they may need to work with your Exchange people to properly configure all the settings.

Next, you enable e-mail by defining an e-mail link for individual site lists and libraries that you want to receive e-mail by going to their **Settings** page and selecting **Incoming e-mail settings** from the **Communications** option group. If this option does not appear, you must see your SharePoint administrator to first turn on e-mail support as defined in the previous paragraph. Either you do not have the necessary permissions to configure this setting or you must have your administrator turn e-mail on through the **Central Administration** site.

■ **Tip** If you have the right to update lists, you should consider adding the e-mail address to the list description if you have e-mail enabled the list. Because the description text appears immediately beneath the list title when displayed in SharePoint, this practice might reduce the number of calls you will get asking for the e-mail addresses of your lists.

To enable a list or library to accept e-mail, you must open the Settings page for that list or library. Then click the option **Incoming e-mail settings** in the **Communications** group. Figure 5-39 shows these settings for a typical list/library. In the first section, **Incoming e-mail**, you must enable e-mail for the list or library. Without this setting, the list or library cannot receive e-mail. In addition, you must identify a specific e-mail address so that SharePoint can route the e-mail to the correct list or library.

Next, you must identify what to do with any attachments in the **E-mail attachment** section. For document, picture, and form libraries, the attachment is the file that you want to add to the library. For most lists, the content you want to add to the list is in the e-mail body, not the attachment, but you can optionally archive the e-mail attachments in the list as well. For most libraries, the **E-mail message** section lets you decide whether you want to save the e-mail itself as another item in the library. For many lists, you can save the e-mail as an attachment.

The **E-mail security** section let you determine whether the library or list can only accept e-mails set to it by users who have update rights to the library or list. This particular option can be useful to prevent spam.

The site at http://office.microsoft.com/en-us/help/HA100823071033.aspx provides details on setting up e-mail for several different types of libraries and lists. The content was written for SharePoint 2007, but it still applies to sending e-mail to SharePoint 2010 libraries and lists.

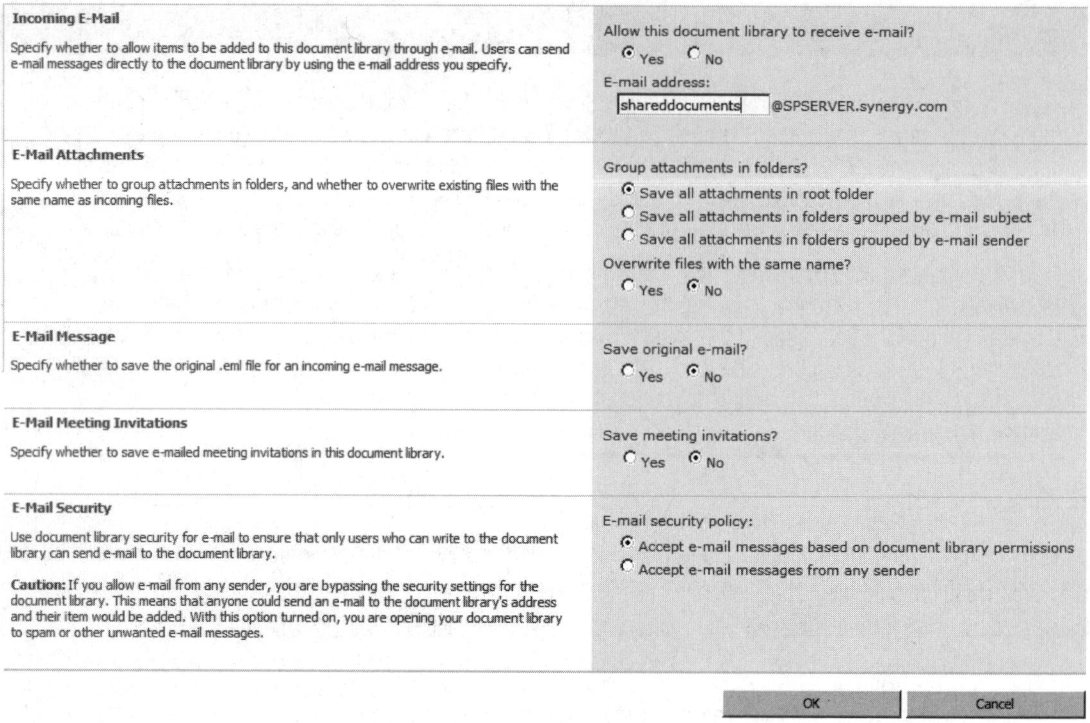

Incoming E-Mail

Specify whether to allow items to be added to this document library through e-mail. Users can send e-mail messages directly to the document library by using the e-mail address you specify.

Allow this document library to receive e-mail?
◉ Yes   ○ No
E-mail address:
[shareddocuments]   @SPSERVER.synergy.com

E-Mail Attachments

Specify whether to group attachments in folders, and whether to overwrite existing files with the same name as incoming files.

Group attachments in folders?
◉ Save all attachments in root folder
○ Save all attachments in folders grouped by e-mail subject
○ Save all attachments in folders grouped by e-mail sender
Overwrite files with the same name?
○ Yes   ◉ No

E-Mail Message

Specify whether to save the original .eml file for an incoming e-mail message.

Save original e-mail?
○ Yes   ◉ No

E-Mail Meeting Invitations

Specify whether to save e-mailed meeting invitations in this document library.

Save meeting invitations?
○ Yes   ◉ No

E-Mail Security

Use document library security for e-mail to ensure that only users who can write to the document library can send e-mail to the document library.

Caution: If you allow e-mail from any sender, you are bypassing the security settings for the document library. This means that anyone could send an e-mail to the document library's address and their item would be added. With this option turned on, you are opening your document library to spam or other unwanted e-mail messages.

E-mail security policy:
◉ Accept e-mail messages based on document library permissions
○ Accept e-mail messages from any sender

[OK]   [Cancel]

Figure 5-39. Viewing an item from a document library through an RSS feed

After you determine whether a list supports e-mail, create a new message in Outlook. You can place the list e-mail address in either the **To** or the **Cc** field. You can send the message to one or more lists, people, or groups from a single message entry. Then refer to Table 5-2 to see how to add content to the lists via your message.

Table 5-2. Sending Content to a SharePoint List

List/Library	Where to Place Content
Announcements	Include your announcement text as an attachment. SharePoint takes your message title as the title of the announcement.
Blogs	Include your blog text in the main body of the message.
Calendars	Send a meeting request or appointment to the list.
Discussion boards	Include your text in the main body of the message.

List/Library	Where to Place Content
Document libraries	Include the document you want to add as an attachment to the e-mail.
Form libraries	Include the form you want to add as an attachment to the e-mail.
Picture libraries	Include the picture as an attachment to the e-mail.

If you want to send an e-mail with both a blog entry and a document file that you will reference within your blog, you can send both with a single e-mail. Include both the blog list and the document library list e-mail address in the **To** field of the message. SharePoint extracts the text from the main body of the message and sends it to the blog site while sending the attachment to the document library. It can do this because each list type can only accept information from specify parts of the e-mail message.

When you are ready to send your content, include the appropriate SharePoint e-mail address in the **To** or **Cc** box, and then click **Send**.

Sending Links via Send To

SharePoint can send a link for any document, image, or form to anyone via e-mail. You can find this option by opening the drop-down list for any item in a library or list. In the drop-down menu, point to **Send To** to open the secondary flyout menu. In this menu, select the option **E-mail a link**. This opens a normal e-mail message with the link to the item in the body of the message.

When the e-mail recipient receives the e-mail message, she can click the link to open and edit the document, resulting in a more efficient, smaller e-mail message than sending the entire file. The user may initially open a read-only version of the document pointed to by the link. However, she can choose to edit the document and of course save her changes back to SharePoint.

Summary

This chapter showed you several ways to use Outlook together with SharePoint, beginning with a look at organizing multiple contacts lists in different SharePoint sites with your Outlook contacts list. By adding links to two or more SharePoint contacts lists, you saw that you can copy and move contacts between any of the lists including the Outlook **Contacts** list itself.

In a similar way, you can use Outlook to consolidate multiple SharePoint calendars with your own Outlook calendar to plan your daily schedule as well as build SharePoint calendars by copying events from your Outlook calendar to them. Outlook lets you overlay two or more calendars so you can see when events conflict and when available time exists. It also shows the relative sequence of events from different calendars.

Next, you looked at combining tasks from multiple SharePoint lists within Outlook. As with contacts and calendars, the ability to consolidate information from multiple tasks lists helps ensure that you do not overlook events from one calendar.

Outlook also lets you work with documents as if they were e-mail messages. It supports the ability to check out documents so you can edit them offline and then resynchronize your changes with the original documents in SharePoint the next time you connect.

Alerts create a notification capability that lets you know when items are added, deleted, or modified in libraries and lists. You can also determine how frequently you want to see the alerts. By monitoring changes within SharePoint libraries and lists, alerts save you a tremendous amount of time that you would otherwise need to spend monitoring each of the libraries and lists for pertinent or interesting changes.

SharePoint libraries and lists have the ability to support RSS feeds as a way to distribute news, blogs, library, list additions, and other information feeds. Recent versions of both IE and Outlook have built-in RSS readers and support independent RSS feed lists, or you can synchronize the feeds that appear in both programs using the **Common Feeds** list.

Finally, you can send e-mails to most blogs, lists, and libraries to update information stored in them. This may require some additional configuration from your SharePoint administrator in both the **Central Administration** site as well as the communication settings of the individual libraries and lists to which you want to send e-mail updates. You can also send an e-mail to others with the URL of an item in a library or list. The recipient of that e-mail can then click that link to open and edit that item without taxing your e-mail servers with large file transfers.

Thus, you can see that Outlook provides many ways to work with several SharePoint features organize your work and personal activities. Outlook can change the way you work with documents, lists, and tasks. It can help you share your thoughts through discussions and blogs. You can use the combination of alerts, RSS feeds, and Outlook to stay informed about changes to lists and libraries.

CHAPTER 6

■ ■ ■

Managing Lists with Access

Many companies have hundreds of unmanaged Access applications running in various departments throughout the organization. While many Office power users find it very easy to create an Access application to quickly meet a need, often those applications suffer from problems like:

"I just looked away a minute and when I turned back my laptop, which I left on the seat beside me in the waiting area, was gone, along with all of our customer order data."

"All I know is that the screen says that it cannot read my C-drive. You do have a backup of my C-drive, don't you?"

"These reports don't match, and I know that my data is correct, so your data must be wrong."

These are just a few of the problems you may encounter when users build important databases on their local machines. Everything from security issues that may or may not involve theft of hardware, simple hardware failure, and inconsistent results caused by duplicate data residing in different databases can ruin your day quickly.

While Access has provided a high level of agility by allowing individuals to build applications quickly, the problems with managing those applications have grown. However, you can get a handle on managing the interface to those applications as well as the data by using Access along with SharePoint.

In this chapter, you will see how using Access stored in a central SharePoint library can provide for a single version of the application interface while making it easy to deploy new upgrades to the application. Also, by storing the data in a SharePoint list, you can leverage SharePoint's ability to link with Access tables to support a single version of the data, provide for a single place to create backups, and protect the data with permissions while providing physical security by storing the data in a centrally located server back in your company headquarters.

In chapter 1, I mentioned that SharePoint includes five default Access web applications as templates: Assets Web Database, Charitable Contributions, Contacts Web Database, Issues Web Database, and Project Web Database. While any or all of these might serve as a starting point for a web application at your organization, you can also use them to develop a web based application via Access to provide an agile development platform. Since these applications require Access services to run, you will need the Enterprise version of SharePoint 2010 to create and use them.

I stated in the beginning of Chapter 2 that you could think of lists in terms used by database systems: items represent rows, and columns represent fields. This chapter will prove how well SharePoint lists translate into databases by demonstrating how you can manage your lists and databases applications using a combination of Microsoft Access and SharePoint.

■ **Note** This text focuses on Access 2010, and while much of what is discussed works with Access 2007, earlier versions of Access do not support the features related to publishing Access Services on the Enterprise edition of SharePoint Server 2010.

Exporting SharePoint Lists to Access

To export a SharePoint list into Access, you can start from SharePoint or Access. Let's first start from SharePoint. Navigate to your SharePoint site, and open the list you want to export. From the **List** ribbon, click **Open with Access** from the **Connect & Export** group as shown in Figure 6-1.

Figure 6-1. Exporting a SharePoint table to Access

A message box, shown in Figure 6-2, prompts you for two pieces of information. First, you must specify a location and name for a new or existing database. Access stores each database as a separate file. Further, it can store the file in any directory. By default, SharePoint and Windows 7 attempts to create a database in your user Documents folder. Also by default, SharePoint wants to use the list name as the database and the table name. You can change either of these defaults by entering a different file name and/or path. You can also use the **Browse** button to locate a different directory. However, you may find the real advantage of the **Browse** button occurs when you need to find an existing database into which you want to add the current SharePoint list.

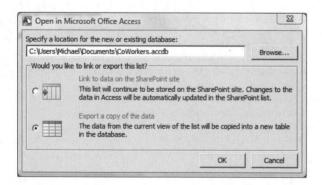

Figure 6-2. You can either export a copy of a SharePoint list to Access or create a link to the list in Access.

If you select an existing database with a different database name than your list, SharePoint still tries to name at least the table in that database with the list name. However, if the database name exists already in the selected directory, SharePoint appends a "1" to the end of the default database name. If a database already exists with that new name, it keeps trying the next sequential number until it finds a valid yet unique database name for the directory. If you attempt to overwrite the default database name that SharePoint selects and try to export the SharePoint list to an existing database name, SharePoint will try to add the selected table to the existing database. If that database already has a table with that name, it will append a "1" to the end of the database name to make it unique. If you attempt to save the same list to the same database again, it adds a new table with the next sequential number to make it unique. Of course, you could override this automatically generated name and save the database with your own unique name. However, you cannot overwrite the table name from this dialog. The important point is that the export option never lets you replace an existing table or database.

So how do you replace an existing Access table in a given Access database with the updated contents of the same SharePoint list? The simple way would be to delete the Access table first, and then export the SharePoint list. This may not always be feasible if you previously established links to other Access tables or use the table as a data source for view definitions, reports, or forms within Access. You have several programmatic alternatives at this point, the details of which are beyond the scope of this book. Most begin by opening the SharePoint list in Access using a table with a different name. Then you can update the original table from the second table using SQL statements.

■ **Note** In this section, I am talking about copying a SharePoint list to Access, not linking the list to an Access table, which is covered in the "Linking SharePoint Lists to Access" section of this chapter.

If you prefer not to manipulate the table with SQL, you can modify the connection properties of each object that uses the original table to point to the new table. The risk here of missing a reference to the original table may be high depending on the complexity of your database.

Synchronizing the Data in Two Versions of an Access Table

Suppose you have two tables called Table1 and Table2, in which Table2 is a more recent copy of Table1 and has changes in it that Table1 does not have. How can you programmatically synchronize the changes from Table2 back to Table1?

From within Access, you can quickly update Table1 to look exactly like Table2 if you make a few assumptions. First, assume that if Table1 and Table2 use any other related tables for lookup values, nothing in those tables has changed that would require those tables to be updated first. Second, assume that Table1 uses a unique ID field consisting of perhaps a sequential number and that its value has no additional meaning other than to define the rows of the table uniquely. Third, both tables have the same column definitions.

The first step updates all of the fields in Table1 with values from Table2 where the unique ID field in Table1 equals Table2. The complexity of this SQL UPDATE expression comes from the SET clause, which must include an expression for every field in the table.

```
UPDATE Table1
INNER JOIN Table2
ON Table1.ID = Table2.ID
SET Table1.[Field1] = [Table2].[Field1],
Table1.[Field2] = [Table2].[Field2],
Table1.[Field3] = [Table2].[Field3];
```

Next, you eliminate any records in Table1 that do not have a corresponding ID value in Table2.

```
DELETE *
FROM Table1
WHERE Table1.ID NOT IN (SELECT Table2.ID FROM Table2);
```

Finally, you add any records from Table2 that do not exist in Table1.

```
INSERT INTO Table1
SELECT *
FROM Table2
WHERE Table2.ID NOT IN (SELECT Table1.ID FROM Table1);
```

At this point, the data in Table1 should exactly match the data in Table2.

■ **Tip** To change the Access table used by a form, open the **Property Sheet** for the form. Click the **Data** tab and then locate the **Record Source** property. Open the drop-down list for this field and select the new table.

■ **Caution** If you update an object such as a report or form with a new record source, beware of fields deleted or renamed from the original table schema. This can cause the form to fail unless you remove such fields from the form or table or associate it with a different table field.

Getting back to the second decision you must make in Figure 6-2, you must decide whether you want to link the SharePoint list data with the Access table or export a copy of the list data to the table. The main advantage of linking data from Access to SharePoint involves editing. When you link the list and table, changes made to a record/item in Access automatically update the SharePoint list. Linking your SharePoint list to Access eliminates the complexity caused by list updates when you only export a copy of the list to Access.

There are other advantages of linking the SharePoint list to an Access table. However, first let's continue to look at what happens when you copy the list to an Access table.

After you click **OK** in Figure 6-2, SharePoint takes a few moments to transfer the selected columns to Access. After completing the transfer, Access opens and displays the new table, as shown in Figure 6-3.

■ **Note** In Access 2010, you may need to double-click the table name in the list of Access Table Objects to open the table.

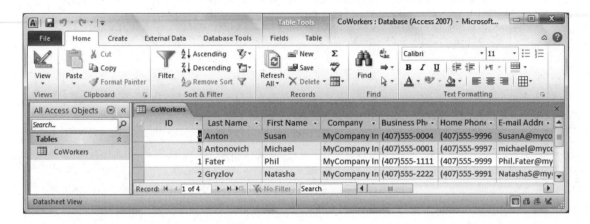

Figure 6-3. SharePoint list shown as an Access table

Notice that when copying a SharePoint list to Access, only the rows and fields included in the SharePoint view appear in the table. Thus, you can use a custom view to determine not only the items/rows transferred to Access, but also the columns/fields transferred.

■ **Tip** Use the **copy data** option when you want to archive selected items from the list. To perform the archive, first define a new view in SharePoint to filter on the records you want to archive. Then switch to this view when you display the list. This view does not have to be the default view, but it must be the current view. Then select **Open with Access** as before, selecting **Export a copy of the data**. Place this data in a database where you want to store archived data. You could use a different database each time you download the list, perhaps including the date to identify the archived date range, or you could add sequentially numbered tables or tables that include a date in the name for a single archived database.

After transferring the data, you can save the database in one of the more recent Access data formats:

- Access 2007

- Access 2002–2003

- Access 2000—(Only indirectly possible since you could create a blank database using the Access 2000 format if you went into **Access Options** (from the **File** menu) and changed the Default file format for **Blank Databases** in the **General** page of the options to Access 2000.)

■ **Note** While there does not seem to be a selection for defining whether to save your database in Access 2007 or Access 2010 format, there are some differences between databases created by each of these versions of Access. In fact, depending on the features of Access 2010 you use, Access 2007 may not open the saved database. This is especially true of any web related features you might use in Access 2010 in preparation to publishing the database to SharePoint, but other changes can also affect your ability to open your Access 2010 database in Access 2007. For complete details on the features that can cause you problems and steps on how to resolve those problems, refer to the following article on Microsoft's MSDN site: `http://msdn.microsoft.com/en-us/office/ cc907897.aspx`.

Thus, you can share list data with those unfortunate associates who do not have access to your SharePoint site.

However, what if, after you copy data to an Access table, you decide to transfer it back to SharePoint? Can you do that? Yes, you can export data from Access not only to Excel, but also to a SharePoint list.

Figure 6-4 shows the Access's **External Data** Ribbon. Within the **Export** section, find the button **More** and select **SharePoint List** from the drop-down menu of additional options.

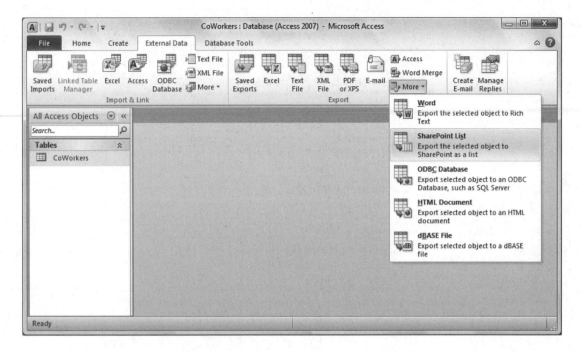

Figure 6-4. External Data tab in the Access Ribbon

When you click this button, a dialog box opens. You must first specify the name of the SharePoint site where you want to publish the data. In Figure 6-5, I have selected the site address `http://vanguard`, the URL of the top-level site of my SharePoint server.

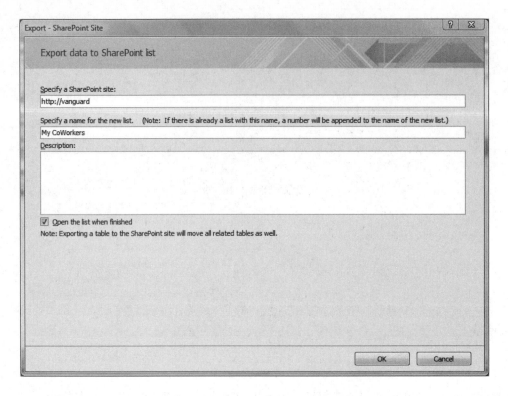

Figure 6-5. The dialog box prompts for SharePoint site and list names

Next, you must specify the name of the list into which you want to copy the Access data. Note that you can only export your Access table to a new SharePoint list. If you attempt to specify the name of an existing list, SharePoint adds "_1" to the end of the list name. If SharePoint already has a list with "_1" at the end of the name, it adds it again making it "_1_1".

■ **Note** This naming convention is different from that used when copying data from SharePoint to Access.

In addition, the check box at the bottom of this figure lets you immediately open the new list after you create it. Personally, I like to see the list after creating it to verify that everything transferred correctly. It's a "Trust but Verify" rule I encourage developers to adopt. If you feel lucky and trust Access to transfer your table to a SharePoint list, I suppose you could leave this option unchecked.

The note at the bottom of this screen informs you that Access exports any tables related to the exported table to their own SharePoint lists. In fact, not only does Access upload all related tables to individual SharePoint lists, but SharePoint also automatically converts the foreign key fields in the parent table to lookup type fields to ensure that the user can select values only from the child table. In addition, SharePoint 2010 now supports true referential integrity. If you defined referential integrity between your tables in Access, the process of exporting the tables to SharePoint retains your referential integrity settings between the lists.

For example, suppose you have two tables in Access. The first table, **Departments**, lists each department in your organization with related information about that department, such as the department name, department head, and perhaps the department's primary phone number. In the second table, **CoWorkers**, you list employees in your organization. Besides the obvious fields such as the employee's name, phone numbers, start date, and others, you include the department from the **Departments** table. Let's also assume that you have formalized this relationship between these two tables using the **DeptID** column in both tables. First, you should define the relationship between the two tables defining which fields from each table should define the line.

Tip: The column name in the two linked tables does not have to be the same. However, I recommend using the same column name for a field found in any table if it represents the same data in the same format with the same values.

After you define the relationship between the two tables, you can then go back and modify the table definition of the child table, CoWorkers, to define the lookup properties of the linking column.

■ **Caution** Just defining the department field in CoWorkers to be a lookup field from the Departments table is not really defining referential integrity. You need to define the relation formally between the two tables in Access.

When you attempt to export just the **CoWorkers** table to SharePoint as a new list, SharePoint recognizes the relationship between the **CoWorkers** and **Departments** tables and uploads both tables as new lists on the selected site. Opening the **CoWorkers** list settings, you can see that the **DeptID** field definition uses a lookup field type that points to the **DeptID** field in the **Departments** list. Furthermore, since you defined referential integrity while in Access, you should find the same relationship defined in the **Relationship** section of the **DeptID** column. If you selected to cascade deleted records from the primary table to the child table in Access, SharePoint adopts this same property between the uploaded lists.

Saving Your Export Steps

When you click **OK**, another dialog box, shown in Figure 6-6, appears asking whether you want to save your export steps.

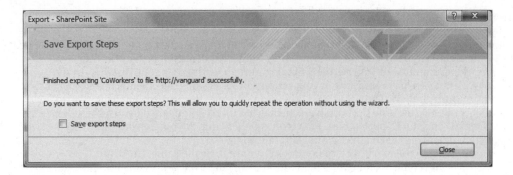

Figure 6-6. *Prompting to save export steps*

If you plan to perform this export only one time, you may not want to select this option. If, however, you think you might perform this task frequently, you may want to save these steps. If you select this option, Access displays the dialog box shown in Figure 6-7.

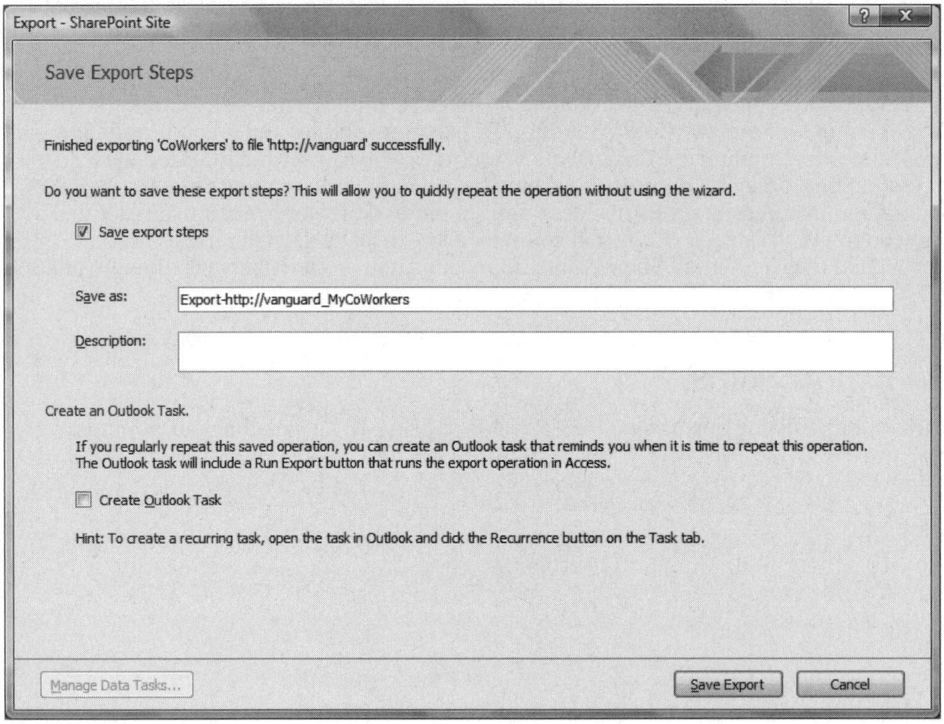

Figure 6-7. *Defining the name and description of the export steps*

This Access dialog box asks you to enter a name and a description to identify your export steps. You must enter a name, because Access uses this name to identify this set of export steps from others you may define, as you will see shortly. While Access considers the description optional, it appears in Access's list showing available exports and can help further identify different exports.

You also have the option of creating an Outlook task. While you cannot rerun the export directly from this task, you can use the task as a reminder to run the export on a future date. You can even set up a reoccurring reminder to run the task periodically.

When you click **Save Export**, SharePoint performs the export, creates the saved steps in Access, and creates the task in Outlook. This process shows another example of the power of SharePoint and Office integration, as it updates three separate MS Office products with one action.

Transfer Issues

When you return to Access, you may see another table in the **Navigation Bar** called **Move to SharePoint Site Issues**. Open this table to examine any problems with the export to SharePoint. Figure 6-8 shows the issues generated when moving the **My Work Contacts** table back to SharePoint.

Issue	Reason	Object Type	Object Name	Field Name
Field values will not be auto-generated.	SharePoint only supports AutoNumber for their ID field.	Table	CoWorkers	ID
Field will not be moved.	Certain fields (like 'binary' fields and SharePoint 'read-only'	Table	CoWorkers	Encoded Absol
Field will not be moved.	Certain fields (like 'binary' fields and SharePoint 'read-only'	Table	CoWorkers	Item Type
Field will not be moved.	Certain fields (like 'binary' fields and SharePoint 'read-only'	Table	CoWorkers	Path
Field will not be moved.	Certain fields (like 'binary' fields and SharePoint 'read-only'	Table	CoWorkers	URL Path
Field will not be moved.	Certain fields (like 'binary' fields and SharePoint 'read-only'	Table	CoWorkers	Workflow Insta
Field will not be moved.	Certain fields (like 'binary' fields and SharePoint 'read-only'	Table	CoWorkers	File Type

Figure 6-8. Issues generated when moving a table back to SharePoint

Issues with Auto Increment Fields

The first issue in this list refers to the field **ID**. In Access, this field is called an auto increment field because each time you add another record to the table, Access automatically increments by one the value used when it added the last record and uses this new value for the new record. While SharePoint will accept the values from this column when it converts the table to a SharePoint list, if your Access table has gaps in the auto increment field values (because you deleted items after creating the table entries), these gaps are closed in the generated SharePoint list. In other words, if you had a short list of 10 items and deleted item 5 from the Access table before uploading the table to SharePoint, SharePoint renumbers the items to fill in the gap using values from 1 through 9 rather than 1 through 10. It then will use 10 for the next value added in SharePoint.

Auto Increment Fields

Every table in relational databases should have a primary key. Most relational systems do not allow you to update existing individual data records without a primary or unique key to identify which record to update. When possible, you should always use existing table fields to create a "natural" key. However, at the same time, you should avoid long "natural" keys or keys that require the concatenation of many individual fields. One solution to long keys uses a "created" key called an *autonumber field*. Access uses this field type to create a unique integer field for each record. You should add this field to the table schema before adding any records to the table. In addition, only one field per table can be an auto increment field, and you cannot set a field to be auto increment after you defined the table even if you have not added data to the table.

The start value for a new table typically begins with 1, and each record added to the table increments this value by 1. While you can no longer use your own increment value in Access, you can use a Random value for the ID. However, a random generated ID value does not translate to SharePoint the same way as an auto increment will. While the ID field does transfer, it will not generate a new random ID for new values added in SharePoint. If you delete a record, the database does not reuse that number. In addition, auto increment fields generally cannot be edited.

In addition to serving as indexes, auto increment fields often make ideal choices as relational fields between tables. Since you cannot edit this field, you cannot easily break the referential link.

When used, the auto increment field should not imply any significance other than to provide a unique identifier for a record that may or may not also serve as a linking field between two tables.

Due to all of the preceding characteristics of auto increment fields, you normally cannot include this field when you copy a table with one of these fields to another table, regardless of whether you create a new table or intend to append to an existing table.

Surprisingly, the import of a list from SharePoint to Access does appear to import the ID field. You can prove this by taking an issue tracking list created in SharePoint and deleting a few items from the middle of the list. Then import the list into Access. If you open the Access table in design mode, you will discover that Access defined the ID field as an autonumber field. However, when you open the corresponding Access table, you will see a gap in the ID sequence exactly representing the positions of the deleted items from SharePoint.

However, exporting the table back to SharePoint does not transfer the autonumber field. If you were to export the issue table with the deleted records from the middle of the table, the new SharePoint list displays a new ID field with no gaps in the sequence. In other words, the transfer back to SharePoint reassigns new ID values to all items, closing the previous gap.

■ **Caution** Based on the way the SharePoint and Access treats the **ID** field when they transfer information back and forth, I would not recommend using the autoincrement **ID** field in the issue tracking list as a lookup field or a linking field to another list, because the values could change if someone exports the list to Access and then imports it back to SharePoint.

Issues with Validation Rules

The second transfer issue refers to a validation concern with the **Employee Number** field in the table **CoWorkers**. In SharePoint, this field has a maximum of five characters. When you export the list to Access, the SharePoint size restriction on the field becomes an Access validation rule. If you then export the table from Access back to SharePoint, SharePoint does not always convert the Access validation rule to a column validation formula, much less a Maximum number of characters setting.

Another issue refers to read-only fields that originated in the SharePoint list. While the transfer of the list to Access includes these fields, Access does not normally display them when displaying the table, although you can see them in the table's design view. As read-only fields that SharePoint generates for each list, Access cannot export these fields back to SharePoint.

■ **Caution** Review the issue list when you transfer an Access table back to a SharePoint list. Some issues you cannot do anything about. However, if the transfer drops validations that you need on fields, you should open the list settings and see whether the SharePoint column properties support a similar style of validation.

Transferring Referential Tables

Another example of issues that you may have previously encountered when you transferred data from Access back to SharePoint 2007 occurred when you had two or more related tables in Access. If you established referential integrity definitions between these tables, and you attempt to export them back to SharePoint, you observed one or more of the following issues:

- SharePoint 2007 had no way to enforce referential integrity.

- SharePoint 2007 could not block or cascade deletes to related records.

- SharePoint 2007 could not cascade updates to related records.

In SharePoint 2010, the move of tables from Access back to SharePoint does retain the referential relationship in the resulting SharePoint lists if you move all the tables at one time using the **SharePoint** command in the **Move Data** group of the **Database Tools** ribbon. However, for this to work correctly, you must explicitly reference each of the fields to be used as shown in Figure 6-9 and you must define the relationship between the tables as shown in Figure 6-10. These settings are also necessary if you want to publish your Access database successfully to SharePoint's Access Services, which I examine later in this chapter in the section "Deploying Your Access Application to SharePoint – Option 2."

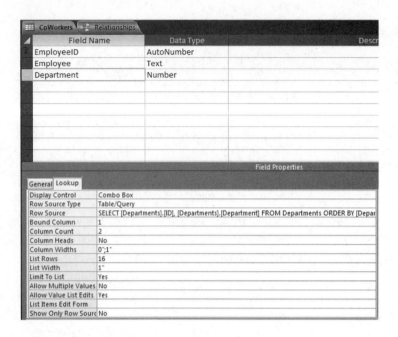

Figure 6-9. Defining the lookup query expression by explicitly naming fields

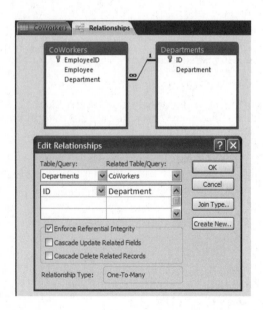

Figure 6-10. Defining the relationship between the tables before moving them to SharePoint

Dealing with Duplicate Lists

Figure 6-11 shows the lists in my SharePoint site. Notice that because I added the list **My Work Contacts** a second time, SharePoint adds a "_1" suffix to the list name to make it unique. I now have essentially two lists with the same name and content, less any minor changes made while in Access.

Figure 6-11. SharePoint lists after exporting tables back from Access

If this happens to you and you want to keep both lists, you should rename one of them to avoid confusion. However let's assume that you don't want to keep both. You could delete the original list and rename the new list back to the original name by deleting the "_1". This technique represents a manual way to update a SharePoint list using Access, but it can lead to problems if the original SharePoint list appears on web pages or if other lists reference it as a lookup because these references will point only to the URL of the original list, not to the new list. Therefore, a better way to deal with updates is to link the Access table to the SharePoint list so you can perform continuous synchronization between them. The "Linking SharePoint Lists to Access" section in this chapter explores this method.

The Outlook Task for the Export Steps

If you created a task in Outlook for the export steps earlier in this chapter, you can open your **Tasks** panel to see the task with the name you defined. In Figure 6-12, you can see that this task does not currently have a due date and has a status of **Not Started**.

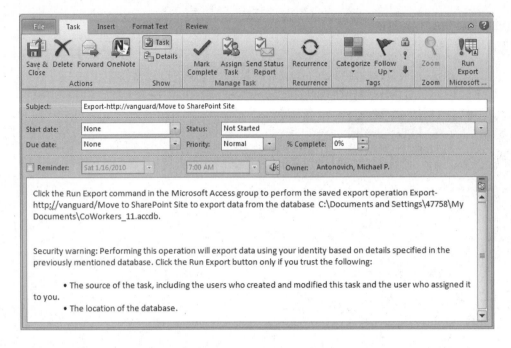

Figure 6-12. Details of the export task in Outlook

If Outlook did not automatically open the task when it created it, you can double-click it in your Outlook tasks list to view the details shown in Figure 6-12. You can now define a start date and a due date as well as set a reminder to perform the task. In the **Task** Ribbon, click the **Recurrence** option in the **Options** group to define a recurrence schedule if you must perform this export on a regular basis.

■ **Tip** You may want to set up tasks to remind you to archive old data from lists, such as issue tracking lists, to prevent such lists from growing too large with completed tasks, thereby degrading performance.

Unfortunately, you cannot run the export task directly from the Outlook task. However, Access automatically includes text in the task instructing you on how to execute the saved export operation from within Access.

Reusing Saved Export Steps

To execute a saved export, open Access and click the **External Data** tab of the **Access** Ribbon. In the **Export** group, click the **Saved Exports** option to display a window like the one shown in Figure 6-13.

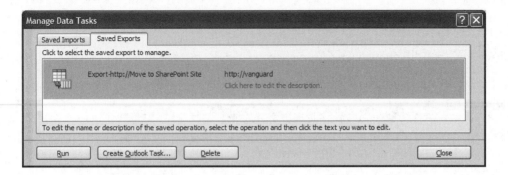

Figure 6-13. Saved Exports tab in the Manage Data Tasks dialog box in Access

In this tabbed window, you can see all your saved imports and exports. Click the **Saved Exports** tab and select the export you want to run. Notice that you can create an Outlook task from here if you did not do so when you created the original export. You can also delete any of the saved exports you no longer need as well as edit the name or the description of the saved export by clicking its respective text. If you did not include a description when you originally saved the export, click beneath the SharePoint server name on the text **Click here to edit the description**. A text box appears in which you can enter a description.

Importing a SharePoint List Directly from Access

You began this section by exporting the SharePoint list by opening the list in SharePoint. However, you can perform the same operation directly from Access without first going to SharePoint. Start by opening Access and then follow these steps:

1. If you get the **Getting Started** screen, select **Blank Database** from the Available Templates group.

2. On the right side of the page, define a filename for the database and click **Create**.

3. Build your database tables in Access

4. Select the **External Data** tab in the **Access** Ribbon.

5. Click the **More** button from the **Import & Link** group to open a drop-down of addition import options.

6. Select **SharePoint list** button.

This action opens the dialog box shown in Figure 6-14, which is similar to the dialog box shown earlier in Figure 6-2. You must specify the SharePoint Server site address. Then you can choose to either import the source data, thereby creating a new Access table, or create a linked table. Let's stick with the import option for now. I will talk about linking lists and tables in the "Linking SharePoint Lists to Access" section later in this chapter.

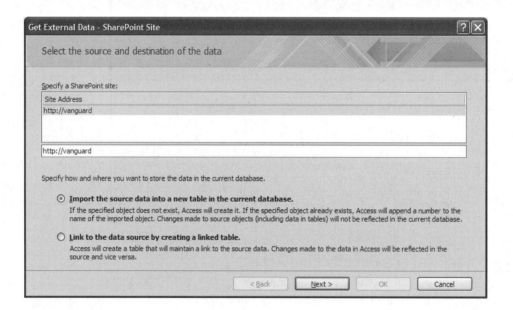

Figure 6-14. Selecting the source and destination of data

The next dialog box displays all lists in the selected SharePoint site. Each list has a separate check box, which allows you to select multiple lists to import at one time rather than exporting them one at a time as you did when starting from SharePoint. Notice that after selecting a list, the **Items to Import** column displays a drop-down list from which you can select a view to use. Remember that not only do views control which columns SharePoint exports to Access, but the view's filter also defines which items (rows) to transfer. Figure 6-15 shows an example of transferring three lists using selected views.

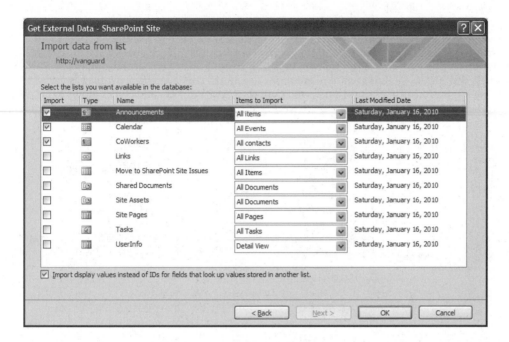

Figure 6-15. Importing multiple SharePoint lists using selected views

Access then allows you to save the import steps just as you did when you exported data from Access. If you choose to save your import steps, you must specify a name for the operation. By default, Access creates a name that begins with "Imports -" followed by the name of the first list. You can also create an Outlook task to remind you to perform this operation later. When you click **OK**, Access imports the lists.

Note that the list of objects that Access could import includes all the SharePoint libraries as well as the lists. When importing into Access from a library, Access only imports the metadata for each library item. The actual document itself does not transfer to Access. However, if you only want to manipulate the metadata from the library, this may be okay. For example, after importing the metadata from the **Purchase Orders** library into an Access table, you could easily create an Access report using the table as the data source. For example, this report might sum the purchase amounts by department for each month in the most recent fiscal period.

Linking SharePoint Lists to Access

In the examples discussed in the previous section, you imported a copy of the SharePoint list data into an Access table. Before continuing with some other ways to work with SharePoint data from Access, let's see how linking to the SharePoint lists differs from simply copying the data into an Access table.

Because you have already seen how to begin a transfer of a list from SharePoint to Access in the previous section, let's pick up the transfer at the point where you have to decide whether to link to SharePoint or simply copy the data. Figures 6-2 and 6-14 illustrate arriving at this point in the process beginning from SharePoint or Access, respectively. However, rather than copying the list data to the Access table, select the option **Link to data on the SharePoint Site**.

For this illustration, suppose I started from the **MyCoWorkers** list to transfer and link to Access. However, remember that the **MyCoWorkers** list could use a lookup reference to select the department to which the coworker belongs. Since SharePoint now supports relational integrity between lists, it does recognize when transferring a list with a lookup to Access that it should also transfer the lookup list. This process mirrors the way Access includes relational tables when transferring data back to SharePoint. Figure 6-16 shows that the link process has transferred both the **MyCoWorkers** and **Depts** tables to Access.

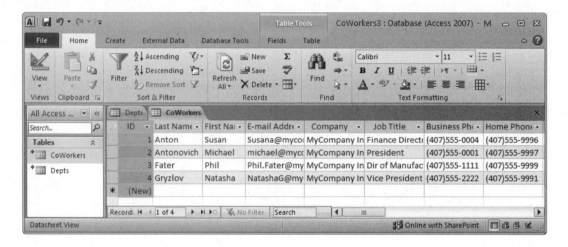

Figure 6-16. *Employees and Depts lists loaded into Access*

In addition, you should see a banner immediately below the ribbon that asked if you want to save your changes to the server, as shown in Figure 6-17.

Figure 6-17. *Save changes back to SharePoint*

When you click on the button **Save to SharePoint Site**, Access displays a list of the document libraries in your current site. For now, save your database in the **Share Documents** folder of your library.

Editing Linked Data

When you link rather than copy a SharePoint list to an Access table, you can edit items in either SharePoint or Access, and the changes automatically appear in the other.

■ **Tip** As a standard practice, you probably don't want to use Access to edit individual elements of data in a SharePoint list. However, you might want to use Access and its linking ability to make mass updates to data, move data between lists, or even move data between lists on different servers. It also could provide a way to link data from a SharePoint list to other databases.

As long as everyone works on different items/rows, no one knows that others might be editing the same list. However, when two or more people edit the same item at the same time, a conflict situation arises. As expected, the first person to save her changes to the item succeeds. The second person to save his changes sees an error message such as the one shown in Figure 6-18.

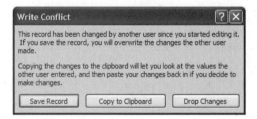

Figure 6-18. Edit conflict on a list linked to SharePoint

In this case, Access raises the message box because it recognizes that one or more columns in the row have changed since you began editing it. Access gives you three options to resolve this conflict. First, you could save your record anyway. This option blindly overrides the previous changes to the fields with your values. An objection to this option might be that you do not know which fields the other person updated, much less the changes she may have made.

The second option lets you copy your changes to the clipboard while updating the record in Access with the most recent values. You can use the **Clipboard Viewer** or paste the clipboard contents into an instance of WordPad to see and evaluate the changes. If you still want to use your values, you can reenter the fields with your values and save the record by navigating to another record. Figure 6-19 shows an example of conflict data from the **Depts** table. I added the conflicting data to the clipboard and then displayed it in a WordPad document.

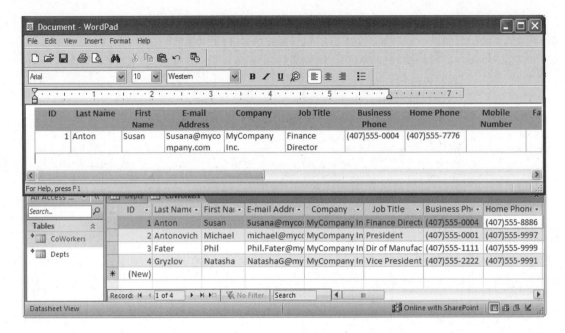

Figure 6-19. Contents of an update conflict added to the clipboard and viewed in WordPad

The third and final option drops your changes. When you select this option, Access updates the table with the values entered by the other person and ignores all your changes.

You might be thinking that you could avoid conflict problems if you check out the list before you begin making changes. Unfortunately, the Check Out feature does not exist for lists. However, if you link to the metadata associated with a document library, you can check out items in a document library. This prevents anyone else from making changes to the metadata.

■ **Note** You could simulate the behavior of Check In and Check Out by using SharePoint event handlers and a custom field, but that would require some coding that is outside the scope of this book.

Using Access to Make Mass Updates

SharePoint has trouble making mass updates to lists. As an example, suppose you have an Inventory list of items you sell, and you need to increase all of the prices of all items by 10 percent. What are the new item prices? How much does your inventory value change? You could open your list and edit each item to update the price for the item. If modifying the price of each of your product records sounds like a lot of work, you are right. You might even need to pull out your calculator to determine the new price, and update the metadata using the **Datasheet View** of the list.

However, if you have more than a few records, a faster way to update the price for all items in your Inventory list begins by linking the list to an Access table. From within the Access table, a single update statement can increment the product price by 10 percent for all items in both the table and the linked list. When finished, you can simply delete the Access table, and the data in the SharePoint list shows the new product prices. Notice that extended inventory value in the last column is a calculated value that multiples the item's price by the number of items in the inventory.

■ **Note** The rest of the section requires some introductory knowledge of creating and using SQL Queries in Access.

Let's begin by looking at the Inventory list before making any changes. Figure 6-20 shows the first several products in the list.

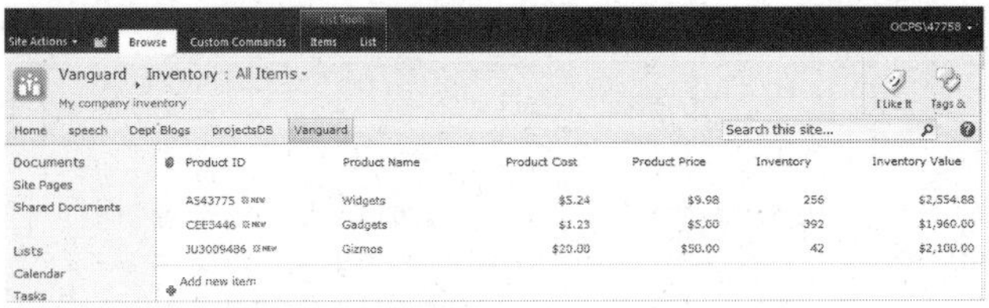

Figure 6-20. Original purchase amounts in the Purchase Orders library

Next, open Access and create a blank database named Inventory. From the **External Data** ribbon, select the **SharePoint List** option from the **More** drop-down in the **Import & Link** section. In the subsequent dialog boxes, define the SharePoint site and select **Inventory** from the list of objects that you can import into Access. Be sure to link the SharePoint list to the Access table. After you have loaded the list into an Access table, you can create a query to update the data.

To create a new query, select the **Create** ribbon. Then select **Query Design** from the **Macros & Code** section. The first step in creating a query displays a dialog box to select the tables you want to include in the query. In this case, select the newly added **Inventory** table by clicking it and then clicking **Add**. If you have other tables to include in your query, you could add them here. If you do not, close this dialog box by clicking the **Close** button.

Next, scroll through the list of fields until you find the field **Product Price**. Double-click the field to select it and add it to the grid in the lower half of the query builder screen. By default, Access assumes that you want a SELECT query. However, you need to use an UPDATE query to change the values of the **Product Price** field. Therefore, click the **Update** button in the **Query Type** group of the **Design** ribbon. This also changes the other information you must provide for the selected field so you can add an update formula. Next, you can specify a filter criterion so that your update only acts on a subset of the rows in the table. If you want to change all the rows, do not include a filter. However, you must supply a formula to increase the **Product Price** field values. Figure 6-21 shows the formula needed to add 10 percent to the product price.

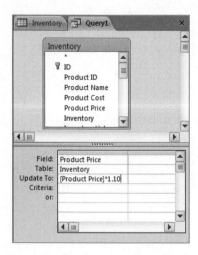

Figure 6-21. Adding 10 percent to the product price

To run the query, click the **Run** option in the **Results** group of the **Design** ribbon. When you run an **UPDATE** query, Access reminds you that you cannot undo the changes made by the query to the linked table. Therefore, the first dialog box that Access pops up lets you cancel the update by clicking **No** or proceed with your action query by clicking **Yes**.

The second dialog box that Access displays tells you how many rows it will update in the table. Again, you can cancel the update by clicking **No** now. If you click **Yes**, Access performs the update to the table. Because you linked the SharePoint list to Access, the changes also apply to the columns in the **Inventory** list on your SharePoint site. If you open the SharePoint site and view the **Inventory** list, you will see that it also updated the **Product Price** fields. Figure 6-22 shows the items in the list, so you can verify that the first item now has a product price of $10.98 rather than $9.98 representing the original price plus a 10 percent increase.

Figure 6-22. Updated purchase amounts in the SharePoint Purchase Orders library

Use Multivalve Fields in Lists

Multivalued fields allow a single field to have more than one value. Microsoft added this capability to the most recent version of Access as well as to SharePoint. Many people believe that this feature violates data normalization rules, which call for atomicity of field values. However, it also serves as an easily solution to problems in which you want to associate a single record or item in a list with multiple values from another list.

■ **Note** Atomicity means that a field should have one and only one value.

If a record in a table has a field that needs more than one value for any field, data normalization requires that you remove that field and make a related but separate table for it. On that basis, people do not believe that a database field should have more than one value. However, simple lists do not have to follow such rules. Therefore, it may have been SharePoint's use of multivalued fields that drove the change in Access, not the other way around. Or maybe they are not related at all.

Rather than debate the pros and cons of multivalued fields, let's look at an example of a SharePoint list that uses them and see how you can enter and maintain that data. You will also look at how SharePoint and Access exchange data with these field types.

Creating a Multivalued Column in SharePoint

In SharePoint, you have two ways to create a multivalued field. The first way uses the choice column type. From the discussion on this column type, you might recall that you must specify the possible values for this field when you define it. You can then display the values as radio buttons, a drop-down list, or check boxes on the default edit form when adding or modifying items in the list. When displayed with check boxes, the user can select one or more of the values. If the user selects multiple values, SharePoint displays them in the **Standard View** concatenated together with a semicolon to separate them.

Alternatively, you could use a lookup column type to create a multivalued field by clicking the **Allow multiple values** check box when defining the field. The key advantage to using this method lies with the ease in which you can maintain the list used to supply values to the lookup. The disadvantage of this method derives from SharePoint's inability to allow the user to define the relationship type between the two lists. While the user can select from **Restricted delete** or **Cascade delete** when you allow the new list to select a single value from the lookup list, only cascade deletes (and updates) are allowed when your new list allows the user to select multiple values.

Figure 6-23 shows a new list column I added to the **CoWorkers** list using the lookup column type to define employee skills from the **Skills** table. Each employee can have one or more skills. Actually, unless you make this field required, you could have an employee with no skills, but then he probably would not remain an employee for long. Right?

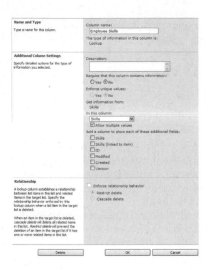

Figure 6-23. *Defining a multivalued column*

To create a multivalued column, you must select the **Allow multiple values** check box in the **Additional Column Settings** group. If you do not select this option, the user can only select one skill from the list. This might be okay if the field description asks for the employee's primary skill rather than her skills in general. However, as soon as you select this check box, SharePoint disables the ability to enforce relationship behavior, otherwise known as referential integrity.

Lookup fields always display in the add/modify form SharePoint automatically generates for a list, using a dual list box sometimes referred to as *mover boxes*. They got this name because they help you move one or more values from one list to the other. Mover boxes also generally take less space on a form than the corresponding radio buttons or check boxes for situations that have more than just a few options. The list box on the left shows the available values from which you can select. The list box on the right shows the values you have already selected. Buttons between the two list boxes help facilitate moving items from one list to the other. Figure 6-24 shows an example of how SharePoint implements a lookup field.

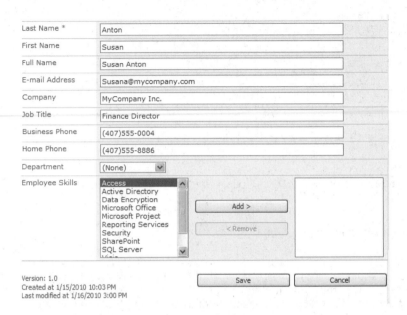

Figure 6-24. Mover boxes used to select values from a lookup list

To add a skill, you can double-click the skill name in the skill box on the left side. You can also click the value and then click the **Add** button found between the lists. Both methods add the skill to the list box on the right side containing your selected skills.

You can also select multiple skills from the available skill list by clicking the first skill, and then pressing the Shift key while you click the last skill you want to select. This technique selects not only the two skills you clicked, but also all the skills between them. If you hold the Ctrl key instead of the Shift key, you will add to the selection only the skills you clicked.

You can also remove selected items from the right side of selected list box by following the same techniques to remove individual or groups of values.

When you click **OK**, SharePoint adds or modifies the item and shows the updated list as shown in Figure 6-25.

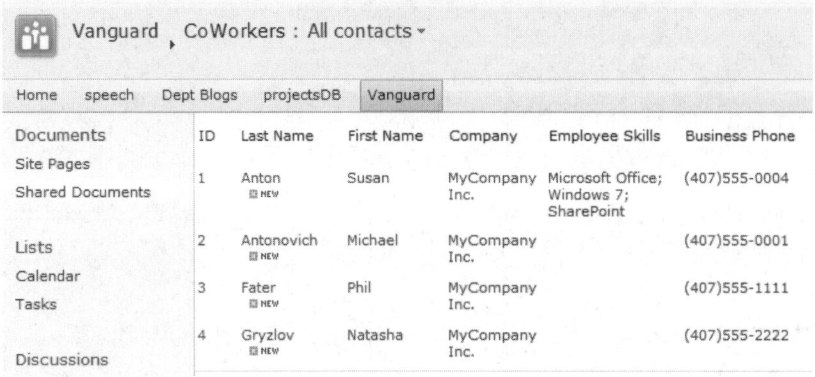

	ID	Last Name	First Name	Company	Employee Skills	Business Phone
Vanguard CoWorkers : All contacts ▾						
Home speech Dept Blogs projectsDB Vanguard						
Documents	1	Anton ☑ NEW	Susan	MyCompany Inc.	Microsoft Office; Windows 7; SharePoint	(407)555-0004
Site Pages						
Shared Documents						
	2	Antonovich ☑ NEW	Michael	MyCompany Inc.		(407)555-0001
Lists						
Calendar	3	Fater ☑ NEW	Phil	MyCompany Inc.		(407)555-1111
Tasks						
	4	Gryzlov ☑ NEW	Natasha	MyCompany Inc.		(407)555-2222
Discussions						

Figure 6-25. Employees list with multivalued Skills column

Notice that the selected skills for Susan Anton appear in the **Employee Skills** field separated with semicolons. Another thing to notice about this list focuses on the column header, **Skills**. In Chapter 2, you learned that the column headers have drop-down menus that usually allow you to temporarily sort or filter the list. In the case of the Employee Skills column, when you open this drop-down menu, you see text at the top of the menu that says `This column type cannot be sorted`. This occurs because you cannot sort multivalued list items. After all, which of the multiple items in the list should have priority for sorting? Figure 6-26 shows this drop-down menu.

Figure 6-26. Drop-down menu for a multivalued column

■ **Note** This drop-down only lists skills to filter by that appear in at least one of the list's items.

Notice, however, that you can filter the list by individual values even in the multivalued field. For example, if you select the value **SharePoint**, SharePoint refreshes the list, applying the filter to display only those employees with SharePoint as a skill. Opening the drop-down menu for the **Employee Skills** column a second time displays an option to clear the filter from the column, and thus displaying all employees again. When a column has an active filter, a funnel-shaped icon appears in the header to the right of the name.

■ **Note** You cannot select more than one filter for a column at a time. However, you can select filters on two or more columns at once.

■ **Tip** If you switch to the **Datasheet View**, you can create custom filters that can include more than one filter for a single column.

In addition to the **Employee Skills** column, suppose you added a choice type column, named **Language**, so you can track the languages each employee knows. Since an employee might know multiple languages, you decide to make this column a multivalued column as well.

Figure 6-27 shows this field after you have added it to the list and specified values for each employee. On your screen, you might notice that the values display in a different color for the **Employee Skills** as opposed to the **Language** column even though they are both multivalued columns. When you create a multivalued column using the choice column type, the way you define the field fixes the possible values. However, the **Employee Skills** column links to the **Skills** list, building the list of possible values dynamically. This difference creates as a hyperlink value rather than just text. In either case, you cannot sort on a multivalued column no matter how you create it. You can verify this by clicking the column header to open the drop-down menu. However, you can again filter the lists by individual values used in the multivalued column.

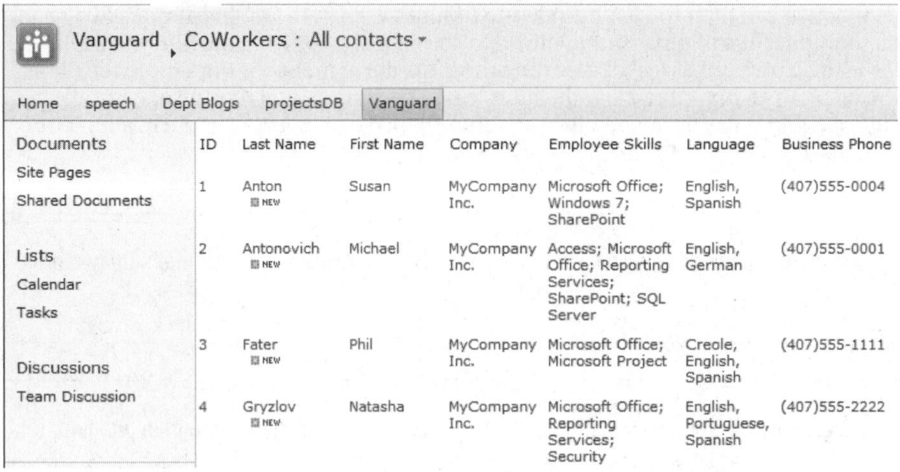

Figure 6-27. Employees list with Skills and Language multivalued columns

At first, you may think that either method of adding a multivalued column should result in the same end-user experience. The primary difference between the two methods is that users with the rights to add and modify items in a list can maintain the skills lookup list, but they cannot add or modify the items in the language choice list unless they also have the Manage Lists permission. However, that is not the only difference.

Opening a List with Multivalued Columns in Access

Let's open the **CoWorkers** list in Access to see how Access treats these two column types.

1. Open the **CoWorkers** list in SharePoint.

2. Select **Open with Access** from the **Connect & Export** group of the **List** ribbon.

At this point, Access opens a dialog box asking whether you want to link to the data in SharePoint or export a copy of the data (see Figure 6-2). Let's see what happens when using each method, beginning with exporting a copy.

3. Select **Export a copy of the dat**a and click **OK**.

After a few moments, Access opens with a copy of the employee data as shown in Figure 6-28. If the table does not immediately open, you may need to open the **CoWorkers** table from the **Navigation** panel by double-clicking it.

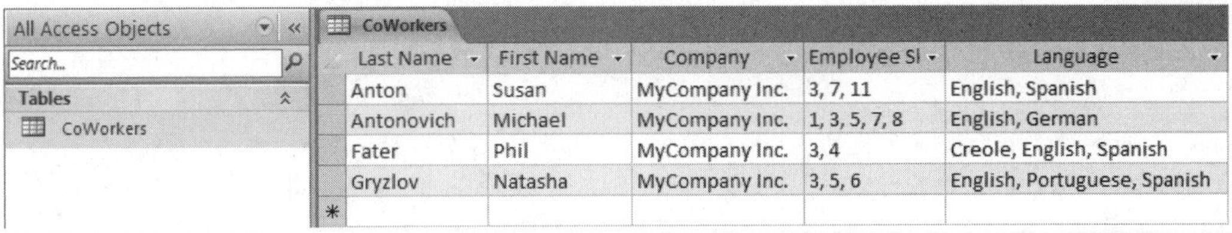

Figure 6-28. Employees table after copying the list

You should first notice that Access replaced the skills in the **Skills** column with their corresponding skill ID, making it rather difficult to interpret the **Skills** column in any useful manner. This does not happen to the **Language** column defined as a choice type column. Thus, when copying a list, Access treats lookup columns differently from choice columns. Furthermore, if you click in the **Skills** column of any row in the Access table, the drop-down only includes the ID values already used for that employee. Thus, the drop-down for each of the employees differs. Nor can you manually enter other ID values, even if you know what skills each ID value represents. Figure 6-29 shows a typical skills drop-down for an employee.

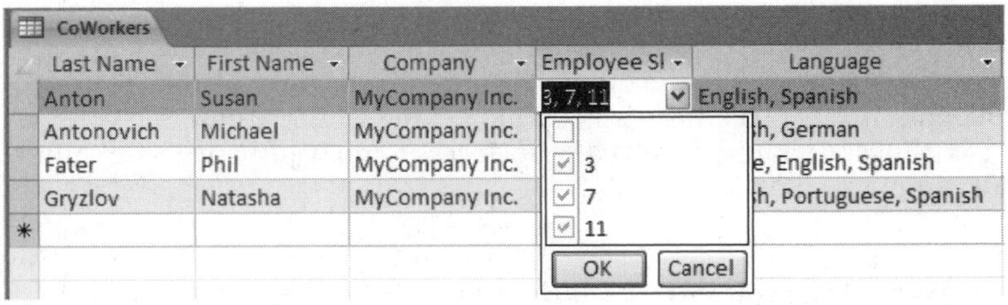

Figure 6-29. Skills drop-down list that appears when you copy the Employees table

On the other hand, the **Language** column displays the selected languages just as it did within SharePoint, except commas separate the values rather than semicolons. In addition, if you edit this field by opening the drop-down list of values for any employee, you will see the complete list of possible values exactly as defined in SharePoint. Using this drop-down, you can modify the languages associated with any employee by clicking the check box before each language. However, changes to any of these columns do not resynchronize with the original SharePoint list because you chose the copy option to create this table.

Instead of choosing **Export a copy of the data** when you open the SharePoint list in Access, open Access using the **Link to data on the SharePoint site** option. When you select this option, SharePoint not only creates a link in Access from the **CoWorkers** table to the **CoWorkers** list in SharePoint, but also includes links to all the lookup tables. Figure 6-30 shows that in addition to the **CoWorkers** table, Access also creates tables linked to **Skills** and **Depts**. As a result, when you open the CoWorkers table, you now see the skill names, not the skill ID values. Furthermore, if you click in the **Skills** column for any employee and open the drop-down menu, you see all available skills from the **Skills** list.

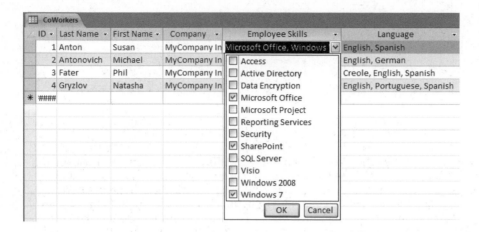

Figure 6-30. The skills drop-down is complete when linking to the Employees list.

For this reason alone, you may choose to use the links option rather than the copy option to view SharePoint lists in Access. But wait, there is more.

When you link to the SharePoint list rather than copy from it, you can make changes in either SharePoint or Access and have your changes appear in the other platform. When you copy the list from SharePoint to Access, changes you make in either platform remain only in the platform in which you make them. This means that by using links to your lists, you can use Access to manage your SharePoint lists, even those with multivalued columns.

Some Reasons Not to Use Multivalued Columns

The first argument against using multivalued columns comes from the inability to sort by them. You cannot easily resolve this problem because you would need to decide which value in a multivalued set controls the sort.

Filtering poses a different problem. While you may be able to filter the records in a table using a "contains" filter, the filtering string must uniquely identify the value you want and no other value. For example, if you used the two languages French and French Creole, you might encounter problems if you attempted to filter or search the records for employees who could speak French. A "contains" filter on the text "French" would return employees who spoke either French or French Creole.

Another potential problem occurs when you want to link the **CoWorkers** table to another table on a multivalued field. For example, suppose you have a table of projects that includes a field that defines the skills needed by the project. You might want to relate these two tables to see which employees you could assign to each project based on matching their skills to the skills needed for the project. However, if you define the **Skills** field in either or both tables as multivalued fields, you cannot use that field to link the tables.

Before leaving this discussion on multivalued fields, let's take a quick look at the schema for these fields in Access. Figure 6-31 shows the field properties for the **Skills** field. In the **Lookup** tab, you can see that the row source uses a **SELECT** statement that pulls data from the **Skills** table. It defines the bound column as the ID column (remember that the copy option shows only the ID values), but defines the width of the first column as 0 so that the skill name (**Title**) appears, not the ID. Notice also the property **Allow Multiple Values** must show **Yes** to allow multiple values in the field.

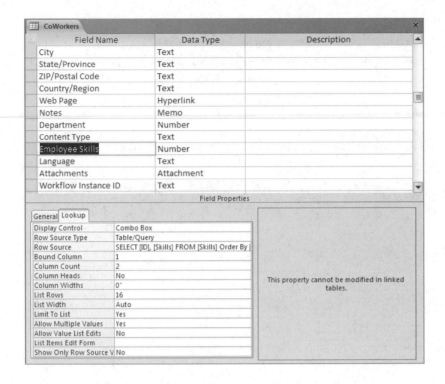

Figure 6-31. Skills field definition in the Access version of Employees

Although powerful in the right circumstances, I recommend that you exercise caution when using multivalued columns, with full knowledge of the limitations they impose.

Creating Access Forms and Reports from a SharePoint List

Once you bring your first list into Access, a natural question might be, "Can I create forms and reports from the list data?" The answer is yes.

Suppose you start with the **CoWorkers** list. If you remember from earlier discussion in this chapter, the **CoWorkers** list uses two fields that define their values using items found in two other lists, the **Depts** and the **Skills** lists. Thus, when you link the **CoWorkers** SharePoint list to Access, it also links these two lists, as you saw in the last section.

Creating a Simple Form

With the three employee-related tables linked into Access, you can generate a simple form for displaying and using just the data from the **CoWorkers** table. The fastest way to create a new form for a single table uses the **Form Wizard**, which you can find by opening the **Create** ribbon and looking for **Form** in the **Forms** group.

■ **Tip** By default, Access generates a form for whichever table you have open or have selected from the left-side **Navigation** panel. If you do not have a table selected or open, the **Form Wizard** appears grayed-out and unavailable.

Figure 6-32 shows an example of a default form generated by Access for the **CoWorkers** table. Like all Access forms, you can further customize the form after using the wizard to build the base form.

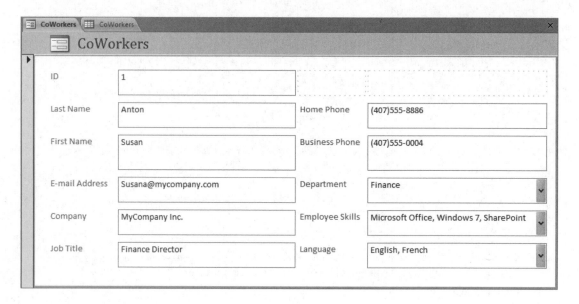

Figure 6-32. A simple form for the Employees table

■ **Tip** If you do not like the default form generated by Access using the **Form Wizard**, you can abandon this form by closing it without saving it. Create a new form using the **Form Design** option from the **Forms** group of the **Create** ribbon. You could also generate a form, save it, and then use **Form Design** to edit the appearance and/or functionality of the form.

Notice that all fields originally created as lookup or choice fields in SharePoint now appear as dropdown lists. Of course, only the **Employee Skills** and **Department** drop-downs link to other tables in the Access database, while the **Language** drop-down references a fixed selection of values. In addition, the fields for **Employee Skills** and **Languages** display the multivalued format discussed earlier in this chapter when you click open their drop-down lists.

■ **Note** The Department column does not display check boxes before the possible values because it is a single value lookup field.

If you like the way a form appears, you can save it for future use by right clicking the highlighted tab at the top of the form and selecting **Save** from the menu that appears. This action opens a simple dialog box that prompts for the form name. Access supports form names that have any combination of letters and numbers. However, you should never use special characters. I do not recommend using spaces in table or field names either, although it is possible if you then delimit those names with square brackets when you reference them.

As to how long table or field names should be, you should always use as many characters as necessary to fully describe your Access tables and forms, up to the limit of 64 characters. Don't, however, make long names just because you can. You can even save a form or report with the same name as the table on which you base it, although that can lead to some confusion. In fact, the icon before the object name may be your only clue if you display the table and form in the **Navigation** panel grouped by **Tables and Related Views** rather than by **Object Type**, as shown in Figure 6-33.

All Tables	ID	Last Name	First Name	E-mail Addr	Company	Job Title
Search...						
CoWorkers	1	Anton	Susan	Susana@myco	MyCompany In	Finance Direct
CoWorkers	2	Antonovich	Michael	michael@myco	MyCompany In	President
CoWorkers	3	Fater	Phil	Phil.Fater@my	MyCompany In	Dir of Manufac
Depts	4	Gryzlov	Natasha	NatashaG@my	MyCompany In	Vice President
Depts	(New)					
Skills						
Skills						

Figure 6-33. A saved form appears in the Navigation panel with its own icon.

In addition to the basic form shown in Figure 6-32, Access provides wizards to help you create several other types of forms, including the following:

- Split Form

- Multiple Items

- PivotChart

- PivotTable

- Modal Dialog

- Datasheet

- Several variations of forms with tabs for sub reports.

It is beyond the scope of this book to examine each of these form types. However, let's look at two form variations beginning with the Split Form.

Creating a Split Form

The Split Form gives you two views of the same data on the same form. Figure 6-34 shows a Split Form for the **CoWorkers** table, in which the top portion of the form shows the fields laid out similarly to those of Figure 6-32. However, the bottom of the form displays the table records in a grid format, in which each record displays as a row in the grid.

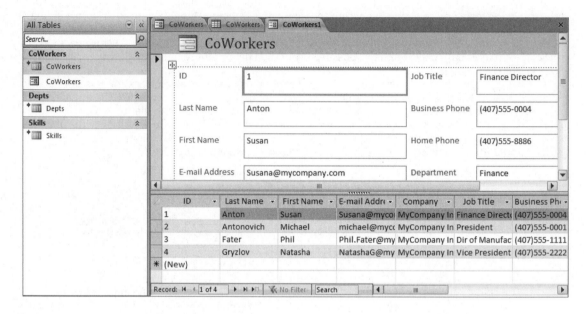

Figure 6-34. A Split Form provides two ways to edit records.

You can change the record shown in the top portion of this form by scrolling through the records using the grid in the lower portion and clicking anywhere in the row of the desired record. Once you select the record, you can then edit the fields in either portion of the form. When you move off the record, Access automatically saves the changes you made to that record.

If you do not like the way a form generated by the wizard looks, you can edit the form design by right-clicking the form's highlighted tab and selecting **Design View** from the drop-down menu. You can also select **Design View** from the **View** drop-down menu found in the **Views** group of the **Home** ribbon.

Figure 6-35 shows the top portion of your original **CoWorkers** form displayed in **Design View**. A form like a report in Access consists of a series of bands. In a form, the default bands include a **Form Header**, **Detail**, and **Form Footer** section. (Not shown by default are the **Page Header** and **Page Footer** bands. You probably will use these latter two bands infrequently when designing forms. However, you may find them quite useful when designing reports.) While the Form Header band only appears once at the beginning of a report no matter how many pages the report runs, the Page Header repeats at the top of each new page in the report. Developers often use this band to define column headings.

Similarly, the Page Footer occurs at the bottom of each page and may include information such as the page number, report name, or the report's generation date. Note that you do not need to use each of these bands. In fact, you can create a form that only uses the **Detail** band. You can turn on or off any of these bands, as well as access other band features, by right-clicking the band's title bar and de-selecting the band from the drop-down menu.

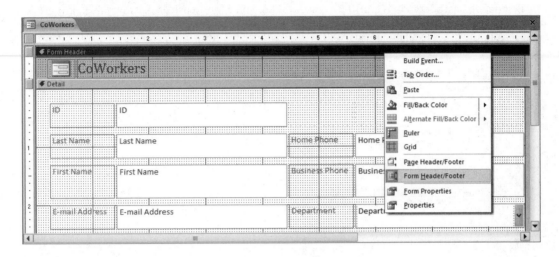

Figure 6-35. Design View lets you customize your form's appearance.

Creating a Custom Form Using a Subform

The last form type I will briefly explore here is the custom form, which uses a subform to display data from a related table. You would use this type of form to show a parent-child relationship between two tables. For example, suppose you want to display a list of employees by department. In this case, the **Depts** table acts as the parent, as each employee belongs to only one department but each department can have multiple employees.

To begin a form that displays this relationship, create a simple form for the **Depts** table. Then after the **Form Wizard** finishes, choose the **Design View** for the form. Next, find the **Subform** icon in the **Tools** group of the **Design** Ribbon, as shown in Figure 6-36.

Figure 6-36. The Design Ribbon with the Subform tool selected

After selecting this design tool, move back into the form and draw a rectangle to represent the area where you want the subform to appear. When you release the mouse button, Access prompts for more information to tie the main portion of the form to the subform using a series of dialog boxes.

The first dialog box, shown in Figure 6-37, asks whether you want to use an existing table or query or if you want to use an existing form. I recommend that you create the subform first and then just reference it from the list of available forms. In this case, choose the previously created CoWorkers form.

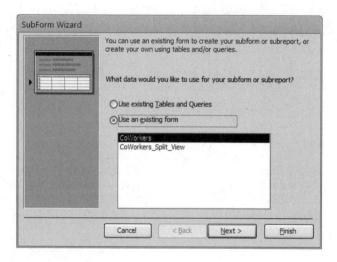

Figure 6-37. Creating your subform from tables, queries, or existing forms

■ **Tip** Use tools and wizards as much as possible to reduce the amount of work you must perform manually.

If you have not created a subform ahead of time, you can always go directly to a table or query. In that case, you must begin by selecting the table or query you want to use in the subform. Then select the fields you want to appear in the subform. Figure 6-38 shows an example of the dialog box that lets you select fields from the list of available fields in the selected table or query and move them into the **Selected Fields** list. The order in which you select fields for this list determines the order in which the fields appear in the subform. Therefore, select the order carefully. While Access lets you rearrange fields in **Design View** mode, you can save yourself time by giving the order of the fields some thought before you select them rather than spending time later moving them around.

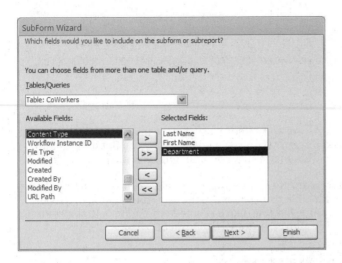

Figure 6-38. Selecting the fields to include in the subform

After you have defined the fields in your subform, you still need to define how you want to link the main form to the subform. Access attempts to help by providing some suggestions in the next dialog box of the wizard. However, if nothing in this list seems correct to you, you can define your own connection.

Figure 6-39 shows the dialog box used to define your own link between the main form and the subform. In this case, you want to use the **ID** field as the connecting field between the **Depts** table and the **Department** field in the **CoWorkers** table. Remember that, when you bring a list from SharePoint over to Access, the lookup columns in the list contain the ID of the record in the lookup table.

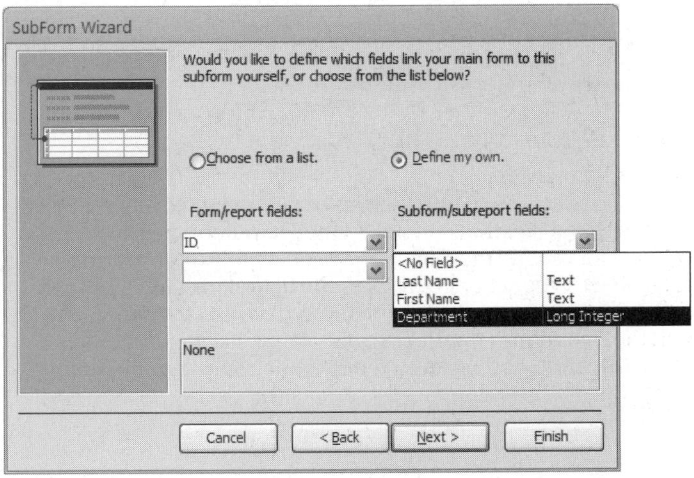

Figure 6-39. Defining the link between the main form and the subform

■ **Caution** When you define your own link, the field type on both sides of the link must be the same. In other words, if you select an integer field on the main form side, you must select an integer field on the subform side. On the other hand, the names of the fields do not matter.

While you can build links between the main form and subform using more than one field, I strongly recommend using single fields for primary and foreign keys between tables. If you do not have a natural unique single field to serve as the key, you may want to use an autonumber field on the primary side of the relationship.

After you finish defining the link between the form and subform, you are ready to save the subform. However, you must supply a name for it. As with table names, you can use any combination of letters and numbers as long as the total length of the name has less than 64 characters. Figure 6-40 shows an example of the completed form displaying the employees within a department.

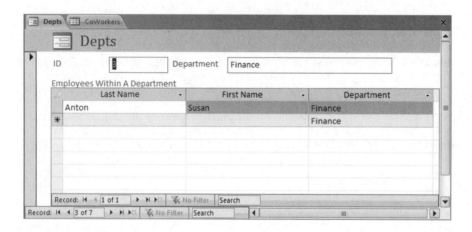

Figure 6-40. Example of finished Split Form

So why did you go through all of this trouble to create an Access form based on tables that represent links to lists in SharePoint? The answer rests with the fact that you linked the SharePoint lists to Access. Because the Access tables represent links, you can modify the data in the Access table or any forms created from those tables, and Access synchronizes your changes back to the SharePoint list. The next time someone opens the SharePoint list, she will see your changes. Thus, you have an alternative way to maintain your lists. Rather than go through the SharePoint interface to edit your lists, you can create a series of Access forms and organize them into an Access application that anyone can use to maintain your SharePoint lists.

Creating a Simple Report

In a similar fashion, you can create Access reports to display data from multiple SharePoint lists. In fact, the technique for designing reports uses many of the same concepts and similar wizards that you used when creating forms. For illustration purposes, the report shown in Figure 6-41 displays the employees in each department.

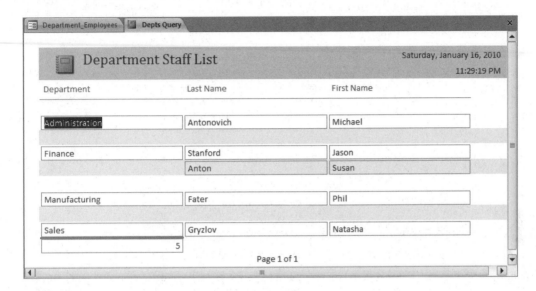

Figure 6-41. Sample of an Access report created from linked SharePoint lists

Again, I want to emphasize that learning how to use Access to create forms and reports goes beyond what we have time for here. There are many books available for Access that can provide you with further assistance in learning how to create forms and reports.

Can Recycle Bin Recover Deleted List Records?

By now, it should not come as a surprise that, when you delete a record in an Access table that links to a SharePoint list, SharePoint also deletes the record from that list. Access warns you that, when you delete a record, it is deleted permanently. However, that does not take into account the fact that you linked Access to SharePoint. Remember, unlike deleting a record from a stand-alone table in Access, when you delete just about anything in SharePoint, SharePoint sends it to the Recycle Bin. Therefore, if you happen to delete the wrong record while in Access, you can recover it through SharePoint.

To recover a deleted record, open SharePoint and navigate to the site. You do not need to go first to the list that links to the Access table. Just follow these steps:

1. Scroll down through the **Quick Launch** area on the left to **Recycle Bin** found at the bottom.

2. Click **Recycle Bin**.

3. When the Recycle Bin opens, it shows all the items deleted in the last 30 days (by default). Locate the deleted record (see Figure 6-42).

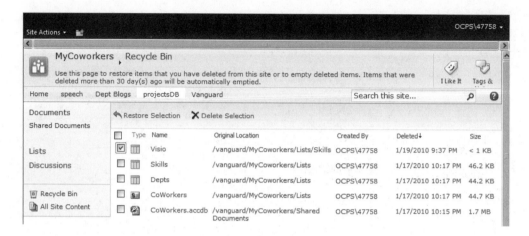

Figure 6-42. Recovering a deleted Access record using the SharePoint Recycle Bin

4. Click the check box to the left of the record you want to restore.

5. Click the **Restore Selection** button at the top of the recycle list.

If you now return to the list, the deleted record again appears in the list. Furthermore, if you go to Access and open the table corresponding to the linked list, you see that the deleted record appears there as well.

Deploying Your Access Application to SharePoint – Option 1

Now that you have seen how Access and SharePoint can share individual lists and tables, you are now ready to address the larger issue of what you can do with Access applications themselves. One of the reasons most IT departments shutter at the thought of the number of Access applications running wild within their companies is that these applications are totally unmanageable—and multiple copies of the data exist throughout the organization on laptops that can be easily stolen or compromised

The first part of this chapter addressed one way in which SharePoint can help manage the data from these applications. You saw how easily you can upload Access tables to SharePoint and then link to those lists. SharePoint then becomes the owner of the data. You can then allocate permissions to access the data through SharePoint totally independent of Access. Thus, if a laptop is stolen or compromised, unless the thieves also know the original owner's user name and password, they cannot access the SharePoint site to get to the data. Thus, moving the tables from Access to SharePoint accomplishes the following data management goals:

- Establishes one version of the truth, one copy of the data

- Provides for an easy way to backup the data on a regular basis

- Protects access to the data with user based permissions

- Tracks versions of the data

- Provides for a Recycle Bin to recover accidentally deleted data

However, the application itself still resides on a user's desktop (or laptop), making it difficult to push out new versions of the application because it is almost impossible to tell where all the copies of the application exist. Sometimes, the developer may even lock the application so that while others can run the application, they cannot get to the source of the forms, reports, queries, or macros to make changes. At first, this may sound like a good idea to protect the integrity of the application's logic. However, when the developer leaves the company, no one can get into the application to make needed changes. What you still need is a way to manage the application's interface including the following goals:

- Maintain a single version of the application

- Provide a way to easily deploy and upgrade the application

- Centrally deploy the application so users can easily get to it

In this section, I will show you a way to achieve all of these goals using the tools available in all versions of SharePoint that support Access services (which, at the time of SharePoint 2010 release, appears to be limited to the Enterprise version) and Microsoft Office 2010.

Moving All Access Tables to SharePoint

The first part of this chapter showed how you could move individual tables or tables grouped together through referential integrity from Access to SharePoint. However, depending on the complexity of your application, you may still need to move multiple tables or groups of tables manually to transfer everything from a single Access application to SharePoint. However, there is a faster way to move all tables from a single Access database to a SharePoint site by following a few simple steps.

First, open your Access application and display the **Database Tools** ribbon, as shown in Figure 6-43. In the **Move Data** group, select **SharePoint** to move all tables in the current database to SharePoint lists. Notice that you could also move your Access data to a centrally managed SQL Server or even a centrally managed Access Database. However, these other options do not provide some of the functionality that SharePoint lists provide, such as versioning and the ability to easily recover data from a recycle bin.

Figure 6-43. Access 2010 provides a command to move all tables to SharePoint at once.

■ **Note** You must use at least the Access 2007/2010 format for the **SharePoint** option to appear enabled in the **Move Data** group.

When you click on this command, Access opens a dialog box to ask where you want to move your data (see Figure 6-44). In the text box, you can enter any existing SharePoint site. In the list box, you see a list of the previously referenced SharePoint sites that you can select and add the tables from the current database.

I generally recommend that you move your Access tables to a new site created just for that one application. This eliminates the potential problems that would occur if you tried to upload tables having names that already exist as lists in the desired site. As you saw earlier, Access would then attempt to add a prefix to the name to insure that it was unique. If you plan to consolidate tables that exist in multiple applications so you only have to maintain one copy of the list in SharePoint, you may want to store the lists for groups of applications in one site.

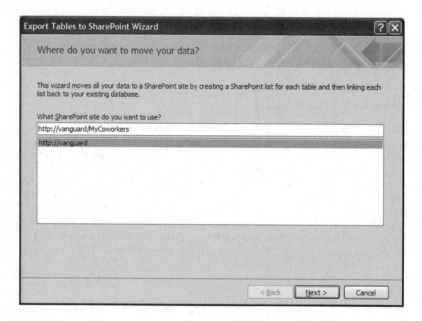

Figure 6-44. Access lets you choose the site to load your Access data.

Access first builds the list definitions in SharePoint based on the table schema in Access. This process includes not only the definition of the columns in the list, but also the validations and any referential integrity between lists. It then uploads the data from the Access table to the newly created SharePoint lists. Depending on the amount of data in your Access tables, this process can take some time. Once Access finishes exported the tables to SharePoint, the dialog shown in Figure 6-45 informs you that the transfer completed successfully.

Figure 6-45. Access notifies you of a successful upload of the data.

If you click the **Show Details** check box at the bottom of this dialog, the export wizard tells you the names of the lists created on the site as shown in Figure 6-46. It also tells you that it created a backup copy of the Access database

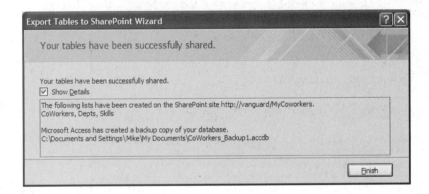

Figure 6-46. The dialog details tell you what lists it created in SharePoint.

Moving the Access Database to SharePoint

You may have also noticed a banner immediately beneath the Access ribbon that asks you to save your changes to the server. This notification, shown in Figure 6-47, is not referring to changes in the table data just transferred. Rather, it asks you to save your Access database to SharePoint.

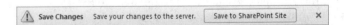

Figure 6-47. Access prompts you to save the database to SharePoint.

While you could choose any site in which to store your Access database, most people will store the database in a library on the same site as the lists created from the database's tables. This practice makes it easy to associate the application with the lists used by the application because they all reside in a single site.

However, there are good reasons to store the applications in a separate site, including:

- Providing a single site from which users can access all applications rather than having to navigate from one site to another.

- Providing unique permissions to the application site that allow select users or groups the ability to edit the applications while limiting them to read and update access to the data in the site containing the lists.

You must create the library first. In Figure 6-48, you see that after clicking the **Save to SharePoint Site** button in Figure 6-47, the **Save Dialog** lets you select the site and library where you want to store the Access database. In this case, you are using a Shared Documents library.

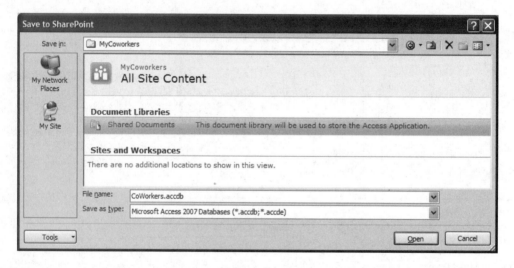

Figure 6-48. *Use the Save Dialog to select a library in which to save the Access database.*

After saving the Access database in the library, you can delete your local copy of the application used to upload the production version to SharePoint. You no longer need it to run the application or to access the data. Furthermore, you can get all other users of the application to remove their local (and now redundant) copies of the application from their local drives. All users can open the database by clicking on the database name or by using the drop-down menu associated with the application.

You now have a single application that all users can access, as shown in Figure 6-49, rather than multiple copies scattered on computers throughout your organization. If you need to update the database to add a new feature or correct a problem, you only need to deploy the new version to one library. Similarly, all users of the application use the same application code since it resides now in only one location, but they all also access and update a central data source.

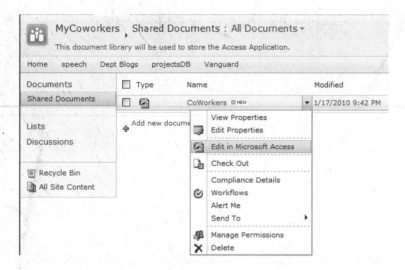

Figure 6-49. All users can now open the Access database from a single location.

Clicking on the Access database name in the library opens the dialog shown in Figure 6-50. Users that do not have edit rights must open the document in Read Only mode. If you have edit rights to the library, you can open the database in Edit mode. However, when you do that, you must supply a location where a local copy of the database can be stored while you edit it.

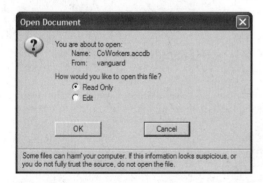

Figure 6-50. Users can open the Access database in Read Only mode or Edit mode depending on permissions.

When opened in Read Only mode, the users sees a banner at the top of the opened database (Figure 6-51) that tells them that they can only change data in linked tables. Since you started by linking all the tables to SharePoint lists, this warning does not present a problem. The banner further goes on to say that to make design changes, they must save a copy of the database. Of course, if they do not have edit rights, they cannot resave the database with their changes back to the SharePoint library. Only users who have edit rights in the first place can choose Edit from the dialog in Figure 6-50 make changes to the forms, reports, etc. and save their changes back to the library.

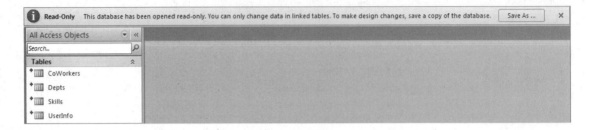

Figure 6-51. Notice that user can only edit linked tables when opening the Access application from the library.

In either case, users can make changes to the data in the linked tables. Access sends changes made to any record in the table to the linked list as soon as you move off the record. Anyone else viewing the record from the SharePoint list will see the change the next time they refresh their page. In addition, users can make changes directly to the data in the SharePoint lists. These changes also appear the next time someone opens a form, report, or view of the table from the Access application.

Overall, this is not a bad solution to managing Access applications for your organization. The one major flaw of this option is that when two or more people download a copy of the application at the same time to make changes to forms, reports, or macros, the last person to save their changes will overwrite the changes of the other simultaneous editors. However, the second option can even address that problem.

Deploying Your Access Application to SharePoint – Option 2

While the method of deploying an Access application to SharePoint in Option 1 solves many of the problems that concern IT departments, such as having an unknown number of copies of the application as well as copies of the data floating through the organization, it still requires each user to have Access on their desktop. If you deploy a version of Microsoft Office that includes Access, this may not be a concern. However, there is still a concern about simultaneously editing the database objects by two or more people. Therefore, if you want to deploy Access applications for others to use who may not have Access on their desktop or if you have many people with edit rights to the database objects, you may want to consider deploying your application to a SharePoint 2010 server supporting Access Services.

Unlike option 1, you do not need to first move all of your Access tables to SharePoint lists as a separate step. While the tables still become SharePoint lists, Access moves them for you when you select the option to publish your Access application to Access Services. To deploy your application, following these steps:

1. Open your Access application.

2. Open the **File** drop-down menu and select **Info** (as shown in Figure 6-52).

3. From the options in the center column, select Publish to Access Services.

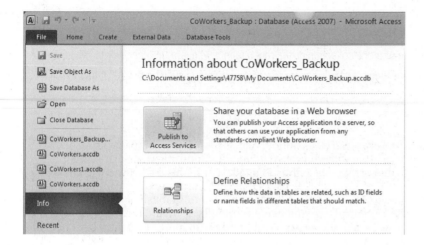

Figure 6-52. Access applications must be published to the Access Services.

When you publish an access application, you need to name the site where you want it published. This site cannot exist prior to publishing. In other words, you cannot add your Access application to an existing site. Figure 6-53 shows that you must enter the server URL as well as the site name. Note that the server URL is the path of the site less the site's name itself.

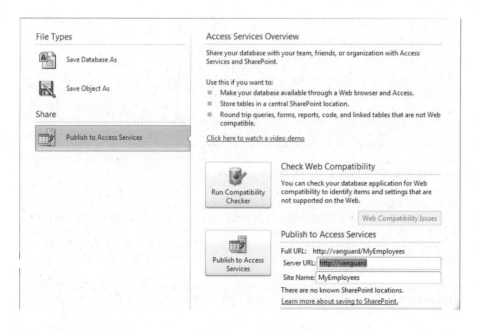

Figure 6-53. Specify the server and the site name for publishing the Access application.

■ **Caution** You can only publish an Access application to be a subsite of an existing site. You cannot publish an Access application to be the root site of a site collection or the root site in a wildcard. In other words, while you can publish to something like: `http://vanguard/` or `http://vanguard/sites/MyProjects`, you cannot publish to `http://vanguard/sites/`.

When you click the **Publish to Access Services** button, Access performs a compatibility check to identify items that may not be compatible with the web. If it finds anything, the wizard stops the publishing process and displays a dialog that says **Publish Failed**. Within this dialog, you will find a link called **Web Compatibility Issues**. Click this link to display a table of all the issues that are preventing the current application from publishing to Access services. The columns in this table identify the type of element that caused the problem, the control type and name within that element, the property where you can find the problem, and a description of the issue. With this information, you can go back to your original Access application and fix the problem.

After addressing each of the issues in the Web Compatibility Issues table, you can retry the wizard to publish your application to Access Services. If you successfully fixed all the issues, you should see the dialog shown in Figure 6-54 that says **Publish Succeeded.**

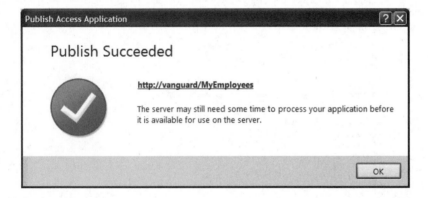

Figure 6-54. Publish succeeded dialog provides a link to the new site.

If you click the link on this dialog, you can open your new application site within your browser, as shown in Figure 6-55. Note that all of the database objects appear in this screen. The wizard has already built the SharePoint lists along with all the corresponding validation and referential integrity. It also converts all of the other database objects into XML representations of those objects. At this point, you could delete your original Access database because you will no longer need it. All the information that defines the application now resides in SharePoint.

Now you can make changes to the schema for the application directly from this screen. SharePoint applies these changes immediately to the list definitions in real time. However, you will also need to build web forms, web reports, web queries, and web macros that you can use on the web. You cannot simply display the forms or reports based on the XML definitions uploaded when you published the application.

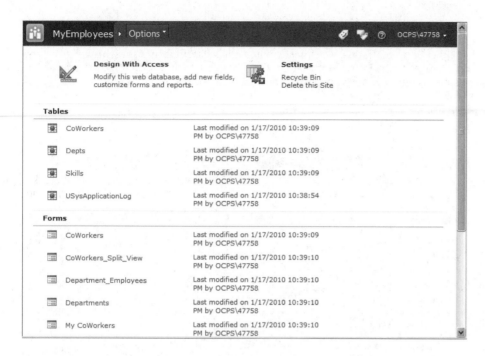

Figure 6-55. List of objects in the published site of the Access application

To make changes to any of these objects, click on the **Options** button at the top of the page to open the drop-down menu and select **Open in Access**. This option uses your local Access client to open the database. You can now use the **Create** ribbon to define new web based forms, reports, macros, and queries such as the one shown in Figure 6-56.

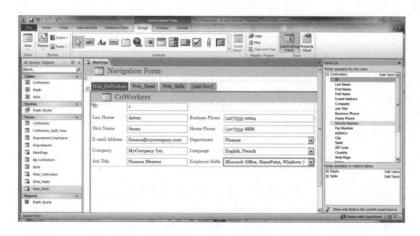

Figure 6-56. Build a Navigation form using web forms created from the Access Services application.

After creating web versions of the forms and reports you want to use on the web, you are almost ready to save your changes. However, first you may want to change the default form that appears when someone goes to the application site. In this example, I created a navigation form using the web forms of the other tables in the database as the individual tab elements. To get the navigation form to appear when the application starts, open the **File** drop-down menu and select **Options**. This selection displays the **Access Options** dialog shown in Figure 6-57. Select the **Current Database** group of options. Find the property **Web Display Form** and using the drop-down, select the form that you want to use as the default form when the application starts.

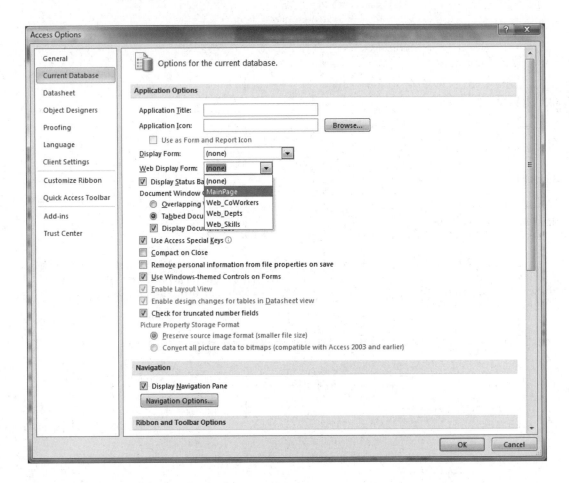

Figure 6-57. *Set the default web page for Access Services.*

These changes are not written back to the SharePoint site immediately. You must open the **File** drop-down menu, as shown in Figure 6-58, and from the **Info** group, click the **Sync All** button. As an application developer, this behavior benefits you as it allows you to make changes in your local client version of the objects. You can then test and debug them before publishing them back with the **Sync All** option.

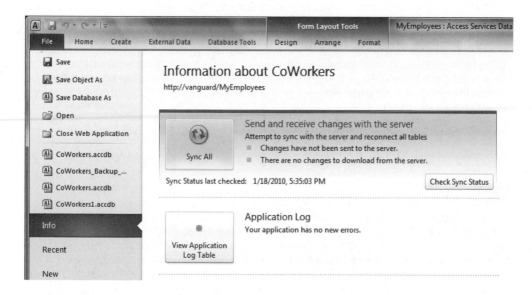

Figure 6-58. Sync changes to Access objects back to Access Services

You can now close your Access client and return to the SharePoint site where you published your application and refresh the page. The page should now show the web page you selected to serve as the default page for the application, as shown in Figure 6-59.

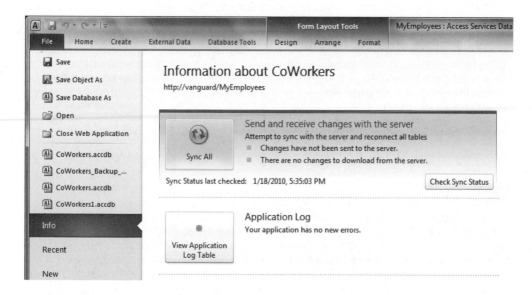

Figure 6-59. Default page of Access Application displayed in a browser

In the **Options** drop-down from the top of the page, you can also manage your site permissions. For example, you can break inheritance for this site and define unique permissions for who can make changes to the application, who can edit the data in the lists, and even who can only view information.

You can also choose **Settings** from the **Options** drop-down. From the context menu, you can tell SharePoint to open your Access client to edit any of the objects (assuming you have the necessary permissions). In addition, you can open any web object and view that object directly within the browser. For example, you can click on the names of any of the web forms created for the application and select **View <form name>** to open that form in the browser. Similarly, the context menu for tables have two options, one to open the table as a list allowing you to modify the data, and one to export the table's data to Excel.

Summary

In this chapter, you saw how to use Access to work with SharePoint lists. You began by performing simple tasks to export SharePoint lists to Access and to publish Access tables to SharePoint. You learned that by linking lists from SharePoint to Access, you could edit data from either platform. Furthermore, within Access, you could build forms to edit the linked tables. You also looked at using multivalued fields, a new and somewhat controversial feature to Access, as it violates the first rule of data normalization—to keep all data fields atomic by supporting multivalued fields.

Until this point, you had performed all editing while remaining online with the SharePoint server. However, the advantage of using Access to manage your lists comes from its ability to work with lists offline. I showed you how to take Access tables offline and then resynchronize your changes with SharePoint's list values. Of course, any time more than one person can modify data from two or more platforms, conflicts can and will occur if multiple people attempt to update the same record at the same time. Therefore, I also demonstrated how to resolve conflicts.

Finally, you looked at two options on how to publish your Access applications to SharePoint. By publishing Access applications to SharePoint, you can alleviate many of the concerns IT departments have with using Access within the organization.

In summary, Access is a powerful tool for quickly building applications. Of course, you may still need to build some applications using a more robust programming language. However, if you can use Access to build a percentage of the simpler applications quickly, your department (and SharePoint) can look like heroes.

■■■

CHAPTER 7

Managing SharePoint Lists from Excel

Along with MS Word, MS Excel is one of the oldest products in the Microsoft Office Suite. Microsoft developed Excel in the early days of PCs as competition for the wildly successful Lotus 1-2-3 program, which was one of the great early productivity tools that helped justify using PCs in many business offices. However, even before the introduction of Lotus, VisiCalc and MultiPlan (an early predecessor to Microsoft Excel) tested the spreadsheet waters. Their ability to work with rows and columns of numbers took advantage of a paradigm well known to accountants and finance departments.

These early competitors hoped to make PCs respectable in corporate environments where large mainframe computers ruled the day. Of course, Microsoft Excel is now as synonymous with Microsoft Office as Microsoft Word. In conjunction with Microsoft Outlook, these three products form the central core around which most office users spend the majority of their day. Therefore, when Microsoft introduced SharePoint, integrating collaboration features with these three Office products seemed to be a no-brainer. Why force users already familiar with several of your other products to learn a new product paradigm?

For Microsoft Word, Outlook, and even the relatively new kid on the block, Access, integration with collaboration has been a priority with SharePoint. However, is the same true for Excel? In this chapter and the next, you will explore how SharePoint works with Excel.

Exporting a List from SharePoint to Excel

The last several chapters have covered exporting lists from SharePoint to Outlook and Access. Therefore, it should not surprise you that you can export a SharePoint list to Excel. In fact, if you have been checking out the options in SharePoint's list and document ribbons, you probably already have a good idea of how to start.

To show that document libraries act very much like lists, let's start with the **Purchase Orders** library. You used this library when you were learning how to use library metadata in other Microsoft Office applications. You created a custom view to sum the **Purchase Amount** column by department to produce a report within SharePoint showing how much each department spent during a specified time defined by a filter.

Begin, as always, by navigating to the library or list you want to use from your SharePoint site. Next, open the **Library** ribbon for the **Purchase Orders** library. Figure 7-1 shows this ribbon. Notice that while it has the options **Connect to Outlook** and **Export to Excel**, it does not have an option you might expect, **Open with Access**.

Figure 7-1. Opening the Export to Excel menu option

■ **Note** Access can only open lists, not libraries.

This difference between lists and libraries is important in terms of how you work with them. I will mention other differences as you proceed through this chapter.

Take a closer look at Figure 7-1. When you hover over the commands with your mouse, the **Connect to Outlook** option includes descriptive text that talks about synchronizing items and working with them offline; however, the **Export to Excel** option uses no such language in its description. Rather, it simply refers to the ability to analyze items within Microsoft Excel. You will see a little later in this chapter what this difference in terminology means with respect to your ability to collaborate.

■ **Caution** The button to Export to Excel is enabled even if your local machine does not have Excel installed. If you don't have Excel installed and you try to export a list by clicking on this button, you will get an error message stating that you are missing a Microsoft SharePoint Foundation-compatible application.

The Role of the IQY File

After selecting the **Export to Excel** option, a dialog box pops up with the title **File Download**. Figure 7-2 shows this dialog box. It asks whether you want to open or save a file with the rather odd extension of `.iqy.` This file type represents a Microsoft Office Excel Web Query File. If you click **Save**, the **Save As** dialog box appears, letting you select where to save this file. However, by itself, the **Save** option does not open the file in Excel or even open Excel. It merely saves a file to your local hard drive. Interestingly, if you double-click this file after saving it, it opens Excel and begins the process of retrieving data from the SharePoint library. If you open the IQY file using Notepad, you will discover that this small file contains some very cryptic text; you should be able to read enough of it to learn that this file contains information pointing back to your SharePoint site and specifically to the library you want to export to Excel.

Figure 7-2. The File Download dialog box saves the Excel Web Query File that retrieves the SharePoint List.

Regardless of whether you try to open the query file immediately or decide to later open the copy of the query file saved to your local hard drive, you will first see a security notice generated by Excel. This security warning occurs because the query file attempts to command Excel to make a connection with another server. With ever-increasing concerns about viruses, Trojan horses, and other nasty things getting into your computer, all software vendors by default lock down connections between machines but allow you to decide which connections to allow and when to allow them. Figure 7-3 shows the **Microsoft Excel Security Notice** dialog box that appears when the IQY file tries to connect Excel to SharePoint.

Figure 7-3. Microsoft Excel Security Notice dialog box before making a data connection

In any situation when you attempt to connect to another server, always verify that you trust the connected source. If you have any doubts about a content source, click the **Disable** button. However, if the server resides inside your corporate firewall, you can probably safely click the **Enable** button to continue.

Choosing How to Display Your Imported List

If you already had a workbook open with Excel, you will see an additional set of dialogs that do not appear if you begin with Excel closed. So let's assume you have a workbook open in your local Excel. Since Excel is not sure what you want to do with the new imported data, it displays another dialog box, the **Import Data** dialog box, shown in Figure 7-4. Here you must make two decisions on how to display your imported list data. In the top portion of this dialog box, you must choose from four options on how to view your data:

- Table

- PivotTable Report

- PivotChart and PivotTable Report

- Only Create Connection

Figure 7-4. The Import Data dialog box lets you decide how and where to place your data.

By default, most lists export to tables. The second half of the dialog box lets you choose whether to place the list in an existing worksheet, a new worksheet, or a new workbook. If you start the export process with Excel open, you can select any of these options.

Before clicking **OK** to begin the actual export of data to Excel, you can click the **Properties** button in this dialog box. This button opens a dialog box named **Connection Properties**. At the top of the dialog box, you can find the connection name along with an optional description. The rest of the dialog box consists of two tabbed pages.

In the first tab, you cannot edit most of the data fields. However, you should find two enabled fields in the **Refresh** control area. The first field lets you to enable background refresh, which allows you to continue to use Excel while the query executes. Unless you have a very large list from which to refresh your Excel data, the query execution time may not matter much to you.

The second option that you can set is to **Refresh the data when opening the file**. If you do not select this option, Excel stores a local copy of the current data when you save the spreadsheet and displays that same data the next time you open the spreadsheet, regardless of what changes have occurred in the original SharePoint list. Of course, you could always manually refresh the data by clicking the **Refresh** button in the **External Table Data** group of the **Table Tools Design** Ribbon.

However, by selecting this option, you could save time and reduce uncertainty of the current data values by telling Excel to refresh the data automatically each time you open the spreadsheet.

■ **Note** Excel does not automatically refresh data from a SharePoint list. That accounts in part for the use of the term "export" in the SharePoint menu selection **Export to Excel**. Thus your first clue: SharePoint does not maintain a continuous link to the data in Excel.

The second tab, titled **Definition**, contains information about the connection between Excel and the SharePoint list so that manual refreshes of the data know how to access the list data. You can also save a copy of the connection definition by clicking the **Export Connection File** button and selecting a location to save the file. The Authentication settings button lets you select the type of authentication you want to use with Excel Services. Unless you plan to use something other than Windows Authentication, you do not need to worry about this setting.

■ **Caution** Do not change the connection definition unless you have a deep understanding of how to define connection strings. Even then, think twice.

When you click **OK** on the Import Data dialog to begin the import of data into Excel, Excel uses the information in the IQY file to import the list data into a spreadsheet. For the **Purchase Orders** library, Figure 7-5 shows the resulting worksheet after exporting and opening the list data within Excel.

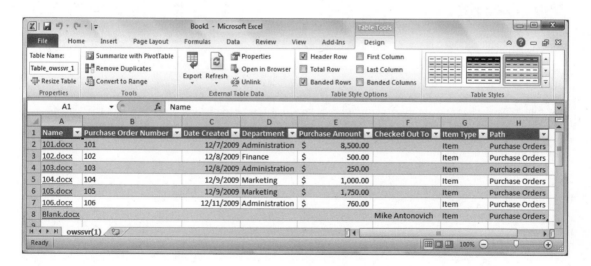

Figure 7-5. The Excel worksheet displays the exported SharePoint list.

■ **Tip** Once you have exported the data to an Excel spreadsheet, you can remove unwanted columns that the process brings along from the list or library, such as Checked Out To, Item Type, and Path.

How Views Affect the Data Exported to Your List

When you export a list to a spreadsheet, the items you export as well as the specific columns you export depend very much on the view open at the time you choose to export. For example, looking at the data in Figure 7-5, suppose you had a view that included only purchases by the Administration department, which included three columns: **Purchase Order Number**, **Date Created**, and **Purchase Amount**. Then the export to Excel would include only the Administration department items with the three selected columns.

You may have noticed that the data in this worksheet is not just simple spreadsheet data. Rather, it appears structured within a table, with each column representing a separate column and each row representing a separate list item. Your other clue that this is not just a collection of cells with data in them should have been the title of the Ribbon, **Table Tools**.

Using Hyperlinks in Your List

If you include in your export one of the instances of the **Name** column, it remains linked to the document in the shared documents library. Therefore, Excel displays that column as a hyperlink. It also means that you can click the document name, and through the URL associated with the hyperlink, the document opens using the appropriate Microsoft Office product, which would be MS Word in this case.

■ **Note** Clicking a link to the document can only open the original document if a) you have an appropriate application that can open the document installed on your desktop, and b) if you have an active network connection. Opening a link will not work if you are offline.

Figure 7-6 shows a dialog box that may pop up when you click the hyperlinked **Name** field in this example. When accessing an internal SharePoint site at your company, you probably can trust the files to be virus free. However, you should have a virus-scanning program on your local desktop computer or on your SharePoint network to ensure that harmful programs cannot hide in your files when you open them from a shared location.

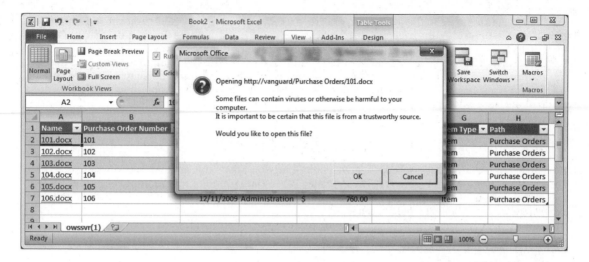

Figure 7-6. The warning dialog box that pops up when opening a document from a SharePoint library

When you open a document, it appears no different than if you opened it directly from the SharePoint library. In the case of a MS Word document, the Document Management panel may also open (as discussed in Chapter 3). With the document open, you can make changes and then close the document. You can then save those changes, and Excel sends them back to the SharePoint library because you effectively performed a remote edit directly to that file. Remember, the file itself does not become a part of your Excel worksheet.

However, although you have the document open for editing, you have not checked it out. You can verify this by looking back at the document library from within SharePoint; notice that the document icon does not contain the green box with the arrow in the lower-right corner, indicating a checked-out document. Therefore, someone else could check out and edit the same document while you edit it. For that reason, I do not recommend editing documents linked to an Excel list as a regular practice.

■ **Tip** The above concern about editing documents from your Excel spreadsheet is true unless you go into **Document Library Settings** for the SharePoint library first, select **Version Settings**, and change the **Require Check Out** option to **Yes**. If you do this first, then when you attempt to open the document from Excel and someone else did not check it out first, you can open the document to read it. While opening it, SharePoint prompts you to check the document out before you can edit it. On the other hand, if someone else had already checked out the document and you attempt to open it, you will get the **File in Use** notification dialog box that allows you to open the document in **Read-Only** mode or be notified when the document becomes available for editing.

If you make changes to the document, MS Word asks you to save your changes if you attempt to close the document with unsaved changes. You can open, edit, and save the document. MS Word will even save changes to any of the metadata back to the SharePoint library. However, the changed metadata will not appear in any of the exported columns to Excel. The key point to remember is that you can either export a SharePoint list or library to Excel or export an Excel spreadsheet to a SharePoint list. You can even refresh the Excel data from SharePoint by using the **Refresh All** option in the **Connections** group of the **Data** ribbon in Excel.

Other Table Tools in Your Excel Workbook

You can export your changed spreadsheet to a new SharePoint list. You can do this by opening the **Table Tools** ribbon, as shown in Figure 7-7. The **External Table Data** group only contains two options under the **Export** button. One supports exporting the current table from Excel to a SharePoint list and the other exports the table to a Visio Pivot Diagrams.

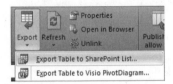

Figure 7-7. External table data ribbon options

■ **Note** If you do not have Visio installed, the option to export to Visio Pivot Diagrams will be grayed out and unselectable.

The **Refresh** button in this group lets you refresh the Excel data using the original connection created to transfer the data to Excel. However, neither of these options let you synchronize data changes in Excel back to SharePoint.

Furthermore, you can only export Excel tables to lists, not to libraries. That means Excel's export option cannot re-create a new library in SharePoint from the purchase orders, even though the items originally came from a library. However, it can create a standard list in which the item's **Name** field displays as a hyperlink, letting you open the Word document almost as you would in a library. I say "almost" because since it is a list, you do not have the ability to check out documents while you edit them. Thus, if you start with a SharePoint library and export it to an Excel table, you can only import it back into SharePoint as a new list, not as a replacement for the existing library or even as a new library.

The **Refresh** button, mentioned previously, allows you to refresh the data in the Excel spreadsheet with data from the source SharePoint library or list, updating changes to the items and columns displayed. This includes not only items that have changes, but also new items and removed items. This refresh, however, overwrites any changes you made in the Excel worksheet with the current information from the SharePoint library.

■ **Note** When you click the **Refresh** button, SharePoint only updates the rows and columns in the Excel table that match a column from SharePoint. If you added rows inside the Excel table, the Refresh button will remove them, but if you add rows outside of the Excel Table (below it), Refresh will not affect those rows even if it needs to push them down to add more rows from the SharePoint list. On the other hand, columns insert into the table are ignored by a refresh. If you deleted columns from your Excel spreadsheet, the refresh will not restore those columns. This functionality may be good or bad depending on what you wanted the refresh to really do.

The **Properties** button allows you to select some of the properties that affect how the table responds to new and deleted rows.

The **Open in Browser** button opens the library or list page from the SharePoint site.

The **Unlink** button permanently removes the connection from the worksheet. While the worksheet remains intact with all its data after you select this option, you can no longer update the data from the SharePoint library or list by clicking the **Refresh** button.

■ **Caution** When you unlink a table from its corresponding SharePoint library or list, you cannot restore the link or the connection.

The crucial concern about exporting your lists to Excel comes down to the lack of synchronization of changes. While you can refresh your Excel table as often as you like by using the **Refresh** button in Excel to get the latest and greatest values from the SharePoint list, this process is one-way only—and a manual process at that, unless you use the **Refresh the data when opening the file** option mentioned earlier. In addition, this refresh process overwrites any changes to the Excel data you made from within Excel, as it completely replaces the Excel data with data from the SharePoint list. The consequences of the refresh option also limit your ability to reorganize the information in the spreadsheet.

■ **Note** Excel 2003 had the ability to update SharePoint lists. However, with both Office 2007 and Office 2010, this feature was been deprecated in favor of using Access 2007. I will return to this issue in the section "What Happened to Synchronization?" later in this chapter to show a way to resolve this limitation.

Exporting Data from an Excel 2007/2010 Spreadsheet into a Custom List

In the last section, you saw that when you export a SharePoint list to Excel, you can manually update the Excel spreadsheet with changes made in SharePoint, but you cannot update SharePoint with changes made directly in the Excel spreadsheet. Let's now look at what you can do when you start from Excel 2007/2010.

For the example shown here, I have created an Excel table that lists the 30 brightest stars in the evening skies. The table includes the name of the star, the name of the constellation in which you can find the star, and the star's apparent magnitude.

Absolute vs. Relative Brightness for the Layman

Apparent magnitude defines the relative brightness of the stars when you view them. However, similar stars appear to vary in brightness when you look at them not only because some are bigger or hotter, but also because they exist at different distances from the Earth. If you could place all stars at the same distance from the Earth, about the same distance as the sun, you could then refer to their absolute brightness.

Figure 7-8 shows the beginning of this worksheet.

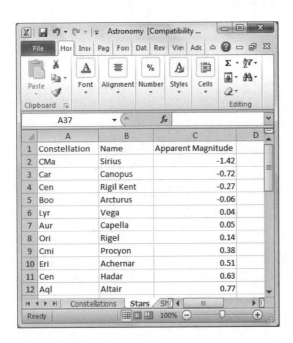

Figure 7-8. Portion of the 30 Brightest Stars spreadsheet

Defining a Table Within Your Excel Worksheet

Before you can export this Excel worksheet to SharePoint, you need to define the data that you want to transfer as a table. A table can include all the data in a worksheet or just a subset of the data. To define a table within a worksheet, follow these steps:

1. Go to the **Insert** Ribbon and select **Table** from the **Tables** section.

2. Select the cells you want to include in the table. Do this by clicking in any corner of the data block you want to use and, while holding the left mouse button down, drag through the data to the diagonal corner.

3. When you reach the diagonal corner, release the mouse button. Excel circumscribes the selected data with a dotted border and lightly shades the cells of the selected range.

4. After releasing the mouse button, a pop-up dialog box appears showing you the range of the selected cells, as displayed in Figure 7-9. You can edit this range manually. However, if you carefully chose your starting and ending point when dragging through the data, this range should accurately represent the data you want to use.

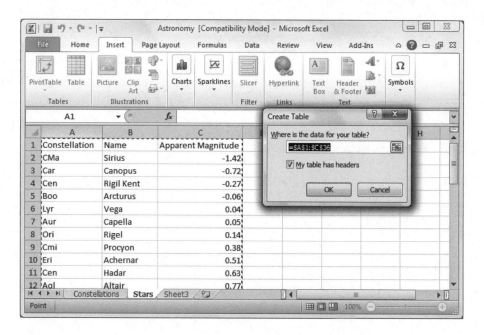

Figure 7-9. Defining the cell range you want to export to create a table

---

■ **Caution** While it is possible to define multiple data ranges for some commands, the **Create Table** command does not support multiple data ranges.

In addition to defining the cell range for the table, you can determine whether your data range includes headers. When copying data to SharePoint, the headers from the Excel data range become the column names. Therefore, including them lets you determine the column names. If you do not include column names in your cell range, then SharePoint generates a set of default names for its columns such as Column1, Column2, etc.

Exporting the Excel Table

Once you have defined a table, a new tab appears above the **Excel** Ribbon named **Table Tools**. This tab contains only a single sub-tab named **Design**. This Ribbon displays only those commands that act on tables not worksheets. In this Ribbon, locate the **External Table Data** section and click the lower portion of the **Export** button. This button's action displays a drop-down menu of the types of exports that Excel supports for tables. In Figure 7-10, you can see that this workbook supports two exports, one for SharePoint and one for Visio. In this case, you want to export the table to a SharePoint list, so select the first option.

Figure 7-10. Exporting the table to a SharePoint list

Before Excel can export the table, it needs additional information. First, it needs the address of the SharePoint site. For this example, I will again use the top-level site on my SharePoint server named Vanguard. Figure 7-11 shows this dialog box.

Figure 7-11. Defining the SharePoint server to publish to and providing a table name

Immediately beneath the **Address** field, you see a check box that asks whether you want to create a read-only connection to the SharePoint list. This option may be confusing; you may think that if you do not select it, you will get a read-write connection. Actually, if you do not select this option, no connection between the SharePoint list and the Excel worksheet will exist after Excel publishes the data to SharePoint so that Excel can read changes to the list data. The thing to remember is that this statement is from Excel's point of view. Therefore, you need to check this box to create a one-way data synchronization that allows Excel to read changes made in the SharePoint list and update the Excel worksheet. Unfortunately, it does not allow Excel to write changes made in Excel back to SharePoint.

Next, you must supply a name for the new SharePoint list (even though the dialog refers to your "table"). This name cannot be the name of any existing list in your SharePoint site. If a list already exists with the name you supply, Excel displays a message that says, "The specified list name is already in use on this server. You must rename the list before publishing it to the server."

■ **Note** You must have permission in SharePoint to create lists to export data from Excel to SharePoint.

You can also supply a list description. This description appears when you display the lists on the site. Therefore, supply a meaningful description that will help site users determine what type of data to expect in the list.

The second page of this dialog box, shown in Figure 7-12, displays how it associates each table field with a data type recognized by SharePoint. Excel tries to assign appropriate data types to each field. However, if it does not, you may need to cancel the current operation, return to the data in the worksheet, and change the data formatting of individual cells to a type that converts to the SharePoint data type you want.

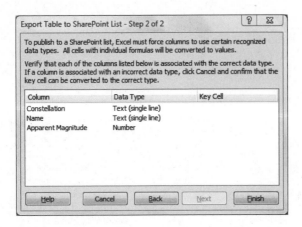

Figure 7-12. *Verifying the data types selected for the SharePoint columns*

■ **Note** You cannot directly change the data types shown in the **Export Table to SharePoint List** dialog box. You can only change the underlying Excel cell formatting to affect the selected data types.

To begin the actual data export, click the **Finish** button. Depending on the size of your table, this operation can take from a few seconds to a few minutes. When it finishes exporting the data, the dialog box shown in Figure 7-13 tells you whether it was able to publish the table successfully or not. If the publishing task succeeds, this dialog box also contains a clickable hyperlink to display the new SharePoint list.

Figure 7-13. *Dialog box announcing the successful publishing of the table*

■ **Tip** You may want to click this link before you click **OK.** This way you don't not have to manually open SharePoint and navigate to the new list to verify the data transfer. Just remember to come back and click the **OK** button to finish the publishing process.

Viewing the Exported Excel Data in the New SharePoint List

Figure 7-14 shows the lists in my SharePoint site. Notice that the list **Stars** appears along with the description supplied in the **Export Table** dialog box from Figure 7-11.

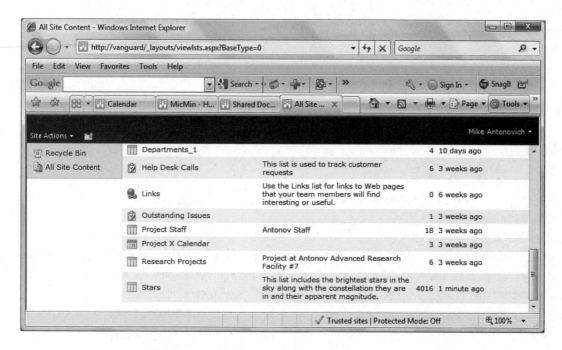

Figure 7-14. The All Site Content page displaying all lists in the current site

If you click the **Stars** list, SharePoint opens the list using the default view as shown in Figure 7-15. Notice that the transfer adds two columns at the beginning of the list that define the item type and allow attachments.

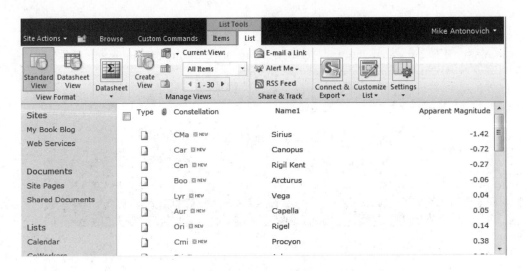

Figure 7-15. The Stars data after being imported to a SharePoint list

---

■ **Tip** If all the values in a column typically remain empty or unimportant (such as Type or Attachment in the above list), you should consider modifying the view to eliminate that column from displaying in the default view and most, if not all, other views you might subsequently create. Even the mandatory list column, Title (which you could rename to something more useful), can be skipped in a view that is used to export data to Excel.

Note that SharePoint changes the name of the column defining the star names. In Excel, you identified this column in the header as **Name**. However, SharePoint reserves this name and therefore renames the column by adding a "1" to the end of the column name. If you do not like this, you can go to the list properties and change the column name to something more meaningful, such as **Star Names**.

If you did not check the box to create a read-only connection to the SharePoint list, you cannot synchronize any changes you make in this SharePoint list back to the Excel spreadsheet. If you did select this option, you can make changes to the SharePoint list, and then with the Excel spreadsheet open, navigate to the **Table Tools Design** Ribbon in Excel. In the **External Table Data** group, click the **Refresh** button and select the option **Refresh** or **Refresh All** as shown in Figure 7-16. These options use the stored connection information between the SharePoint list and Excel created when you exported the original SharePoint list to Excel. You can now reuse this connection to update Excel with the current values in the SharePoint list.

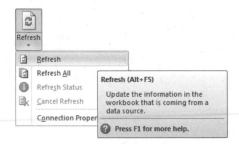

Figure 7-16. The Refresh options available when using a read-only connection to SharePoint

While you can update the Excel table with changes made to the SharePoint list that you exported from Excel, you cannot make changes to the Excel table and automatically synchronize those changes to the SharePoint list. As mentioned before, Microsoft deprecated this feature in Excel 2007. One solution would be to downgrade your Office installation and use Microsoft Excel 2003, which can synchronize data changes in both directions. However, if you think of downgrading your copy of Microsoft Office as something on par with giving up your fully loaded BMW for a Yugo Koral 45, read on to the next sections.

A Quick Look at Excel 2003 and Synchronization

Because I have mentioned several times that Excel 2003 provides different functionality with SharePoint 2003/2007 than Excel 2007/2010, you may be discouraged about Excel's role in SharePoint 2010's collaborative future. Before presenting a solution for the Excel 2007/2010 and 2010 user, let's take a quick look back at Excel 2003 and SharePoint 2003/2007.

Exporting a SharePoint 2007 List to Excel 2003

In SharePoint 2003 and 2007, you could export a list to Excel 2003 by selecting the SharePoint list you wanted to use and choosing **Export to Spreadsheet** from the **Actions** menu. As before, your computer first displays a dialog box asking whether you trust the source when SharePoint tries to send the IQY file. Click **Open** to allow your computer to download the file.

Excel may also prompt you with a similar question about whether you trust the query used to import external data. Since you trust the source in this case, click **Open** to continue.

You might see one more dialog box asking you for your user name and password to access the data on SharePoint, depending on the integration of your network security. After you click **OK** on this dialog box, you should see the list appear in an Excel worksheet, as shown in Figure 7-17. Notice that during this process, you only have the option of selecting where to load the list, such as into a new workbook or a new worksheet, or where on an existing worksheet to place the list if you have Excel open before you start the export from SharePoint. Excel 2003 also does not support the **PivotChart** option found in Excel 2007 and Excel 2010.

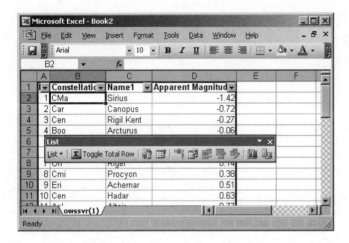

Figure 7-17. Excel 2003 uses the List toolbar to work with synchronized lists.

The **List** toolbar in Excel 2003 allows you to work with the downloaded list. Let's look first at the third and fourth buttons from the left.

The third button synchronizes the Excel list with the SharePoint list. When you click this button, it sends changes made to data rows in Excel back to SharePoint and changes to SharePoint items overwrite the existing data in Excel. If someone makes changes to both the SharePoint item and the Excel row of the same item, the synchronize action displays a Resolve Conflicts and Errors dialog box showing both sets of changes and allows you to determine which set of changes you want to keep.

The fourth button lets you discard your changes and refresh your Excel list with current data from the SharePoint list. Use this option if you made accidental changes to the Excel list or changes that you do not want to keep.

The first button in the toolbar opens a drop-down list of options that allow you to:

- Insert rows and columns into the list.

- Delete rows and columns from the list.

- Sort the list.

- View and edit the list data with an Excel-generated form.

- Publish the list to SharePoint.

- Resize the list.

- View the list on the server.

- Convert the list back to a normal range of data.

- Unlink the list (from SharePoint).

- Define other data range properties and connection properties.

Exporting Excel 2003 Worksheets to SharePoint

One of the first differences you will notice when starting an export from Excel 2003 is how to begin the process. In Excel 2007 and 2010, you have to define the range of cells you want to use as a table before you can export the data to SharePoint. In Excel 2003, the proper terminology defines a **list** instead. You still must select the range of data you want to define in your Excel list the same as you do in Excel 2007 and 2010. However, to create the list, open the **Data** drop-down menu. From this menu, select **List** and then **Create List** as shown in Figure 7-18.

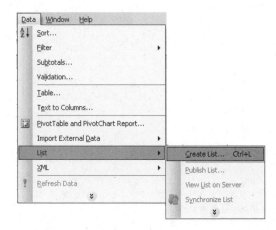

Figure 7-18. Creating a List in Excel 2003 before you can export data to SharePoint

The **Create List** option opens a dialog box that confirms the data range you want to use for the list. You can manually adjust this list by either entering a new range directly or clicking the button to the right of range and dragging through the range of cells you want to use. You should always include headers as the first row of the list. As mentioned, SharePoint uses these headers as your column names. Otherwise, SharePoint creates default names for the columns: Column1, Column2 . . . Column$N$. Figure 7-19 shows that this dialog box looks similar to the one used in Excel 2007 and 2010 except that it replaces the word "Table" with "List."

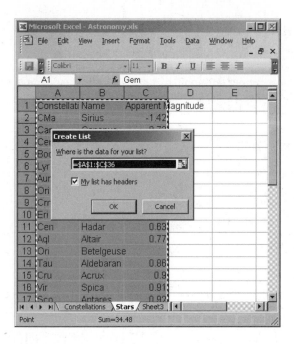

Figure 7-19. Confirming the list data range and whether it has headers

Having defined a list, you can now use the **List** toolbar. Open the **List** drop-down menu to find and select the **Publish List** option as shown in Figure 7-20.

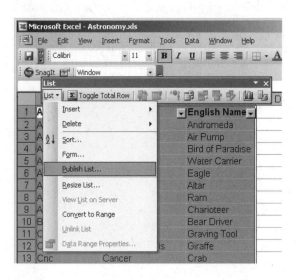

Figure 7-20. Using the Publish List option from the List toolbar to publish to SharePoint

The rest of the process for publishing the list parallels what you saw earlier using Excel 2010. The next dialog box that appears asks you for the site address where you want to publish your list. Instead of a check box asking you to create a read-only connection to the SharePoint list, Excel 2003 displays a check box asking whether you want to link to the new SharePoint list. If you do not select this check box, you cannot synchronize changes between the two lists after the publication process completes. If you do select it, you can synchronize data in both directions.

If the publication of your Excel 2003 worksheet succeeds, you should see a dialog box similar to the one in Figure 7-21.

Figure 7-21. Successfully published Excel worksheets display a link to the new list.

What Happened to Synchronization?

As mentioned at the end of the last section, Microsoft chose to deprecate the ability for Excel to synchronize data with a SharePoint list. Excel proponents are quick to point out that a large number of Office users feel very comfortable working with Excel spreadsheets and manipulating its data. Access supporters counter that they have a superior development platform that allows for the easy creation of forms and reports. After carefully considering where to place its efforts, apparently Microsoft made the decision to deprecate synchronization from Excel 2007 as well as Excel 2010. Of course, this is just an opinion.

The fact is that, out of the box, Excel (since 2007) no longer supports synchronization. However, not all is lost. Another alternative is available.

Microsoft published an add-on for Excel 2007 that allows it to synchronize data with the corresponding SharePoint list. Fortunately, this add-on still works for Excel 2010, although it appears to work slightly different for Excel 2010. The major caveat is that you may first need to save the Excel spreadsheet using the older 2003 format, load the add-on from Microsoft, and then open the spreadsheet again to use the add-on.

You can currently find this add-on at the following address (it's a long URL; be sure to enter it as a single line):

```
www.microsoft.com/downloads/details.aspx
?FamilyId=25836E52-1892-4E17-AC08-5DF13CFC5295&displaylang=en
```

```
or just enter
```

```
http://tinyurl.com/yvw8g5
```

This site includes full instructions on how to download and install this add-on, so I will skip that process. Instead, I will show how you can use the add-on to upload a new table to a new SharePoint list and then maintain the list data from either SharePoint or Excel.

One more note: you should read the "Publishing and Synchronizing Excel 2007 Tables to SharePoint Lists" article at msdn.microsoft.com/en-us/library/bb462636(office.11).aspx.

Linking a List in Excel to SharePoint

I will assume that you have successfully installed the Excel add-on mentioned in the previous section. In fact, I will start with a basic spreadsheet shown in Figure 7-22 that contains some data on NASA's fleet of space shuttles from the past 30 years.

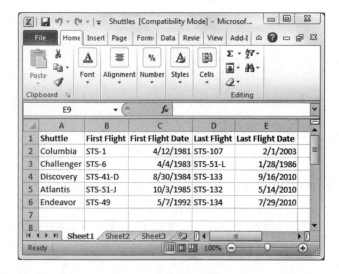

Figure 7-22. Shuttle list created in Excel 2010 but saved in 2003 format

The worksheet contains a simple set of data consisting of four columns and five rows. (If you are a space enthusiast who is wondering what happened to the *Enterprise* and the *Buran*, note that I am only including manned shuttles that have actually flown into space.) However, you cannot simply point at a spreadsheet and upload the data from it into a SharePoint list. I suppose this apparent limitation derives from the fact that a worksheet by itself does not have any boundaries. How many rows does it really have? How many columns does it really have? You can resolve these questions by selecting the columns and rows you want to define as a list and then formatting them as a table within Excel 2010. To do this, follow these steps:

1. Click in one of the corners of the spreadsheet and, while pressing the left mouse button, drag through the cells to the diagonal corner.

2. Click the **Insert** ribbon.

3. Select the **Table** option in the **Tables** group of the **Insert** Ribbon.

4. A small dialog box appears allowing you to verify the data range you selected in Step 1 for the table. You can also select whether this data range includes headers as its first row. These headers, when present, define the names of the columns in the SharePoint list.

When you click **OK**, you have defined a limited area of a worksheet by selecting a table. You can have other data on the spreadsheet that is not part of this table. In fact, you can have several different tables defined on the same worksheet. If you click anywhere within the table you want to publish, a new ribbon tab named **Table Tools Design** appears. Click this tab to open this ribbon. The add-on mentioned at the beginning of this section creates a new group named **SharePoint**. This group has a single button labeled **Publish and allow Sync**.

In SharePoint 2007, you could simply click this button to publish your Excel table to SharePoint. However, the pre-release version of SharePoint 2010 and Excel 2010 will fail during the publish process with a message indicating that the list does not exist. This provides a possible clue to a workaround (assuming this problem will eventually be addressed). Before clicking the Publish and allow Sync button, export the Excel table to your SharePoint 2010 site as described in the section "Exporting the Excel Table" of this chapter. This process publishes the tale to a SharePoint list but does not provide for synchronization. Once it has been published to SharePoint, click the **Publish and allow Sync** button to create the synchronization between the Excel table and SharePoint.

Excel then opens a dialog box that asks where you want to publish your table. Even though you already published the table using the Export option, you must still enter the URL of the site where you published your table into the **Address** field. (In Figure 7-23, this site is http://vanguard.) Then supply the list name previously used in the Export of the table in the **Name** field along with a description. Remember that at this point you are identifying the site and list name of the table you just exported to SharePoint, not a new site or list name.

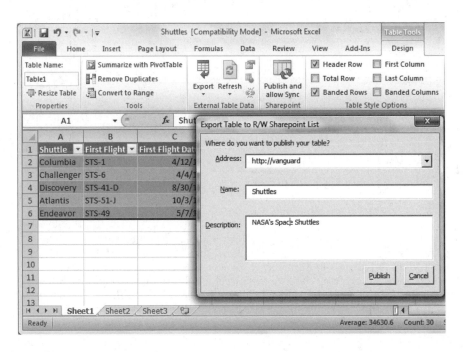

Figure 7-23. Using Publish and allow Sync to publish Excel 2007/2010 spreadsheets to SharePoint 2010

When you click **Publish**, Excel identifies the existing list in SharePoint and adds the synchronization capability between Excel and SharePoint. Perhaps by the time you read this, the problem with this add-on will get resolved so that you can publish and synchronize with this one button rather than having to first export the table and then synchronize it as two separate processes. In any case, you should now be able to go to SharePoint and open the list as shown in Figure 7-24.

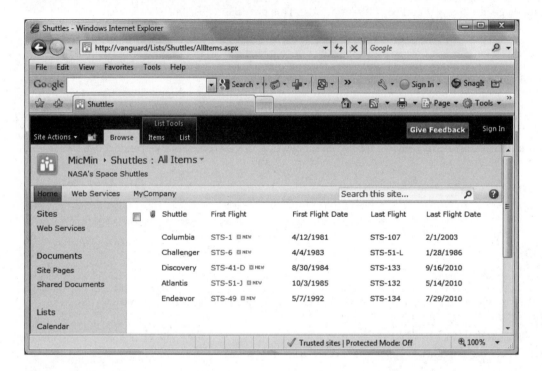

Figure 7-24. Published Excel spreadsheet table displayed in a SharePoint list

Suppose you discover that you have to make a change to the data for one of the shuttles, such as changing the last flight date. You can open the Excel spreadsheet of your shuttle information to find and edit the specific cell. In fact, you can make several changes. However, when you are done making changes, you can now synchronize your changes back to the SharePoint list by right clicking anywhere within the table. This opens the drop-down menu shown in Figure 7-25. Find the **Table** option in this menu. As you hover over this menu option, a submenu flies out to display options specific to tables. Look for and select the option **Synchronize with SharePoint**.

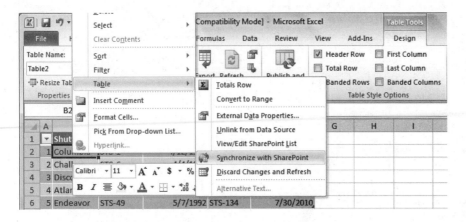

Figure 7-25. Synchronizing Excel changes with SharePoint

■ **Note** Once published to SharePoint, a new column appears at the start of the spreadsheet in Excel called ID, which is read-only. This ID remains read-only so SharePoint and Excel can identify which rows to link together.

When you select this option, Excel synchronizes its changes with SharePoint and vice versa. As long as no one tries to edit the same item/row, this process completes after a few seconds. If a conflict occurs, a dialog box appears with both sets of changes, and you can select how you want to resolve the conflict.

■ **Note** With this add-on to allow synchronization, you can no longer click the **Refresh** button in the **External Table Data** section of the **Table Tools Design** Ribbon. All synchronization, both ways, occurs through the Synchronize with SharePoint option just described.

If you have been making changes in Excel and decide before you synchronize those changes that you really want to discard them and refresh your spreadsheet with the data from the SharePoint list, you can right-click anywhere within the table and select the **Table** option, as shown in Figure 7-26. Then click the **Discard Changes and Refresh** button.

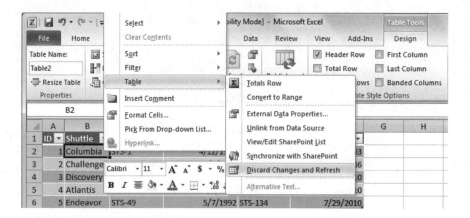

Figure 7-26. Discarding your Excel changes and refreshing from SharePoint

This action updates the Excel table with values from the SharePoint list. You cannot select which of your changed Excel values SharePoint will update. Therefore, the dialog box shown in Figure 7-27 reminds you that refreshing your data from the SharePoint list erases any changes you made in the Excel table, preventing you from updating SharePoint with any of them. In other words, unlike synchronizing, this option performs a one-way overwrite of everything in your Excel table using data from the SharePoint list, just as the old **Refresh** button would.

Figure 7-27. Refresh replaces all Excel data with SharePoint data.

Summary

In this chapter, you examined the basic collaboration features between SharePoint and Excel 2010. You started by exporting the metadata from a document library to an Excel worksheet. If you include a SharePoint column that also includes a link to the document itself, you can open the document from Excel by clicking the link.

At first, it may seem that the collaboration between these two products works like SharePoint's collaboration with other Office products such as MS Word, but you quickly discovered that it actually has at least one serious limitation. While you can export data from SharePoint to Excel and you can refresh Excel with changes made in SharePoint, you cannot send changes made to the Excel worksheet back to the SharePoint list. The synchronization between these two products only works in one direction.

Looking back at Excel 2003, you see that SharePoint did support bidirectional synchronization of changes made on either platform. Fortunately, although Microsoft chose to deprecate bidirectional synchronization between SharePoint and Excel, Microsoft does provide an add-on to Excel that restores this capability. In the last section of this chapter, you saw how to use this add-on with Excel to synchronize changes between Excel and SharePoint.

Perhaps Microsoft hopes that users will switch from Excel to Access for manipulating SharePoint lists while also creating additional functionality through forms and reports. However, SharePoint still has a special role for Excel, as you will see in the next chapter. SharePoint combines Excel spreadsheets with a new service called Excel Services that allows the publication of spreadsheets across the Web. It also provides limited functionality to users of these spreadsheets, even if those users do not have Excel on their desktops.

CHAPTER 8

■ ■ ■

Publishing Excel with Excel Services

You saw in Chapter 7 that Microsoft Office Excel does not, by itself, bring as much capability to the table of collaboration as Word, Outlook, or Access. Because Microsoft has decided to deprecate synchronization between Excel and SharePoint lists, your initial impression may be that the only value Excel can offer might lie in its ability to help you create lists from other data sources. Perhaps if you can export other data into an Excel format or maybe read it into Excel, you might subsequently export it to a new SharePoint list. Similarly, you might transfer the data from a SharePoint list to an Excel worksheet so that you can save it perhaps as a CSV file that other applications might then import. Not to say that these capabilities do not add value, but for a tool as popular as Excel has become, you may expect more.

The good news is that there is more. The bad news is that to use the features discussed in this chapter, you need to be running the Enterprise version of SharePoint Server 2010 with Excel Services turned on. You cannot run Excel Services on SharePoint Foundation 2010 alone. Therefore, if you are fortunate enough to have the Enterprise version, you will want to read this chapter, which examines how to publish Excel spreadsheets to SharePoint. Then, from within SharePoint, you'll be able not only to view the data already in the worksheet, but also to update the data in the worksheet while protecting your format and calculation formulas with parameters. Some of the other benefits of publishing an Excel spreadsheet using SharePoint's Excel Services include the following:

- You can now make your spreadsheet available to anyone who has access to your SharePoint site through a browser. Users with access do not need to have Excel on their desktops.

- You can publish just the parts of your spreadsheet that you want others to see. You can hide your staging data and formulas.

- You can limit viewers' interaction with your spreadsheet to selected cells with parameters.

I will also demonstrate how you can create dashboards with Excel and work with data cubes. Finally, the chapter will close with a brief look at using the Report Center together with Excel Services, KPIs, and more.

Configuring Excel Services

Typically, the task of configuring Excel Services falls to your SharePoint administrator. However, you may be curious about how to turn Excel Services on in case you need to go to your SharePoint administrator with additional requests to expand your use of Excel Services to new sites and libraries. Therefore, this section briefly lists the steps required to accomplish this task. First, your SharePoint administrator must open your SharePoint **Central Administration** site.

1. Select **Central Administration** from the left navigation panel.

2. Select **Manage service applications** from the Application Management group in the main panel.

3. On the Service Applications page, click **Excel Services**.

4. On the next page, click **Trusted File Locations**. You need to tell SharePoint the location of the library that holds the Excel files so that IIS trusts opening and displaying those files.

5. On the **Excel Services Trusted File Location** page, check for your site location. Note that if your SharePoint administrator has already added a parent site and selected **Yes to Trust Children**, you may not have to do a thing. Otherwise, click **Add Trusted File Location**.

6. On this page, the **Address** section expects the URL of the document library or network folder where you will store the Excel files you plan to access. With whatever address you enter, you must select a location type. If you plan to store your Excel files in a SharePoint document library, select **Microsoft SharePoint Foundation**. If you are using a network folder or a web folder, use the UNC or HTTP option, respectively.

7. You can leave most of the other options on this page on their default settings. However, you should change the setting **Allow External Data** to the option **Trusted data connection libraries only and embedded**.

8. Click the **OK** button to complete your definition of the Trusted File Location.

■ **Note** If you have different sites that need their own document library for storing Excel files for use with Excel Services, you must repeat the preceding steps, creating a Trusted File Location for each one.

At this point, your administrator has enabled Excel Services for your document library. If you plan to use simple Excel workbooks with self-contained data, you are set to continue. However, if you want to use an Excel workbook that connects to an external data source, first you must create a data connection library. In addition, data connection libraries are only available for sites built with the Enterprise edition of SharePoint Server 2010. I will talk more about working with data connections later in this chapter.

Publishing an Excel Form to Excel Services

Before you publish your spreadsheets to Excel Services, you should know that Excel Services supports all the layout and formatting features found in Excel, but only when you save your spreadsheets in .xlsx or .xlsb format. What the user sees after you publish your spreadsheet visually matches what you designed within Excel. Therefore, do not be afraid to create visually appealing layouts with formatting to emphasize different aspects of your spreadsheet. All of your formatting work translates to Excel Services.

To publish a form to Excel Services, you only need to add it to the document library defined when you activated Excel Services and specified as a Trusted File Location. You can do this from SharePoint by adding a new document to the document library, or you can publish the workbook from within Excel to your SharePoint library. Let's look first at simply adding a new workbook to the document library.

Adding an Excel Workbook to Your Document Library from SharePoint

For this method, suppose you previously created and saved a workbook that calculates the month-by-month interest and principal portion of a loan payment. Figure 8-1 shows a portion of this spreadsheet.

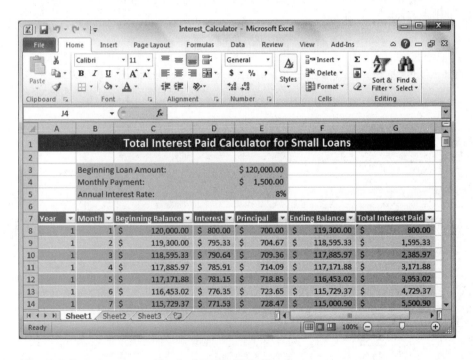

Figure 8-1. An interest paid calculator built in Excel

You can begin by opening the document library where you want to store your Excel workbook. For the purpose of this example, suppose you plan to store your Excel workbook in the **Shared Documents** library of a site named Vanguard. Simply open the library and click the **Upload Document** option in the **New** group of the **Documents** ribbon.

This option opens the **Upload Document** dialog box you saw earlier in this book in Figure 1-24, that allows you either to locate the file you want to upload by using the **Browse** button or to upload multiple files by clicking the **Upload Multiple Files** link. For a single workbook, you could also just enter the file name by typing it in the **Name** text box, but to ensure that you do not misspell the name, I recommend using the **Browse** button to select the file using the standard Windows **Open File** dialog box.

With the file to upload selected, click the **OK** button to continue. SharePoint now loads the file, and it appears in the **Shared Documents** library looking like any other file. You can now view the file either by directly clicking its name in the library list or, if you display the library using the **Standard View**, by positioning your mouse over the file name to display the drop-down menu arrow to the right of the file name and selecting **View in Web Browser**.

■ **Caution** Clicking directly on the file name in the library may open the Excel workbook in your web browser or in your local copy of Excel, depending on the setting of the library. To find out how your library has been set up, open **Settings** for your library and choose **Advanced Settings**. Then in the section titled **Opening Documents in the Browser**, select the option **Open in the browser** or **Use the server default (Open in the browser)** to open your Excel document within the web browser by default.

When you open the workbook within your browser using Excel Services, it should look similar to Figure 8-2. Note that it resembles the workbook opened in Excel.

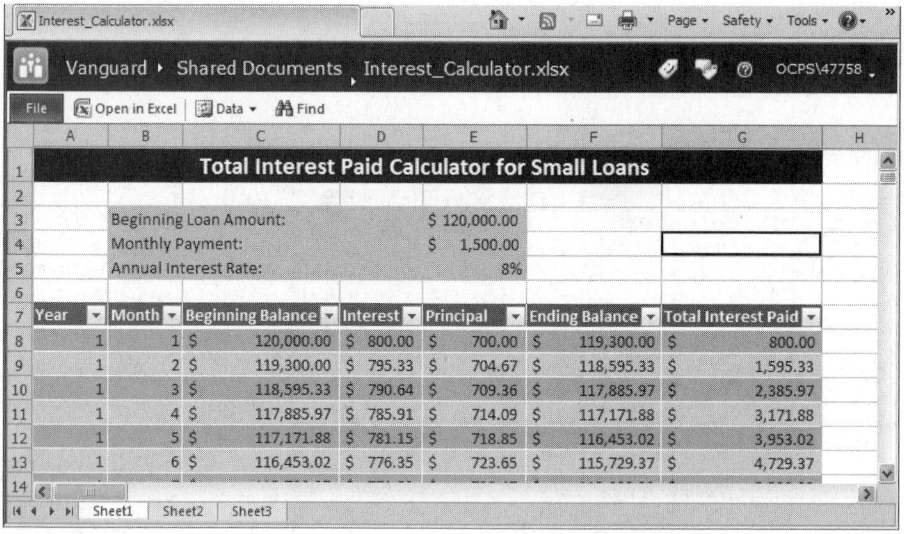

Figure 8-2. A simple total interest paid calculator displayed with Excel Services

Navigating Around Your Worksheet

SharePoint 2010 opens your entire workbook and lets you scroll around without the windowing effect that SharePoint 2007 used. In 2007, your workbook view defaulted to 75 rows by 20 columns at a time. You then could use arrows located in the upper right of the browser window to navigate through the rest of your spreadsheet. In SharePoint 2010, you can simply use the horizontal and vertical scroll bars as you would within Excel to navigate through the entire workbook.

On the top left of the Excel grid, you see three options. The first of these options lets you open the workbook in your local Excel client if you have Excel installed on your local computer.

The second option provides a drop-down menu where you can refresh selected or all connections in the workbook or recalculate the entire workbook. Refreshing a connection instructs the spreadsheet to read the data from its external data connection, check for new values, and update the spreadsheet appropriately. Recalculating the workbook recalculates cells based on formulas, but it does not check whether any data in its data source has changed.

The third option set provides the ability to find text strings anywhere within the spreadsheet. For example, you can look for a specific text string representing characters or even numbers in the values of the spreadsheet cells. Unfortunately, you cannot search using Boolean expressions on cell values. Nor can you search within the formulas used to calculate the cells.

You can even navigate between worksheets of your workbook if you have more than one sheet by using the controls in the lower-left corner of the grid. Notice that just like within Excel, you can move to the first, previous, next, or last worksheet in your workbook using the first four controls. You can also click the worksheet tabs in this section to jump directly to any of the worksheets in the workbook.

What you cannot do is directly edit any of the cell values in the grid. When you simply load your spreadsheet into a library that has Excel Services enabled, you can only view the spreadsheet.

Why You Need Parameters to Make Your Excel Form Interactive

Providing a static spreadsheet to view in the browser may have its place, but for most spreadsheets you want users to be able to change data, sort it, or even filter the data to better serve their needs. After all, spreadsheets are all about what-if analysis and making business decisions after evaluating data.

While you cannot provide total access to all the features spreadsheet users might normally use directly within Excel, you can at least provide the option to change values associated with specific cells while viewing the spreadsheet. Besides, anyone who really needs to have total control over the design of the spreadsheet and change the formatting, structure, or even the formulas used by the spreadsheet can always click the **Open in Excel** option mentioned earlier and work with the spreadsheet using their desktop copy of Excel. Just be sure to limit these permissions to people you trust so that only they can save changes to the workbook back to the library.

When you define parameters for your Excel worksheet, users can enter values for each of the parameters and then recalculate the worksheet the same as if they entered the values directly in the spreadsheet. Basically, a parameter defines an input value that updates a named cell, which in turn updates all dependent cells. In the next section, you will see how to define parameters that allow users to "update" the browser view of the spreadsheet.

Defining Parameters for Your Excel Form

When you decide to publish a spreadsheet with Excel Services, you must decide which field(s) users would most likely need to manipulate. As an example, let's return to our example of the simple interest calculation program mentioned earlier. Suppose we determine that the user only needs to vary three values:

- The initial loan amount

- The loan interest rate

- The monthly payment

With these three pieces of information, you can calculate each month's payment, determining the portion that pays the interest due and the amount used to reduce the loan's principal amount. You can then create a running total of these two numbers to display by month the amount in interest you paid to the bank for the privilege of borrowing the money and the remaining amount due on the loan. It then makes sense to define one row in the table for each month, with the columns representing the various calculated sums. In fact, once you have designed the formulas that you need to calculate for the first month, you can copy them for any number of months.

In the sample spreadsheet created for the examples in this chapter, I stopped the calculations after 30 years for the loan. But that does not mean that it will take 30 years to pay off the loan or that you will necessarily pay off the loan on the last month of the last year. It just provides a workspace for the calculations. In working with loans, you really need four pieces of information: the three specified previously and the length of the loan. You can specify any three, but you cannot force the fourth to a specific value without calculating it. A variation on this theme would be to create a spreadsheet in which you start with an initial loan amount, an interest rate, and a fixed number of months to pay off the loan, and then calculate the amount of the monthly payment you need to make given the other three constraints. This latter example illustrates how a bank determines your monthly mortgage payment amount when you buy a house for $200,000 with a 30-year 6% annual interest rate loan. By running the interest calculator as defined here, you could see how much sooner you could pay off your loan by making an extra $200 per month payment and how that reduces the total amount of money you ultimately pay to the bank.

To create a parameter, you first need to create a named range, or in this case a named cell. To do that, click the cell you want, such as the **Beginning Loan Amount** from Figure 8-1. Then simply go to the **Name box** to the left and immediately above the column headers of the grid. By default, the **Name Box** currently displays the cell reference. Once you click in the **Name** box, to select the cell reference, you can simply type the name you want to give to the cell, replacing the cell reference. For example, after clicking in the loan amount cell (E3), you might enter the name **Beginning_Amt**.

You can repeat this process for each cell you want to define with a name. In fact, you can name any cell or cell range and then use those names in your formulas rather than the cell reference. This technique makes returning to your spreadsheet months later and attempting to figure out what your formulas mean a lot easier. Naming a cell or a cell range does not mean that it will become a parameter for your spreadsheet, but to create a parameter, you must begin with a named cell.

■ **Note** As you will see later, you can create named cell ranges that you can then use in the Excel web part SharePoint provides to display a portion of a spreadsheet, but a cell range cannot be a parameter.

Another way to define the name for the cell begins again by selecting the cell or cell range you want to use. Then open the **Formulas** ribbon. In the **Defined Names** group, select the button **Define Name**. A dialog box appears, shown in Figure 8-3, that lets you define a name. Names can consist of up to 255 characters. However, as with any object name, you should use only as many characters as necessary to clearly and uniquely identify the object. A name must begin with a letter, underscore, or backslash. Excel treats the name **Interest** the same as **interest**, so do not try to differentiate cell names merely based on case. You cannot name a cell the same as another cell reference. You cannot include spaces in a name. However, using an underscore in place of a space makes the name just as readable.

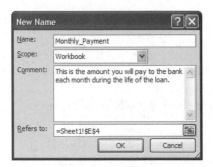

Figure 8-3. Naming a cell or cell range

Next in the dialog box, select a scope. By default, Excel assumes the entire workbook as the scope of the name. However, you can limit the name's scope to just the current worksheet.

The third item in the dialog box lets you document the cell by adding a comment. While adding a comment to a name might define why the cell or range was important enough to name, this information does not appear anywhere on the spreadsheet itself. However, you can see your comments when you open the **Name Manager** dialog box, also found in the **Defined Names** group of the **Formulas** ribbon.

The last option identifies the cell or cell range that the name references. You can change this value either by entering the cell or range reference manually or by clicking the button to the right of this field, which lets you select the cell or range by clicking and dragging (if you want to define a range) through the cells you want to reference. When you finish, click **OK** to create the name.

If you forget what names you have already used or which cell or cell range they apply to, you can view a dialog box that shows all the defined names within the current workbook by clicking the **Name Manager** button. Figure 8-4 shows an example of the **Name Manager.**

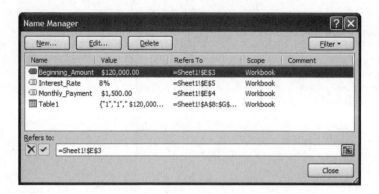

Figure 8-4. The Name Manager shows all named cells and ranges.

You can also use the **Name Manager** to edit properties of a name or delete a name. You can even create a new name definition by clicking the **New** button.

Ideally, you should define named cells that you want to use as parameters before you begin creating your spreadsheet. A good practice groups these parameter cells in a single place, perhaps at the top of the spreadsheet as shown in this example, or on a different worksheet dedicated to prompting for parameters. Then as you lay out the rest of your spreadsheet, you can reference the named cells and named cell ranges in your formulas rather than using cryptic cell references.

Publishing Your Excel Workbook

Once you have finished building your spreadsheet, first save it before you begin the steps to publish it to SharePoint. You can choose from two different ways to publish your spreadsheet. You have already seen one way earlier in this chapter: you can simply open the library where you want to publish your Excel files and upload the file to the library.

However, you can also publish the workbook from within Excel itself. Open the **Files** menu in Excel and select **Save & Send**. From the first column of share options, select Save to SharePoint. This action displays some features of publishing your workbook to Excel Services on the right side of the page as shown in Figure 8-5.

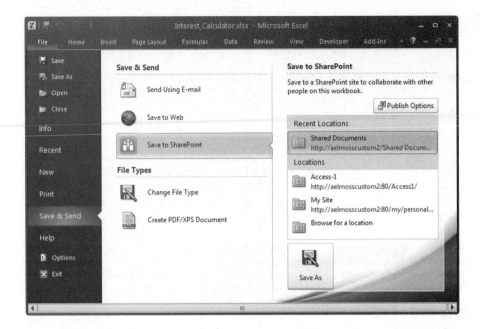

Figure 8-5. Publishing the Excel worksheet to Excel Services

You could save the spreadsheet by clicking the **Save As** button and supplying the name of the site where you want to publish the spreadsheet and its name. However, you would end up with an uneditable spreadsheet, just as if you had used the upload option from within SharePoint. Instead, click the **Publish Options** button at the bottom of the **Save As** window before uploading the file. This button opens the **Publish Options** dialog box shown in Figure 8-6.

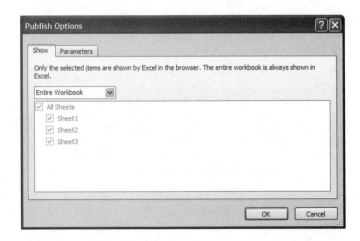

Figure 8-6. The Show page of the Excel Services Publish Options dialog box determines what users see.

This dialog box consists of two tabbed pages. The first page lets you define what parts of the workbook you want to display. By default, the Entire Workbook option displays all worksheets and items. Therefore, there are no additional options to select in the drop-down list displayed beneath the text **Entire Workbook**.

If you only want to display selected worksheets from the workbook, open the drop-down menu and select **Sheets**. This option displays each worksheet in the workbook with a check box before it. Uncheck the box for sheets you do not want to publish from the document. You can select individual worksheets or return to the **All Sheets** option to select them all automatically.

A third option in the drop-down, **Items in the Workbook**, lists tables and named ranges in the workbook. Thus, you can limit publication to a section of a worksheet defined by a specific table or a named cell range and ignore anything else that might appear in the workbook.

For this example, leave the option **Entire Workbook** selected and click the second tab, named **Parameters**. Excel does not assume that any of the named cells should be parameters. Thus, the parameter list begins empty as shown in Figure 8-7, and you must click the **Add** button to begin adding named cells that you want to use as parameters to the list.

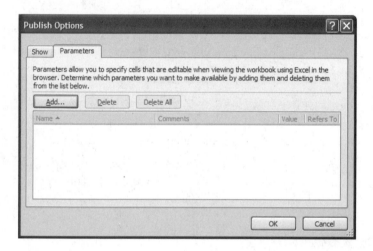

Figure 8-7. *The Parameters page of Excel Services Publish Options shows which named ranges to treat as parameters.*

When you click the **Add** button, you see a list of all the named cells. If you have named ranges or named tables, these do not appear. Only individual cells can serve as parameters. Thus, if you have 20 cells that you want to let users update when they interact with your spreadsheet online, you need to have 20 separate named cells. You cannot simply create a single named range and use it as your parameter. I know that this would make your development life easier. In fact, in some cases, it may even make sense when the values form a series. However, the parameter feature does not support that capability at this time.

On the other hand, as shown in Figure 8-8, you can select all the parameters you want to add at one time. You do not have to select them individually. When you are finished, click **OK**.

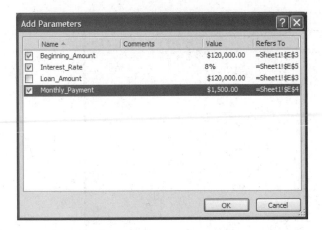

Figure 8-8. Selecting the named ranges you want to use as parameters

Click **OK** twice to return to the **Save & Send** page. It is now time to click **Save As** on this page. In the main **Save As** dialog box, click **My Network Places** along the left side. If you previously published a document to the library where you want to save the Excel spreadsheet, you probably will find a reference to the library here. If so, double-click it to select and open the library. If you have folders already set up for different types of files, open the folder by double-clicking it also. When you reach the folder where you want to save your file, enter a file name that you want to use. By default, Excel assumes that the SharePoint file name will match the name of the file on your local file system if you previously saved the file locally. Also make sure that you save the file as an Excel workbook (***.xlsx**) file.

If you have not previously saved anything to the document library where you want to save the workbook, you must enter the URL of the library directly into the **File Name** box. Figure 8-9 shows an example of entering the URL. Notice that when you enter the URL, you must include the server name as well as all folders up to and including the name of the library where you want to save the file.

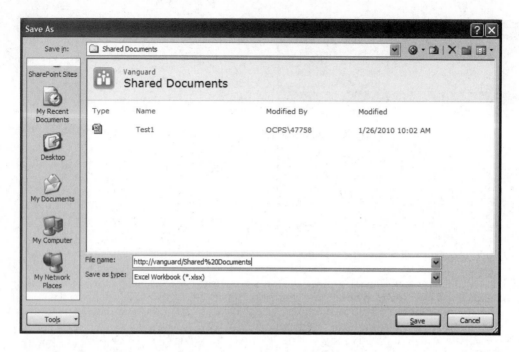

Figure 8-9. Entering the URL of the document library in SharePoint where you want to publish the workbook

---

■ **Tip** How do you know the URL you need to enter? Simple. Open SharePoint and navigate to the document library where you want to save your workbook. With the library open, capture the URL from the **Address** bar at the top of your browser. This URL contains some additional information at the end to display the contents of the library. Therefore, you can remove anything after the name of the library itself, but leave the last slash at the end of the URL so that Excel knows that you have only defined a directory, not a file.

After you select the library name from your **Network Places** or have manually entered the URL for the library, press the Enter key. This displays the contents of the library. Again, navigate through any subfolders if necessary to open the folder where you want to save the workbook.

Once you have saved your workbook to SharePoint, you can open it in your browser by going to the SharePoint library, locating the workbook file, right-clicking the file to open the drop-down menu, and selecting **View in Web Browser**. After the few moments it takes Excel Services to open the workbook and format the web page, you should see a page that looks like Figure 8-10.

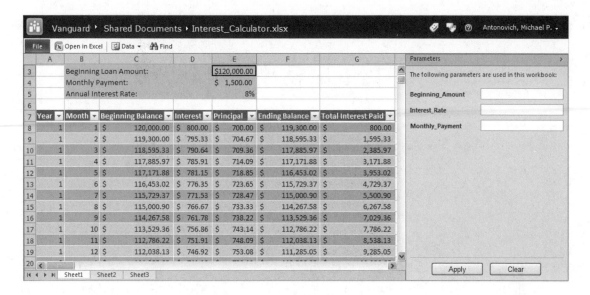

Figure 8-10. Initial values for the interest paid calculator

Notice that, unlike the first time when you uploaded an uneditable version of the spreadsheet, this time you get a panel on the right side that displays the parameters you defined. If you want to change any of the parameters, simply enter the new values you want to use in the text boxes to the right of the parameter names. You do not have to enter all the parameters, only those you want to change from their current values.

■ **Tip** If you do not include the cells referenced by your parameters in a visible part of the spreadsheet, you will not easily know which parameters changed. Therefore, you may want to include them in your displayed range as shown here.

Then click the **Apply** button at the bottom of the **Parameters** panel to recalculate the spreadsheet using your new parameter values. Figure 8-11 shows the screen updated after changing the monthly payment amount from $1,500 to $1,300.

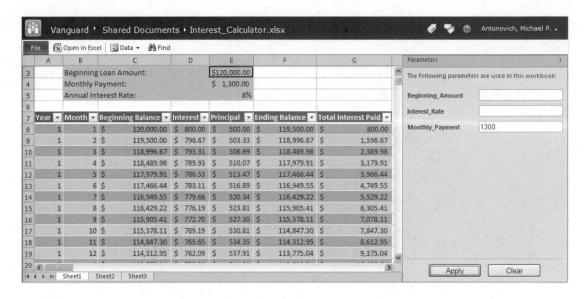

Figure 8-11. Updated values for the interest paid calculator using parameter values

The rest of the page works the same as described earlier. The one remaining item to note is that by publishing your Excel workbook using this method, you use an entire page to display it. You cannot include any other web parts on the page. You cannot add a header or other text that might help explain to users how to use the parameters for the Excel spreadsheet. Fortunately, Microsoft has added a web part that allows you to include an Excel spreadsheet on any web page that has web zones where you can add web parts.

■ **Caution** If recalculating the workbook does not appear to update the cells you expect, contact your SharePoint administrator to find out whether the field **Type of Toolbar** is set to **None** or **Navigate only**. Another possible setting to check is the **Calculate Workbook** setting.

Viewing Uploaded Excel Documents

Once you have published an Excel workbook to a SharePoint library, you can open it either in the web browser itself or in Excel. To select how you want to open the workbook, open the workbook's drop-down menu as shown in Figure 8-12.

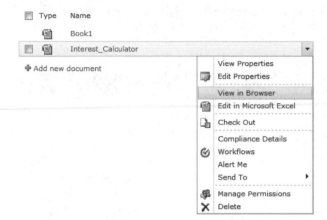

Figure 8-12. To view an Excel document, open the document's drop-down menu.

■ **Note** If you have Microsoft Web Applications installed on your system, you will also see in this drop-down list an Edit in Browser option, which opens the spreadsheet in a browser and uses Microsoft Excel Web App to edit the spreadsheet based on your permissions for the library where you stored the Excel document.

Users who have Excel installed on their local machines can gain access to the full functionality of the spreadsheet by opening the Excel document in Edit mode. When a spreadsheet is opened this way, users can edit any cells within it, not just the cells identified as parameters. They can also make changes to the spreadsheet. If those users also have the necessary permission to write files back to the library, they can then save those changes back to the document in the document library. You can control this ability through the option **Permissions for this document library** under the **Permissions and Management** section of **Library Settings**, found in the **Settings** group of the **Library** ribbon. On the other hand, you manage the permissions of an individual file by selecting **Manage Permissions** as shown in the item's dropidown menu in Figure 8-12.

Also, under **Settings**, you can control access by selecting **Advanced Settings** and changing the option for **Opening Documents in the Browser** setting to either **Open in the browser** or **Use the server default**. Then, if the user simply clicks the document from the library, it will open by default in their browser rather than in their local copy of Excel.

Using the Excel Page Web Part

Viewing an Excel workbook from a SharePoint library either in the browser using Excel Services or by downloading and opening it in a local copy of Microsoft Excel provides a quick way to view the spreadsheet. However, it does not let you include the workbook with other SharePoint features. Fortunately, SharePoint provides a web part that allows you to include an Excel workbook or portion of a worksheet inside any web page.

Suppose you start with a simple web page such as the one shown in Figure 8-13. In this page, you want to add a spreadsheet web part to the Left text area to display the interest-paid calculator beneath the Shared Documents list. Start by going to Site Actions and editing the page.

Figure 8-13. Beginning with a basic web page with two web part zones

Place your cursor beneath the Shared Documents library and click the left mouse button to set the insertion point. Next, open the **Insert** ribbon under the **Editing Tools** and click **Web Part**. The page refreshes and display three areas immediately beneath the ribbon, named Categories, Web Parts and About the Web Part. In the first area, Categories, click **Office Client Applications**. Next, click the web part **Excel Web Access**. Finally, click the Add button beneath the third section to add this web part as shown in Figure 8-14.

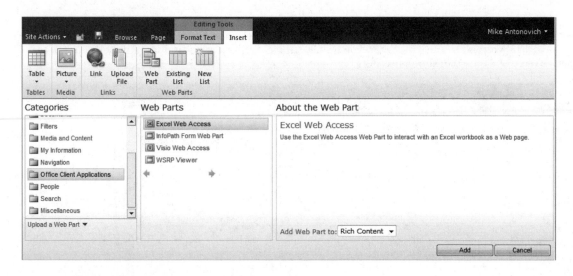

Figure 8-14. Adding a web part from the available parts list

You will now see a new web part at the top of the Left zone, titled **Excel Web Access**. The initial contents of this web part tells you that you must select a workbook for the web part to display by opening the tool pane for the web part and editing the Workbook property. Do this by opening the **Edit** drop-down menu and selecting **Edit Web Part**. You can also simply click the link in the web part: **Click here to open the tool pane**.

When the tool pane opens, as shown in Figure 8-15, in the first text box after the label **Workbook**, enter the URL of the workbook from the library where you published it. If you do not remember the name, or if you want to make sure that you get the path correct, click the button with the ellipses to the right of the text box.

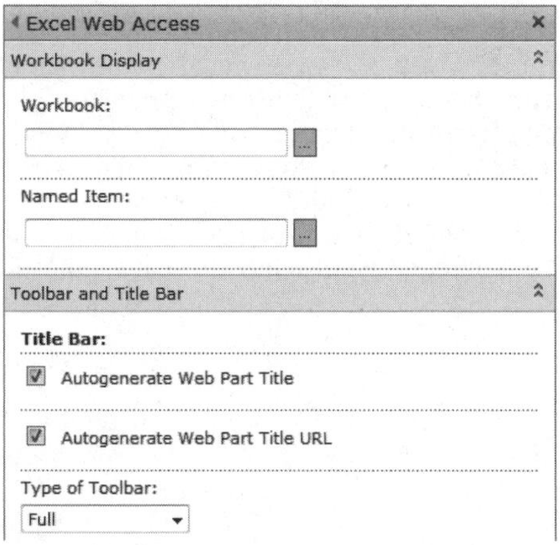

Figure 8-15. Defining the properties of the Excel Web Access web part

Clicking the ellipses button for the URL displays the **Select a Link** dialog box shown in Figure 8-16. Use this dialog box to navigate through your SharePoint site to locate the folder containing the spreadsheet you want to display. When you find it, double-click it, or click it once and then click **OK** to place the URL in the **Workbook** text field.

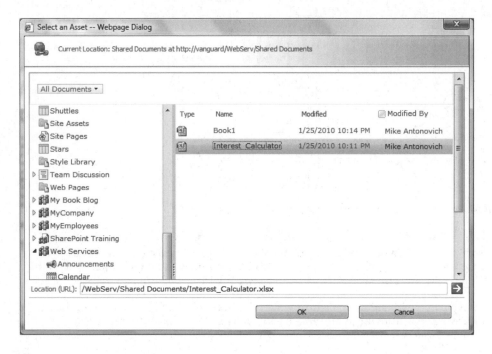

Figure 8-16. Navigating to your workbook

Under **Named Item** in the tool pane, you can also choose a specific named item from the workbook to display. When you do this, only that named area appears within the web part when you display it. This feature eliminates the user's ability to move around the workbook to other areas on the worksheet or to different worksheets in the workbook. You create a named item in the same way that you created named cells for parameters earlier in this chapter. While in Excel, select the range of cells you want to treat as a single object for display purposes and give it a name. Then, when you add the workbook to the web part, use the **Named Item** field to select the named range. Unlike the **Workbook** field, which lets you search for the workbook, the **Named Item** field does not provide you with an easy list to select from available named ranges in the current workbook.

By default, the Excel web part automatically generates a title for itself. To replace this title with your own, you might think that you could simply change the **Title** property in the **Appearance** section of the tool pane. After all, this technique works for many other web parts. However, it will not work here unless you also uncheck the option **Autogenerate Web Part Title** in the **Toolbar and Title Bar** section as well. If you do not uncheck this option, the web part continues to auto-generate its title, overwriting the changes you make to the **Title** field in the Appearance group of properties when you attempt to apply your changes.

■ **Caution** Always turn off the **Close** option in the **Appearance** section of a web part if you do not want users to accidentally remove web parts from the page. If you close a web part, it is still part of the page definition and you can recover a closed web part. If you delete a web part on the other hand, it is gone and you will have to start over with a new instance of the template if you need it. To recover a closed web part, click the **Add a Web Part** button at the top of any web part zone. In the dialog that appears, instead of selecting one of the web part templates, click the **<<add text here>>** link at the bottom of the dialog. This displays a panel to the right of the page. The first link in the panel is **Closed Web Parts** with a number in parentheses after it. If the number here is greater than zero, you have at least one closed web part in the current page. Click the **Closed Web Parts** link to display the closed web parts. You can then select any of the closed web parts and click **OK** to reopen the web part at the top of the current web part zone. You can also specify a web part zone, but even if you open the web part in the current web part zone, you can always drag it to a different position in the current or different web part zone.

Figure 8-17 shows an example of how you might include a web part in the middle of a web page while including other web parts around it. In this case, a Content Editor web part appears above the Excel web part to describe the Excel web part and explain its use.

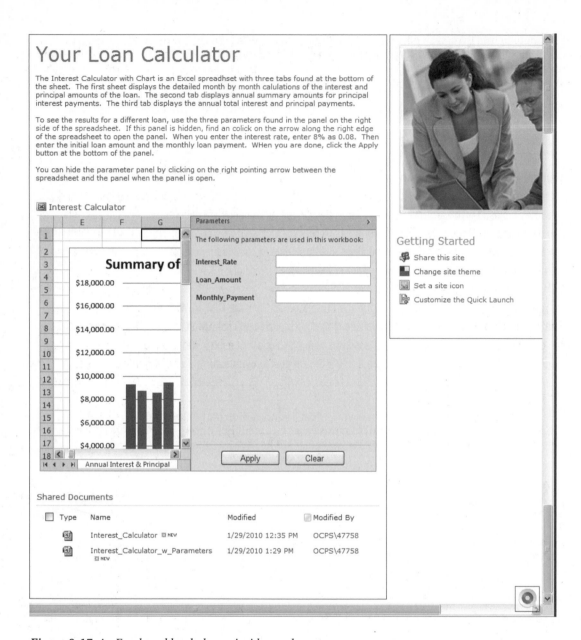

Figure 8-17. An Excel workbook shown inside a web part

Viewing Data from External Sources in Excel Using a Data Connection

In all the Excel examples so far, we have entered data directly into the cells of the worksheets. However, you can create Excel worksheets that display and manipulate data from external data sources. Primarily these external sources will be databases such as Access and SQL Server. However, you can connect to many other data sources as well.

For this section, let's use the PUBS sample database provided for SQL Server 2008.

■ **Tip** If you have Visual Studio, you can create the PUBS database for SQL Server 2008 from `C:\Program Files\Microsoft Visual Studio 10\SDK\v3.5\Samples\Setup\InstPubs.sql`. If you do not have Visual Studio, you can also download PUBS for SQL Server 2000 from Microsoft's Download Center at the following site (be sure to enter the URL as one line even though I show it on two lines here):

`www.microsoft.com/downloads/details.aspx?`

`FamilyID=06616212-0356-46A0-8DA2-EEBC53A68034&displaylang=en`

or simply enter

`tinyurl.com/yzx6lz`

If you begin with the original SQL 2000 PUBS database, you may need to set the compatibility level, using the command `EXEC sp_dbcmptlevel 'Pubs','100'` for SQL Server 2008 or `EXEC SharePoint_dbcmptlevel 'Pubs', '90'` for SQL Server 2007.

The AuthorRoyalty View

Let's take a closer look at the **AuthorRoyalty** view in case you want to try re-creating it on your machine. I created a view in the PUBS database so that I could retrieve data for each book and then calculate the sales for the book along with the royalty due to each author. The information I need spans five tables within PUBS, beginning with the **Sales** table. This table identifies the book by only a **title_id** value. Therefore, I link this ID to the **title_id** value in the **Titles** table. Then the **Titles** table forms a many-to-many relationship with the **Authors** table. Therefore, you need a connecting table named **TitleAuthor** between these two tables to create two one-to-many relationships. Then if you also want to know in which states books were sold, you need to link the **Sales** table to the **Stores** table using the **stor_id** field found in both tables.

Next, you need to look at the fields you want in the spreadsheet and see whether those fields exist as individual fields in the tables selected or you need to calculate some of them. While the **Sales** table provides the quantity of books sold by title, you need to get the price of the book from the **Title** table to calculate the value of the books sold. Similarly, to calculate the author's royalty, you need to multiply the value of the books sold by the author's royalty percentage, which you can find in the **Authors** table.

After thoroughly researching which fields you need to generate the report you want, you can write the view definition as follows:

```
USE [PUBS]
GO
/****** Object:  View [dbo].[AuthorRoyalty]
*******Script Date: 01/20/2008 13:39:41 ******/
SET ANSI_NULLS ON
GO
SET QUOTED_IDENTIFIER ON
GO
CREATE VIEW [dbo].[AuthorRoyalty]
AS
SELECT stores.stor_name
     , stores.state
     , sales.ord_date
     , sales.qty
     , titles.title
     , titles.type
     , titles.price
     , titles.royalty
     , authors.au_lname
     , authors.au_fname
     , sales.qty * titles.price AS Amount
     , sales.qty * titles.price * titles.royalty / 100 AS AuthorRoyalty
  FROM dbo.sales INNER JOIN
       dbo.stores ON sales.stor_id = stores.stor_id INNER JOIN
       dbo.titles ON sales.title_id = titles.title_id INNER JOIN
       dbo.titleauthor ON titles.title_id = titleauthor.title_id INNER JOIN
       dbo.authors ON authors.au_id = titleauthor.au_id

GO
```

Once a view is created, you can access it from a database using the same methods you would to access a table. If you need a special view for your Excel table and do not feel comfortable defining the view yourself, contact your database administrator for further assistance.

Creating an External Connection

Start a new Excel workbook and open the **Data** ribbon as shown in Figure 8-18. In the **Connections** group, click the **Connections** button.

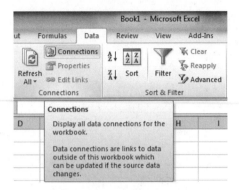

Figure 8-18. Beginning a connection definition

This button opens the **Workbook Connections** dialog box, which shows any connections currently defined for the workbook. As you can see in Figure 8-19, this dialog box initially contains no defined connections for a new workbook.

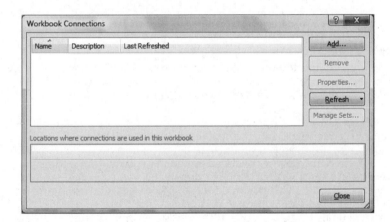

Figure 8-19. Initially, the workbook displays no connections.

To create a connection, click the **Add** button. This action displays a list of all existing connections within your workbook, your computer, and your network. Figure 8-20 shows the existing **Data Connections** dialog box. If a connection already exists on your network or on your computer that you can use, you can save time by reusing it. As you can see in this figure, none of the existing connection definitions point to the databases and tables that you want.

Figure 8-20. Select from existing connections or browse for more.

When you click the **Browse for More** button, the **Select Data Source** dialog box appears. In addition to displaying the same connections seen in the **Existing Connections** dialog box, it adds two additional options:

- Connect to New Data Source.odc

- New SQL Server Connection.odc

If you double-click either of these, it opens an additional dialog box where you can define a new connection. While it is possible to create a data connection from the **Connect to New Data Source.odc** option, I recommend using the **New SQL Server Connection.odc** option directly if your data resides in a SQL Server database.

You can use the **Connect to New Data Source.odc** option when creating a connection to non-SQL Server data sources. For example, you can create ODBC data connections to many applications including Crystal Reports, dBase, and Access. However, you should use OLE DB connections whenever available for your data source. Therefore, check the **Other/Advanced** option in the **Data Connection Wizard** first to see whether you have access to an OLE DB driver. For example, here you may find the latest data link driver for Microsoft Access 2010, called **Microsoft Office 12.0 Access Database Engine OLE DB Provider**. There are also OLE DB providers for SQL, Analysis Services, OLAP Services, Oracle, and more. If you do not see the provider you need in this list, contact your system administrator to see if he or she can locate and install a driver that you can use.

Choosing the **New SQL Server Connection.odc** option, shown in Figure 8-21, takes you directly to the **Data Connection Wizard,** where you can enter the information needed to create a connection to SQL Server.

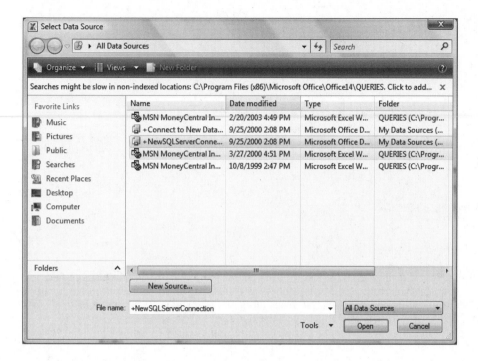

Figure 8-21. Creating a new SQL Server connection

The first page of the **Data Connection Wizard** prompts for the name of the server you want to access. This is the SQL Server name, not necessarily the name of the machine on which SQL Server runs, although they are often the same. You can enter the server name as **localhost** when creating the connection from the machine on which SQL Server runs. However, you cannot use these connections from other machines, because localhost will not resolve to the correct server. Therefore, always enter the name of the server.

You can supply credentials to SQL Server either by using your Windows Authentication information or by supplying a specific user name and password. Using Windows Authentication generally provides a more secure method of defining your connection. In this authentication mode, you do not include your user name and password in the connection information, and the operating system does not send unencrypted user names and passwords across the network. Figure 8-22 shows the dialog box that prompts for your server information.

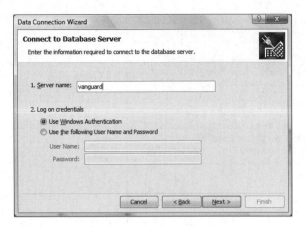

Figure 8-22. Selecting the database server

When you click the **Next** button, the **Data Connection Wizard** contacts the server you specified and uses the logon credentials you indicated. If it succeeds in connecting to the server, it returns in the next page with information asking you to which database, table, or cube you want to connect.

The first prompt uses a drop-down list to display all the databases on the referenced server. It initially selects the default database for the server. However, opening the drop-down list, you can select any of the databases on the server.

Once you have selected a database, you can select the specific table, view, or cube you want to use. Figure 8-23 shows that after selecting the PUBS database, I select a view named **AuthorRoyalty**. Because you can only select a single table for a connection to an Excel worksheet, you may find that views provide the only way to access fields from multiple tables. This is important especially in a normalized database where you want to display descriptive text for users to read, rather than ID values that serve as pointers back to their parent tables.

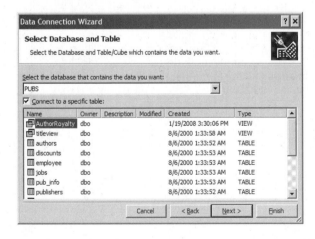

Figure 8-23. Selecting the table or view

After you have selected the table or view you want to use in the connection, the next page of the wizard prompts you for a file name for the data connection. As with most files, you should choose a file name long enough to fully describe the content or purpose of the file, while trying to keep the name as short as possible. One advantage data connection files have over most other files is a *friendly name*. The friendly name appears in dialog boxes such as the **Workbook Connections** and the **Existing Connections** dialog boxes, making it easier to identify which connection file you want to use. Figure 8-24 shows the final page of the **Data Connection Wizard**.

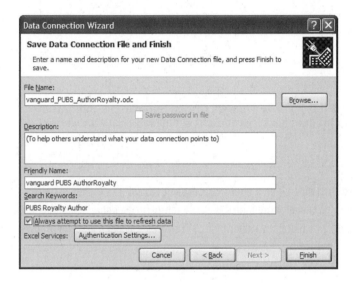

Figure 8-24. *Saving the data connection file*

The option **Always attempt to use this file to refresh data** ensures that this connection file is always used by every workbook when it refreshes its data source, thus using any recent updates to the connection file.

Click the **Finish** button after completing this last page of the **Data Connection Wizard**. You then return to the **Workbook Connections** dialog box, where you see the name of the new connection listed. Click the **Close** button on this dialog box.

Importing the SharePoint List to a Workbook

You should now see the **Existing Connections** dialog box. If you do not, open the **Existing Connections** dialog box from the **Data** ribbon. You can find it in the **Get External Data** group. Click the connection you just created followed by the **Open** button. You now can import the data from your external connection into Excel. First, you must choose how you want to view the data, selecting from the options **Table**, **PivotTable Report**, and **PivotChart and PivotTable Report**. Figure 8-25 shows the **Import Data** dialog box.

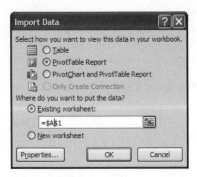

Figure 8-25. Placing data in a PivotTable Report

Your first inclination might be to select **Table** because you want to view the columns and rows of the data. However, Excel Services in SharePoint does not support external data ranges. Fortunately, it does support pivot tables.

■ **Note** Why doesn't Excel Services support external data when it does support pivot tables? The technical details are beyond the scope of this book, but this behavior is well documented on the Internet. In essence, the difference lies in the way pivot tables organize and sort data as a hierarchy rather than as a two-directional collection of rows and columns.

Fortunately, with a little work, you can make most pivot tables look similar to the original tables or views from which they started. The following discussion describes one way to reformat the pivot table.

After exporting the view data to a PivotTable Report, your Excel screen displays the pivot table on the left and the **PivotTable Field List** panel on the right, as shown in Figure 8-26. The **PivotTable Field List** panel consists of five areas. The largest area lists all the fields from the table or view used to create the pivot table. Each field has a check box before it. You must select each field that you want to use from the view or table.

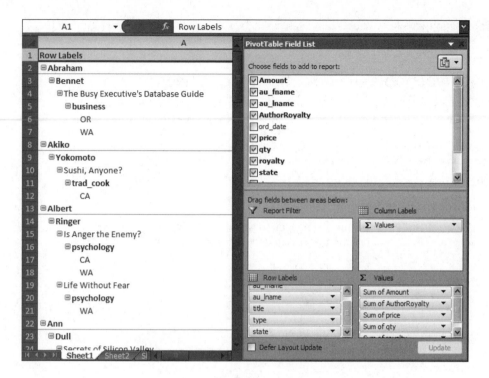

Figure 8-26. The default layout of data in a pivot table

If you simply go down the list of fields, selecting them in the order displayed, the pivot table assumes that you want to create a hierarchy with the fields in that order. If you select the fields in a different order, the hierarchy that Excel builds changes accordingly.

For example, if you select **Title** before **State** and then book **Type**, Excel assumes that you want to display different states within each book title and different book types within each state. Depending on the author, this could mean that while the pivot table lists each book separately, two books classified as Business may be separated by a book classified as Fiction just because you defined the book's **Title** higher on the hierarchy.

On the other hand, if you select the **Type** field before selecting the book's **Title**, all books of the same type for an author appear together. Similar arguments would determine whether you wanted to see all the books written by each author or if you preferred to group all books of a specific type regardless of the author. This hierarchical approach to the data distinguishes pivot tables from regular tables.

If you decide that you want to create a different hierarchy after you have selected the fields, you do not have to start over again. Simply find the field in either the **Row Labels** or **Values** box and click it to display the drop-down field menu. Options in the menu allow you to move the field up or down in the list, or even directly to the top or bottom. You can also click and drag fields up and down the list with your mouse to move fields and you can drag fields between the other three areas or remove fields from display entirely.

As to the different areas where pivot tables place fields by default, Excel assigns label and date type fields to **the Row Labels** bin. It then assigns numeric type data automatically to the **Values** bin and assumes that you want to sum the values here. This may not be what you want. You can move all the fields from the **Values** bin to the **Row Label**s bin. In all cases, be aware of any implied hierarchy in the order of the fields in the **Row Labels** area.

Formatting a Pivot Table to Look Like a Worksheet

When you have the fields you want to display selected and in the order you want, you can begin formatting the pivot table so it looks more like a spreadsheet. Begin by selecting the **PivotTable Tools Options** ribbon. Then from the **PivotTable** section, click **Options**. The **PivotTable Options** dialog box, shown in Figure 8-27, consists of five tabs. Select the tab **Layout and Format** if it does not appear by default. On this page, locate the following two options and check them if necessary:

- **Autofit column widths on update**

- **Preserve cell formatting on update**

Then click the **Data** tab and set the drop-down value to **None** for the property **Number of Items to retain per field**. You generally should not retain items deleted from the data source without a good reason.

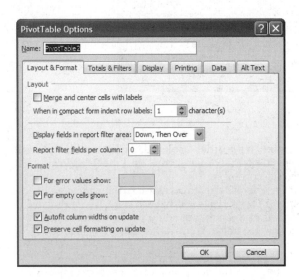

Figure 8-27. Setting the pivot table options

Also on the **Options** ribbon, the **Show** group on the right allows you to turn the field list on or off, hide or show the expand/collapse buttons associated with each unique group value, and hide or show the field headers. Typically, I prefer to hide the field headers because they display the original field names from the table or view. Unless you created meaningful alias names for all the fields, these names may be somewhat cryptic. Therefore, rather than display these names to the user, I hide the headers, and then insert another row at the top of the pivot table and enter my own column headers there.

Next, open the **PivotTable Tools Design** ribbon and locate the **Layout** group. Using the buttons in this group, make the following changes:

In **Subtotals**, select the option **Do Not Show Subtotals**, unless you want to create subtotals for groups.

In **Grand Totals**, select **Off for Rows and Columns**, unless you want grand totals for columns, in which case select **On for Columns Only**.

In **Report Layout**, select **Show in Tabular Form** to create the appearance of a normal column and row table.

On this ribbon, you can also select a pivot table style if you prefer. When you choose a pivot table style, you can use the **PivotTable Style Options** group to determine whether special formatting should apply to headers and whether to apply row or column banding to make the table more readable.

Once you've made all of these changes, your pivot table might look similar to Figure 8-28.

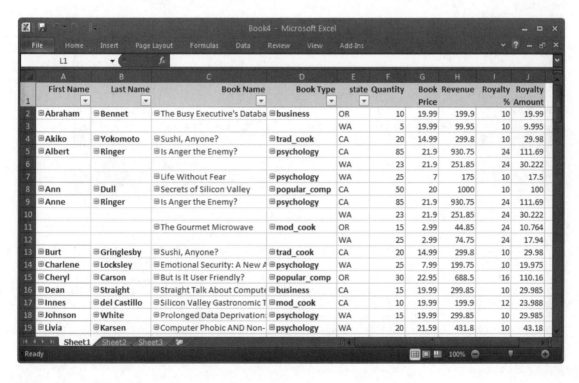

Figure 8-28. The formatted pivot table shown in Excel

Publishing Your Formatted Workbook

To publish your workbook, click the **File** tab and click the **Save & Send** option to display the page shown in Figure 8-29. Click **Save to SharePoint** to display the SharePoint options in the right panel.

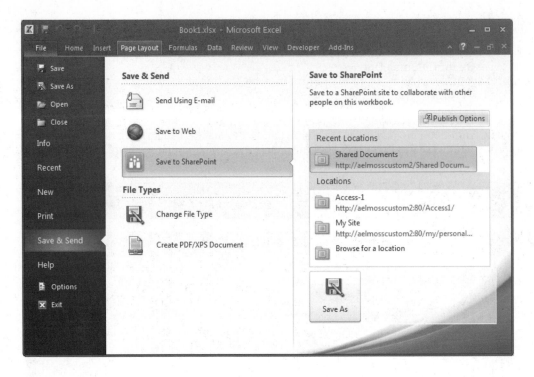

Figure 8-29. Publishing an Excel workbook to SharePoint

Before saving the workbook to SharePoint, click the button **Publish Options** located in the upper right section of Figure 8-29. Clicking this option displays the **Publish Options** dialog, which consists of two tabs. The **Show** tab lets you select the worksheets you want to publish. By default, Excel publishes the entire workbook. However, you can choose from the drop-down menu to publish individual sheets or even named items from the workbook. The second tab, **Parameters**, lets you select parameters to publish. When you finish setting parameters, click **OK** to exit this dialog.

To finish publishing your Excel spreadsheet, click the large Save As button at the bottom of Figure 8-29. In the Save As dialog that appears next, you must specify the library where you want to save the document as shown in Figure 8-30. This library must be one that your SharePoint administrator previously defined as a trusted library using Excel Services.

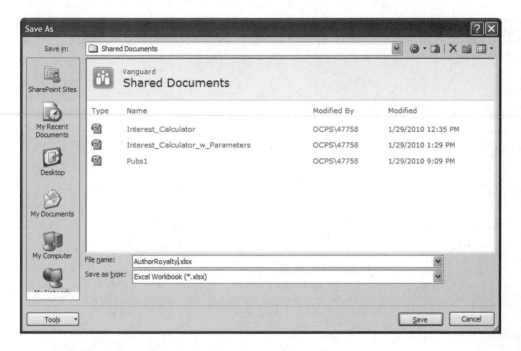

Figure 8-30. Selecting a location to save the workbook

When you click **Save**, Excel sends the workbook to SharePoint and opens the workbook in your browser as shown in Figure 8-31. If you already have a workbook in the selected library with the same name as the current workbook, Excel prompts you to replace the existing workbook. Select **Yes** to replace the current workbook when publishing an update.

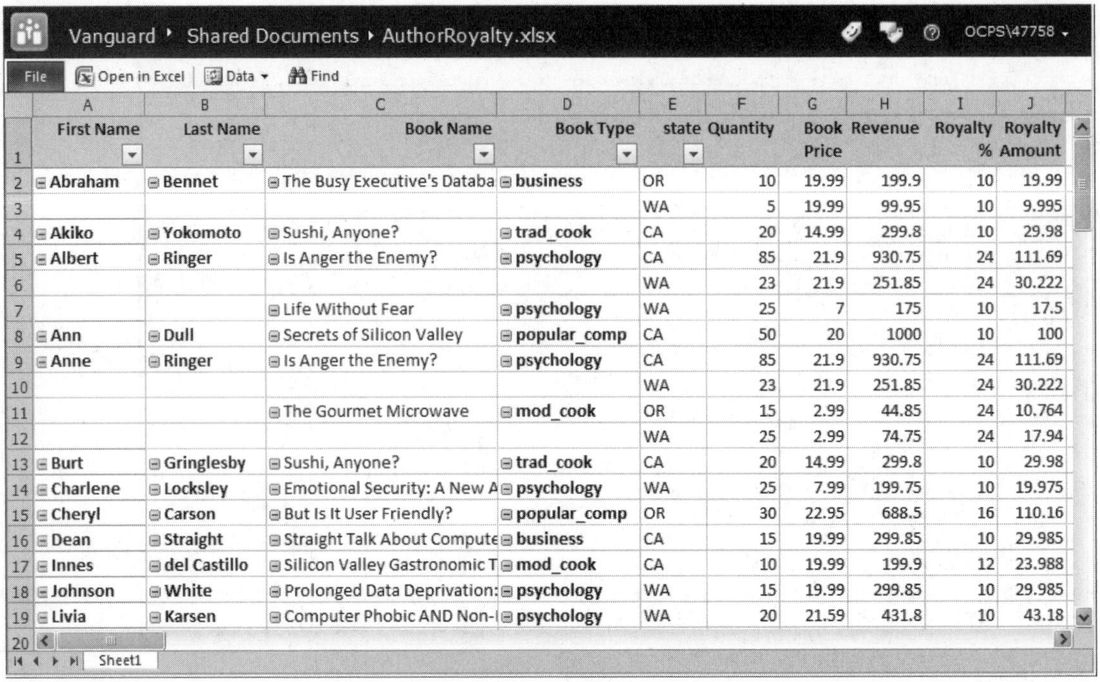

	First Name	Last Name	Book Name	Book Type	state	Quantity	Book Price	Revenue	Royalty %	Royalty Amount
2	Abraham	Bennet	The Busy Executive's Databa	business	OR	10	19.99	199.9	10	19.99
3					WA	5	19.99	99.95	10	9.995
4	Akiko	Yokomoto	Sushi, Anyone?	trad_cook	CA	20	14.99	299.8	10	29.98
5	Albert	Ringer	Is Anger the Enemy?	psychology	CA	85	21.9	930.75	24	111.69
6					WA	23	21.9	251.85	24	30.222
7			Life Without Fear	psychology	WA	25	7	175	10	17.5
8	Ann	Dull	Secrets of Silicon Valley	popular_comp	CA	50	20	1000	10	100
9	Anne	Ringer	Is Anger the Enemy?	psychology	CA	85	21.9	930.75	24	111.69
10					WA	23	21.9	251.85	24	30.222
11			The Gourmet Microwave	mod_cook	OR	15	2.99	44.85	24	10.764
12					WA	25	2.99	74.75	24	17.94
13	Burt	Gringlesby	Sushi, Anyone?	trad_cook	CA	20	14.99	299.8	10	29.98
14	Charlene	Locksley	Emotional Security: A New A	psychology	WA	25	7.99	199.75	10	19.975
15	Cheryl	Carson	But Is It User Friendly?	popular_comp	OR	30	22.95	688.5	16	110.16
16	Dean	Straight	Straight Talk About Compute	business	CA	15	19.99	299.85	10	29.985
17	Innes	del Castillo	Silicon Valley Gastronomic T	mod_cook	CA	10	19.99	199.9	12	23.988
18	Johnson	White	Prolonged Data Deprivation:	psychology	WA	15	19.99	299.85	10	29.985
19	Livia	Karsen	Computer Phobic AND Non-I	psychology	WA	20	21.59	431.8	10	43.18

Figure 8-31. The Excel workbook displayed using Excel Services in SharePoint

Introduction to Status Indicators (KPIs)

Key performance indicators (KPIs) provide a visual communication tool that shows progress toward a goal. Between SharePoint Server 2007 and SharePoint Server 2010, Microsoft decided to rename KPIs, now calling them *status indicators*. Each item in a Status list measures one item, and each item has a desired goal value. The list can then show the current value of that item and compare it to the goal. Based on ranges of values defined by the person building the status indicator, you can then display a color-coded status icon illustrating how well the current value compares to the desired value.

Project teams, managers, and businesses use status indicators to gain a quick visual check on the progress of their projects, to determine whether employees are meeting production goals or whether sales are meeting expectations. Status indicators can quickly illustrate whether you are ahead, behind, or on schedule with whatever business factors the status indicator measures.

Status Types Defined

There are four basic types of status indicators available within SharePoint, based on the source of the data used to create them. While the data source may differ, the basic look and method of using status indicators does not.

- SharePoint lists: You can use existing SharePoint lists to develop status indicators. For example, suppose you track issues at your company using an issue-tracking list. By using simple counts, you can compare the number of outstanding issues to a desired goal for your help desk to see how well they handle incoming calls. For more complex issues, you could track the time needed to resolve issues by your programming staff and compare the average elapse time to a desired goal.

- Excel workbooks: You can link a status indicator to an Excel workbook stored in a SharePoint library. Updated workbook data can then drive the current value in the status indicator. Using the Excel web part on the same page, you can display a detailed list of the data backing up the status indicator or you can use the **Details** link when defining the status indicator to point to another page where you display the spreadsheet.

- SQL Server Analysis Services: Analysis Services can also provide information to create status indicators. This method can supply tracking data from systems maintained in SQL Server. With a little work, you can build performance information into a table and then use that information through Analysis Services to create SQL performance status indicators.

- Manual data: If you do not have a formal way to collect data using one of the preceding methods, you can always manually enter the goal and its current value in this status indicator type.

Creating a Status List

Creating a status list follows many of the same steps used when creating other list types. You begin by going to the site where you want to create the status list, which in this case is the same team site in which we have been working our other examples. Once you have it opened, click **Site Actions** and then select **View All Site Content**. If your current screen displays the **Quick Launch** menu, you might be able to click the **View All Site Content** link directly from the top of this menu.

Next, click **Create** on the **All Site Content** page. On the **Create** page, locate the **Status List** template. Th options page for this template asks for the same basic information as most other lists, including the list name, description, and navigation options as shown in Figure 8-32.

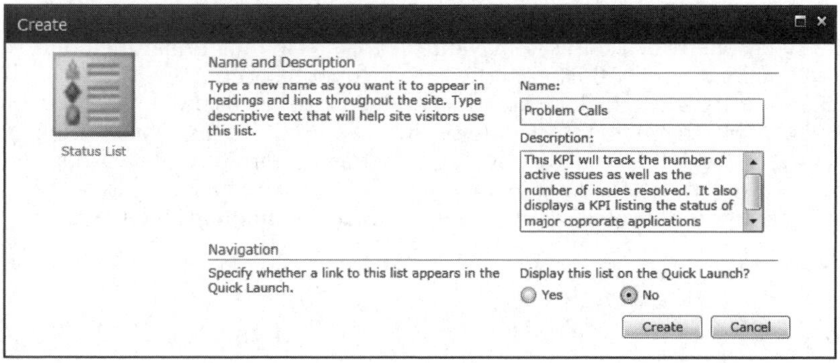

Figure 8-32. Creating a KPI list

Supply a name for the list and enter an optional description. For the example here, I want to create a status list to track problem calls. Therefore, I suggest the name **Problem Calls**. After providing a description for the list, choose the **No** radio button under the question **Display this list on the Quick Launch?** Finally, click the **Create** button to build the list.

Opening the status list settings, you can see that the default columns for each item include a column named **Indicator**, which describes the status indicator. The **Goal** column represents the minimum acceptable value for the item that represents success for the status indicator. The **Value** column represents the current measured value for the item. Finally, the **Status** column displays an icon that visually indicates whether the item has achieved the desired goal.

Creating a Status List with Manually Entered Information

To see how to define a status indicator, click the down arrow to the right of the **New** option in the list's menu bar. Figure 8-33 shows that this menu lets you select from the four different data sources for the status indicator. If you click the **New** button, not the drop-down arrow, SharePoint assumes you want to create the default status indicator type, one using a SharePoint list. Let's begin instead with the simpler (but manually entered) type, by selecting **Fixed Value based Status Indicator**.

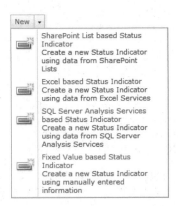

Figure 8-33. Selecting the type of indicator

While SharePoint calls the first property of a status item **Name**, it appears in the **Indicator** column when you display the status list. You must supply this property. You can optionally enter the **Description** property to explain the purpose of the indicator; I recommend using this property. In addition, you might want to indicate whether high values or low values represent success. Then, using the optional **Comments** section, enter an explanation of how you measure the current value for this item and perhaps even how you selected the status range values. Figure 8-34 shows the first part of the page defining the properties of a status item. These first three properties are common to all four status indicator types.

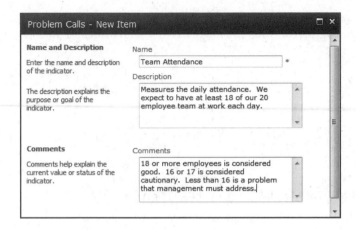

Figure 8-34. *Defining the Name and Description properties of the indicator and entering Comments*

Next, you must enter the current value for the indicator. Because you have selected a manual indicator, you must open and edit this item each time the value changes. Since this example tracks team attendance, you may find yourself doing this daily.

Figure 8-35 also shows that you have to define the rules for the status icon. You can choose to represent better values by higher or lower values. In the case of attendance, higher values represent better values. Therefore, let's assume that you have met your attendance goal when 18 or more employees out of 20 come into work each day. If only 16 or 17 employees arrive, you want to raise a warning to management. If fewer than 16 employees arrive, you want to display the danger icon.

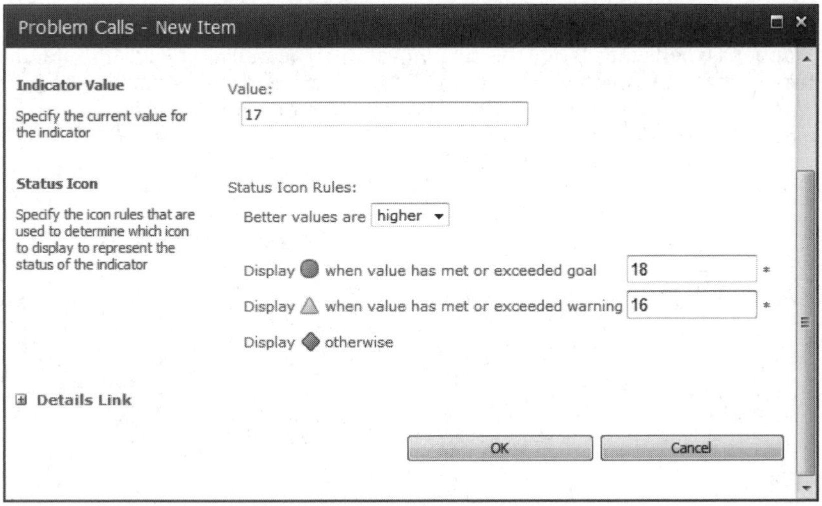

Figure 8-35. *Defining the indicator value and status rules*

After defining the status, click **OK** to see how it appears when you display the list. Figure 8-36 displays the status list with this single indicator, showing that you might have the start of an absentee problem.

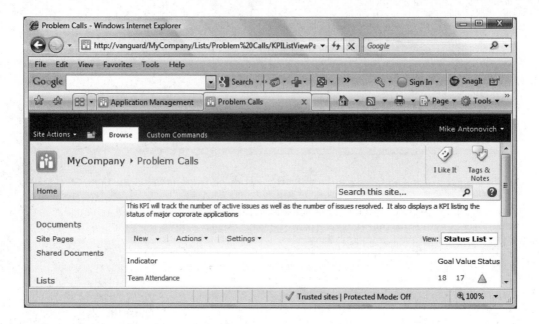

Figure 8-36. *Viewing the resulting indicator in the list*

If you want to see what happens when you change the current value of the indicator, click the status item and select **Edit Indicator** not from the ribbon, but from the line of commands immediately above the indicator as shown in Figure 8-37. Note that there are only two other options, one to delete the indicator and another to manage its permissions.

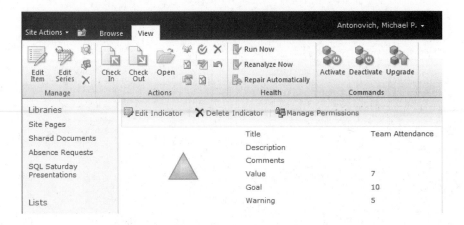

Figure 8-37. Edit, delete, or manage permissions of the indicator

Creating a Status List Using a SharePoint List

Let's now look at a status indicator that uses a SharePoint list. I've created a SharePoint list that tracks the number of active application systems. Suppose I define success as having at least 90% of our systems running, and failure as having less than 80% of our systems running. (OK, I know that may be low for your organization. Of course, you can enter your own numbers.)

Rather than track this information manually, suppose that you have a SharePoint list named **Systems Supported** that includes an item for each application. Furthermore, suppose that this list has a field named **Status** defined as a choice field type with four possible values: **OK**, **Being Repaired**, **Down**, and **Retired**. You can use this list to supply the data for the status indicator. That way, by maintaining the status in the list **Systems Supported**, SharePoint can update the status indicator automatically.

Figure 8-38 shows the full properties list for this status item. The new options begin with the **Indicator Value** section. In this area, you must enter the name of the SharePoint list and view that you want to use to calculate the status value. Notice that you can then calculate the current KPI value in one of three ways:

- Simply total the number of list items in the selected view.

- Calculate the percentage of list items with a specific value in the view based on a Boolean expression.

- Calculate using all list items in the view.

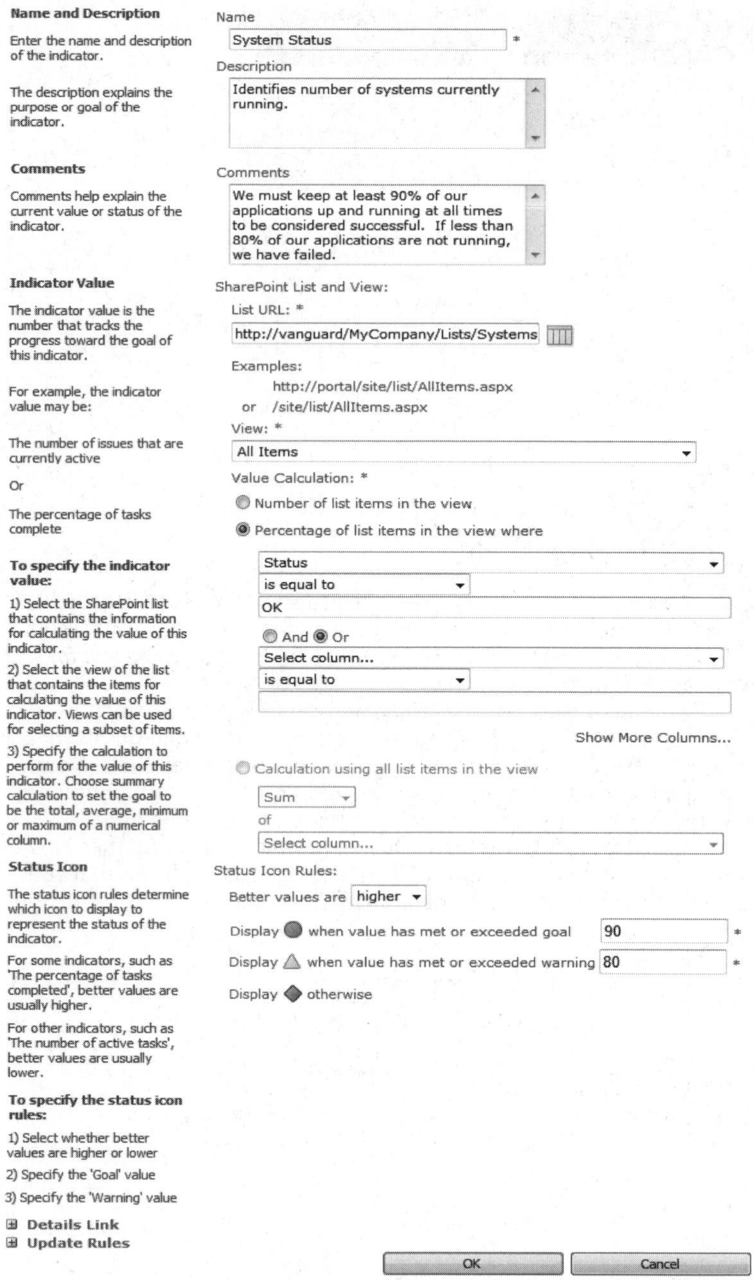

Name and Description

Enter the name and description of the indicator.

The description explains the purpose or goal of the indicator.

Comments

Comments help explain the current value or status of the indicator.

Indicator Value

The indicator value is the number that tracks the progress toward the goal of this indicator.

For example, the indicator value may be:

The number of issues that are currently active

Or

The percentage of tasks complete

To specify the indicator value:

1) Select the SharePoint list that contains the information for calculating the value of this indicator.

2) Select the view of the list that contains the items for calculating the value of this indicator. Views can be used for selecting a subset of items.

3) Specify the calculation to perform for the value of this indicator. Choose summary calculation to set the goal to be the total, average, minimum or maximum of a numerical column.

Status Icon

The status icon rules determine which icon to display to represent the status of the indicator.

For some indicators, such as 'The percentage of tasks completed', better values are usually higher.

For other indicators, such as 'The number of active tasks', better values are usually lower.

To specify the status icon rules:

1) Select whether better values are higher or lower

2) Specify the 'Goal' value

3) Specify the 'Warning' value

⊞ **Details Link**
⊞ **Update Rules**

Name

`System Status` *

Description

`Identifies number of systems currently running.`

Comments

`We must keep at least 90% of our applications up and running at all times to be considered successful.  If less than 80% of our applications are not running, we have failed.`

SharePoint List and View:

List URL: *

`http://vanguard/MyCompany/Lists/Systems` 🔲

Examples:

　　http://portal/site/list/AllItems.aspx
　or /site/list/AllItems.aspx

View: *

`All Items` ▾

Value Calculation: *

◯ Number of list items in the view

◉ Percentage of list items in the view where

　　`Status` ▾
　　`is equal to` ▾
　　`OK`

　　◯ And ◉ Or
　　`Select column...` ▾
　　`is equal to` ▾
　　`　　`

　　　　　　　　　　　　Show More Columns...

◯ Calculation using all list items in the view
　　`Sum` ▾
　　of
　　`Select column...` ▾

Status Icon Rules:

Better values are `higher` ▾

Display ⬤ when value has met or exceeded goal `90`　*

Display △ when value has met or exceeded warning `80`　*

Display ◆ otherwise

　　　　　[　　OK　　]　　　　[　　Cancel　　]

Figure 8-38. Defining an indicator based on a SharePoint list

The Details link allows you to turn the status indicator name into a hyperlink for the current KPI item that displays details about the current KPI value. The Update Rules link lets you decide whether to recalculate the indicator value for every viewer. This can be especially useful when using a SharePoint list in which the selected view displays only the current user's data. You can also choose to update the status value manually by clicking the Update option in the Status indicator's drop-down menu. This option can be useful if the background data that supports the indicator value is dynamically changing.

In this case, you want to calculate the percentage of systems that have a **Status** field value of **OK**. However, if you had a list that included the amount of time a system was down, you could sum the down time across all systems for the time period represented by the view.

Creating a Status List from an Excel Workbook

Next, if you use an Excel workbook to supply your indicator values, you must supply the URL of the workbook published on your SharePoint site using Excel Services. Then you must enter the address of the cell to use for the value or reference the cell by a cell name. If you click the icon to the right of the value, the pop-up window displays the workbook and lets you select the cell to use not just for the **Indicator Value**, but also for the **Indicator Goal** and the **Indicator Warning** values. In fact, you can click the workbook icon next to any of these three values on the main property page for the status indicator to return to the workbook to verify or select new cells to use for these values. This does not mean that you must use cell values for the **Indicator Goal** or **Indicator Warning**. You can enter manual numbers for these values as well. Figure 8-39 shows just this portion of the status indicator's properties, as we have already discussed the other properties of the status indicator for the previous status types.

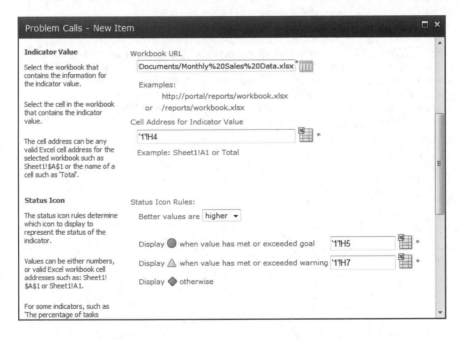

Figure 8-39. Defining an indicator based on an Excel workbook

Creating Dashboards with Excel and Status Indicators

What is a dashboard? Within SharePoint, you can define a dashboard as any web page that displays business information. Often dashboards use graphics to display data, but they do not have to include graphics. What they must do is show trends that can help identify problems, opportunities, or decision points. Some people might refer to this ability as an at-a-glance health check for a business of its key indicators. However, the fact is you can use dashboards for tracking project progress, employee satisfaction, customer purchasing trends, and many more things. The value of a good dashboard lies in its ability to help management make decisions that benefit the organization.

Building a Dashboard from the Dashboard Template in the Report Center

So how can you create a dashboard in SharePoint? First, open your team site and click the option **View All Site Content** in the **Site Actions** menu. Next click **Create** at the top of the **All Site Content**. Then select the **Library** filter and click on the **Report Library** option. You must supply a name for the library along with an option description. As with most other objects, you can also determine whether the object appears in the page's Quick Launch area. Because it's a library, however, you can also determine whether SharePoint creates a new version every time that you edit the file. Once you have the **Reports** library open, display the **Documents** ribbon. In the **New** group, click on the lower half of the **New Document** option. Do not just click the top half of the **New** option, because SharePoint may assume that you want to add a report to the library. From the drop-down menu, click the option **Web Part Page with Status List**. SharePoint Server 2007 called this option the Dashboard page.

As shown in Figure 8-40, you begin defining your dashboard by supplying a page name and a page title. You can also optionally enter a description. Notice that you cannot edit the next two fields in the **Location** section. SharePoint defines the document library as a reports library, and you cannot change it unless you have multiple reports-type libraries. Unless you have defined a folder structure for this library (remember earlier discussions about creating folders to better organize your files), the folder also defaults to the top-level folder. Of course, if you have defined a folder structure, you can select any of your existing folders from this drop-down. This is another reason why you should plan your folder structure before beginning to add documents to your libraries.

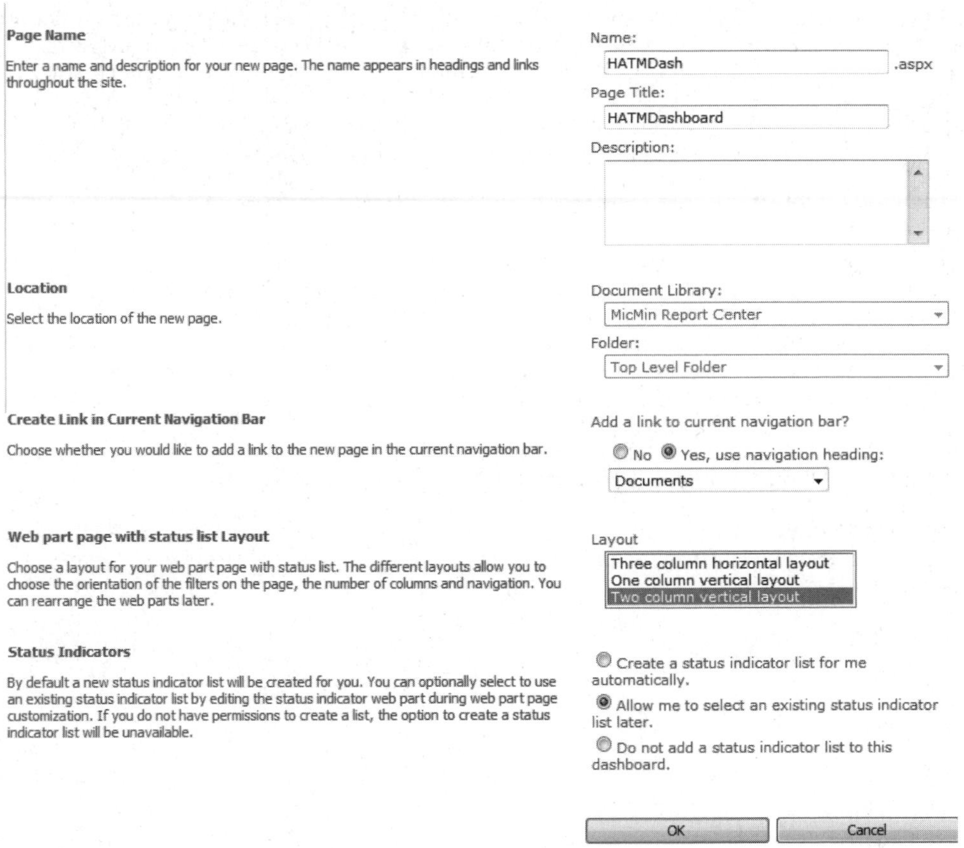

Page Name

Enter a name and description for your new page. The name appears in headings and links throughout the site.

Name:

| HATMDash | .aspx |

Page Title:

| HATMDashboard |

Description:

| |

Location

Select the location of the new page.

Document Library:

| MicMin Report Center | ▼ |

Folder:

| Top Level Folder | ▼ |

Create Link in Current Navigation Bar

Choose whether you would like to add a link to the new page in the current navigation bar.

Add a link to current navigation bar?

◯ No ◉ Yes, use navigation heading:

| Documents | ▼ |

Web part page with status list Layout

Choose a layout for your web part page with status list. The different layouts allow you to choose the orientation of the filters on the page, the number of columns and navigation. You can rearrange the web parts later.

Layout

| Three column horizontal layout |
| One column vertical layout |
| Two column vertical layout |

Status Indicators

By default a new status indicator list will be created for you. You can optionally select to use an existing status indicator list by editing the status indicator web part during web part page customization. If you do not have permissions to create a list, the option to create a status indicator list will be unavailable.

◯ Create a status indicator list for me automatically.

◉ Allow me to select an existing status indicator list later.

◯ Do not add a status indicator list to this dashboard.

[OK]   [Cancel]

Figure 8-40. Creating a two-column dashboard document

■ **Tip** Of course, if you do procrastinate building out your folder structure until after you have already created documents, not all is lost. You can simply switch to the Windows Explorer view of your library by using the option **Open with Windows Explorer** in the **Actions** drop-down menu. There you can drag and drop documents between folders and even create new folders.

In the next section, **Create Link in Current Navigation Bar**, you can determine whether to create an entry in the **Quick Launch** menu. Here you have three options for which section to add the dashboard: **Documents, Lists,** and **Discussions**. Just think of these three options as categories where you can store these special web pages for now.

In the **Dashboard Layout** section, you can choose from three layouts, which differ by the number of columns in the layout. Each layout represents a page template specially designed for dashboards and combines by default status lists, Excel web parts, text areas, contact information of the person creating the page, and more.

The last option lets you create a new status list automatically. If you let SharePoint generate a new status list for you, it names the list using a combination of the current page name followed by the text "Status Indicator Definitions." That is not a bad default. You can also create a dashboard using an existing Status list, or you could decide not to include a status list at all on the dashboard. What? A dashboard without KPIs?

Actually, despite calling this web page a dashboard and leading you to think that it is something special, it is not. The dashboard template provides nothing that you cannot re-create starting from a blank web part page with the same web part zones.

So why create the dashboard this way? It can save you a little time by pre-positioning common web parts used by dashboards on a web page and then automatically placing that page in a separate navigation group in the **Quick Launch** menu.

Organizing Web Parts in the Dashboard Web Part Zones

So let's continue looking at what you get when you create a two-column dashboard. Figure 8-41 shows the initial two-column web page. This page actually places each of the web parts in its own web part zone. These zones include

- Top Left zone

- Top Right zone

- Filter zone

- Middle Left zone

- Middle Right zone

- Bottom Left zone

- Bottom Right zone

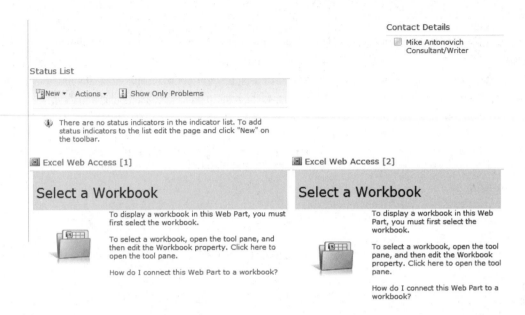

Figure 8-41. The default dashboard page created by SharePoint

You can just imagine what you would get with a three-column dashboard. Actually, don't imagine, go ahead and try it. You can always delete the page if you do not want to keep it.

If you do not want to use all of these web parts, no problem; just edit the page and close them. If you do not like the way SharePoint lays out the page, just edit the page and drag and drop the web parts to locations you do like. Do you want different web parts? Just click **Add a Web Part**, found at the top of each web part zone, and select from the list of available web parts. Remember that you can create "new" web parts by defining new lists using any of the list templates available. While Microsoft provides a collection of commonly used web parts with SharePoint, you can go online and find free or relatively inexpensive web parts to do all sorts of things. One site you definitely want to check out is www.codeplex.com, a Microsoft Open Source community site with wide selection of tools and utilities, and in this case, SharePoint web parts. In addition, if you still cannot find the web part that will do what you want, you can always go down the hall to the den of programmers the company keeps around for emergencies and ask them to build a web part for you using Visual Studio. If your company does not employ a den of programmers, you can find many consultants through the Internet who can gladly build that web part for you.

Adding KPIs to Your Dashboard

Let's continue by modifying the Key Performance Indicators web part found in the Middle Left web part zone. If you do not already have the page in **Edit** mode, select **Edit Page** from the **Site Actions** drop-down menu. With the page in **Edit** mode, open the drop-down menu associated with the **Edit** button and select the option **Modify Shared Web Part** (if you are using Web Pages) or **Edit Web Part** if you are using Wiki Pages for your content. When you do this, an option panel opens to the right of the page.

■ **Note** If you click **Modify Shared Web Part** (or Edit Web Part from a Wiki Page) and do not see the option panel, it may be that your screen is not wide enough. You could go out and buy a new 24" wide-screen panel. As much fun as that might be, however, the less expensive solution is to look for the horizontal scrollbar at the bottom of window. You should see that you can drag the button in the bar to the right to bring the option panel into view.

Figure 8-42 shows the top portion of the option panel. This section usually includes most of the unique properties for the current web control. Most option panels also have sections named

- Appearance
- Layout
- Advance

SharePoint leaves these other sections closed until you choose to see one by clicking the box with the plus sign to the left of the section name.

Figure 8-42. Selecting a KPI list to display

First, you must define the KPI list you want to display in the web part's first option. You can enter the relative URL for this list beginning with the root of your site. Alternatively, you could click the icon to the right of the field for a simpler way to create this reference. This icon lets you search your site for the KPI list as shown in Figure 8-43. When you find the list you want to use, double-click it, or click it once and click **OK** to select the list.

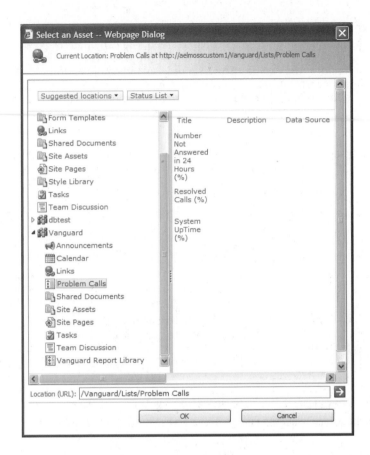

Figure 8-43. Navigating to the KPI list rather than entering its URL manually

The second option, **Change Icon**, lets you do exactly that. You can choose from four different icon styles for your visual status indicators, as shown in Figure 8-44. You have already seen the default indicators in several illustrations. The **Checkmarks** consist of colored circles with either a checkmark, exclamation point, or X in their centers. The **Flat** icons consist of plain colored circles with no symbols. Finally, the **Traffic Lights** consist of black boxes with a green, yellow, or red "bulb" in them. If you want to see these for yourself, select any of the icon types and then click the **Apply** button at the bottom of the option panel. The **Apply** button updates the contents of the edited web part but leaves the option panel open.

Figure 8-44. Changing the KPI status icon

Figure 8-45 shows the configured KPI list: **Problem Calls**, which you built earlier. Notice that the list, even in **Edit** mode, displays the list's menu selections. Right from this screen, you can open the **New** drop-down menu and add a new indicator to the list. You can also open the **Actions** menu and change the icons, reset the order of indicators, and update their values. The reset order of indicators option places the indicators in alphabetical order. The last feature, to update values, can be especially useful when working with data that changes frequently. If you have manually entered KPI values, this option does not allow you to change the values.

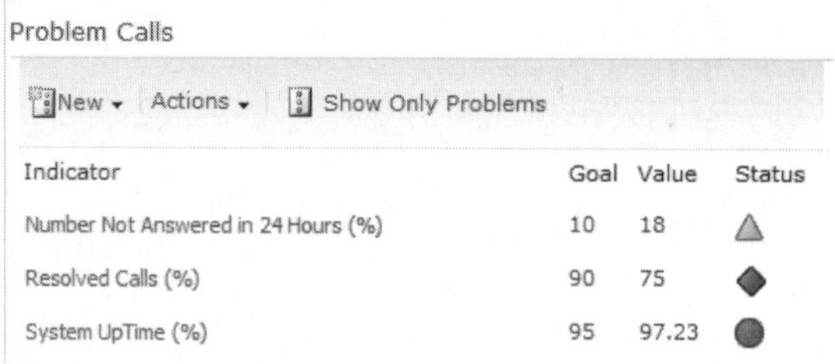

Problem Calls

New ▾ | Actions ▾ | Show Only Problems

Indicator	Goal	Value	Status
Number Not Answered in 24 Hours (%)	10	18	△
Resolved Calls (%)	90	75	◆
System UpTime (%)	95	97.23	●

Figure 8-45. Displaying the KPI list

The last option in the list's menu lets you limit the display to only problem indicators. If you have a long list of indicators, for which most are OK, you can help management focus on problem issues by displaying only the indicators that need attention.

■ **Note** The status list menu remains visible after you publish the page, so that users viewing the page also have access to it. Using permissions, you can control which users can change the status list, making the list read-only for the vast majority of users.

As you move your mouse over the indicators, a drop-down box appears to the right of the indicator text. You can open this menu to edit the properties of the item, assuming you have the appropriate permissions. You can also move individual indicators up and down in the list, creating a custom order.

Finally, I have made several other changes to the dashboard, resulting in the page shown in Figure 8-46. These additions include

- Adding some basic text as a title in a Content Text web part in the Upper Left zone

- Adding the graphical results of a survey on employee morale to the Middle Right zone

- Adding references to published Excel workbooks to the two Excel web parts in the Lower Left and Lower Right zones

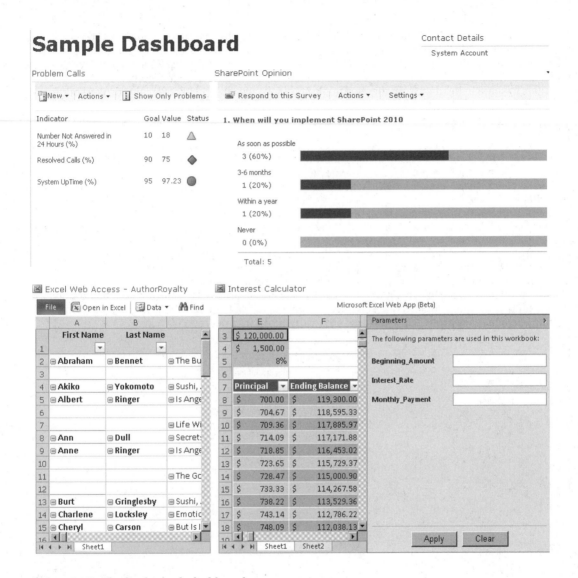

Figure 8-46. The final sample dashboard page

Summary

This chapter started by asking whether Excel was the weakest link in the Microsoft Office lineup of products in terms of collaboration with SharePoint. In the previous chapter, you saw that SharePoint has deprecated a key feature of sharing data between two systems, synchronization. While I did show a way to recover from this weakness, you may still feel that Excel does not contribute to collaboration as thoroughly as some other products.

To demonstrate that there is still a lot you can do, I launched this chapter by showing how you can publish a static Excel workbook to a SharePoint site. Once a workbook is published, a service called Excel Services can open and display it in your browser with virtually no loss of visual fidelity compared to Excel itself. This feature allows users of your site who do not have Excel installed on their local computers to share in the data from the workbook, at least by viewing it. However, a static workbook does not allow interaction.

To allow a published workbook to become a little more dynamic, I next introduced the concept of *parameters*. Visitors to your site can supply their own values to the parameters and then recalculate the spreadsheet using those values.

Then you looked at Report Center sites. A new feature examined here called KPIs provides a way to quickly and visually show important measurable factors in an organization. When management sets a goal level for each factor, they can then measure the actual value of the factor and compare it to the goal. Depending on how well the actual value compares to the goal, the KPI list can display a status icon that at a glance shows which key factors have been met and which need further attention by management.

The chapter closed by showing how to display Excel workbooks on a web page along with other web parts, such as the KPI list, to give management a *dashboard*, a single-screen view of the status of factors important to the success of their organization. While SharePoint provides a dashboard template that can give you a head start in building such a web page, I ended by showing that you could create the same basic web page from a blank web page that has access to the same web parts.

Therefore, with the help of Excel Services, Excel may not be the weakest link after all. It certainly displays some interesting abilities that you might be able to take advantage of in your organization to help management view protected versions of your workbooks. The decision is yours.

CHAPTER 9

■ ■ ■

An Introduction to Creating Forms with InfoPath

I know many people who have installed Microsoft Office 2010 or even 2007 on their desktop machines. On practically a daily basis, they open and use Microsoft Outlook and Microsoft Word. They may even use Excel, PowerPoint, and occasionally Access. Nevertheless, many of them have never noticed a largely undiscovered tool named InfoPath, which first became part of the Office Suite in 2003 and which Microsoft has significantly enhanced since then.

InfoPath is important to your SharePoint implementation because it brings an easy-to-use form design tool based on XML (Extensible Markup Language) to the desktop and your browser. With it, you can gather data from users without having to write applications, and you can then save that data in XML files, databases, or SharePoint lists.

The reason InfoPath works well with SharePoint is that it is based on XML technology just like the rest of Office 2010. When InfoPath saves a form, it creates an XSN file. This file acts like a cabinet (CAB) file to hold a collection of files needed by the form. These files include XML Schema Definition (XSD) files and Extensible Stylesheet Language (XSL) files that provide a formal definition of the XML data, such as element names, data types, and attributes for each field used in a form. InfoPath also uses XSL Transformation (XSLT) files to define different views of the same data or subsets of the data. Because the form data is stored in XML, you can start building a form from an existing XML data schema, or you can begin with a blank form and let InfoPath build the data schema for you.

Perhaps all these strange-sounding technologies scare some people away from using InfoPath. However, you really do not need an in-depth knowledge of these technologies to create and use InfoPath forms, as I will show in this chapter.

You will explore InfoPath's design environment, which includes a rich set of controls for building forms that can be displayed through your browser and thus within SharePoint. It includes all the popular controls needed for forms, ranging from standard text boxes, lists, and date pickers to repeating and optional sections, attachments, hyperlinks, and more. Rather than building ASP.NET pages to collect data over your internet, you can skip most of the programming tasks for simple data-gathering applications by creating an InfoPath form and then publishing it in a library on your site. Users can access your form template and fill in their data online. You can then save the data collected by an InfoPath form locally in an Access table, a SQL Server database, or even a SharePoint list.

InfoPath also lets you add workflows to forms using Windows Workflow Foundation and then publish the forms through SharePoint. Workflows allow you to define a work process for the form. For example, after you fill in an absence request form, you probably need to submit that form to your supervisor. He or she must then sign the document before forwarding it to your department secretary. The secretary then enters the information into your payroll system. You can automate this entire process to pass the form from one person to next, sending e-mails to each recipient that notify that person of a task to complete. Moreover, because SharePoint tracks workflows, you can always tell the status of a document in the workflow. Together with SharePoint, InfoPath improves the efficiency of your work processes.

In this chapter, you will see how easy it is to create an InfoPath form from scratch, as well as how to take existing Word and Excel documents and convert them to InfoPath forms. You will also look at how to work with different data sources. This gives you the foundation you need to publish these forms within SharePoint (the subject of Chapter 10), so that all users of your site can access these forms and fill them in. The advantage of publishing your forms on SharePoint so users can fill them in using their browser is that they do not need to have InfoPath installed on their desktop. Of course, the person creating the form must have InfoPath and a license to create content on the Enterprise edition of SharePoint. For additional questions about licensing at your organization, contact your Microsoft representative.

Why You Should Use InfoPath

I do not know many organizations that do not collect data for their business from customers, potential customers, suppliers, partners, or even their own employees. Forms have always provided a standardized way to collect information, ensuring that all employees collect all necessary information in a consistent manner. Sometimes companies simply store this information on the paper form used to collect it. Often, however, someone must enter this data into a computer system.

Using paper forms to collect information exposes the process to several types of errors. First, if the user handwrites the data into the original form, there could be a problem interpreting the handwriting. Second, even if the data entry clerk can clearly read the data on the form, she still could create errors when she enters the data into a computer system through simple typing mistakes. For example, suppose someone fills in an application form for a car or home loan. Whether because of the applicant's poor writing or a typing error made by a data entry clerk, bad data sent to the credit bureau can result in the denial of the loan request.

In addition, many business processes use a collection of forms to complete a transaction such as buying that car or home. Typically, several fields appear on all of these forms, such as the names of the people involved in the transaction, their addresses, phone numbers, work locations, and perhaps other fields as well. Each time the person collecting this information has to reenter the information, there is one more chance to enter the data incorrectly. With fully integrated electronic forms, once the person collecting the data enters the information, subsequent forms can retrieve the data and pre-fill repeated fields, making the entire process run faster and with less chance of errors.

As mentioned in the first section, you can publish InfoPath forms through the Internet, allowing people not just inside your company, but also outside your company to view, print, and fill in the form. With the increasing use of mobile devices such as BlackBerry handhelds, you might want to create forms that users can fill in via one of these mobile devices. Users can even fill in InfoPath forms offline. Once they download a form, they can disconnect from the Internet and fill in the form at their leisure. Once they complete the form, they can reconnect to the Internet and submit it.

In a similar way, InfoPath forms also support Tablet PC users by allowing them to write with their tablet pens to fill in the form fields directly. InfoPath can then automatically convert this "ink" into text. You can even allow Tablet PC users to add hand-drawn sketches to illustrate information; these can be included in a traffic accident report used by the police.

Another benefit of using a tool like InfoPath forms comes from the ability to share the resulting data with other Office applications. You can even send forms via e-mail and Outlook, export the data to MS Excel, and then pump the data into an Access or SQL Server database.

By having users fill in forms electronically, you can help ensure that they enter correct data by validating the data as they enter it. By using validation rules on individual form fields, you can prevent bad data from getting into your database. The cost of correcting data-entry errors increases dramatically the further through the process the bad data travels. Therefore, flagging bad data as users enter it can save time and money by prompting users to correct their mistakes immediately.

Completing forms online rather than on paper also appeals to those interested in going "green." For others, a more compelling benefit might be that the use of less paper for forms saves money. Your company can buy less paper, cut printing costs, and not have to build and maintain storage facilities to keep the completed forms.

Because InfoPath forms allow you to display and hide different sections of a report, you might be able to combine several similar forms into a single form and then provide a way for users to hide the portions they don't need to work with. Different views on the same data allow you to collect all the data needed with a single form, and then, through different views, show subsets of the data to different users within your organization based on what they need to see rather than sending them the entire form.

Exploring the InfoPath Interface

One huge change from Office 2007 to Office 2010 is that Microsoft has split InfoPath into two programs. You use the first one, InfoPath Designer, to build your forms. Then you and others can use InfoPath Filler to fill in those forms. In fact, you can create an InfoPath form that can only be filled out using InfoPath Filler. The primary function of InfoPath Filler is to let the user fill in an existing form that someone has created using InfoPath Designer; it would be used either because the form is not being publishing in SharePoint or because it requires features that a web browser cannot display. This chapter will focus on InfoPath Designer.

InfoPath Features That a Web Browser Cannot Display

If you must use any of the following features in your InfoPath form, you cannot display the resulting form in a web browser. In these cases, to use the form you must open it using InfoPath Filler.

Objects:

- Vertical Label
- Ink Picture
- Signature Line

Containers:

- Repeating Recursive Section
- Scrolling Region
- Horizontal Repeating Table
- Repeating Choice Group

- Horizontal Region

- Master/Detail

Let's first examine the InfoPath Designer interface. When you open InfoPath Designer, the backstage for InfoPath displays the **New** group as shown in Figure 9-1. In the center portion of the screen, the **New** group displays four categories of form templates:

- Popular Form Templates

- Advanced Form Templates

- InfoPath 2007 Form Templates

- Template Parts

We will explore portions of each of these template groups as we progress through this chapter and the next. You will also see additional groups added to this page as we develop and save forms we develop.

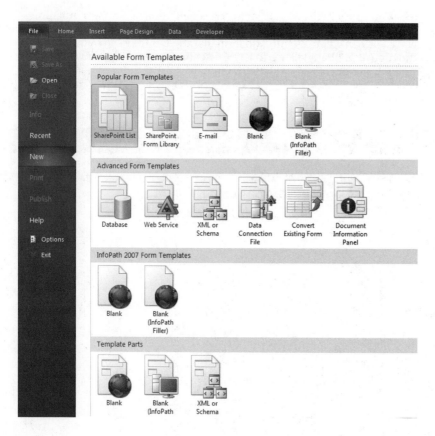

Figure 9-1. The initial form templates provided by InfoPath

Modifying a Form Used with a SharePoint List

To begin our exploration of InfoPath, one of the easiest things you can do is to modify the form used by a SharePoint list. As you have seen many times in prior chapters, SharePoint builds a default form for editing the items in a SharePoint list. The default form is functional, but have you ever wanted to edit the form, add fields, change the layout, or change the theme? With InfoPath, you can accomplish all those things.

From the **New** page in the backstage area, click **SharePoint List** in the **Popular Form Templates** group. This template lets you start from an existing list form, add rules, modify the form layout, and change the formatting. InfoPath first needs to get the location of the SharePoint site that has the list you want to customize. Figure 9-2 shows the first page of the wizard that prompts for the site location.

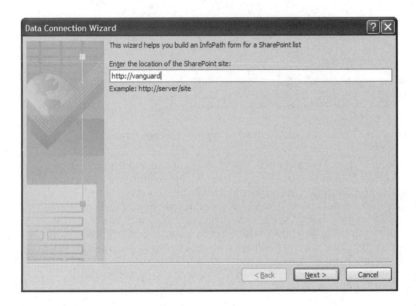

Figure 9-2. Identify the SharePoint site location.

On the second page of the **Data Connection Wizard** (Figure 9-3), you can choose between creating a new list for the site and working with one of the existing lists. Notice that you cannot customize all lists. For example, you cannot customize calendar or status lists. However, you can customize many of the other list types.

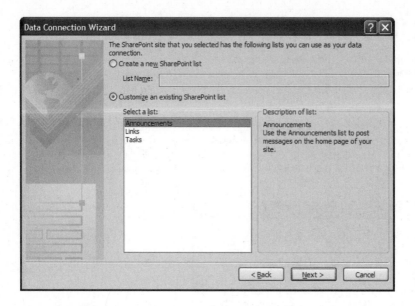

Figure 9-3. *Select an existing SharePoint list for which you want to create a custom form.*

When you click **Next**, InfoPath attempts to connect with the SharePoint site and list that you specified. This could take a few seconds. Depending on the permissions of your site, you may also see a dialog prompting for your user name and password to connect to the SharePoint site.

The initial form that InfoPath generates for you to customize is not exactly the same as the default edit form used by the list (see Figure 9-4). InfoPath generates the form you begin with based on the columns in the list, creating a single-column form. Think of this form as a starting point that already has the columns that currently exist in the list. This form actually consists of a two-column table in which the first column contains the column label and the second column contains the column value. Each row of the table represents a column from the list. However, since this form is a table, you can easily rearrange the rows to put the fields in a different order.

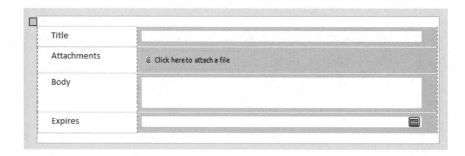

Figure 9-4. *InfoPath creates a starting form for your customization.*

To the immediate right of the form, you should see a panel with the title **Fields**. This panel begins with a list of all the fields defined for the selected list. While the line at the top of this form says that you can drag a field from the list to the form to add it, you may want to wait a bit before doing that. Because all of the columns appear in a table on the form, you must first create an empty location where you drag the field. You will see how to do that in a moment, but first look at the options below the list.

A link with the text **Show advanced view** appears immediately below the field list. When you click this link, the field list changes to a tree view of the fields. Using the check box below the list, you can display the field types as well. However, let's return to the basic view as shown in Figure 9-5.

Figure 9-5. *The Fields panel shows the available columns in the selected list.*

Because I selected the **Announcements** list, the list includes a column that defines a date when the announcement should expire. When using the Announcements list, you can create a view that displays only those events that have an expiration date in the future. However, because there is no start date, the announcement would begin appearing in the view as soon as you created it. If you want to enter an announcement that will not begin appearing until a later date, you need another date column, which I will call **Publish Date**, that defines the first date on which you want the announcement to appear.

Although you could go back to the list, select **List Settings**, and add this new column, you can use InfoPath to redesign the edit form and add the new column all at one time. To begin, click the **Add Field** option under the **Actions** section of the **Fields** panel.

■ **Note** InfoPath enables the **Add Field** option only when displaying the basic view as shown in Figure 9-5. If your Fields panel looks different and the link below the field list says **Show basic view**, click this link to return to the basic view.

This option opens the **Add Field or Group** dialog shown in Figure 9-6. Here you can define both a display name and a column name for the new field. In fact, as you type in the **Display Name** field, InfoPath automatically generates the column name. It automatically eliminates blanks and other characters that SharePoint does not allow in a column name.

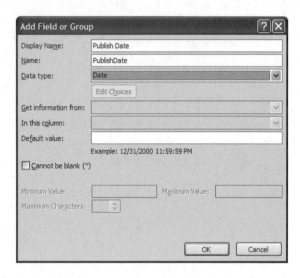

Figure 9-6. The dialog used to define a new column for the current list

Next, you can select the data type from the drop-down list of types. Depending on which data type you select, the rest of the field properties are enabled or disabled as appropriate for that column type. In this case, because we selected a **Date** data type, the only other options we can specify are the **Default value** and the check box that determines whether the user can leave the date blank.

After entering all the parameters to define the field, click **OK** to create it. You will see the new field in the **Fields** panel added immediately. However, you really do not have a place in the current form where you can add this field.

In this case, suppose you want to add the Publish Date field directly above the Expires field. You need to insert a new row above this row. Because the form consists of a table, you can select the **Expires** row by clicking just outside and to the left of the row. After selecting it, switch to the **Layout** ribbon that appears as a sub-tab under **Table Tools**. In the **Rows & Columns** group, click the **Insert Above** button to add a new blank row immediately above the **Expires** row as shown in Figure 9-7.

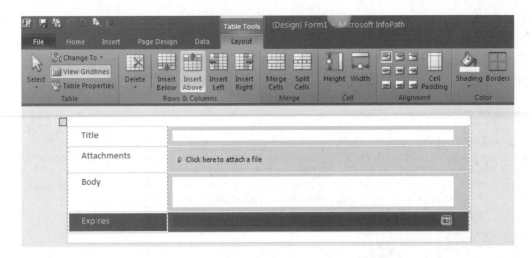

Figure 9-7. To insert a new row in the form above the Expires field, first select the Expires row.

To add the new **Publish Date** column, click and drag the column from the **Fields** panel to the first column of the new row. When you release the mouse button, you should see the **Display Name** property for the column displayed in the first column of the table and a date type field in the second column, as shown in Figure 9-8. Note that the date type field includes a button on the right side of the field that when clicked displays a popup calendar to help you select the date.

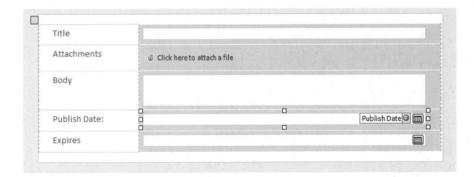

Figure 9-8. The new Announcements form with the addition of a Publish Date column

Now suppose you want to make sure that for every announcement added to the list, the publish date occurs before the expiration date. Because these are simple date fields, you would have no way to enforce this rule. However, InfoPath lets you define validation rules for your form fields. First, click in the field for which you want to add a rule. Then you can click the **Add Rule** button in the **Rules** group of the **Home** ribbon as shown in Figure 9-9.

Figure 9-9. *Add a rule to the form.*

This command displays a drop-down list of possible rule expressions as shown in Figure 9-10. For example, if you start from the **Publish Date**, you could choose the **Is After** option because you want to raise an error when the **Publish Date** is after the **Expires** date. As you position your mouse over your desired **IF** expression, a second menu appears next to the first that shows you the actions and formatting you can use. In this case, let's begin by selecting the **Show Validation Error** action.

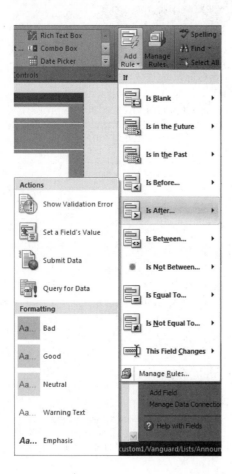

Figure 9-10. *Select an If condition to fire the rule.*

In the **Rule Details** dialog, you can enter an absolute value to which you can compare the **Publish Date** field, or you can click the function button to select a field as shown in Figure 9-11.

■ **Caution** You must select the field from the **Insert Formula** dialog by clicking the **Insert Field** or **Group** button and then selecting the field. You cannot simply enter the name of the field in the text box shown in Figure 9-11.

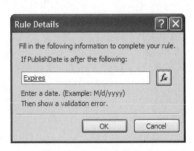

Figure 9-11. Complete the rule details.

Now complete the definition of the rule by clicking the **OK** button. Next, you can go through the **Add Rule** command a second time selecting the same **IF** expression, but this time select **Bad** under formatting. This option will format the field value with red text on a light red background, making it obvious to the user that the value is incorrect. When the user corrects the problem, the field style reverts to the default black text on a white background so you do not have to create a special rule for corrected values.

Rather than select the **Add Rule** command, you can also select the **Manage Rules** button in the **Rules** group to open a panel along the right side of the screen that shows all of the currently defined rules for the selected field as shown in Figure 9-12.

Figure 9-12. The Rules panel for the selected field, Publish Date

Using this panel, you can click in the text box after the label **Details for:** to define a user-friendly name for your new rule. Of course, you could leave the default rule names provided by InfoPath. Next, you must define a condition to trigger the rule. Remember that validation triggers consist of Boolean expressions that must evaluate to **True** for invalid conditions. When a field returns **True** from the validation expression, InfoPath surrounds the field with a dashed red box to show you that the field has an invalid value. However, you should also define a screen tip that displays when the Boolean expression returns a value of **True**. In the screen tip, you can tell the user why the value is not valid.

Although InfoPath Forms Services cannot display validation messages, defining them in your form definition does not create a fatal error condition when you display the form, because web-based forms simply ignore this extra information. On the other hand, if the Design Checker identifies an error, you should fix the indicated error before publishing the form template.

After defining your form rules, you can test them by using the **Preview** option, found in the **Form** group of the **Home** ribbon, as shown in Figure 9-13.

Figure 9-13. Use the Preview command to check how the form would appear in a browser.

This command opens a new window and displays your form as it would appear in a browser. You can test different field values in the form to see if the validations, actions, and formatting options you selected work as expected. Figure 9-14 shows an example of a preview of the **Announcements** form in which the Publish Date is after the Expires date. InfoPath identifies this error condition, surrounds the field with a dashed red box, and displays the screen tip box telling you that `the Publish Date must be less than the Expires Date`.

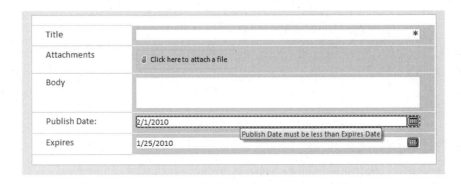

Figure 9-14. Previewing the form shows a validation error on Publish Date.

At any point, you can publish your form to SharePoint. While you could go directly to the **Publish** option in the **Backstage**, you can also access the publish options by opening the Info page as shown in Figure 9-15. In fact, since we are publishing an updated form for an existing list, the **Quick Publish** option may be your fastest and easiest choice. However, before actually publishing the form, you may want to first run the **Design Checker** to ensure that no incompatibilities exist between your form and your SharePoint web site.

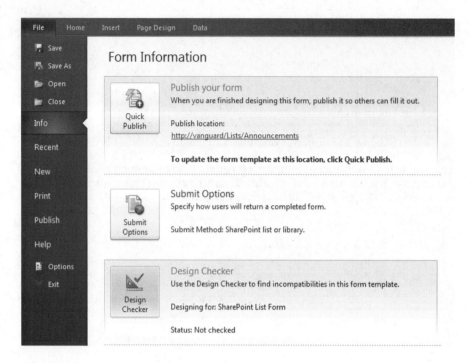

Figure 9-15. *Use the Design Checker to find incompatibilities with your SharePoint web site.*

When you click the **Design Checker** button, InfoPath checks for incompatibilities with the web server where the list is located. Upon completing the check, it opens a panel along the right side of the screen, named Design Checker. Here it will list any error that you would need to correct before publishing the form back to the SharePoint list. If it finds no errors, it displays the text shown in Figure 9-16.

Figure 9-16. Design Checker reports any incompatibilities.

You are now ready to publish the form. Since you built this form as a SharePoint list form, you can use the **Quick Publish** feature in **Backstage's** Info page shown in Figure 9-17. In the **Publish your form** section, you can see that InfoPath already knows the **Publish location**. All you need to do is click the **Quick Publish** button to publish the form in one step.

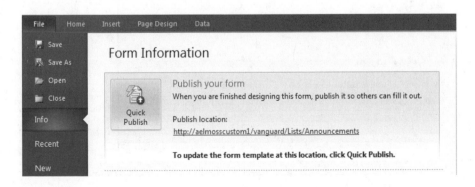

Figure 9-17. Use the Quick Publish option to publish a list form back to the site.

InfoPath then connects to the SharePoint server and locates the site and list. It then uploads the form, publishing it as the default form that users will see when they add a new item to the list or edit an existing item. If, as in this case, you added fields to the list, InfoPath also takes care of adding those fields to the list. However, if you have other list views, you will need to edit each view manually to identify where you want to add the new field. After the upload completes, InfoPath displays one last dialog, telling you that it succeeded in publishing the form. It also provides a link in the dialog that lets you open the list in your browser if you do not already have the list open.

Figure 9-18. The dialog that appears after publishing completes lets you open the list in the browser.

To test the new form, click the link in Figure 9-18. Within a few moments, the list appears. Then either add a new item to the list or click an existing item to edit it; either way, you'll see the new uploaded form as shown in Figure 9-19.

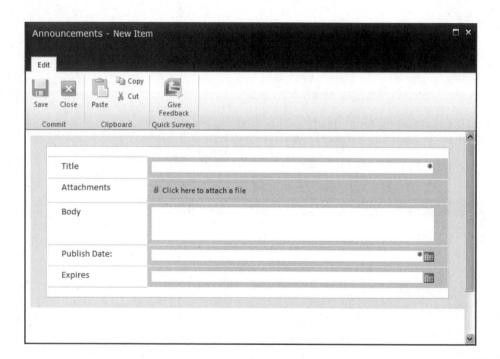

Figure 9-19. View your published list form.

Now that you have seen how easily you can create a new form to edit your SharePoint lists, you might also want to look at the SharePoint Form Library template to build forms that users can fill out and save to the library. Perhaps you want to create a form that colleagues can use within Outlook to fill in data and submit information back to you. Rather than spending time here looking at these similar templates, let's see how to create a new form from a blank template.

Creating a Form from a Blank Template

To create a form from a blank template, you again begin by clicking the File tab to open InfoPath's **Backstage** area as shown in Figure 9-20. Within the **Popular Form Templates** group, select the **Blank** template. In the right side panel, InfoPath tells you that when you create a blank form, you can publish that form to either SharePoint or a network location. Click the **Design this Form** button to open a new blank form.

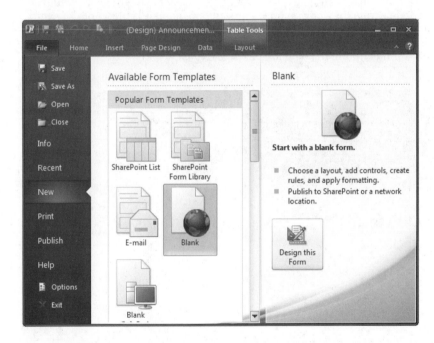

Figure 9-20. InfoPath's New page in the Backstage area

■ **Note** After you have created a form and saved it, you can reopen the form by using the **Recent** area of the **Backstage**. This option displays a list of the recent templates you have worked with, in the main part of the page. You can click any of these templates to reopen them and continue working on them. If it has been some time since you last worked on the template, you may need to click **Open** in the **File** menu to navigate to the network or SharePoint location where you saved the template.

The redesign of SharePoint to use Ajax has eliminated in InfoPath 2010 and SharePoint 2010 many of the control limitations of SharePoint Server 2007 when creating forms.. Therefore, you no longer have to remember to check a box like the **Enable browser-compatible features only** check box. The controls you see in InfoPath when creating your new form are all available within SharePoint 2010.

As you can see in Figure 9-21, the blank template consists of a title area at the top of the page and a body section. If you click anywhere within the body section, a new ribbon, named **Table Tools – Layout** appears at the top of the window. This body section is just a single-cell table. While you can use the **Split Cells** command in the **Merge** group of the **Layout** ribbon to divide the body area into smaller cells to help lay out your page, there is another option that you may want to try first.

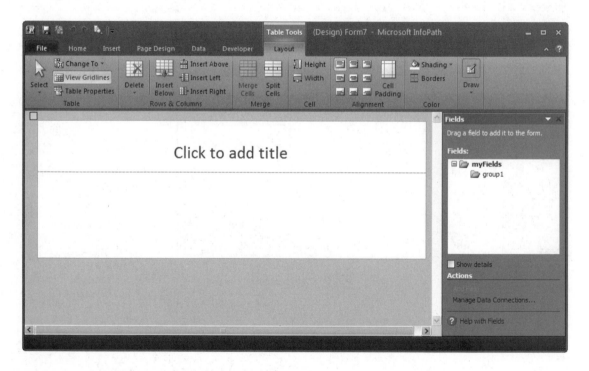

Figure 9-21. InfoPath's blank SharePoint form template

Click the **Page Design** ribbon. Then, from the **Page Layouts** group, click the **Page Layout Templates** button. This option opens a dialog offering the following starting page layouts:

- Title Only: This option corresponds to the default layout.

- Title and Heading: This option adds a header row beneath the title area and above the body table area.

- Title and Body: This option includes a text area between the title and the body areas where you can provide addition information to the user filling in the form.

- Color bar: This page layout is similar to the **Title Only** layout but with the addition of narrow column along the left side of the form that you can display in any color to add a little style to your form.

- Offset Body: In this layout, the body section of the form is offset a small amount from the left edge of the form but otherwise appears similar to the **Title Only** form.

Figure 9-22 shows the **Page Layout Templates** dialog.

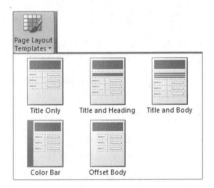

Figure 9-22. *InfoPath's Page Layout Templates dialog*

If you want to change your form layout before you begin, you should first select and delete the default form. Otherwise, selecting a form from the **Page Layout Templates** inserts the template into the existing form template. (You could use this method to build a form quickly that consists of a series of form templates that each have their own heading and body section.)

To delete the current template so you can begin with one of the **Page Layout Templates** in Figure 9-22, click anywhere within the default template. A small square appears in its upper left. Click in this square to select the entire template. If you right-click this square, the drop-down menu show options that you can perform on the entire template. The Delete option opens a fly-out menu of three sub-options. Select **Table** from this fly-out to delete the entire form, as shown in Figure 9-23.

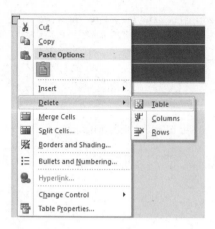

Figure 9-23. Delete the default template to begin your form with a different template.

Now you can go back to the **Page Layout Templates** dialog to select the layout that you want to use. For this example, we will build a form used by employees to request time off from work. Therefore, let's use the **Title and Body** page layout to start our form design.

To begin adding content to your form, you may want to provide a title at the top of the form. Click the text **Click to add title** and enter the title `Request for Absence Form`. The page template preformats the title area with a larger version of the Calibri font. However, you can select your text and change any of the font characteristics including the font type, size, color, and any of the other font styling options.

■ **Note** While it is often tempting to underline titles, remember that underlined text on a web page often indicates to users that the text acts as a hyperlink. For this reason, you probably do not want to underline your form titles. Rather than underline, use other font characteristics to make your title stand out, such as a bold font using one of your site branding colors. In addition, I recommend using a generic font like Arial, which appears similar to Calibri so that all viewers of your site see the form exactly as you designed it even if they do not have the font Calibri on their local system.

The body text area provides an ideal place to display instructions for the user to fill in the form. In the case of this Request for Absence Form, you can provide an instruction paragraph such as the following:

`You must fill in a Request for Absence and submit the completed form to your supervisor in advance of any planned absence. Do not use this form for sick-time or other emergency leave situations. You can only make requests for absence in units of full or half days.`

At this point, your form should look similar to Figure 9-24. Note that the area beneath the body text says **Add tables**. In the next section, you will begin building the interactive portion of the form using tables in this area.

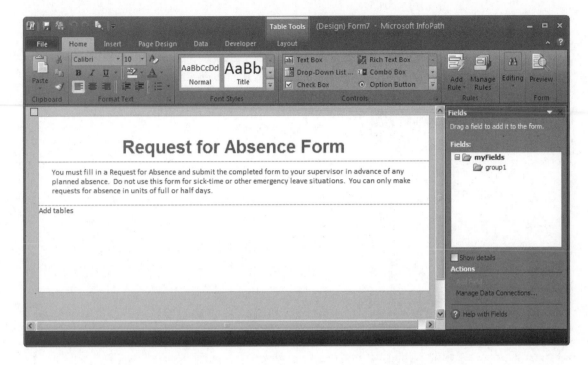

Figure 9-24. The start of a new form using the Title and Heading page template

Next, you need to start building the rest of the form. While you could simply start adding text along with the various input controls for the users to enter data, it would be difficult to arrange the input fields and controls on the form neatly. Moreover, even after you managed to add spaces or tabs to try to position each item where we wanted it, a simple change of the font type or size could instantly rearrange the form.

Tables can provide the underlying structure for a form that can retain the relative positions of text and fields even as you change fonts. Tables also provide an ordered row and column structure that most forms require. Once placed on a form, a table's cells can be merged and split to create different areas to display information and to prompt for different types of text. You can also add more rows and columns to a table as you need to expand or shrink the number of fields on the form. However, you may want to consider how you want to lay out the controls on the form first and then begin with a table that best matches your overall control layout.

Figure 9-25 shows the **Table** dialog available from the **Insert** ribbon. Note that InfoPath offers three basic table layouts:

- Two Column

- Single Column

- Four Column

InfoPath also provides a selection of different styles that run horizontally within each basic layout. The individual columns also provide a unique combination of headings as you examine the style from left to right. The first column provides both a main heading and a subheading before the start of the table. The second column provides just a main heading at the top of the table. The third column provides just a subheading and the last column provides only the table with no headings.

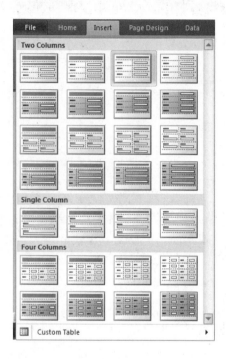

Figure 9-25. InfoPath offers a wide selection of table templates or the ability to custom-define a table.

Of course, you can always use multiple tables for different sections of your form if the structure from one section changes greatly from the previous section. In fact using multiple tables can save time over trying to split or merge columns of a single table to achieve the same visual layout of controls. In addition, you can place one table inside the cell of another table.

As you build your form from top to bottom, you might start with a table template that includes both a main heading and a subheading for the first set of controls. Then, in the next section of controls, you may only want a subheading before the start of the table. In the third section, you may also want to begin your table with a subheading but you might want a different number of columns. In this way, you can easily build your form from the top down, for each data section adding individual tables that already have the exact number of columns you need.

However, if the predefined table templates still do not meet your needs, you can click the option **Custom Table** at the bottom of the **Table** dialog to build your own unique table. Figure 9-26 shows the custom table dialog.

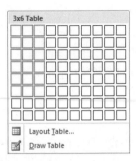

Figure 9-26. Custom-define a table by dragging through the grid of boxes.

In this dialog, you can use your mouse to drag through the grid of squares to indicate the number of columns and rows you want in the table. For example, if you want a three-column table, a table template not shown in Figure 9-25, you can drag through three of the columns and several of the rows as shown in Figure 9-26. Does it matter how many rows you add to the initial table? No. With any table, you can add another row by placing your cursor in the rightmost cell of the last row and pressing the **Tab** key to add another row moving the cursor to the first column in that new row.

If your table has a large number of rows, rather than inserting rows individually, you may want to build your initial table with all the rows you expect to need. From the dialog in Figure 9-26, click the **Layout Table** option to display a dialog that lets you enter the number of columns and rows you want in the created table. Figure 9-27 shows the **Insert Table** dialog about to create a three-column table with 50 rows.

Figure 9-27. For larger tables, define the number of columns and rows directly.

■ **Tip** Do you want to increase the height of the cell? Place the cursor after the last character in the cell and press **Shift+Enter**.

■ **Tip** To change the color of a table cell, place the cursor in the cell and right-click. Select the option **Borders and Shading.** Click the **Shading** tab and select a new color (or even no color if your form uses a background color or image).

■ **Tip** To change the color or style of a border on the table, click anywhere within the table. You should see a small gray square in the upper-left corner of the form. Right-click this square and select **Borders and Shading**. Click the **Borders** tab. Select the line style, color, and width of the line. Then set the table's border lines, by either using the buttons in the **Presets** section or clicking the buttons or ndividual lines in the border diagram.

How Do You Decide How Many Columns You Need?

When laying out your form using tables, you need to determine how many columns your table needs. To determine how many columns you need, you need to know what goes into a column. Let's suppose you plan to add a few text boxes with labels before them to aid users in knowing what information to place in each text box. Typically, you should place the label before the text box in a separate column from the text box itself. This technique gives you more control over the spacing between the label and the text box. Thus, you already need two columns for one field.

Then, if you want two text boxes on the same line, such as for first and last name, you might need three or four columns depending on whether each text box has its own label. In such cases, some form designers recommend that you place a spacer column between the two sets of columns. By adding a spacer column, you can easily control the amount of space between the text box of the first column set and the label of the second column set, even when you use right-justified label text.

Thus, you can see that the number of columns you need for a typical form can grow quite rapidly. You may need as many as five table columns in one row of two data columns and eight table columns for three data columns in the next row. How can you create a table to handle the situation in which every row requires a different number of columns? By splitting and merging cells or by inserting individual tables for each row.

No matter which table template you select for your form, it seems that you always have a portion of the form that requires an exception to the number of columns. Whether you need more or fewer columns for a line, it may be more effort to create multiple tables just for one exceptional row. This situation is where the **Merge Cells** and **Split Cells** options from the **Merge** group of **Table Tools Layout** can quick let you change the number of columns in a single row or even the number of rows within a single column of one row.

To merge cells, you select two or more cells by clicking the first cell and dragging through the cells you want to include. You can select cells vertically, horizontally, or both at the same time when you merge cells. When you merge the cells, the interior cell walls disappear, and you end up with a single large cell. You might do this to insert a sub form, image or other large object inside the structure of your table.

Similarly, you can split cells horizontally or vertically. Simply select the cell you want to split, and select the number of rows and columns into which you want to split the cell. You can even select several cells at once and redefine the number of rows and columns the selected cells should have. For example, you could select three columns and two rows of cells by dragging through them and then select the **Split Cells** option. In the **Split Cells** dialog, you could then specify two columns and three rows to alter the layout of selected cells completely as long as you select the check box **Merge cells before split**. This option takes the cells in the original three columns and two rows and creates a single large cell. It then splits this cell into the two columns and three rows that you specified.

■ **Caution** If you plan to restructure your cells by splitting and merging cells, you might want to do that before adding text to the cells.

Finally, the **Layout** ribbon also allows you to add rows and columns to the table in case you misjudged your requirements when creating the table. Of course, if you merely want to add another row to the end of your table, just place the cursor in the rightmost cell of the last row in the table and press that **Tab** key. Similarly, you can delete rows by dragging through them to select them and pressing the **Delete** key or by right-clicking in any cell and selecting **Delete** and then **Columns** or **Rows** to remove the current column or row.

To begin our simple Request for Absence form, let's add a four-column table. In this table, we will use columns 1 and 3 to hold field labels and columns 2 and 4 to hold field values. Figure 9-28 shows the start of the table. It includes the field labels, but where do we get the field values?

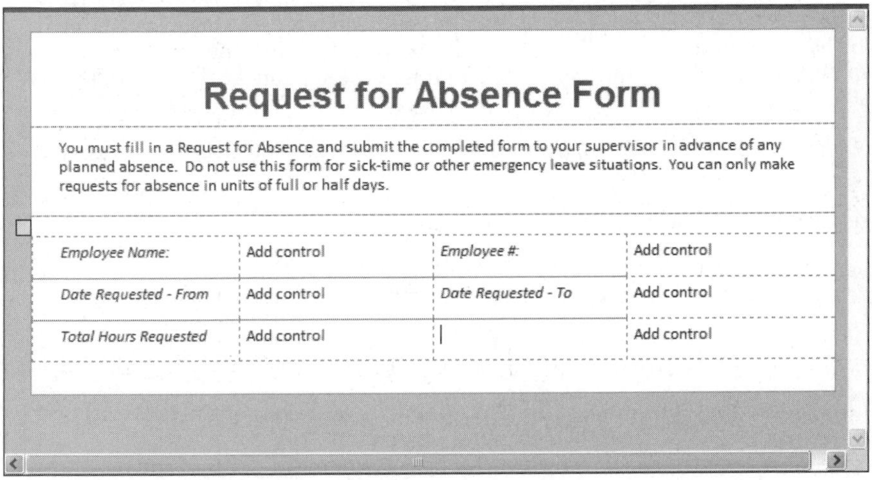

Figure 9-28. The initial table with labels added

The Task Group: Controls

The **Controls** group of the **Home** ribbon displays all the controls that you can place on your form. Figure 9-29 shows the available controls you can use out-of-the-box. InfoPath divides these controls into three groups: **Input**, **Objects**, and **Containers**. Input controls allow the user to enter data or select data. Object controls either perform an action, as the button control does, or hold specific files such as pictures. You use containers to hold other controls.

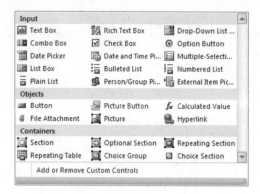

Figure 9-29. InfoPath's control dialog

I will not spend a lot of time talking about each of these controls here. The purpose of most of these controls should be obvious to most of you, especially among the Input controls. The use of even the object controls should be easy to determine based on each one's name. The **Container** controls allow you to group other input and object controls into sections. You might use sections to do any of the following:

- Determine which controls to display to a user based on entries in previous controls.

- Identify optional sections that the user can include or ignore.

- Provide for a repeating set of input objects or even an entire table where the number of repeated items is unknown, such as the number of detail records in a single order.

- Allow the user to choose which section to include in a form.

Let's continue building the Request for Absence form by adding the text box control in the second column of the first row to allow the user to enter their employee name.

To add a control to the table, you can begin by clicking in the cell where you want to add the control. Then open the **Controls** dialog from Figure 9-29 and double click the **Text Box** control. To view the properties of any control, right-click the control after adding it to the form (you can double-click or click and drag the control to position it on the form within a cell of a table). From the drop-down menu, select the **Properties** option at the bottom of the list. (All controls have a Properties option.) A Properties dialog appears, as shown in Figure 9-30.

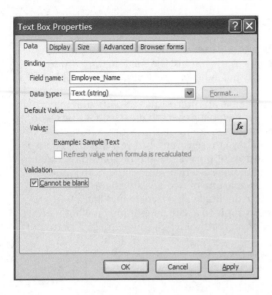

Figure 9-30. The Data page of the Text Box Properties dialog

The **Properties** dialog box has many userselectable properties. Therefore, it separates the properties by type and places them on separate tabbed pages. Most controls have similar properties. The **Data** page has the most differences from one control to another.

On the **Data** page of this dialog, you begin by defining the field name to which you want to bind this control. If you did not start with an existing data source, InfoPath will create a XML schema to manage the data for the form. As you will see later in this chapter, you can then map the XML schema to list columns to make it easy to examine and work with the collected data.

The second item you must specify is the **Data Type** for the current field. The drop-down list for this property shows all the available data types that InfoPath supports. Keep in mind that selecting the proper data type can be part of your data validation. For example, if you want users to enter a quantity such as a number of items ordered consider using the integer data type rather than just a simple number or even a string. By defining the data type as an integer, you make sure the user cannot enter characters, nor can they enter a decimal value. Similarly, when dealing with dates, do not use the Date/Time type unless time is important for the information tracked. If you only use the date, choose the Date type.

While the Text Box control does not let you define a format for the data, many of the other data types do. For example, Date and Date/Time data types allow you to select from a list of available date and time formats for your data. For numeric data, you can define the number of decimal places and the thousands separator (also known as a digit-grouping symbol). If the field represents a monetary value, you can also select the currency symbol you want to use.

Next, you can provide a default value. You can either supply an absolute value as the default by entering it in the text box, or create a function by using the function button to calculate the default value. While you can define the default value to be a function of one or more other fields in the current form instance, you should be aware that the user might enter data in a different sequential order, leaving the dependent fields undefined. Furthermore, for a new form instance, the referenced fields will not have values yet unless they, too, have default values. For example, suppose you have two dates on a form representing a date range. You could default the start date to today. Then you could default the end date of the range as the start date plus 14 days or two weeks. Because the referenced field for the end date calculation has a default value that you can calculate, both dates can successfully use a calculated default value.

Finally, the **Text Box** dialog also lets you determine whether a user will be able to leave the current field blank. If you select this check box, a red asterisk appears to the right of the field on the form as a reminder that the field must have a value. Other controls may have these as well as additional properties on the Data page of the properties dialog.

For example, the Check Box and Option Button controls have an interesting property that may surprise you. When you add a Check Box control to a form, you would expect that each check box would support a Boolean value of **True** or **False**, or perhaps the integer variation on this, 1 or 0. However, if you open the **Properties** dialog box and select the Data tab, you have these values, but you can also change the data type associated with the check box. In fact, the control supports several types of values, ranging from text to integers, dates, and even hyperlinks. You still can only save two values, and both values must have the same data type. However, if you would rather save one of two possible dates, depending on whether the user selects the option, or one of two possible decimal values, you can. Figure 9-31 shows an example where a check box returns the discount to apply to a sale depending on whether the buyer has a frequent buyer card. In this case, the frequent buyer cardholder gets an extra 20% on top of the 10% off sale price.

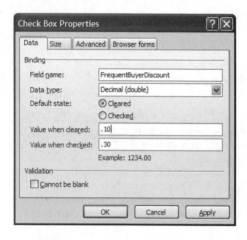

Figure 9-31. An example of the data properties for a check box data control

Similarly, the Option Button control returns a single value no matter how many buttons you associate with the instance of this control. By default, these buttons return an integer ranging from 1 to *n*, where *n* represents the number of option buttons in the group. However, you can return letters, text strings, whole numbers, decimals, or dates instead.

Another interesting feature of controls, *conditional formatting*, lets you change the appearance of the control's contents based on a condition that you define as a Boolean expression. You can access this feature by adding a new rule using the **Add Rule** option in the **Rules** group of the **Control Tools Properties** ribbon. Figure 9-32 shows that rules can consist of validations, formatting, or actions. In this case, choose **Formatting**.

Figure 9-32. Add a formatting rule to the input control Hours_Requested.

The first step in building a formatting rule is to define the condition that must exist before applying the new formatting. In our Request for Absence form, one of the fields that we will need is a text box formatted to hold an integer number representing the number of hours requested. Suppose your company has a rule that generally grants any requests for less than 8 hours. We could create a rule that compares the value of the field Hours_Requested. When that value is less than or equal to 8 hours, we want to change the font color of the field value to green. Therefore, we define the condition expression as shown in Figure 9-33.

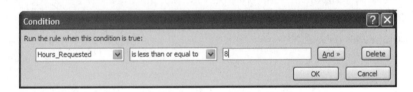

Figure 9-33. Define a condition for the formatting rule.

■ **Tip** You can use conditional formatting to make fields read-only or even invisible based on a predefined condition, an option found at the bottom of the **Formatting** area.

Figure 9-34 shows that after defining the rule condition, you can then use the buttons in the **Formatting** area to define a special style for the field.

Figure 9-34. Define a formatting definition for the Number of Hours field.

You can define more than one conditional formatting rule. For example, you might use another color to indicate requests of more than one day but not more than a week. Finally, you might format anything longer than a week with a third color.

At first you might not give much thought to the order in which you define these rules. However, InfoPath executes these rules sequentially from the top of the Rules list. Therefore, if you defined the first two rules in a different order, you will not get the desired result. In fact, if the rule comparing the number of hours to 40 occurs before the rules comparing the number of hours to 8, the second rule never fires because all number less than 8 are also less than 40 and therefore only the first rule fires. Therefore, you have to make sure that InfoPath executes the 8-hour rule first by placing it physically before the 40-hour rule, as shown in Figure 9-35. If you enter the rules in a different order, you can use the drop-down menu that appears when you position your mouse over any of the rules to move a rule up or down in the list.

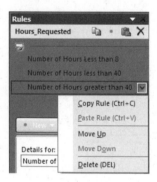

Figure 9-35. Define the order in which the rules fire.

As you can see in this figure, you can also delete existing rules if you no longer need them. You can also copy and paste rules that are similar and may be easier to modify than to create from scratch.

Using a similar technique, you can also apply data validation rules to any field. Using data validation to identify bad data values at the form level before submitting data to the data source allows the user entering data into the form to correct problems immediately. Updating bad data after submitting it to a data source or even at a later time generally requires more time and expense than immediately addressing it.

A validation rule also requires a Boolean expression. In this case, you must create a Boolean expression that identifies values that you do not want to accept rather than the correct values. You might think of this as testing for failure, and I suppose it is. You can then define a tooltip to explain the problem. When the user enters a value for which the Boolean validation expression returns **True**, InfoPath surrounds the offending field with a red dashed box. As the user places the mouse over the offending field, the tooltip then indicates why InfoPath has flagged the value as shown in Figure 9-36.

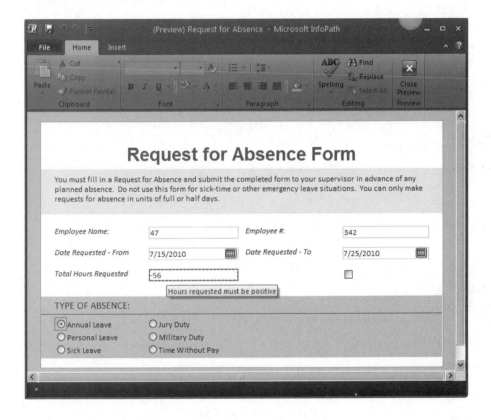

Figure 9-36. *Data validation traps bad data as it's entered.*

The last feature of controls I'll examine here is the ability to add rules to your form that can display messages, set values of other controls, and even execute other actions based on the values entered into the control. You begin defining an action rule much as you did for the last two features, by defining a Boolean condition in the rules manager to specify when you want the rule to fire. Then you can define an action. Possible actions include the following:

- Set a field's value.

- Perform a query for data.

- Submit data.

- Send data to another web part.

Each action requires additional configuration data. For example, to set a field's value, you must identify the field on the current form you want to set and the value you want use. You can use an absolute value or create a calculated value from other fields on the form.

As with conditional formatting, you can specify multiple action, but must carefully specify the order of the actions. However, unlike conditional formatting, you can disable and enable actions without having to delete and read action rules.

The Task Group: Data Sources

The **Data Sources** task group lets you examine your data sources. In the case where you build the data source while you build the form, the **Data Source** panel displays the name of each field you added along with selected properties of the field, as shown in Figure 9-37.

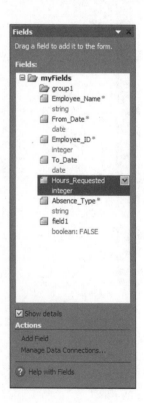

Figure 9-37. View the data source structure.

If you use a different data source, such as an Access or SQL database, you will see the fields used in those respective databases.

The Task Group: Design Checker

The **Design Checker** panel is especially useful when you design a web-based form used with InfoPath Forms Services. It identifies and lists any errors on your form that prevent your form from working properly. It also lists warnings such as the definition of validation messages for some of your form's fields. To run the **Design Checker**, go to the Info page of the **BackStage** area (**File** menu) and click the **Design Checker** button as shown in Figure 9-38.

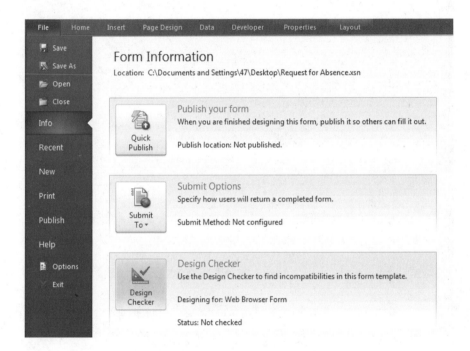

Figure 9-38. Selecting the Design Checker from the Backstage

As an example, InfoPath Forms Services cannot display validation messages.

■ **Note** For those of you who may be wondering what InfoPath Forms Services is, SharePoint Server includes several services to allow users to interact with objects that range from InfoPath Forms to Excel worksheets and even Access applications. These services are bundled with the Enterprise version of SharePoint Server 2010 and can be configured through Central Administration.

Therefore, defining such messages in your form's field definitions creates a warning message. The reason InfoPath does not flag validation messages as a fatal error condition is that when InfoPath displays the form as a web-based form, it simply ignores this extra information. On the other hand, if the Design Checker identifies a fatal error such as an unsupported control type, you must fix the indicated error before publishing the form template. Figure 9-39 shows sample results of the Design Checker in which it found no incompatibilities.

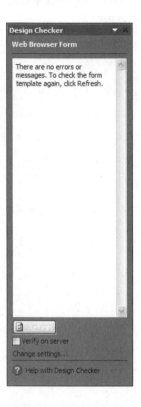

Figure 9-39. *Design Checker identifies errors and warnings before publishing a form.*

By default, the Design Checker validates the form as if it were running within a generic web browser. However, if you click the link **Change Settings**, you can change the compatibility settings to validate the form against earlier InfoPath editions or against the new InfoPath Filler application included with Office.

Steps to Build the Request for Absence Form

Here are the steps to re-create the Request for Absence form shown earlier in Figure 9-8:

1. Open InfoPath and select the **Blank** template from the **Popular Form Templates** in the **New** page of the **BackStage** area.

2. With a blank form open, make sure to display the **Page Layout Templates** in the **Page Layouts** group of the **Page Design** ribbon.

3. Use the default page layout or select the layout by right-clicking the small box in the upper left corner of the page layout and selecting Delete ➤ Table. Then choose a page layout such as the Title and Heading layout.

4. Click in the row that says **Click to add title** and enter `Request for Absence Form`.

5. Using the options in the **Format Text** group of the **Home** ribbon, make the text Arial Bold 22 pt and centered.

6. Click in the second row where it says **Click to add heading** and enter the following text:

   `You must fill in a Request for Absence and submit the completed form to your supervisor in advance of any planned absence. Do not use this form for sick-time or other emergency leave situations. You can only make requests for absence in units of full or half days.`

7. With your mouse pointer still in this second row, click **Shading** in the **Color** group of the **Table Tools Layout** ribbon and select one of the lighter shades of gray to fill in this row's background.

8. Click where the form says **Add tables**. Then open the **Insert** ribbon and select a four-column table grid with no heading.

9. In the first column, first row, enter the text `Employee Name:`

10. In the first column, second row, enter `Date Requested - From:`

11. In the first column, third row, enter `Total Hours Requested`

12. In the third column, first row, enter `Employee #:`

13. In the third column, second row, enter `Date Requested - To:`

14. In the second column of the first row, add a **Text Box** from the **Controls** panel found in the **Controls** group of the **Home** ribbon.

15. Right-click the new control and select **Text Box Properties** from the drop-down menu.

16. In the **Data** page of the **Text Box Properties**, enter the field name `Employee_Name` and indicate that the field cannot be blank. Click **OK** when done.

17. In the fourth column of the first row, add a **Text Box** from the **Controls** panel found in the **Controls** group of the **Home** ribbon.

18. Right-click the new control and select **Text Box Properties** from the drop-down menu.

19. In the **Data** page of the **Text Box Properties**, enter the field name `Employee_ID` and indicate that the field cannot be blank. Click **OK** when done.

20. In the second column of the second row, add a **Date Picker** from the **Controls** panel found in the **Controls** group of the **Home** ribbon.

21. Right-click the new control and select **Date Picker Properties** from the drop-down menu.

22. In the **Data** page of the **Date Picker Properties**, enter the field name `From_Date` and indicate that the field cannot be blank. Also, change the data type to: `Date (date)`. Click **OK** when done.

23. In the fourth column of the second row, add a Date Picker from the Controls panel found in the Controls group of the Home ribbon.

24. Right-click the new control and select Date Picker Properties from the drop-down menu.

25. In the **Data** page of the **Date Picker Properties**, enter the field name `To_Date`. Also, change the data type to `Date (date)`. Click **OK** when done.

26. In the second column of the third row, add a Text Box from the Controls panel found in the Controls group of the Home ribbon.

27. Right-click the new control and select Text Box Properties from the drop-down menu.

28. In the **Data** page of the **Text Box Properties**, enter the field name: `Hours_Requested` and indicate that the field cannot be blank. Also, change the data type to `Whole Number (integer)`. Click **OK** when done.

29. Next, open the Control Tools Properties ribbon and select Manage Rules from the Rules group.

30. Click in the field **To-Date**. Then click **New** in the **Rules** panel to start a new **Validation** rule. Provide a name for the rule, such as **Date Sequence Validation**. Then click the word **None** under **Condition** to open the **Condition** dialog. Create the condition: `To_Date is less than From_Date`. Then click the **And** button and enter the rule: `To_Date is not blank`, because you want to allow this field to be blank if the absence is only for one day. Click **OK** to complete the condition.

31. For the screen tip, enter the text `Enter a date on or after From_Date`.

32. Next, click the **Hours_Requested** field.

33. Click **New** in the **Rules** panel to start a new **Validation** rule. Let's call this one `Number of Hours Less than 0`. Then enter the condition: `Hours_Requested is less than 0`. Provide the screen tip: `Hours requested must be positive`.

34. Click **New** in the **Rules** panel to start a new **Formatting** rule. Let's call this one `Number of Hours Less than or equal to 8`. Then in the formatting section select bold and change the font color to green.

35. Click **New** in the **Rules** panel to start a new **Formatting** rule. Let's call this one `Number of Hours Less than or equal to 40`. Then in the formatting section select bold and change the font color to yellow.

36. Click **New** in the **Rules** panel to start a new **Formatting** rule. Let's call this one Number of Hours Greater than 40. Then in the formatting section select bold and change the font color to red.

37. Now, to allow the user to enter the type of absence, click below the last row of the current table and then select a **Two-column table with SubHeading** from the **Tables** panel drop-down in the **Tables** group of the **Insert** ribbon.

38. Change the heading to Type of Absence: and, with the text selected, click the left-aligned button in the **Home** ribbon's **Format Text** group.

39. Click in the first column of the first row of this table and click the **Option Button** control from the **Control** drop-down in the **Home** ribbon.

40. In the dialog that pops up for the number of option buttons to insert, select 6 and click **OK**. Notice that all the buttons appear in the first cell with no text after them. However, if you hover over any of them, they all have the same field name. Therefore, you can right-click any of them and select **Option Button Properties** from the drop-down menu.

41. Click and drag the button on the bottom to column 2, row 3 of the table. Click to the right of the option button and directly enter the text Time Without Pay.

42. Click and drag the button on the bottom to column 2, row 2 of the table. Click to the right of the option button and directly enter the text Military Duty.

43. Click and drag the button on the bottom to column 2, row 1 of the table. Click to the right of the option button and directly enter the text Jury Duty.

44. Click and drag the button on the bottom to column 1, row 3 of the table. Click to the right of the option button and directly enter the text Sick Leave.

45. Click and drag the button on the bottom to column 1, row 2 of the table. Click to the right of the option button and directly enter the text Personal Leave.

46. Click to the right of the option button in row 1, column 1 and directly enter the text Annual Leave.

47. Eliminate any extra blank lines in row 1, column 1 so all the cells are only as high as the option button itself.

48. Right-click the option button in row 1, column 1 and select **Option Button Properties** from the drop-down menu. In the **Data** page, change the name to **Absence_Type**. Change the **Value when selected** to 1. Click **OK** to finish changing this option button.

49. Right-click the option button in row 2, column 1 and select **Option Button Properties** from the drop-down menu. In the **Data** page, change the **Value when selected** to 2. Click **OK** to finish changing this option button. Notice that the name property has already been set to be the same as the previous option button. All option buttons defined together as a group must have the same name.

50. Right-click the option button in row 3, column 1 and select **Option Button Properties** from the drop-down menu. In the **Data** page, change the **Value when selected** to 3. Click **OK** to finish changing this option button.

51. Right-click the option button in row 1, column 2 and select **Option Button Properties** from the drop-down menu. In the **Data** page, change the **Value when selected** to 4. Click **OK** to finish changing this option button.

52. Right-click the option button in row 2, column 2 and select **Option Button Properties** from the drop-down menu. In the **Data** page, change the **Value when selected** to 5. Click **OK** to finish changing this option button.

53. Right-click the option button in row 3, column 2 and select **Option Button Properties** from the drop-down menu. In the **Data** page, change the **Value when selected** to 6. Click **OK** to finish changing this option button.

54. When you are done changing the properties of the option buttons, you may want to adjust the row height or column widths. You may also want to add shading to some of the rows or columns. However, you have completed the essentials of your Request for Absence form.

Wow! That was a lot of work, but you have completed the Request for Absence form, and you did it without writing a single line of code. Chapter 10 covers how to publish forms such as this one in detail.

Other Available InfoPath Templates

While we focused in this section on created an InfoPath form from the blank template, InfoPath provides several other interesting form templates from which to choose.

- Web Service: This template assumes that you want to design a form that queries and submits data to a *web service*. You can think of a web service as an application that uses XML to transfer information between a client and a server.

- Database: This template lets you build a form template that queries and submits data to an Access or SQL database.

- XML or Schema: This template starts a form by using an existing XML document or XML schema as the data source.

- Data Connection File: This template enables you to use a SharePoint data source that you previously defined in a data connection file when creating your form.

- SharePoint List: By starting with this template, you can create a custom form that users will see when viewing or editing items in a SharePoint list. This form provides a great way to customize the plain form that SharePoint auto-generates when users add new items to a list or edit the properties of an existing item.

- Document Information Panel: Similar to SharePoint List, the template lets you customize the form used to edit the properties of a Microsoft Office document stored in a SharePoint document library.

- E-mail: This template lets you create a form that you want to send to users through e-mail and allow them to complete the form and send it back.

InfoPath 2010 also provides templates to create forms compatible with InfoPath 2007.

Finally, InfoPath 2010 allows you to convert Word forms and even Excel forms into InfoPath forms using the **Convert Existing Form** template that is the focus of the next section.

Migrating Your Existing Word Forms into InfoPath

Suppose you already have a form created using Word. You may have spent a great deal of time creating the formatting of that form to make it look exactly the way you want. Alternatively, maybe you found the perfect form template on Microsoft's template site, but the site only had a Word version of it. In either case, you definitely do not want to re-create that form from scratch. So how can you import that Word form into InfoPath without a lot of extra work?

I am going to start with a form template downloaded from Microsoft's site named **Petty Cash Receipt** (office.microsoft.com/en-us/templates/TC010197861033.aspx?pid=CT101423521033) and shown in Figure 9-40. While this form is basic, it demonstrates the concepts you need to convert a Word template to an InfoPath form. The original version of this form template includes three receipts on a page. I have removed the two extra receipts so you can focus on a single copy of the form.

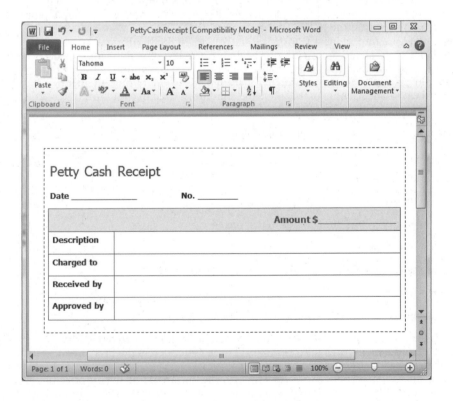

Figure 9-40. The Petty Cash Receipt form in MS Word

■ **Note** I have replaced the fields that were in this template for **Date**, **No.**, and **Amount** with simple underlines because InfoPath will not convert these fields as=is. You must identify the fields with underlines as hints. The need for this step will become apparent when I describe how InfoPath determines the location of fields in a Word document.

When you have a Word template exactly as you would like it, save it as a template file (with the extension `.dot` or `.dotx`) in a directory where you can find it later, and then close Word.

Next, open InfoPath's **Backstage** area (click the **File** button) and click the **New** section to display InfoPath's templates. Click the **Convert Existing Form** option in the **Advanced Form Templates** section. This option lets you import Microsoft Word document or Microsoft Excel spreadsheets. Finally, click the **Design this Form** button. This action opens the **Import Wizard**. From this wizard, you can import either an Excel workbook or a Word document. In this case, select **InfoPath importer for Word documents** as the source and click **Next**.

The second page of the **Import Wizard** prompts for the name of the file to import. You can either enter the file name directly or use the **Browse** button to locate the file through Windows' standard **Open** dialog box. First, let's click the **Options** button to look at the **Options** dialog box.

The **Options** dialog box lets you import just the form layout. You might do this if you want to custom-define the form's fields. The second option imports both the form layout and the form fields, converting the fields as best it can based on the field properties in Word. The last option imports the basic form layout, but lets you customize the conversion of the form fields when it brings them into InfoPath. Choose this option when one or more of the following conditions exist in your Word document:

- You must convert existing Word form fields to InfoPath controls.
- You must detect repeating tables.
- You must detect rich text areas.
- You must convert empty underlined areas to text boxes.
- You must convert empty spaces after colons to text boxes.
- You must convert empty table cells to text boxes.
- You must convert table cells containing label text to text boxes.
- You must convert brackets around multiple spaces to text boxes.
- You must convert brackets around single spaces to check boxes.

For the purpose of this demonstration, select the custom conversion option to convert empty underline areas, areas after colons, and empty table cells to text boxes as defined in the **Petty Cash Receipt** template. Click **OK** to close the **Import Options** dialog.

Next, enter the Word template you want to use or click the **Browse** button to find the file on your available drives. After specifying the file to import and selecting your options, click the **Finish** button to begin the conversion. When the conversion finishes, the wizard displays one last page, informing you whether the conversion completed successfully or not.

■ **Note** You cannot have the template open in Word while you convert it to an InfoPath form.

A conversion can also complete successfully but with issues. When this happens, you can review these issues using the **Design Checker** and correct them in InfoPath. Figure 9-41 shows the results of converting the **Petty Cash Receipt** form.

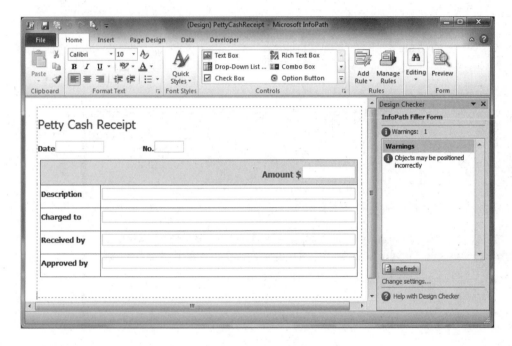

Figure 9-41. Convert the Petty Cash Receipt form into an InfoPath form.

■ **Tip** When InfoPath converts underline characters to fields, it names the fields generically: **Field1**, **Field2**, and so on. However, when InfoPath converts a blank area after a colon to a field, it uses the text to the left of the colon as the field name.

Once you have converted your Word template to InfoPath, use the **Design Checker** to see whether you need to resolve any problems. In this case, the only message in the **Design Checker** states that objects may be positioned incorrectly. In addition to possibly repositioning some of the form field, you might also want to go into some of the fields to add data validation, conditional formatting, or other rules. Other than that, you are ready to publish your form.

Migrating Your Existing Excel Workbook into InfoPath

As with MS Word forms, you may have existing forms in Excel that you want to use with InfoPath. Or maybe you found the perfect form template on Microsoft's template website, but the site only had an Excel version of it. In either case, you definitely do not want to re-create that form from scratch. So how can you import that Excel workbook into InfoPath without starting from a blank form?

I am going to start with an Excel form template downloaded from Microsoft's site, named **Donation Receipt** (office.microsoft.com/en-us/templates/TC060891481033.aspx?pid=CT101423521033), shown in Figure 9-42. While this form is basic, it demonstrates the concepts needed to convert an Excel template to an InfoPath form. The original version of this form template includes three receipts on a page. I have removed the two extra receipts in order to work with just a single copy of the form. Do not be afraid to modify the forms you download before you convert them to InfoPath. A page may contain duplicates of the form because they were designed to print as many copies of the form as possible on a standard 8.5" × 11" sheet of paper.

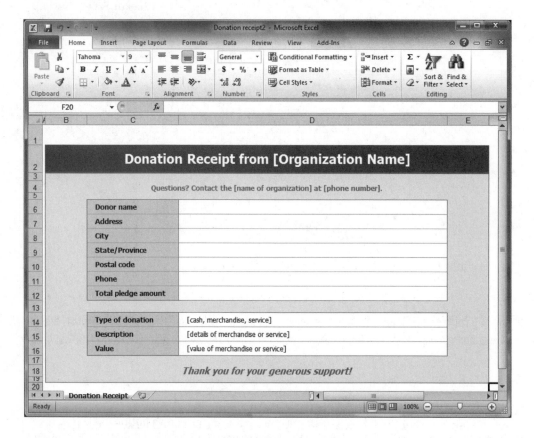

Figure 9-42. *The Donation Receipt form as an Excel document*

■ **Note** The Excel form contains several cells that have prompting text enclosed in brackets ([ ]). The InfoPath **Import Wizard** will not convert these areas to fields, but simply leave them as text. To convert them to fields, you must remove the text, at least in the three cells at the bottom of the form. You can leave the placeholders in the header and subheader text for users to replace when they fill in the form.

When you have an Excel workbook exactly as you would like it, save it as an Excel template (with extension .xlsx) in a directory where you can later find it, and then close Excel.

Next, open InfoPath's **Backstage** area (click the **File** button) and click the **New** section to display InfoPath's templates. Click the **Convert Existing Form** option in the **Advanced Form Templates** section. This option lets you import Word documents or Excel spreadsheets. Finally, click the **Design this Form** button. This action opens the **Import Wizard**. From this wizard, you can import either an Excel workbook or a Word document. In this case, select **InfoPath importer for Excel documents** as the source and click **Next**.

The second page of the **Import Wizard** prompts for the name of the file to import. You can either directly enter the file name or use the **Browse** button to locate the file though Window's standard **Open** dialog box. First, let's click the **Options** button to look at the **Options** dialog box.

The **Options** dialog box gives you three options. The first is to import just the form layout. You might do this if you want to custom define the form fields. The second option imports both the form layout and the form fields, converting the fields as best it can based on the field properties in Excel. The last option imports the basic form layout, but lets you customize the conversion of the form fields when it brings them into InfoPath. Choose this option when one or more of the following conditions exist in your Excel document:

- You have repeating tables.

- You have cells containing formulas that you want to convert to text boxes.

- You have cells containing numeric data rather than just string data.

- You have cells referenced by formulas in other cells.

- You have empty cells within a grid that displays cell borders.

■ **Tip** If you have a complex form, InfoPath may not be able to determine which empty cells to convert to text boxes. In Excel, you can provide InfoPath with hints by turning on the borders for cells that you want to convert to text boxes. This provides the same guidance to InfoPath that underlines, brackets, and colons do in a Word document.

After specifying the file to import and selecting your options, click the **Finish** button to begin the conversion. When the conversion finishes, the wizard displays one last page, informing you whether the conversion has completed successfully or not.

■ **Note** You cannot have the template open in Excel while you convert it to an InfoPath form.

A conversion can complete successfully but with issues. When this happens, review these issues using the **Design Checker** and correct them in InfoPath. Figure 9-43 shows the results of converting the **Donation Receipt** form.

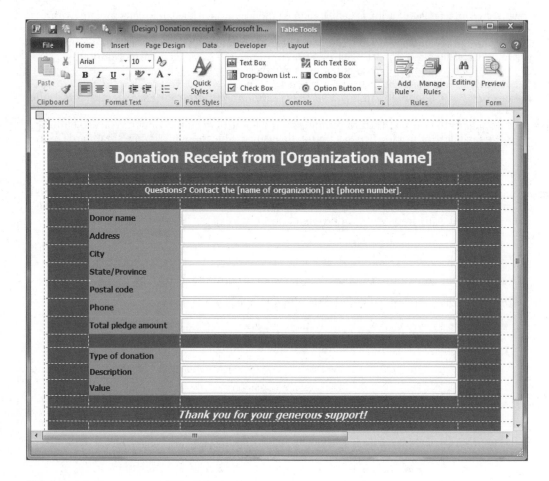

Figure 9-43. *Raw converted Excel form*

You can see in Figure 9-43 that during the conversion process, several unexpected things occurred that you might want to modify. First, the conversion process changed the background colors of the form's cells. Second, the form appears to include a few additional columns and rows. With a little work, you can select the excess table rows and columns and delete them. Then, to change the background color of cells to match the original, begin by selecting cell ranges that you want to change. Then right-click the selected cells and click **Borders and Shading** in the drop-down menu. In the dialog box that appears, you may have to click the **Shading** tab to pick the color used to shade the cells. From this page, you can either select one of the existing colors or click the **More Colors** option at the bottom of the color list. This selection opens the **Color Picker** dialog box. Here you can select a color from a larger list of defined colors, or you can custom blend a color using the area on the right to mix the color you want. When you find a color you like, be sure to click the button **Add to Custom Colors** so you can reuse the same color for other cell areas that you may still need to select. With these changes, the InfoPath form now looks like the one shown in Figure 9-44, which closely resembles the original Excel workbook form.

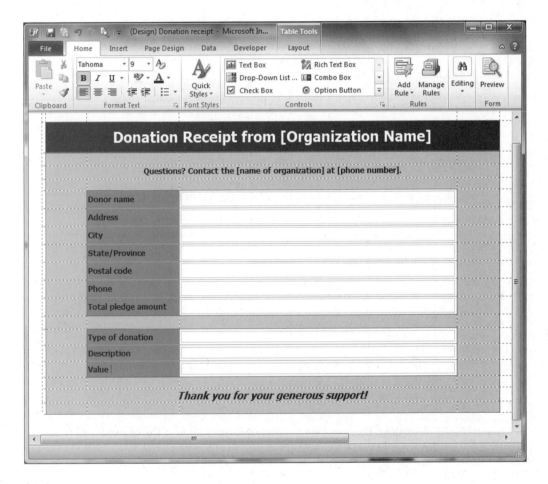

Figure 9-44. After cleaning up the InfoPath form

■ **Note** InfoPath converts all blank cells to text boxes. However, you can change the control type by right-clicking the control and selecting a different control type from the secondary slide-out menu that appears when you position your mouse over **Change to**.

Defining InfoPath Views

InfoPath allows you to define multiple views in the same form against different subsets of the data. Views can serve multiple purposes, including the following:

- You have a very large form and decide to divide it into smaller pages to make it more manageable to those entering data.

- You have a workflow attached to the form and the approver needs read-only access to most of fields, with perhaps the ability to update a comment field and to accept or reject the form.

- You have different people who work on different sections of the form, and they only need to see the part of the form for which they are responsible.

- You have different people who have access to the form, but who do not need to see all the data in the form. Perhaps they do not have the rights to see all the data.

- You want to define a separate print view for a form perhaps to change the controls used to represent the data, thus making the output easier to read and use. You can hide this view from the users entering data, but who may want to use it automatically when they attempt to print the form.

You may have additional reasons for wanting multiple views. However, no matter what the reason, the technique for building those views begins the same way. I suggest you first build the master form that collects all the possible data that you might want to collect. Once you have a master form, which is a view in itself, you can create additional views that display subsets of that master form or even allow users to enter or edit subsets of data.

Before creating another view of an existing form, let's look at the view properties of a form. You can find the view properties of your primary data collection form in all additional views you create.

Viewing Properties

To view the properties of a form, open the Request for Absence form created at the beginning of this chapter. With this form open, click the **Page Design** ribbon option and select **Properties** from the Views group. You should see a dialog box similar to the one in Figure 9-45. This dialog box consists of a set of four tabbed pages that allow you to configure several visual and print features.

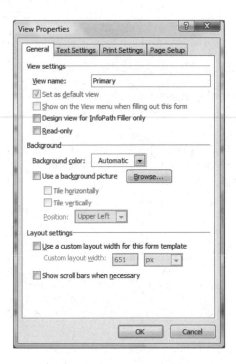

Figure 9-45. The General tab of the View Properties dialog box

The **General** tab includes basic settings for the view beginning with the **View name**. By default, InfoPath names the views **View_1**, **View_2**, and so on. However, these default names do not really describe the purpose of the page. Even if you plan to have only a single view or maybe a view for editing data and a view for printing it, providing a more descriptive name can help you later remember why you created multiple views for the same data source.

Note that you can create a view that allows all InfoPath features, including features not generally available when displaying a form in a web browser, by selecting the option **Design view for InfoPath Filler only**. Using this capability on one of your views means that you can create one view for web browsers and a separate view for users who work with the form directly from the InfoPath Filler installed on their desktops.

As you add more views, you can select which view to use as the default view, as well as whether you want to display a menu of available views to the user during data entry. Finally, the **View settings** section allows you to define a view that provides read-only access to the data.

In the **Background** section, you can define a background color for the form or even paint the background with an image. When using an image for the background, you may need to tile the background. A common tiling technique defines a horizontal ribbon image that, when tiled, vertically gives the illusion of a larger background image that repeats to create a page of any length.

In the **Layout settings** section, you can define the page width based on pixels, inches, centimeters, or point. You probably want to use this option when creating a view for printing data and therefore choose inches or centimeters. You can also choose to use scrollbars when necessary within the form.

The **Text Settings** page in the **View Properties** dialog box lets you change the font and font characteristics for any controls listed in the list box on the left. When you change the font settings through this dialog box, you update the font in every instance of the selected control throughout your form for the current view. For controls that appear frequently throughout your form, this method of changing the font characteristics saves time over changing them for each control instance.

The **Print Settings** page allows you to set the print characteristics of the view. The first option on this page lets you select another view to use instead of the current default view when the user attempts to print. You can also change the print orientation, include headers and footers, define the number of copies, and select to print all or a range of pages. When you're defining headers and footers, InfoPath includes autotext to display the date and/or time you print the form. You can also include page numbering for longer views.

The **Page Setup** page lets you preset the printer that the current view uses as well as the paper and margins. Thanks to this page, users do not have to worry about how to select a network printer or which paper tray to use, or how large to make the margins. You can preset all these options for them so they only need to print the view and then go to the printer to retrieve it.

Generating Your Second View

Now that you know the basic properties of views, let's create a second view for the Request for Absence form that shows only the names of the people who will be absent, the dates they have requested, and the total number of hours.

To create a new view, open the **Page Design** ribbon and click **New** from the **Views** group. Figure 9-46 shows the dialog that InfoPath begins with to ask for the name of the new view. I will call this second view **Management Absence Summary**. After supplying a name, click the **OK** button to begin defining the view.

Figure 9-46. The Views task panel lets you add a new view with this dialog.

The following list steps through the creation of this second view:

1. Change the title text to **Management Absence Summary**.

2. From the **Insert** ribbon, select the **Custom table** option from the **Tables** drop-down and create a table with six columns and two rows.

3. Switch to the **Data** ribbon and click the Show Fields option in the Form Data group to display the fields associated with this form.

4. Drag the **Employee_ID** field to the first cell in the second row.

5. Drag the **EmployeeName** field to the second cell in the second row.

6. Drag the **AbsentFrom** field to the third cell in the second row.

7. Drag the **AbsentTo** field to the fourth cell in the second row.

8. Drag the **HoursRequested** field to the fifth cell in the second row.

9. Drag the **AbsenceType** field to the sixth cell in the second row. With all fields now added to the second row, you might want to resize some of the cells. Also, notice that by dragging the fields from the **Data Source** panel into the cell, you automatically get the name of the field, not just the field's control. You can edit these labels if necessary. At the very least, you will need to select them and drag them into the first row.

10. Right-click each of the date cells and select **Change Control** from the drop-down menu. In the submenu, select **Text Box**. This changes the display type of these two fields.

11. Right-click each of the cells in the second row and select **Text Box Properties** from the drop-down menu. In the pop-up dialog box, click the **Display** tab and check the option **Read-only**.

12. Open the **Controls** panel and add a text box control to the **Absence Type** cell after the other controls. By default, InfoPath names this control **Field1**. Change the name of this field to **AbsenceDescription** by using the text box properties.

13. Select the **AbsenceType** text box and then open the **Manage Rules** drop-down menu from the **Rules** group of the **Table Tools Layout** ribbon.

14. Click the **New** button to begin a new rule.

15. Define the condition: `AbsenceType is greater than 0`. Also, click the check box for **Hide this control**. You want to use this conditional format to hide the **AbsenceType** control when the form displays. You do not want to see the integer value that this field holds. Rather, you want to see text that describes the absence type. However, you cannot do this directly in this field. However, you can use the **AbsenceType** field to create a set of rules that place appropriate user-friendly text in the text box named **AbsenceDescription**.

16. Select **New** from the **Rules** panel again and select an **Action** type rule.

17. Next, define the condition: **Absence Type is equal to 1**.

18. Click the **Add Action** button. In the **Action** dialog box, select the action **Set a field's value**. For the **Field**, click the button to the right of the text box, select **AbsenceDescription**. In the **Value** text box, enter the text `Annual Leave`, since this text represents the type of leave associated with the type value of **1**.

19. Click **OK** twice to save your first rule.

20. Repeat the last four steps to add rules for the other five option buttons defined as follows:

    - 2: Personal Leave
    - 3: Sick Leave
    - 4: Jury Duty
    - 5: Military Duty
    - 6: Time Without Pay

21. Close the **Rules** dialog box when you have completed defining all six rules.

Now let's test the new view. Switch to the **Home** ribbon and click **Preview** from the **Form** group. In preview mode, InfoPath shows a simulation of the form as it would appear in a browser. Make sure the current view has been set to the initial view (View 1 in this example unless you renamed it). Enter data for the form as if you were filling out the complete form. Rather than saving the data, switch to the **Management Absence Summary** view of the data using the drop-down in the **Page Views** group. You should see a form that looks something like Figure 9-47.

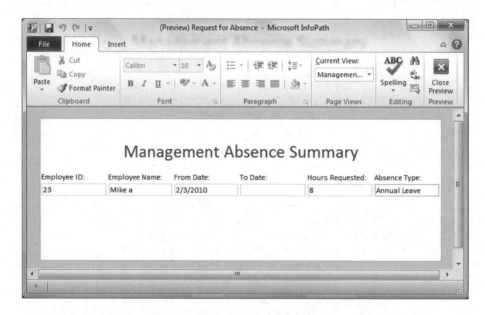

Figure 9-47. The management summary view of absences

Notice that only one text box appears in the **Absence Type** column. The text box **AbsenceDescription** appears with the text assigned to it by the rule created in the **AbsenceType** text box control, which we hid.

I hope that this simple example gives you some ideas of how you can create different views from the same form.

Building Data Connections for Forms

In the first part of this chapter, you saw how to create a basic form that generates XML data files when you submit the form's data. However, you can also create an InfoPath form that uses SQL or Access tables as both the source and the destination for data from a form. To do that, you need to create a data connection from the form to the database. Actually, if you plan to use the form with InfoPath Filler, you need two connections, one to select data from the database to build the form, and a second to update the database. This section explores the steps needed to create a data connection to a SQL Server database.

To begin, select the option **Design a Form Template** from the **Getting Started** menu when you open InfoPath. This opens the dialog box shown in Figure 9-48.

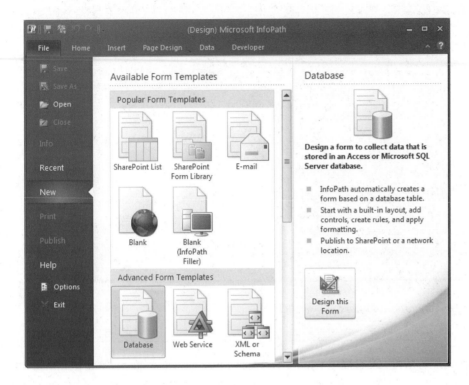

Figure 9-48. Begin a form template with a SQL Server data connection.

In this dialog box, select the **Database** form template. By default, InfoPath creates a web-compatible form, which means that it can read data from the database, but it cannot submit data back to it. You must change the form view properties to design the view for InfoPath Filler if you want to both display data and save changes to the data.

When you click **Design this form**, the **Data Connection Wizard** opens. At this point, your only option appears at the top of the form, allowing you to select the SQL Server or Access database you want to use as your form's data source. Click the **Select Database** button to continue.

InfoPath then opens the **Select Data Source** dialog box, shown in Figure 9-49. This dialog box shows existing connections, if any, that have an extension of `.odc`. If you do not know the details behind these existing connections, you probably need to create a new connection by double-clicking either **+NewSQLServerConnection.odc** or **+Connect to New Data Source.odc**.

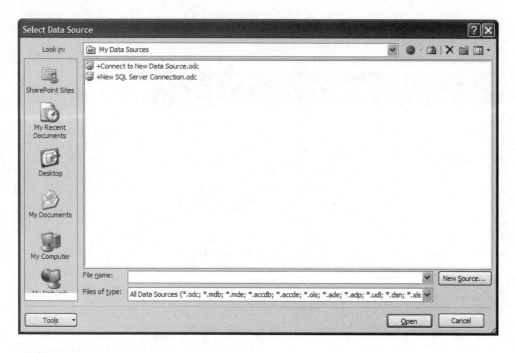

Figure 9-49. The list of available data sources

■ **Note** If you want to connect to an Access database, you should double-click the option **+Connect to New Data Source.odc**. This action opens a dialog box that lets you select from a variety of data sources you have already defined on your machine. While it may be tempting to select a data source other than SQL Server or Access just because you may see it on this list, these other sources will not work with InfoPath at this time.

For this example, you will use the PUBS database running on SQL Server 2005 and will therefore select the option **+New SQL Server Connection.odc**. This action opens another dialog box, titled **Welcome to the Data Connection Wizard**, as shown in Figure 9-50.

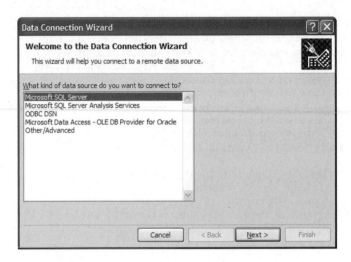

Figure 9-50. Choose the type of data source you want to create.

You need to know the name of the SQL Server you want to connect to before you continue. If you are not sure, check with your database administrator. If you are running SQL Server on your development machine, you could reference the server with the generic name of localhost. However, if you then publish your form on a network share rather than your local machine, the form will not be able to resolve the reference to localhost. It is always better to name the specific server you want to use, as shown in Figure 9-51.

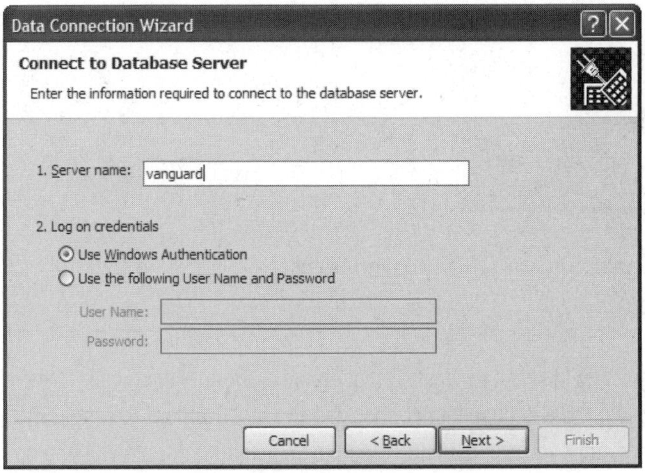

Figure 9-51. Define a database server connection.

If you use a central Domain Controller to log in to your machine and validate users on your corporate network, or even if you are running everything on a high-powered desktop workstation, you can continue to use Windows Authentication as your logon credentials. You can also use a specific SQL Server user name and password if your SQL Server security has been set to mixed mode. However, when you use SQL credentials, the operating system passes your logon information over the network using clear text, making it much less secure than Windows Authentication, which does not. If you do use a SQL Server user name and password, at least use a strong password. *Strong passwords* incorporate at least three of the following types of characters: uppercase letters, lowercase letters, numbers, and symbols. Passwords should have at least 8 characters; Microsoft recommends 14 characters or more. Most importantly, do not simply use words, no matter how long, that could be "discovered" using a dictionary attack.

After you've specified a database server, the **Data Connection Wizard** goes to the server and retrieves the names of all the databases defined on that server. It then populates a drop-down list on the next screen of the wizard with these database names. You must select which database you want to use in this connection. When you select the database you want, the wizard populates the list in the bottom half of this screen with the names of the tables in the database. Figure 9-52 shows the wizard defining a connection to the table **Authors** in the database **PUBS**.

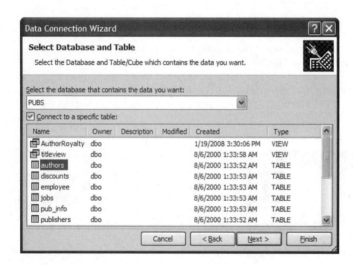

Figure 9-52. The dialog box for selecting the database and table you want to use.

■ **Note** When working with InfoPath, you must eventually select at least a single table to work with on your form. However, you can create a generic connection to just the database by not checking the box **Connect to a specific table**. Then, each time you select the connection, before you can continue creating your form, InfoPath will pop up a dialog box asking you to select a table.

When you click **Next**, the wizard displays the dialog shown in Figure 9-53, asking you to provide a name for the data connection. By default, the wizard combines the name of the server, the database, and the selected table to define the connection name. While I do not recommend changing this default since it is very logical, you may want to provide a description and a user friendly name, which then appear in your **Data Sources** list shown back in Figure 9-49.

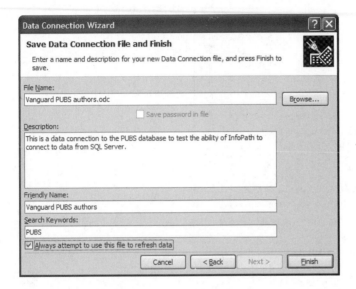

Figure 9-53. *The dialog box for saving the data connection file*

Next, the wizard can display the available fields in the selected table if you click the check box as shown in Figure 9-54. By default, InfoPath selects all the fields in the table. However, you should deselect any fields that you do not need to use, to keep your queries to the database as small as possible. In this same dialog, you can add another table, remove a table, or modify a table.

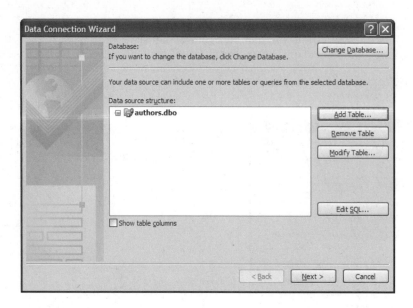

Figure 9-54. The Data Connection Wizard showing one table selected

If you want to include other tables in the form, click the **Add Table** button in Figure 9-54. In this case, to connect the **Authors** table with the **Titles** table, we need to use the joining table, **TitleAuthor**, as shown in Figure 9-55.

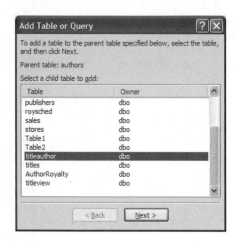

Figure 9-55. Don't forget to include the linking tables between many-to-many relationships.

After you select the table and click **Next**, InfoPath will check whether the data has referential integrity definitions. If so, it will make a recommendation for which field to use to link the two tables, as shown in Figure 9-56. If this is not the correct relationship, you can click the **Remove Relationship** button and click the **Add Relationship** to build your own link between the two tables.

Figure 9-56. Select the existing relationship between the tables or define your own.

You can continue to add more tables to your form view. Figure 9-57 shows the three tables needed to link authors with their titles.

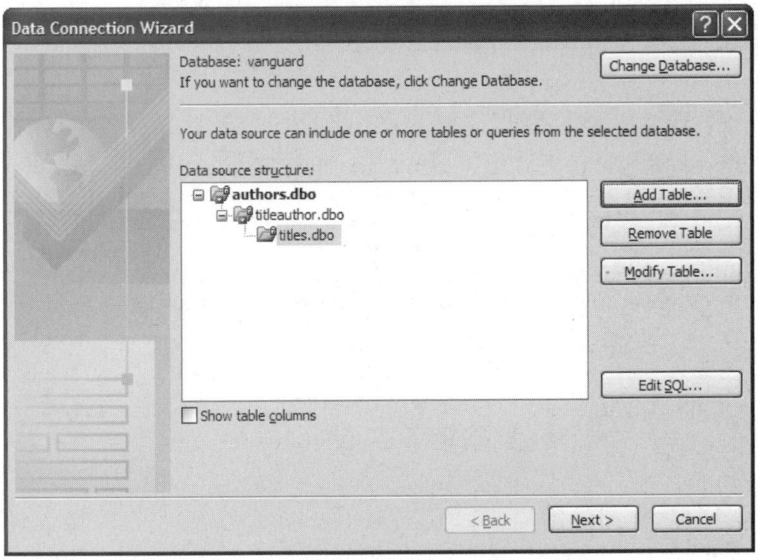

Figure 9-57. An example with three linked tables

After you finish building the view needed for the form and click the **Next** button, the wizard prompts you to save the data connection file. You can accept the default file name or provide your own. In either case, you should include your own description as well as a friendly name for the connection. You can also supply keywords that can help you search for the connection you want. However, most people do not have enough connections to make this a required step. More importantly, choose a name for the file that clearly defines what data it accesses. Figure 9-58 shows the file name selected for this example's connection.

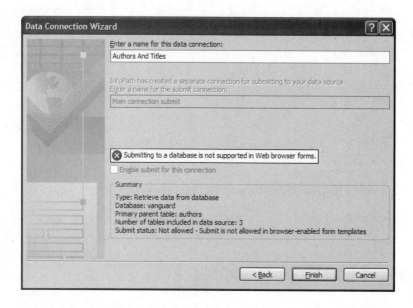

Figure 9-58. Set the data connection name.

When you click **Finish**, InfoPath returns you to the first screen of the **Data Connection Wizard**. However, now the lower portion of the screen displays the data source structure. If you see only the table name, make sure to select the check box **Show table columns**. You should see the fields in the table, each with a check box before it. Check the box of each field you want to use in your form. If you do not need the field, do not check it. Including only the fields you need in your form helps the query execute faster when retrieving data. Figure 9-59 shows an example of selecting only a few of the available fields from the **Authors** table.

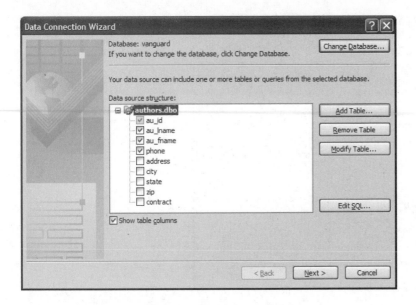

Figure 9-59. *Select fields to retrieve from the table.*

Notice that the field **au_id** has a selected check box before it, but that InfoPath dims the check box so that you cannot select or deselect it. This occurs because you must include primary key fields when you want to either select specific records to display or update data. Without the primary key, you cannot submit any changes you make to the fields of a displayed record, because SQL Server would not know which record to update.

When you click **Next**, the wizard displays one final screen. This screen lets you enter a name for the primary data connection used to select data from the database for the form. If you defined a non-web-based form, you can also supply a name for the submit connection. Figure 9-60 shows this dialog box.

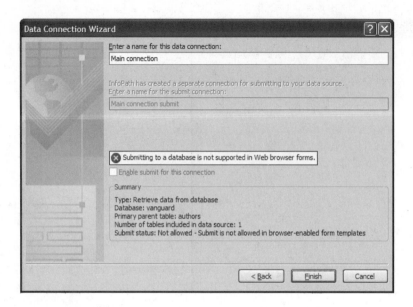

Figure 9-60. Name the retrieve and submit data connections.

At this point, you have finished defining your connection for the current form. However, you can reuse the connection for additional forms. In that case, simply select the connection from the list shown earlier in Figure 9-49. If the connection points to the database in general (no table selected), you first need to select a table. Then the rest of the process continues from the point at which you select the fields you want to use and enter the name of one or more data connections. The next section continues the story of creating your SQL-based form at the point just after you have finished using the **Data Connection Wizard**.

Connecting InfoPath Forms to Data

Once you've made it through the definition of the data connection, InfoPath generates a default form for working with the data. This default form, shown in Figure 9-61, has three sections.

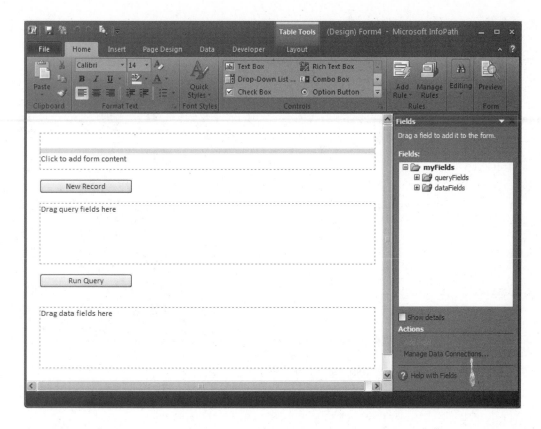

Figure 9-61. *Start by picking a query field(s) for the form's data retrieval.*

The top section uses the **Title and Table** layout control you saw earlier. Here you can enter a title for the form. You can also include content for the form here. However, before doing that, let's look at what you can do with the other two sections.

The second section is called the *query section* because here you can drag fields that you want to use to query the database. Your first thought might be to use the primary key for the main table as the query field. In this case, you probably want to drag the primary key for the **Authors** table, **au_id**, from the list of query fields in the **Fields** panel to the query section of the form. While using the primary keys to query the data is not a bad choice, you can actually use any field to query the database. Using fields that correspond to indexes in the database helps the performance of the query.

In the third section, you place data fields. Again, InfoPath provides an easy way to do this. Simply expand the `Fields` in the **Fields** panel on the right. If you want to include all the fields, simply drag the table `Authors` to the third section, as shown in Figure 9-62. However, if you only want a subset of the available fields, open `d:Authors` to access the individual fields, dragging each one individually over to the third section of the form.

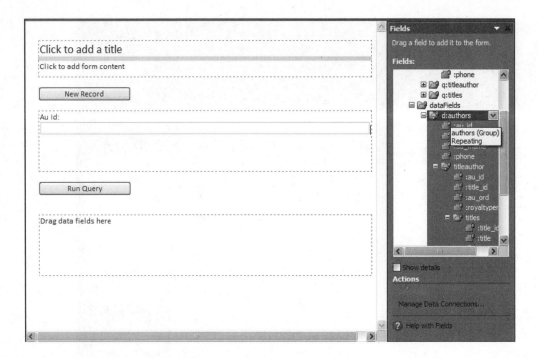

Figure 9-62. Pick data fields to display in the form.

Notice that after you drag the entire table to the third section, InfoPath automatically places the data in a repeating section because there could be more than one row displayed.

On the other hand, there are times when you might want to use the repeating section with controls: if you want to work on a single record at a time, for example, if you have a large number of fields, or if any of the fields consist of large text areas. Initially, InfoPath adds all the controls vertically down the form. If you want to provide additional structure to this section, perhaps by adding a table within the section to position the individual controls, you must do that manually.

No matter how you lay out the fields, you can control many of the properties of the controls as you saw earlier; specifically, you can convert the control types of some fields or add conditional formatting, rules, and data validation. Figure 9-63 shows the resulting form template designed to display a list of employees with their vacation and sick leave balances.

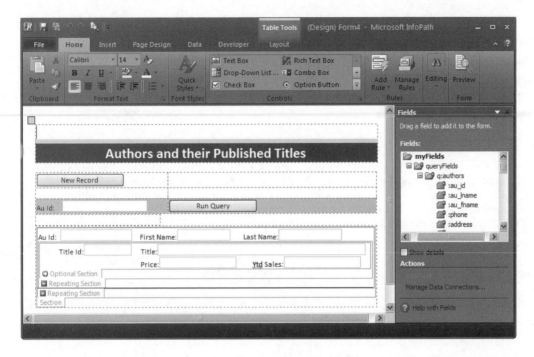

Figure 9-63. *Use a table with invisible borders to rearrange the form controls into a final form.*

To see how this template works, click the **Preview** button in the toolbar. This opens a new window that displays the form as it would appear when someone opens it. In Figure 9-64, you can see the result of entering a single **Author ID** value. When you click the **Run Query** button, the select query built into the **Data Connection Wizard** uses the fields defined in the query section of the report to return a filtered set of data. Since the **Author ID** serves as the primary key to the table, supplying a valid key value returns a single record.

Authors and their Published Titles

New Record

Au Id: 213-46-8915   Run Query

Au Id: 213-46-8915   First Name: Marjorie   Last Name: Green
    Title Id: BU1032   Title: The Busy Executive's Database Guide
                         Price: $19.99   Ytd Sales: $4,095
    Title Id: BU2075   Title: You Can Combat Computer Stress!
                         Price: $2.99   Ytd Sales: $18,722

Figure 9-64. *Query the form data using a single field, the table's primary key, Au Id.*

■ **Caution** You may see a popup dialog after clicking **Run Query** in Figure 9-62 if you are testing your form before publishing, as your local copy of the form tries to access data on a network SQL Server installation. Assuming you trust both your form and the SQL Server, you can merely click **Yes** to close this dialog and execute the query. You should not see this dialog if you click the **Run Query** button after publishing the form as long as the connection is trusted through SharePoint.

Perhaps a more interesting result appears when you click the **Run Query** button without entering any value for the **Author ID**. In this case, the query performs no filtering on the data retrieved, thus returning the entire table as shown in Figure 9-65. I would not recommend doing this on a large table with millions of records. In fact, InfoPath warns that returning all the records for a table can take some time. On the other hand, it can be quite useful for a small set of data.

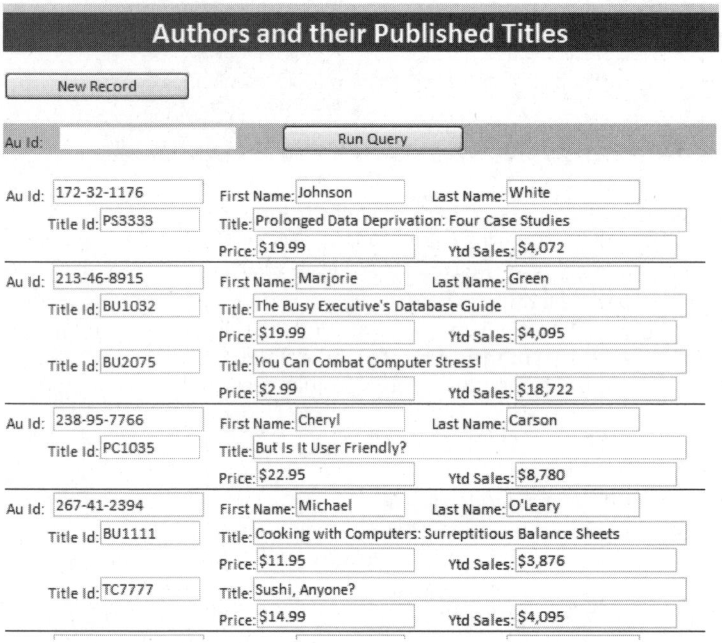

Figure 9-65. Retrieve the entire table when no query field value is specified.

However, even if you have millions of records, you could add query fields to limit records to a reasonable number. In the case of your employee file, you might want to see employees only from a specific department.

■ **Tip** As you can see by the examples provided, the query values must exactly match values in the table. You can get around this limitation by creating a view in the database that combines the data you want, including the addition of calculated fields. For example, if you want to list employees with more than 100 hours of combined vacation and sick time, you could create a Boolean field in the view that resolves to **True** if the sum of vacation and sick hours exceeds 100. Then, in your InfoPath form, you can include this field in the query section and check for a value of **True**.

Creating and Reusing Form Sections with Template Parts

Most programmers practice code reusability. Form designers can also benefit from reusing common groups of controls, especially when those controls require extensive formatting. InfoPath provides a way to build groups of controls that you can later reuse in other templates. In this example, you will build a template for a mailing address so you can use it in a variety of forms, including the order shipment page of an order manifest. In fact, this page uses the template part twice, once for the mail-to address and once for the bill-to address.

You start the process of building a template part similar to that of building a template form. Open the **New** page of the **Backstage** when you start InfoPath. From the **Template Parts** section, select the **Blank** template. Then click the **Design this Form** button as shown in Figure 9-66.

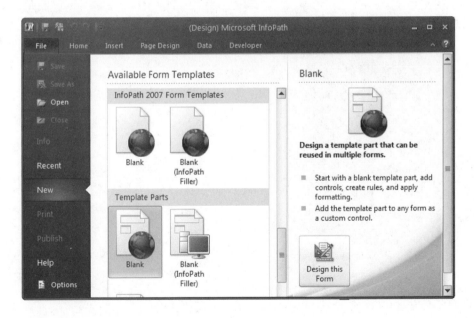

Figure 9-66. *Design a template part.*

■ **Note** When designing a template part, you must begin with a blank template or an existing XML schema. However, you can change the binding for the template part controls after you add it to another form to bind the controls to other data sources.

When InfoPath opens the blank template design area, you should notice that you have all the design tools to create a form layout, add controls to that layout, define data sources, and run your design through the **Design Checker**. You do not have the ability to create multiple views for the template part. However, in any form that you add the template part, you can create alternative views. You also do not have the options associated with publishing the form, because you cannot publish a template part, since it is not meant to represent an entire form by itself.

Figure 9-67 shows the completely designed template part. (You can also find this web part template in the free book code download at www.apress.com with the name `TemplateGroup_MailToAddress.xtp`.) It contains several required fields and one optional field. While most of these fields consist of simple text boxes with a little added formatting, the **State** field uses a drop-down listbox that includes the names of all the states. You can add information for a drop-down manually (as was done for this example), read it from the form's data source, or use an external data source. You can even change the data source after you drop the template part onto a form that you later design. Therefore, you might create a minimal list box, one with only a few entries for testing purposes, if you know that the data source for the form you plan to build later can retrieve values for the list either from the data source itself or from another external data source.

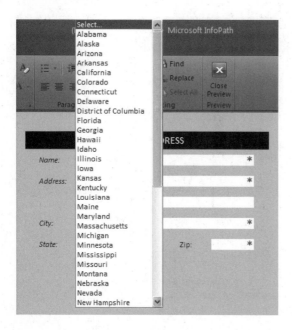

Figure 9-67. The completed template part showing a drop-down state list

When you have finished the template part, test it using the preview mode. Then save the completed part to a directory of your choice.

■ **Tip** If you plan to design a large number of forms, keeping your reusable template parts in a separate directory on your design machine (or a network share if you are only one of several form designers), helps organize your template parts.

After you have saved it, open the **Controls** panel from the **Controls** group of the **Home** ribbon and click the hyperlink beneath the list: **Add or Remove Custom Controls**. This action opens the dialog box shown in Figure 9-68.

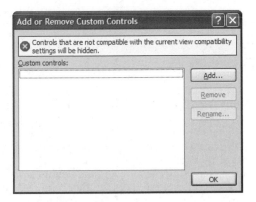

Figure 9-68. The Custom Controls list page

Click the **Add** button to add the control you just created.

■ **Note** You must save the template part first. This dialog box does not assume that you want to add the currently open template part.

From the resulting menu, you can add either a template part or an ActiveX control. In this case, you want to select the **Template Part** option and click **Next**.

The dialog box next asks for the file location of the template part. Enter the full directory path where you saved the completed part manually, or use the **Browse** button to locate and select the file. When you click the **Finish** button, the final page of the dialog box shows the name assigned to the custom control and the version. Clicking the **Close** button on this page closes the dialog box and returns you to the **Add or Remove Custom Controls** page shown in Figure 9-69, where you can see that you have added your custom template part successfully.

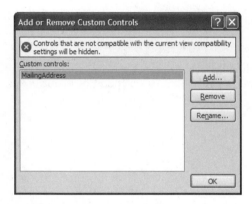

Figure 9-69. *The Add or Remove Custom Controls dialog box showing the new template part*

The next time you open InfoPath to design a new form, or even to modify the design of an existing one, you will see in the **Custom** section of the **Controls** panel the new template part you created and saved. Figure 9-70 shows the **Addresses** page of the **Order Shipping Information** form. On this page, you need to have two possible addresses. The first is the customer's mailing address, and the second is the customer's billing address. Many businesses provide centralized ordering services for their remote locations. Therefore, while you might ship an order to one address, you may need to send the bill for the order to an entirely different address.

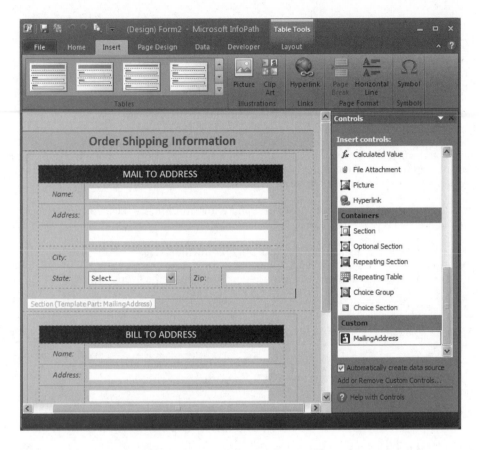

Figure 9-70. Completed Addresses page for the Order Shipping Information form

---

■ **Note** You can also view all of the controls available from the Controls group of the Home ribbon by clicking the More button in the bottom-right corner of the Controls list box.

In this case, you added the same custom template part twice to the same form. However, you can also add this same control to other forms. In each case, you can customize the formatting of the fields, the label data, the binding information for the controls, and even the data source for the drop-down list box. Template parts can be as simple as this one or significantly more complex. The point is that they provide reusability within form design, which also results in uniformity in the way similar information appears and works.

Summary

In this chapter, you explored some of the basic features of InfoPath. You started by seeing how you can create new forms for any of the SharePoint lists giving them their own special "flavor"—or perhaps a better word is branding.

You then saw how to use the same basic techniques to build an InfoPath form from a blank template. You can also now build forms that use external data sources to display data from SQL Server or Access. You even learned how to create reusable form template parts that can save you time in the future for those groups of fields that seem to appear in every form you create. While we did not publish the forms to SharePoint yet, you will learn how to do that in the next chapter. However, by changing the view properties of any of the forms you created here, you can create forms that can include additional features. as long as you save them on a network drive and access them using the InfoPath Filler application.

InfoPath provides more features than I could cover in such a short amount of space. Fortunately, books like *Pro InfoPath 2007*, by Philo Janus (Apress, 2007) can help you further explore the details of InfoPath.

The next chapter dives deeper into using InfoPath with SharePoint, allowing you to use lists to both populate your drop-down form lists and submit data. You will also look more closely at form libraries within SharePoint to store your forms and then use Forms Services to display the forms within a browser.

■ ■ ■

CHAPTER 10

Publishing InfoPath Forms in SharePoint Libraries

In the last chapter, you saw how easily you can build InfoPath forms. When building those forms, the chapter focused primarily on using forms created and saved in a single location, even if that location was on your local computer or in a regular SharePoint document library. However, up until this point, unless you had a copy of InfoPath 2010 installed on your machine, you could not open and use that form. Furthermore, you really don't want to send a copy of the form to everyone who needs it because, for example, making updates to the form would become difficult if everyone at your company had their own copy of the form. Rather, you should publish the form to a common location such as a network file share so that other people in your organization can access it.

However, even if these users have access to the network file share, perhaps not everyone that needs to enter data into that form has a copy of InfoPath installed on their computers. To be truly available to everyone, you need to create forms that do not require the users to have InfoPath on their machines. SharePoint together with Forms Services provides such a solution. You can store InfoPath forms in SharePoint libraries and then open them via InfoPath Forms Services. However, there is a cost to provide this ability to display forms using your web browser: you must limit your design options slightly by avoiding the use of some of InfoPath's features that Forms Services and browsers in general do not support.

In this chapter, we will look further at publishing forms, both to network file shares and form libraries, using SharePoint to allow more users to access them.

Publishing InfoPath Forms to a Network File Share

The easiest way to publish your InfoPath forms, especially if you are a small company and everyone has InfoPath on their desktop, is to publish them to a simple network file share. A *network file share* is any directory on your network that people in your organization can access from their local computers.

Anyone with InfoPath on their local computer can open the published forms and enter data using them. They can save a copy of their data back to the same directory or to any other directory. Let's see how this works by using one of the forms created in the last chapter, the **Request for Absence Report**.

If you previously saved your InfoPath form to a network file share that others could access while you were designing it, you may not need to do much of anything. In fact, all anyone else would need to do is to navigate to the network share where you saved the InfoPath form (the one with the .xsn extension) and double-click on its name to open it. Figure 10-1 shows the **Request for Absence** form stored on a mapped drive.

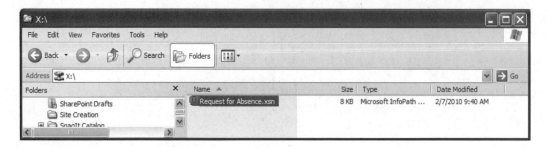

Figure 10-1. Save your InfoPath form to a mapped network drive.

As long as the users have InfoPath Filler 2010, the second of the two InfoPath programs in Microsoft Office 2010, installed on their local machine, it will open the .xsn file ready for them to start filling in the form. The first time they open an InfoPath form, they may see a dialog asking if they want to set Microsoft Office as the default program for opening and editing .xml files. Unless they are using another program to edit .xml files, they should click the **OK** button in this dialog.

You could even start directly from InfoPath Filler 2010 by going to the **Open** page in the **File** menu (Backstage area), as shown in Figure 10-2. This page shows previously opened forms. However, it also has a button, **Find a Form**, that you can use to display the **Open** dialog. From this dialog, you can navigate to the directory or file share that has the file you want, select it, and open it.

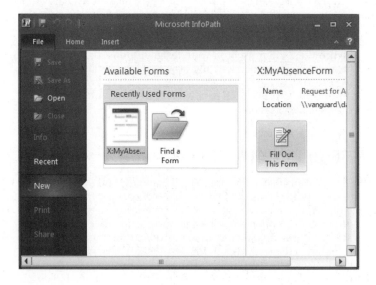

Figure 10-2. InfoPath can open a form stored on a shared network drive.

However, what if you did not store the form on a network drive while designing it? One way to get it to a network drive would be to copy the file from your local drive to the network drive the next time you connect to the network. At that point, other users could access the form as I just described as long as they had InfoPath Filler 2010 installed on their local computer.

There is one more way you can publish your form to the network drive. You could open the form using InfoPath Designer 2010. Then from the backstage area, select the **Publish** page. On this page, find the area titled **Publish a form to a network location or file share,** shown in Figure 10-3, and click the button **Network Location**.

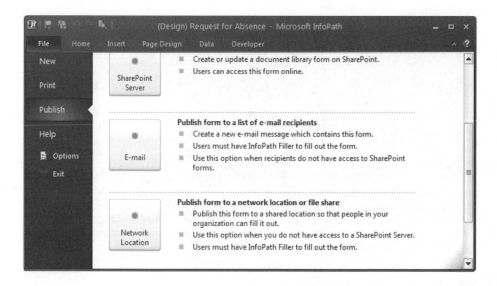

Figure 10-3. Use InfoPath to publish a form to a network location.

The publishing wizard opens a dialog that begins by prompting for the path and file name where you want to store the form. Note that in Figure 10-4, I have entered the path using a mapped drive letter.

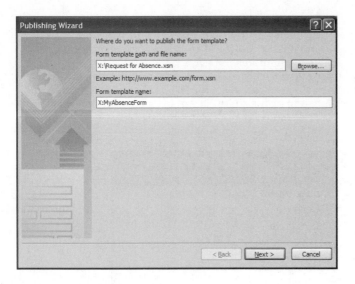

Figure 10-4. Publishing Wizard prompts for the form path and file name.

Some companies define standard mapped drives for employees to use when accessing special network shares such as a location where they can find the company's on-line forms. However, unless everyone who needs to access this form directory maps the URL to the directory with the same drive letter, they could have problems accessing the file. Therefore, when you click **Next** in the **Publishing Wizard**, you can add an alternate path, as shown in Figure 10-5.

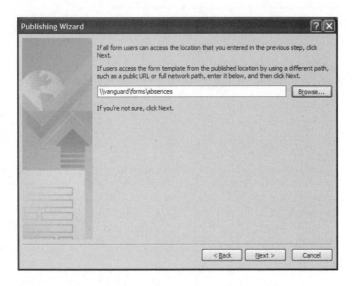

Figure 10-5. Provide an alternate path to let others easily access the form.

When you click **Next** on this page, the Publishing Wizard displays a summary page with the information used to define where you want to publish the form. From this page, you can still return to the previous screens to correct any of the paths or file names entered. On the other hand, if everything is correct, you can click the **Publish** button at the bottom of the form to complete the publishing of the form to the network share.

Notice the reference to **Security Level** on this page. By default, InfoPath sets the security level for a form to **Domain** if you are connected to a network when you create the form. Domain security allows forms to access content stored in the form itself, as well as the following:

- Data in the same domain as the form

- Data in domains included in the trusted sites zone in Internet Explorer

- Content in the local computer and local intranet zone of Internet Explorer

InfoPath defaults to a **Restricted** security level when you create a form while not connected to a network. Restricted security limits the form to accessing content only from within the form itself. This means the form cannot use any of the following features:

- Custom dialog boxes

- Custom task panes

- Data connections

- Human workflow services

- Linked pictures

- Microsoft ActiveX controls

- Managed code and script

- Print view for Microsoft Office Word 2003

- Roles based on Active Directory services

- Rules associated with opening forms

Finally, the **Full Trust** security level allows a form to access data in itself, in the same domain as the form, and in other domains where it has access. It also provides access to files and settings on the computer. You can grant Full Trust to a form if you digitally sign a form with a trusted root certificate. Your system administrator can help generate certificates that allow you to install and use Full Trust forms.

To open the form after publishing it, navigate to the network share and double-click on the .xsn file as mentioned earlier or open the form template directly from InfoPath Filler. After filling in the form, you might ask, "How do I save my data?"

Good question. To save your form data, open the **File** menu and select **Save As** to display the **Save** dialog shown in Figure 10-6. In this dialog, you can see that I am still pointing to the network share using my mapped drive X:. You do not have to store the data from the form in the same directory as the form definition itself. In fact, in many cases you will want to use a different directory so you can define more limited rights to the form's source directory than to the data directory where users need read-write capabilities. However, for the purposes of this example, I will use the same directory. Notice also in Figure 10-6 that the form's source file does not appear. That is because the **Save** dialog filters the directory contents on the extension .xml, and the form source has an extension of .xsn. However, you can view the full directory listing by showing all files to see that both files are still there.

Figure 10-6. Save a data file from a form to the shared network drive.

One other concern about saving your form data this way is that the user is responsible for defining the file name. In this example, I created a file name that combined the user's name, the start date of the absence request, and the number of hours requested. It would be great if everyone used this format every time they saved their data so that you can easily sort the file names to see when people were out of the office and for how long. However, that expectation is not realistic. We will return to this question in a moment, but first, let's look a little more at the file just saved from InfoPath Filler.

If you use Windows explorer to view the files in the mapped drive, as shown in Figure 10-7, you will see that you do indeed have two files stored there. The .xsn file is the form definition file that you published to this location. The second file with the .xml extension is the data file you just saved. Did you notice the difference in the file sizes?

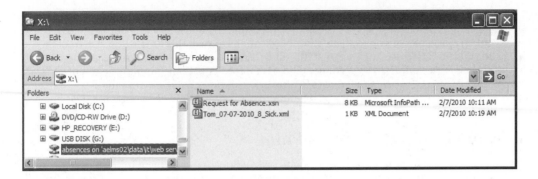

Figure 10-7. Windows Explorer shows both the form source and form data file.

The data file created by InfoPath Filler is substantially smaller than the form definition file. The reason for this difference is that when InfoPath Filler saves the data from the form, it saves only the data, not the form itself. However, it does retain a reference to the path and file name of the form used to create the data in the beginning of the file. If we were to open the .xml file with Notepad (or your favorite XML editor), you would see the data stored by InfoPath Filler. Figure 10-8 shows the opened .xml file.

```
Tom_07-07-2010_8_Sick.xml - Notepad
File  Edit  Format  View  Help
<?xml version="1.0" encoding="UTF-8"?>
<?mso-infoPathSolution solutionVersion="1.0.0.10"
productVersion="14.0.0" PIVersion="1.0.0.0"
href="file:///\\vanguard\absences\Request%20for%20Absence.xsn"
name="urn:schemas-microsoft-com:office:infopath:X-MyAbsenceForm:-myXSD-2010-01-31T15
-57-22" ?>
<?mso-application progid="InfoPath.Document" versionProgid="InfoPath.Document.3"?>
<my:myFields xmlns:xsi="http://www.w3.org/2001/XMLSchema-instance"
xmlns:my="http://schemas.microsoft.com/office/infopath/2003/myXSD/2010-01-
31T15:57:22" xmlns:xd="http://schemas.microsoft.com/office/infopath/2003"
xml:lang="en-us">
        <my:Employee_Name>Tom Richards</my:Employee_Name>
        <my:From_Date>2010-07-07</my:From_Date>
        <my:Employee_ID>342</my:Employee_ID>
        <my:To_Date xsi:nil="true"></my:To_Date>
        <my:Hours_Requested>8</my:Hours_Requested>
        <my:Absence_Type>3</my:Absence_Type>
</my:myFields>
```

Figure 10-8. Examine the xml behind a form data file.

Notice that the first several elements of this XML file provide the operating system with information to identify the type of file. It also identifies the specific form file in the fourth line that I used to generate the data file. That information explains why you can double-click on a data file and the operating system knows which form to use to display the data and where to find that form.

In the lower half of this figure, the element **my:myFields** defines the data section of this file. Each of the sub-elements defines one of the data fields from the form and includes the value of that field. Therefore, it would be possible for you to write other applications to read this XML file and extract the form data. While you could also use XSLT against this data to create other display formats, a far easier approach would be to create different views of the data within InfoPath. For example, you might use the default view of the form to collect data that needs to appear on several related documents. Then create these other documents as alternate views using that data so the user only needs to enter the data once.

Publish Your Form Data to SharePoint

While being able to use your form from a network share provides a great starting point, you saw that one of the potential problems is that the user can save the data after filling in the form in any directory he wants using any naming convention he pleases. You can and probably will lose data this way. It would be much better if you could at least save your form data to a SharePoint library. Let's open the **Request for Absence** form stored in the network share and see how to automatically save the form data to a SharePoint library. Figure 10-9 shows that when you right-click on the form name in the network share, the drop-down dialog contains a command, **Design**, which opens the form using InfoPath Designer 2010.

Figure 10-9. Open the form definition file from the shared network drive using the Design command.

Once you have the form open, click on **File** and go to the **Info** page, as shown in Figure 10-10. Notice the description under the section titled **Submit Options**. It implies that the submit options could allow you to define how users will return completed forms.

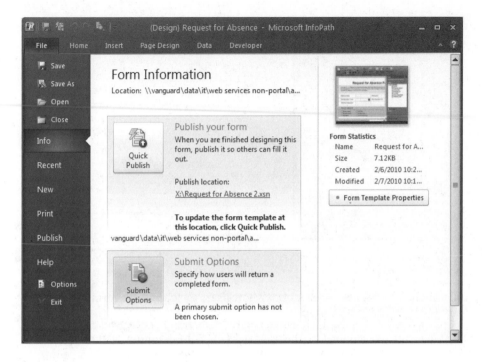

Figure 10-10. Go to the Backstage Info page to change the form's submit options.

When you click the **Submit Options** button in Figure 10-10 for the first time, InfoPath opens the dialog shown in Figure 10-11 to ask where you want to submit the form.

Figure 10-11. The Submit Options drop-down menu.

For this example, choose **Submit Options**. Initially the **Submit Options** dialog shown in Figure 10-12 has no values selected or entered. That explains why the user had to use the **Save** option from the file menu to save the data.

511

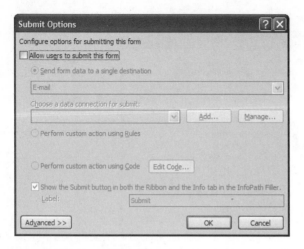

Figure 10-12. The Submit Options dialog.

The first thing you want to do is to click the check box **Allow users to submit this form**. This option adds a **Submit** button to the **Home** ribbon of InfoPath Filler when the form is opened. It also enables some of the other options on this dialog page, as shown in Figure 10-13. Immediately, you can choose from three radio buttons to define the action when the user clicks the **Submit** button. Of these radio buttons, let's choose the first one: **Send form data to a single destination**.

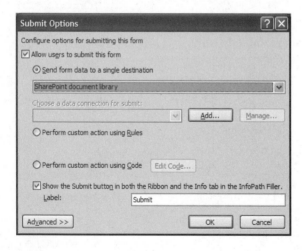

Figure 10-13. Turn Submit on and designate a SharePoint document library as the single destination.

Even with this option, you have several options to choose from when defining that single destination:

- E-mail

- SharePoint document library

- Web Service

- Web Server (HTTP)

- Hosting environment

- Connection from a data connection library

This short introduction to using InfoPath will not go into each of these options. For now just know that each destination prompts for its own specific information needed to send the data to the destination of your choice. For example, the E-mail option needs you to define the standard To:, Cc:, Bcc:, and Subject: fields for the message. You can also provide a brief introduction text that appears in the body of the e-mail. The form data itself becomes an attachment to the e-mail. While I will not go into the details here, you can define the contents of these e-mail fields with data from the form.

In our case, however, you want to define the destination of the data as a SharePoint document library. After making this selection, you must define where it can find that library by clicking the **Add** button in the section **Choose a data connection for submit**.

In the **Data Connection Wizard**, you begin by defining the URL to the document library where you want to save InfoPath's xml data file. The URL must include the full URL of the site and library. This should make sense considering that InfoPath does not know anything at all about your SharePoint site.

Figure 10-14 shows the first page of the **Data Connection Wizard** with the Shared Documents library of our default site as the target location for saving the form data. Next, we need to examine the file name that InfoPath will use when saving the data.

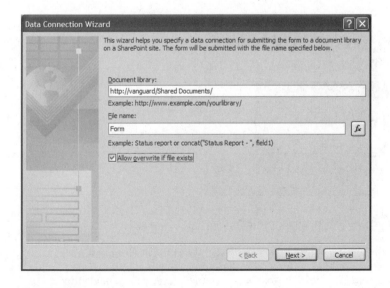

Figure 10-14. Identify the SharePoint document library.

In Figure 10-14 you can see that the default file name is simply **Form**. This file name is very generic and does not tell you much about the contents of the data file. However, more importantly, you could never have more than one file in the SharePoint library with this name. In fact, with the option **Allow overwrite if file exists** turned on, you would overwrite any previous form data with the new form data each time you open the form and submit data. Of course, turning off this check box does not improve the situation much because it still limits you to one file with the name **Form** in your SharePoint library. However, in this case, SharePoint only saves the first submitted data file, rejecting any subsequent submissions because they have the same name and it does not allow overwriting the data file.

To solve this problem, you need to build the file name dynamically using information that returns a unique value. You can do this by clicking the function button (**fx**) to the right of the file name text box to open the **Insert Formula** dialog. In this dialog, you can enter a formula in the large text box or you can use the leftmost of the three buttons below the text box to insert field values from the form to create the file name.

The middle button below the text box lets you use a predefined set of formulas to act on any data from the form. In addition, some formulas allow you to access dynamic information such as the current date—**Today**() and **Now**())—as well as the user name of the person filling in the form—**Username**().

For this example, let's build a file name that consists of a combination of the employee's name, the starting date for the absence, and the total number of hours requested. All three items can be gathered from the form's fields. To combine them into a single file name, you use the **concat**() function. This function lets you combine two or more individual items by listing them as arguments to the function separated with commas. Even though the fields I selected consist of three different data types (string, date, and number), the concat() function performs all the hard work of combining each of these fields into a single string that you can use as a file name. In addition to the three fields, I am also adding a single underline character between each of the field values to help make them readable. You can see the resulting formula in Figure 10-15.

After entering the formula to create a file name, click the **Verify Formula** button to check that you did not make any formatting errors when defining the formula. If you get a dialog box that tells you that the formula does not contain any errors, you can click the **OK** button to the **Insert Formula** dialog to 'lock-in' your formula.

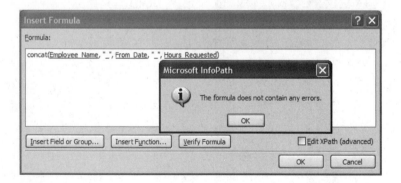

Figure 10-15. Build a custom and dynamic file name for the data file.

Figure 10-16 shows the **Data Connection Wizard** page again with both the document library location and the file name defined. You should give some consideration as to whether you want to allow the user to overwrite a file if it exists. In the Request for Absence example, a user can go back into an existing data file for the form and change the type of absence and resave the data without needed to create a new file. However, if the user tries to change the start date of the absence or the number of requested hours, InfoPath creates a new file based on your file naming convention that uses these two pieces of information. Note also that if you create a second file with a different name, InfoPath does not delete the original data. In fact, it has no way to know whether the two data files are related. Therefore, you must define a naming convention that allows or blocks addition data files from being created when you edit the original file.

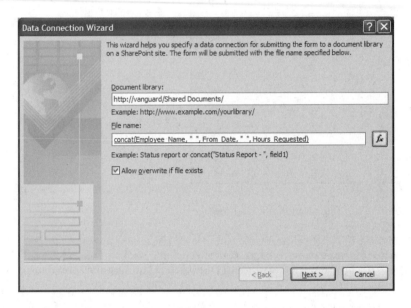

Figure 10-16. Specify whether InfoPath can overwrite a file with the same name.

When you click the **Next** button of the **Data Connection Wizard**, InfoPath shows you one additional screen, Figure 10-17, that lets you verify the information you entered in the first screen and lets you define a name for this data connection. If you only have a single data connection for the form, you can leave the default name. However, if you need to have multiple data connections for the form, you might want to create a more meaningful name so you can identify the purpose of each one. For example, you could change the name **Main Submit** to **Submit Data to SharePoint Library**.

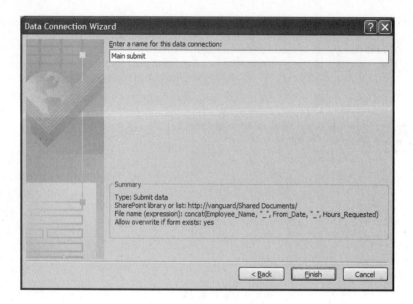

Figure 10-17. Summary/verification of data connection information.

If you notice any problems with the data in the **Summary** section such as perhaps forgetting to check (or uncheck) the **All overwrite if form exists** check box, you can click the **Back** button to correct your mistake. When you finish, click the **Finish** button on this last page of the **Data Connection Wizard**. This action returns you to the **Submit Options** dialog in Figure 10-18 where you can set some additional properties.

You should click the check box to show the **Submit** option in both the **Home** ribbon and the **Info** tab of the backstage page of InfoPath Filler. You can even change the name of the **Submit** option to something else such as '**Save Me Now**' or '**Please Keep Me**' or whatever you may prefer.

Next, click the **Advanced** button at the bottom of the dialog if you do not see additional options. With the **Advanced** properties opened, you can choose to display a message when the submission fails. In the text box associated with this option, you can define exactly what you want the message to say. Unfortunately, there is no way to create a "smart" message that tells the user why his submission failed. Therefore, you might leave the message as is or perhaps add a few helpful hints on common mistakes such as:

- Check your network connection.

- Check that your file name is unique.

- Check that your network cable is securely attached.

- Check that your wireless connection is turned on.

You can also display a message when the submission succeeds. Finally, you can select one of three actions for InfoPath to take when the submission ends. You can automatically close the form. Use this option if the user typically only enters a single instance of the form at any one time. The second option opens a new form after saving the current data. Use this option if the user must enter a series of data sets using the same form. The final action is to leave the form open. Use this option if you have a lengthy form that users might want to save periodically while they enter their data to make sure they do not lose all of their data. After you have completed the **Submit Options** dialog, click the **OK** button to save all your choices. This is also a good time to save a copy of your form back to its source location by clicking **Save** from the **File** menu.

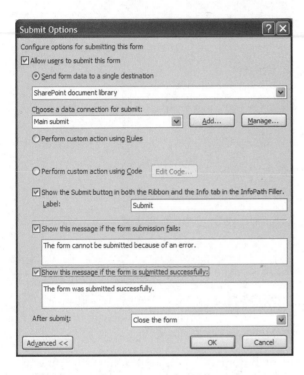

Figure 10-18. Define additional Submit Options.

Now you can test your new version of the Request for Absence form. In Figure 10-19 I have entered 32 hours of personal leave for employee Natasha. Notice that now I have a **Submit** button in the **Home** ribbon that I can click after completing the form.

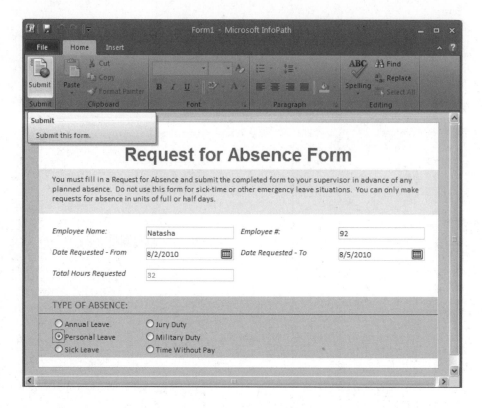

Figure 10-19. Use the Submit button from the Home ribbon to save new form data.

A few moments after you click the **Submit** button for the form, the message box shown in Figure 10-20 appears telling you that the form was submitted successfully. When you click the **Ok** button of this message box, InfoPath closes both the message box and the form as requested.

Figure 10-20. Use a message to indicate success or failure of the submit.

■ **Caution** If you are testing your form locally before submitting it to SharePoint, you may see a warning dialog when InfoPath attempts to access the server to save the data. After publishing the form, you will no longer see this warning.

Going out to the Shared Documents library that I specified as the destination for my data in the Data Connection Wizard, I see in Figure 10-21 that I now have one document in the library. Notice that the name of the document includes the employee name, the beginning date of the absence, and the number of hours that the employee has requested. You can see how useful having this information in the data file name might be when you need to identify individual data files. However, let's see what happens when you make a change to the data.

Figure 10-21. Example of a generated data file name

To edit the data file, position your mouse over the data file name until you see the drop-down arrow to the right of the file name. Click on this arrow to open the file's menu shown in Figure 10-22. You can edit the data file by clicking the option **Edit in Microsoft InfoPath**.

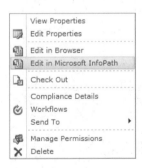

Figure 10-22. Edit the data directly from the SharePoint library from the item's drop-down menu.

If you remember that I previously stated that the data file only contains the data for the form instance, not the form itself, then how does it know how to find the form? Figure 10-8 showed the contents of a typical data file. In it, you saw that one of the xml elements included a reference back to the form. Therefore, when you click on the data file document in your SharePoint library, SharePoint can open InfoPath and read the xml of the data file to determine where to find the form definition. Thus, you see the data file opened in Figure 10-23 using the same form definition that you used to create the data file originally.

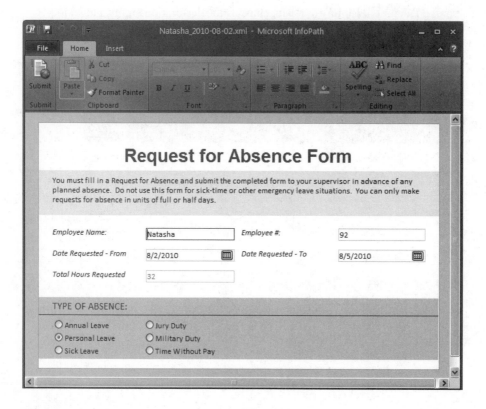

Figure 10-23. SharePoint opens InfoPath Filler from a data file in a document libary.

Suppose you make a small change to this data file by changing the **Requested To** date to 8/4/2010 instead of 8/5/2010 and, therefore, change the **Total Hours Requested** field from 32 hours to 24 hours. When you click the **Submit** button on this changed form or click on the **Submit** button in the **Info** page of the **Backstage** area, InfoPath saves a second copy of the dataset with a new file name, as shown in Figure 10-24. Although the employee name and the first date of the request had not changed for this new version of the form's data, the total number of hours requested did change, thus resulting in a new file in the Shared Documents folder.

Figure 10-24. Resubmitted data creates a second file when the Hours Requested change.

Using InfoPath Forms Services for Customers Without InfoPath

Suppose you do not want to publish your forms to a network file share because it requires that the form users have InfoPath on their desktop, and not everyone in your organization has InfoPath installed. If you have InfoPath Forms Services installed on your SharePoint server, you can publish your templates to document libraries. Users can then access the forms from the library just like they would access other document types.

You can specify in the library whether to attempt to open the file using the appropriate client application or to open it in the user's web browser. Of course, if you do not have Forms Services, you can still publish your form to the library, and users can open the form using their local copy of InfoPath. But with Forms Services, you can give users the choice of whether they want to open the document in InfoPath or directly within their browser.

■ **Note** Users working with the SharePoint 2010 Enterprise edition do not have to worry about Forms Services because the Enterprise edition includes the necessary services. However, if you use the standard edition or use Microsoft SharePoint Foundation 2010, you may want to contact your Microsoft representative to see if you can add Forms Server to support InfoPath forms.

Publishing to a SharePoint Server

Using the **Request for Absence Report** again from the previous section, let's republish the form, but instead of choosing the network share option, choose the SharePoint option from the **Publish** page of the **Backstage** area, as shown in Figure 10-25.

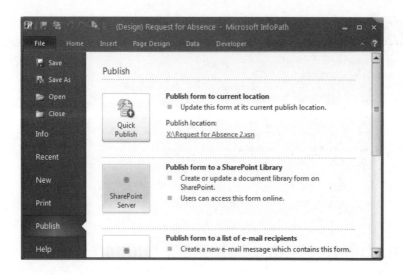

Figure 10-25. Publishing a form to SharePoint

Next, enter the SharePoint site where you want to publish the form. You need to enter the URL of the library for the site you want to use. If you navigate to it in a separate browser window, you can copy the URL from the address bar at the top of your browser as long as you drop the name of the library itself and anything to the right of the library name. Figure 10-26 shows the first page of the **Publishing Wizard**, where you can specify the name of your SharePoint site or InfoPath Forms Services site.

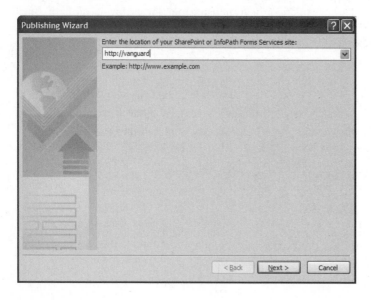

Figure 10-26. Identifying the site where you want to publish the form

On the next page of the wizard, shown in Figure 10-27, it asks you to indicate whether you want users to fill out the form using a browser or if you want them to download the form and open it with a local copy of InfoPath.

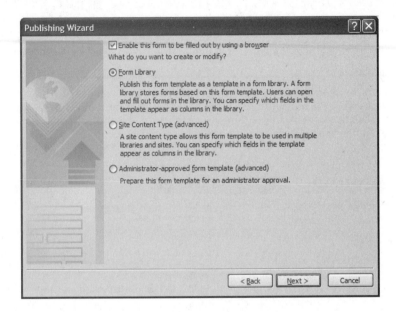

Figure 10-27. Identifying how you want to publish the form

Validating Your Form Before Publishing

Before beginning the process of publishing your form, you should have InfoPath verify that the form does not contain any features that browsers do not support. You can do this by selecting **Design Checker** in the **Info** page of the **Backstage** area. This command displays the **Design Checker** panel along with any incompatibilities with the selected server where you published the form. If you have not published the form yet, you can select the link **Change Settings** at the bottom of the **Design Checker** panel to open the **Compatibility** page of the **Form Options** dialog. Select if necessary the option **Web Browser Form** as the Form Type. To verify the compatibility of the form with InfoPath Forms Services on your specific server, enter the name of your SharePoint server in the text box in the **Server Validation** section. For example, I would enter http://vanguard for my server. When I save the form, InfoPath automatically adds the rest of the URL, transforming my entry to http://vanguard/_vti_bin/FormsServices.asmx. Click **OK** to accept your changes to **Form Options**. Finally, make sure to select the check box **Verify on server**.

You can then click the **Refresh** button immediately above the check box to check your form for incompatibilities against your form server. It may take a few moments for InfoPath to verify your form. However, when it finishes, it displays a set of errors and messages. You must fix errors before you can publish the form if you want Forms Services to be able to open the form. However, messages tell you of noncritical concerns that you can ignore or address without affecting whether Forms Services can open the form. For example, a message warning you that dialog box validation messages will not show merely reminds you that dialog box validation messages can only appear when you open the form with InfoPath Filler.

Next, on this same page of the wizard, you must select from three choices for how you want to publish your form. The first option lets you publish the form to a form library. If your form only has declarative functionality, you can publish the form usually without assistance to a form library and begin using it as long as your SharePoint administrator has activated Forms Services for the site.

■ **Note** *Declarative functionality* meanshat the form supports basic conditional formatting that may change the form's appearance, alter the visibility of individual controls, or change the read-write state of controls.

When you publish a form to a form library, I generally recommend that you get started by saving each template to a new library. However, you will see in the section "Working with a Library That Has Multiple Content Types" that you can publish more than one template to a single library using content types, which the second option on this page of the wizard foreshadows.

■ **Tip** When deciding whether to make more than one template available in a single library, ask the users of the library if that makes sense to them. For example, while you might include a gas-mileage-only expense form in the same library as more extensive trip expense forms, you probably would not include either of these in a library with a vacation or absence request form.

Finally, use the last option on this page when you have a form that requires administrator approval. Form templates that use managed code or data connections usually require the assistance of your SharePoint administrator to set up. These forms also typically require **Full Trust** or at least **Domain Trust** to run, since the data is not self-contained in the form and may not even be on the same server.

For this example, I will run you through publishing the **Request for Absence Report** to a standard form library, since it does not used managed code or reference external data.

On the next page of the wizard, shown in Figure 10-28, you can choose to publish the form to either a new library or an existing library. If you choose to publish to an existing library, you can select from the available libraries found on the SharePoint server listed at the bottom of this page of the wizard.

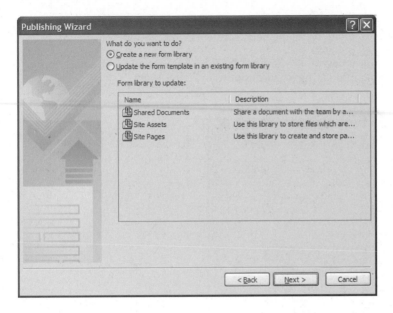

Figure 10-28. Create a new document library at the same time you publish the form.

You may be tempted to try to publish your form to an existing document library by clicking the second option button in Figure 10-28 and then selecting a library from the list. However, if you do not first configure the document library to accept InfoPath forms, it rejects the update. You can only update existing document libraries that already have an InfoPath form defined as the default content type. On the other hand, this list may also display form libraries to which you can directly publish your form. Unfortunately, there is no easy way to differentiate from this list which libraries you defined as document libraries and which you defined as form libraries.

■ **Tip** When I am ready to publish a new form, I generally create a corresponding form library for it before publishing the form since form libraries by default support InfoPath forms.

So you might think that you can simply cancel the **Publishing Wizard** at this point, switch to SharePoint, and manually create a new library. If you create a new document library from within SharePoint, you do not get an InfoPath document as a default template type. This is because unlike Word, Excel, and several other template options that SharePoint does include, it does not include a blank InfoPath form as an option. While you could accomplish this task by creating a new content type first, building the document library, adding the content type to the library, and then making that content type the default for the library, that entails just a few too many steps for me.

You could also create a form library, which is essentially a specialized document library designed to handle XML data created from form templates. A form library uses a Microsoft InfoPath document as its default template type. You could then update the template of that form.

However, the easiest method of publishing a new form is to just select the first option shown earlier in the section in Figure 10-28, and let InfoPath do all the necessary work to create a new form library based on the InfoPath form you want to publish.

In fact, choosing that option prompts you for the name of the form library along with a description. You can see this on the next page of the **Publishing Wizard**, shown in Figure 10-29.

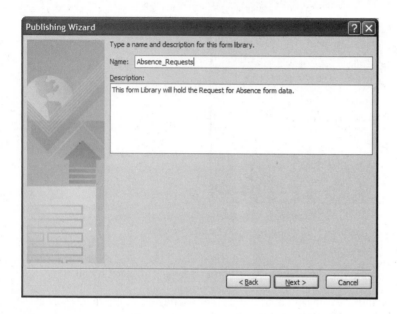

Figure 10-29. Providing a name and description for a new document library

Defining Metadata for the Document Library

When creating a new form library, SharePoint wants to know what additional columns you want to associate with the library. SharePoint gives you the option of adding any of the fields from the InfoPath form as columns. Displaying the major form fields as columns makes it easier to scan through the saved data files after using the form to see important information without having to open each data file individually. It also makes it easy to download the data perhaps through an Excel spreadsheet or Access database that you can use elsewhere.

■ **Tip** Recall from Chapter 7, which covered managing SharePoint lists in Excel, that you can export the metadata from a document library to a spreadsheet. Since the metadata from this library represents data from completing the forms, you can use the resulting Excel spreadsheet to process the data to display groupings, subtotals, totals, averages, and so on.

Figure 10-30 shows that InfoPath recognizes most of the simple data fields and automatically adds them to the list of potential columns in the document library it creates. If you want to check whether the form has any additional fields that you might want to display as a column, click the **Add** button to the right of the dialog box.

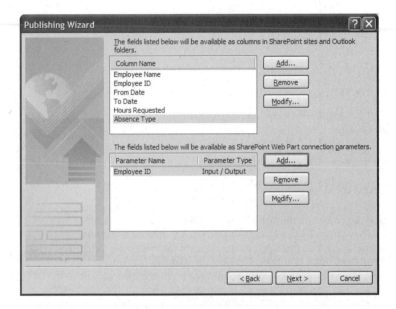

Figure 10-30. Selecting form fields to appear as columns in the library

When you click the **Add** button in the top-half of this form, the **Select a Field or Group** dialog box appears, as shown in Figure 10-31. If you scroll through the list of available fields, you can select any field from the form not already included in the column list. Notice that you can also use this opportunity to rename any form field that may have an abbreviated or complex name with a more descriptive column name when added to the library.

In the second half of this form you can select fields from the form that can be used as connection fields to other lists in the SharePoint site where you save the form library. If you know that you will not need to create connections between this library and any other library or list, you can ignore this feature. In Figure 10-30, I have selected the **Employee ID** field as a field that you could potentially use to connect this library with other libraries and lists.

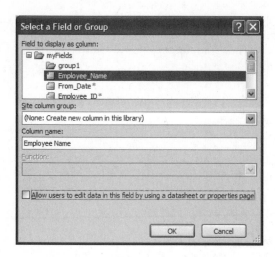

Figure 10-31. Adding a column or changing its name

If you decide not to include any of the columns that InfoPath preselected, you can remove them from the column list before you build the library by selecting them in the list shown earlier in Figure 10-30 and then clicking the **Remove** button. You can even update the column names of the fields that InfoPath preselected by clicking the column name and then clicking the **Modify** button.

The check box at the bottom of the page determines whether the user can edit the data in the select column after it appears in a SharePoint list using the datasheet mode or even the edit (properties) page. You should note, however, that any rules you define within your form do not get translated to the SharePoint list.

When you have all the columns defined that you want to extract from the form, click the **Next** button on the page to proceed to the confirmation page of the **Publishing Wizard**, shown in Figure 10-32. This page displays a summary of the configuration information for the library. If you click **Publish** to continue, InfoPath builds the new document library in SharePoint.

■ **Tip** If you want to manipulate the data in the SharePoint library that holds the form data using a workflow, you must click the check box to allow users to edit the data in the field.

528

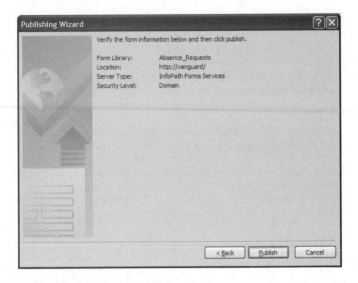

Figure 10-32. Verify action parameters before publishing the form.

It may take a few seconds for InfoPath to create the new document library. However, when it finishes, it refreshes this page of the wizard, giving you the option to open the document library. Figure 10-33 implies that you can open the form immediately in a browser, but if you just created a new library for this form, you may have a few additional library settings to look at first.

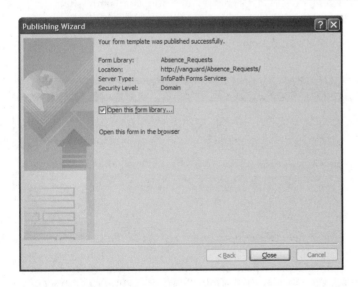

Figure 10-33. Verify the published form by opening it or sending it in an e-mail.

Additional Library Settings

Open the **Library** ribbon and from the **Settings** group click **Library Settings**. Then select **Advanced Settings** under the **General Settings** group. You will see that the **Document Template** has been set to `Absence_Requests/Forms/template.xsn`. The first part of this name is the name of the form library. Think of the next part of the path, `Forms`, as a directory where the library stores all its templates. Then the file name, `template.xsn`, is the name of the default template, which in this case is an InfoPath template, based on its extension of `.xsn`.

So how do you know that this file is the form that you began with? You could click **New** back on the **Library Tools Documents** ribbon to show that the default new document for this library opens a blank copy of the form. You could also click the **Edit Template** link immediately beneath the **Template URL** on the **Advanced Settings** page. Because the extension of the current template is `.xsn`, this action opens the template in InfoPath. It first pops up a dialog box to tell you that you can update the form template. However, if you make changes, you must save the form and then republish it to this library to update it. Republishing the form does not affect any of the existing data records created with the older version of the form.

■ **Caution** The fact that the existing data records are not affected by publishing a new version of the form is not the same as saying that the data will work with the new form. Deleting or renaming fields can cause an apparent loss of data when the new form attempts to display an old data file.

If you click the **Close** button in Figure 10-33 after selecting the option to open the document library, SharePoint opens the new library, as shown in Figure 10-34. Of course, the library starts out empty. So you may be wondering what happened to the form that you published to this library. It is there. However, rather than becoming an entry in the library, as would happen if you simply tried to upload a document to the library, it has become the default template for the library.

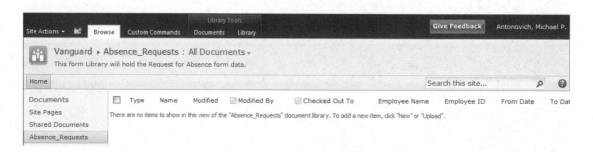

Figure 10-34. *New document library for a form showing the custom columns from the form*

While you are in the **Advanced Settings** page, look at the next section, named **Opening Documents in the Browser** (Figure 10-35). This setting lets you choose whether to open documents in a browser or client application for those documents that support both modes. By default, SharePoint uses the server default, which is defined as the browser window in this server. Therefore, for a form library, you could keep the default value or, if necessary, you could change the default setting to **Open in the browser.** In either case, SharePoint will then use Form Services so that users can fill in your InfoPath form online.

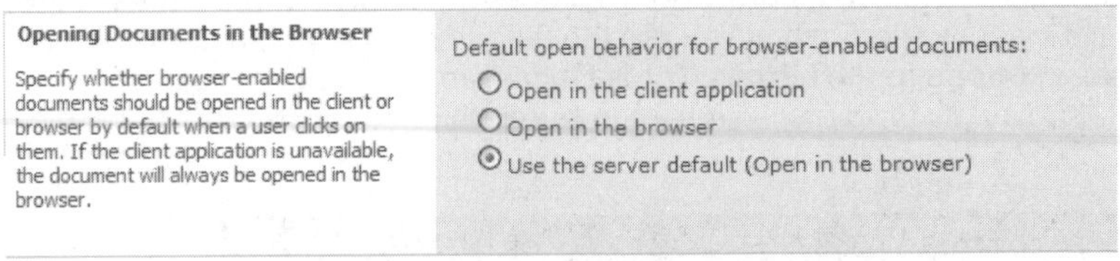

Figure 10-35. Changing the default display in your browser

Finally, if you plan to add more than one form to this library, you need to change the setting for the first option, **Content Types**. By changing the value of this option to **Yes**, you allow the library to support multiple content types, where each content type is a different form. If you plan to use only a single form type within this library, leave this setting at **No**, although setting it to **Yes** will not hurt anything either.

With the **Custom Send To Destination** setting, you can set a name and URL to which to send a copy of the form, generally to another SharePoint library on the current or even another SharePoint site. You may want to do this if you need to have users send a copy of their form data to a second location after they have saved it to the library. Other options include the ability to turn on or off the **New Folder** command in the **New** menu and the ability to determine whether to include this library in search results. Figure 10-36 shows the top portion of the **Advanced Settings** page.

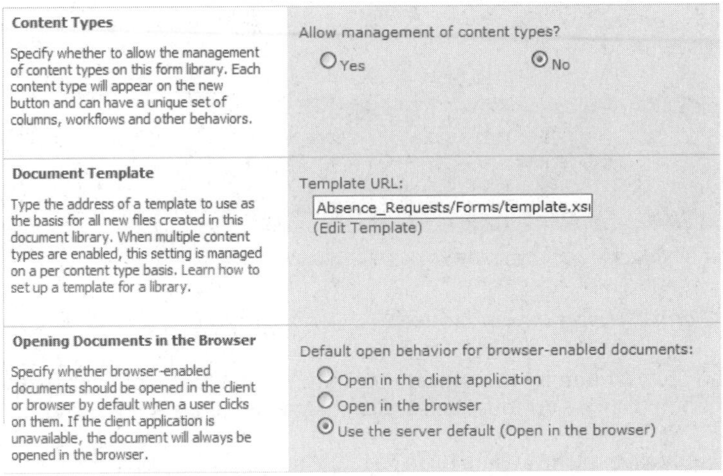

Figure 10-36. Decide whether you want to manage multiple content types in the current library.

Using the Published Form

Click **OK** to save your changes in the **Advanced Settings** page. Then click the library name in the breadcrumb area to display the library list again. So if the form itself does not appear in the library, what does appear in the library? Let's see what happens when you use the default form template to enter some data. Click the **New Document** option in the **Library Tools Documents** ribbon to open an instance of the form. Figure 10-37 shows the form displayed not in InfoPath but in the browser.

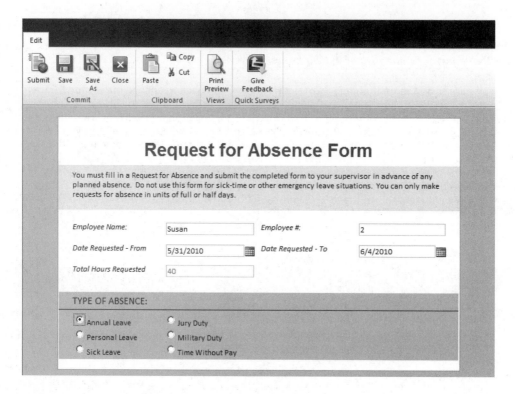

Figure 10-37. Display the form using Forms Services in your browser.

The appearance of the form in the browser mimics the appearance of the form within InfoPath, with the addition of an **Edit** ribbon. This ribbon displays options such as **Save**, **Save As**, **Close**, **Views**, and **Print View**.

The **Save** and **Save As** buttons simply save the form data to an XML file in your form library. When entering data into a new form, both **Save** and **Save As** prompt you for a file name for the XML file. However, after you have saved the form data, you can edit the data and save it again using the same name with the **Save** button or use the **Save As** button to create a second item with the updated data. Saving the form data with either of these two buttons does not close the form.

The **Submit** button allows you to define more options when saving the form data including allowing developers to add custom code to the form's submit event. Submitting options also let you easily define rules that the data must pass before it saves the data. You can also define alternate destinations for the data such as a web service or backend database and, you can even automatically define the XML file name using information from the form data itself. We will explore some of these options in the next section, **Changing Submit Options for a Form**.

■ **Tip** For entering data into a form, you typically do not need the **Views** command. You definitely do not need the **Views** command if you only have a single view for a form.

Changing Submit Options for a Form

If you want to change the options displayed on the ribbon, you need to open the **Info** page of the **Backstage** area and locate the section **Advanced** form options. Then click the **Form Options** button to open a dialog box that lets you set many of the form's options. Because of the number of options, InfoPath groups the options by category. The categories appear in a list along the left side of this dialog box. Select the **Web Browser** category if not already selected. In this area, you can select which commands appear in the ribbon. You can also define whether separate **Toolbars** appear at the top, the bottom, or both the top and bottom if the InfoPath ribbon is unavailable. If you choose to use both top and bottom toolbars, you cannot choose different commands for the top toolbar compared to the bottom toolbar.

Configuring Submit Options for a Form

To use the **Submit** command in the toolbar, you have to configure the submit options for the form. You can find these options by selecting **Submit Options** from the **Info** page of the **Backstage** area. You can configure submit options to send a copy of the form data to:

- E-mail

- A separate SharePoint document library

- A web service

- A hosting environment

- A connection from a data connection library

The **Submit Options** dialog box also provides options to create custom actions using either rules or code. You can even use a data connection option to specify the document library you want to employ and define a file name based on fields within the form, such as the employee's name and the date of her absence. This would eliminate the need for the user to remember the file naming convention discussed in this section.

Saving the Data from a Form

After completing the form as shown in Figure 10-37, you need to save your data. You can click the **Save** or **Save As** option. Both options open the **Save As** dialog box if you began with an instance of a new form. The **Save As** dialog box, shown in Figure 10-38, assumes that you want to save the data from the form into the current library. However, it prompts for a file name. You can enter any name here. Defining a naming convention may help you locate different instances of the form data. For example, Susan filled in the **Request for Absence Report**, shown previously in Figure 10-37, to take a week off beginning May 31, 2010. Therefore, by combining the user's name with the date she requested to have off, you create a meaningful name that helps to identify the user and the date she requested to have off.

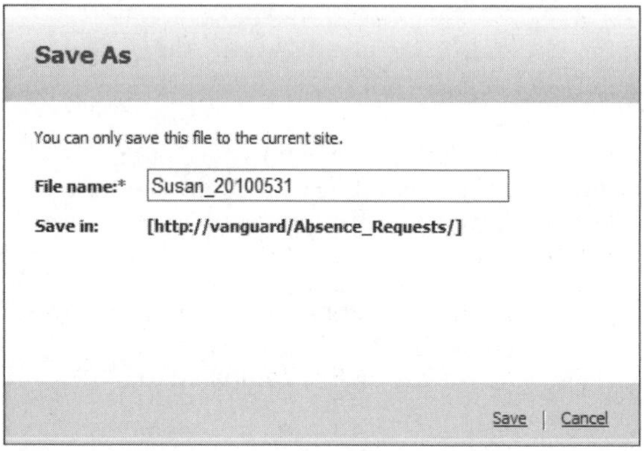

Figure 10-38. Save the data from filling in a form using Forms Services.

When you click **Save**, InfoPath Forms Services saves a copy of the form data in the library. When you look at the library's contents, you now see an entry having the name just entered in the **Save As** dialog box as the file name. You also see some other common library columns such as:

- **Type**
- **Modified** (which displays the date modified)
- **Modified By**
- **Checked Out By**

In addition to these columns, you can see the other columns that you selected earlier in the **Publishing Wizard**. If you decide you want to change which columns appear in the list, you can select **Library Settings** from the **Settings** group of the **Library** ribbon. In the **Columns** section, click the option **Add from existing site columns** found beneath the list of currently used columns.

Figure 10-39 shows the first entry in the library.

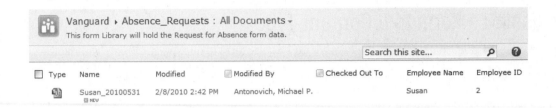

Figure 10-39. This library shows a new item containing the form's output data file.

Like entries in other libraries, you can position your mouse over the item **Name** field to display a drop-down list of options. This list, shown in Figure 10-40, includes options to view and edit the properties, manage permissions, edit the form data, delete the entry, send the data to another location, and check out the file.

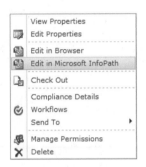

Figure 10-40. This item drop-down lets you open the form data in InfoPath for Forms Services.

To verify that this file is only the data, select the **Edit Properties** option in the file's drop-down menu. The only editable property is **Name**. While you can change the main part of the name, you cannot change the extension, which you can see defaults to .xml. If you were to select the option **Edit in Browser**, this XML file would look similar to the one shown earlier in Figure 10-37.

Notice also that the drop-down menu has two **Edit** options for editing the data. If you use the first edit option to open a copy of the data file in your browser using Microsoft Office InfoPath, you can make changes to the data on the form and then click **Save**, not **Save As**, unless you want to create a second data instance with a new name. The second option lets you edit the data file using a copy of Microsoft Office InfoPath from your desktop. If you make changes to the data on the form using InfoPath, you must select **Save** from the **File** menu in InfoPath to save the data changes back to the data file.

In either case, it may at first appear that the metadata for the data file does not update. Remember that SharePoint uses web pages, and you may need to click your browser's **Refresh** button before the metadata reflects changes made to the data.

■ **Tip** If you want to use the XML in another process, you can download a copy of the XML data file by using the file's drop-down menu and selecting **Send to ➤ Download a Copy**.

Publishing a Form to a Content Type

In the previous section, you published the Request for Absence form to one specific library within the site. However, what if you wanted to use the form in several sites of the current site collection? In this section, you will see how to publish a form to a site content type. With a site content type, you can easily add the form as a content type to any library in the site or its subsites. Therefore, if you have a form that users need to access from many different sites, publishing the form as a content type may be the fastest way to make it available across multiple libraries. It will also let you manage future changes from a central location.

Just like publishing a form to a specific library, you need to begin with the form open in **Design** mode in InfoPath. Then select the **Publish** page from the **File** menu. Then click the **SharePoint Server** button in the **Publish form to a SharePoint Library** section. On the first page of the **Publishing Wizard**, InfoPath may ask you for the location of the SharePoint site. On the next page of the wizard, select the option **Site Content Type (advanced)**, as shown in Figure 10-41.

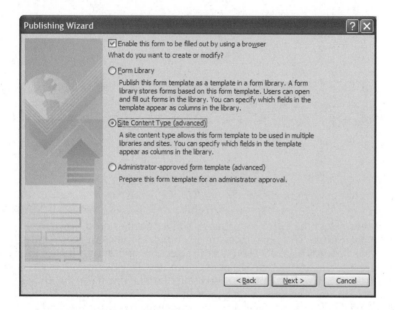

Figure 10-41. Publish your form as a content type to your SharePoint site.

When you click **Next**, the wizard asks what you want to do. You can create a new content type if you never published this form before as a site content type. However, you should select the **Update an existing site content type** option if you previously published the form and need to republish it due to changes. Notice that when you update a content type, SharePoint must update all libraries that use that content type. If you have used it in several libraries, this process could take some time. However, it also shows how you can manage multiple libraries that use the content type from one place.

> ■ **Note** Content types allow you to store different types of documents within the same document library in which each content type has its own unique set of columns or metadata. Each content type can have its own workflows that act only on files of that content type, not all files in the library. This allows you to publish multiple forms to the same content library in which each form has its own metadata and workflows.

On the bottom-half of the page of this wizard, shown in Figure 10-42, you must select what you want to base the content type on. For a new form, select the generic content type **Form**.

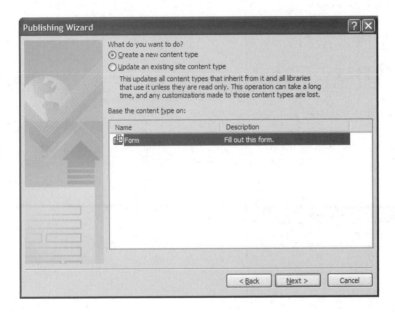

Figure 10-42. Create a new content type or update an existing one.

As with all objects, when you add a site content type, you must provide a name and description for that content type. You must supply a unique name. You should enter the description, although optional, to help users identify what the content type supports. Figure 10-43 shows the minimal entries for these two properties, assuming that you began with the **Request for Absence** form as the source for the content type.

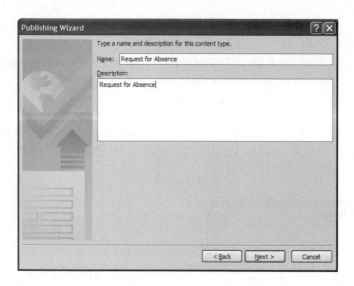

Figure 10-43. Provide a name and description for a new content type.

Next, Figure 10-44 shows that you must specify the name of the site where you want to publish the form. For this example, I will publish the form in the root web of my SharePoint site collection, so I enter the URL `http://vanguard/`.

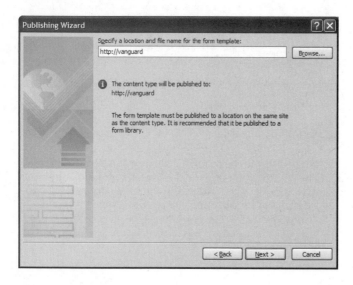

Figure 10-44. Specify the site where you want to publish the content type.

When you click **Next**, SharePoint displays the names of all the libraries that you can access from the requested site (see Figure 10-45). Note that the availability of the form directly relates to the site hierarchy. When you add a content type to a site, all child sites also have access to that content type. Therefore, if you want all of your SharePoint sites to use a specific form, you need to add that content type to the highest site level from which you want to use it. For that reason, you may want to publish the content type to your top-level site.

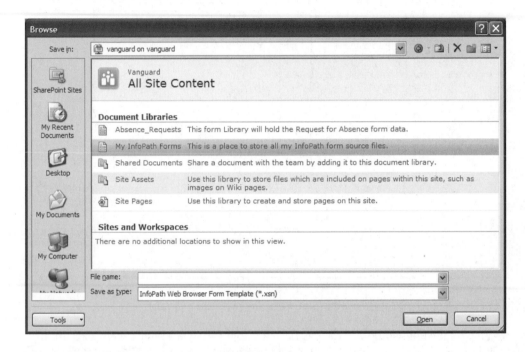

Figure 10-45. Select an initial library to use a content type.

Notice that both form libraries and document libraries appear in Figure 10-45. This can be confusing, as you have to remember which libraries you created as document libraries as opposed to form libraries. When you save the form template source (in XSN format), you should save it in a document library so others can open and edit that source document. On the other hand, you should use form libraries when you publish the form to save the data files from the form. A document library can hold any type of file. However, SharePoint customized the form library to work with XML documents based on one or more form templates defined as content types for that library. The form library stores a single copy of the form template (XSN) and multiple copies of the associated data files (XML) for each time someone uses it.

After you select a document library where you want to store the source, Figure 10-46 shows that you must enter a name for the form template. You can name the template anything you want.

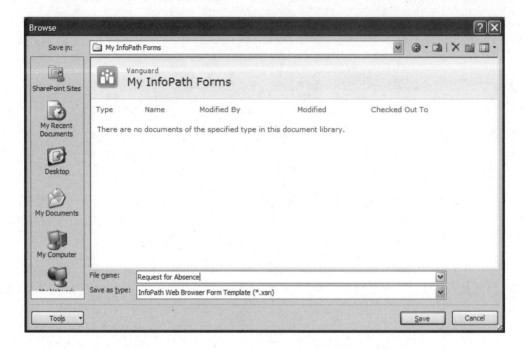

Figure 10-46. *Publish the content type to a form library so others can work with it.*

On the next page of the **Publishing Wizard**, you have the opportunity to define which fields from the form you want to use as columns or metadata in the libraries where you will use this content type. You do not have to select all the fields. However, remember from earlier chapters that you can export metadata from a SharePoint library to an Excel spreadsheet. This capability can be very useful to perform analysis of the collected data without having to resort to a programming language to extract the data from the XML files.

Using the buttons shown in Figure 10-47, you can include additional form fields as columns, remove some of the columns, and modify the column names, perhaps providing a more descriptive name if the form's field names are not particularly user-friendly.

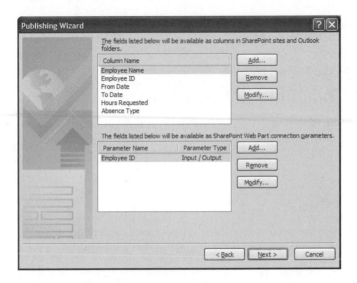

Figure 10-47. Select the form fields you want to publish as columns in a library.

When you are finished defining which fields you want to display as columns, click the **Next** button to proceed to the last page of the **Publishing Wizard** before InfoPath actually publishes the content type. Figure 10-48 shows a summary of the collected parameters. If everything looks correct, complete the publishing of the content type by clicking the **Publish** button.

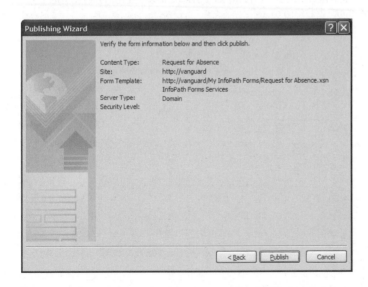

Figure 10-48. Verify your settings before publishing the content type.

The actual publishing process may take a few seconds. However, when it completes, two links appear on this page that let you either manage the content type or open the content type as a form in your browser to review how it looks.

Installing and Using Site Collection Content Types

After you publish a form as a content type, you have to specify the form library where you want to use that content type. However, published content types become available to all libraries in not only the current site where that library resides but also all child site libraries. So how can you tell an existing library to use your new content type?

Adding a Content Type to a Library

Open the specific library where you want to use the content type. Select the option **Library Settings** from the **Settings** group of the **Library** ribbon. If you have not previously gone into the **Advanced Settings** to allow the library to manage content types, you need to do that first. While there, decide whether you want SharePoint to open your form content types using the content type's client application (InfoPath in this case) or to open the form in your web browser.

When you close the **Advanced Settings** page, you should see a section within the **Settings** page with the title **Content Types**. Initially, a form library supports a blank form content type, meaning a blank InfoPath form. However, by clicking the link **Add from existing site content types**, you can add other available content types to the library, as shown in Figure 10-49. While you can view content types from all groups, you can find forms created in InfoPath and loaded as a site content type in the Microsoft Office InfoPath group. After finding the content type you want to use, you can either double-click its name to add it or single-click it and click the **Add** button. You can add multiple content types to the current library while on this page before clicking **OK** to exit.

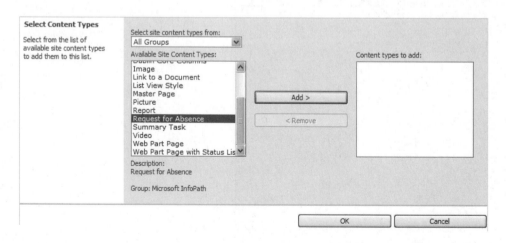

Figure 10-49. Add an available content type to another library/list.

Returning to the **Settings** page, you should see your new content types listed in the **Content Types** area. Notice that by default, all content types activated have a check in the column **Visible on New Button**. This means that when you open the library's **New Document** command from the **Documents** ribbon, you can choose from these content types to create a new document. However, if the user simply clicks the **New Document** button itself, he will get an instance of the default document or form identified by the **Default Content Type** column.

Changing the Default Content Type

To change the default content type, click the hyperlink beneath the content type table **Change new button order and default content type**. Figure 10-50 shows the **Content Types** section of the **Settings** page with the second hyperlink at the bottom of the image used to change the content type order and default content type.

Content Types

This document library is configured to allow multiple content types. Use content types to specify the information you want to display about an item, in addition to its policies, workflows, or other behavior. The following content types are currently available in this library:

Content Type	Visible on New Button	Default Content Type
Form	✔	✔
Request for Absence	✔	

Add from existing site content types

Change new button order and default content type

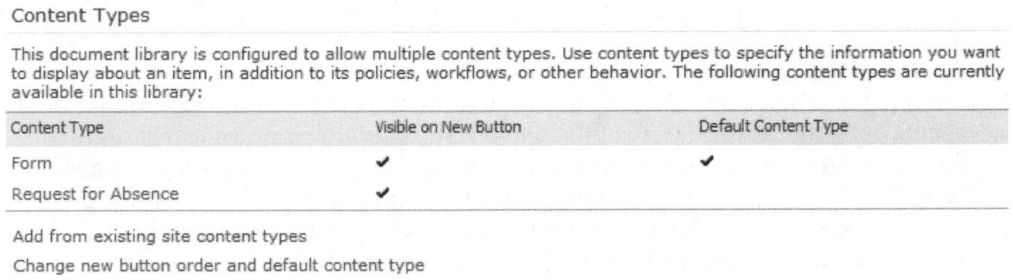

Figure 10-50. Libraries can have multiple content types but only one default type.

When you go to the page that displays the active content types for the current library, you can identify the order of the content types by the numbers in the drop-down boxes on the right side of the screen. These numbers define the order of the content types when you open the **New Document** drop-down list. The content type, identified as number 1, becomes the default content type used by the library. Figure 10-51 shows the process of making the **Request for Absence** form the default content type by moving it to the first position in the list.

Figure 10-51. Select the default content type by moving it to the top of the list.

When you return to the library list and click the **New Document** command, you see all the available content types for the library. Figure 10-52 shows that this library has two possible content types to choose from, but that the content type at the top of the list, **Request for Absence**, acts as the default content type.

Figure 10-52. Choose a content type from the New drop-down menu.

Working with a Library That Has Multiple Content Types

If you have defined multiple content types for a library, you probably also have unique columns that refer to each of those content types. This probably also means that for any given row in the library, only a few of the columns actually have values. While a few of those columns may be common across more than one content type, most are unique to a single content type. Rather than create a confusing display in which the user has to horizontally scroll through blank columns to find the data she needs for a specific item in the library, you might consider creating individual views for each content type.

When you create individual views for each content type the library uses, you can customize the columns used, the sort criteria, filters, and other view properties. To display only the items for one specific content type in each view, look for a field in each content type that always has a value for that content type but no other content types. You can compare that field to a blank or zero depending on the field type, thus determining whether to include that item in the view. If you do not have a unique column you can reference to identify the content type, you may need to consider adding either a custom column that you can manually update or, better yet, a field in the form of each content type that includes a default value to identify the form. However, it will probably be rare that a content type does not contain at least one required field that can serve as the filter field for the view.

Building Custom Workflows for InfoPath Forms Using SharePoint Designer

SharePoint Designer 2010 is not a part of the SharePoint Server 2010 or SharePoint Foundation 2010 installation. While it looks like SharePoint Designer will not be part of any of the Microsoft Office 2010 packages, it is available as a free download from Microsoft (download can be found at: `sharepoint2010.microsoft.com/product/related-technologies/Pages/SharePoint-Designer-2010.aspx`), so there is no excuse not to download it and try it. SharePoint Designer 2010 is a great tool for working with SharePoint that most administrators and designers typically require. While SharePoint Designer 2010 can trace its roots back to the days of Microsoft FrontPage, it provides much more functionality than FrontPage. One of those areas of relatively new functionality pertains to the creation of workflows for InfoPath forms published to a web page.

What Is a Workflow?

Let's begin by first briefly defining the term workflow. A *workflow* is a repeatable process that uses specific resources to perform defined actions when certain conditions exist. You can see an example of a process that requires a workflow when an employee at a company requests vacation time. The employee begins the process by filling in a form requesting specific time off, detailing the number of hours and which days he wants off. Upon completion, the employee typically needs to e-mail or carry the form to his immediate supervisor for approval. Of course, the supervisor has several options on how to act on the request:

- The supervisor can approve the request and forward it on to the clerical staff to enter the information into the company's payroll system.

- The supervisor can reject the request and send a notification of the rejection back to the employee with or without explanation as to why she rejected it.

- If the request for time off is over a specific number of hours or exceeds the number of hours that the employee currently has available, the request may need to be forwarded to the next level of management, where the process of approval or rejection begins again.

These steps define one of several different variations of the process, or workflow, that a vacation request might go through. Within SharePoint, you want to model this workflow so the document passes from the employee to his immediate supervisor or manager and eventually to the payroll department. In terms of publishing web pages, a similar workflow might route pages from the creator, to editors, to reviewers, and finally to approvers.

The example of the vacation request workflow illustrates a relatively simple sequential workflow. However, you can model complex workflows with intricate branching conditions and actions performed by individuals and by the computer system. The key advantage of software-driven workflows is that the users can focus on the tasks and not get distracted by thinking about the process steps.

Perhaps you have not thought of attaching workflows to your libraries and lists before, but when you begin to publish forms on your site, the need for workflows becomes apparent. In many business situations, you must route a completed form to one or more additional parties for review, additional data, or approval. Sure, you could simply save the form or other document in a SharePoint library and then separately notify the next person that she needs to access the document to do her part of the process. However, there are problems with this manual technique of passing documents along a process, some of which include the following:

- The more steps/people that become involved in the process, the harder it becomes to track the status of the document.

- Directly notifying the next person to process the document means that you manually have to create an e-mail to him, but, before that, you must know to whom to send it.

- If you must perform an action, you must know exactly what action to perform and how to respond to any result.

Automated workflows improve efficiency by taking the guesswork out of what to do next. Furthermore, SharePoint Designer's ability to create workflows with no coding makes it easy for anyone familiar with creating rules in products like Outlook to handle e-mail to apply similar skills to building a workflow.

Beginning a Simple Approval Workflow

To illustrate the concept of building a workflow for a form, let's build a simplified approval workflow for our Request for Absence form. I will keep this process simple while showing how easy it is for you to build workflows for your libraries.

To begin a new workflow, open SharePoint Designer from your **Start** menu. Before you can start a new workflow, you have to select the site where you want to work. Like all the other Office 2010 products, you can open the **File** drop-down menu to access the **BackStage** options. In the list on the left side, select **Sites**, as shown in Figure 10-53. Notice that you can use SharePoint Designer to create a new Blank site, add a subsite to your current MySite, customize an existing site, and more. In this case, you want to open an existing site to create a workflow for the Request for Absence form created earlier. Actually, you will create an XML workflow on the XML data saved by the Request for Absence form. If you did not select the check box back on Figure 10-30 to allow the user to edit the data added to the SharePoint library as a column, you will be able to change the data in the XML file outside of the form. However, it will allow us to build a workflow that can approve or reject the individual requests.

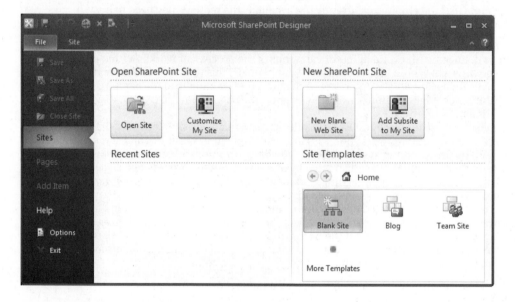

Figure 10-53. Open a site with SharePoint Designer 2010.

On the **Sites** page, click the **Open Site** button. This opens the **Open Site** dialog, which is very similar to the standard **Open** dialog you use to open any file. However, in this case, rather than enter a file name, you want to enter the site name in the text box at the bottom of the dialog. For my system, I would enter `http://vanguard` and then click the **Open** button.

SharePoint Designer then opens a page, as shown in Figure 10-54, where you can view and manage most of the important site settings. The major categories include:

- Site Information
- Permissions

- Customization
- Settings
- Subsites

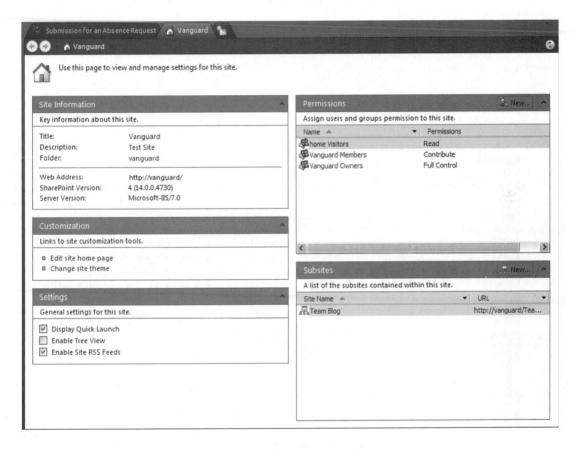

Figure 10-54. SharePoint Designer's site information page

SharePoint Designer may display a message informing you that it is downloading data from the server. This process takes a varying amount of time depending on the speed of your network and the site size. When it finishes, you will see on the screen all the site objects in the navigation menu along the left side of the screen. One of these options is **Workflows**. If you click on this option, you will see in the main portion of the screen a list of all the currently defined workflows for the site. You could go into these workflows and edit them, but I will show you how to create a new workflow for the site, specifically for the Request for Absence library. To do this, you need to click on the **List Workflow** button in the **New** group of the **Workflows** ribbon, as shown in Figure 10-55, because you want to create a workflow for a specific list. Other buttons in this group let you create workflows used for multiple lists or site workflows that you do not even need to associate with a list at all.

Figure 10-55. Select the list or library for which you want to build a workflow.

Clicking the **List Workflow** button displays all the lists in the current site. Notice that lists include libraries such as pages, forms, and documents. If you remember, I warned you earlier that everything is a list. From this list, select the list for which you want to create the workflow, Absence_Requests in this case. After selecting a list, SharePoint Designer opens the dialog box shown in Figure 10-56. In this dialog, you must provide a name for the workflow. You can also provide an optional description to go along with the site to define what it does. When you display the available workflows for an object, this description appears.

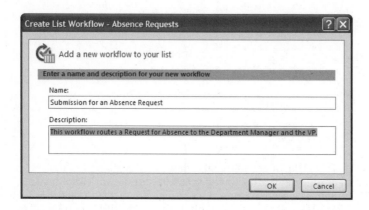

Figure 10-56. Create a new workflow using SharePoint Designer.

When you click **OK**, you can begin the first step of the workflow, as shown in Figure 10-57. SharePoint Designer provides a default name for each step beginning with "Step" followed by a sequential number. However, you can change the step name to something more meaningful such as **Send E-mail to HR**. To change the step name, click on it and enter the new name.

Figure 10-57. Rename the workflow steps.

Defining Workflow Details

Each step consists of one or more sets of details. Each detail consists of a condition and an action that you want the workflow to perform when the condition evaluates to **True**. Condition statements are optional. If you want to execute a specific action every time the workflow runs, you can skip the condition and go directly to the **Actions** button. In fact, for our Absence Request workflow, we want to execute an action immediately after starting the workflow to notify the department manager of the absence request. Therefore, let's first look at the available **Actions** .

When you click the **Actions** button from the **Insert** group of the **Workflow** ribbon, a drop-down list of possible actions appears, as shown in Figure 10-58. As you can see from the list, you have quite a set of actions available. In fact, there are so many actions that the drop-down includes a scroll bar to show all of them.

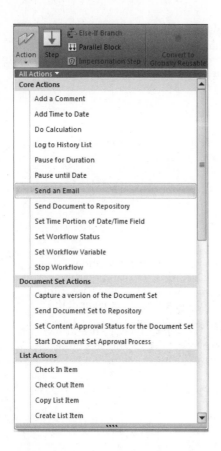

Figure 10-58. Select Send an Email from the available actions drop-down list.

In this case, you want to send the user's immediate supervisor a notification of the absence request. Therefore, the first action you want the workflow to perform when a user saves a new item to the list is to send an e-mail to the person's immediate supervisor. Therefore, select **Send an Email** as your first option.

Configuring an E-mail Message

This option first displays the command for sending the e-mail, as shown in Figure 10-59. The command consists of the word (command) Email followed by the underlined text **these users**. This text represents a clickable area in the command that you can think of as placeholder text that you replace with data. This text is a hyperlink that, when clicked, allows you to define not only who should receive the email but the subject of the email and the body contents of the email.

Figure 10-59. Create an action that sends an e-mail message.

Clicking the link for this placeholder opens a dialog box to define the e-mail message shown in Figure 10-60. Here you can enter the e-mail address of a person directly, or you can click the button to the right of the text box on the **To:** line to select from the users or user groups known to the SharePoint site. Let's assume for this example that the Absence Request form is used in a department site. In fact, the department manager is the site owner. You could enter the department manager's e-mail address directly, but if the department manager changes, you would have to go back into the workflow to change the e-mail address to the new department manager's address. On the other hand, if the site Owners group contains the department manager as a group user, you could simply reference the Owners group. In fact, this defines a better solution because when the department manager changes, you need only change the Owners group membership to "correct" the workflow. This same argument applies to selecting users for the **CC:** line of the e-mail.

■ **Tip** By default, the FROM: address for the e-mail can be set in the Central Administration ➤ System Settings ➤ E-Mail and Text Messages (SMS) ➤ Configure outgoing e-mail settings. Then update the From Address field.

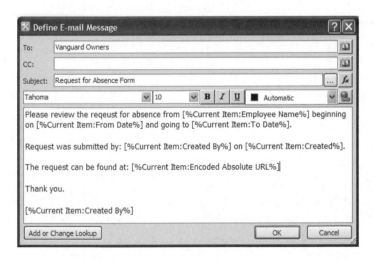

Figure 10-60. Define the properties and content of the e-mail message.

■ **Tip** You can click the lookup button to the right of the To: and CC: fields in the E-mail Message dialog to open a picker list of options that include SharePoint users and groups and the user who created the current item. You can even select the option Workflow Lookup for a User from the left side of the picker list to pick from various data sources including other columns in the current item.

Next, you can enter a text string to appear in the **Subject** field. You can enter a simple text string, as shown in Figure 10-60, or you can click the ellipses button (the one with the three dots) found to the right of the **Subject** field. This opens a dialog box that lets you combine text with values that you look up from a variety of data sources ranging from fields in the current item to fields in other lists. If you choose to use a value from another list, you must identify the item and the field from the list that you want to use.

In fact, the body of the message in Figure 10-60 shows several reference fields. In the first paragraph of the body, the string [%**Current Item:Employee Name%**] retrieves the value from the **Employee Name** column of the current item and inserts it into the string. Similarly, it also retrieves values from the column **From Date** and the column **To Date**. In this way, you can create a custom message that tells the e-mail recipient more than just that she has something to approve on the portal. You can provide specific information to tell her exactly what she needs to approve. You can even provide a link to the list so that the user does not have to try to remember the URL and then navigate to the required list, all of which takes extra time for the approver.

When you click **OK**, SharePoint Designer returns you to the **Step** page, shown in Figure 10-61, where you can add more actions.

Figure 10-61. Actions without a condition always execute.

Adding Multiple Actions

If you did nothing else in this step, the workflow would send the e-mail and immediately proceed to execute the next step in the workflow without giving the department manager time to look at the request. Fortunately, you can have multiple steps, each with individual actions, or you can have a single step with multiple actions. In this case, let's add a second action to create a task for the department manager. To do this, click the **Actions** button a second time, and click the option **Assign a To-do Item**, as shown in Figure 10-62.

Figure 10-62. Add a second action to a step.

When you click the link **a to-do item**, the **Custom Task Wizard** appears that tells you that it will add an item to the Tasks list for each user you include in the command. It also tells you that until all of the to-do items are completed, the workflow remains paused. A workflow executes step-by-step from the beginning through completion unless you tell it to stop or pause. A to-do item is one of the ways you can cause a workflow to pause. Another common way to pause the workflow is to monitor a field for changes in value.

On the second and final page of the wizard, you can enter a name for the task and a short description of what it must do. Next, click the link **these users** to display the **Select Users** dialog. This dialog shows a list of all the users defined in the site's user groups as well as some other basic user groups such as:

> User who created current item
>
> NT AUTHORITY\authenticated users
>
> NT AUTHORITY\LOCAL SERVICE
>
> SHAREPOINT\system

You can select as many users or groups as you may want. However, when you have multiple users assigned to a task, they must all complete the task before the workflow can continue. When you click **OK**, your step command should look similar to Figure 10-63.

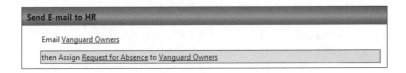

Figure 10-63. To-do tasks cause the workflow to pause until all users complete the task.

Next, we are going to check the number of hours requested. If the person requests less than 40 hours, the corporate policy is to approve the request. If the person requests more than 40 hours, you need to have the vice president approve or reject the request. As an action, you need to send an e-mail to the vice president for these requests. If you do not put a pause or wait action at the end of this step, the workflow would continue executing without giving the vice president time to even look at the absence request. Therefore, you need to add an action telling the workflow to wait at this point. To do this, you can add a second action to this step called **Wait for Field Change in Current Item**. In this case, we want to wait until the vice president changes the **Approval Status** for the request from its initial value of **Pending** to either **Approved** or **Rejected**. They can do this from the drop-down menu for the item in the request library. Also, if the request is less than 40 hours, you want to send an e-mail back to the person who created the request.

Figure 10-64 shows one possible way to complete this step. It sends the vice president an e-mail and then pauses the workflow until the status of the Request for Absence changes to anything other than **Pending**. If the person requests less than 40 hours, the **Else** portion of this step immediately sends an e-mail approving the request.

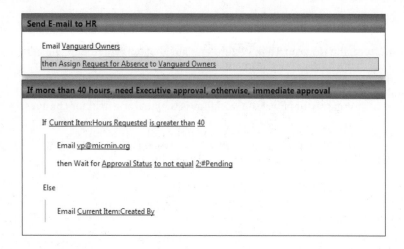

Figure 10-64. *One way to define the step to send an e-mail to an approver.*

Adding Additional Steps

For the last step of this workflow, let's send an e-mail message back to the person who created the Request for Absence to tell them whether the request was approved or rejected.

For this step in the workflow, you need to define a condition that checks whether the **Approval Status** field of the current item equals **Approved**. When it does, you can send an e-mail back to the person who created the item, informing him that the request has been approved.

Begin by clicking the **Conditions** button and select the option **If current item field equals value**, as you did for the condition in the second step of this workflow. Then select the field **Approval Status** and compare it to the value **Approved**.

Next, create an action that sends an e-mail. In the e-mail dialog box, click the **Select Users** button on the far-right side of the **To:** field and select **User who created current item** from the list of available users and groups list, as shown in Figure 10-65.

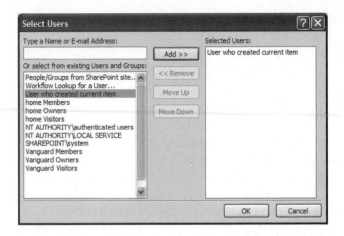

Figure 10-65. Use dynamic properties to define an e-mail's To: field.

In this step, you need to have a second condition, because the approver can either accept or reject the item. The first condition/action set defines what to do when the vice president approves the request. Next you must define what you want the workflow to do when the vice president rejects the request.

To do this, click the hyperlink **Else If Branch** found in the **Insert** group. Then click the **Conditions** button and define the Boolean expression that compares the **Approval Status** to the value of **Rejected**. Next, click the **Actions** button to send the user who created the current item an e-mail informing him that the approver has rejected the item.

■ **Tip** An interesting process you can create places all pending items of a specific type in an initial pending list. When a user creates an item in this list, it starts a modified approval workflow. In this workflow, add an action to the Approved step to copy the list item to a different list, an approved item list, followed by another action to delete the current item from the current list. If the approver rejects the item, you can leave the item in the pending list.

Figure 10-66 shows one possible way to build the final step in this approval workflow.

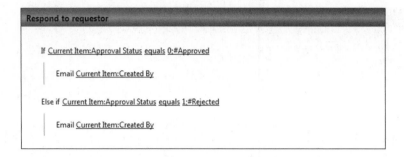

Figure 10-66. Define the approver's possible actions.

When you finish defining your workflow, you must save and publish it by clicking the **Publish** button in the **Save** group or the **Workflow** ribbon. At this point, you can close SharePoint Designer and return to your browser to test the workflow on some of the Absence Requests you may already have in the Absence Request library (list).

■ **Tip** If you ever create your workflow steps out of order, you can easily rearrange their order by first selecting the step by clicking on its header. Then click the **Move Up** or **Move down** option in the **Modify** group of the ribbon. If you miss a step, just add the step to the end of the steps. Then using the previous tip, move it up in the list of steps to the spot where it belongs. If you decide you no longer need a workflow step, open the drop-down list of step options as described in the previous tips and select the **Delete Step** option.

How to Run the Workflow

The default workflow created with SharePoint Designer creates a workflow for a list that you must start manually. To start the workflow, you need to open the list or library. Then from the item's drop-down list, select the option **Workflows**. This displays the available workflows for that item in an area at the top of the screen, as shown in Figure 10-67. Notice that three of these four workflows are the default workflows provided by SharePoint. However, the fourth workflow, **Submission for an Absence Request**, is the workflow you just created and saved in the last section.

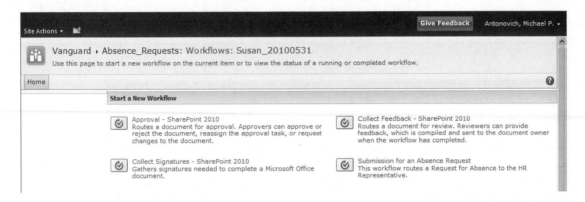

Figure 10-67. Start a workflow manual for a list item.

Click **Submission for an Absence Request** to start the workflow. A dialog pops up for the workflow task with two buttons. The first button starts the workflow, and the second button cancels the workflow. In this case, you want to click the **Start** button. Returning to the library, you can see that the status of the item has changed to started.

If you remember, the first step of the workflow creates a task for the department manager who is the site owner. Therefore, if you open the tasks list, you should see a new task has been created for the site owner, as shown in Figure 10-68.

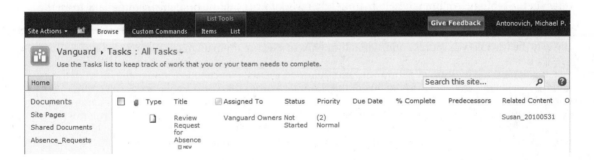

Figure 10-68. Display of task added by the workflow

The purpose of the task is to alert the department manager that someone wants to request an absence. Perhaps they received an e-mail about the task because they previously created an alert for tasks created in this list and assigned to them. Maybe they subscribed to the RSS feed for this list. On the other hand, perhaps you configured the task list to send an automatic e-mail to the person assigned a new task. In any case, the department manager can click on the task to see the screen shown in Figure 10-69. Notice that the task displays a link to the absence request that she can click on to review the details of the request. After reviewing the request, she can then complete the task by clicking the complete button. If she clicks the **Cancel** button, SharePoint closes the task, but leaves the workflow in a suspended state. She can also click the option **Delete Item**. This action puts the task in the Recycle Bin but leaves the workflow in a suspended state as well.

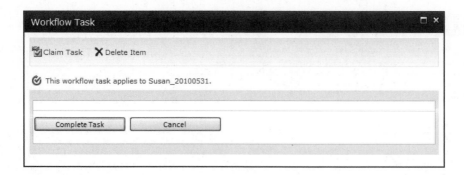

Figure 10-69. Complete a task.

If the department manager clicks the **Complete Task** button, the workflow proceeds with the next step, which in this example checks the number of requested hours to determine whether the vice president needs to approve the request.

Restructuring Your Conditions

If you add a conditional branch that you later decide you no longer need, you can click the down-pointing arrow to the upper-right of any of the existing conditional branches as you click on the condition to display a drop-down menu. From this menu, you can move conditional branches up or down in the sequence of branches. Remember that workflows evaluate branches sequentially from top to bottom by default. The first branch that returns a **True** result for its condition gets to execute its actions. You also have options in this menu to add new branches, delete the current branch, or change the way the workflow executes conditional branches to execute them all in parallel rather than sequentially.

If you have a condition or action with multiple statements, you can also change the order of the actions by clicking anywhere on the line of the statement other than on a hyperlink to select the condition or action. To the right appears a drop-down button that, when clicked, displays a menu letting you move the current action or condition up or down or even delete it. Therefore, even if you miss a condition or action, you can simply add it to the bottom of the list of actions or conditions in the appropriate conditional branch, and then move it to the position where it needs to appear.

■ **Tip** One of the conditions you can use compares the file size to a specific range in kilobytes. You can use this condition to automatically set the approval status to **Approved** or **Rejected** along with sending appropriate e-mail messages to users attempting to add large files to lists. Another condition you can use compares the file type to a specific type. By including a series of conditions joined with an **OR** connector, you can limit the ability of users from uploading specific file types to lists and libraries.

When you finish defining the steps in your workflow, save the workflow by clicking the **Publish** button in the **Save** group of the **Workflow** ribbon. This action saves the workflow to SharePoint, and, in this case, it specifically attaches it to the list specified when you started the workflow definition. The next timea user adds an item to the list, she can manually start the workflow. However, any time a process is manual, the user may forget to initiate the workflow. Can we tell the workflow to start automatically?

Configuring the Workflow Settings

To modify the settings of an existing workflow, click the **Workflow Settings** button in the **Manage** group of the **Workflow** ribbon. This action shows the page in Figure 10-70. Designer separates the workflow's settings into five groups. Here you can change the name of the workflow, change its description, associate the workflow with a different task or history list, and change its start option. This **Start Options** section has the options we want to change to start the workflow automatically.

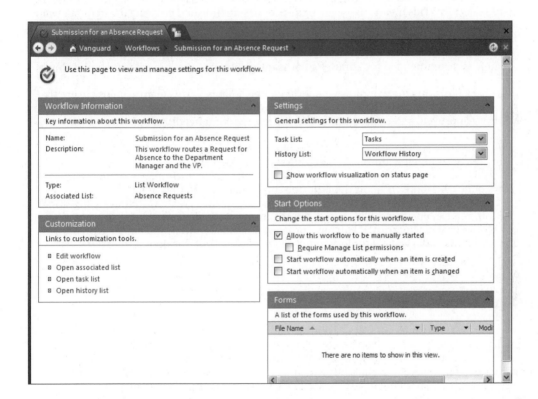

Figure 10-70. The Workflow Settings page

Note that by default, SharePoint Designer sets the workflow to start manually by checking the first check box. Use this option only if you do not need to start the workflow when an item is added or changed, and only if the average user knows when to and when not to start a workflow. For example, you may want the user to be able to create items in a list or library while she works on them over several sessions without starting a workflow until she finishes working on the item. Only at that time will she want to start the workflow on the completed item. You can also limit the users who can start a workflow to only those who have Manage List permissions.

■ **Note** This is similar to an **Approval** workflow for web pages in which the user typically needs control over when to start the workflow, as they may work on changes to the page over a series of days and only when all changes have been made will they want the workflow to begin.

The third check box tells SharePoint to start the workflow automatically whenever someone creates a new item in the select list. This means that even if the user has not finished entering the item but wants to save what he did so he can finish it later, the mere fact that he saves his temporary work fires off the workflow. If users typically complete the entry of all data for the form in a single session, maybe you do want to select this option to start the workflow when they create the item. Starting workflows upon creating a new item is recommended for libraries such as image libraries that typically are built using a single upload.

The fourth check box starts the workflow whenever an item changes. This feature helps ensure that users do not make changes to items without starting an approval process. Otherwise, users might submit an initial item, get it approved, and then return to edit the item without needing approval of their changes.

Either of these last two options start the workflow automatically. In fact, you can select any or all of these options including combining automatic workflows with manual starts.

While this section introduces you to the ability of SharePoint Designer to create workflows, you can create workflows quite a bit more complex than the one shown here. If you find that you need to perform actions that SharePoint Designer does not support, you can also create workflows using Visual Studio. In addition, you can create workflows that you can install at the site's collection level and then apply across multiple lists and libraries. If you have programming skills and would like to learn more about creating workflows using Visual Studio, you may want to check out this book: *Office 2010 Workflow*, by Mark Collins (Apress).

Summary

In this chapter, you looked at different ways to publish a form created with InfoPath. You started by looking at publishing the form to a network share. This solution may work for those organizations in which only a few people need to use the form and have InfoPath installed on their desktop computers. The major limitation of this method is that the form and its data are static files. Furthermore, forms published this way cannot participate in large automated workflows without substantial custom development, and who has time for that?

Next, you looked at publishing a form directly from InfoPath to a SharePoint library. You can even create a new library for the form at the same time that you publish it. You can also use this method to update the form template of existing libraries. When publishing a form to a library, you can include fields from the form as column data in the library, making it easy to see the form's information. By exporting the library metadata to an Excel spreadsheet using techniques discussed in Chapter 7, you can further analyze the data collected from the forms using a tool you are familiar with.

If you need to use a form with more than one library or more than one site, you can publish the form as a content type to a site. Content types published to a site become available to libraries not only in that site but also in any child sites. By publishing to the top-level site of the site collection, you can make the content type available to all sites in the collection.

Finally, I introduced you to the use of SharePoint Designer to create workflows. While SharePoint Designer replaces Microsoft FrontPage as Microsoft's web page designer, SharePoint Designer offers more than just web page creation. It supports the ability to create workflows visually that you can associate with specific lists/libraries in your SharePoint site. It uses a non-programming approach with point-and-click options to build the workflow. SharePoint Designer then attaches the workflow to the selected list so you do not have to do any configuration to make the workflow operate with your form in your SharePoint library.

There are many other features and capabilities to building workflows in SharePoint Designer such as prompting for parameters when your workflow begins and the use of variables within the workflow. In addition, as mentioned at the beginning of the workflow section, SharePoint Designer lets you create workflows that you can apply to more than just a single list. You can even build workflows not associated with a list that you can manually execute at any time. However, it is my hope that you see the potential of building workflows using SharePoint Designer not just for your form libraries associated with InfoPath but for any of your lists and libraries.

CHAPTER 11

■■■

Peer-to-Peer Collaboration with SharePoint Workspace

If you are wondering what SharePoint Workspace is, you are not alone. SharePoint Workspace is the successor to Microsoft Office Groove 2007. You say that does not help much either? Well, Groove 2007 probably should have gotten the award as the newest and least-known addition to the Microsoft Office 2007 Suite. SharePoint Workspace provides you with a personal collaboration area where you can bring together small teams from within or even outside your company. You do not even need SharePoint to use it, but you must have a version of Office that includes SharePoint Workspace. You can even invite friends and neighbors into your shared folder, your shared workspace, or even a shared SharePoint site. Depending on the type of workspace you create, you can:

- Share documents

- Create calendars

- Participate in discussions

- Create forms to manage lists

- Track issues

- Plan meetings

- Share pictures

- And more

The fact that you can do all of these things without involving your IT department or hiring outside consultants puts you in control of sharing information with people outside of your normal network, extending your ability to collaborate with anyone having Internet access. You do not have to worry about firewalls, servers, or security. In addition, since you can invite anyone to join your workspace-based collaboration site and share your files, you can communicate with anyone inside or outside of your company. You can even use your Workspace account between multiple computers as a way to share files and sites between your machines at work and at home.

With all that said, perhaps the greatest advantage of SharePoint Workspace is that it allows you to collaborate with temporary employees or consultants who need to share files and be involved in meetings. Because of their short-time status, your IT department may choose not to add them to the authenticated users of your corporate network, but SharePoint Workspace can help you collaborate with them anyway.

Digging into SharePoint Workspace

First, you should know that you might already have SharePoint Workspace loaded on your computer. Together with OneNote, SharePoint Workspace is now part of Microsoft Office Professional Plus 2010. If you have not installed it yet, go back to your installation disks and modify your options to install it. If you have one of the other versions of Microsoft Office 2010 that does not include SharePoint Workspace, you can still obtain it as a stand-alone application.

Once installed, you can choose from two ways to begin using Workspace:

- Create your own workspace and invite others to it.

- Be invited to participate in someone else's workspace.

Actually, you must do one other thing first. You must create a SharePoint Workspace account with at least one identity so others can find you or so you can create a workspace for yourself. Your Workspace account resides on your computer and holds your identity along with references to workspaces to which you belong, contact information for other members in your workspace, "keys," and information about the devices you use.

Creating Your Workspace Account

When you first start using SharePoint Workspace, the **Account Configuration Wizard** opens, as shown in Figure 11-1, giving you the option of creating a new Workspace account or using an existing account, perhaps from another computer. Let's assume for now that you want to create a new account.

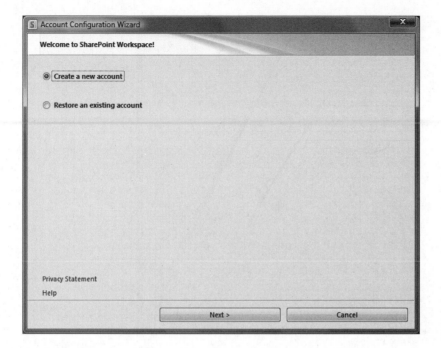

Figure 11-1. Create a SharePoint Workspace on your computer.

The second option allows you to restore an existing account. Once you have created an account on one machine, you can save the account definition file and restore it to another machine effectively adding your existing account to that machine.

When you create a new account, the next screen, shown in Figure 11-2, asks you for your name and e-mail address to create a new account. You can also create an account using an **Account Configuration Code**. This latter option, shown as the second option button in Figure 11-2, relates to corporations who may be hosting a Groove server internally and who have an administrator who supplies new accounts. Let's assume this is not the case and just enter your name and e-mail address. The account wizard uses this information to create an account to identify you and to allow you to access the workspaces where you become a member.

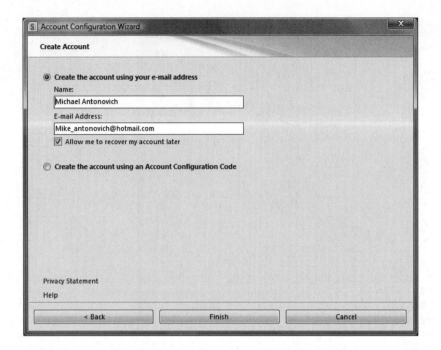

Figure 11-2. Enter your name and e-mail address to uniquely identify your account.

After a few moments, your account creation is complete and the **Workspace Launchbar** appears.

After you create your account, you can open the **Workspace Launchbar** either from the **Start** menu or from the icon that SharePoint Workspace added to the **Quick Launch** bar in the bottom right of your desktop. Using either method, the Workspace Launchbar looks like Figure 11-3. As with all other Microsoft Office products, the Workspace Launchbar has a ribbon.

■ **Tip** If you already have Workspace installed on your computer, you can create a new account any time by clicking the **Workspace** icon in the **Quick Launch** bar of your computer and selecting the **New Account** option. This command opens the wizard described in the "Creating Your Workspace Account" sidebar.

Figure 11-3. The SharePoint Workspace Launchbar dialog

The **File** ribbon lets you open the backstage area. The **Home** ribbon shows your current workspaces divided into four categories. The first category, **New**, shows all recently created workspaces. The **Active** category shows workspaces where at least one member is currently logged in. The **Unread** category lists workspaces that have unread items, and the **Read** category shows workspaces with no unread items. The **Home** ribbon also includes options to search your workspace and to add new contacts. The **View** ribbon defines how the Workspace displays information.

You can now create your own workspace and invite others to join it. Begin by returning to the **Home** ribbon and clicking on the **New** button in the **Workspaces** category. This action displays the drop-down menu shown in Figure 11-4. Notice that you can choose from three types of workspaces. Let's begin with the simplest workspace, the **Shared Folder**.

Figure 11-4. Create a Shared Folder workspace.

The **Shared Folder** workspace lets you share one of the folders on your system with other people and computers. At first, you might think that this feature is no different from using a network file share, and perhaps if you only want to share your folder with other people in your company a network file share would suit your needs. However, if you want to share files with people outside of your company or between a work computer and a home computer, the Shared Folder lets you bridge your shared folder with the outside world.

After clicking the **Shared Folder** option from the **New Workspace** drop-down menu, the first dialog that appears asks you to provide a name for the Shared Folder, as shown in Figure 11-5. Note that the name supplied here does not have to be same name as the folder itself; you can provide any name that uniquely identifies the folder.

Figure 11-5. Provide a name for the Shared Folder workspace.

■ **Tip** Choose your Shared Folder name carefully because this name becomes the default name for the folder on the computer of all the other contacts for this shared workspace.

Next, you can assign this folder name as an alias to an existing folder on your computer or you can create a new folder with this name on your computer's desktop or any other location, as shown in Figure 11-6. Again, you should consider your options carefully because, after you create the workspace links and invite others to join your workspace, you cannot move the folder to another location without having to reinvite all of the users to the new location. For this example, I will choose an existing folder.

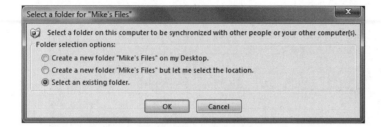

Figure 11-6. Select an existing or new folder for the Shared Folder workspace.

When you click **OK**, Workspace displays a dialog that lets you browse for the folder you want to share, as shown in Figure 11-7. For this example, I selected a folder named Chapter 11 in my **Documents** folder.

Figure 11-7. Dialog to select the specific folder to use when using an existing folder

When you click **OK**, Workspace opens a modified Windows Explorer-like view of the selected folder with the addition of a panel of options on the left side. This panel, shown in Figure 11-8, begins with the name assigned to the folder. It then lists all of the current people who have the workspace open. Of course, since I just created this workspace, I am the only one currently in it. Looking at the other options, you can see that you can invite other people and computers to join your workspace. You can also show the properties of the shared folder, determine whether to synchronize the files in the folder with others, and set the way Workspace downloads changes made to any of the files in the folder.

In the second area, you can open a chat window with others currently active in the workspace. Again, since I just created this workspace, there are no others to chat with yet. Finally, the third area lets you set various properties of the shared folder. You can mark the entire folder read or unread and you can set alerts for this folder. If you click on any of the files in the right window, this panel changes to show the name, type, and size of the select file. You can also mark the individual file as read or unread. If you select multiple files, the panel tells you how many files you selected and the total size of the selected files.

Figure 11-8. Your selected folder as seen through your Shared Folder workspace

Of course, the whole purpose of a shared folder is to allow someone else to share the folder with you. Therefore, click the **Invite someone** option in the **Synchronization Tasks** portion of the panel. You could also go back to the Launchbar and select **Add Contact** from the **Actions** group of the **Home** ribbon. Either method opens the dialog shown in Figure 11-9. In the **To** field, enter the e-mail address of the person you want to invite to your workspace. If you have more than one person to invite, click the **Add More** option to the right of the **To** field. This action opens a dialog box that lets you add as many additional recipients as you want. For each one, you must identify an e-mail address, either business or personal. You can also supply a city and state value for each recipient. The **Search for User** button allows you to search your Outlook Contacts list for a user based on a partial entry of the user's name.

Next, you must assign the user a role. You have three roles to choose from: Manager, Participant, and Guest. By default, people you invite to your workspace receive the role **Participant**, which permits them to do anything on the site except change the roles of other members. In other words, they can add and remove tools and invite new members to your workspace. People with the **Guest** role do not have any of these permissions, and can only read information from the workspace. Finally, anyone allotted the **Manager** role can do everything a Participant can as well as modify the permissions assigned to each of the roles. Keep in mind that you will assign everyone in the current invitation the selected role. If you want to give some people a different role, you must send them a separate invitation so that you can select the desired role for them.

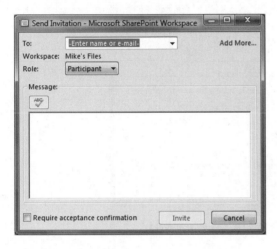

Figure 11-9. Form used to send an invitation to someone to become a member of your workspace

Next you can enter a message to the people you are inviting to your workspace perhaps telling them why you are inviting them. After you enter your message, click the small button in the upper-left corner above the message area to spell check it. You should always spell check messages before you send them so simple spelling errors do not embarrass you.

The last option in the panel is a check box that asks whether you require acceptance confirmation before the invited person can join the workspace. You can choose to select this check box or leave it blank. If you leave it blank, Workspace displays the dialog in Figure 11-10 anyway.

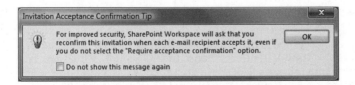

Figure 11-10. The Invitation Acceptance Confirmation message

If you do not want to keep seeing this reminder every time you invite another person to one of your workspaces, click the box at the bottom of this dialog to not show this message again. At this point, Workspace generates an e-mail similar to the one shown in Figure 11-11 to each invitee. As each person accepts the invitation, you will receive an e-mail reconfirming the invitation.

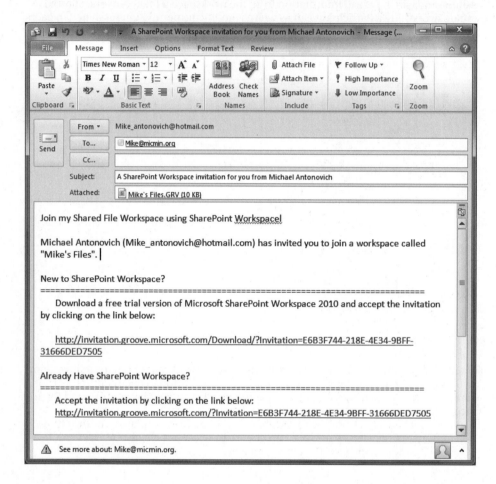

Figure 11-11. The message SharePoint Workspace generates to send as an invitation to your workspace

As shown in Figure 11-11, the invitee can accept the invitation in two different ways. If he has never used SharePoint Workspace and does not have a copy of it, he can choose the first option, which allows him to download a free trial version of SharePoint Workspace. If the invitee already has SharePoint Workspace, he can accept the invitation to the workspace using the second link. This action shows the dialog in Figure 11-12.

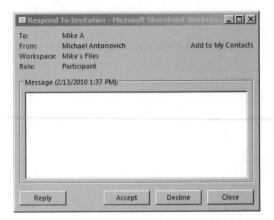

Figure 11-12. The dialog that the invitee sees allowing him to accept or decline the membership invitation

Note that the invitee can accept or decline the invitation to join the workspace using the buttons at the bottom of the dialog. He can also include a message back to you.

No matter whether he accepts or declines, Workspace sends a message back to you to confirm the acceptance. SharePoint Workspace tries to send this message back via the Groove infrastructure. Therefore, you should monitor your SharePoint Workspace account for incoming messages. In the meantime, the invited person does not see the shared workspace. In fact, he receives the message shown in Figure 11-13 when he sends the acceptance back.

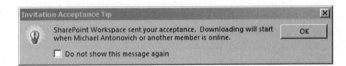

Figure 11-13. Confirmation to the invitee that his acceptance has been sent to the workspace owner

Incoming messages and other actions that you must respond to appear in a box displayed in the lower-right corner of the screen when you hover your mouse over the **SharePoint Workspace** icon in the notification area of the task bar. When a message first appears, it slides up above the **Quick Launch** bar. If you miss the arrival of the message, you can go back and click on the SharePoint Workspace icon to show all messages that require a response, as shown in Figure 11-14.

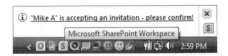

Figure 11-14. Message in the workspace owner's task bar

When you see the incoming message with the invitee's acceptance, click it to open and confirm the invitation. Within the confirm dialog box, as shown in Figure 11-15, click the **Confirm** button to complete the process. As each invitee accepts your invitation to your workspace, his name appears in the **Workspace Members** list on the left-side panel beneath the name of the shared folder.

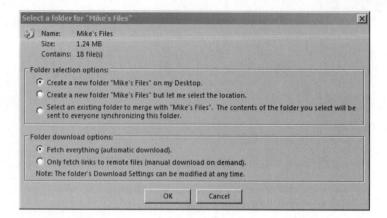

Figure 11-15. After the owner confirms the invitee's acceptance, the invitee determines where to create the shared folder.

In addition, Workspace begins to transfer a copy of the fields to the invitee's computer. The invitee has the option of creating a file with the shared folder's name on their desktop or at some other location. He can also choose to merge the shared folder with the contents of another folder on his machine. However, if he does this, Workspace shares the contents of this folder with all of the other workspace members. This may be exactly what you need to do to perform an initial synchronization of files with all members of the workspace. The other set of options in this dialog lets the invitee determine whether he wants to download everything automatically or whether he just wants to see links to files and then download only those that he wants to open. Users with slow connections may prefer this second option.

After Workspace finishes transferring the folder, the invited member can view the contents of the folder just as if it were any other folder on his computer, as shown in Figure 11-16. Because it looks like any folder, the user can drag files from other folders directly into this shared folder. He can also create new files in this folder using any application including the entire Microsoft Office suite. For example, in Figure 11-16, the invitee can click and drag the Word document named Doc1.docx over to Mike's Folder. When he drops the file here, I, as manager of the shared folder, can open the folder and see the file Doc1.docx. If the workspace had other members, they would be able to see the new Word document as well.

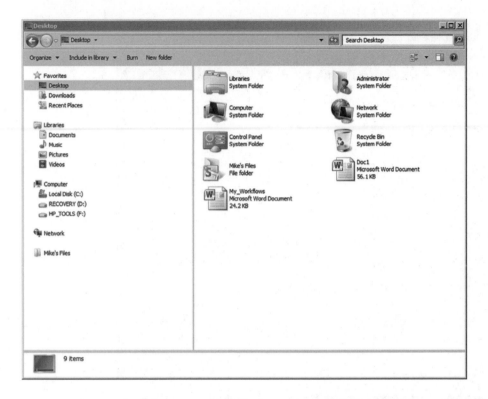

Figure 11-16. Use Windows Explorer to drag files from other directories to the new shared folder.

When I (and others) open SharePoint Workspace, not only do I see the new Word document, but Workspace marks the file with an overlay icon of a folder with a green circle to indicate that the file is new and has not yet been read, as shown in Figure 11-17. After I read the file (or even if I do not read it), I can click the option in the **Files and Folders** section of the panel on the left to mark the file as read. If you need to go back to review any file in a shared folder, you can select the file and then mark it as unread so it places the folder icon with the green circle back over the lower-left portion of the file icon.

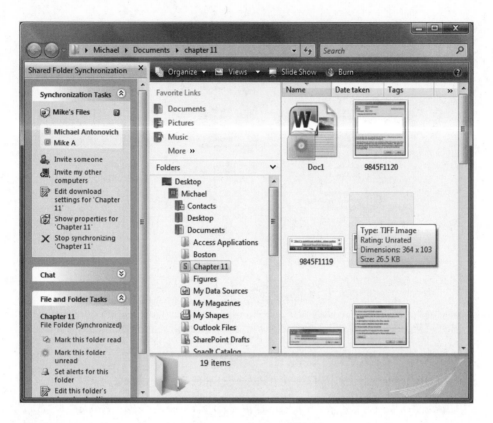

Figure 11-17. Changed or new additions to the shared folder show the Unread icon over their default icon.

Adding Your Account to Other Computers

In the previous section, you saw how easy it is to invite others to join your Shared Folder workspace. If you have multiple computers, you can also add your account to each computer so that you can share the same folder no matter which computer you are using, for example, you could include your account on both your home and work computer so that you can see the shared workspaces wherever you are. SharePoint Workspace makes it easy to add your account information to other computers by clicking the option **Invite my other computers** from the **Synchronization Tasks** section of the panel on the left side of the page, as shown in Figure 11-17. Clicking this option displays the dialog shown in Figure 11-18.

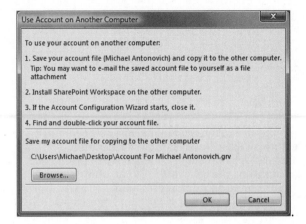

Figure 11-18. Instructions on how to transfer your SharePoint Workspace account to another machine

This dialog gives you instructions on how to copy the account file from your current computer on to another computer, which, of course, must have SharePoint Workspace installed on it. You can quickly set up multiple computers to use your account to view and work with any of the workspaces created by SharePoint Workspace. Clicking **OK** displays the **Save Account As dialog** asking you for the file name to use for the account, as shown in Figure 11-19.

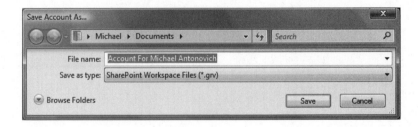

Figure 11-19. Save your SharePoint Workspace account to a file that you can transfer to another machine.

It suggests a file name that includes your user name, but you can change the name and even change the location where Workspace creates the file. When you click **Save**, Workspace prompts you for one more piece of information, as shown in Figure 11-20. It needs a password to protect the account information so that, should anyone else get a copy of your account file, they will not be able to install it on their computer.

Figure 11-20. *Provide a password to protect your account file.*

Copy the file created here to the other computer. Then to add the account file to a new computer, start SharePoint Workspace and select the option **Restore an Existing Account** in the **Account Configuration Wizard** as shown in the "Creating Your Workspace Account" sidebar. When prompted, refer to the account field copied to the new computer supplying the password. You can now reference your shared folder from multiple computers using your common account information.

Creating a Groove Workspace

Now that you know how to create a Shared Folder workspace, let's look at the next level, a Groove workspace. A Groove workspace differs from a Shared Folder workspace in that it adds several more tools that you can share with other members of the workspace. Going back to the Launchpad, open the **New** drop-down menu and select **Groove Workspace**, as shown in Figure 11-21.

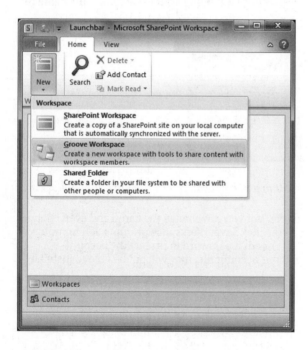

Figure 11-21. *Create a Groove workspace.*

In the next dialog that appears, you have the opportunity to name your workspace. Perhaps more importantly, you can create your workspace in the 2010 style or revert to a compatible 2007 style to allow potential members who may not have migrated to 2010 yet to join and contribute.

Then, SharePoint Workspace creates your workspace. For the example here, I will use the 2010 style. If you need to use the 2007 style, please refer to my previous book *Office and SharePoint 2007 User's Guide* (Apress, 2008). Figure 11-22 shows the open workspace.

Figure 11-22. A New Documents folder begins with a Root Folder in the Groove workspace.

Notice the panel on the left side of the screen. The first section, named **Content**, lists the available tools that you can use in this workspace. By default, Groove Workspace includes three tools: Documents, Discussion, and Calendar. However, a Groove workspace provides additional tools that you can add to your workspace from the **Workspace** ribbon. I will discuss those tools in more detail a little later.

The second panel section, named **Members**, displays a list of the members currently active in the workspace in the **In Workspace** group. If a member is currently on her computer and connected to the Internet, but does not have the workspace open, her name appears in the **Online** group instead. Finally, if the user is not connected to the Internet, her name appears in the **Offline** group.

Of course, you will not see any members other than yourself until you start to invite other people to become members of your workspace. Even if they are already members of your **Shared Folder** workspace, you must reinvite them to your Groove workspace. In fact, each invitation applies only to one specific workspace, so, if you have more than one Groove workspace, you must invite members to each one. To invite a person to your workspace, right-click on the **Members** group header in the left panel and select **Invite to Workspace** from the available commands, as shown in Figure 11-23. You can also click on **Invite Members** from the **Workspace** ribbon.

Figure 11-23. Invite other members to your workspace.

Because you have seen how to invite others to your workspace site in the Shared Folder section of this chapter, I will skip over the details here because the process is the same. Let's instead continue on to the initial content tools provided in the Groove workspace.

Documents Tool

The Documents content tool, like the Shared Folder workspace, allows you to drag files and even folders from your local desktop or mapped drives and drop them into the workspace's Root Folder. This tool makes it easy to share non-SharePoint documents with other members of your workspace. In addition to the typical properties you expect from a directory of files, it has a **Modified By** column to tell you the name of the last person who modified the file. Unlike Groove 2007, the new version of Groove Workspace immediately updates the **Modified By** column with the name of the member as soon as she opens a file to edit it. It also displays a small green icon in the first column of the detail row to indicate that the new version of the file is unread. Then, when the other member saves her changes, Workspace shows a small page-like icon with a down pointing arrow to indicate that a new version is available. To get the latest version, open the **Error Tools Resolve** ribbon and click the **Get Available Updates** command, as shown in Figure 11-24. Groove Workspace generally does not synchronize file changes back to the original folder from which you copied the file. If you want a local copy of the file, you must copy the file back from the workspace to the local drive yourself.

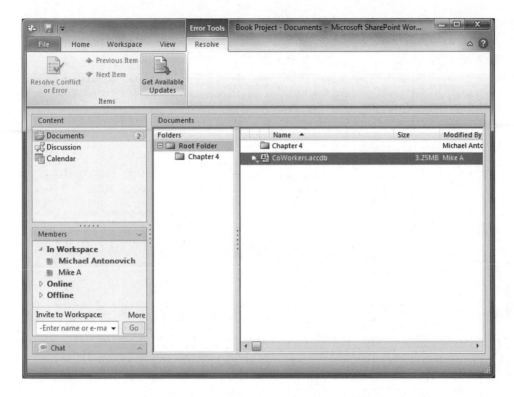

Figure 11-24. Update your Documents folder with changes made by other workspace members.

Discussion Tool

The Discussion tool lets you hold multiple discussions with members of your workspace. Each discussion begins with a single topic. Generally, the purpose of a topic is to introduce the subject of the discussion, such as a question, an observation, an opinion, or just about anything. Once posted to the discussion area, other members of the workspace can add their own comments called **Replies** to the **Topic**. Then the original person who posted the topic might reply to the reply and someone else might reply to them just as a discussion amongst peers might occur in a meeting room, but without having to be physically in the same location. Even more interesting is that the discussion does not limit participation to people who are active at the time of the posting of the original topic. People might log into your workspace and reply to a topic hours or even days after you post the original topic. Figure 11-25 shows a typical set of discussion topics with threaded replies.

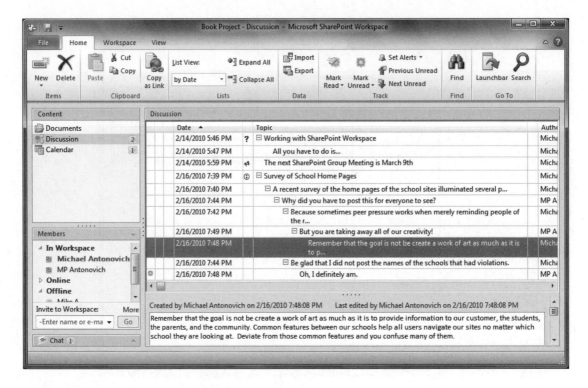

Figure 11-25. Discussion threads with indented replies

Discussions can branch into many different threads as members of the workspace reply to different replies within the discussion topic. As you can see, this tool works in a similar way to the **Discussion Board** list discussed in Chapter 2. You might even think of the **Discussion** tool as a structured chat feature that does not require members to be online, much less to be in the workspace to participate. Of course, resyncing of these responses only occurs when the member returns to an online state.

In some other ways, the **Discussion** tool creates an environment that resembles a blog, in that each member can post new topics in a particular discussion at any time. Members can also return to existing topics to add responses to the topic or even to add responses to responses. Workspace tracks responses in a tree-like structure, indenting each response level a small amount to show the relationship. A small box with a plus or minus sign appears to the left of each topic or response that has a child response. You can click this box to alternately show and hide the rest of the tree beneath that point. If you have no interest in a topic, you can minimize the space it uses by clicking the box to close all responses in that branch. Finally, discussion entries support rich text formatting as well as the ability to add hyperlinks to the text and spell checking, as shown in Figure 11-26.

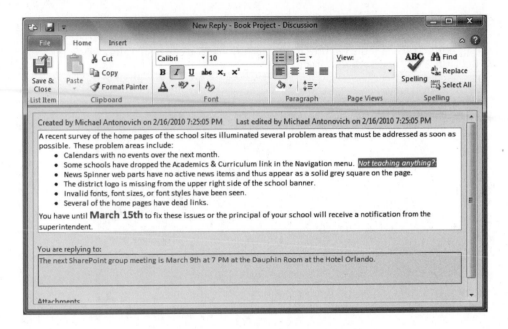

Figure 11-26. Create a Discussion reply with custom formatting of text.

Before leaving the Discussion tool, here are a few other suggestions on things you can do with it:

- Only managers can delete discussion topics and replies. So, unless you are a manager in the workgroup, be careful what you post.

- You can display the **Reading Pane** for the topics on the bottom or on the right side of the window, or you can turn it off completely. To change the position of the reading pane, open the **View** ribbon and look for the **Reading Pane** command in the **Layout** group.

- When you have a highly branched discussion topic, you can quickly open or close all of the branches by using the **Expand All** or **Collapse All** options in the **Lists** group of the **Home** ribbon.

- There are several other views available for the **Discussion** tool. However, only the '**by Topic**' view displays the topics and replies as threaded.

- Once you post a topic or reply, you cannot edit the contents of the message.

- If the text for a reply or topic is long, the list may truncate the text after a point with ellipses (…). To see the full text, click on the topic or reply and view the full text in the **Reading Pane**.

- You can also search for replies or topics with specific word phrases.

- You can mark individual topics and replies as read or unread.

Calendar Tool

The Calendar tool supports a subset of the features found in Outlook. You can display its calendar in month, as shown in Figure 11-27, week, or day mode.

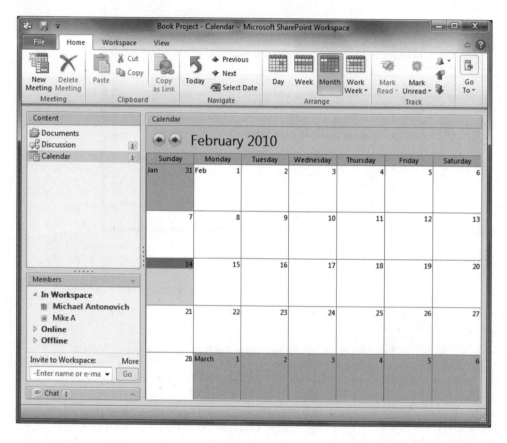

Figure 11-27. The Groove Workspace Calendar tool

You can add meetings to the calendar defining a subject, a start date and time, an end date and time, and details about the appointment. Meetings in Groove Workspace roughly correspond to what you call appointments in Outlook's calendar. With this version of Groove Workspace, you can even create recurring events just as you currently do in Outlook. That is a great feature for teams who have regular meetings every day, every week, or even every other week. In fact, you should be able to schedule most regularly defined periods. You can even select attendees from the current members of your workspace. Figure 11-28 shows a completed meeting entry.

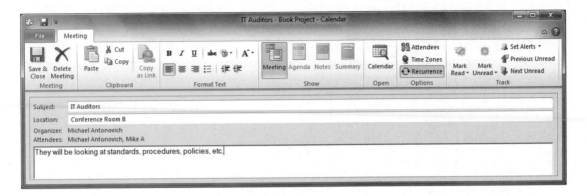

Figure 11-28. Defining a meeting in Groove Workspace looks a lot like defining a meeting in Outlook.

If you go back and edit any individual meeting occurrence (not a meeting series), you can also show separate pages within the meeting where you can define the agenda, add notes during the meeting, and even create a summary of what happened after the meeting. These additional options appear in the **Show** group of the **Meeting** ribbon. Groove Workspace does not enable these options if you edit a meeting series.

Perhaps you may be somewhat disappointed to learn that you cannot transfer appointments between Outlook and your Groove workspace and keep them synchronized. However, if you need to track appointments related to the members in your workspace, especially if those members work outside of your organization, this tool might meet your needs.

Chat Tool

While **Chat** is not specifically a Groove Workspace tool like the first three described above, it is a very useful feature that you might want to explore in more detail, even before trying out some other tools. You can chat with any member currently in your workspace. If he is online, but not in the workspace, you can send that user a message by right-clicking his name in the **Members** portion of the panel and then clicking **Send Member Message**. You can also send messages to offline members. However, they will not receive the message until after the next time they go online. The **Chat** header in the left panel will flash when it receives new chat messages.

The **Chat** area only uses a few of the features in the ribbons at the top of the workspace, such as **Properties** and **Alerts** in the **Workspace** ribbon. However, you do have a button beneath the text box where you enter your chat message that allows you to spell check it before you send it.

What may not be obvious is that there is another button on the bottom right of the Chat area, which displays as a down-pointing arrow similar to the one used on a drop-down list. However, clicking on this button opens a menu of formatting options, as shown in Figure 11-29.

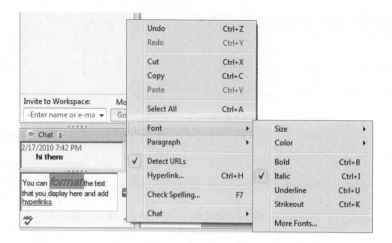

Figure 11-29. Defining a font style for text in a Chat message

You can cut and paste text, change the font style of selected text and paragraphs, add hyperlinks, check spelling, and even manage the chat transcript to print, delete, or search it. The one feature that you may wish you had is the ability to copy the transcript of the chat to a file. However, you can overcome even this minor problem by selecting all of the text in the top control of the Chat area with your mouse, copying it to the clipboard, and then pasting it in Notepad or your choice of text editor.

Overall, the Chat area is a functional tool. It allows you to communicate with other members of your workspace in real time. In many ways, it is very similar to using an instant-messaging program.

Now that we have seen the classic default tools for your workspace, let's open the **Workspace** ribbon and click on the **Add** command to see what other tools you have available.

Notepad Tool

The **Notepad** tool allows you to record text notes. To open this tool, just right-click anywhere in the blank section of the Content panel. A popup menu lets you add a new tool to the content area and change the view order of the tools. As you position your mouse over the **Add New Tool** menu item, a flyout menu appears with a list of the available tools. Once you have added the Notepad to your content area, you can begin adding notes. You can also achieve the same result by going to the **Workspace** ribbon and selecting **Add** from the **Tools** group and then selecting the specific tool you want to add.

Each note must have a name which you might think of as a title. Within the body of the note, you can add only text. However, unlike using the Notepad tool in the operating system, this Notepad lets you style individual words (or characters) in the text as well as add hyperlinks within the text. It also allows you to specify different line justifications by paragraph and to create indented and bulleted sections. In addition to using the ribbon option, you can access any of the styling features including hyperlinking to other sites, spell checking of your text by right-clicking anywhere in the text area while editing your note, and selecting the appropriate option from the pop-up menu.

Figure 11-30 shows a typical example of a note within the Notepad. Notice the three buttons in the upper left. The first button opens and closes the page list. Each note uses a separate page within Notepad. Using the page list, you can quickly locate and open notes based on their name. You can also navigate through your notes by using the second and third button in this area.

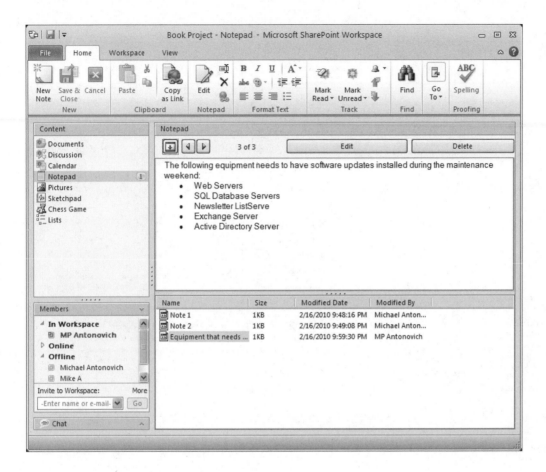

Figure 11-30. *Add notes to the Notepad tool.*

Pictures Tool

The **Pictures** tool lets you include images saved in JPG and BMP formats to your workspace and share them with other members. Once it is loaded into your Groove workspace, you can rename the image, export another member's image to your local hard drive, delete the image from your workspace, and navigate between images. You cannot edit images directly within Groove Workspace. Figure 11-31 shows a typical **Pictures** tool with several pictures in it.

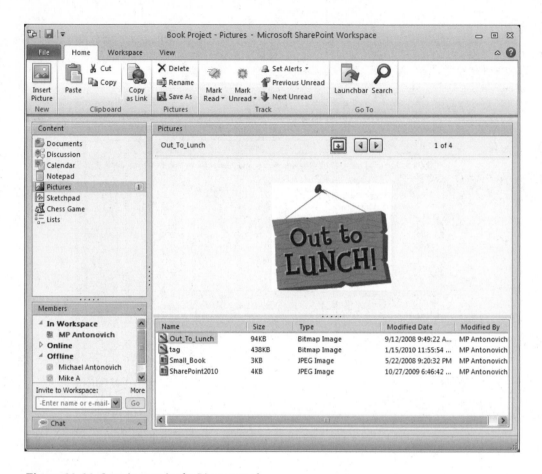

Figure 11-31. Save images in the Pictures tool.

Sketchpad Tool

The **Sketchpad** tool allows you to create simple sketches using drawing tools such as Pencil, Line, Rectangle, Ellipse, Polygon, and Textbox. One interesting feature of this tool is that it lets you begin with a background image (JPG or BMP) and then draw over the top of it. You may find this capability useful to annotate images that you share with other members. However, the tool does not provide a way to export the final sketch. Even the copy-and-paste feature only works within Sketchpad, although you can copy and paste your sketch additions from one sketch page to another. In addition, there is no undo feature and there is no easy way to fill a free-form area with a color. However, other than those concerns, Sketchpad could prove useful for creating some simple illustrations to explain a point. Figure 11-32 shows an example of a sketchpad image that may suggest to other team members the design for a needed report.

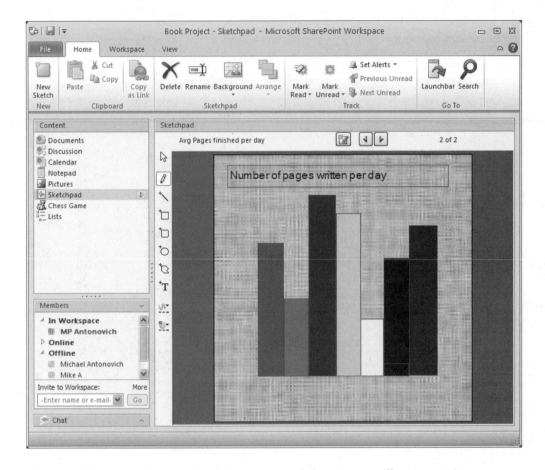

Figure 11-32. Use the Sketchpad tool to create a quick drawing or to illustrate a point.

■ **Tip** If you have a third-party screen capture application or if you use Vista, you can use the Snipping tool to capture the screen and crop the image before saving the image to a file or pasting it into another application.

Chess Tool

Honestly, this is not so much a tool as a way for members to spend some quality downtime playing a simple game of chess with each other after a hard day working on their project tasks. Figure 11-33 shows an example of a game in progress between two workspace members. It is White's turn and Black is about to lose.

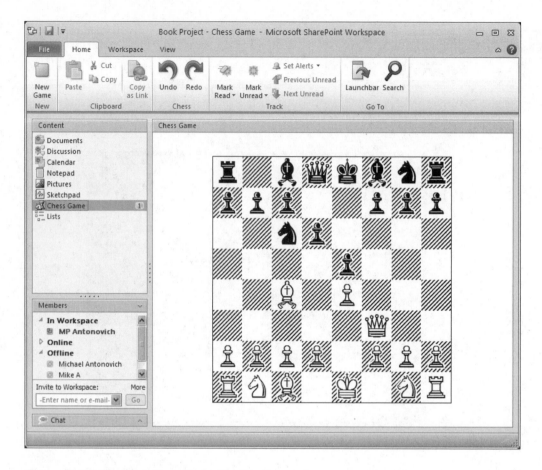

Figure 11-33. The Chess Game tool—Black is about to lose.

By the way, this tool is a very simple implementation of chess that does not validate your move, does not know when you place the opponent's king in check, and it does not know when the checkmate occurs.

Lists Tool

Lists are the last tool that you can use in a Groove workspace that I will cover. It is perhaps the most complex tool within the workspace because it lets you create custom document forms using InfoPath that members of your workspace can fill in to create the list. You can complete most form designs without resorting to coding or development skills. Lists support several different types of fields, styles, and views. Groove Workspace imports data from a list data archive (.gax) which is the same format that the workspace uses to export list data. Therefore, you do have a way to transfer data from one list to another. The list tool cannot read data from other formats, but you can create multiple views to sort and display the data.

The first thing that appears when you create a new list is a window informing you that SharePoint Workspace Lists use Microsoft Office InfoPath to create data input form, as shown in Figure 11-34. When designing a form, you can include multiple view, transforms, sorts, and filter.

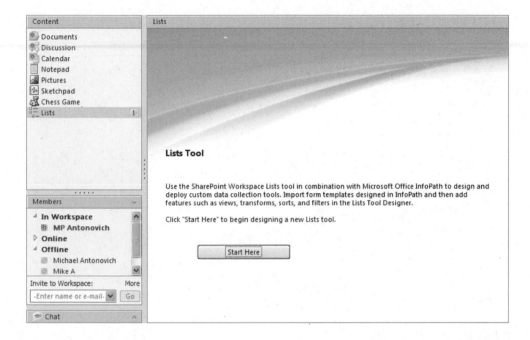

Figure 11-34. The Lists tool initial screen tells you that it uses InfoPath to create the data collection form.

When you click the **Start Here** button to begin a new list, you see the dialog that appears in Figure 11-35. You can define various settings for the list such as the default view, what field to use for search results, whether the user can create new items or change list views, and more. Obviously, you might not know how you want to set these fields when you first begin defining a form for a list. Fortunately, you can return to this dialog at any time by clicking on the **Enter Designer** button in the **Designer** group of the **View** ribbon. In addition, you can select the form and any of the views to open additional dialogs that let you change their individual properties. If you are familiar with XSL Transforms, you can define transforms for the form conditions:

- On New Record
- On Edit Record
- On Save Record

For views, you can not only define basic view properties, but also you can define filters, sort orders, and group definitions. You can also create user-friendly column headers rather than using the field names from the form.

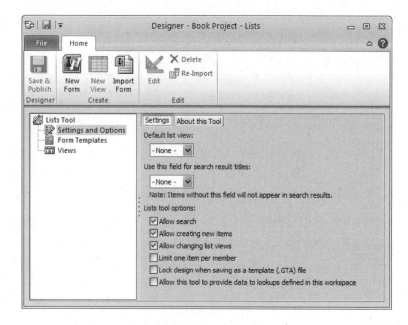

Figure 11-35. The Designer tool for Lists

If you are starting a new form, you can click the **New Form** button in the **Create** section of the **Home** ribbon, as shown in Figure 11-35. You can also import an existing form by using the **Import Form** button in the same group. You should note that you can only import forms created with InfoPath and stored as an **InfoPath Form Template (*.xsn)**. Figure 11-36 shows a simple form designed in InfoPath specifically for use with a list in your workspace. Because we covered creating InfoPath forms in Chapter 9, I will not cover the steps used to create this form.

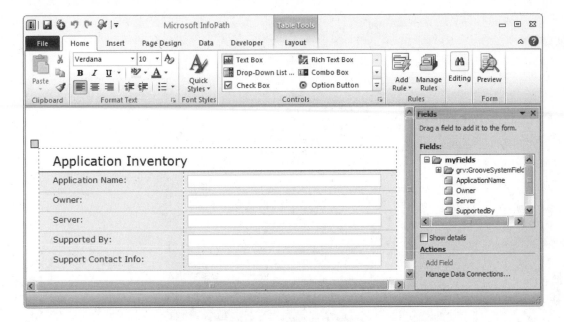

Figure 11-36. The completed InfoPath form design for the Application Inventory list

Rather than publishing the form to SharePoint or a Network share as you saw in Chapter 9, you will publish this form directly to your workspace by opening the **Publish** page in the **Backstage** area and clicking on the **SharePoint Workspace** button, as shown in Figure 11-37. Take note of the instructions under the title **Save for SharePoint Workspace**. This information applies to a choice you must make when you get back into your SharePoint workspace.

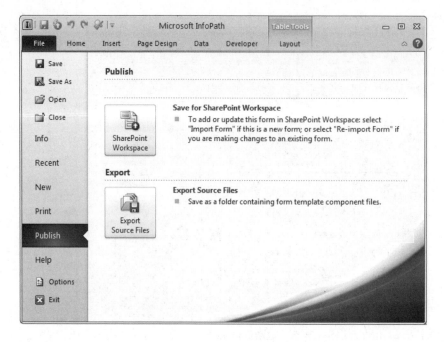

***Figure 11-37.** Publish your form back to your workspace.*

Even though you want to publish the form back to SharePoint Workspace, you must still provide a name for the form. Therefore, InfoPath displays the **Save As** dialog, as shown in Figure 11-38. You do not need to navigate to the folder or drive where you want to save the form. In fact, you want to leave the default provided by InfoPath and just change the **File Name** for the form. Then click **Save**.

Figure 11-38. Save your form to the Workspace folder.

After clicking **Save**, you should get a message informing you that the InfoPath has successfully saved the form. You should now be back in your SharePoint workspace. However, before you can begin using your form, you must still import your new form to associate it with the list. From the **Home** ribbon, select the **Import Form** button from the **Create** group. This command opens the **Open File** dialog, as shown in Figure 11-39. Again, you do not need to change any of the location references from the default Workspace folder shown. Simply select the form that you just created in InfoPath.

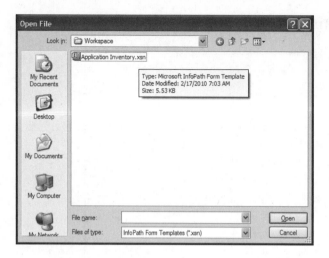

Figure 11-39. From your workspace, open the InfoPath form to use with the list.

After opening the form, you will see the **Designer** again. You first saw this dialog in Figure 11-35, but this time it opens to the **Preview** tab to show you the form. Of course, you can go to any of the other tabs to set properties or transforms. You can also go to the views associated with the form to set the view properties as suggested previously. When you finish setting the properties of the form in the **Designer** dialog, click **Save & Publish** in the **Designer** group of the **Home** ribbon to complete the process, as shown in Figure 11-40.

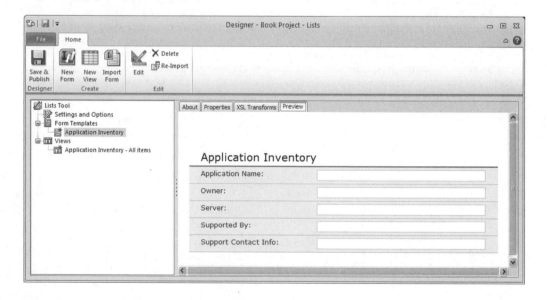

Figure 11-40. Preview of form used with list

The next time you open the list from the left panel, SharePoint Workspace displays the list columns, as shown in Figure 11-41. Of course, the list begins as an empty list. To add your first item to the list, click the **New** button in the **Items** group of the **Home** ribbon.

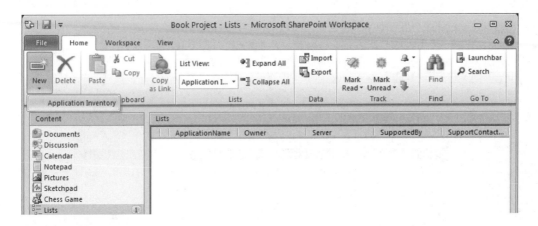

Figure 11-41. Add a new list item.

This command shows you the form you designed for this list. Simply fill in the form and click the **Save & Close** button in the **List Item** group of the **Home** ribbon, as shown in Figure 11-42.

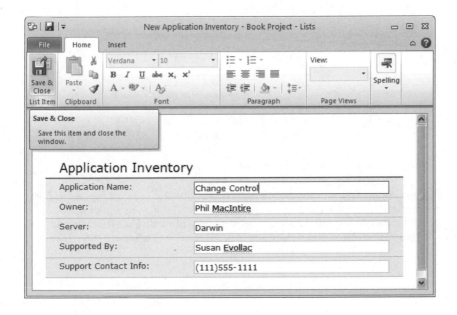

Figure 11-42. Save your list item.

After adding a second list item, your list should look similar to Figure 11-43 with the top portion of the page displaying the list items and the bottom portion of the page displaying the edit form with the column values of the currently selected list item.

Figure 11-43. The list shows both the list of items and the edit form for the currently selected item.

That is how you can not only create a list within Groove Workspace, but also create a form with one or more views that you can use to enter and see the data in the list. However, that is not all that the SharePoint Workspace application can do for you. There is one more type of workspace that you can create and use. Just to make it confusing, Microsoft decided to call this specific workspace the SharePoint Workspace.

■ **Caution** While Groove Workspaces can exceed 2 GB, performance may suffer and you will no longer be able to invite new members to your workspace.

Working with Your SharePoint Files Within SharePoint Workspace

With SharePoint Workspace, you can now create an offline version of a SharePoint site that you can work on when not connected to the network and then synchronize your changes back with the network version of the site the next time you connect. If you use SharePoint for your public-facing Internet sites, you already have the ability to navigate to those sites from any computer in the world that has Internet access, log into those Internet sites in SharePoint, and manage the content remotely. However, what about those internal sites that you might use for collaboration within your corporate firewall?

■ **Note** You can only synchronize with sites created in SharePoint Server 2010 and SharePoint Foundation 2010, not MOSS 2007.

Unless your organization supports VPN or some other connectivity tool to let you drill through the corporate firewall, you can only maintain those sites from computers within your corporate firewall. If you have more work to do on a site than you can finish before the end of your normal workday, you would have no choice but to stay late to finish the task. However, with a SharePoint Workspace, you can make a copy of the collaboration site to your laptop, disconnect from the network, and go home. Once there, you can finish the work you need to accomplish on your disconnected copy of the site on your laptop. Then, in the morning when you get into the office again, you can synchronize your changes with the version of the site in SharePoint. So let's see how you can do this.

First, open the **SharePoint Workspace Launchpad**. From the **New** command in the **Home** ribbon, select the option to create a **SharePoint Workspace**.

■ **Caution** Yes, I know it gets confusing when the name of the product is SharePoint Workspace and the tool you need to use to work with your SharePoint sites offline is also called SharePoint Workspace. In this section, I hope, through connotation, you will understand to which one I am referring.

The first dialog you see begins the process of creating a new SharePoint Workspace on your computer, as shown in Figure 11-44. To do that, you must enter the name of the workspace.

■ **Tip** If you know the network will be down for maintenance, create a SharePoint Workspace of the site you are currently working in so that you can continue working right through the network downtime rather than sitting around and talking with your friends. Right!

Figure 11-44. Select the SharePoint site you want to synchronize.

If you click the **Configure** button, the **Configure Settings** dialog shows you the name of the libraries and lists in the selected site, as shown in Figure 11-45. At this point, you can select each library and list and select in the **Download** drop-down list how you want to configure that library or list. By default, SharePoint downloads the content for all the lists and libraries. However, for a large site, this may take a very long time and may require a large amount of space on your local machine. Therefore, you can also choose to download only the headers within that library or list or you can skip the content of that library or list entirely if it is not an object you need to work with while disconnected from the network.

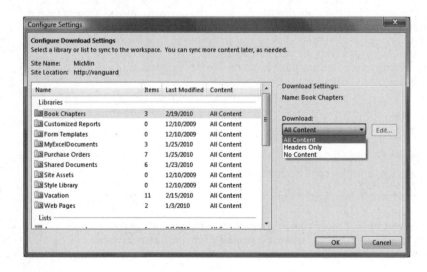

Figure 11-45. Configure the download settings for each object in the SharePoint site.

■ **Tip** You can prevent items from a SharePoint library from being shared with offline clients such as this by opening the SharePoint library with your browser and going to **Library Settings**. From the **Advanced Settings** section, you can locate the **Offline Client Availability** setting and set it to '**No**' to prevent items from this library being downloaded into SharePoint Workspace.

When you click the **OK** button, SharePoint Workspace begins the initial synchronization between your SharePoint site and your local workspace. If you choose to download all the content for all the libraries and lists, this could take several minutes. While SharePoint builds your workspace on your local machine, called initialization, and then downloads the content into this structure, you can monitor the progress, as shown in Figure 11-46.

■ **Tip** You can also create a SharePoint Workspace directly from your site by clicking on **Sync to SharePoint Workspace** from the **Site Actions** menu.

Figure 11-46. Synchronization in progress for a new SharePoint Workspace

After the synchronization process completes, you can click on the **Open Workspace** button at the bottom of the dialog. Perhaps you notice that the SharePoint Workspace skips some of the lists in the site such as calendars, surveys, site page libraries or wikis lists and libraries containing InfoPath forms. These objects appear at the bottom of the **Content** panel on the left side of the window under the heading **Available on Server**. As long as you still have a connection to your network, you can still access these lists and libraries by clicking on the list or library name. In the right side of the window, the message: This list type is not supported by SharePoint Workspace appears. Beneath this message appears a link, Open the list in a browser, which lets you open a browser window to access the content of the selected list or library.

If you open the **Sync** ribbon, you see three commands. **Sync Status** displays a dialog that informs you whether the last synchronization with each object succeeded or failed. It indicates success with the word **Synchronized**. When synchronization fails, the **Status** column generally displays a message about the failure such as:

An unknown error occurred while attempting to synchronize this tool.

As indicated by this error message, every object you synchronize between SharePoint and SharePoint Workspace is called a tool. The Groove Workspace used the same terminology for objects you created there.

The **Change Sync Settings** option opens a dialog that lets you change the settings of the current tool, as shown in Figure 11-47. All tools support the option to disconnect or reconnect with the server even while your machine remains connected to your network. However, libraries, referred to as folders here, also allow you to change the settings of the folder in terms of where to maintain the contents of that folder. It simply toggles between the current setting, which may be to download the content to your local machine, and a new setting of keeping the content for the folder on the server and removing the folder from the workspace.

Figure 11-47. Toggle the Folder Download Settings in SharePoint Workspace.

The most important **Sync** command, though, is the first button, which has two options. The first option lets you synchronize the contents of the currently selected tool. Remember that means the currently selected library or list. The second option lets you synchronize the contents of the entire workspace at once. You can synchronize your individual libraries and lists at any time. If someone has made changes to the contents of those objects, SharePoint Workspace downloads the latest version. However, let's see what happens when you edit some of the content in a downloaded library.

Editing Content in SharePoint Workspace

Just like working in SharePoint itself, when you work in SharePoint Workspace, you should check out a document before you begin to edit it when still connected to your network. If you are not connected to your network, you do not need to check out a document and, in fact, you cannot check out the document because you cannot share the SharePoint Workspace with other members. Only you can be a member of your copy of your SharePoint site. Perhaps you already suspected this because you could not find an option to invite other members to this workspace in any of the ribbons.

However, let's assume for the moment that you are still connected to the network and you want to check out a Word document before you begin to edit it. To do this, click the **Check Out** option in the **SharePoint** group of the **Home** ribbon. You can now double-click the name of your checked-out document to open and edit it in Microsoft Word.

When you finish your editing, you will want to save your changes. If you do not first select **Save** from Word's **File** menu but instead just try to close Word, Word displays a dialog asking whether you want to save your changes.

Next the dialog shown in Figure 11-48 informs you others cannot see your changes until you check the document back in. If you click **'No'**, the document remains checked out to you and stored in your SharePoint Drafts folder.

Figure 11-48. Word's reminder to check in your changes

If you click **'Yes'**, the **Check In** dialog appears letting you provide version comments for this newest version, assuming your library tracks versions. After providing comments, click **OK** to save your changes. This saves your changes to both your local copy and to the SharePoint site.

Alternatively, you could also choose the option to **Save to SharePoint** from the **Share** page of the **Backstage**, as shown in Figure 11-49. Selecting this option saves your changes directly to SharePoint (remember you are still connected to the network), bypassing your local SharePoint Workspace copy.

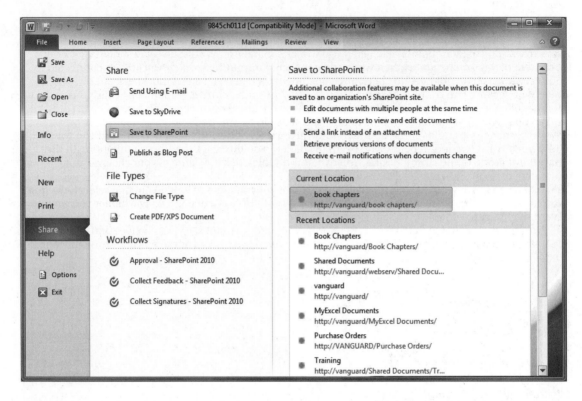

Figure 11-49. Publish your changes directly back to SharePoint, bypassing SharePoint Workspace.

If you open your SharePoint Workspace, your most recent changes would not appear. In fact, in order to get a copy of the update document back into your local copy, you must use the **Sync** option in the **Sync** ribbon to synchronize the workspace or at least the tool containing the document, as shown in Figure 11-50.

Figure 11-50. The synchronization commands from the Sync ribbon

Other Options in the SharePoint Workspace

While selecting any of the libraries in your site, you can click on the **Add Documents** option in the **Home** ribbon to add new documents to your folder. This opens the **Add Files** dialog shown in Figure 11-51.

Figure 11-51. Add files from your computer to a synchronized SharePoint library.

You can also add new documents by dragging and dropping them into the SharePoint Workspace folder from another open Windows Explorer window.

You can create additional subfolders by using the **New Folder** command in the **Home** ribbon. This command creates the new folder within whatever folder you currently have selected in the **Folders** panel. SharePoint Workspace also synchronizes these new folders back to the site.

If you delete a document from the SharePoint Workspace folder, SharePoint also deletes it from the synchronized site. However, SharePoint places the deleted document in the **Recycle Bin** allowing you to recover the file if you made a mistake. After recovering the file, though, it does not immediately appear within the SharePoint Workspace site unless you select the **Sync** tool option discussed earlier.

Working with Lists in the SharePoint Workspace

Working with lists in the SharePoint Workspace functions a little differently from working with libraries. For example, you cannot add items to the list from a folder on your desktop. That would not make sense anyway. However, you can add new items to the list by using the **New** command in the **Items** group of the **Home** ribbon. You can also delete items from a list using the **Delete** command in the same group.

Like the library items, the SharePoint site moves the deleted list item from the list to the **Recycle Bin** where you can recover it if you deleted the item by mistake. Also like the library, you must **Sync** the tool, in this case the list, to copy the recovered list item from SharePoint back to your SharePoint Workspace.

Figure 11-52 also shows that lists in a SharePoint Workspace include all the defined views created in the original SharePoint site. In fact, you can change your view of the list by selecting the view you want from the drop-down list beneath the words **List View** in the **Lists** group of the **Home** ribbon. Also, notice in this figure that your SharePoint Workspace shows the traditional list view at the top of the page and an edit form for the list in the lower portion of the page. You can make changes to the list items in this edit form and have those changes synchronized immediately back to SharePoint if you remain connected to the network, or you can synchronize them the next time you reconnect to the network.

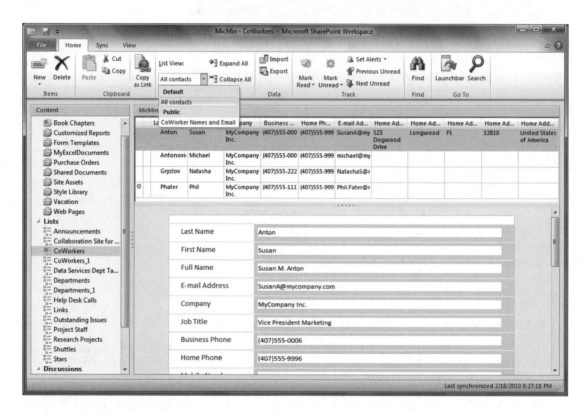

***Figure 11-52.** A SharePoint list synchronized in a SharePoint Workspace*

Working with Discussion Groups in SharePoint Workspace

Working with discussion groups in the SharePoint Workspace functions very much like the list described in the previous section. For example, you can add discussions (topics) and messages (replies) to the discussion list. Of course, unlike a discussion list in a regular SharePoint site, there is no interaction in a discussion list in SharePoint Workspace since you cannot share your SharePoint Workspace with other users. However, you can still add new items to the list by using the **New** command in the **Items** group of the **Home** ribbon. You can also delete items from a list using the **Delete** command in the same group. Like the library items, the SharePoint site moves the deleted item from the list to the **Recycle Bin** where you can recover it if you deleted the item by mistake. Of course, since SharePoint Workspace synchronizes any new topic or reply you create back to your SharePoint site immediately if you are connected with the network, others could immediate reply to your topic or reply. If you then periodically synchronize your discussion group, you still can have a discussion with other members of your SharePoint site.

Figure 11-53 shows a discussion group in a SharePoint Workspace. The SharePoint Workspace shows the traditional threaded discussion view at the top of the page and an edit form for the list in the lower portion of the page that displays the fields for the currently selected topic or reply. However, in this case, you cannot make changes to the items using this edit form.

Figure 11-53. A SharePoint Discussion Group synchronized in a SharePoint Workspace

Properties for SharePoint Workspace

Before leaving your SharePoint Workspace, let's look at some of the properties that you can set for this application. As for the other Microsoft Office 2010 applications, you access the properties for this application by opening the **File** tab and selecting the **Options** page. The **SharePoint Workspace Options** dialog then appears, as shown in Figure 11-54. The panel along the left side divides the options into major groups. The only group I want to look at here is the **General** group.

The **General** group begins with the common options that allow you to change the application's color scheme. You can also set the **ScreenTip style**. However, what I am interested in are the options unique to a SharePoint Workspace. You can find these by clicking on the **Preferences** button located in the **SharePoint Workspace Options** section.

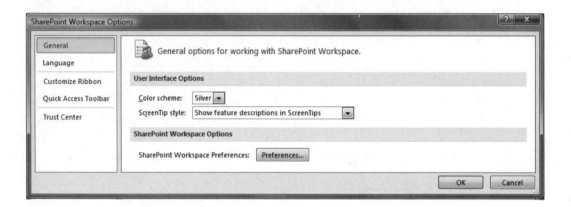

Figure 11-54. The SharePoint Workspace options page

The **Preferences** dialog consists of a six-tab page, as shown in Figure 11-55. The first tab, **Identities**, displays information about the person who created the current SharePoint Workspace which should be you. You can click the **Edit** button to add/edit additional information about yourself including where you work, your address, and your other contact information for both your business and personal views. You can choose to list your contact information in the **Public Workspace Contact Directory** or just the local network directory so that others can find you and invite you to join their workspaces. Of course, you may want to maintain your privacy and not publish more than your name. In any case, others can always invite you to their workspace if they know your e-mail address, as you saw earlier in this chapter.

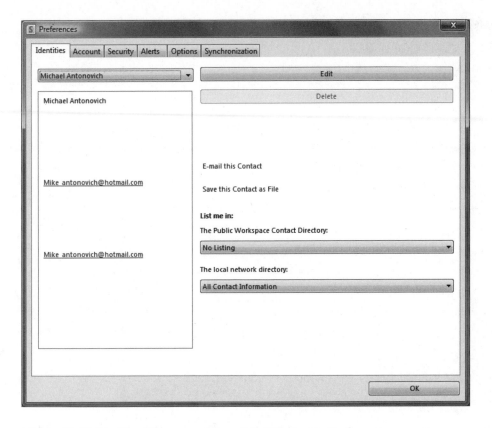

Figure 11-55. The Identities page of SharePoint Workspace Preferences

Figure 11-56 shows the second tab of the **Preferences** dialog that lets you save your account information to a file so you can transfer the account to another machine. Whether you are planning to move to another machine or not, it is good practice to keep a copy of your account information in an offline file just in case your computer crashes and you need to install your account on a reformatted machine.

If you are moving your account off the current machine, you may want to delete the account information from the current machine so that others cannot access your workspace through your account. Remember that you do not need to log into SharePoint Workspace when you start your computer because the account information file takes care of that for you automatically. Therefore, you do not want to leave this information on a machine that you are no longer going to use.

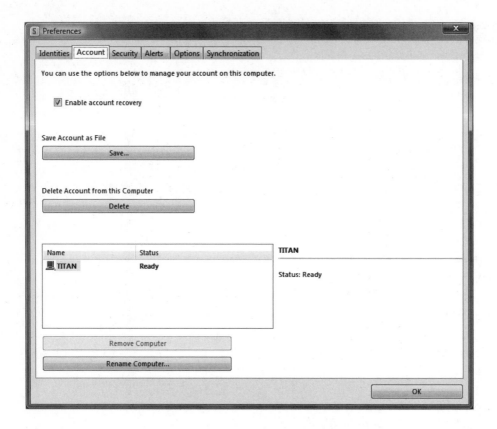

Figure 11-56. The Account page of SharePoint Workspace Preferences

Figure 11-57 shows the third tab of the **Preferences** dialog that lets you view and change some of the security settings related to the current installation of SharePoint Workspace. First, it shows you the digital fingerprint that uniquely identifies you across the entire world. You can also set communication policies. If you intend to include only employees at your company as contacts and members of your workspace, you may choose a more relaxed security. However, if you plan to use SharePoint Workspace outside of a local firewall, you may want to select a more restrictive policy.

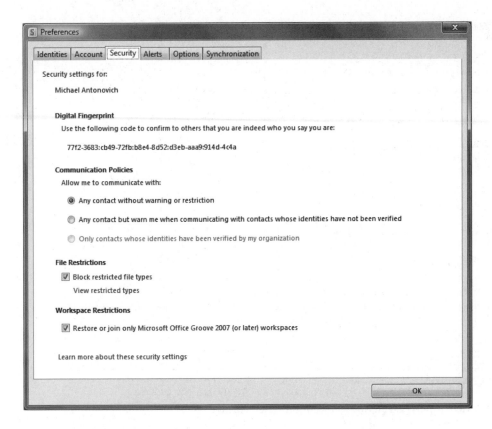

Figure 11-57. The Security page of SharePoint Workspace Preferences

The **File Restrictions** section lets SharePoint Workspace block files with specific extensions from your workspace. You can see the list shown in Figure 11-58 by clicking the hyperlink **View Restricted Types**. You cannot edit this list.

The final option, when selected, limits your system from joining any earlier version of Groove Workspace than Microsoft Office Groove 2007.

Figure 11-58. Restricted file types

The fourth tab shown in Figure 11-59 defines the default alert level that SharePoint Workspace uses when adding unread information to any of your workspaces, even those you may not currently have open. Table 11-1 shows the levels defined by SharePoint Workspace.

Table 11-1. Alert Levels

Alert Level	Alert Description
Off	Workspace displays no alerts for new or modified content
Medium	Workspace highlights new or modified content with an icon
High	Workspace highlights new or modified content with an icon and displays an alert
Auto	Similar to High but allows automatic removal of ignored unread alerts

On the bottom half of the Alerts page, you can define how long in days unread alerts remain active before SharePoint Workspace automatically removes them. If you change either the alert level or the number of days to display unread alerts, you must click the **Apply** button. If you decide you no longer want your custom changes to these two properties, you can click the **Restore Default** to return to the out-of-the-box defaults of the **Auto** level and retention of unread alerts for four days.

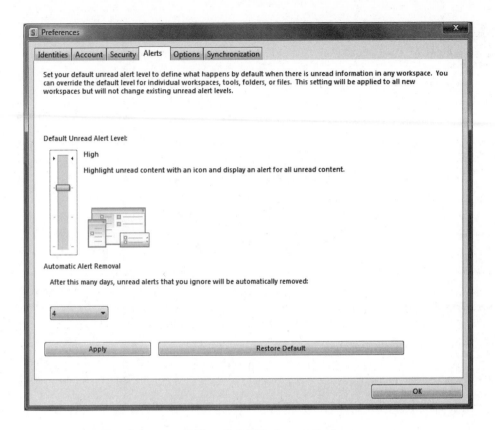

Figure 11-59. *The Alerts page of SharePoint Workspace Preferences*

Figure 11-60 shows the **Options** tab. It provides you with settings to determine whether SharePoint Workspace launches on startup of your system. You can ignore incoming messages from people you do not know and you can set your inline presence indicator to display to everyone or just members of your workspace. However, perhaps the most important setting is whether to scan incoming and outgoing files for viruses. After all, when sharing data with others, the inadvertent passing of viruses from one system to another can cause serious damage to your system.

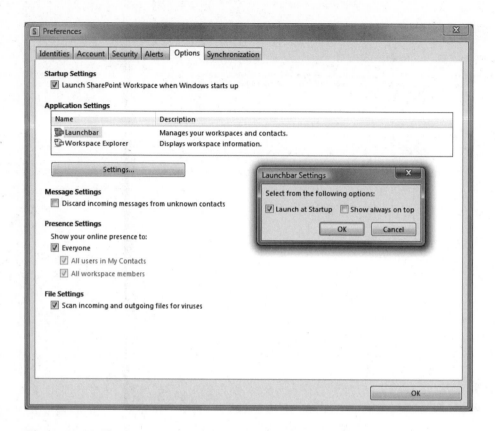

Figure 11-60. The Options page of SharePoint Workspace Preferences

The last tab in the **Preference** dialog is called **Synchronization**. Figure 11-61 shows that it allows you to share some information between computers such as Internet Explorer Favorites. It also allows you to create shortcuts in **Documents** to your **File Sharing** workspaces.

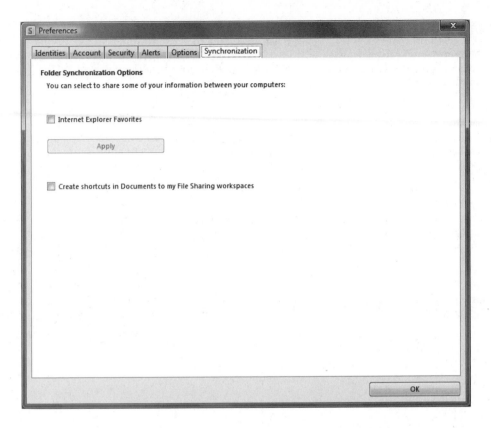

Figure 11-61. The Synchronization page of SharePoint Workspace Preferences

Summary

In this chapter, you looked at one of the newest additions to the Microsoft Office family of tools, SharePoint Workspace, previously known as Groove. SharePoint Workspace allows you to build your own personal collaboration network without needing a server or any special administration tools. As a peer-to-peer collaboration application that only requires Internet access to work, SharePoint Workspace allows you to create collaboration workspaces that include not only people that you work with, but also anyone with Internet access.

SharePoint Workspace supports three types of workspaces. The first workspace type is a simple shared folder workspace. This workspace allows you to share files of any almost any type (see the restricted file types in Figure 11-58). You can then invite other people with Internet access to become members of your workspace. These other people must have their own copy of SharePoint Workspace. While Microsoft will provide a temporary trial copy of SharePoint Workspace for them to use, if you plan on using the workspace for an extended period of time, these invited members may need to purchase a copy of SharePoint Workspace to continue participating in your workspace.

The second type of workspace corresponds to the legacy workspace created in Groove 2007 and is therefore called a Groove workspace. This workspace has many of the tools that sound a lot like similar tools in SharePoint or even Office itself. However, Groove Workspace does not provide integration with SharePoint. Nor does it integrate its tools such as its calendar with the corresponding Microsoft Office products such as Outlook as SharePoint does.

The third and final workspace type is called a SharePoint workspace and this workspace does synchronize with any SharePoint 2010 site. After creating your local workspace version of the site, you can disconnect from the network and work on the libraries and list of the site. The next time you connect to your network, SharePoint Workspace synchronizes your changes to the site. However, working offline increases the potential danger of having two or more people edit the same document at the same time. The ability to check out a SharePoint document before you disconnect from the library may limit other SharePoint users from accessing and changing documents in libraries while you have it open in your SharePoint workspace, but it does not help protect lists since you cannot lock a list. While your SharePoint Workspace recognizes potential conflicts when you attempt to save your changes, you must then determine how to reconcile your changes with those made by someone else.

Microsoft has greatly improved SharePoint Workspace since Groove 2007. SharePoint Workspace can provide an invaluable aid in sharing documents as well as calendars, issue lists, discussions, and other features with people you work with. Especially interesting is its ability to work outside of your corporate firewalls, allowing you to provide collaboration capability with external workers and consultants. SharePoint Workspace then allows you to bring a copy of a site home with you to work on documents in your library or list items rather than being chained to your desk at the office, thus making SharePoint Workspace an auxiliary tool to augment your SharePoint implementation and management.

■ ■ ■

CHAPTER 12

Additional Supporting Libraries

This last chapter examines three final library types that I have not touched on previously. You typically do not use these three libraries by themselves, but rather you use them in a support capacity with other SharePoint and Microsoft Office functionality. You will find two of these libraries only in SharePoint Enterprise edition. Therefore, if you work with a SharePoint Foundation site, you will not be able to use these libraries, but you may want to read the sections covering these libraries anyway to see what you are missing. I hope that the included figures will help you gain a good understanding of how these libraries could benefit your organization.

The first library type is a special implementation of a document library used for records management that only SharePoint Enterprise edition supports. However, you might be interested in records management if you need to archive time sheets, absence requests, purchase requests, performance evaluations, and other documents that your department or company must retain. Typically, records management provides long-term storage for documents created originally in other libraries.

The second library type is the picture library, which you first saw in Chapter 3. I will give you a deeper look at it here. While the most common use of a picture library may be to support content pages, you can maintain picture libraries that are nothing more than libraries of pictures that anyone can view. For that reason, I will show you the different ways you can upload and view your pictures in this library.

The final library type you will examine is the slide library. You will only find this library in SharePoint Enterprise edition. It works specifically with PowerPoint slide presentations. If you have groups of people who must work together on presentations, a SharePoint slide library may be the best way for them to share slides and easily build new presentations based on pulling together slides from other presentations along with their own slides.

So let's get started by looking at creating a records management system.

Creating a Records Management System to Archive Your Documents

Increasingly, today's organizations spend more time managing records than they did just a few years ago. Regardless of whether the reason for retaining more records comes from the fear of litigation or the need to meet new government requirements, organizations retain more records today than ever before and they must manage these records so that they can be easily retrieved when needed. To meet this need, SharePoint Enterprise adds a Records Center template to the list of Enterprise sites. You might argue that even the basic SharePoint features already serve as a central repository for records by providing departments and management with a single place to create, process, and store data.

SharePoint's collaboration features facilitate the easy creation of multiple sites for departments and project groups, with each one potentially supporting multiple document libraries. However, flexibility can also bring chaos. In fact, it might not take long before you find your organization's records scattered across multiple sites.

A Records Center provides a central repository for long-term storage of records after the department or project no longer actively needs them. In addition to determining what to do with documents from a department or project after projects complete, you may also require records retention as part of your organization's auditing and/or compliance requirements. You might also need to archive records for historical reporting or even tax purposes. Regardless of why you think you need a centralized store for your long-term retention of records, SharePoint's Records Center site can help.

To keep the illustrations relatively simple, let's focus on one type of document in a single document library. Suppose your organization has decided that it needs to archive each Request for Bid (RFB) document on your new SharePoint site. Let's see how a Records Center site can satisfy this need.

Creating Site Columns

Assuming that the need to store RFB documents is a new requirement, you have the opportunity to think through how you want to handle them. For example, rather than letting each manager create his own RFB format each time he needs to send out a new RFB, you could provide a common template that everyone could use. You could then create a library that uses that template as its default document type. Furthermore, by using a common RFB, you could create metadata specific to the RFB so that, when you display that metadata in a library, you could quickly view key information about each RFB record. Finally, after a project ends or the item ordered arrives and you accept it, you can archive the original RFB into a Records Center.

Let's start the process by creating a set of site columns that you can reuse when defining content types. Remember that you can add site columns to libraries as metadata so that when you display a list of the items in the library, you can quickly see important information about each item. Suppose you want to create the following site columns to associate with each Request for Bid:

- **RFB_Number**
- **RFB_Due_Date**
- **RFB_Responder_Name**
- **RFB_Response_Amount**

To create these new site columns, follow these steps:

1. Open the **Site Actions** menu.
2. Select **Site Settings**.
3. Click **Site Columns** in the **Galleries** column of the **Site Settings** page.
4. In the **Site Column Gallery**, click **Create**.
5. Enter the column name and select a column type.
6. Enter other information as needed to define the column such as defaults, valid value ranges, etc.

For example, you might define the **RFB_Number** column as a numeric field, the **RFB_Due_Date** field as a date and time field, the **RFB_Responder_Name** as a single line of text, and the

RFB_Response_Amount as currency. As you enter your first column definition, you must choose to place your new columns in an existing column group or create a new group. Using a new group might make it easier to locate columns related to a common content type. Figure 12-1 shows the creation of the **RFB_Group** for RFB-related columns at the same time that you define the properties for the **RFB_Number** column.

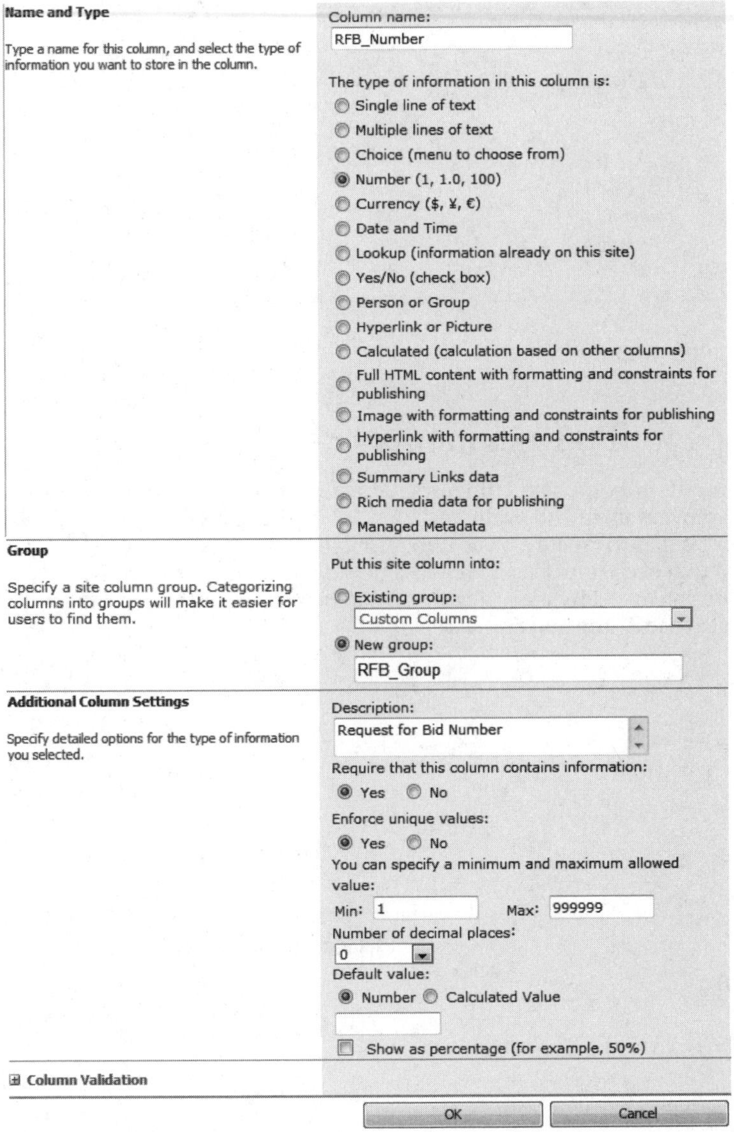

Name and Type

Type a name for this column, and select the type of information you want to store in the column.

Column name:

[RFB_Number]

The type of information in this column is:
- ◎ Single line of text
- ◎ Multiple lines of text
- ◎ Choice (menu to choose from)
- ◉ Number (1, 1.0, 100)
- ◎ Currency ($, ¥, €)
- ◎ Date and Time
- ◎ Lookup (information already on this site)
- ◎ Yes/No (check box)
- ◎ Person or Group
- ◎ Hyperlink or Picture
- ◎ Calculated (calculation based on other columns)
- ◎ Full HTML content with formatting and constraints for publishing
- ◎ Image with formatting and constraints for publishing
- ◎ Hyperlink with formatting and constraints for publishing
- ◎ Summary Links data
- ◎ Rich media data for publishing
- ◎ Managed Metadata

Group

Specify a site column group. Categorizing columns into groups will make it easier for users to find them.

Put this site column into:
- ◎ Existing group:
  [Custom Columns ▼]
- ◉ New group:
  [RFB_Group]

Additional Column Settings

Specify detailed options for the type of information you selected.

Description:
[Request for Bid Number]

Require that this column contains information:
- ◉ Yes ◎ No

Enforce unique values:
- ◉ Yes ◎ No

You can specify a minimum and maximum allowed value:

Min: [1]   Max: [999999]

Number of decimal places:
[0 ▼]

Default value:
- ◉ Number ◎ Calculated Value
[ ]

☐ Show as percentage (for example, 50%)

⊞ Column Validation

[OK]   [Cancel]

Figure 12-1. Create a new site column group while adding a site column.

Similarly, define the rest of the site columns, reusing the **RFB_Group** to organize them. After you finish adding all the fields, you should see all the new columns you added to the **RFB_Group** by selecting just that group in the **Site Column Gallery**. Figure 12-2 shows the new site columns in the **RFB_Group**.

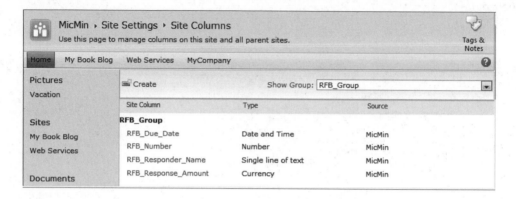

Figure 12-2. *New site columns in the RFB_Group*

Creating a Content Type for RFB Documents

Using a common form for RFB documents not only saves time when creating a new RFB by providing a predefined format, but also helps employees fill in and evaluate forms due to the consistency with which the data appears. Therefore, your next step is to create a basic RFB template using Word that you can then add to the SharePoint library, so that each time a user creates a new document she begins with a common company-wide form for entering the RFB details. Figure 12-3 shows an example of a simple word template for the company Howl at the Rising Sun Software, Inc.

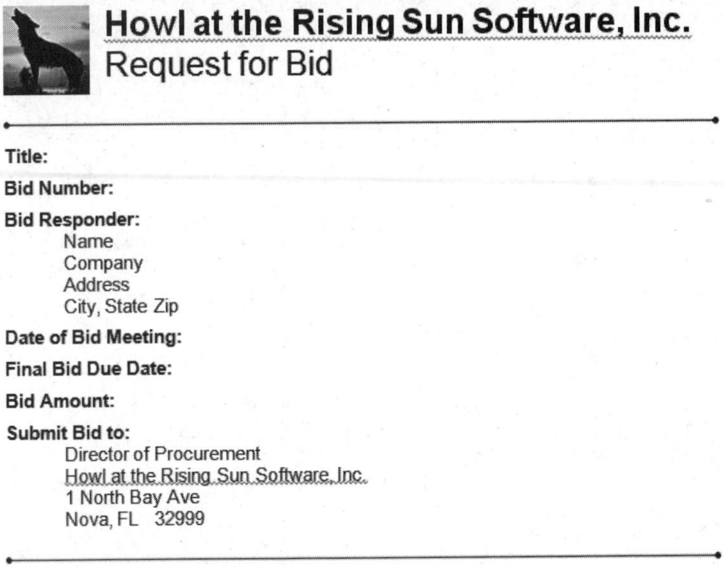

Howl at the Rising Sun Software, Inc.
Request for Bid

Title:

Bid Number:

Bid Responder:
    Name
    Company
    Address
    City, State Zip

Date of Bid Meeting:

Final Bid Due Date:

Bid Amount:

Submit Bid to:
    Director of Procurement
    Howl at the Rising Sun Software, Inc.
    1 North Bay Ave
    Nova, FL   32999

Figure 12-3. Word template for the RFB document.

To use this Word template as the default template in SharePoint, follow these steps:

1. Open the **Site Actions** menu.

2. Select **Site Settings**.

3. From the **Site Settings** page, select **Site content types** from the **Galleries** section, as shown in Figure 12-4.

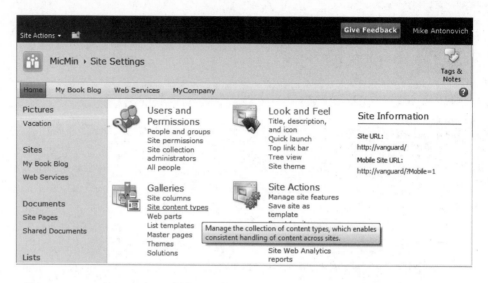

Figure 12-4. Create a new site content type.

4. From the **Site Content Type Gallery**, select the **Create** link in the header area of the gallery, as shown in Figure 12-5.

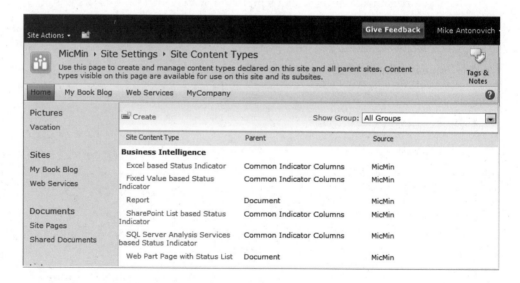

Figure 12-5. Create a new content type from the Site Content Type Gallery.

5. Within the **New Site Content Type** dialog box, enter a name for your new content type. For example, you may want to abbreviate the name for the content type as RFB.

6. Next, supply a description for the content type so everyone knows the purpose of the new content type.

Notice that, in this section, you can also determine from which content group and specific content type you want to inherit the new content type. In the case of the RFB, the most logical content type to inherit from is the **Document** type in the **Document Content Types** group.

You can also determine in which group to place the new content type, including creating a new content type group if you feel that the differences in the new content type warrant its own group.

7. To finish the definition of the content type, click the **OK** button. Figure 12-6 shows the definition of the RFB content type.

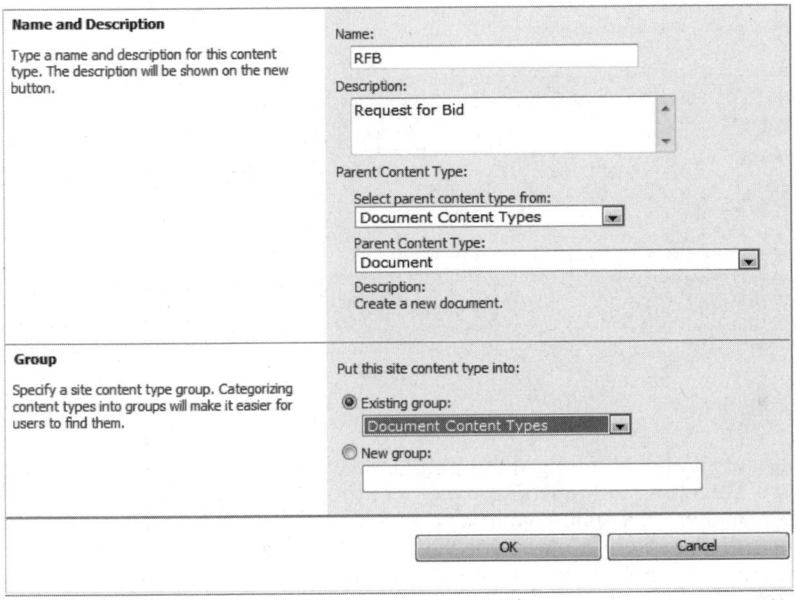

Figure 12-6. Define the site content type RFB.

You should now see a content type definition page similar to Figure 12-7. On this page, you can define additional settings for this content type.

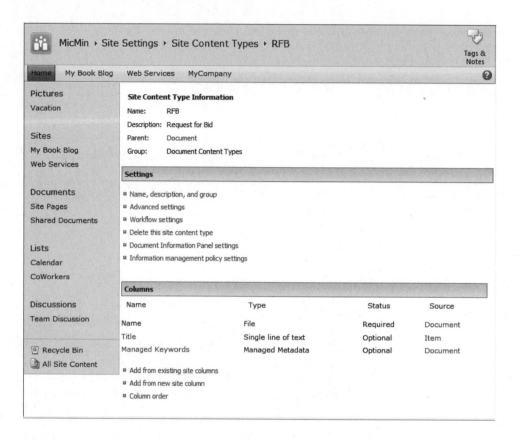

Figure 12-7. Initial site content type definition

The most important additional setting at this point is the one that associates the Word template with the content type. Therefore, before setting any other properties, click the **Advanced Settings** link found in the **Settings** section. This option opens a page that allows you to associate a new or existing document template with the current content type. Figure 12-8 shows the RFB content type being associated with a document template previously created and saved as `C:\SharePoint2010Book\Chapter 12\RFB_Template.dotx`. (You find this file in the book download.)

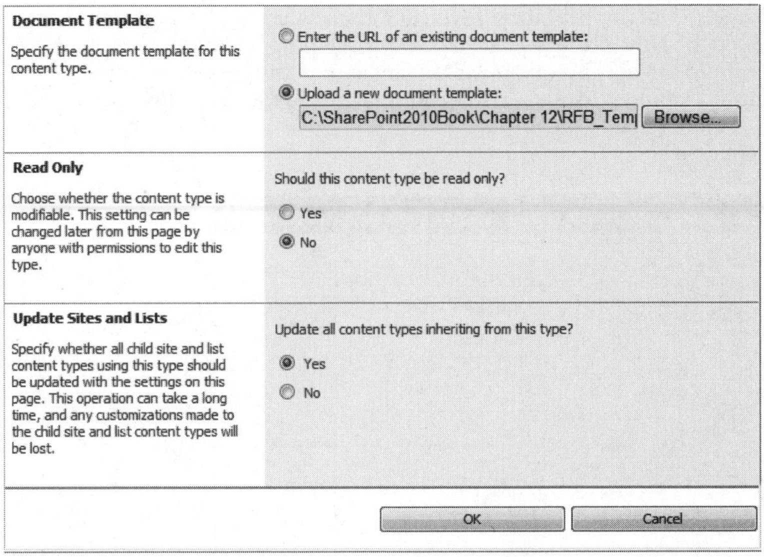

Figure 12-8. Associate a document template with the content type.

You can also determine at this time whether anyone can modify the content type and whether you want sites and lists that use this content type updated. When you create a new content type, the setting of this latter option does not matter. However, if you modify an existing content type on which other content types have been based, you can use this option to determine whether to cascade changes made here to content types in child sites and lists.

■ **Tip** When you update the RFB form, and I know you will someday because all forms are updated eventually, you would want to cascade the update to child sites and lists.

When you are done, click **OK** to return to the **Site Content Type: RFB** page. Alternatively, simply click the breadcrumb **Site Content Type Gallery** found at the top of the image to return to the gallery. You should now see the new content type listed in your selected type group.

Creating a Site Library to Collect RFB Documents

Now that you have site columns defined along with a content type for the documents you plan to create, you can associate them with an existing document library or create a new one. Let's assume you want to create a separate document library to hold RFB documents created by your department. Go to the department or project site where you want to create the library, which must be in the same site collection as the content type, since SharePoint scopes content types to site collections. There you can open the **Site Actions** menu and select **View All Site Contents**. From the All Site Content page, click

Create. On the Create page, click on the **Document Library** type and then select a new document library. In either case, you should see the **New Library** page, as shown in Figure 12-9. This page allows you to assign a name and description to the new library as well as navigation and version history settings. In the **Document Template** section, select an existing template from the drop-down list such as a Word document.

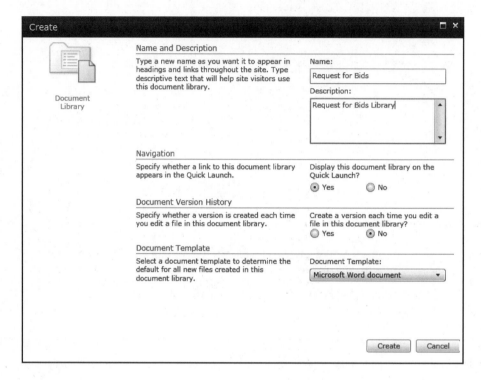

Figure 12-9. Create the working library.

SharePoint creates the library and displays the empty library list, but you still have configuration settings to apply to the library. Therefore, with the new library open, select the option **Library Settings** from the **Settings** group of the **Library** ribbon. Select **Advanced Settings** from the **General Settings** option group. In the resulting settings page, locate the section titled **Content Types** and select the option to allow management of content types, as shown in Figure 12-10.

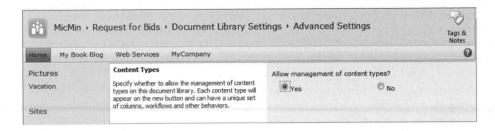

Figure 12-10. Turn on management of content types for the working library.

Click **OK** to accept your changes in the **Advanced Settings** page. Returning to the **Settings** page for the library, look again at the section called **Content Types**. This section lists the content types this library can use. By default, document libraries support the **Document** content type. If no template has been associated with this content type, it opens the Word file `template.doc`, which displays a default blank Word document when the user clicks the **New** button. Figure 12-11 shows the customization page for the Request for Bids library.

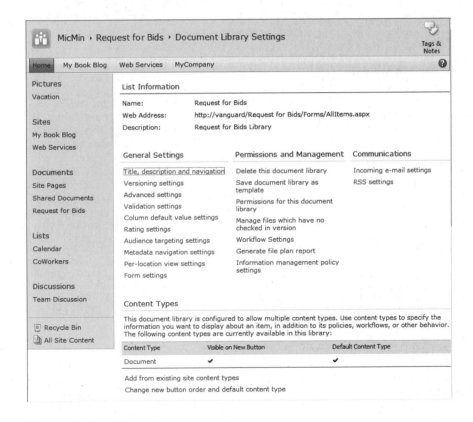

Figure 12-11. Add a new content type.

To add a new content type, click the option **Add from existing site content types** at the bottom of this section. The subsequent page shows the available content types. Scroll through this list, select the RFB content type created earlier, and click **Add**. Figure 12-12 shows that you want to add the content type RFB to the current library. When you click **OK**, SharePoint adds this content type to the library.

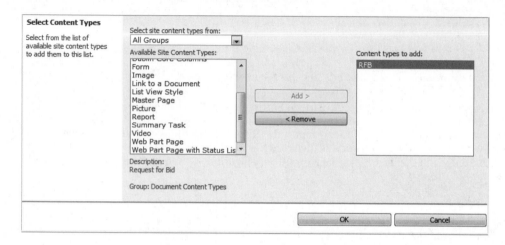

Figure 12-12. Select the content type to add.

After adding this new content type, the blank Word document content type, **Document**, still appears as the default type. While the drop-down menu for the **New** button in the library now shows both content types, **RFB** and **Document**, clicking the **New** button assumes that you want to create an instance of the default content type. Rather than default to a blank Word document, you want to default to a blank RFB form that already has your organization's header on it as well as formatted sections for the RFB contents.

SharePoint provides two ways to promote your RFB form to become the default type replacing the blank Word document. You could simply delete the default content type. If you never want users to create a generic Word document in this library, this may be your best choice. However, if you want to leave your options open, you could change which content type acts as the default. You can do this by clicking the link **Change new button order and default content type**, as shown in Figure 12-13.

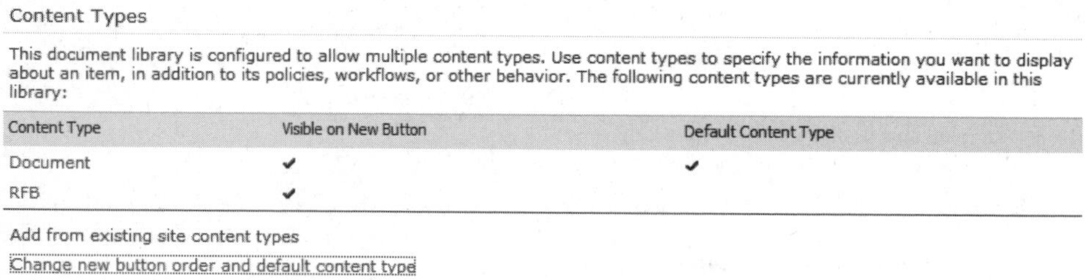

Content Types

This document library is configured to allow multiple content types. Use content types to specify the information you want to display about an item, in addition to its policies, workflows, or other behavior. The following content types are currently available in this library:

Content Type	Visible on New Button	Default Content Type
Document	✔	✔
RFB	✔	

Add from existing site content types

Change new button order and default content type

Figure 12-13. View the content types for the library.

The page to change the content type order works much like the page used to change the order of columns in a view. You see a separate row for each content type. To the left of the content type name there is a check box that lets you determine whether users of the library can see that content type. To the right of the content type name, you see the relative order of the content types. The first content type becomes the default content type. Therefore, the second way to make the RFB content type the default type for this library requires that you simply change its numeric position to 1, as shown in Figure 12-14.

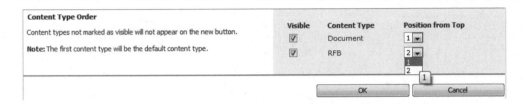

Figure 12-14. Change the default content type for the library.

■ **Tip** You can also remove the original blank Word Document content type by unchecking the check box in the **Visible** column for the **Document Content Type**.

When you return to your library's **Standard View** and open the **New** drop-down menu, you will see that it supports two different content types, **RFB** and **Document**. Figure 12-15 shows this drop-down menu. Notice that the order of the content types matches the order selection made in Figure 12-14. From this drop-down, you can select either content type or even create a new folder. However, if you simply click the **New** button rather than open the drop-down list, SharePoint uses the default content type and opens the RFB template, allowing you to create a new bid.

Figure 12-15. Select from content types when adding a new document.

Before you leave this document library, you have one more thing to do. If you already went back to the **Standard View** to see the **New** menu, return to the **Settings** page for the library. Scroll down to the **Columns** section. I mentioned that you could create site columns that you could apply to libraries. Beneath the list of current columns used by the library, click the link **Add from existing site columns**.

This link displays the window shown in Figure 12-16. To see only the columns associated with Request for Bids, select the **RFB_Group**.

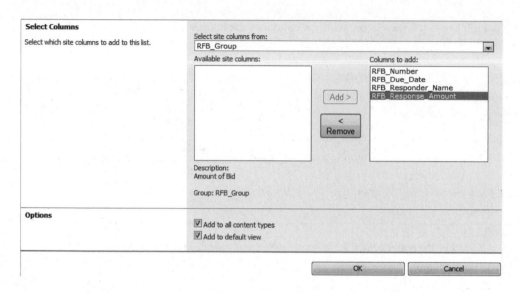

Figure 12-16. Add columns to library metadata from the site columns group RFB_Group.

You can now add each of the columns one at a time from the list on the left to the list on the right by clicking it once to select it and clicking the **Add** button. You can also double-click a column name to move it from one box to another. If you have several columns to select, you might find it faster to begin by clicking the first column name. Then, while holding down the **Shift** key, click the last column name, followed by clicking the **Add** button.

After you have added all four columns to the second list box, consider the two options at the bottom of the dialog box. The first option, **Add to all content types**, adds the selected site columns to each of the content types in the library. If you do not want to do this, remove the check from the check box. In this example, you probably would not want to add these columns to the Document content type. The second option adds the site columns to the default view.

If you do not want to add the site columns to all content types, you can still add the site columns to specific content types by performing the following steps:

1. From the library's **Settings** page, click the content type you want to modify.

2. From the **List Content Type** page, click the link **Add from existing site or list columns** beneath the **Columns** list.

3. The **Select Columns** group defaults to **List Columns** to display any columns included in the list, but not in the current content type. If this list shows the **RFB** columns, move them to the list box on the right the same way as previously described.

4. Click the **OK** button to complete the addition of the columns to the content type.

■ **Tip** If you already added the site columns to the Document content type, you can open that Document content type and, from its list of columns, select each column one at a time and, from its properties page, click the **Remove** button.

You should now see the RFB columns included in the **Columns** section, as shown in Figure 12-17.

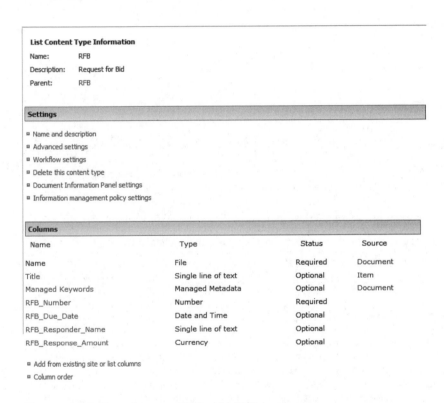

List Content Type Information

Name:	RFB
Description:	Request for Bid
Parent:	RFB

Settings

- Name and description
- Advanced settings
- Workflow settings
- Delete this content type
- Document Information Panel settings
- Information management policy settings

Columns

Name	Type	Status	Source
Name	File	Required	Document
Title	Single line of text	Optional	Item
Managed Keywords	Managed Metadata	Optional	Document
RFB_Number	Number	Required	
RFB_Due_Date	Date and Time	Optional	
RFB_Responder_Name	Single line of text	Optional	
RFB_Response_Amount	Currency	Optional	

- Add from existing site or list columns
- Column order

Figure 12-17. Site columns added to the RFB content type

If you return to the **Settings** page for the library using the breadcrumbs at the top of the page, you will also see the new columns in the **Columns** section, as shown in Figure 12-18. The **Used In** column shows which content types use each of the user-defined columns.

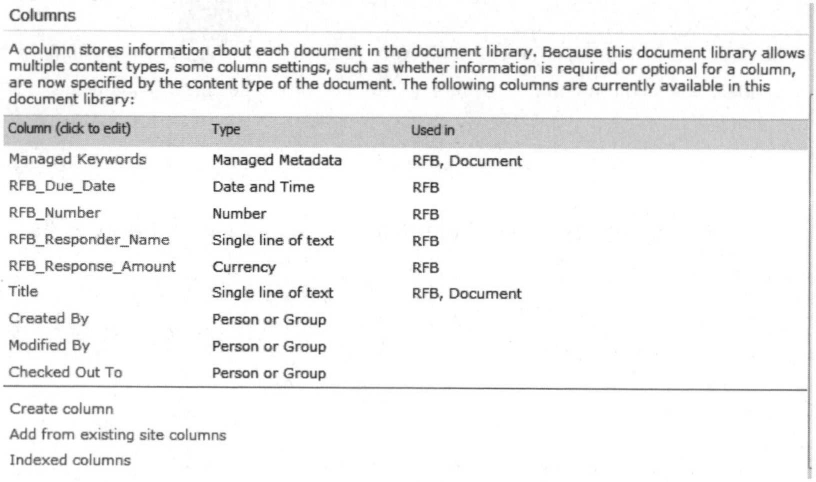

Columns

A column stores information about each document in the document library. Because this document library allows multiple content types, some column settings, such as whether information is required or optional for a column, are now specified by the content type of the document. The following columns are currently available in this document library:

Column (click to edit)	Type	Used in
Managed Keywords	Managed Metadata	RFB, Document
RFB_Due_Date	Date and Time	RFB
RFB_Number	Number	RFB
RFB_Responder_Name	Single line of text	RFB
RFB_Response_Amount	Currency	RFB
Title	Single line of text	RFB, Document
Created By	Person or Group	
Modified By	Person or Group	
Checked Out To	Person or Group	

Create column
Add from existing site columns
Indexed columns

Figure 12-18. Library metadata after adding site columns to only the RFB content type

Now that you have a document library for creating documents based on your custom content type for bid requests, let's look at the next step: creating the **Records Center** site.

■ **Note** You may need the help of your SharePoint administrator to complete this portion of the setup, as you may not have administrative rights to the **Central Administration** site.

Creating the Records Center Site

If you have the necessary permissions to create new sites, open the **Site Actions** menu and select **New Site**. From this **Create** page, filter the list by **Content & Data**, or from the **All Categories** group select the **Records Center** site type, as shown in Figure 12-19. You can immediately enter a title for this site on the right side of the **Create** page or you can click the **More Options** button where you can enter all the site properties in one place. When the **New SharePoint Site** page appears, enter a title and description for the new site. The title appears in the header of the site. The description also appears in the header when supplied.

Next, supply a **URL** name for the site. Developers often use an abbreviated version of the site title for the URL, leaving out spaces or replacing them with underscores. Using shorter URL names makes it easier to enter them later when creating links to the site or referencing the site to upload objects.

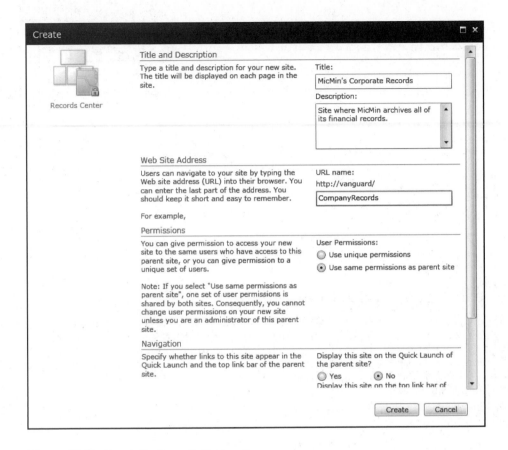

Figure 12-19. Create the Records Center site.

For this subsite, you can choose to use the same user permissions as the parent site, or you can define unique permissions. While you may choose to create your Records Center as the top level of a separate site collection, if you have a small installation, you may choose to create the Records Center as a subsite, as shown here. In either case, most site administrators will probably decide to create unique permissions for the Records Center primarily because fewer people need access to the Records Center, and even those who do typically require more rights than they usually have on other sites.

Finally, as with any subsite, you can define the navigation options, including whether to include the site in the top link bar of the parent site. If you select **No** for this option, you can still locate and enter the Records Center site by displaying **Site Settings** for the current site and looking under **Sites and Workspaces**. Figure 12-20 shows the initial appearance of the Records Center.

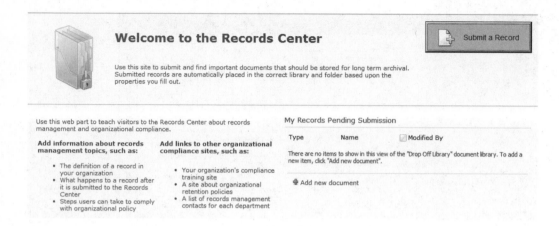

Figure 12-20. The initial Records Center site home page

Creating the External Service Connection

The next step in configuring the Records Center site that you just created involves creating an **External Service Connection**. You must perform this step from the **Central Administration** site for the Records Center site. Open a second browser window and log in to the **Central Administration** site. Switch to the **General Application Settings** page using General Application Settings menu option from the left navigation menu. On this page, select **Configure send to connections** under the **External Service Connections** section, as shown in Figure 12-21.

■ **Note** You may need your SharePoint Administrator's help with this step.

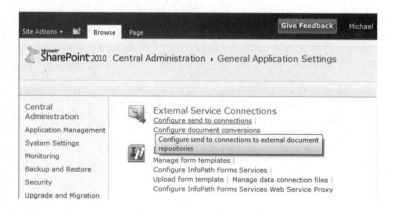

Figure 12-21. Define an External Service Connection for the Records Center.

On the **Configure Send To Connections** page, enter a **Display Name** such as **Records Center**. Your end users will use this name to send documents to the Records Center. Then enter the URL for the Records Center site. The generic version of this URL is `http://server/portal/_vti_bin/officialfile.asmx`. The `server` portion, of course, refers to your SharePoint server's name, and `portal` refers to the site collection. The last portion of this URL refers to a program file that directs items sent to the Records Center to a web service that builds the Records Center folder for the archived file. You cannot just copy files from other site libraries into the Records Center. Instead, each file sent to the Records Center generates its own folder identified by the date and time that you created it. This folder contains the archived document, along with a folder for properties and audit history.

Be sure to click the check box that allows manual submission of a document from the item's **Send To** drop-down menu. You can also choose whether you want to simply copy the document or move the document to the Records Center. If you need to keep a copy of the document in the current library even after moving a copy to the Records Center, you can select **Copy**. You can also move the document but leave a link in the original library so people can still open the document from the Records Center. In the **Explanation** box, you can include a message that appears with the link left in the library so users will know that the original document is in the Records Center.

Finally, click the **Add Connection** button to create the new connection. Note that you can return to an existing connection definition at any time and make changes to these settings. Figure 12-22 shows the **Connection Settings** definition for my Records Center named `CompanyRecords`.

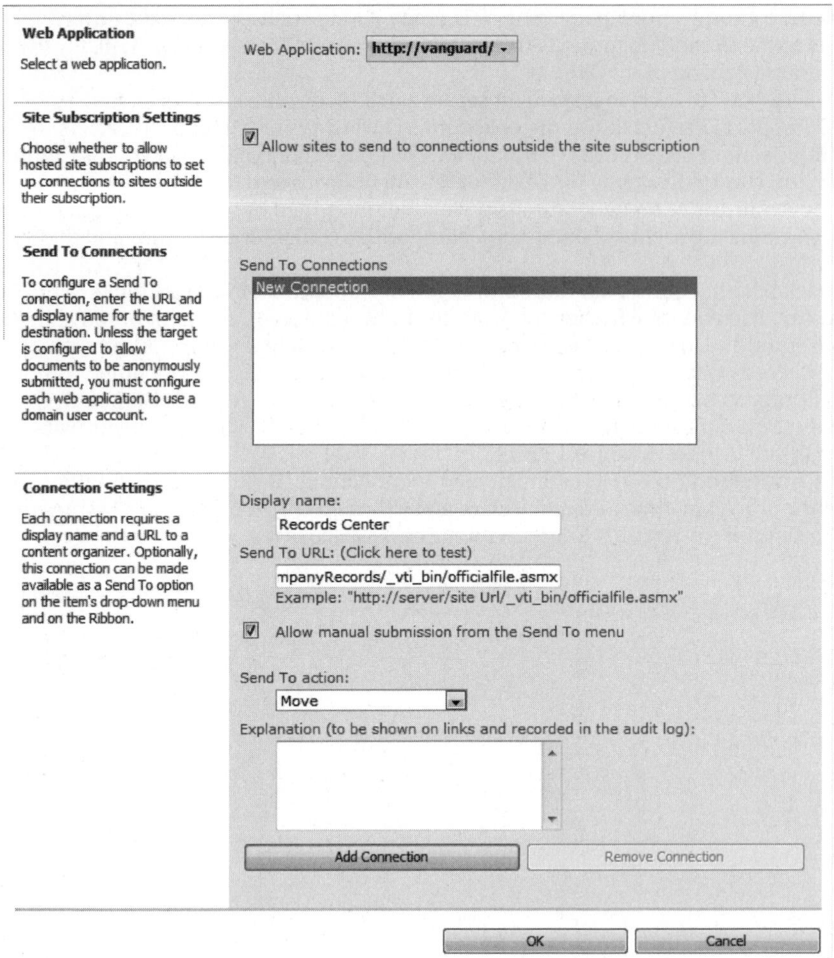

Figure 12-22. Define the connection URL and display name.

Notice that this external connection only allows you to route records from other sites to your Records Center. It does not tell the Records Center what to do with those records that it receives. We must do that within the Records Center itself.

Adding the Site Content Type for RFBs into the Records Center

Before you can use the Records Center, you must add the RFB content type to it so that it recognizes the document type when you send an instance to it. Open the Records Center site and create a new document library called **Bids**. Select **Library Settings** from the **Settings** group of the **Library** ribbon. In the **Content Types** area, click the link **Add from existing site content types**. Add the RFB content type here just as you added the content type to your working site. When you are done, you should see your RFB content type as one of the content types in the Bids library, as shown in Figure 12-23.

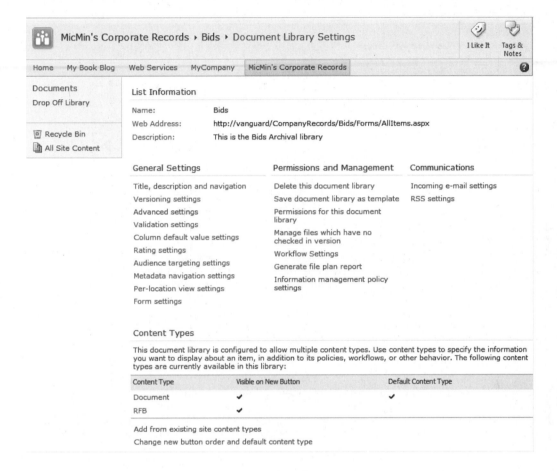

Figure 12-23. Add the RFB content type to the Bids library.

Creating a Policy for the Archival Library

While still in the Bids library, click on the link **Information management policy settings** in the **Permissions and Management** column at the top of the **Settings** page. If you have not previously created a policy for a content type, a value of **'No'** appears in the **Retention Policy Defined** column for that content type. To create a policy, click on the **Content Type Name** in the **Content Type** column. The **Edit Policy** screen for the selected content type appears as shown in Figure 12-24.

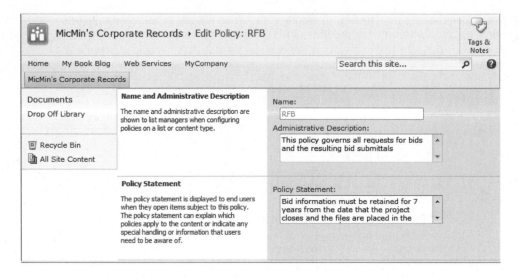

Figure 12-24. Begin a new policy definition.

Begin the policy definition by providing a name and description for the policy. The policy statement describes in text the handling of the file or other information that users might be interested in.

■ **Note** The policy statement does not actually create an action against the file.

The **Retention** section, shown in Figure 12-25, defines a retention period for the items in the library. If your company requires you to keep bid requests for seven years after you archive the file, select the **Enable Expiration** check box. This action opens a dialog that lets you define the retention period. For example, you could define the retention period as a time period based on the file's last modified date plus seven years.

Retention

Schedule how content is managed and disposed by specifying a sequence of retention stages. If you specify multiple stages, each stage will occur one after the other in the order they appear on this page.

Note: If the Library and Folder Based Retention feature is active, list administrators can override content type policies with their own retention schedules. To prevent this, deactivate the feature on the site collection.

☑ Enable Retention

Specify how to manage retention:

Event	Action	Recurrence
Modified + 7 years	Move to Recycle Bin	No
Add a retention stage...		

Figure 12-25. Enable expiration actions in a policy.

You can also specify what happens when the item does expire. The first option lets you perform an action such as delete. This moves the file to the Record Center's **Recycle Bin**, where the administrator for the site can permanently delete it or restore it if necessary. You can also start a workflow for the document based on the workflows defined for the site.

Other options include the ability to assign barcodes to each document or item, which you could then use to track printed copies of the document. You can also provide labels and barcodes with the document that it includes when you print it.

You might also want to check the **Enable Auditing** option, as shown in Figure 12-26, which tells SharePoint to audit specific events, such as each time someone views the items in the list, edits them, checks them out, or moves, copies, or deletes them.

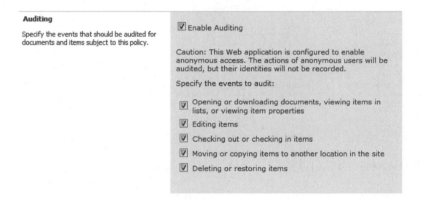

Figure 12-26. Enable auditing in a policy.

Creating a Record Routing Rule

You still have not told the Records Center what to do with incoming documents. Therefore, the last step in setting up your Records Center involves creating record routing instructions. Without records routing, SharePoint would not know what to do with records sent to the Records Center. Actually, it would just leave them in the Drop Off library that SharePoint created as part of the Records Center site template. However, then someone would have to manually route those records to the desired archival library. You can take care of that task automatically by using routing rules. You can have as many record routing rules as you have content types defined. Each rule can then treat each content type individually, sending it to a separate archival library with its own policy. In this simple example, you only have a single archival library, Bids, but you can have any number.

The record routing rule associates a content type with a specific library in the Records Center. By default, SharePoint leaves any content type without a specific routing rule in the Drop Off library, but you can create new routing rules by selecting **Manage Records Center** from the **Site Actions** menu while in the Records Center site.

Figure 12-27 shows the **Records Center Management** page. Initially, the Records Center site includes some default web parts on this page that provide you with step-by-step instructions on how to plan and use the Records Center. You can remove these after you are familiar with their operation. However, the important web part has the title **Content Organizer Rules** found at the bottom of the first column, as shown in Figure 12-27.

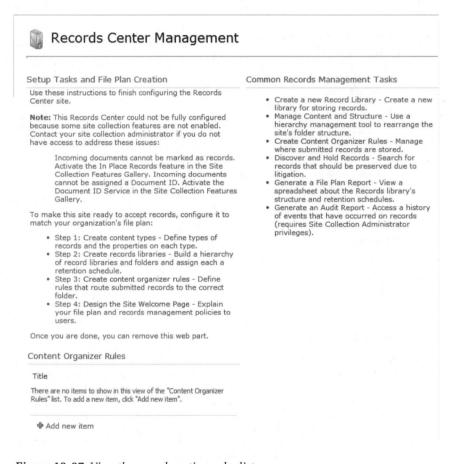

Figure 12-27. *View the record routing rules list.*

To create a new rule, click the link **Add new item** at the bottom of this web part. When the next screen, as shown in Figure 12-28, opens, it allows you to define a new record routing rule. The first property you must supply is the **Title**. While you can provide any name you would like for the rule, I recommend using the name of the content type or something that clearly identifies the content type you want to process.

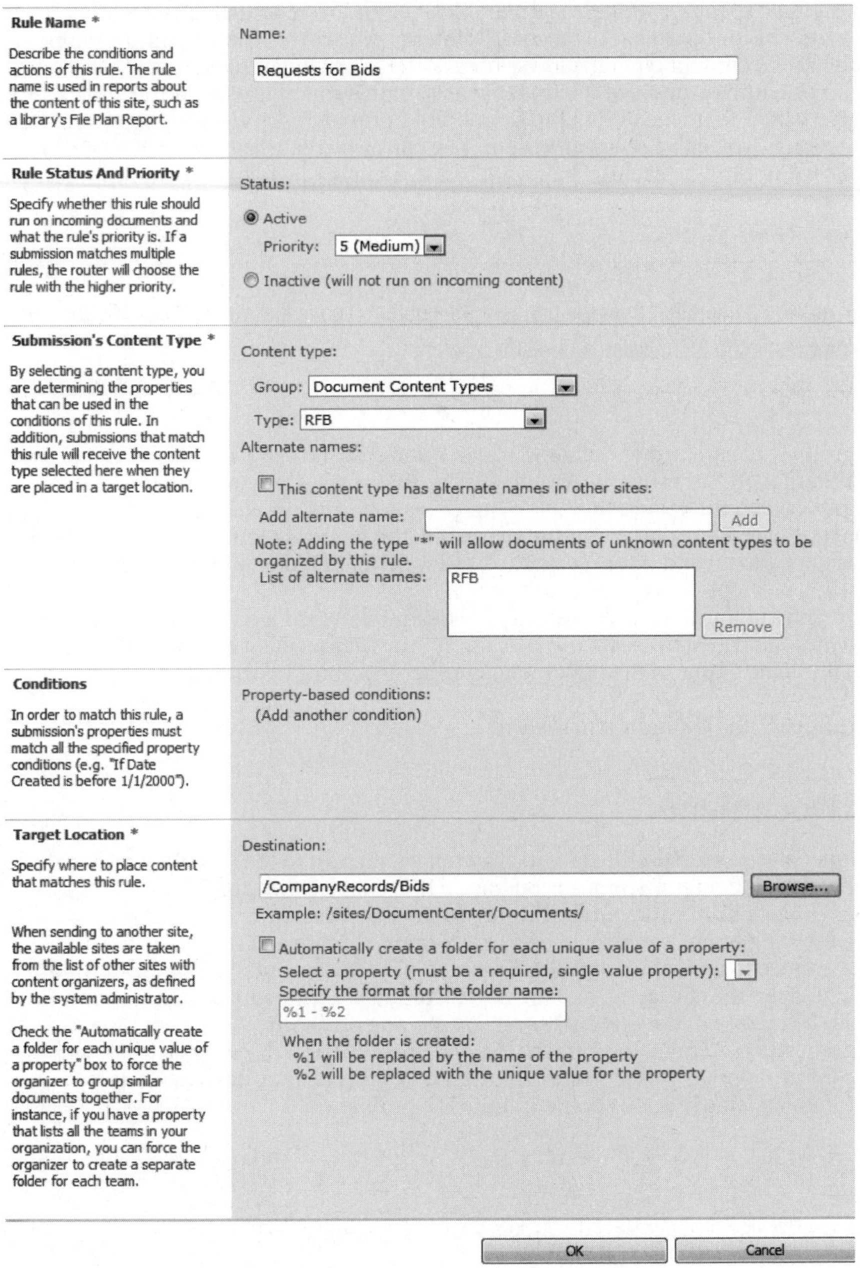

Rule Name *

Describe the conditions and actions of this rule. The rule name is used in reports about the content of this site, such as a library's File Plan Report.

Name:

Requests for Bids

Rule Status And Priority *

Specify whether this rule should run on incoming documents and what the rule's priority is. If a submission matches multiple rules, the router will choose the rule with the higher priority.

Status:

⦿ Active

   Priority: 5 (Medium) ▾

○ Inactive (will not run on incoming content)

Submission's Content Type *

By selecting a content type, you are determining the properties that can be used in the conditions of this rule. In addition, submissions that match this rule will receive the content type selected here when they are placed in a target location.

Content type:

   Group: Document Content Types ▾

   Type: RFB ▾

Alternate names:

☐ This content type has alternate names in other sites:

Add alternate name: [   ] [Add]

Note: Adding the type "*" will allow documents of unknown content types to be organized by this rule.

List of alternate names: | RFB

[Remove]

Conditions

In order to match this rule, a submission's properties must match all the specified property conditions (e.g. "If Date Created is before 1/1/2000").

Property-based conditions:
   (Add another condition)

Target Location *

Specify where to place content that matches this rule.

When sending to another site, the available sites are taken from the list of other sites with content organizers, as defined by the system administrator.

Check the "Automatically create a folder for each unique value of a property" box to force the organizer to group similar documents together. For instance, if you have a property that lists all the teams in your organization, you can force the organizer to create a separate folder for each team.

Destination:

/CompanyRecords/Bids [Browse...]

Example: /sites/DocumentCenter/Documents/

☐ Automatically create a folder for each unique value of a property:
   Select a property (must be a required, single value property): [▾]
   Specify the format for the folder name:
   %1 - %2

   When the folder is created:
   %1 will be replaced by the name of the property
   %2 will be replaced with the unique value for the property

[OK]   [Cancel]

Figure 12-28. Define a new record routing rule.

The second thing you must specify is the rule status, which can be active or inactive. If a rule is active, you can specify a priority for the rule. The Records Center only uses the Priority setting when more than one rule matches the content type. It allows you to determine which rules to run first.

Next, you define the content type upon which this rule acts. In this example, you can see that I specified the content type as RFB that I created in the Document Content Types group. If you have alternative content type names, you can also specify them. You can also create a general rule by using an alternate type of "*". This feature can be useful if you want to use a single rule to handle multiple content types.

■ **Tip** The reason you can provide a title other than the name of the content type is that you can specify the content type you want to process in the Submission's Content Type area.

In the Conditions group, you can further define where to route a document based on values in the available fields in the content type. For example, we can use the **RFB_Due_Date** to route the RFB to different archival folders based on the year of the RFB. With other columns, we could route the RFB document based on the type of bid, the dollar amount of the bid, the division requesting the bid or other criteria. In this case, I will not add an additional condition, as I want all RFB documents for now to go into a single archival folder.

The last group in the rules definition lets you specify the destination location. You must create this location first, which is why you needed to create the Bids library earlier. You can also create folders automatically based on the value of one of the document's properties. You can even use a property to create the folder name.

After defining the rule, click the **OK** button to save lit.

Archiving Your Documents

Now that you have completed the setup for the Records Center, let's return to the working library where you can create an original RFB document. Suppose you have a RFB called New Laptop Computers. You can now test the archival process from your working library to the Records Center.

If you configured everything correctly, you can open the working library and position your mouse over the file you want to archive to open the drop-down menu for the document. Position your mouse over the **Send To** option to open the submenu, as shown in Figure 12-29. This submenu now contains the entry Records Center. If you do not see this entry or if you see an entry with a different name, then you did something different when defining the **External Service Connection** discussed earlier. Since you must configure this information in the Central Administration site, you may need to contact your SharePoint administrator for assistance at this point, if there is a problem.

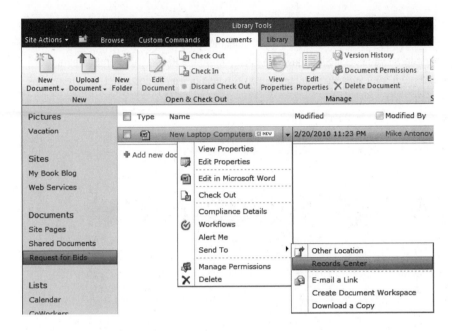

Figure 12-29. Send a document to the Records Center.

Select the **Records Center** option to begin the archival process. You may first see a pop-up message asking if you want to move the document to the Records Center. Remember, you defined the rule to move, not copy, the document. After a few seconds, the pop-up dialog box shown in Figure 12-30 tells you that you successfully sent the copy of the file to the Records Center.

Figure 12-30. Message upon successful addition of document to the Records Center

■ **Note** A copy of the file remains in the working library only if you selected **Copy** when defining the external connection in Central Administrator. If you specified to move the document to the Records Center, SharePoint automatically removes the document from your working library. You can also move the document and leave a link in the library to the new location.

If you now go to the Records Center, you should see the file in the RFB archival library, as shown in Figure 12-31.

Figure 12-31. Archived document folder

This brief introduction to using the Records Center only covers the basics of how to build and use a Records Center to archive your documents to a central location. You may need to consider many additional factors before creating a Records Center for your organization.

Creating a Picture Library in SharePoint

You can use picture libraries in SharePoint to share pictures with other users of your site. They also let you view, organize, share, and edit common graphics. The ability to create a slide show from a picture library may let you share your pictures with coworkers. However, a very important purpose of a picture library is to supply files to display on your site pages that contain images, icons, or pictures of any sort. To do this, you must first store the picture files in your picture library, where SharePoint web pages can find them.

To create a picture library within your SharePoint site, if you do not already have one, go to the **Site Actions** menu and select **View All Site Content**. From the All Site Content page, click the **Create** option at the top of the page. From the navigation panel on the left side of the page, click on **Library** in the **All Types** section. The **Picture Library** appears as one of the options on the right side of the page, as shown in Figure 12-32. Select it and then click the **More Options** button to provide the properties of your new library.

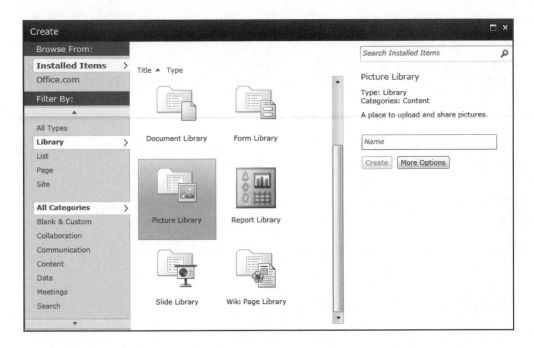

Figure 12-32. *Select Picture Library from the Libraries group.*

When creating a new picture library, as with any other library, list, or web page, you must name it. Names consist of alphanumeric strings that can include spaces, although some people would agree with me in not recommending spaces. I suggest replacing spaces with underscores for readability. In any case, the name must be unique within the current site. You can also provide an optional description, and, if you do, it appears when you open the library above the library's menu.

Next, choose whether you want the picture library to appear in the **Quick Launch** area. Typically, if you have a picture library primarily to share pictures with other members of your team, you would add it to the **Quick Launch** area so that others can access it easily. However, if your picture library only exists to serve pictures to your site pages or to provide icons for pages, other members of your site probably have no need to regularly access the library, and thus you should not include it in the **Quick Launch** area. If you use a picture library for both purposes, I would suggest that you rethink your design and split your pictures into two or more libraries so that only pictures you really want other members to share exist in libraries that appear in the **Quick Launch** area.

■ **Tip** You can also control access through permissions to picture libraries used within the pages of your site so that others cannot modify or delete those images.

Finally, you can determine whether SharePoint tracks versions of your pictures each time you save a new picture with the same name. If the image consists of time-sensitive information that someone might need to go back to earlier versions to view, then include versioning. However, for most uses, tracking picture versions does not make sense, especially considering the size requirements of most pictures. Remember that each version is stored as a copy of the entire picture. Figure 12-33 shows the properties screen of a new picture library.

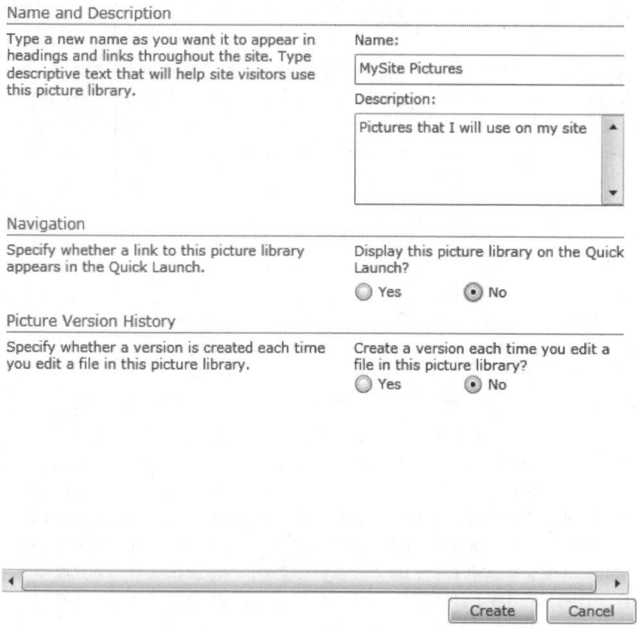

Figure 12-33. *Set the properties of the picture library.*

Keeping the Size of Your Images Under Control

The first and most obvious goal is to keep your images as small as possible. Different formats of the same image can result in greatly different file sizes. Usually, JPG or GIF files result in the smallest files. If you need an image that is only 100 pixels square, don't save an image created from your digital camera that is 3500 by 2900 pixels, and then just let the page formatting "shrink" the image down. This process may display a smaller image, but the physical image size in bytes remains the same. In addition, it is not just the physical storage on your server that need concern you. The larger your image files become, the longer it takes to download those images to a browser, making your web site appear slower than it should, especially for those people with slower web connections.

Another technique to reduce the size of your image files is to reduce their color depth. Often the color depth of digital camera images far exceeds what is necessary when displaying the image on a web page.

Usually, you can reduce the color depth from 32 bit to 16 bit or even less with no perceptible difference in the image. If you work with GIF files representing drawings rather than photographs, you can reduce the color depth down to 256 colors or less.

One tool to help you modify the sizes of your images is the Microsoft Office Picture Manager. It can handle most of your resizing and image modification needs.

Once you have created your picture library, you can open it either by clicking its name in the **Quick Launch** menu if you placed it there or by clicking **View All Site Content** in the **Quick Launch** menu and locating your library within the **Picture Library** group.

Within your picture library, you may want to organize your pictures into different folders and perhaps even different subfolders. To create a folder, click the **New** button in the menu bar, as shown in Figure 12-34. Notice that the new drop-down menu only has this one option. You cannot create a new picture from within a SharePoint library because SharePoint does not host its own graphics design tool.

Figure 12-34. *Add structure to your library by adding folders.*

When you create a new folder, you must name it. Folder names can have up to 128 alphanumeric characters and can contain blank spaces. While you can place periods within a folder name to represent a hierarchy, you cannot put that period at the start or the end of the name. Nor can you put two period characters consecutively in the name. SharePoint also does not allow most special characters. However, because you have to replace blank spaces with the string "%20" in URL references to the library, you may want to avoid blank spaces or replace them with underscore characters, as shown in Figure 12-35. After entering a name, click **OK** to create the folder.

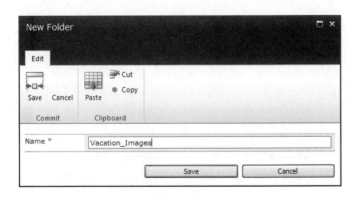

Figure 12-35. *Create names for folders.*

You do not have to define your folder structure fully before starting to use your picture library. While you may not anticipate every need for the picture library and thus not be able to fully build out the file structure for the library ahead of time, leaving the file structure up to the users could also result in a very disorganized structure, maybe even one in which all pictures appear in just one folder.

Deciding when to add a picture to an existing folder and when to create a new folder for the picture is a lot like saving a file in your local or network drive. Get a group of people together, and you typically end up with several different suggestions for the structure. Some members of your SharePoint site might feel it best to separate images by topic. Others might want to save images by how they use them within the site, such as by page. Still others might want to save images based on who uploaded them.

Of course, even within a single folder in your picture library, you could add a custom column to categorize your pictures. Then define separate views to filter your pictures based on the value in that custom column. This method allows you to define multiple sets of ways that you can categorize your pictures by simply changing the supporting metadata for the picture library and defining appropriate views.

The best recommendation I can give you is that any organization is better than no organization, as long as you follow it consistently. Choose a method to structure your pictures within a library, publish the method so anyone using the library knows how to store and search for images, and then stick with that method. You might even include your file structure logic in the description of the library where every site member can read it.

Uploading Pictures to SharePoint

Now that you have a picture library, you probably want to save pictures to it. Accessing the **Upload** menu of the open picture library shows that you have two options for uploading pictures: one for uploading individual images and one for uploading multiple images. While you can navigate to the folder where you want to upload your images before beginning to upload, you can select the picture folder from within the **Select Picture** dialog. In reality, you can select either option because even the **Upload Picture** option allows you to upload multiple images, and the **Upload Multiple Pictures** option does not fail if you only select a single image to upload. Figure 12-36 shows the **Upload** menu.

Figure 12-36. Upload pictures individually or in groups.

■ **Caution** This feature may not be available to users who are attempting to access their site directly from the server on which they have installed SharePoint. The easy solution is to access your site/server from another networked machine.

Uploading Single Images

From the upload page shown in Figure 12-37, you can upload a single image by manually entering its fully qualified name. A more reliable way to reference a picture you want to upload to ensure that you not only spell it correctly, but also get the syntax for the URL correct begins with the **Browse** button. Clicking the **Browse** button displays a standard **Choose File** dialog box common to many Windows applications. From here, you can navigate through the directories of not only your local machine, but also the directories of any network drive that you have rights to view.

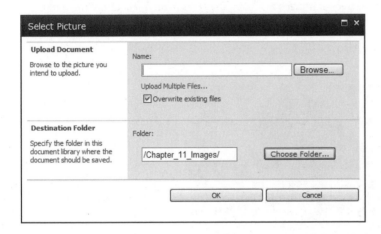

Figure 12-37. Enter the URL for the picture or locate it with Browse.

When you find the file you want, click the file name and then click the **Open** button or just double-click the file name. The **Choose File to Upload** dialog box passes the URL for the image back to the **Select Picture** dialog box.

Before clicking **OK**, you can choose to check the box next to **Overwrite existing files** if you want to override any pictures in the library automatically with the same name. If you do not check this box, and SharePoint discovers that the file you are uploading either has already been uploaded or at least has the same name as a file already in the library, the upload fails with an error. The error message identifies the file by name. You can simply rename one of the images and try to upload the picture again.

■ **Caution** When you select the option to overwrite existing files, SharePoint does not check to see which version of the file has the latest date. Therefore, using this option could inadvertently allow you to replace a more recent version of a file with an earlier one.

Notice also that you can choose the destination folder for the image. Using the **Choose Folder** button, you can display the hierarchy of the Picture library and select the folder where you want to place the uploaded image. By default, SharePoint assumes it is the folder you were in when you click the **Upload** command.

Selecting a single file to upload opens a page that lets you immediately update the default metadata associated with the picture in the current picture library. Figure 12-38 shows this page. You can change the name of the file used by the library, and not have to keep the same name as the original file. You can also specify a title for the picture. Next, you can specify the date and time you took the picture. Not all pictures need this type of information, but, to relate pictures to specific times, you can document that information here. SharePoint uses the description field as alternative text when you place the picture on a web page and the viewer of the web page has turned graphics off. Applications for the seeing impaired can sometimes read the alternative text associated with pictures. In either case, a good description of the image could help people who do not see the picture. Finally, you can specify keywords for the picture that the search engine can use to locate specific images.

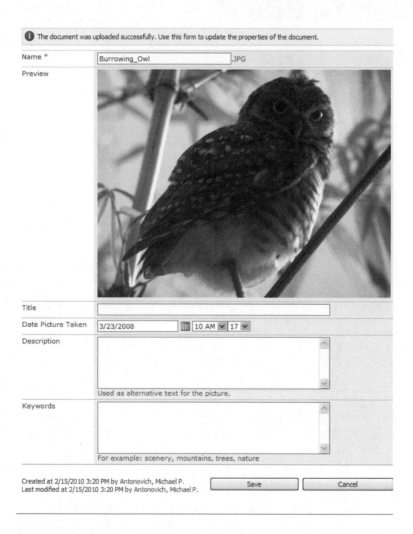

Figure 12-38. Define a picture's metadata as soon as you upload it.

■ **Tip** You can also create content types for picture libraries just as with other libraries. Those content types can have unique column definitions that can include, remove, or modify the default columns used by the default picture library.

Uploading Multiple Images

If you want to upload multiple files, rather than enter a file name in the first text box or click the **Browse** button, click the option **Upload Multiple Files**. This option opens the dialog shown in Figure 12-39.

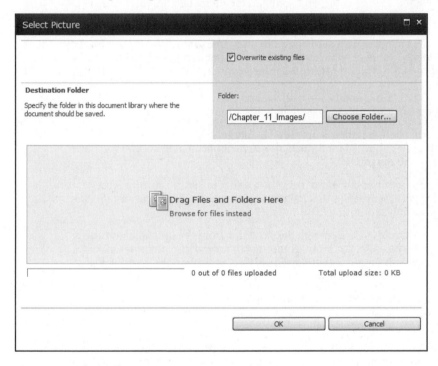

Figure 12-39. Drag files and folders from multiple directories on your local machine when uploading multiple files.

This dialog begins in a similar way to the one used to upload a single file. However, rather than providing a text box and **Browse** button to identify that single file, the **Upload Multiple Files** dialog provides an area where you can drag other files and even folders from another open instance of Windows Explorer. In fact, you can select files from multiple individual folders and drag them into this text box. If you do not have Windows Explorer open, just click the **Browse for files instead** link to open an instance of Windows Explorer so you can locate and select the files you want to upload.

Notice that the text below the area where you drag your files continuously updates to let you know how many files you have uploaded and the total upload size. This upload size could be important if your

SharePoint administrator has placed upload limits on your system. If you need to upload more files than allowed by your upload size limit, you can split the upload into groups of files where each group is less than the upload size limit.

After you have identified all the files you want to upload, you can click the **OK** button to start the upload. You can also get to this same point by selecting the **Upload Multiple Pictures** option from the **Upload** drop-down menu.

Uploading Multiple Images with Microsoft Picture Manager

Depending on your installation, you may instead have access to Microsoft Picture Manager. (Picture Manager is used by default for uploading multiple images when you have it installed.) This is a tool in the Microsoft Office installation. If the people who configured your installation of Microsoft Office included it, you can upload multiple files using it, rather than having to enter a file name in the single file upload text box. You will see this option instead of the screen in the previous section when you click the option **Upload Multiple Files**. Rather than showing a directory tree of the files on your local drive, it opens Microsoft Office Picture Manager, which I will discuss further in the next section. You can also get to this same point by selecting the **Upload Multiple Pictures** option from the **Upload** drop-down menu.

In either case, if you attempt to upload a file with a name that already exists in the library, Microsoft Office Picture Manager pops up an error message that displays four options:

- **Replace File**: This option replaces only the file that raises the current error message. If other files marked for upload also have duplicate names, you will have to address each one separately.

- **Replace All**: This option replaces not only the file that raises the current error message, but also any other files that have a duplicate name in the current upload batch without further prompting.

- **Skip File**: This option skips the current duplicate file from the upload batch and continues with the next file. It continues through the rest of the pictures marked for uploading unless it finds another duplicate. If so, it displays the error dialog box again to let you decide on an action for that file.

- **Cancel Upload**: This option cancels the upload at this point. Files already uploaded remain uploaded, but Microsoft Office Picture Manager will not attempt to upload any of the additional files in the set of selected files.

This ability to handle file name conflicts during upload might be a good reason to use the Microsoft Office Picture Manager, even when you only want to upload a single file. However, there are several other advantages to using this tool to upload your pictures.

Using the Microsoft Office Picture Manager

The ability to preview a thumbnail of the available images in any directory of your local drive is another advantage of the Microsoft Office Picture Manager, as shown in Figure 12-40. The panel on the left lets you navigate to any folder on your local drive and view thumbnails of the pictures found there.

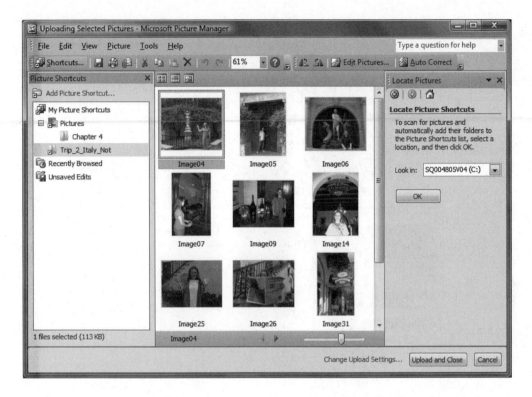

Figure 12-40. Using Microsoft Office Picture Manager to preview and upload pictures

The center panel displays thumbnails of each image found in the selected directory. You can change the size of the thumbnails by using the slide control at the bottom right of this panel. Along the top of the center panel, you should see three icons that allow you to select between three different view modes. The first icon displays each image as a thumbnail with the name of the image immediately beneath it. The second view option, called the **Filmstrip View**, uses the top half of the center panel to display the currently selected image. The rest of the images appear across the bottom half of the panel in a single row. You can move from one image to the next by clicking one of the visible images in the filmstrip area at the bottom, or you can click the left and right pointing arrows found in the control area in the middle of the central panel. An example of Filmstrip View appears in Figure 12-41.

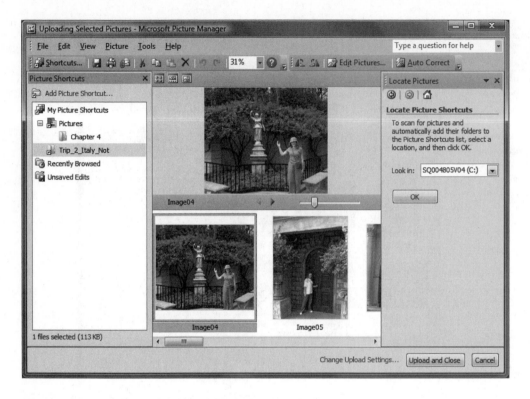

Figure 12-41. Display pictures in a folder using the Filmstrip View.

The third and final option, called the **Single Picture View**, shows only a single picture at a time from the selected library (see Figure 12-42). Beneath the picture, you will find a control bar. Starting from the left side of the control bar, you will see the name of the picture file, navigation buttons that allow you to move to the previous or next image in the directory, and a zoom slide bar that lets you change the size of the displayed image.

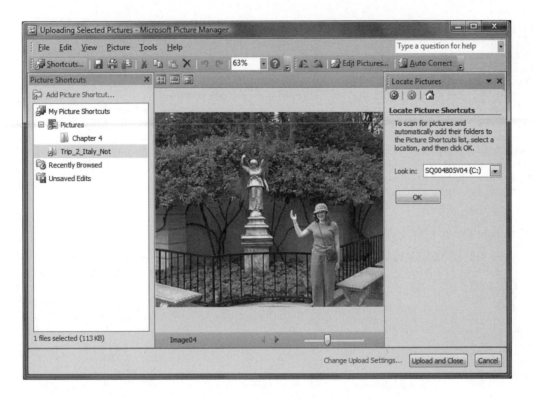

Figure 12-42. Display pictures in a folder using the Single Picture View.

You will most likely select pictures to upload from the **Thumbnail View**. When you click an image, the **Upload** panel on the right side of the screen tracks the number of files you have selected, the name of the library that it will upload the image to, whether it will send the original picture, and whether it will optimize the picture for viewing on the Web. As you might expect, this setting helps reduce the file size for images with millions of colors such as photographs, but it can also substantially reduce the size of even captured screen images. You can easily see the difference in size by alternately clicking the two option buttons in the **Upload Settings** section and checking the value displayed beneath them after the label **Total Transfer**. The **Total Transfer** value can also give you an idea of how "expensive" in terms of file size it would be to display a collection of images on your web pages.

■ **Tip** If you do not see the **Upload** panel, click the text **Change Upload Settings** found at the bottom of the Microsoft Office Picture Manager window to the left of the **Upload** and **Cancel** buttons. You can also select a different panel from the drop-down menu found on the right side of the panel header to the immediate left of the close button.

You can select multiple images to upload in the **Thumbnail View** by clicking the first picture you want, and then, while holding down the **Shift** key, clicking the last picture. This includes all of the intermediate pictures, starting at the topmost picture selected, and then proceeding from left to right, top to bottom, to the bottommost picture.

If you only want to transfer selected pictures from a folder, click the first picture you want, and then, while holding down the **Ctrl** key, click each of the additional pictures you want.

Finally, you can also use the mouse to click and drag through the images. The only limitation, which you may find inconvenient at times, is that you can only select images from a single directory as part of a single upload. If you want to upload images from multiple directories, you must select and upload files from each directory separately.

When you have selected your images, click the **Upload and Close** button to begin the transfer of the files to your SharePoint picture library. Depending on the number of pictures you have selected and their individual sizes, this could take a few seconds to complete.

Using Windows Explorer to Upload Pictures

Another way to upload pictures to your picture library begins by switching the view of your picture library to open it with Windows Explorer. You can find this option in the **Actions** drop-down menu, as shown in Figure 12-43.

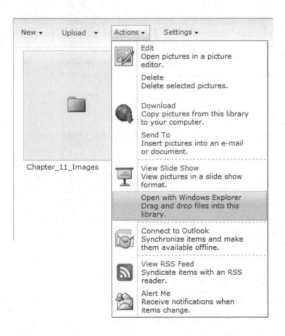

Figure 12-43. Switch to the Windows Explorer view mode.

■ **Caution** This feature may not be available to users who are attempting to access the site directly from the server on which they have installed SharePoint. The easy solution is to access your site/server from another networked machine.

Then open an instance of Windows Explorer from your operating system's **Start** menu. You may want to resize the SharePoint library window and the Windows Explorer window so that you can view both windows side by side. Next, navigate to the directory in Windows Explorer that contains the pictures you want to upload, and select them individually or as a group. With your pictures selected, click and drag the selection over to the SharePoint library area and release the mouse button, as shown in Figure 12-44.

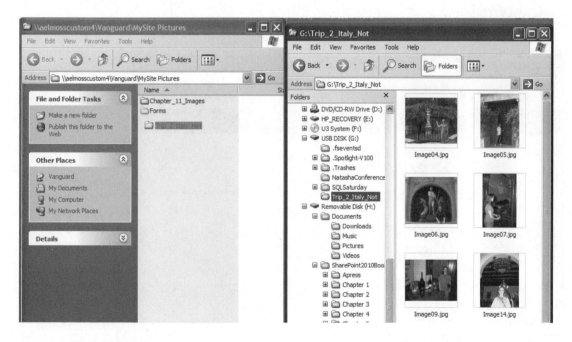

Figure 12-44. Use drag and drop to transfer pictures.

Downloading Images from Your Picture Library

Earlier, I covered how to display pictures from a picture library on a web page. However, if end users of your SharePoint site can view your picture library, they can download the images to their local hard drives. Not only do picture libraries provide an alternative to sending pictures as e-mail attachments to people, but they also have some ability to control the size of the downloaded image. Figure 12-45 shows the **Page Images: Download Pictures** page displayed by selecting the **Download** option in the **Action** menu. Notice that you can download one of three different sizes for the selected pictures: full size, preview size, and thumbnail. This figure shows thumbnails of a picture selected before choosing the **Download** option.

■ **Caution** This feature may not be available to users who are attempting to access their site directly from the server on which they have installed SharePoint. The easy solution is to access your site/server from another networked machine.

■ **Note** You must select the pictures first before you select the **Download** option.

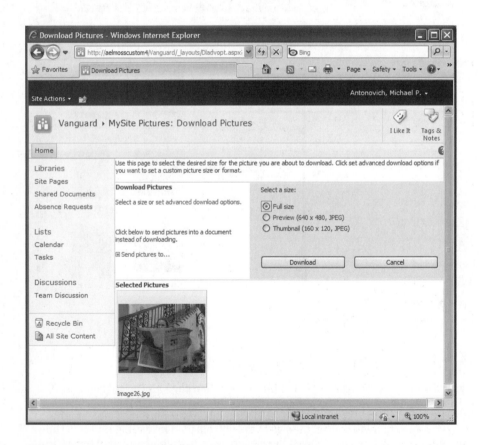

Figure 12-45. Select the size of the pictures to download.

By default, SharePoint downloads the images as saved (Full Size). However, if you click the **Set Advanced Download Options** link, you can choose a different format for the pictures. SharePoint supports converting pictures to the following format types:

- JPEG Interchange Format (*.`jpg`)

- Tagged Image File Format (*.`tif`)

- Windows Bitmap (*.`bmp`)

- Graphics Interchange Format (*.`gif`)

- Portable Network Graphic (*.`png`)

You can choose the final size of the image from a larger selection of predefined sizes. You can also create your own custom-sized image by either specifying the width and height of the image in pixels, which gives you independent scaling of the horizontal and vertical image size, or by specifying a percentage to stretch both the horizontal and vertical size. The page in Figure 12-46 specifies retaining the original format and size of the downloaded images.

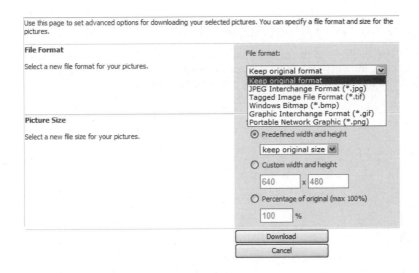

Figure 12-46. Choose a file format for downloaded images.

When you click the **Download** button, you must still identify the directory where you want to place the pictures. You can do this either by entering the directory name in the check box or by locating the directory by clicking the **Browse** button to look for it. If you specify a directory that does not exist, SharePoint displays a message box that allows you to create it.

By default, SharePoint assigns the downloaded pictures the same name they have in the picture library. However, you can rename the pictures as you download them by supplying a base name to which SharePoint adds a numeric value to name each image uniquely. Figure 12-47 shows that it will download the images to a directory named **My Pictures\MySite Pictures**. It also will rename each picture included in the download beginning with the text **Italy_Trip** and then appending a number starting with **01**.

Figure 12-47. Define where to save images and how to name them.

Sending Images to a Microsoft Office Application

Rather than download the image, you could send the image to one of four Microsoft Office applications. Figure 12-48 shows the dialog box that appears after you select one or more of the pictures from the library and then select **Send To** from the **Actions** menu. You can only select one Microsoft Office application at a time. However, you could return to this option several times to resend the image to different applications.

Figure 12-48. Send a picture to an Outlook message.

If you currently have a Microsoft Office file open such as a Word document, the name of the document appears in the drop-down box found beneath the label **Insert into an open file**. In fact, if you have more than one Word or PowerPoint file open, you can insert the graphics into any of them by selecting the one you want from the drop-down list. If you do not have any open Office files, this option appears disabled.

Even if you have a recognized file open, you can still send the selected images to a new Outlook message, Word document, PowerPoint presentation, or Excel spreadsheet. Each possible output destination has its own set of options, which you can display by clicking the **Options** link.

When sending images in an Outlook message, you must first decide whether to send the images as attached files or to embed them into the message. If you embed an image into the message, you get to choose the preview size. Possible output sizes for embedded pictures include

- Thumbnail (160 x 160 px)

- Postcard (448 x 336 px)

- Large Postcard (640 x 480 px)

You can then determine the layout of the images in the message. You can either use a table layout, which allows multiple images in a row, or save a single image to a single row. Figure 12-49 shows an example of the **Options for Sending Pictures** dialog box used to save the selected pictures as previews within the message using the postcard image size and a table layout.

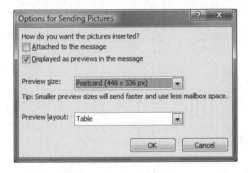

Figure 12-49. Select options for displaying an image in an Outlook message.

■ **Note** The table shows no borders by default. If you want to display borders between and around pictures, right-click between any of the pictures and select **Table Properties** from the pop-up menu. In the **Table Properties** dialog box, select **Borders and Shading**. In the **Borders and Shading** dialog box, click the **Borders** tab if necessary and then select the borders or individual lines you want.

When you send the pictures to a Word document, a PowerPoint presentation, or an Excel workbook, you can set only the image size. You can choose from the following sizes:

- Original size

- Document—Large (1024 x 768 px)

- Document—Small (800 x 600 px)

- Web—Large (640 x 480 px)

- Web—Small (448 x 336 px)

- E-mail—Large (314 x 235 px)

- E-mail—Small (160 x 160 px)

Do not think that you can only use the first three size options just because you want to send the pictures to a Word document. You can use any of these seven sizes when sending a picture to a Word document, PowerPoint presentation, or Excel workbook. SharePoint recommends various sizes for different purposes.

■ **Note** While selecting a size smaller than the original picture commands SharePoint to shrink a larger picture to the size indicated, it would not stretch a smaller picture to a larger size.

Viewing the Pictures in a Picture Library

You have several ways to view the pictures in your library. The first way, shown in Figure 12-50, shows the **Details View** of the pictures that you can display by selecting the **All Pictures** view. As with other menus, this symbol indicates that this item has a second flyout menu. As you position your mouse over this text, you should see a flyout menu with the options **Details**, **Thumbnails**, and **Filmstrip**. This **Details** view only shows the item type (a picture in this case), the picture name, the picture size in pixels, and the file size. These image properties tell you a lot about the picture, but they do not show you what the picture looks like. However, you can easily remedy that by clicking the view drop-down menu in the upper-right corner and selecting the **Modify This View** option. Among the available data columns, you will find these three columns: **Preview**, **Thumbnail**, and **Web Preview**. Each of these columns can display the picture. I suggest using the **Thumbnail** column for most list views because it requires the least amount of space, especially for libraries with larger images. There are also columns to track the date of the picture, keywords used by the search engine, versions, check-in status, and more.

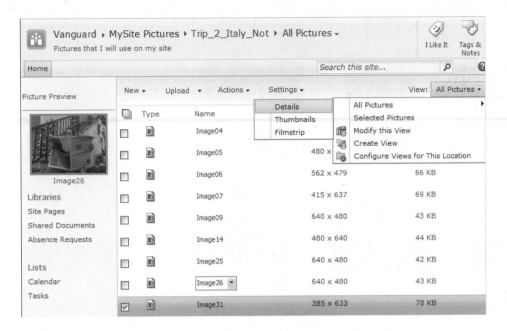

Figure 12-50. *View picture library contents using Detail View.*

■ **Note** If you attempt to edit an image, SharePoint tries to open a picture editor such as Microsoft Office Picture Manager.

To change the picture view, return to the **View** drop-down. This time select **Thumbnails** to see an image like the one shown in Figure 12-51.

Figure 12-51. View picture library contents using the Thumbnails View option.

Notice the check boxes to the left of each item's name that appears below the thumbnail image. You must select one or more of the pictures by clicking these boxes to perform an action on the pictures such as **Delete**, **Download**, or **Send To**.

This figure shows thumbnails of each image in the library in a table-like structure spanning from left to right, top to bottom. If you resize your windows, the number of pictures in each row automatically adjusts based on the available space.

The third view option under **All Pictures**, **Filmstrip**, displays the pictures in a filmstrip mode. This mode displays up to five thumbnail-sized images across the top of the screen. Each of these thumbnails has a check box before the name just like the **Thumbnails View**, allowing you to select images from this view before opening the **Actions** menu to perform an action on them. It then displays one of the images in a larger format in the bottom half of the screen as shown in Figure 12-52. Below this larger image, you will see the image name and a description if you provided one when you uploaded the image.

■ **Note** No matter how wide you can make the window on your monitor, the filmstrip at the top can only display a maximum of five images. Then a vertical bar appears with a green arrow button on the left, the right, or both sides, indicating the presence of additional images. To bring those images into view, click the green arrow to scroll through the filmstrip.

The **Selected Pictures** option in the **View** menu supports the same three subviews as the **All Pictures** option, except that it only displays the images you have selected by clicking the check box before the image names.

Figure 12-52. View picture library contents using Filmstrip View.

The **Explorer View** option, as shown in Figure 12-53, rounds out the list view options. Remember that you can get to the **Explorer View** by selecting **Open with Windows Explorer** from the **Actions** menu. This option shows the pictures using icons representing the file type. This view allows you to copy and paste images between this view and Windows Explorer.

■ **Caution** If you copy and paste pictures from Windows Explorer to your picture library using this method, remember that you may need to go back into each image to add the additional metadata that Windows libraries do not store or provide.

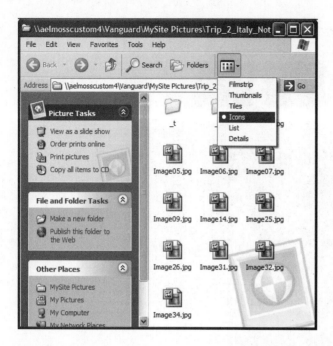

Figure 12-53. *Use Explorer View to drag and drop images between folders.*

When you click an image in the picture library, SharePoint displays it in a preview form that displays not only the picture, but also the supporting metadata for the image, as shown in Figure 12-54. From this view, click **Edit Item** to open the edit form for the picture. There you can change the picture's name, title, date taken, description, and keywords.

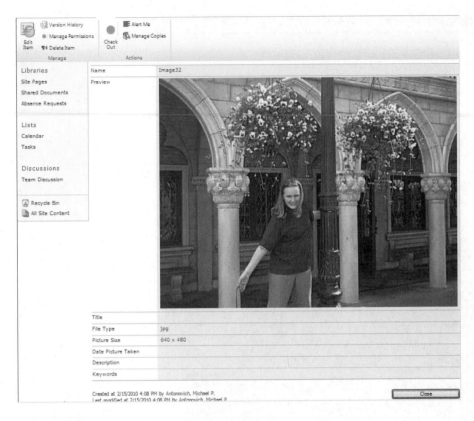

Figure 12-54. Edit preview window for an image

■ **Tip** Keywords can help your search engine find pictures, since basic searches only work on text and would otherwise have no way to identify pictures.

You can also delete the picture, modify the permissions for the picture, manage copies of the picture, check out the picture to exclusively edit it, and set alerts that can tell you when someone else edits or deletes this specific picture.

One last picture viewing option appears in the **Actions** menu of the library. Figure 12-55 shows an example of the picture library after selecting **View Slide Show** from the **Actions** menu.

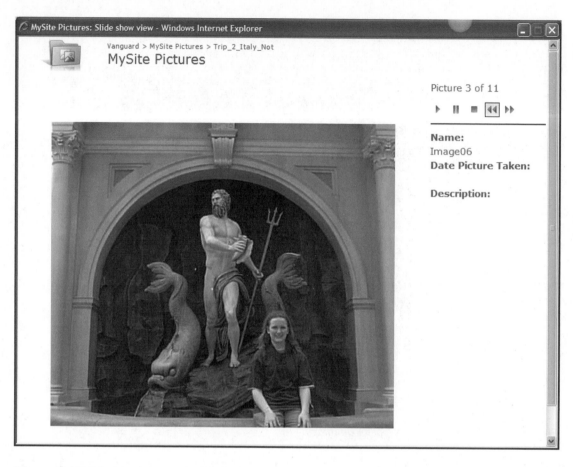

Figure 12-55. Display pictures in a slide show.

While picture libraries work great with static pictures, they do not work well with PowerPoint slides. Therefore, Microsoft adds a special library in SharePoint Enterprise specifically to handle PowerPoint slides. The next section explores that library.

Creating a Slide Library in SharePoint

This chapter closes by looking at the slide library. This library resembles the picture library in that it stores images. However, SharePoint has specifically customized it to store the individual slides from a PowerPoint slide presentation. You can use the slide library to store your slide presentations. However, a more powerful use of this library is to store common slides that your employees can subsequently use in their presentations. Perhaps the slides depict the history of your organization or its products. Maybe you have a set of slides with brief bios of your principal corporate officers. Some slides might represent technical data about your products or services. Whatever the slides may contain, you might want to store the slides in a common shareable location so that others can easily include those slides while putting together a custom presentation or while making a presentation to a potential customer or client.

SharePoint adds slide libraries to the available library types in SharePoint. To create a slide library, begin by clicking the **View All Site Content** option in the **Site Actions** drop-down menu. Next, click the **Create** button near the top left of the page. Then, as shown in Figure 12-56, select **Slide Library** from the **Libraries** group of the **Create** page and then click the **Create** button.

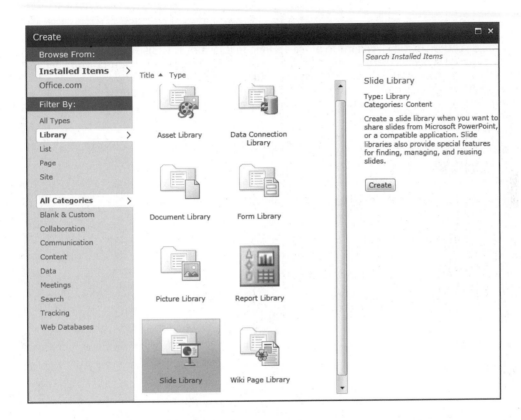

Figure 12-56. Create a slide library for PowerPoint slides.

The settings page for the new library then appears. You must specify a name for the library. If you also include a description, that description appears beneath the library name when you open the library.

As with other libraries, you can decide to include the library in the **Quick Launch** menu. If you want most users to access this library, you probably want to add it to the **Quick Launch** menu. However, even if you do not include it there, you can also get to the library by clicking the **View All Site Content** option in the **Quick Launch** menu and then looking for the library under the section **Document Libraries**.

■ **Note** I know you are probably saying to yourself that there should be a section titled **Slide Libraries**. At the very least, you might have expected to find the slide library under the picture libraries, which it closely resembles. For that reason, take special note that slide libraries fall into the **Document Libraries** grouping when viewing **All Site Content**.

Finally, you can choose to track versions to images added to this library. Unlike picture libraries, which often do not need versions, many people find tracking versions of slides important. If you need to track slide versions, select **Yes** under the **Slide Version History** section.

Figure 12-57 shows a library created to store slides from a recent SQL Saturday presentation. This library does appear in the **Quick Launch** menu but does not track versions of the slides.

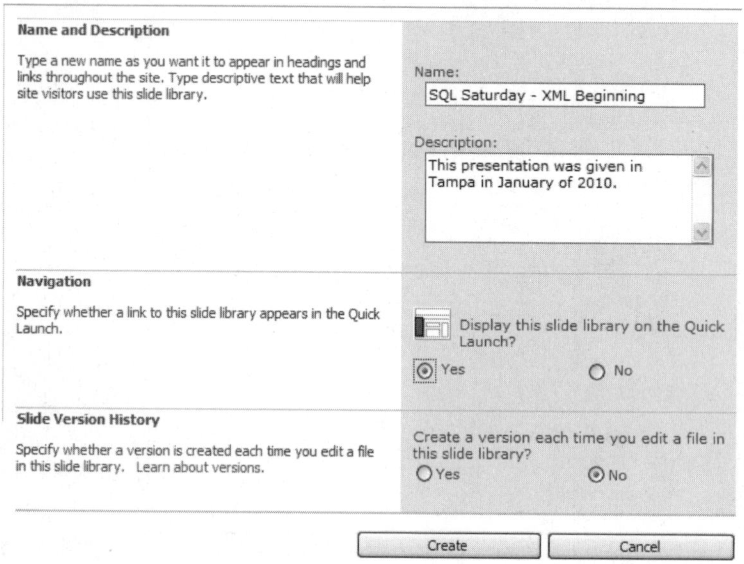

Name and Description

Type a new name as you want it to appear in headings and links throughout the site. Type descriptive text that will help site visitors use this slide library.

Name:

SQL Saturday - XML Beginning

Description:

This presentation was given in Tampa in January of 2010.

Navigation

Specify whether a link to this slide library appears in the Quick Launch.

Display this slide library on the Quick Launch?

◉ Yes   ○ No

Slide Version History

Specify whether a version is created each time you edit a file in this slide library.   Learn about versions.

Create a version each time you edit a file in this slide library?

○ Yes   ◉ No

Create   Cancel

Figure 12-57. Define metadata for a slide library.

After clicking the **Create** button, you will see your new empty slide library. Before you start uploading slides into your library, you might want to think about the structure that you want to create for your slides. Do you really want to store all your slides under a single folder or list? Would it make more sense to group some slides together, separating them from other slides? Of course, you could create separate slide libraries to store slides for different purposes. However, you can achieve the same results while making it easier to transfer slides between areas by using a folder structure for your slides, much as you create a folder structure to store files on your hard drive.

When you click the **New** option in the library menu bar, as shown in Figure 12-58, the only option that you will see, **New Folder**, allows you to create a new folder from your current location in the library. Starting from the library root, you can create a set of folders for different types of slides.

Figure 12-58. Organize your slides with folders.

When you select this option, SharePoint presents you with a very simple form to enter the name of the folder. Folders have no additional properties other than their names. In Figure 12-59, I show the **New Folder** dialog for a folder named XML_For_DBAs_Beginner.

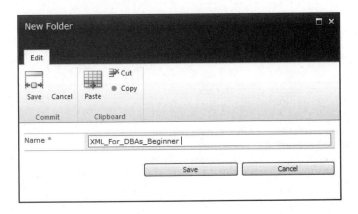

Figure 12-59. Folders must have names.

You can add other folders under the library root in a similar fashion. By double-clicking a folder, you can open it and add a subfolder within it.

Uploading Pictures to Your Slide Library from PowerPoint

While you do not have to complete your entire folder structure before beginning to add pictures to the folders, you should have at least a good idea of the initial folders you need. Once you have your folders, you have two ways to publish your slides from PowerPoint. You can start from your slide library and upload them, or you can start from PowerPoint and publish them.

■ **Caution** This section requires that you have Microsoft PowerPoint installed on your computer along with associated Active X control support for your browser.

Uploading Your Slides

The first way to load slides into your new slide library begins by selecting the option **Publish Slides** from the **Upload** menu. This option begins the process of copying slides from an existing PowerPoint presentation to the library, as shown in Figure 12-60.

Figure 12-60. Upload your PowerPoint slides to your library.

When you start from SharePoint, it opens an instance of PowerPoint on the client machine and pops up the **Browse** dialog box to help you locate the PowerPoint presentation file and open it. After you select a presentation, the **Publish Slides** dialog box appears that displays all the slides in the presentation as a list consisting of a small thumbnail of each slide, the name of the file that contains the slide, and a short description of the slide.

■ **Note** SharePoint takes the slide description from the slide title area, which is another good reason for descriptive titles.

To the left of each thumbnail, a small check box allows you to select which slides you want to upload. If you want to upload all the slides, click the **Select All** button at the bottom of the window. If you decide to change your selection, you can either unselect the slides by clicking their check boxes again or simply click the **Clear All** button to restart. Once you have selected the images that you want to publish, you can verify the name of the slide library you will add them to by checking the contents of the **Publish To** box at the bottom of the dialog box. If you need to change this library, you can manually update this text or use the **Browse** button to navigate to a different location.

Finally, click the **Publish** button to transfer the PowerPoint slides to SharePoint. Figure 12-61 shows several slides being published to the **SQL_Saturday** library.

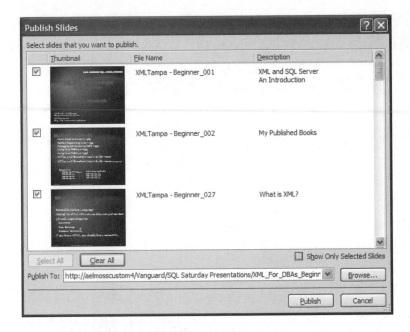

Figure 12-61. Select which slides you want to publish.

Publishing Your Slides from PowerPoint

The second way to transfer slides into your library begins from PowerPoint and publishes the slides to SharePoint. To do this, open your PowerPoint presentation and then, from the **Share** page of the **Backstage** area, click **Publish Slides**. The **Publish Slides** panel tells you that you are about to publish slides to a slide library to provide:

- A location where you can share your slides with other people to use
- Track and review changes to slides
- Locate the latest version of a slide
- Receive an e-mail notification via an alert when a slide changes

Figure 12-62 shows this panel.

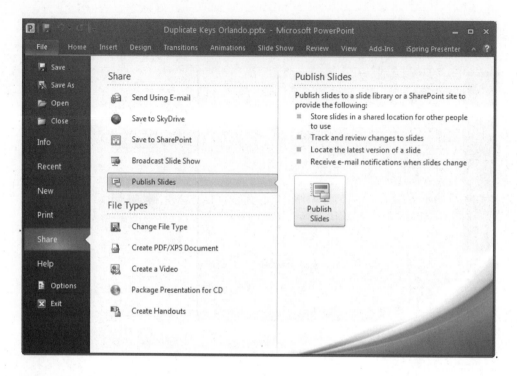

Figure 12-62. Publish slides directly from Publisher 2007.

PowerPoint then opens the same dialog box shown earlier in Figure 12-59 that displays all the slides in the current slide show. To select a slide, you must click the check box to the left of each slide to indicate which ones you want to publish. You do not have to publish all slides in the presentation deck, but you must select at least one before the **Publish** button at the bottom of the dialog box activates.

Before you can publish the slides, you must specify where you want to publish them. When you start from the slide library, SharePoint provides this information to you. However, starting from PowerPoint means that you must enter the URL of an existing SharePoint library in the **Publish To** text box. If you do not know the exact name of the library, you can enter just the root URL to the SharePoint site and then use the **Browse** button to drill down further into the site to locate the folder. However, the folder must already exist. The **Publish Slides** dialog box cannot create a new slide folder for you automatically. When you click **Publish**, PowerPoint transfers the slides from your local presentation deck to the specified SharePoint library.

■ **Caution** You must first create the folder in the SharePoint library where you want to publish your slides. Entering a URL to a folder that does not exist will not create that folder.

Viewing and Performing Actions on Your Slides

Once you have published the slides in the library, they appear in the library list, as shown in Figure 12-63. Like most lists, you can customize this list by opening the view drop-down menu and selecting the **Modify This View** option. However, the default view provides several useful pieces of metadata about the slides.

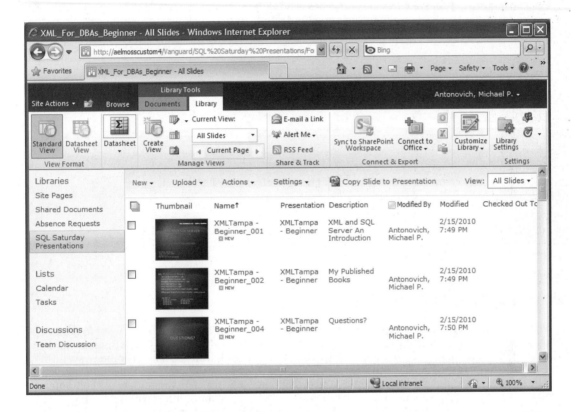

Figure 12-63. View your published slide library.

The list begins with a small thumbnail image of the slide. Following this column, you can find the slide name, taken from the title area of the slide. Immediately after this column, you can find the name of the presentation that contains the original slide along with a number that uniquely identifies the slide. The number is not the order of the slide in the presentation. Rather it is the order of the slide's creation. Also on this default view, you can see who last modified the slide, when she modified it, and the name of the person who has the slide checked out if applicable.

■ **Tip** Slide libraries also use content types. Therefore, you can create your own content type definition for slide libraries.

As with picture libraries, a check box precedes each slide, allowing you to select on which slides you want to perform specific actions. When you open the **Actions** menu, as shown in Figure 12-64, you will not find as many options as for the picture library.

Figure 12-64. View available actions for slide libraries.

For example, you can delete slides from your library by selecting which slides you want to remove and then selecting the **Delete Slides** option from the **Actions** menu. Notice that the **Actions** menu does not provide options to edit slides, change their permissions, or work with them in any other way. I will come back to that in a moment.

The **Actions** menu does contain an option to change the view to a **Datasheet View** to allow you to make mass changes quickly to multiple properties in one or more of the pictures without having to edit the properties of each image individually. It also includes the **Windows Explorer** view. This view allows you to move slides easily between folders in your slide library. However, if you attempt to move them to a directory on your local disk drive, SharePoint will create a separate PowerPoint presentation file for each slide copied.

■ **Tip** To move an image from one library folder to another, click the image in the **Windows Explorer** view and press **Ctrl+C**. Then navigate to the destination folder and paste it there by pressing **Ctrl+V**. You can also use the **Windows Explorer** view to delete folders that you no longer want. Some people also find it easier to manage their folder/directory structure using the **Windows Explorer** view.

So if the **Actions** menu does not provide options to work with individual images in the library, how can you work with these images? Simply position your mouse over the name of the image you want to work with. An arrow for a drop-down menu appears to the right of the name. Click this arrow to display the item menu, as shown in Figure 12-65.

Figure 12-65. Edit an individual slide from the library.

From this menu, you can view and edit the item's properties, manage its permissions, edit it using Microsoft Office PowerPoint (this option requires you to have PowerPoint installed on your local machine), delete the item, download the slide, and send the slide to an e-mail address or other location. You can also check out the image just as you would check out a Word document before editing it, so that others cannot edit the slide while you have it checked out. Finally, there is an option that allows you to create an alert to receive an e-mail when someone changes or deletes this slide.

As useful as all these features may sound, the real power feature is still in the library menu bar. The **Copy Slide to Presentation** feature allows you to copy slides from your library to a new or existing PowerPoint presentation.

Copying Slides from Your Slide Library to PowerPoint Presentations

As mentioned at the beginning of this discussion on slide libraries, you may want to use slide libraries to store commonly reused slides so that anyone in your organization creating a new PowerPoint presentation can import the existing slide rather than create the slide from scratch. To do this, refer back to the library menu bar and the option **Copy Slide to Presentation**, as shown in Figure 12-66.

Figure 12-66. Select a slide to copy to a PowerPoint slide presentation.

Before selecting this option, select the slides you want to insert into the new or existing presentation by checking the box to the left of each desired slide. You could also first open the PowerPoint presentation into which you want to add the slide(s) from the library. When you click **Copy Slide to Presentation**, SharePoint opens the dialog box shown in Figure 12-67. In this dialog box, you can specify whether you want to add the selected slide(s) to a new presentation or an open presentation. If you want to copy the slides to an existing presentation, the drop-down box displays the names of all presentations you currently have open. While typically you will only have one presentation open, the one you want to add the slide into, you could have several presentations open and then add the slides to each of the presentations by repeating the process described here, selecting a different presentation from the drop-down list each time. This technique is always a good way to start a new presentation that uses several existing slides from one or more other presentations stored in the slide library.

Figure 12-67. Define how to copy slides.

You can also decide to keep the source presentation format (hidden by the drop-down list in Figure 12-67). This option retains the formatting of the slide as seen in the slide library. However, because this formatting may differ from the formatting used in the presentation, you may want to deselect this option so that PowerPoint reformats the slide using the current master format scheme used by the presentation into which you are copying the slide.

The last option in this dialog box allows PowerPoint to retain a link to the slide library so that it can notify you when changes occur to the slide in the SharePoint slide library.

When you click **OK**, SharePoint copies the selected slides from the library to the end of the referenced presentation. At this point, you can use all the features of PowerPoint to manipulate the slide further and to reposition the copied slides within the presentation.

Figure 12-68 shows a single slide copied from the sample slide library SQL_CASE_Statements to the end of an existing presentation. After adding slides to a presentation, you can click the slide and drag it to a new position within the presentation.

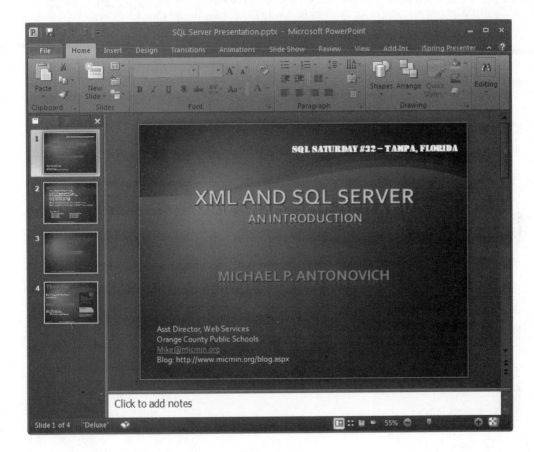

Figure 12-68. PowerPoint appends slides to the end of the show.

Summary

In this chapter, you examined three supporting SharePoint libraries. The first library, the Records Center, is the most complex library implementation presented in this book, although it starts from the basic document library. It requires coordination between at least two different sites, a working document site and an archival site, with libraries in each using content types, site columns, and configuration settings made through SharePoint's **Central Administration** site. However, it provides organizations with a powerful tool to archive documents to protect their most important information.

In learning how to build a records management system, you saw how to create reusable site columns. You also created a Word-based site content type and then made it the default content type for the library. To create the Records Center site, you needed to define an External Service Connection through the **Central Administration** site. You set up a policy on what to do with records after adding them to the Records Center, and you also saw how to create a record routing rule.

You then took a second look at the picture library, which you employed in earlier chapters as the source for images used on web pages. The chapter dived deeper into its ability to serve as a central warehouse for your organization's images, which you can share and view online through the built-in **Filmstrip View** modes. You also looked at the use of the Microsoft Office Picture Manager tool and how you can use it to add and edit pictures in the picture library. Finally, you saw how to export pictures to several Microsoft Office products, changing the picture type as well as some of its other characteristics.

However, the picture library does not solve all of your organization's image needs, especially if your organization uses Microsoft PowerPoint to create both internal and external presentations. The slide library adds features to the basic picture library specifically to support PowerPoint slides. You can use it to store and display slide presentations. However, its real power comes into play when you use it to share common slides with other people who can download them when building their own PowerPoint presentations.

Finally, that wraps up this book introducing you to how you can begin to integrate your use of Microsoft Office products with SharePoint. I know that there are many other topics we could have covered that time and space did not permit. Perhaps over time I will include them in my blog at `http://www.micmin.org/blog.aspx`. I hope you gained an appreciation for how to integrate the Microsoft Office tools that you already know with SharePoint. SharePoint collaboration will change the way you and the rest of your organization work. The ability to share and work with document libraries and lists from any location where you have Internet access lets you work anywhere, any time. This universal access to your information gives your organization the ability to decentralize the way your staff works, increasing their productivity while maintaining the integrity of the information they use. In the office, at home, or on a business trip, you are no longer far from your corporate data when you integrate your daily activities through SharePoint.

Index

■H

■M

■P

■Q

You Need the Companion eBook

Your purchase of this book entitles you to buy the companion PDF-version eBook for only $10. Take the weightless companion with you anywhere.

We believe this Apress title will prove so indispensable that you'll want to carry it with you everywhere, which is why we are offering the companion eBook (in PDF format) for $10 to customers who purchase this book now. Convenient and fully searchable, the PDF version of any content-rich, page-heavy Apress book makes a valuable addition to your programming library. You can easily find and copy code—or perform examples by quickly toggling between instructions and the application. Even simultaneously tackling a donut, diet soda, and complex code becomes simplified with hands-free eBooks!

Once you purchase your book, getting the $10 companion eBook is simple:

❶ Visit **www.apress.com/promo/tendollars/**.

❷ Complete a basic registration form to receive a randomly generated question about this title.

❸ Answer the question correctly in 60 seconds, and you will receive a promotional code to redeem for the $10.00 eBook.

eBookshop

Apress®
THE EXPERT'S VOICE™

233 Spring Street, New York, NY 10013

Offer valid through 11/10.

HEATH

¡DIME!

DOS

FABIÁN A. SAMANIEGO
University of California, Davis
Emeritus

M. CAROL BROWN
California State University, Sacramento

PATRICIA HAMILTON CARLIN
University of Central Arkansas, Conway

SIDNEY E. GORMAN
Fremont Unified School District
Fremont, California

CAROL L. SPARKS
Mt. Diablo Unified School District
Concord, California

CONTRIBUTING WRITERS
Francisco X. Alarcón
Fanny Guía

000025

McDougal Littell
Evanston, Illinois • Boston • Dallas

Director, Modern Languages
Roger D. Coulombe

Managing Editor
Sylvia Madrigal

Editors
Pedro Urbina-Martin

Project Manager
Lori Díaz

D.C. Heath Modern Language Consultants
Daniel Battisti
Dr. Teresa Carrera-Hanley
A.-Lorena Richins Layser
Bill Lionetti

Design and Production
Product Section Head, Modern Languages: Victor Curran
Senior Designer: Pamela Daly
Design Staff: Paulette Crowley, Daniel Derdula, Carolyn J. Langley,
    Joan Paley, Martha Podren
Permissions Editor: Dorothy B. McLeod
Photo Supervisor: Carmen Johnson
Photo Coordinator: Connie Komack
Book Designer: Angela Sciaraffa
Cover Design: Marshall Henrichs
Section Head, Production: Patrick Finbarr Connolly
Production Coordinator: Holly Schuster

Author Team Manager:
J. Thomas Wetterstrom

Cover Illustration
Background: Para el mercado by Mujeres Muralistas; photograph © 1992
    by Timothy Drescher.
Foreground: Photographs of students by Nancy Sheehan,
    © D.C. Heath and Company.

International Standard Book Number: 0-669-43330-6

7 8 9 10—VHP—99

REVIEWERS AND CONSULTANTS

María Brock
Miami Norland
 Senior High School
Miami, FL

Marie Carrera Lambert
Iona College
Eastchester High School
Eastchester, NY

Karen Davis
Southwest High School
Fort Worth, TX

Patricia McFarland
Concord Carlisle High School
Concord, MA

Joseph Moore
Tiffin City Schools
Tiffin, OH

Dr. Linda Pavian Roberts
Waverly Community Schools
Lansing, MI

Robin A. Ruffo
Chaparral High School
Scottsdale, AZ

Paul Sandrock
Appleton High School West
Appleton, WI

Roman J. Stearns
Arroyo Jr. Sr. High School
San Lorenzo, CA

Stephanie M. Thomas
Indiana University
Bloomington, IN

Gladys Varona-Lacey
Ithaca College
Ithaca, NY

Dr. Virginia D. Vigil
Northern Arizona University
Flagstaff, AZ

Marcos Williams
Landon School
Bethesda, MD

Richard V. Teschner
University of Texas at El Paso
El Paso, TX

Héctor Enríquez
University of Texas at El Paso
El Paso, TX

Guillermo Meza
University of Nevada
Reno, NV

LINGUISTIC
CONSULTANT

William H. Klemme
Indiana University
Fort Wayne, IN

FIELD TEST USERS
¡DIME! UNO

Dena Bachman
Lafayette High School
St. Joseph, MO

Cathy Boulanger
L. Horton Watkins High School
St. Louis, MO

Janice Costella
Stanley Intermediate School
Lafayette, CA

Karen Davis
Southwest High School
Fort Worth, TX

Beatriz DesLoges
Lexington High School
Lexington, MA

Amelia Donovan
South Gwinnett High School
Snellville, GA

Velda Hughes
Bryan Senior High School
Omaha, NE

Sarah Witmer Lehman
P. K. Yonge Laboratory School
Gainesville, FL

Alita Mantels
Hall High School
Little Rock, AR

Ann Marie Mesquita
Encina High School
Sacramento, CA

Linda Meyer
Roosevelt Junior High School
Appleton, WI

Joseph Moore
Tiffin City Schools
Tiffin, OH

Craig Mudie
Dennis-Yarmouth Regional
   High School
South Yarmouth, MA

Sue Rodríguez
Hopkins Junior High School
Fremont, CA

Janice Stangl
Bryan Senior High School
Omaha, NE

Teresa Hull Tolentino
Seven Hills Upper School
Cincinnati, OH

Grace Tripp
McCall School
Winchester, MA

Carol B. Walsh
Acton-Boxborough Regional
   High School
Acton, MA

Margaret Whitmore
Morton Junior High School
Omaha, NE

ATLAS

EL MUNDO

Groenlan

Alaska (E.U.)

Canadá

NORTEAMÉRICA

Estados Unidos

OCÉANO ATLÁNTICO

Trópico de Cáncer

Hawai (E.U.)

OCÉANO PACÍFICO

México

Cuba

Bahamas

República Dominicana

Puerto Rico

San Cristóbal y Nevis

Jamaica

Belice

Haití

Dominica

Guatemala

Honduras

Santa Lucía

Barbados

El Salvador

Costa Rica

Granada

San Vicente y Granadinas

Nicaragua

Trinidad y Tobago

Ecuador

Islas Galápagos (Ec.)

Panamá

Colombia

Venezuela

Guyana

Suriname

Guayana Francesa

Ecuador

Kiribati

SUDAMÉRICA

Perú

Brasil

Samoa Occidental

Bolivia

Tonga

Trópico de Capricornio

Paraguay

Chile

Uruguay

Argentina

Islas Malvinas

Los países de habla española

Escala de kilómetros

0   1000   2000   3000

0   1000   2000   3000

Escala de millas

OCÉANO ÁRTICO

Islandia

Noruega

Suecia Finlandia
Estonia
Letonia
Lituania

Dinamarca
Reino
Irlanda Unido Holanda
Alemania Polonia Belarús
Bélgica
Ucrania

EUROPA

Francia Suiza
Andorra Italia
España Cerdeña
Portugal
Grecia

Marruecos
Túnez Malta
Chipre Líbano
Israel

Argelia Libia
Egipto

Mauritania
Malí Níger
ÁFRICA Sudán
Gambia
Burkina
Faso
Benin
Costa Nigeria
Sierra de
eona Marfil Chad
Liberia Togo
Ghana Camerún
Guinea República
Ecuatorial Centroafricana
Gabón Uganda
Congo Rwanda
Zaire Burundi
Tanzanía

Angola
Zambia Malawi
Mozambique
Namibia Zimbabwe Madagascar
Botswana

Swazilandia
Lesotho
Sudáfrica

❶ Checoslovaquia
❷ Austria
❸ Hungría
❹ Eslovenia
❺ Croacia
❻ Bosnia & Herzgovina
❼ Yugoslavia
❽ Albania
❾ (República de) Macedonia

Kazajstán

Georgia
Azerbaiyán
Uzbekistán
Armenia Turkmenistán Tayiskistán

Siria
Iraq Irán Afganistán
Jordania
Kuwait
Arabia Bahréin Pakistán
Saudita Qatar
Emiratos
Árabes Omán
Unidos
Yemen
Eritrea
Djibouti
Etiopía

Somalia

Rusia

ASIA

Mongolia

Kirguistán

China

Corea del
Norte
Japón
Corea
del Sur

Taiwán

Bhután
Nepal
India Myanmar
Bangladesh Lao

Tailandia
Cambodia Viet Nam Filipinas

Brunei
Malasia
Singapur Indonesia

OCÉANO
PACÍFICO

Nauru

Sri Lanka

Maldivas

Seychelles

OCÉANO
ÍNDICO

Comoras

Mauricio

Papua-Nueva
Guinea

Islas
Salomón

Vanuatu

AUSTRALIA

Nueva Zelándia

ANTÁRTIDA

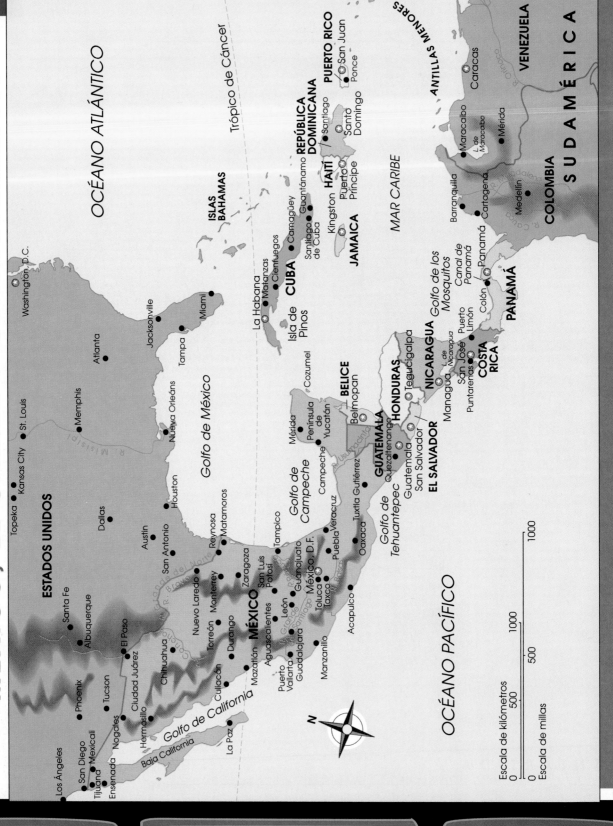

MÉXICO, EL CARIBE Y CENTROAMÉRICA

OCÉANO ATLÁNTICO

Trópico de Cáncer

OCÉANO PACÍFICO

ESTADOS UNIDOS

Los Ángeles
San Diego
Tijuana
Mexicali
Ensenada
Nogales
Santa Fe
Phoenix
Albuquerque
Tucson
El Paso
Ciudad Juárez
Hermosillo
Chihuahua
Culiacán
Durango
Torreón
Mazatlán
Aguascalientes
Guadalajara
León
Guanajuato
Toluca
Taxco
Manzanillo
Puerto Vallarta
Acapulco
Baja California
La Paz
Golfo de California
R. Bravo del Norte
R. Grande
R. Balsas
Zaragoza
Nuevo Laredo
Monterrey
San Luis Potosí
San Antonio
Austin
Dallas
Kansas City
Topeka
St. Louis
Memphis
Atlanta
Jacksonville
Tampa
Miami
Nueva Orleáns
Houston
Matamoros
Reynosa
Tampico
Veracruz
Puebla
MÉXICO México, D.F.
Oaxaca
Tuxtla Gutiérrez
Washington, D.C.
R. Misisipi

Golfo de México

Golfo de Campeche

Golfo de Tehuantepec

Mérida
Cozumel
Campeche
Península de Yucatán

ISLAS BAHAMAS

La Habana
Matanzas
Cienfuegos
CUBA
Camagüey
Santiago de Cuba
Isla de Pinos

JAMAICA
Kingston

HAITÍ
Puerto Príncipe
Guantánamo
REPÚBLICA DOMINICANA
Santiago
Santo Domingo

PUERTO RICO
San Juan
Ponce

MAR CARIBE

ANTILLAS MENORES

R. Usumacinta

BELICE
Belmopán
GUATEMALA
Quezaltenango
Guatemala
San Salvador
EL SALVADOR
HONDURAS
Tegucigalpa
NICARAGUA
Managua
L. de Nicaragua
Golfo de los Mosquitos
Puerto Limón
San José
Puntarenas
COSTA RICA
Canal de Panamá
Colón
Panamá
PANAMÁ

COLOMBIA
Barranquilla
Cartagena
Medellín
R. Magdalena
R. Cauca

VENEZUELA
Maracaibo
L. de Maracaibo
Mérida
Caracas
R. Orinoco

SUDAMÉRICA

N

Escala de kilómetros
0 500 1000
Escala de millas
0 500 1000

SUDAMÉRICA

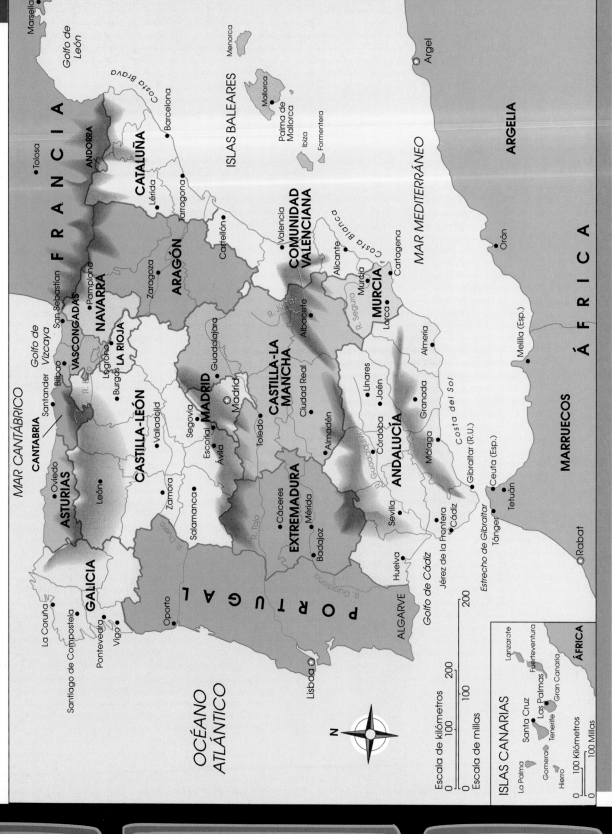

ESPAÑA

FRANCIA

PORTUGAL

MARRUECOS

ARGELIA

Á F R I C A

OCÉANO ATLÁNTICO

MAR CANTÁBRICO

MAR MEDITERRÁNEO

Golfo de León

Golfo de Vizcaya

ISLAS BALEARES

Costa Brava

Costa Blanca

Costa del Sol

Golfo de Cádiz

Estrecho de Gibraltar

Comunidades

GALICIA
ASTURIAS
CANTABRIA
VASCONGADAS
NAVARRA
LA RIOJA
CASTILLA-LEÓN
ARAGÓN
CATALUÑA
MADRID
CASTILLA-LA MANCHA
EXTREMADURA
COMUNIDAD VALENCIANA
MURCIA
ANDALUCÍA
ALGARVE

ANDORRA

Ciudades y lugares

Marsella
Tolosa
San Sebastián
Pamplona
Barcelona
Lérida
Tarragona
Castellón
Menorca
Mallorca
Palma de Mallorca
Ibiza
Formentera
Argel
Orán
Melilla (Esp.)
Zaragoza
Valencia
Alicante
Murcia
Cartagena
Logroño
Burgos
Bilbao
Santander
Oviedo
León
Valladolid
Segovia
Escorial
Ávila
Guadalajara
Madrid
Toledo
Albacete
Lorca
Almería
Granada
Jaén
Linares
Ciudad Real
Almadén
Córdoba
Zamora
Salamanca
Cáceres
Mérida
Badajoz
Sevilla
Málaga
Jérez de la Frontera
Cádiz
Huelva
Gibraltar (R.U.)
Ceuta (Esp.)
Tetuán
Tánger
Rabat
Lisboa
Oporto
Vigo
Pontevedra
La Coruña
Santiago de Compostela

R. Ebro
R. Júcar
R. Segura
R. Tajo
R. Duero
R. Guadiana
R. Guadalquivir

N

Escala de kilómetros
0   100   200

Escala de millas
0   100   200

ISLAS CANARIAS

ÁFRICA

La Palma
Gomera
Hierro
Tenerife
Santa Cruz
Gran Canaria
Las Palmas
Fuerteventura
Lanzarote

0   100 Kilómetros

0   100 Millas

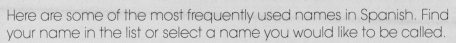

¿Cómo te llamas tú?

Here are some of the most frequently used names in Spanish. Find your name in the list or select a name you would like to be called.

Chicos

Alberto (Beto)	Javier
Alejandro (Alex)	Jerónimo
Alfonso	Joaquín
Alfredo	Jorge
Andrés	José (Pepe)
Antonio (Toni, Toño)	Juan (Juancho)
Arturo (Tudi)	Julio
Benjamín	Lorenzo
Bernardo	Lucas
Carlos	Luis
César	Manuel (Manolo)
Clemente (Tito)	Marcos
Cristóbal	Mariano
Daniel (Dani)	Mario
David	Martín
Diego	Mateo
Eduardo (Edi)	Miguel
Emilio	Nicolás (Nico)
Enrique (Quico)	Octavio
Ernesto	Óscar
Esteban	Pablo
Federico (Fede)	Patricio
Felipe	Pedro
Fernando (Nando)	Rafael (Rafa)
Francisco (Cisco,	Ramiro
Paco, Pancho)	Ramón
Gabriel (Gabi)	Raúl
Germán	Ricardo (Riqui)
Gilberto	Roberto (Beto)
Gonzalo	Rodrigo (Rodri)
Gregorio	Rubén
Guillermo (Memo)	Salvador
Gustavo	Samuel
Hernán	Sancho
Homero	Santiago (Santi)
Horacio	Sergio
Hugo	Teodoro
Ignacio (Nacho)	Timoteo
Jacobo	Tomás
Jaime	Víctor

Chicas

Adela	Guadalupe (Lupe)
Adriana	Inés
Alicia	Irene
Amalia	Isabel (Chavela)
Ana	Josefina (Pepita)
Anita	Juana (Juanita)
Ángela	Julia
Antonia (Toni)	Laura
Bárbara	Leonor
Beatriz (Bea)	Leticia (Leti)
Berta	Lilia
Blanca	Lucía
Carla	Luisa
Carlota	Marcela (Chela)
Carmen	Margarita (Rita)
Carolina	María
Catalina	Mariana
Cecilia	Maricarmen
Clara	Marilú
Concepción (Concha,	Marta
Conchita)	Mercedes (Meche)
Cristina (Cris, Tina)	Mónica
Débora	Natalia (Nati)
Diana	Norma
Dolores (Lola)	Patricia (Pati)
Dorotea (Dora)	Pilar
Elena	Ramona
Elisa	Raquel
Eloísa	Rebeca
Elvira	Rosa (Rosita)
Emilia (Emi)	Sara
Estela	Silvia
Ester	Sofía
Eva	Soledad (Sole)
Florencia	Sonia
Francisca (Paca,	Susana (Susanita)
Paquita)	Teresa (Tere)
Gabriela (Gabi)	Verónica (Vero)
Gloria	Victoria (Vicki)
Graciela (Chela)	Yolanda (Yoli)

CONTENIDO

U N I D A D 2

¡Qué chévere!

UNIDAD 4

Era una ciudad muy...

Caracas, 1940

UNIDAD 6 ¡Hagamos una excursión! 274

Featured country: COSTA RICA

xix

¿Cómo pasan el tiempo?

¡ En una semana empezamos !

¿ Qué piensas tú ?

1. ¿Crees que estas fotos se sacaron en la misma ciudad o en distintas ciudades? ¿Por qué crees eso?

2. En efecto, todas las fotos se sacaron en dos ciudades distintas: El Paso, Texas y Caracas, Venezuela. ¿Puedes identificar cuáles son de El Paso y cuáles son de Caracas? ¿Qué semejanzas ves entre las dos ciudades? ¿Qué diferencias? ¿Cómo explicas estas semejanzas? ¿diferencias?

3. ¿En qué día del año crees que se sacaron las fotos en la página anterior? ¿Por qué crees eso? ¿De qué estarán hablando estos estudiantes?

4. ¿Qué están haciendo los jóvenes en las fotos de arriba? ¿Son actividades que tú y tus amigos hacen?

5. ¿Qué actividades te gusta hacer durante el año escolar? ¿durante las vacaciones de verano? ¿durante las vacaciones de invierno?

6. En **¡DIME!** UNO, los estudiantes expresaron sus impresiones de los jóvenes de otros países y descubrieron cómo son en realidad. ¿Creen tú y tus amigos que los jóvenes de Venezuela son similares o diferentes de ustedes? ¿Por qué?

7. ¿Qué crees que vamos a hacer en esta lección?

1

Buenos días, amigos, y ¡bienvenidos! Es un gran placer conocerlos, y un verdadero privilegio presentarles mi ciudad— El Paso, Texas.

2

El Paso es una ciudad con una larga historia . . .

cuatro siglos de historia — el doble de la edad de EE.UU. En El Paso de hoy, todavía vemos la influencia de diversas gentes y culturas como . . .

3

la influencia indígena,

la de los conquistadores españoles,

En El Paso, 60% de la población somos de origen mexicano y nos criamos bilingües.

Además, El Paso está en la frontera mexicana a unos cuantos pasos de nuestra ciudad gemela, Ciudad Juárez. Sólo el Río Grande, o el Río Bravo como lo llaman en México, separa las dos ciudades.

la de los vaqueros del suroeste norteamericano,

y por supuesto, la de México.

4 ¿Quieren saber cómo pasamos el tiempo?

Pues . . . El Paso es una ciudad muy animada y hay mucho que hacer aquí.

En primer lugar, el clima es fenomenal. ¡Hace sol 360 días al año! En el verano, cuando hace calor, mis amigos y yo nos divertimos mucho.

También hago cosas divertidas con mi familia. Por ejemplo, nos gusta ir a las montañas de Nuevo México. No quedan lejos de aquí.

Allí nos gusta acampar— incluso en invierno.

En el campamento mi actividad favorita es cocinar al aire libre. ¡Me encanta! Lo que no me explico es, si papá y Daniel insisten en que no les gusta mi comida, ¿por qué siempre se la comen?

5

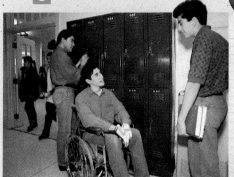

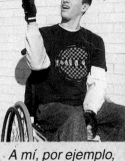

Ah, . . . pero quieren saber algo de mi escuela, ¿verdad? Mi hermano y yo vamos a El Paso High School. Estudiamos mucho, porque los profesores son muy exigentes. Nos dan mucha tarea.

Pero hay otras cosas que hacer.

A mí, por ejemplo, me encantan los deportes, el baloncesto en particular. Soy miembro de un equipo de baloncesto.

A Daniel le gusta el teatro y no es mal actor.

Se puede decir que los dos somos "estrellas", ¿no?

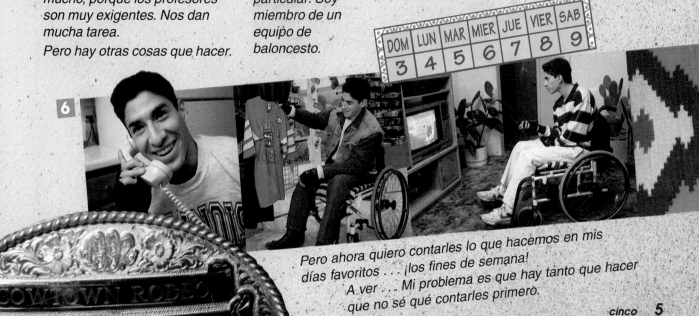

DOM	LUN	MAR	MIER	JUE	VIER	SAB
3	4	5	6	7	8	9

6

Pero ahora quiero contarles lo que hacemos en mis días favoritos . . . ¡los fines de semana! A ver . . . Mi problema es que hay tanto que hacer que no sé qué contarles primero.

7

Bueno, Daniel y yo pasamos mucho tiempo con nuestras amigas Tina y Margarita. A Daniel y a Tina les gusta mucho jugar tenis.

A Margarita y a mí nos gusta ir de compras.

También nos paseamos en el parque o en bicicleta.

Y con frecuencia salimos a tomar refrescos o a comer algo en un restaurante.

Daniel y yo vamos mucho al cine.

8

Sí, . . . hay mucho que hacer y nos gusta hacer de todo — leer, nadar, dormir, bailar, cantar, cocinar, comer, hablar, desayunar, escribir, escuchar, estudiar, hacer ejercicio, jugar, lavar, pasear en bicicleta, tocar el saxofón, ver la tele . . .

3 ¿Qué dice?

A. **PARA EMPEZAR . . .** Indica si los siguientes comentarios son ciertos o falsos. Si son falsos, corrígelos.

1. El Paso tiene una historia de 200 años más o menos, como EE.UU.
2. La cultura indígena y la española influyeron mucho en la historia de El Paso.
3. La mayoría de la población de El Paso es bilingüe.
4. El Paso está a unas cuantas millas de Ciudad Juárez, México.
5. En El Paso llueve mucho y casi siempre hace frío.
6. Nuevo México está muy cerca de El Paso.
7. La ciudad gemela de El Paso es Ruidoso.
8. El Río Grande y el Río Bravo son dos ríos muy cerca de El Paso.

B. **¿QUÉ DECIMOS . . . ?** Identifica a la persona que hace estos comentarios.

Daniel   **Papá**   **Tina**   **Margarita**

1. "¡Bravo, Martín! ¡Qué talento!"
2. "Aquí estamos aprovechando los últimos días de vacaciones".
3. "¡Ay, sí! ¡Me encantaría tener otro mes de vacaciones!"
4. "¡Aguafiestas! ¡Déjanos gozar de la última semana!"
5. "¿Viven por aquí cerca?"
6. "Yo sí, a unas cuadras. Nos mudamos para acá en julio".
7. "¡Híjole, cuentas y cuentas y más cuentas!"
8. "¡Qué va! ¡Sus preguntas no tienen fin!"

C. **Actividades favoritas.** Tu compañero(a) quiere saber más de tus gustos. Contesta sus preguntas.

MODELO   bailar
    Compañero(a): **¿Te gusta bailar?**
    Tú: **Sí, me gusta bailar.** o
           No, no me gusta bailar. o
           Sí, me encanta bailar.

1. hacer la tarea
2. practicar deportes
3. ir a fiestas
4. estudiar
5. salir los fines de semana
6. escribir composiciones
7. ir de excursión
8. ir al cine
9. escuchar música clásica
10. ir de compras

REPASO

Gustar and encantar

Talking about likes and dislikes:

me gusta(n)	no me gusta(n)
te gusta(n)	no te gusta(n)
le gusta(n)	no le gusta(n)
nos gusta(n)	no nos gusta(n)
les gusta(n)	no les gusta(n)

No me gusta bailar.
Me gustan mucho los deportes.

Talking about what you really like, or love:

me encanta(n)	nos encanta(n)
te encanta(n)	
le encanta(n)	les encanta(n)

Le encantan los tacos.
Nos encanta acampar.

See **¿Por qué se dice así?,**
page G2, section 1.1.

REPASO

Indirect object pronouns

me	nos
te	
le	les

Me gusta correr.
Les encanta el teatro.

To clarify or emphasize: **a mí, a ti, a él, a ella,** etc.

Nunca les escribo **a ellos** pero siempre les escribo **a ustedes**.
Pues, **a mí** sí me gusta.

See **¿Por qué se dice así?,**
page G2, section 1.1.

CH. Gustos. La familia de Isabel es muy activa. Según ella, ¿qué les gusta hacer a todos?

yo

MODELO   **A mí me gusta pasear en bicicleta.**

1. mi hermano Luis

2. mi papá

3. yo

4. mi mamá

5. mis abuelitos

6. mi hermana Elena

7. papá y Miguel

8. yo

9. mi mamá

REPASO

Actividades

bailar   cantar

cocinar   comer

desayunar   escribir

escuchar   estudiar

hablar   hacer ejercicio

jugar   lavar

leer   tocar la guitarra

nadar   ver la tele

pasear en bicicleta

D. Le encanta. ¿Conoces los gustos de las otras personas? Di qué les gusta a tus amigos en la clase.

 EJEMPLO **A Martín y a Margarita les gustan los deportes.**

a [. . .] y a [. . .]
a mí
a mi amigo(a) [. . .]
al (a la) profesor(a)
a [. . .] y a mí

| los exámenes |
| la música rock |
| las películas románticas |
| la televisión |
| los deportes |
| la natación |
| los museos |
| el fútbol americano |

---REPASO---

Present tense:
Regular verb endings

-ar	-er, -ir
-o	-o
-as	-es
-a	-e
-amos	-emos, -imos
-an	-en

Yo **hablo** por teléfono, mamá **lee** el periódico y papá **prepara** la comida.

See **¿Por qué se dice así?**, *page G4, section 1.2.*

E. ¿Con qué frecuencia? Pregúntale a tu compañero(a) con qué frecuencia hace estas cosas.

 EJEMPLO   practicar karate
Tú: **¿Con qué frecuencia practicas karate?**
Compañero(a): **Nunca practico karate.** o
                   Practico karate todos los días.

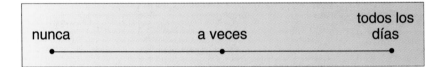

| | | todos los |
| nunca | a veces | días |

1. asistir a conciertos
2. escuchar la radio
3. viajar en autobús
4. abrir regalos
5. comprar ropa nueva
6. cocinar
7. comer en restaurantes mexicanos
8. leer novelas de aventura
9. pasear en bicicleta
10. sacar fotos

F. Siempre ocupados. Según Silvia León, ¿qué hacen los miembros de su familia a estas horas?

Enrique y yo

MODELO   **Enrique y yo estudiamos a las nueve de la noche.**

1. Enrique

2. papá

3. mamá y yo

4. mis amigas y yo

5. mamá

6. toda la familia

7. mi hermano y su amigo

8. yo

Asking for and giving the time

¿Qué hora es?

Son las nueve en punto.

Son las seis y cuarto.

Son las once y media.

Son las dos menos veinte.

LECCIÓN 1

G. Los fines de semana. Pregúntale a tu compañero(a) qué hace con sus hermanos y con sus amigos los fines de semana.

 EJEMPLO *Tú:* **¿Tú y tus hermanos limpian la casa?**
Compañero(a): **No, nunca limpiamos la casa los fines de semana.**

VOCABULARIO ÚTIL:

asistir a clases	jugar [. . .]	¿ . . . ?
bailar	leer novelas	
comer pizza	practicar deportes	
correr	practicar el piano	
escribir cartas	trabajar	
estudiar	ver televisión	
hablar por teléfono	visitar a los abuelos	

REPASO

**Requesting information:
Question words**

¿Adónde?	**¿Cuándo?**
¿Dónde?	**¿Cuánto(a)?**
¿Cómo?	**¿Cuántos(as)?**
¿Cuál(es)?	**¿Por qué?**
¿Qué?	**¿Quién(es)?**

Note that all question words require a written accent.

See **¿Por qué se dice así?,**
page G7, section 1.3.

H. ¿Qué pasa? ¿Qué dicen tú y un(a) amigo(a) cuando se encuentran en el pasillo?

Amigo(a): Hola. ¿ _____ estás?
Tú: Bien, gracias, ¿y tú? ¿_____ tal?
Amigo(a): Regular. Tengo mucho que estudiar.
Tú: ¿_____ tienes que hacer?
Amigo(a): Tengo que escribir una composición.
Tú: ¿Para _____?
Amigo(a): Para el señor Guzmán.
Tú: ¿De _____ páginas es la composición?
Amigo(a): ¡Cinco! ¡Caramba! ¿_____ lo voy a hacer?
Tú: Te ayudo. ¿_____ vas a estudiar?
Amigo(a): Esta tarde después de las clases. ¿_____ te encuentro?
Tú: En la biblioteca.
Amigo(a): Después, ¿_____ no comemos algo?
Tú: ¡Excelente! Me encantan los nachos.
Amigo(a): ¿_____ vamos?
Tú: Al Café del Sol. Son muy buenos allí.

I. Amiga por correspondencia. Vas a escribirle una carta a tu nueva amiga por correspondencia. ¿Qué preguntas piensas hacerle?

MODELO edad: ¿número de años?
¿Cuántos años tienes?

1. escuela: ¿nombre?
2. clases: ¿hora?
3. estudiar: ¿lugar?
4. amigos: ¿personalidad?
5. familia: ¿número de personas?
6. actividades: ¿los fines de semana?
7. música: ¿grupos favoritos?
8. deportes: ¿preferencias?

CHARLEMOS UN POCO MÁS

A. **Encuesta.** Usa la cuadrícula que tu profesor(a) te va a dar para entrevistar a varias personas en la clase. Pregúntales si les gusta hacer las actividades indicadas en los cuadrados. Pídele a cada persona que conteste afirmativamente que firme el cuadrado apropiado. No se permite que una persona firme más de un cuadrado.

EJEMPLO   pasear en bicicleta

      Tú: **¿Te gusta pasear en bicicleta?**
      Compañero(a):   **Sí, me encanta.**
      Tú: **Bien. Firma aquí, por favor.**

      tocar el piano

      Tú: **¿Te gusta tocar el piano?**
      Compañero(a):   **No, no me gusta.**
      Tú: **¡Qué lástima!**

B. **¡Charada!** En grupos de tres, preparen una lista de seis actividades que a todos les gusta hacer. Luego trabajando con otro grupo, dramaticen la primera actividad en su lista para ver si los otros pueden adivinar la actividad. Túrnense hasta dramatizar todas las actividades en sus listas.

C. **¿Y tu profesor(a)?** Con un(a) compañero(a) de clase, escribe una lista de cinco o más actividades que crees que hace tu profesor(a) durante el fin de semana. Después, hazle preguntas al profesor(a) para verificar tu lista.

EJEMPLO   *Tú escribes:*   **calificar exámenes**
           Tú preguntas: **¿Califica usted exámenes los fines de semana?**

CH. ¿Cuándo juega fútbol Beto?   Tu profesor(a) te va a dar un dibujo de varias personas que hacen distintas actividades en distintos días. El problema es que en algunos dibujos faltan los nombres y en otros faltan las fechas. Pregúntale a tu compañero(a) los nombres o las fechas que te faltan y dale la información que le falte a él o a ella. Cuando terminen, escriban una oración para describir cada dibujo.

 EJEMPLO   *Tú:*   **¿Cómo se llama el chico que juega fútbol?**
 Compañero(a):   **Se llama Beto. ¿Cuándo juega fútbol?**
 Tú: **Beto juega fútbol el sábado por la mañana.**

Dramatizaciones

A. Hola.   Te encuentras con un(a) amigo(a) en el supermercado. Dramatiza esta conversación.

- Salúdense.
- Pregúntale qué está haciendo y dile lo que haces tú.
- Hablen de otras actividades que les gusta o no les gusta hacer.
- Despídanse.

B. Mucho gusto.   Acaban de presentarte a un(a) nuevo(a) estudiante. Salúdalo(a) y luego preséntaselo(la) a tus amigos. Hablen de sus actividades favoritas y de sus familias. Decidan qué van a hacer esta tarde. Dramatiza la situación con tres compañeros de clase.

1. Enrique

2. papá

3. mamá y yo

4. mis amigas y yo

5. mamá

6. toda la familia

7. mi hermano y su amigo

8. yo

Asking for and giving the time

¿Qué hora es?

Son las nueve en punto.

Son las seis y cuarto.

Son las once y media.

Son las dos menos veinte.

LECCIÓN 1

G. Los fines de semana. Pregúntale a tu compañero(a) qué hace con sus hermanos y con sus amigos los fines de semana.

 EJEMPLO

Tú: **¿Tú y tus hermanos limpian la casa?**

Compañero(a): **No, nunca limpiamos la casa los fines de semana.**

VOCABULARIO ÚTIL:

asistir a clases	jugar [. . .]	¿ . . . ?
bailar	leer novelas	
comer pizza	practicar deportes	
correr	practicar el piano	
escribir cartas	trabajar	
estudiar	ver televisión	
hablar por teléfono	visitar a los abuelos	

REPASO

**Requesting information:
Question words**

¿Adónde?	**¿Cuándo?**
¿Dónde?	**¿Cuánto(a)?**
¿Cómo?	**¿Cuántos(as)?**
¿Cuál(es)?	**¿Por qué?**
¿Qué?	**¿Quién(es)?**

Note that all question words require a written accent.

See **¿Por qué se dice así?**,
page G7, section 1.3.

H. ¿Qué pasa? ¿Qué dicen tú y un(a) amigo(a) cuando se encuentran en el pasillo?

Amigo(a): Hola. ¿ _____ estás?

Tú: Bien, gracias, ¿y tú? ¿_____ tal?

Amigo(a): Regular. Tengo mucho que estudiar.

Tú: ¿_____ tienes que hacer?

Amigo(a): Tengo que escribir una composición.

Tú: ¿Para _____?

Amigo(a): Para el señor Guzmán.

Tú: ¿De _____ páginas es la composición?

Amigo(a): ¡Cinco! ¡Caramba! ¿_____ lo voy a hacer?

Tú: Te ayudo. ¿_____ vas a estudiar?

Amigo(a): Esta tarde después de las clases. ¿_____ te encuentro?

Tú: En la biblioteca.

Amigo(a): Después, ¿_____ no comemos algo?

Tú: ¡Excelente! Me encantan los nachos.

Amigo(a): ¿_____ vamos?

Tú: Al Café del Sol. Son muy buenos allí.

I. Amiga por correspondencia. Vas a escribirle una carta a tu nueva amiga por correspondencia. ¿Qué preguntas piensas hacerle?

MODELO edad: ¿número de años?
¿Cuántos años tienes?

1. escuela: ¿nombre?
2. clases: ¿hora?
3. estudiar: ¿lugar?
4. amigos: ¿personalidad?
5. familia: ¿número de personas?
6. actividades: ¿los fines de semana?
7. música: ¿grupos favoritos?
8. deportes: ¿preferencias?

IMPACTO CULTURAL
Excursiones

Antes de empezar

A. Ciudad fronteriza. Una ciudad fronteriza es una ciudad que está en la frontera *(línea que divide dos naciones)* con otro país. A veces vemos dos ciudades fronterizas, una en cada nación, lado a lado, la una con la otra. Contesta estas preguntas para ver cuánto sabes de ciudades fronterizas.

1. ¿Hay ciudades fronterizas en Estados Unidos? ¿Con qué países tienen fronteras?
2. ¿Conoces algunas ciudades fronterizas? ¿Cuáles? ¿Las has visitado alguna vez?
3. ¿Te gustaría vivir en una ciudad fronteriza? ¿Por qué sí o por qué no?

B. Anticipar. Mira las fotos en esta lectura y escribe tres preguntas que crees que la lectura va a contestar. Luego escribe otras dos preguntas que no estás seguro si la lectura va a contestar pero que te gustaría tener la información.

EL PASO DEL NORTE
UNA BREVE HISTORIA

que dividen naciones / hacen hacer

conexiones

eventos / relacionada

área cercana

viñas de uvas

hombres de negocio

mejorar

Las líneas fronterizas* que se trazan* entre los países muchas veces no llegan a cumplir* su función de separación. Éste es el caso del suroeste de Estados Unidos donde muchas ciudades de esta región aún conservan lazos* culturales, sociales y económicos con el país vecino, México. Una de estas ciudades es El Paso, en el estado de Texas, que a pesar de hechos* histórico-políticos sigue fuertemente ligada* a su ciudad gemela mexicana, Ciudad Juárez.

Antes de la llegada de los conquistadores de España, la región que ahora ocupan El Paso-Ciudad Juárez en la meseta central de México, estaba ocupada por algunas tribus indígenas americanas como los suma, los manso, los jacome y los jumano. Estas tribus vivían en "rancherías" o pequeños pueblos de más o menos cien personas dedicadas a la agricultura.

En 1534, el conquistador Álvar Núñez Cabeza de Vaca y tres españoles más llegaron a la región de Texas. Ellos creyeron que estas tierras tenían muchas riquezas, pero se desilusionaron al no encontrar nada. Por el contrario, ésta era una zona desértica, de montañas áridas, fuertes vientos y temperaturas extremas.

Sin embargo, en 1581 los frailes franciscanos llegaron a Texas y empezaron a fundar muchas misiones. ① En los alrededores* de El Paso fundaron las primeras dos misiones de Texas en 1682. Los frailes convirtieron esta región del Río Grande en una zona como la del Río Nilo en Egipto. Había muchos cultivos de árboles frutales, viñedos* y trigo. Los españoles dominaron la frontera norte hasta 1821 cuando ocurrió la independencia de México y esta región pasó a formar parte de la nueva nación mexicana.

Durante el período mexicano, la frontera norte siguió siendo una zona agrícola. También en este período, un grupo de comerciantes* que incluye a John G. Heathen y a Stephen F. Austin, empieza la gradual ocupación de la frontera norte por angloamericanos, con la intención de desarrollar* estas zonas de Texas.

R. R. EATING HOUSE & LUNCH COUNTER

En 1836 se proclama la República de Texas y en 1844 se declara la anexión de este estado a Estados Unidos. En 1846, Estados Unidos le declara la guerra a México, la cual termina en 1848 con el Tratado de Guadalupe Hidalgo. En este tratado, se establece que California, Nevada, Utah, casi todo Arizona y Nuevo México y partes de Colorado y Wyoming pasan a ser parte de Estados Unidos por la suma de $15 millones pagados a México.

Desde 1848, las ciudades de Texas como El Paso, se empezaron a poblar* y desarrollar muy rápidamente. Cuando en 1848 se descubrió oro en California, El Paso del Norte se convirtió en "el último lugar de descanso" para comprar todos los víveres necesarios para llegar a California. En 1881, con la llegada de los trenes, **②** El Paso se convirtió en una importante ciudad fronteriza.

Ahora El Paso es una moderna ciudad **③** occidental que, sin embargo, no ha cortado sus lazos con su ciudad hermana del otro lado del Río Grande, o Río Bravo, como lo llaman en México. Hay una gran interdependencia económica, cultural y social entre El Paso y Ciudad Juárez. El Paso conserva sus raíces mexicanas. El bilingüismo en El Paso es un fenómeno extendido por toda la ciudad. **④** Un experto en la historia de estas dos ciudades, Carey McWilliams, dice que el Río Grande no separa a la gente sino que la une.*

tener personas que habitan dicho lugar **③**

combina, junta

Verifiquemos

1. Prepara un diagrama como el siguiente, e incluye toda la información posible bajo cada categoría.

El Paso antes de los españoles

1.
2.

El Paso durante la ocupación española

1.
2.

El Paso bajo México

1.
2.

El Paso moderno

1.
2.

2. ¿Por qué crees que Estados Unidos declaró guerra contra México en 1846?

3. ¿Crees que Estados Unidos pagó suficiente por todo el área que ganó en el Tratado de Guadalupe Hidalgo? ¿Por qué sí o por qué no?

¿ Qué piensas de este collar ?

cumpleaños de Víctor

cumpleaños de mi hermana

cumpleaños de papá

cumpleaños de mamá

¿Qué piensas tú?

1. Estas jóvenes están en un centro comercial. ¿Qué crees que van a hacer?

2. Octubre siempre es muy costoso para Margarita. ¿Por qué?

3. Al comprar regalos para sus padres, su hermana y su amigo Víctor, Margarita tiene que considerar los gustos y las preferencias de cada uno. Basándote en las fotos, ¿qué crees que le va a interesar a cada uno?

4. ¿Qué regalos recomiendas tú para cada persona? Explica por qué.

5. ¿Qué tienes en común con tus mejores amigos? ¿Cómo son diferentes? Descríbete con una sola palabra. Describe a tus mejores amigos con una sola palabra. Describe a cada miembro de tu familia de la misma manera breve.

6. ¿Hay algunas diferencias entre este centro comercial y los centros comerciales en tu ciudad? Explica las diferencias.

7. ¿Qué crees que vas a aprender a decir y hacer en esta lección?

BAILÓ CON UN BULTO

1

En las partes rurales de Texas, Nuevo México, Colorado y Utah, cuando se ve a una persona hacer autostop, no es raro que alguien diga, "Tal vez quiera ir al baile". ¿Por qué dicen eso?, preguntas. Pues, deja contarte algo que pasó hace varios años . . .

2

Imagínate que es una noche oscura y triste de sábado. Un joven soldado, que acaba de regresar a su casa del servicio militar, va manejando su viejo Chevy desgastado, cuando ve a una joven que pide un aventón.

3

El soldado para su coche y le pregunta, "¿Adónde vas?"

"Hay un baile en el pueblo. ¿Puede darme un aventón?"

Como el joven no siente ninguna aprehensión, decide darle un aventón.

Camino al pueblo, la muchacha no habla mucho, pero dice que se llama Crucita Delgado.

El joven queda fascinado con la hermosa muchacha.

4

Cuando llegan al baile la gente tiene mucha curiosidad. Todos conocen bien al joven soldado, pero nadie conoce a la muchacha.

5

Ella es tan hermosa como misteriosa. Tiene la cara pálida y lleva su largo pelo negro en un moño, estilo victoriano. En efecto, todo su vestir parece victoriano: su vestido largo y negro con florecitas de color rosa y azules, su cuello alto, decorado con encaje blanco. Sobre el encaje lleva un broche camafeo. También las medias y los zapatos parecen ser de principios de siglo.

6

El soldado la saca a bailar pero la música es demasiado rápida y ruidosa para ella.

Después de sólo unas cuantas vueltas rápidas, la pobre mujer se cae al suelo. La gente quiere contener la risa pero les es imposible.

Muy avergonzada, Crucita empieza a llorar. Las lágrimas corren sobre las pálidas mejillas de la muchacha. El soldado trata de consolarla, pero está muy desconcertada.

7

Después de un rato, la música empieza de nuevo. Esta vez, es música mexicana. Crucita conoce bien estos bailes y en muy poco tiempo se convierte en la mujer más bella del baile. Toda la gente la mira con admiración.

8

Demasiado pronto termina la música y es hora de ir a casa. Al salir del baile, el soldado pone su chaqueta militar sobre los hombros de Crucita. Él está decidido que quiere mucho verla otra vez. La encuentra encantadora.

9

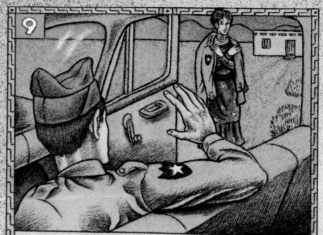

El joven ofrece llevarla a su casa, pero ella insiste en bajarse del coche allá donde él la recogió.

Entonces, para tener buena excusa para volver a verla, el joven soldado insiste en prestarle su chaqueta militar hasta el día siguiente.

10

Por la mañana, bien temprano, el joven se sube al viejo Chevy y vuelve al sitio donde dejó a Crucita. Allí sigue una vereda que conduce a una casa de adobe abandonada.

11

Llama a la puerta varias veces y por fin una viejita contesta. El joven le habla del baile de la noche anterior. La viejita se asusta y le dice, "No es posible. ¡Váyase!" Pero cuando él sigue insistiendo ella le dice, "Bueno, venga. Sígame".

12

Y la viejita le conduce al cementerio, donde le muestra una tumba. Y allí, colgada sobre una lápida, ve su chaqueta militar.

Cuando recoge su chaqueta, puede leer la inscripción en la lápida:

CRUCITA DELGADO
1878–1897
Que Su Alma Alcance
la Paz Eterna

En ese instante, el soldado se dio cuenta que la noche anterior había bailado con un bulto.

¿QUÉ DECIMOS...?

Al andar de compras

1 ¿Le gustan los collares?

Tina y Margarita están de compras en un centro comercial.

Ya casi tengo todo. Tú también, ¿no? ¡Compraste muchísimo!

Sí, ¿verdad? Y todavía tengo que buscarle un regalo a mi mamá.

Estoy tan preocupada porque el lunes es su santo y todavía no tengo nada para ella.

¡Buena idea! A mi mamá le encanta la joyería de fantasía. Le puedo comprar un lindo juego de collar y aretes.

¿Le gustan los collares? Están en oferta en esa joyería.

Descuento de 20%

Gracias, Tina. Siempre tienes ideas tan buenas.

2 Mamá prefiere el rojo.

¿Qué piensas de estos collares? Me encanta el azul.

Pues, mamá prefiere el rojo, pero tiene un vestido blanco y el azul combina bien con el blanco, ¿no?

Claro. Ay, mira, una pulsera y aretes también— un juego completo.

Son perfectos. ¿A cuánto están?

No está mal. ¡Me los llevo! Estoy segura que le van a gustar a mi mamá.

Están en oferta. Todo está rebajado en un veinte por ciento. Deja calcularlo. El juego completo te sale en $24.00 más el impuesto.

3 ¿Qué hacen por aquí?

Estoy tan contenta. Me encantan mis compras, en particular, el regalo para mamá.

¿De compras otra vez? ¿Queda algo en las tiendas para nosotros o ya se lo compraron todo?

¡Hola, Mateo, Daniel!

¿Qué pasa, muchachos? ¿Qué hacen por aquí?

No sé qué me pasa. Echo de menos las vacaciones. No puedo creer que las clases ya comenzaron.

Probablemente lo mismo que ustedes. Yo busco una chaqueta y Mateo ... Cuidado con Mateo porque anda de mal humor.

Tu problema es que tienes química con el profesor "Mataestudiantes".

No, no es eso.

Oye, Daniel. Y esta carta, ¿de quién es?

Es de mi amigo venezolano.

¿Tu amigo venezolano?

4 ¿De qué se escriben?

No sabía que tenías amigos en Venezuela.

Es un amigo por correspondencia. Es muy simpático.

¿Y de qué se escriben?

Hablamos de nuestras familias y amigos y actividades. Por ejemplo, esta vez me dice que juega béisbol, que va frecuentemente al cine y que le gusta comer al aire libre.

Hmmm. ¿Y es guapo? ¿No te pregunta si tienes amigas simpáticas como nosotras?

Lo siento, pero no. Sólo quiere saber qué hago los fines de semana, si salgo frecuentemente, qué películas me gustan, cuál es mi música favorita, si me gustan los deportes y cosas así.

¿Y ya le contestaste?

Todavía no. Pienso hacerlo esta noche.

Pues, le tienes que contar de tus amigas.

A. **PARA EMPEZAR . . .** Indica si estas oraciones son ciertas o falsas a base del cuento "Bailó con un bulto". Si son falsas, corrígelas.

1. Una joven muy hermosa ve a un joven soldado que hace autostop.
2. La joven dice que hay un baile en el pueblo y pide un aventón.
3. El joven queda muy impresionado con Crucita Delgado.
4. La gente del pueblo conoce bien a Crucita Delgado pero nadie conoce al soldado.
5. Crucita está muy de moda en su vestido largo negro de florecitas color de rosa. Claramente es la última moda.
6. Crucita no sabe bailar al ritmo de la música moderna pero baila muy bien a la música mexicana.
7. El joven soldado lleva a Crucita a su casa después del baile y entra a conocer a sus padres.
8. Al día siguiente, cuando llama a la puerta de la casa de Crucita, ella no está allí.
9. Ahora Crucita Delgado es una viejita que vive sola en la casa abandonada.
10. El joven soldado bailó toda la noche con un fantasma.

B. **¿QUÉ DECIMOS . . .?** ¿De qué hablan Daniel y sus amigos: de sus compras, de sus clases o de la carta de Venezuela?

1. "Pienso hacerlo esta noche".
2. "¿A cuánto están?"
3. "Es de mi amigo venezolano".
4. "No sé qué me pasa. Echo de menos las vacaciones".
5. "Estoy segura que le van a gustar a mi mamá".
6. "¿Qué piensas de estos collares?"
7. "Sólo quiere saber qué hago los fines de semana".
8. "Me encanta el azul".

C. **¿Cómo están?** Son las once de la mañana del primer día de clases. ¿Cómo se sienten estos alumnos y profesores?

Lucía

MODELO **Lucía está nerviosa y preocupada.**

VOCABULARIO ÚTIL:

muerto de hambre	listo para las clases	aburrido	triste
emocionado	preocupado	frustrado	solo
cansado	contento	nervioso	tranquilo

1. Marcos

2. Eugenio y Sofía

3. Teodora

4. las profesoras

5. Elena

6. el señor Rubio

7. Clemente, Eva y Lupe

8. Esteban y David

CH. A clase. Nena y Raúl están hablando antes de su clase. ¿Qué dicen?

Nena: Hola, Raúl. ¿Cómo ____?
Raúl: Hola, Nena. Bien, ¿y tú?
Nena: Bien, gracias. ¿Qué ____ haciendo?
Raúl: ____ mirando mi horario. Tengo la clase de química con la señora Rodarte ahora. Ella es muy exigente y yo ____ nervioso.
Nena: ¡Ah! Tú y yo ____ en la misma clase. Podemos estudiar juntos.
Raúl: ¿Y tú no ____ preocupada?
Nena: ¡Qué va! Me encantan las ciencias. ¡Vamos a clase!
Raúl: No sé dónde _están_ mis cosas.
Nena: Allí _a_ tu libro. ¿Qué más necesitas?
Raúl: Nada. Vamos.

REPASO

Describing people: Adjectives

Adjectives must agree in number and gender with the noun(s) they modify.

Elena está **muerta** de hambre.
Él y yo estamos **emocionados** y muy **contentos.**

REPASO

Uses of *estar*

Estar is used . . .

To express conditions:
Pepita **está** enferma.
El gazpacho **está** muy rico.
Tú **estás** muy guapa hoy.

To give location:
El Paso **está** en Texas.
¿Dónde **están** mis libros?

To form the present progressive:
Todos **están** trabajando.
¿Qué **están** haciendo?

See ¿Por qué se dice así?, page G9, section 1.4.

Stem-changing verbs

querer: e → ie

quiero	queremos
quieres	
quiere	quieren

Quiero comprar una pulsera.
¿**Prefieres** la roja?

encontrar: o → ue

encuentro	encontramos
encuentras	
encuentra	encuentran

No **encuentro** los servicios.
Encontramos estos muy caros.

See ¿Por qué se dice así?,
page G11, section 1.5.

REPASO

Stem-changing verbs

The verb **jugar** is the only **u → ue** stem-changing verb.

jugar: u → ue

juego	jugamos
juegas	
juega	juegan

Tú **juegas** muy bien.
¿A qué hora **juegan**?

See ¿Por qué se dice así,
page G11, section 1.5.

D. De compras. Tú y tu compañero(a) están buscando un regalo en un almacén. ¿Qué dicen?

 MODELO camiseta: ¿amarillo o blanco?

Tú: **¿Prefieres la camiseta amarilla o la blanca?**

Compañero(a): **Prefiero la amarilla. ¿Cuánto cuesta?** o
Prefiero la blanca. ¿Cuánto cuesta?

1. pulsera: ¿blanco o morado?
2. pantalones: ¿negro o marrón?
3. reloj: ¿grande o pequeño?
4. aretes: ¿verde o azul?

5. falda: ¿largo o corto?
6. blusas: ¿anaranjado o rosado?
7. collar: ¿amarillo o rojo?
8. zapatos: ¿gris o negro?

E. Todos los días. Según Tere, ¿qué pasa todos los días?

Yo siempre

MODELO **Yo siempre me despierto temprano.**

VOCABULARIO ÚTIL:

acostarse	jugar	almorzar	pensar
despertarse	perder	dormir	levantarse

1. A las 7:30 camino a la escuela y  en mis clases.

2. Mi amigo Samuel siempre en la clase de las 11:00.

3. A mediodía mis amigas y yo  en la cafetería.

4. Después de las clases Micaela y yo

5. Yo siempre

6. En casa, después de comer y estudiar  a las 10:00.

F. ¡A comer! Tú y tu familia acaban de ir de compras y ahora están cenando en un restaurante. Describe lo que pasa en el restaurante.

EJEMPLO **El camarero nos consigue una mesa.**

el camarero	servir (i)	un plato
yo	encontrar (ue)	la cuenta
mi hermano(a)	querer (ie)	una mesa
mamá y papá	pedir (i)	el dinero
un señor	probar (ue)	las pizzas
papá y yo	contar (ue)	la comida
	conseguir (i)	una hamburguesa
		mucha comida
		la especialidad de la casa
		unas sillas

──**R**EPASO──

Stem-changing verbs

pedir: e → i

pido	pedimos
pides	
pide	piden

¿Qué **pides** de postre?
¿**Sirven** buena comida mexicana?

See **¿Por qué se dice así?,**
page G11, section 1.5.

G. ¡Qué negativo! Tienes un(a) amigo(a) que siempre reacciona negativamente. ¿Qué te contesta cuando le haces estas preguntas?

MODELO   hacer
Tú: **¿Qué haces?**
Compañero(a): **No hago nada.**

1. saber
2. decir
3. traer
4. tener
5. ver
6. oír

──**R**EPASO──

Present tense: Irregular verbs

The following verbs have irregular **yo** forms:

conocer	**conozco**
dar	**doy**
decir (i)	**digo**
hacer	**hago**
oír	**oigo**
poner	**pongo**
saber	**sé**
salir	**salgo**
tener (ie)	**tengo**
traer	**traigo**
venir (ie)	**vengo**
ver	**veo**

See **¿Por qué se dice así?,**
page G14, section 1.6.

H. ¿Los conoces? ¿Conoces a todas estas personas de tu escuela? ¿Cómo se llaman?

EJEMPLO   el (la) profesor(a) de historia
Conozco al profesor de historia. Se llama Juan Gómez. o
No conozco a la profesora de historia.

1. el (la) entrenador(a) de volibol
2. el (la) profesor(a) de español
3. el (la) director(a) de la banda
4. el (la) secretario(a) de la escuela
5. el (la) director(a) de la escuela
6. el (la) profesor(a) de inglés
7. el (la) entrenador(a) del equipo de fútbol
8. el (la) profesor(a) de química
9. el (la) enfermero(a) de la escuela

I. Encuesta. ¿Con qué frecuencia hace tu compañero(a) estas actividades?

nunca	muy poco	de vez en cuando	todos los días

 MODELO salir con tus amigos

Tú: **¿Sales con tus amigos frecuentemente?**

Compañero(a): **Sí, salgo frecuentemente.** o **No, nunca salgo con mis amigos.**

1. dar regalos
2. tener que limpiar tu cuarto
3. poner la mesa
4. traer tu almuerzo a la escuela
5. venir a la clase de español
6. ver televisión
7. hacer ejercicios
8. decir tu número de teléfono

CHARLEMOS UN POCO MÁS

A. María quiere leer. Usando el dibujo que tu profesor(a) te dé, pregúntale a tu compañero(a) qué quieren hacer las personas. No mires el dibujo de tu compañero(a).

 EJEMPLO María

Tú: **¿Qué quiere hacer María?**

Compañero(a): **María quiere leer. Pero no puede.**

B. El cuento de Salchicha. Con un compañero(a), escribe un cuento sobre la perrita en el dibujo, Salchicha.

VOCABULARIO ÚTIL:

pelota	comida	perro	pensar
comenzar	perder	pedir	divertirse
acostarse	encontrar	despertarse	comer
jugar	vivir	beber	querer

C. Solamente la verdad. Formen grupos de tres personas. Su profesor(a) les va a dar un juego de nueve preguntas a cada uno. Ustedes deben hacerse las preguntas y contestarlas todas. La idea es que todos deben decir la verdad al contestar todas las preguntas menos una. Al terminar, el grupo tiene que adivinar cuál fue la pregunta que cada persona contestó falsamente.

Dramatizaciones

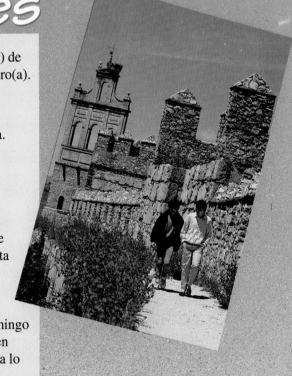

A. ¡Qué problemas! Estás hablando con tu mejor amigo(a) de tus problemas. Dramatiza la conversación con un(a) compañero(a).

- Dile cómo te sientes.
- Menciona algunos de los síntomas.
- Escucha mientras tu amigo(a) te dice lo que él o ella piensa.
- Invita a tu amigo(a) a hacer algo este fin de semana.
- Decidan qué van a hacer y luego despídanse.

B. ¿A qué hora te despiertas? Tú eres un(a) visitante extraterrestre que viene al mundo para conocer la vida de los jóvenes norteamericanos. Pregúntale a un(a) compañero(a) de clase acerca de su vida diaria y sus actividades. Dramatiza esta situación con un(a) compañero(a).

C. Día de las madres. Tú y tu amigo(a) van de compras. Tienen que comprar un regalo para sus madres porque el domingo es el Día de las madres. Dramaticen esta situación. Mencionen varias posibilidades para regalos hasta que cada uno(a) decida lo que va a comprar.

Antes de empezar

A. Mi primer día de clases. Piensa en tu primer día de clases y contesta estas preguntas. Luego discute tus respuestas con dos compañeros de clase.

1. ¿Cuánto recuerdas de tu primer día de clases?
2. ¿Quién te llevó a la escuela?
3. ¿Cómo reaccionaste tú? ¿Te gustó? ¿Lloraste?

B. Puntuación. En grupos de tres, contesten estas preguntas acerca de la falta de puntuación en el poema.

1. ¿Por qué crees que no hay puntuación en este poema?
2. Es fácil ponerle puntuación al poema. ¿Cuántas oraciones completas hay? ¿Cuáles son?
3. Escribe todas las oraciones del poema como oraciones completas. No olvides empezar cada oración con letra mayúscula.

Verifiquemos

A. Interpretemos. Lee el poema en la siguiente página. Luego, indica si estas oraciones son ciertas o falsas para mostrar que entendiste el poema. Explica cada respuesta.

1. El niño entiende inglés.
2. El niño no está tranquilo cuando se va su abuela.
3. La *teacher* entiende el problema del niño.
4. La abuela decide quedarse con el niño durante su primer día de escuela.

B. Expliquemos. En grupos de tres o cuatro, preparen una explicación para la clase de las siguientes partes del poema.

1. mi abuela
   luego me dio
   su bendición
   y se fue

2. yo me quedé
   hecho silla

3. en un mundo
   muy extraño

Este poema es del bien conocido poeta chicano, Francisco X. Alarcón.

First Day of School

frente
a la teacher

apreté
más fuerte
la mano
de mi abuela

la teacher
se sonrió

y dijo algo
raro en inglés

mi abuela
luego me dio

su bendición
y se fue

yo me quedé
hecho silla

en un mundo
muy extraño.

¡Tienes que visitar El Paso!

¿ **Q**ué piensas tú ?

1. ¿Qué están haciendo las personas en los dibujos? ¿Qué crees que van a hacer estas personas al terminar lo que hacen ahora? ¿Por qué crees eso?

2. ¿Cuáles de estas personas hacen lo que hacen porque tienen que hacerlo? ¿Por qué tienen que hacer estas cosas?

3. ¿Qué relación hay entre las personas en los dibujos? ¿Por qué crees eso?

4. ¿Conoces bien a todos tus familiares — abuelos, tíos, primos, etc.? ¿Por qué sí o por qué no?

5. Compara tu respuesta a la pregunta número 4 a la de tus compañeros de clase. ¿Cómo se compara? ¿Por qué crees que unos conocen bien a sus familiares y otros no?

6. ¿Crees que la vida diaria de una familia hispana en un país de habla española es diferente o similar a la vida de una familia hispana en EE.UU.? ¿Por qué?

7. ¿Qué crees que vas a aprender en esta lección?

LA NUERA

Este cuento de Nuevo México habla de la importancia de amar y respetar a los ancianos, un tema que se ve en cuentos de todos los países de habla hispana.

1 Manuel, una persona muy trabajadora, vive en un ranchito con su padre que es viudo. Allí tienen muchos acres de tierra y mucho ganado, vacas y borregas.

2 Durante las Fiestas de San Felipe, Manuel conoce a una joven llamada Dolores.

Empiezan a andar de novios, siempre como se acostumbra, en presencia de una persona mayor de edad. Después de unos meses, Manuel decide que quiere casarse con Dolores.

3 Siguiendo la tradición de la comunidad, Manuel y su padre van a casa de la señorita a pedirles a los padres su mano en matrimonio. Y como la tradición dicta, los padres de la novia esperan una semana antes de dar su respuesta. Aceptan la petición de Manuel.

Como regalo de boda, el padre del novio traspasa todas sus tierras, sus animales, su casa, en fin, todas sus posesiones, a su querido hijo y su futura esposa.

Dolores y Manuel, como dicta la costumbre, le proporcionan al padre de Manuel un cuarto de la casa.

Todo está bien mientras el padre de Manuel esté en condiciones de trabajar.

Después de unos años, Dolores y su marido tienen un niño muy lindo. A la vez, el padre de Manuel empieza a debilitarse.

Dolores se queja constantemente de que su suegro es mucho trabajo para ella.

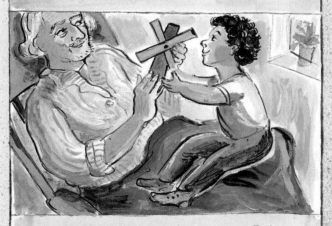

Resulta que la única razón por la que Dolores permite al viejito continuar allí con ellos es que ella siempre puede contar con él para cuidar al bebé. Con el pasar de los años, como uno se puede imaginar, el abuelo y su nieto resultan muy prendidos el uno al otro.

7 Desafortunadamente, dentro de poco el viejo se enferma. Y ahora es su nieto quien lo cuida. Le trae sus comidas, le lava la cara, lo peina y lo afeita. A Dolores le sigue molestando la presencia del anciano.

8 Llega el día en que Dolores proclama que necesita el cuarto del abuelo y le dice a Manuel que su padre tiene que dormir en el granero.

Manuel y su hijo ponen la cama del viejo en el granero, donde hace mucho frío. Dolores no le permite ni una sola cobija. "Va a morirse de frío", le dijo el niño a su mamá y ella le contestó, "Allí está bien. Él está acostumbrado al frío". El nieto se pone muy triste al ver a su abuelo sufrir tanto.

9 Al día siguiente, el nieto encuentra una vieja cobija y va a su padre y le dice, "Por favor, papá, corte esta cobija en dos".

"¿Por qué en dos?" pregunta su padre.

"Para poder darle a mi abuelo la mitad, y la otra la voy a guardar para cuando usted y mamá estén viejos y tengan que dormir en el granero".

10 Al oír eso Dolores se acuerda de un refrán que dice, "Joven eres y viejo serás". A los dos les vino un sentimiento profundo y rápido van a pedirle perdón al viejo. Le juran que nunca van a faltarle el respeto que se merece.

Y la familia pasa diez años maravillosos juntos. De allí en adelante, todos tratan al viejito con mucho cariño y respeto. Y no cabe duda que Dolores y Manuel estarán siempre agradecidos del consejo que les dio su hijo.

Ésta es la carta que Daniel le escribió a su amigo Luis.

El Paso

Mi familia

Querido Luis,

Gracias por tu carta. Estuvo muy interesante. Estoy encantado de tener un nuevo amigo venezolano. Me encantaría conocer tu país algún día. Caracas parece una ciudad fascinante.

Hace siete años que vivo en El Paso. No es tan grande como Caracas, pero es la cuarta ciudad más grande de Texas. Lo único que nos separa de Ciudad Juárez, la cuarta ciudad más grande de México, es el Río Grande, o como dicen en México, el Río Bravo. No tendrías ningún problema aquí porque todo el mundo habla español. Me gusta mucho El Paso; tiene un clima ideal si te gusta el sol y el calor.

Somos cinco en mi familia: mis padres, mi hermano Martín, mi hermana Nena y yo. Todos somos morenos y muy guapos, por supuesto. Mi hermano Martín tiene diecisiete años y, como resultado de un accidente automovilístico hace cinco años, usa silla de ruedas. Es muy activo, sin embargo, sobre todo en el baloncesto. Juega con un equipo especial que ganó el campeonato de Texas el año pasado y dicen que va a ganarlo este año también. Nena tiene trece años. Está muy interesada en el arte—pintura y dibujo. A todos nos gusta acampar y vamos a muchos lugares interesantes.

Mi hermano y yo asistimos a El Paso High School. Aparentemente, es muy diferente de tu escuela. Tú dices que tienes quince clases—pues nosotros solamente tenemos seis. Yo, por ejemplo, tengo historia de Estados Unidos, inglés, álgebra, química, educación física y música. Todas nuestras clases se reúnen todos los días, de lunes a viernes. ¡Y no tenemos clases los sábados, como ustedes! A propósito, toco el saxofón en la orquesta. Tengo que practicar muchas horas pero me gusta.

Mi saxofón

Casi todos mis amigos también van a El Paso High School. Mi mejor amigo se llama Mateo Romero. Es muy simpático y hacemos todo juntos. Jugamos tenis, vamos al cine y a partidos de baloncesto y fútbol americano. También juego tenis con una chica muy divertida que se llama Tina Valdez. A veces los tres nos reunimos con otros amigos para escuchar música o para ir a conciertos. Me fascina toda clase de música, pero mi favorita es la música popular latinoamericana. ¿Cuáles son los cantantes y los "hits" de ahora en Venezuela?

Me gustaría saber más de Caracas y de tus amigos. ¿Cómo son tus amigos? ¿Qué hacen los fines de semana? ¿Tienes una amiga especial? ¿Cómo es el clima en Caracas? ¿Hace buen tiempo todo el año? Escríbeme pronto. Algún día en el futuro tienes que visitarme aquí en El Paso. Y sí, yo tendré que visitarte en Caracas también.

Enfrente de mi escuela

Saludos de tu amigo

Daniel

¡Pobre Mateo! No juega tenis muy bien.

Mi hermano, mis amigos y yo escuchamos música en casa.

CHARLEMOS UN POCO

A. **PARA EMPEZAR . . .** Pon los siguientes hechos en el orden apropiado según el cuento ''La nuera''.

1. Los dos juran que nunca van a faltarle respeto al viejo.
2. Dolores le dice a Manuel que su padre tiene que dormir en el granero.
3. Dolores empieza a quejarse constantemente de que su suegro no hace nada.
4. Manuel y Dolores invitan al padre de Manuel a vivir con ellos.
5. Manuel y Dolores salen juntos durante varios meses, en compañía de personas mayores.
6. El nieto le dice a su padre que corte la vieja cobija en dos.
7. Manuel conoce a una joven llamada Dolores en las Fiestas de San Felipe.
8. Dolores y su marido tienen un niño muy lindo.
9. Como regalo de matrimonio, el padre de Manuel les da todas sus posesiones.
10. Manuel les pide la mano de Dolores a sus padres.

B. **¿QUÉ DECIMOS . . . ?** Selecciona la respuesta apropiada según la carta que escribió Daniel.

1. Hace *(5 / 7 / 15)* años que Daniel vive en El Paso.
2. El Paso es la *(segunda / tercera / cuarta)* ciudad más grande de Texas.
3. *(Daniel / Martín / Mateo)* usa silla de ruedas.
4. *(Daniel / Martín / Luis)* tiene quince clases.
5. Daniel toca un instrumento en *(una orquesta / una banda / un restaurante)*.
6. A Daniel le gusta jugar tenis con *(Mateo / Tina / Mateo y Tina)*.
7. Daniel quiere saber más de *(las clases de Luis / la familia de Luis / el clima de Caracas)*.
8. A Daniel le encantaría *(visitar a Luis en Caracas / vivir con Luis / hablar con Luis por teléfono)*.

C. **¿Y tú?** Tu compañero(a) quiere saber cómo eres. Contesta sus preguntas y luego hazle preguntas a él (ella).

MODELO   romántico
    Compañero(a): **¿Eres romántico(a)?**
    Tú: **Sí, soy romántico(a).** o
                No, no soy romántico(a).

VOCABULARIO ÚTIL:

estudioso	perezoso	tímido	popular
fuerte	débil	tonto	inteligente
simpático	antipático	organizado	desorganizado

REPASO

Adjectives

Adjectives must agree in number and gender with the word(s) they describe.

Carlos es guap**o**, tímid**o** e inteligent**e**.
Alicia y Paula son simpátic**as**, organizad**as** e inteligent**es**.

See **¿Por qué se dice así?**, *page G16, section 1.7.*

LECCIÓN 3

See ¿**Por qué se dice así?**,
page G17, section 1.8.

REPASO

Describing people: Ser

soy	somos
eres	
es	son

Soy inteligente y guapo.
Sí, y **eres** muy modesto también,
¿no?

See ¿**Por qué se dice así?**,
page G17, section 1.8.

REPASO

Describing future plans: Ir

voy	vamos
vas	
va	van

Voy al gimnasio a las dos.
¿**Van** a correr esta tarde?

See ¿**Por qué se dice así?**,
page G17, section 1.8.

CH. Descripciones.   Describe a estas personas.

 EJEMPLO   **Mi mejor amiga y yo no somos ni altas ni bajas;
somos medianas.**

VOCABULARIO ÚTIL:

alto	débil	interesante	serio
atlético	delgado	joven	tacaño
bajo	gordo	moreno	
cómico	guapo	rubio	

1. mi mejor amigo(a) [. . .]
2. mis papás
3. mis amigos [. . .] y [. . .]
4. yo

5. el(la) profesor(a) [. . .]
6. mi hermano(a) [. . .]
7. mi mejor amigo(a) y yo
8. mi gato(a) o mi perro(a)

D. Los domingos.   ¿Adónde van estas personas los domingos?

EJEMPLO   **Mis abuelos van al parque.**

yo
mi familia
mis amigos y yo
mi amigo(a) . . .
mis abuelos

gimnasio
parque
biblioteca
iglesia
café
cine
centro comercial
restaurante
casa de unos amigos
¿ . . . ?

E. El fin de semana.   ¿Qué planes tiene tu compañero(a) para
este fin de semana? Pregúntale si va a hacer las actividades
representadas en este dibujo.

 MODELO   *Tú:*   ¿**Vas a jugar tenis este fin de
semana?**
Compañero(a): **Sí, voy a jugar.** o
No, no voy a jugar.

F. ¡Qué horario! Pregúntale a tu compañero(a) a qué hora tiene sus clases.

 MODELO *Tú:*　　　　　**¿A qué hora tienes la clase de drama?**

Compañero(a): **Tengo drama a las [*dos*].** o
　　　　　　　　No tengo clase de drama.

1.

2.

3.

4.

5.

6.

7.

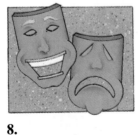

8.

9.

10.

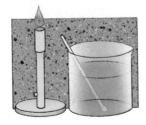

11.

12.

See **¿Por qué se dice así?,** *page G17, section 1.8.*

---

*R*EPASO

Tener

tengo	tenemos
tienes	
tiene	tienen

¿A que hora **tienes** inglés?
¿**Tenemos** que comprarlo?

See **¿Por qué se dice así?,** *page G17, section 1.8.*

LECCIÓN 3

G. ¡Mucho que hacer!   Es sábado y todos en tu familia tienen que ayudar. ¿Quiénes tienen que hacer estas tareas?

EJEMPLO   arreglar tu cuarto
Yo tengo que arreglar mi cuarto. o
Mi hermano tiene que arreglar su cuarto.

1. preparar el almuerzo
2. lavar el coche
3. preparar la comida
4. poner la mesa
5. lavar el perro

6. estudiar
7. limpiar la casa
8. lavar los platos
9. hacer la cama
10. ir de compras

H. Familia y amigos.   Explica cuánto tiempo hace que tú, tu familia y tus amigos hacen estas cosas.

EJEMPLO   **Hace 7 años que mi familia tiene un perro.**

mi amigo . . .
yo
mis amigos . . . y . . .
. . . y yo
mi familia

salir con . . .
trabajar en . . .
saber nadar
ser buenos amigos
cantar en español
asistir a este colegio
estudiar . . .
tener un gato / perro
saber esquiar
¿ . . . ?

I. ¿Cuánto tiempo hace que . . . ?   Pregúntale a tu compañero(a) si hace esto. Si dice que sí, pregúntale cuánto tiempo hace que lo está haciendo.

EJEMPLO   *Tú:*   **¿Vives en *[tu ciudad]*?**
          Compañero(a): **Sí.**
          Tú: **¿Cuánto tiempo hace que vives en . . . ?**
          Compañero(a): **Hace tres años.**

tu amigo . . .
tú
tus amigos . . . y . . .
tú y . . .
tu familia
¿ . . . ?

leer el periódico
trabajar en . . .
tener coche
estudiar español
vivir aquí
tocar el piano
ser buenos amigos
asistir a este colegio
estudiar baile
conocer a tu mejor amigo(a)
tener un gato / perro
ir a esquiar
salir con . . .

REPASO

Hacer in time expressions

To ask how long something has been happening, use:

¿Cuánto tiempo hace que +
[present tense verb]?

To tell how long something has been happening, use:

Hace + *[time]* + **que** +
[present tense verb]

¿Cuánto tiempo hace que viven aquí?
Hace tres años que vivimos aquí.
Hace cuatro meses que estudio español.

*See ¿**Por qué se dice así?**,
page G20, section 1.9.*

CHARLEMOS UN POCO MÁS

A. **¿Quién es?**   ¿Cuánto sabes de las personas que acabas de conocer? Selecciona a una de estas personas y descríbesela a tu compañero(a) sin mencionar el nombre. Tu compañero(a) tiene que adivinar *(decir)* quién es.

 EJEMPLO   *Tú:* **Es guapo. Tiene diecisiete años. Le gusta mucho el baloncesto.**
Compañero(a): **Es Martín Galindo.**

1.

2.

3.

4.

5.

B. **La persona más seria . . .**   Su profesor(a) les va a dar una cuadrícula. En grupos de tres, primero escriban individualmente las respuestas a la pregunta en la primera columna. Luego hagan las preguntas a sus dos compañeros y anoten todas las respuestas. Informen a la clase los casos donde dos o tres personas estuvieron de acuerdo.

C. **Encuesta.** Tu profesor(a) te va a dar un cuestionario para usar al entrevistar a tus compañeros de clase. Pregúntales a varias personas cuánto tiempo hace que participan en estas actividades. Pídeles que firmen en el cuadrado apropiado y que escriban el número de años. Recuerda que no se permite que una persona firme más de una vez.

EJEMPLO   estudiar inglés

Tú:	**¿Cuánto tiempo hace que estudias inglés?**
Compañero(a):	**Hace once años que estudio inglés.**
Compañero(a) escribe:	**once** *(en el cuadrado apropiado)*

Dramatizaciones

"Houston, tenemos un problema."

APOLLO 13

GARY SINISE BILL PAXTON ED HARRIS TOM HANKS KEVIN BACON

HOY PRE-ESTRENO EXCLUSIVO

"A"

LIDO 1
4:30–7:00–9:30

LIDO 2
5:00–7:30–10:30

UNA PELÍCULA DE RON HOWARD

A. **El sábado.** Estás charlando con un(a) amigo(a) de las actividades del sábado que viene. Dramaticen su conversación.

- Saluda a tu amigo(a).
- Pregúntale qué tiene que hacer el sábado que viene.
- Dile lo que tú tienes que hacer.
- Pregúntale qué va a hacer el sábado por la noche.
- Invítalo(la) a ir al cine contigo.

B. **¡Qué interesante!** Estás conversando con un(a) nuevo(a) estudiante que parece ser muy interesante. Para conocerlo(la) mejor, le haces muchas preguntas. Dramatiza la conversación con un compañero(a).

C. **El nuevo estudiante.** Tu amigo(a) quiere conocer al (a la) nuevo(a) estudiante también. Contesta todas las preguntas que tu amigo(a) te hace con la información que ya tienes. También describe al (a la) nuevo(a) estudiante.

Para todo público

Totalmente hablada en español

WALT DISNEY presenta
La Bella y **la Bestia**

Nominada al "Oscar 1992", como: "Mejor película del año" y ganadora de "2 Oscar de la academia 1992", como: "Mejor canción original" y "Mejor música original"

7ª Semana MULTICINE 5 pm. y 8
MARQUÉS UNO 5.15 pm. y 8.30 pm.
CIPRESES UNO Cont. 1pm. a 10 pm.
ALTAMIRA (Pto Ordaz)
CINEMA UNO Y MEDIO
(PORLAMARI)

MEL GIBSON

CORAZÓN VALIENTE

Estrategias para leer:
Prediciendo con fotos, dibujos, gráficos o diagramas

A. **Ilustraciones.** Ciertas lecturas casi siempre vienen acompañadas de fotos, dibujos, gráficos o diagramas. Mira la lista que sigue y piensa en el tipo de lectura que tiende a usar cada tipo de ilustración. Luego indica el propósito de cada tipo de lectura.

Tipo de ilustración	Tipo de lectura	Propósito de lectura
Foto		
Dibujo		
Gráfico		
Diagrama		

B. **Predecir.** Un buen lector siempre usa las ilustraciones para predecir o anticipar el contenido de la lectura y también, para clarificar o confirmar al leer. Antes de leer esta selección, mira las fotos y anota lo que cada foto te hace anticipar.

¿Qué hay en la foto?	Lo que anticipo.	Lo que sé después de leer.
1.		
2.		
3.		
4.		

C. **Confirmar.** Ahora lee la selección. Vuelve a la actividad **B** y completa la tercera columna del cuadro.

D. **Comparar.** Compara tus predicciones en la segunda columna con el verdadero contenido de la tercera columna. ¿Acertaste? ¿Cómo te ayudó el predecir a leer mejor?

the whole enchilada

En Estados Unidos todo el mundo sabe lo que es una enchilada y muchos hasta saben prepararlas. Pero nadie las prepara como Roberto Estrada, dueño de una tortillería y un restaurante en Las Cruces, Nuevo México. ¿Pero por qué son tan diferentes las enchiladas de Roberto Estrada?, te preguntas. Pues, hay varias cosas que hacen que sus enchiladas sean singulares.

En primer lugar, Roberto Estrada prepara enchiladas típicas de Nuevo México. **1** Éstas son muy diferentes de las enchiladas tradicionales de México, **2** las cuales generalmente se preparan rellenas de queso, o de carne, o hasta de mariscos-cangrejo, **3** camarones **4** o langosta **5** y casi siempre se sirven tres enchiladas enrolladas con frijoles refritos y arroz a la mexicana al lado.

En Nuevo México, si pides una enchilada, te van a servir tres tortillas no enrolladas, sino tendidas como un panqueque. Tampoco se rellenan, simplemente se sirven con un poco de queso rallado **6** y cebolla picada **7** encima de cada tortilla. Una enchilada normalmente tiene tres tortillas y también se acostumbra servirlas con frijoles refritos y arroz a la mexicana, . . . ¡pero no si las prepara Roberto Estrada!

¿Por qué no?, dices. Porque las enchiladas de Roberto Estrada se preparan sólo una vez al año en el mes de octubre y son tan grandes que es imposible comer algo más. Son tan grandes que para hacer una sola enchilada de tres tortillas, Roberto usa 250 libras **8** de masa, 75 galones de chile colorado, 50 libras de cebolla picada y 175 libras de queso rallado.

Sin duda, Roberto Estrada prepara las enchiladas más grandes del mundo entero. Siempre las prepara para la fiesta de "The Whole Enchilada" en Las Cruces, Nuevo México. Ya lleva más de 12 años preparando "The Whole Enchilada" y cada año la enchilada parece crecer más y más. Cuando empezó a hacerla medía unos 6 pies de diámetro y servía a 2,000 personas, más o menos. La que hizo más recientemente midió 10 pies de diámetro y sirvió a 8,500 personas.

Recientemente, más de 100,000 personas asistieron a la fiesta de "The Whole Enchilada", y los más de 1,500 voluntarios que ayudaron dicen que les gusta la fiesta no sólo porque acaban por "devorarse la enchilada más grande del mundo entero, sino también porque es como una fiesta de familia". Y de veras que lo es, ya que la mayoría de los voluntarios han servido de voluntarios desde que empezó la fiesta en 1981.

Verifiquemos

1. Preparen un esquema como éste y comparen las enchiladas mexicanas con las de Nuevo México y las de Roberto Estrada.

Enchiladas

Enchiladas mexicanas	Enchiladas nuevo mexicanas	Enchiladas de Roberto Estrada
1.	1.	1.
2.	2.	2.

2. Describe la fiesta de "The Whole Enchilada". ¿Dónde y cuándo es? ¿Cómo la celebran? ¿Quiénes asisten? ¿Cuánto tiempo hace que la celebran?

3. ¿Hay alguna fiesta que celebra un producto particular en tu ciudad? ¿Cuál es? Descríbelo.

ESCRIBAMOS AHORA

Estrategias para escribir:
Planificación

A. Empezar. En *Leamos ahora* leíste de un evento, una fiesta que se celebra cada año en Las Cruces, Nuevo México. ¿Qué información acerca del evento incluyó el autor? ¿Cuál fue el enfoque del artículo? ¿Dónde crees que se publicó este artículo originalmente? ¿Qué eventos anuales se celebran en tu escuela? ¿tu comunidad? ¿tu región?

B. Planificar. Selecciona uno de los eventos que mencionaste en la sección anterior para describirlo en un artículo para el periódico escolar. Será necesario mencionar ciertos datos y tú tendrás que decidir cuáles otros datos van a interesar a tu público. Para ayudarte a planificar, prepara un cuadro como el que sigue. Identifica en el cuadro lo que ya sabes, lo que necesitas investigar y dónde podrás conseguir la información que necesitas.

Evento	Lo que ya sé	Lo que debo investigar	¿Dónde debo conseguir la información?
Título del evento			
Fecha / Hora			
¿Dónde es?			
¿Frecuencia?			
¿Desde cuándo?			
¿Cómo recibió su nombre?			
Actividades específicas			
Mi parte favorita			

C. Organizar.   Antes de empezar a escribir tu artículo, decide cuál información en tu cuadro debes incluir y cuál es opcional. Luego piensa en lo que puede causar que el evento sea interesante y atractivo para tu público. Tal vez quieras usar un marcador para indicar la información que quieres incluir. El título ''The Whole Enchilada'' es muy llamativo porque tiene doble sentido. ¿Puedes pensar en un título llamativo para tu artículo?

CH. Primer borrador.   Ahora, usa la información en tu cuadro y prepara la primera versión de tu artículo. No te detengas demasiado en forma o exactitud; simplemente desarrolla tus ideas. Vas a tener amplia oportunidad para corregir el formato y la estructura.

D. Compartir.   Comparte el primer borrador de tu artículo con dos compañeros de clase. Pídeles sugerencias. Pregúntales si hay algo más que desean saber sobre tu evento, si hay algo que no entienden, si hay algo que puede o debe eliminarse. Dales la misma información sobre sus artículos cuando ellos te pidan sugerencias.

E. Revisar.   Haz cambios en tu artículo a base de las sugerencias de tus compañeros. Luego, antes de entregar el artículo, compártelo una vez más con dos compañeros de clase. Esta vez pídeles que revisen la estructura y la puntuación. En particular, pídeles que revisen el uso de verbos en el presente y de concordancia entre sujeto / verbo y adjetivo / sustantivo.

F. Versión final.   Escribe la versión final de tu artículo incorporando las correcciones que tus compañeros de clase te indicaron. Entrega una copia en limpio a tu profesor(a).

G. Publicar.   Cuando tu profesor(a) te devuelva el artículo, léeselo a tus compañeros en grupos de cuatro. Luego piensen en un título para una libreta que incluya los cuatro artículos. Escriban una breve introducción para la libreta y entréguensela a su profesor(a).

UNIDAD 2

¡Qué chévere!

CARACAS

PLAZA
VENEZUELA
SABANA
GRANDE
CHACAO
CHACAITO
ALTAMIRA

¿ Nos acompañan ?

¿ **Q**ué piensas tú ?

1. ¿Quiénes crees que son los jóvenes en la foto? ¿Qué hora crees que es? ¿Adónde crees que fueron los jóvenes antes de venir a este café? ¿Por qué crees eso?

2. ¿De qué estarán hablando los jóvenes?

3. ¿De qué partes del mundo te recuerdan estas fotos? ¿Por qué? ¿Hay algunas fotos que no relacionas con nada?

4. ¿Crees que todas estas cosas se pueden encontrar en un lugar? ¿Dónde? ¿Están de acuerdo contigo tus compañeros de clase?

5. ¿Crees que todas estas cosas se pueden encontrar en Venezuela? ¿Por qué sí o por qué no?

6. ¿Qué impresiones tienes tú de Venezuela? ¿De dónde vienen tus impresiones?

7. Los autores de **¡DIME!** les preguntaron a estos jóvenes venezolanos si hay algo en particular que quieren que los jóvenes de EE.UU. piensen de ellos. ¿Qué crees que contestaron?

8. ¿Qué quieres tú que los jóvenes de otros países piensen de los jóvenes en EE.UU.?

9. En esta lección, van a repasar mucho de lo que aprendieron en **¡DIME!** UNO y a escuchar lo que estos jóvenes están diciendo. Si consideras esto y tus respuestas a las primeras tres preguntas, ¿qué crees que van a hacer en esta lección?

1

Tegucigalpa es ahora la capital de Honduras, como ya saben ustedes, pero este cuento tiene lugar en tiempos antiguos, cuando era un pueblo pequeño sin mucho contacto con países extranjeros.

2

Es en esos tiempos que vive en el pequeño pueblo de Tegucigalpa, la familia Real—Don Periquito Real, su esposa Misia Pepa y su hijita, Laurita.

Es una familia feliz. Tienen bastante dinero y no tienen que trabajar. No son muy inteligentes pero viven contentos porque viven juntos.

3

La señora Real está muy orgullosa porque habla un poquito de francés e inglés. No los habla muy bien, pero cree que los habla a la perfección. Por eso, se cree superior a la gente del pueblo. Hasta pronuncia el nombre de su hija, Laurita, como en inglés—"Lorita".

La diversión favorita de toda la familia Real es hablar. Hablan constantemente. El padre habla con los hombres del pueblo y la madre habla con sus esposas.

Y Lorita habla todo el día con sus amiguitos.

En la tarde hablan durante horas juntos. Verdaderamente, los vecinos y otros del pueblo los encuentran muy aburridos.

Les gusta mucho a los Real criticar a sus vecinos. Pero peor que eso, también les gusta mucho repetir lo que oyen en casas de sus amigos.

Provocan muchos problemas en el pueblo con sus chismes.

6 Finalmente, la gente decide que la familia Real es incorregible. Y todo el pueblo se pone de acuerdo de no invitarlos más a sus fiestas y reuniones.

Por lo tanto, Misia Pepa, su marido y su hija tienen que quedarse en casa. Interesantemente, no parece molestarles mucho. Simplemente pasan el día hablando entre ellos.

7 Y parecen estar contentísimos hablando juntos todo el día. Hablan durante el desayuno.

Pasan el día en el jardín hablando.

Hablan mientras Misia Pepa prepara la comida.

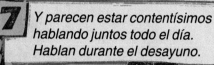

8 ¿CÓMO TE LLAMAS? ¿CÓMO TE LLAMAS?

Y cada tarde los tres se sientan, cada uno en su silla mecedora, y porque no hay nada nuevo que discutir, simplemente repiten, palabra por palabra, de una manera automática, lo que oyen durante el día. Así se pasan los días, las semanas enteras y los meses.

9 Poco a poco empieza a tener lugar una transformación notable en los tres personajes. La nariz de los tres crece hasta convertirse en un grotesco pico muy duro. Luego, sus brazos empiezan a cambiar y se convierten en alas de colores brillantes: amarillo, rojo y verde.

10 Y actualmente, en Honduras y en muchas partes de Sudamérica, hay muchos pajaritos muy graciosos, que repiten todo lo que oyen. Y, ¿cómo les llaman? "Periquitos o loritos reales", ¡por supuesto!

¿QUÉ DECIMOS...?

Al charlar entre amigos

1 ¡Chévere!

Unos amigos se encuentran en el centro de Caracas.

Mira, Diana, allí están Luis y Salvador. Vamos a saludarlos.

Ven, Chela, y te presentamos.

¡Meche, Diana! ¿Qué tal?

Les presento a nuestra nueva vecina, Chela.

¡Chévere!

Es un placer. Salvador Méndez. Así que eres la nueva vecina de Meche y Diana, ¿eh?

Sí, acabo de mudarme de Maracaibo.

Chela Fuentes. Encantada.

Mucho gusto. Luis Miranda.

¿Ah, sí? Mis padres dicen que es una ciudad muy interesante pero no la conozco. ¿Nos acompañan?

Sí, siéntense. Las invitamos a unas arepas.

Gracias.

¡Qué amables!

3 | **Salúdalo de mi parte.**

Los amigos caminan en el Parque Central.

¿Por qué no vamos al Parque Central? ¿Lo conoces?

No, conozco muy poco de Caracas. Vamos.

¿Héctor? ¿Quién sabe? Parece estar bien. No lo veo muy a menudo porque está muy ocupado.

¿Qué tal tus clases, Diana? ¿Son buenas?

Regulares. A mí me gustaría estar ya en la universidad — como tu hermano Héctor. ¿Y cómo está él?

Pues, salúdalo de mi parte, por favor.

Y tú, Chela, ¿tienes hermanos?

¿A su hermana?

Sí, tengo un hermano pequeño y una hermana que va a la Universidad Simón Bolívar.

¿De veras? Mi hermano también estudia allí. A lo mejor la conoce.

¿Y por qué no?

4 | **Estamos todos juntos.**

Chela, ¿también vas a nuestro colegio?

¿Quieres estudiar juntos?

Sí, mañana es mi primer día.

Luis, ¿ya hiciste la tarea para la clase de inglés?

¡Y está en nuestra sección!

Not yet pero la voy a hacer esta noche.

No, fíjate que no puedo. Tengo que salir con mis padres.

¡Qué chévere! Entonces vamos a estar todos juntos este año.

A. **PARA EMPEZAR...** Después de leer la leyenda "La familia Real", completa estas oraciones.

1. La familia Real es . . .
   a. *rica / pobre.*
   b. *inteligente / no muy inteligente.*
   c. *interesante / aburrida.*
   ch. *contenta / triste.*

2. La señora Real . . .
   a. es *modesta / orgullosa / chismosa.*
   b. habla *alemán / francés / inglés / japonés.*
   c. habla lenguas extranjeras *no muy bien / bien / muy bien.*

3. Los Real provocan muchos problemas porque . . .
   a. critican a sus *vecinos / hijos.*
   b. *repiten / olvidan* todo lo que oyen.
   c. cuentan *chismes / historias.*

4. Los Real pasan el tiempo . . .
   a. *hablando / jugando* en el jardín.
   b. *trabajando / hablando* mientras preparan la comida.
   c. *durmiendo / hablando* en sus sillas mecedoras.

5. La transformación de los Real incluye . . .
   a. una nariz *aristocrática / grotesca.*
   b. brazos convertidos en *alas / serpientes.*
   c. colores *oscuros / brillantes.*

B. **¿QUÉ DECIMOS . . .?** Di a quién o a quiénes describen estas oraciones.

Luis   **Meche**   **Diana**   **Salvador**   **Chela**

1. Prefiere las arepas de pollo.
2. Todavía no hace su tarea para la clase de inglés.
3. Mañana es su primer día de clases.
4. Tiene un hermano en la universidad.
5. Es de Maracaibo.
6. Prefiere las arepas de queso.
7. Va a salir con sus padres esta noche.
8. Es la vecina de Meche.
9. No conoce Maracaibo.
10. Acompañan a sus amigos a comer arepas.

C. Todos los días. ¿Con qué frecuencia ves a estas personas?

MODELO tu médico(a)
Lo (La) veo raras veces. o
Nunca lo (la) veo.

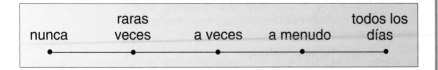

| nunca | raras veces | a veces | a menudo | todos los días |

1. tus amigos(as)
2. tu profesor(a) de español
3. tus padres
4. el (la) director(a) de la escuela

5. tu dentista
6. tu mejor amigo(a)
7. tus abuelos
8. el (la) entrenador(a) de baloncesto

CH. Lo olvida todo. Tu compañero(a) tiene una memoria muy mala. Siempre olvida todo. Para ver que olvidó hoy, hazle preguntas mencionando todos los objetos en el dibujo.

MODELO *Tú:* **¿Tienes tu almuerzo?**
Compañero(a): **Sí, lo tengo.** o
No, no lo tengo.

REPASO

Direct object pronouns

me	nos
te	
lo, la	los, las

Direct object pronouns usually precede conjugated verbs.

Siempre **nos** escuchan.
No **la** veo nunca.

See **¿Por qué se dice así?,**
page G22, section 2.1.

D. Planes.   Pregúntale a tu compañero(a) sobre sus planes para el fin de semana.

 MODELO   *Tú:*   **¿Vas a escuchar la radio?**
Compañero(a):   **Sí, la voy a escuchar.** o
Sí, voy a escucharla.

ver comer leer hacer jugar llamar escuchar visitar	la radio papas fritas a tus amigos televisión tenis pizza a tus abuelos el periódico volibol la tarea tus videos tu comida favorita tus discos

E. Lo sabe todo.   Tu abuelo(a) siempre sabe lo que están haciendo todos a esta hora. ¿Cómo contestas sus preguntas?

 MODELO   preparar la cena (mamá)
Abuelo(a):   **Tu mamá está preparando la cena, ¿verdad?**
Tú: **Sí, está preparándola.** o
Sí, la está preparando.

1. ayudar a tu mamá (hermanita)
2. lavar el perro (hermano)
3. comer papas (Gabi y sus amigos)
4. hacer la tarea (tú)
5. tomar café (papá)
6. ver televisión (Gabi y sus amigos)
7. leer el periódico (papá)
8. escuchar tus discos favoritos (tú)

F. Escuelas rivales.   Tú y un(a) amigo(a) son de escuelas rivales. Cada uno(a) cree que su escuela es mejor. ¿Qué dicen cuando comparan las dos instituciones?

 MODELO   escuela
Tú: **Nuestra escuela es fantástica.**
Compañero(a):   **Su escuela es horrible.**

1. profesores	5. director(a)
2. equipo de fútbol	6. entrenadores
3. estudiantes	7. clases
4. biblioteca	8. gimnasio

G. Geografía. Tu profesor(a) quiere saber quién tiene los parientes que viven más lejos de su ciudad. Pregúntales a varios compañeros de clase dónde viven sus parientes. Luego en grupos de cuatro, decidan quién tiene los parientes que viven más lejos.

 MODELO tíos

> *Tú:* **¿De dónde son tus tíos?**
> *Compañero(a):* **Mi tío es de [*lugar*] y mi tía es de [*lugar*].**

1. madre (madrastra)
2. padre (padrastro)
3. hermanos (hermanastros)
4. abuelos maternos
5. abuelos paternos
6. tíos
7. primos

H. Después de las clases. Estás ayudándole a tu profesor(a) a limpiar la sala de clase y encuentras varias cosas. Pregúntale a tu profesor(a) si son de él (ella). Tu compañero(a) va a hacer el papel de tu profesor(a).

MODELO *Tú:* **Profesor(a), ¿es su cuaderno?**
   Profesor(a): **No, es de Mónica.**

Mónica

1. Sergio   2. Pilar y Hugo   3. Natalia   4. Jaime

 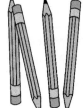 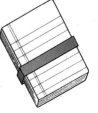

5. Adriana   6. Julio y Berta   7. Gerardo   8. Tere

REPASO

Possessive adjectives

mi	tu
mis	tus

Mis abuelos son de California.
¿De dónde es **tu** madrastra?

See **¿Por qué se dice así?,** *page G24, section 2.2.*

REPASO

Possessive adjectives: Summary

mi	nuestro(a)
mis	nuestros(as)
tu	
tus	
su	su
sus	sus

See **¿Por qué se dice así?,** *page G24, section 2.2.*

REPASO

Possession with *de*

de { nosotros, nosotras
usted, ustedes
él, ellos
ella, ellas
[nombre] }

No es **de él**, es **de ellas**.
Ésos no son **de nosotras**, son **de ustedes**.

See **¿Por qué se dice así?,** *page G24, section 2.2.*

CHARLEMOS UN POCO MÁS

A. La sala de clase.   Tu profesor(a) les va a dar un dibujo a ti y a tu compañero(a). Los dos dibujos son similares pero no son idénticos. Para descubrir cuántas diferencias hay, pregúntale a tu compañero(a) si lo que ves en tu dibujo aparece en el suyo. Recuerda que no se permite mirar el dibujo de tu compañero(a) hasta terminar la actividad.

EJEMPLO   *Tú:*   **¿Ves a dos muchachos estudiando?**
          Compañero: **Sí, los veo. o No, no los veo.**

B. No son mis zapatos.   Alicia y su hermano(a) empacaron rápidamente para las vacaciones con la familia. Ahora están desempacando y tienen que decidir de quién es cada prenda de ropa. Pregúntale a tu compañero(a) de quién son estas prendas. Él (Ella) te va a contestar usando la información en el dibujo que tu profesor(a) le va a dar.

EJEMPLO   *Tú:*   **¿Son los zapatos de mamá?**
          Compañero(a):   **No , no son sus zapatos.**

o

          Tú: **¿Son tus botas?**
          Compañero(a):   **Sí, son mis botas.**

C. ¿Lo vas a comprar? Tú y tu amigo(a) ganaron un premio de un millón de bolívares. Claro, quieren comprarle regalos a sus familias y sus amigos. Estudien este anuncio y decidan qué les gustaría comprar y para quién.

 EJEMPLO **Me gusta mucho la guitarra. La voy a comprar para mi hermano, [*nombre*].** o
Me gustan los videos. Voy a comprarlos para papá. o
Los videos son buenos. Los compro para papá.

CH. Las más interesantes. Tú eres reportero(a) con el periódico escolar y cada semana escribes una descripción de la familia para una sección del periódico titulada **Las familias más interesantes de [*tu comunidad*].** Entrevista a un(a) compañero(a) y consigue suficiente información para escribir un artículo sobre su familia.

Dramatizaciones

A. De compras. Estás en una tienda de discos compactos con un(a) compañero(a). Quieres comprar cinco discos compactos para regalarles a tus cinco mejores amigos. Ves muchos que te gustan pero tu compañero(a) casi nunca está de acuerdo con tu selección. Dramaticen esta situación.

B. En la Casa Blanca. El presidente de Estados Unidos y su esposa están planeando una fiesta en la Casa Blanca y quieren invitar a famosos actores y actrices, artistas y deportistas. Tú y tu compañero(a) tienen que decidir a quiénes van a invitar. Dramaticen la conversación.

C. Prefiero mi reloj. Tu amiga, Carmelita, tiene un problema muy serio. Ella siempre insiste en que todas sus cosas son mejores, más grandes o más costosas que las de otras personas. Tú y un(a) amigo(a) deciden que es necesario hablar con Carmelita sobre su mala actitud. Al hablar, compara algunas de tus cosas con las de Carmelita. Dramatiza la situación con dos compañeros(as) de clase.

IMPACTO CULTURAL
Excursiones

Antes de empezar

A. **El mapa.** Localiza estos lugares en el mapa: el Mar Caribe, Venezuela, Colombia, Brasil, Guyana, los Andes, el río Orinoco, el Lago de Maracaibo.

B. **Impresiones.** Antes de leer esta lectura sobre Venezuela, indica cuáles son tus impresiones sobre el país. Luego, después de leer la selección, vuelve a estas preguntas y decide si necesitas cambiar algunas de tus impresiones iniciales.

1. Venezuela está en . . .
   - **a.** Norteamérica.
   - **b.** Sudamérica.
   - **c.** Centroamérica.
   - **ch.** Europa.

2. El clima en la mayor parte de Venezuela es . . .
   - **a.** muy variado.
   - **b.** muy árido.
   - **c.** tropical.
   - **ch.** frío.

3. La población venezolana incluye . . .
   - **a.** chinos.
   - **b.** canadienses.
   - **c.** japoneses.
   - **ch.** europeos.

4. La economía de Venezuela está basada principalmente en . . .
   - **a.** la exportación de frutas tropicales.
   - **b.** la exportación de café.
   - **c.** la producción de petróleo.
   - **ch.** la exportación de azúcar.

5. El origen del nombre de la nación de Venezuela es . . .
   - **a.** la ciudad italiana "Venecia".
   - **b.** una tribu de indígenas llamados "venezolanos".
   - **c.** un general español.
   - **ch.** una mujer llamada Venezuela.

Venezuela

¡Un país para querer!

En la parte norteña de Sudamérica, se encuentra una perla frente al Mar Caribe: Venezuela. Su territorio está frente a las Antillas en el Mar Caribe y es vecino de Colombia, Brasil y Guyana. Es un país extenso con un clima tropical ideal. Su población es una mezcla de indígenas, de descendientes de conquistadores españoles y de negros traídos del África como esclavos. Además, tiene una numerosa población europea de origen alemán, francés, inglés, holandés, italiano y portugués.

Aunque Venezuela no es un país muy grande, es más grande que Texas pero más pequeño que Alaska, y su geografía es muy variada. Hay montañas y clima frío en los Andes; y llanuras, grandes ríos y clima tropical en el resto del país. Casi una mitad del país es de terreno montañoso y en gran parte de Venezuela la temperatura no varía mucho de 80° F.

En las montañas, cerca del pueblo Icabarú se encuentran las famosas minas de diamantes de la Gran Sabana. Cerca de allí también está uno de los espectáculos naturales más impresionantes de todo el mundo, el Salto Ángel, **1** la cascada más alta del mundo. Con una caída de más de media milla, es quince veces más alta que las cataratas del Niágara.

Los llanos de la parte central y sur, donde corren los ríos Orinoco y Apure, es un área difícil que sufre inundaciones seis meses del año y sequías los otros seis meses. Al noroeste, en el Golfo de Venezuela y en el Lago de Maracaibo, es donde navegaron Alonzo de Ojeda y Américo Vespucio cuando le dieron el nombre de Venezuela, o la pequeña Venecia, a la región. Esto porque vieron que los indígenas vivían en casas puestas sobre pilotes en el agua de las inundaciones. **2**

Venecia

Venezuela tiene ciudades muy bellas, con características especiales. A Caracas, ❸ la capital, se le llama "la ciudad de la eterna primavera". Es una ciudad muy moderna y cosmopolita con sus hermosos parques, varias universidades, hermosos centros comerciales y gran actividad política, económica y cultural. El Centro Cultural junto con la Plaza Bolívar son dos de los sitios más populares de los turistas en Caracas. Otras hermosas ciudades de Venezuela son Mérida en los Andes, Maracaibo frente al lago del mismo nombre, Barquisimeto en los llanos centrales, Puerto La Cruz y Cumaná en la costa del Mar Caribe, y Ciudad Bolívar y Puerto Ordaz en la parte sur en las márgenes del río Orinoco.

La economía venezolana está basada principalmente en petróleo. ❹ Se ha calculado que hasta un 85 por ciento de la economía de la nación depende de la producción de petróleo. Por eso, cuando baja el precio de este producto el país tiene problemas económicos. Actualmente, el país hace todo lo posible por introducir otros comercios como la producción del café, cacao, azúcar, frutas tropicales, maderas, caucho, hierro, acero, carbón, aluminio, oro y piedras preciosas.

Venezuela es especial por la gran variedad y diversidad de sus habitantes ❺ y por la gran variedad de diversiones que ofrece, por la riqueza de su tierra y del mar y por la magia del trópico. Es por todo eso que los venezolanos dicen: "Venezuela: ¡Un país para querer!"

Verifiquemos

1. Prepara un diagrama de Venezuela, como el siguiente, e incluye toda la información posible bajo cada categoría.

Venezuela

En las montañas	En los llanos	En la capital	La economía
1. minas de diamantes	1. Río Orinoco	1. Caracas	1. petróleo
2.	2.	2.	2.
3.	3.	3.	3.

2. Dibuja el Salto Ángel o la vista que en tu imaginación vieron Alonzo de Ojeda y Américo Vespucio al nombrar Venezuela.
3. Explica el título de esta lectura.
4. Si tú pudieras visitar Venezuela, ¿qué te gustaría ver y hacer?

Otras culturas y yo

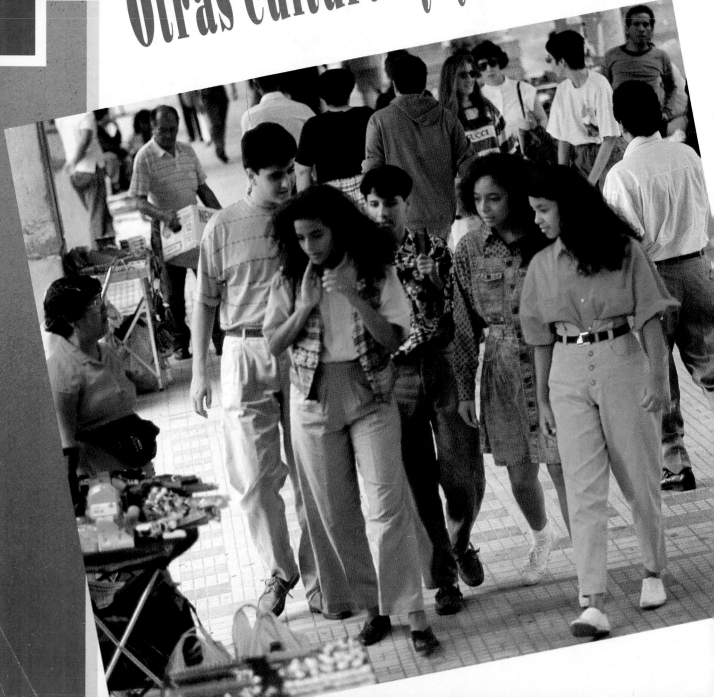

¿ **Q**ué piensas tú ?

1. ¿Qué ciudad crees que es la ciudad en la foto? ¿Por qué crees eso?

2. ¿Qué puedes decir de la vida de la gente que vive en esta ciudad a base de la foto?

3. Nombra los países que reconoces en esta página. ¿Qué representa cada dibujo, algo típico o estereotípico de la cultura de estos países? ¿Por qué crees eso?

4. ¿Qué es un estereotipo? ¿Cómo empiezan los estereotipos?

5. ¿Son los estereotipos una representación verdadera y exacta de la cultura que representan? ¿Por qué crees eso? En tu opinión, ¿son buenos o malos los estereotipos? ¿Por qué?

6. ¿Puedes describir una sola cultura representativa de Estados Unidos? ¿de Sudamérica? ¿de otras partes del mundo? ¿Por qué sí o por qué no?

7. ¿Cuáles son algunos elementos que deben considerarse al describir la cultura de un pueblo o un país?

8. En esta lección, los estudiantes que conociste en la primera lección van a hablar de cómo pasaron el verano. ¿Cuáles son algunos temas que crees que vas a repasar en esta lección?

EL PÁJARO DE LOS SIETE COLORES

Todos los países del mundo tienen sus cuentos y leyendas con sus héroes y villanos y otros personajes interesantes, divertidos, fantásticos o mágicos. Hay leyendas japonesas, alemanas, inglesas, griegas y norte-americanas, . . . y, por supuesto, hay leyendas hispanas.

Esta leyenda venezolana cuenta cómo los buenos hechos merecen y reciben la buena fortuna.

Había una vez . . .

. . .un hombre ciego y sus tres hijos. Todos sabían que al padre no le volvería la vista hasta escuchar el canto del pájaro de los siete colores.

Por eso, el hijo mayor decidió salir en busca del pájaro de los siete colores.

Llegó a la orilla de un río donde vio a un niño ahogándose. La madre del niño le pidió auxilio, pero el jóven le dijo que no porque tenía demasiada prisa, y siguió su camino.

5

Más adelante el hijo mayor llegó a la casa de una señora pobre. Ella le pidió dinero para poder enterrar a su esposo recién muerto. Pero él le dijo que no. Dijo que tenía muy poco dinero y siguió adelante.

6

Poco después, el hijo mayor llegó a un lago encantado. Como tenía mucha sed, tomó el agua del lago y se quedó encantado. Se quedó profundamente dormido.

Cuando el hijo mayor no regresó, el segundo hijo salió en busca del pájaro de los siete colores pero le pasó lo mismo que a su hermano mayor.

7

Entonces, el tercer hijo decidió salir en busca del pájaro de los siete colores. Cuando llegó al río, inmediatamente se echó al agua y le salvó la vida al niño que se ahogaba. Luego continuó su búsqueda.

Al llegar a la casa de la señora pobre, el hijo menor le dio todo su dinero para enterrar al muerto y de nuevo continuó su camino.

8

Al poco tiempo, el hijo menor llegó a una casa donde vivían tres hermanas, las dueñas del pájaro de los siete colores.

Cuando les contó a las jóvenes lo de su padre, la hija menor inmediatamente se montó en el caballo con él y regresaron rápidamente a la casa del ciego.

9

Tan pronto como llegaron, el pájaro empezó a cantar y en seguida le volvió la vista al padre.

Al hablar de lo que hicimos

1 Una actividad especial.

Buenos días, jóvenes. Atención, por favor. Hoy vamos a empezar nuestro estudio de geografía con una actividad especial. Esta actividad es para hacerlos reflexionar sobre el contacto que tenemos con otras culturas en la vida diaria.

Bueno..., trabajando en grupos, quiero que preparen una lista de lo que hicieron durante las vacaciones que tiene que ver con otras culturas. ¿Está claro? Bien. Ahora, en grupos de cuatro, por favor.

Pues somos cuatro. ¿Empezamos?

No entiendo. Yo ni salí de Caracas.

No importa, Meche. Hiciste algo, seguramente. Por ejemplo, ¿no comiste en algún restaurante chino?

Pues, sí. Y también en uno italiano. ¡Ah!, y en otro mexicano.

¿Qué hiciste tú, Salvador?

Pues vi una película francesa.

Ay, también leí una novela sobre el espía inglés, James Bond. Fue muy interesante.

Ay, ¡qué culto! Ja, ja.

Pues, y tú, ¿qué hiciste? ¿Viste una telenovela argentina?

No, en realidad, vi algunos programas norteamericanos en la televisión. Y también fui a visitar a mis tíos en Bogotá.

¡Ah! ¡Se me olvidó! Mis primos alemanes vinieron a visitarnos.

¡Y ahora lo recuerdas!

¿Y tú, Chela? ¿Qué hiciste?

¿Adónde fuiste?

¡Chévere! ¿Y por qué Brasil?

Yo también hice un viaje.

¿No les dije? Estuve en Brasil.

Espera. Espera un momento, por favor.

Mi padre es científico ambiental y nos llevó en un viaje por el río Amazonas.

¡Cuéntanos todo! ¿Dónde empezaste el viaje? ¿Cuánto tiempo duró? ¿Cuántas personas fueron? ¿Qué viste? ¿No te dio miedo?

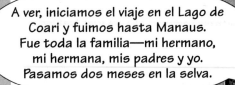

A ver, iniciamos el viaje en el Lago de Coari y fuimos hasta Manaus. Fue toda la familia—mi hermano, mi hermana, mis padres y yo. Pasamos dos meses en la selva.

¿Viste animales salvajes?

¡Ay, sí, muchos! Vimos guacamayas, jaguares, capibaras, tapires y muchos caimanes.

¿No te asustaron?

No, para nada, sólo las pirañas me asustaron.

¡Pirañas! ¿Y había culebras?

¡Huy! ¡Qué tonto eres!

Sí, vimos varias anacondas y boas.

¿De veras? Me encantan las serpientes.

¡Salvador! ¡Quítate! ¡Yo las odio!

Por favor, escriban un informe sobre el contacto más interesante que tuvieron con otra cultura durante las vacaciones.

Silencio, por favor. Como veo que todavía no terminaron, les voy a dar una tarea relacionada con este tema para la próxima clase.

Animales del Amazonas

En general se dice:	En Venezuela se dice:

anaconda	tragavenado

boa	tragavenado

capibara	chigüire

cocodrilo	caimán

jaguar	tigre

piraña	caribe

serpiente	culebra

tapir	danto

CHARLEMOS UN POCO

A. **PARA EMPEZAR . . .** Indica si las siguientes oraciones son ciertas o falsas según la leyenda ''El pájaro de los siete colores''. Si son falsas, corrígelas.

1. Para poder ver, el hombre ciego tenía que escuchar el canto del pájaro de los siete colores.
2. Dos de los tres hijos salieron de la casa en busca del pájaro de los siete colores.
3. El hijo mayor no ayudó a nadie.
4. El hijo mayor se quedó profundamente dormido cuando tomó el agua del lago encantado.
5. El segundo hijo también se quedó profundamente dormido cuando tomó el agua del lago encantado.
6. El tercer hijo hizo lo mismo que el hermano mayor.
7. El pájaro de los siete colores vivía en una casa con tres viejitas.
8. El hijo menor encontró el pájaro de los siete colores y lo mató para poder llevarlo a la casa de su padre.
9. Tan pronto como oyó el canto del pájaro de los siete colores, le volvió la vista al padre.

B. **¿QUÉ DECIMOS . . .?** Según el diálogo, ¿quién hizo estas cosas?

Luis	Meche	Salvador	Chela

1. Comió en un restaurante chino.
2. Leyó una novela sobre James Bond.
3. Vio jaguares, caimanes, anacondas y pirañas.
4. Recibió a sus primos alemanes.
5. Hizo un viaje a Brasil.
6. Vio una película francesa.
7. Comió en un restaurante italiano.
8. Visitó a unos parientes en Colombia.
9. Viajó por el río Amazonas.
10. Vio unos programas norteamericanos en la tele.

C. El fin de semana. Los compañeros de clase de Herlinda hicieron muchas cosas el fin de semana pasado. Según Herlinda, ¿qué hicieron?

Blanca y Shotaro

MODELO   **Blanca y Shotaro estudiaron.**

REPASO

Preterite: -ar verb endings

-é	-amos
-aste	
-ó	-aron

¿**Alquilaste** un video?
Sí, pero primero **limpié** mi cuarto y
estudié un rato.

See **¿Por qué se dice así?,**
page G27, section 2.3.

1. yo

2. Beto

3. mis amigos y yo

4. Luz

5. la profesora

6. José y Felipe

7. Eugenio y Pepita   **8.** Enrique

LECCIÓN 2

Preterite: *-er, -ir* verb endings

-í	-imos
-iste	
-ió	-ieron

¿**Vieron** televisión anoche?
No. **Salimos** a cenar.
Comí unas arepas exquisitas.

See ¿**Por qué se dice así?**,
page G27, section 2.3.

REPASO

Preterite:
Regular verb endings

	-ar	-er, -ir
Yo	-é	-í
Tu	-aste	-iste
el	-ó	-ió
nos ellos	-amos	-imos
ellas	-aron	-ieron

See ¿**Por qué se dice así?**,
page G27, section 2.3.

CH. Una fiesta.   Ayer Pepe celebró su cumpleaños. Según él, ¿qué pasó en la fiesta?

MODELO   **Yo recibí muchos regalos.**

mis amigos y yo	tomar	pastel
mamá	recibir	pizza
yo	leer	limonada
los invitados	romper	café
papá	ver	tarjetas
mis hermanos	abrir	regalos
Óscar	comer	piñata
		la tele

D. Durante el verano.   Pregúntale a un(a) compañero(a) si hizo estas cosas durante el verano.

 MODELO   practicar deportes
    Tú: ¿**Practicaste deportes?**
    Compañero(a): **Sí, practiqué deportes todos los días**.

1. comer en un restaurante italiano
2. viajar a otro estado
3. viajar a otro país
4. jugar tenis
5. asistir a un concierto
6. escribir cartas
7. leer un libro interesante
8. pasear en bicicleta
9. ver muchas películas
10. visitar a sus abuelos
11. trabajar
12. correr mucho

E. Ocupados.   ¿Qué dice Roberto que él y su familia hicieron ayer?

Rubén y Timoteo

 MODELO   **Rubén y Timoteo caminaron en el parque.**

1. Irma

2. Irma y Marta

3. Rubén

4. mamá

5. yo

6. Susana y yo

7. papá

8. Marta y Timoteo

F. ¿Qué hicieron allá? Tú y unos amigos fueron a otros países durante el verano. ¿Adónde fueron y qué hicieron allá?

> MODELO   Gabriel: Segovia (ir al cine mucho)
> **Gabriel fue a Segovia. Fue al cine mucho.**

1. Julieta y Patricia: París (ir a muchas fiestas)
2. Enrico: Roma (ir a visitar a sus parientes)
3. Rosita y Jorge: Buenos Aires (ir de compras todos los días)
4. Carlota y yo: Guadalajara (hacer tres excursiones al lago Chapala)
5. Eduardo y Eva: Madrid (ir a la Biblioteca Nacional)
6. Tú: Cuzco (hacer una excursión a Machu Picchu)
7. Carmen y Héctor: México, D.F. (hacer excursiones a las pirámides)
8. Tú y yo: Venezuela (hacer una excursión por el río Orinoco)

REPASO

**Preterite:
Three irregular verbs**

Ir/Ser	Hacer
fui	hice
fuiste	hiciste
fue	hizo
fuimos	hicimos
fueron	hicieron

See **¿Por qué se dice así?,**
page G27, section 2.3.

Adjectives of nationality

Adjectives whose singular masculine form ends in **-o**:

argentino	hondureño
boliviano	italiano
brasileño	mexicano
colombiano	noruego
coreano	paraguayo
cubano	peruano
chileno	puertorriqueño
chino	ruso
dominicano	salvadoreño
ecuatoriano	sueco
europeo	suizo
filipino	uruguayo
griego	venezolano
guatemalteco	

Adjectives whose singular form ends in **-a**, **-e**, or **-í**:

canadiense	marroquí
costarricense	nicaragüense
estadounidense	paquistaní
israelita	vietnamita

Adjectives whose singular masculine form ends in a consonant:

alemán	holandés
danés	inglés
escocés	irlandés
español	japonés
francés	portugués

See **¿Por qué se dice así?**,
page G30, section 2.4.

G. Fiesta internacional. Conociste a estas personas en una fiesta internacional. Identifícalas.

MODELO **Ellas se llaman Margaret y Christy. Son canadienses.**

Margaret y Christy

1. Ricardo

2. María

3. Tomás

4. Tereza

Canadá

NORTEAMÉRICA

Estados Unidos

México

OCÉANO ATLÁNTICO

SUDAMÉRICA

Bolivia

Brasil

Argentina

5. Claude y Pierre

6. Heidi

7. Olga e Ivan

8. Jie

9. Yushiko y Miyoshi

10. Marcella

OCÉANO ÁRTICO

Suecia

Inglaterra

Dinamarca

Alemania

Francia

Italia

España

Grecia

Comunidad de Estados Independientes

Rusia

ASIA

Corea del Norte

China

Corea del Sur

Japón

OCÉANO PACÍFICO

India

ÁFRICA

AUSTRALIA

H. ¿Mi nacionalidad?   ¿De dónde eres? Tu profesor te va a asignar un país pero no te va a decir cuál es. Hazles preguntas a tus compañeros para descubrir tu nacionalidad.

 MODELO   *Tú:*   ¿Soy boliviano(a)?
           Compañero(a): **No, no eres de Bolivia.**   o
                        Sí, eres de La Paz.

CHARLEMOS UN POCO MÁS

A. Hecho en el Japón. En grupos de cuatro decidan cuántas prendas de ropa u objetos en sus bolsos están hechos en el extranjero. Preparen una lista de los objetos y su origen.

EJEMPLO   **zapatos: argentinos**   **bolígrafo: coreano**

B. ¿Eres danés? Tu profesor(a) te va a dar una tarjeta de identidad y un mapa de Europa. La tarjeta indicará tu nuevo nombre y país de origen.

- Preséntate a varios compañeros de clase.
- Diles tu nuevo nombre.
- Pregúntales el suyo.
- Pregúntales su nacionalidad y diles la tuya.
- Pregúntales si viajaron a otro país este verano.
- Diles que tú viajaste a [*nombre de un país vecino a tu país de origen*].
- Escribe tu nombre en el mapa en tu país de origen y en el país que visitaste. Haz lo mismo con los nombres de tus compañeros de clase.

C. ¿Quién hizo esto? Tu profesor(a) te va a dar una cuadrícula con una actividad indicada en cada cuadrado. Pregúntales a tus compañeros de clase si hicieron estas actividades durante el verano. Cada vez que recibas una respuesta afirmativa, pídele a esa persona que firme en el cuadrado apropiado. Recuerda que no se permite que la misma persona firme más de un cuadrado.

Dramatizaciones

A. ¡Yo también! Tu compañero fue de vacaciones con su familia por una semana durante el verano. Tú no saliste de tu ciudad en todo el verano. Pregúntale a tu amigo sobre sus vacaciones: ¿adónde fue?, ¿con quién?, ¿qué hizo?, ¿qué vio?, etc. Al contestar sus preguntas, trata de impresionarlo con todas las actividades que hiciste tú. Dramaticen esta situación. Usen su imaginación e inventen actividades creativas.

B. Contactos culturales. El gobierno federal quiere saber cuántos productos del extranjero usan los jóvenes en Estados Unidos. Tú eres un(a) investigador(a) de la C.I.A. que está entrevistando a jóvenes en tu escuela. Entrevista a dos personas. Dramatiza la situación con dos compañeros de la clase.

IMPACTO CULTURAL
Nuestra lengua

Antes de empezar

A. Jerga. Cada país o región tiene su lenguaje especial o jerga. Por ejemplo, en algunas partes de EE.UU. los jóvenes dicen *bad* cuando algo es muy bueno.

1. ¿Cuáles son algunas palabras en inglés que usas tú para referirte o dirigirte directamente a un(a) amigo(a) pero no a un adulto?
2. ¿Cuáles son algunas palabras en inglés que tú y tus amigos usan entre ustedes cuando quieren decir que algo es muy bueno o muy especial?

B. Direcciones. Prepara una lista en español de varias maneras de dar direcciones cuando no recuerdas el número exacto o no sabes el nombre de la calle.

Peligro a Descanso. Pedro Valera, un estudiante venezolano, conversa con Steve, su nuevo amigo norteamericano. ¿De qué hablan?

Steve: **Hola, Pedro. ¿Cómo estás?**

Pedro: **Bien, mi vale, ¿y tú?**

Steve: **Pues, no muy bien. Estoy preocupado por el examen de mañana.**

Pedro: **¿Tú también? Memo y yo vamos a estudiar juntos esta noche. ¿Quieres acompañarnos?**

Steve: **¡Por supuesto! ¿Dónde van a estar?**

Pedro: **En casa de Memo. Vive cerca de mí, en Perico a El Muerto #320.**

Steve: **¡Ay! Siempre me pierdo en esa parte de la ciudad. ¿Por qué no usan el nombre de las calles? Es mucho más fácil.**

Pedro: **Es que es la parte más antigua de Caracas. Y es tradicional nombrar las esquinas. Todas las esquinas en esa sección tienen nombres: Angelitos, Peligro, Descanso, Las Monjas, San Jacinto . . .**

Steve: **Sí, es interesante, pero confuso.**

Pedro: **Bueno, entonces te esperamos a eso de las nueve.**

Steve: **Bien, mi vale. Hasta más tarde.**

Verifiquemos

A. ¿Qué dijo? Contesta estas preguntas para mostrar que entendiste el diálogo.

1. ¿Qué quiere decir "mi vale"?
2. ¿Por qué siempre se pierde Steve en la parte de Caracas donde viven Pedro y Memo?
3. La dirección de Memo no es como las direcciones en Estados Unidos. ¿Por qué no?
4. "Perico" y "El Muerto" no son nombres de calles. ¿De qué son nombres?
5. Con un(a) compañero(a), selecciona uno de los nombres mencionados en el diálogo. Luego usen su imaginación para explicar por qué creen ustedes que recibió este nombre el lugar.
   Perico   El Muerto   Angelitos   Peligro   Descanso   Las Monjas
6. ¿Por qué dice Steve "mi vale" al despedirse?

¡ Pirañas !

¿ Qué piensas tú ?

1. ¿Dónde hay selvas tropicales? ¿Dónde crees que está esta selva tropical? ¿Por qué crees eso?

2. ¿Por qué hay tanto interés actualmente en preservar las selvas tropicales?

3. ¿Reconoces estos animales y plantas? ¿Son muy comunes? ¿Qué tienen en común?

4. ¿Se preocupan tú y tus amigos por el medio ambiente? ¿Por qué?

5. En tu opinión, ¿qué preocupaciones sobre el medio ambiente tienen los jóvenes en otras partes del mundo?

6. ¿Qué soluciones propones tú para estos problemas?

7. En esta lección, vamos a leer la composición que escribió Chela para su clase de geografía sobre su viaje por el río Amazonas. ¿Qué crees que vamos a repasar en la lección?

EL LEÓN Y LAS PULGAS

En el siglo veinte, empezamos a darnos cuenta que tenemos que proteger la tierra—los ríos, lagos y costas, las plantas y los animales.

1

El cuento "El león y las pulgas" nos ayuda a entender lo que puede pasar si no cuidamos nuestro mundo.

2

Hace muchísimo tiempo, los animales de la selva africana proclamaron al león "rey de todos los animales", por ser el animal más majestuoso, más poderoso, más hermoso y más fuerte de todos los animales.

3

Desafortunadamente, con el pasar del tiempo, el león se volvió orgulloso y tiránico. A tal extremo llegó su tiranía, que del respeto y la admiración inicial, los animales pasaron a sentir miedo y terror de su monarca.

La única excepción fueron las pulgas, esos fastidiosos insectos que no sentían ni miedo ni respeto por el rey, ni por ningún otro animal.

Pues bien, las pulgas decidieron demostrarles a todos los demás animales que ellas eran más poderosas que el invencible león. Con esta idea, una pequeña colonia de pulgas se estableció en el lustroso y elegante pelaje dorado del león.

Con la excelente y noble sangre del león, la pequeña colonia empezó a crecer rápidamente y se extendieron por todas las partes del cuerpo del rey. Las pulgas vieron en el león un magnífico y delicioso banquete que les permitió tener una fiesta continua, día tras día.

Desgraciadamente, las pulgas picaron tanto al león que éste finalmente se enfermó y acabó por morirse.

El día que murió el león, las pulgas tuvieron una gran fiesta. A pesar de ser tan pequeñas, feas e insignificantes, ¡ellas ganaron! ¡Vencieron al animal más poderoso de la selva!

Pero, ¿ganaron realmente? Una vez que murió el león, las pulgas perdieron el espléndido banquete de todos los días y, poco a poco, ellas empezaron a morir.

Las pulgas no se dieron cuenta que al matar al león, perdieron la fuente de su alimentación.

Hay una moraleja en este cuento para todas las gentes del mundo, ¿no? ¿Puedes ver algunos paralelos con tu vida personal? ¿con el bienestar de tu ciudad? ¿de tu país?

¿QUÉ DECIMOS AL ESCRIBIR...?

De una excursión

Chela acaba de escribir su informe para la clase de
geografía. Antes de pasar a la próxima página para
leerlo, mira el mapa y examina su ruta por el río
Amazonas. ¿Qué te parece?

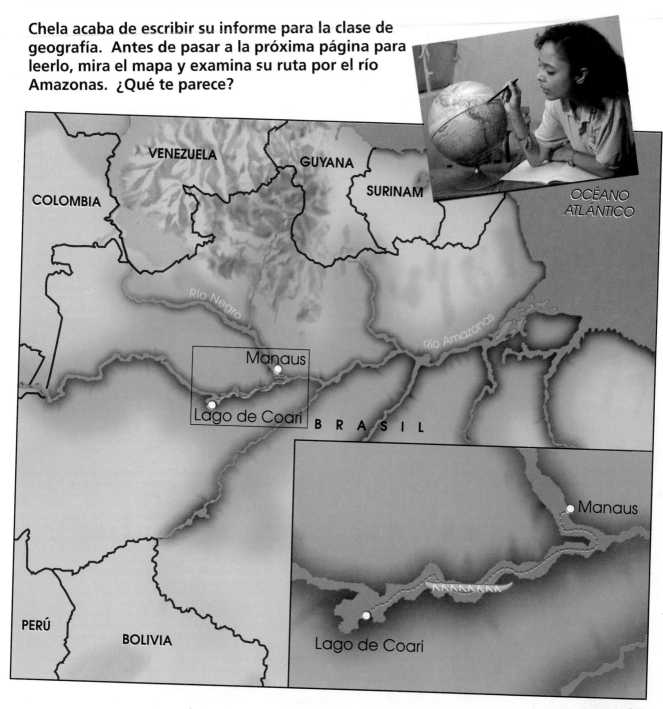

1

     Durante las vacaciones hice un viaje con mi familia por el río Amazonas. Mi padre es científico ambiental y tuvo que hacer algunas investigaciones sobre el estado de la selva y el pantano del río. Esta área es muy importante porque la selva produce oxígeno y absorbe contaminantes. La salud de la selva afecta el bienestar del mundo entero.

2

     No sabía que el río Amazonas era tan interesante. Es el río más largo de Sudamérica (6.450 kilómetros) y el segundo más largo del mundo. Sólo el río Nilo es más largo. Nosotros desembarcamos en uno de los tributarios más importantes, el río Negro, que desemboca en la ciudad de Manaus. ❶

❶

❷

❸

3

     Me gustó mucho la ciudad de Manaus. Es el puerto más grande de esa región. De allí se exportan muchos productos de la selva, como la nuez❷ del Brasil, el caucho❸ y varias clases de madera dura.❹

❹

4

    Fue una sorpresa encontrar a diversas poblaciones a lo largo del río. Además de los indígenas, vimos a personas de varios grupos étnicos—norteamericanos, europeos, negros, japoneses y gente de raza mixta. La riqueza del país atrae a personas de negocio, de distintas partes del mundo, interesadas en establecer sus negocios allí. Pero el desarrollo de la selva tropical ya está causando problemas ambientales.

5

    Los científicos se preocupan por el efecto de la explotación de la selva tropical en el medio ambiente. Por ejemplo, la minería del oro y otros metales contamina el agua. Además, muchos agricultores cortan y queman los árboles para criar ganado y cultivar la tierra. Estas prácticas sostienen la economía de la región, pero destruyen el equilibrio natural y amenazan algunas poblaciones indígenas.

6

    Muchas especies de plantas y animales que vimos en nuestro viaje sólo viven en las selvas del Amazonas y hoy se encuentran en peligro de extinción por la destrucción de la selva. Sería terrible verlos desaparecer—¡aun las anacondas y las pirañas!

CHARLEMOS UN POCO

A. **PARA EMPEZAR . . .** Pon las siguientes oraciones en orden cronológico según la leyenda ''El león y las pulgas''.

1. Las pulgas tuvieron una gran fiesta para celebrar su victoria.
2. El león se volvió orgulloso y tiránico.
3. Pronto, las pulgas se dieron cuenta de que al matar al león, perdieron su fuente de alimentación.
4. Las pulgas decidieron demostrar que ellas eran más poderosas e invencibles que el león.
5. Los animales de la selva proclamaron al león ''rey de todos los animales''.
6. Pero las pulgas perdieron el espléndido banquete de todos los días y empezaron a morir.
7. Las pulgas picaron tanto al león que se enfermó y se murió.
8. Los animales pasaron a sentir miedo y terror de su monarca.

B. **¿QUÉ DECIMOS . . .?** Completa estas frases según el informe de Chela.

1. El río más largo de Sudamérica es . . .
   a. el río Amazonas.
   b. el río Orinoco.
   c. el río Nilo.

2. El río más largo del mundo es . . .
   a. el río Amazonas.
   b. el río Orinoco.
   c. el río Nilo.

3. Un puerto importante en el Amazonas es . . .
   a. Maracaibo.
   b. Guayaquil.
   c. Manaus.

4. Tres productos de la selva son . . .
   a. el plástico, el cristal y la madera.
   b. el caucho, la madera y las nueces.
   c. las nueces, la madera y el cristal.

5. El desarrollo de la selva pone en peligro . . .
   a. las ciudades grandes.
   b. a la población indígena.
   c. la industrialización.

6. Unos animales salvajes del río Amazonas son . . .
   a. las pirañas y las anacondas.
   b. los leones y los elefantes.
   c. los tigres y las gorilas.

C. ¡Qué diferentes! ¿Cómo se comparan estos animales de la selva?

el tucán

el caimán

MODELO   ser / largo

El caimán es más largo que el tucán.

1. ser / grande
2. tener / colores
3. ser / fuerte
4. tener / dientes
5. ser / pequeño
6. ser / lindo
7. tener ojos / grandes
8. ser / feroz

CH. Amigas. Éstas son Manuela y Carmen. Compara sus edades y di cuál de ellas es mejor o peor en estas actividades.

Carmen, 15 años   Manuela, 16 años

EJEMPLO   **Manuela juega fútbol mejor que Carmen.**

LECCIÓN 3

**Unequal comparisons:
*más que/menos que***

Tú eres **más** alto **que** yo.
Epi tiene **menos** dinero **que** yo.

*See **¿Por qué se dice así?**,
page G32, section 2.5.*

**Unequal comparisons:
*mayor/menor, mejor/peor***

Tú eres **mayor que** yo.
Sí, pero soy **menor que** Francisco.

Eva habla español **mejor que** yo.
Sí, pero habla inglés **peor que** tú.

*See **¿Por qué se dice así?**,
page G32, section 2.5.*

See ¿**Por qué se dice así?**, *page G32, section 2.5.*

Equal comparisons:
tan/como, tanto/como

1. **tan** + adj. + **como**

   Ella es **tan** alta **como** tú.
   Ellos son **tan** inteligentes **como** nosotros.

2. **tanto (-a, -os, -as)** + noun + **como**

   No tengo **tanto** dinero **como** ustedes.
   Leí **tantas** novelas **como** tú.

D. Parecen gemelos. Pedro y Paco no son parientes pero son increíblemente parecidos. Compáralos.

MODELO   ser guapo   tener libros
         Pedro es tan   **Pedro tiene tantos**
         guapo como Paco.   **libros como Paco.**

1. ser delgado
2. tener zapatos
3. ser simpático
4. tener camisetas
5. ser estudioso
6. ser alto
7. tener discos
8. ser fuerte

E. Materiales escolares. Meche necesita comprar materiales escolares para sus clases. ¿Cómo se comparan los precios de este almacén con los de esta papelería?

MODELO   lápices
        Los lápices del almacén son más baratos que los lápices de la papelería.
                  o
        Los lápices de la papelería son más caros que los lápices del almacén.

	Almacén Bolívar	Papelería Torres
lápices	5 Bs	10 Bs
reglas	25 Bs	20 Bs
cuadernos	60 Bs	60 Bs
carpetas	20 Bs	25 Bs
bolígrafos	35 Bs	40 Bs
papel	160 Bs	150 Bs
borradores	30 Bs	30 Bs
mochila	725 Bs	715 Bs
papel de computadora	480 Bs	485 Bs

1. reglas
2. cuadernos
3. carpetas
4. bolígrafos
5. papel
6. borradores
7. mochila
8. papel de computadora

F. ¡Qué impresionante! Gabi acaba de regresar de un viaje al pantano del Amazonas. ¿Cómo describe su experiencia?

EJEMPLO **Los productos de la selva tropical son importantísimos.**

el río Amazonas	lindo
las plantas	rico
los animales	alto
la selva	largo
los problemas	importante
las frutas	interesante
la gente	feroz
los árboles	malo
los productos	simpático
	largo

G. Es el más . . . ¿Conoces estos animales salvajes? Asocia los dibujos con la palabra que mejor describe cada animal.

MODELO rápido
El leopardo es el animal más rápido de la selva.

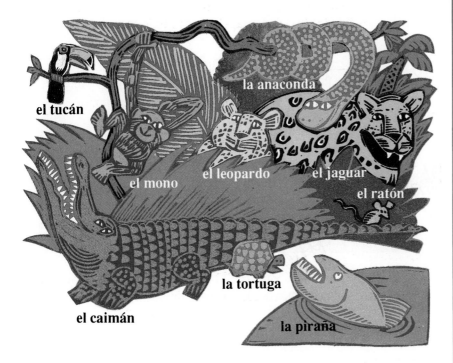

el tucán
la anaconda
el mono
el leopardo
el jaguar
el ratón
el caimán
la tortuga
la piraña

1. bonito
2. pequeño
3. largo
4. grande
5. feo
6. lento
7. peligroso
8. fuerte

H. Sudamérica. Mañana tu compañero(a) va a tener un examen sobre Sudamérica en la clase de geografía. Ayúdalo(la) a prepararse para el examen.

 MODELO ¿Cuál es el país con costas en dos océanos?
Colombia

1. ¿Cuáles son las montañas más importantes de Sudamérica?
2. ¿Qué río pasa entre dos capitales al desembocar en el Océano Atlántico?
3. ¿Cuál es el país más grande de Sudamérica?
4. ¿Qué países tienen una costa en el Océano Pacífico?
5. ¿Cómo se llama el río que pasa por toda Venezuela?
6. ¿Cuál es el país más largo de Sudamérica?
7. ¿Cómo se llama el lago que está entre dos países?
8. ¿Qué países no tienen costa?
9. ¿Qué países están en el ecuador?
10. ¿Cuál es el pico más alto de los Andes?

CHARLEMOS UN POCO MÁS

A. El Orinoco. Tú y tu compañero(a) están mirando las fotos en el álbum de Jacinto. Él y su familia hicieron un viaje por el río Orinoco durante el verano. Escriban subtítulos para cada foto explicando lo que Jacinto y su familia vieron en su viaje. Compartan sus subtítulos con otros compañeros de clase.

B. Nuestro continente.   Con un(a) compañero(a) de clase, compara Sudamérica con el mapa de Norteamérica que tu profesor(a) les va a dar. Menciona el tamaño, número de países, cordilleras y ríos principales, etc.

C. Un informe.   Con un amigo o una amiga, prepara un informe sobre un país de habla española. Comparen el país con Estados Unidos: tamaño, población, características físicas, ciudades principales, etc. Será necesario buscar información en la enciclopedia o en otras fuentes. Presenten su informe a la clase.

CH. Países.   Tu profesor(a) te va a dar el mapa de un país de Sudamérica o Centroamérica. Tú tienes que identificar el país, escribir el nombre del país y su capital en el lugar apropiado y luego localizar el país en el mapa del (de la) profesor(a).

Dramatizaciones

A. Un viaje a Brasil.   Tú eres reportero(a) del periódico de tu escuela. Ahora tienes que entrevistar a Chela Fuentes o a su hermano. Tu compañero(a) hará el papel de Chela o su hermano. La entrevista es para conseguir toda la información posible sobre su viaje de este verano a Brasil. Dramatiza esta situación con tu compañero(a). Usa tu imaginación para recrear el viaje de Chela.

B. Otro viaje.   Ahora, como reportero(a) del periódico de tu escuela, tienes que entrevistar al (a la) profesor(a) de geografía sobre su viaje a México este verano. Pasó una semana en la capital y otra en Guadalajara. Pídele que compare las dos ciudades o una de las dos con una ciudad en EE.UU. Tu compañero(a) hará el papel del (de la) profesor(a). Dramaticen esta situación.

LEAMOS AHORA

Estrategias para leer:
Ojear y anticipar

A. Ojear. Ojear es mirar rápidamente una lectura para encontrar información específica. Cuando ojeamos, siempre es necesario saber exactamente qué información necesitamos. Ojea ahora los primeros dos párrafos de esta lectura para encontrar la siguiente información.

1. Prepara una lista de todas las acciones o actividades mencionadas en los primeros dos párrafos.
2. Mira el cuarto y el quinto párrafo ahora. ¿Hay algunas palabras que se repitan más de dos o tres veces? ¿Cuáles son?
3. Las palabras en esta lista son palabras afines con el inglés. ¿Cuál es su significado? Todas estas palabras caen en dos categorías principales, *Plantas y sus productos* y *Medicinas y enfermedades*. Ponlas en la categoría apropiada.

anticoagulante	filodendro
aspirina	medicina
cafeína	músculos
cáncer	planta
cirugía	SIDA
coco	sufrir
cola	tropical
fibra	vainilla

B. Ojear y comparar. Ahora lee las siguientes preguntas. Luego ojea los últimos dos párrafos de la lectura y compáralos con los primeros dos.

1. ¿Qué tipo de verbos se usan en los primeros dos párrafos que no se usan en los últimos dos?
2. ¿Para qué se usan estos verbos usualmente?

C. Anticipar el tema. Considera toda la información que ya tienes: la repetición de ciertas palabras en la lectura, las categorías de vocabulario en la lectura y el tipo de verbos o actividades que hay en los primeros párrafos.

1. ¿Qué relación hay entre todas estas cosas y el título de la lectura?
2. En tu opinión, ¿qué crees que vas a aprender en esta lectura? Sé específico(a).

La selva tropical y yo

Por la mañana te levantas rápidamente y te bañas. Luego te pintas (si eres chica) y te vistes. Tomas un cafecito, cereal y fruta antes de coger el autobús escolar. La mañana pasa rápidamente y al mediodía un amigo te invita a ir a almorzar en su coche. Tú pides una hamburguesa, una Cola y, de postre, un helado de vainilla. Regresan al colegio y al terminar las clases, decides caminar a casa con otros amigos. En camino tú compras un dulce de chocolate y tus amigos compran chicle. **1**

En casa, haces la tarea después de cenar y luego ves la televisión un rato. Tu madre te pide que le des un poco de agua a la planta en tu cuarto antes de acostarte. Tú tienes un pequeño dolor de cabeza y decides tomar una aspirina. Luego te acuestas y te duermes en seguida.

¿Es una descripción representativa de tu vida diaria? Es probable que tú no tomes café por la mañana, o a lo mejor tú no vas al colegio en el autobús escolar sino en tu propio coche. Fuera de eso, es probable que no haya grandes diferencias.

Bueno, pero ¿qué tiene que ver todo esto con la selva tropical?, te preguntas. Es una pregunta válida . . . y la respuesta es bien sencilla. Tiene **todo** que ver con la selva tropical. ¿Cómo? ¿Dices que no entiendes? Pues veamos. Examinemos tu rutina diaria.

Probablemente duermes en una cama pintada de laca o barniz, **2** pinturas hechas de la resina de varios árboles de la selva tropical. Es probable también, que duermas en una almohada **3** rellena de fibra de los *árboles kapok* que crecen sólo en la selva tropical. En el

---

Verifiquemos

A. Decide qué palabra o frase mejor completa estas oraciones.
1. *Barniz* y *laca* son (camas / pinturas / árboles tropicales).
2. Muchas *almohadas* están rellenas de (jabón / palo de rosa / productos de árboles tropicales).
3. El *palo de rosa* se usa para producir (aroma / color / fibra).
4. El *annatto* es un árbol que se usa para producir (aroma / color / fibra).
5. El *caucho* es esencial para el buen funcionamiento de (bicicletas / restaurantes / televisores).

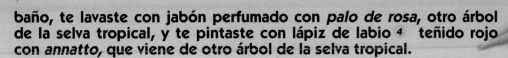

baño, te lavaste con jabón perfumado con *palo de rosa,* otro árbol de la selva tropical, y te pintaste con lápiz de labio **4** teñido rojo con *annatto,* que viene de otro árbol de la selva tropical.

Si para el desayuno comes "granola", ésta consiste de *coco y anacardo* **5** que también vienen de la selva tropical, como la *banana* que le pusiste encima. El *café* que tomas y el *azúcar* que le pones, también son productos de la selva tropical. El autobús que te lleva a la escuela, o tu propio coche, viaja en llantas **6** de *caucho,* producto de otro árbol de la selva tropical, como también lo son las suelas **7** de zapatos deportivos que probablemente llevas hoy mismo.

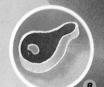

La carne en tu hamburguesa es *carne de res* **8** *barata* que viene de ganado **9** criado en la selva tropical recientemente destruida. La *cola* que bebes viene de una planta rica en cafeína y la *vainilla* en tu helado también viene de la selva tropical. Y sí, tienes razón. El *chocolate* y el *chicle* también. El *chocolate* viene de productos del árbol *cacao* y el otro del *árbol chicle.*

Pero hay más. La planta en tu cuarto probablemente es un *filodendro* de la selva tropical y la *aspirina* que tomaste viene de otra planta tropical. Y no es todo. En la televisión viste, tal vez, un programa sobre grandes avances que se están haciendo en el campo de medicina relacionados a plantas y animales de la selva tropical. Éstos incluyen *liana,* una planta que produce un anticoagulante; *curare,* otra planta que relaja los músculos durante cirugía del corazón; otras tres plantas que parecen tener buen efecto en personas que sufren de SIDA; y varias otras plantas que parecen ser buenas para los pacientes de cáncer.

Ahora, ¿cómo contestas tu propia pregunta? ¿Cómo afecta la selva tropical a tu vida diaria?

B. Contesten estas preguntas en grupos pequeños e informen a la clase de sus conclusiones.

1. ¿Qué relación hay entre las selvas tropicales y la medicina?

2. ¿Cuáles son cinco ejemplos de contacto diario que todas las personas en su grupo tienen en común con la selva tropical?

ESCRIBAMOS AHORA

Estrategias para escribir:
Obtener información y preparar un informe

A. Empezar. En esta unidad, Chela y sus compañeros de clases tuvieron que pensar en todos los contactos que tuvieron con otras culturas durante el verano. ¿Cuáles son algunos contactos que mencionaron? ¿Cuáles son algunos contactos que tú tuviste con otras culturas durante el verano?

B. Torbellino de ideas. En grupos de cuatro, preparen una lista de todos los contactos que ustedes tuvieron con otras culturas durante el verano.

C. Organizar. Ahora usa la información de tu lista de ideas para preparar un cuestionario similar al que sigue pero con un mínimo de diez preguntas. Usa tu cuestionario para entrevistar a tus compañeros de clase y obtener información acerca de los contactos que ellos tuvieron con otras culturas durante el verano.

Actividad	¿Quién?	¿Dónde?	¿Cuánto tiempo?	¿Qué cultura?
¿Visitaste un país extranjero?				
¿Viste una película francesa / alemana / japonesa?				
¿ . . . ?				

CH. Primer borrador. Ahora, usa la información que obtuviste en tu encuesta y prepara un informe escrito. Incluye conclusiones en categorías apropiadas, según la información que tengas: un contraste entre hombres y mujeres, el porcentaje de individuos que participaron en la encuesta, los contactos más y menos comunes, interesantes, etc.

D. Compartir. Comparte el primer borrador de tu informe con dos compañeros de clase. Pídeles sugerencias. Pregúntales si hay algo más que desean saber sobre tu encuesta, si hay algo que no entienden, si hay algo que puede o debe eliminarse. Dales la misma información sobre sus informes cuando ellos(as) te pidan sugerencias.

E. Revisar. Haz cambios en tu informe a base de las sugerencias de tus compañeros. Luego, antes de entregar el informe, compártelo una vez más con dos compañeros de clase. Esta vez pídeles que revisen la estructura y la puntuación. En particular, pídeles que revisen el uso de verbos en el pretérito.

F. Versión final. Escribe la versión final de tu informe incorporando las correcciones que tus compañeros(as) de clase te indicaron. Entrega una copia en limpio a tu profesor(a).

G. Publicar. Cuando tu profesor(a) te devuelva el informe, léeselo a tus compañeros en grupos de cuatro. Luego cada grupo debe preparar una lista de la información más interesante y válida que escuchó.

UNIDAD 3

Queridos televidentes . . .

RADIO CARACAS TELEVISION

TELECARIBE

VENEZOLANA DE TELEVISION

Hoy va a llover y ...

ISLA DE MARGARITA **32°**

COSTA CENTRAL **28°**

MARACAIBO **38°**

BARQUISIMETO **29°**

CARACAS **25°**

PUERTO LA CRUZ **32°**

MÉRIDA **12°**

CIUDAD BOLÍVAR **42°**

PUERTO AYACUCHO **42°**

CARACAS
ESTA NOCHE
19°
MAÑANA
24°

DESPEJADO   NUBLADO

LLUVIA   LLOVIZNA

¿ **Q**ué piensas tú ?

1. ¿En qué parte(s) del mundo crees que se sacaron estas fotos? ¿Por qué crees eso?

2. Si te decimos que todas las fotos se sacaron el 15 de julio, ¿van a cambiar tus respuestas a la primera pregunta? ¿Cómo? ¿Por qué?

3. ¿Crees que todos los lugares representados en las fotos están poblados? ¿Por qué? En tu opinión, ¿cómo es el estilo de vida en todos estos lugares? ¿Por qué crees eso?

4. ¿Qué efecto tiene el tiempo en el estilo de vida de una gente? ¿Qué influencia tiene el tiempo en la cultura de una gente? ¿Por qué crees eso?

5. ¿Cómo puedes explicar la gran extensión de influencia hispana por todo el mundo? ¿Te sorprende esta extensión? ¿Por qué?

6. En esta lección, vamos a repasar mucho de lo que aprendiste en **¡DIME!** UNO. ¿Puedes decir cuáles son tres cosas que vamos a repasar?

1

TÍO TIGRE Y TÍO CONEJO

Los cuentos de Tío Tigre y Tío Conejo están entre los más populares de la tradición oral de las Américas. Se dice que tienen su origen con los trabajadores de las grandes haciendas y plantaciones. En estos cuentos, el pequeño y astuto Tío Conejo siempre vence al grande, fuerte y bobo Tío Tigre.

2

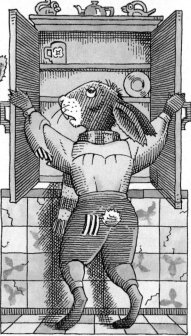

Ese día, el primer día de invierno, hizo mucho frío durante el día. También hizo viento y llovió continuamente. "¡Ay!" pensó Tío Conejo mientras pensaba en preparar la cena, "éste va a ser un invierno horroroso. Va a hacer un frío de mil demonios".

Buscó algo que comer en el aparador pero no encontró nada. "Y voy a sufrir mucha hambre también".

Pero como a Tío Conejo no le gustaba trabajar, "el trabajo es para los bobos" decía, tuvo que pensar cuidadosamente en cómo iba a sobrevivir el invierno.

3

Tío Conejo salió a caminar y pensar en su dilema. En el camino descubrió un abrigo de lana muy elegante.

"Con este hermoso abrigo, voy a estar muy cómodo durante el invierno".

Y como no vio a nadie en el camino, se puso el abrigo y siguió caminando.

4

Un poco más tarde, Tío Conejo se encontró con Tío Tigre.

"¿Dónde conseguiste ese hermoso abrigo?" preguntó Tío Tigre.

"Lo hice yo mismo", respondió Tío Conejo. "¿No sabe usted que yo tejo abrigos de lana?"

"¿Ah, sí?" dijo Tío Tigre. "¿Podría tejerme uno a mí? Me gustaría mucho tener un abrigo como éste".

5

Tío Conejo se quedó pensando un rato, luego dijo que sí, pero con una condición...

"Usted tiene que traerme toda la lana que voy a necesitar y también algo de comer mientras trabaje en su abrigo", dijo al ingenuo tigre. "No voy a tener tiempo para ir de compras y tejer también"

Tío Tigre quedó contentísimo. "Voy a tener el abrigo más hermoso de todos", se dijo.

ARROZ

FRIJOLES NEGROS

6

Y así pasaron los días con Tío Conejo tejiendo y Tío Tigre trayéndole más y más lana y comida. Día tras día durante todo el invierno Tío Tigre le llevaba lana, huevos, salchichas, pan y otras comidas a Tío Conejo. Y todas las tardes el pobre bobo salía de la casa de Tío Conejo sin su abrigo de lana.

Los días pasaron a semanas, las semanas a meses, y pronto, sin darse cuenta Tío Tigre, llegó la primavera.

7

Sí, terminó el invierno y llegó la primavera. Y el pobre Tío Tigre flaco y cansado de tanto trabajar todo el invierno, ya no necesitaba un abrigo. Y Tío Conejo, gordito y calientito bajo toda esa lana, sobrevivió un invierno más. ¡Pobre Tío Tigre!, ¿verdad? ¡Nunca gana! ¡Así es la vida!

¿QUÉ DECIMOS...?

Al hablar de un incidente

1 Vamos a leerlos en la radio.

Luis y su hermanita, Irene, esperan a su papá en el canal de televisión donde trabaja.

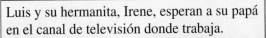

¿Cuánto tiempo falta? Ya tengo hambre.

Faltan quince minutos. Déjame hacer la tarea.

¿Tienes mucha tarea?

Sí, para la clase de composición.

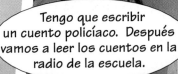

¿De veras? A ver.

Irene, ¡por favor!

Tengo que escribir un cuento policíaco. Después vamos a leer los cuentos en la radio de la escuela.

¿En la radio? ¡Qué divertido!

¿Divertido? ¡No tengo ni idea de lo que voy a escribir!

Pues, papá te puede ayudar, estoy segura.

Espero que sí.

Y ahora el reporte del tiempo. Hoy hacia el oriente del país hizo una temperatura de 32° centígrados. En el occidente hizo aún más calor con temperaturas que llegaron hasta los 38° en la zona de Maracaibo.

Por el contrario, en la ciudad de Mérida hizo frío, registrándose una temperatura mínima de 12°. El sur del país estuvo nublado y con lluvias aisladas.

Aquí en la zona metropolitana de Caracas, la temperatura llegó a los 25° por la tarde. Esta noche va a hacer más fresco, bajando hasta los 19°. Mañana se anticipa una temperatura máxima de 24° con posibilidades de llovizna.

Y ahora más noticias. Primero quiero contarles un incidente muy curioso que ocurrió hoy día. Un empleado municipal, José Rivera, descubrió algo insólito al vaciar un basurero en el Parque los Caobos. Entre la basura encontró una bolsa con cien mil bolívares. Entrevisté a José Rivera después de su descubrimiento.

3 | ¡No lo pude creer!

Señor Rivera, díganos cuándo descubrió el dinero.

Se cayó de una bolsa de papel común y corriente. ¡Imagínese!

Pues, sabe usted, lo encontré poco después de llegar al trabajo a eso de las nueve de la mañana.

¿Qué pensó al encontrarlo?

¿Cómo lo encontró?

Pues, no lo pude creer, sabe. ¡Tanta plata! ¿Y por qué aquí?

CHARLEMOS UN POCO

A. **PARA EMPEZAR . . .** Pon los siguientes incidentes en el orden que ocurrieron en el cuento "Tío Tigre y Tío Conejo".

5 **1.** "¿Dónde conseguiste ese hermoso abrigo?" preguntó Tío Tigre.

8 **2.** "Sí, pero con una condición . . ."

3 **3.** En el camino, descubrió un abrigo de lana muy elegante.

10 **4.** "Voy a tener el abrigo más hermoso de todos".

6 **5.** "Lo hice yo mismo", respondió Tío Conejo.

9 **6.** "Usted tiene que traerme toda la lana y algo de comer mientras trabaje".

1 **7.** Ese día hizo mucho frío, hizo viento y llovió continuamente.

12 **8.** Y Tío Conejo, gordito y calientito, sobrevivió un invierno más.

7 **9.** "¿Podría tejerme uno a mí?"

11 **10.** Pronto terminó el invierno y llegó la primavera.

2 **11.** "Éste va a ser un invierno horroroso. Va a hacer un frío de mil demonios y voy a sufrir mucha hambre".

4 **12.** Se puso el abrigo y siguió caminando.

B. **¿QUÉ DECIMOS . . .?** ¿Quién hizo estos comentarios: Irene, Luis, Diego Miranda o José Rivera?

| Irene | Luis | Diego | José |

1. ¿Cuánto tiempo falta?

2. Díganos cuándo descubrió el dinero.

3. Mañana se anticipa una temperatura máxima de 24 grados.

4. ¡Tanta plata! ¿Y por qué aquí?

5. Bueno, papá está terminando. Voy a buscarlo.

6. El sur del país estuvo nublado.

7. Tengo que escribir un cuento policíaco.

8. Se cayó de una bolsa de papel.

9. ¿Y ya tiene planes para el dinero?

10. Esta noche va a hacer más fresco.

C. ¿Qué tiempo hace? Describe el tiempo que hace hoy en estas ciudades.

> MODELO   Los Ángeles 27°C (80°F)
> **En Los Ángeles hace veintisiete grados. Hace calor.**

1. Caracas 23°C (72°F)
2. Chicago 7°C (45°F)
3. la Ciudad de México 20°C (68°F)
4. San Francisco 24°C (75°F)
5. Madrid 13°C (55°F)
6. Quebec 0°C (32°F)
7. San Juan 31°C (88°F)
8. Guadalajara 18°C (65°F)

CH. Pronóstico. ¿Qué tiempo va a hacer mañana en estas ciudades?

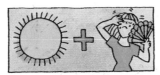

Miami

> MODELO   **En Miami va a hacer sol y mucho calor.**

1. París

2. Managua

3. Moscú

4. Londres

5. Santiago

6. El Cairo

7. Tokio

8. Berlín

9. Nueva York

10. nuestra ciudad ¿ . . . ?

REPASO

Weather expressions

hace calor

hace frío

hace fresco

hace ___ grados

hace sol

hace buen tiempo

hace mal tiempo

hace viento

Llueve.
Está lloviendo.
(Va a llover.)

Llovizna.
Está lloviznando.
(Va a lloviznar.)

Nieva.
Está nevando.
(Va a nevar.)

Está nublado.

D. Los sábados. Según Pepita, ¿qué hizo su familia el sábado pasado?

mamá

MODELO   Por la mañana . . .
Por la mañana, mamá tomó café.

Por la mañana . . .

1. yo

2. mi hermano

3. todos nosotros

Por la tarde . . .

4. papá

5. papá y mi hermano

6. mamá

Por la noche . . .

7. mis amigas y yo

8. mamá y papá

E. Concierto. El director de la escuela acaba de aprobar un concierto de rock para este fin de semana y todos ya están informados. ¿Cuándo lo supieron?

MODELO   Pablo: durante la clase de geografía
Pablo lo supo durante la clase de geografía.

1. Héctor y Lisa: después de la clase de álgebra
2. tú: durante el almuerzo
3. yo: en el trabajo
4. el profesor Rubio: entre la clase de español e inglés
5. Mario y yo: después de las clases
6. los señores Flores: ayer por la mañana
7. Martín: en la clase de arte
8. el profesor de historia: antes de las clases

F. Gustos diferentes. Hoy es el almuerzo del Club de español. Todos los socios y todos los profesores trajeron algo para comer. ¿Qué trajeron estas personas?

MODELO   **Óscar trajo pizza.**   Óscar

1. mi hermana y yo
2. profesora Valdivia
3. tú
4. profesor de español

5. Jorge y Ana
6. Beto
7. Silvia
8. Marta y tú

G. Una familia aburrida. La familia de Sergio nunca quiere hacer nada. ¿Qué dice Sergio del fin de semana pasado?

MODELO   papá / no querer / ir / cine
Papá no quiso ir al cine.

1. mis abuelos / no querer / asistir / concierto
2. mamá / no querer / alquilar / video
3. mis hermanas / no querer / cantar / nuevo / canción
4. Norberto y Miguel / no querer / ir / partido / fútbol
5. mi prima Luisa / no querer / tocar / piano
6. mi hermano y yo / no querer / aprender / nuevo / baile
7. ustedes / no querer / ver / programa / televisión
8. tú / no querer / asistir / clase / karate

Preterite of *saber*

supe	supimos
supiste	
supo	supieron

Lo **supimos** esta mañana.
No **supe** tu dirección.

See **¿Por qué se dice así?**, *page G37, section 3.1.*

Preterite of *traer*

traje	trajimos
trajiste	
trajo	trajeron

¿Quién **trajo** los discos?
Yo los **traje**.

See **¿Por qué se dice así?**, *page G37, section 3.1.*

Preterite of *querer*

quise	quisimos
quisiste	
quiso	quisieron

Ellas no **quisieron** hacerlo.
Yo no **quise** venir.

See **¿Por qué se dice así?**, *page G37, section 3.1.*

Preterite tense: Irregular verb endings and stems

-e	-imos
-iste	
-o	-ieron

-u stem: andar   **anduv-**

       estar   **estuv-**

       haber   **hub-**

       tener   **tuv-**

       poder   **pud-**

       poner   **pus-**

       saber   **sup-**

-i stem: querer   **quis-**

      venir   **vin-**

-j stem: decir   **dij-**

      traer   **traj-**

See **¿Por qué se dice así?**, *page G37, section 3.1.*

Demonstratives

cerca: **este**   **esta**

     estos   **estas**

lejos: **ese**   **esa**

     esos   **esas**

más **aquel**   **aquella**

lejos: **aquellos**   **aquellas**

See **¿Por qué se dice así?**, *page G39, section 3.2.*

Demonstrative pronouns

Demonstratives require written accents when they replace a noun.

Esta lámpara es más grande que **ésa**. Me gustan esos sofás pero prefiero **aquéllos**.

See **¿Por qué se dice así?**, *page G39, section 3.2.*

H. ¡Qué fiesta!   ¿Por qué salió mal la fiesta de Paulina?

MODELO   Graciela / no traer / refrescos
       Graciela no trajo los refrescos.

1. Gerardo / no poder / encontrar / casa
2. los invitados / no querer / bailar
3. Florencia / andar / y llegar tarde
4. no haber / bastante pizza
5. Paulina / no poner / discos / favorito
6. comida / estar / malísimo
7. hermanos de Paulina / no decir / nada / invitados
8. Mateo / no saber de / fiesta
9. Daniela y Pilar / venir tarde
10. mamá de Paulina / no tener tiempo para preparar / nachos

I. ¡Mejor!   Los dependientes de Galería Azul están comparando la ropa que venden con la de una tienda rival. ¿Qué dicen?

MODELO   **Esta blusa es mejor que aquélla.** o
       Esta blusa es más grande que ésa.

| mejor   peor   más [??] que . . . |

1.   **2.**   **3.**   **4.**   **5.**

6.   **7.**   **8.**   **9.**   **10.**

J. En la mueblería.   Tu familia quiere comprar nuevos muebles. ¿Qué comentarios hacen tú y tu hermano(a)?

MODELO   sofá: largo
    Tú: **¿Te gusta ese sofá?**
    Hermano(a): **Sí (No), es más largo que aquél.**

1. cama: duro   4. lámpara: bonito   7. mesa: elegante
2. silla: moderno   5. estante: alto   8. televisor: grande
3. mesitas: bajo   6. sillones: cómodo   9. alfombra: hermoso

CHARLEMOS UN POCO MÁS

A. El sábado pasado.   Prepara por escrito una lista de lo que hiciste el sábado pasado a las 9:00 y las 11:00 de la mañana, a la 1:00, las 3:00, las 5:00 y las 7:00 de la tarde y a las 9:00 y las 10:00 de la noche. Pregúntales a dos compañeros lo que hicieron ellos a esas horas. Luego díganle a la clase qué actividades todas las personas en su grupo hicieron al mismo tiempo.

B. Hoy en la costa . . .   Todos los domingos un canal de televisión en tu ciudad invita a estudiantes del colegio a ser locutores. Hoy tú y un(a) compañero(a) van a dar el reporte del tiempo. Prepara la presentación con tu compañero(a). Usen el pronóstico que su profesor(a) les va a dar o uno de un periódico local.

C. ¡Caricaturistas!   Tú y tu compañero(a) son famosos caricaturistas. Acaban de crear esta tira cómica y ahora van a escribir el diálogo. Cuando lo completen, léanle su diálogo a la clase.

CH. ¿Ésta o ésa? Tú y tu compañero(a) van de compras para el regreso a la escuela. Decidan qué van a comprar. Comenten sobre todos los objetos en el dibujo. Digan lo que les gusta y lo que deciden comprar.

EJEMPLO *Tú:* **Me gusta esta mochila negra.**
Compañero(a): **Prefiero ésa amarilla.**

Dramatizaciones

A. Entrevista. Hace un mes, alguien se robó una famosa máscara de oro del Museo de Antropología. Tu compañero(a), un(a) detective célebre, acaba de encontrar la máscara. Entrevístalo(la) y consigue todos los detalles de cómo la encontró. Dramaticen la entrevista.

B. ¡Qué fracaso! Anoche su equipo de béisbol perdió. ¡Fue un fracaso total! Ahora tú y tus amigos están discutiendo el partido, tratando de decidir por qué perdieron tan mal. Cada persona ofrece distintas razones por el fracaso. Dramaticen la discusión.

Vocabulario útil

receptor(a)
lanzador(a)
primera base
segunda base
tercera base
jardinero(a) corto(a)
jardinero(a) ⎫
guardabosque ⎭

IMPACTO CULTURAL
Excursiones

Antes de empezar

A. El mapa. Estudia el mapa de Chile y contesta estas preguntas. Revisa tus respuestas después de leer la lectura.

1. El gran desierto de Atacama está en el . . .
- **a.** norte de Chile.
- **b.** sur de Chile.
- **c.** este de Chile.
- **ch.** oeste de Chile.

2. El valle central de Chile representa . . .
- **a.** una mitad del país.
- **b.** un tercio del país.
- **c.** un cuarto del país.
- **ch.** una parte insignificante del país.

3. Hay muchos lagos y volcanes en el . . .
- **a.** norte de Chile.
- **b.** sur de Chile.
- **c.** este de Chile.
- **ch.** oeste de Chile.

4. La cordillera de los Andes está en el . . .
- **a.** norte de Chile.
- **b.** sur de Chile.
- **c.** este de Chile.
- **ch.** oeste de Chile.

5. Chile tiene fronteras con . . .
- **a.** Perú, Bolivia y Brasil.
- **b.** Bolivia, Paraguay y Argentina.
- **c.** Argentina, Bolivia y Perú.
- **ch.** Bolivia, Perú, Argentina y Uruguay.

B. Impresiones. Antes de leer esta lectura, indica cuáles son tus impresiones sobre Chile. Luego, después de leer la selección, vuelve a estas preguntas y decide si necesitas cambiar algunas de tus impresiones iniciales.

1. Chile está en . . .
- **a.** Norteamérica.
- **b.** Sudamérica.
- **c.** Centroamérica.
- **ch.** Europa.

2. Chile es tan largo como . . .
- **a.** California y Arizona.
- **b.** Texas, Nuevo México, Arizona y California.
- **c.** Nuevo México y Texas.
- **ch.** Arizona y Nuevo México.

3. La población chilena consiste principalmente en . . .
- **a.** indígenas.
- **b.** indígenas y negros.
- **c.** mexicanos.
- **ch.** europeos.

4. El clima en Chile es . . .
- **a.** muy consistente en todo el país, frío.
- **b.** muy consistente en todo el país, tropical.
- **c.** muy similar al clima de California y la Florida.
- **ch.** muy variado como en EE.UU.

Chile

Tierra de contrastes

Chile, un país que mide unas dos mil seiscientas millas de largo, una distancia mayor que la que hay entre Chicago y San Francisco, se extiende desde Perú y Bolivia en el norte hasta Tierra del Fuego en el punto sur de Sudamérica. En el este, su frontera con Argentina está formada por la majestuosa cordillera de los Andes, y la del oeste por el Océano Pacífico.

Dentro de esos bordes hay cuatro regiones que verdaderamente forman una tierra de contrastes: el desierto en el norte, el valle central, las montañas y lagos en el sur y la cordillera de los Andes en el este.

El desierto de Atacama en el norte es el desierto más árido del mundo entero. La atmósfera es tan clara y pura allí que acaba por ser el sitio ideal para los astrónomos. Han construido varios observatorios en el desierto, el más famoso siendo el observatorio Cerro La Silla, el segundo más grande y más sofisticado del mundo. **1**

En la cordillera de los Andes, a unas 80 millas (129 km) está Portillo, uno de los centros de esquí más populares con esquiadores profesionales. **2** Es aquí donde los mejores esquiadores del mundo pasan la temporada, que dura de mayo a octubre, manteniéndose en forma para las competencias mundiales de enero y febrero.

En contraste, en el valle central se dice que existe el mejor clima y la tierra más fértil del mundo entero. El promedio de la temperatura en el valle es 59°F (15°C) y es allí donde se produce y de donde exportan unos de los vinos más exquisitos del mundo. Tres cuartos de la población de Chile vive en el valle central. **3**

Al sur del valle central está una región de Chile llamada "la Suiza de Sudamérica". Es una región montañosa, de hermosos lagos y bosques. Es difícil decidir cuál de los muchos lagos de esta región es el más hermoso. ¿Será el lago Laja, con la impresionante reflexión del volcán Antuco, o tal vez es el lago Esmeralda con el volcán Osorno a la distancia? **4** ¿Qué opinas tú? En esta región también viven los araucanos, los indígenas de Chile.

Esta tierra de contrastes está habitada por una gente muy variada. **5** Basta con ver sólo los nombres de algunos de sus líderes nacionales como O'Higgins, el héroe de la independencia de Chile y Cochrane, el fundador de la marina chilena. Entre los últimos presidentes de esta república están Alessandri (origen italiano), Frei (origen suizo), Allende Gossens (origen alemán), Pinochet (origen francés) y Aylwin (origen inglés). En Santiago, la capital, es común que las tiendas o fábricas lleven nombres como Küpfer, Haddad, Bercovich, Luchetti y Mackenzie. Todos son chilenos.

Y todo hace que Chile sea de veras una tierra de muchos contrastes.

Verifiquemos

1. Pasa a la pizarra y dibuja el mapa de Chile. Indica las cuatro secciones principales de este país.
2. ¿Por qué es ideal el desierto de Atacama para el estudio de astronomía?
3. ¿Por qué van tantos de los mejores esquiadores del mundo a esquiar en Portillo?
4. ¿Por qué vive tres cuartos de la población chilena en el valle central?
5. ¿Por qué se le llama al sur de Chile "la Suiza de Sudamérica"?
6. Describe a la población de Chile.
7. Explica el título de esta lectura.

Después de unos avisos comerciales

CAMPAMENTO CANAIMA

AYUDANOS A MANTENER LA LIMPIEZA
GRACIAS...

U.S.B.

CRUCE A LA DERECHA →

Venezuela
Tierra nuestra

Para conservar un grato recuerdo de tu viaje . . .

☞ Conserva el ambiente:
Cuida tus playas.

☞ Conserva la limpieza:
Cuida tus paisajes.

☞ Conserva la belleza:
Cuida tus parques.

☞ Conserva tu vida:
Maneja con cuidado.

☞ Conserva el orden:
Cumple las leyes.

☞ Conserva amistades:
Respeta a los demás.

turismo para todos

PIEL PERFECTA
15
Máxima protección contra el sol

N U N C A SALGAN SIN LA LOCIÓN QUE MÁS PROTECCIÓN OFRECE. PÓNGANSE PIEL PERFECTA.

ADVERTENCIA:
Se ha comprobado que los rayos ultravioletas son dañinos para la piel.

¿ **Q**ué piensas tú ?

1. ¿Para quién es el cartel de Venezuela? ¿Qué recomienda que las personas hagan? ¿Cómo sabes esto?

2. ¿Cómo sería un cartel para atraer a turistas a tu ciudad? ¿Qué dibujos o fotos tendría?

3. Es probable que no entiendas cada palabra en las fotos, el cartel y el anuncio para *Piel perfecta.* ¿Puedes adivinar lo que dicen? ¿Qué te ayuda a entender las palabras que no conoces?

4. ¿Qué atracciones se mencionarían en propaganda para atraer a turistas a Venezuela que no se mencionarían en anuncios para tu estado? ¿Por qué no se mencionarían en tu estado?

5. ¿Qué tipo de lenguaje se usa en letreros, en anuncios para viajeros y en anuncios para vender objetos? ¿Qué tipo de lenguaje se usa para dar consejos o hacer recomendaciones?

6. En esta lección, vamos a repasar mucho de lo que aprendiste el año pasado. ¿Puedes nombrar dos o tres cosas que vamos a repasar y practicar en esta lección?

TRES CONSEJOS

Este cuento es muy popular en los Estados Unidos, en México y en Sudamérica. Relata lo importante que es seguir los consejos de los ancianos.

Había una vez un hombre muy pobre que tuvo que dejar a su esposa y a su hijo para buscar trabajo. Pasó muchos años caminando de pueblo en pueblo buscando trabajo y fortuna.

Un día, en el camino a otro pueblo, encontró a un viejecito. Decidió hacerle una consulta. "Usted parece ser un hombre muy sabio", le dijo. "Por favor, déme algún consejo para mejorar mi situación".
"Bueno", dijo el viejo. "Más vale dar que recibir, si te lo puedes permitir. Los consejos nos cuestan poco a nosotros, los viejos. Escúchame. Hay tres consejos que te puedo dar".

"Primero, no dejes camino principal por vereda".

"Segundo, no preguntes lo que no te importa".

"Y tercero, no hagas nada sin considerar las consecuencias."

4

Se despidieron, y el hombre pobre continuó el camino al siguiente pueblo donde pasó la noche.

5

Al día siguiente, empezó su viaje a otro pueblo con otros tres caminantes. Pero cuando ellos decidieron tomar una vereda para acortar el camino, el hombre recordó el primer consejo del viejo sabio, "No dejes camino principal por vereda", y decidió seguir por el camino principal.

Cuando llegó al pueblo, le dijeron que unos bandidos habían matado a sus compañeros de camino. El hombre dio gracias a Dios que siguió el consejo del viejito.

6

Unos meses más tarde, después de haber visitado varios pueblos más, el hombre llegó a un rancho muy próspero. El propietario lo recibió cortésmente y le dio trabajo.

Al día siguiente, cuando el hombre conoció a la dama de la casa, vio que era muy, muy flaca y parecía estar muy triste. Pero otra vez, el hombre recordó el consejo del anciano, "No preguntes lo que no te importa", y no preguntó nada acerca de la dama.

Con ese hecho, el propietario decidió que este hombre tenía que ser el hombre de más confianza en el mundo entero. Lo puso a cargo del rancho y ofreció pagarle una fortuna.

7 Años después, cuando ya había acumulado una pequeña fortuna, el hombre decidió regresar a casa por su mujer y su hijo. Ya hacía más de diez años que no los veía.

8 Cuando llegó a su casa, miró por la ventana y vio a un hombre durmiendo en la cama. Creyó que su esposa se había casado con otro. Su primera reacción fue querer matar al desconocido. Pero recordó el consejo del viejo sabio, "No hagas nada sin considerar las consecuencias", y no hizo nada.

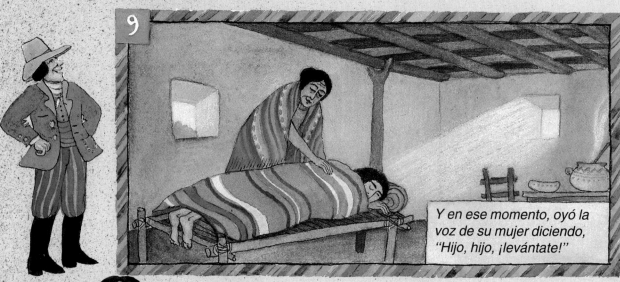

9 Y en ese momento, oyó la voz de su mujer diciendo, "Hijo, hijo, ¡levántate!"

10 Su mujer y su hijo, ya todo un hombre, estaban contentísimos de verlo. Él les contó de su puesto en el rancho y les enseñó toda su fortuna.

11 Al día siguiente los tres se fueron a vivir al rancho que el hombre dirigía. En camino, el hombre le dijo a su hijo, "Siempre presta atención a los consejos de los ancianos, porque ellos son muy sabios".

Al dar mandatos

1 ¡Compre *Doña Arepa*!

María, no sé qué hacer. Los niños no quieren comer. Hasta dejan la arepa en el plato sin comer.

Perdone, señora. Usted necesita . . .

¡DOÑAAAAA AREPAAAAA! ¡La mejor harina para hacer arepas en casa!

Cómalas con mantequilla o rellénelas con jamón . . .

. . . con queso o con lo que a sus niños más les apetezca.

Déles arepas *Doña Arepa*.

Tienen un sabor incomparable.

¡Nunca queda ni una sola miguita con arepas hechas con *Doña Arepa*!

Busque *Doñaaaa Arepaaaa* en su tienda favorita hoy mismo. ¡Compre lo mejor! ¡Compre *Doñaaaa Arepaaaa*!

2 ¡Pónganse *Piel perfecta*!

Lourdes y César se encuentran por casualidad.

Hola, César, ¿cómo estás? Hace tanto tiempo que no te veo. ¿Qué es de tu vida?

¡Ay, cuidado, Lourdes! No ves que estoy quemado. Ayer pasé toda la tarde en la playa y mírame ahora. ¡Me duele todo!

¡Pero César! ¿Por qué no te pusiste loción protectora? Sabes que tienes que protegerte de los rayos dañinos del sol.

Usa *Piel perfecta*.

Ustedes también. Para evitar las quemaduras del sol, nunca salgan sin la loción que más protección ofrece. ¡Pónganse *Piel perfecta*!

3 Mira lo que hiciste.

¡Hija, ven acá! Mira lo que hiciste.

¿Qué papá?

Desenchufaste un cable y apagaste la cámara.

Lo siento, papá.

¿Quién te dio permiso para entrar aquí?

¿Cuántas veces tengo que decirte que cuando estoy trabajando, no entres aquí? De aquí en adelante, haz lo que te digo.

Sí, papá.

Nadie, papá. Es que yo venía . . .

De otra forma, no vuelves al canal. ¿Entiendes?

Sí, papá.

Y además . . .

(Sr. Miranda, Sr. Miranda. La cámara . . .)

(¡Ah! Irene, sal de aquí.)

Perdonen ustedes la interrupción. Tuvimos un problema técnico.

4 Permanezcan con nosotros.

A continuación les traemos una nueva serie, "Nuestra Venezuela". Todo el mundo debe ver este interesantísimo programa informativo . . .

. . . sobre nuestro país y su futuro.

Luego vean en este mismo canal la sensacional telenovela "Doña Perfecta".

Esta noche jueguen a "Venezuela y punto" con Pepe Muñoz . . .

. . . y permanezcan con nosotros para el último noticiero del día. No se pierdan nuestra excelente programación. Por ahora, me despido de ustedes deseándoles una noche muy agradable.

CHARLEMOS UN POCO

A. **PARA EMPEZAR . . .** ¿A cuál(es) personaje(s) del cuento "Tres consejos" se refiere cada comentario?

los tres caminantes

el viejito

el propietario   la mujer y su hijo   el hombre pobre

1. Tuvo que dejar a su esposa y a su hijo para buscar trabajo.
2. "Usted parece ser un hombre muy sabio".
3. Caminó de pueblo en pueblo buscando trabajo y fortuna.
4. "Más vale dar que recibir, si te lo puedes permitir".
5. Decidieron tomar una vereda para acortar el camino.
6. "No dejes camino principal por vereda".
7. Unos bandidos los habían matado.
8. Lo recibió cortésmente y le dio trabajo.
9. "No preguntes lo que no te importa".
10. Lo puso a cargo del rancho y ofreció pagarle una fortuna.
11. Al acumular una pequeña fortuna, decidió regresar a casa.
12. "No hagas nada sin considerar las consecuencias".

REPASO

Regular affirmative *tú* commands

Infinitive	Command
-ar	**-a**
-er, -ir	**-e**

Recuerda llamarme esta tarde.

Come las arepas. Son excelentes aquí.

Pide un refresco para mí.

See **¿Por qué se dice así?**, *page G41, section 3.3.*

B. **¿QUÉ DECIMOS . . .?** Siempre oímos muchos mandatos en la televisión. Completa los mandatos que acabas de escuchar.

1. Rellene sus arepas con . . .
2. Usa *Piel perfecta* . . .
3. Perdonen ustedes . . .
4. No se pierdan . . .
5. Busque *Doña Arepa* en . . .
6. Pónganse . . .
7. Permanezcan con nosostros para . . .
8. Esta noche jueguen a . . .

el último noticiero.
Piel perfecta.
jámon y queso.
"Venezuela y punto".
para protegerte de los rayos dañinos.
su tienda favorita.
nuestra excelente programación.
la interrupción.

C. ¡Escucha y obedece!   Tienes que cuidar a un niño difícil.
¿Qué le dices?

MODELO   **Ponte la chaqueta ahora mismo.**

1.

2.

3.

4.

5.

6.

7.

8.

9.

10.

REPASO

**Irregular affirmative *tú*
commands**

di**go**	di
pon**go**	pon
sal**go**	sal
ten**go**	ten
ven**go**	ven
hago	haz
voy	ve
soy	sé

*See ¿***Por qué se dice así?**,
page G41, section 3.3.

REPASO

**Pronouns and affirmative
commands**

Object and reflexive pronouns
always follow and are attached to
affirmative commands.

Teresa, **dame** los libros.
Pepito, **ponte** los zapatos.

*See ¿***Por qué se dice así?**,
page G41, section 3.3.

Regular negative *tú* commands

Infinitive	*Command*
-ar	**-es**
-er, -ir	**-as**

These endings are added to the stem of the **yo** form of present tense verbs.

No llam**es** a casa todos los días.
No hag**as** eso.
No pid**as** dinero constantemente.

See **¿Por qué se dice así?**, *page G43, section 3.4.*

Irregular negative *tú* commands

Infinitive	*Negative **tú** command*
dar	**no des**
estar	**no estés**
ir	**no vayas**
ser	**no seas**

See **¿Por qué se dice así?**, *page G43, section 3.4.*

Pronouns and commands

In negative commands, object and reflexive pronouns always precede the verb, but they follow and are attached to affirmative commands.

Memo, no **me** llames.
No **la** leas ahora.

Teresa, da**me** los libros.
Pepito, pon**te** los zapatos.

See **¿Por qué se dice así?**, *pages G41–G45, sections 3.3 and 3.4.*

CH. La primera cita. Pablo está dándole consejos a su hermanito que va a salir por primera vez en una cita. ¿Qué le dice?

 MODELO   no ponerse nervioso
No te pongas nervioso.

1. no llegar tarde
2. no entrar en el restaurante primero
3. no sentarse primero
4. no decir cosas tontas
5. no pedir el plato más barato
6. no comer con la boca abierta
7. no poner los brazos en la mesa
8. no dejar una propina muy pequeña
9. no salir del restaurante primero
10. no volver a casa muy tarde

D. Examencito. ¿Qué consejos recibes antes de un examen?

 MODELO   no perder / autobús
No pierdas el autobús.

1. no hablar / durante / examen
2. no olvidar / lápiz
3. no ser / deshonesto
4. no mirar / papeles / otro / estudiantes
5. no dar / respuestas a / tu / amigos
6. no salir / antes de la hora
7. no ir / baño / durante / examen
8. no estar / nervioso

E. Nuevo(a) amigo(a). Un(a) nuevo(a) compañero(a) de clase acaba de mudarse a una casa cerca de ti. ¿Qué dice cuando tú le ofreces ayuda?

 MODELO   ayudarte (sí)
Tú: **¿Te ayudo?**
Compañero(a): **Sí, ayúdame.**

traer unos sándwiches (no)
Tú: **¿Traigo unos sándwiches?**
Compañero(a): **No, gracias, no los traigas.**

1. preparar limonada (sí)
2. poner la lámpara allí (no)
3. cambiar el reloj (sí)
4. sacar estas cosas de las maletas (no)
5. hacer la cama (no)
6. arreglar los libros (sí)
7. limpiar el piso (no)
8. llamarte más tarde para salir (sí)

F. ¿Qué hago?   Tú estás teniendo muchos problemas y decides hablar con un(a) consejero(a) en tu escuela. Dile tus problemas. ¿Qué consejos te da?

EJEMPLO   *Tú:*   **Siempre hago las mismas cosas.**
          Consejero(a):   **Cambia de rutina.**

Problemas

Sacar malas notas.
No saber bailar.
Ser muy tímido(a).
Siempre estar cansado(a).
No tener amigos.
Estar aburrido(a).
Estar triste.
Tener muy poco dinero.
Nunca querer levantarme.
Siempre hacer las mismas
   cosas.
No poder dormir.
¿ . . . ?

Consejos

'Leer un libro interesante.
No pensar en tus problemas.
Ver una película.
Hacer ejercicio.
Salir más.
No ver tanta televisión.
Asistir a una clase.
No beber café en la noche.
No trabajar tanto.
Trabajar más.
Poner música tranquila.
Participar en más actividades
   sociales.
Cambiar de rutina.
No ir directamente a casa
   después de las clases.
No acostarse tan tarde.
¿ . . . ?

G. Me duele.   Tú eres un paciente en la oficina de un(a) doctor(a), tu compañero(a). Escucha lo que te dice y hazlo.

MODELO   levantar los brazos
         Compañero(a): **Levante los brazos.**
         Tú: *(You raise your arms.)*

1. levantar el brazo derecho, el brazo izquierdo
2. bajar el brazo izquierdo, el brazo derecho
3. levantar y doblar la pierna derecha,
   la pierna izquierda
4. saltar en el pie derecho tres veces,
   en el izquierdo
5. bajar la cabeza, levantarla
6. abrir la boca, cerrarla
7. tocar el pie izquierdo, el pie derecho
8. doblar la cabeza a la izquierda,
   a la derecha
9. tocar la nariz con la mano izquierda,
   con la derecha
10. saltar en el pie izquierdo diez veces,
    en el derecho

Regular *Ud. / Uds.* commands

Infinitive	Command	
	Ud.	**Uds.**
-ar	**-e**	**-en**
-er, -ir	**-a**	**-an**

Estudi**en** esto para mañana.
No beb**a** el agua allí.
No abr**an** la boca.

See **¿Por qué se dice así?**,
page G45, section 3.5.

Ud. / Uds. commands: Irregular stems

Ud. / Uds. commands add their endings to the stem of the **yo** form of present tense verbs.

Pien**sen** en sus primos.
No pong**an** los pies en la mesa.
Dig**a** lo que necesita hoy.

See **¿Por qué se dice así?**, *page G45, section 3.5.*

Pronouns and Ud./Uds. commands

Remember that object and reflexive pronouns always follow and are attached to affirmative commands. In negative commands, they precede the verb.

Acuéstese temprano.
No las pongan en la mesa.

Note that a written accent is necessary when a pronoun is attached to the verb.

See **¿Por qué se dice así?**, *page G45, section 3.5.*

H. ¡Promoción!   Tú preparas un anuncio para el almacén donde trabajas. ¿Qué dices en el anuncio para vender los productos?

MODELO   comprar nuestros productos
Compre nuestros productos.

1. venir a nuestro almacén para todas sus necesidades
2. buscar los mejores precios aquí
3. no salir sin probar nuestras comidas riquísimas
4. traer a toda la familia a comer aquí
5. lavar la ropa con nuestro detergente mágico
6. no olvidar nuestras revistas y nuestros libros
7. visitar nuestra tienda las veinticuatro horas del día
8. descubrir las mejores ofertas de la ciudad

I. ¡Vivan una vida sana!   Tus compañeros de clase quieren tener buena salud. ¿Qué les dices?

MODELO   lavarse los dientes después de comer
Lávense los dientes después de comer.

1. hacer ejercicio
2. hacerlo tres veces a la semana
3. no comer comida con muchas calorías
4. dormir bastantes horas
5. participar en una variedad de actividades
6. practicar deportes
7. no practicarlos cuando hace mucho sol
8. no bañarse al sol sin bronceador
9. ponerse bronceador frecuentemente
10. no acostarse muy tarde

J. En el restaurante.   Tú y un(a) amigo(a) van a comer a un restaurante. Dramatiza la situación al leer el diálogo con dos compañeros(as).

Camarero(a):	(Pasar) ustedes.
Tú:	Gracias.
Camarero(a):	(Seguirme), por favor. ¿Está bien esta mesa?
Amigo(a):	Sí, perfecta.
Camarero(a):	Bueno, (sentarse), por favor.
Tú:	Gracias. (Darnos) la carta, por favor.
Camarero(a):	Sí, aquí la tienen. ¿Les traigo algo para empezar?
Amigo(a):	Sí, (servirnos) los entremeses variados.
Tú:	Me muero de sed. (Traerme) un refresco, por favor.
Camarero(a):	¿Qué van a comer?
Amigo(a):	(Decirnos), ¿cuál es la especialidad de la casa?
Camarero(a):	Pues, (pedir) el pescado. Está muy fresco hoy.
Tú:	Bueno, el pescado para mí.
Amigo(a):	Para mí, no. (Servirme) el arroz con pollo.

CHARLEMOS UN POCO MÁS

A. El pájaro de papel. Tu profesor(a) les va a dar a unas personas de la clase las instrucciones para construir un pájaro de papel colorido. A los demás les va a dar papel colorido, un grapador, tijeras, hilo y las ilustraciones que acompañan las instrucciones. En grupos pequeños, la persona con las instrucciones les va a decir a los otros lo que tienen que hacer con los materiales para construir un pájaro de papel. Mientras escuchan a su compañero(a), deben mirar bien las ilustraciones para comprender las instrucciones.

MODELO **Corten el papel en seis tiras de una pulgada por nueve pulgadas de tamaño.**

B. El premio. Tu profesor(a) de español ganó un premio extraordinario y tiene que asistir a un banquete formal para recibirlo. Dale consejos acerca de lo que debe hacer para prepararse y cómo debe portarse.

C. Clase, levanten las manos . . . Tú y tu compañero(a) van a enseñarle a una clase de tercer grado a hacer algo—por ejemplo, cómo hacer ejercicios, cómo bailar, cómo ponerse un suéter. Decidan qué van a enseñar a hacer y practíquenlo con sus compañeros de clase.

CH. ¿Eres un Picasso? En la cuadrícula que te va a dar tu profesor(a), hay dibujos en unos cuadrados pero faltan en otros. Tu compañero(a) tiene los dibujos que faltan en tu cuadrícula, y tú tienes los que faltan en la suya. Tu compañero(a) te va a describir los dibujos que faltan en tu cuadrícula y te va a decir dónde debes ponerlos. Dibújalos hasta llenar la cuadrícula. Describe los dibujos que faltan en la cuadrícula de tu compañero(a). Pueden alternar sus descripciones.

EJEMPLO **Dibuja un(a) . . . entre . . . y . . .**
Baja tres cuadrados y dobla a la . . .

Dramatizaciones

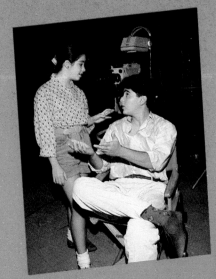

A. Un producto nuevo. Tú y tu compañero(a) trabajan para una estación de televisión en la sección de publicidad. Hoy tienen que preparar un anuncio para un producto nuevo. Prepárenlo y preséntenselo a la clase.

B. ¿Una ensalada de frutas? Tu profesor(a) de ciencias domésticas tiene una llamada telefónica de emergencia y pide que tú y un(a) compañero(a) lo (la) sustituyan. Decidan qué receta van a enseñarle a la clase a preparar hoy. Dramaticen su presentación con la clase entera.

Antes de empezar

A. Hojeando. Lee rápidamente al buscar esta información en la lectura. No es necesario que entiendas o recuerdes toda la información. Sólo concéntrate en encontrarla.

1. ¿Cómo se llama la maestra?
2. ¿Dónde enseñó?
3. ¿Quién es José Vasconcelos?
4. ¿De qué fue amante la maestra?
5. ¿Cuál fue el incidente más trágico de su vida?
6. ¿Quién es Gabriela Mistral?
7. ¿Cuántos libros escribió?
8. ¿Cuál fue el premio más prestigioso que ella recibió?

B. La idea principal. Selecciona la frase que mejor exprese la idea principal de cada párrafo.

Párrafo 1   **a.** el norte de Chile
           b. la juventud chilena
           c. dedicación a la enseñanza
           ch. las señoritas de Santiago

Párrafo 2   **a.** los 31 años
           b. fama internacional
           c. José Vasconcelos
           ch. reforma educacional

Párrafo 3   **a.** éxito en educación
           b. excelente trabajo como maestra
           c. manera de expresar amor
           ch. amor a Dios

Párrafo 4   **a.** amor trágico
           b. los 17 años
           c. suicidio
           ch. tristeza y soledad

Párrafo 5   **a.** triunfos literarios
           b. "Los sonetos de la muerte"
           c. *Desolación, Ternura, Tala* y *Lagar*
           ch. Amor intenso e íntimo

Párrafo 6   **a.** Premio Nóbel de Literatura
           b. tres escritores
           c. una escritora de Hispanoamérica
           ch. honor

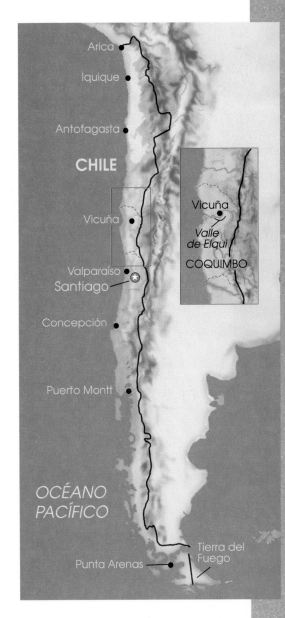

Arica
Iquique
Antofagasta
CHILE
Vicuña
Valparaíso
Santiago
Concepción
Puerto Montt
OCÉANO
PACÍFICO
Punta Arenas
Tierra del Fuego
Vicuña
Valle de Elqui
COQUIMBO

Maestra y amante de la humanidad

Nació en 1889 en el Valle de Elqui, provincia de Coquimbo, en el norte central de Chile. Su verdadero amor era la enseñanza, y se dedicó a educar a la juventud chilena. Fue maestra rural. Enseñó en escuelas primarias y secundarias. Sirvió como directora de escuelas y llegó a ser directora del Liceo de Señoritas de Santiago.

A los treinta y un años ya tenía fama internacional como educadora. En 1922, el famoso reformista de la educación mexicana, el Ministro de Educación José Vasconcelos, la invitó a México para cooperar en la reforma educacional de ese país.

Pero a pesar de todos estos éxitos en educación, Lucila Godoy Alcayaga es recordada no tanto por su excelente trabajo como maestra sino por la manera en que expresó su amor: amor al hombre, al universo, a Dios, a la naturaleza, a la justicia, a los humildes, a los abandonados y a los niños.

Este amor nació de un incidente trágico en la vida de la joven Lucila. Cuando ella sólo tenía diecisiete años, amó a un hombre que se suicidó, al parecer, por honor. Ella pudo haberse consumido en la tristeza de este trágico amor, tan trágico que ella nunca se casó. Pero la manera en que Lucila Godoy Alcayaga pudo sobrevivir el dolor, la tristeza y la soledad que sentía fue por expresarlos en poesía, bajo el nombre literario de Gabriela Mistral.

La poeta chilena Gabriela Mistral tuvo su primer gran triunfo literario ocho años después de la muerte de su amado cuando, en 1914, recibió el primer premio de los Juegos Florales de Santiago por "Los sonetos de la muerte". En 1922, se publicó su mejor libro, *Desolación*. En él expresa la tristeza y soledad que siente por la pérdida de su amado. En su segundo libro, *Ternura* (1924), canta el amor al hombre, a los niños, los humildes, los perseguidos y los abandonados. En su tercer libro, *Tala* (1938), se vuelve hacia el hombre, la humanidad, Dios y la naturaleza. En su último libro, *Lagar* (1954), el amor hacia todo lo creado es más intenso e íntimo.

Gabriela Mistral recibió el Premio Nóbel de Literatura en 1945. Antes de ella, sólo dos escritores de la lengua española habían recibido este honor, y ninguno había sido de Hispanoamérica.

LOS QUE NO DANZAN

Una niña que es inválida
dijo: "¿Cómo danzo yo?"
Le dijimos que pusiera
a danzar su corazón . . .

Luego dijo la quebrada:
"¿Cómo cantaría yo?"
Le dijimos que pusiera
a cantar su corazón . . .

— DESOLACIÓN

TAMBORITO PANAMEÑO

Panameño, panameño,
panameño de mi vida,
yo quiero que tú me lleves
al tambor de la alegría.

— TALA

Verifiquemos

1. Describe a Gabriela Mistral, la maestra.
2. Describe a Gabriela Mistral, la poeta.
3. ¿Por qué crees que Lucila Godoy Alcayaga usó el nombre literario Gabriela Mistral?
4. ¿Qué efecto tuvo la muerte de su amante en Gabriela Mistral?
5. ¿Por qué es especialmente significativo que Gabriela Mistral recibió el Premio Nóbel de Literatura en 1945?
6. Explica el título de esta lectura.

Había una vez . . .

¿ **Q**ué piensas tú ?

1. ¿Conoces algunos de estos lugares? ¿Cuáles? ¿Dónde están? ¿Qué sabes de ellos?

2. Imagínate que acabas de regresar de una excursión a uno de estos lugares. ¿Cómo lo describirías a tus amigos?

3. ¿Conoces otros monumentos o lugares misteriosos como éstos? ¿Cuáles? ¿Dónde están? Descríbelos.

4. ¿Cuáles son algunas explicaciones de lugares como éstos? ¿Son creíbles estas explicaciones? ¿Las crees tú? ¿Por qué sí o por qué no?

5. ¿Qué explicación puedes dar tú de estos tres lugares?

6. ¿Hay algunos lugares u objetos misteriosos en tu ciudad? ¿en tu estado?

7. ¿Por qué interesan tanto estos lugares misteriosos?

8. En esta lección, van a leer un cuento misterioso que escribió Luis para un programa de radio en su escuela. ¿Qué crees que vas a aprender en esta lección?

PARA EMPEZAR

Escuchemos un cuento peruano

LA CASA EMBRUJADA

1 Los cuentos de casas embrujadas con tesoros enterrados abundan por todo el mundo. Este cuento es de Perú.

2 Había una vez una casa embrujada en la plaza central de un pueblo peruano. Todos los habitantes del pueblo le tenían mucho miedo a esa casa.

¿Por qué?
Porque constantemente oían gemidos y quejidos.

Con frecuencia aparecían objetos volando por la casa.

También se rompían las cosas sin ninguna razón.

Y lo peor de todo, aunque nadie vivía en la casa, se oían los pasos de alguien que subía y bajaba las escaleras...

3 Un día, una joven costurera con su sirvienta Ildefonsa y un perrito enfermizo, Salguerito, llegaron al pueblo. Buscaban una casa que alquilar. Como ni la costurera ni Ildefonsa creían en fantasmas, decidieron alquilar la casa embrujada porque se alquilaba a muy buen precio.

4

En seguida, empezaron los problemas. ¡El pobre perro! No importaba si dormía dentro o fuera, a medianoche el fantasma de la casa le tiraba de la cola y de las orejas.

Tanto lo asustaba que sólo en la cocina quería dormir, siempre al pie de la estufa.

5

Pero no se limitaba al perro el fantasma. Malicioso como era, se pasaba mucho tiempo en el taller de la costurera. Jugaba con la máquina de coser. Se perdían las tijeras u otras cosas.

6

Las dos mujeres sentían la presencia de una persona que las seguía a todas partes de la casa.

7

El cura del pueblo vino y les dijo a las señoras que el fantasma no era asunto del diablo, sino del previo dueño de la casa.

8

Entonces, las mujeres invitaron a su casa a un hombre de nombre Florián, que era experto en encontrar a los fantasmas.

Florián se puso a buscar al fantasma por todas partes. Buscó de rincón en rincón. Dos años enteros estuvo buscando al fantasma y no lo encontró.

Durante todo ese tiempo, Salguerito siempre lo miraba, ladraba y corría a la cocina a echarse al pie de la estufa.

Al final, Florián se fue diciendo que en esa casa no había fantasmas.

9 Poco después, un día domingo cuando Ildefonsa estaba en la cocina preparando la comida y Salguerito dormía en su lugar favorito, al pie de la estufa, Ildefonsa vio algo raro donde estaba Salguerito.

10 Intrigada, Ildefonsa se puso a escarbar con un cuchillo... Y Salguerito escarbó con sus patitas.

11 De repente, apareció una olla llena de un magnífico tesoro—una olla repleta de monedas de oro y plata, de joyas y piedras preciosas.

12 Dicen que ese domingo, a medianoche, la costurera, Ildefonsa y Salguerito salieron del pueblo no sólo llevándose el tesoro, sino también al fantasma, porque después de ese día, no volvió a verse ni a oírse el fantasma en la casa.

Nadie sabe adónde se fueron.

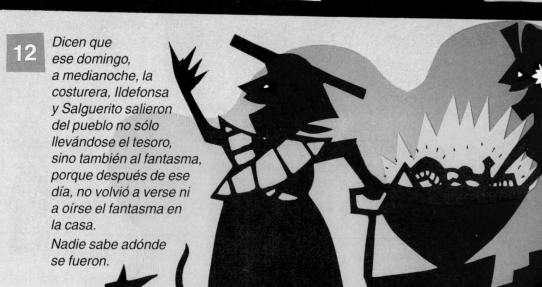

Éste es el cuento policíaco que escribió Luis para leer en la radio. ¿Puedes resolver el misterio?

Había una vez una viejita que no confiaba en nadie. Tenía mucho dinero ahorrado que guardaba en su colchón porque no confiaba en los bancos y no quería entregarles su dinero. Todos los días se levantaba temprano, se sentaba a la mesa y contaba su dinero.

Un día, su nieta supo que guardaba una fortuna en un lugar secreto y se puso muy agitada. Le dijo: —¡Abuelita! ¡Tienes que poner tu dinero en un lugar seguro! ¿Por qué no lo llevamos al banco?

La abuelita le contestó: —¡Paciencia, hija! Yo no llegué a los 75 años sin haber aprendido algo. Ese dinero era de tu abuelo y tengo que guardarlo con mucho cuidado. Pero, . . . sí voy a considerar tu sugerencia.

La nieta añadió: —Por favor, abuelita. Piénsalo bien.

La abuela pensó y pensó. —Tal vez mi nieta tenga razón. Tal vez deba meter mi dinero en el banco—. Entonces un día cuando hacía muy buen tiempo, la abuela tomó una decisión. Decidió ir al banco a depositar su dinero. Con mucho cuidado, lo sacó del colchón y lo metió en una bolsa de papel. Salió camino al banco, pero como hacía tan buen tiempo, se sentó a comer en el parque. Mientras comía, tomaba el sol y pensaba en su decisión.

Cuando terminó de comer, siguió al banco. Al llegar, entró y se acercó a una caja. Saludó al cajero y le presentó la bolsa de papel, diciendo:

—Ésta es toda mi fortuna. Quiero guardarla aquí en su banco.

—Cómo no, señora—, respondió el cajero y abrió la bolsa.

¡Y qué sorpresa tuvo cuando en la bolsa no encontró nada más que los restos del almuerzo de la abuelita! Cuando le mostró la bolsa a la abuelita, ésta empezó a gritar:

—¡Ave María purísima! ¡Mi dinero! ¡Mi dinero! ¿Qué pasó con mi dinero? ¡Dios mío! ¿Qué voy a hacer?

CHARLEMOS UN POCO

A. **PARA EMPEZAR . . .** Indica a quién(es) o a qué se refieren estas descripciones del cuento ''La casa embrujada''.

la costurera   Ildefonsa

el fantasma   Salguerito   Florián

1. Gemía y se quejaba constantemente.
2. Buscaba una casa que alquilar.
3. Tan asustado estaba que sólo quería dormir al pie de la estufa.
4. Jugaba con la máquina de coser.
5. Era experto en encontrar a los fantasmas.
6. Se oían sus pasos cuando subía y bajaba las escaleras.
7. Vio algo raro donde estaba Salguerito.
8. Salieron del pueblo y no volvieron.
9. Dos años estuvo buscando al fantasma y no lo encontró.
10. Se puso a escarbar con sus patitas.

B. **¿QUÉ DECIMOS . . .?** Pon en orden cronológico los sucesos del cuento de la viejita.

1. Decidió ir al banco con su dinero.
2. Hacía muy buen tiempo.
3. Había una viejita que no confiaba en nadie.
4. No encontró el dinero.
5. La abuela pensó y pensó.
6. Guardaba mucho dinero en un colchón.
7. El cajero abrió la bolsa.
8. Su nieta le dijo: ''¿Por qué no lo llevamos al banco?''
9. Comió en el parque.
10. Dijo que quería abrir una cuenta.

Imperfect tense: -*ar* verbs

-aba	-ábamos
-abas	
-aba	-aban

De niño, yo **estudiaba** mucho.
Nosotros nunca **comprábamos** nada allí.

See ¿Por qué se dice así?,
page G48, section 3.6.

Imperfect tense: -*er* / -*ir* verbs

-ía	-íamos
-ías	
-ía	-ían

Primero **leíamos** el periódico.
¿Dónde **vivías?**

See ¿Por qué se dice así?,
page G48, section 3.6.

C. **¿Quieres ir al cine?** ¿Qué hacían tú y tus amigos cuando llamó Mario para invitarlos a salir?

> MODELO Beto: trabajar
> **Beto trabajaba.**

1. Marisol: limpiar su cuarto
2. tú y Alfredo: preparar la cena
3. Lorena y Martín: estudiar para un examen
4. tú: mirar un video
5. Pilar: lavarse el pelo
6. Chavela y yo: no estar en casa
7. Alonso: hablar con su abuela
8. yo: pasear en bicicleta
9. Elisa: escuchar la radio
10. nosotros: jugar fútbol

CH. **Entrevista.** Cuando eras niño(a), ¿hacías estas cosas? Contesta las preguntas de tu compañero(a).

> MODELO correr mucho
> *Compañero(a):* **¿Corrías mucho?**
> *Tú:* **Sí, corría todos los días.** o
> **No, no corría mucho.**

1. beber leche
2. comer pizza
3. salir a jugar
4. aprender muchas cosas nuevas
5. recibir cartas
6. escribir tarjetas
7. dormirse en clase
8. hacer ejercicio
9. leer cuentos
10. subir a los carros chocones
11. vivir en esta ciudad
12. asistir a conciertos de rock

D. **¡El tiempo pasa volando!** Solé está describiendo unas viejas fotos de su familia. ¿Qué dice?

> EJEMPLO abuelos / vivir / esta casa
> **Mis abuelos vivían en esta casa.**

1. nosotros / visitarlos / todos los veranos
2. padre / llevarnos / playa todos los días
3. hermanas y yo / nadar y / jugar / playa todo el día
4. yo / tener / cinco años / esa foto
5. mamá / no gustarle / playa
6. ella siempre / llevar sombreros / grandes
7. abuela y mi mamá / preferir / sombreros grandes

E. El sábado. ¿Qué hacían estas personas el sábado pasado?

MODELO **Maribel / instalar / software**
Maribel instalaba software.

1. nosotros / comunicarse / red

2. Luisa y Pablo / programar / software

3. Ramón / conectarse / Internet

4. Gloria / leer / correo electrónico

5. mis amigos y yo / instalar / impresora láser

6. el secretario / desconectarse / red

7. Dolores / usar / audífonos y micrófono

8. Lucas / dibujar / ratón

Computación

software hardware

correo electrónico

Internet

instalar

conectarse desconectarse
via módem

red

programar

Reflexive pronouns

me acuesto	**nos** acostamos
te acuestas	
se acuesta	**se** acuestan

Nos acostamos muy tarde anoche.
¿**Te** peinaste esta mañana?

See ¿Por qué se dice así?,
page G49, section 3.7.

F. Todos los días. Tu compañero(a) está haciéndote preguntas de una encuesta que encontró en una revista. ¿Qué le respondes?

 MODELO afeitarse / peinarse
Compañero(a): **¿Qué haces primero, te afeitas o te peinas?**
Tú: **Me afeito antes de peinarme.** o
Me peino antes de afeitarme.

1. oír la radio / despertarse
2. tomar café / levantarse
3. ponerse la bata / ponerse las zapatillas
4. lavarse los dientes / cepillarse el pelo
5. arreglarse / vestirse
6. bañarse / peinarse
7. desayunar / arreglarse
8. ponerse los pantalones / ponerse los calcetines
9. acostarse / dormirse
10. lavarse los dientes / quitarse la ropa

G. Cuando era niño . . . El abuelo de Andrea está contándole lo que hacían él y su familia los domingos cuando era niño. ¿Qué dice?

EJEMPLO **Mamá se acostaba tarde.**

yo	desayunar	a las 10:30
mamá	levantarse	temprano
mis hermanitos	acostarse	rápidamente
mis padres	bañarse	a las 9:00
mi hermana	afeitarse	tarde
papá y yo	vestirse	lentamente
	almorzar	al mediodía
		a las 8:00

CHARLEMOS UN POCO MÁS

A. Nuestro álbum. Tú y un(a) compañero(a) están viendo las fotos que sacaron el verano pasado. Escriban subtítulos para cada foto. Digan quiénes son las personas en las fotos y qué hacían estas personas. Luego en grupos de 4 a 6, lean los subtítulos a las otras personas en su grupo.

 EJEMPLO **Son mamá y papá. Preparaban unas hamburguesas para nosotros el cuatro de julio.**

Ejemplo

1.

2.

3.

4.

5.

6.

7.

B. Encuesta. Usa el cuestionario que te va a dar tu profesor(a) para entrevistar a varias personas de la clase. Pregúntales si hacían estas cosas relacionadas a computación hace tres años. Pídeles a las personas que contesten afirmativamente que firmen el cuadrado apropiado. Recuerda que no se permite que una persona firme más de una vez.

MODELO **¿Usabas monitores a color?**

C. Me levanto a las seis.   Prepara una lista de cinco actividades de tu rutina diaria al prepararte para ir a la escuela. Luego compara tu lista con la de dos compañeros. Escribe en la pizarra las actividades en tu lista que no aparecen en las listas de tus compañeros.

CH. ¡Al revés!   Tu profesor(a) dice que cuando era estudiante de secundaria, siempre tenían una "Semana Loca" en su colegio. Según el (la) profesor(a), ¿qué hacían durante esa semana?

Dramatizaciones

A. ¿Más fácil o más difícil?   Tú y tu compañero(a) están tratando de decidir si hace cinco años era más fácil o más difícil usar computadoras. Dramaticen su conversación.

B. Probablemente jugaba a . . .   Tú y tus compañeros están tratando de imaginarse cómo era y qué hacía su profesor(a) de español cuando era estudiante de secundaria. Dramaticen esta discusión.

LEAMOS AHORA

Estrategias para leer:
Predecir el contenido

COLOMBIA

Bogotá

Quito

ECUADOR

PERÚ

Lima

A. Título e ilustraciones. La mayor parte del tiempo leemos para conseguir nueva información o más información sobre algún tópico. Con frecuencia, el título de un artículo anuncia el tema de la lectura y le da una idea al lector del tipo de información que se va a encontrar en el artículo.

1. Hay dos palabras afines en el título de esta lectura. Estas dos palabras te dicen que la lectura es de una _____ y que hay algún _____ relacionado a este lugar.

2. Ahora mira las fotos que acompañan la lectura. Es probable que no sepas el significado de la palabra *Pascua* en el título, pero en las fotos hay objetos que tú ya conoces. ¿Dónde están estas gigantescas esculturas? Bien. Entonces ya sabes que el artículo contiene información sobre _____ .

Isla de Pascua

Océano Pacífico

3.700 kilómetros

B. Predecir el contenido. Una buena manera de prepararte para leer es tratar de predecir el contenido de la lectura. Prepárate para predecir el contenido de esta lectura por crear tres columnas en una hoja de papel y poner como título de las columnas:

1. **Lo que sé**
2. **Lo que no sé.**
3. **Lo que aprendí.**

Luego sigue este modelo al completar el formulario con toda la información que ya tienes a mano sobre la Isla de Pascua y la información que te gustaría saber.

CHILE

Santiago

Lo que sé	Lo que no sé	Lo que aprendí
1. La Isla de Pascua está en Sudamérica.	1. ¿De qué país es la Isla de Pascua?	

C. ¡A confirmar! Ahora lee el artículo dos veces, por lo menos. La primera vez, léelo sin parar, para tener una buena idea del mensaje principal. La segunda vez, llena la tercera columna en el formulario que preparaste en el ejercicio **B**. Una parte de lo que leíste va a confirmar lo que ya sabías, otra parte va a contestar algunas de las preguntas que escribiste en la segunda columna y otra parte va a incluir información que no anticipaste del todo.

La Isla de Pascua y sus misterios . . .

La Isla de Pascua—un lugar remoto y lleno de misterio, en el Océano Pacífico—continúa siendo un punto de interés para los arqueólogos e historiadores . . . ¡Allí se encuentra el secreto de sus antiguos habitantes, de los constructores de los formidables *moais* . . . esos gigantescos monolitos de piedra, dispersos por toda la isla, que constituyen uno de los misterios más grandes de todos los tiempos!

Según comenta el arqueólogo Eduardo Edwards, "el primer contacto que tuvieron los pascuenses con los hombres blancos europeos fue en 1722 en un domingo de Pascua de Resurrección de ese año, el navegante holandés Jacob Roggeween descubrió la isla y sus grandes estatuas de piedra . . . ¡pero ya en aquel entonces los nativos no sabían nada de ellas . . . desconocían su origen!

Poco a poco los científicos fueron concibiendo la idea de que los habitantes de la Isla de Pascua no eran en realidad descendientes de la cultura original que la habitó, sino que era un pueblo que había llegado posteriormente. Pero . . . ¿qué pueblo fue el primero en habitar la isla? Muchos historiadores se inclinan a creer que fueron los de la Polinesia, pues entre los habitantes de la isla existía una leyenda que narraba episodios de una guerra entre dos grupos humanos, en la que los polinesios exterminaron al grupo anterior. Además, los misioneros y los primeros europeos en llegar a Pascua encontraron mucha similitud entre sus habitantes y los del resto de la Polinesia . . . incluso hasta en el lenguaje.

Sin embargo, no todos los científicos piensan igual. Por ejemplo, en el año 1956 el famoso especialista noruego Thor Heyerdahl planteó la teoría de que el origen de los pascuenses era peruano. Según él, "algún grupo peruano-incaico podría haber partido de Perú en una balsa, llegado a la Isla y subyugado a sus habitantes hasta convertirlos en trabajadores que, bajo sus órdenes, tallaban las gigantescas estatuas". No obstante, las corrientes actuales de la ciencia parecen aceptar el origen polinesio de los habitantes del lugar . . . lo que todavía deja muchas preguntas sin contestar.

Según los estudios del polen realizados por el paleontólogo John Slenley de Inglaterra, "en la parte interior alta de la isla existían abundantes bosques, mientras que en la zona más baja—entre los 50 y 200 metros de altura—se encontraba una extensa sabana". Otras exploraciones permitieron suponer que los antiguos pascuenses cortaban madera para la construcción de botes.

Ni la historia, ni la arqueología han descubierto quiénes fueron los creadores de los aproximadamente 600 *moais* en la Isla de Pascua. ¡Algunos pesan más de 60 toneladas!

"Los Siete *Moais*", como los identifican los nativos. ¿Por qué si todos los demás *moais* fueron ubicados de espaldas al mar, únicamente éstos recibieron una orientación diferente?

Todo esto parece indicar que los antiguos habitantes de la isla fueron destruyendo los bosques, y a medida que lo hacían, la tierra se fue secando, el clima fue cambiando y la gente que vivía en el interior ya no tuvo agua, viéndose obligados a regresar a la costa.

Nada se sabe de certeza al respecto, pero sin duda los *moais* son prueba del nivel tecnológico de aquellos hombres que fueron capaces de elevar esos gigantescos monolitos de piedra. ¡Y mientras los científicos continúan trabajando para responder todas las preguntas que hoy nos seguimos haciendo sobre la Isla de Pascua y sus misterios . . . los *moais* siguen allí, en su sitio, ¡como testigos del pasado, que los hombres de hoy se esfuerzan por conocer!

¿Qué representará la corona de este *moai*?

El único *moai* sentado en toda la isla.

El *ahu Tahai* es uno de los templos más bellos e importantes que aún se conservan en la Isla de Pascua.

Verifiquemos

A. Formulario. Ahora repasa la información en el formulario que preparaste en los ejercicios **B** y **C** y contesta estas preguntas.

1. ¿Confirmó el artículo toda la información que habías escrito en la primera columna? ¿Resultó incorrecto algo que escribiste en la primera columna?

2. ¿Contestó la lectura todas tus preguntas en la segunda columna? Si no, ¿dónde podrías encontrar más información sobre la Isla de Pascua?

3. ¿Qué aprendiste en esta lectura que no habías anticipado del todo?

B. ¡A compartir! Ahora compara tu formulario con el de dos o tres compañeros de clase. Escribe en la tercera columna de tu formulario todo lo que aparezca en la tercera columna de sus formularios que no aparece en la tuya.

ESCRIBAMOS AHORA

Estrategias para escribir:
Selección de información para incluir en un artículo informativo

A. Empezar. En la sección **Leamos ahora,** aprendiste estrategias para ayudarte a predecir y recordar información de un artículo. Veamos cómo puedes usar estrategias similares al prepararte para escribir un artículo informativo.

1. ¿Qué escribiste en cada columna del formulario anterior antes de leer el artículo sobre la Isla de Pascua?
2. ¿Cómo te ayudó esta información a encontrar y recordar la nueva información que leíste?
3. Si tuvieras que preparar un formulario similar para ayudarte a organizar información para un artículo que vas a escribir, ¿cuáles serían algunos títulos que podrías usar en las columnas de ese formulario?

B. Al seleccionar el tema. Selecciona un lugar o sitio en tu comunidad o estado que sería de interés para algunos lectores. Tal vez necesites buscar información sobre el lugar que seleccionaste. Puedes visitar el sitio, llamarlo por teléfono o escribir una carta a algún departamento de turismo para pedir información.

C. Organizar. Ahora prepara un formulario similar al que sigue. Puedes usar los mismos títulos para tus columnas o crear tus propios títulos.

¿Qué se sabe de mi tópico?	En mi opinión, ¿qué más se quiere saber?	¿Qué más quiero yo que se aprenda del tópico?
1. Nombre del sitio.	2. Origen del nombre.	3. ¿Por qué se considera importante este sitio?

Tu artículo probablemente va a incluir información apropiada para cada columna de tu formulario, pero es probable que no necesites usar toda la información que consigas sobre el sitio. Usa un marcador para indicar en tu formulario toda la información que en tu opinión tiene que incluirse. Si quieres, puedes usar marcadores de diferentes colores para indicar si la información debe estar en el primer, el segundo o el tercer (etc.) párrafo.

CH. Primer borrador.   Ahora usa la información en tu formulario para escribir un artículo sobre el lugar o sitio que seleccionaste. Decide si ilustraciones o fotos harían tu artículo más interesante o informativo. Si decides que sí, indica dónde las pondrías y de qué sería cada foto.

D. Compartir.   Comparte el primer borrador de tu artículo con dos compañeros de clase. Pídeles sugerencias. Pregúntales si hay algo más que desean saber sobre tu sitio, si hay algo que no entienden, si hay algo que puede o debe eliminarse. Dales la misma información sobre sus sitios cuando ellos te pidan sugerencias.

E. Revisar.   Haz cambios en tu artículo a base de las sugerencias de tus compañeros. Luego, antes de entregar el informe, compártelo una vez más con dos compañeros de clase. Esta vez pídeles que revisen la estructura y la puntuación. En particular, pídeles que revisen las formas de verbos en el pretérito y en el imperfecto.

F. Versión final.   Escribe la versión final de tu artículo incorporando las correcciones que tus compañeros de clase te indicaron. Si decidiste que es apropiado tener ilustraciones o fotos, inclúyelas. Puedes usar fotos o ilustraciones de alguna revista o periódico o simplemente puedes dibujarlas tú mismo(a). Entrega una copia en limpio a tu profesor(a).

G. Publicar.   Cuando tu profesor(a) te devuelva el informe, júntate con tres compañeros de clase que escribieron sobre un sitio diferente. Combinen los cuatro artículos en un libro. Decidan en un título para su libro y preparen un contenido con el nombre de cada autor y el título de su artículo. Entreguen los libros para que su profesor(a) permita a toda la clase que los vea.

Era una ciudad muy...

Caracas, 1940

¿ Era de abuelita la cajita ?

¿ Qué piensas tú ?

1. Compara las fotos de esta página. ¿Qué están haciendo en cada foto? ¿Cuándo crees que las sacaron? ¿Por qué crees eso?

2. ¿Qué semejanzas y diferencias observas en el lugar? ¿en la gente? ¿en la actividad?

3. ¿Qué están haciendo la abuela y las dos chicas en la foto a la izquierda? ¿Qué estará diciéndoles la abuela? ¿Por qué crees eso?

4. ¿Hay reuniones a las cuales asisten varias generaciones de tu familia? En estas reuniones, ¿de qué hablan tus padres, tíos y abuelos por lo general?

5. ¿Recuerdas algo específico de cuando tenías cinco años? ¿diez años? ¿Qué hacías a esas edades? ¿Qué te gustaba y no te gustaba? ¿Cómo te comportabas cuando te sentías contento(a)? ¿triste? ¿Cómo te comportabas cuando tenías visitas?

6. ¿Cuál es tu memoria más temprana? ¿Cuántos años tenías en aquel entonces?

7. Piensa en todo lo que hemos dicho y di qué crees que vas a aprender en esta lección.

EL SOMBRERÓN

Los guatemaltecos nos cuentan esta triste historia del Sombrerón.

Dicen que hace muchos años que no lo ven, gracias a Dios, pero que en otros tiempos sí lo veían de vez en cuando; aunque nadie quería verlo porque inevitablemente, les traía mala suerte.

Era un hombrecito muy pequeño—tan pequeñito que cabía en la palma de una mano. Llevaba un sombrero enorme y zapatitos con espuelas de plata . . .

. . . y tenía una guitarra que tocaba cuando cantaba para despertar la admiración de las niñas bonitas. Y siempre iba acompañado de sus cuatro mulas de carga.

En un pequeño pueblo vivía Celina, una niña muy buena y muy bonita. Aun cuando tenía no más de cinco años, la gente no se cansaba de admirarla cada vez que la veían. Cuánto más crecía, más linda se ponía. ¡Sus ojos eran tan grandes y hermosos!

¡Y su pelo era tan largo y ondulado!

Además de ser bonita, Celina era muy trabajadora. Siempre ayudaba a su mamá a hacer tortillas para vender.

Una tarde, aparecieron cuatro mulas amarradas al poste del alumbrado eléctrico. "¡Dios nos libre!" comentó una mujer. "¡Debemos esconder a las niñas! ¡Son las mulas del Sombrerón!"

6

Pero esa noche, y noche tras noche, Celina no podía dormir bien porque oía una música muy linda —la voz de alguien que cantaba acompañado de una guitarra. Lo raro era que la madre de Celina no oía nada.

7

Celina ya no podía controlar su curiosidad. Tenía que conocer al dueño de esa voz. Una noche salió a espiar y vio que era el Sombrerón. Mientras él bailaba y cantaba tocando su guitarra, enamoraba a la niña.

8

Tan grande fue el amor que Celina sentía que pronto dejó de comer y ya no podía ni dormir ni sonreír.

9

La madre de Celina consultó a sus vecinos y todos le dijeron lo mismo. "Está enamorada del Sombrerón".

10

Los vecinos la aconsejaron que llevara a la niña lejos de la casa y que la encerrara en una iglesia. Todo el mundo sabía que los fantasmas no podían entrar en las iglesias.

11

Ese día, cuando llegó la noche, el Sombrerón no encontró a la niña en ninguna parte. La buscó toda la noche pero fue en vano. Al amanecer, se fue silencioso y triste.

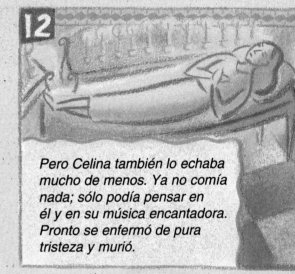

12

Pero Celina también lo echaba mucho de menos. Ya no comía nada; sólo podía pensar en él y en su música encantadora. Pronto se enfermó de pura tristeza y murió.

13

La noche antes del entierro, cuando la mamá de Celina y todo el pueblo estaban en el velorio de la niña, todos oyeron un llanto espantoso. Era el Sombrerón llorando el dolor que sentía por la pérdida de su Celina.

14

Por la mañana, cuando salieron de la casa, la gente del pueblo vio una maravilla. ¡Era como un milagro! ¡Había un reguero de lágrimas cristalizadas, como diamantes, sobre las piedras de la calle!

Al hablar de la niñez

1 Son cosas del pasado.

Meche y Diana están en casa de su abuela, ayudándola con la limpieza.

Abuelita, ya pasé un trapo a los muebles y pasé la aspiradora.

Yo saqué la basura y limpié las ventanas. ¿Qué más hay que hacer?

Saquen las cosas, límpienlas y pónganlas en orden.

Pues, a ver. Este armario está muy desorganizado. Hace años que nadie lo arregla. ¿Por qué no empiezan aquí?

¿Quién sabe, niñas? Son cosas del pasado — de cuando ustedes eran pequeñas, de cuando su papá era un niño y hasta de cuando yo era joven.

¿Qué cosas tienes aquí, abuelita?

2 ¿Te acuerdas de esto?

¡Ay, Meche! ¿Te acuerdas de esto?

¡Claro que sí! ¡Mi osito de peluche! ¡Dámelo!

Ese osito era tu juguete favorito. No te separabas de él cuando venías a visitarme. ¡Cómo lo querías! ¡Decías que ibas a guardarlo para siempre!

¡Mira, Meche! Nuestro juego de damas.

¡Siempre jugaban a las damas cuando llovía! ¡Cómo les gustaba! Y pobre Mechita — nunca ganaba.

¿De quién era esta cajita, abuelita? Parece muy vieja.

3 Allí guardaba mis cosas.

Esa caja es muy vieja. Era mía cuando yo tenía tu edad. Allí guardaba mis tesoros más queridos.

¿Qué tesoros ponías ahí, abuelita?

4 | Parece una jaula.

Imperfect: *ser, ver, ir*

ser	ver	ir
era	veía	iba
eras	veías	ibas
era	veía	iba
éramos	veíamos	íbamos
eran	veían	iban

See ¿Por qué se dice así?,
page G51, section 4.1.

CHARLEMOS UN POCO

A. **PARA EMPEZAR . . .** Después de leer el cuento "Las lágrimas del Sombrerón", indica si estas oraciones son verdaderas o falsas. Si son falsas, corrígelas.

1. El Sombrerón siempre traía mala suerte.
2. El Sombrerón era más pequeño que un hombre pero más grande que un niño.
3. El Sombrerón siempre llevaba puesto un sombrero grande e iba acompañado de sus cuatro mulas de carga.
4. Celina era una niña muy hermosa de menos de cinco años.
5. Primero Celina oyó al Sombrerón cantar, luego lo vio bailar y tocar la guitarra.
6. Celina se enamoró totalmente del Sombrerón, pero él no se enamoró de ella.
7. Cuando Celina se fue del pueblo, el Sombrerón se puso tan triste que se enfermó y se murió.
8. Cuando el Sombrerón supo de la muerte de Celina, lloró lágrimas que se convirtieron en diamantes.
9. Todo el pueblo oyó al Sombrerón llorar por Celina.
10. La maravilla fue que las piedras de la calle se convirtieron en diamantes.

B. **¿QUÉ DECIMOS . . .?** ¿Quiénes hacían estas actividades en el pasado?

Diana   **Meche**   **Abuela**   **Papá**

1. Guardaba sus cosas especiales en una cajita.
2. Jugaba con un osito de peluche.
3. Recibía cartas de amor.
4. Jugaban a las damas mientras llovía.
5. No se separaba de su juguete favorito.
6. Construyó una jaula.
7. Nunca ganaba cuando jugaban a las damas.
8. Tenía muchas joyas.

C. ¡Muy diferente! Nuestras vidas cambian mucho cuando nos mudamos de una ciudad a otra. ¿Cómo era la vida de este estudiante antes de mudarse a tu ciudad?

MODELO mi vida / ser / muy distinto
Mi vida era muy distinta.

1. siempre / ir / escuela / 7:00
2. escuela / ser / muy pequeño
3. haber / 350 estudiantes
4. después / clases / mis amigos y yo / ir / cine
5. allí / nosotros ver / bueno / películas
6. por / noche / yo / hacer / tarea
7. a veces / familia / ver televisión
8. mi vida / ser / muy divertido

CH. Álbum. Tú le estás enseñando unas viejas fotos en el álbum de tu familia a un(a) amigo(a). ¿Qué dices de las personas en las fotos?

EJEMPLO **Mis padres eran más jóvenes.**

		películas cómicas
		a la escuela
mis hermanos y yo		más jóvenes
mis padres	**ser**	muy guapo
papá	**ver**	pequeño
mamá	**ir**	televisión muy poco
todos		a su trabajo todos los días
yo		a visitar a los abuelos

D. ¡Qué trabajo! Tu compañero(a) quiere saber quiénes en tu familia hacían los quehaceres diarios cuando eran niños. Contesta sus preguntas.

MODELO lavar la ropa
Compañero(a): **Cuando eras niño(a), ¿quién lavaba la ropa?**
Tú: **Mamá lavaba la ropa.** o
Mamá y yo lavábamos la ropa.

1. sacar la basura
2. poner la mesa
3. cortar el césped
4. pasar un trapo a los muebles
5. pasar la aspiradora
6. lavar los platos
7. hacer la cama
8. planchar la ropa
9. lavar el carro
10. preparar la comida

Quehaceres domésticos

limpiar la casa

hacer la cama

sacar la basura

lavar los platos

cortar el césped

pasar un trapo

lavar la ropa

poner la mesa

barrer el patio

planchar la ropa

lavar el carro / coche

pasar la aspiradora

preparar la comida

limpiar las ventanas

Imperfect: Habitual actions

De niño **iba** al cine todos los sábados.
Siempre **lavábamos** el carro los sábados por la mañana.

See **¿Por qué se dice así?,** *page G53, section 4.2.*

Imperfect: Age and habitual actions

Yo **tenía** seis años y mi hermano **tenía** cuatro.

Cuando papá **tenía** quince años, **trabajaba** en un almacén.

See **¿Por qué se dice así?**, *page G53, section 4.2.*

E. Recuerdos. ¿Qué dice Sonia al describir su álbum de fotos?

4 años

MODELO   **Cuando tenía cuatro años, jugaba con mi osito de peluche.**

1. 4 años   **2.** 6 años   **3.** 7 años

4. 8 años   **5.** 9 años   **6.** 10 años

7. 11 años   **8.** 12 años

F. En primaria. Tu compañero(a) quiere saber con qué frecuencia te gustaba hacer estas cosas cuando estabas en la escuela primaria. Contesta sus preguntas.

MODELO   descansar
    Compañero(a): **¿Te gustaba descansar?**
    Tú: **Sí, descansaba todos los días.** o
            No, raras veces descansaba.

			todos los
nunca	raras veces	muchas veces	días

1. hablar por teléfono
2. jugar con amigos
3. comer pizza
4. ver televisión
5. limpiar la casa
6. hacer la tarea
7. ir al cine
8. pasear en bicicleta

G. ¿Cuándo?   ¿Qué hora era cuando hiciste estas cosas ayer?

MODELO   Te despertaste.
    Eran las seis y cuarto cuando me desperté. o
    Cuando me desperté, eran las seis y cuarto.

1. Te levantaste.
2. Desayunaste.
3. Saliste para la escuela.
4. Llegaste a la escuela.
5. Almorzaste.
6. Regresaste a casa.
7. Cenaste.
8. Te acostaste.

H. Entrevista.   Tu compañero(a) quiere saber cuándo aprendiste a hacer estas cosas. Contesta sus preguntas.

MODELO   tocar el piano
    Compañero(a): **¿Cuándo aprendiste a tocar el piano?**
    Tú: **Hace [¿ ?] años.** o
            Nunca aprendí a tocar el piano.

1. jugar tenis
2. escribir tu nombre
3. contar hasta 100
4. caminar
5. leer
6. poner la mesa
7. hacer la cama
8. tocar la guitarra

I. ¿Hace cuánto tiempo?   Las computadoras han cambiado nuestra vida personal. ¿Cómo?

MODELO   escribir: máquina / computadora
    Hace 10 años escribíamos a máquina.
    Hoy escribimos con computadoras.

1. comunicar: teléfono / módem
2. escribir notas: papel / correo electrónico
3. dibujar: lápiz / ratón
4. hacer amigos: persona / Internet
5. instalar software: diskettes / disco compacto
6. programar: programador / yo

Imperfect: Telling time in the past

Eran las siete cuando llamó.
No, **era** la una menos cuarto cuando sonó el teléfono.

See **¿Por qué se dice así?,** *page G53, section 4.2.*

Hacer to express *ago*

To express the concept of *ago*, Spanish uses the following formula:

hace + *[time]* + *[past tense]*

Hace cien años conducíamos caballos, no autos.

Hace dos días aprendí a usar el Internet.

See **¿Por qué se dice así?,** *page G54, section 4.3.*

A. Quehaceres. Tú eres reportero(a) para el periódico de tu colegio y tienes que escribir un artículo sobre los quehaceres más comunes de los estudiantes durante el verano. Usa el formulario que tu profesor(a) te va a dar para entrevistar a tres compañeros de clase. Luego, en grupos de cuatro, decidan cuáles quehaceres eran los más comunes y díganselo a la clase.

MODELO   *Tú:*   **¿Con qué frecuencia lavabas el carro de tu papá?**

Compañero(a):   **Lo lavaba cada sábado. o Nunca lo lavaba.**

Tú escribes: **cada sábado** *(en el cuadro apropiado)*

B. ¿Angelitos o diablitos? ¿Recuerdas cómo eras en la escuela primaria? Primero escribe las respuestas a estas preguntas en una hoja de papel. Luego, hazle las mismas preguntas a tu compañero(a) y comparen sus respuestas.

1. ¿Cómo se llamaba tu maestro(a) favorito(a)?
2. ¿Por qué te gustaba?
3. ¿Eras buen(a) estudiante?
4. ¿Cuánto estudiabas?
5. ¿Qué notas recibías?
6. ¿Qué hacías cuando recibías una mala nota? ¿Les decías a tus padres?
7. ¿Tenían que disciplinarte de vez en cuando? ¿Por qué?
8. ¿Quién era tu mejor amigo(a)? ¿Cómo era?
9. ¿Te gustaba practicar deportes? ¿Cuáles?
10. ¿Cuáles eran tus actividades favoritas los fines de semana?

C. ¿Hace mucho tiempo? Usa la cuadrícula que tu profesor(a) te va a dar para entrevistar a varias personas de la clase. Pregúntales cuánto tiempo hace que hicieron las actividades en cada cuadrado y pídeles que firmen el cuadrado apropiado. Recuerda que no se permite que una persona firme más de un cuadrado.

MODELO   *Tú:*   **¿Cuánto tiempo hace que sacaste la basura?**

Compañero(a):   **Ya hace tres días.**

CH. ¡Vacaciones! Princesa y Necio son dos gatos que siempre acompañaban a sus dueños en las vacaciones de verano. Cada verano iban al mismo lugar y hacían las mismas cosas. ¿Adónde iban y qué hacían? Con un compañero, describe los dibujos a continuación para contestar la pregunta. Muestren creatividad, pero limítense al español que ya saben bien.

1.

2.

3.

4.

5.

6.

7.

8.

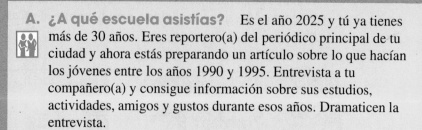

Dramatizaciones

A. **¿A qué escuela asistías?** Es el año 2025 y tú ya tienes más de 30 años. Eres reportero(a) del periódico principal de tu ciudad y ahora estás preparando un artículo sobre lo que hacían los jóvenes entre los años 1990 y 1995. Entrevista a tu compañero(a) y consigue información sobre sus estudios, actividades, amigos y gustos durante esos años. Dramaticen la entrevista.

B. **¿Mejor o peor?** Tú y un(a) amigo(a) están comparando sus vidas cuando asistían a la escuela primaria. Hablan de sus personalidades, profesores, clases favoritas y actividades. Dramatiza la conversación con un(a) compañero(a).

C. **¿Qué es?** Tú descubriste una caja grande en el patio de la casa de tu amigo(a). La caja tiene algo que hace muchos años era muy importante para tu amigo(a). Claro, tú quieres saber todos los detalles de por qué era tan importante este objeto. Dramatiza la situación con un(a) compañero(a).

IMPACTO CULTURAL
Excursiones

Antes de empezar

A. Mapa y fotos. Estudia las fotos y el mapa sobre la cultura de los incas. Luego contesta y completa estas frases. No es necesario leer la lectura todavía.

1. ¿Por cuáles países de Sudamérica se extendía el Imperio de los Incas?
   - **a.** Ecuador, Perú, Bolivia, Argentina y Chile
   - **b.** Brasil, Paraguay y Uruguay
   - **c.** Colombia, Venezuela y Brasil
   - **ch.** Perú, Ecuador, Venezuela y Colombia

2. Un *quipu* probablemente es para . . .
   - **a.** llevar dinero.
   - **b.** llevar algo para comer.
   - **c.** calentarse las manos.
   - **ch.** contar.

3. Los edificios que construyeron los incas eran muy . . .
   - **a.** pequeños.
   - **b.** abiertos.
   - **c.** sólidos.
   - **ch.** frágiles.

4. Los incas construyeron las terrazas para . . .
   - **a.** jugar deportes.
   - **b.** construir más edificios.
   - **c.** sembrar flores y decorar sus edificios.
   - **ch.** cultivar diferentes comidas.

5. Machu Picchu probablemente fue . . .
   - **a.** una fortaleza.
   - **b.** un centro religioso.
   - **c.** la capital de los incas.
   - **ch.** un refugio para el Inca y sus nobles.

B. Impresiones. Antes de leer del Imperio de los Incas, indica si en tu opinión estos comentarios son ciertos o falsos. Si no sabes, usa tu sentido común para decidir.

C F **1.** El Imperio de los Incas estaba en Centro y Sudamérica.
C F **2.** En 1500, los españoles encontraron toda la historia de los incas en tres volúmenes muy impresionantes.
C F **3.** Machu Picchu son las ruinas de una cultura muy civilizada.
C F **4.** Los incas fueron excelentes agricultores.
C F **5.** Los incas no tenían buenos ingenieros ni buenos arquitectos.
C F **6.** Muchas tradiciones incaicas se practican actualmente en Perú.

EL IMPERIO DE LOS INCAS

El Imperio de los Incas empezó con Manco Capac, el primer Inca, en el año 1100 y terminó con la muerte de Atahualpa en el año 1533. Se extendió en los Andes por una distancia de más de 2,500 millas (la distancia de Phoenix a Nueva York, más o menos), por los actuales territorios de Ecuador, Perú, Bolivia, Chile y Argentina. Cuando llegaron los españoles, el imperio incaico tenía entre 3.5 y 7 millones de habitantes.

Entre ellos, había muchas tribus diferentes que habían sido conquistadas por los incas. Y todas las tribus en el imperio incaico tenían que aprender a hablar quechua, la lengua oficial de los incas. En efecto, *Inca* era el nombre del rey y *quechua* el nombre de su gente.

La capital de los incas fue la ciudad de Cuzco **①** que está situada casi en medio del imperio, en la parte sudoeste de Perú. En esta ciudad se encuentran los restos más impresionantes de lo que fue este gran imperio. Allí se pueden ver restos de edificios, casas, templos, fortalezas y andenes o terrazas para la agricultura incaica. Los incas no tuvieron una escritura verdadera, pero desarrollaron el *quipu,* un sistema de números que usa nudos en cuerdas de diferentes colores. **②** El *quipu* también se usó para grabar historia y versos. Esa tradición vive todavía entre la población quechua de Perú y Bolivia.

Los incas fueron excelentes arquitectos e ingenieros. Ellos planificaron muy cuidadosamente sus ciudades. Hicieron edificios de piedras de distintas formas: cuadradas, rectangulares y poligonales como la famosa Piedra de los doce ángulos. **③** Tan superior fue la arquitectura de los incas que, después de 500 años o más, todavía se conservan muchas de sus estructuras, a pesar de los muchos terremotos que ocurren en el área.

Alrededor de la ciudad de Cuzco, los incas construyeron fortalezas para defenderse de sus enemigos. La fortaleza de Sacsahuamán es una de las fortalezas más impresionantes. **④** Los incas utilizaron piedras inmensas para construirla, pero no usaron ni cemento ni mortero para unir estas piedras. A pesar de esto, es imposible meter el filo de un cuchillo entre estas piedras.

Unos de los más famosos restos arqueológicos del mundo entero son las ruinas de Machu Picchu. **⑤** Estas ruinas están en la selva a tres horas de la ciudad de Cuzco, muy cerca de la zona del Río Urubamba, una de las fuentes del Amazonas. Machu Picchu no fue descubierta hasta el año 1911 por el profesor estadounidense Hiram Bingham. No se sabe definitivamente qué fue esta maravilla incaica. Una teoría dice que fue una fortaleza, otra que fue un centro religioso y todavía otra, que sirvió de refugio a los últimos incas que huían de los españoles.

La economía de los incas dependía intensamente de la agricultura. Cultivaban maíz, papas, calabazas, frijoles, chiles, cacahuates, tomates, camotes, aguacates y otras plantas. Por todo Cuzco, y en particular en Machu Picchu se conservan los más hermosos andenes o terrazas que los incas construyeron para poder trabajar la tierra montañosa. **⑥**

Actualmente, la ciudad de Cuzco está habitada por los descendientes de los incas. Los cuzqueños son *mestizos* como casi todos los habitantes del Perú. **⑦** Pero los cuzqueños han conservado la antigua cultura indígena. Su lengua es el *quechua*, la lengua de los antiguos peruanos. Su religión es una mezcla de catolicismo con viejas creencias religiosas indígenas. Los cuzqueños, como los descendientes más directos de los incas, conservan sus viejas tradiciones y costumbres.

Verifiquemos

1. Vuelve a las actividades **A** y **B** de **Antes de empezar** y decide si tus respuestas originales fueron correctas o no.
2. Dibuja la Piedra de los doce ángulos. ¿Por qué usaron los incas este tipo de piedra para construir sus edificios?
3. Prepara un diagrama del Imperio de los Incas, como el siguiente, e incluye toda la información posible bajo cada categoría.

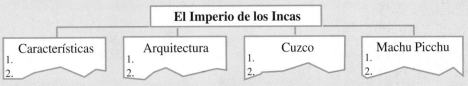

El Imperio de los Incas

Características	Arquitectura	Cuzco	Machu Picchu
1.	1.	1.	1.
2.	2.	2.	2.

4. ¿Qué aspecto del imperio incaico te gustaría estudiar más? ¿Por qué?

Ahora les voy a contar.

¿ Qué piensas tú ?

1. Las fotos a la izquierda son de un periódico venezolano. Cada una es de incidentes que ocurrieron la semana pasada. Descríbele una de las fotos a tu compañero(a) y luego que él o ella te describa la otra a ti. Incluyan todos los detalles posibles sobre el sitio y lo que pasaba antes, durante y después del incidente.

2. ¿Qué hacías tú esta mañana antes de la primera clase, cuando sonó el timbre? ¿Dónde y con quién estabas? ¿Había otras personas cerca de ustedes? ¿Qué hacían?

3. Imagínense que hubo simulacro contra incendios ayer, poco antes del almuerzo. Describe detalladamente lo que tú y tus amigos hacían antes de empezar el simulacro y lo que hicieron cuando oyeron el timbre.

4. Compara las fotos de Caracas. ¿Cuáles son las diferencias? ¿Cómo explicas esas diferencias?

5. ¿Hay diferencias de este tipo en tu ciudad? ¿en otras ciudades del estado?

6. Piensa en todo lo que hemos dicho y di qué crees que vas a aprender en esta lección.

EL GALLO DE LA CRESTA DE ORO

Este cuento venezolano es semejante a un cuento popular de Estados Unidos.

1

Había una vez unos viejitos muy, muy pobres. Lo único que tenían era su ranchito. La viejita un día sembró una mata de tomate, porque cuando no hay mucho de comer, los tomates siempre son buenos.

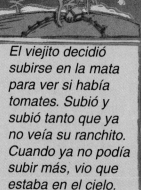

2

Inmediatamente la mata de tomate empezó a crecer y al día siguiente ya llegaba al techo. Al tercer día, la mata llegó a las nubes.

3

El viejito decidió subirse en la mata para ver si había tomates. Subió y subió tanto que ya no veía su ranchito. Cuando ya no podía subir más, vio que estaba en el cielo.

Miró alrededor y no vio nada más que unas piedritas y un gallo con la cresta de oro. Recogió las piedritas y al gallo también y volvió al ranchito.

4 A la viejita le gustaron mucho las piedritas porque eran perfectas para moler la masa. Cuando se puso a moler, ¡algo mágico pasó! Cada vez que molía con las piedritas, salían toda clase de comidas buenas. Los viejitos estaban contentísimos, pues ya no tendrían que pasar hambre.

5 Un día llegó un señor y pidió posada. Los viejitos lo invitaron a pasar la noche y a cenar con ellos.

6 Cuando llegó la hora de comer, la viejita sacó sus piedritas mágicas y se puso a moler. El hombre vio que salía todo tipo de comida: arepas, pollo frito, guayaba y toda clase de dulces. El hombre, muy impresionado, quería comprar las piedritas mágicas pero los viejitos no querían venderlas.

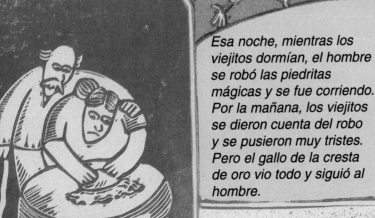

7 Esa noche, mientras los viejitos dormían, el hombre se robó las piedritas mágicas y se fue corriendo. Por la mañana, los viejitos se dieron cuenta del robo y se pusieron muy tristes. Pero el gallo de la cresta de oro vio todo y siguió al hombre.

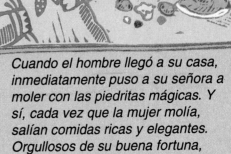

8 Cuando el hombre llegó a su casa, inmediatamente puso a su señora a moler con las piedritas mágicas. Y sí, cada vez que la mujer molía, salían comidas ricas y elegantes. Orgullosos de su buena fortuna, invitaron a muchos amigos y vecinos a comer.

¡LADRÓN!

Mientras todos comían un sabrosísimo banquete de comida elegantísima, apareció el gallo de la cresta de oro y gritó: "¡Quiquiriquí, ladrón! ¡Danos las piedras que nos robaste!"

El hombre, enfurecido, cogió al gallo del cuello y lo tiró en una olla llena de agua.

Pero el gallo se tomó toda el agua, salió de la olla y otra vez denunció al hombre. "¡Quiquiriquí, ladrón, ladrón!"

El hombre se enojó tanto que otra vez cogió al gallo del cuello y lo tiró en el horno. Pero el gallo de la cresta de oro era muy astuto y simplemente botó toda el agua que había tomado en la olla y apagó el fuego. Luego salió del horno y, como antes, denunció al hombre diciendo: "¡Quiquiriquí, ladrón, ladrón!"

Entonces, el gallito de la cresta de oro cogió las piedritas mágicas y se fue volando hasta la casa de los viejitos.

Los invitados veían y oían todo y no lo podían creer. Asustados, todos salieron corriendo, hasta el señor y su mujer.

Allí los tres, el gallito de la cresta de oro y los dos viejitos, vivieron felices muchos, muchos años.

¿QUÉ DECIMOS...?

Al hablar del pasado

1 | Mira lo que apareció.

2 ¿Tenías un ratón?

Esta jaulita era para mi ratoncito, Miguelín.

¿De veras tenías un ratoncito?

¿Por qué un ratón, papá?

Cuando tenía diez años, un vecino me lo regaló. Estaba en su jardín y no lo quería matar. Yo lo llevé a casa.

¿Y qué dijo la abuela? ¿No se asustó?

Papá y yo le construimos la jaula y yo le puse el nombre de "Miguelín".

Bueno, al principio no sabía qué pensar, pero después se acostumbró.

3 Lo quería mucho.

¿Qué hacías con el ratoncito, papá?

Pues, todos los días le daba de comer y beber.

Y de vez en cuando lo sacaba de la jaula y jugaba con él en el patio.

¿Y lo tocabas?

Claro que sí.

Era muy suave. Yo lo quería mucho y lo cuidaba muy bien.

Cada dos días le limpiaba la jaula y le cambiaba la paja. Me divertía mucho con él.

¿Y qué pasó con Miguelín?

Un día fui a darle de comer a mi ratoncito...

... pero la jaula estaba vacía y la puerta estaba abierta.

Busqué a Miguelín por todos lados pero nunca lo encontré. No sé lo que le pasó.

¡Ay, qué triste, papá! ¿Qué hiciste?

Saben que lloré por varios días. Pero su abuelita me convenció de que para Miguelín era mejor estar libre.

Y en efecto, tenía razón. Todo salió bien.

¿Cómo? ¿Qué pasó?

Explícanos, papá.

Pues, hubo un concurso literario y escribí un cuento sobre Miguelín. ¿Y saben qué pasó?

¿Qué pasó?

Dinos.

Gané un premio. Y con el dinero del premio me compré un perrito.

CHARLEMOS UN POCO

A. **PARA EMPEZAR . . .** ¿Quién hizo esto en el cuento "El gallo de la cresta de oro"?

la viejita **el viejito** **el gallo** **el hombre**

1. Sembró una mata de tomate.
2. Decidió subirse en la mata.
3. Recogió unas piedritas en el cielo.
4. Se puso a moler y algo mágico pasó.
5. Quería comprar las piedritas.
6. Se robó las piedritas.
7. Invitó a muchos amigos a comer.
8. Apareció de repente y acusó al ladrón.
9. Trató de matar al gallo de la cresta de oro.
10. Denunció al ladrón dos veces más.
11. Devolvió las piedritas al ranchito.
12. Vivieron muchos años muy felices.

B. **¿QUÉ DECIMOS . . .?** Según la historia de Miguelín, ¿en qué orden ocurrieron estas cosas?

1. Buscó a Miguelín en todas partes.
2. Su papá y él le construyeron una jaula.
3. Escribió un cuento y ganó un premio.
4. Un vecino le regaló un ratoncito al papá de Meche y Diana.
5. Todos los días le daba de comer y de beber.
6. Compró un perrito.
7. Le dio el nombre de Miguelín.
8. No encontró al ratoncito y lloró mucho.
9. Llevó al ratoncito a casa.
10. Un día vio que la jaula estaba vacía.

C. Diferentes.
Teo y Alicia nunca hacen la misma cosa al mismo tiempo. ¿Qué hacían los dos ayer a estas horas?

 MODELO **A las ocho y media, Teo dormía mientras Alicia desayunaba.**

hora	Teo	Alicia
8:30	dormir	desayunar
9:00	ver televisión	arreglarse
9:30	leer el periódico	ir de compras
11:00	comer	mirar una película
12:00	jugar fútbol	almorzar
2:30	tomar refrescos	jugar tenis
4:30	pasear en bicicleta	descansar en casa
6:00	lavar el carro	cortar el césped
8:00	hacer un sándwich	leer una novela

CH. ¡Pero no llamaron!
Según Margarita, ¿qué hacían los miembros de su familia cuando llegaron unos amigos sin llamar?

 MODELO **Mamá preparaba la comida.**

Imperfect: Continuing actions

Past actions viewed as continuing or in progress are expressed in the imperfect.

Mamá **leía** el periódico mientras papá **veía** la tele.

¿Con quién **hablabas**?

*See ¿**Por qué se dice así?**, page G55, section 4.4.*

Preterite: Interrupted continuing actions

When a past action viewed as continuing or in progress is interrupted by another action, the latter is expressed in the preterite.

El teléfono **sonó** mientras comíamos.
Ellas caminaban en el parque cuando me **vieron**.

See **¿Por qué se dice así?**,
page G55, section 4.4.

Preterite: Completed actions

When a past action is viewed as completed, it is expressed in the preterite.

Carlota me **llamó** esta mañana.
Ya le **escribí** a abuelita.

See **¿Por qué se dice así?**,
page G57, section 4.5.

Preterite: Focus on beginning or end of past actions

When focused on the beginning or end of a past action, the verb is expressed in the preterite.

¿Ya **conociste** a la nueva estudiante?
Ellas **terminaron** primero.

See **¿Por qué se dice así?**,
page G57, section 4.5.

D. Un día terrible. Según Eduardo, ¿qué hacían él y su familia cuando ocurrieron estas interrupciones el sábado pasado?

MODELO hermana estudiar: entrar Juanita
Mi hermana estudiaba cuando entró Juanita en su cuarto.

1. mamá cocinar: llamar vecina
2. yo jugar fútbol: empezar llover
3. mis hermanos dormir: gritar papá
4. abuelita pasar la aspiradora: desenchufarla Juanita
5. nosotros cenar: llegar mis tíos
6. yo hacer ejercicio: sonar teléfono
7. abuelito cantar: empezar a llorar el bebé
8. mamá barrer la cocina: encontrar un ratón

E. Nos divertimos. ¿Qué hicieron tú y tus amigos la última vez que fueron a un centro comercial?

 EJEMPLO **Mi amigo José comió pizza.**

		pizza
		una camiseta
	comer	refrescos
yo	comprar	juegos de video
mi amigo [. . .]	beber	una película
mi amiga [. . .]	ver	los amigos
todos nosotros	hablar	las amigas
mis amigos [. . .] y [. . .]	jugar	hamburguesas
[. . .]	mirar	limonada
	buscar	ropa
		discos compactos
		[. . .]

F. Hace mucho tiempo. Tu compañero(a) quiere saber cuándo conociste a estas personas. Contesta sus preguntas.

MODELO el profesor de inglés
Compañero(a): **¿Cuándo conociste al profesor de inglés?**
Tú: **Lo conocí hace una semana.**

1. el(la) director(a) de la escuela
2. el(la) profesor(a) de español
3. tu amigo(a) [¿ ?]
4. tu doctor(a)
5. tu dentista
6. el(la) entrenador(a) del equipo de fútbol
7. el(la) secretario(a) de la escuela
8. tus vecinos

G. ¡Fiesta! Hubo una fiesta en casa de Chela. Según ella, ¿qué pasó?

EJEMPLO **Florencia preparó más limonada.**

yo	dormirse	canciones románticas
mamá	servir	en el comedor
Florencia	tocar	más pastel
Rubén y Lucas	pedir	el tango y el cha-cha-chá
Ramiro y yo	preparar	en el sofá
mis tíos	conseguir	discos populares
Rosario	bailar	más limonada
	comer	toda la noche
		tapas

REPASO

Preterite: e → i, o → u stem-changing -ir verbs

Stem-changing **-ir** verbs in the preterite undergo a one-vowel change only in the **usted/él/ella, ustedes/ellos/ellas** forms.

¿Qué **pidieron** ustedes?
Yo **serví** el postre y ella **sirvió** las bebidas.

Note: There are no **-ar, -er** stem-changing verbs in the preterite.

*See ¿***Por qué se dice así?**, *page G60, section 4.6.*

CHARLEMOS UN POCO MÁS

A. Los fines de semana. Cuando Julio era joven, él y su papá hacían varias cosas juntos durante los fines de semana. Usen los horarios que su profesor(a) les va a dar para identificar las cinco cosas que ellos hacían juntos. No se permite mirar el horario de su compañero(a) hasta terminar esta actividad.

EJEMPLO **El sábado a las seis y media de la tarde, el papá de Julio cenaba en casa. ¿Qué hacía Julio?**

B. Antes y ahora. Escribe siete u ocho actividades que siempre hacías cuando eras estudiante en la escuela primaria y compáralas con lo que haces ahora. Luego pregúntale a tu compañero(a) si hacía las mismas actividades. Informen a la clase de todo lo que hacían en común.

EJEMPLO *Tú escribes:* **En la escuela primaria siempre comía en casa; ahora como en la cafetería con frecuencia.**

Tú preguntas: **¿En la escuela primaria, siempre comías en casa?**

Compañero(a): **No. Comía en el colegio.** o
Sí, comía en casa.

C. ¿Sí o no? Con tu compañero(a), prepara de ocho a diez preguntas para hacerle a tu profesor(a). Quieres descubrir qué tipo de estudiante era cuando asistía a la escuela secundaria. Luego háganle las preguntas a su profesor(a).

CH. Lo pasábamos muy bien. Con un compañero, prepara una lista de todo lo que ustedes y sus familias hacían en el parque cuando eran más jóvenes. Si no iban al parque, describan lo que hacían estas personas.

Dramatizaciones

A. ¡Era mi favorito! Tú y un(a) amigo(a) están conversando del objeto favorito que más recuerdan de su niñez. Tu amigo(a) te hace muchas preguntas para saber la importancia de tu objeto y tú le haces muchas preguntas a tu amigo(a). Dramaticen esta conversación.

B. Animales domésticos. Tú y un(a) amigo(a) están hablando de los animales domésticos que tenían cuando eran niños. Dramaticen la conversación.

IMPACTO CULTURAL
Tesoros nacionales

Antes de empezar

A. Al anticipar. Estudia cuidadosamente las fotos de la fortaleza, del camino y del puente en las siguientes páginas. ¿Cuánto puedes decir de la gente que los construyó? ¿Qué conocimientos debían tener para poder construirlos? ¿Qué habilidades necesitaban los trabajadores? ¿Qué herramientas usaron?

B. La idea principal. Identifica la idea principal de los primeros cuatro párrafos al hojear la lectura y selecciona la frase que mejor la exprese.

Párrafo 1   **a.** la caída del imperio incaico
      b. la grandeza del imperio incaico
      c. el terreno difícil de los Andes
     ch. los grandes líderes del imperio incaico

Párrafo 2   **a.** el noveno Inca
      b. Alejandro Magno
      c. Napoleón
     ch. la extensión del imperio incaico

Párrafo 3   **a.** la importancia de los caminos y puentes que se siguen usando
      b. las fortalezas de Koricancha y Sacsahuamán
      c. la importancia de Cuzco
     ch. lo impresionante del imperio incaico

Párrafo 4   **a.** la leyenda de una hermosa mujer de Ica
      b. la honestidad de la mujer nativa peruana
      c. los canales de irrigación
     ch. las terrazas o andenes de agricultura

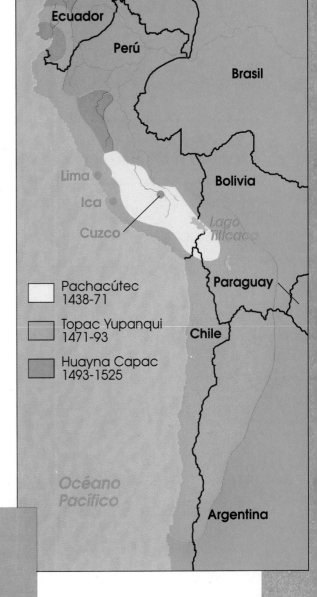

Venezuela
Colombia
Ecuador
Perú
Brasil
Lima
Ica
Cuzco
Lago Titicaca
Bolivia
Paraguay
Chile
Argentina
Océano Pacífico

Pachacútec 1438-71
Topac Yupanqui 1471-93
Huayna Capac 1493-1525

EL NOVENO INGA
PACHACVTI INGA
YPANQVI

Reynobas ta chile 9 de to basucor sellon pachagni

Pachacútec el gran Inca

El Imperio de los Incas
tuvo trece reyes o Incas

MANCO CAPAC

SINCHI ROCA

LLOQUE YUPANQUI

MAYTA CAPAC

CAPAC YUPANQUI

INCA ROCA

YAHUAR HUACA

VIRACOCHA INCA

PACHACÚTEC (1438-71)

TOPAC YUPANQUI (1471-93)

HUAYNA CAPAC (1493-1525)

HUASCAR (1525-32)

ATAHUALPA (1532-33)

En cierto sentido, la ascendencia y caída de la civilización incaica es más impresionante que la de las grandes civilizaciones de Mesopotamia o del Egipto. ¿Por qué? Porque los incas crearon su imperio, no de extensos valles con magníficos ríos, sino de difíciles montañas con vastos cañones y de tierras casi imposibles de conquistar y cultivar. Sin embargo, bajo estos grandes líderes, el imperio se fue expandiendo, poco a poco, hasta cubrir los Andes desde más allá de Quito en Ecuador hasta más allá de Santiago de Chile.

De los muchos grandes líderes, el más responsable por las grandezas que todavía sobreviven en Perú es Pachacútec, el noveno Inca.[1] Tan grandes e impresionantes fueron las conquistas y hazañas de este Inca que se dice que Pachacútec es el nativo americano más grande en toda la historia del continente. Aun se le ha comparado con el macedonio, Alejandro Magno, y con el emperador francés, Napoleón. Cuando Pachacútec llegó a ser el Inca, su reino se extendía no más de 80 millas; cuando murió en 1471, el imperio ya tenía una extensión de más de 500 millas.

Fue Pachacútec quien hizo reconstruir la capital de Cuzco hasta que llegó a ser la imponente ciudad que encontraron los españoles. Bajo su dirección, se construyeron imponentes fortalezas, como las de Sacsahuamán y Koricancha,[2] y grandes templos y palacios como los de las hermosas ciudades de Cuzco y Machu Picchu. Bajo Pachacútec también se construyeron los primeros caminos del imperio,[3] caminos que transcurren en lo alto de los Andes y que incluyen puentes[4] que todavía siguen renovándose y usándose.

Pachacútec mandó construir canales de irrigación para proveer de agua las terrazas o andenes para la agricultura. Estos canales eran perfectas obras de ingeniería. Una leyenda dice que Pachacútec se enamoró de una hermosa mujer de Ica, una ciudad en la costa de Perú. Pero esta mujer amaba a otro hombre. Cuando ella le confesó a Pachacútec que amaba a otro, el Inca se impresionó por la honestidad de la mujer y le ofreció lo que deseara. Ella pidió un canal de irrigación para su pueblo y Pachacútec lo mandó a construir. El impresionante canal de Pachacútec todavía se usa en la ciudad de Ica.

Pachacútec conquistó muchos pueblos⑥ y tenía fama de ser muy severo con sus enemigos. Pero también protegió a todos en su imperio y respetó las tradiciones y creencias de su gente.

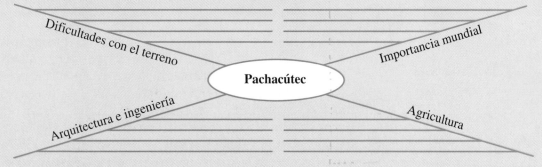

Verifiquemos

1. Prepara un esquema araña, como el modelo, de las dificultades, la importancia mundial y las grandes hazañas en arquitectura, ingeniería y agricultura del noveno Inca, Pachacútec.

Dificultades con el terreno

Importancia mundial

Pachacútec

Arquitectura e ingeniería

Agricultura

2. Con un(a) compañero(a) de clase, escribe un minidrama de la conversación de Pachacútec y la mujer de Ica, cuando ésta le confesó que tenía otro amante. Presenten su minidrama a la clase.

¡... y todo cambió!

TRAYECTORIA CRONOLÓGICA

	800 a. de J.C.–1200 d. de J.C.	1400	1500	1600	1700
DEL MUNDO	**753 a.de J.C.** La fundación de Roma		**1492** Cristóbal Colón llega a las Antillas	**1620** El *Mayflower* llega a Nueva Inglaterra	
DE PERÚ		**1200** La fundación de la dinastía de los incas	**1438–1532** Extensión del Imperio de los Incas	**1531** La llegada de los españoles **1535** Fundación de Lima	

Caracas

Lima

Buenos Aires

ANTICIPEMOS

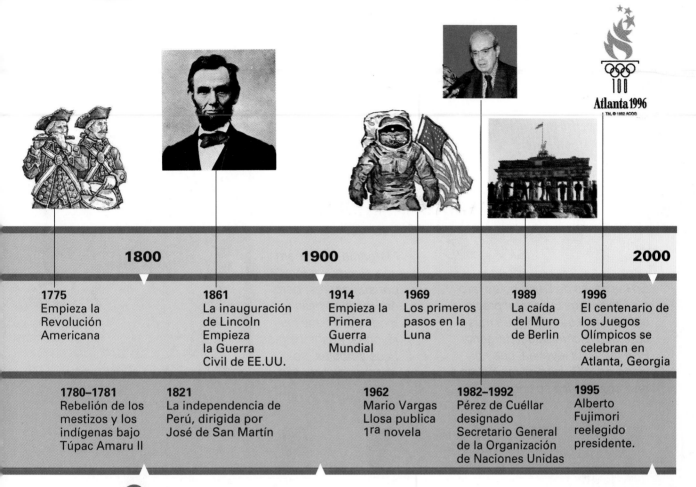

1800	1900	2000

1775
Empieza la
Revolución
Americana

1861
La inauguración
de Lincoln
Empieza
la Guerra
Civil de EE.UU.

1914
Empieza la
Primera
Guerra
Mundial

1969
Los primeros
pasos en la
Luna

1989
La caída
del Muro
de Berlin

1996
El centenario de
los Juegos
Olímpicos se
celebran en
Atlanta, Georgia

1780–1781
Rebelión de los
mestizos y los
indígenas bajo
Túpac Amaru II

1821
La independencia de
Perú, dirigida por
José de San Martín

1962
Mario Vargas
Llosa publica
1ra novela

1982–1992
Pérez de Cuéllar
designado
Secretario General
de la Organización
de Naciones Unidas

1995
Alberto
Fujimori
reelegido
presidente.

¿Qué piensas tú?

1. Con un(a) compañero(a), estudia la trayectoria cronológica de Perú y prepara una narración breve sobre la historia de Perú.

2. Ahora con tu compañero(a), estudia la trayectoria cronológica del mundo entero y prepara una narración breve de lo que pasaba en el resto del mundo durante los momentos históricos que mencionaste en tu narración sobre la historia de Perú.

3. Compara las tres ciudades en las fotos. ¿Cuáles son algunas semejanzas? ¿algunas diferencias?

4. Localiza las tres ciudades en un mapa y explica por qué crees que estas tres ciudades importantes sudamericanas se fundaron en ese local. En tu opinión, ¿por qué llegaron a ser ciudades de gran importancia en sus países?

5. ¿Cuáles son las ciudades principales de tu estado? ¿Puedes contar algo sobre la historia de tu ciudad o sobre la capital de tu estado? ¿Cuándo y cómo se fundaron? ¿Por qué se fundaron allí?

6. Piensa en todo lo que hemos dicho y di qué crees que vas a aprender en esta lección.

LA CAMISA DE MARGARITA PAREJA

1

En las calles de Lima, no es raro oír a los viejos criticar un precio alto con la expresión: "¡Es más caro que la camisa de Margarita Pareja!" Esta leyenda, que nos viene de la Ciudad de los Reyes en Perú, explica su origen.

2

Margarita Pareja era una hija muy mimada por sus padres, pero era también bella y modesta. Todos los jóvenes, hasta los más ricos y nobles, se enamoraban de ella.

3

Vivía en Lima en esos tiempos, un don Honorato, el hombre más rico, más avaro y más orgulloso de toda la ciudad.

4

Don Honorato tenía un sobrino que se llamaba Luis Alcázar. Este joven esperaba heredar toda la fortuna de su tío, pero en los tiempos de que hablamos, Luis Alcázar vivía más pobre que una rata.

Cuando en una procesión por la ciudad, Luis vio a la linda, la hermosa Margarita, se enamoró de ella al instante; a ella le pasó lo mismo. Tan enamorados estaban que no les importaba nada más. Ni la pobreza en la cual vivía Luis tenía importancia para los dos enamorados.

Luis le pidió al padre de Margarita la mano de su hija. Pero el padre se puso furioso. No quería tener como yerno a tal pobretón.

El tío de Luis— tan orgulloso como era—se puso aún más furioso. "Este don Raimundo insultó a mi sobrino, ¡el mejor joven de toda la ciudad de Lima!"

Y la hermosa Margarita también se puso furiosa. Se arrancó el pelo . . . y dijo que ya no quería ni comer ni beber absolutamente nada. Con el pasar de los días, la hermosa Margarita se ponía más y más pálida y flaca. ¡Parecía que iba a morir!

El padre de la joven consultó a médicos y a curanderos, pero todos le dijeron que no había remedio para un corazón destrozado. Pero tanto amaba don Raimundo a su hija, que por fin decidió aprobar la boda de Luis y la hermosa Margarita.

Antes de consentir de su parte, don Honorato, el tío de Luis, insistió en una condición: don Raimundo tenía que prometer que ni ahora ni nunca le daría ni dote ni dinero a su hija. Margarita tendría que ir a casa de su marido con sólo la ropa que llevaba puesta y nada más.

Don Raimundo no estaba del todo contento con esta condición. Pidió, por lo menos, poder regalar a su hija una camisa de novia.

Don Honorato consintió y don Raimundo así tuvo que jurar: "Juro no dar a mi hija más que la camisa de novia".

Al día siguiente tuvo lugar la boda. La hermosa Margarita llevaba su camisa nueva y su padre cumplió su juramento. Ni en vida ni en muerte dio a su hija nada más.

Pero, ¡Dios mío! ¡Qué camisa! La bordadura que adornaba la camisa era de puro oro y plata. Y el cordón que ajustaba el cuello era una cadena de brillantes que valía una fortuna.

Y por eso es que todavía ahora, cuando se habla de algo caro, dicen los viejitos de Lima: "¡Es más caro que la camisa de Margarita Pareja!"

Éste es el cuento de Miguelín que escribió el padre de Meche y Diana.

MIGUELÍN

Miguelín era un ratoncito muy aventurero. Vivía en una jaula muy cómoda y estaba bastante contento. Pero quería conocer el mundo. Un día, el muchacho que lo cuidaba no cerró bien la puerta. Entonces, Miguelín sacó el hocico y miró a su alrededor. No vio a nadie y decidió salir. Se fue a la calle donde encontró a un ratón anciano y muy sabio.

—Perdone, señor. Tengo ganas de conocer el mundo. ¿Adónde debo ir? —preguntó Miguelín.

—Pues, mira, chico. Aquí estás muy bien. La vida es tranquila y segura. Pero si insistes en conocer el mundo, no hay como Caracas. Súbete a ese carro y puedes llegar fácilmente.

Así fue como Miguelín llegó a la gran ciudad de Caracas. Quedó asombrado. Había gente por todas partes y edificios enormes. Tenía mucho cuidado porque había muchísimo tráfico. Pero también había muchos cafés al aire libre donde encontraba migajas debajo de las mesas.

Durante varios días, Miguelín caminaba y caminaba. Lo miraba todo y se divertía mucho. Pero luego, empezó a extrañar su vida en el campo. En la ciudad había pocos árboles y aunque la comida era muy rica le causaba dolores de estómago. Y lo peor de todo eran los gatos feroces que querían atraparlo. Un día cuando Miguelín buscaba comida, unos gatos lo atacaron. Como él no tenía casa donde esconderse, tuvo que correr y correr hasta encontrar un lugar seguro. Decidió que ya no le gustaba la ciudad y empezó a sentirse muy triste y desesperado. Quería regresar a su casa.

En ese momento, Miguelín oyó una voz. Era una ratoncita que lloraba. Miguelín la buscó y por fin la encontró detrás de un árbol. Se le acercó y le preguntó:

—¿Por qué lloras? ¿Te puedo ayudar?

—¿Quién eres tú?

—Yo soy Miguelín. ¿Y tú?

—Me llamo Minerva y estoy muy triste aquí en la ciudad. Quiero regresar al campo donde estaba muy contenta y llevaba una vida muy tranquila en mi casa.

—¿Tú también? Yo vine a la ciudad hace poco y también quiero regresar. ¿Vamos juntos?

—¡Oh, sí! —dijo la ratoncita.

Y así fue. Miguelín y Minerva regresaron al campo donde encontraron una buena casa y criaron una familia de bellos ratoncitos. Y vivieron muy felices.

CHARLEMOS UN POCO

A. **PARA EMPEZAR . . .** Pon en orden cronológico el cuento de "La camisa de Margarita Pareja".

1. Margarita rehusó comer y se puso muy enferma.
2. Don Honorato era el hombre más rico y más avaro de toda la ciudad.
3. El padre de Margarita le dio una camisa que valía una fortuna.
4. Luis pidió permiso para casarse con Margarita.
5. Margarita Pareja era una joven muy hermosa y modesta.
6. El padre de Margarita juró no dar a su hija más que una camisa de novia.
7. Cuando Luis vio a la hermosa Margarita por primera vez, se enamoró.
8. El padre de Margarita decidió aprobar la boda de Luis y Margarita.
9. Por eso, los viejitos de Lima dicen que algo es más caro que la camisa de Margarita Pareja.
10. Luis Alcázar era el sobrino de don Honorato.
11. Don Honorato dijo que el padre de Margarita insultó a su sobrino.
12. Don Honorato insistió en que Margarita tendría que casarse con sólo la ropa que llevaba puesta y nada más.
13. El padre de Margarita no le dio permiso a Luis para casarse con su hija.

B. **¿QUÉ DECIMOS . . . ?** Según el cuento de Miguelín, indica si las oraciones son ciertas o falsas. Si son falsas, corrígelas.

1. Miguelín estaba muy triste cuando vivía en una jaula.
2. Miguelín salió para conocer el mundo.
3. A Miguelín le gustaba la comida de Caracas.
4. Miguelín empezó a extrañar los árboles del campo.
5. Miguelín y unos gatos se hicieron buenos amigos.
6. Miguelín conoció a una ratoncita en Caracas.
7. Minerva también era del campo.
8. A Minerva le gustaba la vida de la ciudad.
9. Minerva y Miguelín decidieron vivir en Caracas.
10. Miguelín y Minerva tuvieron una familia.

Imperfect: Description of an ongoing situation

The imperfect is used when describing past situations that are viewed as in-progress.

Había un sillón grande en la sala de familia.
La lámpara **estaba** en la mesita.

See **¿Por qué se dice así?,**
page G61, section 4.7.

C. ¡Qué desastre!   Máximo acaba de limpiar su cuarto y ahora todo está en su lugar. ¿Dónde estaban estas cosas antes de limpiarlo según el dibujo?

 EJEMPLO   libros
Los libros estaban en el piso. o
Había libros en el piso.

1. suéter	**3.** camiseta	**5.** mochila	**7.** cuadernos
2. camisa	**4.** sombrero	**6.** libros	**8.** calcetines

CH. ¡Qué emoción!   ¿Cómo se sentían estas personas en las situaciones indicadas?

 EJEMPLO   nosotros: perder los partidos de fútbol
Cuando perdíamos los partidos de fútbol, nos sentíamos muy tristes.

VOCABULARIO ÚTIL:

contento	triste	furioso	aburrido
emocionado	nervioso	preocupado	tranquilo
desesperado	asustado	cansado	asombrado

1. papá: comprar un carro nuevo
2. mamá: encontrar una serpiente en la casa
3. abuelitos: pasar la semana en el campo
4. yo: recibir una carta de amor
5. hermanos: no haber buenos programas en la televisión
6. mi mejor amigo y yo: hacer mucho ejercicio
7. tú: encontrar un perro feroz
8. papá: tener una cita con el dentista
9. Miguelín: unos gatos atacarlo
10. amigos: recibir una mala nota

Imperfect: Description of emotional states

The imperfect is used when describing emotional states in the past.

Todos nos **sentíamos** muy contentos.
Él me **amaba** locamente.

See **¿Por qué se dice así?,**
page G61, section 4.7.

D. ¡Qué diferente! ¿Cómo eran estas personas cuando tenían ocho años?

Manuel   Manuela

EJEMPLO   **Manuel y Manuela eran bajos y morenos. Los dos eran delgados. Les gustaba jugar tenis y jugaban todos los días.**

1. Jaime

2. Rafael

3. Adela

4. Paulina

5. Lorenzo

6. Melinda

7. ¿tú?

8. ¿tu amigo(a)?

E. Un cuento. ¿Qué les pasó a estos cochinillos aventureros?

MODELO haber una vez / familia / cochinillos
Había una vez una familia de cochinillos.

1. todos vivir / contento / rancho
2. un día / 3 cochinillos / salir / casa
3. ver / lancha / cerca / río
4. 2 cochinillos / subir / lancha
5. de repente / lancha / empezar a separarse de la orilla
6. todos / cochinillos / gritar / gritar / pero nadie / oír
7. cochinillo que / estar / la orilla / correr a buscar / abuelo
8. abuelo / ser / sabio
9. abuelo y cochinillo / regresar / río
10. cuando / 2 cochinillos / ver / abuelo / saltar al agua / salvarse

F. Había una vez . . . Éste es el cuento de una chica que se llamaba Adriana. Con tu compañero(a), describe cada dibujo para completar el cuento.

 EJEMPLO ser / día
hacer / tiempo
Era un día de octubre y hacía muy buen tiempo. o
Era un día muy bonito y hacía sol.

1. Adriana / estar en casa
estar / aburrido

2. llamar / amiga Emi
decidir pasear / bicicleta

3. ir / parque
haber / mucha gente

4. en / parque / tomar helados
mirar / lago / lanchas

5. de repente / empezar a llover
decidir regresar / casa

6. en casa / jugar a las damas
divertirse / la tarde

CHARLEMOS UN POCO MÁS

A. En agosto viajaba por . . . ¿Cómo pasaban el verano cuando eran niños tus compañeros de clase? Usa la cuadrícula que tu profesor(a) te va a dar para entrevistarlos. Pregúntales si de costumbre hacían estas actividades en el verano. Pídeles a las personas que contesten afirmativamente que firmen el cuadrado apropiado. Recuerda que no se permite que una persona firme más de un cuadrado.

MODELO   *Tú:*   **¿Ibas al cine?**

B. La familia Elgorriaga. Los fines de semana siempre eran muy interesantes en la familia Elgorriaga. Tu profesor(a) te va a dar un dibujo de las actividades de la familia Elgorriaga pero no aparecen los nombres de todos los miembros de la familia. Dile a tu compañero(a) qué hacían las personas y los animales indicados en tu dibujo y pídele que te diga lo que hacían las personas en su dibujo. Escribe los nombres que faltan en tu dibujo en el blanco apropiado.

C. La vida de . . . Con un compañero(a), crea y escribe una descripción de una semana típica el año pasado en la vida de uno de tus personajes favoritos. Puedes escoger a un personaje histórico, una estrella de cine, un cantante, un deportista o una caricatura cómica, o puedes inventar a un personaje original. Si quieres, incluye dibujos del personaje.

CH. ¿Era muy diferente? ¿Cómo era la vida social de tu profesor(a) cuando era un(a) joven de quince o dieciséis años? ¿Era similar o muy diferente de tu vida ahora? Con tu compañero(a), prepara por escrito una lista de ocho a diez preguntas para hacerle a tu profesor(a).

Dramatizaciones

A. Todos los veranos íbamos a . . . Tú y tu compañero(a) están hablando del lugar favorito adonde iba toda la familia para pasar las vacaciones. Mencionen por qué iban allá y qué hacían para divertirse. Dramaticen esta conversación.

B. ¡Era ideal! Imagínate que antes de venir a este colegio tú vivías en un lugar ideal donde la escuela y la vida eran muy diferentes. Tú le estás explicando a tu compañero(a) cómo era tu vida antes de venir acá. Claro, tu compañero(a) quiere hacerte muchas preguntas. Dramaticen la conversación.

LEAMOS AHORA

Estrategias para leer:
Hacer un resumen

Sumarios. Generalmente cuando leemos lecturas informativas, tratamos de recordar lo que leímos. Los resúmenes nos ayudan a hacer esto.

La forma más fácil de hacer un sumario es empezar por tomar buenos apuntes al leer. Luego, hay que escribir una oración que resuma la lectura entera y una oración que resuma cada párrafo de la lectura.

Para hacer un resumen de la lectura *Los enigmáticos diseños del Valle de Nasca*, el lector probablemente empezó por sacar estos apuntes muy generales:

Tema	Comienzo	Desarrollo	Conclusiones
diseños nascas	enormes diseños geométricos y de animales	descubiertos por Kroeber y Mejía en 1926 y estudiados por Reiche en los años 1940	creados por una gran civilización precolombina

Luego el lector escribió el siguiente sumario en una oración:

Los diseños nascas, enormes dibujos geométricos y de animales, fueron descubiertos en 1926 por Alfred Kroeber y Toribio Mejía y estudiados en 1940 por María Reiche. Fueron creados por una de las más grandes civilizaciones precolombinas.

Ahora para preparar un sumario, empieza por leer el artículo una vez sin parar para tener una idea general del contenido. Luego, prepara un cuadro de cuatro columnas como el anterior. Completa el cuadro al leer cada párrafo detenidamente, haciéndote estas preguntas cada vez:
(1) ¿De qué se trata el párrafo? (2) ¿Cómo comienza?
(3) ¿Cómo se desarrolla? (4) ¿Cómo termina?

Usa la información en tu cuadro para escribir un sumario de una oración para cada uno de los seis párrafos de la lectura. Luego, compara tus sumarios con los de dos o tres compañeros. Revísalos si encuentras que no incluiste alguna información importante o si incluiste información insignificante.

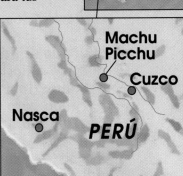

LOS ENIGMÁTICOS DISEÑOS DEL VALLE DE NASCA

La figura de este mono es de dimensiones tan grandes como las de un terreno de fútbol.

Sabemos que el pueblo nasca, como las grandes civilizaciones precolombinas de regiones situadas más al norte: los mochicas, los maya y los aztecas, fue caracterizado por la construcción de templos, pirámides y complejos acueductos subterráneos. Sabemos también que sus habitantes crearon cerámicas que son obras de exquisita belleza y a la vez fueron feroces guerreros que les cortaban la cabeza a sus enemigos y las exhibían como trofeos.

Pero no es por eso que recordamos la cultura nasca. No. Es por los fabulosos diseños trazados en las rocas y arenas del desierto . . . enormes triángulos, trapecios y espirales que cubren incontables hectáreas de una tierra tan árida como la de un paisaje lunar . . . animales estilizados de tamaños tan inmensos que sólo pueden ser contemplados desde un avión.

¿Cuándo se descubrieron las líneas de Nasca? Sabemos que en 1926, dos prestigiosos arqueólogos—el norteamericano Alfred Kroeber y el peruano Toribio Mejía—observaron algunas líneas en el desierto peruano pero pensaron que eran intentos prehistóricos de irrigación. Luego, durante la década de los años treinta, unos pilotos comenzaron a observar en sus vuelos que las líneas formaban figuras. Pero no fue hasta los años cuarenta que el mundo comenzó a tomar conciencia de estos dibujos, gracias en parte a los esfuerzos de María Reiche, una maestra escolar de matemáticas, de origen alemán. Tanto se interesó María Reiche en estas figuras que dedicó el resto de su vida a estudiarlas.

¿Dónde vivieron los nascas? ¿En el desierto? El descubrimiento en la región sudeste de Perú de una ciudad perdida de 2,000 años de antigüedad está arrojando una nueva luz sobre los famosos dibujos del desierto peruano. "Indudablemente ésta fue una gran civilización . . . En muchos aspectos, los nascas fueron verdaderos genios", dice la arqueóloga Helaine I. Silverman (de la Universidad de Illinois, en Estados Unidos), quien descubrió los restos de lo que ella considera "el mayor núcleo de población de la cultura nasca".

Ahora sabemos que el trazado de los diseños nascas no dependió de un alto nivel de habilidades tecnológicas. Niños de las escuelas peruanas han duplicado algunas de las mayores figuras geométricas, utilizando estacas, cuerdas y montañas de rocas. Una explicación para las elaboradas figuras de animales es que ellas fueron ampliadas a base de los diseños familiares encontrados en los tejidos, utilizando para ello el mismo sistema de rejillas.

La arqueóloga Silverman no tiene duda de que "las figuras fueron elaboradas para rendir culto a los dioses . . . básicamente pienso que todo el mundo nasca se entregaba con dedicación al trazado de estas líneas y figuras que hoy tanto admiramos".

Esta ave mide más de 200 metros de largo. ¿Sabes cuántos pies hay en 200 metros?

¿Son las figuras nascas diseños de tejidos familiares ampliados?

Los nascas crearon cerámicas de exquisita belleza.

Verifiquemos

Estudia el esquema que sigue sobre el pueblo nasca. Luego prepara un esquema similar sobre cada uno de los siguientes temas.

I. El pueblo nasca
II. Las líneas nascas
III. Descubrimiento de las líneas de Nasca
IV. El trazado de los diseños nascas

I. El pueblo nasca
A. Vivieron hace 2000 años
B. Fue una gran civilización
   1. Templos
   2. Pirámides
   3. Acueductos subterráneos
C. Practicaron diferentes profesiones
   1. Artistas
      a. Cerámica de exquisita belleza
      b. Dibujos de nasca
   2. Guerreros
      a. Feroces
      b. Les cortaban la cabeza a enemigos
      c. Exhibían cabezas como trofeos

ESCRIBAMOS AHORA

Estrategias para escribir:
Decidir en un punto de vista

A. Empezar. Un buen escritor siempre piensa cuidadosamente antes de decidir en el punto de vista que va a representar. Por ejemplo, en un artículo sobre un partido de fútbol, ¿crees que el equipo que ganó va a describir el partido de una manera diferente de la del equipo que perdió? ¡Claro que sí! Cada equipo va a describirlo desde su propio punto de vista.

Ahora repasa todos los cuentos y leyendas que has escuchado y leído en **¡DIME!** DOS. Piensa en los personajes indicados aquí y escribe una oración sobre lo que tú crees que cada personaje opina de lo ocurrido en el cuento. Los comentarios de *La familia Real* ya están escritos.

Cuento/Leyenda	Personaje 1	Personaje 2
1.2 Bailó con un bulto	El joven soldado	Crucita Delgado
1.3 La nuera	El abuelo	El nieto
2.1 La familia Real	**Papá Real:** Somos una familia muy simpática y amistosa. Nos encanta charlar pero la gente del pueblo no es muy amistosa.	**Gente del pueblo:** Son muy raros, aburridos y chismosos. Tuvimos que dejar de invitarlos porque hablan constantemente y no dicen nada.
2.2 El pájaro de los siete colores	El hijo mayor	El hijo menor
2.3 El león y las pulgas	El león	El líder de las pulgas
3.1 Tío Tigre y Tío Conejo	Tío Tigre	Tío Conejo
3.2 Los tres consejos	Esposo	Esposa
3.3 La casa embrujada	La costurera	El perro
4.1 El Sombrerón	El Sombrerón	Madre de Celina
4.2 El gallo de la cresta de oro	El gallo	El ladrón
4.3 La camisa de Margarita Pareja	Margarita Pareja	El padre de Margarita

B. Planear. Ahora tú vas a escribir uno de los cuentos mencionados en la actividad **A** desde el punto de vista de uno de los personajes. Al empezar a planear tu cuento, selecciona uno de los cuentos y el personaje que tú vas a representar. Luego en dos columnas, prepara una lista de todos los eventos principales en tu cuento y cómo ve esos eventos tu personaje.

Cuento: _____

Personaje: _____

Eventos:	Punto de vista de mi personaje:

C. Primer borrador. Ahora, usa la información de las listas que preparaste en la actividad **B** para escribir el primer borrador de tu cuento. No olvides que estás relatando el cuento desde el punto de vista de un personaje particular.

CH. Compartir. Comparte el primer borrador de tu cuento con dos compañeros de clase. Pídeles sugerencias. Pregúntales si es lógico tu cuento, si hay algo que no entienden, si hay algo que puedes o debes eliminar. Dales la misma información sobre sus cuentos cuando ellos te pidan sugerencias.

D. Revisar. Haz cambios en tu cuento a base de las sugerencias de tus compañeros. Luego, antes de entregar el cuento, compártelo una vez más con dos compañeros de clase. Esta vez pídeles que revisen la estructura y la puntuación. En particular, pídeles que revisen el uso de los verbos en el pretérito y el imperfecto.

E. Versión final. Escribe la versión final de tu cuento incorporando las correcciones que tus compañeros de clase te indicaron. Entrega una copia en limpio a tu profesor(a).

F. Publicar. Junten todos los cuentos en un solo volumen titulado, **¡DIME! DOS: Otro punto de vista.** Guarden su primer "libro" en la sala de clase para leer cuando tengan un poco de tiempo libre.

Recomiendo que . . .

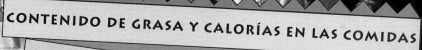

CONTENIDO DE GRASA Y CALORÍAS EN LAS COMIDAS

ALIMENTO	PORCIÓN	GRASA (Gm.)	CALORÍAS
FRUTAS Y VEGETALES			
Maíz	1 mazorca	1.0	100
Manzana	1 mediana	00.5	80
Uvas	10	00.07	15
CEREALES, GRANOS Y PASTA			
Arroz blanco, cocido	1/2 taza	0.13	100
Avena	3/4 taza	1.8	110
Granola	1/3 taza	0.0	88
Pasta, cocida	1/2 taza	0.0	80
CARNES, PESCADO, HUEVOS Y AVES			
Chuletas de cerdo	3 oz.	15.8	233
Huevo	1 grande	5.6	80
Langosta	3 oz.	0.46	83
Pollo, carne oscura	3 oz.	8.3	76
PANES Y GALLETAS			
Pan	1 pedazo	1.0	75
Galletas de trigo	4	1.4	36
LECHE Y PRODUCTOS DE LA LECHE			
Leche	1 taza	8.1	150
Queso parmesano	1 cda.	1.5	33

¡ Hagan más ejercicio !

"Te recomiendo la leche más completa pero sin grasa"

Millie García
L.N. Ph.D
Nutricionista.

Mi Vaquita

Mi Vaquita, la leche que tiene todas las vitaminas, proteínas y minerales necesarios para tu buena salud, y la de tu familia. Además, Mi Vaquita tiene un bajo contenido de sodio y colesterol. Es la económica leche en polvo que se disuelve al instante. Es 100% natural, deliciosa y fácil de digerir. Por eso la usamos en casa y la recomiendo profesionalmente.

Mi Vaquita. Lo mejor de la leche y sin grasa. Naturalmente mejor.

Valle Arriba Centro Atlético

La nueva forma de estar en forma

- Las más modernas instalaciones: circuito de máquinas Body Master, sala de pesas libres, centro cardiovascular, canchas múltiples, gimnasia olímpica, sauna vapor
- Supervisión profesional
- Asesoramiento médico especializado
- Restaurante
- Tienda de deportes
- Peluquería unisex

Visítenos en la Av. Principal Colinas de Valle Arriba (frente al segundo retorno), Urb. Colinas de Valle Arriba

telfs. 238.35.46/238.38.66/238.50.28

El ejercicio aeróbico

Primer paso para una vida mejor

El ejercicio aeróbico desarrollado hace relativamente pocos años por un especialista norteamericano, el doctor Kenneth Cooper, no sólo ha demostrado ser un elemento clave para mejorar nuestra condición física, sino una valiosa herramienta para adquirir una mejor calidad de vida

¿ Qué piensas tú ?

1. ¿Para qué son estos anuncios?

2. ¿Qué resultados prometen los anuncios?

3. ¿Qué hacen los jóvenes en la foto del parque? ¿Cómo crees que se sienten los padres o los profesores de estos jóvenes sabiendo que están allí, en el parque?

4. Si un(a) amigo(a) se pasa todo el día frente al televisor comiendo y viendo la tele, ¿qué consejos podrías darle?

5. ¿Qué recomendaciones puedes darle a una persona para que tenga buena salud?

6. Por todo el mundo, nosotros, los estadounidenses, tenemos la reputación de estar obsesionados por la buena salud y un buen estado físico. En tu opinión, ¿tienen las mismas actitudes hacia esto en otros países? ¿Por qué crees eso?

7. ¿Qué vocabulario se necesita para hacer sugerencias o recomendaciones?

8. ¿Qué crees que vas a aprender a decir en esta lección?

EL HIJO LADRÓN

En este cuento guatemalteco, vamos a ver cómo un ladrón se convirtió en sub-alcalde protector de su pueblo.

En un pueblecito guatemalteco vivía una viuda honrada. Era madre de cuatro hijos, varones todos y de temperamento muy diferente. Uno era sastre, otro zapatero, otro carpintero y el menor . . . era ladrón. Era inteligente el más joven, pero nada le interesaba y prefería la vida fácil del robo. La viuda sufría mucho por este hijo. Siempre le decía, "Hijo, es necesario que trabajes como tus hermanos. No es bueno que seas ladrón".

Un día el alcalde del pueblo publicó este anuncio:

La Honorable Alcaldía Municipal busca un hombre muy inteligente que pueda proteger al pueblo de ladrones y asesinos. La persona que desee ocupar este puesto debe pasar tres pruebas pertinentes.

Cuando vio el anuncio, el hijo ladrón le preguntó a su madre, "¿No es lógico que un ladrón como yo sea el mejor candidato?" Su madre contestó, "Es posible que tengas razón, mi hijo". Inmediatamente el hijo ladrón reaccionó diciendo, "Pues, mamá, ve y pregunta cuáles son las tres pruebas". Y así lo hizo la buena mujer.

Para probar si el sistema de seguridad del pueblo era adecuado, el futuro sub-alcalde tenía que intentar robar cuatro mulas cargadas de plata y protegidas por un capitán y cuatro soldados.

El hijo ladrón se fue a hablar inmediatamente con su hermano, el zapatero. "Es preciso que tú me hagas un par de botas de primera categoría. Es importante que sean excelentes". Y así lo hizo su hermano.

Cuando los soldados salieron con las mulas cargadas de plata, el ladrón los esperaba oculto. Puso una de las hermosas botas en medio del camino. Los soldados la encontraron y dijeron, "¡Es curioso que sólo una bota esté aquí! ¡Qué lástima, porque es una maravilla!" Y la dejaron en el camino.

Al poco rato, se encontraron con la segunda bota y el capitán dijo, "¡Dios mío! ¡La otra bota! El que llegue primero a la primera bota se hace dueño de las dos". Y todos se fueron corriendo a buscar la primera bota.

Y en ese momento el hijo ladrón aprovechó para robarse las mulas y la plata.

El alcalde se enfureció tanto que puso, como segunda prueba, una segunda carga de mulas protegidas esta vez por diez soldados fuertes y valientes.

El ladrón fue de prisa a ver a su hermano, el sastre. "Es preciso que tú me hagas una sotana de fraile".
Y así lo hizo su hermano.

Los soldados encontraron al falso fraile en el camino diciendo a grandes gritos, "El fin del mundo está muy cerca. Arrepiéntanse".

Los soldados oyeron esto y aterrorizados, le pidieron la bendición al falso fraile. Éste les dio una botella de agua bendita para beber inmediatamente. Los soldados pidieron otra, porque les gustó, y luego una botella más para cada uno.

No sabían que en realidad el "agua bendita" era un té para dormir y pronto todos se quedaron profundamente dormidos.

Otra vez el hijo ladrón robó fácilmente la valiosa carga.

Esta vez el alcalde se puso furioso, pero empezó a admirar la inteligencia del ladrón. Como tercera prueba, dijo que el ladrón tenía que entrar en su propia casa y robar las sábanas de la cama en que dormía.

Esta vez el ladrón fue a ver a su hermano, el carpintero. "Hermano mío, es necesario que tú me hagas un muñeco grande como un hombre".

Y así lo hizo el carpintero.

Esa noche, cuando todos en casa del alcalde estaban dormidos, el ladrón subió al segundo piso, al dormitorio del alcalde mismo, y puso el muñeco contra la ventana para dar la impresión de ser un hombre a punto de entrar en el dormitorio. Entonces se ocultó a un lado del balcón e hizo un ruido muy fuerte. El alcalde se despertó y cuando vio al "hombre" en la ventana, pensó que alguien lo quería matar. Salió de la casa gritando y pidiendo ayuda.

El ladrón entró en el dormitorio por la ventana, quitó las sábanas de la cama, las dobló cuidadosamente y se las llevó.

El alcalde se dio cuenta de los talentos del joven y lo invitó a ser sub-alcalde protector del pueblo. El nuevo protector tuvo mucho éxito en su puesto durante muchos años.

¿QUÉ DECIMOS...?

Al dar consejos y expresar opiniones

1 ¡Despiértate!

Luis y Meche están en su última clase del día.

¿QUÉ DECIMOS...?

Al dar consejos y expresar opiniones

1 ¡Despiértate!

Luis y Meche están en su última clase del día.

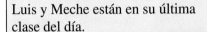

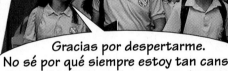

2 ¡No seas así!

Meche y Diana están en camino a casa.

No sabes lo que me pasó en clase hoy. Otra vez me dormí. Luis tuvo que despertarme. ¡Qué vergüenza! ¡Imagínate! No sé qué voy a hacer. Ojalá que no me pase otra vez.

¿No dormiste bien anoche? ¿A qué hora te acostaste?

No es eso. Dormí más de ocho horas.

Entonces, es posible que necesites hacer más ejercicio. El ejercicio te da energía, ¿sabes?

Supongo que tienes razón.

Escúchame, Meche. Mañana empiezo mi nuevo trabajo como instructora de ejercicios aeróbicos. ¿Por qué no me acompañas?

No seas así, Meche.

No sé, estoy demasiado cansada. Además, tengo mucha tarea este fin de semana.

3 ¡Es necesario que hagas ejercicio!

Meche está dormida en su cuarto.

¿Qué te pasa, hija?

No es posible que tengas tanto sueño a esta hora. ¿No dormiste bien anoche?

¿Qué almorzaste?

Sí, mamá. Pero no tengo energía para nada. Hasta me dormí en clase hoy.

Unas papitas fritas, nada más.

¡Meche! Es importante comer comida nutritiva. Y también es necesario que hagas ejercicio todos los días. ¿Por qué no vas mañana con Diana a su clase de ejercicios aeróbicos?

Pero, allí también tienen piscina. Puedes nadar. Eso sí te gusta.

Ay, no me gusta saltar tanto . . . y menos en compañía de otros.

Bueno, sí. Déjame pensarlo, mamá. Quizás vaya con Diana mañana.

4 ¡No comas eso!

Luis está con su mamá en la cocina.

Luis, ¿qué buscas? Ya casi es la hora de la comida.

¿Un refresco y chocolate? ¡Por favor, hijo! No comas más eso. Me dices que no quieres engordar más y mira lo que estás comiendo.

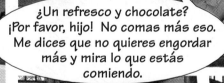

Tienes razón, mamá. Debo tener más cuidado. Voy a ponerme a dieta. Tengo que adelgazar si quiero que las muchachas me presten más atención.

Sólo un refresco, mamá.

¿Por qué no te haces socio del Club Atlético? Creo que tienen piscinas, pesas y clases de ejercicios aeróbicos.

Excelente idea, mamá. Además, es probable que el ejercicio me ayude a dormir mejor de noche, ¿no?

Sí, claro. Además, es mejor que salgas de casa por la tarde y que no veas tanta televisión. Y además, tampoco es bueno que comas tanta chuchería.

Mira la hora que es, hijo. Ven. Ayúdame a poner la mesa.

A. **PARA EMPEZAR . . .** Pon las oraciones en orden cronológico según el cuento de ''El hijo ladrón''.

1. El hijo ladrón le preguntó a su madre, ''¿No es lógico que un ladrón como yo sea el mejor candidato?''
2. Como prueba, dijo que el ladrón tenía que entrar en su propia casa y robarse las sábanas de la cama en que dormía.
3. El futuro sub-alcalde tenía que intentar robar cuatro mulas cargadas de plata y protegidas por un capitán y cuatro soldados.
4. En un pueblecito guatemalteco vivía una viuda con sus cuatro hijos.
5. El alcalde del pueblo anunció que buscaba un sub-alcalde.
6. El hijo ladrón robó fácilmente la carga valiosa.
7. En realidad el ''agua bendita'' era un té para dormir y pronto todos se quedaron dormidos.
8. Los soldados encontraron una sola bota en el medio del camino.
9. ''Mamá'', dijo el hijo, ''ve y pregunta cuáles son las tres pruebas''.
10. El alcalde invitó al ladrón a ser sub-alcalde del pueblo.
11. Como segunda prueba tenía que robar una segunda carga de mulas protegidas esta vez por diez soldados.
12. Uno era sastre, otro zapatero, otro carpintero y el menor . . . era ladrón.
13. ''El que llegue primero a la primera bota se hace dueño de las dos''.

B. **¿QUÉ DECIMOS . . .?** ¿Quién recibe estos consejos? ¿Meche o Luis?

| Meche | Luis |

1. No es bueno que veas tanta televisión.
2. Es necesario que hagas más ejercicio.
3. No te comas ese chocolate ahora.
4. Es mejor que salgas de casa por la tarde.
5. Es importante comer comida nutritiva.
6. No es bueno que comas tantos dulces.
7. ¿Por qué no te haces socio del Club Atlético?
8. ¿Por qué no me acompañas a la clase de ejercicios aeróbicos?

C. El futuro. ¿Cómo reaccionas a estos pronósticos sobre tu futuro?

MODELO   Vas a trabajar en otro país.
        ¡Chévere! Ojalá que trabaje en otro país. o
        ¡Ay, no! Ojalá que no trabaje en otro país.

1. Vas a recibir honores en la universidad.
2. Vas a practicar muchos deportes.
3. Vas a salir con personas importantes.
4. Vas a vivir en una mansión.
5. Vas a tener que trabajar mucho.
6. Vas a participar en los Juegos Olímpicos.
7. Vas a casarte pronto.
8. Vas a inventar algo nuevo.
9. Vas a descubrir una nueva medicina.
10. Vas a comer en restaurantes elegantes todos los días.

CH. Esperanzas. ¿Qué esperanzas tienen Yolanda y Rafael para el Año Nuevo?

 MODELO   nosotros / ganar / todo / partidos
        Ojalá que nosotros ganemos todos los partidos.

1. tú / tener / bueno / suerte
2. entrenador / escogerme para / equipo / béisbol
3. yo / aprender a tocar / guitarra
4. profesores / no exigir / mucho / tarea
5. tú y yo / asistir a / mucho / conciertos
6. nuestro / familias / hacer / viaje / interesante
7. Trini / prestarme / más atención
8. todo / estudiantes / sacar / bueno / notas

D. ¿Bueno o malo? Estás en una nueva escuela. ¿Qué esperas?

MODELO   clases no ser difíciles
        Ojalá que las clases no sean difíciles.

1. profesores dar buenas notas
2. haber un club de español
3. estudiantes ir al patio a comer
4. padres no ir a hablar con el director
5. clases no ser difíciles
6. mejor amigo(a) y yo estar en la misma clase
7. profesores saber hablar español
8. haber bailes todos los fines de semana
9. nadie verme llegar tarde
10. saber todo lo que me pregunte la profesora
11. director ser muy simpático
12. estar muy contento(a) en esta escuela

**Present subjunctive:
Regular verb endings**

-ar	-er, -ir
-e	-a
-es	-as
-e	-a
-emos	-amos
-en	-an

Ojalá que mamá lo **compre**.
Ojalá que me **escriba** hoy.
Ojalá que **tengan** el dinero.

*See **¿Por qué se dice así?**,
page G66, section 5.1.*

**Present subjunctive:
Verbs with irregular stems**

dar	estar	ir
dé	esté	vaya
des	estés	vayas
dé	esté	vaya
demos	estemos	vayamos
den	estén	vayan

saber	ser	ver
sepa	sea	vea
sepas	seas	veas
sepa	sea	vea
sepamos	seamos	veamos
sepan	sean	vean

haber: haya

Ojalá que no **sepa** mi número.
Ojalá que **estemos** todos aquí.
Ojalá que **haya** más boletos.

*See **¿Por qué se dice así?**,
page G68, section 5.2.*

Impersonal expressions

Certainty:
Es cierto   Es seguro
Es claro

Es cierto que hace mucho frío.
Es claro que vamos a ganar.

Other impersonal expressions:
Es bueno   Es necesario
Es curioso   Es posible
Es dudoso   Es preciso
Es fantástico   Es probable
Es importante   Es terrible
Es mejor   Es triste

Es bueno que hagas tanto ejercicio.
Es terrible que vean tanta televisión.

See **¿Por qué se dice así?,**
page G69, section 5.3.

E. Recomendaciones. Tu amigo(a) no tiene mucha energía.
¿Qué le recomiendas?

 EJEMPLO   **Es malo que tomes mucho helado.**

1.   2.   3.   4.

5.   6.   7.   8.

F. Invitados.   Tus padres están limpiando la casa porque hoy
vienen unos invitados a cenar. ¿Qué sugieres hacer tú para
ayudarles y qué te contestan?

 MODELO   limpiar el cuarto de baño
                  Tú: **¿Limpio el cuarto de baño?**
                  Mamá (Papá): **Claro. Es necesario que limpies el
                                   cuarto de baño.**

1. pasar la aspiradora   6. poner la mesa
2. hacer las camas   7. pasar un trapo a los muebles
3. cortar el césped   de la sala
4. barrer el patio   8. preparar los entremeses
5. lavar las ventanas   9. sacar la basura

G. ¡Qué talento!   Tu clase de español va a hacer un programa cultural. ¿Cómo van a participar todos?

 MODELO   tocar la guitarra
Es probable que [. . . y . . .] toquen la guitarra. o
Es probable que [. . .] y yo toquemos la guitarra.

1. bailar	**6.** organizar el programa
2. escribir el programa	**7.** comprar los refrescos
3. tocar el piano	**8.** traer las sillas
4. recibir al público	**9.** estar en el programa
5. hacer los anuncios	**10.** ir por la comida

H. Problemas.   Toda tu familia dice que tú das muy buenos consejos. ¿Qué consejos das cuando tus parientes te dicen sus problemas?

 MODELO   no dormir bien
ser / importante hacer ejercicio
Pariente: **No duermo bien.**
Tú: **Es importante que hagas ejercicio.**

1. necesitar perder peso
ser / recomendable ponerse a dieta
2. no tener energía
ser / mejor nadar todos los días
3. siempre tener sueño
ser / importante descansar bastante
4. no poder meter goles
ser / recomendable practicar más
5. no conocer a nadie
ser / importante hacerse socio de un club
6. no saber bailar
ser / recomendable ir a una clase de baile
7. estar aburrido(a)
ser / preciso salir más

I. El mundo.   ¿Qué opinas tú de estas situaciones mundiales?

 EJEMPLO   Hay mucha contaminación en el mundo.
Es una lástima que haya mucha contaminación en el mundo.

1. Pocas personas en Estados Unidos hablan otra lengua.
2. Muchas personas europeas hablan dos o tres lenguas.
3. Algunos países no practican la democracia.
4. Muchas personas no saben nada de la política.
5. Las familias latinoamericanas son muy unidas.
6. Muchas personas no prestan atención al medio ambiente.
7. Cada año hay menos árboles en la selva.
8. Hay poco crimen en algunas ciudades mundiales.

CHARLEMOS UN POCO MÁS

A. Galletitas de fortuna. Tú trabajas en una panadería china donde tu responsabilidad es escribir fortunas para poner en las galletitas de fortuna. Es importante siempre escribir fortunas positivas y negativas. Escribe unas quince fortunas. Luego léeselas a un(a) compañero(a) para ver si reacciona positiva o negativamente.

 EJEMPLO *Tú escribes y lees:* **Hoy vas a conocer a un millonario.**
Tu compañero(a): **Ojalá que conozca a un millonario hoy.**

B. ¡Necesito sus consejos! ¿Tienes algún problema ahora? Pues, ésta es tu oportunidad para recibir consejos de tus compañeros de clase. Escribe una breve descripción de tu problema en media hoja de papel pero no firmes tu nombre — todos los problemas deben ser anónimos. Tu profesor(a) va a recoger todos los problemas y va a leerlos uno por uno. Entonces, toda la clase va a dar consejos.

 EJEMPLO *Problema:* **Mis padres no me permiten salir de noche durante la semana.**
Clase: **Es mejor que pidas permiso para salir una o dos veces al mes, nada más.** o
Es posible que tus padres tengan razón. Debes quedarte en casa a estudiar.

C. ¡Un desfile! La semana que viene la banda de la escuela va a marchar en un desfile por las calles principales de tu ciudad. Tú y tu amigo(a) son los directores estudiantiles de la banda. Ahora están preparando una lista de consejos que van a tener que darles a los miembros de la banda. Preparen su lista y léansela a la clase.

 EJEMPLO **Es importante que todos los músicos practiquen mucho.**

Dramatizaciones

A. ¡Ojalá ganemos! Tú y tu amigo(a) son candidatos en las elecciones de su escuela. Ahora están haciéndose recomendaciones sobre lo que deben hacer si van a ganar. Dramaticen su discusión.

B. Una excursión a . . . Tú y dos amigos son el(la) presidente, el(la) vice-presidente y el(la) secretario(a) del club de español. Ahora están planeando una excursión para todos los miembros. Decidan adónde van, qué van a hacer y todo lo que es necesario hacer antes de salir en su viaje. Dramaticen su conversación.

IMPACTO CULTURAL
Excursiones

Antes de empezar

A. Probablemente . . . Antes de leer la lectura, indica cuáles de las siguientes posibilidades es la más probable, en tu opinión.

1. Los musulmanes conquistaron y controlaron gran parte de la Península Ibérica por casi 800 años, desde 711 hasta 1492.
   a. Obviamente, hay mucha influencia árabe en la cultura española.
   b. Hay muy poca influencia árabe en España por falta de tolerancia religiosa de parte de los musulmanes tanto como de los cristianos.

2. Durante los 800 años de la época musulmana, tres diferentes grupos étnicos y religiosos tuvieron que convivir, o vivir juntos.
   a. Fue una época muy difícil durante la cual hubo muy poco progreso en España porque los tres grupos constantemente estaban guerreando.
   b. Gracias a la tolerancia de los árabes, los tres grupos pudieron trabajar juntos y lograron hacer grandes avances en educación, ciencias y literatura.

3. Fuera de España, los árabes no tuvieron buenas relaciones con los países europeos.
   a. Por eso, los musulmanes nunca compartieron sus conocimientos científicos y técnicos con los países del occidente.
   b. Sabían mucho de las ciencias y el comercio y compartían sus conocimientos con los muchos visitantes de otros países europeos a España.

4. En la arquitectura árabe de esa época son notables los motivos florales, geométricos o caligráficos, el arco de herradura y las paredes cubiertas de azulejos.
   a. Pero cuando los reyes católicos, Fernando e Isabel, reconquistaron España en 1492, destruyeron todos los edificios árabes, en particular los palacios y templos musulmanes.
   b. Por eso en la España de hoy podemos ver grandes mezquitas y hermosos palacios musulmanes.

Estados islámicos en la Península Ibérica

OCÉANO ATLÁNTICO

León · Pamplona · GASCUÑA · Narbonne

Zamora · Zaragoza · Barcelona

Duero · Salamanca

Madrid

Toledo

Lisboa

Córdoba

Sevilla · Guadalquivir

Granada · MAR MEDITERRÁNEO

Islas Baleares

Ceuta

0 ___ 100 millas
0 ___ 100 kilómetros

☐ Estados islámicos
☐ Estados cristianos

B. ¡Por siglos y siglos! Los árabes invadieron y controlaron la mayor parte de España por casi 800 años. Trata de imaginar cómo cambiaría EE.UU. si un país hispano, digamos México, invadiera y controlara nuestro país por 800 años.

1. ¿Por qué no podría México haber invadido EE.UU. hace 800 años? ¿Cuántos años tiene EE.UU.?
2. ¿Cómo era México hace 800 años? ¿Cómo era Estados Unidos?
3. ¿Sería diferente EE.UU. después de 800 años de dominación mexicana? ¿Cómo? Sé específico(a); menciona la religión, la educación, las comidas, la arquitectura, las artes, etc.

España,
*tierra de moros**

Grupos musulmanes* de Asia y África invadieron y conquistaron la Península Ibérica en el año 711 d. de J.C. trayendo con ellos su gran cultura, sin duda una de las más extraordinarias en la historia del mundo. En un largo período que duró ocho siglos, es decir, hasta 1492, los árabes dejaron en la Península una riquísima herencia de conocimientos* científicos, filosóficos y artísticos. Durante este período se fundaron las primeras universidades de la Península y de Europa, y varias ciudades españolas, como Granada,❶ Sevilla,❷ y Toledo,❸ se convirtieron en las ciudades más avanzadas del continente europeo.

Gracias a la tolerancia religiosa de los árabes, esta etapa* de dominio árabe en España se caracterizó por la convivencia* entre principalmente tres diferentes grupos étnicos y religiosos: los judíos,* los musulmanes y los cristianos. En muchos casos hubo fusión de culturas, como la de los españoles cristianos y los árabes, creando un nuevo grupo: los hispanoárabes.

Los sabios* hispanoárabes imitaron a sus maestros árabes y crearon bibliotecas y escuelas como la famosa escuela de traductores de la ciudad de Toledo. En ésta se reunían musulmanes, judíos y cristianos para traducir al latín y al hebreo los conocimientos de matemáticas, astronomía, medicina, física y química aprendidos de la cultura árabe. Hacia 1218, el rey cristiano Alfonso IX de León fundó la Universidad de Salamanca,❹ la primera de España.

Esta etapa de la historia española significó una apertura* hacia el resto del mundo debido en parte al florecimiento agrícola e industrial y de actividad comercial. Por medio de estas relaciones comerciales, empezaron a propagarse* rápidamente numerosos adelantos* científicos y técnicos que llegaban a la Península del Oriente musulmán.

musulmanes
1
árabes que creen en Islam

entendimientos

período
vivir juntos
israelitas

eruditos/
personas
que saben
mucho

entrada
y salida

reproducirse
progresos

En las letras, la cultura árabe fue una de las más literarias de todos los tiempos. Cultivaron la poesía y el canto,* los cuales eran muy importantes para la educación. En la poesía hispanoárabe se incorporaron elementos de la poesía árabe como los temas de guerra y amor. En poemas bilingües llamados *muwashshahas,* intercalan versos árabes y *jarchas.** En prosa, los escritores hispanoárabes tuvieron mucho interés por los cuentos y fábulas orientales. Aun en la lengua española, el árabe ha tenido una gran influencia, empezando con la expresión "ojalá" (*Washah Allah* = quiera Dios) y continuando a un sinnúmero de palabras de agricultura, ciencias y arquitectura: *alfalfa, algodón, acequia, albaricoque, almendra, alcohol, alquimia, álgebra, alhaja, alcázar, alfombra, almohada* . . .

En la arquitectura, los hispanoárabes también se inspiraron en ejemplos orientales. En los edificios construidos en esta época se pueden notar los motivos florales, geométricos o caligráficos.⑤ También el arco de herradura* y las paredes cubiertas de azulejos.* Los ejemplos más hermosos de arquitectura son la mezquita* de Córdoba ⑥ y el palacio de Medina az-Zahra de los siglos VII y IX. De los siglos XI y XII están la mezquita de Sevilla con su famosa Giralda y, en la misma ciudad, la llamada Torre de Oro ⑦ junto al río Guadalquivir. De los siglos XIII–XIV se conserva en Granada el famoso palacio de la Alhambra ⑧ y el Generalife.

el arte de cantar

canciones cortas en español

horseshoe
ladrillo de colores
edificio religioso

Verifiquemos

1. Vuelve a la actividad **A** de **Antes de empezar** y decide si tus respuestas originales fueron correctas o no.
2. Dibuja una puerta en la forma de arco de herradura. ¿Por qué crees que los árabes construyeron estos tipos de puertas? ¿Crees que fue por motivos de seguridad o artísticos?
3. Haz un esquema araña, como el de la página 201 de **Unidad 4**, indicando las contribuciones de los árabes en *(a)* educación *(b)* arquitectura *(c)* literatura y *(ch)* lengua.
4. ¿Qué aspecto de la civilización árabe te interesa más? ¿Por qué?
5. Compara la convivencia de los distintos grupos étnicos de la España musulmana con la convivencia multicultural de Estados Unidos de hoy.

¡Recomiendo que comas aquí!

VERDELECHO Restaurante Naturista

PLATOS PRINCIPALES

	CALORÍAS
PIMIENTOS RELLENOS CON LEGUMBRES Y ARROZ SALVAJE	215
Bs. 800	
PECHUGA DE PAVO CON SALSA DE NUECES	947
Bs. 1050	
PECHUGA DE POLLO CON COULIS DE TOMATES	448
Bs. 930	
GULASH DE LEGUMBRES CON SPAETZLI	945
Bs. 745	
FILETE DE ATÚN CON SALSA "NAIGUATA"	320
Bs. 1110	
LOS PLATOS ANTERIORES SON SERVIDOS CON VEGETALES FRESCOS, ARROZ O PAPAS	56 / 103 Cada Ración

ENTRADAS FRÍAS

	CALORÍAS
TERRINA DE COLIFLOR Y BRÓCOLIS SOBRE ENSALADA DE VEGETALES CHINOS	340
Bs. 870	
PLATO DE FRUTAS TROPICALES CON QUESO RICOTTA	239
Bs. 555	
ENSALADA DE ATÚN "VERDELECHO"	264
Bs. 870	

ENTRADAS CALIENTES

QUICHE PROVENÇALE SOBRE PURÉ DE TOMATES	349
Bs. 555	
OMELETTE DE ESPÁRRAGOS U HONGOS	289/279
Bs. 625	
CREPE DE ESPINACAS, BERROS Y HIERBAS	402
Bs. 415	

POSTRES

TORTA DE PIÑA	Bs. 410	143
TORTA DE FRUTAS	Bs. 410	283
COCTEL DE FRUTAS CON QUESO RICOTTA	Bs. 325	115
GELATINA DE FRESAS	Bs. 315	24

SOPAS

GAZPACHO ANDALUZ	98
Bs. 470	
SOPA DE LENTEJAS CON PLÁTANOS	163
Bs. 415	
CALDO DE POLLO CON LEGUMBRES	165
Bs. 415	

Restaurante Naturista VERDELECHO

¿ Qué piensas tú ?

1. ¿Cuáles comidas reconoces en este menú? ¿Puedes adivinar qué son algunas de las otras comidas?

2. Tu mejor amigo está a dieta porque quiere perder peso. ¿Qué comidas del menú le recomendarías? Otro amigo sólo quiere comer comida saludable. ¿Qué comidas le recomendarías a él? ¿Por qué?

3. Si un amigo venezolano viene a visitarte, ¿cuáles son algunas cosas de la ''cultura norteamericana'' que vas a tener que explicarle? ¿Qué le puedes recomendar que vea y haga en tu ciudad? ¿Qué restaurante le puedes recomendar? ¿Cuáles selecciones del menú le recomendarías? ¿Por qué?

4. ¿A quién le pides consejos cuando los necesitas? ¿A quién le das consejos, aun cuando no te los piden?

5. ¿De qué país crees que son estos tres edificios? ¿Por qué crees eso? ¿Para qué crees que se usaron los edificios originalmente? ¿Por qué crees eso? ¿Por qué crees que hay diferencias tan grandes en la arquitectura de estos edificios? ¿Qué puede haber causado estas diferencias?

6. ¿Qué sabes tú de la invasión de España por los árabes? ¿Cuándo ocurrió? ¿Cuánto tiempo estuvieron los árabes en España? ¿Qué más puedes decir de esta época?

7. Piensa en cómo contestaste estas preguntas y di qué crees que vas a aprender en esta lección.

ASTURIAS
ESPAÑA
ÁFRICA

LA PROFECÍA DE LA GITANA

PARA EMPEZAR
Escuchemos una leyenda española

Entre las leyendas españolas hay muchas que tratan del largo conflicto entre los moros, del norte de África, y los habitantes de la Península Ibérica, que hoy se llama España. Este cuento del siglo VIII, es del príncipe moro, Abd al-Aziz. Relata como se salvó de los soldados de don Pelayo, un noble que vivía en lo que hoy es la provincia de Asturias.

1

Era el año 718 y continuaba en el norte de la Península Ibérica el conflicto entre los soldados de don Pelayo, un noble cristiano, y los del príncipe moro, Abd al-Aziz.

En esta batalla, el ejército de don Pelayo acababa de ganar su primera batalla contra el príncipe moro, Abd al-Aziz.

2

Todos los soldados moros que no murieron en la batalla fueron hechos prisioneros por don Pelayo. Sólo el príncipe y su criado escaparon.

3

Los dos moros estaban casi muertos de fatiga, de hambre y de sed. Pero por miedo de ser descubiertos, decidieron no buscar ayuda, sino escaparse a las montañas donde podrían pasar la noche.

4

Después de caminar hasta la noche, llegaron a una montaña donde descubrieron una cueva inmensa.

El criado dijo, "Ya está bastante oscuro. Sugiero que nos quedemos aquí. Es difícil que nos encuentren".

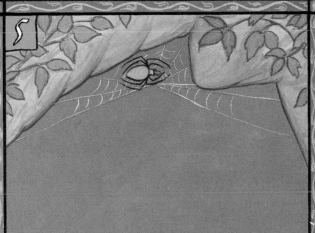

5

El príncipe miró la entrada de la cueva dudosamente, hasta que vio una araña.

"Bien", dijo, "con esta araña aquí, estoy seguro que Alá nos va a proteger".

6

"¿Quizás pienses que estoy loco?" continuó el príncipe. "No, amigo. Es que todavía recuerdo lo que me dijo una gitana en Granada hace seis meses".

"¿Y qué le dijo la gitana?" preguntó el criado.

7

Ella me dijo, "Recomiendo que siempre cuides a las arañas. Sí, sí . . . ¡Insisto en que siempre las respetes y las protejas!"

Como era un consejo algo raro, le pregunté a la gitana por qué me recomendaba eso. Ella contestó, "Porque algún día una araña te va a salvar la vida".

8

Pero el criado estaba tan cansado que se durmió mientras el príncipe hablaba. Viendo eso, el príncipe también se acostó y se durmió.

9

A la mañana siguiente los dos hombres se despertaron al oír voces y pasos cerca de su cueva. "¡Los soldados de don Pelayo!" dijo el príncipe en voz baja.

10

"Vamos a buscar aquí", gritó uno de los soldados.

"Es inútil", contestó otro. "¡Nadie ha entrado allí!"

"¿Y cómo lo sabes?" dijo el primero y empezó a caminar hacia la entrada de la cueva.

11

"¿No tienes ojos? ¿No ves la telaraña que cubre la entrada de un lado al otro? ¡Es imposible que alguien haya entrado aquí!"

"Tienes razón", dijo el primero.

"Vámonos".

12

Y los soldados empezaron a bajar la montaña diciendo, "Tenemos que confesarle a don Pelayo que el príncipe moro y su fiel criado son más listos que nosotros".

13

El príncipe y su compañero, dentro de la cueva, no podían creerlo. "Es la araña providencial de la gitana", dijo el príncipe. "Es un milagro".

Durante la noche, la araña había construido una cortina que cubría la entrada de la cueva.

¿QUÉ DECIMOS...?

Al sugerir o recomendar algo

1 No tengo ganas.

2 Es un buen comienzo.

Bueno, es un buen comienzo. Pero el ejercicio no es suficiente para la buena salud.

Es también importante la nutrición.

...pan, productos lácteos como la leche y el queso. Y sugiero que eviten las comidas grasosas y los dulces.

Les recomiendo que sigan todos una dieta balanceada de frutas, vegetales, carne, ...

¡Ay, no! ¡Ay!

Y es bueno beber por lo menos dos litros de líquido cada día.

¿Esto incluye el café?

En realidad, no deben tomar mucho café. Es preferible que beban jugos y agua. El café puede quitarles el sueño—otro factor importantísimo para la buena salud.

Es recomendable que durmamos ocho horas.

Es buena excusa para no terminar la tarea.

¡Qué lista eres!

3 **Recomiendo que sigas mis consejos.**

¡Ayyy! ¡Me duele todo el cuerpo! Nunca voy a llegar a casa. Apenas puedo caminar.

Yo tampoco. Sobre todo me duelen las piernas.

Y tengo un hambre feroz. Pero no me gusta nada la idea de comer tantos vegetales y frutas.

Las papitas fritas también son vegetales, ¿no?

Ay, Luis, sí, son vegetales, pero las papitas fritas tienen mucha grasa y sal. Es mejor que no las comas.

¡Uf! Otra de mis comidas favoritas que no debo comer. ¡Qué barbaridad!

Pues, si te importa la salud, recomiendo que sigas mis consejos.

Está bien, Diana.

A propósito, Luis, ¿por qué no viene tu hermano, Héctor, a estas clases?

No sé.

4 | Clara Consejera lo sabe todo.

Un poco más tarde…

Es simpático pero un poco joven, ¿no crees?

Para ti, quizás, pero no para mí. ¿No te parece muy guapo y fascinante?

Diana, ¿qué piensas de Luis?

Bueno, no es para tanto. Es buen mozo. ¿Por qué? ¿Te gusta?

Hmmm. No sé qué aconsejarte. Pero mira, ¿por qué no le escribes a Clara Consejera?

¿Clara? ¿La consejera del periódico? ¡Qué buena idea! Lo voy a hacer ahora mismo.

Muchísimo. Pero ni me hace caso. Para él, simplemente soy otra amiga. No sé qué hacer para llamarle la atención.

Ella siempre da excelentes consejos y contesta en seguida. Es muy buena.

CHARLEMOS UN POCO

A. **PARA EMPEZAR . . .** Di si las siguientes frases son ciertas o falsas, según el cuento "La profecía de la gitana". Si son falsas, corrígelas.

1. Don Pelayo vivió a fines del siglo VIII.
2. Don Pelayo protegió el norte de la península contra la invasión de los moros.
3. El príncipe moro, Abd al-Aziz, ganó una batalla muy importante contra don Pelayo y sus soldados.
4. Los soldados del príncipe Abd al-Aziz que no murieron en la batalla fueron hechos prisioneros.
5. Sólo el príncipe y su criado escaparon.
6. El príncipe y su criado le pidieron ayuda a una familia que vivía en el campo.
7. Los dos moros decidieron pasar la noche en una cueva en las montañas de Asturias.
8. Una gitana le había dicho a Abd al-Aziz que iba a morir de picada de araña.
9. Los soldados de don Pelayo encontraron la cueva donde estaban el príncipe y su criado.
10. Abd al-Aziz y su criado fueron capturados en la cueva.
11. Los soldados no pudieron ver al príncipe y a su criado porque ellos cubrieron la entrada de la cueva con una cortina de metal.
12. En efecto, una araña les salvó la vida al príncipe y a su criado.

B. **¿QUÉ DECIMOS . . .?** ¿Qué le aconseja Diana a su clase de ejercicios aeróbicos?

1. El café puede . . .
2. El sueño es . . .
3. El ejercicio no es suficiente . . .
4. Es bueno beber . . .
5. Es recomendable que duerman . . .
6. Es importante . . .
7. Les recomiendo que sigan todos . . .
8. Sugiero que eviten comidas . . .

a. dos litros de líquido cada día.
b. grasosas y los dulces.
c. importantísimo para la salud.
ch. la nutrición.
d. una dieta balanceada.
e. para la buena salud.
f. quitarles el sueño.
g. ocho horas.

C. ¿Eres buen consejero? ¿Qué aconsejas que estas personas hagan ahora en preparación para su futura carrera?

Mario quiere ser mecánico.

EJEMPLO **Aconsejo que Mario trabaje en una gasolinera.**

1. Román quiere ser veterinario.

2. Tomasina quiere ser ingeniera.

3. Bárbara y Carlos quieren ser maestros.

4. Miriam y Rafael quieren ser cocineros.

5. Pablo quiere ser jugador de fútbol.

6. Paco y Matilde quieren ser reporteros.

7. Mi amiga quiere ser escritora.

8. Matías y Germán quieren ser músicos.

Expressions of persuasion

aconsejar
insistir en
pedir (e → i)
preferir (e → ie, i)
querer (e → ie)
recomendar (e → ie)
sugerir (e → ie, i)

Aconsejamos que ustedes no vean esa película.
Mamá **insiste en** que no salga contigo.
Prefiero que tú me llames.

See **¿Por qué se dice así?,** *page G73, section 5.4.*

LECCIÓN 2

CH. ¡Marciano! Un(a) marciano(a) acaba de mudarse a la Tierra y necesita consejos. ¿Qué consejos le das cuando hace preguntas? Tu compañero(a) debe hacer el papel del (de la) marciano(a).

 MODELO   vivir en la ciudad
　　　　　　Marciano(a): **¿Sugieres que viva en la ciudad?**
　　　　　　Tú:　　　　　**Sí, recomiendo que vivas en la ciudad.**
　　　　　　　　　　　　　　　　　　　　o
　　　　　　　　　　　　　No, no recomiendo que vivas en la ciudad. El campo es mejor.

1. estudiar en la escuela
2. practicar deportes
3. ver mucha televisión
4. comprar un coche
5. trabajar en el centro
6. salir a comer frecuentemente
7. aprender karate
8. visitar los museos
9. estudiar español

D. Entrevista. Xochitl tiene una entrevista con el señor Pérez para trabajar como instructora de ejercicios aeróbicos. ¿Qué consejos recibe antes de la entrevista?

 MODELO   entrenador / recomendar / practicar / todo / ejercicios
　　　　　　El entrenador recomienda que practique todos los ejercicios.

1. mamá / pedir / llegar a tiempo
2. papá / insistir en / hablar cortésmente
3. yo / querer / no estar / nervioso
4. su / amigos / sugerir / escuchar bien
5. su / hermano / aconsejar / ser / atento
6. Sofía / aconsejar / pensar antes de responder
7. su / padres / recomendar / hacer / bueno / preguntas
8. su / abuela / sugerir / preparar una demostración

E. Problemas. Estas personas quieren tus consejos. ¿Qué les dices para ayudarles con sus problemas?

Rubén

 EJEMPLO   **Sugiero que sigas una buena dieta.** o
　　　　　　Recomiendo que no comas pastel. o
　　　　　　Aconsejo que pierdas peso.

1. la señora Blanco

2. el señor Torres

3. José

4. Rita

5. Patricia y Esteban

6. el director

7. Flaquito y Flaquita

8. Marta

Present subjunctive: Stem-changing -ar and -er verbs

empezar	poder
e → ie	o → ue
empiece	pueda
empieces	puedas
empiece	pueda
empecemos	podamos
empiecen	puedan

Quiero que **empieces** esta tarde.
No creo que **podamos** hacerlo.

See **¿Por qué se dice así?**,
page G75, section 5.5

Present subjunctive: Stem-changing -ir verbs

pedir	servir
e → i	e → i
pida	sirva
pidas	sirvas
pida	sirva
pidamos	sirvamos
pidan	sirvan

Recomiendo que **pidas** las arepas.
Es probable que **sirvan** arepas de
pollo hoy.

See **¿Por qué se dice así?**,
page G77, section 5.6.

Present subjunctive Stem-changing -ir verbs

divertir	dormir
e → ie, i	o → ue, u
divierta	duerma
diviertas	duermas
divierta	duerma
divirtamos	durmamos
diviertan	duerman

Quiero que te **diviertas**.
Es imposible que **duerman** aquí.

See **¿Por qué se dice así?**,
page G77, section 5.6.

F. ¡Terrible! ¡Fantástico! ¡Importante! El(La) director(a) está anunciando algunos cambios en tu escuela para el año que viene. ¿Qué opinas de los cambios?

MODELO Los estudiantes no van a poder venir a la escuela en autobús.
Es terrible que no podamos venir a la escuela en autobús.

1. Las clases van a empezar a las 7:00 de la mañana.
2. Todos vamos a almorzar en casa.
3. Todos vamos a perder peso al hacer más ejercicio.
4. Los profesores van a jugar fútbol con los estudiantes.
5. Todos vamos a sentarnos en sillones en la biblioteca.
6. Los estudiantes van a volver a la escuela por la noche.
7. Los materiales escolares van a costar más dinero.
8. Los estudiantes van a poder hacer más recomendaciones.

G. ¡A comer! Acabas de comer en un nuevo restaurante. ¿Qué les recomiendas a tus amigos?

EJEMPLO **Sugiero que pidan la especialidad de la casa.**

(no) recomendar		la carne asada
(no) aconsejar	servir	la especialidad de la casa
sugerir	conseguir	una mesa cerca de la cocina
es posible	pedir	el gazpacho
es bueno	almorzar	los entremeses variados
		un(a) camarero(a) cortés

H. Consejos locos. Tú y un(a) amigo(a) tienen varios problemas y le piden consejos al señor Bocaloca. ¿Qué le dicen y qué consejos les da?

MODELO siempre terminar tarde / comenzar más tarde
Tú: **Siempre terminamos tarde.**
Bocaloca: **Comiencen más tarde.**
Amigo(a): **¿Usted quiere que comencemos más tarde?**

1. no poder dormir / dormir en el piso
2. sacar malas notas / no pensar tanto
3. no poder despertarse / acostarse más tarde
4. estar aburridos(as) / no divertirse tanto
5. querer hacer algo nuevo / repetir su rutina
6. ser muy flacos(as) / perder peso
7. querer llamar la atención / seguir mis consejos
8. preferir recibir buenos consejos / conseguir otro consejero

CHARLEMOS UN POCO MÁS

A. Sugiero que tú . . .   Tú y tu compañero(a) tienen que ayudar a limpiar la sala de clase. Antes de empezar, van a dividir el trabajo. Usen el dibujo que les va a dar su profesor(a) para decidir lo que cada uno quiere que el otro haga.

B. En el café.   Un(a) amigo(a) de Venezuela está visitándote en EE.UU. Tú lo (la) llevas a comer a tu restaurante favorito. Recomiéndale varias cosas para comer. Él (Ella) va a decirte si le gusta o no le gusta lo que recomiendas o si prefiere comer otra cosa.

EJEMPLO   *Tú:*   **Recomiendo que pidas el melón.** o
                    Sugiero que pruebes el melón.
          Compañero(a):   **Pues, no me gusta ¿Qué más hay?** o
                    Bueno, lo voy a probar.

C. Comida saludable.   ¿Normalmente comen ustedes comida saludable? Para saberlo, prepara una lista de toda la comida saludable que puedes nombrar. Tu compañero(a) va a preparar una lista de todo lo que los jóvenes típicos comen durante la semana. Luego su profesor(a) les va a dar un esquema como el siguiente, para que combinen las dos listas.

Comida saludable

1 _____
2 _____
3 _____
4 _____
5 _____
6 _____
7 _____

Comida saludable que comemos todos

1 _____
2 _____
3 _____
4 _____
5 _____
6 _____
7 _____

Comida típica de jóvenes

1 _____
2 _____
3 _____
4 _____
5 _____
6 _____
7 _____

Dramatizaciones

A. Tú puedes recomendarle que . . .   Su profesor quiere darles un examen mañana pero tú y dos compañeros quieren convencerle que no les dé el examen. Ahora están hablando de cómo van a convencerle. Dramaticen su conversación.

B. Quiero que vayas conmigo.   Tú estás tratando de convencer a tu amigo(a) de acompañarte a una clase de baile. Pero tu amigo no quiere ir. Dramaticen su conversación.

C. ¡Por favor!   Tú y tu amigo(a) están discutiendo cómo pueden convencer a sus padres que les den permiso de ir al cine esta noche. Dramaticen la conversación.

IMPACTO CULTURAL
Tesoros nacionales

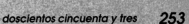

Antes de empezar

A. Impresiones. ¿Cuánto sabes de la España de la segunda mitad del siglo XX? Indica si en tu opinión, estos comentarios son ciertos o falsos. Luego, después de leer la lectura, revisa tus respuestas.

C F 1. Actualmente el Generalísimo Franco es el rey de España.

C F 2. Franco es considerado un dictador.

C F 3. La España de Franco fue muy liberal y progresista.

C F 4. Franco creía que España era única y superior moralmente.

C F 5. El gobierno militar del General Franco afectó todos los aspectos de la vida de los españoles: la educación, la política y la vida social.

C F 6. Las costumbres y modas de otros países eran bien recibidas en la España de Franco.

C F 7. Desde 1975, la vida en España cambió mucho.

C F 8. Ahora no se permite criticar al gobierno en España.

C F 9. Hoy en día en España, sólo se permite la música clásica y la música tradicional española; no se permite ni música rock ni salsa.

C F 10. Ahora, los españoles tienen la responsabilidad de seleccionar entre lo bueno y lo malo que la vida les ofrece.

B. Sumarios. Ahora lee el tercer párrafo y el último de **La España de Franco y la España de hoy** y selecciona el mejor sumario de los siguientes.

Tercer párrafo:

1. El gobierno de Franco fue una dictadura sumamente autoritaria y católica.
2. En las escuelas primarias, durante la época de Franco, los niños aprendían que España era única y superior moralmente.
3. El gobierno militar de Franco impuso la religión católica en todas las escuelas españolas.

Último párrafo:

1. Lamentablemente, el gobierno español actual no controla el crimen tan bien como lo controlaba Franco.
2. La libertad permite escoger entre lo bueno y lo malo y, desafortunadamente, algunas personas van a escoger lo malo.
3. En la época de Franco todo era bueno, ahora todo es malo porque los españoles no son responsables.

La España de Franco y
la España de hoy

Por medio de

observador

salieron

paralización

manera de actuar

personas que siguen

con devoción

El Generalísimo Francisco Franco (1892-1975), **❶** participó en 1936 en un movimiento militar **❷** que empezó la Guerra Civil en España. Tras* el triunfo de 1939, llegó a ser jefe de Estado y se mantuvo en este puesto hasta que murió en 1975.

Soy Roberto R. y soy testigo* de los años que gobernó el Generalísimo Francisco Franco. Nací en 1939 , el mismo año en que terminó la Guerra Civil Española y Franco y la Falange, su partido político, empezaron a gobernar España. Alrededor de 4.000.000 de españoles se exiliaron* en 1939, entre ellos maestros, artistas famosos como Pablo Picasso, escritores y políticos. Por 35 años España vivió un estado de estancamiento* político, cultural y económico.

El gobierno militar del General Franco constituyó una dictadura. La ideología falangista era sumamente autoritaria y católica, y se impuso en todos los aspectos de la vida de los españoles, desde la educación en las escuelas y universidades hasta el comportamiento* y actividades políticas y sociales. Cuando yo estaba en la escuela primaria, nosotros teníamos un libro llamado *España es así.* Este libro decía que España era católica desde el año 589 y siempre sería así. Decía que España era diferente al resto de los países de Europa porque España era única y superior moralmente. Por esta razón recitábamos "España Grande y Libre" y teníamos una clase de religión obligatoria.

La moral era muy importante en la época de Franco y por esta razón sus seguidores* desempeñaron un papel paternalista. Nuestros profesores nos enseñaban que las costumbres y modas de otros países eran malas para España. Debíamos evitar las malas tentaciones para mantener la pureza de nuestras mujeres. Por eso, había policías en las playas **❸** y piscinas públicas para dar multas a las personas que usaban trajes de baño impropios. Las piscinas públicas tenían diferentes horarios para hombres y mujeres. Se estableció la Censura para las revistas, periódicos y películas. Aun prohibió el divorcio. La mujer debía quedarse en casa y representar fielmente* su papel de esposa y madre.

BARCELONA
SEDE OLIMPICA 1992

actividades

④

imposible

usos más recientes

⑤

el privilegio de seleccionar

abusan

ofrece

¡Qué diferente es la España de hoy! En 1975 Francisco Franco murió y España volvió a abrir sus puertas al mundo. Ahora España participa con el resto de los países de Europa en acontecimientos* culturales, políticos, sociales y económicos. Muchas ciudades de España se han convertido en capitales de acontecimientos internacionales importantes en las artes, los deportes ④ y las ferias. Ahora la educación en las escuelas y universidades es más abierta. La crítica, incluso del propio gobierno español actual, forma parte importante de la educación. Durante el gobierno de Franco, la crítica del falangismo era algo inconcebible.*

Libres de la Censura falangista, la libertad de expresión y acción se ha generalizado en todos los aspectos. Ahora nosotros los españoles podemos adoptar las modas* en el vestido y la música como todos los europeos. Las mujeres pueden usar el traje de baño de su gusto sin ningún problema. ⑤ Podemos escuchar rock y salsa, y no solamente música clásica sino también música tradicional española.

En la época de Franco todo esto estaba muy bien controlado. Ahora el español tiene derecho de escoger* entre lo bueno y lo malo que la vida le ofrece en una España libre. Lamentablemente, siempre hay personas que se aprovechan* de esa libertad y optan por lo malo. Es responsabilidad de todo español usar los derechos que la libertad les otorga,* para su propio bien y el bien de su país.

Verifiquemos

1. Vuelve a las actividades **A** y **B** de **Antes de empezar** y decide si tus respuestas originales fueron correctas o no.

2. Compara mediante un esquema la España de Franco y la España de hoy en los siguientes aspectos:

	España de Franco	España de hoy
La educación	1. 2.	1. 2.
Las modas	1. 2.	1. 2.
La mujer	1. 2.	1. 2.
La música	1. 2. …	1. 2. …

3. ¿Crees que la dictadura de Franco tuvo algunos aspectos positivos? Explica tu respuesta.

¡Temo que esté enamorado de mí!

¿ **Q**ué piensas tú ?

1. Piensa en los jóvenes en estas dos páginas. ¿Qué están pensando? ¿De qué se preocupan? ¿Qué los contenta?

2. En tu opinión, ¿qué esperanzas tienen?

3. ¿De qué crees que tienen miedo estos jóvenes? ¿Qué les enoja? ¿Qué los entristece?

4. ¿Crees que estos jóvenes son muy diferentes de ti y de tus amigos? ¿Por qué y cómo?

5. Toma el tiempo necesario para preparar una lista de todas las expresiones que usas para expresar tus sentimientos y emociones. Compara tu lista con las de dos compañeros de clase y añade expresiones que te falten.

6. ¿De qué vas a poder hablar al terminar esta lección?

LAS ÁNIMAS

Esta leyenda española trata de un indiano que se hizo muy rico con el oro y la plata de las Américas.

1

Había una vez en Andalucía una viejita con una sobrina linda y buena pero muy perezosa.

La vieja temía morir y dejar a la pobre sobrina sin esposo. ¿Quién iba a querer casarse con ella? No sabía ni hilar, ni coser, ni bordar, . . . ¡no sabía hacer nada!

2

Un día llegó al pueblo un indiano muy rico y guapo, que quería casarse. La tía fue inmediatamente al caballero y le dijo que ella tenía una sobrina con tantos talentos que tendría que escribir un libro para contarlos. Él le contestó que le gustaría mucho conocerla.

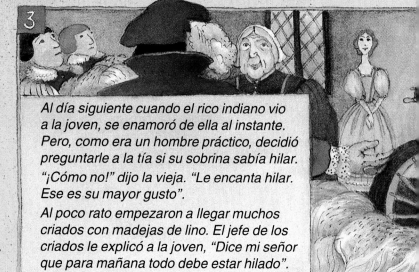

3

Al día siguiente cuando el rico indiano vio a la joven, se enamoró de ella al instante. Pero, como era un hombre práctico, decidió preguntarle a la tía si su sobrina sabía hilar.

"¡Cómo no!" dijo la vieja. "Le encanta hilar. Ese es su mayor gusto".

Al poco rato empezaron a llegar muchos criados con madejas de lino. El jefe de los criados le explicó a la joven, "Dice mi señor que para mañana todo debe estar hilado".

4

La muchacha se puso a llorar porque ella no sabía hilar.

"Ay. Cuánto siento no saber hilar", dijo, porque ella también se había enamorado del guapo indiano.

En ese instante aparecieron tres ánimas buenas, vestidas de blanco, y se pusieron inmediatamente a trabajar. Cuando todo el lino estaba transformado en hilo fino, desaparecieron.

Cuando a la mañana siguiente llegó el rico caballero indiano, quedó muy impresionado.

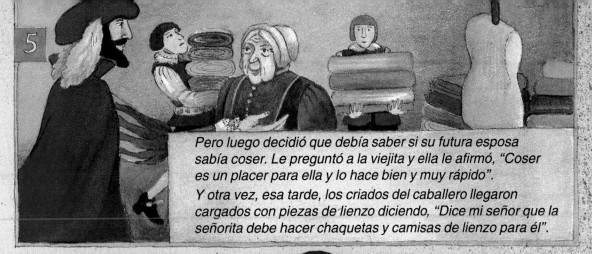

5

Pero luego decidió que debía saber si su futura esposa sabía coser. Le preguntó a la viejita y ella le afirmó, "Coser es un placer para ella y lo hace bien y muy rápido".

Y otra vez, esa tarde, los criados del caballero llegaron cargados con piezas de lienzo diciendo, "Dice mi señor que la señorita debe hacer chaquetas y camisas de lienzo para él".

6

Y otra vez la muchacha que no sabía nada de cortar ni coser se puso a llorar.

Pero por la noche las tres ánimas volvieron y en poco tiempo todo el lienzo estaba transformado en chaquetas y camisas.

El caballero indiano no podía creer que tenía una novia tan lista.

7

Pero luego el rico caballero quería saber si la joven sabía bordar. Con este fin, mandó docenas de chalecos con sus criados, diciendo uno de ellos, "Mi señor los quiere bordados, todos diferentes y de todos los colores".

8

Y otra vez la muchacha comenzó a llorar. No sabía bordar tampoco.

Y como en las otras ocasiones las tres ánimas aparecieron y en poco tiempo tenían todos los chalecos bordados.

"Nos gusta mucho hacer este trabajo", dijeron las ánimas, "pero queremos que usted nos invite a la boda".

"¡Sí, con mucho gusto!" contestó la muchacha.

Cuando el indiano vio todos los chalecos bordados y en tan poco tiempo, pensó que tenía la novia más capaz de toda España y decidió casarse al instante.

Pero la muchacha, aunque contenta de que su novio la amaba, se sentía muy triste.

"¿Cómo puedes estar triste?" le preguntó su tía.

"Estoy preocupada de que mi futuro marido no sepa la verdad". Su tía le contestó, "Sí, hija. A mí también me inquieta que él piense que tú puedes hacerlo todo".

Llegó el día de la boda. Cuando todos estaban sentados disfrutando de un banquete espléndido, llegaron las tres ánimas. Eran tan viejas y feas que todos los invitados las miraron con la boca abierta.

La muchacha las presentó a su nuevo marido diciendo, "Son tres tías mías muy especiales".

El novio les habló con mucho cariño. A la primera le dijo, "Debo preguntarle, ¿por qué tiene un brazo corto y un brazo largo?"

"Los tengo así por lo mucho que he hilado", le contestó.

A la segunda le preguntó, "¿Por qué tiene los ojos tan saltones y colorados?"

Ésta le contestó, "He pasado la vida cortando y cosiendo".

Y a la tercera, "¿Por qué tiene el cuerpo tan torcido?"

Ella le contestó, "Estoy así de tanto inclinarme para bordar".

El novio, tan enamorado de su nueva esposa, le dijo, "De aquí en adelante, no quiero que tú hiles, ni cortes, ni cosas, ni bordes jamás en tu vida".

Y al decir esto, las tres ánimas desaparecieron y el caballero y su esposa fueron muy felices.

De nuestras emociones

¿Qué opinas de estas cartas

que recibió Clara Consejera?

Querida Clara Consejera:

Espero que me pueda ayudar con mi problema. Estoy muy enamorada de un amigo mío, pero él no se da cuenta de mi amor. No me considera más que una amiga aunque nos vemos muy a menudo. Estamos en el mismo colegio y a veces me acompaña a casa después de las clases. Sin embargo, me trata como a una hermana.

Fui a una clase de ejercicios aeróbicos y ahora estoy poniéndome en línea, pero el muchacho de mis sueños no se fija en mí. ¿Qué debo hacer? Ayúdeme. Temo que nunca me vaya a hacer caso. ¿Qué me aconseja, Clara Consejera? Yo sé que me puede ayudar.

Sola y triste

Querida Clara Consejera:

Tengo un problema romántico. Estoy enamorado de la hermana de una amiga mía. Ella es mayor que yo y me trata como a un niño. Me molesta que no me vea como hombre. Asisto a su clase de ejercicios aeróbicos (ella es instructora) y sigo todos sus consejos pero no me da resultados con ella.

Además, cuando trato de hablar a solas con ella, siempre está su hermana menor. Tengo miedo de que su hermana esté enamorándose de mí. Ella es muy simpática, pero no me atrae igual que su hermana mayor. Por eso necesito sus consejos. ¿Cómo puedo llamar la atención de la hermana mayor? ¿Y qué debo hacer con la hermana menor para no lastimarla y no causar problemas entre las dos?

Hay otra complicación también. Ya le dije a un amigo de El Paso, Texas en EE.UU. que tengo novia y es posible que él venga a visitarme este verano. ¿Qué le voy a decir si viene?

Espero que me pueda contestar pronto porque no veo ninguna solución.

Desesperado

Querida Clara Consejera:

Tengo un problema un poco complicado. Pero estoy segura que Ud. me puede ayudar.

Éste es mi problema. Un joven, estudiante universitario, me interesa mucho, pero nunca lo veo porque estudio en el colegio todavía. Conozco a su hermano menor y siempre le pregunto por mi amor, pero él nunca me dice mucho.

Además, temo que el hermano menor esté enamorado de mí. Esto a pesar de que mi hermana menor está loca por él. ¿Qué puedo hacer para desenredar esta situación?

¿Cómo puedo interesar al hermano mayor? ¿Debo escribirle una carta y declarar mis sentimientos? ¿O debo hablar con el hermano menor? ¿Qué recomienda que haga? Ayúdeme, por favor.

Confundida

CHARLEMOS UN POCO

A. **PARA EMPEZAR . . .** Combina las tres columnas con hechos de la leyenda de "Las ánimas".

La tía	tenía un brazo corto y uno largo	en poco tiempo bordaron todo.
La sobrina	ni hilaba, ni cosía, ni bordaba;	cargados de lienzo.
El indiano	fue al caballero diciendo	de cortar ni de coser.
El ánima	empezaron a llegar	la joven sabía bordar.
Las tres viejitas	aparecieron vestidas de blanco y	fueron muy felices.
Los criados	quería saber si	más capaz de toda España.
	dijo que no sabía nada	por lo mucho que hilaba.
	pensó que tenía la novia	se pusieron a trabajar.
	desaparecieron y el caballero y su esposa	que tenía una sobrina muy hábil.
	volvieron a aparecer y	no sabía hacer nada.

B. **¿QUÉ DECIMOS . . .?** ¿Quién tiene estos problemas?

Sola y triste

Desesperado

Confundida

1. ¿Debo escribirle una carta y declarar mis sentimientos?
2. ¿Y qué debo hacer con la menor para no lastimarla?
3. El chico de mis sueños no se fija en mí.
4. Me molesta que no me vea como hombre.
5. Me trata como a una hermana.
6. Sigo todos sus consejos pero no me da resultados.
7. Temo que el hermano menor esté enamorado de mí.
8. Un joven, estudiante universitario, me interesa mucho.

Present subjunctive: With and without a subject change

With subject change:
Me alegro de que todos **estén** aquí.
Siento que no **puedas** venir.

Without subject change:
Me alegro de **estar** aquí.
Siento no **poder** venir.

See **¿Por qué se dice así?,**
page G80, section 5.7.

Present subjunctive: Expressions of anticipation or reaction

alegrarse de	sentir
esperar	temer
gustar	tener miedo (de)

Mis padres **temen** que yo **sufra** un accidente.
Papá **espera** que yo **haga** mis quehaceres.

See **¿Por qué se dice así?,**
page G80, section 5.7.

C. En el autobús. Al viajar en autobús escuchas varias conversaciones. Selecciona el comentario en la segunda columna que mejor complete cada comentario de la primera columna.

A	**B**
1. Perdí cinco kilos.	**a.** ¡Tengo miedo de que saque una mala nota!
2. Vi una serpiente en el parque.	
3. Invité a muchas personas a cenar.	**b.** Me molesta que siempre perdamos.
4. Andrés tuvo un examen difícil hoy.	**c.** ¡Ay! Espero que no haya más.
5. Perdí todo mi dinero.	**ch.** Me alegro de que estés más delgado. ¡Estás guapísimo!
6. El equipo rival ganó el partido.	**d.** Buena suerte. A mí no me gusta preparar la comida.
	e. Siento no poder darte nada.

CH. ¡Lo teme! ¿Qué opinan tus padres cuando tú haces estas cosas? ¿Cómo reaccionan?

EJEMPLO   **Mamá teme que yo viaje en avión.** o
Le gusta a mamá que yo vuele.

1.

2.

3.

4.

5.

6.

7.

8.

D. Chismes. Tú y tu compañero(a) están hablando de personas que conocen. ¿Qué dicen?

 MODELO   la profesora / furioso (calmarse)

> *Tú:* **La profesora está furiosa.**
> *Compañero(a):* **Tienes razón. Espero que se calme.**

1. Susana / cansado (dormir más)
2. Ramón / gordo (perder peso)
3. Gloria y Carlota / aburrido (salir más)
4. Marcos / triste (pensar en algo alegre)
5. Esteban y Yolanda / nervioso (calmarse)
6. muchos estudiantes / preocupado por sus notas (estudiar más)
7. el director / flaco (comer más)
8. Timoteo / enfermo (guardar cama)

E. Las noticias. Estás leyendo los titulares del periódico.
¿Cómo reaccionas?

 EJEMPLO   Hay miles de habitantes sin casa.
           **Estoy preocupado(a) de que haya miles de
           habitantes sin casa.**

1. Hay más contaminación en el lago.
2. Va a nevar todo el día mañana.
3. El equipo local va a tener un nuevo entrenador.
4. La directora del colegio quiere cancelar las clases mañana.
5. El ballet folklórico viene a nuestra ciudad.
6. El cine local da una nueva película romántica.
7. El almacén más grande tiene grandes ofertas este fin de
   semana.
8. La situación económica está peor.

F. Yo, ¿consejero(a)? ¿Qué les aconsejas a estas personas
cuando te cuentan sus problemas?

 EJEMPLO   Mis hermanos siempre me molestan y no puedo
           estudiar en casa.
           (Recomiendo que . . .)
           Recomiendo que estudies en la biblioteca. o
           Recomiendo que les expliques tus sentimientos.

1. Mis padres no me permiten salir cuando yo quiero.
   (Sugiero que . . .)
2. Me interesa una chica en mi clase de inglés.
   (Recomiendo que . . .)
3. Quiero romper con mi novio pero temo lastimarlo.
   (Aconsejo que . . .)
4. Mis padres me tratan como un bebé.
   (Sugiero que . . .)
5. El chico de mis sueños no se fija en mí.
   (Recomiendo que . . .)
6. Mis padres insisten en que limpie mi cuarto pero yo odio
   limpiarlo.
   (Aconsejo que . . .)
7. Estoy loco por mi profesora de arte.
   (Sugiero que . . .)
8. Tengo una familia muy grande y nunca estoy a solas.
   (Recomiendo que . . .)
9. Mis padres insisten en que mi hermanito siempre me acompañe.
   (Sugiero que . . .)
10. Papá nunca me permite usar su carro.
    (Recomiendo que . . .)
11. Mamá insiste en que siempre regrese a casa a las diez de la
    noche.
    (Aconsejo que . . .)

A. Temo que... Pregúntales a tres compañeros de clase qué temen en estos lugares.

EJEMPLO   en la calle
    Tú: **¿Qué temes en la calle?**
    Compañero(a): **Temo que alguien me robe la cartera.** o
                      Tengo miedo que mi coche no funcione.

1. en la escuela	**6.** en la clase de español
2. en las fiestas	**7.** en la oficina de la directora
3. en la oficina del médico	**8.** en la clase de matemáticas
4. en un restaurante elegante	**9.** en el parque
5. en un carro	**10.** en la ciudad

B. El problema es que ... ¿Qué les dices a tus amigos cuando hablas con ellos y se presentan estas situaciones? Con un(a) compañero(a), prepara un minidrama para cada una de estas situaciones.

EJEMPLO   Tú invitaste a una amiga a ir al parque a comer contigo hoy día. El problema es que ya es hora de ir por ella pero hace mucho viento y parece que va a llover.
    Tú: **(Rin, rin.) ¡Hola, Patricia! Mira, es probable que no podamos ir al parque hoy.**
    Compañero(a): **¿No? ¿Por qué? ¿No te sientes bien?**
    Tú: **No, no es eso. Es que hace mucho viento y temo que vaya a llover.**

1. Estás con unos amigos en casa y te piden un helado. El problema es que no hay helado en la heladera.
2. Hablas con tu mejor amigo(a) por teléfono y te dice que tiene una cita con tu amiga(o) el sábado. El problema es que tú ibas a invitarlo(la) al cine el sábado.
3. Tus amigas vienen por ti para ir a la fiesta. El problema es que tus padres dicen que tú no puedes salir esta noche.
4. Tú le dijiste a tu novia(o) que sabes tocar la guitarra. Él (Ella) te pide que la toques para su papá. El problema es que no sabes tocar ningún instrumento.
5. Hablas con un(a) amigo(a) por teléfono. Te invita a salir a pasear en su carro. El problema es que tienes un examen de matemáticas mañana.
6. Estás comiendo en casa de una buena amiga. Su mamá te sirve rosbif. El problema es que tú eres vegetariano(a).
7. Esta noche después del partido de fútbol todos tus amigos van a una pizzería. El problema es que tú tienes que adelgazar.
8. Dos hermanas te invitan a pasar el fin de semana con su familia en las montañas. El problema es que es el fin de semana que tus abuelos vienen a visitarte.

C. Querida Clara Consejera. Tú tienes un problema serio y necesitas consejos. Escríbele una carta a Clara Consejera explicándole el problema. Menciona lo que temes y lo que te alegra de tu situación. Luego léele la carta a tu compañero(a) y él (ella) te va a dar consejos. Cuando él (ella) te lea su carta, dale consejos tú.

Dramatizaciones

A. ¡Qué horror! Tú tienes un amigo(a) que está muy deprimido(a). Decides hablar con un(a) consejero(a) para pedir consejos de cómo debes ayudar a tu amigo(a). Dramatiza esta situación con un compañero(a) de clase haciendo el papel del (de la) consejero(a).

B. Consejos por teléfono. Tú eres el (la) locutor(a) en un programa de radio que da consejos. Esta noche recibes tres llamadas de amigos en tu escuela. Uno tiene problemas en la escuela, otro con un animal doméstico y el otro con su familia. Dramatiza la situación con tres amigos.

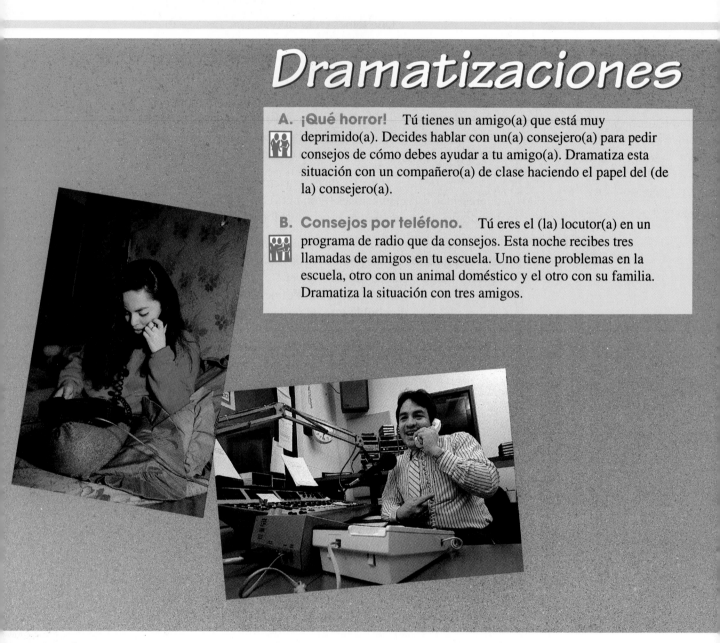

LEAMOS AHORA

Estrategias para leer:
El pensar al leer

A. **El pensar al leer.** Los buenos lectores siempre piensan al leer. Piensan al anticipar o predecir, al hacer comparaciones y al crear imágenes visuales imaginarias. También piensan al explicar o interpretar el texto, al confirmar sus interpretaciones y al arreglar o reajustar sus interpretaciones.

Para reflexionar en cómo piensas tú al leer, prepárate para sacar apuntes de lo que piensas al leer este artículo. Tendrás que expresar tus pensamientos en frases como las que siguen.

Al anticipar o predecir:	"El título me hace anticipar que este artículo va a ser de . . ."
	"En la siguiente parte creo que va a explicar cómo . . ."
Al describir:	"Creo que esto describe a . . ."
	"Ahora lo veo en mi imaginación. Hay . . ."
Al comparar:	"Esto es como cuando yo / nosotros / mi hermano . . ."
	"Esto me hace pensar en . . ."
Al interpretar:	"Otra manera de decir esto es . . ."
	"Esto probablemente quiere decir . . ."
Al confirmar la comprensión:	"No entiendo esto porque . . ."
	"Creo que esto quiere decir que . . ."
Al reajustar:	"Necesito leerla otra vez porque . . ."
	"Esta palabra nueva probablemente quiere decir . . ."
	"Necesito buscar esta palabra . . ."

B. **¡A sacar apuntes!** Ahora al leer este artículo sobre Antonio Banderas, hazlo con papel y lápiz en mano. Usa las sugerencias en el margen al anotar lo que piensas. Éstas son sugerencias y nada más. Tú debes sacar apuntes de todo lo que estés pensando al leer el artículo.

Antonio Banderas
Un galán latino en Hollywood

Anticipar
Confirmar
comprensión

Comparar
Describir

Con sus películas *Los reyes del mambo*, *Entrevista con un vampiro* y *Desesperado*, Antonio Banderas se ha convertido en el nuevo galán latino de Hollywood. ¿Cómo era de niño y cómo reacciona Antonio ahora frente a tanto éxito? Esto fue el tema de una entrevista que tuvo Lola Díaz de *Cambio 16* con Antonio.

Predecir

Según Lola, Antonio dice que de niño era muy tímido. "Miedoso y extremadamente tímido". Dice que en el colegio siempre hablaba bajito porque tenía la sensación de que su voz sonaba rara y diferente. Nunca quería sobresalir, prefería estar al fondo, perdido en las masas. Sin embargo, ¡ahora es actor por excelencia en Hollywood!

Comparar
Describir

A pesar de parecer tenerlo todo: amor, belleza, juventud y éxito, Antonio dice que a veces le da miedo estar tan feliz. En su propia percepción, Antonio se siente muy inseguro en el fondo, y es precisamente esa inseguridad que le causa el miedo.

Comparar
Describir

Lola Díaz le preguntó si no le daba cierto miedo el hacer una película en Hollywood. "Yo siempre tuve mucho miedo antes de ir allí", dijo, pero fue "mucho más fascinante de lo que uno se pueda imaginar. Ellos me alquilaron un chalé en un barrio pegado a Beverly Hills, me pusieron un coche con chófer y me traían y me llevaban a todo tipo de fiestas y de cenas y siempre me trataron a cuerpo de rey. Luego, después de siete meses, me fui acostumbrando bastante a ese mundo. Hollywood no me da ningún miedo, todo lo contrario. Lo que estoy deseando es que me ofrezcan algo".

Comparar
Describir

Según Antonio, lo único que ha querido durante toda su vida es conquistar un espacio de libertad. "Mi espacio de libertad", dice, "comienza cuando el director en escena dice *acción*, y termina cuando dice *corte*. Ésa es la única verdad . . . que debo trabajar. Todo lo que hay alrededor, el dar o recibir un Óscar, el que te admiren, el que te consideren especial o el que te inviten a las fiestas más importantes no significa nada".

Confirmar
comprensión
Reajustar

Interpretar

El popular actor dice que lo único que es importante para él es que "cuando salgo a la pantalla la gente me crea". En otras palabras, lo más importante para este joven actor es que en los ojos de su público siempre pueda dejar de ser Antonio Banderas y llegar a ser el personaje que representa.

Confirmar
comprensión
Reajustar

Los hermanos César y Néstor Castillo (Armand Assante y Antonio Banderas) con Desi Arnaz (Desi Arnaz hijo), en el centro. De la película *Los reyes del mambo.*

Banderas con Salma Hayek. De la película *Desesperado.*

Verifiquemos

A. **¿Cómo piensas tú?** Compara tus apuntes con los de dos o tres compañeros de clase. ¿Son los apuntes de tus compañeros más completos que los tuyos a veces? ¿Cuándo son más completos los tuyos?

B. **Título.** Explica el título de esta lectura.

C. **Cambios.** Según este artículo, Antonio Banderas cambió mucho en algunos aspectos y no cambió en otros. Prepara un diagrama como el que sigue e indica cómo era Antonio antes, cómo es ahora y en qué aspectos no ha cambiado.

ANTONIO BANDERAS

Antes	Todavía	Ahora
1.	1.	1.
2.	2.	2.
3.	3.	3.
. . .	. . .	. . .

ESCRIBAMOS AHORA

Estrategias para escribir:
Entrevistas

A. Empezar.   El artículo sobre Antonio Banderas es interesante porque nos permite verlo no sólo como estrella de Hollywood sino también como una persona común y ordinaria. Nos dice algunas cosas que recuerda de su juventud y de cómo se siente ahora que es estrella. Es un poco sorprendente saber que de niño era muy tímido y es fascinante cuando dice que, a pesar de ser tan famoso, sólo se siente libre mientras actúa.

Lola Díaz, la escritora del artículo, consiguió toda esta información en una entrevista, después de planear las preguntas que le quería hacer a Antonio.

Antes de escribir un artículo corto sobre un hispano en tu escuela o comunidad, vas a tener que entrevistar a la persona que seleccionaste. Como Lola Díaz, tienes que planear tu entrevista cuidadosamente. Vas a necesitar hacer preguntas sobre actividades específicas y también sobre lo que piensa y siente la persona que seleccionaste. En preparación para tu entrevista, estudia el artículo de Antonio Banderas con un(a) compañero(a) de clase y traten de adivinar qué preguntas le hizo Lola Díaz a Antonio para conseguir toda la información. Preparen una lista por escrito de todas las preguntas que creen que preparó Lola Díaz.

B. Planear.   Lo primero que tienes que hacer es hablar con la persona que vas a entrevistar para decidir la fecha, la hora y el lugar de la entrevista. Luego debes preparar un formulario similar al que sigue para ayudarte a organizar tus preguntas.

Información	Necesito confirmar. . .	Necesito preguntar. . .
Nombre		
Edad		
Profesión		
Descripción		
Familia		
Experiencias . . .		
Lo que piensa de . . .		
Lo que siente . . .		

C. Para sacar apuntes. Al entrevistar a la persona que seleccionaste, debes sacar muchos apuntes en la entrevista. Es importante ser lo más exacto posible, en particular al citar *(escribir exactamente)* lo que la persona dice. Durante la entrevista lo más importante es sacar muchos apuntes. Ahora puedes organizar tus apuntes y decidir si vas a usar toda la información o sólo parte de la información. Por ejemplo, si todos tus lectores ya saben los datos biográficos de la persona que seleccionaste, probablemente es mejor que no incluyas esa información en tu artículo.

CH. Primer borrador. ¿Cómo empezó Lola Díaz su artículo? Empezó por hacer algunos comentarios sobre Antonio Banderas ahora, la estrella de Hollywood. Luego habló de sus recuerdos del pasado y finalmente, volvió a hablar de los éxitos de Antonio actualmente. Al repasar tus apuntes y organizar tu primer borrador, recuerda que no es siempre necesario escribir la información cronológicamente. Con frecuencia hay otras maneras más interesantes de presentar la información.

D. Compartir. Comparte el primer borrador de tu artículo con dos compañeros de clase. Pídeles sugerencias. Pregúntales si es lógico tu artículo, si hay algo que no entienden, si hay algo que puedes o debes eliminar. Dales la misma información sobre sus artículos cuando ellos te pidan sugerencias.

E. Revisar. Haz cambios en tu artículo a base de las sugerencias de tus compañeros. Luego, antes de entregar el artículo, compártelo una vez más con dos compañeros de clase. Esta vez pídeles que revisen la estructura y la puntuación. En particular, pídeles que revisen el uso del subjuntivo y la concordancia: verbo / sujeto y sustantivo / adjetivo.

F. Versión final. Escribe la versión final de tu artículo incorporando las correcciones que tus compañeros de clase te indicaron. Si es posible, incluye una foto de la persona que entrevistaste. Entrégale una copia en limpio a tu profesor(a).

G. Publicar. Junten todos los artículos en un solo volumen. En grupos de cuatro, decidan en un título apropiado para el volumen. Luego, cada grupo puede sugerir un título y la clase puede votar para decidir cuál van a usar. Guarden su segundo ''libro'' en la sala de clase para leer cuando tengan un poco de tiempo libre.

¡Hagamos una excursión!

¡Vamos a Aguirre Springs!

¿Qué piensas tú?

1. Los dos muchachos en la foto son Martín y su hermano Daniel. ¿Qué está haciendo Martín ahora? ¿Tiene todo lo que necesita? ¿Qué le falta? ¿Qué está haciendo su hermano Daniel? ¿Cuál es la manera más fácil para que Martín consiga lo que necesita?

2. Imagínate la conversación entre los dos hermanos. ¿Qué crees que va a decir Daniel si quiere descansar y no tiene ganas de hacer nada?

3. ¿Qué está haciendo el padre de los muchachos? ¿Qué crees que está diciendo?

4. ¿Qué está leyendo la chica en el dibujo? ¿Cómo sabes? ¿Qué va a decir si acepta la invitación? ¿Qué va a decir si quiere ir pero no puede? ¿si puede ir pero no quiere?

5. ¿Qué dices al extender una invitación informal, por ejemplo al cine o a un partido de baloncesto? ¿Qué dices al extender una invitación más formal, como a salir con una chica o un chico a una fiesta? ¿Hay diferencias en los dos tipos de invitaciones?

6. ¿Qué dices cuando te invitan a hacer algo que quieres hacer? ¿a hacer algo que no quieres hacer? ¿a hacer algo que sospechas que tus padres no te vayan a permitir hacer?

7. ¿Qué crees que vas a aprender a hacer y decir en esta lección?

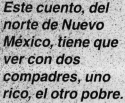

LA CENIZA

Este cuento, del norte de Nuevo México, tiene que ver con dos compadres, uno rico, el otro pobre.

Para uno de ellos, la vida parecía pasar muy serena. No tenía que trabajar mucho.

El otro compadre tenía una vida muy difícil. Trabajaba de sol a sol, pero ganaba muy poco.

Un día, el compadre pobre y su esposa estaban discutiendo sus problemas.

"¿Por qué no vas a ver a nuestro compadre?" sugirió la mujer.

"Es posible que pueda decirte el secreto–cómo mejorar nuestra fortuna".

"¡Lo dudo!", dijo su marido. "¡No creo que él quiera ayudarnos! Pero, sí, puedo hablar con él".

Y el compadre pobre se fue a visitar a su compadre rico. "Trabajo muy duro todo el día", le dijo, "pero la mayor parte del tiempo mi esposa y yo nos acostamos con hambre. Quiero vivir como tú. ¿Es posible que me digas tu secreto? ¿Cómo puedo hacerme rico?"

El compadre rico le contestó, "Sólo porque eres tú, te voy a ayudar. Voy a decirte mi secreto. Yo me hice rico vendiendo ceniza. Tú debes hacer lo mismo". (Por supuesto, el compadre rico no estaba diciendo la verdad, pero el pobre se lo creyó todo.)

Esa noche el compadre pobre y su esposa empezaron inmediatamente a llenar sacos de ceniza.

No dejaron de trabajar hasta la madrugada, cuando el carro estaba cargado de sacos de ceniza. El compadre pobre le dio un beso a su mujer y se fue a vender ceniza. Su esposa pensó, "Estoy segura que va a volver rico, como su compadre".

Algunas gentes eran bondadosas con el pobre hombre.

Otras se asombraban.

Pero la mayoría se reía de él. "Es probable que esté loco", decían. Pero aunque no vendía ni siquiera un puñado de ceniza, el pobre hombre seguía de puerta en puerta por días, luego por semanas y aún por meses.

Poco a poco, el pobre hombre reconoció que su compadre lo había engañado. Y como echaba terriblemente de menos a su familia, decidió volver a casa. Como ya no tenía sentido seguir cargando los sacos de ceniza, empezó a arrojar la ceniza. ¡Hacía una cochinada!

En ese momento llegó un oficial, y, muy enojado, se lo llevó a la cárcel.

9

No salió de la cárcel hasta un año después. El pobre hombre estaba muy cambiado y se sentía totalmente fracasado. Pensaba, "¿Cómo es posible que sea tan desafortunado?"

Cuando una señora vio al pobre hombre en la calle, le dio lástima y le regaló un **nicle** para ayudarlo.

Con el nicle el pobre compró una máscara de diablo pensando, "Creo que mis hijos deben saber cómo es el diablo".

10

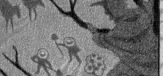

En el largo camino a casa, el pobre hombre se preparaba para pasar la noche cuando oyó acercarse unos caballos.

No queriendo ser visto por nadie, se puso la máscara de diablo y se subió a un árbol. Dos ladrones a caballo se detuvieron debajo del árbol y empezaron a enterrar unos sacos llenos de monedas de oro.

El compadre los veía con tanta curiosidad que perdió el equilibrio y se cayó al suelo.

"¡El diablo!", gritó uno. "Creo que viene por nosotros", dijo el otro y los dos ladrones se fueron corriendo horrorizados.

11

El pobre hombre no sabía qué hacer. Por fin decidió cargar los sacos de monedas de oro en los caballos y llevárselos a casa.

Así es que el compadre pobre llegó a casa hecho un hombre rico—con dos caballos finos y sacos de oro.

Cuando el compadre rico vino a ver a su compadre, éste quería saber cómo llegó a ser tan rico tan pronto. El compadre que había sido pobre simplemente señaló la ceniza en la hoguera y sonrió.

1 Vamos a acampar.

El Sr. Galindo y sus hijos se preparan para una excursión.

Martín, dudo que necesites tanta práctica. Además, te necesitamos. Ven, ayúdanos con las maletas y tráeme los sacos de dormir.

Sí, papá. Te los traigo en seguida.

¡Quíhubole, Martín! Sr. Galindo, ¿qué tal?

Hola, Mateo.

¿Qué hacen ustedes? ¿Y dónde está Daniel?

Hola, Mateo. Vamos a acampar este fin de semana.

¿De veras? ¡Qué padre! ¿Adónde van?

Vamos a Aguirre Springs, en la sierra, cerca de Las Cruces. ¿Por qué no nos acompañas, Mateo?

¿Te puedo decir más tarde?

Sí, Mateo, ven con nosotros.

Híjole, me encantaría, pero es posible que tenga que trabajar. Además, les tendría que pedir permiso a mis papás.

Claro, Mateo. Espero tu llamada.

Ya está todo, ¿no?

Sólo falta la comida— pero eso lo dejamos para mañana.

¡Quíhubole, Tina, Margarita!

¡Hola! ¿Qué tal?

Hola, chicas.

Buenas tardes, muchachas.

¡Hola!

¿Adónde van con tantas cosas?

A Aguirre Springs, a acampar.

Ayyy, ¿en el invierno? ¿Están locos? Hace mucho frío, ¿no?

¡Qué va! Somos fuertes. Además, nos vamos a abrigar bien.

Bueno, que les vaya bien... en el fffffríííooo.

Ya, ya, vámonos, Margarita. Tenemos prisa. Que les vaya bien. Hasta luego.

Sí, que les vaya bien . . . en el fffffríííooo.

3 ¿Por qué no vamos nosotras?

Tina, ¿por qué no vamos nosotras también?

A mis papás les encanta acampar.

Si mis padres tienen que trabajar este fin de semana, no creo que podamos ir. Pero voy a preguntárselo.

¡Pues, vamos!

¡Ay, esa Margarita! ¡Qué exagerada! Y siempre es así. Nunca cambia.

¿Cómo la aguantas?

No es para tanto...

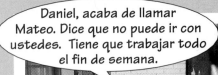

Daniel, acaba de llamar Mateo. Dice que no puede ir con ustedes. Tiene que trabajar todo el fin de semana.

¡Ay, Nena! ¿Ya colgaste? Quería hablar con él.

Lo siento. La comida ya está y mamá dice que vengan a comer.

4 ¡Eres un genio!

En la carretera a Nuevo México. . .

Ni yo tampoco, papá. Creo que todos los fusibles están bien. No veo ninguno fundido.

¡No comprendo por qué no funciona este carro!

Ven, hijo. Ayúdame aquí. ¿Ves ese desarmador grande? Pásamelo, por favor.

¿Éste, papá?

Sí. Gracias.

Sabes, no creo que sea nada del motor tampoco. ¡Caramba! Ya va a anochecer pronto. Y dudo que haya una gasolinera por aquí.

Ay, Martín. ¿Tú qué sabes de carros? La batería sólo tiene dos años y tiene garantía de cinco.

No te preocupes, papá. No puede ser nada serio. Andábamos bien hace poco y el carro no es tan viejo. ¿Revisaron la batería?

De todos modos, si las terminales están sucias...

Dame ese cepillo, Daniel.

¡Martín, eres un genio! Una de las terminales está bastante corroída.

Gracias.

Ahora, pruébalo, Daniel.

Perdón, Daniel. ¿Qué decías? ¿Me lo puedes repetir?

CHARLEMOS UN POCO

A. **PARA EMPEZAR . . .** Según el cuento de "La ceniza", ¿quién hizo o dijo lo siguiente: el compadre rico, el compadre pobre o la esposa del pobre?

1. Trabajaba de sol a sol, pero ganaba muy poco.
2. "Es posible que pueda decirte el secreto — cómo mejorar nuestra fortuna".
3. "¿Es posible que me digas tu secreto? ¿Cómo puedo hacerme rico?"
4. "¡No creo que él quiera ayudarnos! Pero, sí, puedo hablar con él".
5. "Yo me hice rico vendiendo ceniza. Tú debes hacer lo mismo".
6. "Estoy segura que va a volver rico, como su compadre".
7. "¿Cómo es posible que sea tan desafortunado?"
8. Señaló la ceniza en la hoguera y sonrió.

B. **¿QUÉ DECIMOS . . .?** Pon las siguientes oraciones en orden cronológico, según el diálogo.

1. Daniel admite que Martín tenía razón.
2. El carro ya no anda.
3. Las chicas hablan de ir también.
4. Los Galindo empacan el carro.
5. Unas chicas saludan a los Galindo.
6. Los Galindo entran en la casa para comer.
7. Martín juega baloncesto.
8. Mateo llama para decir que tiene que trabajar.
9. Papá invita a Mateo a acompañarlos.
10. Martín sugiere que revisen la batería.

REPASO

Extending, accepting and declining invitations

Extending invitations:
¿Me (Nos) acompañas?
¿Quieres acompañarme?

Accepting invitations:
¡Claro que sí!
¡Cómo no!
¡Qué divertido!
¿Cuándo quieres ir?

Declining invitations:
Lo siento pero ya tengo planes.
Gracias, pero tengo que trabajar.

C. **¿Me invitas?**  ¿Qué dices y qué te contesta tu compañero(a) cuando lo (la) invitas a hacer estas cosas?

MODELO   correr (practicar el piano)
　　　Tú:　　　　　　**Voy a correr. ¿Me acompañas?**
　　　Compañero(a):　**Gracias, pero tengo que practicar el piano.** o
　　　　　　　　　　　Lo siento pero tengo que practicar el piano.

1. jugar tenis (limpiar mi cuarto)
2. alquilar un video (estudiar para un examen)
3. pasear en bicicleta (ayudar a mi mamá)
4. ir de compras (cortar el césped)
5. tomar un café (hacer mi tarea)
6. ir al zoológico (lavar el coche)
7. acampar (visitar a mis abuelos)
8. cenar en un restaurante (escribir una composición)

CH. Una visita. Tu primo está visitándote y tú y él reciben varias invitaciones. ¿Cómo respondes?

 MODELO   *Compañero(a):*   **¿Quieren acompañarme a la fiesta?**

           Tú: **¡Qué divertido! ¡Claro que sí!** o **Lo siento, pero ya tenemos planes.**

1.

2.

3.

4.

5.

6.

7.

8.

D. En cinco años. ¿Cómo va a ser tu vida en cinco años?

MODELO ¿Vas a estudiar en la universidad?
Es probable que estudie en la universidad. o
Es imposible que estudie en la universidad. o
Es dudoso que estudie en la universidad.

1. ¿Vas a tener un trabajo?
2. ¿Vas a ganar mucho dinero?
3. ¿Vas a vivir en la misma ciudad?
4. ¿Vas a salir con los mismos amigos?
5. ¿Vas a vivir con tu familia?
6. ¿Vas a viajar mucho?
7. ¿Vas a tener un carro elegante?
8. ¿Vas a escuchar música clásica?
9. ¿Vas a asistir a muchos conciertos?
10. ¿Vas a leer el periódico todos los días?

E. Secretos. Tú sabes los secretos de muchos amigos. ¿Qué opinas de sus problemas?

EJEMPLO Beltrán está cansado durante el día. Es dudoso que . . .
Es dudoso que duerma bastante.

VOCABULARIO ÚTIL:
acostarse: temprano / tarde
comer: demasiado / poco
dormir: bastante / poco
estudiar: mucho / poco
hacer ejercicio: mucho / poco
levantarse: temprano / tarde
salir: mucho / poco
tomar: mucho / poco

1. Bárbara y Alicia están muy delgadas.
   Está claro que . . .
2. Ernesto está muy gordo.
   Es obvio que . . .
3. Guillermina tiene mucha tarea.
   Es posible que . . .
4. Pepe y Daniela llegan tarde a la escuela.
   Es cierto que . . .
5. Zacarías tiene poca energía.
   Es dudoso que . . .
6. Micaela conoce a pocas personas.
   Es probable que . . .
7. Dionisio y Florencia sacan malas notas.
   Es evidente que . . .
8. Federico está perdiendo peso.
   Dudo que . . .

F. Opiniones. Tú quieres saber la opinión de tu compañero(a) sobre estos temas controversiales. ¿Qué les preguntas y qué te contestan?

MODELO   Hay vida en otros planetas.

> *Tú:*   **¿Crees que haya vida en otros planetas?** o
> **¿Crees que hay vida en otros planetas?**
>
> *Compañero(a):*   **Sí, creo que hay vida en otros planetas.** o
> **No, no creo que haya vida en otros planetas.**

1. Los padres saben más que los hijos.
2. La educación universitaria es importante.
3. Vamos a tener una sociedad perfecta algún día.
4. Los perros son más inteligentes que los gatos.
5. Es mejor vivir en la ciudad que en el campo.
6. Debemos cortar los árboles en la selva.
7. Hay bastante petróleo en este país.
8. Debemos limitar la población del planeta.

G. Muy de moda. A Rosario le encanta su ropa internacional y siempre habla de ella. ¿Qué dice?

MODELO   collar mexicano: primos
> **Me encanta este collar. Mis primos me lo trajeron de México.**

1. suéter peruano: tío Felipe
2. falda puertorriqueña: papá
3. blusas guatemaltecas: abuelos
4. sombrero boliviano: amiga Susana
5. zapatos argentinos: tías
6. chaqueta panameña: primo Pepe
7. pantalones uruguayos: mamá
8. pulsera española: amigo Joaquín

Expressions of doubt: *Creer*

In negative statements, the verb **creer** is followed by the subjunctive. In affirmative statements, it is followed by the indicative. In questions, it may be followed by the subjunctive or the indicative.

¿Crees que **puedan** hacerlo?
¿Crees que **pueden** hacerlo?
No, no creo que lo **puedan** hacer.
Pues, yo sí creo que lo **pueden** hacer.

See **¿Por qué se dice así?,** *page G82, section 6.1.*

Double object pronouns: Placement

When two object pronouns occur in a sentence, the indirect object pronoun always comes first.

No **me lo** explicó.
¿**Nos las** vas a mandar?

See **¿Por qué se dice así?,** *page G84, section 6.2.*

Double object pronouns with commands

When used with commands, object pronouns follow and are attached to affirmative commands, and they precede negative commands.

Vénde**melas.**
Dá**melo** por favor.
No **te las** pongas.
No **me los** traigas.

See **¿Por qué se dice así?,**
page G84, section 6.2.

Double object pronouns with infinitives

Object pronouns precede conjugated verbs or may follow and be attached to infinitives.

¿Te dio su dirección?
Va a dár**mela** más tarde.
Me la va a dar más tarde.

See **¿Por qué se dice así?,**
page G84, section 6.2.

Object pronouns with -ndo verb forms

Object pronouns may precede the conjugated verb or follow and be attached to the **-ndo** verb form of the present progressive.

Ernesto está haciéndo**melo.**
¿Te las están preparando ahora mismo?

See **¿Por qué se dice así?,**
page G84, section 6.2.

H. ¡Qué generoso! Estás de compras con tu tío(a) que quiere comprarte muchas cosas. ¿Qué le dices?

 MODELO *Tío(a):* **¿Te compro ese libro?**
Tú: **Sí, cómpramelo.** o
No, gracias, no me lo compres.

I. De visita. Tú y tu hermano(a) acaban de llegar al pueblo de tu prima Angélica. ¿Cómo contestan ustedes las preguntas que les hace su tío(a)?

 MODELO monumentos
Tío(a): **¿Ya les enseñó Angélica los monumentos?**
Tú: **No, nos los va a enseñar mañana.** o
No, va a enseñárnoslos mañana.

1. iglesia
2. colegios
3. biblioteca
4. teatros
5. plazas
6. parque
7. centro comercial
8. fuentes

J. Ahora mismo. Tú amigo(a) es candidato(a) para presidente del Club de español. Tú y varios amigos están ayudándole. ¿Qué le dices cuando te pregunta cuándo se van a hacer estas cosas?

 MODELO escribir la carta (Rafael)
Presidente: **¿Cuándo me va a escribir la carta Rafael?**
Tú: **Te la está escribiendo ahora mismo.** o
Está escribiéndotela ahora mismo.

1. buscar la información (Alicia)
2. escribir el artículo para el periódico (Teodoro)
3. conseguir los números de teléfono (Blanca)
4. preparar los cheques (Gonzalo)
5. hacer la lista de miembros (Flora)
6. traer los casetes (Adán)

CHARLEMOS UN POCO MÁS

A. ¿Me acompañas? Hay muchas cosas que quieres hacer este fin de semana. Dile a tus compañeros qué vas a hacer e invítalos a acompañarte. Tus compañeros van a responder que sí a tres o cuatro de tus invitaciones.

B. Excusas. Tus amigos van a invitarte a acompañarlos a varios lugares el sábado. Tú no quieres salir el sábado. Por eso tienes que darles excusas.

C. Es dudoso. Usa el cuestionario que tu profesor(a) te da para entrevistar a tus compañeros de clase. Pídeles que firmen la línea apropiada. Recuerda que no se permite que una persona firme más de una vez.

EJEMPLO *Tú:* **¿Vas a vivir en Europa?**
Compañero(a): **Es probable que viva en Europa.**

CH. **¿Por qué?** Después de mirar estos dibujos, tú y tu compañero(a) deben decidir por qué ocurre cada situación.

Sergio

EJEMPLO **Es obvio que Sergio se levanta tarde.** o
Es probable que Sergio se levante tarde.

1. Susana

2. Tomás y Memo

3. Rodrigo

4. Conchita y Lupe

5. Rosario

6. Alegra

7. Diego

8. Eduardo

Dramatizaciones

A. **El baile.** Hay un baile en la escuela el viernes por la noche. Tu amigo(a) va a invitarte al baile. Pero como no sabes bailar, no quieres ir. Decidan qué van a hacer. Dramaticen esta situación.

B. **¿Qué pasa con Ricardo?** Tú y tu amigo(a) están muy preocupados porque Ricardo, otro amigo, está haciendo cosas muy extrañas. Hoy, por ejemplo, lleva puesta una camisa amarilla con pantalones rojos y ahora, está comiendo sopa con tenedor. Traten de explicar las acciones raras de su amigo.

IMPACTO CULTURAL
Excursiones

Antes de empezar

A. **Yo digo que** . . . ¿Cuánto sabes de Costa Rica? Indica si crees que estos comentarios son ciertos o falsos. Si no estás seguro(a), adivina usando lo que ya sabes de Latinoamérica.

Los autores

Yo digo que . . .

Sí **No**	**1.** Costa Rica, como los otros países latinoamericanos, tiene una historia muy violenta.	**Sí**	**No**
Sí **No**	**2.** En Costa Rica es posible nadar en el Océano Atlántico por la mañana y en el Pacífico por la tarde del mismo día.	**Sí**	**No**
Sí **No**	**3.** En Costa Rica, la mayor parte de la población vive en el Valle Central.	**Sí**	**No**
Sí **No**	**4.** El clima de Costa Rica varía mucho, frío en las montañas, calor en el Valle Central y templado en las costas.	**Sí**	**No**
Sí **No**	**5.** En Costa Rica hay selva tropical con toda especie de animales.	**Sí**	**No**
Sí **No**	**6.** La selva tropical en Costa Rica siempre ha sido protegida por el gobierno federal.	**Sí**	**No**
Sí **No**	**7.** El gobierno federal costarricense, como el de EE.UU., ha establecido un sistema de parques nacionales para proteger la ecología.	**Sí**	**No**
Sí **No**	**8.** Costa Rica tiene una larga tradición de democracia.	**Sí**	**No**
Sí **No**	**9.** La constitución de Costa Rica no permite tener ejército.	**Sí**	**No**
Sí **No**	**10.** En 1987 el presidente de Costa Rica recibió el Premio Nóbel de la Paz.	**Sí**	**No**

B. **Los autores dicen** . . . Ahora lee la lectura y vuelve al formulario de la actividad **A** e indica si los comentarios son ciertos o falsos según los autores.

Parques Nacionales

OCÉANO PACÍFICO

NICARAGUA

MAR CARIBE

ALAJUELA

GUANACASTE

HEREDIA

Volcán Poas

Volcán Irazú

San José   CARTAGO   LIMÓN

SAN JOSÉ

PANAMÁ

PUNTARENAS

COSTA RICA

COSTA RICA
Rica en todo sentido

En medio de una zona llena de conflictos y guerras, Costa Rica constituye un verdadero paraíso de gente alegre y pacífica y de bosques tropicales con una gran variedad de plantas y animales.

Costa Rica es un país muy pequeño, más o menos del tamaño de West Virginia. Una persona puede viajar a la capital, San José, que está en el Valle Central, y decidir si quiere nadar en el Atlántico o el Pacífico esa misma tarde. ❶

En Costa Rica se distinguen tres regiones naturales: las costas del Pacífico y el Atlántico, las zonas montañosas con sus volcanes como el Irazú (11.260 pies) y el Poas ❷ (9.000 pies), y la región del Valle Central ❸ donde vive la mayoría de los habitantes. ❹ El país tiene una tierra muy fértil creada por la actividad de los volcanes. En estas diferentes regiones hay una variedad de climas pero sin llegar a los extremos, es decir, ni hace mucho frío ni mucho calor.

Debido a la gran variedad de terrenos y al buen clima, Costa Rica tiene una gran diversidad de especies de plantas y animales. Por ejemplo, por pequeño que es el país, hay más de ochocientas cincuenta especies de pájaros, muchos de ellos de bello plumaje, como los loros, los picaflores ❺ y, claro, el quetzal, ❻ el más famoso del país. También hay 1239 especies de mariposas de hermosos colores y una variedad de reptiles, gatos silvestres, primates y marsupiales. Entre los animales nativos americanos más curiosos están los perezosos ❼ y los armadillos. También tiene una gran variedad de flora con sus más de ochocientas especies de helechos, mil doscientas especies de orquídeas ❽ y dos mil variedades de árboles.

Lamentablemente todas estas especies de animales están en peligro de extinción debido a la deforestación de los bosques tropicales. **9** En 1950, el 72 por ciento de Costa Rica estaba cubierto de bosques. En 1973, era el 49 por ciento, en 1978 el 34 por ciento y en 1985 el 26 por ciento. Si continúa así, para el año 2000 todos los bosques de Costa Rica serán destruidos. Por eso, en un esfuerzo para mantener su riqueza natural, el gobierno ha creado un sistema de parques nacionales **10** que cubren el 11 por ciento de su territorio. En estos parques habitan por lo menos un ejemplar de cada especie de plantas y animales.

Además de sus riquezas naturales, Costa Rica se distingue por su fuerte tradición democrática. Sólo ha tenido dos períodos violentos en su historia: uno de 1917 a 1919 bajo un dictador militar y otro durante su Guerra Civil en 1948-49. En 1949, después de la Guerra Civil, se adoptó una nueva constitución en la que se prohibió el establecimiento de un ejército nacional. Sólo hay una Guardia Nacional con cuatro mil miembros y la Guardia de Asistencia Rural con tres mil miembros no profesionales.

Debido a este estado de paz, Costa Rica ha concentrado sus esfuerzos en la educación de sus ciudadanos. Así, esta nación goza de uno de los más altos índices de alfabetismo de Latinoamérica. También Costa Rica ha contribuido internacionalmente para lograr la paz en Centroamérica, especialmente el expresidente Óscar Arias. **11** Éste recibió el Premio Nóbel de la Paz en 1987, por su esfuerzo en traer la paz a los países de Centroamérica.

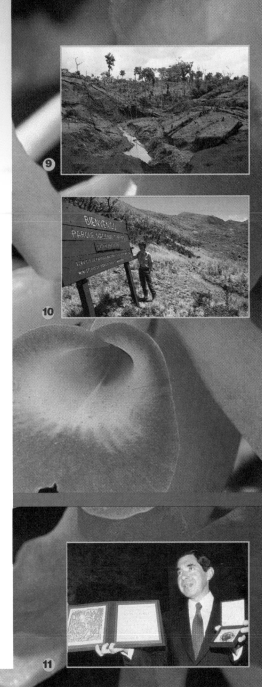

Verifiquemos

1. Prepara un esquema como el que sigue y compara Costa Rica con EE.UU. en las áreas indicadas.
2. ¿Crees que es importante que Costa Rica haya establecido un sistema de parques nacionales para proteger los bosques tropicales? ¿Por qué?
3. ¿Qué podrías hacer tú para protegerlos?

Costa Rica	Estados Unidos
1. gobierno	1. gobierno
2. geografía	2. geografía
3. educación	3. educación
4. ejército	4. ejército

He oído de «La cueva».

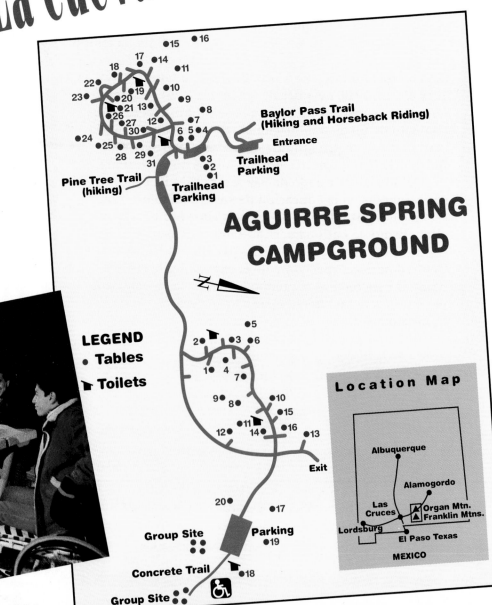

Baylor Pass Trail
(Hiking and Horseback Riding)

Entrance

Trailhead Parking

Pine Tree Trail (hiking)

Trailhead Parking

AGUIRRE SPRING CAMPGROUND

LEGEND

- **Tables**
- **Toilets**

Exit

Group Site

Concrete Trail

Group Site

Parking

Location Map

Albuquerque

Alamogordo

Las Cruces

Organ Mtn.
Franklin Mtns.

Lordsburg

El Paso Texas

MEXICO

¿ Qué piensas tú ?

1. ¿De qué es el mapa? ¿Puedes describir el área? ¿Es un desierto? ¿Hay montañas? ¿playas? ¿lagos? ¿Qué se puede hacer en este lugar? ¿Cómo lo sabes?

2. Si tú estuvieras en la entrada a este lugar, ¿qué dirías para dirigir a alguien al primer campamento número 1? ¿al número 7? ¿a los servicios más cercanos? ¿al comienzo del camino Pine Tree? ¿al camino para personas en sillas de ruedas?

3. ¿Qué busca el hombre en el dibujo? ¿Dónde ha buscado ya?

4. ¿Dónde sugieres que busque? ¿Por qué?

5. Cerca de donde tú vives, ¿adónde puede ir una familia a pasar el fin de semana? ¿Cuál es el atractivo de ese lugar?

6. ¿Conoces algunos cuentos, leyendas o misterios relacionados a algún lugar cerca de donde vives tú? Si conoces alguno, cuéntaselo a la clase.

7. ¿Qué crees que vas a aprender a hacer y decir en esta lección?

EL RICO

Este cuento, que nos viene del norte de Nuevo México, tiene sabor de un melodrama típico — con un rico malvado, un hombre pobre pero honesto y una bellísima y virtuosa heroína. Y como en todos los cuentos de esta índole, el malvado lleva su merecido.

1

Hace muchos años, en un pueblito tranquilo, vivía un joven que era dueño de la mayor parte de las propiedades de la región. También se le consideraba el hombre más rico del país. La gente lo llamaba "el rico". Lo único que le faltaba era una esposa.

2

Camino abajo, a una corta distancia, vivía otro hombre llamado don Gonzalo. Don Gonzalo le debía al rico una cantidad considerable de dinero.

3

Un día, el rico fue a visitar a don Gonzalo y le dijo, "He decidido casarme con tu hija, la bella Angelita". Pero antes de poder contestar don Gonzalo, Angelita reaccionó diciéndole a su padre, "¡Yo también he decidido! No tengo ninguna intención de casarme con ese malvado". El rico se puso furioso y le dijo a don Gonzalo, "Pues, yo he determinado que, si no me da la mano de su hija, les voy a quitar la casa y el terreno".

Cuando Angelita y su padre trataron de razonar con el rico, él reaccionó diciendo, "¿No han oído lo que he dicho? Yo pienso tomar lo que legítimamente es mío. Van a perder su ranchito y tendrán que vivir en la calle con los mendigos". Don Gonzalo se puso muy triste. No quería perder lo poco que tenía. Se vio obligado a firmar unos papeles en los que daba su consentimiento.

El día de la boda, el rico andaba algo nervioso. Quería tener una boda perfecta para impresionar a su nueva esposa. Él llamó al criado encargado de los otros criados y le preguntó, "¿Han hecho todo lo que les dije?" Éste le contestó, "Sí, señor. Hemos limpiado la casa de arriba abajo y hemos preparado el cochinillo asado. Y sí, la costurera ha hecho un hermosísimo túnico de novia y un velo".

Luego, el rico llamó a una criada y le dio una larga lista de instrucciones. La pobre muchacha salió volada e hizo exactamente lo que le pidió el rico.

7 Primero, fue a la casa de Angelita y le dijo, "Mi patrón me ha mandado por lo que le pertenece legalmente". Como Angelita sabía que su padre le debía mucho dinero al rico, decidió empezar a pagarle mandándole su burra.

8 Cuando ya era hora de empezar la celebración y la novia todavía no llegaba, el criado encargado de los otros fue a hablar con la criada. Ésta le dijo, "He hecho exactamente lo que el patrón pidió. He metido lo que legalmente le pertenece al patrón por la puerta de los sirvientes para que nadie la vea".

"La he subido a la alcoba en el piso de arriba".

"La he vestido con el túnico y el velo de novia".

"Y ya está lista para llevarla a la sala de baile". En ese instante le gritó el rico a la criada que bajara con su novia. Claro, la criada sacó a la burra del dormitorio donde estaba y la llevó al baile.

9 Toda la gente se reía a carcajadas. Había algunos que estaban desmorecidos de risa.

El rico se sentía como un idiota y no volvió a molestar a Angelita.

1 ¿Por dónde vamos ahora?

Por fin llegamos.

¿Por dónde vamos ahora, Daniel?

Según este mapa, hay tres sitios distintos.

Para llegar al primero, hay que doblar a la derecha por el primer camino. Para el segundo y el tercero, sigue derecho en el camino principal. El primero parece el sitio más popular. Hay más de treinta lugares.

Bueno, vamos al primero, entonces. ¿Está bien?

2 Ayúdame a armar la carpa.

Daniel, ¿has visto las zanahorias y el apio?

Sí, creo que están en la hielera.

¿Te los traigo?

3 Vamos a «La cueva».

CHARLEMOS UN POCO

A. **PARA EMPEZAR . . .** Pon en orden lo que dijo la criada cuando el criado encargado le preguntó si había seguido las instrucciones que le dio el patrón.

1. ''He metido lo que legalmente le pertenece al patrón por la puerta de los sirvientes para que nadie la vea''.
2. ''Y ya está lista para llevarla a la sala de baile''.
3. ''He hecho exactamente lo que el patrón pidió''.
4. ''La he subido a la alcoba en el piso de arriba''.
5. ''La he vestido con el túnico y el velo de novia''.

B. **¿QUÉ DECIMOS . . .?** ¿Quién dijo estas cosas: Daniel, Martín o papá?

Daniel   **Martín**   **Papá**

1. ''Por fin llegamos. ¿Por dónde vamos ahora?''
2. ''Hay que doblar a la derecha por el primer camino''.
3. ''¿Has visto las zanahorias y el apio?''
4. ''Mejor tráeme toda la hielera y así no te molesto más''.
5. ''Ah, también, pon la linterna ahí encima de la mesa''.
6. ''Ven acá. Ayúdame a armar la carpa''.
7. ''¿Qué vamos a hacer mañana?''
8. ''He oído hablar de la cueva, pero realmente no recuerdo los detalles''.
9. ''En la escuela hicimos una excursión al museo de la universidad''.
10. ''Pues, yo he oído otras cosas de la cueva''.
11. ''Lo único que vieron en lo oscuro de la cueva fueron los ojos brillantes de un puma''.
12. ''Casi me muero de miedo''.

C. ¿Por dónde vamos?   La familia Galindo está en ''Aguirre Spring Campground''. Quieren visitar «La cueva» y almorzar allí. ¿Qué direcciones reciben? Pon las direcciones en orden cronológico según el mapa.

REPASO

Giving directions

Dobla a la derecha (izquierda).
Sigue derecho.
Camina media (una, dos, . . .) cuadra(s).
Toma el autobús (metro, tren).
Pasa por el parque.
Cruza la calle.

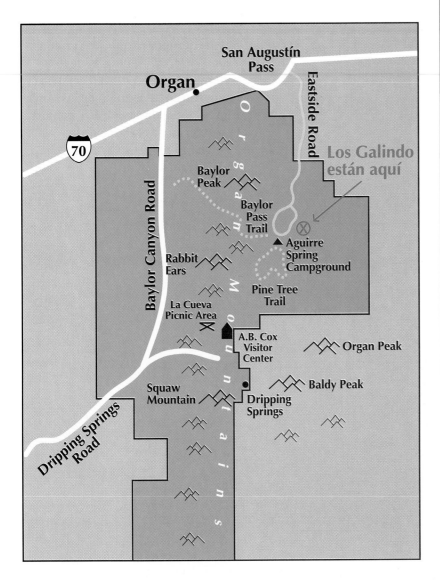

1. Entonces, doblen a la izquierda en el camino Baylor Canyon.
2. Doblen a la izquierda y sigan adelante unas millas.
3. Luego, doblen a la izquierda y sigan unas dos millas más y allí están las mesas.
4. «La cueva» está detrás de las mesas.
5. Pasando el pueblo de Organ, sigan una milla más.
6. Salgan por el camino principal del campamento y regresen a la carretera 70.
7. Sigan todo derecho unas seis millas hasta llegar a otro camino.

CH. ¿Cómo llego? Estás en el aeropuerto de una nueva ciudad y necesitas direcciones para llegar a varios lugares. Pregúntale a tu compañero cómo llegar a los lugares indicados.

 EJEMPLO   hotel

Tú: **¿Puedes decirme cómo llegar al hotel?**

Compañero(a): **Sal del aeropuerto por la Avenida de la Libertad. Dobla a la derecha y camina media cuadra. Dobla a la izquierda en la Avenida de las Flores. Sigue dos cuadras y dobla a la izquierda en el Paseo de la Justicia. El hotel está a la derecha en la esquina.**

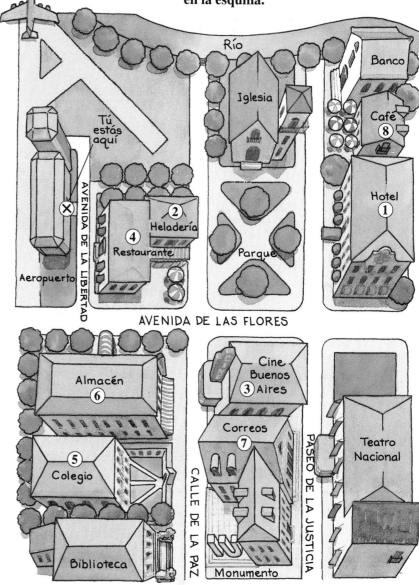

D. Quehaceres. Al volver de una excursión durante el fin de semana, tu madre o padre quiere saber los quehaceres que has hecho. ¿Qué te preguntan y qué les contestas?

MODELO   limpiar la casa
Madre (Padre): **¿Ya limpiaste la casa?**
Tú: **Todavía no he limpiado la casa pero voy a hacerlo en seguida.**

1. lavar el carro
2. pasar la aspiradora
3. sacar la basura
4. limpiar los baños
5. cortar el césped
6. pasar un trapo
7. lavar los platos
8. preparar la cena

E. Para sobresalir, yo . . .   ¿Qué han hecho tú y tus amigos para salir bien en la escuela este año?

MODELO   Pedro y Mario: dormir ocho horas cada noche
Para sobresalir, Pedro y Mario han dormido ocho horas cada noche.

1. yo: leer todas las lecciones
2. Pepe y Hernando: responder a todas las preguntas
3. Federica: aprender los elementos químicos
4. Irma y yo: traer cosas interesantes a la clase
5. tú: asistir a todas las clases
6. tú y Constanza: comer un buen desayuno
7. nosotros: salir solamente los fines de semana
8. los hermanos Sánchez: pedir ayuda a los profesores

F. Ocupados.   Estás de vacaciones en Centroamérica. Tu familia quiere saber qué han hecho tú y tus compañeros de viaje. ¿Qué les dices cuando les hablas por teléfono?

EJEMPLO   **Yo he descubierto muchas cosas fascinantes.**

| el guía
yo
mi amigo(a) [. . .]
todos nosotros
[. . .] y [. . .] | descubrir
ponerse
hacer
escribir
romper
ver | mucha ropa nueva
unas películas
mucho ejercicio
muchas cosas fascinantes
un nuevo hotel
muchas cartas
varios museos
el brazo
un tour de la capital |

**Present perfect tense:
-*ar* verbs**

he
has
ha   } + **-ado** verb form
hemos
han

No **hemos comprado** los regalos todavía.
¿**Has estudiado** para el examen?

See **¿Por qué se dice así?,**
page G86, section 6.3.

**Present perfect tense:
-*er* and -*ir* verbs**

he
has
ha   } + **-ido** verb form
hemos
han

No **he comido** todavía
¿**Has recibido** mi regalo?

See **¿Por qué se dice así?,**
page G86, section 6.3.

Irregular past participles

abrir	**abierto**
decir	**dicho**
descubrir	**descubierto**
escribir	**escrito**
hacer	**hecho**
morir	**muerto**
poner	**puesto**
resolver	**resuelto**
romper	**roto**
ver	**visto**
volver	**vuelto**

Todavía no **han descubierto** al ladrón.
No **hemos visto** a Carlos.

See **¿Por qué se dice así?,**
page G86, section 6.3.

G. Antes de salir. ¿Qué ha hecho cada miembro de la familia de Javier en preparación para su viaje a Miami?

yo

MODELO **Yo me he despertado a las cinco.**

1. mi hermanita   **2.** Ana   **3.** mi papá

4. Ana   **5.** yo   **6.** mi mamá

7. mi hermanita   **8.** Ana y mi mamá

H. Mandón. Tu hermano(a) mayor siempre te dice qué hacer cuando tú ya lo has hecho. ¿Cómo le contestas?

MODELO   escribir tu composición
    Hermano(a): **Escribe tu composición.**
    Tú: **Ya la he escrito.**

1. hacer la tarea
2. leer el libro de historia
3. limpiar tu cuarto
4. poner la mesa

5. lavar el carro
6. barrer el piso
7. sacar la basura
8. pasar un trapo a los muebles

I. ¿A quién? Acabas de empezar tu nuevo puesto de camarero(a) pero a veces tienes problemas recordando quién pidió qué. ¿Qué les preguntas a los clientes?

MODELO carne: ¿señora o niños?
      La carne, ¿se la sirvo a la señora o a los niños?

1. ensalada: ¿señorita o señor?
2. entremeses: ¿niños o todos?
3. pollo: ¿señora o niña?
4. arepas: ¿señorita o señor?
5. sopa: ¿señor o señora?
6. hamburguesa: ¿niño o niña?
7. papas: ¿niños o adultos?
8. postre: ¿señorita o señor?
9. el café: ¿señor o señora?
10. la tortilla española: ¿niña o señorita?

Double object pronouns: 3rd person

In sentences with two object pronouns, when both pronouns begin with the letter **l**, the first one (**le** or **les**) becomes **se**:

Yo le di el libro ayer.
↓
Yo ~~le~~ lo di ayer.
↓
Yo **se lo** di ayer.

¿**Se los** vendió?
Nosotros **se la** escribimos.

See **¿Por qué se dice así?,** *page G89, section 6.4.*

J. Llorón. Tú y tu hermano(a) están cuidando a un niño difícil. Cada vez que el niño necesita algo, tu hermano(a) quiere que tú lo hagas. ¿Qué te dice que hagas y cómo le contestas?

MODELO cantar una canción
    Hermano(a): **Cántale una canción.**
    Tú: **No quiero. Cántasela tú.**

1. contar un cuento
2. servir una taza de leche
3. traer sus juguetes
4. buscar un libro
5. dibujar unos animales
6. dar una banana
7. preparar su comida
8. hacer unas figuritas

K. ¿Qué pasó? Anoche hubo una tormenta y en las casas de muchos de tus amigos se cortó la electricidad. Hoy, todo el mundo quiere saber qué pasó en su telenovela favorita, *Vidas y sueños.* ¿Qué dicen cuando les preguntas cómo supieron lo que pasó?

EJEMPLO Manuel me lo explicó a mí.

yo		a Manuel
Manuel		a ti
Irma	decir	a nosotros
nosotros	explicar	a Irma
tú	contar	a Tomás y Paulina
ellos	repetir	a mí
Tomás y Paulina		a ellos

CHARLEMOS UN POCO MÁS

A. Al salir de . . .   Tu profesor(a) va a darles a ti y a tu compañero(a) un plano de una ciudad. Tú necesitas ir a ciertos lugares indicados en tu mapa y tu compañero(a) necesita ir a otros lugares indicados en el suyo. Pídele direcciones a los lugares indicados y dile cómo llegar a los lugares donde él o ella quiere ir. Marquen la ruta a cada destinación empezando cada vez desde la casa.

B. ¿Qué han hecho?   Mira los dibujos aquí. Con un compañero(a) decidan qué ha pasado en cada dibujo. Luego escriban una breve descripción para cada dibujo.

1. Marcos

2. Pámela, David y Juan

3. Linda y Marcela

4. Luis

5. yo

6. tú

C. ¡De veras! ¿Hay algo que quieres saber de alguna persona en la clase? Con un(a) compañero(a), prepara de ocho a diez preguntas para hacerle a una persona en la clase [hasta puede ser su profesor(a)] sobre lo que ha hecho en los últimos cinco años. Luego entrevisten a la persona.

EJEMPLO   **¿Ha(s) visitado México?**
¿Ha(s) vivido en otro estado?

Dramatizaciones

A. ¿Dónde está?   Tu compañero(a) quiere ir a varios lugares en tu pueblo pero no sabe dónde están. Dile cómo llegar allí cuando te pida direcciones específicas. Dramaticen esta situación.

B. He visitado a mi tía.   Te encuentras con un(a) amigo(a) que no has visto desde hace dos años. Tú quieres saber qué ha hecho en los últimos dos años y tu amigo(a) quiere saber qué has hecho tú. Dramaticen esta situación.

Antes de empezar

A. Diminutivo. En español, usamos el diminutivo, es decir, la terminación **-ito(s)/-ita(s)**, para expresar afecto o cariño. Por ejemplo, decimos *abuelita* en vez de *abuela* y *perritos* en vez de *perros*. ¿Puedes dar el diminutivo de estas palabras?

hermano   prima   abuelos
hermanas   perro   gata

¿Cuáles son algunas maneras que tú usas en inglés para expresar afecto o cariño con tus familiares?

B. ¡Es de Texas! Con frecuencia podemos identificar el origen de unas personas por su habla. Por ejemplo, si una persona dice "you all" con frecuencia sabemos que es de Texas o por lo menos del suroeste. ¿Cuáles son otras marcas lingüísticas en inglés que identifican el origen de ciertas personas?

Los "ticos"

Dos muchachos conversan en el patio de un colegio de San José.
Luis es de Costa Rica y Miguel es de Venezuela.

Luis: **Miguel, ¿puedes esperarme un momentico? . . . porque todavía tengo que llamar a mi primo para desearle "feliz cumpleaños".**

Miguel: **Sí, perfecto. No hay problema. Dime, Luis, ¿por qué no vamos a cenar algo antes de la película?**

Luis: **¡Qué buena idea! Conozco un sitio chiquitico que queda muy cerca del cine. Sé que te va a gustar.**

Miguel: **¡¡Chévere!! Pero dime, Luis, ¿qué es eso del "tico"? ¿Es una costumbre nueva de todos los jóvenes aquí? Suena muy bien, eh.**

Luis: **¡Qué va, Miguel! ¿No sabes que en mi país todos somos "ticos"?**

Verifiquemos

1. Luis usa dos palabras que le suenan un poco raro a Miguel. ¿Cuáles son? ¿Cuál es su significado?
2. ¿Es una nueva costumbre de todos los jóvenes en Costa Rica usar el "tico"? Explica tu respuesta.
3. ¿Qué diría Luis: poquito o poquitico, ratito o ratico, cortito o cortico? ¿Cómo lo sabes?
4. ¿Cuál es la regla que explica lo que dicen los costarricenses en comparación con el resto de los hispanohablantes?

¡ Qué susto !

¿ Qué piensas tú ?

1. Daniel le escribió una carta a un amigo, contándole lo que pasó en Aguirre Springs. ¿Qué crees que dice en su carta?

2. Si Martín escribe una carta describiendo el viaje a Aguirre Springs, ¿cómo va a variar su versión de la de su hermano? ¿de la versión de su padre?

3. Mira el dibujo ahora. ¿Qué pasó? ¿Qué está pasando ahora? ¿Quién creen los padres que es el culpable?

4. ¿Qué dice cada hijo para explicar su inocencia? ¿Quién crees tú que es el culpable? ¿Por qué?

5. ¿Has hecho algo ridículo alguna vez? ¿Cómo te sentiste? ¿Qué le dijiste a tus padres o a tus amigos cuando les contaste lo que te pasó?

6. ¿Qué crees que vas a aprender a decir y hacer en esta lección?

CAIPORA, EL PADREMONTE

1 Parece que todas las culturas del mundo tienen mitos y fábulas para explicar el gran poder de la naturaleza. Éste es el caso en el mito brasileño: Caipora, el Padremonte.

Cada mañana, muy temprano, dos compadres — uno se llamaba Toño y el otro Chico — iban juntos al monte a cortar leña.

El monte era una belleza: claro y oscuro, con matas y árboles de todo tipo . . . y además, el canto de los pájaros y las bandadas de mariposas de colores brillantes.

2 Toño cortaba con cuidado las ramas más bajas, para no lastimar mucho a los árboles. Él siempre respetaba todas las plantas y jamás molestaba a los animalitos del bosque.

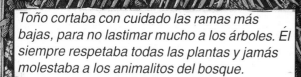

El compadre Chico cortaba troncos. Él no respetaba la naturaleza. Quebraba ramas sin necesidad. Y a veces mataba un animal, sólo para practicar la puntería.

3

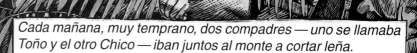

Un día, el compadre Chico no fue al monte. Toño entró solo en el bosque. Le pareció que todo era diferente. Los animales — todo el bosque en efecto — parecían estar inquietos y temerosos. Se oían ruidos extraños y se sentía un viento frío. Un gris oscuro y misterioso parecía predominar.

4

De repente, Toño vio en lo oscuro del bosque una aparición espantosa. ¡Era el Caipora, el Padremonte! El leñador se quedó paralizado de miedo. Era enorme, verde de pies a cabeza. Tenía las piernas fuertes y grandes, el cuerpo cubierto de pelos gruesos y los brazos tan largos que casi tocaban el suelo. Tenía también cabeza de zorro y lo peor de todo, tenía los pies volteados con los dedos hacia atrás.

5

De pronto, Caipora preguntó, "¿Tienes una pipa ahí, muchacho?" "¿Pipa? ¿Yo?", contestó el leñador. "Sí, aquí en mi mochila". Y le dio al monstruo su pipa. Caipora agarró la pipa y se fue trotando. El leñador se secó el sudor de la frente y dijo: "¡Uf! Tengo que trabajar para olvidar esta experiencia".

6

Ese día el compadre Toño volvió con la carreta cargada de leña de la mejor calidad.

Al día siguiente usó la leña como siempre, para fabricar carbón para vender en el pueblo. Cuando terminó el proceso, Toño decidió que sin duda esta leña produjo el mejor carbón que jamás había fabricado. Con este carbón, Toño muy pronto se hizo rico y no tuvo que ir más al bosque.

7 Cuando su compadre Chico supo de la buena fortuna de su compañero, insistió en saber el secreto de su riqueza. Toño decidió no darle muchos detalles de su encuentro con el monstruo del bosque. Simplemente le dijo, "Pienso que mi suerte fue por causa del encuentro, pero no estoy seguro . . ."

8 Un buen día el compadre Chico se encontró con el Caipora. En seguida le ofreció una pipa muy elegante, casi gritando de codicia. "Caipora, ¿puedes darme carbón? Mira, te doy mi mejor pipa".

9 El Caipora se enfureció. De sus ojos salían chispas verdes de odio.

"¡Eres tú — el matador de árboles y de animales!" Entonces el Padremonte agarró al codicioso violentamente.

10 Y desde ese día, apareció en el bosque un nuevo espanto: un hombre vuelto al revés que vaga entre los árboles como alma en pena.

Al regresar a casa, Martín les escribió una carta a sus primos en Monterrey, México.

Queridos primos:

Saludos de El Paso. Espero que todos estén bien. ¿Cómo está tía Gabriela? Mamá le manda recuerdos.

El fin de semana pasado mi papá, mi hermano y yo fuimos a Nuevo México a acampar en las montañas, los Órganos, cerca de Las Cruces. Nos divertimos muchísimo. Es un gran lugar para acampar. Ojalá algún día podamos ir allí todos juntos.

El segundo día fuimos a un sitio de excavaciones arqueológicas. Es una cueva que tiene una historia de siete mil años. Todo fue muy interesante, pero lo más fascinante fue lo que aprendimos sobre un señor del siglo pasado.

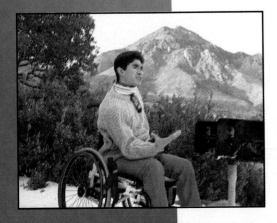

Era un señor bien excéntrico a quien todo el mundo llamaba el Ermitaño. Se pasó casi toda la vida viviendo solo en las montañas. Cuando el Ermitaño ya era viejo, se instaló en la cueva que visitamos.

La gente de Las Cruces le advirtió que era peligroso vivir solo allí, pero él no les hizo caso. Muchas personas del pueblo siguieron insistiendo hasta que, para complacerlos, dijo que iba a prender un fuego frente a la cueva cada noche para señalar que estaba bien. Una noche la gente del pueblo no vio la señal acostumbrada y todos se alarmaron. Al día siguiente salieron a buscarlo y lo encontraron muerto. Nadie sabe cómo murió, pero como te puedes imaginar, abundan las explicaciones.

Tengo que contarles una cosa chistosa que nos ocurrió la primera noche en el campamento. Después de cenar, mientras tomábamos chocolate, mi hermano nos empezó a contar otro cuento sobre esa misma cueva. Se trataba de un puma que vivía en la cueva y que una noche atacó a unos jóvenes universitarios.

El cuento era tan fantástico que yo sabía que él lo iba inventando. Sin embargo, los dos pasamos un gran susto cuando de repente, oímos unos ruidos extraños, como de un animal grande, cerca de nosotros. ¡Casi nos morimos de miedo! ¡Qué sorpresa llevamos cuando supimos que eran dos compañeras de clase! Ellas sabían que íbamos a estar allí, y vinieron al campamento con sus padres. Cuando oyeron a Daniel contar su cuento, decidieron asustarnos. ¡Qué malas!, ¿no?

¿Qué nos cuentan de nuevo? ¿Y cuándo vienen a visitarnos? Podemos ir a pasar la noche en « La cueva ». Escríbanos pronto.

Un fuerte abrazo de su primo,

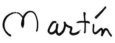

CHARLEMOS UN POCO

A. **PARA EMPEZAR . . .** Pon estas oraciones en orden según el mito brasileño ''Caipora, el Padremonte''.

1. Un día, Toño vio en lo oscuro del bosque, una aparición espantosa. ¡Era Caipora!
2. Cuando su compadre Chico le ofreció su pipa, casi gritando de codicia, Caipora lo convirtió en un nuevo espanto: un hombre vuelto al revés.
3. Caipora le pidió su pipa al leñador y éste se la dio.
4. Con el carbón que fabricó de la leña que cortó ese día, Toño se hizo rico, y no tuvo que ir más al bosque.
5. Toño cortaba con cuidado para no lastimar mucho a los árboles. Su compadre Chico cortaba los troncos.
6. Tenía también cabeza de zorro y lo peor de todo, tenía los pies volteados con los dedos hacia atrás.
7. Dos compadres, Toño y Chico, iban siempre al monte a cortar leña.
8. Tenía las piernas fuertes y grandes, el cuerpo cubierto de pelos gruesos y los brazos tan largos que casi tocaban el suelo.

B. **¿QUÉ DECIMOS . . .?** Di si son ciertos o falsos estos comentarios sobre la carta que escribió Martín. Si son falsos, corrígelos.

1. Martín escribió una carta a sus abuelos en México.
2. Martín y su familia fueron a acampar a las montañas en Texas.
3. Lo pasaron bien.
4. La cueva que visitaron era muy vieja.
5. Muchas personas vivieron en «La cueva».
6. El Ermitaño llegó a la cueva cuando era joven.
7. El Ermitaño tenía miedo de vivir en la cueva.
8. Cada noche el Ermitaño les daba una señal a sus amigos.
9. El Ermitaño todavía vive en la cueva.
10. Daniel contó un cuento de espantos sobre la cueva.
11. Daniel y Martín se asustaron cuando oyeron los ruidos de un puma.
12. Dos compañeras de clase también fueron a acampar al mismo lugar.

LECCIÓN 3

-ar	-er, -ir
-aba	-ía
-abas	-ías
-aba	-ía
-ábamos	-íamos
-aban	-ían

De niño, yo **estudiaba** mucho.
Nosotros **vivíamos** en San Antonio.
Yo siempre **me dormía**
inmediatamente.

See **¿Por qué se dice así?**,
page G92, section 6.5.

C. En mi niñez. Cuando Isabel era niña, siempre iba al parque
con su familia en el verano. Según ella, ¿qué hacían allí?

EJEMPLO **Angelita tomaba helado.**

CH. El verano pasado. El año pasado, la familia de Isabel pasó las vacaciones en México. Según ella, ¿qué hicieron?

MODELO   mis hermanos y yo: bailar en una discoteca
Mis hermanos y yo bailamos en una discoteca.

1. Simón: tomar el metro por primera vez
2. mamá y yo: comer en la Zona Rosa el último día en la capital
3. toda la familia: ver el Ballet Folklórico un domingo por la tarde
4. mi hermano: asistir a un partido de jai alai con papá
5. mis abuelos: visitar el Museo de Antropología un domingo por la tarde
6. papá y Angelita: comprar artesanías en Puebla
7. yo: subir al restaurante de la Torre Latinoamericana con mi tía
8. Simón y José: escuchar un concierto en la universidad
9. toda la familia: cenar en Coyoacán
10. José: ir al museo de Frida Kahlo

D. ¡Los Canguros! ¿Qué pasó ayer cuando tú y un(a) amigo(a) vieron a su grupo rock favorito? Para contestar, completa este diálogo.

Tú: ¡Imagínate! Ayer (vi / veía) a Los Canguros en persona.

Amigo(a):   ¡En persona! ¿Dónde (estuvieron / estaban)? ¿Qué (pasó / pasaba)? ¿Dónde (estuviste / estabas)?

Tú: Pues, (fui / iba) de compras al centro comercial con mi hermano. Él (necesitó / necesitaba) unos zapatos nuevos y yo (quise / quería) comprar una camiseta.

Amigo(a):   Sí, sí. Pero ¿dónde (encontraron / encontraban) a Los Canguros?

Tú: Pues, (fuimos / íbamos) a entrar en el almacén cuando de repente (oímos / oíamos) su música.

Amigo(a):   Ay, ¿sí? Y, ¿qué (hicieron / hacían) ustedes entonces? ¿(Supieron / sabían) dónde buscarlos?

Tú: ¡Claro que sí! (Salimos / Salíamos) a buscarlos en seguida. (Estuvimos / Estábamos) muy emocionados y . . .

Amigo(a):   ¡Por favor! Finalmente, ¿dónde los (vieron / veían)?

Tú: (Estuvieron / Estaban) en frente de la tienda de música tocando para el público. Además, la tienda (vendió / vendía) sus discos a un precio muy reducido.

Amigo(a):   ¿(Compraste / Comprabas) unos discos?

Tú: ¡Qué va! (Compré / Compraba) todos los discos de ellos que todavía no (tuve / tenía) en casa.

Amigo(a):   ¡Caramba! ¿Cuánto (gastaste / gastabas)?

Tú: Pues, te puedo decir que no (compré / compraba) la camiseta.

REPASO

The preterite

-ar	-er, -ir
-é	-í
-aste	-iste
-ó	-ió
-amos	-imos
-aron	-ieron

Trabajé toda la noche.
¿Ya **comiste**?
Salió esta mañana a las 10:00.

See **¿Por qué se dice así?**, *page G92, section 6.5.*

REPASO

Preterite: Irregular verbs

Irregular endings

-e	-imos
-iste	
-o	-ieron

Irregular stems:

-u stem	
andar	**anduv-**
estar	**estuv-**
haber	**hub-**
poder	**pud-**
poner	**pus-**
saber	**sup-**
tener	**tuv-**

-i stem	
querer	**quis-**
venir	**vin-**

-j stem	
decir	**dij-**
traer	**traj-**

See **¿Por qué se dice así?**, *page G92, section 6.5.*

E. Una fábula. Con un(a) compañero(a), decide el orden correcto de las oraciones de este cuento.

1. —Antes de matarme, —dijo ella, —déjenme gritar una cosa.
2. —Bueno, —le dijeron los ladrones, —pero rápido. Tenemos mucha prisa.
3. Al ver que ni su hija ni su perro venían, la viejita les pidió un favor a los ladrones.
4. Después de robar sus cosas, los ladrones entraron donde estaba la viejita y la iban a matar.
5. Ella gritó: —¡Ay, cuándo en mis Tiempos, Lucía!
6. Ese día su hija Lucía y su perro Tiempos estaban dormidos en otro cuarto y no oyeron nada.
7. Había una vez una mujer que era muy vieja.
8. Lucía y Tiempos oyeron y salieron pronto.
9. También tenía un perro que se llamaba Tiempos.
10. Tenía una hija que se llamaba Lucía.
11. Una vez vinieron a la casa de la vieja dos hombres malos que pensaban robarle.
12. Y el perro atacó a los ladrones.

F. Examen. Ernesto tuvo una experiencia muy interesante. ¿Qué pasó?

MODELO   Ernesto / estar / muy preocupado.
            Ernesto estaba muy preocupado.

1. tener / examen / clase de química al día siguiente
2. pasar / todo / tarde estudiando
3. a / siete / amigo Andrés / llamar
4. Andrés invitarlo / ir al cine, pero Ernesto / decir / que no
5. más tarde / amiga Valentina / venir / casa
6. ella invitar / Ernesto a salir para tomar / refresco
7. otra vez / Ernesto declinar / invitación
8. en la mañana / entrar / laboratorio de química
9. sentirse / bien preparado
10. haber / un mensaje / pizarra: ''No hay examen hoy''

G. Una caminata. Ramona y Jacobo Vargas fueron a acampar. Basándote en los dibujos, cuenta lo que pasó.

1. levantarse / hacer buen (mal) tiempo / sentirse

2. decidir caminar / montañas / caminar millas

3. de repente / comenzar / llover / hacer viento

4. ver cueva / decidir buscar refugio / correr

5. llegar / ver ojos / asustarse

6. (¿ . . . ?)

H. ¡Qué día! Tu compañero(a) te está describiendo el tiempo. ¿Qué opinas?

MODELO *Compañero(a):* **Hace viento.**
         Tú: **¡Es un mal día!** o
                ¡Es un buen día! o
                ¡Es un gran día!

1.   **2.**   **3.**   **4.**

5.   **6.**   **7.**   **8.**

LECCIÓN 3

Adjectives: Shortened forms

bueno	**buen**
grande	**gran**
malo	**mal**
primero	**primer**
tercero	**tercer**
alguno	**algún**
ninguno	**ningún**

Éste es mi **primer** examen.
Simón Bolívar fue un **gran** hombre.

*See **¿Por qué se dice así?**,
page G95, section 6.6*

trescientos veintitrés **323**

I. Encuesta. Entrevista a tu compañero(a) sobre sus actividades de la semana pasada. Luego él (ella) te va a entrevistar a ti.

EJEMPLO   ver programa de televisión

Tú: **¿Viste algún programa de televisión?**

Compañero(a):   **No, no vi ningún programa de televisión.** o
Sí, vi [. . .]

1. recibir carta
2. tocar instrumento musical
3. oír cuento
4. conocer a persona nueva
5. hacer viaje
6. ir a restaurante
7. comprar cosa interesante
8. leer libro de aventura

CHARLEMOS UN POCO MÁS

A. ¿Cómo era?   Ayer visitaste a un primo que asiste a la universidad.

Ahora vas a describir su apartamento a tu compañero(a). Usa el dibujo que tu profesor(a) te va a dar de una sala amueblada. Tu compañero(a) va a recibir un dibujo de la misma sala sin muebles. Dile a tu compañero(a) exactamente dónde están todos los muebles para que él (ella) pueda dibujarlos. No se permite ver su dibujo antes de terminar esta actividad. Empieza por decir: **El apartamento estaba en el primer piso. La sala no tenía muchos muebles. Había . . .**

Vocabulario útil:

a la derecha de	debajo de	enfrente de
a la izquierda de	encima de	detrás de
al lado de	sobre	en
cerca (lejos) de	delante de	entre

B. Encuesta.   Tu profesor(a) te va a dar una cuadrícula con una actividad

indicada en cada cuadrado. Pregúntales a tus compañeros de clase si hacían estas actividades durante su niñez. Pídeles a las personas que contesten afirmativamente que firmen en el cuadrado apropiado. Recuerda que no se permite que una persona firme más de un cuadrado.

EJEMPLO   llorar

¿Llorabas mucho?

C. ¿Qué hicieron?   Tú y tu amigo(a) van a entrevistar a otra pareja de

estudiantes sobre sus actividades la semana pasada. Preparen por escrito de ocho a diez preguntas sobre las actividades más comunes de sus amigos. Luego háganselas a otra pareja y contesten las preguntas que ellos van a hacerles a ustedes.

EJEMPLO   **¿Estudiaste química con [*nombre*]?** o
¿Estudiaron química tú y [*nombre*]?

CH. ¡Fue fascinante! Con tu compañero(a), escribe un cuento basado en estos dibujos del viaje de Mercedes y su familia a Los Ángeles.

lunes

martes

miércoles

jueves

viernes

sábado

domingo

Dramatizaciones

A. ¡Qué susto! Tu amigo(a) acaba de regresar de visitar a sus abuelos en otra ciudad. Durante su visita su abuelo tuvo un susto muy grande. Ahora tú quieres saber todos los detalles de la visita. Dramatiza la conversación con un compañero(a).

B. Íbamos a una cueva. El (La) director(a) de la escuela quisiera saber lo que pasó cuando tú y dos amigos fueron a acampar en la lluvia. Cada persona tiene una versión distinta de ese fin de semana. Dramatiza esta situación con dos compañeros. Uno puede hacer el papel de director(a).

C. ¿Escargot o caracoles? Tú y un(a) amigo(a) están discutiendo lo que ocurrió cuando los miembros del Club de francés fueron a un restaurante elegante y comieron una comida típica. Dramaticen su conversación.

Estrategias para leer:
Leer un poema

A. ¡Es como la música! El leer poesía es, de varios puntos de vista, como escuchar música. En efecto, hay varias características de música en la poesía. Como una canción, un poema tiene palabras, imágenes, ritmo y significado. Los buenos lectores siempre escuchan la música dentro de un poema. También se hacen preguntas sobre el significado de las palabras en el poema y de cómo las usa el poeta. Para leer y entender *nocturno sin patria* por Jorge Debravo, un poeta costarricense, tú también tendrás que escuchar la música del poema y pensar sobre el significado de las palabras del poeta.

Escucha el poema y contesta estas preguntas:
1. ¿Tiene rima el poema?
2. ¿Cuáles palabras y sonidos se repiten en el poema?
3. ¿Dónde empieza y termina cada oración?
4. Describe el ritmo del poema. ¿Es lento o rápido? Es tranquilizante o vibrante?
5. Describe los sonidos del poema. ¿Son abruptos y fuertes o son lentos y suaves?
6. ¿Qué emociones te hacen sentir o te sugieren el ritmo y los sonidos de este poema?

Palabra	Significado	Simbolismo	Lo que veo...	Lo que siento...
cuchillo	un utensilio para cortar	defensores de fronteras	el cuchillo corta y puede matar	miedo furia peligro
patria				
aire				
salvajes				
arrancar				
traje				
punta				

B. El significado. Piensa en las palabras del poema. ¿Cuál es su significado? ¿Cómo las usa el poeta? ¿Literalmente? ¿Simbólicamente? ¿Qué sientes al ver estas palabras de *nocturno sin patria?* ¿Sabes su significado? ¿Sabes el significado que le da el poeta?

Este poema tiene cinco estrofas. Lee el poema ahora y trata de decir en pocas palabras el significado de cada estrofa. La primera ya está completada.

Estrofa	Significado según el poeta
1ra	Lo que al poeta no le gusta
2da	_____

¿Qué impresión tienes ahora en cuanto al mensaje principal del poeta? Contesta simplemente por completar una de estas dos frases:
1. En mi opinión, el poeta no cree que . . .
2. En mi opinión, el poeta cree que . . .

poeta social

Jorge Debravo (1938–1967), el poeta costarricense, publica su primer libro de poesía, *Milagro abierto*, en 1959. En los diez años que siguen, salen otras cinco colecciones, las cuales se publican de nuevo en un solo tomo en 1969 bajo el nombre de su primera publicación. Desde entonces, han salido cuatro más colecciones: *Nosotros los hombres*, 1966, *Canciones cotidianas*, 1967, *Los despiertos*, 1972, y *Antología mayor*, 1974.

Debravo es considerado uno de los poetas más involucrados en el drama social. Su poesía trata de temas sociales: la protesta, la miseria del pueblo, la angustia . . . Como él mismo ha dicho:

> *He tomado partido . . . Todos los hombres somos hermanos. Comprendo, sin embargo, que a algunos habrá de obligarlos a comportarse como hermanos. Porque hay hombres que todavía no son humanos. Debemos enseñarles a serlo . . .*
>
> *Mi poesía no se sujeta a ninguna norma ideológica preconcebida. Nace simplemente, dice lo que se ha de decir y no calcula los intereses que resultarán favorecidos o golpeados.*

nocturno sin patria

Yo no quiero un cuchillo en manos de la patria.
Ni un cuchillo ni un rifle para nadie:
la tierra es para todos,
como el aire.

Me gustaría tener manos enormes,
violentas y salvajes,*
para arrancar* fronteras* una a una
y dejar de frontera solo el aire.

Que nadie tenga tierra
como se tiene traje:
que todos tengan tierra
como tienen el aire.

Cogería* las guerras* de la punta*
y no dejaría una en el paisaje*
y abriría la tierra para todos
como si fuera el aire . . .

Que el aire no es de nadie, nadie, nadie . . .
Y todos tienen su parcela de aire.

no doméstico, rudo
sacar con violencia / límite de un estado

Tomaría / estado de combate /
de la cabeza / mundo

Verifiquemos

1. Explica lo que el poeta quiere decir cuando dice "Yo no quiero un cuchillo en manos de la patria".
2. ¿Le gustan las fronteras al poeta? ¿Por qué sí o por qué no?
3. ¿Qué relación hace el poeta entre la tierra y un traje? ¿entre tierra y aire?
4. ¿Cómo es posible "Que el aire no es de nadie, nadie, nadie . . .", pero sin embargo "todos tienen su parcela de aire"? Explica el último verso del poema.
5. La introducción dice que Jorge Debravo escribe sobre temas sociales. ¿Es verdad en *nocturno sin patria?* Explica.

Estrategias para escribir:
Escribir un poema

A. Reflexionar. En *nocturno sin patria* de Jorge Debravo, el poeta habló de algo en el mundo que no está bien; dijo lo que haría para cambiarlo y, finalmente, habló de cómo sería el mundo después de este cambio. Aunque *nocturno sin patria* no rima, está lleno de imágenes vivas y el ritmo del poema ayuda a expresar los sentimientos del poeta. Ahora tú vas a escribir un poema corto sobre algo que quieres cambiar.

B. Empezar. Primero, debes pensar en un tema. Piensa en algo que te preocupa: la ecología, la escuela, la familia, los animales . . . No tiene que ser un asunto tan grande como ''la falta de fronteras en el mundo entero'' de Jorge Debravo. Sólo debe ser algo de interés personal para ti. Selecciona un tema que te permita describir lo que no está bien y lo que tú puedes cambiar.

C. Torbellino de ideas. Tu poema va a tener tres estrofas. En la primera vas a describir el problema y decir qué es lo que no está bien. En la segunda estrofa vas a decir lo que vas a cambiar o cómo vas a solucionar el problema. En la tercera hablarás del resultado después del cambio. Prepara listas de palabras que te ayudan a expresar cada una de estas ideas. Usa un marcador para seleccionar las palabras más vivas.

El problema	La solución	El resultado
No quiero . . . No me gusta . . .	Voy a . . .	Va a . . .
Palabras expresivas: 1. 2. 3. . . .	1. 2. 3. . . .	1. 2. 3. . . .

CH. Primer borrador. Escribe el primer borrador de tu poema. Si quieres, vuelve a mirar *nocturno sin patria* y estudia el formato. Fíjate que no hay una oración completa en cada verso o línea del poema. También nota que no es necesario tener rima, pero sí debe tener ritmo.

D. Compartir. Lee los poemas de tus compañeros y que ellos lean el tuyo. Pídeles que hagan un breve resumen de tu poema para ver si lo entendieron. También pídeles sugerencias para hacerlo más claro y más efectivo. Haz el mismo tipo de comentarios sobre sus poemas.

E. Revisar. Haz cambios en tu poema a base de las sugerencias de tus compañeros. Luego, antes de entregar el poema, dáselo a dos compañeros de clase para que lo lean una vez más. Esta vez pídeles que revisen la estructura y la puntuación. En particular, pídeles que revisen la concordancia: verbo / sujeto y sustantivo / adjetivo.

F. Versión final. Escribe la versión final de tu poema incorporando las correcciones que tus compañeros de clase te indicaron. Presta mucha atención al formato. Piensa en la versión final como una obra de arte que tiene atractivo visual tanto como auditivo.

G. Publicar. Cuando tu profesor(a) te devuelva tu poema, prepáralo para publicar. Dibuja una ilustración apropiada (o recorta unas de revistas) para cada estrofa de tu poema. Pongan todos los poemas en un cuaderno. ¡Éste será el primer libro de poemas de la clase! Denle un título a su primer libro de poesía.

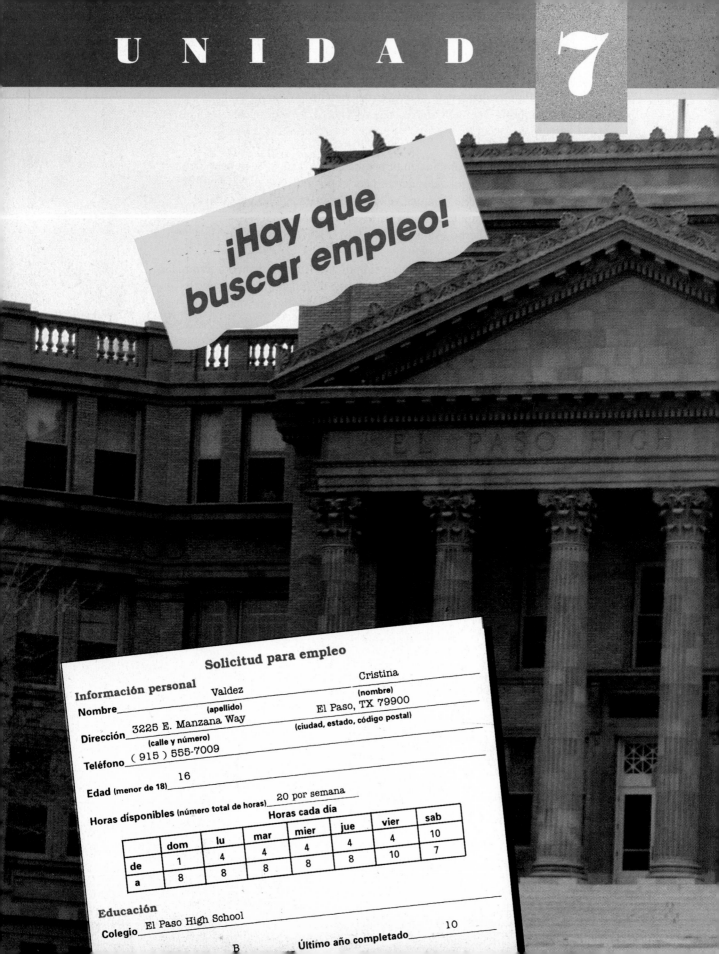

¡Hay que buscar empleo!

Solicitud para empleo

Información personal

Nombre _____ Valdez _____ Cristina _____
             (apellido)   (nombre)

Dirección _3225 E. Manzana Way_ _El Paso, TX 79900_
          (calle y número)   (ciudad, estado, código postal)

Teléfono (915) 555-7009

Edad (menor de 18) _16_

Horas disponibles (número total de horas) _20 por semana_

Horas cada día

	dom	lu	mar	mier	jue	vier	sab
de	1	4	4	4	4	4	10
a	8	8	8	8	8	10	7

Educación

Colegio _El Paso High School_

B _____ Último año completado _10_

Si trabajo, puedo comprarme un . . .

Exclusive Auto, c.a. Su Garantía

Haga su sueño realidad. Le ofrecemos el Carro Importado de su preferencia, garantizado en talleres especializados. Y lo más importante: FINANCIAMIENTO AL 8% ANUAL.

ACCORD
Desde $14,000.00

MAZDA MX 6
Desde $20,000.00

Teléfonos: 376-1200
368-1400

Mercedes Benz 450 SLC

Se vende por motivo de viaje. Deportivo rojo, $7,000.00. Detalles: 612-1023 cualquier hora.

Vendo Camioneta Cherokee Limited

Año 92, color rojo atardecer, full equipo. Favor llamar por el precio: 396-2311, señor Mariátegui.

DODGE EDICIÓN ESPECIAL

Tremenda ocasión, año 1978, poco uso, perfecto de motor, carrocería y cauchos. Con vidrios, maleta, asientos eléctricos. Teléfono: 432-1693 mañanas y tardes, Manuel Luis.

Se vende Suzuki Samurai

$9,000.00.

Año 94, full equipo, como nueva.

Informes: ☎ 962-1798, señora Sabanes.

¿ Qué piensas tú ?

1. ¿Tienes un carro? ¿Quién hace los pagos? Si no tienes carro, ¿te gustaría tener tu propio carro? ¿Quién te lo compraría?

2. ¿Cuál de los carros en estos anuncios te gustaría tener? ¿Por qué?

3. ¿Hay muchos gastos en mantener un carro? Explica. Prepara una lista de los costos mensuales para mantener tu carro o el que seleccionaste de estos anuncios. Compara tu lista con la de dos compañeros de clase. ¿Han sido realistas? ¿Han considerado el costo de gasolina, aceite y seguro?

4. ¿Recibes ''dinero de bolsillo'' de tus padres? ¿Qué haces para ganar dinero ''extra''? ¿Te pagan tus padres cuando haces tareas adicionales en casa?

5. ¿Qué gastos esperan tus padres que pagues con tu propio dinero? ¿Ropa? ¿Diversiones? ¿Regalos de cumpleaños y de Navidad?

6. ¿Cómo ganan dinero los jóvenes en tu ciudad? ¿Qué tipo de trabajo hay para jóvenes? ¿Pagan estos puestos? ¿Cuánto pagan? ¿Ganarías suficiente en uno de estos puestos para pagar el carro que seleccionaste en la pregunta número 2?

7. ¿Qué crees que vas a aprender en esta lección?

EL COLLAR DE ORO

Unos cuentos tratan de lo mágico y de lo sobrenatural, otros del triunfo de la bondad sobre la maldad y otros de individuos listos e inteligentes que se burlan o aprovechan de personajes tontos. Este cuento de una bruja mala, su hija tonta y una joven buena e inteligente, trata de todos estos temas.

Hace muchos años, había un hombre y una mujer que tenían muchos hijos. Eran muy pobres, y muchas veces no había comida para todos y tenían que acostarse con hambre. Un día, el padre de la familia decidió enviar a su hija mayor a buscar trabajo. Zenaida, la hija, era muy trabajadora y siempre estaba lista para ayudar a la familia.

En aquellos días no era fácil conseguir trabajo, pero una vieja le ofreció trabajo a Zenaida. "Si trabajas bien", dijo la vieja, "voy a pagarte bien. Unos dos o tres reales por semana".

La vieja hacía trabajar a la muchacha todo el día y parte de la noche.

Tenía una hija que era tan mala y fea como su madre.

Después de escuchar sus conversaciones y observar sus ritos, Zenaida se dio cuenta de que podían ser brujas.

4 Zenaida trabajó para la vieja bruja y su hija por una semana, luego por dos, y tres . . . , y la vieja no le pagó ni uno, ni dos, ni tres reales por semana. ¡No le pagó nada!

Por fin, la muchacha le dijo a la vieja, "Ya hace más de un mes que trabajo para usted. ¿Cuándo me va a pagar?"

La vieja contestó, amenazando a la pobre muchacha. "No me enojes", dijo. "Si me enojas, te voy a castigar".

5 Esa noche, Zenaida encontró un collar de oro en el pasillo cerca de su cuarto. Se lo puso y a medianoche se fue de casa de las brujas.

6 Caminó la mayor parte del día y a punto de meterse el sol, llegó a un castillo muy grande. Tocó a la puerta y salió un viejito. Zenaida le explicó su situación y le dijo que andaba buscando trabajo. El viejito tenía muchos cuartos que necesitaban limpiarse y le dio trabajo.

7 Cuando el viejito vio el collar de oro que llevaba la muchacha, le preguntó de dónde era. Zenaida le explicó lo de la bruja al anciano y él dijo que sabía de quién hablaba. Dijo que la bruja le había robado una espada con diamantes y perlas y dos sacos de oro.

Zenaida se puso furiosa y dijo que ella sabía exactamente dónde estaban. Dijo, "Yo misma voy por ellos en seguida".

8 Cuando llegó a la casa de la bruja, entró sin hacer ruido y encontró la espada y los sacos de oro. Ya estaba por salir cuando se topó con la vieja. La bruja agarró a Zenaida y gritó, "Ahora no te me escapas. Por robar mi collar, mis diamantes y mi oro, te voy a castigar".

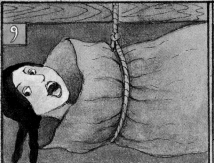

9 Zenaida tuvo que pensar pronto y sugirió, "¿Por qué no me mete en un saco y me cuelga de una de las vigas de la cocina? Entonces, puede irse al monte a buscar un buen palo para golpearme". "¡Qué buena idea!", pensó la vieja y metió a Zenaida en un saco, la colgó de una viga en la cocina y se fue a buscar un buen palo.

Tan pronto salió la vieja, entró su hija al cuarto. Dentro del saco, Zenaida se puso a cantar, "¡Oh, si ves lo que yo veo, te va a fascinar! ¡Oh, si ves lo que yo veo, te va a fascinar!" Muy curiosa, la hija de la bruja insistió en ver lo que Zenaida veía. Pero Zenaida le dijo que para ver la maravilla, ella tenía que estar colgada del saco también. La hija no pudo controlar su curiosidad e insistió en cambiar de lugar con Zenaida.

Fuera del saco, por fin, Zenaida cogió la espada y el oro y se fue corriendo. Cuando la bruja llegó con su palo, ¡oyó a su hija gritando suspendida en el saco!

10 El viejito estaba tan contento de ver su espada y su oro, que le dio a Zenaida uno de los sacos de oro. Zenaida regresó a su familia y todos, con excepción de la mala bruja y su hija, vivieron felices para siempre.

¿QUÉ DECIMOS...?

Al hablar de cómo ganar dinero

1 ¡Súbanse y damos una vuelta!

¡Qué aburrido! No hay nada que hacer esta tarde.

¡Mira! ¡Es Daniel!

¡Y Mateo está manejando!

Hola.

¿Qué tal, chicas?

¿De quién es este carro?

Es mío. ¿Les gusta?

¡Ay, qué suave! ¿Dónde lo compraste?

Un amigo de mi papá me lo vendió hoy mismo.

¡Es absolutamente fantástico! ¿Te costó mucho?

Bastante. Tres mil dólares.

¿Pagaste tres mil por un carro? ¿Dónde conseguiste tanto dinero?

Sí... y su papá le prestó el resto.

Pues, hace tiempo que trabajo. He estado ahorrando mi dinero.

¿Y qué? Vamos, muchachas. Súbanse y las llevo a dar una vuelta.

2 ¡Un convertible de lo más llamativo!

Es magnífico tu carro, Mateo. Gracias.

De nada. Nos vemos.

¡Y manejen con cuidado! Adiós.

Hasta luego.

Hasta pronto.

¡Cuánto me gustaría tener mi propio carro! Ah, sí... para poder llevar a mis amigos a pasear y no tener que caminar a la escuela.

Anda, Tina. ¡Y dices que yo no soy realista! No hay manera que tú compres tu carro a menos que ahorres mucho dinero.

Momento, momento. Antes de hacerte ilusiones, ¿por qué no hablas con tus padres?

Y sé exactamente lo que quiero— un convertible rojo de lo más llamativo y un radio también...

Ya lo sé. Pero si trabajo mucho en casa... quizás...

Bueno, sí. Tienes razón.

3 ¿Me puedes pagar algo?

Mamá, he estado pensando. Si hago más quehaceres en casa, ¿me puedes pagar algo?

Hija, en esta familia no es costumbre pagar los quehaceres.

Ya lo sé, ¿pero si hago mucho más?

Pues, depende de lo que hagas.

¿Si limpio el baño, paso la aspiradora, sacudo los muebles, por ejemplo?

¿Por todo eso? No sé. Unos veinte dólares, tal vez. Pero no por hora, por semana.

¿Y si lavo el carro también?

Es que quiero comprarme un carro.

Ay, no sé, hija. Es mejor que hables con tu papá. Dime, hija, ¿por qué de repente tienes tanto interés en ganar dinero?

¡Ay, Tina!

4 ¡No te burles de mí!

¡Ay, Tina! Casi nunca nos vemos ya. A propósito, ¿cuánto dinero tienes guardado ya?

¿Qué tal, Tina? Ven. Vamos a dar un paseo en bicicleta. Luego podemos ir de compras a Cielo Vista. Hay buenas ofertas hoy.

No puedo, Margarita. Tengo demasiado que hacer. Después de aspirar el carro, todavía tengo que limpiar el baño y mi cuarto. Además, si gasto mi dinero, no voy a poder comprar mi carro.

A ver... al terminar las tareas de hoy, voy a tener setenta y cinco dólares, más o menos.

¡No te burles de mí! No entiendes lo difícil que es. Parece que trabajo y trabajo y ¿para qué? Nunca voy a tener suficiente dinero.

¡Setenta y cinco! Sólo te hacen falta dos mil novecientos veinticinco, ¿no?

Margarita, ¡eres un genio! Obviamente, es la solución. Con mi talento, estoy segura de poder conseguir un buen puesto y ganar los tres mil en un par de meses.

Tienes razón. Si sigues como vas, creo que vas a terminar la universidad antes de poder comprarte un carro. ¿Por qué no te consigues otro trabajo?

CHARLEMOS UN POCO

A. **PARA EMPEZAR . . .** Di si los siguientes comentarios son ciertos o falsos según el cuento, "El collar de oro". Si son falsos, corrígelos.

1. Zenaida tuvo que salir a buscar trabajo porque era la única hija y sus padres eran muy pobres.
2. Una vieja le ofreció trabajo a Zenaida diciendo, "No puedo pagarte mucho si trabajas conmigo".
3. La vieja hizo trabajar mucho a la muchacha, día y noche.
4. La vieja tenía una hija hermosa y muy inteligente.
5. La vieja y su hija eran brujas.
6. Cuando Zenaida pidió su salario, la vieja la amenazó diciendo, "Si me enojas, te voy a castigar".
7. Esa noche, Zenaida se escapó con un hermoso collar de perlas.
8. Zenaida consiguió trabajo con un viejito a quien le habían robado una espada y tres sacos de oro.
9. Zenaida intentó traerle la espada y el oro al viejito pero la vieja bruja la captó y la mató.
10. La bruja y su hija vivieron felices para siempre y la familia de Zenaida continuó en la pobreza.

B. **¿QUÉ DECIMOS . . . ?** Completa los comentarios de Tina, su mamá y sus amigos.

Tina **Mamá** **Margarita** **Mateo**

1. "¿Por todo eso? . . .
2. "Estoy segura de poder . . .
3. "Súbanse y las llevo . . .
4. "No hay manera que tú compres tu carro . . .
5. "¿Pagaste tres mil . . .
6. "Nunca voy a tener . . .
7. "Si hago más quehaceres en casa, . . .
8. "Vas a terminar la universidad . . .

a. por un carro?"
b. a dar una vuelta".
c. a menos que ahorres mucho dinero".
ch. ¿me puedes pagar algo?"
d. Unos veinte dólares, tal vez".
e. suficiente dinero".
f. antes de poder comprarte un carro".
g. conseguir un buen puesto".

C. Consejos. Todos tus amigos te consideran un(a) excelente consejero(a) y siempre vienen a ti con sus problemas. ¿Qué consejos les das cuando vienen con estos problemas?

MODELO tener sueño
        Compañero:(a): **Tengo sueño.**
        Tú: **Si tienes sueño, debes dormir más.**

VOCABULARIO ÚTIL:

conseguir un trabajo   llamar a un(a) amigo(a)
hacerte miembro de un club   salir
dormir más   usar los anteojos
estudiar todas las noches   tomar clases
evitar el café   usar bronceador
hacer más ejercicio

1. estar aburrido   6. sacar malas notas
2. no saber bailar   7. no poder dormir
3. dolerme los ojos   8. siempre quemarme al sol
4. no tener amigos   9. no tener energía
5. no tener ganas de estudiar   10. querer un carro

CH. Esperanzas. Estas personas acaban de conseguir trabajo. ¿Qué piensan comprar con el dinero que van a ganar?

Leticia

MODELO **Si gana bastante dinero, Leticia piensa comprar zapatos.**

1. Pancho   2. Pepe   3. yo   4. Gregorio

5. tú   6. Luisa   7. Marcos y yo   8. Ana y Juan

9. Débora   10. Esteban y Lupe

Making speculations: *Si*

The expression **si** is followed by the indicative when used in the present tense:

Si quieres, puedo ir contigo.
Si llama Carlos, no estoy aquí.

See **¿Por qué se dice así?**, *page G96, section 7.1.*

D. Soñador(a).   Tú eres un(a) gran soñador(a). ¿Qué te imaginas que va a pasar si haces estas cosas?

> EJEMPLO   sacar buenas notas
> **Si saco buenas notas, puedo asistir a la universidad.** o
> **Si saco buenas notas, voy a conseguir un buen trabajo.**

1. ganar mucho dinero
2. practicar muchos deportes
3. conseguir un trabajo en un restaurante
4. limpiar toda la casa
5. quedarme en casa
6. escribir muchas cartas
7. comprar un saco de dormir
8. viajar a Venezuela
9. comprar un carro
10. tomar clases de ejercicios aeróbicos

E. Quehaceres.   Tú y tu compañero(a) tienen que limpiar la escuela. Ahora tienen que negociar para ver quién va a hacer qué.

> EJEMPLO   **Yo lavo el piso de la cafetería si tú limpias los baños.**

---

limpiar los baños
barrer el pasillo
cortar el césped
lavar las pizarras
limpiar los borradores
arreglar los estantes
limpiar los pupitres
pasar un trapo a los escritorios de los profesores
sacar la basura
lavar las ventanas
limpiar el laboratorio
lavar el piso de la cafetería

F. ¿Cuántas veces?   ¿Con qué frecuencia haces estas cosas?

> EJEMPLO   salir a comer / mes
> **Salgo a comer [número] veces por mes.**

1. ir al cine / mes
2. asistir a la clase de español / semana
3. peinarse / día
4. practicar deportes / semana
5. ir a acampar / año
6. hablar por teléfono / día
7. alquilar un video / mes
8. lavarse los dientes / día

Negotiating: Si

The expression **si** is often used in negotiating:

Yo lavo el carro **si** tú limpias el interior.

Si tu sacas la basura, yo preparo los sándwiches.

See **¿Por qué se dice así?**, *page G96, section 7.1.*

The preposition *por*: Per / By

Los tomates están a seis **por** un dólar.

Siempre alquilamos tres videos **por** semana.

See **¿Por qué se dice así?**, *page G97, section 7.2.*

G. Intercambios. Tú y tu compañero(a) tienen varias cosas que intercambiar. Decidan cómo van a hacer sus intercambios.

EJEMPLO *Tú:* **Te doy mi reloj por tu mochila.**
Compañero(a): **No, te doy mi collar por tu reloj.**

**The preposition *por*:
In exchange for**

Me dio cinco dólares **por** la mochila.
¡Pagué demasiado **por** este carro!

*See **¿Por qué se dice así?**,*
page G97, section 7.2.

TÚ

COMPAÑERO(A)

H. ¿Tanto? ¿Sabes el valor de estas cosas? ¿Cuánto pagarías por cada una?

EJEMPLO un viaje a Europa
Pagaría dos mil dólares por un viaje a Europa.

1. un módem
2. un radio
3. boleto para un concierto de rock
4. un viaje de esquí
5. una impresora láser
6. una cena con tu artista favorito(a)
7. un disco duro
8. un carro
9. una semana en San Juan, Puerto Rico
10. una bicicleta

LECCIÓN 1

The preposition *por*: Duration of time

Vamos a estar allá **por** un mes.
No comí nada **por** días.

See ***¿Por qué se dice así?***, *page G97, section 7.2.*

I. Vacaciones. Tú y tus amigos van a viajar durante las vacaciones de verano. ¿Cuánto tiempo van a estar de vacaciones?

 EJEMPLO   **Mario va a estar en Italia por tres semanas.**

mi familia y yo	Italia	3 semanas
yo	India	1 semana
mi amigo(a) . . .	Egipto	1 mes
mis amigos . . . y . . .	Australia	2 meses
tú	Guatemala	3 meses
	Paraguay	10 días
	Rusia	2 semanas
	¿ . . . ?	5 días
		¿ . . . ?

CHARLEMOS UN POCO MÁS

A. Si gano la lotería . . . Usa la encuesta que tu profesor(a) te va a dar para entrevistar a tus compañeros de clase. Haz cada pregunta a tres personas y anota sus respuestas. No hagas más de una pregunta a la misma persona. Al terminar, compara tu información con la de tus compañeros de clase.

 EJEMPLO   ganar la lotería
Compañero(a):   **¿Qué vas a hacer si ganas la lotería?**
Tú: **Si gano la lotería, voy a viajar a España.**

B. Entrevista. Prepara una lista de diez situaciones problemáticas y típicas. Luego, pregúntale a un compañero(a) qué hace en cada situación en tu lista. Informa a la clase las respuestas más creativas que recibes.

 EJEMPLO   *Tú escribes:*   **Ves al novio de tu mejor amiga con otra persona.**
          Tú preguntas: **¿Qué haces si ves al novio de tu mejor amiga con otra persona?**
          Compañero(a) dice: **Si veo al novio de mi mejor amiga con otra persona, inmediatamente se lo digo a mi amiga.** o
                                Si veo al novio de mi mejor amiga con otra persona no digo nada. o . . .

C. Subtítulos. Con un(a) compañero(a), escribe subtítulos para estos dibujos. Después en grupos de seis, lean sus subtítulos, decidan cuáles son los mejores y leánselos a la clase.

1. Sergio

2. Luisa y Paco

3. los hermanos

4. Rosario y Sra. Ortiz

5. Gloria y Beatriz

6. Ricardo

Dramatizaciones

A. Si ganamos diez mil . . .   Tú y dos compañeros son finalistas en la lotería y tienen la posibilidad de ganar 10, 25, 50, 75, 100 mil o 1 millón de dólares. Hablen de lo que piensan hacer si ganan cada cantidad de dinero. Todos tienen que estar de acuerdo. Dramaticen su conversación.

B. El carro.   Tú quieres usar el carro de tu hermano(a) este fin de semana pero él (ella) no quiere prestártelo. Tú mencionas varias razones por las cuales lo necesitas pero tu hermano(a) siempre tiene una excusa para no prestártelo. Dramaticen esta situación. Tu compañero(a) va a tomar el papel de tu hermano(a).

IMPACTO CULTURAL
Excursiones

Antes de empezar _____

A. Mi ciudad. ¿Cuánto sabes de tu ciudad? Contesta estas preguntas con un(a) compañero(a) de clase para saber cuánto saben del lugar donde viven.

1. ¿Cuándo se fundó su ciudad? ¿Por qué se fundó en ese sitio? ¿Cuál era la industria principal?
2. ¿De dónde viene el nombre de su ciudad?
3. ¿Cuál es la importancia de tu ciudad en el estado? ¿Es la más grande? ¿la más pequeña?
4. ¿Cuáles son las industrias principales en tu ciudad ahora?
5. ¿Cuáles son las atracciones turísticas de tu ciudad?
6. ¿Te gusta vivir donde vives o preferirías vivir en otra ciudad? ¿Por qué?

B. Ciudad vecina. Muchas ciudades en EE.UU. tienen ciudades vecinas. Con un(a) compañero(a), contesta estas preguntas para ver cuáles son las ventajas o desventajas de tener una ciudad vecina.

1. ¿Tiene tu ciudad una ciudad vecina? Si no, ¿cuáles son dos ciudades vecinas en tu estado?
2. ¿Cuál de las dos ciudades es la más grande?
3. ¿Cuál de las dos ciudades tiene las mejores diversiones? ¿los mejores restaurantes? ¿los mejores centros comerciales? ¿las mejores escuelas?
4. ¿Cuál ofrece más oportunidad de empleo? Explica por qué.
5. ¿En cuál de las dos ciudades te gustaría vivir? ¿Por qué?

Palacio Municipal, Ciudad Juárez

Ciudad Juárez: ¿Ciudad gemela?

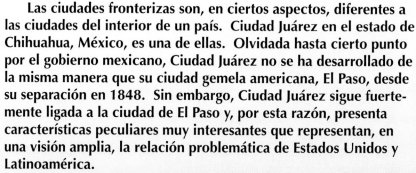

Las ciudades fronterizas son, en ciertos aspectos, diferentes a las ciudades del interior de un país. Ciudad Juárez en el estado de Chihuahua, México, es una de ellas. Olvidada hasta cierto punto por el gobierno mexicano, Ciudad Juárez no se ha desarrollado de la misma manera que su ciudad gemela americana, El Paso, desde su separación en 1848. Sin embargo, Ciudad Juárez sigue fuertemente ligada a la ciudad de El Paso y, por esta razón, presenta características peculiares muy interesantes que representan, en una visión amplia, la relación problemática de Estados Unidos y Latinoamérica.

Gobernada por distintos gobiernos desde 1848, el desarrollo de Ciudad Juárez y El Paso ha sido desigual. El Paso se ha convertido en una ciudad americana moderna con una economía muy diversificada. Ciudad Juárez impresiona por sus contrastes de extrema pobreza de la mayoría de la población que vive en los barrios o las "colonias", **1** y de extrema riqueza de los ricos que viven en áreas exclusivas como Campestre. **2** Esta brecha entre ricos y pobres se ha cerrado un poco desde los años cincuenta, debido al desarrollo gradual de la clase media.

Para incentivar el desarrollo de Ciudad Juárez, el gobierno mexicano ha invertido millones de pesos para desarrollar el turismo en el área. Miles de turistas americanos cruzan la frontera para visitar los modernos centros comerciales, **3** museos de arte e historia, restaurantes y hoteles que se han construido en toda la frontera.

Así como miles de turistas americanos cruzan la frontera hacia Ciudad Juárez, miles de mexicanos visitan El Paso. **4** (Cada año más de 40 millones de mexicanos cruzan la frontera entre El Paso y Ciudad Juárez legalmente.) Indudablemente, el comercio entre las dos ciudades es muy intenso. Como dice un prominente ciudadano de esta ciudad americana, "El Paso y Ciudad Juárez son dos gemelas que se encuentran en la caja registradora".

A pesar de todos los mexicanos que cruzan la frontera por turismo o por comercio, **5** cientos de ellos llegan a El Paso para quedarse. Ellos son los "ilegales" que van en busca de una vida mejor en Estados Unidos. Éste es un problema muy serio en la frontera y muy difícil de controlar por el intenso tráfico que existe en el área. El problema se hace peor debido a que en invierno, el Río Grande—o Río Bravo, como se llama en México—no consta más que de un chorrito de agua. Esto permite que los ilegales puedan saltar sin aun mojarse los zapatos.

Una solución parcial para el problema de la migración a EE.UU. ha sido el desarrollo industrial en la frontera de El Paso—Ciudad Juárez. En 1965 se estableció la industria "maquiladora" *(twin plant program)* en esta área. De acuerdo a este plan de desarrollo industrial, compañías americanas se establecen en la frontera, en suelo mexicano, y dan trabajo a miles de trabajadores mexicanos. Ambos países se han beneficiado hasta cierto punto, pero también existen serios problemas como la explotación de los trabajadores mexicanos por las industrias americanas y la pérdida de trabajos en EE.UU. cada vez que una compañía americana se establece en suelo mexicano.

¿Cómo va a afectar la situación de las ciudades gemelas el Tratado de Libre Comercio entre Canadá, EE.UU. y México? **6** Esto es difícil de predecir. Lo único que es seguro es que estas dos ciudades siempre vivirán la una para la otra, buscándose siempre, como dos hermanas gemelas separadas por la fuerza.

Verifiquemos

1. Con un(a) compañero(a), preparen un diagrama como el siguiente. Hagan una comparación entre su ciudad, Ciudad Juárez y su ciudad gemela, El Paso, Texas. Decidan primero qué es o qué van a comparar, e indiquen cuáles serán las subcategorías. La primera, industria, ya está señalada.

Mi ciudad	**Ciudad Juárez**	**El Paso**
1. Industria	1. Industria	1. Industria
2.	2.	2.

2. Explica el título de la lectura.
3. ¿Cuáles son las razones principales por las cuales Ciudad Juárez y El Paso se desarrollaron desigualmente?
4. ¿Conoces tú otras ciudades fronterizas? ¿Cuáles son?

¡Tal vez pueda trabajar!

Club de deportes solicita Instructor de natación para cursos sabatinos

Requisitos:
- Experiencia comprobada
- Disponibilidad inmediata
- Conocimientos del idioma español

Ofrecemos:
- Remuneración competitiva
- Grato ambiente de trabajo

Favor dirigirse con referencias comprobables a Club Deportivo La Onda.

PROGRAMADORES EXPERTOS

Si manejas
C ++ para multimedia

sabes de
HTML
A/V digital

y conoces
QUICKTIME CR/VRML
OPEN GL/MPEG/DIRECTOR

envíanos tus datos personales

SR GERENCIA DE PERSONAL
Ref 1184

**Casilla de Correo 2860
(1000) Correo Central**

Si tienes trabajos o demos adjúntalos en:
PC: diskettes o CD-ROM
MAC: diskettes, removibles hasta 88Mb, ópticos de 128 Mb o CD-ROM

Conjunto de rock solicita Guitarrista

Con experiencia y dispuesto a "trabajar duro" para tocar la buena música.

Interesados favor de llamar al
396-0231

Preguntar por Gisela o Jaime.

Trabaja con Turismo

Oportunidad de trabajo se presenta en compañía de Programación Turística

Debes reunir los siguientes requisitos:
- Entre 15 y 18 años
- Disponibilidad de hacer trabajos de investigación breves
- Conocimiento en procesador de palabras (no indispensable)
- Capacidad para mantener relaciones interpersonales

Interesados dirigirse a 2032 Sacramento Blvd.

Urge

¿ **Q**ué piensas tú ?

1. ¿Crees que todos los jóvenes en estas fotos reciben un salario por lo que están haciendo? Si no, ¿cuáles sí y cuáles no? ¿Cuánto crees que gana cada uno? ¿Te interesaría hacer algunos de estos trabajos? ¿Cuáles? ¿Por qué?

2. ¿Estás capacitado(a) para hacer algunos de estos trabajos? ¿Cuáles? ¿Por qué crees que no estás capacitado(a) para todos?

3. En la primera lección, preparaste una lista de todos los gastos que tendrías si tuvieras carro. Ahora prepara una lista de tus otros gastos mensuales: ropa, materiales escolares, diversión, etc. Combina este total con el de tener carro. ¿Ganarías lo suficiente en cualquiera de estos puestos (*trabajos*) para pagar todos tus gastos? ¿Cuántas horas tendrías que trabajar por semana?

4. ¿Dónde crees que vas a estar y qué crees que estarás haciendo en diez años? ¿Serán tus gastos mensuales iguales a lo que son ahora? ¿Por qué crees eso?

5. ¿Qué condiciones influyen el costo de vida?

6. ¿Qué tipo de puesto esperas tener cuando ya seas un adulto? ¿Qué habilidades debes tener para conseguir tal puesto? ¿Qué puede influir en tu preferencia de puesto? ¿Tus padres? ¿Tus notas en la escuela? ¿La manera en que quieres vivir? ¿ . . . ?

7. ¿Qué crees que vas a aprender en esta lección?

PARA EMPEZAR

Escuchemos unos refranes

Todas las culturas tienen un sinnúmero de dichos populares que expresan la verdad o el conocimiento de algún sabio del pasado. Estas perlas de la lengua, llamadas "refranes" en el mundo hispanohablante, siempre son vivas, con frecuencia sencillas y todas creativas. Escuchemos ahora algunos refranes de México y del suroeste de Estados Unidos.

Quizás conozcas a algunas personas que creen que lo saben todo. Sí, los que llamamos "sabelotodos" porque siempre se rehúsan a ver o escuchar la evidencia. Simplemente insisten en que ya lo saben todo. Pues, dos buenos refranes para estas personas son:

No hay peor ciego que el que no quiere ver. y...
El peor sordo es el que no quiere oír.

O tal vez tengas algún amigo que habla continuamente. Sí, uno de esos que "habla hasta por los codos". A pesar de hablar incesantemente, estas personas nunca tienen nada que decir. Son aburridísimas. De estas personas se puede decir:

Habló el buey y dijo mu.

Y quizás sepas de alguna persona que lo critica todo. Son las personas que llamamos "criticones" porque constantemente se la pasan criticando. En inglés se dice de estas personas que "el que vive en una casa de vidrio no debe tirar piedras". En español decimos:

El que al cielo escupe, en la cara le cae.

x

4

Tal vez tengas amigos que son inteligentes pero que tienden a no pensar antes de actuar. Son las personas que siempre parecen atraer algún desastre. A veces los llamamos "bobos". De estas personas se puede decir:

La mala suerte y los tontos caminan del brazo.

5

Cuando nos encontramos con un amigo o un conocido en un lugar inesperado, en inglés decimos que "el mundo es muy pequeño". En Nuevo México se dice:

Las piedras rodando se encuentran.

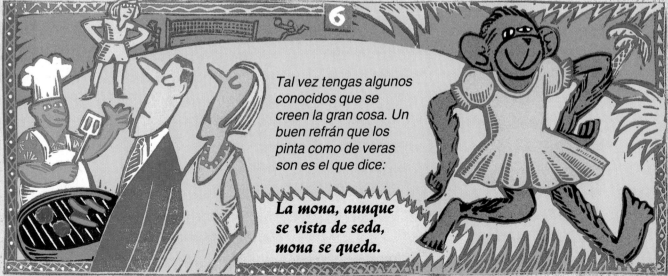

6

Tal vez tengas algunos conocidos que se creen la gran cosa. Un buen refrán que los pinta como de veras son es el que dice:

La mona, aunque se vista de seda, mona se queda.

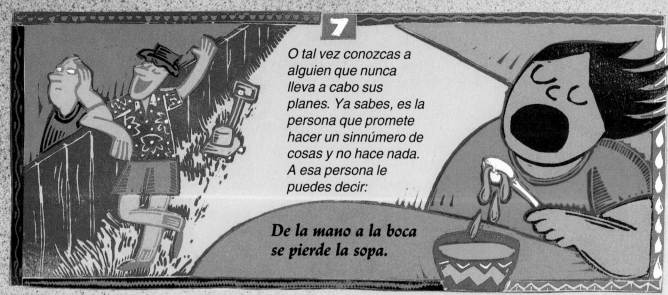

7

O tal vez conozcas a alguien que nunca lleva a cabo sus planes. Ya sabes, es la persona que promete hacer un sinnúmero de cosas y no hace nada. A esa persona le puedes decir:

De la mano a la boca se pierde la sopa.

8

Algunos refranes son muy apropiados para animar a alguien que se siente desanimado. Por ejemplo, hay uno que dice:

Donde una puerta se cierra, cien se abren.

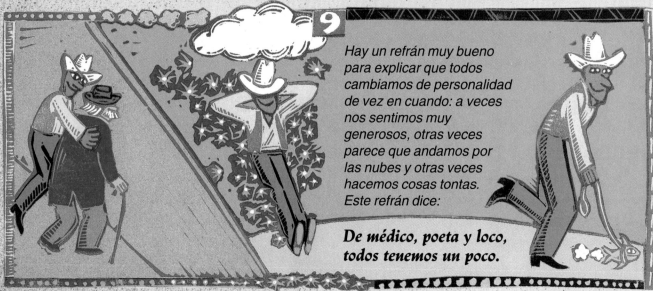

9

Hay un refrán muy bueno para explicar que todos cambiamos de personalidad de vez en cuando: a veces nos sentimos muy generosos, otras veces parece que andamos por las nubes y otras veces hacemos cosas tontas. Este refrán dice:

De médico, poeta y loco, todos tenemos un poco.

¿QUÉ DECIMOS...?

Al hablar de posibilidades de empleo

1 Un trabajo que pague bien.

Mamá, lo he pensado mucho y he decidido que debo tratar de conseguir trabajo fuera de casa. Si no lo hago, voy a ser una viejita cuando compre mi carro.

No sé, mamá—uno que pague bien. ¿Qué me recomiendas?

Vamos, hija. No es para tanto. Pero, estoy de acuerdo. Si tanto quieres un carro, es mejor que busques trabajo. ¿Qué clase de trabajo quieres?

Ay, no sé, hija. Es bien difícil conseguir trabajo estos días. ¿Por qué no hablas con tus amigos? Quizás uno de ellos sepa de un buen puesto. Ah, y también puedes mirar los anuncios clasificados del periódico.

Bueno, ya me voy, mamá.

Es cierto. Mateo trabaja. Quizás necesiten a alguien allí.

Adiós, hija.

2 Quizás pueda ser gerente de ventas.

Algo interesante— donde pueda usar mi talento creativo.

Mateo, busco trabajo. Yo también pienso comprarme un carro tan pronto como tenga suficiente dinero. ¿Necesitan personas donde tú trabajas?

Lo dudo, Tina, porque acaban de despedir a varias. ¿Qué quieres hacer?

Puedes solicitar con «Viva El Paso». Ellos emplean a muchos jóvenes para el espectáculo.

¡Ah, sí! ¡Sería perfecto!

Tal vez puedas trabajar para una compañía como secretaria.

Anda, Margarita. En realidad, me gustaría. Pero sólo es durante el verano y yo necesito trabajar todo el año.

¿Sabes escribir a máquina?

Y además, si tienes clases todo el día, ¿cómo vas a trabajar en una oficina?

Eso sí sería bueno, pero ...

No, no sé ni mecanografía ni taquigrafía.

Quizás pueda ser gerente de ventas en un almacén. Los gerentes no tienen que estar allí todo el día—sólo los dependientes.

¿no necesitas años de experiencia para ser gerente? Cuando lleguemos a tu casa, ¿por qué no vemos los clasificados?

3 | **Buscan personas que hablen español.**

No veo ningún puesto para mí.

Ay, aquí hay uno que paga muy bien. Dice que se puede ganar hasta mil quinientos la semana.

Ni yo tampoco.

¿De veras? Déjame verlo.

A ver: vendedores, puestos inmediatos, por hora... ¡Ay, caramba! Requieren personas que tengan auto.

Ay, mira. Solicitan una persona para lavar y planchar.

Ay, Margarita, dice que tienes que ser mayor de edad.

Pues, sabes hablar por teléfono, ¿no? Buscan personas que hablen español para hacer llamadas. Sólo pagan cinco dólares la hora pero...

Si eso es lo que hago en casa. ¡Híjole! Parece que sólo estoy capacitada para hacer trabajo doméstico.

4 ¿Has encontrado algo?

¿Cómo te va, hija? ¿Has encontrado algo?

Nada, mamá. Parece que no hay puesto para mí.

Así me lo imaginaba, hija.

A ver, pásame el periódico. Quizás yo vea algo. Un buen trabajo que no requiera experiencia. ¿Qué tal este restaurante? Buscan meseros y lavaplatos.

Mira éste, el El Paso Times busca personas para repartir periódicos.

Yo quería algo más interesante.

¿Más limpieza? Estoy hasta aquí con la limpieza.

El trabajo, trabajo es, hija. No siempre puedes contar con que sea interesante.

CHARLEMOS UN POCO

A. **PARA EMPEZAR . . .** En tus propias palabras, explica el significado de cada uno de estos refranes.

1. La mona, aunque se vista de seda, mona se queda.
2. De la mano a la boca se pierde la sopa.
3. La mala suerte y los tontos caminan del brazo.
4. El peor sordo es el que no quiere oír.
5. Donde una puerta se cierra, cien se abren.
6. El que al cielo escupe, en la cara le cae.
7. Las piedras rodando se encuentran.
8. No hay peor ciego que el que no quiere ver.
9. Habló el buey y dijo mu.
10. De médico, poeta y loco, todos tenemos un poco.

B. **¿QUÉ DECIMOS . . .?** ¿Quién dice lo siguiente: Tina, Margarita o mamá?

1. ''He decidido que debo tratar de conseguir trabajo fuera de casa''.
2. ''Quizás uno de tus amigos sepa de un buen puesto''.
3. ''Yo también pienso comprarme un carro''.
4. ''¿Por qué no vemos los clasificados?''
5. ''Quizás pueda ser gerente de ventas en un almacén''.
6. ''Requieren personas que tengan auto''.
7. ''Pues, sabes hablar por teléfono, ¿no?''
8. ''Solicitan una persona para lavar y planchar''.
9. ''Quizás yo vea algo. Un buen trabajo que no requiera experiencia''.
10. ''El *El Paso Times* busca personas para repartir periódicos''.

C. Marte. Estás imaginando la vida en el planeta Marte. ¿Qué dices?

MODELO el planeta ser rojo
     Tal vez el planeta sea rojo.

1. haber criaturas exóticas
2. criaturas no tener pelo
3. vivir en cuevas
4. comer árboles
5. todo el mundo dormir de día
6. todos salir de noche
7. gente usar carros eléctricos
8. marcianos construir edificios bajo la tierra
9. no haber agua
10. marcianos hablar una lengua rara

Expressing probability and improbability: *Tal vez*

When expressing doubt, **tal vez** is followed by the subjunctive:

Tal vez **vengan** mañana.
Tal vez **tengas** que hacerlo tú.

See **¿Por qué se dice así?,** *page G99, section 7.3.*

CH. Vacaciones. ¿Qué planes tienes para las vacaciones?
Contesta las preguntas de tu compañero(a).

MODELO dormir mucho: un poco
Compañero(a): **¿Piensas dormir mucho?**
Tú: **No sé. Tal vez duerma un poco.**

1. leer muchos libros: uno o dos
2. nadar en el océano: en el río
3. hacer ejercicio: correr un poco
4. practicar deportes: tenis y volibol
5. ir a acampar: a Aguirre Springs
6. asistir a un concierto: al concierto de Los Lobos
7. aprender karate: judo
8. viajar a otro país: a Canadá

D. ¡Fiesta! Hay una gran fiesta este fin de semana y tú estás muy
emocionado(a). ¿Qué estás pensando?

MODELO quizás / ser / mejor fiesta del año
Quizás sea la mejor fiesta del año.

1. quizás / todo / mi / amigos / ir
2. quizás / la / decoraciones / ser / bonito
3. quizás / haber / banda / fantástico
4. quizás / banda / tocar / mi canción / favorito
5. quizás / yo / bailar / todo / noche
6. quizás / servir / refrescos / rico
7. quizás / yo / conocer / persona / interesante
8. quizás / todo / nosotros / salir a comer / después

E. Tu escuela ideal. ¿Qué características tiene la escuela de tus
sueños?

MODELO **Prefiero una escuela que tenga una montaña rusa,
que no permita exámenes y que le dé buenas notas
a todo el mundo.**

VOCABULARIO ÚTIL:
no dar notas
emplear profesores excelentes
tener una montaña rusa
requerir mucho recreo
permitir salir para comer
tener clases al aire libre
estar en el campo
dar muchas películas
hacer muchas fiestas
¿ . . . ?

> **Expressing probability and
> improbability: *Quizás***
>
> When expressing doubt, **quizás** is
> followed by the subjunctive:
>
> Quizás no **quieran** ir.
> Quizás **estén** enfermos.
>
> *See* **¿Por qué se dice así?,**
> *page G99, section 7.3.*

> **Describing unknown entities:
> Adjective clauses**
>
> The subjunctive is used when
> referring to unknown entities.
>
> Mis padres quieren **una casa** que **sea**
> más grande.
> Busco **un novio** que **sea** guapo y que
> **tenga** mucho dinero.
>
> *See* **¿Por qué se dice así?,**
> *page G100, section 7.4.*

F. En el mercado. La familia de María va de compras a un mercado al aire libre. Según ella, ¿qué buscan todos?

MODELO   hermano / buscar / suéter / ser / de su talla
Mi hermano busca un suéter que sea de su talla.

1. Luisa / querer / bicicleta / andar bien
2. yo / buscar / saco de dormir / servir para el frío
3. Everardo / necesitar / guitarra / tener / bueno / tono
4. papás / desear / televisor / estar en / bueno / condiciones
5. Pablo y Diana / querer comprar / discos compactos / no ser / viejo
6. abuelita / buscar / joyas / combinar con / su nuevo / blusa
7. hermanita / necesitar / jaula / servir / para un canario
8. papá / querer encontrar / carpa / ser / bastante grande para todos

G. ¿Quiénes? Pregúntale a un(a) compañero(a) si conoce a personas con estas características.

MODELO   saber hablar ruso
Tú: **¿Conoces a alguien que sepa hablar ruso?**
Compañero(a):   **No conozco a nadie que sepa hablar ruso.** o
                         Sí, conozco a alguien que sabe hablar ruso. Se llama [*nombre*].

1. vivir en México
2. usar el Internet
3. trabajar de noche
4. hablar tres lenguas
5. tener familia en otro país
6. repartir periódicos
7. manejar muy rápido
8. ahorrar dinero
9. ser famoso
10. contar cuentos de espantos

H. Anuncios. Tú y un(a) amigo(a) están mirando los anuncios clasificados para encontrar un empleo. Dile a tu compañero(a) qué tipo de persona buscan estos lugares.

MODELO   **Servicio Varela busca un(a) mecánico(a) que tenga cinco años de experiencia.**

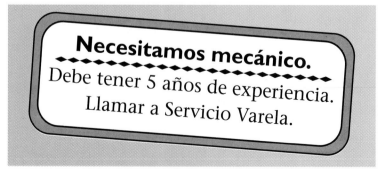

Necesitamos mecánico.
Debe tener 5 años de experiencia.
Llamar a Servicio Varela.

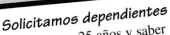

Solicitamos dependientes

Deben tener 25 años y saber usar computadoras. Se prefieren personas con experiencia. Llamar a Pueblito Mexicano.

Buscamos

Administrador de redes

Debe tener 2 años de experiencia y saber cómo instalar hardware. Llamar a MicroTec. 55–99–32

Corporación importante busca recepcionista.

Tiene que hablar y escribir inglés y saber cómo instalar software. Llamar a Empresas Rodarte, 55–72–98

Mercado González

Jóvenes para ayudar a los clientes. Deben ser responsables. Llamar entre 9 y 5.

VENDEDORES

Puestos inmediatos para 5 personas. Deben tener buena presencia. Tiempo parcial (15-20 horas). Llamar a **Mundo Digital** entre 9 y 5.

Empleamos dependientes

Deben saber jugar varios deportes. Llamar a Deportes Ratón.

CHARLEMOS UN POCO MÁS

A. Encuesta. Usa el cuestionario que tu profesor(a) te va a dar para entrevistar a dos compañeros de clase. Pregúntales si creen que su profesor(a) hace las cosas en la lista y anota sus respuestas, marcando la columna apropiada. En grupos de seis, resuman en tablas todas las respuestas que recibieron.

 EJEMPLO escribir a máquina

Tú: **¿Crees que el(la) profesor(a) no escribe a máquina?**

Estudiante #1: **Tal vez escriba a máquina.** o **Es verdad que escribe a máquina.**

B. Anuncios clasificados. Su profesor(a) va a darle a cada uno de ustedes o un anuncio clasificado o una descripción de habilidades. Si recibes un anuncio, úsalo para encontrar a una persona que pueda hacer el trabajo. Si recibes una descripción de habilidades, úsala para encontrar a alguien que te quiera emplear. Cuando encuentren a la persona que buscan, siéntense y tengan una entrevista para decidir si van a trabajar juntos o no.

C. Quiero una casa que . . . ¿Cómo es la casa de tus sueños? Descríbesela a tu compañero(a). Tu compañero(a) va a anotar lo que describes y después va a escribir un anuncio clasificado en busca de tal casa.

EJEMPLO **Deseo una casa que tenga cien cuartos. También quiero que sea . . .**

Dramatizaciones

A. Tal vez . . . Tú y un(a) amigo(a) van de compras a su centro comercial favorito a buscar ropa para la escuela. Desafortunadamente, tu amigo(a) está muy negativo(a) hoy y sólo tiene comentarios negativos que hacer. Tú tratas de ser lo más positivo(a) posible. Dramaticen esta situación.

B. Agencia de motos. Tu compañero(a) quiere comprar la motocicleta de sus sueños. Tú quieres vender una moto. Dramaticen esta situación.

IMPACTO CULTURAL
Tesoros nacionales

Antes de empezar

A. **Héroes nacionales.** En grupos de tres o cuatro, definan lo que es un héroe nacional. ¿Cómo se determina quién puede serlo? ¿Qué características debe tener tal persona? ¿Qué tipo de hazañas debe haber hecho? ¿Cuáles son algunos héroes nacionales de EE.UU.?

B. **Abraham Lincoln.** ¿Cuánto sabes del presidente número 16 de Estados Unidos? Con un(a) compañero(a), contesta estas preguntas.
1. ¿Dónde nació Abraham Lincoln?
2. ¿Qué puedes contar de la niñez de Lincoln?
3. ¿Qué estudió Lincoln, en preparación para una carrera con el gobierno?
4. ¿Con quién se casó Abraham Lincoln?
5. ¿Cuál fue la hazaña más importante en la vida de Lincoln?
6. ¿Dónde y cómo murió Abraham Lincoln?

BENITO JUÁREZ
EL GRAN HÉROE DE MÉXICO

murieron sus padres

Por muchas razones, se dice que Benito Juárez es el Abraham Lincoln de México. Juárez fue un indígena de la Nación Zapoteca del estado de Oaxaca en México. Nació el 21 de marzo de 1806 en el Pueblo de Guelatao, Oaxaca. Quedó huérfano* desde los tres años y vivió con su tío Bernardino Juárez hasta la edad de doce años. En estos años Benito trabajó en labores del campo. Tuvo una educación mínima porque en su pueblo no había escuelas. Benito no hablaba español. Su tío le enseñó un poco de español y le hizo entender la importancia de saber hablar español para salir adelante.

protector

Entusiasmado con la idea de educarse, dejó su pueblo en 1818 para ir a la capital del estado. En Oaxaca, Benito conoció a su mentor y padrino* Don Antonio Salanueva. Éste lo ayudó a ingresar en la escuela; pero en las escuelas no se enseñaba gramática española, solamente se recitaba de memoria el catecismo. También había mucha injusticia contra los indígenas pobres como Benito. Éstos tenían que estudiar en departamentos separados de los niños "decentes" que eran hijos de buenas familias.

para ser abogado

Por estas razones, Benito decidió estudiar en el seminario, y en 1828, cuando se abrió el colegio civil llamado Instituto de Ciencias y Artes, Benito pasó a estudiar leyes* a esta institución. En 1834 recibió su título de abogado.

tuvo / puestos

Efectivamente, Juárez fue un liberal del partido republicano de México que luchó por la democracia y el progreso de México. Combatió contra las fuerzas conservadoras del país como la Iglesia, los oligarcas y el ejército que por mucho tiempo dominaron el país y los mantuvieron en virtual atraso y pobreza. En vida, Juárez desempeñó* varios cargos* públicos, entre los más importantes fueron los de gobernador del estado de Oaxaca, Ministro de Justicia y Educación Pública de México y finalmente, el de presidente de la República.

Los cambios que logró* Juárez en sus gobiernos fueron no solamente revolucionarios, sino que se caracterizaron por dar una lección genuina de honestidad, energía y buena administración. A pesar de los sangrientos eventos que ocurrieron durante sus períodos de gobierno, como la guerra civil o la guerra de la reforma y la intervención extranjera* en México de Francia, Juárez actuó siempre con rectitud* cuidando del bienestar de su país.

Entre muchas cosas, Juárez se preocupó mucho por la educación de todos los ciudadanos mexicanos. Instituyó la educación pública gratis y obligatoria para todos. Se preocupó también por el desarrollo económico del país y abrió las puertas de México al mercado mundial. Disminuyó* la inmensa burocracia y trató de pagar la deuda* externa. Terminó de construir el Ferrocarril Mexicano [1] iniciado por el gobierno anterior que era muy importante para la unión y el desarrollo del país.

Cuando murió Benito Juárez el 19 de julio de 1872, miles de ciudadanos fueron a su entierro.* Aún muchos años después de su muerte, muchos mexicanos iban en peregrinación a visitar su tumba en la Ciudad de México. En su honor ahora, se puede ver su nombre en muchos lugares de toda la nación mexicana, [2] desde la Institución de Ciencias y Artes donde recibió su título de abogado y que ahora lleva su nombre, hasta la Ciudad Juárez (antes El Paso del Norte) donde Benito Juárez se estableció para luchar desde allí contra las fuerzas francesas cuando éstas invadieron su país.

pudo hacer

de otros países justicia

Hizo menos cuenta

funeral

Verifiquemos

1. ¿Por qué se dice que Benito Juárez es el Abraham Lincoln de México? Para contestar, prepara un diagrama como el que sigue y haz una comparación de la vida de Abraham Lincoln y Benito Juárez en las tres áreas señaladas. En los dos extremos pon las diferencias y en el área que los dos óvalos comparten, pon lo que estos dos expresidentes tienen en común.

NIÑEZ **EDUCACIÓN** **GRANDES HAZAÑAS**

Abraham Lincoln
1.
2.
3.
...

1.
2.
3.
...

Benito Juárez
1.
2.
3.
...

2. ¿Qué problemas tuvo el Presidente Juárez con Francia? ¿con Estados Unidos?
3. ¿Qué evidencia hay que el Presidente Juárez fue y sigue siendo amado de la gente mexicana?

¡Buscamos a alguien con experiencia!

¿ **Qué** piensas tú ?

1. ¿Qué características crees que buscaba la persona que emplea a cada uno de estos jóvenes? ¿Qué otras habilidades debe tener una persona interesada en estos puestos?

2. De lo que sabemos de Tina, ¿cuáles de estos puestos son buenos para ella? ¿Por qué crees eso?

3. Con un(a) compañero(a) de clase, dramatiza la entrevista que Tina tuvo para conseguir uno de estos puestos. Tú puedes hacer el papel de entrevistador(a) y tu compañero(a) el de Tina.

4. ¿Qué habilidades o características tienes que te hacen pensar que eres un(a) buen(a) candidato(a) para estos puestos? ¿Tendrías problemas al trabajar cinco o seis días por semana? Explica.

5. ¿Te gustaría trabajar mientras estás en el colegio? ¿Por qué?

6. ¿Creen tus amigos que debes conseguir empleo ahora? ¿tus padres? ¿tus profesores?

7. ¿Qué crees que vas a aprender en esta lección?

LOS ÁRBOLES DE FLORES BLANCAS

Esta leyenda mexicana viene de la región que hoy conocemos como el estado de Oaxaca.

En el siglo XV el joven rey Cosijoeza acaba de ocupar el trono de los zapotecas en la bella ciudad de Juchitán, en el actual estado de Oaxaca. Era bondadoso, sabio y valiente. Era también un guerrero muy astuto que, a la vez, le gustaba gozar de la belleza de la naturaleza. En sus jardines gozaba en particular de unos árboles de flores blancas, árboles que solamente se encontraban en Juchitán.

Una tarde, cuando el joven rey paseaba por los jardines, vinieron unos emisarios de su enemigo, el rey azteca Ahuizotl.
Los emisarios explicaron: "Nuestro rey quiere que le mandes unos árboles de flores blancas. Quiere plantarlos a lo largo de los canales de su ciudad, Tenochtitlán".
Después de pensarlo, el joven rey dijo: "No es posible. Se prohíbe sacar estos árboles de mi reino".

Cosijoeza sabía que su enemigo Ahuizotl mandaría a sus guerreros aztecas a apoderarse de los árboles de las flores blancas y del reino zapoteca. Reunió a sus jefes guerreros y les dijo que otra vez tenían que pelear para salvar sus vidas y su reino del poder de los aztecas. Y los jefes prepararon las fortificaciones y las flechas envenenadas.

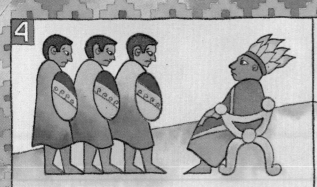

4

Tres meses más tarde, el ejército azteca volvió vencido a Tenochtitlán, la capital azteca. Su rey Ahuizotl se puso muy furioso.

Resolvió hacer uso de la astucia para obtener los árboles de las flores blancas y la derrota de los zapotecas. Llamó a Coyolicatzín, su hija más hermosa y más amada, y le explicó su plan.

5

Como el plan pedía, la princesa salió secretamente de la ciudad con dos criados. Después de un viaje largo y difícil, llegaron los tres a un bosque cerca del palacio del rey zapoteca y allí pasaron la noche.

Al día siguiente, cuando el joven rey paseaba por el bosque vio a esa joven bella, hermosamente vestida y adornada con joyas preciosas.

La invitó a su palacio donde su madre la cuidó con cariño. En pocos días el joven rey se enamoró completamente de la misteriosa joven.

Cuando Cosijoeza le dijo a la bella joven que quería casarse con ella, ésta le contestó: "Es muy difícil que yo pueda ser tu esposa, pues mi padre es el rey azteca, Ahuizotl".

6

Coyolicatzín volvió a Tenochtitlán, y pocos días después vinieron unos emisarios del rey zapoteca, cargados de riquezas para el rey azteca. Vinieron a pedir la mano de la bella Coyolicatzín. Como su plan dictaba, el rey azteca aceptó los regalos del joven rey y anunció que la hermosa Coyolicatzín sería la esposa del rey zapoteca.

Las bodas de la princesa azteca y el rey zapoteca se celebraron con gran esplendor y alegría en Juchitán, la capital zapoteca, y el rey se sintió el más feliz de todos los hombres.

Pero como el plan del rey azteca pedía, la princesa poco a poco iba descubriendo los secretos del ejército zapoteca.

Aprendió los secretos de las fortificaciones.

Y, más importante, aprendió cómo se hacían las flechas envenenadas.

Pero la princesa descubrió algo más también. Descubrió que amaba con todo el corazón a su esposo y a los zapotecas y sabía que nunca sería capaz de traicionarlos. Finalmente, con lágrimas de amor, le contó todo a su esposo.

El joven rey, con palabras muy cariñosas, perdonó a su esposa, y en gratitud por su lealtad, envió como regalo al rey azteca unos árboles de flores blancas.

Hoy día se pueden ver árboles de esta clase en Tenochtitlán, la vieja capital de los aztecas, que ahora se llama la Ciudad de México.

¿QUÉ DECIMOS AL ESCRIBIR...?

Una solicitud de empleo

Éstos son algunos de los anuncios que vio Tina. ¿Para cuáles tiene las calificaciones que se buscan? ¿Cuáles no debe solicitar? ¿Por qué?

2 VENDEDORES SE BUSCAN

- De 25 a 35 años
- Profesionales de la venta
- Teléfono y coche propio
- Área de trabajo: El Paso y Juárez
- Indispensable: buenos informes y referencias

Interesados, llamar al teléfono 762-4360, preguntando por el señor Cuadros, hoy de 10:00 AM a 5:00 PM.

BILINGÜE

¡Urgente! Se necesita recepcionista bilingüe (inglés/español). Con experiencia, para trabajar en oficina de empleos.

Responsabilidades:

> Entrevistar a futuros empleados
> Contestar el teléfono
> Escribir a máquina

Una gran oportunidad para personas responsables y maduras. Llamar a TEMPS en Las Cruces.

791-2432

SE SOLICITAN PERSONAS

Para trabajar en restaurante de comida rápida.

Se ofrece:
- **Ambiente agradable**
- **Horas flexibles**
- **Entrenamiento pagado**
- **Uniformes**
- **Comidas gratis**
- **Pago atractivo**

Se requiere
- **Buena presencia**
- **Puntualidad**
- **Buenas referencias**

Solicite en persona en La Hamburguesa Gorda

Centro Comercial Cielo Vista

OPERADORES/AS

Con experiencia en aguja sencilla, para coser bolsas, faldas y pantalones. Con permiso de trabajo o residencia. Le garantizamos $4.75 la hora.

616 S. Santa Fe
El Paso, TX

SE NECESITAN

secretarias bilingües, operadoras de terminales, taquimecanógrafas. Trabaje para empresa importante.

Escriba con "currículum" a 534 Mesa St.

tel. 791-9139

BUENOS DÓLARES $$$$

REPARTA PERIÓDICOS

Lunes a domingo de 3 AM a 6 AM.

Se puede ganar hasta $550 al mes.

Llamar entre las 8 AM y 5 PM al:

762-6164.

Éste es el formulario que llenó Tina al solicitar un trabajo. ¿A cuál de los anuncios respondió?

Solicitud para empleo

Información personal

Nombre_____ Valdez _____ Cristina _____
         (apellido)   (nombre)

Dirección___ 3225 E. Manzana Way _____ El Paso, TX 79900 _____
             (calle y número)   (ciudad, estado, código postal)

Teléfono___ (915) 555-7009 _____

Edad (menor de 18)___ 16 _____

Horas disponibles (número total de horas)___ 20 por semana _____

Horas cada día

	dom	lu	mar	mier	jue	vier	sab
de	1	4	4	4	4	4	10
a	8	8	8	8	8	10	7

Educación

Colegio___ El Paso High School _____

Promedio de notas___ B ___ Último año completado___ 10 ___

Experiencia Trabajos más recientes (pagados o voluntarios)

El verano pasado trabajé como ayudante en un campamento para niños.

Durante el año escolar, soy ayudante de oficina de la escuela.

Referencias

Sra. Olga Urrutia, El Paso HS

Sr. Ernesto Padilla, Campamento Coronado

Miss Leona Mendenhall, El Paso HS

Actividades

Miembro del Club de francés, miembro del coro, miembro del equipo de tenis.

CHARLEMOS UN POCO

A. **PARA EMPEZAR . . .** ¿A quién describe o quién dice esto en el cuento azteca de ''Los árboles de flores blancas''?

Cosijoeza

Ahuizotl   Coyolicatzín

1. Acaba de ocupar el trono de los zapotecas en la bella ciudad de Juchitán, en el actual estado de Oaxaca.
2. ''Es muy difícil que yo pueda ser tu esposa, pues mi padre es el rey azteca, Ahuizotl''.
3. Reunió a sus jefes guerreros y les dijo que otra vez tenían que pelear para salvar sus vidas y su reino.
4. Perdonó a su esposa, y en gratitud por su lealtad, envió como regalo al rey azteca unos árboles de flores blancas.
5. Poco a poco iba descubriendo los secretos del ejército zapoteca.
6. Era también un guerrero muy astuto que, a la vez, le gustaba gozar de la belleza de la naturaleza.
7. Descubrió que amaba con todo el corazón a su esposo y a los zapotecas, y sabía que nunca sería capaz de traicionarlos.
8. Resolvió hacer uso de la astucia para obtener los árboles de las flores blancas y la derrota de los zapotecas.

B. **¿QUÉ DECIMOS . . .?** ¿Descubre Tina esta información al leer los anuncios clasificados? ¿Sí o no?

1. Se busca recepcionista que sepa inglés y español.
2. Una empresa busca secretarias bilingües.
3. Los operadores de máquinas de coser ganan más de $5.00 por hora.
4. Se ofrecen comidas gratis en La Hamburguesa Gorda.
5. Una persona de dieciséis años puede conseguir el trabajo de vendedor.
6. Para trabajar de cajero se necesita saber inglés.
7. Los cajeros ganan más que los operadores.
8. Se buscan personas para repartir periódicos entre las ocho y las cinco.
9. Nadie busca ayuda para limpiar la casa.
10. Se necesita coche para ser vendedor.

LECCIÓN 3

When stating rules and
regulations: Impersonal *se*

Se prohíbe hablar inglés en la clase.
No se permite fumar.

See **¿Por qué se dice así?,**
page G103, section 7.5.

When referring to non-specific
people or things: Impersonal *se*

No se habla inglés allí.
¿Dónde **se venden** televisores?

See **¿Por qué se dice así?,**
page G103, section 7.5.

C. En la biblioteca. ¿Qué les dice el (la) bibliotecario(a) a los estudiantes que no se portan bien?

 MODELO hablar

No hables, por favor. Se prohíbe hablar aquí.

1. comer
2. hacer ruido
3. tomar refrescos
4. escuchar música

5. escribir en nuestros libros
6. cantar
7. correr
8. dormir

CH. España. Un(a) amigo(a) va a visitar Madrid con su familia y tiene muchas preguntas para ti. Contesta sus preguntas.

 MODELO almorzar a las 12:00

Compañero(a): **¿Almuerzan a las doce?**
Tú: **No, allí no se almuerza a las doce.**

comer paella
Compañero(a): **¿Comen paella?**
Tú: **Sí, allí se come paella.**

1. hablar inglés
2. comer al aire libre
3. viajar en metro
4. dar un paseo por la noche

5. cenar temprano
6. tomar helado
7. servir cochinillo asado
8. llegar a la hora exacta

D. ¿Dónde? Tú acabas de mudarte a esta ciudad. Pregúntale a tu compañero(a) dónde puedes conseguir los objetos en el dibujo.

 EJEMPLO *Tú:* **¿Dónde se alquilan videos?**
Compañero(a): **Se alquilan videos en [*nombre de tienda*].**

VOCABULARIO ÚTIL:
vender   comprar   alquilar

E. Empleos. Tú y tu compañero(a) trabajan en el departamento de anuncios clasificados del periódico. Hoy están preparando una página de anuncios modelos para sus clientes. Prepárenlos.

EJEMPLO   **Se solicitan empleados que sean responsables.**

buscar requerir solicitar necesitar	operadores secretario(a) empleados cajero(a) persona vendedores programador(a)	poder trabajar de noche hablar inglés tener experiencia ser responsable tener buena presencia saber escribir a máquina tener conocimiento de redes conocer bien la ciudad

F. Mesero principal. Tú eres mesero en un restaurante. Hoy estás entrenando a un mesero nuevo. ¿Qué le dices de estos objetos?

MODELO   **Este platillo es para el postre.**

postre

1. leche

2. ensalada

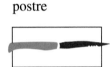
3. café

4. carne

5. sopa

6. comida

7. pescado

8. helado

G. ¡Qué necio! Tu hermanito(a) es muy curioso(a). Te hace preguntas constantemente. ¿Qué te pregunta y qué le contestas tú?

EJEMPLO   estudiar todo el día
Hermanito(a):   **¿Por qué estudiaste todo el día?**
Tú: **Lo hice para salir bien en el examen.**

VOCABULARIO ÚTIL:
no escuchar tus preguntas
conversar con mis amigos
ganar dinero
salir bien en el examen
hacer ejercicio

conservar energía
perder peso
planear una fiesta
ganar el partido
ver las noticias

1. practicar el cabezazo
2. apagar la lámpara
3. prender la tele
4. correr
5. no comer el postre

6. hablar por teléfono
7. trabajar el sábado
8. ir al café
9. cortar el césped
10. cerrar la puerta

The preposition *para:* Purpose

¿Eso? Es **para** cortar manzanas.
Estas pastillas son **para** tu dolor de estómago.

*See ¿**Por qué se dice así?**,*
page G104, section 7.6.

The preposition *para*:
Intended recipient

¿**Para** quién es ese regalo?
El collar es **para** ti, mi amor.

See **¿Por qué se dice así?**,
page G104, section 7.6.

H. ¡De vuelta!   Acabas de volver de un viaje a México donde compraste mucho. ¿Para quiénes compraste estos recuerdos?

EJEMPLO   **El plato es para mi abuela.**

I. Profesiones.   ¿Dónde trabajan estas personas?

MODELO   **Los bomberos trabajan para la ciudad.**

políticos	
enfermeros	sus clientes
abogados	el restaurante
bomberos	el gobierno
camareros	las compañías
maestros	el hospital
secretarios	las escuelas
médicos	la ciudad
cocineros	

The preposition *para*:
Employer

Trabajamos **para** una compañía de
  petróleo.
Tu mamá trabaja **para** la
  universidad, ¿no?

See **¿Por qué se dice así?**,
page G104, section 7.6.

CHARLEMOS UN POCO MÁS

A. Se habla español. Su profesor(a) va a darle a cada uno de ustedes o un anuncio clasificado o una descripción de un servicio que buscan. Si recibes un anuncio, úsalo para encontrar a una persona que necesite el servicio que tú ofreces. Si recibes una descripción de lo que buscas, úsala para encontrar a alguien que ofrezca ese servicio. Cuando encuentren a la persona que buscan, siéntense y decidan si van a hacer negocio juntos.

  EJEMPLO   **Busco flores para el cumpleaños de mi madre.**

B. Letreros. Con un(a) compañero(a), diseña y escribe cinco letreros para la escuela o la clase. Luego en grupos de tres o cuatro, comparen sus letreros y decidan cuál es el más creativo. Preséntenselo a la clase.

C. Simplemente hay que . . . Hoy, Clara Consejera, la consejera del periódico escolar, no está. Tú y tu compañero(a) están sustituyéndola. ¿Qué consejos les dan a estas personas?

 EJEMPLO   bailar bien
Para bailar bien hay que practicar mucho.

1. perder peso

2. aprender español

3. tener dinero

4. sacar buenas notas

5. no tener sueño

6. ganar el partido

7. comprar un coche

8. hacer un viaje

Dramatizaciones

A. Los requisitos.   Tú eres el (la) recepcionista para una compañía internacional. Tu compañero(a) está interesado(a) en trabajar con la compañía. Quiere saber cuáles son los requisitos para conseguir empleo en la compañía. Dramaticen esta situación.

B. ¿Para quién?   Sólo falta una semana para Navidad y tú necesitas comprar regalos para tu familia y tus amigos. Estás ahora en un almacén grande pidiéndole consejos a un(a) dependiente. Dramaticen esta situación. Tu compañero(a) va a hacer el papel del (de la) dependiente.

Estrategias para leer:
El hacer preguntas

El hacer preguntas. En la **Unidad 6,** aprendiste a hacer preguntas para ayudarte a entender un poema. El hacer preguntas es una estrategia muy valiosa para entender todo tipo de lectura. Hay varios tipos de preguntas que un buen lector se puede hacer, dependiendo del tipo de lectura. Por ejemplo, algunas preguntas sólo se pueden contestar . . .

1. con información *específica* que viene de una sola oración en la lectura.
2. con una *combinación* de información que sólo se puede hacer después de leer varios párrafos.
3. si el lector cuenta con su *propia experiencia* o *pasado.*
4. si hay una *interacción* entre autor y lector basada en una combinación de lo que el lector ya sabía y lo que acaba de aprender en la lectura.

El artículo que sigue se publicó en el *Sacramento Bee,* basado en un artículo que originalmente se publicó en Texas, en el *Dallas Morning News.* Antes de leer este artículo, estudia las preguntas que siguen con un(a) compañero(a). En una hoja de papel, indiquen si son preguntas que sólo se pueden contestar con información *específica,* con una *combinación* de información, si el lector cuenta con su *propia experiencia* o *pasado* o si hay una *interacción* entre autor y lector.

Preguntas	Tipo	Respuestas
¿Cómo se llama la alumna que da el discurso de fin de curso?		
¿Quiénes son los otros jóvenes mencionados en el artículo?		
¿Qué hicieron estos jóvenes?		
¿Bajo qué circunstancias asistieron a la escuela secundaria estos jóvenes?		
¿Por qué crees que estas noticias fueron de interés periodístico en Dallas, Texas?		
¿Por qué fueron de interés periodístico en Sacramento, California?		

Ahora, lean el artículo individualmente. Al leer, tengan presente estas preguntas y anoten toda la información que les ayude a contestarlas. Tal vez sea necesario leer el artículo varias veces para encontrar todas las respuestas.

Para el MIT:
Cinco estudiantes de El Paso sobresalen y brillan

Liliana Ramírez, Albert Martínez, Enrique Arzaga, Alicia Ayala y David Villarreal

sin ventajas

grupo de jóvenes con mal fin

no recordaron

van en camino

éxito

piden entrar en

descubrir

dinero para sus estudios

conserje

El PASO, Texas—La conocen como la escuela bajo el *freeway* (autopista), y está entre la Carretera Interestatal 10 y la frontera con México, en un barrio de cantinas, taquerías y tiendas de "pesos por dólares".

"Ysleta High School", la pobre y desvencijada* Escuela Secundaria Ysleta, también está localizada en una zona de El Paso donde abundan las pandillas.* Pero hoy existe una nueva pandilla en Ysleta. A cinco de sus estudiantes recién graduados se les olvidó* lo pobre que son o que deberían ser pandilleros y ahora se encaminan* a asistir al prestigioso Instituto Tecnológico de Massachusetts (MIT) este otoño.

"Es un admirable logro",* afirmó John Hammond, el director asociado de admisiones de MIT, señalando que de los 7,000 estudiantes que solicitan* a MIT cada año sólo 600 consiguen matricularse. Cerca del ocho

por ciento de los 4,300 estudiantes subgraduados son hispanos.

"Nosotros reclutamos a todos estos cinco jóvenes", continuó Hammond. "Ellos pasaron por todo el proceso de admisiones, individualmente, debido a sus propios méritos, antes de darnos cuenta* siquiera que venían de la misma escuela secundaria".

Los cinco estudiantes de Ysleta cada uno ganaron becas* de más de $20,000 dólares al año. Alicia Ayala, la hija de un aseador de edificios* pensionado fue la estudiante que dio el discurso oficial en la graduación de su generación. "Soy una mujer hispana, pero eso no quiere decir que no pueda hacer grandes cosas", dijo ella. "Yo tengo muchos planes".

Luego está el caso de Liliana Ramírez quien no hablaba inglés cuando su familia se mudó de México a EE.UU. hace

apenas* dos años y medio. Y
David Villarreal, un adelantero
del equipo de básquetbol que
valora* más sus éxitos*
académicos que sus victorias
deportivas. Y Enrique Arzaga,
que cree que "cualquiera que no
lo haga y luego le eche la culpa
a la escuela o al medio ambiente
simplemente está buscando
excusas". Y ahí está Albert
Martínez, a quien le fascinan
las computadoras y que también
canta como tenor en el coro de
la escuela y trabaja medio tiempo en la noche limpiando edificios. Su madre, Dolores, es
viuda y también limpia edificios.
"La mayor parte de mi vida, me
he privado* de muchas cosas",
dijo Albert, que bien podría
hablar en nombre de sus cuatro
compañeros.

"Nosotros siempre tuvimos
que limitarnos y contentarnos
con poco. Pero yo nunca
aprendí lo que significa ser un
'desventajado'.* Comparados
con cualquiera, mi madre y yo
somos pobres. Pero yo no. Yo
tengo otras riquezas".

El director de la escuela,
Roger Parks no intenta dar
excusas por la realidad de
Ysleta. Reconoce que el treinta
y seis por ciento de los estudiantes no terminan la escuela
secundaria. "Esta cifra* es tan
alta como la de cualquier otra
escuela de El Paso". También
apunta* que "el sesenta y ocho
por ciento de nuestros estudiantes
provienen de familias que son
consideradas económicamente
desventajadas".

"Nuestro estereotipo es ser
'la escuela bajo el *freeway*'",
dijo Parks, "pero nunca hemos
aceptado las limitaciones que
otra gente nos impone. Lograr*
que cinco de nuestros estudiantes
entren a MIT quizás nunca se
vuelva a repetir, pero nosotros
siempre tendremos estudiantes
de este calibre".

Cada año más o menos una
docena de los estudiantes más
sobresalientes de Ysleta pueden
en realidad escoger a qué universidad asistir—Cornell, Rice,
Yale, Harvard, Stanford, West
Point. MIT de Cambridge,
Massachusetts, hasta tiene una
persona que funge* como reclutador voluntario en busca de
estudiantes sobresalientes, y
muchas veces los encuentra en
Ysleta.

sólo

da más valor / triunfos

no he tenido

uno sin oportunidades

número

indica

Conseguir

actúa

Verifiquemos

1. Compara Ysleta High School con tu escuela. ¿Cuáles son las semejanzas? ¿las diferencias?
2. ¿Hay escuelas en tu ciudad semejantes a Ysleta High School? ¿Cuáles son y cuáles no son las semejanzas?
3. ¿Cuál de los cinco jóvenes te impresionó más? ¿Por qué?
4. ¿Qué piensas del director de la escuela, Roger Parks? ¿Crees que es un buen director? ¿Por qué?
5. ¿Cómo explicas tú que una escuela tan pobre produzca no sólo a cinco estu- diantes que sean aceptados a M.I.T. en el mismo año, sino también a otros que puedan ser aceptados en Cornell, Rice, Yale, Harvard, Stanford y West Point?

ESCRIBAMOS AHORA

Estrategias para escribir:
Narrativa—Ensayo personal

A. Empezar. El ensayo personal te permite compartir tus pensamientos y experiencias personales con otros. Este tipo de ensayo tiene varios usos: el narrar un cuento, el describir o explicar algo, o el persuadir a alguien que piense de cierta manera o que haga algo. En esta escritura, tú vas a narrar una anécdota de tu niñez.

Primero tendrás que seleccionar un incidente de tu niñez. Puede ser algo divertido, triste, conmovedor, misterioso, raro u otro tipo de incidente. Para ayudarte a decidir, prepara una lista de incidentes de tu niñez que recuerdas. Categoriza esos incidentes en un cuadro como el que sigue.

Divertido	Triste	Conmovedor	Misterioso	Raro	Otro

B. Organizar. Primero, selecciona uno de los temas que incluiste en la lista que preparaste en la actividad **A.** Piensa acerca de la información que vas a necesitar para poder contar este incidente en detalle: quiénes participaron; dónde ocurrió el incidente; cuál fue el orden cronológico; por qué fue divertido, triste o conmovedor . . . Tal vez te ayude organizar todos los incidentes en orden cronológico o tal vez prefieras organizarte usando otras de las técnicas que hemos mencionado en otras unidades: hacer un torbellino de ideas, usar racimos, hacer esquemas, etc.

C. Primer borrador. Al empezar a escribir tu ensayo, piensa en una oración que comunique el tema y el resultado que esperas lograr. Por ejemplo, podrías empezarlo: ''Cuando yo empecé a asistir a la escuela, a la edad de cinco años, descubrí algo sorprendente''. Desarrolla tu cuento usando tus apuntes y lo que hiciste en **B** para organizar el tema. Recuerda tu primera oración a lo largo de escribir este ensayo y asegúrate de que todo lo que digas esté relacionado a lo que dices en la primera oración.

CH. Compartir. Lee el ensayo personal de dos compañeros y comparte con ellos el tuyo. Pídeles que hagan un breve resumen de tu ensayo para ver si lo entendieron. También pídeles sugerencias para hacerlo más claro y más efectivo. Haz el mismo tipo de comentarios sobre sus ensayos.

D. Revisar. Haz cambios en tu ensayo a base de las sugerencias de tus compañeros. Luego, antes de entregarlo, dáselo a dos compañeros de clase para que lo lean una vez más. Esta vez pídeles que revisen la estructura y la puntuación. En particular, pídeles que revisen la concordancia — verbo / sujeto y sustantivo / adjetivo — y el uso del pretérito y del imperfecto.

E. Versión final. Escribe la versión final de tu ensayo incorporando las correcciones que tus compañeros de clase te indicaron. Presta mucha atención al formato. Piensa en la versión final como uno de varios cuentos que se van a publicar en un libro de anécdotas.

F. Publicar. Cuando tu profesor(a) te devuelva tu ensayo, prepáralo para publicar. Dibuja una o dos ilustraciones apropiadas (o sácalas de revistas) para ilustrar lo interesante de tu anécdota. Luego pongan todos los ensayos en un cuaderno y decidan cúal es el título más apropiado para un libro de anécdotas sobre la niñez de toda la clase.

UNIDAD 8

¡Voy a Venezuela!

¿ Cuándo saldrás ?

JUNIO

d	l	m	m	j	v	s
			1	2	3	4
5	6	7	8	9	10	11
12	13	14	15	16	17	18
19	20	21	22	23	24	25
26	27	28	29	30		

TERCERA EDAD

Si has cumplido 60 años aprovecha esta oportunidad y VISITA EXPAÑA.

Salida a **Tenerife** días 3-10 y 17 de febrero, 23 y 30 de marzo

Salida a **Madrid** y **Santiago** días 22-26 y 29 de enero, 18-25 de marzo

Reserve en cualquiera de nuestras tres direcciones

CASABLANCA AGENCIA DE VIAJES

Colinas de Bello Monte
Av. Miguel Ángel

Sabana Grande
C/ El Recreo

Av. Urdaneta
Ibarras a Pelota

EN 1993... EL COSTA RIVIERA LLEGA A LA GUAIRA

Atrévase a conquistar el Caribe: REPÚBLICA DOMINICANA, PUERTO RICO, SANTO TOMÁS, TRINIDAD y LA GUAIRA, VENEZUELA.

Descubra el Costa Riviera y viva una aventura en cada puerto. Disfrute de la exótica magia del Caribe mientras goza de las más sofisticadas comodidades y el acogedor servicio de nuestra tripulación.

*Mil ambientes a bordo
*Manjares a toda hora
*La más excitante vida nocturna
*Diversión y más diversión

TIPO DE ACOMODACIÓN

Interna, cama baja y litera, ducha y toilette. Por persona $750*

Interna, dos camas bajas, ducha y toilette. Por persona $900*

Externa, dos camas bajas, ducha y toilette. Por persona $1000*

3er y 4° adulto ocupando el mismo camarote. Por persona $500*

Niños menores de 12 años acompañados por dos adultos en el mismo camarote. Por niño $350*

*MÁS IMPUESTOS

Costa Tours Línea "C"
Centro Comercial Bello Campo, Local 24
Tel.: 32.38.31 - 32.38.32

¿ Qué piensas tú ?

1. ¿Qué estación es? ¿otoño? ¿invierno? ¿Qué crees que esperan con anticipación estos jóvenes? ¿Por qué crees eso?

2. Sabiendo lo que sabes de estos jóvenes, ¿cómo crees que van a pasar el verano?

3. ¿Para qué son los anuncios en esta página? ¿Cuál te llama la atención? ¿Por qué te atrae?

4. ¿Qué podrá hacer y ver una persona que haga el viaje a La Guaira en Venezuela? ¿Cómo viajarán? ¿Qué lugares visitarán?

5. ¿Qué puedes decir de alguien que decida hacer un viaje a España? ¿Cuánto tiempo durará el viaje? ¿Cuándo van a salir?

6. ¿Qué planes tienes tú para el verano? ¿Tienes algunos planes específicos para el año próximo?

7. ¿Qué crees que vas a aprender en esta lección?

1

El nopal es un cacto muy bien conocido en las Américas, pero sin duda abunda más en México. Es una bella planta verde con flores rojas.

Esta leyenda mexicana explica el origen de esta planta que figuró en el escudo azteca y después en el escudo de la República de México.

2

Hace muchos siglos los aztecas vivían en el norte de México. Cerca del año 800 d. de J.C., sus dioses les hablaron diciendo: "Pronto irán al sur, donde encontrarán una nueva tierra más grande y bonita que la de aquí. Un día verán un águila hermosa posada en una planta desconocida. El ave tendrá una serpiente en el pico. Y allí construirán una gran ciudad".

3

Los aztecas obedecieron el mandato de sus dioses, pero el viaje fue largo y difícil y duró por muchos siglos. No fue hasta el año 1300 cuando los primeros aztecas llegaron al gran valle de México. De las montañas que rodeaban el valle, vieron el lago de Texcoco con sus islas grandes y pequeñas.

4

"Aquí viviremos", anunció el supremo sacerdote, "hasta que nuestros dioses nos den una señal indicando dónde debemos construir nuestra ciudad". Pero, como toda la tierra alrededor del lago ya estaba ocupada por otras tribus, los aztecas tuvieron que establecerse en una de las islas grandes del lago.

5

Con los aztecas vino su dios Huitzilopochtli, el dios de la guerra. Lo veneraban más que a los otros dioses. Y como este dios exigía sacrificios humanos, los aztecas hacían guerra sin cesar contra sus vecinos quienes antes habían vivido en paz y armonía.

6

Lejos, al norte, vivía la buena hermana del dios Huitzilopochtli con su esposo y su hijito Cópil. Pertenecían a una tribu pacífica.
"Cuando yo sea mayor", dijo el chico, "voy a hacer prisionero a mi tío para que no pueda causar tanta aflicción".
"No puedes hacerlo, hijito", dijo su madre.
"Tu tío es muy fuerte y poderoso".
"Sí, lo haré", respondió el muchacho.

Pasaron años y más años. Cópil se convirtió en un joven valiente, hermoso, hábil, bueno e inteligente. Y tenía todavía en el corazón el deseo de vencer a su tío y proteger a las otras tribus pacíficas.
Con mil hombres valientes, se puso en marcha en el largo viaje hacia el valle de México.
Cuando llegaron al gran bosque que rodeaba al lago de Texcoco, Cópil dijo: "Descansaremos aquí, y mañana llevaremos a cabo nuestros planes".

7

Pero el dios azteca tenía espías y ya sabía las intenciones de Cópil.
Llamó a sus sacerdotes y les dio este mandato terrible: "Irán al campamento de mi sobrino Cópil. Lo matarán y me traerán su corazón como ofrenda".

8

9

Los sacerdotes hicieron exactamente lo que les pidió su dios. Entonces Huitzilopochtli les mandó enterrar el corazón de Cópil entre rocas y mala hierba de una isla en el centro del lago.

10

A la mañana siguiente, todos vieron lo que había pasado durante la noche.

Una bella planta verde con magníficas flores rojas había crecido en el sitio donde enterraron el corazón de Cópil. Pero lo verdaderamente asombroso fue que posada en esta planta vieron un águila con una serpiente en el pico.

11

De repente todo el mundo oyó la voz del dios Huitzilopochtli: "La profecía de los dioses está cumplida. Aquí fundarán su ciudad y la llamarán Tenochtitlán".

Y el dios anunció que ya había vuelto a su habitación en el cielo de donde iba a guiar el futuro de la ciudad.

12

Tenochtitlán creció y prosperó y lo sigue haciendo todavía bajo el nombre de Ciudad de México. Y a la vez, esa bella planta verde llamada nopal, con magníficas flores rojas, sigue recordándonos del joven y valiente Cópil.

¿QUÉ DECIMOS...?

Al hacer planes para el futuro

1 ¡Podremos hacer tantas cosas!

Tina y Margarita andan de compras en Stanton Street.

> ¡Increíble! ¡Sólo faltan dos semanas para las vacaciones!

> Pero, chica, no olvides, voy a seguir trabajando. Si trabajo tiempo completo durante el verano, podré comprar mi carro en septiembre.

> Que bien lo sé. Pronto podremos nadar, jugar tenis, ir de compras...

> ¿Tan pronto? ¡En septiembre! Tina, te felicito. No sabía que te faltaba tan poco. Pues, hace poco que cumplí los dieciséis años. Y ahora yo también podré trabajar.

> ¡Mira! Creo que solicitaré con «Viva El Paso». ¿Qué tal te parece?

> Pero, fíjate. Tú estarás trabajando de noche y yo de día. ¡Nunca nos veremos!

> Por eso mismo lo haré. Y además, como el espectáculo es de noche, no tendré que levantarme temprano y podré hacer todas mis cosas favoritas durante el día.

> ¡Sería perfecto para ti, como eres tan dramática!

> Vamos, chica, no es para tanto. Necesito entrar aquí. Busco un pañuelo azul y verde. Creo que aquí es donde los vi.

¡Hola, Tina, Margarita! ¿Qué hacen por aquí?

Andamos de compras, como siempre.

Sí, y estamos también hablando de nuestros planes para el verano. Las dos pensamos trabajar. Yo voy a estar en «Viva El Paso». Y ustedes, ¿tienen planes?

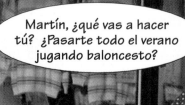

Yo tengo que trabajar, pero claro, también voy a jugar tenis todos los días.

Y tú, Daniel, ¿qué vas a hacer?

No sé. Ya veremos.

Pues, yo puedo jugar contigo, Mateo. Pienso trabajar sólo de noche.

Martín, ¿qué vas a hacer tú? ¿Pasarte todo el verano jugando baloncesto?

Pues sí. Nuestro equipo jugará en el campeonato del estado este julio. Después de eso, no sé.

Supongo que iré a acampar con mi familia, como de costumbre. Queremos llevar a mi mamá y a Nena a la cueva cerca de Las Cruces. Esta vez iremos todos juntos. Bueno, todos menos Daniel.

¿Cómo que todos menos Daniel? ¿Qué vas a hacer tú, Daniel?

¿Por qué no pasamos allí a tomar algo y les cuento mis planes?

Vamos, Daniel. Me muero de curiosidad. ¿Qué vas a hacer este verano?

Pues en agosto, voy a ir a un campamento de música por dos semanas.

¡No andes con rodeos, Daniel! ¿Qué vas a hacer durante junio y julio?

Bueno, en junio tendré que hacer todos los preparativos …

¡Por Dios, Daniel! ¿Los preparativos para qué?

Para mi viaje.

¿Adónde vas?

A Venezuela, a visitar a mi amigo, Luis.

¡No me digas! ¿Por cuánto tiempo? ¿Cuándo sales?

Mira, Daniel, mira lo que te compré para tu viaje.

A fines de junio y no regreso hasta principios de agosto. ¡Estaré allí cinco semanas!

¡Ay, qué envidia! ¡Cinco semanas en Sudamérica! Bueno, entonces te tendré que hacer una lista de las cosas que quiero que me traigas.

Ah, gracias.

CHARLEMOS UN POCO

A. **PARA EMPEZAR . . .** Pon estas escenas en orden cronológico según lo que escuchaste en el cuento "El origen del nopal".

1. A la mañana siguiente, todos vieron una bella planta en el sitio donde enterraron el corazón de Cópil.
2. Cópil, el sobrino de Huitzilopochtli, dijo, "Voy a hacer prisionero a mi tío para que no pueda causar tanta aflicción".
3. Pero los sacerdotes mataron a Cópil y enterraron su corazón en una isla.
4. Para satisfacer a Huitzilopochtli, los aztecas hacían guerra sin cesar contra sus vecinos que antes habían vivido en paz y armonía.
5. Hace muchos siglos que vivían en el norte de México los aztecas.
6. En el año 1300, los primeros aztecas llegaron al gran valle de México con Huitzilopochtli, el dios de la guerra.
7. En esta planta vieron un águila con una serpiente en el pico y allí construyeron su ciudad, Tenochtitlán, que ahora es la Ciudad de México.
8. Sus dioses les dijeron, "Un día verán un águila hermosa posada en una planta desconocida. El ave tendrá una serpiente en el pico. Y allí construirán una gran ciudad".
9. Con mil hombres valientes, se puso en marcha en el largo viaje hacia el valle de México.

B. **¿QUÉ DECIMOS . . .?** ¿Quiénes harán estas cosas durante el verano?

Tina   **Margarita**   **Daniel**   **Martín**   **Mateo**

1. Irá de compras.
2. Seguirá trabajando.
3. Irá al campamento de música.
4. No tendrá que levantarse temprano.
5. Jugará tenis.
6. Participará en un campeonato.
7. Hará un viaje largo.
8. Participará en "Viva El Paso".

C. Este fin de semana. ¿Qué hará tu compañero(a) este fin de semana?

MODELO   asistir a un concierto
Asistirá a un concierto.

1. trabajar el sábado
2. correr por las tardes
3. sacar muchas fotos en el zoológico
4. pedir una pizza
5. aprender a tocar la guitarra
6. repartir periódicos como siempre
7. ir a acampar con su familia
8. competir en el campeonato de béisbol

CH. El verano.   ¿Qué planes tienen Esteban y sus amigos para el fin de semana?

Quico y Carmen

MODELO   **Quico y Carmen pasearán en bicicleta.**

1. mis amigos y yo

2. Lilia y Juana

3. Leticia

4. yo

5. Pablo y Soledad

6. todos nosotros

7. Mariela

8. yo

Talking about the future: The future tense

The future tense has one set of endings for **-ar**, **-er**, and **-ir** verbs. These endings are attached to the infinitive.

veré	veremos
verás	
verá	verán

Te **veré** en San Francisco.
¿**Correrán** ustedes?

*See ¿**Por qué se dice así?**, page G107, section 8.1.*

D. ¡Fiesta internacional! Tu colegio va a tener una fiesta internacional este fin de semana y todos tendrán que participar. ¿Qué harán estas personas? Usa tu imaginación.

EJEMPLO **Mis amigos Linda y David bailarán en Moscú.**

	cantar	Londres
mis padres	descansar	Madrid
mi amigo(a) [. . .]	asistir a un concierto	Acapulco
el(la) profesor(a)	ir de compras	Buenos Aires
mis amigos [. . .] y [. . .]	pasear	Caracas
[. . .] y yo	comer	Moscú
¿ . . . ?	visitar	París
	bailar	San Juan
	¿ . . . ?	¿ . . . ?

E. Posesiones. Tu compañero(a) de clase quiere saber si tendrás todo esto en unos diez años. Contesta sus preguntas.

MODELO *Compañero(a):* **¿Tendrás una lancha?**
Tú: **No, pero tendré un(a) . . .**

Talking about the future: Future tense of irregular verbs

Irregular verbs in the future tense use the same endings as regular future tense verbs; only the stems are irregular.

poner	**pondr-**
salir	**saldr-**
tener	**tendr-**
venir	**vendr-**
decir	**dir-**
hacer	**har-**
haber	**habr-**
poder	**podr-**
querer	**querr-**

tendré	**tendr**emos
tendrás	
tendrá	**tendr**án

¿**Tendrás** muchos hijos?
No. **Tendré** sólo un hijo.

See **¿Por qué se dice así?,**
page G109, section 8.2.

F. **¿Sí o no?**   Algunos estudiantes quieren que se suspendan las clases la semana que viene. ¿Qué opinas tú? ¿Qué crees que dirán estas personas?

MODELO   tus padres
Mis padres dirán que sí. o
Mis padres dirán que no.

1. tus amigos
2. el (la) director(a)
3. los estudiantes de francés
4. el (la) profesor(a) de español
5. el (la) secretario(a) de la escuela
6. el (la) entrenador(a)
7. los miembros de la banda
8. los profesores de ciencias
9. el enfermero
10. la consejera

G. Proyectos.   Tu mejor amigo dice que va a hacer muchos cambios el próximo año. ¿Qué cambios hará?

MODELO   ponerse en línea
Se pondrá en línea.

1. hacer más ejercicio
2. ponerse a dieta
3. salir más
4. hacerse socio de un club atlético
5. decir la verdad siempre
6. venir a clases todos los días
7. saber usar la computadora mejor
8. poder salir más en coche

H. El futuro.   ¿Puedes predecir el futuro de estas personas?

EJEMPLO   **Mi amiga Manuela será artista de cine.**

mi amiga [. . .]	querer ser presidente
yo	tener muchos hijos
el (la) profesor(a)	ser doctor(a)
mis amigos [. . .] y [. . .]	sacar buenas notas en la universidad
[. . .] y yo	cantar con una banda
mi amigo [. . .]	ser artista de cine
el (la) director(a)	tener su propia compañía
	hablar tres lenguas
	trabajar para NASA como astronauta
	saber más español que la profesora
	vivir en otro país

Talking about the future: *Decir*

diré	diremos
dirás	
dirá	dirán

¿**Dirás** la verdad?
Yo no **diré** nada.

See ¿**Por qué se dice así?**,
page G109, section 8.2.

CHARLEMOS UN POCO MÁS

A. Año Nuevo. Prepara por escrito una lista de ocho a diez resoluciones para el Año Nuevo. Luego pregúntales a varios compañeros de clase qué resoluciones tienen ellos y diles las tuyas. Decide cuál es la resolución más interesante entre todas y escríbela en la pizarra.

B. Este verano. En grupos de cuatro discutan lo que harán este verano. Luego preparen un dibujo de sus actividades. Usen el dibujo para contarle a la clase los planes de todos en su grupo.

C. Predecir el futuro. Tú y tu compañero(a) son editores del periódico escolar. Hoy es el 5 de enero y están preparando una edición humorística enfocada en el futuro. Escriban subtítulos cómicos para estas fotos, indicando lo que harán o lo que serán estas personas en el futuro.

CH. Las aventuras de Riso. Tu profesor(a) va a darles a ti y a dos compañeros dibujos que muestran las actividades de una semana en la vida de Riso. Pongan los dibujos en un orden apropiado y escriban un cuento narrando las aventuras de este joven. Luego en grupos de seis, léanse los cuentos.

Dramatizaciones

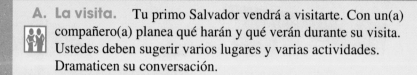

A. La visita. Tu primo Salvador vendrá a visitarte. Con un(a) compañero(a) planea qué harán y qué verán durante su visita. Ustedes deben sugerir varios lugares y varias actividades. Dramaticen su conversación.

B. ¿Quién será . . . ? El (La) director(a) de la escuela y un(a) consejero(a) están discutiendo el futuro de unos estudiantes en tu clase de español. Tú y tu compañero(a) van a hacer estos papeles. Dramaticen la conversación.

IMPACTO CULTURAL
Excursiones

Antes de empezar

A. Torbellino de ideas. Con dos compañeros de clase, haz un torbellino de ideas sobre Argentina. Simplemente escriban todo lo que saben de Argentina en dos minutos. Su profesor(a) va a controlar el tiempo.

B. Datos y más datos. ¿Sabes algo de la historia de Argentina? Para ver cuánto sabes, indica si estos comentarios son ciertos o falsos. Luego, después de leer la lectura, vuelve a contestar las preguntas, pero esta vez, del punto de vista del autor.

Tú		Argentina	Autor	
sí	no	**1.** Argentina es relativamente diferente de los otros países latinoamericanos.	sí	no
sí	no	**2.** Como México, Perú y Brasil, Argentina tiene una población indígena muy grande.	sí	no
sí	no	**3.** Argentina es un país muy industrializado.	sí	no
sí	no	**4.** Ya no hay muchos gauchos en Argentina.	sí	no
sí	no	**5.** En Argentina hay muchísimos europeos, especialmente españoles e italianos.	sí	no
sí	no	**6.** Los argentinos están muy orgullosos de sus tradiciones nativas. Por eso no aceptan lo extranjero, en particular lo europeo.	sí	no
sí	no	**7.** En Argentina, el 95 por ciento de la población sabe leer y escribir.	sí	no
sí	no	**8.** En 1982, hubo una guerra entre Argentina e Inglaterra.	sí	no

Argentina

Una búsqueda de la paz y la democracia

1

2

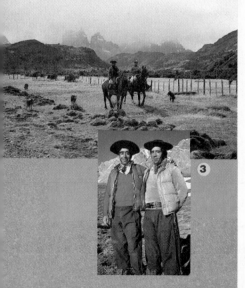

3

Situado al extremo sudeste del continente americano, el territorio de Argentina está compuesto en su mayor parte por fértiles tierras bajas llamadas *pampas*. Éstas son ideales para la agricultura y la ganadería. En su área andina, donde se levanta el Aconcagua, la cumbre más alta del hemisferio, hay extensos depósitos de minerales y reservas de gas natural. También es autosuficiente en petróleo, ha desarrollado significativamente su capacidad hidroeléctrica **1** y posee uno de los más desarrollados programas de energía nuclear, inclusive la bomba nuclear.

Un triste capítulo en la historia de este gran país es la manera en que trató a sus indígenas. Unos cincuenta años después de ganar su independencia, el gobierno argentino empezó una campaña contra la población indígena, hasta que, para fines del siglo XVIII, todos los grupos indígenas habían sido virtualmente exterminados. **2**

Otro grupo argentino que casi desapareció, éste por la llegada de la industrialización, fue el de los gauchos **3** o vaqueros argentinos. Mestizos en su mayoría, los gauchos eran una gente independiente e individualista que amaba la vida del campo. Vivían en la pampa y trabajaban de vez en cuando para los hacendados. Su importancia fue disminuyendo con el comienzo de la refrigeración y la exportación en masa del ganado. Poco a poco este grupo se vio obligado a abandonar su vida independiente y limitarse a las grandes haciendas e integrarse en la sociedad rural argentina.

A mediados del siglo XIX, Argentina abrió sus puertas a Europa. Miles de inmigrantes europeos llegaron a puertos argentinos y continuaron llegando hasta la primera mitad del siglo presente. En su mayoría fueron españoles e italianos, pero también había muchos franceses, polacos, rusos y alemanes. Aunque la mayoría de estos inmigrantes eran campesinos, los argentinos estaban decididos a crear una sociedad predominante urbana, europea, y lo lograron. Basta ver sus grandes ciudades modernas. Aún en su música y baile más representativo, el tango, **4** se ve ese gran predominio de lo europeo.

Con una población de 32,608,687 habitantes (censo 1990)[5] Argentina es uno de los países latinoamericanos con el más bajo índice de analfabetos. Efectivamente, el 95 por ciento de su población es alfabeta. Además, el 86 por ciento de su población es urbana y la mayoría pertenece a la clase media. El 90 por ciento de la población argentina es raza blanca de descendencia europea.

A pesar del alto nivel de educación de sus ciudadanos y de su deseo de lograr paz y estabilidad, Argentina ha tenido que sobrellevar en las últimas décadas gobiernos militares que han manchado su historia con lamentables asesinatos. Un ejemplo de esto es la llamada "guerra sucia" que ocurrió entre 1976-79, entre el gobierno militar y las guerrillas. En esta guerra murieron y desaparecieron miles de inocentes. Las madres y abuelas de estos "desaparecidos" fueron llamadas "Las Madres de la Plaza de Mayo",[6] porque estas mujeres se reunían en esta plaza con las fotos de sus "desaparecidos" para reclamarle al gobierno.

Otro hecho lamentable fue la guerra de las Malvinas o Falkland, ocurrida en 1982. Después de esta humillante derrota ante Inglaterra, se inició en Argentina una nueva era de democratización y revitalización económica. Grandes problemas persisten, pero como todo país latinoamericano, Argentina sigue su búsqueda de la paz y la democracia.

Verifiquemos

1. Vuelve a la actividad **B** de **Antes de empezar** e indica otra vez si los comentarios son ciertos o falsos. ¿Cómo se comparan las opiniones del autor con las tuyas?

2. Compara la manera en que los indígenas fueron tratados en Argentina con el tratamiento que recibieron en EE.UU.

3. Prepara una lista de todo lo que hace que Argentina sea un país moderno y progresista.

¡No deberías llevar tanto!

¿ **Q**ué piensas tú ?

1. ¿Qué consejos de último momento crees que le va a dar su hermana a Daniel? ¿su padre? ¿su madre?

2. ¿Qué harías tú si fueras testigo al robo y al accidente de bicicleta en estos dos dibujos?

3. ¿Cómo reaccionarías si tú fueras el chofer del carro? ¿la víctima del robo? ¿el ciclista?

4. Si pudieras cambiar una cosa en tu persona, ¿qué cambiarías? ¿Por qué cambiarías eso? ¿Qué efecto tendría tal cambio?

5. Si pudieras cambiar algo en tu escuela, ¿qué cambiarías? ¿Qué efecto tendría el cambio en los estudiantes?

6. Si un(a) amigo(a) tuyo(a) estuviera por hacer algo peligroso o deshonesto, ¿qué harías para convencerlo(la) que no lo hiciera?

7. ¿Qué crees que vas a aprender en esta lección?

Esta leyenda de la Argentina cuenta las aventuras del señor Sapo, el primer astronauta entre los animales, y explica por qué los sapos de hoy llevan manchas oscuras en la piel.

Una vez en tiempos muy remotos, todas las aves fueron invitadas a una fiesta en el cielo. En seguida, cada una de ellas empezó a hablar de lo que haría para participar en el programa.

Los ruiseñores, las calandrias, los canarios y los sinsontes cantarían.

Los loros y los tucanes contarían chistes.

Los flamencos bailarían.

Y las águilas y los cóndores demostrarían la acrobacia aérea.

Sólo el cuervo negro no fue invitado porque no tenía ningún talento; no sabía ni cantar ni bailar.

Le habría gustado mucho tocar su guitarra, pero tocaba con más entusiasmo que talento y no les gustaba a las otras aves escucharlo.

Pero nada de esto molestó al cuervo. Él le dijo a su amigo, el sapo, que practicaría mucho y el día de la fiesta, simplemente iría.

"Ah, sí", respondió el sapo, "a mí me gustaría tanto volar con las aves al cielo y participar en tal fiesta".

El cuervo se burló del sapo diciendo, "¡No seas ridículo! No tienes ni alas ni plumas, . . . además, eres muy feo. Sólo van los que pueden volar a gran altura y tienen plumaje hermoso".

Pero el sapo decidió que si no iba, se perdería una oportunidad única. Por eso, cuando el cuervo puso su guitarra en el suelo y se dirigió al río para beber agua, el sapo se metió en la guitarra sin ser visto.

¡Y qué fiesta! El coro de cantores cantó hermosas melodías. Los chistes fueron bien cómicos. Los danzantes entretuvieron a los invitados. Y la demostración de acrobacia aérea fue increíble. El señor Sapo lo encontró todo muy divertido.

Cuando todas las aves empezaron a bailar, el sapo no pudo resistir acompañarlas. Cantó y bailó con tal agilidad, entusiasmo y alegría, que todos aplaudieron ruidosamente. Lo único que inquietaba al sapo fue la posibilidad que el cuervo lo viera y se enojara con él. Y sí, ¡el cuervo lo vio!

7

Al terminar la fiesta, el sapo se metió otra vez en la guitarra sin que nadie lo viera . . . o por lo menos es lo que pensaba el sapo. El hecho es que su amigo, el cuervo, lo vio.

8

Mientras regresaba a la tierra guitarra en mano, el cuervo, deliberadamente, dio vuelta a su guitarra y el aventurero sapo salió proyectado por la boca de la guitarra en dirección al suelo que estaba muy distante. El pobre sapo temía morirse de miedo o de chocar con las rocas en el suelo.

9

Por fin llegó a la tierra y chocó fuertemente, pero no contra las rocas. No murió, gracias a Dios, pero se golpeó mucho. Y cuando sanaron las heridas que le resultaron de sus aventuras, le quedaron en su lugar unas manchas iguales a las que tienen los sapos de hoy.

Sí, ¡es verdad! Y todavía hablan estos sapos con orgullo del viaje extraordinario de su antepasado ilustre.

1 Yo llevaría más.

Te traje dos, por si acaso.

Ah, gracias.

Mira, hay otra dentro de ésta. Es posible que las necesite todas.

¿Qué más recomienda mamá que empaque?

Ropa para salir: Pantalones . . . saco . . . camisas blancas . . . corbatas . . . y zapatos.

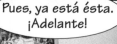

¡Ojalá que salgamos mucho!

Ah, también llevaré mi traje.

Pues, ya está ésta. ¡Adelante!

¿Cuál sería mejor?

Dicen que no hace frío en Caracas pero no lo creo.

No sé. Lleva las dos.

Ya no hay más en la lista. Pero, ¿no debes llevar ropa para el frío? Yo llevaría por lo menos una chaqueta.

Ah, ¿y si hace calor?

Y una toalla para la playa, ¿no? Ah, ¡y tu loción protectora!

Buena idea. ¿Me las traes?

Ah, sí. Luis dice que hay playas cerca. Debo llevar el traje de baño y las sandalias.

3 ¡No olvides...!

Hijo . . . ¿Recordaste tu cepillo de dientes y la pasta?

Gracias, mamá. ¡Nena, tráeme la pasta dental y mi cepillo!

Aquí lo tienes todo Daniel— toalla, loción protectora, pasta y cepillo.

Ah, también necesito mi cepillo para el pelo y mi peine. ¿Me los traes?

Ay, no olvides el champú y tu rasuradora eléctrica.

¡Nenaaa!

Sí, señor. A la orden.

Voy. Ahora te los traigo.

4 No puedo cerrarla.

Bueno, mamá. Ya estoy listo.

Pero, hijo, ¿qué has hecho? ¿Cuánto llevas?

¡Dos maletas! ¡Dios mío! Es imposible que ponga todo en dos.

Solamente permiten dos maletas en los vuelos internacionales.

Debes llevar sólo lo esencial.

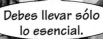

No puedo cerrarla, Daniel.

Siéntate encima, así. Allí está. A ver . . . todo está listo otra vez.

Increíble, pero lo hicimos.

Sí puedes, Nena.

Ya ves. Esta vez sí estoy listo.

CHARLEMOS UN POCO

A. **PARA EMPEZAR . . .** Según el cuento ''Las manchas del sapo'', ¿quién dice que haría o le gustaría hacer lo siguiente?

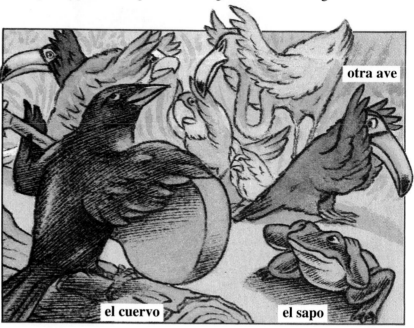

otra ave

el cuervo

el sapo

1. Le gustaría volar al cielo y participar en la fiesta.
2. Contaría chistes.
3. Practicaría mucho.
4. Demostraría acrobacia aérea.
5. Le habría gustado tocar su guitarra.
6. Bailaría.
7. Decidió que no se perdería una oportunidad única.
8. Cantaría.

B. **¿QUÉ DECIMOS . . .?** Di si son ciertos o falsos estos comentarios sobre los preparativos de Daniel. Si son falsos, corrígelos.

1. Nena no ayuda a su hermano.
2. Mamá le hizo una lista de cosas para empacar.
3. Daniel empaca ropa para salir.
4. Daniel decide no llevar chaqueta.
5. Daniel busca varias cosas en el baño.
6. Daniel empaca cuatro maletas.
7. Sólo permiten una maleta en los vuelos internacionales.
8. Al final, es fácil cerrar las maletas.

C. ¡A comer! Si tú y tu familia estuvieran en el restaurante
"Chihuahua Charlie's" en Cd. Juárez, ¿qué pedirían para comer?

Speculating: The conditional

Conditional verb endings:

pediría	pediríamos
pedirías	
pediría	pedirían

¿**Pedirías** la comida más cara?
¿Qué **pedirían** ustedes?

See ¿**Por qué se dice así?**,
page G111, section 8.3.

SOPAS	ENSALADAS
Crema de frijol	Ensalada mixta
Sopa de cebolla	Ensalada César
Sopa de tortilla	
ENTREMESES	**POSTRES**
Enchiladas	Pastel
Tacos de pollo	Flan
ChimiCharlie's	Helado con cajeta
Combinación	Café

MODELO Mi tía [*nombre*]
Mi tía Paula pediría la ensalada César y flan.

1. mi abuelita
2. mis hermanitos
3. mi tío [*nombre*]
4. yo
5. papá
6. mis primos
7. mamá
8. todos nosotros

CH. De viaje. ¿Qué llevarías y que no llevarías en un viaje a
Sudamérica? Contesta las preguntas de tu compañero(a).

 EJEMPLO *Compañero(a):* **¿Qué llevarías?**
Tú: **Llevaría camiseta y . . .** o
  No llevaría . . .

VOCABULARIO ÚTIL:

llevar	camisetas	ropa interior
empacar	ropa formal	cámara
comprar	sandalias	champú
	traje de baño	perro
	computadora	bicicleta
	cepillo y pasta	piyamas
	toalla	loción protectora
	rasuradora	

Speculating: The conditional of irregular verbs

Irregular verbs in the conditional use the same endings as regular verbs and have the same irregularities in the stem as irregular verbs in the future tense.

poner	**pondr-**
salir	**saldr-**
tener	**tendr-**
venir	**vendr-**
decir	**dir-**
hacer	**har-**
haber	**habr-**
poder	**podr-**
querer	**querr-**

podría	**podríamos**
podrías	
podría	**podrían**

¿**Podrían** venir temprano?
Yo **podría** hacerlo esta tarde.

See **¿Por qué se dice así?,**
page G111, section 8.3.

REPASO

Giving advice/orders: Affirmative *tú* commands

Affirmative **tú** commands are formed by dropping the **-s** of the **tú** form of the present indicative.

Escríbeme, por favor.
Invita a tus padres.

There are eight irregular forms:

decir	**di**
poner	**pon**
salir	**sal**
tener	**ten**
venir	**ven**
hacer	**haz**
ir	**ve**
ser	**sé**

See **¿Por qué se dice así?,**
page G113, section 8.4.

D. ¿Yo, director(a)?   Si fueras director(a) de la escuela, ¿qué sería diferente?

 MODELO   los estudiantes / tener menos clases
Los estudiantes tendrían menos clases.

1. yo saber / los nombres de todos los estudiantes
2. haber / más asambleas
3. nosotros venir / más tarde
4. nosotros salir / más temprano
5. haber / muchos días de fiesta
6. los estudiantes hacer / poca tarea
7. los profesores siempre dar / buenas notas
8. los estudiantes poder / hablar en todas las clases
9. yo tener / una oficina enorme
10. ¿ . . . ?

E. Entrevista.   Un(a) amigo(a) tiene una entrevista para un nuevo trabajo. ¿Qué consejos le das?

 MODELO   hablar mucho
Amigo(a): **¿Debo hablar mucho?**
Tú: **Sí, habla mucho.** o
           No, no hables mucho.

1. prestar atención
2. ser cortés
3. llegar a tiempo
4. hacer muchas preguntas
5. decir la verdad
6. llevar ropa informal
7. hablar lentamente
8. pedir café
9. ¿ . . . ?

F. Sugerencias.   A veces los padres de los estudiantes le hacen sugerencias ridículas al profesor Soto. ¿Qué sugerencias le hicieron recientemente?

MODELO   dar menos exámenes
Dé menos exámenes.

1. enseñar bailes típicos
2. tocar más música en clase
3. traer dulces a clase
4. preparar comida en clase
5. ir con nosotros a un restaurante
6. dar buenas notas
7. pedir más películas
8. hacer un viaje con los estudiantes
9. ¿ . . . ?

G. Abuelos.   Tus abuelos acaban de limpiar su casa y encontraron muchas cosas tuyas. ¿Qué quieres que te traigan?

MODELO   *Abuelo(a):*   **¿Te traemos el osito de peluche?**
         Tú: **Sí, tráiganmelo, por favor.**   o
                    No, no lo traigan.

REPASO

Giving advice/orders: Negative *tú* commands

Negative **tú** commands are formed by using the **tú** form of the present subjunctive.

No me **llames.**
No **te pongas** esa camisa.

The following verbs have irregular forms:

dar	**digas**
estar	**estés**
ir	**vayas**
ser	**seas**

See **¿Por qué se dice así?,**
page G113, section 8.4.

REPASO

Giving advice/orders: *Ud./Uds.* commands

Ud./Uds. commands use the **Ud./Uds.** forms of the present subjunctive.

No vuelva muy tarde.
Digan la verdad.

The following verbs have irregular forms:

dar	**dé(n)**
estar	**esté(n)**
ir	**vaya(n)**
ser	**sea(n)**

See **¿Por qué se dice así?,**
page G114, section 8.4.

REPASO

Commands and object pronouns

Direct and indirect object pronouns follow and are attached to affirmative commands and precede negative commands.

Píde**selo** a tu papá.
No **me lo** expliquen, por favor.

See **¿Por qué se dice así?,**
page G114, section 8.4.

Present subjunctive forms

Verb endings are added to the stem of the **yo** form of the present indicative.

-ar		-er, -ir	
-e	-emos	-a	-amos
-es		-as	
-e	-en	-a	-an

Ojalá que todos **recibamos** una *A*.
Ojalá que yo no **tenga** que ir.

The following verbs have irregular forms:

dar	dé, des, dé, . . .
estar	esté, estés, esté, . . .
haber	haya, hayas, haya, . . .
ir	vaya, vayas, vaya, . . .
saber	sepa, sepas, sepa, . . .
ser	sea, seas, sea, . . .
ver	vea, veas, vea, . . .

See ¿Por qué se dice así?,
page G116, section 8.5.

Expressing doubt

Doubt:
Duda que **podamos** hacerlo.
No creo que **quiera** venir.

Certainty:
Yo sé que **puede** hacerlo.
Creo que **quiere** venir.

See ¿Por qué se dice así?,
page G117, section 8.5.

H. A finales del año. Sabes lo que normalmente pasa a finales del año escolar. ¿Qué esperanzas tienes para este año?

 MODELO Hay actividades especiales.
Ojalá que haya actividades especiales. o
Ojalá que no haya actividades especiales.

1. El (La) director(a) visita las clases.
2. Los profesores hacen fiestas en clase.
3. Muchas clases tienen exámenes difíciles.
4. Hacemos excursiones.
5. Hay un banquete.
6. Los profesores piden mucho trabajo.
7. El coro y la banda dan conciertos especiales.
8. Tenemos que trabajar muchísimo.

I. No lo creo. ¿Cuánto sabes de Sudamérica? ¿Qué opinas de estos comentarios?

VOCABULARIO ÚTIL:
Es cierto que . . .
Creo que . . .
Dudo que . . .

MODELO Es posible esquiar en Chile.
Es cierto que se puede esquiar en Chile. o
Creo que se puede esquiar en Chile. o
Dudo que sea posible esquiar en Chile.

1. Hay ruinas importantes en Perú.
2. El clima de Venezuela cambia mucho.
3. Chile es un país largo.
4. Venezuela produce mucho petróleo.
5. Los descendientes de los incas hablan quechua.
6. El viejo Imperio de los Incas se limita a Perú y Ecuador.
7. Leones y elefantes viven en la selva sudamericana.
8. El Río de la Plata es el río más largo de Sudamérica.

J. Mis nuevos amigos. ¿Cuál es tu emoción frente a las actividades de tus nuevos amigos de **¡DIME!** DOS?

VOCABULARIO ÚTIL:

Es bueno que	Es triste que
Me alegro (de) que	Es malo que
Es terrible que	Es interesante que

Diego Miranda

 MODELO **Es terrible que Diego Miranda se enoje con su hija.**
o . . .

1. Martín

2. Diana

3. Tina

4. Daniel

5. Miguelín

6. Meche

7. Margarita

8. Luis

REPASO

Expressing anticipation or reaction

Esperamos que todos **vengan.**
Me alegro que no **haya** clases hoy.
Ojalá que **se diviertan**.

*See ¿**Por qué se dice así?,** page G117, section 8.5.*

*R*EPASO

Persuading

Quiero que **vengas** sola.
Sugieren que lo **hagamos** aquí.
Recomienda que tú la **escribas**.

See ¿Por qué se dice así?,
page G117, section 8.5.

K. ¡Es rico(a)!   Tu compañero(a) tiene mucho dinero y mucho tiempo libre este verano. ¿Qué recomiendas que haga?

 MODELO   ser importante que / comer . . .
Es importante que comas en restaurantes elegantes.

1. sugerir que / viajar a . . .
2. recomendar que / ir a . . .
3. querer que / comprar . . .
4. ser necesario que / asistir a . . .
5. preferir que / visitar . . .
6. aconsejar que / comer . . .
7. insistir en que / dar . . .
8. ser preciso que / conocer . . .

L. El verano.   ¿Qué deseos, temores, preferencias y probabilidades ves para el verano?

 EJEMPLO   **Ojalá que mi familia viaje a otro país.**

		ir a la playa
creo		venir a visitar
es importante	mis amigos	practicar deportes
espero	mi amigo(a) [. . .]	viajar a otro país
temo	mi familia	no estar aquí
prefiero	mis abuelos	leer muchos libros
dudo	mi hermano(a)	divertirse
es probable	todos	salir frecuentemente
ojalá	¿ . . . ?	dormir tarde
¿ . . . ?		conseguir un trabajo
		¿ . . . ?

CHARLEMOS UN POCO MÁS

A. Encuesta.   Usa la cuadrícula que te dará tu profesor(a) para entrevistar a tus compañeros de clase. Pregúntales si harían estas cosas en diez años. Pídeles a las personas que contesten afirmativamente que firmen el cuadrado apropiado. Recuerda que no se permite que una persona firme más de una vez.

 MODELO   *Tú:*   **¿Vivirías en otro país?**
Compañero(a):   **No. Yo sólo viviría en EE.UU.** o
Sí, viviría en *[país]*.

B. Compraríamos mucho. Tú y un(a) amigo(a) están discutiendo lo que comprarían si ganaran diez mil dólares en la lotería. ¿Comprarían algunas de las cosas en el dibujo, u otras cosas?

C. ¿Cómo llego a Correos? Tu compañero(a) es un(a) nuevo(a) profesor(a) que no conoce tu ciudad. Necesita ir a varios lugares este fin de semana. Usa el mapa que tu profesor(a) te va a dar para decirle cómo llegar a esos lugares. Tu compañero(a) va a escribir los nombres de cada edificio que visita en su mapa. Recuerda que no se permite ver el mapa de tu compañero(a) hasta terminar la actividad.

CH. Opiniones. ¿Qué opinan tú y tu amigo(a) de estos titulares del periódico? Discútanlos y compartan sus opiniones con la clase.

La basura cósmica: Peligro para los vuelos espaciales

Costa Rica–líder en conservación de bosques tropicales

Nuestros amigos: ¡Los ratones!

¡El arte falso inunda el mercado!

Mantenga su auto como nuevo

Joven habla cuatro lenguas. Recibe $150,000 mensuales

¡Ya estamos listos para vivir en el planeta Marte!

¿Nos invadirán los extraterrestres?

Dramatizaciones

A. Conferencia mundial. Tú y tres compañeros de clase son representantes de cuatro países distintos. Hoy van a participar en un panel de las Naciones Unidas que va a hablar sobre lo que las Naciones Unidas debería hacer para mejorar el mundo y para mejorar la vida en sus países. Dramaticen la conferencia.

B. Mejoremos el colegio. Tú y dos amigos han sido seleccionados para representar a todos los estudiantes de su escuela en un comité de padres, estudiantes, profesores y el (la) director(a). El comité preparará un informe sobre lo que los administradores deberían hacer para mejorar la escuela. Dramaticen la primera reunión del comité.

C. Consejos. Tu abuelo(a) va a recibir un premio prestigioso del Congreso de los EE.UU. por su trabajo con jóvenes delincuentes. Con un compañero(a) haciendo el papel de tu abuelo(a), dramatiza una conversación donde tu abuelo(a) pide tus opiniones sobre el problema de la delincuencia y lo que tú harías para eliminarla.

IMPACTO CULTURAL

Nuestra lengua

Antes de empezar

A. Dialecto: una definición. El diccionario define "dialecto" como una variedad regional de una lengua. Dice que esta variedad puede basarse en diferencias en la pronunciación, el vocabulario o la gramática.

1. ¿Puedes pensar en algunos ejemplos de dialecto en inglés basados en pronunciación?
2. ¿Puedes pensar en algunos ejemplos de dialecto en inglés basados en vocabulario? ¿en gramática?

B. En el mundo de hispanohablantes. El español es la lengua nativa de 362 millones de personas en más de veintiuna naciones. Obviamente, el español tiene muchos dialectos también.

1. ¿Cuáles son algunos dialectos que conoces tú?
2. En tu opinión, ¿deben aceptarse y respetarse todos los dialectos? ¿Por qué sí o por qué no? ¿Aceptas y respetas tú los dialectos en inglés que identificaste en la actividad anterior?

El voseo

Dos amigas argentinas conversan en su colegio.
Un muchacho de Chile las ve y empieza a conversar con ellas.

Rosita:	**¡Vos no sabés la cantidad de dinero que gasté hoy!**
Ana María:	**Sí che, ya me imagino vos siempre gastando.**
Rosita:	**Claro, linda, ¡cómo vos no comprás nunca nada!**
Jorge:	**¡Qué argentinas se ponen ustedes dos cuando se enojan! . . . ¡ja, ja, ja!**

Verifiquemos

1. ¿Por qué encuentra Jorge cómica y muy argentina la manera de hablar de sus amigas?
2. ¿Cuáles son algunas diferencias en el habla de las dos amigas que tú observas?
3. ¿Es el habla de Rosita y Ana María un dialecto? Explica tu respuesta.

Ayer fuimos a . . .

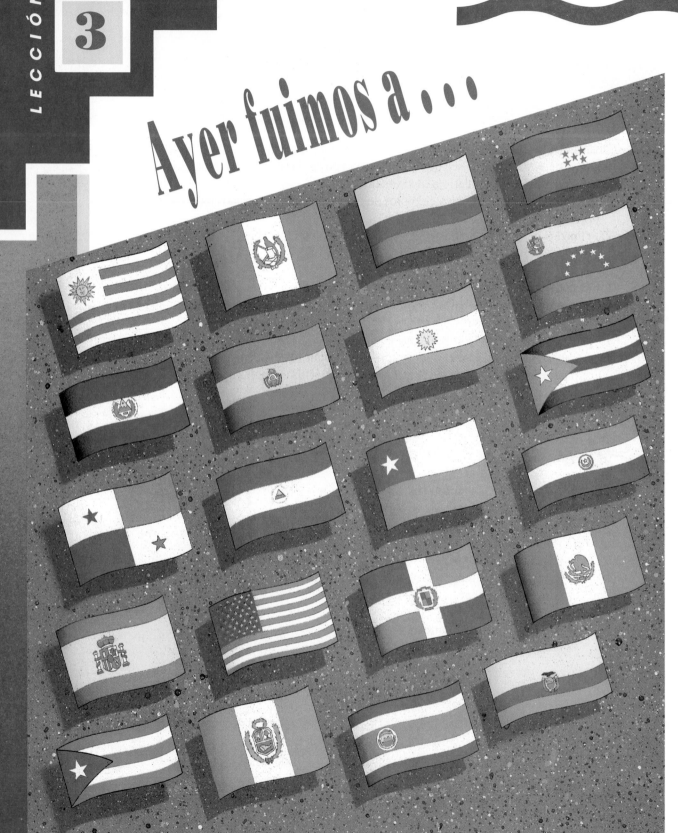

Sr. Galindo

Nena

el profesor
de geografía

Diana

Mateo

Abuelita

Tina

¿ **Q**ué piensas tú ?

1. ¿Reconoces algunas de estas banderas?
¿Cuáles? ¿Puedes adivinar de qué países
son algunas de las que no reconoces?

2. ¿Sabes cuál es el significado del símbolo
en la bandera mexicana? ¿del símbolo en
otras de las banderas?

3. El regalo en esta página es para una de
las personas en las fotos. ¿Qué podría
ser? ¿Para quién será? ¿Qué sería un
buen regalo para cada una de las
personas en las fotos?

4. ¿Cuál de todas las leyendas y todos los
cuentos que has escuchado este año es tu
favorito? ¿Por qué?

5. ¿Sabes algunos cuentos o algunas
leyendas de tu propia cultura? En grupos
de tres o cuatro, traten de narrar uno de
los cuentos o las leyendas que
identificaron en la pregunta anterior.

6. ¿Por qué crees que una cultura inventa
cuentos y leyendas como los que has
escuchado en **¡DIME!** DOS?

7. ¿Qué crees que vas a aprender en esta
lección?

LA CALANDRIA

La música de los mariachis es la música nacional de México. "La calandria" es una canción que cuenta la triste historia de un engaño amoroso. ¿Qué relación a la vida verdadera ven ustedes en lo que le pasa a este pobre pájaro?

1 En una jaula de oro, pendiente de un balcón, se hallaba una calandria, cantando su dolor.

2 Hasta que un gorrioncillo a su jaula llegó... "Si Ud. puede sacarme, con Ud. yo me voy".

3 El pobre gorrioncillo de ella se enamoró; el pobre como pudo los alambres rompió.

4 Y la ingrata calandria después que la sacó, tan luego se vio libre, voló, voló y voló.

5 El pobre gorrioncillo
todavía la siguió,
a ver si le cumplía
lo que ella prometió.

6 La malvada calandria
esto le contestó:
"Yo a Ud. no lo conozco,
ni presa he sido yo".

7 Y triste el gorrioncillo,
luego se regresó,
se paró en un manzano,
lloró, lloró y lloró.

8 Y ahora en esa jaula,
pendiente de un balcón,
se encuentra el gorrioncillo,
cantando su dolor.

¿QUÉ DECIMOS AL ESCRIBIR...?

De un viaje que hicimos

Ésta es la primera carta
de Venezuela que recibió
la familia Galindo.
¿Reconoces algunos
de los lugares?

Luis y yo en el
centro de Caracas

VENEZUELA Bs. **12**

25 Años de la Fundación del Niño

Los Galindo
1753 Gus Moran Drive
El Paso, Texas

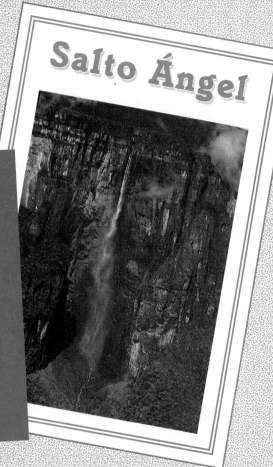

Salto Ángel

Venezuela

Auyán-tepui

14 de julio

Queridos Papá, Mamá, Martín y Nena:

Saludos desde Caracas. ¿Cómo les va a todos? ¿Ya fueron a acampar a los Órganos o a Ruidoso? Martín, ¿qué tal el equipo este año? ¿Han ganado muchos partidos? Escríbeme pronto y cuéntame todo.

¡Caracas es una ciudad fantástica! ¡Hay tanto que hacer! Conocemos lugares nuevos todos los días y casi siempre tomamos el metro. ¡Me encanta! Es mucho más interesante que el autobús y la comida aquí es riquísima, mamá. Ayer fuimos a comer a una arepera, un restaurante que se especializa en arepas — una comida típica de Venezuela. Son muy sabrosas. Probé varios tipos: de pollo, de carne y de queso — y me encantaron todas.

La primera semana visitamos dos universidades, la Central y la Simón Bolívar. Fuimos de compras cerca de la Plaza Bolívar, la plaza principal de Caracas. También fuimos a un parque. Luis me contó que cuando era niño, su familia iba al parque todos los domingos y se divertían mucho. Son muy bonitos los parques aquí. Todo es tan verde y la ciudad está rodeada de montañas.

Universidad
Simón Bolívar

Centro Comercial
Concresa

También fuimos a un centro comercial super moderno. No he visto nada que se compare. Cielo Vista Mall ni se le acerca. Es enorme. Estoy seguro que a Margarita le encantaría. Ojalá que volvamos allí porque todavía tengo que comprarles regalos a todos.

La semana pasada hicimos una excursión en caravana y luego tomamos el sobrevuelo al Salto Ángel. ¡Qué impresionante! Pasamos por los tepuyes, unas montañas planas típicas de esta región. Me fascinó. El Salto Ángel es la catarata más alta del mundo.

Ayer Luis y yo fuimos a visitar a su tía en un pueblo muy pintoresco que se llama El Hatillo. Me gustó mucho el pueblo y saqué muchas fotos. Cuando estábamos allí, hubo una boda en la plaza. ¡Imagínense! La tía de Luis es muy simpática. Esa noche nos preparó una cena fantástica.

En el futuro espero visitar otras ciudades como Maracaibo en la costa y Mérida en los Andes.

Bueno, se me hace tarde y mañana Luis quiere salir a correr bien temprano. Escríbanme pronto.

Con mucho cariño,

Daniel

Luis y yo en
el Hatillo

CHARLEMOS UN POCO

A. **PARA EMPEZAR . . .** Decide si las siguientes oraciones son ciertas o falsas según la triste historia de ''La calandria''. Si son falsas, corrígelas.

1. Un gorrioncillo estaba en una jaula de oro.
2. La calandria le pidió ayuda al gorrioncillo para escaparse de la jaula.
3. La calandria no prometió hacer nada por el gorrioncillo.
4. El gorrioncillo se enamoró de la calandria y ella se enamoró de él.
5. El gorrioncillo abrió los alambres de la jaula y la calandria se escapó.
6. La calandria invitó al gorrioncillo que la siguiera.
7. La calandria cumplió con la promesa que le hizo al gorrioncillo.
8. El gorrioncillo y la calandria volvieron muy contentos a la jaula de oro.
9. El gorrioncillo se fue a un manzano a llorar.
10. La calandria volvió muy triste a la jaula de oro y lloró, lloró y lloró.

B. **¿QUÉ DECIMOS . . .?** ¿Dónde hizo Daniel las siguientes cosas: en el centro de Caracas, en El Hatillo o en el Salto Ángel?

Caracas

el Hatillo

Salto Ángel

1. Cenó con la tía de Luis.
2. Comió en una arepera.
3. Sacó muchas fotos.
4. Fue a un parque.
5. Vio unas montañas planas.
6. Vio una boda en la plaza.
7. Tomó el metro.
8. Vio la catarata más alta del mundo.

See **¿Por qué se dice así?**,
page G119, section 8.6.

REPASO

Discussing past activities: Preterite

Is used to:
- Describe completed single actions or a series of actions
- Focus on an action beginning
- Focus on an action coming to an end

Ellos **ganaron** anoche.
Corrió cuando me **vio**.
Pobrecito, se le **cayó** el taco.

See **¿Por qué se dice así?**,
page G119, section 8.6.

REPASO

Discussing past activities: Imperfect

Used to talk about:
- Continuing actions
- Ongoing situations
- Physical or emotional states
- Habitual actions
- Age (with **tener**)
- Telling time

Allí, **trabajábamos** día y noche.
De niña siempre **estaba** enferma.
En esa foto yo **tenía** tres años.
Eran las ocho y todos **estaban** durmiendo.

See **¿Por qué se dice así?**,
page G119, section 8.6.

C. ¡Qué divertido! Según Inés, ¿qué pasó una noche muy especial al final del año escolar?

 MODELO   yo / divertirse / mucho / sábado pasado
Me divertí mucho el sábado pasado.

1. yo / jugar / volibol / equipo / escuela / este año
2. nosotras / ganar / campeonato / ciudad
3. escuela / hacer / banquete para nosotras / cafetería
4. mis padres / ir / banquete
5. yo / recibir / trofeo
6. todos / pasarlo bien
7. después / haber / baile
8. Jaime / invitarme / bailar
9. después / él y yo / salir / baile / y / ir / a comer
10. yo / llegar / casa / tarde pero contenta

CH. Ocupados. Eran las ocho de la noche. Según Felipe, ¿qué hacían todos los miembros de su familia?

EJEMPLO   **Papá se bañaba en el baño.**

D. De niño(a). ¿Con qué frecuencia hacía tu compañero(a) estas actividades durante el verano cuando era niño(a)?

MODELO   ir a la playa

> *Tú:*   **Cuando eras niño(a), ¿ibas a la playa?**
>
> *Compañero(a):*   **Sí, siempre iba a la playa en [. . .]** o
> **A veces iba a la playa.** o
> **No, nunca iba a la playa; iba a [. . .]**

1. alquilar muchos videos
2. caminar en el bosque
3. acampar en las montañas
4. ver mucha televisión
5. asistir a partidos de béisbol
6. ir al cine
7. pasear en bicicleta
8. nadar en la piscina

E. El cuento de Puma.   Puma es un gato aventurero. ¿Qué le pasó un día? Para saberlo, pon las oraciones en orden cronológico y pon los verbos en la forma apropiada. El cuento empieza así:

MODELO   **Había una vez un gato que se llamaba Puma.**

- Caramba. En ese momento, la puerta del garaje (**cerrarse**).
- En el mismo patio Puma (**ver**) un ratón y (**empezar**) a correr detrás de él.
- Puma lo (**seguir**).
- Un día (**hacer**) buen tiempo y Puma (**sentirse**) muy bien.
- (**Haber**) una vez un gato que (**llamarse**) Puma.
- Gato y ratón (**correr**) y (**correr**).
- Pobre Puma. El garaje (**estar**) oscuro y él (**estar**) atrapado.
- Por fin, el ratón (**ver**) un escape y (**entrar**) en un garaje.
- Primero (**ir**) al jardín del vecino para saludar a su amigo, pero el gato vecino (**dormir**) al sol del patio.
- Por eso, (**decidir**) salir de la casa en busca de aventuras.

F. Fin de semana. Usa el vocabulario que acompaña cada dibujo para contar lo que estas dos chicas hacían para pasar el tiempo un fin de semana típico.

ser / sábado / no haber clases

MODELO **Era sábado y no había clases.**

1. Sofía / levantarse a las siete / hacer buen tiempo

2. llegar amiga Luisa / decidir hacer una excursión

3. preparar comida / ir en bicicleta al parque

4. hacer sol / haber muchas personas / divertirse

5. comer / empezar a llover / decidir regresar

6. llegar a casa / ver TV / tomar algo / estar cansado

G. Indeciso(a). Tu compañero(a) es una persona muy indecisa. Pregúntale si piensa hacer estas cosas durante el fin de semana.

VOCABULARIO ÚTIL:

hacer un viaje
visitar a los parientes
nadar mucho
jugar tenis
ir a acampar
aprender a tocar un instrumento

estudiar
asistir a una clase
pasear en bicicleta
trabajar
dormir mucho
¿ . . . ?

 EJEMPLO *Tú:* **¿Vas a nadar este fin de semana?**
Compañero(a): **No, pero quizás nade hoy por la tarde.**

H. El año que viene. ¿Qué crees que van a hacer tú, tu familia y tus mejores amigos el año que viene?

EJEMPLO **Tal vez Ana y Raúl jueguen volibol.**

VOCABULARIO ÚTIL:

jugar baloncesto, fútbol, etc.
estudiar química, álgebra, etc.
tener seis clases
sacar buenas notas
trabajar en la oficina
ir a todos los partidos

ser miembro del Club de español
cantar en el coro
tocar en la orquesta
salir mucho
¿ . . . ?

REPASO

Expressing doubt: *Quizás* and *tal vez*

Quizás no **haya** clase hoy.
Tal vez **tengamos** que regresar.

See **¿Por qué se dice así?,**
page G121, section 8.7.

CHARLEMOS UN POCO MÁS

A. Las aventuras de . . . Tú y tu compañero(a) van a crear un cuento basado en los dibujos que su profesor(a) les va a dar. Primero decidan en qué orden van a poner los dibujos. Luego desarrollen su cuento y, finalmente, cuéntenselo a la clase.

B. Había una vez . . . Con un compañero(a) de clase, escriban un cuento o leyenda breve que explique uno de los fenómenos que siguen o algún otro que ustedes escojan. Ilustren su cuento con dibujos o fotos de revistas. Compartan su cuento con el resto de la clase.

- ¿Por qué vuelan los pájaros?
- ¿Por qué sale el sol cada día?
- ¿Por qué son verdes los pinos?
- ¿Por qué los perros son nuestros mejores amigos?
- ¿Por qué hay siete días en una semana?
- ¿Por qué hay desiertos?

C. Quizás visites . . . Tomás vivirá con una familia en Costa Rica este verano. Está muy preocupado. Usa este dibujo y con un(a) compañero(a) traten de convencer a su amigo de que tal vez le guste Costa Rica.

Dramatizaciones

A. ¡Premios! Es el fin del año escolar. Tú estás en un comité con el (la) director(a) de la escuela y un(a) profesor(a). Ustedes tres tienen que decidir quiénes van a recibir los siguientes premios. Sólo pueden nombrar a una persona para cada premio pero puede ser profesor(a) o estudiante. Dramatiza la situación con dos compañeros que harán el papel de director(a) y profesor(a).

El (La) más cómico(a)	El (La) más deportivo(a)
El (La) más estudioso(a)	El (La) más dramático(a)
El (La) más activo(a)	El (La) más indeciso(a)
El (La) más ¿ . . . ?	

B. ¡No metas la pata! Tú y tres amigos van a preparar una breve sátira mostrando lo que han aprendido en la clase de español este año. Luego presentarán la sátira a la clase. La sátira puede ser sobre algo cultural o lingüístico.

Estrategias para leer:
Interpretación de imágenes

A. **El papel de las imágenes.** Si tuvieras que seleccionar un animal como símbolo de ti mismo, ¿qué animal seleccionarías? ¿Por qué? ¿Qué cualidades comparten tú y el animal? ¿Cómo son similares el movimiento, la "personalidad" y el comportamiento del animal con los tuyos?

B. **Metáforas.** Muchos escritores literarios usan comparaciones inesperadas entre dos objetos, para hacer sus ideas o imágenes más vivas. Una comparación que dice que una cosa *es* otra cosa es una *metáfora.* En este poema, vas a encontrar una metáfora que empieza en los primeros dos versos *(líneas)* del poema y se mantiene hasta el último verso.

Lee el título del poema y mira los dibujos. ¿A qué cosa que vuela se refiere el poeta? Ahora lee los primeros dos versos del poema. ¿Cuáles son las dos cosas que Alarcón está comparando?

C. **Para anticipar.** Antes de leer el poema, piensa un poco en los pájaros. Prepara una lista de todas las cualidades y características de los pájaros que se te ocurran. ¿Tienen todos los pájaros las mismas cualidades? Después de leer el poema, vuelve a leer tu lista. ¿Mencionó el poeta todo lo que hay en tu lista? ¿Mencionó el poeta algunas cualidades o características de pájaros que no se te ocurrieron a ti?

CH. Interpretación de imágenes. Ahora lee el poema completo. Léelo otra vez y, aún una tercera vez. Fíjate en la riqueza de imágenes visuales. Prepara un cuadro similar al que sigue. Escribe en una columna los símbolos que el poeta menciona en cada estrofa *(agrupación de cinco versos)* y en otra lo que las imágenes creadas por estos símbolos representan para ti.

Símbolos que veo . . .	Imágenes de "palabras". . .
1ra estrofa: pájaros	Las palabras en libros pueden llevarte a todas partes como los pájaros que vuelan a todas partes.
2da estrofa: nubes, viento, árboles	Las palabras pueden describir lo imaginario, lo que sentimos, lo que vemos.

1. En tu opinión, ¿cuáles de los símbolos fueron los más fáciles de interpretar? ¿Por qué?
2. ¿Cuáles imágenes te gustaron más? ¿Por qué?
3. ¿Hay algunas imágenes que no supiste interpretar? ¿Cuáles?
4. Piensa en el poema completo. ¿Es posible que Alarcón esté usando "palabras" como una metáfora para otra cosa? ¿Qué podría ser esa cosa? ¿Por qué crees eso?

Para volar

por
Francisco X. Alarcón

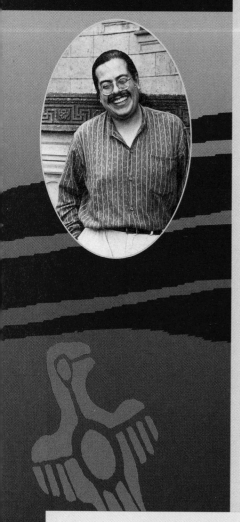

las palabras
son pájaros
que siguen
a los libros
y la primavera

a las palabras
les gustan
las nubes
el viento
los árboles

hay palabras
mensajeras
que vienen
de muy lejos
de otras tierras

para éstas
no existen
fronteras
sino estrellas
canto y luz

hay palabras
familiares
como canarios
y exóticas
como el quetzal

las palabras

son

Verifiquemos

1. ¿Qué son las palabras, según el poeta? ¿Qué siguen las palabras? ¿Qué les gusta a las palabras?
2. ¿De dónde vienen las palabras mensajeras? ¿Qué no existe para las palabras mensajeras? ¿Qué sí existe?
3. ¿Con qué tipo de palabras compara el poeta los canarios? ¿El quetzal? ¿Por qué?
4. Aunque el poeta no lo dice directamente, ¿qué les pasa a las palabras que resisten el frío?
5. ¿Adónde se van las palabras que no resisten el frío? ¿Qué les pasa a las palabras difíciles de traducir?

pájaros

unas resisten
el frío
otras se van
con el sol
hacia el sur

hay palabras
que se mueren
enjauladas
difíciles
de traducir

y otras
hacen nido **1**
tienen crías **2**
les dan calor
alimento **3**

les enseñan
a volar
y un día
se marchan
en parvadas **4**

las letras
en la página
son las huellas **5**
que dejan
junto al mar

6. Pon en orden cronológico el proceso de las palabras que hacen nido:
   a. enseñan a las crías a volar
   b. dejan impresiones de sus pies en la playa
   c. les dan un lugar cómodo y calentito para vivir a las crías
   ch. se van, todas en grupo
   d. hacen nido
   e. les dan de comer a las crías
   f. tienen crías
7. ¿Qué opinas tú: son las palabras como los pájaros? Explica tu respuesta.

ESCRIBAMOS AHORA

Estrategias para escribir:
Metáforas en poemas

A. Empezar. En *Para volar,* Alarcón usa los pájaros como metáfora para las palabras. A pesar de ser muy sencillo en forma, es un poema lleno de imágenes visuales fuertes que comparan a los pájaros con las palabras. Ahora, después de dos años de estar aprendiendo a comunicar en español, tú vas a seleccionar tu propia metáfora para desarrollar en un poema sobre el significado que una ''lengua'' tiene para ti. Puedes, por ejemplo, comparar las lenguas a los caminos. En ese caso, podrías pensar en los diferentes tipos de caminos que hay, adónde van los caminos, de qué están hechos, qué se puede ver al viajar por un camino, quiénes usan los caminos, etc. Y claro, tendrás que pensar en cómo cada una de estas cualidades y características puede representar algo importante de las lenguas.

B. Seleccionar. Primero debes seleccionar una metáfora. Puedes usar la de camino / lengua o, si prefieres, puedes seleccionar una propia. Para ayudarte a decidir, trabaja con tres o cuatro amigos y preparen una lista de cosas que se pueden comparar con una lengua. De la lista, selecciona una o dos cosas que te interesen a ti y empieza a preparar una lista de cualidades y características que podrías usar en tu poema.

C. Organizar. Ahora organiza tus ideas. Usa un cuadro como el que sigue, u otra manera de organizar tus ideas para el poema que prefieras. Usa un marcador para ayudarte a agrupar ideas similares o enumera *(ordena)* tus ideas en el orden en que piensas usarlas en tu poema.

Símbolos: caminos	Imágenes: lenguas
Van a todas partes.	Comunican con todo el mundo.

CH. Primer borrador.   Escribe ahora la primera versión de tu poema. Tal vez quieras usar *Para volar* como modelo. Trata de usar palabras vivas y descriptivas que le ayuden al lector de tu poema a ''ver'' lo que tú te imaginas. Dale un título apropiado a tu poema. Debe ser un título que sugiera la metáfora que piensas desarrollar.

D. Compartir.   Lee el poema de dos compañeros y que ellos lean el tuyo. Pídeles que hagan un breve resumen de tu poema para ver si lo entendieron. También pídeles sugerencias para hacerlo más claro y más efectivo. Haz el mismo tipo de comentario sobre sus poemas.

E. Revisar.   Haz cambios en tu poema a base de las sugerencias de tus compañeros. Luego, antes de entregarlo, dáselo a dos compañeros de clase para que lo lean una vez más. Esta vez pídeles que revisen la forma y la estructura. En particular, pídeles que te digan si has sido consistente en el uso de tu metáfora.

F. Versión final.   Escribe la versión final de tu poema incorporando las correcciones que tus compañeros de clase te indicaron. Presta mucha atención al formato. Piensa en la versión final como uno de varios poemas que se van a presentar en una sala de exhibiciones.

G. Publicar.   Cuando tu profesor(a) te devuelva tu poema, prepáralo para publicar. Escríbelo en una hoja de papel especial de 8 1/2 x 14 o más grande. Luego dibuja varias imágenes visuales apropiadas (o usa dibujos de revistas) para ilustrar los símbolos o las imágenes de tu poema. Las ilustraciones pueden estar en el margen, todo alrededor del poema o en el fondo del poema. Entrega tu creación artística para que tu profesor(a) pueda usarla para decorar la sala de clase a principios del año próximo. Considera tu obra maestra un mensaje literario personal para una futura clase de estudiantes de español.

¿POR QUÉ SE DICE ASÍ?

Manual de gramática

LECCIÓN 1

1.1 THE VERBS GUSTAR AND ENCANTAR

In **¡DIME!** UNO you learned that the verb **gustar** expresses likes and dislikes and that the verb **encantar** is used to talk about things you really like, or love. Both verbs are always preceded by an indirect object pronoun.

Indirect Object Pronouns			
a mí	**me** gusta(n)	**nos** gusta(n)	a nosotros(as)
a ti	**te** gusta(n)	**os** gusta(n)	a vosotros(as)
a usted	**le** gusta(n)	**les** gusta(n)	a ustedes
a él, a ella	**le** gusta(n)	**les** gusta(n)	a ellos, a ellas

¿**Te** gusta?   *Do you like it?*
Le gusta la música.   *He (She) likes music.*
Nos encanta bailar.   *We love to dance.*

■ If more than one thing is liked or loved, the verb is in the plural.

Me encant**an** las vacaciones.   *I love vacations.*
Le gust**an** los deportes.   *He (She) likes sports.*
No nos gust**an** los huevos.   *We don't like eggs.*
Les encant**an** sus clases.   *They really like their classes.*

Note that **encantar** is not used negatively.

■ The formula **a** + [*a name or pronoun*] is frequently used to clarify or emphasize who is doing the liking or disliking.

To clarify:
¿Le gusta **a Rafael**?   *Does Rafael like it?*
A **ellos** no les gusta.   *They don't like it.*

To emphasize:
¡Tú sabes que **a mí**   *You know that I love desserts!!*
   me encantan los postres!
Pues, ¡**a todos nosotros**   *Well, we all love them.*
   nos encantan!

Vamos a practicar

a. ¿Te gusta? ¿Cuáles de estas actividades te gustan y cuáles no? ¿Hay algunas que te encantan?

MODELO   correr
> **Me gusta correr.** o
> **No me gusta correr.** o
> **Me encanta correr.**

1. limpiar la casa
2. hacer la tarea
3. viajar
4. trabajar
5. bailar
6. escribir poemas
7. ir al cine
8. hablar por teléfono

b. Actividades favoritas. Éstas son las actividades favoritas de ciertas personas. ¿Qué puedes decir tú de las personas y sus actividades favoritas?

MODELO   a Roberta: tocar la guitarra
> **A Roberta le encanta tocar la guitarra.**

1. a Toni: asistir a conciertos
2. a Ernesto y a mí: preparar la comida
3. a Andrea: llevar ropa elegante
4. a todos nosotros: escuchar música
5. a Elisa y a Víctor: practicar los deportes
6. a mamá: ver televisión
7. a mí: ir a fiestas
8. a ti: pasear en bicicleta

c. Siempre de moda. Hortensia siempre lleva ropa muy elegante y siempre dice lo que piensa de la ropa de los demás. ¿Qué piensa de esta ropa?

MODELO   pantalones morados
> **Le gustan esos pantalones morados.**

> sudadera marrón
> **No le gusta esa sudadera marrón.**

1. camisa anaranjada
2. calcetines verdes
3. suéter rojo
4. zapatos blancos
5. chaqueta azul
6. sombrero negro
7. traje amarillo
8. camisetas rosadas

ch. Preferencias.   ¿Qué opinan los miembros de tu familia de estas bebidas y comidas?

EJEMPLO   **A mi mamá le gustan las albóndigas.**

a mi mamá		las hamburguesas
a mi hermano(a)		el café
a mis hermanos(as)	gustar	las albóndigas
a mí	no gustar	la salsa picante
a [¿ . . . ?] y a mí	encantar	los postres
a mi papá		la ensalada
a [¿ . . . ?]		las papas fritas

1.2 *PRESENT INDICATIVE TENSE: REGULAR VERBS*

You have learned that there are three types of verbs: **-ar**, **-er**, **-ir** and that these verbs are conjugated in the present indicative tense by replacing the **-ar**, **-er**, **-ir** endings with the ending corresponding to the subject. The following chart shows the present tense endings.

Present Tense			
	-ar mirar	*-er* leer	*-ir* asistir
yo	mir**o**	le**o**	asist**o**
tú	mir**as**	le**es**	asist**es**
usted	mir**a**	le**e**	asist**e**
él, ella	mir**a**	le**e**	asist**e**
nosotros(as)	mir**amos**	le**emos**	asist**imos**
vosotros(as)	mir**áis**	le**éis**	asist**ís**
ustedes	mir**an**	le**en**	asist**en**
ellos, ellas	mir**an**	le**en**	asist**en**

Siempre **miramos** los   *We always watch the same*
   mismos programas.   *programs.*
¿Qué **lees**?   *What are you reading?*
¿**Asiste** a la universidad? *Does he attend the university?*

Vamos a practicar _____

a. Los fines de semana.   ¿Qué hacen estas personas los fines de semana?

EJEMPLO   **La profesora califica exámenes.**

	asistes a conciertos
	salen con sus amigos
la profesora	charlamos mucho
tú	camino en las montañas
Beto y Jaime	llevan ropa elegante
yo	come pizza
el director	visitas a los parientes
mis padres	preparamos comida especial
Clara y yo	practica deportes
ustedes	alquilo videos
	leen revistas y libros
	califica exámenes

b. Nueva amiga.   Óscar acaba de conocer a Paula y quiere saber más de ella. Completa su conversación con estos verbos.

ayudar   bailar   invitar   nadar
pasar   pasear   practicar   trabajar

Óscar: ¿_____ tú muchos deportes durante el verano?
Paula: Sí, _____ todos los días. Además, mis amigos y yo _____ en bicicleta.
Óscar: ¿_____ también?
Paula: No, solamente en la casa. Mis hermanos y yo _____ a mamá con la casa.
Óscar: ¿Y de noche? ¿Qué haces?
Paula: _____ tiempo con mis amigos. A veces ellos me _____ a una discoteca y nosotros _____ toda la noche.

c. Mi colegio.   ¿Cómo describe Febe su rutina en el nuevo colegio?

MODELO   todo / días / (yo) asistir a / colegio Central
         Todos los días asisto al colegio Central.

1. (ellos) abrir / puertas / 7:00 / y yo / entrar / en seguida
2. (yo) aprender mucho / en todo / mi / clases
3. en / clase de inglés / profesora hacer / mucho / preguntas y todo / nosotros / responder
4. (nosotros) leer / libros / interesante / y escribir / mucho / composiciones
5. mediodía / todos / comer / cafetería
6. durante / recreo / (nosotros) beber / refrescos / patio
7. mi / amigos y yo / salir / colegio / 4:00
8. ¿qué / hacer tú / en / colegio?

ch. Después de las clases. ¿Qué hacen estas personas al salir de la escuela?

el director

MODELO **El director limpia la casa.**

VOCABULARIO ÚTIL:

bailar	beber	comprar	correr	descansar
escribir	hablar	lavar	pasear	sacar

1. Rebeca y Daniela

2. la profesora

3. mis amigos y yo

4. yo

5. Santiago

6. Nena

7. Enrique y Jacobo

8. Rafa y Bea

9. Consuelo y Noemí

10. David y Hernando

Question words are used to request information. Note that all question words have written accents.

Question Words			
¿Adónde?	*Where (to)?*	**¿Cuándo?**	*When?*
¿Dónde?	*Where?*	**¿Cuánto(a)?**	*How much?*
¿Cómo?	*How, what?*	**¿Cuántos(as)?**	*How many?*
¿Cuál(es)?	*Which, what?*	**¿Por qué?**	*Why?*
¿Qué?	*What?*	**¿Quién(es)?**	*Who?*

■ Some question words have more than one form.

¿Quién es tu amiga?	*Who is your friend?*
¿Quiénes son esas chicas?	*Who are those girls?*
¿Cuál es tu carro?	*Which (one) is your car?*
¿Cuáles son sus deportes favoritos?	*What are your favorite sports?*
¿Cuánto dinero tienes?	*How much money do you have?*
¿Cuánta leche bebes?	*How much milk do you drink?*
¿Cuántos libros hay?	*How many books are there?*
¿Cuántas personas asistieron?	*How many people attended?*

■ When **quién(es)** is used as the direct or indirect object, **a** must precede it.

¿A quién vas a llamar?	*Who(m) are you going to call?*
¿A quiénes les das regalos?	*Who(m) do you give gifts to?*

■ Both **qué** and **cuál** correspond to the English word *what.* They are not always interchangeable, however.

Qué asks for a definition or explanation.

¿Qué es un ''capibara''?	*What is a ''capibara''?*
¿Qué hay de nuevo?	*What's new?*

Cuál asks for a selection.

¿Cuál es la fecha hoy?	*What's the date today?*
¿Cuál es tu nombre?	*What is your name?*
¿Cuál es tu dirección?	*What is your address?*
¿Cuál es tu teléfono?	*What is your phone number?*

■ Question words that appear in statements still require the written accent.

Quiere saber **cómo** es Lima.	*He wants to know what Lima is like.*
No se a **qué** colegio asiste.	*I don't know what school he goes to.*

¿POR QUÉ SE DICE ASÍ?

Vamos a practicar

a. Nueva ciudad.   Acabas de mudarte a una nueva ciudad. ¿Qué preguntas le haces a un nuevo amigo?

MODELO   ¿_____ escuelas secundarias hay aquí?
          ¿Cuántas escuelas secundarias hay aquí?

1. ¿_____ es el alcalde *(mayor)*?
2. ¿_____ es el medio de transporte más rápido?
3. ¿_____ tiempo hace en el verano?
4. ¿_____ son los restaurantes — caros?
5. ¿_____ son las mejores tiendas para comprar ropa?
6. ¿_____ está la oficina de correos?
7. ¿_____ hay más festivales municipales — en verano o en invierno?
8. ¿_____ te gusta vivir en esta ciudad?

b. ¡Cuántas preguntas!   Acabas de recibir una carta de tu nueva amiga por correspondencia y le dices a tu mamá que tiene muchas preguntas. Ahora tu mamá quiere saber qué información pide tu amiga. ¿Qué le dices a tu mamá?

MODELO   ¿A qué escuela asistes?
          Mi amiga quiere saber a qué escuela asisto.

1. ¿Cuántas clases tienes?
2. ¿Cuál es tu clase favorita?
3. ¿Qué haces después de las clases?
4. ¿Con quiénes estudias?
5. ¿Adónde vas los fines de semana?
6. ¿Cuántos años tienes?
7. ¿Cómo es tu familia?
8. ¿Cuándo practicas deportes?

c. Conversando.   Patricio habla por teléfono. ¿Qué preguntas le hace su amigo?

MODELO   ¿ _____ ?
          Estoy *bien* gracias, ¿y tú?
          ¿Cómo estás?

Amigo: ¿_1_?
Patricio: No voy al cine contigo *porque tengo que estudiar.*
Amigo: ¿_2_?
Patricio: Tengo que estudiar *química.*
Amigo: ¿_3_?
Patricio: Voy a estudiar *en la biblioteca.*
Amigo: ¿_4_?
Patricio: Voy a estudiar *con Lisa.* Es muy inteligente.
Amigo: ¿_5_?
Patricio: El examen es *el lunes.*
Amigo: ¿_6_?
Patricio: El profesor se llama *López.*
Amigo: ¿_7_?
Patricio: Es muy *exigente* pero es *bueno.*
Amigo: ¿_8_?
Patricio: Después del examen voy *al gimnasio.*

LECCIÓN 2

1.4 THE VERB ESTAR

The verb **estar** *(to be)* has the following forms:

estar	
estoy	estamos
estás	estáis
está	están

The verb **estar** is used in the following ways:

■ To talk about conditions: health, taste, current appearance

Estoy muy cansado.	*I'm very tired.*
El postre **está** rico.	*The dessert is delicious.*
Estás muy guapo hoy.	*You look very handsome today.*

■ To indicate location of people and things

¿Dónde **están** las papas?	*Where are the potatoes?*
Estamos en la misma clase.	*We're in the same class.*
Está a la derecha.	*It's on the right.*

■ To form the progressive, with the **-ndo** form of verbs

¿Qué **están** haciendo?	*What are you doing?*
Estamos cantando una nueva canción.	*We're singing a new song.*
Abuelita **está** leyendo el periódico.	*Grandma is reading the newspaper.*

Vamos a practicar

a. ¡Qué día!   ¿Cómo están estas personas?

MODELO   Tengo que hacer mil cosas hoy.
        Estoy muy ocupado.

VOCABULARIO ÚTIL:

aburrido	cansado	contento	rico	triste	furioso
guapo	listo	nervioso	ocupado	emocionado	

1. Irma tiene examen hoy.
2. No dormí bien anoche.
3. Llevas ropa muy elegante hoy.
4. A mí me encanta este helado.
5. Los novios van a su boda.
6. Los jugadores perdieron el partido.
7. Saqué una "A" en el examen.
8. El novio de Cristina salió con su amiga.
9. No tenemos nada que hacer.
10. Estudié mucho para el examen.

b. Un tour. Hay ocho autobuses de turistas haciendo un tour por la ciudad de El Paso y sus alrededores. Di dónde están todos ahora.

MODELO   el profesor Ramírez (la Universidad de Texas)
El profesor Ramírez está en la Universidad de Texas.

1. Rebeca e Iris (Centro Cívico)
2. la doctora Fuentes (el Museo de Historia)
3. tú (la Plaza San Jacinto)
4. Francisco y Mariano (el Parque Chamizal)
5. Beto (el Estadio del Sun Bowl)
6. yo (Ciudad Juárez)
7. nosotras (la Misión Ysleta)
8. ustedes (el parque de diversiones ''Western Playland'')

c. El sábado. Es el sábado y todos están ocupados. ¿Qué están haciendo estas personas?

Mamá

MODELO   **Mamá está limpiando la casa.**

1. Enrique y Sandra   **2.** la señora Martínez   **3.** Jorge

4. Clara y Micaela   **5.** Ana   **6.** yo

7. Papá   **8.** Carlos

Some verbs in Spanish have irregular stems. (The stem is the infinitive minus the **-ar,** **-er,** or **-ir** ending.) In these verbs, the stressed vowel of the stem changes from **e → ie,** **o → ue,** or **e → i** in all forms except **nosotros** and **vosotros.** You should learn which verbs are stem-changing verbs.

Stem-Changing Verbs		
e → ie **empezar**	**o → ue** **contar**	**e → i** **pedir**
emp**ie**zo emp**ie**zas emp**ie**za	c**ue**nto c**ue**ntas c**ue**nta	p**i**do p**i**des p**i**de
empezamos empezáis emp**ie**zan	contamos contáis c**ue**ntan	pedimos pedís p**i**den

¿A qué hora **empieza** la clase?	*What time does class begin?*
Siempre me **cuentas** tus problemas.	*You always tell me your problems.*
Allí **pedimos** papas fritas.	*We order french fries there.*

Following is a list of common stem-changing verbs:

e → ie			
cerrar	divertir(se)	pensar	querer
comenzar	empezar	perder	recomendar
despertar(se)	entender	preferir	sentar(se)
			sentir

o → ue			
acostarse	costar	encontrar	probar
almorzar	doler	morir	recordar
contar	dormir	poder	volver

e → i			
conseguir	repetir	servir	vestir(se)
pedir	seguir		

Jugar is the only verb in which the stem vowel changes from **u → ue** in all present indicative forms except **nosotros** and **vosotros.**

Norma **juega** muy bien.	*Norma plays very well.*
Jugamos todos los días.	*We play every day.*

Vamos a practicar

a. Los sábados. Micaela acaba de escribir una carta sobre sus actividades. Personaliza la carta un poco más usando *yo* como sujeto en vez de *nosotros*.

Querida amiga:

Siempre *empezamos* los sábados a las diez de la mañana con un buen desayuno. (Los fines de semana *dormimos* tarde, por supuesto.) Después *limpiamos* la casa y *lavamos* el carro. Al terminar, *almorzamos* y si *podemos*, *salimos* a caminar en el parque. *Seguimos* en el parque hasta la hora de merendar. Entonces *caminamos* a un café donde *pedimos* algo de beber. A veces *probamos* los entremeses también. Luego *volvemos* a casa. Después de cenar, *vemos* televisión o *jugamos* a las cartas. *Nos acostamos* tarde porque los domingos también *nos despertamos* tarde. *Nos divertimos* mucho los fines de semana.

---

b. ¡Examen de español! Este fin de semana Micaela y sus amigos tienen que estudiar para un examen de español. Todos quieren hacer otras cosas pero no pueden. ¿Qué quieren hacer?

Raúl

MODELO **Raúl quiere ir al cine pero no puede.**

1. Juanita y Pancho

2. Aurelio

3. ustedes

4. yo

5. Amalia y Marcos

6. tú

7. Cecilia

8. nosotros

9. Dulce, María y Silvia

10. Armando

¿POR QUÉ SE DICE ASÍ?

c. ¡Desorganizada!   Jorge acaba de llegar a casa. Completa la conversación que tiene con su hermana.

Jorge: ¡Hola hermana! ¿Qué me __1__ (contar)?

María: Hola. ¿Sabes? No __2__ (poder) encontrar mi regla.

Jorge: ¡Caramba, María! Tú siempre __3__ (perder) todo. ¿Te __4__ (ayudar) a buscarla?

Un poco después

María: Yo no la __5__ (encontrar).

Jorge: Ni yo tampoco. Pues, __6__ (poder) comprar otra. Por lo menos, las reglas no __7__ (costar) mucho.

María: Pero yo no __8__ (querer) usar mi dinero.

Jorge: ¿Por qué no le __9__ (pedir) dinero a mamá?

María: ¿Me acompañas?

Jorge: Sí, __10__ (poder) ir juntos.

1.6 *PRESENT TENSE: IRREGULAR VERBS*

Some verbs have irregular forms in the present tense. The following verbs have irregular **yo** forms:

conocer	**conozco**
dar	**doy**
decir (i)	**digo**
hacer	**hago**
oír	**oigo**
poner	**pongo**
saber	**sé**
salir	**salgo**
tener (ie)	**tengo**
traer	**traigo**
venir (ie)	**vengo**
ver	**veo**

Note that **decir**, **tener** and **venir** are also stem-changing verbs and that **oír (oigo, oyes, oye, oímos, oís, oyen)** is irregular throughout its conjugation.

Vamos a practicar

a. Marta. Ésta es la composición que Julia, la mejor amiga de Marta, escribió sobre Marta. ¿Qué piensa Marta al leer la composición? Para contestar la pregunta, cambia todos los verbos a la forma de *yo*.

> *Tiene* muchísimos amigos. *Conoce* a todo el mundo y siempre *da* buena impresión. *Asiste* a muchas fiestas y *sabe* bailar muy bien. *Sale* con un muchacho muy guapo. Lo *ve* mucho y *hace* muchas cosas con él. Le *dice* a todo el mundo que *tiene* una vida muy feliz.

b. ¡Feliz cumpleaños! Felipe está describiendo las fiestas de cumpleaños de su familia. Para saber lo que dice, completa este párrafo.

> Me encantan las fiestas de cumpleaños. Yo siempre _____ (hacer) mucho para ayudar a mi mamá. Antes de la fiesta, mamá y yo _____ (preparar) un pastel muy rico. Más tarde yo _____ (salir) con papá para comprar los refrescos. Después, yo _____ (traer) unos discos de mi cuarto y _____ (poner) la música. Cuando Paquita, la vecina, _____ (oír) la música, ella _____ (venir) a la fiesta inmediatamente. Durante la fiesta nosotros _____ (comer) y _____ (escuchar) música y _____ (dar) regalos. Yo siempre _____ (dar) regalos muy bonitos. ¡Cuánto me _____ (gustar) las fiestas!

c. ¡Pobres padres! Todos los años los niños en el *kindergarten* dicen cosas muy divertidas los primeros días de clases. Completa estas oraciones para saber algunas de las cosas que dijeron este año.

1. Yo _____ (saber) que _____ (tener) diecinueve años.
2. No duermo bien porque _____ (oír) a mi hermano roncar *(snore)* toda la noche.
3. Yo no _____ (venir) a clase todos los días porque mis padres duermen toda la mañana.
4. Hoy _____ (traer, yo) a mi perro porque necesita una educación. Mamá dice que es tonto.
5. El 4 de julio siempre me _____ (poner) camisa blanca, pantalones rojos y calcetines azules.
6. Yo no _____ (conocer) a mi tía.
7. Yo siempre _____ (hacer) el desayuno para mis padres.
8. Papá dice que yo nunca _____ (decir) la verdad.

L E C C I Ó N 3

1.7 ADJECTIVES

Adjectives are words that describe nouns.

- Adjectives whose singular masculine form ends in **-o** have endings reflecting both *gender* (masculine or feminine) and *number* (singular or plural).

	Singular	Plural
masculine	alt**o**	alt**os**
feminine	alt**a**	alt**as**

- Most other adjectives have endings reflecting *number,* not gender.

Singular	Plural
inteligent**e**	inteligent**es**
fenomenal	fenomenal**es**

- Adjectives must agree with the nouns they describe in number and gender. Adjectives usually follow the noun they describe.

¿Quién es esa chica moren**a**?	*Who is that dark girl?*
El señor brasileñ**o** canta bien.	*The Brazilian man sings well.*
¿Dónde están las carpetas viej**as**?	*Where are the old folders?*
No tengo zapatos azul**es**.	*I don't have blue shoes.*

- An adjective which describes both a masculine and a feminine noun must be in the masculine plural form.

El colegio y las clases son **fantásticos**.	*The school and the classes are fantastic.*

Vamos a practicar

a. Gemelos. Cambia esta descripción de Matilde a una descripción de Matilde y su hermano gemelo, Mateo. Matilde y Mateo son gemelos idénticos.

MODELO   **Tengo unos buenos amigos que . . .**

Tengo una buena amiga que se llama Matilde. Es baja y morena y muy delgada. Es muy simpática e inteligente. Habla tres lenguas. Además, es buena estudiante. Es seria y estudiosa. También es divertida y muy alegre. Es muy buena amiga.

b. No es así. Héctor y Roberto fueron al mismo restaurante para comer anoche, pero tienen impresiones totalmente opuestas. ¿Cómo responde Roberto a los comentarios de Héctor? Selecciona los adjetivos apropiados.

aburrido / antipático / caro / lento / malo / poco / terrible / viejo

Héctor: ¡Qué buen restaurante es el Bodegón!
Roberto: ¡Al contrario! Ese restaurante es ＿＿＿.
Héctor: La comida es excelente y económica.
Roberto: ¡No! La comida es ＿＿＿ y ＿＿＿.
Héctor: Dan mucha comida.
Roberto: Al contrario, dan ＿＿＿ comida.
Héctor: El servicio es muy rápido.
Roberto: ¡Estás loco! El servicio es ＿＿＿.
Héctor: Los camareros son simpáticos y jóvenes.
Roberto: ¡Qué va! Ellos son ＿＿＿ y ＿＿＿.
Héctor: Yo creo que es muy interesante comer allí.
Roberto: Yo no. Yo creo que es ＿＿＿.

1.8 THE VERBS *SER, IR* AND *TENER*

The common verbs **ser**, **ir** and **tener** are irregular. The following chart presents their present tense conjugation.

ser	ir	tener
soy	voy	tengo
eres	vas	tienes
es	va	tiene
somos	vamos	tenemos
sois	vais	tenéis
son	van	tienen

The verb **ser** is used in the following ways:

■ To identify a person, place, idea or thing

Ellas **son** mis primas.	*They are my cousins.*
Caracas **es** una ciudad hermosa.	*Caracas is a beautiful city.*
La educación **es** importante.	*Education is important.*
Sus libros **son** interesantísimos.	*His books are extremely interesting.*

■ To describe inherent characteristics

| El colegio **es** grande. | *The school is big.* |
| Siempre **eres** tan original. | *You are always so original.* |

■ To tell origin or nationality

| **Es** de Maracaibo. | *She is from Maracaibo.* |
| **Somos** venezolanas. | *We are Venezuelan.* |

The verb **ir** is used in the following ways:

- To talk about going places, with **ir a** + *place*

Vamos a El Paso.	*We're going to El Paso.*
Después de las clases, **voy a** mi clase de baile.	*After school, I go to my dance class.*

- To talk about future activities, with **ir a** + *infinitive*

Mañana **van a jugar** fútbol.	*Tomorrow they are going to play soccer.*
¿**Vas a contestar** la carta?	*Are you going to answer the letter?*

The verb **tener** is used in the following ways:

- To talk about possessions, relationships, commitments, and age

Tengo una mochila nueva.	*I have a new backpack.*
Tenemos muchos amigos.	*We have a lot of friends.*
Pepe **tiene** clase a las 9:00.	*Pepe has class at 9:00.*
Mi hermano **tiene** catorce años.	*My brother is fourteen.*

- To talk about obligations with **tener que** + *infinitive*

Tengo que llamarla.	*I have to call her.*
Tienen que practicar.	*They have to practice*

- To form certain idiomatic expressions

tener calor	*to be hot*
tener frío	*to be cold*
tener hambre	*to be hungry*
tener sed	*to be thirsty*
tener cuidado	*to be careful*
tener sueño	*to be sleepy*
tener ganas de	*to feel like*
tener prisa	*to be in a hurry*
tener miedo (de)	*to be afraid (of)*
tener razón	*to be right*
tener suerte	*to be lucky*

No **tengo ganas de** ir.	*I don't feel like going.*
Los niños **tienen sueño.**	*The children are sleepy.*
Nosotros **tenemos razón;** ellos no.	*We're right; they're not.*
Yo **tengo calor,** pero ellos dicen que **tienen frío.**	*I'm hot, but they say they are cold.*
Nadie **tiene prisa,** ¿verdad?	*No one's in a hurry, right?*
¿**Tienes miedo de** caminar solo?	*Are you afraid to walk alone?*

Vamos a practicar

a. Amigas por correspondencia. Josefina acaba de escribirle una carta a su nueva amiga por correspondencia. Para saber lo que dice, completa su carta con **ser.**

Querida Susana:

   Yo _____ tu nueva amiga por correspondencia. Mi nombre _____ Josefina Delgado. _____ (yo) alta y rubia. Mi familia _____ de Italia pero vivimos en Nicaragua. Mis dos hermanos _____ estudiantes universitarios y mi hermanita y yo _____ estudiantes del Colegio San Juan. Mi papá _____ arquitecto y mi mamá _____ ingeniera. Los dos _____ muy trabajadores y buenos papás. ¿Cómo _____ tú? ¿Cómo _____ tu familia? Escríbeme pronto. Tengo muchas ganas de conocerte.

Tu nueva amiga,
Josefina

---

b. Planes. Todos tus amigos tienen planes para mañana. ¿Qué van a hacer?

MODELO   Andrés: parque (jugar tenis)
          Mañana Andrés va al parque. Va a jugar tenis.

1. María y Teresa: museo (ver artesanías)
2. tú: Restaurante Ofelia (probar la comida)
3. los Perón: aeropuerto (salir de viaje)
4. yo: cine (ver la nueva película)
5. la profesora: gimnasio (hacer ejercicio)
6. nosotros: tienda (comprar ropa)
7. ustedes: discoteca (bailar)
8. Luis: biblioteca (buscar un libro)

c. Obligaciones. Varios estudiantes están hablando en el patio de la escuela antes de empezar las clases. ¿Qué dicen?

MODELO   Iris / tener que / escribir / composición
          Iris tiene que escribir una composición.

1. Olga / tener / matemáticas / 10:00
2. yo / tener que / estudiar / después de / clases
3. Felipe / no tener / mochila
4. tú / tener / nuevo / computadora / ¿no?
5. Horacio / tener miedo / perros / grande
6. nosotros / tener / práctica de fútbol / 4:00
7. profesores / tener que / hablar / con el director / este / mañana
8. tú y yo / tener / francés / 1:30
9. Raquel y Mario / tener / mucho / libros / interesante
10. yo / tener ganas de / ir / cine

ch. **En el pasillo.**   Paco y Sara se encuentran en el pasillo de la escuela antes de las clases. Para saber lo que dicen, completa su conversación con la forma apropiada de **estar**, **ir**, **ser** o **tener**.

Paco: ¡Hola, chica! ¿Cómo _____?

Sara: Regular. _____ un poco preocupada porque _____ un examen en la clase de historia y _____ que estudiar mucho.

Paco: ¿Quién _____ el profesor?

Sara: _____ una profesora nueva — la señora Bustamante.

Paco: ¿Cómo _____? No la conozco.

Sara: _____ alta y _____ el pelo negro.

Paco: ¿A qué hora _____ la clase?

Sara: _____ mañana a las 2:00.

Paco: Entonces, _____ tiempo para estudiar.

Sara: Sí. _____ a la biblioteca a estudiar ahora mismo.

1.9 *HACER IN EXPRESSIONS OF TIME: PRESENT TENSE*

To tell how long someone has been doing something, Spanish uses the verb **hacer** in the following structure:

$$\boxed{\textbf{hace} + \textit{[time]} + \textbf{que} + \textit{[present tense]}}$$

Hace dos semanas **que** asiste a la universidad.

Hace tres años **que** vivo aquí.

Hace un año **que** estudiamos español.

He has been attending the university for two weeks.

I've lived here for three years.

We've been studying Spanish for a year.

To ask how long someone has been doing something, Spanish uses the following structure:

$$\boxed{\textbf{¿Cuánto tiempo hace que} + \textit{[present tense]}?}$$

¿Cuánto tiempo hace que estudias español?

¿Cuánto tiempo hace que toca el piano Pedro?

How long have you been studying Spanish?

How long has Pedro been playing the piano?

Vamos a practicar

a. ¿Y tú? Ahora tu profesor(a) te hace unas preguntas a ti. ¿Qué dices?

> MODELO   estudiar español
> **Hace un año que estudio español.**

1. estudiar inglés
2. tocar (un instrumento)
3. conocer al (a la) director(a) del colegio
4. participar en actividades del colegio
5. vivir en esta comunidad
6. jugar (un deporte)
7. saber leer
8. salir con (una persona)

b. La familia de Leonor. Según Leonor, su familia es muy especial. ¿Por qué?

> MODELO   5 años / tía / cantar ópera
> **Hace cinco años que mi tía canta ópera.**

1. 9 años / mamá / tocar / piano
2. 11 años / papá / jugar fútbol
3. 6 años / hermano / hablar chino
4. 3 años / primos / bailar / ballet folklórico
5. 5 años / yo / practicar karate
6. 15 años / abuelo / escribir poemas
7. 13 años / tío / ser artista
8. 4 años / hermanas / hacer gimnasia

c. ¿Cuánto tiempo? Eres reportero(a) para el periódico escolar. Ahora estás preparando una lista de preguntas para hacerles a los profesores. ¿Qué les vas a preguntar a los profesores que tú tienes que entrevistar?

> MODELO   hablar español
> **¿Cuánto tiempo hace que usted habla español?**

1. vivir en esta ciudad
2. ser profesor(a) de español
3. ser casado(a)
4. tener interés en otras culturas
5. escribir cartas en español
6. tener amigos que hablan español
7. leer novelas en español
8. tocar la guitarra
9. bailar el tango
10. participar en festivales internacionales

LECCIÓN 1

2.1 DIRECT OBJECT PRONOUNS

You have learned that direct objects answer the questions *what?* or *who(m)?* after the verb. You have also learned that direct object pronouns are used to avoid repetition of nouns.

Comemos **arepas.**	*We eat arepas.*
Las comemos con mantequilla.	*We eat them with butter.*
¿Ves a **Luis**?	*Do you see Luis?*
No, no **lo** veo.	*No, I don't see him.*

The direct object pronouns in Spanish are given below.

Direct Object Pronouns			
me	**me**	**nos**	*us*
you (familiar)	**te**	**os**	*you (familiar)*
you (m. formal)	**lo**	**los**	*you (m. formal)*
you (f. formal)	**la**	**las**	*you (f. formal)*
him, it (m.)	**lo**	**los**	*them (m.)*
her, it (f.)	**la**	**las**	*them (f.)*

Like indirect object pronouns, direct object pronouns are placed . . .

■ before conjugated verbs.

¿**Me** quieres?	*Do you love me?*
Te adoro, mi amor.	*I adore you, my love.*

■ either before the conjugated verb or after and attached to an infinitive or the **-ndo** verb form.

Voy a hacer**la** ahora.	
La voy a hacer ahora.	*I'm going to do it now.*
Están mirándo**nos**.	
Nos están mirando.	*They're looking at us.*

■ after and attached to the affirmative command form.

Di**me**.	*Tell me.*
Píde**las.**	*Order them.*

■ A written accent is always required when a pronoun is attached to the **-ndo** verb form or to command forms with two or more syllables.

Estoy **escuchándote**.   *I'm listening to you.*
Salúdalo de mi parte.   *Say hello to him for me.*

Vamos a practicar

a. ¿Los conoces?   ¿Conoces estos lugares?

MODELO   el Museo de Antropología en México
           Lo conozco. o
           No lo conozco

1. el río Misisipí
2. los parques de tu ciudad
3. la Casa Blanca
4. el Teatro Degollado en Guadalajara

5. las pirámides de Egipto
6. el Alcázar de Segovia
7. la catedral de Notre Dame en París
8. las Montañas Rocosas

b. ¡Mamáaa!   Es el primer día de la escuela y Pepita está muy preocupada. ¿Qué dicen ella y su mamá?

MODELO   llevar a la escuela (sí)
          Pepita: **¿Vas a llevarme a la escuela?** o
                   ¿Me vas a llevar a la escuela?
          Mamá: **Sí, voy a llevarte.** o
                 Sí, te voy a llevar.

1. acompañar a la clase (no)
2. esperar después de las clases (sí) ·
3. ayudar con la tarea (sí)
4. visitar en la clase (no)
5. llamar al mediodía (no)
6. buscar a las tres (sí)

c. ¿Estás listo(a)?   Tu mamá te hace estas preguntas durante el desayuno. ¿Qué dices?

MODELO   ¿Tienes tu sándwich?
          Sí, lo tengo. o
          No, no lo tengo.

1. ¿Tienes ti tarea?
2. ¿Estás comiendo el cereal?
3. ¿Quieres más jugo?
4. ¿Vas a llevar a Elena y a Ana hoy?
5. ¿Me estás escuchando?
6. ¿Tienes tus libros?
7. ¿Quieres llevar una manzana?
8. ¿Vas a llamar a tu padre durante el almuerzo?

ch. ¡Qué divertido!   La familia Torres pasa mucho tiempo haciendo sus cosas favoritas. Según Sancho, ¿qué están haciendo ahora?

MODELO   A mamá le gusta leer el periódico.
Está leyéndolo ahora.

1. A Joaquín le gusta jugar tenis.
2. A mis hermanitos les gusta ver televisión.
3. A mamá y a mí nos gusta escuchar música.
4. A mi tía Celia le gusta leer sus revistas favoritas.
5. A mí me gusta hacer la tarea.
6. A papá y a Elena les gusta lavar los carros.
7. A mis abuelitos les gusta tomar chocolate.
8. A mi tío Pepe le gusta tocar la guitarra.

2.2 POSSESSIVE ADJECTIVES

In **¡DIME!** UNO you learned that possessive adjectives are used to indicate that something belongs to someone or to establish a relationship between people or things. You also learned possessive adjectives precede and agree in number and gender with the noun they modify.

Possessive Adjectives			
Singular	Plural	Singular	Plural
mi	mis	nuestro nuestra	nuestros nuestras
tu	tus	vuestro vuestra	vuestros vuestras
su	sus	su	sus

Es para **mi** clase de composición.   *It's for my composition class.*
¡Tú y **tus** ideas!   *You and your ideas!*
Nuestra clase es muy grande.   *Our class is very large.*
Ese niño no come **sus** arepas.   *That boy isn't eating his arepas.*

- Possession can also be expressed with the preposition **de**. This construction is especially useful if the meaning of **su(s)** is not clear from the context.

Su examen es mañana.
El examen **de ellos** es mañana.   *Their exam is tomorrow.*

Sus hermanos están en Perú.   *His brothers are in Peru.*
Los hermanos **de David** están   *David's brothers are in Peru.*
   en Perú.

Vamos a practicar

a. ¡Qué noche! Después de pasar la noche en casa de Amanda, todas las chicas están teniendo problemas en encontrar sus cosas. Según Amanda, ¿qué no encuentran?

Juanita

MODELO **Juanita no encuentra su reloj.**

1. nosotras

2. Noemí y Clara

3. yo

4. Julia

5. Lilia

6. Marta y Eva

7. Enriqueta

8. tú

¿POR QUÉ SE DICE ASÍ?

G25

b. **Su orden.**   Tú y un grupo de amigos están en su restaurante favorito. Cuando el mesero trae la comida, te pregunta si sabes lo que pidieron todos. ¿Qué le dices?

> MODELO   La pizza, ¿es de David y Carlos?
> **Sí, es su pizza.**

1. Los sándwiches, ¿son de Sole y Jorge?
2. La hamburguesa, ¿es de Amalia?
3. El pollo, ¿es de Matías y Yolanda?
4. Los refrescos, ¿son de Édgar y Chela?
5. El pastel de manzana, ¿es de Inés?
6. La sopa, ¿es de Lucas?
7. Las papas, ¿son de Laura?
8. El café, ¿es de Virginia y Roberto?

c. **Álbum de fotos.**   Le estás enseñando un álbum de fotos a una nueva amiga. ¿Qué dicen?

> MODELO   abuela / tía
> *Tú:*   **¿Es tu abuela?**
> *Amiga:* **No, es mi tía.**

1. primos / hermanos
2. mamá / tía
3. hermanos / sobrinos
4. tío / abuelo
5. hermana / prima
6. primo / papá

ch. **Nuestra casa**   Describe la casa donde vives.

VOCABULARIO ÚTIL:
cómodo / incómodo
duro / blando
grande / pequeño
bonito / feo
moderno / viejo
elegante / ordinario

> EJEMPLO   sala
> **Nuestra sala es pequeña.**

1. sofá
2. sillas
3. baños
4. televisor
5. cocina
6. comedor
7. alcobas
8. camas

LECCIÓN 2

2.3 THE PRETERITE OF REGULAR AND THREE IRREGULAR VERBS

The preterite is used to talk about what happened in the past. There are two sets of endings for regular verbs in the preterite: one for **-ar** verbs and one for **-er** and **-ir** verbs.

Preterite of *-ar* and *-er, -ir* Verbs		
pas**ar**	com**er**	sal**ir**
pas**é**	com**í**	sal**í**
pas**aste**	com**iste**	sal**iste**
pas**ó**	com**ió**	sal**ió**
pas**amos**	com**imos**	sal**imos**
pas**asteis**	com**isteis**	sal**isteis**
pas**aron**	com**ieron**	sal**ieron**

Lo **pasé** muy bien.	*I had a great time.*
¿No **comiste** nada?	*Didn't you eat anything?*
Ni **salimos** de Caracas.	*We didn't even leave Caracas.*

Some verbs require a spelling change in the preterite to maintain consistent pronunciation of the verb stem.

- An unaccented **i** between two vowels changes to **y.**

Papá lo **leyó** ayer.	*Dad read it yesterday.*
No **oyeron** las noticias.	*They didn't hear the news.*

Note that this rule affects the **usted / él / ella** and the **ustedes / ellos / ellas** forms of the preterite.

- The letter **c** changes to **qu** before **e** or **i.**

Practiqué el piano una hora.	*I practiced the piano an hour.*

Note that this rule affects the **yo** form of verbs ending in **-car**: practi**car**, califi**car**, expli**car**, etc.

- The letter **g** changes to **gu** before **e** or **i.**

Llegué tarde.	*I got there late.*

Note that this rule affects the **yo** form of verbs ending in **-gar**: lle**gar**, pa**gar**, ju**gar**, obli**gar**, etc.

■ The letter **z** changes to **c** before **e** or **i**.

Comencé mi tarea.   *I began my homework.*

Note that this rule affects the **yo** form of verbs ending in **-zar**: comen**zar**, empe**zar**, almor**zar**, especiali**zar**, etc.

The verbs **ir, ser,** and **hacer,** which are very common, are irregular in the preterite. Note that **ir** and **ser** have identical forms. The context in which they are used always clarifies meaning.

Preterite of *ir, ser,* and *hacer*		
ir	ser	hacer
fui	fui	hice
fuiste	fuiste	hiciste
fue	fue	hizo
fuimos	fuimos	hicimos
fuisteis	fuisteis	hicisteis
fueron	fueron	hicieron

Fuimos a Brasil.   *We went to Brasil.*
El viaje **fue** fantástico.   *The trip was fantastic.*
¿Qué **hicieron** ustedes?   *What did you do?*

Vamos a practicar

a. Ayer.   La familia de Inés hace estas cosas todos los días. Según Inés, ¿qué hicieron ayer?

MODELO   Ayer, yo me **desperté** a las . . .

Yo me **despierto** a las seis y cuarto pero no me **levanto** hasta las seis y media. Primero **desayunamos** y después, mi mamá **prepara** el almuerzo y mis hermanos y yo nos **arreglamos** para las clases. Mi papá nos **lleva** a la escuela. **Llegamos** a la escuela a las ocho y **pasamos** seis horas allí. Después de las clases yo **trabajo** en un café y mis hermanos **practican** deportes. Raúl **juega** fútbol y Micaela, tenis. **Llego** a casa muy cansada a eso de las seis. Todos **cenamos**, y después **estudio** mis lecciones y me **acuesto** temprano.

b. En el parque. León y sus amigos pasaron la tarde en el parque. Según León, ¿qué hicieron?

MODELO   mi / amigos / yo / decidir ir / parque
Mis amigos y yo decidimos ir al parque.

1. yo / aprender/ nuevo juego / y recibir / premio
2. Jaime / descubrir / carros chocones
3. nosotros / subir a los carros / divertirse
4. todos / oír / nuestro / gritos
5. Pablo / comer / mucho / hamburguesas
6. Enrique / Tomás / beber / mucho / refrescos
7. nosotros / salir tarde / y perder el autobús
8. yo / volver / casa / y escribir / carta / mi abuelo

c. Un buen día. Sofía le escribió esta notita a su amiga Ana. Completa la nota con las formas apropiadas de **hacer, ir** y **ser**.

Ayer (1) un día buenísimo. Yo (2) al colegio a pie. (3) muy buen tiempo todo el día. Las clases (4) divertidas. (5) muchas cosas interesantes. Por la tarde, mi clase de biología (6) una excursión al lago. Y tú, ¿qué (7) ? ¿ (8) (tú) a una parte interesante? Escríbeme.

ch. Después de las clases. Antonio y Bárbara están hablando. Para saber lo que dicen, completa su conversación con la forma apropiada del verbo indicado.

1. ir
2. buscar (yo)
3. encontrar
4. ir
5. ver (ustedes)
6. ver (nosotros)
7. gustar
8. ser
9. llegar
10. hacer
11. jugar
12. jugar
13. conocer
14. ganar
15. ser

Antonio: ¿Adónde (1) ayer después de las clases? Te (2) pero no te (3) .
Bárbara: (4) al cine con Verónica.
Antonio: ¿Ah sí? ¿Qué (5) ?
Bárbara: (6) una nueva película de terror.
Antonio: ¿Les (7) ?
Bárbara: Sí, (8) buenísima y muy larga. Yo no (9) a casa hasta las siete. Y tú, ¿qué (10) ?
Antonio: (11) tenis.
Bárbara: ¿Con quién (12) ?
Antonio: Con Manuel, un nuevo amigo que (13) allí.
Bárbara: ¿Quién (14) ?
Antonio: Nadie. (15) un empate.

2.4 ADJECTIVES OF NATIONALITY

The masculine/feminine and singular/plural forms of most adjectives of nationality follow one of three patterns depending on whether the singular forms end in a vowel or a consonant.

■ Adjectives of nationality whose singular masculine form ends in **-o** have a feminine form ending in **-a.** The plural of these adjectives is formed by adding **-s.**

	singular	plural
masculine	colombian**o**	colombiano**s**
feminine	colombian**a**	colombiana**s**

The following are some common adjectives of nationality whose singular masculine form ends in **-o.**

argentino	chino	hondureño	salvadoreño
boliviano	dominicano	italiano	sueco
brasileño	ecuatoriano	mexicano	suizo
colombiano	europeo	paraguayo	uruguayo
coreano	filipino	peruano	venezolano
cubano	griego	puertorriqueño	
chileno	guatemalteco	ruso	

■ Adjectives of nationality whose singular form ends in **-e, -a,** or an accented **-í** have only one form which is both masculine and feminine. The plural of these adjectives is formed by adding **-s** to those ending in **-e** or **-a** and **-es** to those ending in **-í.**

	singular	plural
masculine **feminine** }	canadiens**e** israelit**a** paquistan**í**	canadiense**s** israelita**s** paquistaní**es**

The following are some common adjectives of nationality whose singular form ends in **-e, -a,** or **-í.**

canadiense	marroquí
costarricense	nicaragüense
estadounidense	paquistaní
israelita	vietnamita

- Adjectives of nationality that end in a consonant form the feminine singular by adding **-a**. The plural of these adjectives is formed by adding **-es** to masculine adjectives and **-s** to feminine ones.

	singular	plural
masculine	español japonés	españoles japoneses
feminine	española japonesa	españolas japonesas

The following are some common adjectives of nationality whose singular masculine form ends in a consonant.

alemán	francés	irlandés
escocés	holandés	japonés
español	inglés	portugués

Vamos a practicar

a. Familias internacionales. ¿Cuál es la nacionalidad de las familias de estos estudiantes?

MODELO   Enrique es cubano.
          Su familia es cubana.

1. Benito es italiano.
2. Kwang Mi es coreana.
3. Pierre es francés.
4. Keiko es japonesa.
5. Heinrich es alemán.
6. Gabriela es nicaragüense.
7. Tomás es español.
8. Lisa es estadounidense.

b. Campamento. Sonia acaba de regresar de un campamento internacional. ¿Cómo describe las fotos que sacó?

MODELO   Este señor alto es inglés. Es muy simpático. (señoras)
          Estas señoras altas son inglesas. Son muy simpáticas.

1. Ésta es la directora. Es francesa y muy inteligente. (director)
2. Este chico es peruano. Es muy divertido. (chica)
3. Esta chica es mi mejor amiga. Es rusa y es tímida. (chicas)
4. Este niño es filipino. Es muy cómico. (niños)
5. Los chicos morenos son mis amigos chilenos. (chicas)
6. La joven venezolana es simpática. (jóvenes)
7. Él es mi compañero costarricense. (compañeras)
8. Estos chicos altos son puertorriqueños. (chica)

LECCIÓN 3

2.5 COMPARATIVES

Spanish uses various structures when making equal and unequal comparisons.

Unequal comparisons:

Ellos salen **más que** nosotros.	*They go out more than we do.*
Este disco cuesta **menos que** ése.	*This record costs less than that one.*
Tú hablas **mejor que** yo pero escribes **peor que** yo.	*You speak better than I do but you write worse than I do.*
Ella es **mayor que** tú pero **menor que** yo.	*She is older than you but younger than I am.*

- When making unequal comparisons with **más que** and **menos que**, the thing or quality being compared is often expressed between **más** or **menos** and **que**:

> **más** + [adjective, adverb or noun] + **que**
>
> **menos** + [adjective, adverb or noun] + **que**

Jorge es **más alto que** Alberto.	*Jorge is taller than Alberto.*
Esta cama es **menos dura que** la mía.	*This bed is less hard than mine.*
Ana corre **más rápido que** tú.	*Anna runs faster than you.*
La profesora habla **menos lento que** los estudiantes.	*The teacher talks less slowly than the students.*
La biblioteca tiene **más libros que** revistas.	*The library has more books than magazines.*
Tengo **menos dinero que** tú.	*I have less money than you do.*

- Some unequal comparisons are made with **mejor, peor, mayor** or **menor:**

mejor	*better*	**mayor**	*older*
peor	*worse*	**menor**	*younger*

Esta pizza está **peor que** la otra.	*This pizza is worse than the other one.*
Mi hermano es **mayor que** yo.	*My brother is older than I am.*

Equal comparisons:

¿Es **tan** inteligente **como** yo?   *Is he as intelligent as I am?*
Tú tienes **tantos** libros **como** yo.   *You have as many books as I do.*

■ Equal comparisons are made with **tan . . . como** or **tanto . . . como**, depending on whether the comparison being made refers to an adjective or adverb, or a noun.

> **tan** + [adjective or adverb] + **como**

La película es **tan buena**   *The movie is as good as the*
    como el libro.   *book.*
Julia no come **tan tarde**   *Julia doesn't eat as late as*
    como su hermano.   *her brother.*

> **tanto(a, os, as)** + [noun] + **como**

No hay **tanta limonada**   *There isn't as much*
    como leche.   *lemonade as milk.*
Esta clase tiene **tantos**   *This class has as many boys*
    chicos como chicas.   *as girls.*

Vamos a practicar

a. En la clínica.   Hugo y Paco son hermanos. ¿Cómo se comparan?

Nombre:	Hugo Ruiz	Nombre:	Paco Ruiz
edad:	18	edad:	15
estatura:	175 cm	estatura:	173 cm
peso:	100 kg	peso:	80 kg

MODELO   _____ es más grande que _____.
      Hugo es más grande que Paco.

1. _____ es más bajo que _____.
2. _____ es más alto que _____.
3. _____ es menos gordo que _____.
4. _____ es más pequeño que _____.
5. _____ es menor que _____.
6. _____ es más delgado que _____.
7. _____ es menos grande que _____.
8. _____ es mayor que _____.

b. **¡Casi idénticos!**   Todo el mundo dice que Carlota es la mujer ideal para Luis porque los dos son muy similares en apariencia y personalidad. Son casi idénticos.

MODELO   alto
Carlota es tan alta como Luis.
años
Carlota tiene tantos años como Luis.

1. delgado
2. simpático
3. guapo
4. amigos
5. popular
6. estudioso
7. inteligente
8. clases
9. divertido
10. actividades

c. **Es evidente.**   ¿Cómo se comparan estas cosas?

MODELO   las computadoras y los lápices (moderno)
Las computadoras son más modernas.   o
Los lápices son menos modernos.

1. el autobús y el avión (lento)
2. la serpiente y el elefante (gordo)
3. los coches y las bicicletas (caro)
4. la nota ''F'' y la nota ''A'' (bajo)
5. el perro y el tren (rápido)
6. el agua y la limonada (delicioso)
7. los libros y las revistas (pesado)
8. una pizza y una hamburguesa (caro)
9. la computadora vieja y la computadora nueva (malo)
10. el tigre y las pulgas (feroz)

2.6 *SUPERLATIVES*

You have already learned that the **-ísimo** form of an adjective is used to express a very high degree (*really, extremely, very, very*) of the characteristic that adjective names.

Esta paella está **riquísima**.   *This paella is really delicious.*
Tomasita e Irma son   *Tomasita and Irma are*
   inteligentísimas.   *extremely smart.*
Es **buenísima**.   *It's very, very good.*

To express the *highest* degree of quality, Spanish uses the definite article (**el, la, los, las**) with the thing or quality being compared before the comparative construction.

$$\left.\begin{array}{l} \text{el, la} \\ \text{los, las} \end{array}\right\} \text{[noun]} + \left.\begin{array}{l} \text{más} \\ \\ \text{menos} \end{array}\right\} + \text{[adjective]}$$

Éstas son **las blusas más bonitas**.	*These are the prettiest blouses.*
Tienen **el carro menos elegante**.	*They have the least elegant car.*
El Amazonas es **el río más largo** de Sudamérica.	*The Amazon is the longest river in South America.*

When the thing or quality being compared is *not* mentioned, the definite article alone precedes the comparative structure.

$$\left.\begin{array}{l} \text{el, la} \\ \text{los, las} \end{array}\right\} \left.\begin{array}{l} \text{más} \\ \\ \text{menos} \end{array}\right\} + \text{[adjective]}$$

El Nilo es **el más largo** del mundo.	*The Nile is the longest in world.*
Éstos son **los menos** importantes.	*These are the least important.*

- When referring to the *best / worst* or the *oldest / youngest,* Spanish uses **mejor / peor** and **mayor / menor** preceded by the definite article. Note that **de** is used when the comparison group is mentioned.

Éstos son **los mejores** estudiantes del colegio.	*These are the best students in the school.*
Es verdad. Somos **los mejores.**	*It's true. We're the best.*
Acabo de ver **la peor** película del año.	*I just saw the worst movie of the year.*

Vamos a practicar

a. De viaje. En su viaje por Venezuela, todo lo que ve le impresiona a Leticia. ¿Qué dice cuando regresa a Estados Unidos?

MODELO   montañas: alto
Las montañas son altísimas.

1. hoteles: elegante
2. ciudad: grande
3. edificios: alto
4. comida: rico

5. río: largo
6. gente: simpático
7. cama: cómodo
8. tren: rápido

b. Los Vargas. ¿Cómo son los miembros de la familia Vargas?

Cristina   Teodoro   Papá   Mamá   Abuelita

MODELO   La persona más joven es _____.
La persona más joven es René.

1. La persona mayor es _____.
2. La persona más grande es _____.
3. La adulta más baja es _____.
4. La persona menos joven es _____.

5. La persona más pequeña es _____.
6. La persona más delgada es _____.
7. La persona menos delgada es _____.
8. La persona más alta es _____.

c. Fanfarrón. Máximo cree que todo lo que tiene y hace es lo mejor. ¿Qué dice?

MODELO   yo / tener / clases / interesante / escuela
Yo tengo las clases más interesantes de la escuela.

1. yo / tener / carro / rápido / ciudad
2. mis hermanos y yo / ser / jóvenes / inteligente / escuela
3. yo / ser / estudiante / estudioso / clase
4. mi hermano / ser / jugador / fuerte / equipo
5. yo / tener / amigos / simpático / mundo
6. yo / ser / hijo / listo / familia
7. mi novia / ser / chica / bonita / escuela
8. yo / tener / familia / famosa / ciudad

d. Mi familia. ¿Cómo describes a los miembros de tu familia?

MODELO   alto
Mi tía (mamá / hermana / prima) es la más alta. o
Mi padre (hermano / tío / primo) es el más alto.

1. delgado
2. bajo
3. estudioso
4. pequeño

5. tímido
6. cómico
7. gordo
8. joven

LECCIÓN 1

3.1 THE PRETERITE TENSE: IRREGULAR VERBS

In **Unidad 2,** you learned three irregular verbs in the preterite: **ir, ser,** and **hacer.** Like the verb **hacer,** the following verbs have irregular stems in the preterite and all take the same irregular preterite verb endings.

estar	**estuv-**	
tener	**tuv-**	
poder	**pud-**	**-e**
poner	**pus-**	**-iste**
saber	**sup-**	**-o**
querer	**quis-**	**-imos**
venir	**vin-**	**-isteis**
decir	**dij-***	**-ieron (-eron*)**
traer	**traj-***	

Estuvo enfermo ayer.	*He was sick yesterday.*
Tere lo **puso** en la mesa.	*Tere put it on the table.*
Supe† el secreto.	*I found out the secret.*
No quisimos† hacerlo.	*We refused to do it.*
Dijimos la verdad.	*We told the truth.*
Trajeron* pizza a la fiesta.	*They brought pizza to the party.*

*Verbs whose stem ends in **j** drop the **i** and add **-eron** to the **ustedes / ellos / ellas** ending.
†Note that in the preterite tense, **saber** means *to find out* and **no querer** means *to refuse.*

The verbs **dar** and **haber** are also irregular in the preterite.

dar	**haber**
di	Present tense:
diste	**hay** *(there is / there are)*
dio	Preterite tense:
dimos	**hubo** *(there was / there were)*
disteis	
dieron	

Me **dieron** un regalo especial.	*They gave me a special gift.*
¿Qué le **diste** a Elena?	*What did you give Elena?*
Hubo una gran fiesta ayer.	*There was a great party yesterday.*
Hubo varios participantes.	*There were several participants.*

Vamos a practicar

a. Buenas intenciones. Todos quisieron leer veinte libros durante el verano. ¿Qué pasó? ¿Lo hicieron?

MODELO Patricia (sí)
**Patricia quiso leer veinte libros
y pudo hacerlo.**

Hortensia (no)
**Hortensia quiso leer veinte libros
pero no pudo hacerlo.**

1. Raúl (sí)
2. Constanza y Edgar (no)
3. tú (no)
4. yo (sí)
5. ustedes (no)
6. nosotros (sí)
7. Elena (sí)
8. Narciso y Silvia (no)
9. usted (sí)

b. ¡Ganó Sara! Hubo elecciones estudiantiles ayer. ¿Cuándo supieron estas personas los resultados?

MODELO el director: primero
El director los supo primero.

1. Sara: inmediatamente
2. los profesores: después de las clases
3. yo: a las tres y media
4. Jacobo y Marisela: después de la clase de música
5. tú: al llegar a casa
6. ustedes: al hablar con Sara
7. Diego: por la noche
8. las secretarias: hoy por la mañana
9. ellos: el día siguiente

c. ¡Pobrecito! Si Federico hace esto todos los días, ¿qué hizo ayer?

MODELO **Ayer caminé a la . . .**

Camino a la escuela. ¡Uf! *Traigo* muchos libros en mi mochila. *Llego* a las ocho y *estoy* allí hasta las tres. *Tengo* que estudiar mucho porque *hay* mucho que aprender. Los profesores *dan* mucha tarea y por eso, no *puedo* ver televisión. ¡Pobre de mí!

ch. ¡Auxilio! Diego está entrevistando a dos personas sobre un accidente. ¿Qué le dicen que vieron?

1. ver	**4.** pasar	**7.** llamar	**10.** haber	**13.** poner
2. poder	**5.** chocar	**8.** venir	**11.** tener	**14.** decir
3. ver	**6.** correr	**9.** hacer	**12.** dar	

Diego: ¿ 1 ustedes el accidente?
Mamá: Yo no 2 ver mucho, pero mi hijo lo 3 todo.
Diego: ¿Ah, sí? ¿Qué 4 , joven?
Hijo: Dos carros 5 en la esquina. Yo 6 a mi casa y mamá 7 a la policía. Muy pronto 8 la policía y la ambulancia.
Diego: ¿Qué 9 ?
Hijo: Pues, 10 una mujer lastimada y 11 que llevarla al hospital. Le 12 un calmante y la 13 en una ambulancia.
Diego: ¡Qué lástima! ¿Va a estar bien?
Mamá: La policía 14 que sí.
Diego: Gracias por la entrevista.

3.2 DEMONSTRATIVES

In **¡DIME! UNO,** you learned that Spanish has three sets of demonstratives: one to point out someone or something *near the speaker,* another to point out someone or something *farther away,* and a third one to refer to someone or something *a good distance* from both the speaker and the listener.

Demonstratives							
	cerca		**lejos**		**más lejos**		
	m.	*f.*	*m.*	*f.*	*m.*	*f.*	
singular	este	esta	ese	esa	aquel	aquella	
plural	estos	estas	esos	esas	aquellos	aquellas	

- Demonstrative adjectives must agree in number and gender with the noun they modify and always go before the noun.

Esta loción es buena.	*This suntan lotion is good.*
¿De quién es **ese** dinero?	*Whose money is that?*
Aquella mujer es preciosa.	*That woman (over there) is lovely.*

■ Demonstratives may be used as pronouns to take the place of nouns. When they do, they reflect the number and gender of the noun they replace and require a written accent.

Este libro es más interesante
    que **ése**.

*This book is more interesting
    than that one.*

Estas arepas son mejores
    que **aquéllas.**

*These arepas are better than
    those.*

■ **Esto** and **eso** are used to refer to concepts, to ideas, and to situations, and also to things unknown to the speaker. They never require a written accent.

¿Qué es **esto**?

What is this?

Eso no puede ser.

That can't be.

Vamos a practicar

a. Fotos.   Felipe le está enseñando a su amigo Alejandro su álbum de fotos. ¿Qué dice?

MODELO   señora / tía Luisa
    Esta señora es mi tía Luisa.

1. chico / amigo Raúl
2. chicos / primos Jorge y Virginia
3. señora / tía Yolanda
4. chica / amiga Linda
5. muchachas / sobrinas Elena y Lilia
6. señor / abuelo materno

b. De compras.   Tú estás de compras en un almacén grande. ¿Qué dices al comparar estas cosas?

MODELO   **Esta guitarra es buena pero
    aquélla es buenísima.**

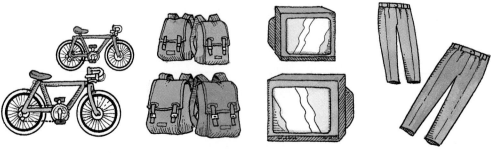

1.   2.   3.   4.

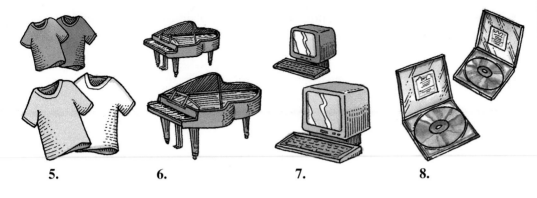

5.   **6.**   **7.**   **8.**

c. Opiniones.   Iris es una persona muy positiva y Samuel es una persona muy negativa. ¿Qué dicen ellos?

> MODELO   libro: interesante / aburrido
>   *Iris:*   **Este libro es interesante.**
>   *Samuel:*   **¿Ése? Es aburrido.**

1. clase: organizado / desorganizado
2. muebles: hermoso / feo
3. noticias: excelente / terrible
4. video: estupendo / horrible
5. idea: muy bueno / ridículo
6. carros: muy bueno / muy malo
7. doctor: simpático / antipático
8. hamburguesas: especial / ordinario

LECCIÓN 2

3.3 AFFIRMATIVE *TÚ* COMMANDS: REGULAR AND IRREGULAR

In **¡DIME!** UNO, you learned that affirmative **tú** commands are used to tell someone you normally address as **tú** to do something. You also learned that regular affirmative **tú** commands use the verb ending of the **usted / él / ella** form in the present tense:

Affirmative *Tú* Commands		
escuch**ar**	**-a**	escucha
com**er**	**-e**	come
abr**ir**	**-e**	abre

Escucha lo que te digo.	*Listen to what I tell you.*
Come tu arepa.	*Eat your arepa.*
Abre la carta.	*Open the letter.*

■ There are eight irregular affirmative **tú** commands and almost all are derived from the **yo** form of the present tense, eliminating the **-go** ending.

Irregular Affirmative *tú* Commands		
Infinitive	*Yo* Present	Command
decir	**di**go	**di**
poner	**pon**go	**pon**
salir	**sal**go	**sal**
tener	**ten**go	**ten**
venir	**ven**go	**ven**
hacer	hago	**haz**
ir	voy	**ve**
ser	soy	**sé**

¡**Di**me la verdad!	*Tell me the truth!*
Haz la tarea ahora.	*Do your homework now.*
Ponlo allí.	*Put it there.*
Ven acá.	*Come here.*

■ Object pronouns are always attached to the end of affirmative commands. Written accents may be required to preserve the original stress of the command.

Escúchame.	*Listen to me.*
Hazlo ahora.	*Do it now.*
Escríbeme pronto.	*Write to me soon.*

Vamos a practicar _____

a. ¡A trabajar!   Es tu primer día de trabajo en un restaurante. ¿Qué te dicen los otros empleados?

MODELO   trabajar más rápido
Trabaja más rápido.

1. venir al trabajo temprano
2. salir después de terminar de limpiar
3. contar los cubiertos
4. tener paciencia
5. saludar a los clientes
6. almorzar a las dos
7. ir a comprar más leche
8. decir gracias por las propinas

b. Procrastinadora. Susana siempre deja para mañana lo que debe hacer hoy. ¿Qué consejos le das?

MODELO Prefiero comenzar el trabajo mañana.
Comiénzalo ahora.

1. Prefiero escribir la composición mañana.
2. Prefiero lavar los platos mañana.
3. Prefiero limpiar la casa mañana.
4. Prefiero lavar el carro mañana.
5. Prefiero hacer la tarea mañana.
6. Prefiero leer el libro mañana.
7. Prefiero ayudarte mañana.
8. Prefiero pagar la cuenta mañana.
9. Prefiero practicar la guitarra mañana.
10. Prefiero aprender las palabras mañana.
11. Prefiero llamar a mi prima mañana.
12. Prefiero pensar en este problema mañana.

3.4 NEGATIVE TÚ COMMANDS: REGULAR AND IRREGULAR

Negative **tú** commands are formed by adding **-es** to *-ar* verbs and **-as** to *-er* and *-ir* verbs. The command ending is added to the stem of the **yo** form of present tense verbs. (The stem is the present tense form minus the **-o** ending.) The formation of negative **tú** commands is summarized in the chart below.

Infinitive	*Yo* Present	*Tú* Command
escuchar	**escuch**o	**no escuches**
pensar	**piens**o	**no pienses**
contar	**cuent**o	**no cuentes**
comer	**com**o	**no comas**
hacer	**hag**o	**no hagas**
abrir	**abr**o	**no abras**
dormir	**duerm**o	**no duermas**
pedir	**pid**o	**no pidas**
decir	**dig**o	**no digas**

No escuches.   *Don't listen.*
No cuentes con él. *Don't count on him.*
No hagas eso.   *Don't do that.*
No pidas papas.   *Don't order potatoes.*

- The following high-frequency verbs have irregular negative **tú** command forms:

Infinitive	Negative *Tú* Command
dar	**no des**
estar	**no estés**
ir	**no vayas**
ser	**no seas**

No les **des** nada.	*Don't give them anything.*
No estés triste.	*Don't be sad.*
No vayas con ellas.	*Don't go with them.*
No seas así.	*Don't be like that.*

- In negative commands, object pronouns always come directly before the verb.

¡No **me** digas!	*You don't say!*
No **la** escribas allí.	*Don't write it there.*
No **te** duermas ahora.	*Don't fall asleep now.*
No **les** hables ahora.	*Don't talk to them now.*

Vamos a practicar

a. ¿Qué hago? Es tu primer día de trabajo en un almacén. ¿Cómo te contestan los otros empleados?

MODELO ¿Trabajo en la caja?
No, no trabajes en la caja.

1. ¿Hablo mucho con los clientes?
2. ¿Voy al banco?
3. ¿Cuento el dinero?
4. ¿Escribo los precios?
5. ¿Organizo las cosas?
6. ¿Limpio el piso?
7. ¿Como al mediodía?
8. ¿Salgo a las cuatro y media?

b. Traviesa. Tienes que cuidar a una niña muy activa. ¿Qué le dices?

MODELO no tocar las fotos
No toques las fotos.

1. no jugar con el perro
2. no salir al patio
3. no ir a la tienda
4. no abrir la nevera

5. no ver ese programa
6. no hablar por teléfono
7. no poner el gato en la mesa
8. no decir nada

c. Consejos. Tu primo va a entrar en una nueva escuela. ¿Qué consejos le das?

1. llegar	**3.** hablar	**5.** dar	**7.** escribir
2. ser	**4.** estar	**6.** ir	**8.** poner

Tengo muchos buenos consejos para ayudarte en la escuela. Primero, nunca __1__ tarde a clase. Y no __2__ descortés, sobre todo con los profesores y no __3__ demasiado. Los días de exámenes, no __4__ nervioso y no le __5__ las respuestas a tus compañeros nunca. No __6__ al patio durante las clases. No __7__ en el pupitre y no __8__ chicle allí tampoco. Pero no te preocupes. Todo va a salir bien y vas a tener mucho éxito.

ch. ¿Te ayudo? Ahora estás en tu fiesta de cumpleaños y tu hermanito quiere ayudarte. ¿Qué le dices?

MODELO ¿Preparo la limonada?
No, no la prepares.

1. ¿Pongo la mesa?	**5.** ¿Paso los entremeses?
2. ¿Sirvo los nachos?	**6.** ¿Corto el pastel?
3. ¿Canto mi canción favorita?	**7.** ¿Traigo el helado?
4. ¿Toco la guitarra?	**8.** ¿Te ayudo?

3.5 USTED / USTEDES COMMANDS

Usted / ustedes commands are used with people you address as **usted** or **ustedes**. Regular affirmative and negative **usted / ustedes** commands are formed by adding **-e / -en** to *-ar* verbs and **-a / -an** to *-er* and *-ir* verbs. As with negative **tú** commands, the command ending is added to the stem of the **yo** form of present tense verbs.

Usted / Ustedes Commands			
Infinitive	**Yo** Present	**Ud.** Command	**Uds.** Command
hablar	hable	**hable**	**hablen**
cerrar	cierre	**cierre**	**cierren**
comer	come	**coma**	**coman**
tener	tenge	**tenga**	**tengan**
abrir	abre	**abra**	**abran**
salir	salge	**salga**	**salgan**

Hable con la Srta. García.	*Talk to señorita García.*
Cierre la puerta, por favor.	*Close the door, please.*
Tenga cuidado.	*Be careful.*
Pidan la paella.	*Order the paella.*
Salgan temprano.	*Leave early.*

■ The following high-frequency verbs have irregular **usted / ustedes** command forms:

Infinitive	*Usted* Command	*Ustedes* Command
dar	dé	den
estar	esté	estén
ir	vaya	vayan
ser	sea	sean

Déme los libros, por favor.   *Give me the books, please.*
Esté aquí a las dos en punto.   *Be here at two sharp.*
Vayan a verlos.   *Go see them.*
Sean buenos.   *Be good.*

■ As with **tú** commands, object pronouns precede the verb in negative commands and are attached to the end of affirmative commands. When attaching pronouns, accents are usually required to preserve the original stress of the infinitive.

Denme la bolsa de papel.   *Give me the paper bag.*
Siéntense, por favor.   *Sit down please.*
No lo **pague.**   *Don't pay it.*
No me **miren.**   *Don't look at me.*

Vamos a practicar

a. **¡Ay de mí!**   En un programa de radio varias personas hablan de sus problemas. ¿Qué les dice el locutor?

MODELO   Yo soy muy flaco porque como poco.
            La solución es fácil. ¡Coma más!

1. Soy muy tímido y hablo poco.
2. Siempre estoy cansada porque duermo poco.
3. Tengo poco dinero porque trabajo poco.
4. Estoy aburrido porque salgo poco.
5. Conozco pocos lugares porque viajo poco.
6. No soy fuerte porque hago poco ejercicio.
7. No converso bien porque leo poco.
8. Toco la guitarra mal porque practico poco.

b. **¡Sean buenos!**   Tienes que cuidar a dos niños. Su mamá te dijo lo que deben hacer. ¿Qué les dices a ellos?

MODELO   Deben venir directamente a casa.
            Vengan directamente a casa.

1. Deben comer unas frutas.
2. Deben tomar leche.
3. Deben salir a jugar un rato.
4. Deben empezar su tarea a las cuatro.
5. Deben hacer toda su tarea.
6. Deben poner la mesa.
7. Deben lavar los platos.
8. Deben limpiar su cuarto.

c. A la tienda. Papá manda a los niños a la tienda. ¿Qué les dice?

MODELO escuchar bien
Escuchen bien.

1. ir a la tienda
2. ser responsables
3. escoger frutas maduras
4. pedir carne fresca
5. pagar en la caja

6. ser simpáticos
7. saludar al cajero
8. dar el dinero al cajero
9. volver a casa directamente
10. ser buenos

ch. Primer día. Hoy Matilde empieza a trabajar de camarera. ¿Cómo contesta sus preguntas la camarera principal?

MODELO ¿Pongo la mesa?
Sí, póngala.

1. ¿Llevo un uniforme blanco?
2. ¿Saludo a los clientes?
3. ¿Traigo el menú?
4. ¿Sirvo las bebidas primero?
5. ¿Escribo la orden?
6. ¿La llevo a la cocina?
7. ¿Les sirvo inmediatamente?
8. ¿Traigo el café con el postre?
9. ¿Llevo el dinero a la caja?
10. ¿Guardo las propinas?

d. Pobre Paulina. Tu tía Paulina necesita consejos. ¿Qué le dices?

MODELO Yo como demasiado chocolate.
¡No coma tanto chocolate!

1. Hablo por teléfono demasiado.
2. Duermo demasiado.
3. Trabajo demasiadas horas.
4. Lloro demasiado.

5. Limpio la casa demasiado.
6. Bebo demasiado café.
7. Leo demasiadas revistas.
8. Veo televisión demasiado.

e. Al contrario. Tú no estás de acuerdo con los mandatos que tu hermano les da a tus amigos. ¿Qué les dices tú?

MODELO Lean mi cuento.
No lo lean.

1. Hagan mi tarea.
2. Preparen mi almuerzo.
3. Traigan los refrescos.
4. Escriban mi composición.

5. Laven mis perros.
6. Coman mi ensalada.
7. Limpien mi cuarto.
8. Saquen la basura.

¿POR QUÉ SE DICE ASÍ?

L E C C I Ó N 3

3.6 *THE IMPERFECT TENSE*

You have already learned to use the preterite tense to talk about things that happened in the past. In this lesson, you will learn another way to talk about the past, using the imperfect tense.

■ In the imperfect tense, **-ar** verbs take **-aba** verb endings and **-er** and **-ir** verbs take **-ía** endings.

Imperfect Tense		
-ar verbs	**-er and -ir verbs**	
bail**ar**	corr**er**	sal**ir**
bail**aba**	corr**ía**	sal**ía**
bail**abas**	corr**ías**	sal**ías**
bail**aba**	corr**ía**	sal**ía**
bail**ábamos**	corr**íamos**	sal**íamos**
bail**abais**	corr**íais**	sal**íais**
bail**aban**	corr**ían**	sal**ían**

The **nosotros** form of **-ar** verbs and all forms of **-er** and **-ir** verbs require written accents.

Bailábamos mucho.	*We used to dance a lot.*
Corrían todos los días.	*They ran every day.*
Salía a las cinco todos los días.	*I would leave at 5:00 every day.*

Note that the imperfect tense may be translated as *"used to," "would,"* or just the simple past tense in English.

Vamos a practicar _____

a. Antes . . .   Sarita está escuchando a sus abuelitos hablar sobre el pasado. ¿Qué comentarios hacen?

MODELO   Ahora yo no bailo pero antes . . .
   Ahora yo no bailo pero antes bailaba todos los días.

1. Ahora tu mamá no estudia . . .
2. Ahora tú no descansas mucho . . .
3. Ahora nosotros no trabajamos . . .
4. Ahora tú no lloras mucho . . .
5. Ahora yo no juego fútbol . . .
6. Ahora tu papá no toca el piano . . .
7. Ahora nosotros no escuchamos la radio . . .
8. Ahora tus padres no bailan . . .
9. Ahora yo no tomo mucho café . . .
10. Ahora tus tíos y tus tías no cantan mucho . . .

b. Y no había luz. ¿Qué estaban haciendo estas personas ayer a las cuatro de la tarde cuando cortaron la electricidad?

MODELO Manuel / leer / correo electrónico
Manuel leía su correo electrónico.

1. Raquel / instalar / monitor
2. tú / aprender / software / nuevo
3. Nela y Timoteo / comunicarse / red
4. nosotros / usar / módem
5. mis papás / desconectarse / Internet
6. yo / comprar / almohadilla
7. usted / abrir / computadora / nueva
8. el bebé / jugar / teclado
9. mi abuelo / escribir / computadora
10. mis hermanos / desconectar / cables

c. Una sorpresa. Hoy, a eso de las tres de la tarde, alguien dejó una docena de rosas muy bonitas en la puerta de la casa de los García. Ahora la señora García quiere saber por qué nadie contestó la puerta. ¿Qué hacían todos?

MODELO Clara: practicar el piano
Clara practicaba el piano.

1. yo: escribir una composición
2. mi papá: trabajar en el garaje
3. mi hermano y yo: estudiar
4. mis hermanas: escuchar música
5. mi abuelo: leer el periódico en la sala
6. mi mamá y mi tía: no estar en casa
7. tú: jugar golf
8. mi abuela: comprar algo especial para mamá
9. mi tío: dormir
10. mis primas: hablar por teléfono

3.7 REFLEXIVE VERBS

In **¡DIME!** UNO, you learned that reflexive pronouns are used when the subject and the object are identical.

Reflexive Pronouns			
yo	**me**	peino	*I comb*
tú	**te**	peinas	*you comb*
usted	**se**	peina	
él / ella	**se**	peina	*he / she / it combs*
nosotros(as)	**nos**	peinamos	*we comb*
vosotros(as)	**os**	peináis	*you comb*
ustedes	**se**	peinan	
ellos / ellas	**se**	peinan	*they comb*

Se sentaron a mi lado.	*They sat down beside me.*
El bebé **se durmió**.	*The baby went to sleep.*
Me levanté tarde hoy.	*I got up late today.*

■ Like direct and indirect object pronouns, reflexive pronouns precede conjugated verbs and negative commands but follow and are attached to affirmative commands. They may also follow and be attached to infinitives and the **-ndo** form of the verb.

Marta **se levanta** muy temprano.	*Marta gets up very early.*
Pues, **apúrate**.	*Well, hurry up.*
Lupe **está bañándose**.	*Lupe is bathing.*
Tuvieron que **acostarse** muy tarde.	*They had to go to bed very late.*
No **se duerman.**	*Don't fall asleep.*

Vamos a practicar

a. Buenos días. ¿Qué pasa por la mañana en la casa de Felipe?

MODELO todo / familia / despertarse / 6:00
Toda la familia se despierta a las seis.

1. primero / mamá / quitarse las piyamas / ponerse / bata
2. yo / bañarse / afeitarse / baño
3. todos / sentarse a / mesa / para desayunar
4. hermano / lavarse / cepillarse / pelo
5. hermanas / peinarse / su cuarto
6. yo / ponerse / jeans / camiseta
7. papá / tener que / lavarse / dientes / porque irse / 8:00
8. mis hermanos y yo / despedirse / irse a / colegio / 8:15

b. De vacaciones. ¿Cómo describe Leonor sus últimas vacaciones en una carta a su amiga Tomasita?

1. levantarse	4. arreglarse	7. sentarse	10. despedirse
2. salir	5. ponerse	8. divertirse	11. vestirse
3. bañarse	6. quemarse	9. caerse	12. acostarse

Cuando estábamos de vacaciones en la Florida, __1__ a eso de las diez de la mañana todos los días. Un poco después mis hermanos y yo __2__ al océano a jugar todas las mañanas. Mientras tanto mis papás __3__ y __4__ para el día. Antes de salir del hotel, mamá __5__ loción protectora para no __6__ en el sol. Entonces, los dos __7__ en la playa a mirarnos. Yo __8__ mucho jugando volibol. Mis hermanitos querían jugar también pero siempre __9__ y mamá les decía que no. Después yo __10__ de mis amigos y todos volvíamos al hotel para __11__. Por la tarde, hacíamos muchas cosas diferentes, y cada noche __12__ cansados pero muy contentos.

L E C C I Ó N   1

4.1 THE IMPERFECT: SER, VER, IR

There are just three irregular verbs in the imperfect.

ser	ver	ir
era	veía	iba
eras	veías	ibas
era	veía	iba
éramos	veíamos	íbamos
erais	veíais	ibais
eran	veían	iban

Éramos muy jóvenes.	*We were very young.*
La **veía** frecuentemente.	*I used to see her often.*
Iban a llamarnos.	*They were going to call us.*

Vamos a practicar

a. Los gustos. Muchas veces los programas que nos gusta ver en la televisión reflejan nuestra personalidad. ¿Cómo eran estas personas de niños y qué tipo de programas veían en la televisión?

MODELO Roque / terrible / películas de terror
Roque era terrible y siempre veía películas de terror.

1. yo / activo / programas de música rock
2. Felipe / serio / programas documentales
3. Julia y Delfina / alegre / programas musicales
4. tú / drámatico / obras de teatro
5. mis tías / sentimental / telenovelas
6. Elena / triste / películas trágicas
7. ustedes / inteligente / películas históricas
8. Marcos y yo / atléticos / programas deportivos

b. Hay que cancelar.   Ayer por la tarde estas personas tenían planes especiales, pero llovió toda la tarde y tuvieron que suspender sus planes. ¿Qué iban a hacer?

MODELO   yo
Iba a ir al parque.

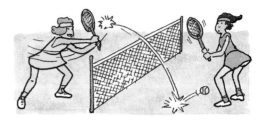

nosotras
Íbamos a jugar tenis.

1. Juana

2. los niños

3. mis amigos y yo

4. Inés y José

5. nosotras

6. tú

7. yo

8. mi familia

The imperfect is used to talk about things that happened in the past. It has several specific uses.

■ The imperfect is used to describe habitual or customary actions. It is often used with expressions such as **todos los días**, **generalmente**, **siempre**, **muchas veces**, and the like.

De niño, **jugaba** fútbol todos los sábados.	*As a kid, I used to play soccer every Saturday.*
Siempre **íbamos** a la biblioteca.	*We always used to go to the library.*
Cuando **llovía**, **veíamos** películas.	*When it rained, we would watch movies.*

■ The imperfect is used to tell time in the past.

Era mediodía y hacía mucho calor.	*It was noon and it was very hot.*
Eran las once de la noche y los niños tenían sueño.	*It was 11:00 at night and the children were sleepy.*

■ The imperfect is used to express age in the past.

Julia **tenía** siete años en 1993.	*Julia was seven in 1993.*
Todavía era fuerte cuando **tenía** setenta y cinco años.	*He was still strong when he was seventy five.*

Vamos a practicar

a. Siempre lo mismo. Andrés Salazar siempre seguía la misma rutina. ¿Qué hacía? Cambia su rutina al pasado.

Todos los días, **se levanta** temprano, **se baña** y **se viste**. Después, **va** a la cocina y **prepara** el desayuno. Mientras **toma** su café, **lee** el periódico. A las 7:30 **sale** para el trabajo. **Trabaja** toda la mañana y **almuerza** a mediodía. Después del almuerzo, **camina** y **conversa** con sus amigos. A las cinco **regresa** a casa y **hace** ejercicios. Después de cenar, **ve** televisión o **alquila** un video. **Se acuesta** a las diez y **se duerme** después de leer un poco.

b. ¡Otra vez! El timbre de tu escuela no funcionó bien todo el día. ¿Qué hora era cuando sonó?

MODELO   8:05
         Eran las ocho y cinco cuando sonó.

1. 8:30	**3.** 10:07	**5.** 12:35	**7.** 1:45
2. 9:45	**4.** 11:50	**6.** 1:20	**8.** 2:57

c. **¡Qué grandes están!** El año pasado, en la reunión de la familia Peralta, Riqui Peralta preguntó las edades de todos. Según él, ¿cuántos años tenían?

MODELO mi tío Alfredo: 35
Mi tío Alfredo tenía treinta y cinco años.

1. mi abuelo: 70
2. papá: 42
3. Pepito y Pepita: 12
4. mi tía Sara: 54
5. mi abuela materna: 63
6. mi primo José: 21
7. yo: 15
8. mamá y mi tía Josefa: 37

ch. **De niño.** David acaba de escribirle a su amigo por correspondencia. ¿Qué le dice de su niñez? Completa su carta con el imperfecto de los verbos indicados.

1. ser
2. ser
3. vivir
4. ir
5. tomar

6. jugar
7. encantar
8. llegar
9. regresar
10. tener

> Querido Samuel,
>
>   Cuando yo (1) niño, mi vida (2) muy diferente. Nosotros (3) en Maracaibo y mi hermana y yo (4) a la playa todos los días de vacaciones. Allí (5) el sol y (6) en el lago. Nos (7) el agua. (8) muy temprano y no (9) a casa hasta muy tarde. Cuando (10) diez años, nos mudamos a Caracas y todo cambió.

4.3 *HACER* TO EXPRESS *AGO*

To express the concept of *ago*, Spanish uses the verb **hacer** in the following structure:

> **hace** + *[time]* + *[preterite or imperfect]*

Hace muchos años **construyó** la jaula.	*He built the cage many years ago.*
Hace dos meses **compraba** leche en polvo.	*I was buying powdered milk two months ago.*

a. De otra parte. Todos los vecinos de la Calle Montemayor vinieron de otra ciudad. Según Pablo, ¿cuánto tiempo hace que se mudaron para acá?

MODELO   5 años: los Bermúdez
> **Hace cinco años vinieron los Bermúdez.**

1. 3 años: la familia Alarcón
2. 7 años: los Méndez
3. 2 años: el señor Fuentes
4. 1 año: los Vega

5. 15 años: la señora Estrada
6. 6 años: mis tíos
7. 1 año: nosotros
8. 11 años: las hermanas Robledo

b. Prodigiosa. Cecilia sólo tiene doce años pero aprendió a hacer muchas cosas a una edad muy temprana. ¿Cuánto tiempo hace que aprendió a hacer estas cosas?

MODELO   2 años / aprender / tocar / guitarra / clásico
> **Hace dos años aprendía a tocar la guitarra clásica.**

1. 5 años / escribir / primer poema / portugués
2. 7 años / empezar / cantar ópera / italiano
3. 8 años / ganar / trofeo / natación
4. 1 año / construir / bicicleta
5. 3 años / aprender / hablar / japonés
6. 4 años / leer / *Don Quijote*
7. 6 años / preparar / primera paella
8. 9 años / comenzar / usar / computadora

L E C C I Ó N 2

4.4   USES OF THE IMPERFECT: CONTINUING ACTIONS

■ Past actions may be viewed as either completed or continuing. Those seen as continuing or in progress are expressed in the imperfect.

Hablaban mientras **caminaban**.	*They were talking while they were walking.*
Hacía su tarea a esa hora.	*He was doing his homework at that hour.*

■ Sometimes a continuing action is interrupted by another action. In this case the continuing action is expressed in the imperfect and the interrupting action is in the preterite.

Abuelita **llamó** mientras **comíamos.**	*Grandma called while we were eating.*
Jugaba muy bien cuando **chocó** con un defensor.	*He was playing very well when he ran into a guard.*

Vamos a practicar

a. Una visita inesperada. Según Rebeca, ¿qué hacían ella y su familia el domingo por la tarde cuando de repente llegaron sus abuelos?

el bebé

MODELO **El bebé tomaba leche.**

1. Claudio

2. Estela y Susana

3. Mamá y yo

4. Papá

5. los gatitos

6. yo

7. mis primos

8. el perro

b. Día de limpieza.   Una vez al año todos los estudiantes de la señora Gutiérrez ayudaban a limpiar la escuela. ¿Qué hacía cada uno?

MODELO   Marta: limpiar las ventanas
Pedro: pintar las paredes
Marta limpiaba las ventanas mientras Pedro pintaba las paredes.

1. Paco: barrer el pasillo
Begoña: limpiar los baños
2. Chavela: sacar la basura
yo: vaciar los basureros
3. tú: pasar la aspiradora
el profesor: mover los muebles
4. la profesora: guardar los libros
Laura y Raúl: pasar un trapo
a los muebles

5. Jacobo: preparar limonada
Esther: hacer sándwiches
6. Concepción: limpiar los escritorios
Mateo: lavar las pizarras
7. Jerónimo: cortar el césped
ustedes: barrer el patio
8. la secretaria: organizar los gabinetes
el director: supervisar

c. ¡Caramba!   Germán dice que nadie pudo terminar lo que hacía porque hubo muchas interrupciones. ¿Qué pasó?

MODELO   yo / escribir una carta / cuando el perro / entrar
Yo escribía una carte cuando el perro entró.

1. Mamá / leer el periódico / cuando Luisito / apagar las luces
2. Toño y yo / estudiar para un examen / cuando Olga / llamar
3. Pablo / hacer la tarea / cuando el perro / desenchufar la computadora
4. Jaime y Gloria / jugar tenis / cuando empezar a llover
5. el bebé / dormir / cuando papá / abrir la puerta
6. nosotros / limpiar la casa / cuando nuestros abuelos / llegar
7. Luisito / ver un programa de niños / cuando papá / cambiar el canal
8. mi tía / calificar exámenes / cuando el bebé / comenzar a gritar

4.5   USES OF THE PRETERITE: COMPLETED ACTIONS AND BEGINNING OR ENDING ACTIONS

The preterite is used to express past actions viewed as a completed whole. Words which specify a limited time period are frequently associated with the preterite. Some typical words are **ayer, el lunes, el fin de semana pasado, un día, una vez.**

Ayer **cenamos** temprano.

Leí la lección antes de la clase.

Hicimos muchas cosas durante las vacaciones: **nadamos**, **visitamos** a los abuelos y **fuimos** a acampar.

Yesterday we ate supper early.

I read the lesson before class.

We did a lot of things during vacation: we swam, visited our grandparents, and went camping.

The preterite is used to focus attention on the beginning or the end of a past action.

Focus on beginning:

Comimos a las 6:00.	*We ate at 6:00.*
De repente **brilló** el sol.	*Suddenly the sun began to shine.*
Irma **habló** a los diez meses.	*Irma started to talk at ten months.*

Focus on end:

Regresó muy tarde.	*He returned very late.*
La clase **terminó** a la una.	*Class ended at one.*
Pasó la tormenta.	*The storm ended.*

Vamos a practicar

a. ¡Otro año más!   El sábado pasado fue el cumpleaños de Antonio. ¿Qué hicieron él y sus amigos para celebrarlo?

MODELO   mis amigos y yo
Fuimos al cine.

1. yo

2. mis amigos y yo

3. el guitarrista

4. el camarero

5. mis amigos

6. yo

7. todos

8. Susana y yo

b. **Una visita especial.**   El viernes pasado el director de la compañía de papá vino a cenar a nuestra casa. Según Rosa, ¿qué hicieron todos en preparación?

1. Carmelita: contar los cubiertos, poner la mesa, limpiar su cuarto
2. Papa: comprar las bebidas, lavar el carro, cortar el césped
3. yo: sacar la basura, pasar la aspiradora, hacer las camas
4. Rogelio: barrer el patio, dar de comer al perro, limpiar las ventanas
5. Mamá: preparar la comida, lavar y secar los platos elegantes
6. los abuelos: pasar un trapo a los muebles, comprar flores, decorar la mesa

c. **¡Ay de mí!**   Catalina pasó un día muy malo ayer. ¿Por qué?

1. salir	**4.** chocar	**7.** seguir	**10.** encontrar
2. terminar	**5.** lastimarse	**8.** llegar	**11.** empezar
3. montarse	**6.** levantarse	**9.** abrir	**12.** regresar

Catalina (1) corriendo del colegio a la 1:00 porque su clase (2) tarde y tenía mucha hambre. (3) en su bicicleta para ir a su casa. En el camino (4) con otra bicicleta pero, por suerte, no (5) . Sin llorar, (6) y (7) rápidamente a casa. Cuándo (8) Catalina, (9) la puerta y no (10) a nadie en la casa. (11) a llorar. Y todavía lloraba cuando su mamá (12) a casa. ¡Pobrecita!

¿POR QUÉ SE DICE ASÍ?

4.6 STEM-CHANGING *-IR* VERBS IN THE PRETERITE: *E → I and O → U*

You have learned that stem-changing verbs that end in **-ir** undergo stem changes in the preterite. In these verbs, **e** becomes **i** and **o** becomes **u** in the **usted /él / ella** and **ustedes / ellos / ellas** forms. There are no **-ar** or **-er** verbs with a stem change in the preterite.

pedir (e → i)	
pedí	pedimos
pediste	pedisteis
pidió	pidieron

morir (o → u)	
morí	morimos
moriste	moristeis
murió	murieron

Murieron pocas personas en el accidente.

Few people died in the accident.

Pidió una hamburguesa pero le **sirvieron** una ensalada.

She ordered a hamburger but they brought her a salad.

The following is a list of common stem-changing **-ir** verbs. Note that the letters in parentheses indicate respective stem changes in the present tense and in the preterite.

e → i (present and preterite)	
conseguir (i, i)	*to get, obtain*
pedir (i, i)	*to ask for*
reírse (i, i)	*to laugh*
repetir (i, i)	*to repeat*
seguir (i, i)	*to follow*
vestirse (i, i)	*to get dressed*

e → ie (present), e → i (preterite)	
divertirse (ie, i)	*to have a good time*
preferir (ie, i)	*to prefer*
sentir (ie, i)	*to feel*

o → ue (present), o → u (preterite)	
dormir (ue, u)	*to sleep*
morir (ue, u)	*to die*

a. Exploradores. ¿Cuándo murieron estos exploradores?

MODELO Vasco Núñez de Balboa, 1519
Vasco Núñez de Balboa murió en mil quinientos diez y nueve.

1. Juan Ponce de León, 1521   **5.** Francisco de Orellana, 1546
2. Diego de Almagro, 1538   **6.** Hernán Cortés, 1547
3. Francisco Pizarro, 1541   **7.** Pedro de Valdivia, 1554
4. Hernando de Soto, 1542   **8.** Alvar Núñez Cabeza de Vaca, 1557

b. Lo de siempre. Ayer fue un día normal en el restaurante donde trabaja Diana. Según esta descripción de su rutina, describe lo que pasó ayer. Cambia los verbos del presente al pretérito.

Llega a las cuatro y **busca** su uniforme. **Se viste** y **sale** a trabajar. **Saluda** a los clientes y ellos la **siguen** a la mesa. Después de darles la carta, Diana les **sirve** agua y **toma** su orden. Para estar segura, **repite** la orden de cada persona. Entonces les **sirve** la comida que **piden**. Ella **se divierte** en su trabajo y **recibe** buenas propinas. Al llegar a casa, **cena, se acuesta** y **se duerme** en seguida, muy cansada pero contenta.

L E C C I Ó N   3

4.7 *USES OF THE IMPERFECT: DESCRIPTION*

■ In addition to describing habitual actions, telling time in the past and talking about age in the past, the imperfect is used when describing an ongoing situation, and physical, emotional or mental states. Generally, possession and physical location are considered ongoing situations and the imperfect is used.

Ongoing situations:

Tenía muchos amigos.	*I had a lot of friends.*
Había muchas carpetas en el pupitre.	*There were a lot of folders on the desk.*
La jaula **estaba** en el jardín.	*The cage was in the garden.*

Physical, emotional or mental states:

Tenía dolor de cabeza.	*I had a headache.*
Ese invierno mamá no **se sentía** bien.	*That winter Mom didn't feel well.*
Yo lo **amaba**, pero él ya no me **quería.**	*I loved him, but he no longer loved me.*
Estaba nerviosísima.	*She was really nervous.*
Estábamos aburridos.	*We were bored.*

■ The imperfect is frequently used to provide the background for other imperfect or preterite actions. It describes what was happening before other actions began.

Había una vez una viejita que no **confiaba** en nadie. Un día **decidió** poner todo su dinero en. . .	*Once upon a time there was a little old lady who didn't trust anybody. One day she decided to put all her money in. . .*

Vamos a practicar

a. ¡Qué cansados!   Nadie durmió bien anoche. ¿Por qué?

MODELO   Patricia: estar nervioso
Patricia estaba nerviosa.

1. Fernando: no estar cansado
2. Estela y Ramón: tener mucha tarea
3. yo: tener que leer un libro muy interesante
4. mi papá: no tener sueño
5. ustedes: estar preocupado
6. nosotros: no sentirse bien
7. Luisita: tener miedo
8. Amalia: pensar en su novio

b. Reacciones.   Describe el estado emocional o físico que las siguientes personas tenían ayer.

MODELO   Sofía y Federico sacaron una F en el examen. (contento / triste)
Estaban tristes.

1. Nosotros corrimos cinco millas. (cansado / furioso)
2. Rosa María y Jaime iban a tomar un examen. (nervioso / aburrido)
3. Leonor vio una serpiente. (asustado / contento)
4. Enriqueta y Rodrigo recibieron buenas notas. (preocupado / emocionado)
5. Alejandro no tenía nada que hacer. (asombrado / aburrido)
6. Elena perdió su dinero. (tranquilo / desesperado)
7. Perdimos el partido. (furioso / contento)
8. Pedro pasó todo el día en el parque. (asustado / tranquilo)

c. En el campamento. Pedro escribió esta descripción. Ahora la quiere cambiar al pasado para usarla en un cuento. ¿Cómo la cambia?

> **Estoy** descansando debajo de un árbol. **Es** un día muy bonito; **hace** mucho sol y un calorcito muy agradable. Algunos compañeros **están** ocupados. Unos **preparan** la comida mientras que otros **ponen** la mesa o **duermen** la siesta. Nadie **habla** y el silencio **es** tranquilizador. Todos **estamos** muy contentos.

ch. La familia Vargas. Vas a escribir un cuento sobre la familia Vargas. Escribe el primer párrafo usando las expresiones que siguen.

MODELO   afuera: hacer mal tiempo, llover
Afuera hacía mal tiempo. Llovía mucho.

1. en la sala: leer el periódico, jugar
2. en una alcoba: dormir
3. en el cuarto de baño: peinarse
4. en la cocina: preparar la cena, hacer limonada
5. en el comedor: poner la mesa
6. en otra alcoba: escribir cartas, descansar

4.8 NARRATING IN THE PAST: IMPERFECT AND PRETERITE

When talking about the past, it is common to use both the imperfect and preterite in the same paragraph. The uses you have been studying determine which one should be used.

The imperfect is used to describe past actions that are . . .	The preterite is used to describe past actions that are . . .
1. viewed as continuous or in progress. 2. habitual.	1. viewed as completed. 2. focused on the beginning or end of the actions.

The difference between the preterite and imperfect is similar to the difference between seeing a series of snapshots and watching a video. The preterite is like a snapshot, which reduces an event to a single moment. The imperfect is more like a video, which captures the ongoing nature of a past event.

Note the use of both the preterite and the imperfect in the following paragraph.

Un día cuando **hacía** muy buen tiempo, la abuela **decidió** ir al banco a depositar su dinero. Con mucho cuidado lo **sacó** del colchón y lo **metió** en una bolsa de papel. **Salió** camino al banco, pero como **hacía** tan buen tiempo, **se sentó** a comer en el parque. Mientras **comía**, **tomaba** el sol y **pensaba** en su decisión.

One day when the weather was good, the grandmother decided to go to the bank to deposit her money. Very carefully she took it out of the mattress and put it in a paper bag. She headed for the bank, but since it was a beautiful day, she sat down to eat in the park. While she ate, she enjoyed the sun and thought about her decision.

Vamos a practicar _____

a. ¡Una sorpresa! David está describiendo una experiencia especial. ¿Qué dice?

Cuando (**era / fui**) niño, cada año en el mes de agosto (**iba / fui**) a visitar a mi abuelo. Él (**era / fue**) viudo y (**vivía / vivió**) solo en un rancho lejos de mi casa. Yo siempre (**tenía / tuve**) que pasar seis horas en el autobús para llegar a su casa. Me (**gustaba / gustó**) estar con él porque (**sabía / supo**) mucho y me (**enseñaba / enseñó**) muchas cosas del rancho. Yo siempre le (**ayudaba / ayudé**) con los quehaceres. (**Limpiaba / Limpié**) los corrales y le (**daba / di**) de comer a los animales.

Un agosto, cuando (**tenía / tuve**) ocho años, (**pasaba / pasó**) algo muy especial. Cuando (**llegaba / llegué**) al rancho, mi abuelo me (**llevaba / llevó**) al corral. Un caballo nuevo (**estaba / estuvo**) allí. (**Era / Fue**) pequeño y negro y muy bonito. ¡Y qué sorpresa! Mi abuelo me (**decía / dijo**): "Este caballo es tuyo". Yo no (**sabía / supe**) qué decir. Mi abuelo me (**ayudaba / ayudó**) a subir y (**empezaba / empezó**) a enseñarme a montar a caballo. (**Pasaba / Pasé**) todo el mes con mi caballo. (**Me divertía / Me divertí**) mucho ese verano.

b. Caperucita Roja. Éste es un cuento muy conocido. Cuéntalo en el pasado.

Hay una niña muy bonita y simpática que siempre **lleva** puesta una caperuza roja, y por eso se **llama** Caperucita Roja. Un día **descubre** que su abuela **está** enferma y **decide** llevarle unas frutas. En una canasta **pone** manzanas, naranjas y bananas y **sale** para la casa de su abuela. **Lleva** puesta su caperucita roja, por supuesto. En el camino un lobo (un animal muy feroz) **se acerca** a la niña y le **pregunta**:

—¿Adónde vas, preciosa?

La niña **responde**:

—A casa de mi abuela. Le llevo estas frutas porque está enferma. —y ella se **va**.

Cuando Caperucita **llega**, **encuentra** a su abuela muy diferente. **Tiene** los ojos, la nariz y la boca muy grandes. En muy poco tiempo **sabe** que no **es** su abuela.

—**Es** el lobo. **Grita** y grita.

En pocos minutos **viene** un cazador y **salva** a la niña. Después **encuentran** a la abuela en el armario. Ella **está** asustada pero bien.

LECCIÓN 1

5.1 PRESENT SUBJUNCTIVE: FORMS AND OJALÁ

The verb tenses you have been using up until now belong to the **Indicative Mode**. Verb tenses in the indicative mode are used to express what we know or believe to be true or factual. There is another mode, the **Subjunctive Mode**, which consists of verb tenses used to talk about things which are not facts, such as hopes, persuasion, doubt, emotion and the like.

Following are the **-ar**, **-er**, and **-ir** endings for the present subjunctive tense.

Present Subjunctive		
-ar **nadar**	**-er** **aprender**	**-ir** **salir**
nade	aprenda	salga
nades	aprendas	salgas
nade	aprenda	salga
nademos	aprendamos	salgamos
nadéis	aprendáis	salgáis
naden	aprendan	salgan

Ojalá que **nademos** hoy.   *I hope we swim today.*
Ojalá que **salgan** temprano.   *I hope they leave early.*

■ Note that the theme vowels of the present subjunctive are the exact opposites of the present indicative:

Theme Vowels		
Verbs	Present Indicative	Present Subjunctive
-ar	-a ⟶	-e
-er, -ir	-e ⟶	-a

Present Subjunctive:
-ar: **-e, -es, -e, -emos, -éis, -en**
-er, -ir: **-a, -as, -a, -amos, -áis, -an**

You may also recognize the subjunctive endings as identical to the endings you learned for **Ud. / Uds.** and **tú** negative commands.

■ The present subjunctive makes use of the stem of the **yo** form in the present indicative.

Yo Present Indicative	Present Subjunctive
trabaj**o**	trabaj**e**, trabaj**es**, trabaj**e**, trabaj**emos** . . .
teng**o**	teng**a**, teng**as**, teng**a**, teng**amos**, teng**áis**, . . .
dig**o**	dig**o**, dig**as**, dig**a**, dig**amos**, dig**áis**, dig**an**

The present subjunctive is always used after the expression **ojalá (que)**, which came to Spanish from an Arabic expression meaning "May Allah grant that." In modern Spanish it means *I hope (that)* . . .

Ojalá que no me **pase** otra   *I hope it doesn't happen to*
  vez.   *me again.*
Ojalá saques buenas notas.   *I hope you get good grades.*

■ Note that the use of **que** is optional after **ojalá.**

■ Two useful expressions are **Ojalá que sí** *(I hope so)* and **Ojalá que no** *(I hope not).*

—¿Vamos a perder?   *Are we going to lose?*
—**Ojalá que no**.   *I hope not.*
—¿Vas a jugar tú?   *Are you going to play?*
—**Ojalá que sí**.   *I hope so.*

Vamos a practicar

a. Galletas.   ¿Qué dicen tus amigos cuando ven sus fortunas en las galletas chinas al terminar de comer en un restaurante chino?

MODELO   Vas a vivir muchos años.
      Ojalá que viva muchos años.

1. Vas a hablar muchas lenguas.
2. Vas a viajar por el mundo entero.
3. Vas a conocer a muchas personas famosas.
4. Vas a cenar en París pronto.
5. Vas a ganar un millón de dólares.
6. Vas a tener buena suerte en el amor.

b. De vacaciones.   ¿Qué deseos tienen tú y tus amigos para las vacaciones de invierno?

MODELO   descansar mucho
      Ojalá que descansemos mucho.

1. recibir muchas cartas   5. salir todos los días
2. esquiar   6. bailar mucho
3. trabajar poco   7. comer bien
4. visitar a muchos parientes   8. viajar a otro país

UNIDAD

5

c. El porvenir. ¿Esperas tener estas cosas en el futuro?

MODELO ¿Un coche grande?
Ojalá que sí. o **Ojalá que no.**

1. ¿Poco dinero?
2. ¿Cinco perros y cinco gatos?
3. ¿Una profesión importante?
4. ¿Un(a) esposo(a) famoso(a)?
5. ¿Una casa en el campo?
6. ¿Muchos hijos?

5.2 PRESENT SUBJUNCTIVE: IRREGULAR VERBS

The following verbs have irregular forms in the present subjunctive.

Present Subjunctive: Irregular Verbs					
dar	estar	ir	saber	ser	ver
dé	esté	vaya	sepa	sea	vea
des	estés	vayas	sepas	seas	veas
dé	esté	vaya	sepa	sea	vea
demos	estemos	vayamos	sepamos	seamos	veamos
deis	estéis	vayáis	sepáis	seáis	veáis
den	estén	vayan	sepan	sean	vean

Ojalá que **vayamos** a Italia.   *I hope we go to Italy.*
Ojalá que **sepan** esto.   *I hope they know this.*
Ojalá que no **sea** mañana.   *I hope it's not tomorrow.*

■ The present subjunctive of **hay** (*haber*) is **haya**.

Ojalá **haya** bastante tiempo.   *I hope there is enough time.*
Ojalá que no **haya** examen hoy.   *I hope there isn't an exam today.*

Vamos a practicar

a. Nuevos alumnos. Pepito y Pepita empezaron la escuela hoy y su mamá está preocupada. ¿Qué dice ella?

MODELO estar bien
Ojalá que estén bien.

1. saber su dirección y teléfono
2. dar la información correcta a la maestra
3. ir directamente al patio para el recreo
4. haber buena comida en la cafetería
5. saber dónde esperarme después de las clases
6. no haber problemas con los otros niños
7. ser buenos
8. estar contentos

¿POR QUÉ SE DICE ASÍ?

b. ¡Una fiesta! Ramona está muy emocionada porque va a una fiesta esta noche. ¿Qué está pensando?

MODELO   haber buena comida
          ¡Ojalá que haya buena comida!

1. todos mis amigos estar allí
2. mi vestido ser bastante elegante
3. todos saber la dirección
4. Pablo ir a la fiesta
5. yo dar una buena impresión
6. haber otras fiestas grandes este año
7. la música ser buena
8. dar regalos a los invitados

5.3 THE PRESENT SUBJUNCTIVE: IMPERSONAL EXPRESSIONS

Impersonal expressions are expressions that do not have a specific subject. The verb **Es** *(It is)* followed by an adjective forms a large number of impersonal expressions in Spanish.

> **Es** + *adjective* = impersonal expression

When impersonal expressions that express a certainty are followed by a conjugated verb, the conjugated verb is always expressed in an indicative tense.

Es cierto que **tiene** mucho dinero.	*It is true that he has a lot of money.*
Es verdad que **llegan** esta tarde.	*It is true that they arrive this afternoon.*
Es verdad que **vino** ayer.	*It is true she came yesterday.*

The following is a list of common impersonal expressions of certainty:

es cierto	*it is certain, true*
es claro	*it is clear*
es obvio	*it is obvious*
es seguro	*it is sure*
es verdad	*it is true*

All other impersonal expressions followed by a conjugated verb require that the conjugated verb be in the subjunctive.

Es terrible que **me duerma** en clase.	*It's awful that I fall asleep in class.*
Es posible que **necesites** hacer más ejercicio.	*It's possible that you need to exercise more.*
Es importante que **entreguen** toda la tarea.	*It's important for you to turn in all your homework.*

■ Note that impersonal expressions are always connected to the conjugated verb with the conjunction **que**. This is always the case when you have a change of subject — two conjugated verbs in a sentence, each with their own subject.

The following is a list of common impersonal expressions that require the subjunctive:

es bueno	*it is good*
es mejor	*it is better*
es fantástico	*it is fantastic*
es terrible	*it is terrible*
es triste	*it is sad*
es curioso	*it is odd*
es dudoso	*it is doubtful*
es posible	*it is possible*
es imposible	*it is impossible*
es probable	*it is probable*
es improbable	*it is improbable*
es importante	*it is important*
es necesario	*it is necessary*
es preciso	*it is necessary*
es recomendable	*it is recommendable*

Vamos a practicar

a. La buena salud. Manuel está estudiando la salud en la escuela y todos los días le dice a su mamá lo que deben hacer para tener buena salud. ¿Qué le dice a su mamá?

MODELO hacer ejercicio (importante)
        Es importante que hagamos ejercicio.

1. ver televisión todo el día (malo)
2. correr (recomendable)
3. practicar deportes (bueno)
4. ir al médico una vez al año (importante)
5. descansar bastante (necesario)
6. cambiar de rutina de vez en cuando (preferible)
7. comer frutas y vegetales (importante)
8. beber muchos líquidos (bueno)
9. caminar mucho (necesario)
10. salir más (recomendable)
11. no fumar (importante)
12. ser activo (mejor)

b. Invitados. La familia Ramírez tiene invitados esta noche. Según la mamá, ¿qué deben hacer todos para ayudarle con las preparaciones?

yo

MODELO   **Es necesario que yo haga las camas.**

1. Gloria

2. Diego

3. Papá

4. Diego y yo

5. Abuelita

6. los niños

7. Papá

8. tú

¿POR QUÉ SE DICE ASÍ?

c. El partido. Hoy hay un partido de fútbol. ¿Qué opina Rosa María del partido?

MODELO   necesario / todos / jugadores / llegar temprano
Es necesario que todos los jugadores lleguen temprano.

1. importante / aficionados / gritar mucho
2. dudoso / otro equipo / ser / muy bueno
3. terrible / Lilia Gómez / estar / enfermo
4. probable / Tania / meter / mucho / goles
5. increíble / haber / tanto / aficionados / aquí
6. bueno / jugadores / escuchar / instrucciones del entrenador
7. fantástico / banda / tocar / hoy
8. probable / nosotros / ganar / partido

ch. Una fiesta. Estás invitado(a) a una fiesta este fin de semana. ¿Cómo contestas estas preguntas de tu hermanito(a)?

EJEMPLO   ¿Van a traer pizza?
Es probable que traigan pizza.

VOCABULARIO ÚTIL:

dudoso	horrible	ridículo	imposible
fantástico	importante	posible	probable

1. ¿Van a tocar música clásica?
2. ¿Va a haber mucha comida?
3. ¿Van a bailar el tango?
4. ¿Vas a saludar a todo el mundo?
5. ¿Va a haber alguien que toque la guitarra?
6. ¿Van a beber leche?
7. ¿Vas a traer los refrescos?
8. ¿Van a ir todos tus amigos?

d. ¡Qué bueno! Hay una nueva escuela en tu ciudad. ¿Cómo reaccionas a estos comentarios sobre la escuela?

EJEMPLO   Sólo hay diez estudiantes por clase.
Es bueno que sólo haya diez estudiantes por clase.
Es dudoso que sólo haya diez estudiantes por clase.

1. Los estudiantes van a casa para almorzar.
2. Los profesores son inteligentísimos.
3. No hay biblioteca.
4. La directora sabe hablar cinco lenguas.
5. Los consejeros conocen bien a todos los estudiantes.
6. Todos tienen que estar en clase a las siete de la mañana.
7. Las clases terminan a las dos de la tarde.
8. El gimnasio es enorme.
9. Los estudiantes siempre hacen excursiones los viernes.
10. Los equipos de fútbol y baloncesto nunca practican.

LECCIÓN 2

5.4 EXPRESSIONS OF PERSUASION

You previously learned that sentences having two conjugated verbs and a change of subject require the conjunction **que** between the two verbs. It may help to think of the two parts of subject-change sentences as a truck and trailer rig with **que** being the connecting hitch. The two parts of the sentence, the one beginning with **que** and the one preceding it, are called the dependent and independent clauses, respectively. Note that like the truck below, the independent clause can function as an independent sentence. The dependent clause depends on the other clause to function, just as the trailer depends on the truck to pull it.

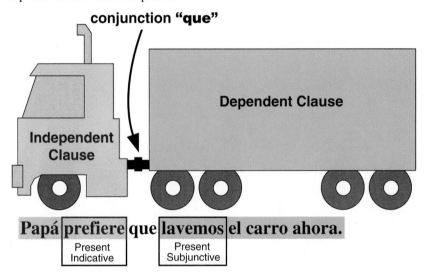

conjunction "que"

Dependent Clause

Independent Clause

Papá | prefiere | que | lavemos | el carro ahora.

Present Indicative

Present Subjunctive

The present subjunctive is used after expressions of persuasion, when someone is advising, insisting on, recommending, suggesting, etc. a certain course of action to someone else.

¿Por qué **insisten en que vaya?**	*Why do you insist that I go?*
Recomiendo que sigan mis consejos.	*I recommend that you follow my advice.*
Sugerimos que eviten las comidas grasosas.	*We suggest that you avoid greasy foods.*

Here are some common verbs of persuasion:

aconsejar	*to advise*
insistir en	*to insist (on)*
pedir (e → i)	*to ask (a favor)*
preferir (e → ie, i)	*to prefer*
querer (e → ie)	*to want (someone to do something)*
recomendar (e → ie)	*to recommend*
sugerir (e → ie, i)	*to suggest*

Vamos a practicar

a. Mucho trabajo. Raúl tiene que ayudar mucho en casa. ¿En qué insisten sus padres?

MODELO lavar los platos
Insisten en que lave los platos.

1. hacer la cama
2. pasar el trapo a los muebles
3. pasar la aspiradora
4. sacar la basura

5. poner la mesa
6. cortar el césped
7. barrer el patio
8. planchar su ropa

b. Están aburridos. Cuando estas personas están aburridas, ¿qué sugieres tú que hagan?

MODELO **Sugiero que corran.**

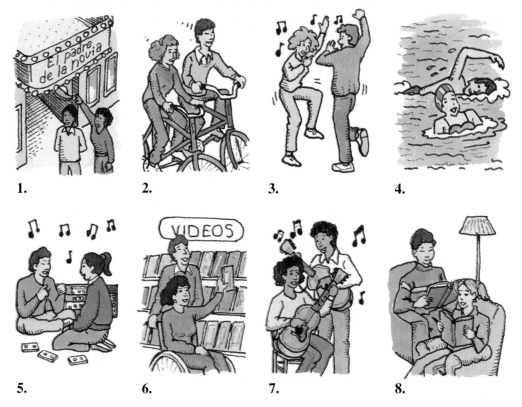

1.

2.

3.

4.

5.

6.

7.

8.

¿POR QUÉ SE DICE ASÍ?

c. Banquete internacional. El club de español va a tener un programa internacional. ¿Qué quiere la profesora que hagan todos?

MODELO recomendar / Pancho / limpiar / sala
    Recomienda que Pancho limpie la sala.

1. querer / tú / escribir / invitación
2. sugerir / Rosa y yo / comprar / refrescos
3. insistir en / todos / llevar / ropa / típico
4. pedir / Carlota y Eugenio / cantar / canciones
5. preferir / yo / recibir / invitados
6. querer / ustedes / poner / mesas
7. recomendar / Hugo / preparar / comida
8. preferir / Soledad y Benito / traer / música
9. aconsejar / nosotros / practicar / bailes
10. querer / todos / llegar temprano
11. pedir / yo / ayudar / con los refrescos
12. sugerir / todos / participar / programa

5.5 PRESENT SUBJUNCTIVE: -AR AND -ER STEM-CHANGING VERBS

The stem-changing **-ar** and **-er** verbs you learned in the present indicative undergo the same pattern of changes in the present subjunctive.

Present Subjunctive: Stem-Changing Verbs	
pensar e → ie	**poder** o → ue
piense	**pueda**
pienses	**puedas**
piense	**pueda**
pensemos	podamos
penséis	podáis
piensen	**puedan**

Es importante que **pienses** mucho.
 It is important for you to think hard.

Es posible que **podamos** salir esta noche.
 It's possible that we can go out tonight.

Vamos a practicar

a. Cambios. El instructor de la clase de aeróbicos tiene unas sugerencias para toda la clase. ¿Cuáles son?

MODELO   recomendar: despertarse temprano
Recomienda que se despierten temprano.

1. aconsejar: empezar el día con ejercicios
2. recomendar: no sentarse por mucho tiempo seguido
3. insiste en: pensar en la salud cada día
4. recomendar: almorzar bien
5. querer: probar nuevos vegetales
6. sugerir: jugar tenis o volibol
7. preferir: acostarse temprano
8. aconsejar: recordar sus consejos

b. ¡Buena salud! Los padres de Susana y Miguel son fanáticos para la buena salud. ¿Qué dice Miguel de sus padres?

MODELO   sugerir / toda la familia / perder peso
Sugieren que toda la familia pierda peso.

1. insistir en / hijos / despertarse / más temprano
2. aconsejar / Susana y yo / comenzar / clase de karate
3. recomendar / abuelos / acostarse / más temprano
4. preferir / yo / sentarse al escritorio / para estudiar
5. querer / bebé / jugar con / otro / juguetes
6. insistir en / niños / pensar más en / lecciones
7. aconsejar / todos nosotros / empezar a / caminar juntos
8. recomendar / Susana / almorzar / comida / nutritivo

c. ¡Anímate! El profesor Martínez está calificando los exámenes finales. ¿Cómo contestaron estos estudiantes la pregunta sobre una chica que se siente muy triste y aburrida?

EJEMPLO   comenzar el día con un buen desayuno.
Aconsejo que comience el día con un buen desayuno. o
Es importante que comience el día con un buen desayuno.

VOCABULARIO ÚTIL:

aconsejar	ser importante	ser necesario
recomendar	ser mejor	sugerir

1. sentarse a planear unos cambios en tu rutina
2. perder un poco de peso
3. probar unos deportes nuevos
4. encontrar una buena clase de aeróbicos
5. empezar unos nuevos proyectos
6. jugar tenis conmigo todos los días
7. almorzar con tus amigos los sábados
8. pensar más en cosas positivas

The **e → i** stem-changing **-ir** verbs you learned in the present indicative undergo the same change in the present subjunctive, but in all persons.

Present Subjunctive: Stem-Changing -ir Verbs	
pedir e → i	seguir e → i
pida	siga
pidas	sigas
pida	siga
pidamos	sigamos
pidáis	sigáis
pidan	sigan

Es probable que **pidan** el cochinillo asado.

It is likely they will order the roast suckling pig.

Es importante que **sigas** mis consejos.

It's important that you follow my advice.

The **e → ie** and **o → ue** stem-changing **-ir** verbs you learned in the present indicative undergo the following changes in the present subjunctive: e → ie, i; o → ue, u.

Present Subjunctive: Stem-Changing -ir Verbs	
divertir e → ie, i	dormir o → ue, u
divierta	duerma
diviertas	duermas
divierta	duerma
divirtamos	durmamos
divirtáis	durmáis
diviertan	duerman

Es probable que **nos divirtamos**.

It's likely that we'll have a good time

Es recomendable que **durmamos** ocho horas.

It's recommended that we sleep eight hours.

Vamos a practicar

a. Un banquete. Estás hablando de un banquete este fin de semana. ¿Qué dices?

VOCABULARIO ÚTIL:

es importante   recomiendo   es dudoso   ojalá

EJEMPLO   nosotros: conseguir una buena mesa.
Ojalá que nosotros consigamos una buena mesa.

1. nosotros: pedir una mesa cerca de la mesa principal
2. ellos: no repetir el programa del año pasado
3. ellos: servir comida rica
4. todos: vestir elegantemente
5. la directora: seguir las recomendaciones de los estudiantes
6. ellos: conseguir unos buenos músicos
7. mis amigos: pedir sus canciones favoritas
8. los profesores: servir los refrescos

b. Una cita. Julio quiere invitar a Susana a salir a comer a un nuevo restaurante. ¿Qué consejos le da su mamá?

Julio: ¿Qué sabes del restaurante Rincón Delicioso? Pienso invitar a Susana.
Mamá: Es muy buena idea que (ir, ustedes) allí. Es un restaurante fabuloso.
Julio: ¿Es necesario que (vestirse, nosotros) formalmente?
Mamá: Es recomendable que (ponerse, tú) saco y corbata porque el restaurante es elegante. Sugiero que (conseguir) una mesa cerca de la ventana. Hay una vista preciosa.
Julio: ¿Qué recomiendas que (pedir, nosotros)?
Mamá: Sugiero que (comenzar) con el gazpacho y que (seguir) con la paella. También recomiendo que (probar) sus albondiguitas.
Julio: ¡Mamá, no podemos comer tanto! Además, es probable que todo (costar) mucho dinero.
Mamá: Es probable que no (costar) demasiado. La comida allí es muy buena pero económica.

c. Mucho sueño. Las siguientes personas dicen que tienen mucho sueño. ¿Qué les aconseja su médico?

MODELO   José: 1
Sugiere que José duerma una hora más.

1. yo: 2
2. Isabel: 3
3. los señores Solís: 1
4. tú y yo: 2
5. el bebé: 5
6. ustedes: 1
7. nosotros: 3
8. tú: 2

¿POR QUÉ SE DICE ASÍ?

ch. Agente de viajes. Alicia, una agente de viajes, siempre tiene el mismo deseo para todos sus clientes. ¿Qué deseos tiene para estos clientes?

MODELO   Margarita / México
Ojalá que Margarita se divierta en México.

1. la familia López / Colombia
2. yo / España
3. los Ruiz / Guatemala
4. mis padres y yo / Europa
5. Samuel / Argentina
6. ustedes / China
7. nosotros / Francia
8. tú / Israel

d. Una carta. Juan Pedro se siente triste y deprimido. ¿Qué consejos le da su prima Eva? Para contestar, completa esta carta con la forma correcta de los verbos entre paréntesis.

Querido primo:

Es triste que (sentirse, tú) tan deprimido. Ojalá que mis consejos te (ayudar).

Primero, sugiero que (dormir, tú) bastante. Es importante que (dormir, nosotros) ocho horas cada noche. También recomiendo que (seguir, tú) una dieta balanceada. Aun al comer en un restaurante es mejor que (pedir, nosotros) comidas nutritivas. Si comes así, es probable que (perder) peso y que (tener) más energía.

Respecto a tus actividades, te aconsejo que no (repetir) lo mismo todos los días. Es posible que no (divertirse, tú) porque no sales bastante. Esto tiene que cambiar. Ojalá que tú y tus amigos (encontrar) algunas actividades nuevas y que (divertirse) mucho.

Un abrazo,
Eva

5.7 *THE PRESENT SUBJUNCTIVE: EXPRESSIONS OF ANTICIPATION OR REACTION*

In sentences with a subject change, the present subjunctive is used in the dependent clause after expressions of anticipation or reaction in the independent clause.

Espero que él **llegue** temprano.	*I hope that he gets there early.*
Sentimos mucho que no **tengan** tiempo.	*We're very sorry they don't have time.*
Estoy contento que **sirvan** pizza.	*I'm glad they serve pizza.*
Me alegro que **estén** aquí.	*I'm happy that they are here.*

■ Remember that the subjunctive is only required when there is a subject change. If there is only one subject, the second verb is not conjugated. It remains in the infinitive form.

Sentimos no **tener** tiempo.	*We're sorry we don't have time.*
¿**Tienes miedo de conocerla**?	*Are you afraid of meeting her?*
Me gusta estar aquí.	*I like being here.*

Here are some common verbs of anticipation or reaction:

alegrarse (de)	*to be happy (about)*
esperar	*to hope*
sentir	*to regret, to be sorry*
temer	*to fear*
tener miedo (de)	*to be afraid (of)*
estar preocupado (de)	*to be worried (about)*
gustar	*to like*
estar contento(a) / alegre / triste / furioso(a)	*to be happy, content / happy, joyous / sad / furious*

Some impersonal expressions also indicate anticipation or reaction:

es bueno
es fantástico
es terrible
es triste

Es triste que no puedan venir.	*It's sad that they can't come.*
Es terrible que estés enferma.	*It's terrible that you're sick.*

a. Reacciones. ¿Qué anticipas o cómo reaccionas en estas situaciones?

MODELO   No podemos jugar fútbol hoy.
         Siento que no podamos jugar fútbol hoy.

VOCABULARIO ÚTIL:
sentir   esperar   temer

1. Hace mal tiempo hoy.
2. No hay examen en la clase de español mañana.
3. Sirven pizza en la cafetería.
4. Tenemos que trabajar después de las clases.
5. Vemos una película en la clase de historia hoy.
6. El director visita la clase de inglés.
7. Hacemos experimentos en la clase de química.
8. Alicia va al médico durante la clase de educación física.

b. ¡Qué negativo! Paco es una persona muy negativa. Nunca está contento. ¿Qué dice bajo estas situaciones?

MODELO   tener que comer vegetales (no gustarle)
         No me gusta tener que comer vegetales.

1. sacar malas notas (tener miedo de)   4. leer tantas páginas (molestarle)
2. no saber bailar (sentir)   5. perder el partido (temer)
3. jugar mal (no gustarle)   6. sentirse mejor (esperar)

c. Una carta. Tú eres el (la) consejero(a) del periódico de tu escuela y recibiste esta carta. Completa la carta con la forma apropiada de los verbos entre paréntesis.

Querido(a) consejero(a):

   Espero que usted (poder) ayudarme con este problema. Me molesta que los profesores siempre (dar) exámenes los lunes cuando estoy cansada. Es terrible que mis amigos y yo (tener) que pasar los fines de semana estudiando y siento que no (poder) divertirnos. ¡No nos gusta (tener) que estudiar tanto! Mis padres insisten en que yo (estudiar) día y noche porque tienen miedo que yo (sacar) malas notas. Pero no les gusta que yo no (divertirse) tampoco. No es justo que los profesores nos (tratar) así. Pido que usted me (sugerir) una solución. Espero (recibir) su respuesta pronto.

                                                  Loca los lunes

LECCIÓN 1

6.1 EXPRESSIONS OF DOUBT

■ The subjunctive forms are used after expressions of doubt. The list that follows includes several common verbal expressions of doubt.

dudar	*to doubt*
es dudoso	*it is doubtful*
es (im)posible	*it is (im)possible*
es (im)probable	*it is (im)probable*
no creer	*not to believe*

Dudo que **necesites** tanta práctica.	*I doubt that you need so much practice.*
No creo que Manuel **esté** allí.	*I don't think Manuel is there.*
Es probable que **tenga** que trabajar.	*I'll probably have to work.*

In negative statements, the verb **creer** expresses doubt and is therefore also followed by the subjunctive. In questions, it may be followed by the subjunctive or the indicative, depending on the degree of doubt being implied.

No creo que **salgan** hoy.	*I don't believe they leave today.*
¿Crees que **es** un puma?	*Do you think it's a puma?*
¿Creen ustedes que **haya** monstruos en la cueva?	*Do you think that there are monsters in the cave?*

■ Expressions of certainty do not require subjunctive forms. The list that follows includes several common verbal expressions of certainty.

es cierto	*it's true*	es evidente	*it's obvious*
es verdad	*it's true*	está claro	*it's clear*
es obvio	*it's obvious*		

Es cierto que **hace** frío.	*It's true that it's cold.*
Es evidente que ya **salieron.**	*It's obvious that they already left.*
Está claro que **vamos** a ganar.	*It's clear that we're going to win.*

In affirmative statements, the verb **creer** expresses certainty and is therefore followed by the indicative.

Creo que **llegan** a las nueve.	*I believe they arrive at nine.*
Creemos que ellas lo **tienen.**	*We believe they have it.*

Vamos a practicar

a. Lo dudo.   Irene está muy negativa hoy y no acepta nada de lo que oye del campamento Aguirre Springs en Nuevo México. ¿Qué dice cuando alguien hace estos comentarios del campamento?

MODELO   Hace calor allí.
Dudo que haga calor allí.

1. Unos animales salvajes viven cerca.
2. No hay que llevar agua para beber.
3. Los sanitarios están cerca.
4. Es interesante visitar «La cueva».
5. Algunas personas suben las montañas.
6. Los arqueólogos hacen excavaciones allí.
7. Las montañas tienen poca vegetación.
8. Llueve mucho en el verano.

b. No puedo.   Gabi siempre tiene excusas para no salir los sábados. ¿Cuáles son algunas excusas que usó Gabi recientemente?

MODELO   salir con mi familia
Es probable que salga con mi familia.

1. visitar a mis primos
2. tener que limpiar la casa
3. trabajar
4. tener que practicar el piano
5. alquilar un video
6. hacer la tarea
7. escribir cartas
8. organizar mi cuarto

c. En preparación.   Julia va a pasar la noche en un campamento por primera vez y tiene muchas preguntas para sus amigos. ¿Qué pregunta?

MODELO   necesitar abrigos
¿Crees que necesitemos abrigos? o **¿Crees que necesitamos abrigos?**

1. llover mucho
2. dormir bien en los sacos de dormir
3. hacer frío por la noche
4. haber mesas donde comer
5. ver animales salvajes
6. tener que caminar mucho

ch. Opiniones.   Unos estudiantes están expresando sus opiniones sobre asuntos escolares. ¿Qué crees tú de estos asuntos?

MODELO   exámenes / ser / necesario
Creo que los exámenes son necesarios. o
No creo que los exámenes sean necesarios.

1. notas / ser / importantes
2. comida de la cafetería / costar / mucho
3. profesores / saber / mucho
4. estudiantes / trabajar / bastante
5. nuestro equipo de fútbol / jugar / bien
6. estudiantes / recibir / notas / justo

d. Al acampar. Paco y Trini son muy buenos amigos pero con frecuencia tienen opiniones opuestas porque Paco es muy escéptico mientras Trini cree todo lo que oye. ¿Qué dicen los dos muchachos cuando oyen estos comentarios?

MODELO   Hay pumas en la cueva.
> *Paco:* **Es dudoso que haya pumas en la cueva.**
> *Trini:* **Es evidente que hay pumas en la cueva**.

1. Podemos beber el agua del río.

2. Un animal grande vive en la cueva.

3. Hay plantas peligrosas alrededor de la cueva.

4. Es posible subir las montañas.

5. Tenemos bastante comida.

6. Los vampiros salen de noche por aquí.

6.2 DOUBLE OBJECT PRONOUNS: 1ST AND 2ND PERSONS

Sentences may contain both a direct and an indirect object pronoun. When this happens, the indirect object pronoun always precedes the direct object pronoun. The two pronouns always occur together and may not be separated by other words.

■ Double object pronouns are placed before conjugated verbs.

¿El café? **Te lo** sirvo.	*The coffee? I'll serve it to you*
Recibimos la carta de David ayer. **Nos la** escribió la semana pasada.	*We got the letter from David yesterday. He wrote it to us last week.*

■ In sentences where there is an infinitive or an **-ndo** verb form, the object pronouns may either precede the conjugated verb, or follow and be attached to the infinitive or the **-ndo** verb form.

Me lo van a explicar. Van a explicár**melo**.	*They are going to explain it to me.*
Te las estoy preparando. Estoy preparándo**telas**.	*I'm preparing them for you.*

■ Object pronouns always precede negative commands and are always attached to the end of affirmative commands.

No **me lo** lea.	*Don't read it to me.*
Léa**melo**.	*Read it to me.*
No **nos la** cantes.	*Don't sing it to (for) us.*
Cánta**nosla**.	*Sing it to (for) us.*

■ When double object pronouns are attached to the end of a verb form, a written accent is always required.

Quiero **comprártelos**.	*I want to buy them for you.*
Están **trayéndonosla**.	*They are bringing it to us.*
Dámelo.	*Give it to me.*

Vamos a practicar

a. ¿Me ayudas? Estás ayudando a mamá a preparar la cena. ¿Qué te dice?

MODELO la sal
Necesito la sal. ¿Me la traes?

1. la leche
2. el ajo
3. el pescado
4. las verduras

5. el aceite de oliva
6. los huevos
7. la cebolla

8. dos manzanas
9. el queso
10. las papas

b. Gracias. Tu abuelito siempre les ofrece ayuda a ti y a tus hermanos. ¿Qué le dicen?

MODELO ¿Les sirvo la limonada?
Sí, sírvenosla. o **No, no nos la sirvas.**

1. ¿Les limpio los cuartos?
2. ¿Les explico la tarea?
3. ¿Les busco los libros?
4. ¿Les doy sus bolígrafos?

5. ¿Les compro esas frutas?
6. ¿Les preparo los sándwiches?
7. ¿Les leo este artículo?
8. ¿Les cuento mi historia favorita?

c. Se me olvidó. Prometiste comprar varios materiales escolares para tu hermano(a) pero olvidaste la lista en casa. ¿Qué pasa cuando regresas a casa?

MODELO *Hermano(a):* **¿Me compraste los bolígrafos?**
Tú: **¡Ay, caramba! Te los voy a comprar el sábado.** o
¡Ay, caramba! Voy a comprártelos el sábado.

1.   2.   3.   4.

5.   6.   7.   8.

ch. **¿Cómo les va?** ¿Qué le dices a Marta cuando ella ofrece ayudarte con las preparaciones para una comida mexicana?

MODELO   la salsa (Felipe)
¿La salsa? Felipe está preparándomela. o
¿La salsa? Felipe me la está preparando.

1. los entremeses (Antonia)
2. el postre (Carla y Rodrigo)
3. la limonada (papá)
4. los frijoles (mi abuelita)
5. la ensalada (Joaquín)
6. los nachos (mi hermano)
7. las tortillas (mi tía)
8. la carne (Francisco y Javier)

L E C C I Ó N   2

THE PRESENT PERFECT TENSE

As in English, the present perfect tense in Spanish is used to talk about what *has happened*. It is formed by combining the present indicative of the verb **haber** with the past participle of the main verb.

- You have already used several *impersonal* forms of the verb **haber**: **hay, hubo, había, haya.**

No **hay** clases hoy.	*There are no classes today.*
Hubo una fiesta ayer.	*There was a party yesterday.*
Antes **había** una estatua en la plaza.	*There used to be a statue in the square.*
Ojalá **haya** mucha gente.	*I hope that there are lots of people.*

- The present indicative of **haber** is used as an auxiliary verb to form the present perfect tense. The present indicative of the verb **haber** is as follows:

Present Indicative	
haber	
he	hemos
has	habéis
ha	han

- The past participle of regular **-ar** verbs is formed by adding **-ado** to the stem of the infinitive. The past participle of **-er** and **-ir** verbs is formed by adding **-ido** to the infinitive stem.

Past Participles		
-ar verbs	**-er** verbs	**-ir** verbs
habl**ado**	com**ido**	sal**ido**
cont**ado**	aprend**ido**	ped**ido**
pens**ado**	le**ído**	divert**ido**

- The present perfect tense is formed by combining the present indicative of the verb **haber** with the past participle of the main verb and is used to talk about past actions with current relevance.

No **han hablado** mucho.	*They haven't talked a lot.*
¿Has comido?	*Have you eaten?*
Nos **hemos divertido**.	*We've had a good time.*

- Some verbs have irregular past participles. Following is a list of the most common ones.

abrir	**abierto**
descubrir	**descubierto**
escribir	**escrito**
decir	**dicho**
hacer	**hecho**
resolver	**resuelto**
volver	**vuelto**
morir	**muerto**
poner	**puesto**
romper	**roto**
ver	**visto**

Me **han dicho** otras cosas.	*They've told me other things.*
Hemos hecho muchos planes.	*We've made a lot of plans.*
¿**Has visto** la nueva película?	*Have you seen the new movie?*

- Object pronouns and reflexive pronouns precede the conjugated form of **haber** when the present perfect tense is used.

¿Dónde **lo** has puesto?	*Where have you put it?*
Les he escrito varias veces.	*I've written to them several times.*
Ya **se** han acostado.	*They've already gone to bed.*

Vamos a practicar

a. ¿Qué pasa?   Son las doce de la tarde el sábado y todos los miembros de la familia de Beatriz están cansadísimos. Según Beatriz, ¿qué han hecho para estar tan cansados?

MODELO   papá: sacar la basura
Papá ha sacado la basura.

1. José: cortar el césped
2. yo: limpiar mi cuarto
3. mi abuela: lavar la ropa
4. mis hermanas: guardar la ropa
5. mamá y yo: preparar el desayuno
6. tú: limpiar el baño
7. papá y José: lavar el coche
8. mamá: pasar la aspiradora

b. ¡Sospechosos!   El detective Blanco está observando a una pareja sospechosa en un restaurante. ¿Qué dice al hablar con su sargento por la radio?

MODELO   sospechosos / pedir / mesa / privado
Los sospechosos han pedido una mesa privada.

1. yo / escoger / mesa / muy cerca de ellos
2. sospechosos / leer / carta muy interesante
3. camarera / servir / entremeses muy caros
4. pareja / recibir / llamada telefónica muy sospechosa
5. mujer / pedir / sopa
6. sospechoso / comer / mucho toda la noche
7. los dos / recibir / paquete / misterioso
8. pareja / salir / restaurante / rápidamente

c. Titulares.   Según estos titulares *(headlines)*, ¿qué ha pasado esta semana?

MODELO   Corporación PASO abre nueva tienda
La Corporación PASO ha abierto una nueva tienda.

1. Gobernador dice que sí
2. Cien personas ven OVNI *(Objeto Volante No Identificado)*
3. Cinco personas mueren en accidente
4. Científico propone nueva teoría
5. Jugador favorito rompe brazo
6. Autora local escribe nueva novela
7. Químicos tóxicos ponen a niños en peligro
8. La temperatura sube a 104 grados hoy
9. Astronautas vuelven a la tierra
10. Presidente resuelve problemas con Congreso

ch. Ya, ya.   Tu mamá quiere saber si hiciste lo que te pidió. Tú no lo has hecho ¿Qué le dices cuando te pregunta si ya hiciste lo que te pidió?

MODELO   ¿Ya lavaste los platos?
Todavía no los he lavado, pero los lavo en seguida.

1. ¿Ya pusiste la mesa?
2. ¿Ya pasaste la aspiradora?
3. ¿Ya barriste el patio?
4. ¿Ya hiciste las camas?

5. ¿Ya pasaste un trapo a los muebles?
6. ¿Ya sacaste la basura?
7. ¿Ya limpiaste los baños?
8. ¿Ya lavaste el perro?

6.4   DOUBLE OBJECT PRONOUNS: 3RD PERSON

In sentences with two object pronouns, when both pronouns begin with the letter **l**, the first one (**le** or **les**) becomes **se**.

Yo le di el libro ayer. → Yo ~~le~~ **lo** di ayer → Yo **se lo** di ayer.
Les pidieron las latas. → ~~Les~~ **las** pidieron. → **Se las** pidieron.

¿Me va a servir la leche?	*Are you going to serve me my milk?*
Sí, **se la** sirvo ahora mismo.	*Yes, I'll serve it to you right away.*
¿Nos enviaron el paquete?	*Did you send us the package?*
Sí, **se lo** enviamos ayer.	*Yes, we sent it to you yesterday.*

- The indirect object pronoun **se** can be clarified by using

a + *[a name or pronoun]*

Pídaselas **a Inés**.	*Ask Inés for them.*
Quiero dárselo **a ustedes**.	*I want to give it to you.*

- Remember that object pronouns precede conjugated verbs but follow and are attached to affirmative commands. They also may follow and be attached to infinitives and present participles.

Se lo vamos a llevar el jueves.
Vamos a llevár**selo** el jueves.
   We'll take it to you on Thursday.

Se lo estoy preguntando ahora mismo.
Estoy preguntándo**selo** ahora mismo.
   I'm asking her about it right now.

Sírva**sela**.	*Serve it to them.*
No **se la** sirva.	*Don't serve it to them.*

Note that written accents are required whenever two object pronouns are added to a word.

Vamos a practicar

a. Sí, papá. Cuando la familia Valenzuela va a acampar, el padre siempre insiste en decirles a todos lo que deben hacer. ¿Qué le dice a su hijo y qué le contesta el hijo?

MODELO   mochila
        Padre: **Hijo, dale la mochila a tu mamá.**
        Hijo: **Sí, papá, se la doy.**

   1. linterna
   2. estufa
   3. sudaderas
   4. saco de dormir
   5. carpa
   6. hielera
   7. abrigos
   8. botas

b. ¡Navidad! Paquita acaba de regresar con muchísimos paquetes del centro comercial. ¿Para quién dice que son todos los regalos?

José

MODELO   **¿El radio? Voy a regalárselo a José.**   o
                ¿El radio? Se lo voy a regalar a José.

1. tía Elena   **2.** abuelita

3. Mario

4. papá

5. abuelito

6. Berta

7. mamá

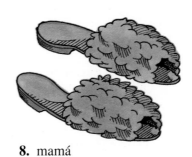

8. mamá

c. El secreto. Elisa tiene un secreto pero todo el mundo lo sabe ya. ¿Cómo lo saben?

MODELO   yo: a Julio
Yo se lo dije a Julio.

1. Julio: a María
2. María: al profesor
3. el profesor: a nosotros
4. nosotros: a Jorge y Sara
5. Jorge y Sara: a ti
6. tú: a Román
7. Román: a Carmen
8. Carmen: a mí

LECCIÓN 3

6.5 PRETERITE AND IMPERFECT: ANOTHER LOOK

You have seen that Spanish uses the preterite and imperfect to talk about something that took place in the past. In **Unidad 4** you learned that each tense has specific uses, as indicated here.

Uses of the Preterite	Uses of the Imperfect
• Completed actions: single action or series of actions *(4.5)* • Focus on beginning of an action *(4.5)* • Focus on an action coming to an end *(4.5)*	• Continuing actions *(4.4)* • Ongoing situations *(4.7)* • Physical or emotional states *(4.7)* • Habitual actions *(4.2)* • Age *(4.1)* • Telling time *(4.1)*

Examples of preterite	Examples of imperfect
Ayer **fui** de compras. **Salí** temprano y **llegué** a buena hora. **Encontré** muchas cosas en oferta. Al mediodía, **almorcé** con una amiga y después **vimos** una película muy interesante. **Volví** a casa a la hora de cenar. *Yesterday I went shopping. I left early and got there at a good time. I found a lot of things on sale. At noon, I ate lunch with a friend and later we saw a very interesting movie. I returned home at supper time.*	Cuando **era** niño, **era** alto y muy fuerte. **Tenía** muchos amigos y todos los días **jugábamos** fútbol después de las clases. Nos **gustaba** mucho el fútbol. Los fines de semana también **nos divertíamos** jugando fútbol. *When I was a child, I was tall and very strong. I had a lot of friends and every day we used to play soccer after school. We liked soccer a lot. On weekends we also had a good time playing soccer.*
Hablé con mamá esta mañana y **dijo** que papá **aceptó** el puesto con la compañía japonesa. Le **hicieron** una oferta tan buena que no **pudo** rechazarla. *I spoke with mom this morning and she said that dad accepted the job with the Japanese firm. They made him such a good offer that he couldn't turn it down.*	**Eran** las once de la noche y **estábamos** en una cueva muy oscura. Mientras **caminábamos**, **oíamos** ruidos muy extraños. ¿Qué animal nos **esperaba**? *It was eleven o'clock at night and we were in a very dark cave. As we were walking, we heard very strange noises. What animal awaited us?*

Examples of the preterite and imperfect	
Los amigos del Ermitaño le **advirtieron** que **era** peligroso vivir allí, pero él no les **hizo** caso. Sin embargo, para complacerlos, **prendía** un fuego cada noche para señalar que **estaba** bien.	*The friends of the Hermit warned him that it was dangerous to live there, but he didn't pay any attention to them. Nevertheless, to placate them, he lit a fire every night to signal that he was all right.*
Daniel nos **contaba** un cuento de espantos cuando de repente **oímos** unos ruidos extraños cerca de nuestra carpa.	*Daniel was telling us a scary story when suddenly we heard strange noises near our tent.*

Vamos a practicar

a. Un sábado terrible. El sábado pasado Federico tuvo interrupciones todo el día. ¿Quiénes lo interrumpieron?

MODELO   mamá / llamarlo / desayunar
Federico dormía tranquilamente cuando su mamá lo llamó a desayunar.

1. oír / teléfono

2. hermanita / colgar / teléfono

3. llegar / amiga Susana

4. empezar / llover

5. hermanita / desenchufar / televisor

6. dormirse

b. Dripping Springs Resort. Al leer esta historia sobre un lugar de recreo en Nuevo México, selecciona el verbo correcto en el pretérito o el imperfecto.

En el siglo diecinueve, el coronel Eugene Van Patten (construyó / construía) un centro turístico al pie de los Órganos, las montañas cerca de Las Cruces, Nuevo México. (Fue / Era) impresionante para esos días; (tuvo / tenía) dieciséis habitaciones, un comedor muy grande y una sala para conciertos. Muchas personas famosas (visitaron / visitaban) el lugar. Se dice que hasta Pancho Villa (durmió / dormía) allí una vez.

El coronel (tuvo / tenía) una esposa indígena y muchos indígenas de la región (vivieron / vivían) y (trabajaron / trabajaban) con ellos. A menudo (dieron / daban) bailes para los turistas y todos siempre (se divirtieron / se divertían) muchísimo.

En 1917, el coronel (perdió / perdía) todo su dinero y (tuvo / tenía) que vender su propiedad a un médico de San Francisco. Poco después la esposa del médico (se puso / se ponía) enferma de tuberculosis y el nuevo dueño (decidió / decidía) establecer un sanitorio para personas con esa enfermedad.

c. Una aventura. Mateo cuenta una aventura que él y su hermana Eva tuvieron al acampar. ¿Qué dicen?

1.	ser	**11.**	estar
2.	ir	**12.**	ponerse
3.	ser	**13.**	empezar
4.	armar	**14.**	comenzar
5.	preparar	**15.**	empezar
6.	comer	**16.**	venir
7.	contar	**17.**	ponernos
8.	hacer	**18.**	ver
9.	decidir	**19.**	estar
10.	descubrir		

Cuando nosotros __1__ niños, nuestra familia siempre __2__ a acampar a las montañas Guadalupe a unas cien millas de El Paso. __3__ un lugar muy pintoresco. Al llegar, nosotros siempre __4__ la carpa y __5__ la cena. __6__ y __7__ cuentos de espantos antes de acostarnos.

Una vez, como __8__ muy buen tiempo, mi hermana y yo __9__ caminar un rato antes de comer. Después de caminar una hora, __10__ que __11__ bastante lejos del lugar del campamento. De repente el cielo __12__ muy oscuro y __13__ a hacer mucho viento. Cuando __14__ a llover, yo __15__ a llorar y mi hermana tuvo que calmarme. Afortunadamente, papá y mi otra hermana __16__ a buscarnos. ¡Qué contentos __17__ cuando los __18__ ! Ellos también __19__ muy contentos de vernos.

Some adjectives have a shortened form before singular nouns. Following is a list of common adjectives that have a shortened form before masculine singular nouns.

bueno	**buen**	*good*	tercero	**tercer**	*third*
malo	**mal**	*bad, evil*	alguno	**algún**	*some*
primero	**primer**	*first*	ninguno	**ningún**	*no, not any, none*

Algún día vamos a Europa.   *Some day we're going to Europe.*
¡Que tengan **buen** viaje!   *Have a good trip!*
No veo **ningún** fuego.   *I don't see any fire.*

- The adjective **grande** *(big, large)* becomes **gran** *(great)* before a noun of either gender.

Es un **gran** jugador.   *He's a great player.*
Es una **gran** idea.   *It's a great idea.*

Vamos a practicar

a. El Club de español.   Muchas personas están hablando de los bailes que presentó el Club de español en el banquete anoche. ¿Qué están diciendo?

MODELO   ¿Viste el _____ baile? (primero)
         ¿Viste el primer baile?

1. Fue un _____ banquete. (grande)
2. José es un _____ guitarrista. (bueno)
3. Fue la _____ fiesta del año. (primero)
4. ¿Sirvieron _____ comida? (bueno)
5. No comí _____ postre, aunque había muchos. (ninguno)
6. Armando fue el _____ bailarín. (tercero)
7. _____ chicas de tu escuela bailaron también. (alguno)
8. Alicia no vino. ¡Qué _____ suerte! (malo)

b. A mediodía.   Estás en la cafetería con un grupo de amigos. ¿Qué comentarios están haciendo?

MODELO   Sra. Barrios / ser / muy bueno / profesora
         La Sra. Barrios es muy buena profesora.

1. hoy / ser / primero / día que Inés / sentarse con Jorge
2. Tomás / ser / malo / jugador de básquetbol
3. nuevo / profesora / ser / tercero / mujer a la izquierda
4. ¿tener (tú) / alguno / libro / interesante?
5. Sr. Uribe / ser / grande / entrenador
6. no haber / ninguno / silla por aquí
7. yo / ir / jugar en / juegos / olímpico / alguno / día
8. director / estar comiendo en / cafetería / por / primero / vez

LECCIÓN 1

7.1 **SI** CLAUSES IN THE PRESENT TENSE

Although *if* (**si**) expresses doubt, it is followed by the indicative, not the subjunctive, when used in the present tense.

Si yo **hago** más de los quehaceres en casa, ¿me puedes pagar algo?	*If I do more of the chores around the house, can you pay me something?*
Si trabajas, puedes comprarte un carro.	*If you work, you can buy (yourself) a car.*

Vamos a practicar

a. Buenas intenciones. ¿Qué planes tienes para el verano?

MODELO   encontrar un trabajo: ir a México para Navidad
Si encuentro un trabajo, puedo ir a México para Navidad.

1. trabajar: ganar mucho dinero
2. ganar mucho dinero: comprar un carro
3. comprar un carro: salir con mis amigos
4. salir con mis amigos: divertirme mucho
5. divertirme mucho: pasar un buen verano
6. pasar un buen verano: regresar contento(a) a las clases

b. A la universidad. Pronto vas a la universidad. ¿Qué consejos te dan tus amigos?

EJEMPLO **Si haces la tarea, vas a entender el curso.**

estudiar	sacar malas notas
asistir a eventos sociales	no dormir bien
hacer muchas preguntas	estar cansado(a)
tomar mucho café	engordar
hacer ejercicio	sacar buenas notas
ver mucha televisión	aprender mucho
comer demasiado	hacer muchos amigos
dormir poco	tener buena salud

7.2 THE PREPOSITION POR

The preposition **por** has several functions in Spanish.

- **Por** expresses the idea of *per,* or *by.*

| ¿Cuánto pagan **por** hora? | *How much do they pay per hour?* |
| Vendemos las flores **por** docena. | *We sell the flowers by the dozen.* |

- **Por** expresses the concept of *in exchange for.*

¿Pagaste tres mil **por** un carro?	*You paid three thousand for a car?*
Te doy mi reloj **por** tu cámara.	*I'll give you my watch for your camera.*
Te vendo este disco **por** tres dólares.	*I'll sell you this record for three dollars.*

- **Por** is used to express duration of time.

Trabajé allí **por** algún tiempo.	*I worked there for a period of time.*
Estuve allí **por** un mes.	*I was there for a month.*
Lo buscaron **por** tres días.	*They looked for it for three days.*

Vamos a practicar

a. **A trabajar.** Estos jóvenes trabajan dos horas después de las clases todos los días. Basándote en su pago, ¿cuánto ganan por día, por semana y por mes?

MODELO   Yoli gana $4.00 por hora.
Gana $8 por día, $40 por semana y $160 por mes.

1. Beto gana $3.50 por hora.
2. Mónica y Patricio ganan $5.50 por hora.
3. Gloria gana $5.00 por hora.
4. Diego y Clemente ganan $4.50 por hora.
5. Eloísa gana $3.00 por hora.
6. Rodrigo y Cecilia ganan $6.00 por hora.
7. Sergio gana $4.00 por hora.
8. Adán y Chela ganan $6.50 por hora.
9. Amalia gana $3.75 por hora.
10. Carolina gana $4.25 por hora.

b. A buen precio. ¿Cuánto pagarías por estas cosas?

$20

EJEMPLO   **Pagaría veinte dólares por el reloj.**

1. $2.000   **2.** $75   **3.** $25

4. $15   **5.** $150   **6.** $20

7. $5.000   **8.** $100.000

c. ¿Qué me dio?   Intercambiaste muchas cosas con tus amigos. ¿Qué recibiste?

MODELO   Lucas: radio (video)
Lucas me dio su radio por mi video.

1. Gustavo: linterna (raqueta de tenis)
2. Julia: jaula y ratoncito (serpiente)
3. Gerardo y Soledad: juego de damas (disco compacto)
4. Valentín: esquíes (guitarra)
5. Norma y Leticia: collares (pulseras)
6. Rosario: aretes (bolígrafos)

ch. Muchas mudanzas.   Felipe ha vivido en muchos lugares. Según él, ¿cuánto tiempo vivió en cada lugar?

MODELO   París: 6 meses
Viví en París por seis meses.

1. Londres: 1 año
2. Buenos Aires: 4 meses
3. Moscú: 3 años
4. Santo Domingo: 2 años
5. Roma: 10 meses
6. Caracas: 4 años
7. Los Ángeles: 1 mes
8. Madrid: 2 años

d. Empleos.   Josefa y sus amigos están hablando de sus empleos. ¿Qué dicen?

MODELO   tú / ganar nueve dólares / hora, ¿no?
   Tú ganas nueve dólares por hora, ¿no?

1. René sólo / poder trabajar dos días / semana
2. Juancho y Luis / tener que trabajar ocho horas / día en verano
3. Maricarmen / no tener que pagar / su comida
4. Gustavo y yo / ganar doce dólares / hora
5. Berta y Ernesto / preferir trabajar / la noche

L E C C I Ó N   2

7.3   PRESENT SUBJUNCTIVE: *QUIZÁS, TAL VEZ*

The subjunctive is used after **quizás** and **tal vez** when the speaker wishes to express probability or improbability.

Quizás haya vida en otro planeta.
Maybe (perhaps) there is life on another planet.

Tal vez tenga que trabajar el domingo.
Perhaps (maybe) I'll have to work on Sunday.

Vamos a practicar

a. Nueva escuela.   Aurora está preocupada porque va a una nueva escuela y tiene muchas dudas. ¿Qué le dices para calmarla?

MODELO   Probablemente los profesores no son simpáticos.
   Quizás sean simpáticos.

1. Probablemente no dan exámenes fáciles.
2. Probablemente no tienen buen equipo de fútbol.
3. Probablemente no hay clase de arte.
4. Probablemente la comida no es buena.
5. Probablemente la banda no toca bien.
6. Probablemente no hacen buenas fiestas.
7. Probablemente no hay biblioteca.
8. Probablemente no tienen Club de español.

b. Excusas.   Nadie quiere asistir a la primera reunión de un nuevo club. ¿Qué excusas dan?

MODELO   visitar a mis abuelos
   No puedo porque tal vez visiten a mis abuelos.

1. tener que trabajar (yo)
2. llamar a mi novio(a)
3. haber un programa importante en la tele
4. llegar mis tíos
5. tener que estudiar (yo)
6. ir de compras (mi mamá y yo)

7.4 PRESENT SUBJUNCTIVE: ADJECTIVE CLAUSES

In **Unidad 5** you learned that some sentences have two clauses: an independent clause and a dependent clause. You learned that like a truck pulling a trailer, the independent clause can function alone, whereas the dependent clause depends on the other clause to function (just as a trailer depends on a truck to pull it).

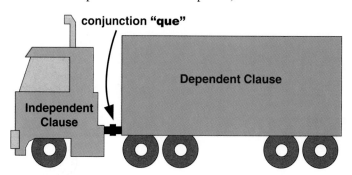

- An adjective clause is a dependent clause that describes a noun in the independent clause.

Tengo dos amigos **que** **hablan francés.**	*I have two friends who speak French.*
Compré una camiseta **que** **combina con mis jeans.**	*I bought a T-shirt that matches my jeans.*

- When the noun described by the clause designates something or someone that may not exist or does not exist, the subjunctive is used.

Busco **un carro** que **sea** bueno y barato.	*I'm looking for a car that is good and inexpensive.*
Necesitan **una persona** que **hable** español.	*They need a person who speaks Spanish.*

- When the noun that an adjective clause describes is real or known to exist, the indicative is used.

Mateo tiene **un carro** que **es** bueno y barato.	*Mateo has a car that is good and inexpensive.*
Conozco a **muchas personas** que **hablan español.**	*I know a lot of people who speak Spanish.*

Vamos a practicar _____

a. **Mi carro.** Jacobo quiere comprarse un carro. ¿Cómo describe el carro de sus sueños?

MODELO ser bonito
Quiero un carro que sea bonito.

1. andar bien
2. no costarme mucho
3. ser nuevo
4. tener radio
5. llevarme a todas partes
6. correr rápido
7. usar poca gasolina
8. tener garantía

b. Nueva ropa. Carmen y Luci andan de compras. ¿Hablan de lo que encuentran o de lo que buscan? Basándote en el dibujo, selecciona el comentario más apropiado.

MODELO a. Allí hay un suéter que combina con mis pantalones.
b. Busco un suéter que combine con mis pantalones.
Respuesta correcta: *b*

1. a. Quiero una camiseta que tenga un dibujo bonito.
b. Veo una camiseta que tiene un dibujo bonito.

2. a. Quiero un vestido que pueda llevar a la fiesta.
b. Allí hay un vestido que puedo llevar a la fiesta.

3. a. Necesito unas botas que sean bastante altas.
b. Ya tengo unas botas que son bastante altas.

4. a. Veo una blusa que le va a gustar a mi mamá.
b. Busco una blusa que le guste a mi mamá.

5. a. Me probé una falda que me llega a las rodillas.
b. No veo ninguna falda que me llegue a las rodillas.

6. a. Necesito unos zapatos que sirvan para jugar tenis.
b. Compré unos zapatos que sirven para jugar tenis.

c. Empleados.   Los jefes están hablando de los empleados y personas que solicitan trabajo. ¿Hablan de personas que ya conocen o que no conocen? Selecciona el verbo apropiado.

MODELO   No encuentro a nadie que (entiende, **entienda**) esta computadora. Hay un empleado en el segundo piso que (**entiende**, entienda) la computadora.

1. Solicitamos una persona que (sabe, sepa) escribir a máquina.
2. Tenemos una secretaria que (escribe, escriba) sesenta palabras por minuto.
3. Conozco a alguien que (busca, busque) trabajo aquí.
4. No hay nadie que (puede, pueda) reparar esta máquina.
5. Buscamos a dos camareros que (pueden, puedan) trabajar de noche.
6. Necesito un joven que (conoce, conozca) bien la ciudad.
7. Encontré a alguien que (es, sea) muy responsable.
8. Quiero emplear a un reportero que (escribe, escriba) bien.
9. Hay un director que (sabe, sepa) hablar japonés en el tercer piso.
10. Tenemos empleados que (llegan, lleguen) puntualmente a la hora del trabajo.

ch. Querido Adolfo.   Homero acaba de mudarse a una nueva ciudad. ¿Qué le cuenta a su amigo?

Querido Adolfo:

   ¿Cómo estás? Estoy bastante contento aunque ahora vivo en una ciudad que no (conocer) muy bien. No hay autobuses que (pasar) cerca de mi casa pero sí hay un metro que (ir) a muchas partes. Todavía hay mucho que hacer. Por ejemplo, necesitamos encontrar una escuela que (quedar) cerca de la casa para mis hermanos. Yo quiero un carro que (poder) usar para ir a mi secundaria y también buscamos a una persona que le (ayudar) a mi mamá con los quehaceres. Pero por lo general, todo va bien. A propósito, ayer conocí a una joven que (vivir) cerca y que (ser) muy guapa. Prometió enseñarme la ciudad. ¿Qué te parece?

   Te escribo más la semana que viene.

                                             Tu amigo,
                                             Homero

LECCIÓN 3

7.5 THE IMPERSONAL SE

- In Spanish, the pronoun **se** represents an indefinite or ''impersonal'' subject that refers to people in general, rather than to specific persons.

Se puede ganar hasta $550 al mes.	*One can earn up to $550 a month.*
¿Cómo **se dice** ''job'' en español?	*How do you say ''job'' in Spanish? (you = one)*
Se busca camarero.	*They're looking for a waiter. (they = no one in particular)*

- When talking about a plural noun, the verb is usually plural.

Se necesitan dos periodistas.	*They need two journalists.*
Se venden treinta y dos mil periódicos por día.	*Thirty-two thousand papers are sold per day.*

- The impersonal **se** is often used in signs and announcements.

Se alquilan bicicletas.	*Bicycles for rent.*
Se habla español.	*Spanish is spoken [here].*
Se prohibe fumar.	*No smoking.*

Vamos a practicar

a. **Multilingüe.**   ¿Dónde se hablan estas lenguas?

MODELO: **En Francia se habla francés.**

Brasil	japonés
Inglaterra	chino
Alemania	ruso
Puerto Rico	italiano
China	portugués
Italia	francés
Japón	español
Rusia	inglés
Francia	alemán

b. ¡Es diferente! Carmen vive en El Paso pero acaba de regresar de un viaje a España. ¿Cómo describe la vida española?

MODELO *Hablan* español con otro acento.
Se habla español con otro acento.

Por la mañana *desayunan* y *van* al trabajo o a la escuela. *Regresan* a casa a almorzar a las dos. Después de almorzar, *toman* una siesta y *vuelven* al trabajo. De noche, *pasean* en las calles. *Cenan* muy tarde y a veces *salen* a ver una película después.

c. Anuncios. Estás leyendo los anuncios clasificados. ¿Qué dicen?

MODELO ofrecer sueldos atractivos
Se ofrecen sueldos atractivos.

1. buscar mecánico
2. requerir personas con experiencia
3. necesitar camareros
4. solicitar cajero
5. ofrecer entrenamiento gratis
6. solicitar dos secretarios bilingües
7. buscar operadores de teléfono
8. necesitar vendedora de ropa femenina

ch. Letreros. Al pasear por la ciudad, ves estos letreros *(signs)*. ¿Qué dicen?

MODELO alquilar / televisores
Se alquilan televisores.

1. reparar / zapatos
2. comprar / neveras usadas
3. solicitar / pintor de casa
4. hablar / inglés
5. vender / uniformes escolares
6. prohibir / fumar
7. vender / computadora casi nueva
8. alquilar / muebles

7.6 THE PREPOSITION *PARA*

The preposition **para** has several uses in Spanish.

■ **Para** expresses the concept of *purpose*.

Para comprar un carro, hay que tener mucho dinero.	*To (In order to) buy a car you have to have a lot of money.*
Súbanse **para** dar una vuelta.	*Get in so we can go for a ride.*
Este vaso es **para** jugo.	*This glass is for juice.*

- **Para** is used to designate the intended recipient of actions or objects.

Este regalo es **para** ti.	*This gift is for you.*
Cantaron **para** nosotros.	*They sang for us.*
No hay trabajo **para** mí.	*There's no job for me.*

- **Para** is used after the verb **trabajar** to indicate *employed by.*

Trabaje **para** una empresa importante.	*Work for an important firm.*
Trabajé **para** mi papá el verano pasado.	*I worked for my Dad last summer.*

Vamos a practicar

a. ¿Para qué? ¿Para qué sirven estas cosas?

MODELO **Las bebidas son para beber.**

la comida	acampar
los libros	beber
la música	cantar
los videos	leer
la carpa	dormir
las canciones	comer
la guitarra	ver
la cama	escuchar
las bebidas	tocar

b. Consejos. Clara Consejera tiene estos consejos para su público.

MODELO dormir mejor / evitar el café
Para dormir mejor hay que evitar el café.

1. perder peso / comer menos
2. no estar cansado / dormir más
3. tener más energía / hacer ejercicio
4. aumentar de peso / comer más
5. divertirse / salir de casa
6. no estar aburrido / ver una película
7. ganar amigos / ser una persona simpática
8. sacar buenas notas / hacer la tarea

c. ¿Para mí? En una celebración familiar, todos van a intercambiar regalos. Según Alejandro, ¿para quién(es) son estos regalos?

abuelos

MODELO **El televisor es para mis abuelos.**

1. hermano **2.** tía Estela **3.** mamá

4. hermana **5.** yo **6.** papá

7. tío Ernesto **8.** padres

ch. Empleos. Leonor y sus amigos están hablando de sus trabajos. ¿Qué dicen?

MODELO tú / trabajar / la tienda de música, ¿no?
Tú trabajas para la tienda de música, ¿no?

1. yo / trabajar / el periódico
2. Magda y Enrique / limpiar casas / ganar dinero
3. Manolo / trabajar / su tío
4. Cecilia y yo / cortar el cesped / los vecinos
5. Adela y Andrés / preferir trabajar / un restaurante
6. tú / trabajar en un campamento / ganar dinero en el verano
7. yo / ahorrar dinero / comprar un carro

d. Anuncio. Encontraste este anuncio en el periódico. ¿Qué dice? Complétalo con **para, por** o **si.**

_____ usted necesita trabajo, no busque más. Venga a trabajar _____ el periódico _El Diario._ Tenemos puestos _____ personas de todas edades y pagamos de $8 a $15 _____ hora. _____ usted trabaja de noche, puede ganar más. _____ pedir una solicitud, llame al 555-4825 o solicite en persona _____ la mañana entre las 8 y las 12.

LECCIÓN 1

8.1 THE FUTURE TENSE: REGULAR FORMS

Spanish has several ways to talk about the future. You already know how to talk about what you are going to do using:

$$\boxed{\textbf{ir a } + \textit{infinitive}}$$

Voy a visitar a mi amigo.	*I'm going to visit my friend.*
No **vamos a estudiar** hoy.	*We're not going to study today.*

You may also use the simple present indicative tense with future meaning.

Mis padres **llegan** mañana.	*My parents arrive tomorrow.*
Nuestro avión **sale** a la una.	*Our plane leaves at one.*

Spanish also has a future tense to talk about what you will do in the future. The future tense has the same set of endings for **-ar**, **-er** and **-ir** verbs. To form the future tense, these endings are added to the infinitive form of the verb.

Future Tense Verb Endings	
-é	-emos
-ás	-éis
-á	-án

nadar		correr		dormir	
nadaré	nadar**emos**	correré	correr**emos**	dormiré	dormir**emos**
nadar**ás**	nadar**éis**	correr**ás**	correr**éis**	dormir**ás**	dormir**éis**
nadar**á**	nadar**án**	correr**á**	correr**án**	dormir**á**	dormir**án**

Margarita **dormirá** mucho.	*Margarita will sleep a lot.*
Mateo y Tina **jugarán** tenis.	*Mateo and Tina will play tennis.*
Correré todos los días.	*I will run every day.*
Nadaremos en el Caribe.	*We will swim in the Caribbean.*

Vamos a practicar

a. Dormilones. Los jóvenes siempre duermen mucho más en el verano. ¿Cuántas horas dormirán tú y tus amigos cada noche?

MODELO   Noé: 12
Mi amigo Noé dormirá doce horas.

1. Beatriz: 9   **4.** tú: 11   **7.** Víctor: 10
2. yo: 10   **5.** nosotros: 9   **8.** ustedes: 13
3. Memo y Beto: 14   **6.** Yoli y Raquel: 12

b. La semana que viene. Raquel dice que la rutina diaria de ella y sus amigos es muy similar. Según Raquel, ¿qué van a hacer ella y sus amigos la semana que viene?

MODELO   Diana comió en un restaurante italiano la semana pasada.
La semana que viene, Diana comerá en un restaurante italiano.

1. Javier y Vicente leyeron una buena novela la semana pasada.
2. Yo jugué volibol tres veces la semana pasada.
3. Ustedes fueron de compras la semana pasada.
4. Tomasa compró una camiseta nueva la semana pasada.
5. Tú alquilaste un video la semana pasada.
6. Pablo y yo asistimos a un concierto la semana pasada.
7. Marcos y Marisela pidieron una pizza la semana pasada.
8. Usted vio una película nueva la semana pasada.

c. Planes. ¿Qué planes tiene la familia de Eva para el sábado, según ella?

Abuelita

MODELO   **Abuelita escribirá cartas.**

1. Mamá   **2.** mis hermanitos   **3.** yo   **4.** Abuelito

5. tía Gloria y Mamá   **6.** Amanda y yo   **7.** mi hermano y su novia   **8.** Papá

ch. Resoluciones.   A fines de año, todo el mundo hace resoluciones personales. ¿Cómo piensas cambiar tu vida y qué piensan hacer estas personas?

> MODELO   perder peso (Paulina)
> Paulina perderá peso.

1. practicar más deportes (ustedes)
2. comer comida más nutritiva (Guillermo)
3. nadar todos los días (yo)
4. aprender karate (Paquita)
5. aprender a tocar la guitarra (tú)
6. evitar los dulces (nosotras)
7. seguir una dieta para adelgazar (Lorenzo y Verónica)
8. leer más (todos)

8.2   THE FUTURE TENSE: IRREGULAR FORMS

Some verbs have irregular stems in the future tense. The verb endings are the same ones you learned for regular verbs.

poner	**pondr-**	pondré, pondrás, pondrá, pondremos, pondréis, pondrán
salir	**saldr-**	saldré, saldrás, saldrá, saldremos, saldréis, saldrán
tener	**tendr-**	tendré, tendrás, tendrá, tendremos, tendréis, tendrán
venir	**vendr-**	vendré, vendrás, vendrá, vendremos, vendréis, vendrán
decir	**dir-**	diré, dirás, dirá, diremos, diréis, dirán
hacer	**har-**	haré, harás, hará, haremos, haréis, harán
haber	**habr-**	habré, habrás, habrá, habremos, habréis, habrán
poder	**podr-**	podré, podrás, podrá, podremos, podréis, podrán
querer	**querr-**	querré, querrás, querrá, querremos, querréis, querrán
saber	**sabr-**	sabré, sabrás, sabrá, sabremos, sabréis, sabrán

Habrá un examen mañana.	*There will be a test tomorrow.*
Podré comprar mi carro.	*I'll be able to buy my car.*
Haremos la tarea en casa.	*We'll do our homework at home.*
Querrán salir el sábado.	*They'll want to go out Saturday.*

Vamos a practicar

a. Encuesta. Algunas personas quieren eliminar los deportes en tu escuela. Hoy va a haber una encuesta para ver cuál es la opinión de la mayoría. ¿Qué crees que dirán estas personas en la encuesta?

MODELO   el (la) profesor(a) de arte
    El (La) profesor(a) de arte dirá que no. o
    El (La) profesor(a) de arte dirá que sí.

1. los entrenadores
2. los miembros de la banda
3. yo
4. el (la) director(a)
5. los atletas
6. el (la) consejero(a)
7. el (la) entrenador(a)
8. tus amigos

b. ¡Qué lástima! Habrá muchos eventos especiales este fin de semana. ¿Por qué no irán estas personas?

MODELO   Habrá un concierto de rock. (Felisa / estudiar)
    Felisa no podrá ir porque tendrá que estudiar.

1. Habrá un partido de béisbol. (César / lavar el carro)
2. Habrá una fiesta. (yo / limpiar la casa)
3. Habrá una película especial. (Adriana / trabajar)
4. Habrá un banquete. (tú / ayudar a tu mamá)
5. Habrá una excursión. (nosotros / hacer la tarea)
6. Habrá una exhibición de arte. (Manuel y Bárbara / escribir una composición)
7. Habrá un concierto de rock. (Rolando / practicar el saxofón)
8. Habrá un baile. (Sandra / cuidar a los niños)

c. ¡Haré tacos! El Club de español va a servir una comida mexicana y todos van a ayudar a preparar la comida. ¿Qué van a hacer estas personas?

MODELO   tú: los nachos
    Tú harás los nachos.

1. nosotros: el ponche
2. el profesor: las enchiladas
3. Diana y León: los tacos
4. yo: los frijoles
5. Édgar: la ensalada
6. ustedes: la salsa
7. Nilda: las tortillas
8. Tina y Esteban: el postre
9. la directora: el arroz
10. Alfredo: el pastel

ch. El año 2050. ¿Qué predicciones tienes para el año 2050?

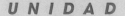

> MODELO   haber / casas / otros planetas
> **Habrá casas en otros planetas.** o
> **No habrá casas en otros planetas.**

1. nosotros / saber / el origen / universo
2. médicos / descubrir / cura para el cáncer
3. carros / poder andar sin gasolina
4. criaturas / otro / planetas / venir a visitarnos
5. nosotros / hacer viajes / otro / planetas
6. mucho / personas / vivir / la luna
7. estudiantes / tener / menos exámenes
8. medio ambiente / ser / menos contaminado

L E C C I Ó N   2

8.3   THE CONDITIONAL: REGULAR AND IRREGULAR VERBS

The conditional has the same set of endings for **-ar**, **-er** and **-ir** verbs. (Note that all endings require a written accent.) To form the conditional, these endings are added to the infinitive form of the verb.

Conditional Verb Endings	
-ía	-íamos
-ías	-íais
-ía	-ían

llevar		ser		conducir	
llevaría	llevaríamos	sería	seríamos	conduciría	conduciríamos
llevarías	llevaríais	serías	seríais	conducirías	conduciríais
llevaría	llevarían	sería	serían	conduciría	conducirían

Para un viaje de un mes, yo **llevaría** más ropa.	*For a month long trip, I would take more clothes.*
Ese trabajo **sería** perfecto.	*That job would be perfect.*
Yo no **conduciría** ese carro.	*I wouldn't drive that car.*

■ The conditional is used to talk about what would happen under certain conditions. The conditions may or may not be mentioned.

■ Irregular verb stems of the conditional are identical to the irregular verb stems of the future tense.

poner	**pondr-**	pondría, pondrías, pondría, pondríamos, pondríais, pondrían
salir	**saldr-**	saldría, saldrías, saldría, saldríamos, saldríais, saldrían
tener	**tendr-**	tendría, tendrías, tendría, tendríamos, tendríais, tendrían
venir	**vendr-**	vendría, vendrías, vendría, vendríamos, vendríais, vendrían
decir	**dir-**	diría, dirías, diría, diríamos, diríais, dirían
hacer	**har-**	haría, harías, haría, haríamos, haríais, harían
haber	**habr-**	habría, habrías, habría, habríamos, habríais, habrían
poder	**podr-**	podría, podrías, podría, podríamos, podríais, podrían
querer	**querr-**	querría, querrías, querría, querríamos, querríais, querrían
saber	**sabr-**	sabría, sabrías, sabría, sabríamos, sabríais, sabrían

¿Qué **dirías** tú?	*What would you say?*
En ese caso, Beatriz no **podría** ir.	*In that case, Beatrice wouldn't be able to go.*
Yo no **saldría** con ellos.	*I wouldn't go out with them.*

Vamos a practicar ⎯⎯⎯⎯⎯⎯⎯⎯⎯⎯⎯⎯⎯⎯

a. ¡Millonarios!   Todos están hablando de lo que comprarían con un millón de dólares. ¿Qué dicen?

MODELO   nosotros: un yate
Nosotros compraríamos un yate.

1. Gregorio: una casa en las montañas
2. Leticia y Matías: un carro nuevo
3. Nati: un avión
4. tú: una computadora
5. Rodrigo: un restaurante
6. yo: una motocicleta
7. todos nosotros: mucha ropa nueva
8. Constanza: joyas elegantes

b. Si yo fuera Tobías . . .   Tobías siempre recibe muy malas notas. Si tú fueras Tobías, ¿qué harías para recibir buenas notas?

MODELO   hacer la tarea
Si yo fuera Tobías, haría la tarea.

1. estudiar más
2. hablar con el (la) profesor(a)
3. pasar más tiempo en la biblioteca
4. no salir tanto
5. leer las lecciones con cuidado
6. no ver mucha televisión
7. hacer muchas preguntas
8. poner más atención a los detalles

c. El mundo ideal. En tu opinión, ¿cómo sería el mundo ideal?

MODELO   haber (mucha/poca) comida para todos.
             Habría mucha comida para todos.

1. todos saber (una/varias) lengua(s)
2. la gente pobre tener (más/menos) dinero
3. haber (poca/mucha) contaminación
4. todos ser (amigos/enemigos)
5. la gente poder viajar (más/menos)
6. haber (más/menos) problemas de salud
7. siempre hacer (buen/mal) tiempo
8. todos querer vivir en (paz/guerra)

8.4 *REPASO: TÚ AND USTED / USTEDES* COMMANDS

You have learned that commands are used to tell someone what to do.

Tú *commands*

- Regular affirmative **tú** commands are formed by dropping the **-s** of the **tú** form of the present indicative.

Habla más despacio, por favor.	*Talk slower, please.*
Piensa lo que haces.	*Think about what you're doing.*
Corre a la escuela.	*Run to school.*
Repite lo que te digo.	*Repeat what I tell you.*

- There are eight irregular affirmative **tú** commands.

decir	**di**	venir	**ven**
poner	**pon**	hacer	**haz**
salir	**sal**	ir	**ve**
tener	**ten**	ser	**sé**

Di la verdad.	*Tell the truth.*
Sal de aquí.	*Get out of here.*
Haz tu tarea.	*Do your homework.*

- Negative **tú** commands are formed by using the **tú** form of the present subjunctive.

Infinitive	*Yo* form	Negative *Tú* command
escuchar	escuchø	no escuches
decir	digø	no digas
dormir	duermø	no duermas

No **juegues** en la casa.	*Don't play in the house.*
No **digas** eso.	*Don't say that.*
No **duermas** tanto.	*Don't sleep so much.*

- The following high-frequency verbs have irregular negative **tú** command forms:

Infinitive	Negative *tú* command
dar	**no des**
estar	**no estés**
ir	**no vayas**
ser	**no seas**

No le **des** mi libro.	*Don't give her my book.*
No estés preocupado.	*Don't be worried.*
No vayas tan tarde.	*Don't go so late.*
No seas travieso.	*Don't be naughty.*

Usted / Ustedes *commands*

- Regular affirmative and negative **usted / ustedes** commands use the **usted / ustedes** forms of the present subjunctive.

Naden todos los días.	*Swim every day.*
Por favor **asista** a nuestro concierto.	*Please attend our concert.*
No vuelvan muy tarde.	*Don't get back too late.*
No se vaya ahora.	*Don't leave now.*

- The following high-frequency verbs have irregular **usted / ustedes** command forms:

Infinitive	*Usted* command	*Ustedes* command
dar	dé	den
estar	esté	estén
ir	vaya	vayan
ser	sea	sean

Commands and object pronouns

Direct and indirect object pronouns follow and are attached to affirmative commands, and precede negative commands.

Hazlo ahora.	*Do it now.*
Levántate* ahora mismo.	*Get up right now.*
Díganselo* a Juan.	*Tell Juan about it.*
No **me mires** así.	*Don't look at me like that.*
No **les sirva** pollo.	*Don't serve them chicken.*
No **me los compren**.	*Don't buy them for me.*

*Note that when adding pronouns to affirmative commands, a written accent may be required to preserve the original stress of the verb.

Vamos a practicar

a. A las montañas. Raquelita va a acampar a las montañas con otra familia. ¿Qué le dice su mamá?

> MODELO llevar ropa elegante
> **Lleva ropa elegante.** o
> **No lleves ropa elegante.**

1. empacar tu saco de dormir
2. olvidar tu chaqueta
3. hacer lo que te dicen
4. ser bueno
5. comer la comida que te sirvan
6. salir sola del campamento
7. dormir cerca del fuego
8. tener cuidado

b. ¿Cómo llego? Un turista quiere visitar el museo y te pide direcciones. ¿Qué le dices?

> MODELO seguir derecho dos cuadras
> **Siga derecho dos cuadras.**

1. doblar a la izquierda en la calle Segovia
2. caminar dos cuadras más
3. no doblar en la primera esquina
4. cruzar la calle
5. ahora doblar a la derecha
6. caminar una cuadra y media
7. no pasar la iglesia
8. entrar en el museo al lado de la iglesia

c. En el campamento. Tú trabajas de consejero(a) en un campamento de verano. Ahora tienes que explicar la rutina diaria a tu grupo de niños. ¿Qué les dices?

> MODELO **Despiértense a las seis y media.** 6:30

1. 6:45 **2.** 6:50 **3.** 7:00 **4.** 7:15

5. 7:45 **6.** 8:30 **7.** 2:30 **8.** 9:30

¿POR QUÉ SE DICE ASÍ?

ch. Hoy en la oficina. Tú eres el (la) jefe(a) de una oficina y tienes que darle instrucciones a tu secretario(a). ¿Cómo respondes a sus preguntas?

MODELOS ¿Preparo el café?
Sí, prepárelo ahora. o
No, no lo prepare todavía.

¿Le escribo la carta al señor Carrión?
Sí, escríbasela ahora. o
No, no se la escriba todavía.

1. ¿Preparo el informe?
2. ¿Llamo al cliente?
3. ¿Le sirvo café al cliente?
4. ¿Le enseño la presentación al cliente?
5. ¿Les traigo el nuevo producto a ustedes?
6. ¿Le doy la lista de los precios al cliente?
7. ¿Pido el almuerzo?
8. ¿Les sirvo el almuerzo?

8.5 REPASO: PRESENT SUBJUNCTIVE—DOUBT, PERSUASION, ANTICIPATION AND REACTION

The subjunctive mode consists of verb forms used after expressions of doubt, persuasion, anticipation or reaction, and so forth.

Forms of the subjunctive

- The present subjunctive verb endings simply reverse the theme vowel of the infinitive.

Present subjunctive theme vowels
-ar → **-e**
-er, -ir → **-a**

- The following verbs are irregular in the present subjunctive.

Present Subjunctive: Irregular Verbs					
dar	**estar**	**ir**	**saber**	**ser**	**ver**
dé	esté	vaya	sepa	sea	vea
des	estés	vayas	sepas	seas	veas
dé	esté	vaya	sepa	sea	vea
demos	estemos	vayamos	sepamos	seamos	veamos
deis	estéis	vayáis	sepáis	seáis	veáis
den	estén	vayan	sepan	sean	vean

- The subjunctive form of **hay** is **haya**.

Uses of the subjunctive

- The subjunctive mode is used in dependent clauses after expressions of doubt. After expressions of certainty, the indicative mode is used.

Dudo que **ganemos** el partido.	*I doubt that we'll win the game.*
Es posible que **llueva**.	*It's possible that it will rain.*
No creo que **vengan**.	*I don't think they're coming.*

Es obvio que **eres** listo(a).	*It's obvious that you're smart.*
Sé que no **hay** clase hoy.	*I know that there's no class today.*
Creo que **vienen** hoy.	*I think they're coming today.*

- The subjunctive mode is used in dependent clauses after expressions of anticipation or reaction.

Esperamos que **vayas**.	*We hope you go.*
Es triste que **tengamos** que salir ahora.	*It's sad that we have to leave now.*
Ojalá que nos **den** dulces.	*I hope they give us candy.*

- The subjunctive mode is used in dependent clauses after expressions of persuasion.

Quiere que **nos divirtamos**.	*She (He) wants us to have a good time.*
Sugiero que **practiquemos**.	*I suggest that we practice.*
¿Recomiendas que **estudie** más?	*Do you recommend that I study more?*

Vamos a practicar _____

a. **Lo dudo.**   Carmelita siempre tiene dudas. ¿Qué dice cuando oye estos comentarios?

EJEMPLO   Habrá un examen difícil mañana.
Dudo que el examen de mañana sea difícil.

1. Ganaremos el campeonato de golf.
2. La familia Pérez irá al Japón este verano.
3. Los profesores calificarán exámenes esta noche.
4. Tendremos una película en la clase de historia.
5. Nos darán refrescos en la clase de español.
6. Habrá una fiesta chévere el sábado.
7. Marta y Ricardo jugarán tenis esta tarde.
8. Todos recibiremos una *A* en la clase de español.

b. Sociología.   Un estudiante universitario está haciendo una encuesta para su clase de sociología. Quiere que tu reacciones a estos comentarios usando una de las siguientes expresiones: **Es dudoso que . . . , Creo/No creo que . . . , Es cierto que . . .**

EJEMPLO   Los profesores califican exámenes todos los días.
No creo que los profesores califiquen exámenes todos los días. o
Es cierto que los profesores califican exámenes todos los días.

1. Los padres saben mucho más que los hijos.
2. El (La) primer(a) hijo(a) es más inteligente.
3. Los hombres hablan más que las mujeres.
4. Hay poca contaminación en el planeta Tierra.
5. Necesitamos mejor transporte público en nuestras ciudades.
6. Los perros son los mejores amigos de los seres humanos.
7. Debemos ayudar a los habitantes de otros países.
8. Las clases de español son las más interesantes.

c. ¡Desastre!   ¿Qué haces tú cuando tienes un problema verdaderamente serio? Para saber lo que hace esta joven, completa la carta que le escribió a Clara Consejera.

Querida Clara Consejera,

Espero que usted me _____ (poder) ayudar con mi problema. Estoy muy preocupada porque mis padres salieron de la ciudad y yo choqué su carro contra un árbol. Es probable que ellos _____ (regresar) la semana que viene y tengo miedo de que _____ (ir) a estar furiosos conmigo. Es terrible que yo no _____ (tener) dinero para arreglarlo pero soy muy pobre. ¿Qué debo hacer? ¿Es mejor que les _____ (decir) la verdad inmediatamente o es preferible que _____ (esperar) hasta que vean el carro? ¡Aconséjeme, por favor!

Es triste que mis padres _____ (tener) que encontrar tan malas noticias al regresar de su viaje, pero me alegro de que _____ (haber) personas como usted para aconsejarme.

Triste y desesperada.

ch. Nuestro club.   Según Luisita, ¿qué recomiendan todos para el Club de español para este verano?

MODELO   los hermanos Quintana / preferir que / el Club de español / ser más activo
Los hermanos Quintana prefieren que el Club de español sea más activo.

1. yo / sugerir que / el Club de español / hacer un viaje a México
2. los estudiantes de francés / pedir que / (nosotros) ir a Europa con ellos
3. la profesora / insistir en que / (nosotros) trabajar para ganar el dinero
4. nosotros / preferir que / nuestro / padres / pagar el viaje
5. los padres / querer que / (nosotros) vender dulces en la escuela
6. el director / recomendar que / el Club / lavar coches
7. tú / aconsejar que / (nosotros) esperar otro año
8. los estudiantes del cuarto año / insistir en que / (nosotros) viajar este año

¿POR QUÉ SE DICE ASÍ?

LECCIÓN 3

8.6 REPASO: PRETERITE AND IMPERFECT

You have learned that the preterite and imperfect are used to talk about the past. The specific uses of each tense are summarized in the following chart. The numbers in parentheses indicate the unit and lesson where each concept was introduced.

Preterite	Imperfect
■ Completed actions: single action or series of actions (4.5) ■ Focus on beginning of an action (4.5) ■ Focus on an action coming to an end (4.5)	■ Continuing actions (4.4) ■ Ongoing situations (4.7) ■ Physical or emotional states (4.7) ■ Habitual actions (4.2) ■ Age (with **tener**) (4.2) ■ Telling time (4.2)

Era la medianoche y todo **estaba** tranquilo. El viejito **entró** en la cocina como **acostumbraba**. **Sacó** algo para comer de la nevera. Se **sentó** en la sala y **empezó** a leer unas páginas de su cuento policíaco favorito. Esta noche **iba** a leer la parte más interesante — la parte donde se sabe quién es el criminal.

Según el cuento, el sospechoso **era** un hombre alto, de pelo gris, que **tenía** unos setenta y dos años. La noche anterior, cuando el viejito **dejó** de leer, los detectives en el cuento **salieron** para la casa del sospechoso para arrestarlo.

Mientras el viejito **leía**, **oyó** un ruido de la calle. En seguida alguien **llamó** a la puerta. El viejito **estaba** preocupado. **Suspiró, se levantó** y **fue** a abrir la puerta. ¡Qué sorpresa! ¿Qué **quería** la policía a esta hora?

It was midnight and everything was quiet. The old man entered the kitchen as he was accustomed to doing. He took out something to eat from the refrigerator. He sat down in the living room and began to read a few pages of his favorite mystery story. Tonight he was going to read the most interesting part — the part where it's revealed who the criminal is.

According to the story, the suspect was a tall, gray-haired man who was about seventy-two years old. The night before, when the old man stopped reading, the detectives set out for the suspect's house to arrest him.

While the old man read, he heard a noise from the street. Immediately, someone knocked at the door. The old man was worried. He sighed, got up, and went to open the door. What a surprise! What did the police want at this hour?

Vamos a practicar

a. ¡Qué vergüenza!   Completa la carta que Xavier le mandó a Narciso para saber cómo él pasó las vacaciones el verano pasado.

Querido Narciso:

¿Cómo estás? Tengo muchas ganas de verte otra vez y pasar el verano juntos. (Nos divertimos, Nos divertíamos) tanto el verano pasado. ¿Recuerdas como cada día (fuimos, íbamos) a la playa y (nadamos, nadábamos) en el océano y (charlamos, charlábamos) con las chicas bonitas?

¿Recuerdas a Diana? ¿Recuerdas esa noche cuando por fin (salí, salía) con ella? —después de invitarla tantas veces. (Fuimos, Íbamos) al restaurante más elegante de la ciudad. ¡Qué noche! Diana (tuvo, tenía) mucha hambre y (pidió, pedía) el plato más caro de toda la carta. Entonces yo (decidí, decidía) pedir el plato más barato.

Mientras (comimos, comíamos) ella y yo (conversamos, conversábamos) sobre los amigos y nuestros pasatiempos favoritos. La conversación (fue, era) tan interesante que yo no (presté, prestaba) atención a lo que (hice, hacía). De repente derramé la sopa y (sentí, sentía) algo caliente sobre mis piernas. ¡Qué vergüenza! (Tuve, Tenía) que regresar a casa sin siquiera bailar con Diana. Quizás este año . . . .

Hasta pronto, mi amigo. ¡Que vengan pronto las vacaciones!

Tu amigo,
Xavier

b. La Cenicienta. ¿Recuerdas este cuento de hadas? Cuenta la primera parte.

Había una vez una joven muy bella que (llamarse) Cenicienta. (Vivir) con su madrastra y sus dos hermanastras. Todas la (tratar) muy cruelmente. Cenicienta siempre (tener) muchos quehaceres y no (poder) salir como sus hermanastras. Un día, la familia (recibir) una invitación muy importante. El rey (ir) a tener un baile grande para encontrar una esposa para su hijo. Todas (estar) muy emocionadas, incluso Cenicienta. Pero su madrastra le (decir) que sólo las dos hermanastras (poder) asistir al baile con ella. Y así (pasar).

Cuando (salir) las tres mujeres muy elegantemente vestidas, Cenicienta (empezar) a llorar y llorar. De repente (aparecer) su hada madrina y le (decir), ''No llores. Tú también vas a ir''. En un momento, el hada madrina (cambiar) el viejo y feo vestido de Cenicienta en un vestido largo y bellísimo. Y le (dar) unos zapatos preciosos de cristal. También (cambiar) la calabaza del jardín en un elegante coche de caballos. Cenicienta (estar) contentísima. ''Ya estás lista, niña'', (decir) el hada madrina, ''pero recuerda que tienes que volver a casa antes de la medianoche''.

c. ¡Qué memoria! ¿Tienes una buena memoria? ¿Cuánto recuerdas del cuento ''*El leon y las pulgas*''? Completa la siguiente reconstrucción del cuento.

VOCABULARIO ÚTIL:

establecerse	querer	ser	empezar
sentir	picar	tener	estar
proclamar	vencer	perder	matar

1. Los animales de la selva africana _____ al león ''rey de todos los animales''.
2. Desafortunadamente, el león también _____ orgulloso y tiránico.
3. En efecto, todos los animales _____ miedo de su monarca.
4. Las pulgas no _____ ni miedo ni respeto por el rey, ni por ningún otro animal.
5. Las pulgas _____ mostrarles a todos los demás animales que ellas _____ más poderosas que el león.
6. Con esta idea _____ en el lustroso y elegante pelaje dorado del león.
7. Pronto la pequeña colonia _____ a crecer rápidamente.
8. Las pulgas _____ tanto al león que éste acabó por morirse.
9. Las pulgas _____ una gran fiesta para celebrar la muerte del león.
10. Desgraciadamente, al matar al león, las pulgas _____ la fuente de su alimentación.

8.7 REPASO: QUIZÁS AND TAL VEZ

The subjunctive is used after **quizás** and **tal vez** when the speaker wishes to express doubt.

Quizás tengamos refrescos.	*Maybe we'll have soft drinks.*
Tal vez venga mi prima.	*Perhaps my cousin will come.*

Vamos a practicar

a. El fin de semana. El abuelito de Gloria quiere saber qué van a hacer todos este fin de semana. ¿Qué le dice Gloria?

Felipe

MODELO **Quizás Felipe vaya de compras.**

1. Mamá

2. yo

3. Papá

4. mi hermanito

5. mis padres

6. Felipe y yo

7. mi hermanita

8. mis hermanitos

b. ¡Qué imaginación! Tú hermanito(a) tiene una imaginación muy activa. ¿Cómo reaccionas a sus comentarios sobre la vida en otro planeta?

MODELO Probablemente los habitantes tienen tres brazos.
             Tal vez tengan tres brazos.

1. Probablemente el césped es azul.
2. Probablemente los habitantes comen aire.
3. Probablemente viven en los árboles.
4. Probablemente hace 200 grados durante el verano.
5. Probablemente nieva todo el invierno.
6. Probablemente los habitantes tienen dos narices.
7. Probablemente hay pocos animales.
8. Probablemente nadie bebe agua.

MATERIAS DE CONSULTA

APÉNDICE 1

EL ABECEDARIO

Note that the Spanish alphabet has four additional letters: **ch, ll, ñ,** and **rr.** *
When alphabetizing in Spanish, or when looking up words in a dictionary or
names in a telephone directory, words or syllables beginning with **ch, ll,** and **ñ**
follow words or syllables beginning with **c, l,** and **ñ,** respectively, while **rr** is
alphabetized as in English.

a	*a*	n	*ene*
b	*be* (*be* grande, *be* larga, *be* de burro)	ñ	*eñe*
		o	*o*
c	*ce*	p	*pe*
ch	*che*	q	*cu*
d	*de*	r	*ere*
e	*e*	rr	*erre*
f	*efe*	s	*ese*
g	*ge*	t	*te*
h	*hache*	u	*u*
i	*i*	v	*ve, uve* (*ve* chica, *ve* corta, *ve* de vaca)
j	*jota*		
k	*ka*	w	*doble ve, doble uve*
l	*ele*	x	*equis*
ll	*elle*	y	*i griega, ye*
m	*eme*	z	*zeta*

* In 1994, the Association of Spanish Language Academies voted to remove the
ch and **ll** from alphabetical listings. However, students should be made aware of
them as there is still an abundant number of resources alphabetized using these
two letters. This change does not affect pronunciation, usage, or spelling.

APÉNDICE 2

I. REGULAR VERBS

Infinitive	cantar	correr	subir
Present indicative	canto	corro	subo
	cantas	corres	subes
	canta	corre	sube
	cantamos	corremos	subimos
	cantáis	corréis	subís
	cantan	corren	suben
Preterite	canté	corrí	subí
	cantaste	corriste	subiste
	cantó	corrió	subió
	cantamos	corrimos	subimos
	cantasteis	corristeis	subisteis
	cantaron	corrieron	subieron
Imperfect	cantaba	corría	subía
	cantabas	corrías	subías
	cantaba	corría	subía
	cantábamos	corríamos	subíamos
	cantabais	corríais	subíais
	cantaban	corrían	subían
Future	cantaré	correré	subiré
	cantarás	correrás	subirás
	cantará	correrá	subirá
	cantaremos	correremos	subiremos
	cantaréis	correréis	subiréis
	cantarán	correrán	subirán
Conditional	cantaría	correría	subiría
	cantarías	correrías	subirías
	cantaría	correría	subiría
	cantaríamos	correríamos	subiríamos
	cantaríais	correríais	subiríais
	cantarían	correrían	subirían

Infinitive	cantar	correr	subir
Commands			
tú	canta	corre	sube
negative tú	no cantes	no corras	no subas
usted	(no) cante	(no) corra	(no) suba
ustedes	(no) canten	(no) corran	(no) suban
Present progressive	estoy cantando	estoy corriendo	estoy subiendo
	estás cantando	estás corriendo	estás subiendo
	está cantando	está corriendo	está subiendo
	estamos cantando	estamos corriendo	estamos subiendo
	estáis cantando	estáis corriendo	estáis subiendo
	están cantando	están corriendo	están subiendo
Present subjunctive	cante	corra	suba
	cantes	corras	subas
	cante	corra	suba
	cantemos	corramos	subamos
	cantéis	corráis	subáis
	canten	corran	suban
Present perfect	he cantado	he corrido	he subido
	has cantado	has corrido	has subido
	ha cantado	ha corrido	ha subido
	hemos cantado	hemos corrido	hemos subido
	habéis cantado	habéis corrido	habéis subido
	han cantado	han corrido	han subido

II. STEM-CHANGING VERBS[1]

Infinitive in *-ar* and *-er*

Infinitive change	pensar **e → ie**	volver **o → ue**	jugar[2] **u → ue**
Present indicative	**pie**nso **pie**nsas **pie**nsa pensamos pensáis **pie**nsan	**vue**lvo **vue**lves **vue**lve volvemos volvéis **vue**lven	**jue**go **jue**gas **jue**ga jugamos jugáis **jue**gan
Present subjunctive	**pie**nse **pie**nses **pie**nse pensemos penséis **pie**nsen	**vue**lva **vue**lvas **vue**lva volvamos volváis **vue**lvan	**jue**gue **jue**gues **jue**gue juguemos juguéis **jue**guen

Infinitive in *-ir*

Infinitive change(s)	servir **e → i**	dormir **o → ue, u**	divertir **e → ie, i**
Present indicative	s**i**rvo s**i**rves s**i**rve servimos servís s**i**rven	d**ue**rmo d**ue**rmes d**ue**rme dormimos dormís d**ue**rmen	div**ie**rto div**ie**rtes div**ie**rte divertimos divertís div**ie**rten
Present subjunctive	s**i**rva s**i**rvas s**i**rva s**i**rvimos s**i**rváis s**i**rvan	d**ue**rma d**ue**rmas d**ue**rma d**u**rmamos d**u**rmáis d**ue**rman	div**ie**rta div**ie**rtas div**ie**rta div**i**rtamos div**i**rtáis div**ie**rtan
Present participle	s**i**rviendo	d**u**rmiendo	div**i**rtiendo

[1] Only the tenses containing stem changes are presented in this section.

[2] This verb is unique. It is the only **u → ue** stem-changing verb.

Preterite	serví	dormí	divertí
	serviste	dormiste	divertiste
	sirvió	durmió	divirtió
	servimos	dormimos	divertimos
	servisteis	dormisteis	divertisteis
	sirvieron	durmieron	divirtieron

III. IRREGULAR VERBS[1]

andar

Preterite: anduve, anduviste, anduvo, anduvimos, anduvisteis, anduvieron

caer

Present indicative: caigo, caes, cae, caemos, caéis, caen
Preterite: caí, caíste, cayó, caímos, caísteis, cayeron
Present subjunctive: caiga, caigas, caiga, caigamos, caigáis, caigan
Present participle: cayendo
Past participle: caído

conocer

Present indicative: conozco, conoces, conoce, conocemos, conocéis, conocen
Present subjunctive: conozca, conozcas, conozca, conozcamos, conozcáis, conozcan

dar

Present indicative: doy, das, da, damos, dais, dan
Preterite: di, diste, dio, dimos, disteis, dieron
Present subjunctive: dé, des, dé, demos, deis, den

decir

Present indicative: digo, dices, dice, decimos, decís, dicen
Preterite: dije, dijiste, dijo, dijimos, dijisteis, dijeron
Future: diré, dirás, dirá, diremos, diréis, dirán
Conditional: diría, dirías, diría, diríamos, diríais, dirían
Commands: di, no digas, (no) diga, (no) digan
Present subjunctive: diga, digas, diga, digamos, digáis, digan
Present participle: diciendo
Past participle: dicho

[1] Only the tenses containing irregular forms are presented in this section.

estar

Present indicative: estoy, estás, está, estamos, estáis, están
Preterite: estuve, estuviste, estuvo, estuvimos, estuvisteis, estuvieron
Present subjunctive: esté, estés, esté, estemos, estéis, estén

haber (impersonal forms)

Present indicative: hay
Preterite: hubo
Future: habrá
Conditional: habría
Present subjunctive: haya

hacer

Present indicative: hago, haces, hace, hacemos, hacéis, hacen
Preterite: hice, hiciste, hizo, hicimos, hicisteis, hicieron
Future: haré, harás, hará, haremos, haréis, harán
Conditional: haría, harías, haría, haríamos, haríais, harían
Commands: haz, no hagas, (no) haga, (no) hagan
Present subjunctive: haga, hagas, haga, hagamos, hagáis, hagan
Past participle: hecho

ir

Present indicative: voy, vas, va, vamos, vais, van
Preterite: fui, fuiste, fue, fuimos, fuisteis, fueron
Imperfect: iba, ibas, iba, íbamos, ibais, iban
Commands: ve, no vayas, (no) vaya, (no) vayan
Present subjunctive: vaya, vayas, vaya, vayamos, vayáis, vayan
Present participle: yendo
Past participle: ido

oír

Present indicative: oigo, oyes, oye, oímos, oís, oyen
Preterite: oí, oíste, oyó, oímos oísteis, oyeron
Present subjunctive: oiga, oigas, oiga, oigamos, oigáis, oigan
Present participle: oyendo

poder

Present indicative: puedo, puedes, puede, podemos, podéis, pueden
Preterite: pude, pudiste, pudo, pudimos, pudisteis, pudieron
Future: podré, podrás, podrá, podremos, podréis, podrán
Conditional: podría, podrías, podría, podríamos, podríais, podrían
Present participle: pudiendo

poner

Present indicative: pongo, pones, pone, ponemos, ponéis, ponen
Preterite: puse, pusiste, puso, pusimos, pusisteis, pusieron
Future: pondré, pondrás, pondrá, pondremos, pondréis, pondrán
Conditional: pondría, pondrías, pondría, pondríamos, pondríais, pondrían
Commands: pon, no pongas, (no) ponga, (no) pongan
Present subjunctive: ponga, pongas, ponga, pongamos, pongáis, pongan
Past participle: puesto

querer

Present indicative: quiero, quieres, quiere, queremos, queréis, quieren
Preterite: quise, quisiste, quiso, quisimos, quisisteis, quisieron
Future: querré, querrás, querrá, querremos, querréis, querrán
Conditional: querría, querrías, querría, querríamos, querríais, querrían
Present subjunctive: quiera, quieras, quiera, queramos, queráis, quieran

saber

Present indicative: sé, sabes, sabe, sabemos, sabéis, saben
Preterite: supe, supiste, supo, supimos, supisteis, supieron
Future: sabré, sabrás, sabrá, sabremos, sabréis, sabrán
Conditional: sabría, sabrías, sabría, sabríamos, sabríais, sabrían
Present subjunctive: sepa, sepas, sepa, sepamos, sepáis, sepan

salir

Present indicative: salgo, sales, sale, salimos, salís, salen
Future: saldré, saldrás, saldrá, saldremos, saldréis, saldrán
Conditional: saldría, saldrías, saldría, saldríamos, saldríais, saldrían
Commands: sal, no salgas, (no) salga, (no) salgan
Present subjunctive: salga, salgas, salga, salgamos, salgáis, salgan

ser

Present indicative: soy, eres, es, somos, sois, son
Preterite: fui, fuiste, fue, fuimos, fuisteis, fueron
Imperfect: era, eras, era, éramos, erais, eran
Commands: sé, no seas, (no) sea, (no) sean
Present subjunctive: sea, seas, sea, seamos, seáis, sean

tener

Present indicative: tengo, tienes, tiene, tenemos, tenéis, tienen
Preterite: tuve, tuviste, tuvo, tuvimos, tuvisteis, tuvieron
Future: tendré, tendrás, tendrá, tendremos, tendréis, tendrán
Conditional: tendría, tendrías, tendría, tendríamos, tendríais, tendrían
Commands: ten, no tengas, (no) tenga, (no) tengan
Present subjunctive: tenga, tengas, tenga, tengamos, tengáis, tengan

traer

Present indicative: traigo, traes, trae, traemos, traéis, traen
Preterite: traje, trajiste, trajo, trajimos, trajisteis, trajeron
Present subjunctive: traiga, traigas, traiga, traigamos, traigáis, traigan
Present participle: trayendo
Past participle: traído

venir

Present indicative: vengo, vienes, viene, venimos, venís, vienen
Preterite: vine, viniste, vino, vinimos, vinisteis, vinieron
Future: vendré, vendrás, vendrá, vendremos, vendréis, vendrán
Conditional: vendría, vendrías, vendría, vendríamos, vendríais, vendrían
Commands: ven, no vengas, (no) venga, (no) vengan
Present subjunctive: venga, vengas, venga, vengamos, vengáis, vengan
Present participle: viniendo

ver

Present indicative: veo, ves, ve, vemos, veis, ven
Preterite: vi, viste, vio, vimos, visteis, vieron
Imperfect: veía, veías, veía, veíamos, veíais, veían
Present subjunctive: vea, veas, vea, veamos, veáis, vean
Past participle: visto

VOCABULARIO

ESPAÑOL-INGLÉS

VOCABULARIO
español-inglés

This **Vocabulario** includes all active and most passive words and expressions in **¡DIME!** (Exact cognates, conjugated verb forms, and proper nouns used as passive vocabulary are generally omitted.) A number in parentheses follows most entries. This number refers to the unit and lesson in which the word or phrase is introduced. The number **(3.1),** for example, refers to **Unidad 3, Lección 1.** The unit and lesson number of active vocabulary—words and expressions students are expected to remember and use—is given in boldface type: **(3.1).** The unit and lesson number of passive vocabulary–words and expressions students are expected to recognize and understand—is given in lightface type: (3.1).

The gender of nouns is indicated as *m.* (masculine) or *f.* (feminine). When a noun designates a person or an animal, both the masculine and feminine form is given. Irregular plural forms of active nouns are indicated. Adjectives ending in **-o** are given in the masculine singular with the feminine ending (**a**) in parentheses. Verbs are listed in the infinitive form, except for a few irregular verb forms. Stem-changing verbs appear with the change in parentheses after the infinitive.

The following abbreviations are used:

adj.	adjective	*m.*	masculine
adv.	adverb	*n.*	noun
art.	article	*past part.*	past participle
cond.	conditional	*pl.*	plural
conj.	conjunction	*poss.*	possessive
dir. obj.	direct object	*prep.*	preposition
f.	feminine	*pres.*	present
fam.	familiar	*pres. perf.*	present perfect
form.	formal	*pres. subj.*	present subjunctive
fut.	future	*pret.*	preterite
imper.	imperative	*pron.*	pronoun
imperf.	imperfect	*refl.*	reflexive
indir. obj.	indirect object	*sing.*	singular
inf.	infinitive	*subj.*	subject

A

a   to
  a *(personal)*
  a caballo   on horseback (6.1)
  a eso de   around, about **(2.2)**
  a gritos   at the top of one's voice (5.1)
  a lo largo de   along, alongside (7.3)
  a lo mejor   probably, maybe, perhaps **(2.1)**
  a mediados de   in the middle of *(time period)* (8.1)
  a medida que   as (3.3)
  a menudo   often **(2.1)**
  a pesar de   in spite of (1.1)
  a propósito   by the way (7.1)
  a punto de   about to (5.1)
abandonado(a)   abandoned (1.2)
abandonado(a) *n.*   one who has been abandoned (3.2)
abandonar   to abandon (8.1)
abierto(a)   open **(3.2)**
abogado *m.*, **abogada** *f.*   lawyer (7.3)
abrazo *m.*   hug (5.2)
abrigar   to cover up, wrap up (6.1)
abrigo *m.*   coat (3.1)
abrir   to open (1.1) *pres. perf.* **(6.2)**
absolutamente   absolutely **(7.1)**
absorber   to absorb (2.3)
abuelito *m.*, **abuelita** *f.*   grandpa, grandma (1.1)
abuelo *m.*, **abuela** *f.*   grandfather, grandmother (1.1)
abundante   abundant (3.3)
abundar   to abound, be plentiful (3.3)
aburrido(a)   boring; bored (1.2)
acá   here (1.1)
acabar de   to have just (1.2) **(1.1)**
acabar por   to end up (by) (1.3)
académico(a)   academic (7.3)
acampar   to camp (1.1) **(1.3)**
acaso *m.*   chance **(8.2)**
accesorio *m.*   accessory (1.1)
accidente *m.*   accident (1.3)
aceite *m.*   oil (6.1)
acento *m.*   accent (7.3)
aceptar   to accept (6.1)
acequia *f.*   irrigation ditch (5.1)
acerca de   about, concerning (1.2)
acercarse   to approach, draw near (6.1) **(3.3)**
acero *m.*   steel (2.1)
acertar   to guess right; to be correct (1.3)
acompañar   to accompany (1.2)
aconsejar   to advise (4.1) **(5.2)**
acontecimiento *m.*   event, happening (5.2)
acordar (ue)   to agree; to remember **(4.1)**
acordarse (ue)   to remember (1.3)
acortar   to shorten (3.2)
acostarse (ue)   to go to bed (1.2)
acostumbrado(a)   accustomed (1.3) **(6.3)**
acostumbrar   to be customary (1.3)

acostumbrarse (a)   to become accustomed (to) (4.2)
acrobacia *f.* **aérea**   aerobatics (8.2)
actitud *f.*   attitude (2.1)
actividad *f.*   activity (1.1)
activo(a)   active (1.1)
actriz *f.* *(pl.* **actrices***)*   actress (2.1)
actual   current, present-day (3.3)
actualmente   nowadays (2.1)
actuar   to act (7.2)
acuerdo *m.*   agreement, accord (2.1)
  de acuerdo   agreed (2.1)
acumular   to amass, accumulate (3.2)
adecuado(a)   adequate (5.1)
adelante   ahead; forward *(sports)* (2.2)
  en adelante   from now on, henceforth (3.2)
adelantero *m.*   forward *(sports)* (7.3)
adelanto *m.*   advance (5.1)
adelgazar   to make thin, make slender **(5.3)**
además   besides; moreover (1.1)
adicional   additional (7.1)
adiós   good-bye (1.1)
adivinar   to guess (1.1) **(8.3)**
adjetivo *m.*   adjective (1.3)
administración *f.*   administration (7.2)
administrador *m.*, **administradora** *f.*   administrator (8.2)
admiración *f.*   admiration (1.2)
admirar   to admire (4.1) **(6.1)**
adobe   sun-dried clay brick (1.2)
¿adónde?   (to) where? (1.1)
adoptar   to adopt (5.2)
adornado(a)   adorned (7.3)
adornar   to adorn (4.3)
adulto *m.*, **adulta** *f.*   adult (2.3)
advertir (ie, i)   to advise, warn **(6.3)**
aeropuerto *m.*   airport (1.3)
aeróbico(a)   aerobic **(5.1)**
afecto *m.*   affection (6.2)
afeitarse   to shave (3.3)
aficionado *m.*, **aficionada** *f.*   fan (5.1)
afines: palabras afines   cognates (3.3)
afirmar   to affirm, assert, state (5.3)
afirmativamente   affirmatively (1.1)
afirmativo(a)   affirmative (2.2)
aflicción *f.*   affliction, grief (8.1)
afortunadamente   fortunately **(5.1)**
agarrar   to grab, clutch (6.3)
agencia *f.*   agency (7.2)
agente *m. f.*   agent (5.2)
agilidad *f.*   agility (8.2)
agitado(a)   agitated, upset (3.3)
agradable   agreeable, nice (3.2)
agradecido(a)   thankful, grateful (1.3)
agrícola   agricultural, agrarian (1.1)
agricultor *m.*, **agricultora** *f.*   farmer (2.3)
agua *f.*   water (2.3)
aguacate *m.*   avocado (4.1)
aguafiestas *m. f.*   wet blanket, party pooper **(1.1)**

aguantar to bear, endure, put up with (6.1)
águila *f.* eagle (8.1)
ahí there (4.1)
ahogarse to drown (2.2); to suffocate
ahora now (1.2)
ahorrado(a) saved **(3.3)**
ahorrar to save **(7.1)**
aire *m.* air (1.2)
aislado(a) isolated **(3.1)**
ajo *m.* garlic (6.1)
ajustar to adjust (4.3)
al (a + el) to the + *m. sing. noun*
   al aire libre outdoors (1.1)
   al fondo in the background (5.3)
   al instante immediately (4.3)
   al lado on the side (1.3)
   al parecer apparently (3.2)
   al revés backwards, inside-out (6.3)
ala *f.* wing (2.1)
alambre *m.* wire (8.3)
alarmar to alarm (6.3)
albaricoque *m.* apricot (5.1)
albóndiga *f.* meatball (1.1)
albondiguita *f.* small meatball (5.2)
álbum *m.* album **(4.1)**
alcalde *m.* mayor (1.1)
alcaldía *f.* mayor's office (5.1)
alcanzar to reach, attain (1.2)
alcázar *m.* fortress; royal palace (2.1)
alcoba *f.* bedroom (2.1)
alegrarse to be glad, be happy **(5.3)**
alegre happy (1.3)
alegría *f.* happiness, joy (3.2)
alemán, alemana (*m. pl.* **alemanes**) German **(2.2)**
alfabeta literate (8.1)
alfabetismo *m.* literacy (6.1)
alfalfa *f.* alfalfa (5.1)
alfombra *f.* rug, carpet (3.1)
algo something **(1.1)**
algodón *m.* cotton (5.1)
algún, alguno some (1.1)
alguna vez at any point, ever (1.1)
alhaja *f.* jewel, gem (5.1)
alimentación *f.* food; nutrition (2.3)
alimento *m.* food, nourishment (8.3)
alma *f.* soul (1.2)
   alma en pena soul in torment (6.3)
almacén *m.* (*pl.* **almacenes**) department store (1.2)
almendra *f.* almond (5.1)
almohada *f.* pillow (2.3)
almorzar (ue) to eat lunch (1.2)
almuerzo *m.* lunch (1.3)
alquilar to rent (1.1)
alquimia *f.* alchemy (5.1)
alrededor (de) around (1.2)
alrededores *m. pl.* outskirts, surroundings (1.1)
alternar to alternate (3.2)

alto(a) high (1.2); tall
altura *f.* altitude; height (3.3)
alumbrado *m.* **eléctrico** electric wiring (4.1)
aluminio *m.* aluminum (2.1)
alumno *m.*, **alumna** *f.* student (1.2)
allí there (1.1)
amable friendly **(2.1)**
amado(a) dear, beloved (7.3)
amado(a) *n.* loved one (3.2)
amanecer *m.* dawn, daybreak (4.1)
amante *m. f.* lover, fan (3.2)
amar to love (1.3)
amarillo(a) yellow (1.1)
amarrado(a) tied (4.1)
ambiental environmental **(2.2)**
ambiente: medio ambiente environment (7.3)
ambos both (7.1)
ambulancia *f.* ambulance (3.1)
amenazar to threaten (2.3)
americano(a) American (1.1)
amigo *m.*, **amiga** *f.* friend (1.1)
amiguito *m.*, **amiguita** *f.* little friend (2.1)
amor *m.* love (3.2)
amoroso(a) related to love; loving (8.3)
ampliado(a) enlarged (4.3)
amplio(a) broad (7.1); wide
amueblado(a) furnished
anacardo *m.* cashew (2.3); cashew tree
anaconda *f.* anaconda (snake) **(2.2)**
analfabeto *m.* illiterate (person) (8.1)
anaranjado(a) orange (1.1)
anciano(a) old, elderly (1.) **(4.3)**
anciano *m.*, **anciana** *f.* elder (3.2)
andar to walk; to function, run (1.2) *pret.* **(3.1)**
   andar de compras to go shopping (1.2)
   andar de novios to date seriously (1.3)
   andar por las nubes to daydream, have one's head in the clouds (7.2)
andén *m.* (*pl.* **andenes**) (foot)path (4.1)
andino(a) Andean, of the Andes (8.1)
anexión *f.* annexation (1.1)
angelito *m.* little angel (2.2)
ángulo *m.* angle (4.1)
angustia *f.* anguish, distress (6.3)
animado(a) lively, bustling, busy (1.1)
ánima *f.* soul, spirit (5.3)
animar to encourage, cheer up; to enliven (7.2)
anoche last night (1.2)
anochecer to get dark, to become nighttime **(6.1)**
anotar to make a note of, jot down (1.3)
anónimo(a) anonymous (5.1)
ante before, in the face of (8.1)
anteojos *m. pl.* eye glasses (7.1)
antepasado *m.* ancestor (8.2)
anterior *adj.* previous (1.2)
antes (de) before (1.2)
anticipación *f.* anticipation **(8.1)**

anticipar to anticipate (1.3)
anticoagulante *m.* anticoagulant (2.3)
antigüedad *f.* antiquity (4.3)
antiguo(a) ancient, old (2.1)
Antillas *f. pl.* West Indies, the Antilles (2.1)
antipático(a) disagreeable, unpleasant (1.3)
antología *f.* anthology (6.3)
antropología *f.* anthropology (2.1)
anunciar to announce (3.3)
anuncio *m.* announcement, advertisement (2.1)
añadir to add **(3.3)**
año *m.* year (1.1)
apagar to turn off; to extinguish **(3.2)**
aparador *m.* cupboard (3.1)
aparecer to appear **(2.1)**
aparentemente apparently (1.3)
aparición *f.* apparition (6.3)
apariencia *f.* appearance (2.3)
apenas scarcely, hardly (5.2)
apéndice *m.* appendage (2.1); appendix
apertura *f.* opening (5.1)
apetecer to be appetizing to **(2.1);** to appeal to, take one's fancy
apio *m.* celery (6.2)
aplaudir to applaud (8.2)
apoderarse to seize, take possession of (7.3)
aprehensión *f.* apprehension (1.2)
aprender to learn (1.1) *pres. subj.* **(5.1)**
apretar to squeeze (1.2)
aprobar to approve, agree with (3.1)
apropiado(a) appropriate (1.1)
aprovechar to profit by; to take advantage of **(1.1)**
apuntar to point out (7.3)
apunte *m.* note (5.3)
    tomar (sacar) apuntes to take notes
aquel, aquella, aquellos, aquellas *adj.* that, those (*over there*) (3.1)
    aquel entonces that time (4.1)
aquél, aquélla, aquéllos, aquéllas *pron.* that one, those (ones) (3.1)
aquí here (1.1)
árabe *m. f.* Arab (5.1)
araña *f.* spider (5.2)
árbol *m.* tree (1.1) **(2.3)**
arco *m.* arch (5.1)
    arco *m.* **de herradura** horseshoe arch, Moorish arch (5.1)
área *f.* area (6.2)
arena *f.* sand (4.3)
arepa *f.* arepa (*griddle cake made of corn*) **(2.1)**
arepera *f.* cafe specializing in arepas **(8.3)**
arete *m.* earring (1.1) **(1.2)**
argentino(a) Argentine, Argentinian (2.2)
árido(a) arid, dry, barren (1.1)
armadillo *m.* armadillo (6.1)
armar to set up **(6.2);** to arm
armario *m.* closet (4.1)

armonía *f.* harmony (8.1)
aroma *m.* aroma, fragrance (2.3)
arqueología *f.* archaeology (3.3)
arqueológico(a) archaeological (4.1)
arqueólogo *m.,* **arqueóloga** *f.* archaeologist (3.3)
arquitecto *m.,* **arquitecta** *f.* architect (1.3)
arquitectura *f.* architecture (4.1)
arrancar to pull up, root out (4.3)
arreglar to arrange; to adjust, fix (1.3)
arreglarse to get ready (3.3)
arrepentirse to repent (5.1)
arriba above; up **(4.1)**
arrojar to throw (4.3)
arroz *m.* rice (1.3)
arruinado(a) ruined (8.2)
arte *m. f.* art (1.3)
artefacto *m.* artifact (6.2)
artesanía *f.* handicrafts (1.3)
artículo *m.* article (2.1)
artista *m. f.* artist (1.3); entertainer
asamblea *f.* assembly (8.2)
ascendencia *f.* rise (4.2)
aseador *m.* **de edificios** building caretaker (7.3)
asesinato *m.* murder, assassination (8.1)
asesino *m.* murderer, killer (5.1)
así so, thus (1.2); like this, in this way
asignar to assign (2.2)
asistencia *f.* help, assistance (6.1)
asistir (a) to attend **(1.1)** *pret.* **(2.2)**
asombrado(a) amazed, astonished **(4.3)**
asombrarse to be amazed, be astonished (6.1)
asombroso(a) amazing, astonishing (8.1)
aspiradora *f.* vacuum cleaner **(4.1)**
aspirar to vacuum (7.1)
astronauta *m. f.* astronaut (6.2)
astronomía *f.* astronomy (3.1)
astrónomo *m.,* **astrónoma** *f.* astronomer (3.1)
astucia *f.* cleverness, guile, cunning (7.3)
astuto(a) astute, intelligent, clever (3.1)
asunto *m.* matter, affair (3.3)
asustado(a) frightened (4.2) **(4.3)**
asustar to frighten (3.3) **(4.2)**
asustarse to be frightened, get scared (1.2)
atacar to attack (4.3)
atención *f.* (*pl.* **atenciones**) attention (2.2)
atento(a) attentive **(5.2)**
aterrorizado(a) terrified (5.1)
atleta *m. f.* athlete (8.1)
atlético(a) athletic (1.3)
atmósfera *f.* atmosphere (3.1)
atracción *f.* (*pl.* **atracciones**) attraction (7.1)
atractivo(a) attractive (6.2)
atraer to attract, draw, lure (2.3)
atrapado(a) trapped (8.3)
atrapar to nab; to trap **(4.3)**
atrás backwards (6.3)
atraso *m.* backwardness (7.2); delay

aun even (2.3)

aún still, yet (3.3)

aunque though, although (2.1)

autobús *m. (pl.* **autobuses***)* bus (2.3)

automovilístico(a) pertaining to automobiles (1.3)

autopista *f.* freeway (7.3)

autor *m.,* **autora** *f.* author (2.1)

autoridad *f.* authority **(3.1)**

autoritario(a) authoritarian (5.2)

autostop: hacer autostop to hitchhike (1.2)

autosuficiente self-sufficient (8.1)

auxilio *m.* help (2.2)

avance *m.* advance (2.3)

avanzado(a) advanced (5.1)

avaro(a) greedy, miserly (4.3)

ave *f.* bird (4.3)

avenida *f.* avenue (6.2)

aventón *m.* ride, lift (1.2)

aventura *f.* adventure (1.1)

aventurero *m.,* **aventurera** *f.* adventurer (4.3)

aventurero(a) adventurous (8.2)

avergonzado(a) embarrassed (1.2)

avión *m. (pl.* **aviones***)* airplane (2.3)

ayer yesterday (2.2)

ayudante *m., f.* helper, assistant (7.3)

ayudar to help (1.1)

azúcar *m.* sugar (2.1)

azul blue (1.1)

azulejo *m.* tile (5.1)

～～～ B ～～～

bailar to dance **(1.1)** *pret.* **(2.2)**

bailarín *m.,* **bailarina** *f. (pl.* **bailarines***)* dancer (6.3)

baile *m.* dance (1.3)

bajar to go down, lower (2.1)

bajo *prep.* under (1.1)

bajo(a) short (1.3); low (8.1)

balanceado(a) balanced **(5.2)**

balcón *m.* balcony (5.1)

baloncesto *m.* basketball (1.1)

balsa *f.* raft (3.3)

banco *m.* bank (3.2)

banda *f.* band (1.2)

bandada *f.* flock (6.3)

bandera *f.* flag **(8.3)**

bandido *m.* bandit (3.2)

banquete *m.* banquet, feast (2.3)

bañarse to take a bath (3.2)

  bañarse al sol to sunbathe **(3.2)**

baño *m.* bathroom (2.1)

barato(a) cheap, inexpensive **(3.2)**

barbaridad *f.* outrage (5.2); nonsense

barniz *m. (pl.* **barnices***)* varnish (2.3)

barrer to sweep **(4.1)**

barrio *m.* neighborhood *(of a town)* (5.3)

basado(a) (en) based (on) (2.1)

basar to base (6.3)

básquetbol *m.* basketball (1.3)

basta con to be enough, to suffice (3.1)

bastante more than enough (2.1); enough (3.1); fairly (5.3)

basura *f.* garbage **(1.3)**

basurero *m.,* **basurera** *f.* garbage collector **(3.1)**

bata *f.* bathrobe (3.3)

batería *f.* battery **(6.1)**

batido m. milkshake (2.1)

bebé *m. f.* baby (1.3)

beber to drink (1.1) *pret.* **(2.2)**

bebida *f.* drink (3.2)

beca *f.* scholarship (7.3)

béisbol *m.* baseball (1.2)

belleza *f.* beauty (4.3)

bello(a) beautiful (4.3)

bendición *f.* blessing (1.2)

bendito(a) blessed, holy (5.1)

beneficiarse to benefit, profit (7.1)

beso *m.* kiss (6.1)

biblioteca *f.* library (1.1)

bibliotecario *m.,* **bibliotecaria** *f.* librarian (7.3)

bicicleta *f.* bicycle (1.1)

bien well (1.1)

bienestar *m.* well-being (2.3)

bilingüe bilingual (1.1)

bilingüismo *m.* bilingualism (1.1)

biología *f.* biology (2.2)

blanco(a) white (1.1)

blando(a) soft (2.1)

blusa *f.* blouse (1.2)

boa *f.* boa constrictor **(2.2)**

bobo *m.,* **boba** *f.* fool (7.2)

bobo(a) foolish, stupid (3.1)

boca *f.* mouth (3.2); entrance (6.2)

boda *f.* wedding **(1.2)**

boleto *m.* ticket (7.1)

bolígrafo *m.* ballpoint pen (2.3)

bolívar *m.* bolívar *(monetary unit of Venezuela)* (2.1)

boliviano(a) Bolivian **(2.2)**

bolsa *f.* bag **(3.1)**

bolsillo: dinero *m.* **de bolsillo** allowance **(7.1)**

bomba *f.* **nuclear** nuclear bomb (8.1)

bombero *m.,* **bombera** *f.* fire fighter (7.3)

bondad *f.* good, goodness (7.1)

bondadoso(a) kind-hearted, good-natured (6.1)

bordadura *f.* embroidery (4.3)

bordar to embroider (5.3)

borde *m.* border (3.1)

borrador *m.* draft (1.3); eraser (2.3)

  primer borrador first draft (1.3)

borrega *f.* yearling sheep or lamb (1.3)

bosque *m.* woods, forest (8.3)

bota *f.* boot (6.2)

botar to throw away (4.2)

bote *m.* rowboat (3.3)
botella *f.* bottle (5.1)
brasileño(a) Brazilian **(2.2)**
¡bravo(a)! bravo! hooray! (1.1)
brazo *m.* arm (3.2)
brecha *f.* breach, gap (7.1)
breve brief (1.1)
brillante bright, shining, brilliant (2.1)
brillante *m.* diamond (4.3)
brillar to shine, be outstanding (7.3)
broche *m.* clasp (1.2)
bromear to joke (6.2)
bronceador *m.* suntan lotion **(3.2)**
bruja *f.* witch, sorceress (7.1)
bueno(a) good (1.1)
buey *m.* ox (7.2)
bulto *m.* ghost, apparition (1.2)
burlarse to laugh at, make fun of **(7.1)**
burocracia *f.* bureaucracy (7.2)
burro *m.*, **burra** *f.* donkey (6.2)
buscar to look for (1.2)
búsqueda *f.* search (2.2)

caballo *m.* horse (4.3)
caber to fit (4.1)
  no cabe duda there is no doubt (1.3)
cabeza *f.* head (3.2)
cabezazo *m.* header *(soccer shot)* (7.3)
cacahuate *m.* peanut (4.1)
cacao *m.* cacao, cocoa (2.1)
cacto *m.* cactus (8.1)
cada each, every (1.1)
cadena *f.* chain (4.3)
caer to fall (1.2)
caerse to fall, fall down (3.3)
café *m.* coffee; café (1.1)
cafeína *f.* caffeine (2.3)
cafetería *f.* cafeteria (1.2); café
caída *f.* fall (2.1)
caimán *m.* (*pl.* **caimanes**) caiman *(South American reptile)* **(2.2)**
caja *f.* cash register (3.2); box
  caja *f.* **registradora** cash register (7.1)
cajero *m.*, **cajera** *f.* cashier **(3.3)**
cajeta *f.* cajeta *(browned, sweetened, condensed milk)* (8.2)
cajita *f.* small box **(4.1)**
calabaza *f.* squash; pumpkin (4.1)
calandria *f.* calandra lark (8.2)
calcetín *m.* (*pl.* **calcetines**) sock (1.1)
calcular to calculate (1.2)
calentarse to warm (4.1)
calentito(a) (nice and) warm (3.1)
calibre *m.* caliber (7.3)

calidad *f.* quality (6.3)
caliente hot (8.3)
calientico(a) warm **(2.1)**
calificación *f.* (*pl.* **calificaciones**) qualification **(7.3)**; grade
calificar to grade (1.1)
caligráfico(a) calligraphic (5.1)
calmante *m.* sedative, tranquilizer (3.1)
calmarse to calm oneself **(5.3)**
calor *m.* heat (1.3)
calorcito *m.* warmth (4.3)
caloría *f.* calorie (3.2)
cama *f.* bed (1.3)
camafeo *m.* cameo brooch (1.2)
cámara *f.* camera **(3.2)**
camarero *m.*, **camarera** *m.* waiter, waitress (1.2)
camarón *m.* (*pl.* **camarones**) shrimp (1.3)
cambiar to change (1.2)
cambio *m.* change (5.2)
caminante *m. f.* traveler (3.2)
caminar to walk (1.2)
caminata *f.* hike (6.3)
camino *m.* road; way (3.2)
  camino a on the way to (1.2)
  camino abajo downhill (6.2)
camisa *f.* shirt (1.1)
camiseta *f.* T-shirt (1.1)
camote *m.* sweet potato (4.1)
campamento *m.* camp (1.1)
campaña *f.* campaign (8.1)
campeonato *m.* championship (1.3)
campesino *m.* farmer (8.1)
campo m. country (4.3); field (7.2); countryside
canadiense *m. f.* Canadian (2.2)
canal *m.* television channel, station **(3.1)**
  canal *m.* **de irrigación** irrigation canal (4.2)
canario *m.* canary (7.2)
canasta *f.* basket (4.3)
cancelar to cancel (4.1)
cáncer *m.* cancer (2.3)
canción *f.* (*pl.* **canciones**) song (3.1)
candidato *m.*, **candidata** *f.* candidate (5.1)
cangrejo *m.* crab (1.3)
cansado(a) tired (1.2)
cansarse (de) to get tired (of) (4.1)
cantante *m. f.* singer (1.3)
cantar to sing **(1.1)**
cantidad *f.* amount, quantity (6.2)
cantina *f.* bar (7.3)
canto *m.* song; singing (2.2); song; the art of singing (5.1)
cantor *m.* singer (8.2)
cañón *m.* (*pl.* **cañones**) canyon (4.2)
capacidad *f.* capacity (8.1)
capacitado(a) qualified, capable **(7.2)**
capaz (*pl.* **capaces**) capable (3.3)
caperucita *f.* small hood (4.3)

caperuza *f.* hood

capibara f. capybara *(a large South American rodent)* **(2.2)**

capítulo *m.* chapter (8.1)

caracol *m.* snail (6.3)

característica *f.* characteristic (2.1)

caracterizado(a) characterized (4.3)

caracterizarse to characterize (7.2)

¡caramba! wow! hey! (1.1)

carbón *m.* coal (2.1); charcoal

carcajada *f.* loud laugh, guffaw (6.2)

cárcel *f.* jail (6.1)

carga *f.* load (5.1)

cargado(a) laden, loaded (5.1)

cargar to carry (6.1); to load

cargo *m.* office *(position)* (7.2)

caricatura *f.* caricature, cartoon (4.3)

caricaturista *m. f.* caricaturist, cartoonist (3.1)

cariño *m.* affection, love (1.3)

cariñoso(a) affectionate, loving (7.3)

carne *f.* meat (1.3)

caro(a) expensive (2.3)

carpa *f.* tent **(6.2)**

carpeta *f.* folder (2.3)

carpintero *m.,* **carpintera** *f.* carpenter (5.1)

carrera *f.* career, profession **(5.2)**

carreta *f.* cart, wheelbarrow (6.3)

carretera *f.* highway **(6.1)**

carro *m.* car (1.2); cart, wagon (6.1)

   carros chocones *m. pl.* bumper cars (2.1)

carta *f.* letter (1.1); menu

cartera *f.* wallet (5.3)

casa *f.* house (1.1)

casado(a) married (1.3)

casarse con to get married to (1.3)

cascada *f.* waterfall (2.1)

casete *m.* cassette (6.1)

casi almost (1.1)

caso *m.* case, event (1.1)

castigar to punish (7.1)

casualidad *f.* chance, accident **(3.2)**

catarata *f.* waterfall (2.1) **(8.3)**

catecismo *m.* catechism (7.2)

catedral *f.* cathedral (2.1)

categoría *f.* category (1.1)

catolicismo *m.* Catholicism (4.1)

católico(a) Catholic (5.1)

caucho *m.* rubber (2.1)

causar to cause (2.3)

cazador *m.,* **cazadora** *f.* hunter (4.3)

cebolla *f.* onion (6.1)

celebración *f. (pl.* **celebraciones)** celebration (7.3)

celebrar to celebrate (4.2)

cementerio *m.* cemetery (1.2)

cemento *m.* cement (4.1)

cena *f.* dinner (1.1)

cenar to eat dinner (1.2)

ceniza *f.* ashes, cinder (6.1)

censo *m.* census

censura censorship (5.2)

centígrado *m.* centigrade **(3.1)**

centro *m.* center (1.2)

cepillarse (el pelo) to brush (one's hair) **(3.3)**

cepillo *m.* brush (6.1)

   cepillo *m.* **de dientes** toothbrush **(8.2)**

cerámica *f.* ceramics, pottery (4.3)

cerca (de) near (1.1)

cerrar (ie) to close (1.2)

certeza *f.* certainty (3.3)

   de certeza with certainty

cesar to cease, stop (8.1)

césped *m.* grass, lawn **(4.1)**

ciego *m.,* **ciega** *f.* blind person (7.2)

ciego(a) blind (2.2)

cielo *m.* sky (4.2); heavens (8.1)

ciencias *f. pl.* science (1.2)

científico *m.,* **científica** *f.* scientist **(2.2)**

ciento *m.* hundred (7.1)

cierto(a) sure, certain (1.1) **(5.1)**

cifra *f.* number (7.3)

cine m. movie theater (1.1)

cirugía *f.* surgery (2.3)

cita *f.* date, appointment (3.2)

ciudad *f.* city (1.1)

   ciudad *f.* **gemela** twin city (1.1)

ciudadano *m.,* **ciudadana** *f.* citizen (6.1)

civilización *f. (pl.* **civilizaciones)** civilization (4.3)

civilizado(a) civilized (4.1)

clarificar to clarify (1.3)

claro of course (1.2)

   ¡claro que sí! of course! (4.1)

claro(a) clear (2.2) **(5.1)**; light *(color)*

clase *f.* class (1.1); type (4.2)

clásico(a) classic, classical **(1.3)**

clasificado(a) classified **(7.2)**

cliente *m. f.* client (3.2)

clima *m.* climate **(1.3)**

cobija *f.* blanket, cover (1.3)

cocina *f.* kitchen (2.1)

cocinar to cook (1.1)

cocinero *m.,* **cocinera** *f.* cook, chef (5.2)

coco *m.* coconut *(fruit)*; coconut tree (2.3)

coche *m.* car (1.3)

cochinada *f.* filthy mess (6.1)

cochinillo *m.* suckling pig (4.3)

cochino *m.* pig **(4.3)**

codicia *f.* greed (6.3)

codicioso(a) *n.* one who is greedy (6.3)

codo *m.* elbow (7.2)

coger to take (hold of); to seize (2.3)

cola *f.* soft drink (2.3); tail (3.3)

colchón *m. (pl.* **colchones)** mattress **(3.3)**

colegio *m.* school (1.1)

colgado(a) hung (1.2)

colonia *f.* colony (2.3); neighborhood, community (7.1)

colorado(a) red (5.3)

colorido(a) colored (3.2)

columna *f.* column (1.3)

collar *m.* necklace (1.1) **(1.2)**

combatir to fight; to struggle (7.2)

combinar to combine, put together (1.2)

comedor *m.* dining room (2.1)

comentario *m.* comment, commentary (1.3)

comenzar (ie) to begin (1.2)

comer to eat (1.1) *pret.* **(2.2)** *pres. perf.* **(6.2)**

comercial *adj.* commercial (1.2)

comerciante *m. f.* merchant, trader (1.1)

comercio *m.* commerce, trade (2.1)

cómico(a) funny (1.3)

comida *f.* food; meal (1.1)

comienzo *m.* beginning (1.1)

comité *m.* committee (8.2)

¿cómo? how? what? (1.1)

cómodo(a) comfortable (2.1)

compacto(a) compact (4.2)

compadre *m.* friend, companion (6.1); godfather

compañero *m.,* **compañera** *f.* partner (1.1); companion

compañía *f.* company (4.2) **(7.2)**

comparación *f.* (*pl.* **comparaciones**) comparison (5.3)

comparar to compare (1.3) **(2.3)**

comparado compared to (4.2)

compartir to divide (up), share (2.3)

competir (i, i) to compete **(8.1)**

complacer to please (6.3)

complejo(a) complex (4.3)

completado(a) completed (7.3)

completar to complete (1.1)

completo(a) complete, whole **(1.2)**

complicado(a) complicated **(5.2)**

comportamiento behavior, conduct (5.2)

comportarse to behave **(4.1)**

composición *f.* (*pl.* **composiciones**) composition (1.1)

comprar to buy (1.1)

compras *f.* purchase, buying
   de compras shopping (1.1)

comprender to understand (2.1)

compuesto de composed of, made up of (8.1)

computadora *f.* computer (1.3)

común common, ordinary (3.3)

comunicarse to communicate with **(3.3)**

con with (1.1)

concebir: concibiendo conceiving (3.3)

concentrarse to concentrate (3.2)

conciencia: tomar conciencia to become aware of (4.3)

concierto *m.* concert (1.1)

concordar (ue) to agree (1.3)

concurso *m.* contest **(4.2)**

condición *f.* (*pl.* **condiciones**) condition (7.2)

cóndor *m.* condor (8.2)

conducir to drive (1.3) *cond.* **(8.2)**; to lead (1.2)

conectarse to log on; connect to **(3.3)**

conejo *m.,* **coneja** *f.* rabbit (3.1)

conferencia *f.* conference, meeting (8.2)

confesar to confess (4.2)

confianza: de confianza trustworthy, reliable (3.2)

confiar to trust, confide in **(3.3)**

confirmar to confirm (1.3)

confundido(a) confused **(5.3)**

confuso(a) confusing (2.2)

congreso *m.* congress; meeting (6.2)

conmigo with me (5.2)

conocer to know, be acquainted with (1.1); to meet

conocido *m.* acquaintance (7.2)

conocido(a) known (1.2)

conocimiento *m.* knowledge (4.2)

conquistador *m.,* **conquistadora** *f.* conquistador (1.1)

consecuencia *f.* consequence (3.2)

conseguir (i, i) to get, obtain (1.2)

consejero *m.,* **consejera** *f.* counselor, adviser **(5.3)**

consejo *m.* advice (1.3) **(3.2)**

consentimiento *m.* consent (6.2)

consentir to consent (4.3)

conservador(a) conservative (7.2)

conservar to preserve, maintain (1.1)

considerar to consider (3.3)

consistente consistent (1.3)

consistir de to consist of (2.3)

consolar to console (1.2)

constantemente constantly (7.3)

constar de to consist of, be composed of (7.1)

constitución *f.* constitution (6.1)

constituir to constitute (3.3)

constructor *m.,* **constructora** *f.* builder (3.3)

construir to build (3.2)

consultar to consult (4.1)

consumirse to consume oneself (3.2)

contacto *m.* contact (2.2)

contaminación *f.* pollution **(5.1)**

contaminado(a) contaminated, polluted (8.1)

contaminante *m.* pollutant (2.3)

contaminar to contaminate, pollute (2.3)

contar (ue) to tell, recount (1.1); to count (1.2)
   contar con to depend on (1.3)

contemplado(a) contemplated; looked at (4.3)

contener to contain (1.2)

contenido *m.* content (1.3)

contentarse to be contented, be satisfied (7.3)

contento(a) happy, content (1.2)

contestar to answer **(1.2)**

contigo with you (1.1)

continente *m.* continent (2.3)

continuación: a continuación following, next, continuation **(3.2)**

continuar to continue (1.3)

continuo(a) continual (2.3)

contra against (1.1)

contrario: al contrario on the contrary **(3.1)**

contraste *m.* contrast (3.1)

contribuir to contribute (6.1)

controlar to control (4.1)
convencer to convince **(4.2)**
conversación *f.* (*pl.* **conversaciones**) conversation (1.1)
conversar to converse, chat (1.3)
convertir (ie, i) to convert (1.1)
convertirse en (ie, i) to convert into (1.2)
convivencia *f.* coexistence (5.1)
cooperar to cooperate (3.2)
corazón *m.* heart (2.3)
corbata *f.* necktie (5.2)
cordillera *f.* mountain range **(2.3)**
cordón *m.* cord, cordon (4.3)
coreano(a) Korean **(2.2)**
coro *m.* chorus, choir (7.3)
corona *f.* crown (3.3)
coronel *m.* colonel (6.3)
corporación *f.* (*pl.* **corporaciones**) corporation (6.2)
correcto(a) correct (5.1)
corregir (i, i) to correct **(4.3)**
correo *m.* mail **(1.1)**
   correo electrónico electronic mail **(3.3)**
correr to run **(1.1)** *pret.* **(2.2)** *imperf.* **(3.3)** *fut.* **(8.1)**
correspondencia *f.* correspondence **(1.1)**
corriente ordinary, common **(3.1)**
corriente *f.* current (3.3)
corroído(a) corroded (6.1)
cortar to cut (1.2)
corte *f.* court (7.3)
cortés courteous **(5.2)**
cortésmente courteously, politely (3.2)
cortina curtain, screen (5.2)
cosa *f.* thing (1.1)
coser to sew (5.3)
cosmopolita cosmopolitan (2.1)
costa *f.* coast (2.1) **(2.3)**
costar (ue) to cost (1.2)
costarricense *m. f.* Costa Rican (2.2)
costo *m.* cost (7.1)
costoso(a) costly, expensive (2.1)
costumbre *f.* custom, habit (1.3) **(7.1)**
costurera *f.* seamstress (3.3)
cotidiano(a) daily (6.3)
creado: todo lo creado all that is created (3.2)
creador *m.,* **creadora** *f.* creator (3.3)
crear to create (3.3)
creatividad *f.* creativity (4.1)
creativo(a) creative (2.2)
crecer to grow (1.3)
creencia *f.* belief (4.1)
creer to believe (1.1)
crema *f.* cream **(8.2)**
cresta *f.* crest of a rooster (4.2)
cría *f.* baby animal (8.3)
criado *m.,* **criada** *f.* servant (5.2)
criado(a) brought up, raised (2.3)
criar to raise (2.3) **(4.3)**
criarse to grow up (1.1)

criatura *f.* creature (7.2)
crimen *m.* (*pl.* **crímenes**) crime **(5.1)**
cristal *m.* crystal, glass (8.3)
cristalizado(a) crystallized (4.1)
cristiano *m.* Christian (5.1)
crítica criticism (5.2)
criticón *m.* (*pl.* **criticones**) critic, faultfinder (7.2)
cronológico(a) chronological **(3.3)**
cruelmente cruelly (8.3)
cruzar to cross (8.2)
cuaderno *m.* notebook (2.1)
cuadra *f.* city block (1.1)
cuadrado *m.* square **(1.1)**
cuadrado(a) square (4.1)
cuadrícula *f.* a pattern of squares **(1.1)**
cuadro *m.* chart, table, diagram (8.3)
¿cuál(es)? which, which one(s)? (1.1)
cualidad *f.* quality (8.3)
cualquier(a) *pron.* anybody, whoever, whichever (7.3)
cuando when (1.2) **(4.1)**
¿cuándo? when? (1.1)
¿cuánto(a)? ¿cuántos(as)? how much?, how many? (1.1)
cuarto *m.* room (1.2)
cubano(a) Cuban (2.2)
cubierto(a) covered (5.1)
cubiertos *m. pl.* place settings (3.2)
cubrir to cover (4.2)
cuenta *f.* bill, check; account (1.1)
   darse cuenta to realize (7.3)
cuento *m.* tale, story (1.2)
cuerda *f.* rope (4.1)
cuerpo *m.* body (5.2)
cuervo *m.* crow (8.2)
   cuervo *m.* **negro** black crow (8.2)
cuestionario m. questionnaire (1.3) **(3.3)**
cueva *f.* cave (5.2) **(6.2)**
cuidado careful (1.2)
cuidado *m.* care (6.3)
   con cuidado with care, carefully (3.3)
cuidadosamente carefully (6.2)
cuidar to take care of (1.3)
culebra *f.* snake **(2.2)**
cultivar to cultivate; to farm (2.3)
cultivo *m.* cultivation (1.1)
cultura *f.* culture (1.1) **(1.3)**
cumbre *f.* summit (8.1)
cumpleaños *m.* birthday (1.2)
cumplido(a) fulfilled (8.1)
cumplir to fulfill, carry out (1.1)
cura *f.* cure (8.1)
cura *m.* priest (3.3)
curandero *m.,* **curandera** *f.* witch doctor; healer (4.3)
curiosidad *f.* curiosity (1.2) **(8.1)**
curioso(a) curious (3.1)
curso *m.* course (*academic*) (7.1)
   fin *m.* **de curso** end of the school year (7.3)

～～CH～～

chaleco *m.*   vest (5.3)
chalé *m.*   chalet (5.3)
champú *m.*   shampoo **(8.2)**
chaqueta *f.*   jacket (1.1)
charlar   to chat, talk (1.1)
cheque *m.*   check (6.1)
¡chévere!   fantastic! **(2.1)**
chica *f.*   girl (2.2)
chicle *m.*   chewing gum (2.3)
chico *m.*   boy (1.1)
chile *m.*   (chile) pepper (4.1)
   chile colorado *m.*   red pepper (1.3)
chileno(a)   Chilean (2.2)
chino(a)   Chinese **(1.3)**
chisme *m.*   gossip, tale (2.1) **(5.3)**
chispa *f.*   spark (6.3)
chiste *m.*   joke (8.2)
chistoso(a)   funny **(6.3)**
chocar   to collide, crash, run into (3.1)
chofer *m.*   driver (8.2); chauffeur
chorrito *m.*   trickle, small stream (7.1)
chuchería   candy, junk food **(5.1)**

～～D～～

dama *f.*   lady (3.2)
damas *f. pl.*   checkers **(4.1)**
danés, danesa (*m. pl.* **daneses**)   Danish **(2.2)**
danzante *m.*   dancer (8.2)
danzar   to dance (3.2)
dañino(a)   harmful, injurious **(3.2)**
dar   to give (1.1) *pres. subj.* **(5.1)**
   dar una vuelta   take a ride **(7.1)**
   dar vuelta   to turn around; to flip (8.2)
   darle de comer   to feed **(4.2)**
   darse cuenta   to realize (1.2)
dato *m.*   fact (8.1)
de   of; from (1.1)
   de acuerdo   agreed (2.1)
   de acuerdo a   according to (7.1)
   de largo   in length (3.1)
   de moda   in fashion (1.1)
   de nuevo   again (1.2)
   de prisa   quickly (5.1)
   de repente   suddenly (4.3)
   de vez en cuando   from time to time (4.1)
debajo de   under, underneath (4.3)
deber   to be obliged; should, must (1.2); to owe (6.2)
debido a   due to, owing to (5.1)
débil   weak **(1.3)**
debilitarse   to become weak (1.3)
década *f.*   decade (4.3)
decente   respectable (7.2); decent

decidir   to decide (1.1)
decir   to say; to tell (1.1) *pres. subj.* **(5.1)** *pres. perf.* **(6.2)** *fut.* **(8.1)** *cond.* **(8.2)**
decisión *f.* (*pl.* **decisiones**)   decision (3.3)
declarar   to declare (1.1)
decoración *f.* (*pl.* **decoraciones**)   decoration (7.2)
decorado(a)   decorated (1.2)
decorar   to decorate (4.1)
dedicación *f.* (*pl.* **dedicaciones**)   dedication (3.2)
dedicado(a)   dedicated (1.1)
dedicarse   to devote oneself (3.2)
defenderse   to defend oneself (4.1)
definitivamente   definitively (4.1)
deforestación *f.*   deforestation (6.1)
dejar   to allow; to let (1.1); to leave (behind) (1.2)
   déjame ver   let me see **(1.2)**
   dejar de + *inf.*   to stop (4.1)
delgado(a)   thin, slender (1.3)
deliberadamente   deliberately (8.2)
delicioso(a)   delicious (2.3)
delincuencia *f.*   delinquency (8.2)
delincuente *m. f.*   delinquent, offender (8.2)
demandar   to demand, ask for (8.1)
demás: los demás   the rest; the others (2.3)
demasiado(a)   too, too much (1.2)
democracia *f.*   democracy (5.1)
democrático(a)   democratic (6.1)
democratización *f.*   democratization (8.1)
demonio: un frío de mil demonios   bitter cold (3.1)
demostración *f.* (*pl.* **demostraciones**)   demonstration **(5.2)**
demostrar   to demonstrate (2.3)
dentista *m. f.*   dentist (2.1)
dentro   within (1.3); inside (3.3)
   dentro de   in, within **(8.2)**
denunciar   to denounce (4.2)
departamento *m.*   department (7.3)
depender (de)   to depend (on) (2.1) **(7.1)**
dependiente *m. f.*   salesclerk (7.2)
deporte *m.*   sport (1.1)
deportista *m. f.*   sportsman, sportswoman (2.1)
deportivo(a)   athletic; pertaining to sports (2.1)
depositar   to deposit **(3.3)**
deprimido(a)   depressed **(5.2)**
derecha *f.*   right, right side (3.2)
derecho *m.*   right *(legal)* (5.2)
derecho *prep.*   straight ahead (6.2)
derecho(a)   right (3.2)
derrota *f.*   defeat (7.3)
desafortunadamente   unfortunately (7.2)
desafortunado   unfortunate (6.1)
desanimado(a)   discouraged, dispirited (7.2)
desaparecer   to disappear (2.3)
desaparecidos *m. pl.*   the missing (ones) (8.1)
desarmador *m.*   screwdriver (6.1)
desarrollar   to develop (1.1)
desarrollo *m.*   development (2.3)

desastre *m.* disaster (7.2)
desayunar to eat breakfast (1.1)
desayuno *m.* breakfast (1.2)
descansar to rest (1.1)
descanso *m.* rest (2.2)
descendencia *f.* descent, origin (8.1)
descendiente *m. f.* descendant (2.1)
desconcertado(a) disconcerted, flustered (1.2)
desconectarse to log off; disconnect from **(3.3)**
desconocer to not know, be ignorant of (3.3)
desconocido *n.* unknown person, stranger (3.2)
desconocido(a) unknown (8.1)
descortés impolite (3.2)
describir to describe (1.1)
descripción *f.* (*pl.* **descripciones**) description **(1.3)**
descubrimiento *m.* discovery (3.1)
descubrir to discover (3.1) *pres. perf.* **(6.2)**
desde from (3.1); since (1.3)
   desde entonces since then (6.3)
desear to desire, wish (3.2)
desembarcar to disembark, to land (2.3)
desembocar to flow into *(river)* **(2.3)**
desempacar to unpack (2.1)
desempeñar to play (a role) (5.2); to fill, hold (an office) (7.2)
desenchufar to disconnect, unplug **(3.2)**
deseo *m.* desire (5.1)
desértico(a) desert-like (1.1)
desesperado(a) desperate **(4.3)**
desfile *m.* parade (5.1)
desgastado(a) worn-out (1.2)
desgraciadamente unfortunately (2.3)
deshonesto(a) dishonest **(3.2)**
desierto *m.* desert (3.1)
desigual unequal, different (7.1)
desilusionarse to be disappointed (1.1)
desmorecido: desmorecidos de risa dying of laughter (6.2)
desolación *f.* desolation; grief (3.2)
desorganizado(a) disorganized (1.2)
despacio slowly (8.2)
despedirse (i, i) to say good-bye (1.1)
despertarse (ie) to wake up (1.2)
despierto(a) *n.* one who is awake (6.3)
después (de) after (3.1)
destinación *f.* (*pl.* **destinaciones**) destination (6.2)
destrozado(a) broken (4.3); destroyed
destrucción *f.* destruction (2.3)
destruido(a) destroyed (2.3)
destruir to destroy (3.3)
desvencijado(a) broken-down; disadvantaged (7.3)
desventaja *f.* disadvantage (7.1)
desventajado(a) disadvantaged (7.3)
desventajado(a) *n.* one who is disadvantaged (7.3)
detalle *m.* detail (3.1) **(4.1)**
detenerse to stop (6.1)
detenidamente slowly, carefully, thoroughly (4.3)

determinar to decide, make up one's mind (6.2); to determine
detrás de behind (4.3)
deuda *f.* debt (7.2)
devorar to devour (1.3)
día *m.* day (1.1)
diablito *m.* little devil (4.1)
diablo *m.,* **diabla** *f.* devil (3.3)
diagrama *m.* diagram (1.3)
diálogo *m.* dialogue (2.2)
diamante *m.* diamond (2.1)
diario(a) daily (1.2) **(2.2)**
dibujar to draw (2.1) **(6.2)**
dibujo *m.* drawing, sketch (1.1)
dictador *m.* dictator (5.2)
dictadura *f.* dictatorship (5.2)
dictar to dictate (1.3)
dicho *past part.* **(decir)** said (6.2)
dicho *m.* saying, proverb (7.2)
diente *m.* tooth (2.3)
dieta *f.* diet **(5.1)**
diferencia *f.* difference (4.1)
diferente different (1.3)
difícil difficult (3.2)
dificultad *f.* difficulty (4.2)
dilema *m.* dilemma (3.1)
diminutivo *m.* diminutive (6.2)
dinero *m.* money (1.2)
   dinero *m.* **de bolsillo** allowance, pocket money **(7.1)**
dios *m.* god (3.3)
   ¡dios mío! my God!, my goodness! (3.3)
dirección *f.* (*pl.* **direcciones**) address (5.1); instructions
directamente directly (3.2)
director *m.,* **directora** *f.* principal; director (1.1)
   director *m.* **asociado** associate director (7.3)
   director *m.* **en escena** stage director (5.3)
dirigir to manage, direct (3.2)
dirigirse (a) to address, speak to (2.2); to go to (8.2)
disciplinar to discipline (4.1)
disco *m.* record (1.2)
   disco compacto compact disc
discoteca *f.* discotheque (1.1)
discurso *m.* speech (7.3)
discutir to discuss (1.2) **(8.1)**; to argue
diseñar to design (7.3)
diseño *m.* design *(pattern)* (4.3)
disminuir to diminish (7.2)
disperso(a) dispersed, scattered (3.3)
disponible available (7.3)
distancia *f.* distance (3.1)
   a la distancia in the distance (3.1)
distinguir to distinguish (6.1)
distinto(a) different, distinct (1.1)
diversidad *f.* diversity, variety (2.1)
diversificado(a) diversified (7.1)
diversión *f.* (*pl.* **diversiones**) diversion, entertainment (2.1)

diverso(a) diverse, different (1.1) **(2.3)**
divertido(a) amusing, fun (1.3)
divertirse (ie, i) to have a good time (1.2) *pres. subj.* **(5.2)**
dividir to divide (5.2)
doblar to turn (3.2); to fold (5.1); to double
doble *m.* double (1.1)
docena *f.* dozen (3.3)
doctor *m.,* **doctora** *f.* doctor (1.2)
doler (ue) to hurt (1.2)
dolor *m.* pain (4.3)
doméstico(a) domestic (3.2)
dominación *f.* domination, rule (5.1)
dominar to rule; to control (1.1)
domingo *m.* Sunday (1.2)
dominicano(a) Dominican (2.2)
dominio *m.* dominion, power, authority (5.1)
don *m.* Don *(title of respect)* (4.3)
¿dónde? where? (1.1)
dorado(a) golden (2.3)
dormido(a) asleep (2.2) **(5.1)**
dormilera: té de dormilera sleep-inducing tea (5.1)
dormilón *m.,* **dormilona** *f.* sleepyhead **(8.1)**
dormirse (ue, u) to go to sleep; to fall asleep (3.3) *pres. subj.* **(5.2)** *fut.* **(8.1)**
dote *m.* dowry (4.3)
drama *m.* drama (6.3)
dramático(a) dramatic (4.1)
dramatizar to dramatize (1.1)
duda *f.* doubt (4.3) **(7.1)**
  no cabe duda there is no doubt (1.3)
dudar to doubt **(6.1)**
dudosamente doubtfully (5.2)
dudoso(a) doubtful **(5.1)**
dueño *m.,* **dueña** *f.* owner (1.3)
dulce *m.* candy (2.3) **(5.1)**; sweet
duplicar to duplicate (4.3)
durante during (1.1); for *(time)* (5.1)
durar to last (2.2)
duro(a) hard (2.3)

～～E～～

ecología *f.* ecology (6.1)
economía *f.* economy (2.1)
económico(a) economic (1.1); economical **(1.3)**
ecuador *m.* equator (2.3)
ecuatoriano(a) Ecuadorian (2.2)
echar de menos to miss **(1.1)**
echar la culpa to blame (7.3)
echarse to throw oneself (2.2)
edad *f.* age (1.1)
edición *f. (pl.* **ediciones)** edition (8.1)
edificio *m.* building (2.3)
educación *f.* education (1.3); good breeding
  educación *f.* **pública** public education (7.2)
educacional educational (3.2)

educador *m.,* **educadora** *f.* educator, teacher (3.2)
educar to educate (3.2)
efectivamente really, in fact (7.2)
efecto *m.* effect (2.3)
ejemplar *m.* specimen, example (6.1)
ejemplo *m.* example (1.1)
ejercicio *m.* exercise (1.1) **(2.3)**
ejército *m.* army (5.2)
el the (1.1)
él he (1.1)
elaborado(a) elaborate (4.3)
elección *f. (pl.* **elecciones)** election (3.1)
electricidad *f.* electricity (3.3)
eléctrico(a) electric, electrical (7.2)
electrónico: correo electrónico *m.* electronic mail **(3.3)**
elefante *m.* elephant (2.3)
elegante elegant (1.1)
elemento *m.* element (6.2)
elevar to erect (3.3); to raise
eliminar to eliminate (8.2)
ella she (1.1)
embrujado(a) haunted (3.3)
emergencia *f.* emergency (3.2)
emisario *m.,* **emisaria** *f.* emissary (7.3)
emoción *f. (pl.* **emociones)** emotion (5.3)
emocionado(a) emotional, excited (1.2)
empacar to pack (2.1)
empate *m.* tie *(in sports)* (2.2)
emperador *m.* emperor (4.2)
empezar (ie) to begin (1.2) *pres. subj.* **(5.2)**
empleado *m.,* **empleada** *f.* employee **(3.1)**
emplear to employ **(7.2)**; to use
empleo *m.* employment; job (7.1) **(7.2)**
empresa *f.* enterprise, business **(7.3)**
en in **(1.1)**
  en adelante henceforth (1.3)
  en busca de in search of (2.2)
  en camino on the way (2.3)
  en cuanto a with regard to, as to (6.3)
  en efecto in fact, actually (1.2) **(4.2)**
  en el fondo at heart, really (5.3)
  en gran parte most (2.1)
  en medio in the middle (5.1)
  en oferta on sale (1.2)
  en peligro in danger (6.1)
  en primer lugar in the first place (1.1)
  en punto on the dot *(time)* (1.1)
  en realidad in reality (2.2)
  en seguida right away (1.1)
  en su camino on her (his) way (2.2)
  en vano in vain (4.1)
  en vez de instead of (6.2)
enamorado(a) in love **(5.3)**
enamorarse de to fall in love with (7.3)
encaje *m.* lace (1.2)
encaminarse to set out for, take the road to (7.3)
encantado(a) delighted (1.1); enchanted (2.2)

encantador(a)   charming (1.2)
encantar   to love, really like (1.1)
encargado(a)   in charge (6.2)
encerrar (ie)   to shut in, lock up (4.1) to enclose
enciclopedia *f.*   encyclopedia (2.3)
encima de   on top of; above (6.2)
encontrar (ue)   to find; to meet (1.1)
encuentro *m.*   encounter, meeting (6.3)
encuesta *f.*   survey (1.1) **(3.3)**
enchilada *f.*   enchilada *(corn tortilla dipped in hot sauce and filled with meat or cheese)* (1.3)
energía *f.*   energy **(5.1)**
   energía *f.* **nuclear**   nuclear energy (8.1)
enfermarse   to become ill (1.3)
enfermedad *f.*   illness; disease (2.3)
   enfermedad venérea   venereal disease (5.2)
enfermero *m.,* **enfermera** *f.*   nurse (1.2)
enfermizo(a)   sickly (3.3)
enfermo(a)   sick (4.3)
enfocado(a)   focused (8.1)
enfrente de   facing, in front of (6.3)
enfurecer   to infuriate **(5.3)**
enfurecerse   to become furious (5.1)
enfurecido(a)   furious (4.2)
engañar   to trick, deceive (6.1)
engaño *m.*   trick, deception (8.3)
engordarse   to gain weight **(5.1)**
enigmático(a)   enigmatic, mysterious (4.3)
enjaulado(a)   caged (8.3)
enojado(a)   angry (6.1)
enojar   to anger (7.1)
enojarse   to get angry (4.2) **(5.3)**
enorme   enormous (4.3)
enrollado(a)   rolled up (1.3)
ensalada *f.*   salad (1.1)
enseñanza *f.*   teaching (3.2)
enseñar   to show; to teach (2.1) **(6.1)**
entender (ie)   to understand (1.2)
entero(a)   entire, whole (1.3)
enterrado(a)   buried (3.3)
enterrar(ie)   to bury (2.2)
entierro *m.*   burial, funeral (4.1)
entonces   then (1.1)
entrada   entrance (5.2)
entrar   to enter (1.1)
entre   among (3.1); between (3.2)
entregar   to deliver **(3.3)**; to hand in
entregarse   to devote oneself (4.3)
entremés *m.* *(pl.* **entremeses)**   appetizer (1.2)
entrenador *m.,* **entrenadora** *f.*   trainer (1.2)
entrenamiento *m.*   training **(7.3)**
entretener   to entertain (8.2)
entrevistador *m.,* **entrevistadora** *f.*   interviewer **(7.3)**
entrevistar   to interview (1.1)
entristecer   to sadden **(5.3)**
entusiasmado(a)   excited, delighted, filled with enthusiasm (7.2)

entusiasmo *m.*   enthusiasm (8.2)
envenenado(a)   poisoned (7.3)
enviar   to send (7.1)
envidia *f.*   envy **(8.1)**
episodio *m.*   episode (3.3)
época *f.*   epoch, period, time (5.1)
equilibrio *m.*   balance (2.3)
equipo *m.*   team (1.2)
ermitaño *m.*   hermit **(6.3)**
escalera *f.*   stairs, staircase (3.3)
escapar   to escape (5.2)
escarbar   to dig (3.3)
escargot *(French)*   snail (6.3)
escena: director *m.* **en escena**   stage director (5.3)
esclavo *m.*   slave (2.1)
escocés *m.,* **escocesa** *f.* *(m. pl.* **escoceses)**   Scottish **(2.2)**
escoger   to select (3.2)
escolar   pertaining to school (1.1)
esconder(se)   to hide (oneself) (4.1) **(4.3)**
escribir   to write (1.1) *pret.* **(2.2)** *pres. perf.* **(6.2)**
   escribir a máquina   to type **(7.2)**
escrito(a)   written (3.1)
escritor *m.,* **escritora** *f.*   writer (3.2)
escritorio *m.*   desk (4.2)
escritura *f.*   writing (4.1)
escuchar   to listen to (1.1) *pret.* **(2.2)**
escudo *m.*   coat-of-arms, shield (8.1)
escuela *f.*   school (1.1)
   escuela primaria *f.*   primary school (3.2)
escultura *f.*   sculpture (3.3)
escupir   to spit (7.2)
ese, esa *adj.*   that (1.2)
ése, ésa *pron.*   that (one) (3.1)
esencial   essential **(8.2)**
esforzarse (ue) por   to strive to (3.3)
esfuerzo *m.*   effort (4.3)
esos, esas *adj.*   those (3.1)
ésos, ésas *pron.*   those (3.1)
espacio *m.*   space (5.3)
espada *f.*   sword (7.1)
espanto *m.*   fright, terror **(6.3)**
espantoso(a)   frightful, terrifying (4.1)
español *m.*   Spanish *(language)* (1.2)
español *m.,* **española** *f.*   Spaniard (2.2)
especial   special (1.1)
especialidad *f.*   specialty (1.2)
especialista *m. f.*   specialist (3.3)
especializar   to specialize **(8.3)**
especie *f.*   species; kind (2.3) **(4.1)**
específico(a)   specific (2.3)
espectáculo *m.*   spectacle, sight (2.1); show, performance (7.2)
esperanza *f.*   hope **(5.1)**
esperar   to wait for (2.1); to hope for (4.3); to expect
espía *m. f.*   spy (2.2)
espiar   to spy (4.1)
espiral *f.*   spiral (4.3)

espléndido(a) splendid (2.3)

esplendor *m.* splendor (7.3)

esposo *m.*, **esposa** *f.* husband, wife (5.1)

espuela *f.* spur (4.1)

esquema *m.* diagram, outline, plan (1.3)

    esquema *m.* **araña** clustering, visual mapping (4.2)

esquí *m.* (*pl.* **esquíes**) ski; skiing (7.1)

esquiador *m.*, **esquiadora** *f.* skier (3.1)

esquiar to ski **(1.3)**

esquina *f.* (street) corner (2.2)

estabilidad *f.* stability (8.1)

establecer to establish (1.1)

establecerse to take up residence (2.3)

establecimiento *m.* establishment, founding, setting-up (6.1)

estaca *f.* stake (4.3)

estación *f.* (*pl.* **estaciones**) television station (3.1); season of the year

estadístico(a) statistical (1.3)

estado *m.* state (1.1)

estadounidense *m. f.* of the United States, American **(2.2)**

estancamiento stagnation, paralysis (5.2)

estante *m.* bookcase (3.1)

estar to be (1.1) *pres. subj.* **(5.1)**

    estar frustrado(a) to be frustrated **(1.2)**

    estar loco(a) to be crazy (5.2)

    estar loco(a) por to be crazy about **(5.3)**

    estar muerto(a) to be dead **(5.2)**

    estar seguro(a) to be sure **(1.2)**

estatua *f.* statue (3.3)

este *m.* east (3.1)

este, esta *adj.* this (1.1)

éste, ésta *pron.* this (one) (3.1)

estereotipo *m.* stereotype (7.3)

estilizado(a) stylized (4.3)

estilo *m.* style (1.2)

estómago *m.* stomach (4.3)

estos, estas *adj.* these (3.1)

éstos, éstas *pron.* these (3.1)

estrella *f.* star (4.3)

estrofa *f.* verse, stanza (6.3)

estructura *f.* structure (4.1)

estudiante *m. f.* student (1.1)

estudiantil pertaining to students (3.1)

estudiar to study (1.1)

estudio *m.* study **(2.2)**

estudioso(a) studious (1.3)

estufa *f.* stove (3.3)

etapa *f.* stage, phase (5.1)

eterno(a) eternal (1.2)

étnico(a) ethnic **(2.3)**

europeo(a) European (2.1)

evidencia *f.* evidence, proof (7.2)

evitar to avoid **(3.2)**

exactamente exactly (6.3)

exagerado(a) exaggerated **(6.1)**

examen *m.* (*pl.* **exámenes**) exam, test (1.1)

excavación *f.* (*pl.* **excavaciones**) excavation (6.1)

excelente excellent (1.1)

excéntrico(a) eccentric (6.3)

exclusivo(a) exclusive (7.1)

excursión *f.* (*pl.* **excursiones**) excursion, short trip (1.1)

excusa *f.* excuse **(5.2)**

exhibición *f.* (*pl.* **exhibiciones**) exhibition (8.1)

exhibir to exhibit (4.3)

exigente demanding (1.1)

exigir to demand, require **(5.1)**

exiliarse to go into exile (5.2)

existir to exist; to be (3.1)

éxito *m.* success (3.2)

exótico(a) exotic (7.2)

experiencia *f.* experience (4.3)

experimento *m.* experiment (5.3)

explicación *f.* (*pl.* **explicaciones**) explanation (6.3)

explicar to explain (1.3)

explotación *f.* exploitation (2.3)

exportar to export (2.3)

expresar to express (3.2)

expresión *f.* (*pl.* **expresiones**) expression (4.3)

expuesto(a) exposed (5.2)

exquisito(a) exquisite (3.1)

extender(se) (ie) to spread (2.3); to extend (3.1)

extendido(a) widespread (1.1); extended

extensión *f.* size; extension; expanse (4.2)

extenso(a) spacious, vast (2.1)

exterminado(a) exterminated (8.1)

exterminar to exterminate (3.3)

externo(a) external (7.2)

extinción *f.* extinction (2.3)

extranjero(a) foreign (2.1)

extrañar to miss, pine for (4.3); to find strange or odd

extraño(a) strange (1.2)

extraordinario(a) extraordinary (3.2)

extraterrestre *adj.* extraterrestrial (1.2)

extremadamente extremely (5.3)

extremo *m.* outer part (7.2)

extremo(a) extreme (1.1)

fábrica *f.* factory (3.1)

fabricar to make (6.3)

fábula *f.* fable; myth; tale (5.1)

fabuloso(a) fabulous (5.2)

falda *f.* skirt (1.2)

falta *f.* lack (1.2)

faltar to be lacking (1.1)

fama *f.* fame (3.2); reputation (4.2)

familia *f.* family (1.1)

familiar familiar (4.3); pertaining to the family (7.3); family member

famoso(a) famous (2.3)

fantasía *f.* fantasy (1.2)
fantasma *m.* ghost, phantom (3.3)
fantástico(a) fantastic (2.1)
fascinado(a) fascinated (1.2)
fascinante fascinating (1.3)
fascinar to fascinate **(1.3)**
fastidioso(a) annoying (2.3)
fatiga *f.* fatigue (5.2)
favorecido(a) favored (6.3)
favorito(a) favorite (1.1)
fecha *f.* date (1.1)
feliz (*pl.* **felices**) happy (1.2)
femenino(a) feminine (7.3)
fenómeno *m.* phenomenon (1.1)
feo(a) ugly (2.1)
feria *f.* fair (5.2)
feroz (*pl.* **feroces**) fierce, ferocious **(2.3)**
ferrocarril *m.* railway, railroad (7.2)
fértil *adj.* fertile (3.1)
fibra *f.* fiber (2.3)
fiel loyal, faithful (5.2)
fiesta *f.* fiesta, party (1.1)
figura *f.* figure (4.3)
figurar to figure, appear (8.1)
figurita *f.* figurine (6.2)
fijarse to pay attention to; to notice; to check **(2.1)**
filipino(a) Philippine **(2.2)**
filo *m.* cutting edge (4.1)
filodendro *m.* philodendron (2.3)
filosófico(a) philosophical (5.1)
fin *m.* end (1.1)
finalista *m. f.* finalist (7.1)
fines de end of (*time period*) (8.1)
fino(a) thin, fine (5.3)
firmar to sign (1.1) **(2.2)**
física *f.* physics (5.1)
físico(a) physical (1.3)
flaco(a) skinny (3.2)
flamenco *m.* flamingo (8.2); a Spanish dance
flan *m.* flan (*custard with a burnt sugar sauce*) (8.2)
flecha *f.* arrow (7.3)
flor *f.* flower (4.1)
flora *f.* flora (6.1)
floral floral (5.1)
florecimiento *m.* flourishing (5.1)
florecita *f.* little flower (1.2)
folklórico(a) folkloric (1.3)
forma *f.* form, shape **(1.2)**; way (4.3)
formado(a) formed (3.1)
formar to form (1.1)
formidable formidable, enormous (3.3)
formulario *m.* form (3.3)
fortaleza *f.* fortress (4.1)
fortificación *f.* (*pl.* **fortificaciones**) fortification (7.3)
fortuna *f.* fortune (2.2) **(3.3)**; luck
foto *f.* photo (1.1)
fotografía *f.* photograph (4.1)

fracasado(a) failed (6.1)
fracaso *m.* disaster, failure (3.1)
fraile *m.* monk (1.1); priest
francés, francesa (*m. pl.* **franceses**) French (1.3) **(2.2)**
franciscano *m.* Franciscan (1.1)
frase *f.* sentence (2.3); phrase
frecuencia *f.* frequency (1.1) **(4.1)**
frecuentemente frequently (1.2)
frente *f.* forehead (6.3); *m.* front
    frente a facing, in front of (1.2)
fresco(a) cool (3.1)
frijol *m.* bean (1.3)
frío *m.* cold (6.1)
    un frío de mil demonios bitter cold (3.1)
frito(a) fried (1.1)
frontera *f.* border (between countries) (1.1)
fronterizo(a) border (1.1)
frustrado(a) frustrated **(1.2)**
fruta *f.* fruit (2.3)
frutal *adj.* fruit, pertaining to fruit (1.1)
    árbol *m.* **frutal** tree that bears fruit (1.1)
fuego *m.* fire (4.2)
fuente *f.* fountain, source (2.3)
fuera outside (3.3) **(7.2)**
    fuera de apart from, except for (2.3); outside (of) (7.1)
fuera were (*imperf. subj. of* **ir**) (6.3)
fuerte strong (1.3)
fuerza *f.* force (7.1)
fumar to smoke (7.3)
función *f.* (*pl.* **funciones**) function (1.1)
funcionamiento *m.* functioning (2.3)
funcionar to function (4.1)
fundador *m.*, **fundadora** *f.* founder (3.1)
fundar to found; to establish (1.1)
fundido(a) blown out (*fuse*) (6.1)
fungir to act, function as (7.3)
furia *f.* fury (6.3)
furioso(a) furious (1.2)
fusible *m.* fuse (6.1)
fusión *f.* fusion, uniting (5.1)
fútbol *m.* soccer (1.1)
futuro *m.* future (1.3) **(3.2)**

gabinete *m.* cabinet **(4.2)**
galán *m.* gentleman, leading man (5.3)
galón *m.* (*pl.* **galones**) gallon (1.3)
galleta *f.* cookie **(5.1)**
galletita *f.* small cookie **(5.1)**
gallo *m.* rooster (4.2)
ganadería *f.* cattle raising (8.1)
ganado *m.* cattle, livestock (1.3)
ganar to win (1.1); to earn (6.1)
garaje *m.* garage (3.3)

garantía *f.* guarantee (6.1)
garantizar to guarantee (7.3)
gasolina *f.* gas (7.1)
gasolinera *f.* service station **(5.2)**
gastar to spend *(time)*; to waste (6.3)
gasto *m.* expenditure, expense **(7.1)**
gato *m.* cat (1.3)
   gato *m.* **silvestre** wild cat (6.1)
gaucho *m.* gaucho *(Argentinian cowboy)* (8.1)
gazpacho *m.* gazpacho *(cold puréed vegetable soup from Spain)* (5.2)
gemelo *m.,* **gemela** *f.* twin brother, twin sister (1.1)
gemelo(a) twin (1.1)
   ciudad gemela twin city (1.1)
gemido *m.* groan, moan (3.3)
generalísimo *m.* supreme commander (5.2)
   Generalísimo Franco General Franco (5.2)
generalizarse to become general or universal; to become widely used (5.2)
generoso(a) generous (6.1)
genio *m.* genius (4.3) **(6.1)**
gente *f.* people (2.3)
genuino(a) genuine (7.2)
geografía *f.* geography (2.1)
geométrico(a) geometric (4.3)
gerente *m. f.* manager **(7.2)**
gigantesco(a) gigantic (3.3)
gimnasia *f.* gymnastics (1.3)
gimnasio *m.* gymnasium (1.1)
gitana *f.* gypsy (fortuneteller) (5.2)
globo *m.* ball; sphere (7.2)
gobernador *m.,* **gobernadora** *(f.)* governor (6.2)
gobernar (ie) to govern (5.2)
gobierno *m.* government (2.2)
gol *m.* goal *(soccer)* (5.1)
golpeado(a) struck down (6.3)
golpear to hit, strike (7.1)
gordo(a) fat (1.3)
gorila *m.* gorilla (2.3)
gorrioncillo *m.* little sparrow (8.3)
gozar to enjoy **(1.1)**
grabar to record (4.1)
gracias thank you (1.1)
gracioso(a) funny, amusing (2.1)
grado *m.* degree *(temperature)* **(3.1)**
graduado(a) graduated (7.3)
gráfico *m.* graph, diagram (1.3)
gramática *f.* grammar (7.2)
gran great (1.1); a lot (2.1); large
grande large, big (1.2)
grandeza *f.* greatness, magnificence (4.2)
granero *m.* granary, barn (1.3)
grapador *m.* stapler (3.2)
grasa *f.* grease **(5.2)**
grasoso(a) fatty, greasy (5.2)
gratis free, at no cost (7.2)
griego(a) Greek **(2.2)**

gris gray (1.2)
gritar to yell (3.3)
grito *m.* shout, yell (2.1)
grotesco(a) grotesque, bizarre (2.1)
grueso(a) thick, coarse (6.3)
gruñido *m.* growl, grunt (6.2)
grupo *m.* group (1.1)
guacamayo *m.* macaw **(2.2)**
guapo(a) good-looking (1.2)
guardabosque *m., f.* outfielder (3.1)
guardar to keep, save (1.3) **(3.3)**
guardia *f.* guard (6.1)
guatemalteco(a) Guatemalan (2.2)
guayaba *f.* guava jelly; guava apple (4.2)
guerra *f.* war (8.2)
guerrero *m.,* **guerrera** *f.* fighter, warrior (4.3)
guerrero(a) *(adj.)* warlike (7.3)
guerrilla *f.* guerrilla forces (8.1)
guía *m. f.* (tour) guide (6.2)
guiar to guide, lead, direct (8.1)
guitarra *f.* guitar (1.1)
guitarrista *m. f.* guitarist (4.2)
gustar to like (1.1)
gusto *m.* pleasure (1.1); taste (5.2); fancy, liking (5.3)

～～～H～～～

haber to have; to be *pret.* **(3.1)** *fut.* **(8.1)** *cond.* **(8.2)**
   había una vez once upon a time (3.3)
hábil skillful (8.1)
habilidad *f.* skill, ability (4.2)
habitación *f.* (*pl.* **habitaciones**) room, bedroom (6.3); dwelling, abode (8.1)
habitado(a) inhabited (3.1)
habitante *m. f.* inhabitant (2.1)
habitar to inhabit (3.3)
habla *f.* language, dialect, speech (6.2)
   habla hispana Spanish-speaking (1.3)
hablar to speak, talk (1.1) *pres. perf.* **(6.2)**
hacendado *m.* land-owner, rancher (8.1)
hacer to do, to make *pret.* (2.1) *pres. perf.* **(6.2)** *fut.* **(8.1)** *cond.* **(8.2)**
   hacer autostop to hitchhike (1.2)
   hacer ejercicio to exercise (1.1) **(5.1)**
   hacer el papel to play the role **(2.1)**
   hacer una consulta to ask for advice (3.2)
   hacer una pregunta to ask a question **(1.2)**
hacerse to become (5.3)
hacia toward (3.1)
hacienda *f.* farm, ranch (3.1)
hada *f.* **madrina** fairy godmother (8.3)
hallar to find
hallarse to find oneself; to be (8.3)
hambre *f.* hunger **(1.2)**
hamburguesa *f.* hamburger (1.1)
hardware *m.* hardware **(3.3)**
harina *f.* flour **(3.2)**

hasta *prep.* until (1.1); up to (2.1)
    hasta cierto punto up to a point, to some extent (7.1)
    hasta luego good-bye, see you later (1.1)
hasta even (1.3)
hay there is, there are (1.1)
hazaña *f.* heroic feat; achievement; deed (4.2)
hebreo *m.* Hebrew (language) (5.1)
hectárea *f.* hectare *(unit of measure)* (4.3)
hecho *m.* event (1.1); deed (2.2); fact
hecho(a) made (2.2)
helado *m.* ice cream (1.2)
helecho *m.* fern (6.1)
hemisferio *m.* hemisphere (8.1)
heredar to inherit (4.3)
herencia *f.* heritage, inheritance, legacy (5.1)
herida *f.* wound, injury (8.2)
hermanastro *m.,* **hermanastra** *f.* stepbrother, stepsister (2.1)
hermanito *m.,* **hermanita** *f.* little brother, sister (1.2)
hermano *m.,* **hermana** *f.* brother, sister (1.1)
hermoso(a) beautiful (3.1)
herradura *f.* horseshoe (5.1)
herramienta *f.* tool (4.2)
hidroeléctrico(a) hydroelectric (8.1)
hielera *f.* ice chest **(6.2)**
hierba: mala hierba weed (8.1)
hierro *m.* iron (2.1)
hijo *m.* son (2.3)
¡híjole! geez! goodness! *(Mexican)* (1.1)
hilar to spin (5.3)
hilo *m.* thread, yarn (3.2)
hispanohablante Spanish-speaking (7.2)
historia *f.* history (1.1); story (4.1)
historiador *m.,* **historiadora** *f.* historian (3.3)
histórico(a) historic, historical; of historical importance (1.1)
hocico *m.* snout *(animal)* **(4.3)**
hoguera *f.* fire (6.1)
hoja *f.* leaf (4.1)
    hoja *f.* **de papel** sheet of paper (3.3)
¡hola! hello!, hi! (1.1)
holandés, holandesa *(m. pl.* **holandeses)** Dutch **(2.2)**
hombre *m.* man (2.1)
hombro *m.* shoulder (1.2)
hondureño(a) Honduran (2.1)
honestidad *f.* honesty (4.2)
honesto(a) honest **(3.1)**
honor *m.* honor, fame **(3.1)**
honorable honorable, worthy (5.1)
honrado(a) honest, honorable, decent (5.1)
hora *f.* hour (1.1)
horario *m.* schedule (1.2)
horno *m.* oven (4.2)
horrorizado(a) horrified (6.1)
horroroso(a) horrible, dreadful (3.1)
hoy today (1.2)
huella *f.* footprint, trace, imprint (8.3)

huérfano *m.,* **huérfana** *f.* orphan (7.2)
huevo *m.* egg (6.1)
huir to flee (4.1)
humanidad *f.* humanity (3.2)
humilde *m. f.* humble (3.2)
humillante humiliating (8.1)

idéntico(a) identical (1.3)
identidad *f.* identity (2.2)
identificar to identify **(2.3)**
ideología *f.* ideology (5.2)
ideológico(a) ideological (6.3)
iglesia *f.* church (1.3)
igual same; alike; equal (3.3)
    igual a like, the same as (8.2)
igualmente likewise (1.1)
ilusión *f. (pl.* **ilusiones)** illusion (7.1)
ilustración *f. (pl.* **ilustraciones)** illustration (3.2)
ilustre illustrious, famous (8.2)
imagen *f. (pl.* **imágenes)** image (5.3)
imaginación *f.* imagination (2.2)
imaginar to imagine (5.1)
imaginario(a) imaginary (5.3)
    lo imaginario that which is imaginary (8.3)
imitar to imitate (5.1)
imperfecto(a) imperfect (4.1)
imperio *m.* empire (4.1)
imponente imposing, majestic (4.2)
imponer to impose (5.2)
importancia *f.* importance (4.2)
importante important (2.3)
importar to be important (2.2) **(5.2)**
    le importa to be important to (3.2)
impresión *f. (pl.* **impresiones)** impression **(1.2)**; imprint (8.3)
impresionante impressive (2.1)
impresionar to impress, make an impression (2.2)
impropio(a) improper, inappropriate (5.2)
impuesto *m.* tax **(1.2)**
incaico(a) Incan (3.3)
incapacitado(a) disabled
incentivar to encourage, stimulate, provide incentive for (7.1)
incesantemente incessantly, unceasingly (7.2)
incidente *m.* incident, occurrence **(3.1)**
inclinarse to be inclined (3.3); to bend (5.3)
incluir to include (1.1)
incluso including (1.1)
incómodo(a) uncomfortable (2.1)
incomparable without equal **(3.2)**
inconcebible unthinkable, inconceivable (5.2)
incontable countless (4.3)
incorporar to incorporate (5.1)
incorregible incorrigible (2.1)

increíble   incredible (5.1)
indeciso(a)   undecided; indecisive **(8.3)**
independencia *f.*   independence (1.1)
indiano *m.*   Spaniard returning prosperous from America (5.3)
indicado(a)   indicated (2.2)
indicar   to indicate (2.1)
índice *m.*   rate (6.1); index
indígena *adj.*   indigenous, native (1.1)
indígena *m. f.*   native, indigenous person (2.1); Indian
individualista   individualistic (8.1)
individualmente   individually (1.3)
individuo *m.*   individual (7.1)
índole *f.*   class, kind, sort (6.2)
indudablemente   undoubtedly (4.3)
industria *f.*   industry (7.1)
industrial   industrial (7.1)
industrializado(a)   industrialized (8.1)
inesperado(a)   unexpected (4.2)
inevitablemente   inevitably (4.1)
influencia *f.*   influence (1.1)
influir   to influence (7.2)
información *f.* (*pl.* **informaciones**)   information (1.1)
informado(a)   informed (3.1)
informar   to inform (1.3)
informativo(a)   informative **(3.2)**
informe *m.*   report **(2.2)**
ingeniería *f.*   engineering (4.2)
ingeniero *m.*, **ingeniera** *f.*   engineer (1.3)
ingenuo   ingenuous, naïve (3.1)
inglés *m.*   English (language) (1.1)
inglés, inglesa (*m. pl.* **ingleses**)   English **(2.2)**
ingrato(a)   ungrateful (8.3)
ingresar   to enter, be admitted to (7.2)
iniciado   initiated, begun (7.2)
iniciar   to initiate, begin **(2.2)**
injusticia *f.*   injustice (7.2)
inmediatamente   immediately (1.2)
inmediato(a)   immediate, next (7.2)
inmenso(a)   immense, enormous (4.1)
inmigrante *m. f.*   immigrant (8.1)
inquietar   to worry, disturb, trouble (5.3)
inquieto(a)   restless, unsettled (6.3); anxious, uneasy
inseguridad *f.*   insecurity (5.3); unsafeness
inseguro(a)   insecure (5.3); unsafe
insignificante   insignificant, unimportant (2.3)
insistir   to insist (1.1) **(5.2)**
insólito(a)   unusual **(3.1)**
inspirarse en   to be inspired by (5.1)
instalar   to install **(3.3)** (6.3)
institución *f.* (*pl.* **instituciones**)   institution (2.1)
instituir   to institute, establish (7.2)
instituto *m.*   institute (7.2)
instrucción *f.* (*pl.* **instrucciones**)   instruction (3.2)
instructor *m.*, **instructora** *f.*   instructor **(5.1)**
insultar   to insult (4.3)
integrar   to integrate (8.1)

inteligente   intelligent (1.3)
intención *f.* (*pl.* **intenciones**)   intention (1.1)
intensamente   intensely (4.1)
intenso(a)   intense (3.2)
intentar   to try, attempt (5.1)
intento *m.*   attempt (4.3)
interacción *f.* (*pl.* **interacciones**)   interaction (7.3)
intercalar   to intercalate, insert (5.1)
intercambiar   to exchange (7.1)
intercambio *m.*   exchange (7.1)
interdependencia *f.*   interdependence (1.1)
interés *m.* (*pl.* **intereses**)   interest **(1.3)**
interesado(a)   interested **(1.3)**
interesante   interesting (1.1)
interesar   to interest (5.3)
interesarse (en)   to be interested (in) (4.3)
internacional   international (3.2)
Internet *m.*   Internet (a world-wide communications network) **(3.3)**
interpretar   to interpret (1.2)
interrumpir   to interrupt (6.3)
interrupción *f.* (*pl.* **interrupciones**)   interruption **(3.2)**
intervención *f.*   intervention (7.2)
íntimo(a)   intimate (3.2)
intrigado(a)   intrigued (3.3)
introducir   to introduce, bring in (2.1)
inundación *f.* (*pl.* **inundaciones**)   flood (2.1)
inútil   useless, fruitless, in vain (5.2)
invadir   to invade (5.1)
inválido(a)   disabled (3.2)
invasión *f.* (*pl.* **invasiones**)   invasion (5.2)
invencible   invincible (2.3)
inventar   to invent (4.3) **(5.1)**
invertir (ie, i)   to invest (7.1); to invert
investigación *f.* (*pl.* **investigaciones**)   investigation **(2.3)**
investigador *m.*, **investigadora** *f.*   investigator (2.2)
invierno *m.*   winter (1.1)
invitación *f.* (*pl.* **invitaciones**)   invitation (5.2)
invitado *m.*, **invitada** *f.*   guest (2.2)
invitar   to invite (1.2)
involucrado(a)   involved (6.3)
ir   to go (1.1) *pret.* (2.1) *imperf.* **(4.1)** *pres. subj.* **(5.1)**
   ir de compras   to go shopping (1.1)
irse   to leave, go; to go away (3.3)
irlandés, irlandesa (*m. pl.* **irlandeses**)   Irish **(2.2)**
irrigación *f.*   irrigation (4.2)
isla *f.*   island (3.3)
israelita *m. f.*   Israeli **(2.2)**
italiano(a)   Italian **(2.2)**
izquierda *f.*   left, left side (6.2)
izquierdo(a)   left (3.2)

~~~~**J**~~~~

jabón *m.*   soap (2.3)
jaguar *m.*   jaguar **(2.2)**
jai alai *m.*   jai alai *(sport)* (6.3)

jamás   never (5.3)
jamón *m.*   ham (3.2)
japonés, japonesa (*m. pl.* **japoneses**)   Japanese **(2.2)**
jardín *m.* (*pl.* **jardines**)   garden (4.2)
jardinero *m.*   fielder (3.1)
   jardinero *m.* **corto**   shortstop (3.1)
jaula *f.*   cage **(4.1)**
jefe *m.,* **jefa** *f.*   head, chief (5.2); leader (7.3); boss
   jefe *m.* **de estado**   head (chief) of state (5.2)
jerga *f.*   slang (2.2)
joven *m. f.* (*pl.* **jóvenes**)   young person (1.2)
joya *f.*   jewel, piece of jewelry (3.3)
joyería *f.*   jewelry; jewelry department or store (1.2)
judío *m.*   Jew (5.1)
juego *m.*   game **(1.2)**
   juego *m.* **de damas**   checkers **(4.1)**
jugador *m.,* **jugadora** *f.*   player (2.3)
jugar (ue)   to play (1.1)
jugo *m.*   juice (5.2)
juguete *m.*   toy **(4.1)**
julio   July (1.1)
junio   June (1.1)
junto a   near (to), next to (8.3)
juntos(as)   together (1.2)
juramento *m.*   oath (4.3)
jurar   to swear, promise (1.3)
justicia *f.*   justice (3.2)
justo(a)   just, fair (6.1)
juventud *f.*   youth (3.2)

la *dir. obj. pron.*   her, it (2.1)
labor *f.*   labor, work (7.2)
laca *f.*   lacquer, shellac (2.3)
lácteo(a)   milky, pertaining to milk (5.2)
lado *m.*   side (4.2)
ladrar   to bark (3.3)
ladrón *m.* (*pl.* **ladrones**)   robber, thief (4.2)
lagar *m.*   wine, olive, or apple press (3.2)
lago *m.*   lake (2.1)
lágrima *f.*   tear (1.2) **(3.2)**
lamentablemente   regrettably, unfortunately (5.2)
lámpara *f.*   lamp **(3.1)**
lana *f.*   wool (3.1)
lancha *f.*   small boat; rowboat (4.3)
langosta *f.*   lobster (1.3)
lanzador *m.*   pitcher (3.1)
lápida *f.*   gravestone (1.2)
lápiz *m.* (*pl.* **lápices**)   pencil (2.3)
   lápiz *m.* **de labio**   lipstick (2.3)
largo(a)   long (1.2)
   a lo largo de   along, alongside (7.3)
las *art.*   the (1.1)
las *dir. obj. pron.*   them (2.1)

lástima: ¡qué lástima!   what a shame (3.1)
lastimado(a)   hurt (3.1)
lastimar   to hurt; to offend **(5.3)**; to bruise, injure (6.3)
latinoamericano(a)   Latin American **(1.3)**
lavaplatos *m. sing.*   dishwasher (7.2)
lavar   to wash **(1.1)**
lavarse   to wash oneself (3.3)
lazo *m.*   tie, connection (1.1)
le   to (for) him, her, or you (1.1)
lealtad *f.*   loyalty (7.3)
lección *f.* (*pl.* **lecciones**)   lesson (2.1)
lector *m. f.*   reader (3.3)
lectura   reading (2.1)
leche *f.*   milk (3.2)
leer   to read (1.1)
legítimamente   legitimately, rightfully (6.2)
lejos (de)   far (from) (2.1)
lengua *f.*   tongue; language (1.3)
lenguaje *m.*   language (2.2)
lentamente   slowly (3.3)
lentes *m. pl.*   eyeglasses (1.1)
lento(a)   slow **(1.3)**
leña *f.*   firewood (6.3)
leñador *m.*   woodsman (6.3)
león *m.* (*pl.* **leones**)   lion **(2.3)**
leopardo *m.*   leopard **(2.3)**
les   to (for) them, you (1.1)
letra *f.*   letter (8.3)
   letra *f.* **mayúscula**   capital letter (1.2)
letras *f. pl.*   literature (5.1)
letrero *m.*   sign, poster (7.3)
levantarse   to get up (1.2)
ley *f.*   law (7.2)
leyenda *f.*   legend (2.1)
libertad   freedom (5.2)
libra *f.*   pound (1.3)
libre   free (8.3)
   libre comercio *m.*   free trade (7.1)
libro *m.*   book (1.1)
liceo *m.*   lycée, high school (3.2)
líder *m. f.*   leader (3.1)
lienzo *m.*   linen (5.3); canvas
ligado(a)   tied, linked (1.1)
limitarse   to limit oneself (3.3)
limonada *f.*   lemonade (2.3)
limpiar   to clean (1.1)
limpieza   cleanliness **(4.1)**
lindo(a)   pretty (1.2)
línea *f.*   line (4.3)
lingüístico(a)   linguistic; pertaining to language (6.2)
   (8.3)
lino *m.*   flax linen (5.3)
linterna *f.*   lantern **(6.2)**
líquido *m.*   liquid **(5.2)**
lista *f.*   list **(1.1)**
listo(a)   ready **(1.1)**; clever
literario(a)   literary (3.2) **(4.2)**

literatura *f.*   literature **(4.2)**
litro *m.*   liter **(5.2)**
lo *dir. obj. pron.*   him, it (2.1)
   lo mismo   the same **(1.2)**
lobo *m.*   wolf (4.3)
localizado(a)   located (7.3)
localizar   to locate (2.1) **(2.3)**
loción *f.* (*pl.* **lociones**)   lotion **(3.2)**
   loción *f.* **protectora**   sunscreen (lotion) **(3.2)**
loco(a)   crazy **(1.3)**
locutor *m.,* **locutora** *f.*   announcer (3.1)
lógico(a)   logical (5.1)
lograr   to succeed, to manage to (5.1); to achieve, attain
   (6.1)
logro *m.*   achievement (7.3)
lorito *m.* **real**   little parrot (2.1)
loro *m.*   parrot (2.1)
los *art.*   the (1.1)
los *dir. obj. pron.*   them (2.1)
lotería *f.*   lottery (7.1)
luchar   to fight (7.2)
luego   then (1.1)
lugar *m.*   place (1.1)
luna *f.*   moon (8.1)
lunar   lunar (4.3); mole
lunes *m.*   Monday (1.1)
lustroso(a)   shiny (2.3)
luz *f.* (*pl.* **luces**)   light (3.3) **(4.2)**

<div align="center">~~~ LL ~~~</div>

llamada *f.*   (phone) call (3.2)
llamar   to call (2.1)
   llamar a la puerta   to knock at the door (1.2)
llamarse   to be named (1.1)
llamativo(a)   flashy, showy **(7.1)**; catchy (title) (1.3)
llano *m.*   plain, prairie (2.1)
llanta *f.*   tire (2.3)
llanto *m.*   weeping, crying (4.1)
llanura *f.*   plain (2.1)
llegada *f.*   arrival (1.1)
llegar   to arrive; to reach (3.1)
   llegar a ser   to become (3.2)
llenar   to fill (3.2)
lleno(a)   filled (3.3)
llevar   to carry; to take (1.1); to wear *pret.* **(2.2)** *cond.*
   (8.2)
   llevar a cabo   to carry out (8.1)
   llevar su merecido   to get one's just desserts (6.2)
llorar   to cry (1.2)
llorón *m.,* **llorona** *f.*   cry baby (6.2)
llover (ue)   to rain (3.1)
llovizna *f.*   mist, fine rain **(3.1)**
lloviznar   to drizzle **(3.1)**
lluvia *f.*   rain **(3.1)**

<div align="center">~~~ M ~~~</div>

macedonio(a)   Macedonian (4.2)
madeja *f.*   skein (5.3)
madera *f.*   wood (2.1)
madrastra *f.*   stepmother (2.1)
madre *f.*   mother (1.2)
madrugada *f.*   dawn, daybreak (6.1)
maduro(a)   mature; ripe (3.2)
maestro *m.,* **maestra** *f.*   teacher (4.1) **(5.2)**
magia *f.*   magic (2.1)
mágico(a)   magical (2.2)
   lo mágico   that which is magic (7.1)
magnífico(a)   magnificent, splendid (2.3)
maíz *m.*   corn (4.1)
majestuoso(a)   majestic (2.3)
mal   bad (1.2)
mala hierba *f.*   weed
maldad *f.*   evil (7.1)
maleta *f.*   suitcase (3.2)
malicioso(a)   malicious, nasty (3.3)
malo(a)   bad (1.3)
malvado *m.*   villain (6.2)
malvado(a)   evil, wicked (6.2)
mamá *f.*   mom (1.1)
mancha *f.*   spot (8.2)
manchar   to stain (8.1)
mandar   to order (4.2); to send (3.2)
mandato *m.*   command **(3.2)**; order (8.1)
mandón, mandona   bossy (6.2)
manejar   to drive (1.2) **(7.1)**
manera *f.*   manner, way (3.2)
mango *m.*   mango *(tropical fruit)* **(2.1)**
mano *f.*   hand (3.2)
   tener a mano   to have at hand
mantener(se)   to maintain, keep (5.2)
   mantenerse en forma   to stay in shape (3.1)
mantequilla *f.*   butter (3.2)
manzana *f.*   apple (2.1)
manzano *m.*   apple tree (8.3)
mañana *f.*   morning (1.2)
mañana   tomorrow (1.1)
mapa *m.*   map (2.2)
maquiladora *f.*   assembly plant (7.1)
máquina *f.*   machine **(7.2)**
   máquina *f.* **de coser**   sewing machine (3.3)
mar *m.*   sea (2.1)
maravilla *f.*   marvel, wonder (4.1)
maravilloso(a)   marvelous (1.3)
marca *f.*   mark (6.2)
marcador *m.*   highlighter (1.3)
marcar   to mark (6.2)
marciano *m.,* **marciana** *f.*   Martian (5.2)
marcha: ponerse en marcha   to start (8.1)
marcharse   to go (away), leave (8.3)
margen *f.* (*pl.* **márgenes**)   border (2.1); margin

mariachi *m.* mariachi (*Mexican band of strolling musicians playing string and brass instruments*) (8.3)
marido *m.* husband (1.3)
marina *f.* navy (3.1)
mariposa *f.* butterfly (6.1)
marisco *m.* seafood (1.3)
marrón brown (1.1)
marroquí *m. f.* (*pl.* **marroquíes**) Moroccan **(2.2)**
marsupial *m.* marsupial (6.1)
más more (1.1)
   más adelante later (2.2)
   más vale + *inf.* to be better to (3.2)
masa *f.* dough (1.3); mass, bulk (8.1)
masas *f. pl.* masses (5.3)
máscara *f.* mask (3.1)
mata *f.* plant (4.2)
matado *past part.* killed (3.2)
matador *m.,* **matadora** *f.* killer (6.3)
"mataestudiantes" *lit.,* ''student killer,'' difficult professor (1.2)
matar to kill (2.3)
matas *f. pl.* thicket, bushes (6.3)
matemáticas *f. pl.* mathematics (1.3)
materia *f.* material (3.2)
materno(a) maternal (2.1)
matricularse to enroll (7.3)
matrimonio *m.* matrimony, marriage (1.3)
máximo(a) maximum **(3.1)**
mayor *adj.* oldest (2.2); greater, older (1.3) **(2.3)**
   mayor parte *f.* most (2.1); the majority
mayoría *f.* majority (1.3)
me me (1.1)
mecánico *m.,* **mecánica** *f.* mechanic (5.2)
mecanografía *f.* typewriting **(7.2)**
mediados: a mediados de in the middle of (*time period*) (8.1)
medianoche *f.* midnight (8.3)
mediante by means of, through (5.2)
medias *f. pl.* stockings (1.2)
medicina *f.* medicine (2.3) **(5.1)**
médico *m.,* **médica** *f.* doctor (2.1)
medio *m.* **ambiente** environment (2.3)
medio *m.* **de transporte** means of transportation **(1.1)**
medio(a) *adj.* half (2.1); middle (7.1)
   medio tiempo half-time (7.3)
mediodía *m.* noon (1.2)
medir (i, i) to measure (1.3)
mejilla *f.* cheek (1.2)
mejor better (1.1)
mejorar to get better, improve (3.2) **(8.2)**
melodía *f.* melody (8.2)
melodrama *m.* melodrama (6.2)
melón *m.* (*pl.* **melones**) melon (5.2)
memoria *f.* memory (2.1)
mencionar to mention (1.2) **(2.3)**
mendigo *m.,* **mendiga** *f.* beggar (6.2)
menor *adj.* youngest (2.2); smaller, younger **(2.3)**

menos less (1.1)
mensaje *m.* message (3.3)
mensajero *m.,* **mensajera** *f.* messenger (8.3)
mensual monthly (7.1)
mentor *m.* mentor (7.2)
mercado *m.* market (7.2)
   mercado *m.* **al aire libre** outdoor (open-air) market **(7.2)**
merecer to deserve (1.3)
merecido *m.* just desserts (*deserving punishment or reward*) (6.2)
merendar to snack (1.2)
mérito *m.* merit (7.3)
mes *m.* month (1.1)
mesa *f.* table (1.2)
mesero *m.,* **mesera** *f.* waiter, waitress (7.2)
meseta *f.* plateau, tableland (1.1)
mesita *f.* little table; nightstand (3.1)
mesonero *m.,* **mesonera** *f.* waiter, waitress **(2.1)**
mestizo *m.* mestizo, person of mixed-race (8.1)
mestizo(a) mestizo, of mixed blood (4.1)
metáfora *f.* metaphor (8.3)
meter to put (in) **(3.3)**; to insert (4.1)
meterse to go into, get into (8.2)
   meterse el sol the setting of the sun (7.1)
metro *m.* subway (8.3)
metropolitano(a) metropolitan (3.1)
mexicano(a) Mexican (2.2)
mezcla *f.* mixture (2.1)
mezquita *f.* mosque (5.1)
mi my (1.1)
miedo *m.* fear **(2.2)**
miedoso(a) fearful (5.3)
miembro *m. f.* member (1.1)
mientras while (1.2)
migaja *f.* small bit of bread **(4.3)**
migración *f.* migration (7.1)
miguita *f.* crumb **(3.2)**
mil *m.* thousand (7.1)
milagro *m.* miracle (4.1)
militar military (1.2)
milla *f.* mile (2.1) **(6.2)**
millón *m.* (*pl.* **millones**) million (7.1)
millonario *m.* millionaire **(5.1)**
mimado(a) spoiled (4.3)
mina *f.* mine (1.1)
minería *f.* mining (2.3)
mínimo(a) minimum **(3.1)**; minimal (7.2)
ministro *m.* minister (7.2)
mío my (1.1)
mirar to watch, look at (1.1)
miseria *f.* poverty, destitution (6.3)
misionero *m.,* **misionera** *f.* missionary (3.3)
misión *m.* (*pl.* **misiones**) mission (1.1)
mismo(a) same (1.1)
misterio *m.* mystery **(3.3)**
misterioso(a) mysterious (1.2)

mitad *f.* half (1.3)
mito *m.* myth (6.3)
mixto(a) mixed (2.3)
mochila *f.* backpack (1.2)
moda *f.* fashion (5.2)
   de moda in fashion (1.1)
módem *m.* modem **(3.3)**
moderno(a) modern (2.1)
mojarse to get wet (7.1)
moler to grind (4.2)
molestar to disturb; to bother (1.3) **(5.3)**
momento *m.* moment (2.2)
monarca *m.* monarch, king (2.3)
moneda *f.* coin (3.3)
monja *f.* nun (2.2)
mono *m.*, **mona** *f.* monkey **(2.3)**
monolito *m.* monolith (3.3)
montaña *f.* mountain (1.1)
   montaña *f.* **de rocas** pile of rocks (4.3)
montañoso(a) mountainous (2.1)
montar to mount (4.2)
   montar a caballo to ride (horseback) (2.2)
monte *m.* woodlands, forest (6.3); mountain
monumento *m.* monument (6.1)
moño *m.* bun *(a Victorian hairstyle)* (1.2); ribbon
morado(a) purple (1.1)
moral morals, morality (5.2)
moraleja *f.* moral (2.3)
moreno(a) dark-haired, dark-complexioned (1.3)
morir (ue, u) to die (1.2) *pret.* **(4.2)** *pres. perf.* **(6.2)**
   morir de miedo to die of fright **(6.2)**
moro *m.* Moor (5.1)
mortero *m.* mortar (4.1)
mostrar (ue) to show (1.2)
motivo *m.* motif (5.1); motive
motocicleta (moto) *f.* motorcycle (7.2)
movimiento *m.* movement (5.2)
mozo *m.* young man (5.2)
muchacho *m.*, **muchacha** *f.* boy, girl (1.1)
muchísimo a (whole) lot (1.1)
mucho much, a lot (1.1)
mudanza *f.* move (7.1)
mudarse to move (1.1)
mueble *m.* (piece of) furniture (3.1)
mueblería *f.* furniture store (3.1)
muerte *f.* death (3.2)
muerto *m.*, **muerta** *f.* dead person (2.2)
muerto(a) dead (1.2)
   muerto de hambre dying of hunger (1.2)
mujer *f.* woman (2.3)
mula *f.* mule (4.1)
   mula *f.* **de carga** pack mule (4.1)
multa *f.* fine, penalty (5.2)
multilingüe multilingual (7.3)
mundial world-wide (3.1) **(5.1)**
mundo *m.* world (1.2)
municipal municipal **(3.1)**

muñeco *m.*, **muñeca** *f.* doll, puppet (5.1)
músculo *m.* muscle (2.3)
museo *m.* museum (1.1)
música *f.* music (1.1)
músico *m.*, **música** *f.* musician (5.2)
musulmán *m.* (*pl.* **musulmanes**) Moslem (5.1)
muy very (1.1)

<center>~~~~~N~~~~~</center>

nacer to be born (3.2)
nación *m.* (*pl.* **naciones**) nation (1.1)
nacional national (3.1)
nacionalidad *f.* nationality **(2.2)**
nacho *m.* nacho *(tortilla chip with cheese and chilis)*
   (1.1)
nada nothing (1.2)
   nada en particular nothing really; nothing special
   (1.1)
nadar to swim **(1.1)** *pres. subj.* **(5.1)** *fut.* **(8.1)**
nadie no one, nobody (2.2)
naranja *f.* orange (4.3)
nariz *f.* (*pl.* **narices**) nose (3.2)
narrar to narrate (3.3)
natación *f.* swimming (1.1)
nativo(a) *adj.* native (3.1)
nativo *m.*, **nativa** *f.* native (3.3)
naturaleza *f.* nature (3.2)
navegante *m. f.* navigator, sailor (3.3)
navegar to navigate (2.1)
Navidad *f.* Christmas (6.2)
necesario(a) necessary (1.1) **(2.3)**
necesidad *f.* necessity (3.2)
necesitar to need (1.2) **(5.1)**
necio(a) bothersome; foolish; stubborn **(7.3)**
negativamente negatively (1.2)
negativo(a) negative **(1.1)**
negocio *m.* business, trade (2.3)
negro(a) black (1.1)
nervioso(a) nervous (1.2)
nevar (ie) to snow (3.1)
nevera *f.* refrigerator (3.2)
ni not even; nor (2.2)
ni siquiera not even (6.1)
nicaragüense *m. f.* Nicaraguan (2.2)
nicle *m.* nickel (6.1)
nido *m.* nest (8.3)
nieto *m.*, **nieta** *f.* grandson, granddaughter (3.3)
ningún, ninguno(a) no, none, not any (1.3)
niñez *f.* childhood; infancy **(4.1)**
niño *m.*, **niña** *f.* boy, girl (2.2)
nivel *m.* level (3.3)
no no; not (1.1)
no obstante nevertheless (3.3)
no sólo . . . sino también not only . . . but also (3.3)
noble noble (2.3)
nocturno *m.* nocturne, relating to night (6.3)

noche *f.*   night (1.1)
nombrar   to name (2.1)
nombre *m.*   name (1.1)
nopal *m.*   Mexican cacti with red flowers (8.1)
norma *f.*   standard, norm, rule (6.3)
norte *m.*   north (1.1)
norteamericano(a)   North American (1.2)
norteño(a)   northern (2.1)
noruego(a)   Norwegian **(2.2)**
nos   us; to (for) us (1.1)
nosotros   we (1.1)
nota *f.*   note; grade (2.2)
notable   remarkable (2.1)
notar   to note **(5.1)**
noticias *f. pl.*   news (3.1)
noticiero *m.*   newscast **(3.2)**
novela *f.*   novel (1.1)
novio *m.,* **novia** *f.*   boyfriend, girlfriend (1.2)
nube *f.*   cloud (4.2)
   andar por las nubes   to be daydreaming, to have one's head in the clouds (7.2)
nublado(a)   cloudy (3.1)
núcleo *m.*   nucleus (4.3)
nudo *m.*   knot (4.1)
nuestro(a)   our (1.2)
nuevo(a)   new (1.1)
   ¿qué hay de nuevo?   what's new? (1.1)
nuez *m.* (*pl.* **nueces**)   nut (2.3)
número *m.*   number (1.1)
numeroso(a)   numerous (1.3)
nunca   never (1.1)
nutrición *f.*   nutrition **(5.2)**
nutritivo(a)   nutritious **(5.1)**

obedecer   to obey (8.1)
objeto *m.*   object (2.1)
obligación *f.* (*pl.* **obligaciones**)   obligation (1.3)
obligado(a)   obliged (3.3); obligated (6.2)
obligar   to force (6.3)
obligatorio(a)   obligatory (5.2)
obra *f.*   work (4.1)
observar   to observe **(4.1)**
observatorio *m.*   observatory (3.1)
obsesionado(a)   obsessed (5.1)
obtener   to get, obtain (7.3)
obviamente   obviously (5.1)
obvio(a)   evident, obvious **(5.1)**
occidental   Western (1.1)
occidente *m.*   West **(3.1)**
océano *m.*   ocean **(2.3)**
ocultarse   to hide (5.1)
oculto(a)   hidden (5.1)
ocupación *f.* (*pl.* **ocupaciones**)   occupation (1.1); job
ocupado(a)   busy (1.1); occupied, inhabited (1.1)

ocupar   to occupy *(space)* (1.1); to occupy, fill (5.1)
ocurrir   to occur (1.1)
odiar   to hate **(2.2)**
odio *m.*   hatred (6.3)
oeste *m.*   west (3.1)
oferta *f.*   offer; bargain (1.2)
oficina *f.*   office (1.1)
ofrecer   to offer (1.2)
oír   to hear (1.2)
ojalá   let's hope that; I hope that **(5.1)**
ojear   to eye quickly, to scan (2.3)
ojo *m.*   eye (2.3)
oligarca *m.*   oligarch (7.2)
olímpico(a)   Olympic **(5.1)**
oliva *f.*   olive (6.1)
olvidar   to forget (2.1)
olla *f.*   pot (3.3)
ondulado(a)   wavy, curly (4.1)
operador *m.,* **operadora** *f.*   operator **(7.3)**
opinar   to form an opinion ; to think (1.1)
opinión *f.* (*pl.* **opiniones**)   opinion (5.1)
oportunidad *f.*   opportunity, chance (5.1)
optar   to choose, decide on, opt for (5.2)
opuesto(a)   opposite (1.3)
oración *f.* (*pl.* **oraciones**)   sentence (1.1) **(2.1)**
orden *m. f.* (*pl.* **órdenes**)   order, sequence (3.2); command **(3.3)**
ordenar   to arrange, put in order (4.2)
ordinario(a)   ordinary (2.1)
organizado(a)   organized (1.3)
organizar   to organize (3.2)
orgullo *m.*   pride (8.2)
orgulloso(a)   proud, haughty (2.1)
oriental   oriental (5.1)
oriente *m.*   East **(3.1)**
origen *m.* (*pl.* **orígenes**)   origin (2.2)
orilla *f.*   bank of a river, shore (2.2) **(4.3)**
oro *m.*   gold (2.1)
orquesta *f.*   orchestra (1.3)
orquídea *f.*   orchid (6.1)
oscurecido(a)   darkened (6.2); obscured
oscuro(a)   dark (1.2) **(6.2)**
osito *m.*   little bear **(4.1)**
   osito *m.* **de peluche**   teddy bear **(4.1)**
otoño *m.*   autumn (8.1)
otorgar   to grant, give (5.2)
otro(a)   other (1.1)
ovalado(a)   oval (8.1)
óvalo *m.*   oval (7.2)
oxígeno *m.*   oxygen (2.3)
¡oye! *fam.*   hey!, listen! (1.2)

P

paciencia *f.*   patience (3.2) **(3.3)**
paciente *m. f.*   patient (3.2)
pacífico(a)   pacific, peaceful (6.1)

padrastro *m.* stepfather (2.1)
padre *f.* father (1.1)
padremonte *m.* Father Woods (6.3)
padrino *m.* godfather, protector (7.2)
paella *f.* paella *(Spanish rice dish seasoned with saffron)* (4.1)
pagado(a) paid **(7.3)**
pagar to pay (3.2)
página *f.* page (1.1)
pago *m.* payment **(7.1)**
país *m.* (*pl.* **países**) country, nation (1.3)
paisaje *m.* landscape, countryside (4.3)
paja *f.* straw **(4.2)**
pajarito *m.* little bird (2.1)
pájaro *m.* bird **(2.2)**
palabra *f.* word (2.2)
　palabras *f. pl.* **afines** cognates (2.3)
paleontólogo *m.*, **paleontóloga** *f.* paleontologist (3.3)
pálido(a) pale (1.2)
palo *m.* stick (7.1)
pampa *f.* pampas, prairie lands in Argentina (8.1)
pan *m.* bread (5.2)
panadería *f.* bakery (5.1)
panameño(a) Panamanian (3.2)
pandilla *f.* gang (7.3)
pandillero *m.* member of a gang (7.3)
panqueque *m.* pancake (1.3)
pantalones *m. pl.* pants (1.1)
　pantalones *m.* **cortos** shorts **(8.2)**
pantalla *f.* screen (5.3)
pantano *m.* marsh (2.3)
pañuelo *m.* handkerchief **(8.1)**
papa *f.* potato (1.1)
papá *m.* dad (1.1)
papel *m.* role **(2.1)**; paper (2.3)
papelería *f.* stationery store (1.1) **(2.3)**
papita *f.* small potato **(5.1)**
　papitas *f. pl.* **fritas** French fries **(5.1)**
paquete *m.* package (6.2)
paquistaní *m. f.* (*pl.* **paquistaníes**) Pakistani **(2.2)**
par *m.* pair (7.1)
para for (1.1)
paraguayo(a) Paraguayan (2.2)
paraíso *m.* paradise (6.1)
paralelo *m.* parallel (2.3)
paralizado(a) paralyzed (6.3)
parar to stop (1.2)
parcela *f.* part, portion (6.3)
parcial partial (7.1)
parecer to appear, seem (1.2) **(1.3)**
　al parecer apparently (3.2)
pared *f.* wall (4.2)
pareja *f.* couple, pair (6.2)
paréntesis *m. pl.* parentheses (5.2)
pariente *m.* relative (1.1)
parque *m.* park (1.2)
párrafo *m.* paragraph (1.2)

parte *f.* part (2.1)
participar to participate (3.2)
particular private (1.2); particular
partido *m.* game (1.2); political party (5.2)
　tomar partido to decide, make up one's mind (6.3)
partir: partido departed, left (3.3)
parvada *f.* flock (8.3)
pasado *m.* past (3.3) **(4.1)**
pasado(a) past (1.3)
pasar to happen; to go past; to spend time (1.1) *pret.* (2.2)
pasatiempo *m.* pastime (8.3)
pascua *f.* Easter (3.3)
Pascua de Resurrección *f.* Easter of Resurrection (3.3)
pasear to walk, stroll (1.1) *pret.* (2.2)
pasillo *m.* hallway (1.1)
paso *m.* pace; step (1.1)
　unos cuantos pasos a few steps (1.1)
pasta *f.* **dental** toothpaste **(8.2)**
pastel *m.* cake (1.2)
paternalista paternalistic (5.2)
paterno(a) paternal (2.1)
patita *f.* paw (3.3)
patria *f.* native land, mother country (6.3)
patrón *m.* (*pl.* **patrones**) master, boss (6.2); patron
paz *f.* peace (1.2)
pedir (i, i) to ask for, to request (1.1) *pres. subj.* **(5.2)** *cond.* **(8.2)**
　pedir perdón to ask forgiveness (1.3)
pegado(a) attached to (5.3)
peinarse to comb one's hair (3.3)
peine *m.* comb **(8.2)**
pelaje *m.* coat, hair (2.3)
pelear to fight (7.3)
película *f.* film, movie (1.1)
peligro *m.* danger (2.2)
peligroso(a) dangerous **(2.3)**
pelo *m.* hair **(1.3)**
pelota *f.* ball (1.2)
pena: alma en pena soul in torment (6.3)
pendiente hanging (8.3)
Península Ibérica Iberian Peninsula (5.1)
pensamiento *m.* thought (5.3)
pensar (ie) to think (1.1) *pres. subj.* **(5.2)**
pensionado retired (7.3)
peor worse (2.2)
pequeño(a) small, little (2.1)
perder (ie) to lose (2.1)
perderse (ie) to get lost (2.2)
pérdida *f.* loss (3.2)
perdido(a) lost (4.3)
perdonar to pardon, excuse (3.2); to forgive (7.3)
peregrinación *f.* (*pl.* **peregrinaciones**) pilgrimage (7.2)
perezoso *m.* sloth (6.1)
perezoso(a) lazy **(1.3)**
perfecto(a) perfect (1.2)
perfumado(a) perfumed (2.3)

perico *m.* parakeet, parrot (2.2)
periódico *m.* newspaper (1.3)
periodístico: de interés periodístico newsworthy (7.3)
periquito *m.* little parakeet (2.1)
perla *f.* pearl (2.1)
permanecer to remain (3.2)
permiso *m.* permission (3.2)
permitir to permit, allow (1.1)
pero but (1.1)
perrito *m.* puppy (1.2)
perro *m.* dog (1.2)
perseguido(a) *n.* one who is persecuted (3.2)
persistir to persist (8.1)
persona *f.* person (1.1)
personaje *m.* person (2.1); character (4.3)
personalidad *f.* personality **(1.1)**
personalizar to personalize (1.2)
pertenecer to belong (6.2)
pertinente pertinent, relevant (5.1)
peruano(a) Peruvian (2.2)
pesar to weigh (3.3) **(6.2)**
pesas *f. pl.* weights **(5.1)**
pescado *m.* fish (3.2)
pesimista *m. f.* pessimist (2.1)
peso *m.* weight **(5.2)**; peso *(Mexican monetary unit)* (7.1)
petición *f.* (*pl.* **peticiones**) request (1.3)
petróleo *m.* oil, petroleum (2.1)
picado(a) chopped, minced
picaflor *m.* humming-bird (6.1)
picante spicy (1.1)
picar to bite (2.3)
pico *m.* peak **(2.3)**; beak (8.1)
pie *m.* foot (2.2)
   a pie on foot (2.2)
piedra *f.* stone (3.3)
   piedra *f.* **preciosa** precious stone (2.1)
piel *f.* skin **(3.2)**
pierna *f.* leg (3.2)
pieza *f.* piece (5.3)
pilote *m.* pile *(bldg.)* (2.1)
pino *m.* pine tree (8.3)
pintado(a) painted (2.3)
pintar to paint (4.2); to depict (7.2)
pintarse to put on make-up (2.3)
pintor *m.*, **pintora** *f.* painter (7.3)
pintoresco(a) picturesque (6.3)
pintura *f.* painting, picture (1.3); paint (2.3)
pipa *f.* pipe (6.3)
pirámide *f.* pyramid (2.1)
piraña *f.* piranha fish **(2.2)**
piscina *f.* swimming pool **(5.1)**
piso *m.* floor (3.2)
piyamas *f. pl.* pajamas (3.3)
pizarra *f.* chalkboard (3.3)
placer *m.* pleasure (1.1)
planchar to iron **(4.1)**

planear to plan (2.1)
planeta *m.* planet (6.1)
planificar to plan (4.1)
planta *f.* plant **(2.3)**
plantación *f.* (*pl.* **plantaciones**) plantation (3.1)
plantar to plant (7.3)
plantear to set forth, state (3.3)
plata *f.* silver **(3.1)**
platillo *m.* saucer (7.3)
plato *m.* plate (1.2)
playa *f.* beach (3.2) **(8.2)**
plaza *f.* town square **(8.3)**
pluma *f.* feather (8.2)
plumaje *m.* plumage, feathers (6.1)
población *f.* (*pl.* **poblaciones**) population (1.1) **(2.3)**
poblar to settle, colonize (1.1)
pobre poor (1.2)
pobreza *f.* poverty (4.3)
poco(a) little
   dentro de poco within a short time, soon (1.3)
   poco a poco little by little (2.1)
   un poco a little (1.2)
poder (ue) to be able (1.1) *pres. subj.* **(5.2)** *fut.* **(8.1)** *cond.* **(8.2)**
poder *m.* power (6.3)
poderoso(a) powerful, mighty (2.3)
podrías *cond.* would be able (2.1)
poema *m.* poem (1.1)
poesía *f.* poetry (3.2)
poeta *m. f.* poet (1.2)
policía *f.* police force; policewoman; *m.* policeman (3.1)
policíaco(a) mystery **(3.1)**
policías *m. f.* policemen, policewomen (5.2)
poligonal polygonal (4.1)
Polinesia *f.* Polynesia (3.3)
polinesio(a) *n.* Polynesian (3.3)
política politics (5.2)
político(a) political (1.1)
pollo *m.* chicken (2.1)
poner to put, place (1.3) *pres. perf.* **(6.2)** *fut.* **(8.1)** *cond.* **(8.2)**
   poner a cargo to put in charge of (3.2)
ponerse to put on (3.3)
   ponerse + *adj.* to become (1.3)
   ponerse a + *inf.* to begin to + *inf.* (5.3)
   ponerse de acuerdo to agree (2.1)
   ponerse en línea to get into shape, slim down **(8.1)**
   ponerse en marcha to start (8.1)
poquísimo very little (4.1)
poquito(a) little (2.1)
por for; by **(1.1) (3.2)**
   por casualidad by accident, coincidence (3.2)
   por ciento *m.* percent (1.2)
   por ejemplo for example (1.2)
   por el contrario on the contrary (1.1) **(3.1)**
   por escrito in writing **(3.1)**
   por eso for that reason, therefore (2.1)

por favor   please (1.1)

por lo menos   at least (1.2)

por lo tanto   so, therefore (2.1)

por si acaso   if by chance, just in case **(8.2)**

por supuesto   of course (1.1)

¿por qué?   why? (1.1)

porque   because (1.2)

portarse   to behave (3.2)

portugués, portuguesa (*m. pl.* **portugueses**)   Portuguese **(2.2)**

posada *f.*   lodging (4.2)

posado(a)   perched (8.1)

poseer   to possess, have (8.1)

posesión *f.* (*pl.* **posesiones**)   possession (8.1)

posibilidad *f.*   possibility (1.2) **(3.1)**

posible   possible (2.3)

positivo(a)   positive **(1.1)**

poste *m.*   post, pole (4.1)

poste *m.* **de alumbrado eléctrico**   electrical pole (4.1)

posteriormente   subsequently (3.3)

postre *m.*   dessert (1.1)

práctica *f.*   practice (1.3)

practicar   to practice (1.1)

práctico(a)   practical (5.3)

precio *m.*   price (3.2)

precioso(a)   beautiful, precious (4.3)

precisamente   precisely (5.3)

preciso(a)   necessary **(5.1)**

es preciso   it's necessary (5.1)

precolombino(a)   pre-Columbian (4.3)

preconcebido(a)   preconceived (6.3)

predecir   to predict (1.3) **(8.1)**

predicción *f.* (*pl.* **predicciones**)   prediction **(8.1)**

predominante   predominant (8.1)

predominar   to predominate, prevail (6.3)

predominio *m.*   predominance (8.1)

preferencia *f.*   preference **(1.1)**

preferir (ie, i)   to prefer (1.2)

pregunta *f.*   question **(1.1)**

preguntarse   to ask oneself, to wonder (1.3)

prehistórico(a)   prehistoric (4.3)

premio *m.*   prize (2.1) **(4.2)**

prenda *f.*   article (of clothing) (2.1)

prendedor *m.*   brooch (1.1)

prender   to ignite, set fire **(6.3)**; to turn on

prendido(a)   close to, fond of (1.3)

preocupado(a)   worried (1.2)

preparación *f.* (*pl.* **preparaciones**)   preparation (5.2)

preparar   to prepare (1.1)

presencia *f.*   presence (1.3)

presentación *f.* (*pl.* **presentaciones**)   presentation (3.1)

presentar   to introduce (1.1); to show (7.1); to present

presidente *m., f.*   president (2.1)

preso *m.,* **presa** *f.*   prisoner (8.3)

prestar   to lend, give **(5.1)**

prestar atención   to pay attention (3.2)

prestigioso(a)   prestigious (3.2)

previo(a)   previous, prior (3.3) **(7.2)**

primario(a)   primary (3.3)

primate *m.*   primate (6.1)

primo *m.,* **prima** *f.*   cousin (1.3)

principal   principal, main (7.1)

principio *m.*   beginning (4.2)

principios de   beginning of (1.2)

prisa *f.*   hurry (1.3)

privarse   to give up, go without (7.3)

privilegio *m.*   privilege (1.1)

probabilidad *f.*   probability (8.2)

probable   probable **(5.1)**

probablemente   probably (1.2)

probar (ue)   to taste (1.2); to prove (5.1)

problema *m.*   problem (1.1)

problemático(a)   problematic (7.1)

proclamar   to proclaim (1.1)

producir   to produce (2.3)

producto *m.*   product (2.1) **(2.3)**

profecía *f.*   prophecy (8.1)

profesión *f.* (*pl.* **profesiones**)   profession (5.1)

profesor *m.,* **profesora** *f.*   professor, teacher (1.1)

profundamente   deeply (5.1)

profundo(a)   deep, profound (1.3)

programa *m.*   program (2.2)

programación *f.* (*pl.* **programaciones**)   programming **(3.2)**

programado(a)   programmed; planned **(8.3)**

programar   to program *(computers)* **(3.3)**

progresista   progressive (5.2)

progreso *m.*   progress (7.2)

prohibido(a)   prohibited (7.3)

prohibir   to prohibit (5.2)

promedio *m.*   average (3.1) **(7.3)**

prometer   to promise (4.3)

prominente   prominent (7.1)

promoción *f.* (*pl.* **promociones**)   promotion (3.2)

pronóstico *m.*   forecast (3.1); prediction

pronto   quickly (1.3)

pronunciar   to pronounce (2.1)

propagarse   to propagate, spread (5.1)

propiedad *f.*   property (6.2)

propietario *m.,* **propietaria** *f.*   owner (3.2)

propina *f.*   tip (3.2)

propio(a)   own (2.3)

proporcionar   to provide (1.3)

propósito *m.*   purpose (1.3)

prosa *f.*   prose (5.1)

prosperar   to prosper, flourish (8.1)

próspero(a)   prosperous (3.2)

protección *f.*   protection **(3.2)**

protector(a)   protective **(3.2)**

proteger   to protect **(3.2)**

protesta *f.*   protest (6.3)

proveer   to provide, supply (4.2)

provenir (ie, i)   to come from (7.3)

providencial   providential (5.2)

provincia *f.* province (3.2)
provocar to provoke (2.1)
próximo(a) next (2.2)
proyectado(a) thrown, hurled (8.2)
proyecto *m.* project (8.1)
prueba *f.* proof (3.3); test, trial (5.1)
publicación *f.* (*pl.* **publicaciones**) publication (6.3)
publicar to publish (3.2); to publicize (5.1)
publicidad *f.* publicity (3.2)
público *m.* public, audience (5.1)
pueblo *m.* town, village (1.1)
puente *m.* bridge (4.2)
puerta *f.* door (1.1)
puerto *m.* port (2.1) **(2.3)**
puertorriqueño(a) Puerto Rican (2.2)
pues well (1.1)
puesto *m.* job, position (3.2) **(7.1)**
puesto(a) placed, set (2.1); in place; on (4.3)
pulga *f.* flea **(2.3)**
pulgada *f.* inch (3.2)
pulsera *f.* bracelet (1.1) **(1.2)**
puma *m.* mountain lion, puma **(6.1)**
puntería *f.* marksmanship, aim (6.3)
punto *m.* point; dot (1.1)
  punto *m.* **de vista** point of view (6.3)
puntualidad *f.* punctuality **(7.3)**
puntualmente punctually (7.2)
puñado *m.* handful (6.1)
pupitre *m.* student desk (3.2)
pureza *f.* purity (5.2)
puro(a) pure (3.1)

Q

que that (1.1)
qué what (1.1)
  ¡qué barbaridad! what an outrage! what nonsense! (5.2)
  ¡qué caballero! what a gentleman! **(5.1)**
  ¡qué culto! how educated! how cultured! **(2.2)**
  ¡qué envidia! what envy! **(8.1)**
  ¡qué fracaso! what a disaster! (3.1)
  ¡qué lástima! what a shame! (3.1)
  ¡qué padre! how great! (6.1)
  ¡qué suerte! what luck! **(1.2)**
  ¡qué susto! what a fright! **(6.3)**
  ¡qué va! no, not at all. (6.2)
  ¡qué vergüenza! how embarrassing! (5.1)
¿qué? what? (1.1)
  ¿qué hay de nuevo? what's new? **(1.1)**
  ¿qué tal? how's it going? (1.1)
  ¿qué va? what's happening? (1.1)
quebrado(a) *n.* one who is broken (3.2)
quebrar (ie) to break, smash (6.3)
quechua *f.* quechua (*indigenous Peruvian language*) (8.2)
quedar to remain (1.2)

quehacer *m.* chore **(4.1)**
quejarse to complain (1.3)
quejido *m.* moan (3.3)
quemado(a) burned **(3.2)**
quemadura *f.* burn **(3.2)**
quemar(se) to burn (oneself) (2.3)
querer (ie) to want, wish (1.1) *pret.* **(3.1)** *fut.* **(8.1)** *cond.* **(8.2)**
querido(a) dear, beloved (1.2)
queso *m.* cheese (2.1)
quetzal *m.* quetzal (*Central American bird with brilliant plumage*) (6.1)
¿quién?, ¿quiénes? who? (1.1)
¡quíhubole! what's happening, what's up **(6.1)**
química *f.* chemistry (1.2)
químico *m.*, **química** *f.* chemist (6.2)
quitar to take away, remove **(5.2)**
quitarse to take off (*clothes*) (3.3)
¡quítate! stop it! **(2.2)**
quizás perhaps **(5.1)**

R

raíz *f.* (*pl.* **raíces**) root (1.1)
rallado(a) grated (1.3)
rama *f.* branch (6.3)
ranchería *f.* a village in which certain Native-American tribes lived and farmed (1.1)
ranchito *m.* small ranch (1.3)
rancho *m.* ranch (3.2)
rápidamente quickly, rapidly (3.3)
rápido(a) fast (1.1) **(1.3)**
raqueta *f.* racket (7.1)
raro(a) strange (1.2)
rasuradora *f.* razor **(8.2)**
rato *m.* short period of time, a while (1.2)
ratón *m.* (*pl.* **ratones**) mouse **(2.3)**
ratoncito *m.* little mouse **(4.2)**
rayo *m.* ray **(3.2)**
raza *f.* race (2.3)
razón *f.* (*pl.* **razones**) reason (1.3)
razonar to reason (6.2)
reacción *f.* (*pl.* **reacciones**) reaction (3.2)
reaccionar to react; to respond (1.2)
reajustar to readjust (5.3)
real *m.* coin of 25 *céntimos*, one quarter of a peseta (7.1)
real magnificent (2.1) royal; real
realidad *f.* reality (2.2)
realista *m. f.* realist **(7.1)**
realizado(a) carried out (3.3)
realmente really (2.3)
rebajado(a) reduced, discounted (1.2)
recepcionista *m. f.* receptionist **(7.2)**
receptor *m.* catcher (3.1)
receta *f.* recipe (3.2)
recibir to receive (1.1)

recién recently (7.3)
reciente recent **(7.3)**
recientemente recently (1.3)
recitar to recite (5.2)
reclamar to reclaim **(3.1)**; to claim, demand (8.1)
reclutador *m.* **voluntario** voluntary recruiter (7.3)
reclutar to recruit (7.3)
recoger to gather (1.1); to pick up (1.2)
recomendable advisable **(5.1)**; commendable
recomendación *f.* (*pl.* **recomendaciones**) recommendation **(5.1)**
recomendar (ie) to recommend (1.2)
reconocer to realize (6.1); to recognize (7.3)
recordar (ue) to remind (8.1); to remember (1.2)
recrear to recreate (2.3)
recreo *m.* recess, recreation (1.1)
rectitud *f.* rectitude, honesty (7.2)
recuerdo *m.* remembrance, souvenir (4.1); memory
red *m.* network **(3.3)**
redondo(a) round (7.2)
reducido(a) reduced (6.3)
referencia *f.* reference **(7.3)**
referirse (ie, i) a to refer (to) (2.2)
reflejar to reflect (4.1)
reflexionar to reflect, think (5.3)
reforma *f.* reform (3.2)
reformista *m. f.* reformer (3.2)
refrán *m.* refrain, saying (1.3)
refresco *m.* soft drink (1.1)
refrito(a) refried (1.3)
refugio *m.* refuge (4.1) **(6.2)**
regalar to give (as a gift) **(4.2)**
regalo *m.* gift (1.1)
régimen *m.* regimen, diet **(5.2)**
región *f.* (*pl.* **regiones**) region (1.1)
registrar to register (3.1)
regla *f.* ruler (*for measuring*) (1.2); rule (6.2)
regresar to return, go back (2.3)
regreso *m.* return (3.1)
reguero *m.* stream (4.1)
regular okay, so-so (1.1)
rehusar to refuse (7.2)
reino *m.* reign, kingdom (4.2)
reír (i, i) to laugh **(4.1)**
reírse (i, i) to laugh (6.1)
   reírse a carcajadas to roar with laughter (6.2)
rejilla *f.* lattice; canework (4.3)
relación *f.* relation, relationship (7.1)
relacionado(a) related (2.2)
relajar to relax (2.3)
relatar to tell (of), relate (3.2)
relativamente relatively (8.1)
reloj *m.* clock; watch (1.2)
rellenar to fill (1.3) **(3.2)**
relleno(a) filled (1.3)
remedio *m.* remedy, cure (4.3)
remoto(a) remote (3.3)

rendir to render (4.3)
   rendir culto to render homage (4.3)
renovar to restore (4.2)
reparar to repair (7.2)
repartir to distribute **(7.2)**
repasar to review, go over (3.3)
repente: de repente suddenly (4.3)
repetir (i, i) to repeat (1.2)
repleto(a) replete, full (3.3)
reporte *m.* report (3.1)
reportero *m.,* **reportera** *f.* reporter (1.3)
representante *m. f.* representative (8.2)
representar to represent (1.3)
república *f.* republic (1.1)
republicano(a) republican (7.2)
reputación *f.* reputation (5.1)
requerir (ie, i) to require **(7.2)**
requisito *m.* requisite **(7.3)**
reserva *f.* reserve (8.1); reservation
residencia *f.* residence (7.3)
resina *f.* resin (2.3)
resolución *f.* (*pl.* **resoluciones**) resolution (8.1)
resolver (ue) to resolve **(3.3)** *pres. perf.* **(6.2)**
respecto a with respect to (5.2)
respetar to respect (1.3)
respeto *m.* respect (1.3)
respirar to breathe **(5.2)**
responder to respond (1.1)
responsabilidad *f.* responsibility (5.2)
responsable responsible (3.2)
respuesta *f.* answer, response (1.2)
restaurante *m.* restaurant (1.1)
resto *m.* rest, remainder (2.1)
restos *m. pl.* remains (4.1)
resultado *m.* result **(5.3)**
resultado(a) resulted (1.3)
resultar to turn out to be (1.3)
resumen *m.* summary (4.3)
resumir to sum up (4.3)
reunión *f.* (*pl.* **reuniones**) meeting, (social) gathering (2.1); reunion (4.1)
reunir to assemble, bring together (7.3)
reunirse to get together, meet (1.3)
revés: al revés backwards, inside-out (6.3)
revisar to look over, examine (3.1)
revista *f.* magazine (1.1)
revitalización *f.* revitalization (8.1)
revolucionario(a) revolutionary (7.2)
rico *m.,* **rica** *f.* rich person (7.1)
rico(a) rich; tasty, delicious (1.2)
ridículo(a) ridiculous (3.1)
rima *f.* rhyme (6.3)
rincón *m.* corner (3.3)
río *m.* river (2.1)
riqueza *f.* riches, wealth (2.1); richness (8.3)
riquezas *f. pl.* riches; resources (1.1)
risa *f.* laughter (1.2)

ritmo *m.*   rhythm (6.3)
rito *m.*   rite, ceremony (7.1)
robar   to rob, steal (3.1)
robo *m.*   robbery, theft (4.2)
roca *f.*   rock (4.3)
rodar   to roll (7.2)
rodeado(a)   surrounded **(8.3)**
rodear   to surround (8.1)
rodilla *f.*   knee (7.2)
rojo(a)   red (1.1)
romántico(a)   romantic (1.1)
romper   to break **(2.2)** *pres. perf.* **(6.2)**
rondar   to prowl around; to haunt (6.2)
ropa *f.*   clothing (1.1)
rosa *adj.*   pink (1.2)
rosa *f.*   rose (3.3)
rosado(a)   pink (1.1)
rubio(a)   blond (1.3)
rueda *f.*   wheel **(1.3)**
ruido *m.*   noise, sound (5.1) **(6.3)**
ruidosamente   loudly (8.2)
ruidoso(a)   noisy, loud (1.2)
ruina *f.*   ruin (8.2)
ruinas *f. pl.*   ruins (4.1)
ruiseñor *m.*   nightingale (8.2)
ruso(a)   Russian **(2.2)**
ruta *f.*   route (2.3)
rutina *f.*   routine **(1.1)**   —

～～S～～

sábado *m.*   Saturday (1.1)
sabana *f.*   savanna, a tropical/subtropical grassland (3.3)
sábana *f.*   sheet *(on a bed)* (5.1)
sabelotodo *m.*   know-it-all (7.2)
saber   to know; to know how (1.1) *pret.* **(3.1)** *pres. subj.* **(5.1)** *cond.* **(8.2)**
sabio *m.*   wise person (7.2)
sabio(a)   wise (3.2) **(4.3)**
sabor *m.*   flavor **(3.2)**
sacar   to take out (1.2)
    sacar apuntes   to take notes (4.3)
    sacar fotos   to take photos (1.1)
sacerdote *m.*   priest, leader (8.1)
saco *m.*   sack, bag (6.1); jacket (5.2)
    saco *m.* **de dormir**   sleeping bag **(6.1)**
sacudir: sacudir los muebles   to dust *(the furniture)* (7.1)
sal *m.*   salt (5.2)
salario *m.*   salary **(7.2)**
salchicha *f.*   sausage (3.1)
salir   to leave (1.1) *pret.* **(2.2)** *imperf.* **(3.3)** *pres. subj.* **(5.1)** *pres. perf.* **(6.2)** *fut.* **(8.1)** *cond.* **(8.2)**
salón *m.* *(pl.* **salones*)*   living room (3.3)
salsa *f.*   sauce (1.1)
saltar   to jump (3.2)
saltón *(pl.* **saltones*)*   bulging (5.3)

salud *f.*   health **(2.3)**
saludable   healthful **(5.2)**
saludar   to greet (1.1)
saludo *m.*   greeting (1.3)
salvadoreño(a)   Salvadoran (2.2)
salvaje   wild, savage **(2.2)**
salvar   to save *pret.* **(2.2)**
sanar   to heal (8.2)
sandalia *f.*   sandal **(8.2)**
sándwich *m.*   sandwich (3.2)
sangre *f.*   blood (2.3)
sangriento(a)   bloody (7.2)
sanitorio *m.*   sanatorium (6.3)
sano(a)   healthy, wholesome (3.2)
santo *m.*   saint's day, birthday (1.2)
sapo *m.*   toad (8.2)
sastre *m.*   tailor (5.1)
sátira *f.*   satire; skit (8.2)
secar   to dry (4.2)
secarse   to dry up (3.3)
sección *f.* *(pl.* **secciones*)*   section **(2.1)**
secretario *m.,* **secretaria** *f.*   secretary (1.2)
secreto(a)   secret **(3.3)**
secundario(a)   secondary (1.1)
sed *f.*   thirst (5.2)
seda *f.*   silk (7.2)
seguida: en seguida   right away, straightaway (5.2)
seguidor *m.,* **seguidora** *f.*   follower (5.2)
seguir (i, i)   to follow; *pres. subj.* **(5.2)**
según   according to (1.1)
seguramente   surely **(2.2)**
seguridad *f.*   security (5.1); safety
seguro *m.*   insurance **(7.1)**
seguro(a)   sure, certain **(1.2)**
seleccionado(a)   selected (8.2)
seleccionar   to select (1.3)
selva *f.*   jungle **(2.2)**
    selva *f.* **tropical** (2.3)   rain forest
semana *f.*   week (1.3)
    fin *m.* **de semana**   weekend (4.2)
sembrar   to plant (4.1)
semejante a   similar to (4.2)
semejanza *f.*   similarity (4.1)
seminario *m.*   seminary (7.2)
sencillo(a)   simple (2.3)
sensacional   sensational (3.2)
sentarse   to sit down (1.2)
sentido *m.*   sense
    doble sentido   double meaning (1.3)
    sentido *m.* **común**   common sense (4.1)
sentimiento *m.*   feeling (1.3)
sentir (ie, i)   to feel (1.2) **(5.2)**
sentirse (ie, i)   to feel (7.2)
señal *f.*   sign, signal **(6.3)**
señalado(a)   indicated (7.1)
señalar   to point out (4.1); to point to (6.1); to mark; to indicate

señor (Sr.) *m.* Mr. (1.1)
señora (Sra.) *f.* Mrs. (1.2)
señorita (Srta.) *f.* Miss (6.2)
separación *f.* (*pl.* **separaciones**) separation (1.1)
separado(a) separated, separate (7.2)
separar to separate (1.1)
separarse to separate; to distance oneself **(4.1)**
sequía *f.* drought (2.1)
ser to be (1.1) *pret.* (2.1) *imperf.* **(4.1)** *pres. subj.* **(5.1)** *cond.* **(8.2)**
   ser listo(a) to be clever or sharp (5.2)
ser *m.* **humano** human being (8.2)
sereno(a) serene, calm (6.1)
serie *f.* series **(3.2)**
serio(a) serious (1.3)
serpiente *f.* snake **(2.2)**
servicio *m.* service (1.3); restroom (6.2)
servir (i, i) to serve (1.2) *pres. subj.* **(5.2)**
severo(a) severe (4.2)
si if (1.2)
sí yes (1.1)
SIDA *m.* AIDS (2.3)
siempre always (1.1)
sierra *f.* ridge (of mountains) **(6.1)**
siesta *f.* nap (4.3)
siglo *m.* century (6.3)
significado *m.* meaning (2.3)
significar to mean (5.1)
significativo(a) significant (3.2)
siguiente following, next (2.1)
silencio *m.* silence (4.3)
silencioso(a) silent (4.1)
silla *f.* chair (1.2)
   silla *f.* **de ruedas** wheelchair **(1.3)**
   silla *f.* **mecedora** rocking chair (2.1)
sillón *m.* (*pl.* **sillones**) easy chair (3.1)
simbolismo *m.* symbolism (6.3)
símbolo *m.* symbol (8.3)
similitud *f.* similarity (3.3)
simpático(a) nice (1.2)
sin without (1.3)
   sin duda without a doubt (1.3)
   sin embargo nevertheless (1.1)
singular unique, extraordinary (1.3)
sinnúmero *m.* a great many, a huge number of (5.1)
sino rather (1.1)
sinsonte *m.* mockingbird (8.2)
síntoma *m.* symptom **(1.2)**
siquiera without even (7.3)
sirviente *m.*, **sirvienta** *f.* servant (3.3)
sistema *m.* system (4.1)
sitio *m.* site, place (1.2) **(6.2)**
situación *f.* (*pl.* **situaciones**) situation (1.1)
situado(a) situated, located (4.1)
sobre on; over; about (1.2)
   sobre todo above all **(1.3)**
sobrellevar to bear, to endure (8.1)

sobrenatural: lo sobrenatural the supernatural (7.1)
sobresaliente outstanding (7.3)
sobresalir to stand out, excel (5.3) **(6.2)**
sobrevivir to make it through, survive (3.1)
sobrino *m.*, **sobrina** *f.* nephew, niece (2.1)
sociedad *f.* society (6.1)
socio *m.*, **socia** *f.* member (3.1) **(5.1)**
sociología *f.* sociology (8.2)
sofisticado(a) sophisticated, advanced (3.1)
software *m.* software **(3.3)**
sol *m.* sun (1.3)
solamente only (1.1)
soledad *f.* loneliness (3.2)
solicitar to apply, solicit **(7.2)**
solicitud *f.* application **(7.3)**
solo(a) alone; single (1.2)
sólo only (1.2)
solución *f.* (*pl.* **soluciones**) solution (3.2)
sombrero *m.* hat (1.1)
sonar (ue) to ring **(4.2)**; to sound (5.3)
soneto *m.* sonnet (3.2)
sonreír (i, i) to smile **(4.1)**
sonreírse (i, i) to smile (1.2)
soñador *m.*, **soñadora** *f.* dreamer
sopa *f.* soup (2.1)
sordo *m.*, **sorda** *f.* deaf person (7.2)
sorprender to surprise (6.2)
sorpresa *f.* surprise (2.3) **(3.3)**
sospechar to suspect **(6.1)**
sospechoso(a) suspicious **(6.2)**
sostener to sustain (2.3)
sotana *f.* cassock, monk's attire (5.1)
sótano *m.* basement (6.2)
su, sus his, her, your; your (*pl.*), their (1.1)
suave smooth, soft **(4.2)**
sub-alcalde deputy mayor (5.1)
subgraduado undergraduate (7.3)
subir to go up; to climb; to get into (2.1)
subterráneo(a) subterranean, underground (4.3)
subtítulo *m.* subtitle, captions (2.3) **(3.3)**
subyugar: subyugado subjugated (3.3)
suceso *m.* event, incident (3.3)
sucio(a) dirty **(6.1)**
sudadera *f.* sweatshirt (1.1)
sudor *m.* sweat (6.3)
sueco(a) Swedish **(2.2)**
suegro *m.*, **suegra** *f.* father-in-law, mother-in-law (1.3)
suela *f.* sole (*of shoe*) (2.3)
sueldo *m.* salary, wages (7.3)
suelo *m.* floor (*of a room*) (1.2); ground (6.1)
sueño *m.* sleep; dream **(5.1)**
suerte *f.* luck (4.1)
suéter *m.* sweater (1.1)
suficiente sufficient, enough (1.1)
sufrir to experience (2.1); to suffer (5.3)
sugerencia *f.* suggestion **(3.3)**
sugerir (ie, i) to suggest **(5.2)**

suicidarse   to commit suicide, kill oneself (3.2)
suicidio *m.*   suicide (3.2)
suizo(a)   Swiss **(2.2)**
sujetarse   to conform to (6.3); to subject oneself to
sujeto *m.*   subject (1.2)
suma *f.*   amount (1.1)
sumamente   extremely (5.2)
sumario *m.*   summary (4.3)
supermercado *m.*   supermarket (1.1)
supervisar   to supervise **(4.2)**
suponer   to suppose (3.3)
supremo(a)   supreme (8.1)
sur *m.*   south (2.1)
suroeste *m.*   southwest (1.1)
suspender   to suspend (4.1)
suspendido(a)   hanging (7.1)
suspirar   to sigh (8.3)
sustituir   to substitute (3.2)
susto *m.*   fright **(6.3)**

〜〜〜T〜〜〜

tabulación *f. (pl.* **tabulaciones***)*   tabulation, tally (7.2)
tacaño(a)   stingy **(1.3)**
taco *m.*   taco *(corn tortilla with filling)* (8.2)
tal   such (8.2)
  tal vez   maybe, perhaps (1.1)
tala *f.*   destruction, devastation (3.2) felling of trees
talento *m.*   talent **(1.1)**
talla *f.*   size *(clothing)* (7.2)
tallar   to carve (3.3)
taller *m.*   (work)shop (3.3)
tamaño *m.*   size (2.3)
también   also (1.1)
tambor *m.*   drum (3.2)
tamborito *m.*   little drum (3.2)
tampoco   neither, not either (1.2)
tan   so (1.2)
  tan pronto como   as soon as (2.2)
tanto *adv.*   so much (2.3)
  tanto como   as . . . as (1.2)
tanto(a)   so much, so many (1.1)
tapas *f. pl.*   appetizers (4.2)
tapir *m.*   tapir **(2.2)**
taquería *f.*   taco restaurant (7.3)
taquigrafía *f.*   shorthand **(7.2)**
taquimecanógrafa *m. f.*   shorthand typist (7.2)
tarde *f.*   afternoon (3.3)
tarde   late (1.1)
tarea *f.*   homework (1.1); task
tarjeta *f.*   card (2.2)
te *dir. (indir.) obj. pron.*   to (for) you (1.1)
  te toca a ti   it's your turn **(1.1)**
te *refl. pron.*   yourself (1.1)
té *m.*   tea (5.1)
  té *m.* **de dormilera**   tea that induces sleep (5.1)

teatro *m.*   theatre (2.1)
técnico(a)   technical **(3.2)**
tecnológico(a)   technological (3.3)
techo *m.*   ceiling; roof (4.2)
tejer   to weave (3.1)
tejido *m.*   weaving (4.3)
telaraña *f.*   spiderweb (5.2)
tele *f. abbrev.*   television (1.1)
telefónico(a)   pertaining to the telephone (3.2)
teléfono *m.*   telephone (1.1)
telenovela *f.*   soap opera **(2.2)**
televisión *f.*   television (1.1)
televisor *m.*   television set (2.1)
tema *m.*   theme, subject (1.3) **(2.2)**
temer   to fear (5.3)
temeroso(a)   fearful, frightened (6.3)
temor *m.*   dread, fear (8.2)
temperamento *m.*   temperament, nature, disposition (5.1)
temperatura *f.*   temperature (2.1) **(2.3)**
templado(a)   mild (6.1)
templo *m.*   temple (3.3)
temporada *f.*   season (3.1)
temprano *adv.*   early (2.1)
temprano(a)   early (4.1)
tender (ie)   to tend (1.3)
tendido   flat, extended (1.3)
tener   to have **(1.1)** *pres. subj.* **(5.1)** *fut.* **(8.1)** *cond.* **(8.2)**
  tener a mano   to have at hand (3.3)
  tener buen efecto   to have a good effect (2.3)
  tener calor   to be hot (1.3)
  tener cuidado   to be careful (1.3)
  tener derecho   to have the right (5.2)
  tener éxito   to succeed, be successful (5.1)
  tener frío   to be cold (1.3)
  tener ganas de   to feel like, to have a mind to (1.1) **(1.3)**
  tener hambre   to be hungry (1.3)
  tener lugar   to take place (2.1)
  tener miedo   to be afraid **(1.3)**
  tener presente   to keep in mind (7.3)
  tener prisa   to be in a hurry (1.3)
  tener que ver (con)   to have to do (with) (2.3)
  tener razón   to be right (1.3)
  tener sed   to be thirsty (1.3)
  tener sentido   to make sense (6.1)
  tener sueños   to have dreams **(1.3)**
  tener suerte   to be lucky **(1.3)**
tenis *m.*   tennis (1.3)
tentación *f. (pl.* **tentaciones***)*   temptation (5.2)
teñido(a)   dyed (2.3)
teoría *f.*   theory (3.3)
tercio *m.*   one third (3.1)
terminar   to end (1.1)
ternura *f.*   tenderness (3.2)
terraza *f.*   terrace *(hillside farming)* (4.1)
terremoto *m.*   earthquake (4.1)

terreno *m.* terrain (2.1)
   terreno *m.* **de fútbol** soccer (football) field (4.3)
territorio *m.* territory (2.1)
terror *m.* terror (2.3)
tesoro *m.* treasure (3.3) **(4.1)**
testigo *m. f.* witness (3.3)
tiempo *m.* time (1.1)
tienda *f.* store (1.1)
tierra *f.* land (1.1); earth (7.2)
tigre *m.* tiger, mountain lion (6.3)
tijeras *f. pl.* scissors (3.2)
timbre *m.* bell (4.1)
tímido(a) timid (1.3)
tío *m.,* **tía** *f.* uncle, aunt (2.1)
típico(a) typical (1.3)
tipo *m.* type (1.3)
tira *f.* strip (3.1)
   tira *f.* **cómica** comic strip (3.1)
tiranía *f.* tyranny (2.3)
tiránico(a) tyrannical (2.3)
tirar to pull (3.3); to throw (7.2)
titulado(a) titled, called (2.1)
titular *m.* title; headline **(5.3)**
título *m.* title (2.1); degree (7.2)
toalla *f.* towel **(8.2)**
tocar to play an instrument (1.1); to touch
   tocar a la puerta to knock on the door (7.1)
todavía still (1.2)
todo(a), todos(as) all (1.1)
tolerancia *f.* tolerance (5.1)
tomar to eat; to drink; to take (2.1)
   tomar apuntes to take notes (4.3)
   tomar conciencia to become aware of (4.3)
   tomar el sol to sunbathe (3.3)
tomo *m.* volume (6.3)
tonelada *f.* ton (3.3)
tono *m.* tone (7.2)
tonto(a) foolish, silly (1.3)
toparse to run into (7.1)
torbellino *m.* brainstorm (2.3)
torcido(a) bent (5.3); twisted
tormenta *f.* storm (6.2)
tortilla *f.* cornmeal or flour pancake (1.3)
   tortilla *f.* **española** Spanish omelet of eggs and potatoes (6.2)
tortillería *f.* tortilla factory (1.3)
tortuga *f.* turtle, tortoise **(2.3)**
totalmente totally (1.3)
tóxico(a) toxic (6.2)
trabajador *m.,* **trabajadora** *f.* worker **(1.3)**
trabajador(a) hard-working (1.3)
trabajar to work (1.1) *pres. subj.* (5.1)
trabajo *m.* work (1.1)
traducir to translate (5.1)
traductor *m.* translator (5.1)
traer to bring (1.2) *pret.* **(3.1)**
tráfico *m.* traffic (4.3)

trágico(a) tragic (3.2) **(4.1)**
traicionar to betray (7.3)
traído(a) brought (2.1)
traje *m.* suit (1.1)
   traje de baño bathing suit (5.2)
tranquilo(a) calm, tranquil (1.2)
tranquilizante soothing, lulling (6.3)
transcurrir to pass (4.2)
transporte *m.* transportation (1.1)
trapecio *m.* trapezoid (4.3)
trapo *m.* cloth, rag **(4.1)**
tras after (2.3)
traspasar to transfer over (1.3)
tratado *m.* agreement, treaty (1.1)
tratado(a) treated (8.1)
tratamiento *m.* treatment (8.1)
tratar to treat (1.3)
tratar de to attempt to, try to (1.2); to deal with, be
   about (5.2)
travieso(a) mischievous, naughty (3.2)
trayectoria *f.* **cronológica** time line (4.3)
trazado *m.* outline (4.3)
trazado(a) outlined, sketched (4.3)
trazar to draw; trace (a line) (1.1)
tren *m.* train (2.3)
triángulo *m.* triangle (4.3)
tribu *f.* tribe (1.1)
tributario *m.* tributary (2.3)
trigo *m.* wheat (1.1)
triste sad (1.2)
tristeza *f.* sadness (3.2)
triunfo *m.* triumph (3.2)
trofeo *m.* trophy (4.1)
tronco *m.* trunk (6.3)
tropical tropical (2.3)
trópico *m.* tropics (2.1)
trotar to trot (6.3)
tu, tus your (1.1)
tú you (1.1)
tucán *m.* (*pl.* **tucanes**) toucan **(2.3)**
tumba *f.* tomb, grave (1.2)
túnico *m.* bride's tunic, blouse (6.2)
turismo *m.* tourism (7.1)
turista *m. f.* tourist (2.1)
turístico(a) tourist(ic) (6.3)
turnar to take turns (1.1)
tuyo(a) your (4.2)

ubicado(a) to be placed, situated (3.3)
último(a) last, final (1.1)
un, una a (1.1)
único(a) only (1.3); unique

unido(a)   united **(5.1)**
uniforme *m.*   uniform (3.2)
unir   to join, unite (1.1)
universidad *f.*   university (1.2)
universitario(a)   pertaining to the university (1.3); university student **(5.3)**
universo *m.*   universe (3.2)
urbano(a)   urban (8.1)
uruguayo(a)   Uruguayan (2.2)
usado(a)   used (7.3)
usar   to use (1.1)
uso *m.*   use (7.3)
usted(es)   you (1.1)
útil   useful (3.1)
utilizar   to use (4.1)

~~~V~~~

vaca *f.*   cow (1.3)
vacaciones *f. pl.*   vacation (1.1)
vaciar   to empty **(3.1)**
vacío(a)   empty (4.2)
vagar   to wander, roam (6.3)
vale: mi vale *m. f.*   my friend *(Venez.)* (2.2)
valer   to be worth (4.3)
válido(a)   valid (2.3)
valiente   valiant, brave (7.3)
valioso(a)   valuable (5.1)
valor *m.*   value (7.1)
valorar   to value (7.3)
valle *m.*   valley (3.1)
vaquero *m.,* **vaquera** *f.*   cowboy, cowgirl (1.1)
variado(a)   varied (5.2)
variar   to vary (2.1)
variedad *f.*   variety (2.1)
varios(as)   several (1.1)
varón *m. (pl.* **varones***)*   man, male (5.1)
vasto(a)   vast, huge (4.2)
vecino *m.,* **vecina** *f.*   neighbor **(1.2)**
vecino(a)   neighboring, nearby (1.1)
vegetación *f. sing.*   vegetation (6.1)
vegetal *m.*   vegetable **(5.2)**
velo *m.*   veil (6.2)
velorio *m.*   wake (4.1)
vencer   to conquer, defeat, beat (2.3)
vencido(a)   beaten, defeated (7.3)
vendedor *m.,* **vendedora** *f.*   salesperson **(7.3)**
vender   to sell (3.1)
venerar   to venerate, worship (8.1)
venéreo(a)   venereal (5.2)
venezolano(a)   Venezuelan (1.2)
venir (ie, i)   to come (1.1) *fut.* **(8.1)** *cond.* **(8.2)**

venta *f.*   sale **(7.2)**
ventaja *f.*   advantage (7.1)
ventana *f.*   window (4.1)
ver   to see (1.1) *imperf.* **(4.1)** *pres. subj.* **(5.1)** *pres. perf.* **(6.2)** *fut.* **(8.1)**
   verse obligado a + *inf.*   to be obliged to + *inf.*, find oneself compelled to + *inf.* (6.2)
verano *m.*   summer (1.1)
veras: de veras   in truth, really (4.2)
verbo *m.*   verb (1.1)
verdad *f.*   truth (1.1)
verdaderamente   truthfully (8.2)
verdadero(a)   real, true (1.1); actual, real (1.3)
verde   green (1.1)
verduras *f. pl.*   green vegetables (6.1)
vereda *f.*   path, trail (1.2); sidewalk
vergüenza *f.*   shame, embarrassment (5.1)
verificar   to verify (1.1)
verso *m.*   verse (4.1); line (of a poem) (8.3)
vestido *m.*   dress (1.2); clothing (5.2)
vestir *m.*   dress, attire (1.2)
vestirse (i, i)   to get dressed (3.3)
veterinario *m.,* **veterinaria** *f.*   veterinarian **(5.2)**
vez *f. (pl.* **veces***)*   time (1.1)
   a veces   at times (1.1)
   de vez en cuando   from time to time (8.1)
   en vez de   instead of (1.2)
viajar   to travel **(1.1)** *pret.* **(2.2)**
viaje *m.*   trip (1.3)
vibrante   vibrant (6.3)
vice-presidente *m., f.*   vice president (5.1)
víctima *f.*   victim (8.2)
victoria *f.*   victory (7.3)
victoriano(a)   Victorian (1.2)
vida *f.*   life **(1.1)**
vidrio *m.*   glass (7.2)
viejito *m.,* **viejita** *f.*   elderly person **(3.3)**
viejo(a)   old (1.3)
viento *m.*   wind (3.1)
   hace viento   it's windy (3.1)
viera   would see *(imperf. subj.)* (8.2)
vietnamita *m. f.*   Vietnamese **(2.2)**
viga *f.*   beam, rafter (7.1)
villano m.   villain (2.2)
vino *m.*   wine (3.1)
viñedo *m.*   vineyard (1.1)
violín *m.*   violin **(1.3)**
virtual   virtual (7.2)
virtualmente   virtually (8.1)
virtuoso(a)   virtuous (6.2)
visión *f.*   view (7.1); vision
visita *f.*   visit (4.2)
visitante *m. f.*   visitor (1.2)
visitar   to visit (1.1) *pret.* **(2.2)**
vista *f.*   view (2.1); sight (2.2)
visto   seen *(past part.)* (6.1)

visualizar   visualize (8.3)
viudo *m.,* **viuda** *f.*   widower, widow (1.3)
víveres *m. pl.*   food (1.1)
vivir   to live **(1.2)**
vivo(a)   lively, vivid (7.2); alive
vocabulario *m.*   vocabulary (5.1)
volado(a) *adv.*   in a rush, hastily (6.2)
volando(a)   flying (3.3)
volar (ue)   to fly (3.3)
volcán *m.* (*pl.* **volcanes**)   volcano (3.1)
volibol *m.*   volleyball (5.2)
volteado(a)   turned around (6.3)
voluntario *m.,* **voluntaria** *f.*   volunteer (1.3)
volver (ue)   to return (1.2) *pres. perf.* **(6.2)**
   volver a + *inf.*   to (*inf.*) again (1.2)
volverse   to become (2.3)
voseo *m.*   the use of **vos** *(Argentina)* (8.2)
voz *f.* (*pl.* **voces**)   voice (3.2) **(4.3)**
vuelo *m.*   flight **(8.2)**
vuelta *f.*   turn (1.2) **(7.1)**

y   and (1.1)
ya   right now (1.1); already (2.1)
ya no   no longer (3.3)
ya que   since, as (1.3)
yerno *m.,* **yerna** *f.*   son-in-law, daughter-in-law (4.3)
yo   I (1.1)

zanahoria *f.*   carrot (6.2)
zapatero *m.,* **zapatera** *f.*   shoemaker (5.1)
zapatilla *f.*   slipper (3.3)
zapato *m.*   shoe (1.1)
zarcillo *m.*   earring **(4.1)**
zona *f.*   zone, area (1.1)
zoológico *m.*   zoo (6.1)
zorro *m.*   fox (6.3)

VOCABULARIO

INGLÉS–ESPAÑOL

VOCABULARIO
inglés-español

This **Vocabulario** includes all active words and expressions in **¡DIME!** (Exact cognates, conjugated verb forms, and proper nouns used as passive vocabulary are generally omitted.) A number in parentheses follows all entries. This number refers to the unit and lesson in which the word or phrase is introduced (and, when there is no more than one number, reentered). The number (**3.1**), for example, refers to **Unidad 3, Lección 1**.

The gender of nouns is indicated as *m.* (masculine) or *f.* (feminine). When a noun designates a person or an animal, both the masculine and feminine form is given. Irregular plural forms of active nouns are indicated. Adjectives ending in **-o** are given in the masculine singular with the feminine ending (**a**) in parentheses. Verbs are listed in the infinitive form, except for a few irregular verb forms presented early in the text. Stem-changing verbs appear with the change in parentheses after the infinitive.

A

(to be) **able** poder (ue) *pres. subj.* (**5.2**) *fut.* (**8.1**) *cond.* (**8.2**)
about a eso de (**3.1**)
above arriba (**4.1**)
   above all sobre todo (**1.3**)
absolutely absolutamente (**7.1**)
(by) **accident** por casualidad (**3.2**)
(to) **accustom oneself** acostumbrarse (**4.2**)
   accustomed acostumbrado(a) (**6.3**)
actually en efecto (**4.2**)
(to) **add** añadir (**3.3**)
(to) **admire** admirar (**6.1**)
advice consejo *m.* (**3.2**)
advisable recomendable (**5.1**)
(to) **advise** aconsejar (**5.2**); advertir (ie, i) (**6.3**)
adviser consejero *m.*, consejera *f.* (**5.3**)
aerobic aeróbico(a) (**5.1**)
(to be) **afraid** tener miedo (**1.3**)
agitated agitado(a) (**4.1**)
(to) **agree** acordar (ue) (**4.1**)
album álbum *m.* (**4.1**)
allowance bolsillo: dinero *m.* de bolsillo (**7.1**)
although aunque (**5.3**)
amazed asombrado(a) (**4.3**)
American estadounidense *m. f.* (**2.2**)
anaconda (snake) anaconda *f.* (**2.2**)
(to) **get angry** enojarse (**5.3**)
(to) **answer** contestar (**1.2**)
anticipation anticipación *f.* (**8.1**)
(to) **appear** parecer (**1.3**); aparecer (**2.1**)
(to be) **appetizing to** apetecer (**2.1**)
application solicitud *f.* (**7.3**)

(to) **apply** solicitar (**7.2**)
(to) **approach** acercarse (**3.3**)
arepa (griddle cake made of corn) arepa *f.* (**2.1**)
around a eso de (**3.1**)
(to) **ask for** pedir (i, i) *pres. subj.*(**5.2**)
   to ask questions hacer preguntas (**1.1**)
asleep dormido(a) (**5.1**)
(to be) **astonished** asombrado(a) (**4.3**)
(to) **attend** asistir (a) (**1.1**) *pret.* (**2.2**)
attentive atento(a) (**5.2**)
authority autoridad *f.* (**3.1**)
average promedio *m.* (**7.3**)
(to) **avoid** evitar (**3.2**)

B

bag bolsa *f.* (**3.1**)
balanced balanceado(a) (**5.2**)
bank of a river orilla *f.* (**4.3**)
bathing suit traje de baño *m.* (**8.2**)
battery batería *f.* (**6.1**)
(to) **be** ser *imperf.* (**4.1**) *pres. subj.* (**5.1**) *cond.* (**8.2**);
   estar *pres. subj.* (**5.1**);
   haber *fut.* (**8.1**) *cond.* (**8.2**)
   (to be) **able** poder (**5.2**)
   (to be) **afraid** tener miedo (**1.3**)
   (to be) **sleepy** tener sueño (**1.3**)
beach playa *f.* (**8.2**)
(to) **become nighttime** anochecer (**6.1**)
(to) **begin** empezar (ie) *pres. subj.* (**5.2**); iniciar (**2.2**)
(to) **behave** comportarse (**4.1**), portarse (**3.2**)
bird pájaro *m.* (**2.2**)
boa constrictor boa *f.* (**2.2**)
(to) **bother** molestar (**5.3**)

box (small) caja, cajita *f.* **(4.1)**
bracelet pulsera *f.* **(1.2)**
Brazilian brasileño(a) **(2.2)**
bread crumb migaja *f.* **(4.3)**
(to) **break** romper **(2.2)** *pres. perf.* **(6.2)**
(to) **breathe** respirar **(5.2)**
(to) **bring** traer *pret.* **(3.1)**
(to) **brush (one's hair)** cepillarse (el pelo) **(3.3)**
building edificio *m.* **(4.3)**
burn quemadura *f.* **(3.2)**
    burned quemado(a) **(3.2)**
business empresa *f.* **(7.3)**
by por **(3.1) (8.2)**

cabinet gabinete *m.* **(4.2)**
cafe (specializing in arepas) arepera *f.* **(8.3)**
cage jaula *f.* **(4.1)**
caiman (South American reptile) caimán *m.* *(pl. caimanes)* **(2.2)**
(to) **calm oneself** calmarse **(5.3)**
camera cámara *f.* **(3.2)**
(to) **camp** acampar **(1.3)**
candy dulce *m.* **(5.1)**
capable capacitado(a) **(7.2)**
captions subtítulo *m.* **(3.3)**
capybara (a large South American rodent) capibara *f.* **(2.2)**
carefully con cuidado **(3.3)**
career carrera *f.* **(5.2)**
(to) **carry** llerar **(2.2)**
cashier cajero *m.*, cajera *f.* **(3.3)**
category categoría *f.* **(7.2)**
cave cueva *f.* **(6.2)**
centigrade centígrado *m.* **(3.1)**
certain cierto(a) **(5.1)**; seguro(a) **(1.2)**
championship campeonato **(1.3)**
chance (if by) casualidad *f.* **(3.2)**; por si acaso **(8.2)**
channel (television) canal *m.* **(3.2)**
cheap barato(a) **(3.2)**
(to) **check** fijarse **(2.1)**
checkers juego *m.* de damas **(4.1)**
childhood niñez **(4.1)**
Chinese chino(a) **(2.2)**
chore quehacer *m.* **(4.1)**
chronological cronológico(a) **(3.3)**
claim reclama **(3.1)**
classified clasificado(a) **(7.2)**
(to) **clean** limpiar **(2.2)**
    cleanliness limpieza **(4.1)**
clear claro(a) **(5.1)**

climate clima *m.* **(1.3)**
cloth trapo *m.* **(4.1)**
cloudy nublado(a) **(3.1)**
coast costa *f.* **(2.3)**
coat saco *m.* **(8.2)**
coincidence por casualidad **(3.2)**
comb peine *m.* **(8.2)**
(to) **come** venir (ie, i) *fut.* **(8.1)** *cond.* **(8.2)**
    come here ven acá **(3.2)**
command orden *m. f.* *(pl. órdenes)* **(3.3)**
common común y corriente **(3.1)**
(to) **communicate with** comunicarse **(3.3)**
company compañía *f.* **(7.2)**
(to) **compare** comparar **(2.3)**
(to) **compete** competir (i, i) **(8.1)**
complete completo(a) **(1.2)**
complicated complicado(a) **(5.3)**
(to) **confide in** confiar en **(3.3)**
(to) **confuse oneself** confundirse **(5.3)**
    confused confundido(a) **(5.3)**
(to) **connect to** conectarse **(3.3)**
contest concurso *m.* **(4.2)**
continuation continuación: a continuación **(3.2)**
contrary (on the) por el contrario **(3.1)**
(to) **convince** convencer **(4.2)**
cookie galleta *f.* **(5.1)**
    small cookie galletita *f.* **(5.1)**
(to) **correct** corregir (i, i) **(4.3)**
correspondence correspondencia *f.* **(1.1)**
counselor consejero *m.*, consejera *f.* **(5.3)**
(to) **count** contar **(1.2)**
country campo **(4.3)**
courteous cortés **(5.2)**
crazy loco(a) **(1.3)**
    (to be) **crazy about** estar loco(a) por **(5.3)**
cream crema *f.* **(8.2)**
crime crimen *m.* *(pl. crímenes)* **(5.1)**
culture cultura *f.* **(1.3)**
curiosity curiosidad *f.* **(8.1)**
custom costumbre *f.* **(7.1)**
(to) **cut** cortar **(4.1)**

daily diario(a) **(2.2)**
(to) **dance** bailar *pret.* **(2.2)**, **(3.3)**
dangerous peligroso(a) **(2.3)**
Danish danés, danesa (*m. pl.* daneses) **(2.2)**
dark oscuro(a) *m. f.* **(6.2)**
(to be) **dead** estar muerto(a) **(5.2)**
    dead/dying of hunger muerto de hambre **(1.2)**

decision decisión **(3.3)**
degree (temperature) grado *m.* **(3.1)**
(to) **deliver** entregar **(3.3)**
(to) **demand** exigir **(5.1)**
demonstration demostración *f.* (*pl.* demostraciones) **(5.2)**
(to) **depend (on)** depender (de) **(7.1)**
(to) **deposit** depositar **(3.3)**
depressed deprimido(a) **(5.2)**
desperate desesperado(a) **(4.3)**
detail detalle *m.* **(4.1)**
development desarrollo **(2.3)**
(to) **die** morirse (ue, u) *pret.* **(4.2)** *pres. perf.*
    (to) **die of fright** morirse de miedo **(6.2)**
diet dieta *f.* **(5.1);** régimen *m.* **(5.2)**
different diverso(a) **(2.3)**
dirty sucio(a) **(6.1)**
(to) **disconnect** desenchufar **(3.2);** desconectarse **(3.3)**
(to) **discover** descubrir *pres. perf.* **(6.2)**
(to) **discuss** discutir **(8.1)**
dishonest deshonesto(a) **(3.2)**
(to) **distance oneself** separarse **(4.1)**
(to) **distribute** repartir **(7.2)**
diverse diverso(a) **(2.3)**
(to) **do** hacer *pres. perf.* **(6.2)** *fut.* **(8.1)** *cond.* **(8.2)**
doubt duda *f.* **(7.1)**
    (to) **doubt** dudar **(6.1)**
    doubtful dudoso(a) **(5.1)**
(to) **draw** dibujar **(6.2)**
    (to) **draw near** acercarse **(3.3)**
dream sueño *m.* **(5.1)**
    (to have) **dreams** tener sueños **(1.3)**
(to) **drink** beber *pret.* **(2.2)**
(to) **drive** manejar **(7.1);** conducir *cond.* **(8.2)**
drizzle llovizna **(3.1)**
    (to) **drizzle** lloviznar **(3.1)**
(to) **dust** pasar un trapo **(4.1)**
Dutch holandés, holandesa (*m. pl.* holandeses) **(2.2)**

<div align="center">~~~ E ~~~</div>

earring arete *m.* **(1.2);** zarcillo *m.* **(4.1)**
East oriente *m.* **(3.1)**
    eastern oriental **(3.1)**
(to) **eat** comer *pret.* **(2.2)** *pres. perf.* **(6.2)**
economical económico(a) **(1.3)**
elderly anciano(a) **(4.3)**
    elderly person viejito *m.,* viejita *f.* **(3.3)**
electronic mail correo electrónico **(3.3)**
(to) **employ** emplear **(7.2)**

employee empleado *m.,* empleada *f.* **(3.1)**
    employment empleo *m.* **(7.2)**
(to) **empty** vaciar **(3.1)**
    empty the trash vaciar el basurero **(3.1)**
energy energía *f.* **(5.1)**
English(person) inglés, inglesa (*m. pl.* ingleses) **(2.2)**
(to) **enjoy** gozar **(1.1)**
(to) **enrage** enfurecer **(5.3)**
enterprise empresa *f.* **(7.3)**
environmental ambiental **(2.2)**
envy envidia *f.* **(8.1)**
essential esencial **(8.2)**
ethnic étnico(a) **(2.3)**
event suceso *m.* **(3.3)**
evident obvio(a) **(5.1)**
exaggerated exagerado(a) **(6.1)**
example ejemplo *m.* **(1.1)**
excel sobresalir **(6.2)**
excuse excusa *f.* **(5.2)**
exercise ejercicio *m.* **(2.3)**
    (to) **exercise** hacer ejercicio **(5.1)**
expenditure gasto *m.* **(7.1)**
expense gasto *m.* **(7.1)**

<div align="center">~~~ F ~~~</div>

(to) **fall asleep** dormirse (ue, u) *pres. subj.* **(5.2) (8.1)**
fame honor *m.* **(3.1)**
fantastic! ¡chévere! **(2.1)**
(to) **fascinate** fascinar **(1.3)**
fast rápido(a) **(1.3)**
fear miedo *m.* **(2.2)**
(to) **feed** darle de comer **(4.2)**
(to) **feel** sentir (ie, i) **(5.2)**
    (to) **feel like** tener ganas de **(1.1)**
    ferocious feroz (*pl.* feroces) **(2.3)**
fierce feroz (*pl.* feroces) **(2.3)**
(to) **fill** rellenar **(3.2)**
flag bandera *f.* **(8.3)**
flashy llamativo(a) **(7.1)**
flat plano(a) *m. f.* **(8.3)**
flavor sabor *m.* **(3.2)**
flea pulga *f.* **(2.3)**
flight vuelo *m.* **(8.2)**
flour harina *f.* **(3.2)**
(to) **flow into (river)** desembocar **(2.3)**
(to) **follow** seguir (i, i) *pres. subj.* **(5.2)**
food alimento *m.* **(8.3)**
fortunately afortunadamente **(5.1)**
fortune fortuna *f.* **(3.3)**

French francés, francesa *m. (pl.* franceses) **(2.2)**
    French fries papitas *f. pl.* fritas **(5.1)**
frequency frecuencia *f.* **(4.1)**
friendly amable **(2.1)**
fright espanto *m.,* susto *m.***(6.3)**
    (to be) **frightened** asustado(a) **(4.3)**
frustrated frustrado(a) **(1.2)**
    (to be) **frustrated** estar frustrado(a) **(1.2)**
funny chistoso(a) **(6.3)**
future futuro *m.* **(3.2)**
(to) **gain weight** engordarse **(5.1)**

game juego *m.* **(1.2)**
    game of checkers juego de damas **(1.2)**
garbage basura *f.* **(3.1)**
    garbage collector basurero *m.,* basurera *f.* **(3.1)**
gasoline gasolina *f.* **(7.1)**
genius genio *m.* **(6.1)**
German alemán, alemana *m.(pl.* alemanes) **(2.2)**
(to) **get better** mejorar **(8.2)**
(to) **get dark** anochecer **(6.1)**
(to) **get fat** engordarse **(5.1)**
(to) **get into shape** ponerse en línea **(5.3)**
(to) **get motivated** animarse **(5.2)**
(to) **give** dar *pres. subj.* **(5.1)**; prestar **(5.1)**
(to be) **glad** alegrarse **(5.3)**
(to) **go** ir *pres. subj.* **(5.1)**
a good guy un buen mozo **(5.2)**
gossip chisme *m.* **(5.3)**
grass césped *m.* **(4.1)**
grease grasa *f.* **(5.2)**
    greasy grasoso(a) *m. f.* **(5.2)**
greater mayor *adj.* **(2.3)**
Greek griego(a) **(2.2)**
to grow crecer **(2.1)**
(to) **guess** adivinar **(8.3)**

habit costumbre *f.* **(7.1)**
hair pelo *m.* **(1.3)**
handkerchief pañuelo *m.* **(8.1)**
(to be) **happy** alegrarse **(5.3)**
hardware hardware *m.* **(3.3)**
(to) **hang** colgar **(6.1)**
harmful dañino(a) **(3.2)**
(to) **hate** odiar **(2.2)**
(to) **have** tener *pres. subj.* **(5.1)** *fut.* **(8.1)** *cond.* **(8.2)**;

haber *fut.* **(8.1)** *cond.* **(8.2)**
    (to) **have a good time** divertirse (ie, i) *pres. subj.* **(5.2)**
    (to) **have a mind to** tener ganas de **(1.1)**
    (to) **have just** acabar de **(1.1)**
headline titular *m.* **(5.3)**
health salud *f.* **(2.3)**
healthful saludable **(5.2)**
hermit ermitaño *m.* **(6.3)**
(to) **hide** esconder(se) **(4.3)**
highway carretera *f.* **(6.1)**
honest honesto(a) **(3.1)**
honor honor *m.* **(3.1)**
hope esperanza *f.* **(5.1)**
    I hope that..., let's hope that... ojalá **(5.1)**
how educated! ¡qué culto! **(2.2)**
how cultured! ¡qué culto! **(2.2)**
how stupid you are! ¡qué tonto eres! **(2.2)**
hunger hambre *f.* **(1.2)**

ice chest hielera *f.* **(6.2)**
(to) **identify** identificar **(2.3)**
(to) **ignite** prender **(6.3)**
(to) **be important** importar **(5.2)**
impression impresión *f. (pl.* impresiones) **(1.2)**
(to) **improve** mejorar **(8.2)**
in en **(1.1)**; dentro de **(8.2)**
in fact en efecto **(4.2)**
incident incidente *m.* **(3.1)**
indecisive indeciso(a) **(8.3)**
inexpensive barato(a) **(3.2)**
infancy niñez *f.* **(4.1)**
informative informativo(a) **(3.2)**
(to) **infuriate** enfurecer **(5.3)**
(to) **initiate** iniciar **(2.2)**
injurious dañino(a) **(3.2)**
(to) **insist** insistir **(5.2)**
(to) **insist upon** insistir (en) **(5.2)**
(to) **inspect** revisar **(6.1)**
(to) **install** instalar **(3.3)**
instructor instructor *m.,* instructora *f.* **(5.1)**
insurance seguro *m.* **(7.1)**
interest interés *m. (pl.* intereses) **(1.3)**
    interested interesado(a) **(1.3)**
Internet (a world-wide communications network) Internet *m.* **(3.3)**
interruption interrupción *f. (pl.* interrupciones) **(3.2)**
interviewer entrevistador *m.,* entrevistadora *f.* **(7.3)**
(to) **invent** inventar **(5.1)**

investigation investigación *f.* (*pl.* investigaciones) **(2.3)**

Irish irlandés, irlandesa (*m. pl.* irlandeses) **(2.2)**

(to) **iron** planchar **(4.1)**

isolated aislado(a) **(3.1)**

Israeli israelita *m. f.* **(2.2)**

Italian italiano(a) **(2.2)**

J

jaguar jaguar *m.* **(2.2)**

Japanese japonés, japonesa (*m. pl.* japoneses) **(2.2)**

job ocupación *f.* (*pl.* ocupaciones); puesto *m.* **(7.1);** empleo *m.* **(7.2)**

jungle selva *f.* **(2.2)**

junk food chuchería **(5.1)**

just in case por si acaso **(8.2)**

K

(to) **keep** guardar **(3.3)**

kind especie *f.* **(4.1)**

(to) **know** saber *pres. subj.* **(5.1)** *cond.* **(8.2)**

knowledgable sabio(a) *m. f.* **(4.3)**

Korean coreano(a) **(2.2)**

L

lamp lámpara *f.* **(3.1)**

lantern linterna *f.* **(6.2)**

(to) **last** durar **(2.2)**

Latin American latinoamericano(a) **(1.3)**

(to) **laugh** reír (i, i) **(4.1)**

    (to) **laugh at** burlarse **(7.1)**

lawn césped *m.* **(4.1)**

lazy perezoso(a) **(1.3)**

(to) **learn** aprender *pres. subj.* **(5.1)**

(to) **leave** salir *pret.* **(2.2)** *imperf.* **(3.3)** *pres. subj.* **(5.1)** *fut.* **(8.1)** *cond.* **(8.2)**

(to) **lend** prestar **(5.1)**

leopard leopardo *m.* **(2.3)**

let me see déjame ver **(1.2)**

life vida *f.* **(1.1)**

light luz *f.* (*pl.* luces) **(4.2)**

pertaining to language lingüístico(a) **(8.3)**

lion león *m.* (*pl.* leones) **(2.3)**

    mountain lion puma *m.* **(6.2)**

liquid líquido *m.* **(5.2)**

list lista *f.* **(1.1)**

(to) **listen to** escuchar *pret.* **(2.2)**

liter litro *m.* **(5.2)**

literary literario(a) **(4.2)**

literature literatura *f.* **(4.2)**

little bear osito *m.* **(4.1)**

(to) **live** vivir **(1.1)**

(to) **locate** localizar **(2.3)**

long largola **(1.1)**

lotion loción *f.* (*pl.* lociones) **(3.2)**

love amor *m.* **(5.3)**

    in love enamorado(a) **(5.3)**

    with much love (salutation in a letter or card) con mucho cariño **(8.3)**

(to be) **lucky** tener suerte **(1.3)**

M

macaw guacamaya *m.* **(2.2)**

machine máquina *f.* **(7.2)**

magical mágico(a) **(2.2)**

mail correo *m.* **(1.1)**

(to) **make** hacer *pres. perf.* **(6.2)** *fut.* **(8.1)** *cond.* **(8.2)**

    (to) **make fun of** burlarse **(7.1)**

    (to) **make the bed** hacer la cama **(4.1)**

    (to) **make thin** adelgazar **(5.1)**

manager gerente *m. f.* **(7.2)**

mango (tropical fruit) mango *m.* **(2.1)**

market (open-air) mercado *m.* al aire libre **(7.2)**

mansion mansión *f.* **(5.1)**

mattress colchón *m.* (*pl.* colchones) **(3.3)**

maximum máximo(a) **(3.1)**

maybe a lo mejor **(2.1);** quizas **(5.1)**

means of transportation medio *m.* de transporte **(1.1)**

medicine medicina *f.* **(5.1)**

(to) **meet** reunirse **(1.3)**

member socio(a) *m. f.* **(5.1)**

(to) **mention** mencionar **(2.3)**

mile milla *f.* **(6.2)**

milkshake batido **(2.1)**

millionaire millonario *m.* **(5.1)**

minimum mínimo(a) *m. f.* **(3.1)**

(to) **miss** echar de menos **(1.1)**

mist llovizna *f.* **(3.1)**

modem módem *m.* **(3.3)**

monkey mono *m.*, mona *f.* **(2.3)**

Moroccan marroquí *m. f.* (*pl.* marroquíes) **(2.2)**

mountain range cordillera *f.* **(2.3)**

mouse ratón *m.* (*pl.* ratones) **(2.3)**

    little mouse ratoncito *m.* **(4.2)**

municipal municipal (**3.1**)
mystery policíaco(a) (**3.1**); misterio *m.* (**3.3**)

(to) **nab** atrapar (**4.3**)
nationality nacionalidad *f.* (**2.2**)
natural natural (**2.3**)
necessary necesario (**2.3**); preciso(a) (**5.1**)
necklace collar *m.* (**1.2**)
(to) **need** necesitar (**5.1**)
negative negativo(a) (**1.1**)
neighbor vecino *m.*, vecina *f.* (**1.2**)
network red *m.* (**3.3**)
newscast noticiero *m.* (**3.2**)
next week la semana que viene
noise ruido *m* (**6.3**)
Norwegian noruego(a) (**2.2**)
nutrition nutrición *f.* (**5.2**)
   nutritious nutritivo(a) (**5.1**)

(to) **observe** observar (**4.1**)
obvious obvio(a) (**5.1**)
occurrence incidente *m.* (**3.1**)
ocean océano *m.* (**2.3**)
(to) **offend** lastimar (**5.3**)
often a menudo (**2.1**)
old anciano(a) (**4.3**)
   older mayor *adj.* (**2.3**)
Olympic olímpico(a) (**5.1**)
on my behalf de mi parte (**2.1**)
(to) **open** abrir *pres. perf.* (**6.2**)
operator operador *m.*, operadora *f.* (**7.3**)
orchestra orquesta *f.* (**1.3**)
order ordén *f.* (**3.3**)
ordinary corriente (**3.1**)
outside fuera (**7.2**)

pajamas pijamas *f.* (**8.2**)
Pakistani paquistaní *m. f.* (*pl.* paquistaníes) (**2.2**)
party pooper aguafiestas *m. f.* (**1.1**)
past pasado *m.* (**4.1**)
patience paciencia *f.* (**3.3**)
payment pago *m.* (**7.1**)
paid pagado(a) (**7.3**)
peak pico *m.* (**2.3**)
penpal amigo por correspondencia (**1.1**)

perhaps a lo mejor (**2.1**); quizás (**5.1**)
personality personalidad *f.* (**1.1**)
Philippine filipino(a) (**2.2**)
photograph fotografía *f.* (**4.1**)
picturesque pintoresco(a) *m. f.* (**8.3**)
pig cochino *m.* (**4.3**)
piranha fish piraña *f.* (**2.2**)
place (in) puesto(a), sitio *m.* (**6.2**)
   (to) **place** poner *pres. perf.* (**6.2**) *cond.* (**8.2**)
planned programado(a) (**8.3**)
plant planta *f.* (**2.3**)
(to) **play the role** hacer el papel (**2.1**)
pocket money dinero *m.* de bolsillo (**7.1**)
pollution contaminación *f.* (**5.1**)
population población *f.* (*pl.* poblaciones) (**2.3**)
port puerto *m.* (**2.3**)
Portuguese portugués, portuguesa (*m. pl.* portugueses) (**2.2**)
position puesto *m.* (**7.1**)
positive positivo(a) (**1.1**)
possibility posibilidad *f.* (**3.1**)
prediction pronóstico *m.*; predicción *f.* (*pl.* predicciones) (**8.1**)
   (to) **predict** predecir (**8.1**)
preference preferencia *f.* (**1.1**)
(to) **preserve** preservar (**2.3**)
previous previo(a) (**7.2**)
prior previo(a) (**7.2**)
prize premio *m* (**4.2**)
probable probable (**5.1**)
   probably a lo mejor (**2.1**)
product producto *m.* (**2.3**)
profession carrera *f.* (**5.2**)
(to) **profit by** aprovechar (**1.1**)
(to) **program (computers)** programar (**3.3**)
   programming programación *f.* (*pl.* programaciones) (**3.2**)
   programmed programado(a) (**8.3**)
(to) **protect** proteger (**3.2**)
protection protección *f.* (**3.2**)
protective protector(a) (**3.2**)
puma puma *m.* (**6.2**)
punctuality puntualidad *f.* (**7.3**)
(to) **put** poner *pres. perf.* (**6.2**); *fut.* (**8.1**) *cond.* (**8.2**)
   (to) **put in** meter (**3.3**)

qualification calificación *f.* (*pl.* calificaciones) (**7.3**)
qualified capacitado(a) (**7.2**)
question pregunta *f.* (**1.1**)
   questionnaire cuestionario *m.* (**3.3**)

R

rag trapo *m.* **(4.1)**
rain lluvia *f.* **(3.1)**
    (fine) rain llovizna *f.* **(3.1)**
(to) **raise** criar **(4.3)**
ray rayo *m.* **(3.2)**
razor rasuradora *f.* **(8.2)**
ready listo(a) **(1.1)**
realist realista *m. f.* **(7.1)**
(to) **realize** darse cuenta de **(5.3)**
recent reciente **(7.3)**
receptionist recepcionista *m. f.* **(7.3)**
(to) **reclaim** reclamar **(3.1)**
recommendation recomendación *f.*
    (pl. recomendaciones) **(5.1)**
reduced rebajado **(1.1)**
reference referencia *f.* **(7.3)**
(to) **reflect upon** reflexionar **(2.2)**
refuge refugio *m.* **(6.2)**
(to) **remain** permanecer **(3.2)**
    remains restos **(3.3)**
(to) **remember** acordar (ue) **(4.1)**, acordarse de **(4.1)**
(to) **remove** quitar **(5.2)**
report informe *m.* **(2.2)**
(to) **request** pedir (i, i) *pres. subj.***(5.2)**
(to) **require** exigir **(5.1)**; requerir (ie, i) **(7.2)**
requisite requisito *m.* **(7.3)**
(to) **resolve** resolver (ue) **(3.3)**
result resultado *m.* **(5.3)**
(to) **return** volver (ue) *pres. perf.* **(6.2)**
ridge (of mountains) sierra *f.* **(6.1)**
(to) **ring** sonar (ue) **(4.2)**
road camino *m.* **(6.2)**
role papel *m.* **(2.1)**
routine rutina *f.* **(1.1)**
(to) **run** correr *pret.* **(2.2)** *imperf.* **(3.3)** *fut.* **(8.1);**
    andar *pret.* **(3.1)**
Russian ruso(a) **(2.2)**

S

(to) **sadden** entristecer **(5.3)**
salary salario *m.* **(7.2)**
sale venta *f.* **(7.2)**
salesperson vendedor *m.,* vendedora *f.* **(7.3)**
same mismo (a) **(1.2)**
sandal sandalia *f.* **(8.2)**
savage salvaje **(2.2)**
(to) **save** salvar *pret.* **(2.2);** guardar **(3.3);** ahorrar
    (7.1)

saved ahorrado(a) **(3.3)**
saxophone saxofon **(1.3)**
(to) **say** decir *pres. subj.* **(5.1)** *pres. perf.* **(6.2)** *fut.*
    (8.1) *cond.* **(8.2)**
    (to) **say goodbye** despedirse de **(3.2)**
(to) **scare** asustar **(2.2),** dar miedo **(2.2)**
    (to) **scare oneself** asustarse **(4.1)**
(pertaining to) **school** escolástico(a) *m. f.* **(8.3)**
scientist científico *m.,* científica *f.* **(2.2)**
Scottish escocés *m.,* escocesa *f.*
    (m. pl. escoceses) **(2.2)**
secret secreto(a) **(3.3)**
section sección *f. (pl.* secciones) **(2.1)**
(to) **see** ver *imperf.* **(4.1)** *pres. subj.* **(5.1)** *pres. perf.*
    (6.2) *fut.* **(8.1)**
sentence oración *f. (pl.* oraciones) **(2.1)**
(to) **separate** separar, separarse **(4.1)**
series serie *f.* **(3.2)**
(to) **serve** servir (i, i) *pres. subj.* **(5.2)**
service station gasolinera *f.* **(5.2)**
(to) **set fire** prender **(6.3)**
(to) **set up** armar **(6.2)**
shampoo champú *m.* **(8.2)**
shape forma *f.* **(1.2)**
shore orilla *f* **(4.3)**
shorthand typist taquigrafía *f.,* **(7.2)**
shorts pantalones *m.* cortos **(8.2)**
show (as in an event) espectáculo *m.* **(7.2)**
showy llamativo(a) **(7.1)**
sign señal *f.* **(6.3)**
    (to) **sign** firmar **(2.2)**
signal señal *f.* **(6.3)**
silver plata *f.* **(3.1)**
(to) **sing** cantar **(1.1)**
site sitio *m.* **(6.2)**
(to) **ski** esquiar **(1.3)**
skin piel *f.* **(3.2)**
sleep sueño *m.* **(5.1)**
sleeping bag saco *m.* de dormir **(6.1)**
sleepyhead dormilón *m.,* dormilona *f.* **(8.1)**
(to) **slim down** ponerse en línea **(5.3)**
slow lento(a) **(1.3)**
smaller menor *adj.* **(2.3)**
(to) **smile** sonreír (i, i) **(4.1)**
smooth suave **(4.2)**
snake serpiente *f.,* culebra *f.* **(2.2)**
snout (animal) hocico *m.* **(4.3)**
soap opera telenovela *f.* **(2.2)**
soft suave **(4.2)**
software software *m.* **(3.3)**
(to) **solicit** solicitar **(7.2)**
soul in torment alma en pena **(6.3)**

sound ruido *m.* (**6.3**)
Spanish español(a) (**2.2**)
(to) **speak** *pres. perf.* hablar (**6.2**)
(to) **specialize** especializar (**8.3**)
    speciality especialidad *f.* (**5.2**)
species especie *f.* (**4.1**)
(to) **spy** espiar (**4.1**)
square cuadrado(a) (**1.1**) (**4.1**)
    a pattern of squares cuadrícula *f.* (**1.1**)
(to) **stand out** sobresalir (**6.2**)
stationery store papelería *f.* (**2.3**)
stingy tacaño(a) (**1.3**)
stop it! ¡quítate! (**2.2**)
straw paja *f.* (**4.2**)
(to) **take a stroll** pasear (**2.2**)
stubborn necio(a) (**7.3**)
study estudio *m.* (**2.2**)
subject tema *m.* (**2.2**)
(to) **substitue** sustituir (**3.2**)
subtitle subtítulo *m.* (**3.3**)
(to) **suggest** sugerir (ie, i) (**5.2**)
suggestion sugerencia *f.* (**3.3**)
(to) **sunbathe** bañarse al sol (**3.2**)
sunscreen loción *f.* protectora (**3.2**)
(to) **supervise** supervisar (**4.2**)
sure cierto(a) (**5.1**); seguro(a) (**1.2**)
    (to be) **sure** estar seguro(a) (**1.2**)
surely seguramente (**2.2**)
surprise sorpresa (**3.3**)
survey encuesta *f.* (**3.3**)
(to) **suspect** sospechar (**6.1**)
suspicious sospechoso(a) (**6.2**)
Swedish sueco(a) (**2.2**)
(to) **sweep** barrer (**4.1**)
(to) **swim** nadar (**1.1**) *pres. subj.* (**5.1**) *fut.* (**8.1**)
swimming pool piscina *f.* (**5.1**)
Swiss suizo(a) (**2.2**)
symptom síntoma *m.* (**1.2**)

(to) **take advantage of** aprovchar (**1.1**)
    (to) **take a trip** viajar (**2.2**)
    (to) **take away** quitar (**5.2**)
    (to) **take out the trash** sacar la busura (**4.1**)
tale chisme *m.* (**5.3**)
talent talento *m.* (**1.1**)
(to) **talk** hablar *pres. perf.* (**6.2**)
tapir tapir *m.* (**2.2**)
taste sabor (**3.2**)
    tasty sabroso(a) *m. f.* (**8.3**)
tax impuesto *m.* (**1.2**)

(to) **teach** enseñar (**3.2**)
tear lágrima *f.* (**3.2**)
technical técnico(a) (**3.2**)
teddy bear osito *m.* de peluche (**4.1**)
(to) **tell** contar (**1.2**) decir *pres. subj.* (**5.1**) *pres. perf.*
    (**6.2**) *fut.* (**8.1**) *cond.* (**8.2**)
temperature temperatura *f.* (**2.3**)
tent carpa *f.* (**6.2**)
terror espanto *m.* (**6.3**)
theme tema *m.* (**2.2**)
tie corbata *f.* (**8.2**)
(to) **think** pensar (**5.2**)
title título *m.* titular *m.* (**5.3**)
(to) **tolerate** aguantar (**6.1**)
toothbrush cepillo *m.* de dientes (**8.2**)
toothpaste pasta *f.* dental (**8.2**)
tortoise tortuga *f.* (**2.3**)
toucan tucán *m.* (*pl.* tucanes) (**2.3**)
towel toalla *f.* (**8.2**)
town square plaza *f.* (**8.3**)
toy juguete *m.* (**4.1**)
tragic trágico(a) (**4.1**)
training entrenamiento *m.* (**7.3**)
(to) **trap** atrapar (**4.3**)
(to) **travel** viajar (**1.1**) *pret.* (**2.2**)
treasure tesoro *m.* (**4.1**)
tree árbol *m.* (**2.3**)
tropical tropical (**2.3**)
(to) **trust** confiar (**3.3**)
turn vuelta *f.* (**7.1**)
    it's your turn te toca a ti (**1.1**)
    (to) **turn off** apagar (**3.2**)
    (to) **turn in** entregar (**3.3**)
turtle tortuga *f.* (**2.3**)
(to) **type** escribir a máquina (**7.2**)
    typewriting mecanografía *f.* (**7.2**)

united unido(a) (**5.1**)
    United States (of the) estadounidense *m. f.* (**2.2**)
university student universitario(a) (**5.3**)
(to) **unplug** desenchufar (**3.2**)
unusual insólito(a) (**3.1**)
up arriba (**4.1**)

(to) **vacuum** pasar la aspiradora (**4.1**)
    vacuum cleaner aspiradora *f.* (**4.1**)
vegetable vegetal *m.* (**5.2**)

Venezuelan venezolano **(1.2)**
veterinarian veterinario *m.*, veterinaria *f.* **(5.2)**
Vietnamese vietnamita *m. f.* **(2.2)**
violin violín *m.* **(1.3)**
(to) **visit** *pret.* **(2.2)** visitar
voice voz *f.* **(4.3)**

waiter mesonero *m.*, **(2.1)**
waitress mesonera *f.* **(2.1)**
(to) **want** querer (ie) *pret.* **(3.1)** *fut.* **(8.1)** *cond.* **(8.2)**
(to) **warn** advertir (ie, i) **(6.3)**
warm calientico **(2.1)**
(to) **wash** lavar **(1.1)**
waterfall catarata *f.* **(8.3);** salto *m.* **(8.3)**
weak débil **(1.3)**
(to) **wear** llevar *pret.* **(2.2)** *cond.* **(8.2)**
wedding boda *f.* **(1.2)**
(to) **weigh** pesar **(6.2)**
    weight peso *m.* **(5.2)**
    weight (for lifting) pesa *f.* **(5.1)**

West occidente *m.* **(3.1)**
    western occidental **(3.1)**
wet blanket aguafiestas *m. f.* **(1.1)**
what a gentleman! ¡qué caballero! **(5.1)**
what a fright! ¡qué susto! **(6.3)**
what envy! ¡qué envidia! **(8.1)**
what luck! ¡qué suerte! **(1.2)**
what's happening, what's up ¡quíhubole! **(6.1)**
what's new? ¿qué hay de nuevo? **(1.1)**
wheel rueda *f.* **(1.3)**
wheelchair silla *f.* de ruedas **(1.3)**
when cuando **(4.1)**
whole completo(a) **(1.2)**
wild salvaje **(2.2)**
wise sabio(a) **(4.3)**
(to) **wish** querer (ie) *pret.* **(3.1)** *fut.* **(8.1)** *cond.* **(8.2)**
within dentro, dentro de **(8.2)**
without equal incomparable **(3.2)**
(to) **work** trabajar *pres. subj.* **(5.1)**
worker trabajador *m.*, trabajadora *f.* **(1.3)**
world wide mundial **(5.1)**
(to) **write** *pret.* **(2.2)** *pres. perf.* **(6.2)** escribir
writing (in) por escrito **(3.1);** escritura *f.* **(4.1)**

ÍNDICE

Gramática / Funciones / Estrategias

ÍNDICE

Gramática / Funciones / Estrategias

This index lists the grammatical structures, their communicative functions, and the reading and writing strategies in the text. Entries preceded by a ● indicate functions. Entries preceded by a ■ indicate strategies. The index also lists important thematic vocabulary (such as household chores, leisure-time activities, weather expressions.) Page references beginning with *G* correspond to the *¿Por qué se dice así?* (**Manual de gramática**) section.

The Jabberwocky lurks.

CRÉDITOS

VIDEO CREDITS

For D.C. Heath & Company

Producers	Roger D. Coulombe
	Marilyn Lindgren

For Videocraft Productions, Inc.

Executive Producer	Judith M. Webb
Project Director	Bill McCaw
Directors	Juan Mandelbaum
	Chris Schmidt
Producer	Mark Donadio
Associate Producers	Krista D. Thomas
Video Editor	Stephen Bayes
Directors of Photography	Gary Henoch
	Jim Simeone
Sound Recordist	James Mase

Graphic Designer	Alfred DeAngelo
Composer	Jonno Deily
Sound Mixer	Joe O'Connell

El Paso

Local Producer	Michael Charske
Local Associate Producer	John Gutiérrez

Venezuela

For Alter Producciones Cinematográficas	Delfina Catalá
	Cristián Castillo
Local Producer	Hilda de Luca
Local Associate Producers	Miguel Cárdenas
	María Eugenia Jacome

TEXT CREDITS

"La Isla de Pascua y sus misterios" from *Mundo 21* is reprinted by permission of Editorial América, S.A.

"nocturno sin patria" by Jorge Debravo from *Nosotros los hombres* is reprinted by permission of Margarita Salazar Madrigal.

"Bailó con un bulto," "La nuera," and "La ceniza" are reprinted from *Cuentos From My Childhood* by Paulette Atencio by permission of the Museum of New Mexico Press.

"Ahora valoro mucho más España" by Lola Díaz is used by permission from *Cambio 16* (No.1.068/11-5-92).

"El rico" and "Caipora, el Padremonte" are adapted by permission from *Cuentos de espantos y aparecidos* by Verónica Uribe.

"Los viejitos y el gallo de la cresta de oro" and "Cuento del pájaro de los siete colores" from *Había una vez 26 cuentos* by Pilar Almoina de Carrera is adapted by permission.

"La profecía de la gitana" and "Las ánimas" are adapted from *Leyendas de España* by Genevieve Barlow and William N. Stivers by permission of National Textbook Company.

"La camisa de Margarita" from *Leyendas latinoamericanas* by Genevieve Barlow is adapted by permission of National Textbook Company.

"Las lágrimas del Sombrerón" from *Cuentos de espantos y aparecidos* by Luis Alfredo Arango is used by permission of Ediciones Ekaré-Banco del Libro, Venezuela.

"La familia Real," "El león y las pulgas, and "El hijo ladrón" from *Aventuras infantiles* by Maricarmen Ohara is reprinted by permission of the author and Alegría Hispana Publications.

"El collar de oro" from *Cuentos From My Childhood* by Paulette Atencio is used by permission of the Museum of New Mexico Press.

"Los árboles de flores blancas," "El origen del

nopal," and "Las manchas del sapo" from *Leyendas latinoamericanas* by Genevieve Barlow are adapted by permission of National Textbook Company.

"Out of poverty, into MIT: 5 El Paso students rise, shine" by Mark McDonald, *Dallas Morning News*, is adapted by permission.

"Good Morning U.S.A." is adapted from SPICE by permission of Stanford Program on International and Cross Cultural Education.

ILLUSTRATION CREDITS

Fian Arroyo: 83

Susan Banta: 15, 32, 33, 232, 304, 320

Ron Barrett: 313

Willi Baum: 295

Diana Bryan: 155

Carlos Castellanos: 11, 30, 84-85, 99(b), 122, 125, 157, 158, 160, 198, 211, 223(rt), 248-249, 285, 306, 325, 343, 347, 364, 379, 397

Marilyn Cathcart: 153, 154

Dan Derdula: 18-19, 34-35, 50-51, 72-73, 106-107, 254-255, 404-405, 438-439

Tom Durfee: 207, 208, 209, 277

Randall Enos: 37, 99(t), 101, 194, 345, 400, 432

David Gothard: 414

Tamar Haber-Schaim: 257, 376, 377, 398

Cynthia Jabar: 50, 439(glosses)

Timothy C. Jones: 159, 195, 212-213, 308, 407, 425, 434

Joni Levy Liberman: 11(side), 44, 69, 177, 180

Judy Love: 12-13, 28-29, 178, 181, 223(center), 247, 264-265, 290, 322-323, 380, 436

Claude Martinot: 13(side), 68, 121, 126, 139, 210, 251, 288, 289, 323(b), 421, 433

Tim McGarvey: 45, 65, 67, 417, 424

Kathy Meisl: 21, 294, 303, 335, 353, 362-363, 366-367, 373, 382-383, 388, 389, 422

Morgan Cain & Associates: 71, 86-87, 95, 102, 127, 145, 161, 183, 199, 235, 291, 403, 418

Cyndy Patrick: 106-107(glosses), 123, 124, 143(t), 375

Sean Sheerin: 202, 203

Anna Veltfort: 75

Joe Veno: G6, G10, G12-G13, G25, G36, G39, G40-G41, G52, G56, G58-G59, G63, G71, G74, G85, G90-G91, G93, G98, G101, G106, G108-G109, G115, G122

Anna Vojtech: 82, 138, 143(center), 378

Para empezar **sections**

Polo Barrera: 170, 171, 172, 426, 427

Ron Barrett: 114, 115, 116

Willi Baum: 224, 225, 226

Gavin Bishop: 92, 93, 94

Diana Bryan: 150, 151, 152

Randall Enos: 58, 59, 60, 188, 189, 190, 354, 355, 356

David Gothard: 22, 23, 24, 408, 409, 410

Hrana Janto: 240, 241, 242

Timothy C. Jones: 278, 279, 280

Paige Leslie Miglio: 314, 315, 316

Cyndy Patrick: 370, 371, 372, 390, 391, 392

Winslow Pels: 204, 205, 206, 296, 297, 298

Elivia Savadier: 76, 77, 78

Beata Szpura: 38, 39, 40

Anna Vojtech: 132, 133, 134, 258, 259, 260, 336, 337, 338

PHOTO CREDITS